VIEWPOINTS
Readings in Canadian History

VIEWPOINTS
Readings in Canadian History

R. DOUGLAS FRANCIS
University of Calgary

DONALD B. SMITH
University of Calgary

THOMSON

NELSON

Australia   Canada   Mexico   Singapore   Spain   United Kingdom   United States

THOMSON
✳
NELSON

Viewpoints: Readings in Canadian History
by R. Douglas Francis and Donald B. Smith

**Associate Vice President,
Editorial Director:**
Evelyn Veitch

Executive Editor:
Anne Williams

Marketing Manager:
Lenore Taylor

Developmental Editor:
Linda Sparks

Permissions Coordinator:
Robyn Craig

Production Editor:
Lara Caplan

Copy Editor:
Karen Rolfe

Proofreader:
Shirley Corriveau

Indexer:
Jin Tan

Production Coordinator:
Ferial Suleman

Design Director:
Ken Phipps

Cover Design:
Andrew Adams

Compositor:
Interactive Composition Corporation

Printer:
Webcom

**Library and Archives Canada
Cataloguing in Publication Data**

Viewpoints : readings in Canadian
history / [edited by] R. Douglas
Francis, Donald B. Smith. —1st ed.

Includes bibliographical references
and index.

ISBN 0-17-641538-6

1. Canada—History—Textbooks.
I. Francis, R. D. (R. Douglas), 1944–
II. Smith, Donald B., 1946–

FC165.V53 2006   971
C2005-906937-6

For information about the photographs featured on the cover, see the Photo Credits (page 585).

CONTENTS

PREFACE

In *Viewpoints* we present a collection of articles suitable for introductory Canadian history tutorials. Based on our *Readings in Canadian History: Pre-Confederation* and *Post-Confederation* volumes, seventh editions, we have selected topics related to major issues explored in Canadian history survey courses. We have included valuable articles of a general nature that deal with the various regions of the country and, whenever possible, ones that reflect new research interests.

Viewpoints includes two or three selections on each of fifteen topics, thereby affording instructors flexibility in choosing readings. Short introductions to each topic set the readings in a historical context and offer suggestions for further reading. We hope that this reader will contribute to increased discussion in tutorials. It is designed to complement course lectures and, where applicable, textbooks, in particular, *Journeys* by R. Douglas Francis, Richard Jones, and Donald B. Smith (Toronto: Thomson Nelson, 2005). We also provide for each topic weblinks to primary sources on the World Wide Web, as well as bibliographies of appropriate secondary sources.

Important reference works for students preparing essays and reports on different aspects of Canadian history include *Dictionary of Canadian Biography*, vols. 1–15, with additional volumes in preparation (Toronto: University of Toronto Press, 1966–); *Historical Atlas of Canada*, vols. 1–3 (Toronto: University of Toronto Press, 1987–93); and the annotated bibliographical guides by M. Brook Taylor, ed., *Canadian History: A Reader's Guide*, vol. 1, *Beginnings to Confederation* (Toronto: University of Toronto Press, 1994); and Doug Owram, ed., *Canadian History: A Reader's Guide*, vol. 2, *Confederation to the Present* (Toronto: University of Toronto Press, 1994). Gerry Hallowell, ed. *The Oxford Companion to Canadian History* (Don Mills, ON: Oxford University Press, 2004), is also very useful.

ACKNOWLEDGEMENTS

We wish to thank the following individuals who offered valuable suggestions for changes to the seventh edition of our two-volume *Readings in Canadian History: Pre-Confederation* and *Post-Confederation*, on which this one-volume collection is based. In preparing past editions we and the publisher sought advice from a number of Canadian historians. Their comments were generously given and greatly improved the original outlines of the collections. We would like to thank, in particular, Douglas Baldwin of Acadia University, Robert A. Campbell of Capilano College, Roger Hall of the University of Western Ontario, and Brent McIntosh of North Island College for their valuable reviews of the fifth edition. Thanks, too, for comments on earlier editions to Douglas Baldwin of Acadia University, Olive Dickason of the University of Alberta, John Eagle of the University of Alberta, Roger Hall of the University of Western Ontario, Hugh Johnston of Simon Fraser University, Wendy Wallace and Paul Whyte of North Island College, and Carol Wilton-Siegel, of York University. Many other individuals made valuable suggestions; we are indebted to John Belshaw of the University of the Cariboo, Barbara Bessamore of the University College of the Fraser Valley, Catherine Briggs of the University of Waterloo, Graham Broad of the University of Western Ontario, Margaret Conrad of Acadia University, Terry L. Chapman of Medicine Hat College, Cynthia Comacchio of Wilfrid Laurier University, Beatrice Craig of the University of Ottawa, Karen Dubinsky of Queen's University, Ross Fair of Ryerson University, Chad Gaffield of the University of Ottawa, Jacqueline Gresko of Douglas College, Ernest Levos of Grant MacEwan College, Marcel Martel of Glendon College — York University, Brent McIntosh of North Island College, Carolyn Podruchny of York University, Paige Raibmon of the University of British Columbia, Thomas Socknat of the University of Toronto, Robert Sweeny of Memorial University, Peter Ward of the University of British Columbia, and Catherine Wilson of the University of Guelph.

Heartfelt thanks also go to Anne Williams, Rebecca Rea, Linda Sparks, and Lara Caplan for their assistance with the completion of *Viewpoints*, and to Karen Rolfe who copy edited the book. A special thanks goes to David Smith who researched the World Wide Web for sources, particularly primary sources, appropriate for each topic. Finally, we wish to thank those Canadian historians who consented to let their writings be included in this reader. Their ideas and viewpoints will greatly enrich the study and appreciation of Canadian history among university and college students taking introductory courses in Canadian history.

Douglas Francis
Donald Smith
Department of History
University of Calgary

The First Nations and European Contact

Captain Bulgar, Governor of Assiniboia and the Chiefs and Warriors of the Chippewa Tribe of Red Lake. Watercolour by Peter Rindisbacher, 1823. Gift-giving ceremonies accompanied First Nations negotiations with Europeans as shown in this council in the Red River, 1823.

The Europeans who came to North America looked upon it as an empty continent, open for settlement. In reality, the First Nations claimed and inhabited almost every part of the "New World," from the Gulf of Mexico to the Arctic coast, from the Atlantic to the Pacific. At the time of European contact, more than 50 First Nations groups lived within the borders of what is now Canada.

In the pre-European period, there was neither a common designation for the country nor a common name for the native inhabitants. The First Nations owed their allegiance to their family, their band, their village, their community, and — in the case of several nations — their confederacy. But they had no concept of a pan-Indian identity. Each group spoke its own language and regarded its own members as "the people." This lack of a perceived common identity contributed to the First Nations' failure to resist the Europeans. Other factors included the reliance of some First Nations groups on European manufactured trade goods, the fur-trade rivalries, the colonial wars, and the catastrophic drop in population that resulted from exposure to European diseases.

Anthropologist Harald Prins in "Children of Gluskap: Wabanaki Indians on the Eve of the European Invasion," looks at the First Nations of what are now the Maritime provinces and northern New England. In "The French Presence in Huronia: The Structure of Franco–Huron Relations in the First Half of the Seventeenth Century," anthropologist Bruce Trigger traces the fortunes of the Hurons, one of the First Nations groups that came into the closest contact with French fur traders in the 17th century. Historian Wendy Wickwire examines accounts of the first meetings between the Nlaka'pamux, the Native people of what is now south-central British Columbia. The fur traders referred to the Nlaka'pamux, who speak a common language, as the "Thompsons," after the major river in their territory.

These three articles raise many important questions. How did the Wabanaki, for example, envision their world before European contact? What was their system of political organization on the eve of the newcomers' arrival? Why did the Hurons' contact with the French have such a dramatic effect on their society? What do the oral traditions of the Nlaka'pamux add to our understanding of the initial contact between the First Nations and the Europeans in what is now British Columbia?

Diamond Jenness's dated *Indians of Canada* (Ottawa: King's Printer, 1932; numerous editions since) must be supplemented by Olive Patricia Dickason, *Canada's First Nations: A History of Founding Peoples from Earliest Times*, 3rd ed. (Toronto: Oxford University Press, 2002); Paul Magocsi, ed., *Aboriginal Peoples of Canada: A Short Introduction* (Toronto: University of Toronto Press, 2002); and Arthur J. Ray, *I Have Lived Here Since the World Began: An Illustrated History of Canada's Native People* (Toronto: Lester Publishing Limited, 1996 [rev. ed. 2005]). Alan D. McMillan and Eldon Yellowhorn have written a useful survey, *First Peoples in Canada* (Vancouver: Douglas and McIntyre, 2004). A good collection of articles on Canada's Native peoples, edited by R. Bruce Morrison and C. Roderick Wilson, is *Native Peoples: The Canadian Experience*, 3rd ed. (Don Mills, ON: Oxford University Press, 2004). Anthropologist Alice B. Kehoe provides an overview in her *North American Indians: A Comprehensive Account*, 2nd ed. (Englewood Cliffs, NJ: Prentice-Hall, 1992). Robert McGhee's *Ancient Canada* (Ottawa: Canadian Museum of Civilization, 1989) reviews what is currently known of Canada's First Nations and Inuit before the arrival of the Europeans.

A good introduction to the subject of early French–Aboriginal relations in the Americas remains Olive Patricia Dickason's *The Myth of the Savage and the Beginnings of French Colonialism in the Americas* (Edmonton: University of Alberta Press, 1984). Other useful introductions include Alfred G. Bailey's older study, *The Conflict of European and Eastern Algonkian Cultures, 1504–1700*, 2nd ed. (Toronto: University of Toronto Press, 1969 [1937]); the short booklet by Bruce Trigger entitled *The Indians and the Heroic Age of New France*, Canadian

Historical Association, Historical Booklet no. 30, rev. ed. (Ottawa: CHA, 1989), and his *Natives and Newcomers: Canada's "Heroic Age" Reconsidered* (Montreal/Kingston: McGill-Queen's University Press, 1985); and the first chapter, entitled "Native Peoples and the Beginnings of New France to 1650," in John A. Dickinson and Brian Young, *A Short History of Quebec*, 2nd ed. (Toronto: Copp Clark Pitman, 1993), pp. 2–26. For specific information on the Huron, see Conrad Heidenreich, *Huronia: A History and Geography of the Huron Indians, 1600–1650* (Toronto: McClelland and Stewart, 1971); and Bruce G. Trigger, *The Huron: Farmers of the North*, 2nd ed. (Fort Worth, TX: Holt, Rinehart and Winston, 1990). An interesting popular account of early First Nations–European contact is Robert McGhee's *Canada Rediscovered* (Ottawa: Canadian Museum of Civilization, 1991). Useful maps appear in R. Cole Harris, ed., *Historical Atlas of Canada*, vol. 1, *From the Beginning to 1800* (Toronto: University of Toronto Press, 1987).

Students interested in pursuing the subject further should consult Cornelius Jaenen, *Friend and Foe: Aspects of French–Amerindian Cultural Contact in the Sixteenth and Seventeenth Centuries* (Toronto: McClelland and Stewart, 1976); Bruce Trigger, *Natives and Newcomers: Canada's "Heroic Age" Reconsidered* (Montreal/Kingston: McGill-Queen's University Press, 1985); and Denys Delâge, *Bitter Feast: Amerindians and Europeans in the American Northeast, 1600–64*, translated from the French by Jane Brierley (Vancouver: University of British Columbia Press, 1993). A model study of ecological history in the early European contact period is William Cronon's *Changes in the Land: Indians, Colonists, and the Ecology of New England* (New York: Hill and Wang, 1983). For valuable secondary studies on early European–First Nations contact in what is now British Columbia see the bibliographical suggestions for Topic Fourteen: The Pacific Coast.

The Europeans' early attitudes to the question of Aboriginal sovereignty are reviewed in Brian Slattery's "French Claims in North America, 1500–59," *Canadian Historical Review* 59 (1978): 139–69, and W.J. Eccles's "Sovereignty-Association, 1500–1783," *Canadian Historical Review* 65 (1984): 475–510. Leslie C. Green and Olive Dickason review the ideology of the European occupation of the Americas in *The Law of Nations and the New World* (Edmonton: University of Alberta Press, 1989).

WEBLINKS

Canada's First Nations: European Contact

http://www.ucalgary.ca/applied_history/tutor/firstnations/contact.html

Contains European contact narratives from the perspective of Aboriginal peoples from each geographic region of Canada.

Canada Heirloom Series: Canada's Native Peoples

http://collections.ic.gc.ca/heirloom_series/volume2/volume2.htm

A detailed illustrated history of First Nations in Canada and their cultures.

Atlas of Canada: Aboriginal Peoples circa 1630, 1740, and 1823

http://atlas.gc.ca/site/english/maps/historical/aboriginalpeoples

Interactive maps detailing the changes in distribution of First Nations in Canada prior to the creation of Indian reserves.

Oneida Indian Nation — Culture & History

http://oneida-nation.net/historical.html

Describes the culture of the Oneida people and contains many pictures of their cultural artifacts.

Champlain Society

http://link.library.utoronto.ca/champlain/search.cfm?lang=eng

The digital collections of the Champlain Society contain numerous early primary source accounts of European contact with the First Nations, including Samuel de Champlain's voyages in New France. Browse the database by subject, and select for example, "Canada — Discovery and exploration," "New France — Discovery and exploration," or "Northwest, Canadian — History — Sources."

The Jesuit Relations

http://puffin.creighton.edu/jesuit/relations/

Translated and transcribed versions of *The Jesuit Relations and Allied Documents*, a very important source of knowledge of the history of New France and interactions between First Nations and emigrated settlers.

Article One

Children of Gluskap: Wabanaki Indians on the Eve of the European Invasion

Harald E.L. Prins

The native people of northern New England and the Maritime Provinces originally referred to their homeland as Ketakamigwa (the big land on the seacoast).[1] The area was thought of as the eastern part of a large island. This island was the earth as they knew it.[2] They referred to it as "top land," surrounded by the "great salt water." It was imagined as the center of a horizontally stratified universe, crowned by a sky-world where the spirits of the dead lived on as stars. Below was the netherworld, the realm of hostile spirits appearing in reptile form. A mysterious life force known as Ketchiniweskwe (great spirit) was thought to govern this universe.[3]

As inhabitants of the region where the skies first turn light in the morning, the native people of the northeastern coastal area were traditionally known as Wabanakiak (the people of the dawn).[4] They believed themselves to be the children of Gluskap, a primordial giant creature who came into being somewhere in the Northeast "when the world contained no other man, in flesh, but himself."[5] The meaning of his name is not certain and is sometimes translated as "good man," "the liar," or as "man out of nothing."[6]

As Gluskap's children, the Wabanakis have been the inhabitants of Ketakamigwa ever since time began. Their descendents today include the people belonging to the Abenaki,

Source: "Children of Gluskap: Wabanaki Indians on the Eve of the European Invasion," in *American Beginnings: Exploration, Culture, and Cartography in the Land of Norumbega*, ed., Emerson W. Baker, Edwin A. Churchill, Richard D'Abate, Kristine L. Jones, Victor A. Konrad, and Harald E. L. Prins (Lincoln: University of Nebraska Press, 1994): 95–117, 325–333. Reprinted with permission of the publisher.

Penobscot, Passamaquoddy, Maliseet, and Micmac tribes. Roaming through their homeland, the original Wabanakis became thoroughly familiar with all the natural features of the landscape, knowing the precise location of each river, lake, cape, and mountain. As hunters, fishers, and gatherers, they took regular stock of the available resources in their habitat and knew in great detail "what the supply of each resource was: deer, moose, beaver, fur-bearers, edible birds, berries, roots, trees, wild grasses. They knew the districts where each was to be found when wanted and, roughly, in what quantities."[7]

Of course, such ecological intimacy was possible only on the basis of a thorough geographic understanding of the immediate environment. But to what extent the Wabanakis' knowledge extended to territories beyond their tribal boundaries remains unclear.[8] It appears that they were familiar with territories as far south as the Hudson River, knew the area west until the St. Lawrence River, and could find their way north to Newfoundland, perhaps even beyond.

HISTORICAL ECOLOGY OF WABANAKI HABITAT

Until the end of the Ice Age about twelve thousand years ago, no human occupied the region now known as New England and the Maritime Provinces. However, when the glaciers retreated, small bands of Paleo-Indians moved into the tundras, preying on big game such as the mastodon, mammoth, musk-ox, and, most of all, large herds of grazing caribou. A few material remains, including flint spearpoints, knives, and scrapers have been found at their ancient camping places and kill sites at locations such as Debert, Munsungun, and Aziscohos lakes.[9] With climatic warming, the tundras of these Paleo-Indian hunting bands transformed gradually into a woodland habitat. The emerging woodlands represented a rich mosaic of tree stands with widely varying compositions. Environmental conditions initially favored white pine, followed by birch, oak, and hemlock. About five thousand years ago, a modern ecological system developed, with warm summers and cold winters marked by up to five months of snow-covered ground. Northern hardwoods such as maple, elm, ash, and beech appeared in the forests, followed later by spruce. Some of these trees, in particular the white pine, were enormous in dimension, measuring up to 5 feet in diameter and reaching more than 150 feet in height.

Broken by swamps, lakes, and ponds, these enormous territories have been drained by several major river systems since the end of the Ice Age. The 240-mile-long Penobscot, for example, collects water of 322 streams and 625 lakes and ponds, draining a total area of 7,760 square miles. The remainder of the territory is drained by the Restigouche, Miramichi, St. John, St. Croix, Kennebec, Androscoggin, Saco, and several other rivers.[10] Typical for this woodlands habitat, which became the homeland of the Wabanakis, is its thriving wildlife, traditionally its abundance of white-tailed deer along with moose and caribou. In addition, black bear, wolves, raccoons, red foxes, lynxes, bobcats, fishers, martens, otters, and skunks have long prospered here, as have rodents like beavers, muskrats, hares, and porcupines. Inland waters, at least seasonally, have formed the natural environment of fish such as salmon, trout, sturgeon, bass, smelt, and alewives; marine life at the coast includes not only an abundance of lobsters and shellfish (in particular, clams and oysters) but also sea mammals such as seals, porpoises, and whales (fig. 1.1). For thousands of years, multitudes of water birds have flocked to the area, again mostly seasonally — loons, ducks, cormorants, herons, geese, and swans. Pheasants, partridges, pigeons, grouse, and turkeys share in the bounty of the land along with hawks, majestic eagles, and birds of prey.

The presence of the Wabanakis in this rich and expansive habitat affected not only the animals they hunted but also the landscape itself. Like many other native groups, the Wabanakis periodically burned the land to improve its natural productivity and aid in hunting.

1.1 Micmac petroglyph at Kejimkujik Lake, depicting hunters lancing a large fish. In Garrick Mallery, "Picture-Writing of the American Indians," *Tenth Annual Report of the Bureau of Ethnology to the Secretary of the Smithsonian, 1888–1889*, 1893, p. 531.

For instance, in the valley of the Penobscot River, "the ground is plaine, without Trees or Bushes, but full of long Grasse, like unto a pleasant meadow, which the Inhabitants doe burne once a yeere to have fresh feed for their Deere."[11]

THE ALNANBIAKS: THE REAL PEOPLE

The following description of the Wabanakis is an ethnohistorical composite, based on information winnowed from an array of archaeological, oral traditional, historical documentary, and ethnographic sources. As an assemblage, it reconstructs their culture as it existed when they first encountered Europeans on their shores. At this time, there may have been some thirty thousand Wabanakis living in northern New England and the Maritime Provinces.[12] They all spoke closely related languages or dialects belonging to the larger Algonquian family. Generally, these people referred to their own kinfolk as the Alnanbiaks, the Ulnooks, or some other term to express the idea of "real people" or "truly humans." These Wabanakis were divided into several major ethnic groups, also known as nations or tribes. Members of each particular ethnic group shared a territorial range and could be distinguished from the members of other groups primarily by a limited set of cultural features, including obvious identifications such as defined styles of dress and speech. The various Wabanaki groups maintained close relations, which allowed them to cope with mutual conflict resulting from intertribal competition for valued resources in their territories.[13]

In the early seventeenth century, French visitors to the region reported that the Wabanakis were divided into three such major groupings from northeast to southwest: the Souriquois, Etchemins, and Armouchiquois. Later these ethnonyms, as first recorded by Samuel de Champlain, were generally replaced by the terms Micmac, Maliseet-Passamaquoddy, Penobscot, and Abenaki (fig. 1.2). Although they were all linked to each other directly or indirectly by ties of kinship and friendship, they formed distinctive bands ranging in size from as few as fifty members to more than one thousand. These bands were formed primarily on the basis of voluntary association between related kin groups. Although individual status differences did exist, the social structure of these tribal communities was fundamentally egalitarian.

Accordingly, their political organization was based on democratic principles, and decisions concerning the commonweal were based on consensus among the members. Their chiefs, known as sagamores, were leaders who were recognized as first among equals. "They have Sagamores, that is, leaders in war; but their authority is most precarious. . . . The Indians follow them through the persuasion of example or of custom, or of ties of kindred and alliance."[14] Responsible for the well-being and general security of their communities, these Wabanaki sagamores presided over the warriors. One such chieftain was Chief Mentaurmet, the sagamore of Nebamocago, the largest of three Wabanaki villages in the Sheepscot River valley. When a party of strangers arrived, Chief Mentaurmet received them, accompanied by "about forty

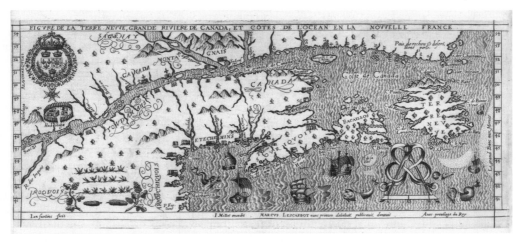

1.2 Extract from Marc Lescarbot, *Figure de la Terre Neuve, grand riviere de Canada, et côtes de l'ocean en la Nouvelle France,* in his *Histoire de la Nouvelle France,* 1609. Courtesy of Library and Archives Canada, NMC 97952.

powerful young men stationed around [his wigwam] like a bodyguard, each one with his shield, his bow and arrows upon the ground in front of him."[15]

Under leadership of these sagamores, the bands usually moved seasonally within their own districts, from their particular hunting areas to their favourite fishing, clamming, sealing, and fowling sites. Dispersing in small family groups during the fall, bands rejoined in the spring, usually near rapids or falls where they lived on the basis of an abundance of spawning fish. At these tribal gatherings, sometimes many hundreds of people assembled at one site, exchanging information, making new friendships, finding spouses for their children, and engaging in barter.

In charge of the collective pursuit of subsistence, allied sagamores made formal agreements with each other about territorial divisions within each tribal range. "These sagamies divide up the country and are nearly always arranged according to bays or rivers."[16] The territorial arrangements between the chieftains, each with his own following, enabled the kin groups to optimally exploit the ecological diversity of their allocated territory. These were usually situated along tributaries of the various rivers such as the Kennebec or Penobscot or in bays such as Passamaquoddy. This way, regional bands could carefully adjust their food-collecting strategies to the seasonal rhythms of resident game animals, fish runs, and plant growth cycles without running into conflict with their neighbors.[17]

MATERIAL CULTURE

As a Stone Age people, the Wabanakis tapped into the ever-shifting storehouse of nature for all their immediate supplies. Using primarily raw materials such as stone, bone, wood, and leather, they fabricated most of their own tools and weapons, including wooden bows and arrows, flint knives and scrapers, stone axes, bone fishhooks, long spears, and wooden clubs, as well as bark baskets, basswood fiber nets, rawhide snares, and traps. For example, bows were made of spruce or rock maple and were then polished with flaked stones or oyster shells and strung with moose sinew. Arrow shafts were made of white ash or young alders fitted with eagle feathers as flight-stabilizers and tipped with bone or flint points. Tribesmen fashioned lances from beech wood, equipping them with a sharply pointed moose bone, and crafted large cedar shields for protection.[18]

For winter travel, the Wabanakis used snowshoes made of white ash or beech, corded with leather thongs. To transport goods over the snow and ice, they used toboggans. As soon as the rivers became ice-free in the spring, they turned to their lightweight birch-bark canoes, which could seat as many as six or seven persons. Sometimes, these boats were made of spruce bark or even moose hide.[19] Especially on long-distance journeys, their seaborne craft were occasionally equipped with mast and sail, "which was . . . of bark but oftener of a well-dressed skin of a young Moose."[20]

Tree bark (white birch, as well as spruce) was used not only for the Wabanakis' canoes but also for covering their lodges. In addition to bark, they also used animal skins or woven mats as cover. Well accommodated inside, these wigwams were sometimes lined with "mats made of Rushes painted with several colours."[21] For added warmth, the Wabanakis used deerskins to line their winter quarters. Hemlock twigs or balsam fir needles usually covered the wigwam floor, on top of which were mats, hides, or soft sealskins, all spread around the central fireplace. In addition to the conical wigwam, which typically served as a one-family dwelling, the Wabanakis also built large communal or ceremonial lodges, sometimes measuring over one hundred feet long and thirty feet broad. The great wigwam at Nebamocago in the Sheepscot Valley, for example, could seat "fully eighty people"[22] (fig. 1.3).

1.3 W.R. Herries, painting of a small Maliseet camp on the banks of a river, 1850s. Courtesy of Library and Archives Canada, C115891.

Although the Wabanakis were familiar with pottery (since about three thousand years earlier), more popular were the many different types of birch-bark containers, which were "sowed with threads from Spruce [spruce] or white Cedar-roots, and garnished on the outside with flourisht works, and on the brims with glistering quills taken from the Porcupine, and dyed, some black, others red." They also made "dishes, spoons, trayes wrought very smooth and neatly out of the knots of wood, [and] baskets, bags, and matts woven with Sparke, bark of the Line-Tree [bass wood?] and Rushes of several kinds, dyed as before, some black, blew, red, yellow, [as well as] bags of Porcupine quills, woven and dyed also."[23]

TRADITIONAL HUNTERS, FISHERS, AND GATHERERS

Until the period of European contact in the sixteenth and early seventeenth centuries, the traditional Wabanaki mode of subsistence based on hunting, fishing, and gathering persisted in the territories east of the Kennebec River. In aboriginal northeastern North America, this river formed the northern boundary of an indigenous horticulture complex, which had originated in the highlands of Meso America some four thousand years ago.[24]

Beyond this ecological boundary, climatic conditions did not favor an indigenous Neolithic revolution. Accordingly, longstanding food-collecting strategies persisted among eastern Wabanaki groups identified as Etchemin (Maliseet-Passamaquoddy) and Souriquois (Micmac).[25] Early Europeans described them as "a nomadic people, living in the forest and scattered over wide spaces, as is natural for those who live by hunting and fishing only."[26] In the pursuit of game, in particular moose, deer, and caribou, Wabanaki tribesmen chased the animals with the help of packs of hunting dogs. Among others, bear, beaver, and otter were also favored targets. Moreover, especially during the summer months, the Wabanakis also hunted water fowl and other birds.

When they were on the coast, they searched for harbour seal and gray seal, which supplied them not only with soft hide but also with meat and oil. This oil was highly valued as grease for their hair and bodies and was also considered "a relish at all the feasts they make among themselves."[27] Sometimes, they also hunted whales or feasted on stranded whales.[28] During their stay on the coast, "when the weather does not permit going on the hunt," they went digging for clams at the muddy flats.[29] Other shellfish were also enjoyed, in particular lobster, "some being 20 pounds in weight." Surplus lobster caught during the summer months was dried and stored for winter food. Lobster meat was also good for bait, "when they goe a fishing for Basse or Codfish."[30]

In addition to traps or weirs, made of wooden stakes and placed in a shallow stream or small tidal bay, Wabanaki fishers used nets, hooks, and lines. Harpoons served to take porpoise and sturgeon, and special three-pronged fish spears enabled the Wabanakis to catch salmon, trout, and bass. Taking their canoes on the water at night, they lured the fish with torches of burning birch bark. This way, a man could spear up to two hundred fish during one trip.[31]

Adding to their diversified diet, the Wabanakis tapped the sweet sap of the maple tree and harvested greens, wild fruits, nuts, seeds, and last but not least, edible roots and tubers. On the basis of such intimate knowledge of nature, some Wabanakis became specialists in herbal medicine. Benefiting from the medicinal qualities inherent in certain roots, leaves, and bark, these Wabanakis brewed select teas or prepared poultices to be used as remedies.[32]

Among these hunters and gatherers, the burden of labor seems to have fallen disproportionately on the shoulders of native women. As one outside observer noted:

> Besides the onerous role of bearing and rearing the children, [women] also transport the game from where it has fallen; they are the hewers of wood and drawwers of water; they make and repair the household utensils; they prepare food; they skin the game and prepare the hides like fullers; they sew garments; they catch fish and gather shellfish for food; often they even hunt; they make the canoes . . . out of bark; they set up the tents wherever and whenever they stop

for the night — in short, the men concern themselves with nothing but the more laborious hunting and the waging of war. For this reason almost everyone has several wives.[33]

Those Wabanakis who were migratory hunters, fishers, and gatherers moved every six weeks or so and could set up a village within hours. Among their favourite haunts was a site known to them as Kenduskeag, located on a tributary to the Penobscot (at Bangor). Drawn by the abundance of eel that could be taken here, a regional band of about three hundred members returned to this location each fall, setting up eighteen seasonal lodges and constructing fish weirs. Although there were other seasonal villages as large as Kenduskeag, most of these temporary villages were much smaller. On the shores of the Bay of Fundy, for example, one such Wabanaki encampment consisted of no more than eight wigwams.[34]

CORN PLANTERS IN SOUTHERN MAINE

Generally, the larger tribal communities existed in the region west of the Sheepscot. This area was inhabited by people originally named Armouchiquois (perhaps a derogative, meaning dogs) by their Souriquois neighbors.[35] In contrast to the eastern Wabanaki groups, who maintained a mode of subsistence based exclusively on hunting, fishing, and gathering, these Armouchiquois planted vegetable gardens. Having adopted the horticultural complex of tribes to the south shortly before the arrival of Europeans in the area (probably in the fifteenth century A.D.), these western Wabanaki groups grew hard flint corn, kidney beans, and squash, as well as tobacco, in their village gardens. Although precise estimates for the actual acreage under cultivation are unavailable, an average village with a population of four hundred "would have utilized between 330 and 580 acres of planting fields to insure subsistence maintenance over half a century."[36]

Using a technique called slash-and-burn, the Armouchiquois cleared fertile plains in river valleys. By stoking fires around the bases of standing trees, they burned the bark, thereby killing the trees. Later, they felled the dead trees with stone axes. As one tree toppled, it usually knocked down several others. Later, all this wood was removed by burning. Men cleared the land, and women took charge of the gardens. In May or early June, they planted the fields. With digging sticks, they made long rows of holes, about three feet apart. In each hole they put several corn and bean kernels. Several weeks later, they planted squash seeds in between the growing plants. As a result, the cornstalks became beanpoles, and the leaves of the squash vines smothered weeds. Once harvested, much of the corn was stored for the winter in large holes in the ground. Lined with dwarf-rush mats and covered with earth, each of these "barns" could hold some six to ten bushels. Meanwhile, the Armouchiquois continued to rely on traditional food-collecting strategies as well (fig. 1.4).[37]

In addition to the usual meals of roasted or boiled meat, fowl, fish and so forth, the corn-growing Armouchiquois feasted on thick corn chowder mixed with clams, fish, meat, or other ingredients. When they traveled, they preferred a simple fare of parched cornmeal mixed with water, known as *nocake*, their equivalent of fast food. Supplementing the corn, they also ate beans and a large variety of edible wild plants. Finally, in the summer, "when their corne [was] spent," squash was "their best bread."[38]

Clearly, horticulture not only permitted high population densities than in areas inhabited by migratory food collectors but also allowed for more permanent settlement patterns. Reluctant to leave their village gardens unprotected during periods of conflict, these Wabanaki corn growers had little alternative but to defend their settlements against hostile raiders. For instance, one fortified Armouchiquois village, located at the mouth of the Saco River, included "a large cabin surrounded by palisades made of large trees placed by the side of each other, in which they take refuge when their enemies make war upon them."[39]

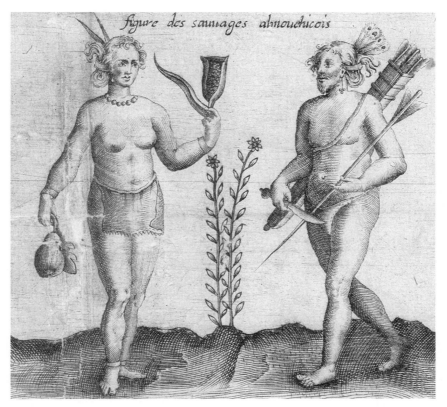

figure des sauuages abnouchicois

1.4 Armouchiquois man and woman. The woman has an ear of corn and a squash; the man carries a quiver on his back and holds an arrow in one hand and a European knife in the other. Detail from Samuel de Champlain, *Carte Geographique de la Nouvelle France*, 1612. Courtesy of John Carter Brown Library at Brown University.

REGIONAL TRADE NETWORKS

Although the Wabanaki bands were mostly self-sufficient communities, their highly mobile way of life enabled them to easily cross territorial boundaries. During periods of peace, for instance, periodic expeditions to neighboring villages took place. However, when intertribal relations turned hostile, the bands could strike against their enemies. Although foot travel was not uncommon, they mostly used their swift canoes, which made travel much faster and easier (fig. 1.5).[40]

Etchemin and Souriquois hunting groups living east of the Kennebec traded with the Armouchiquois from Saco and elsewhere, who supplied them with surplus produce from their gardens, "to wit, corn, tobacco, beans, and pumpkins [squash]."[41] On their long-distance trading journeys, Wabanaki tribesmen in general bartered such things as beautiful furs, strong moose-hide moccasins, dressed deerskins, and moose hides with the Narragansett and other southern neighbors. These trade goods were exchanged for luxuries such as wampum (blue and white beads made of quahog shell). Wampum was a specialty of the Narragansett of Rhode Island.

1.5 Detail showing Micmac canoes from Jean-Baptiste Louis Franquelin, *Carte pour servir à l'éclaircissement du Papier Terrier de la Nouvelle-France*, [1678]. Original in Bibliothèque Nationale, 125-1-1. Reproduced from a photograph in Library and Archives Canada, NMC 17393.

"From hence they [neighboring tribes] have most of their curious Pendants & Bracelets; from hence they have their great stone-pipes, which will hold a quarter of an ounce of Tobacco . . . they make them of greene, & sometimes of black stone [with Imagerie upon them]. . . . Hence likewise our Indians had their pots wherein they used to seeth their victuals."[42]

PERSONAL APPEARANCES

Described as "of average stature . . . handsome and well-shaped,"[43] the Wabanakis were generally "betweene five or six foote high, straight bodied, strongly composed, smooth skinned [and] merry countenanced."[44] Their robust life-style and ordinarily protein-rich diet made them a healthy people. Moreover, they made regular use of sweat baths, followed by massage, and "afterwards rubbing the whole body with seal oil" or other animal fat in order to "stand heat and cold better." By greasing themselves, they were also protected against "mosquitos, [which then] do not sting so much in the bare parts."[45] According to one early European traveler to the region, "You do not encounter a big-bellied, hunchbacked, or deformed person among them: those who are leprous, gouty, affected with gravel, or insane, are unknown to them."[46]

Their personal fashions, including hairstyle and ornamentation, not only reflected individual taste but also served as cultural markers indicating social divisions based on ethnic affiliation, rank, age, gender, or marital status. Decorative devices, such as headdresses, could involve colorful arrangements with bird feathers, wampum, dyed porcupine quills, or moose hair.[47]

Among eastern Wabanaki groups, in particular the Souriquois and Etchemin, adult men typically tied "a knot of [their hair], with a leather lace, which they let hang down behind."[48] Sometimes, a few bird feathers were woven into these topknots. When a warrior died, his relatives "upon his head stuck many feathers," before his burial.[49] In contrast to the adult men, boys wore their hair "of full length." They tied it "in tufts on the two sides with cords of leather." Some of them had their hair "ornamented with coloured Porcupine quills."[50]

At times, these eastern Wabanakis differed from their corn-growing neighbors west of the Sheepscot, who were clearly recognizable by their distinct hairstyle. Typically, these Armouchiquois shaved "their hair far up on the head," leaving it very long at the back, which they combed and twisted "in various ways very neatly, intertwined with feathers which they attach[ed] to the head."[51] Farther south, in Massachusetts Bay, tribesmen commonly wore their hair "tied up hard and short like a horse taile, bound close with a fillet . . . whereon they prick[ed] feathers of fowls in a fashion of a crownet."[52]

Sagamores were sometimes distinguished by their own particular headgear. Their prerogative was a bird with an aggressive reputation, described as a "black hawk" (probably the eastern kingbird). Viewed as a symbol of their bravery, the dead bird's "dried body" was affixed to the topknot in their hair. Although most Wabanaki men plucked out their scant facial hair, some chieftains distinguished themselves by growing beards.[53]

Among the eastern Wabanakis, in particular the Souriquois, adult women generally wore their hair loose on their shoulders. However, those who were not yet married wore theirs "also full length, but tie[d] it behind with the same cords." They beautified themselves by making "ornamental pieces of the size of a foot or eight inches square, all embroidered with Porcupine quills of all colours." One visitor described the ornament: "It is made on a frame, of which the warp is threads of leather from unborn Moose, a very delicate sort; the quills of Porcupine form the woof which they pass through these threads. . . . All around they make a fringe of the same threads, which are also encircled with these Porcupine quills in a medley of colours. In this fringe they place wampum, white and violet."[54]

In addition to wearing wampum necklaces and bracelets, Wabanaki men as well as women also pierced their ears, often in several places. Special pendants "as formes of birds, beasts, and fishes, carved out of bone, shells, and stone" hung from their pierced ears, in which they sometimes also stuck "long feathers or hares' tails."[55]

As noted earlier, Wabanaki tribesmen also used paint to distinguish themselves. "When they goe to their warres, it is their custome to paint their faces with a diversitie of colours, some being all black as jet, some red, some halfe red and halfe black, some blacke and white, others spotted with diver kinds of colours, being all distinguished to their enemies, to make them more terrible to their foes."[56] For instance, whereas Etchemin tribesmen at Pemaquid painted "their bodies with black; their faces, some with red, some with black, and some with blue,"[57] Souriquois mariners on the southern Maine coast were reported to have had "their eyebrows painted white."[58]

The Wabanakis, as well as their southern neighbors, also marked their skin with red and black tattoos. Among the Souriquois, and probably among the other native groups as well, women tattooed the skin of their husbands or lovers. At the Massachusetts coast, for instance, tribesmen had "certaine round Impressions downe the outside of their armes and brestes, in forme of mullets [stars] or spur-rowels [and] bearing upon their cheeks certaine pourtraitures of beasts, as Beares, Deares, Mooses, Wolves, &c, some of fowls, as of Eagles, Hawkes, &c."[59] These designs probably represented their animal guardian spirits of family totems. The Wabanakis believed that wearing such tattoos endowed them with special spirit power.

Garments were made by the women, who dressed the hides by scraping them and rubbing them with sea-bird oil. Next, the women cut the supple leather and stitched the pieces together as robes, mantles, breechclouts, leggings, or moccasins. Finally, the leather was painted or "ornamented with embroidery," using dyed moose hair or flattened porcupine quills. In addition to making a "lace-like pattern" or "broken chevrons," they also "studded [their clothing] with figures of animals," which were probably symbolic as well.[60] Small, funnel-sized copper objects, made of thin sheets rolled into form, were also used to embellish their clothing. Sometimes, the "leather buskins" of Wabanaki children were also decorated with these "little round pieces of red copper."[61]

During the warmer seasons, Wabanaki men usually donned a mantle made of smoothly dressed white moose hide or tanned deerskin, along with a soft leather breechclout, leggings, and moose-hide or sealskin moccasins. Usually, the moose-hide moccasins were made from old and greasy leather coats, which the women "embellish with dye & and edging of red and white Porcupine quills."[62] Occasionally, the men also wore coats made of wild goose or turkey feathers. When the weather turned cold, they were warmly dressed in thick fur robes made of beaver, otter, raccoon, or even bear skins. Black wolves were also highly valued; these furs were "esteemed a present for a prince" among the native peoples of the region.[63]

PLACE-NAMES: TURNING THE LANDSCAPE INTO A MAP

Native place-names in Wabanaki territories generally convey essential geographic information, describing the distinctive features of a locality such as its physical appearance, its specific dangers, or its precious resources. A name might, for instance, note where certain animals could be hunted, fish netted, or plants harvested. Specifically, *Shawokotec* (for Saco) referred to "the outlet of the river," *Pemaquid* signified "it is situated far out," *Machias* described "bad little falls," *Olamon* was the spot where "red ochre" for paint could be found, *Passamaquoddy* was attractive as "the place with plenty of Pollock," *Kenduskeag* was the "eel-weir place," and *Cobossecontee* (near Gardiner) was the place where "sturgeon could be found."[64]

Such place-names show how thoroughly familiar the Wabanakis were with the particular challenges and opportunities of their habitat. Ranging widely throughout northeastern North America, Wabanaki tribespeople depended dearly on such topographic marking points for their physical survival. Accumulating over hundreds, perhaps even thousands, of years, their individual experiences were committed to collective memory not only in the form of place-names but also in the form of tribal lore, tales, legends, songs, and, ultimately, myths. Thus embedded in their cultural fabric, place-names contain vital elements of ecological knowledge. Indeed, the purpose of place-names was "to turn the landscape into a map which, if studied carefully, literally gave a village's inhabitants the information they needed to sustain themselves."[65]

On their journeys, moving swiftly in their lightweight birch-bark canoes, the Wabanakis were guided by this knowledge. Place-names might indicate where to expect such difficulties as swift currents, dangerous rapids, and gravel bars or might suggest which fork to take or where to portage to a connecting travel route. Such information was crucial, especially when traveling for purposes of long-distance trade or raiding parties, but also during regular seasonal migrations. To this day, many place-names in New England and the Maritimes still contain elements of ancient Wabanaki toponyms.

Beyond the previously mentioned ecological toponyms, some place-names may derive from certain political realities in traditional Wabanaki society. For instance, early seventeenth-century European records reveal that Wabanaki tribesmen inhabiting the Maine coast in that period referred to the region from Cape Neddick to Schoodic Point (the end) as *Mawooshen* (also spelled *Moasson*).[66] Under this name, they apparently understood an area "fortie leagues in bredth, and fiftie in length, [comprising] nine rivers, [namely the] Quibiquesson, Pemaquid, Ramassoc, Apanawapeske, Apaumensek, Aponeg, Sagadehoc, Ashamahaga, Shawokotec."[67] Although we may always remain in the dark about the precise meaning of *Mawooshen*, it probably refers not to a stretch of land but to the confederacy of allied villages under a regional grand chief known as the Bashabes.

Other place-names make sense only in the context of native culture — place-names whose meanings are expressed in the context of the Wabanakis' particular worldview as recounted in myth. Traditional native storytellers attributed many topographic features in the landscape to the legendary activities of Gluskap, their culture-hero, who shaped the earth in a particular way so as to make it "a happy land for the people."[68] According to one story, rivers such as the Penobscot were formed when Gluskap killed the monster frog that had caused a world drought. The released waters streamed down the mountainsides toward the sea. Gluskap paddled along the coast in his canoe and entered all the rivers emptying into the ocean. "He inspected them. Wherever there were bad falls he lessened them so they would not be too dangerous for his descendants. He cleared the carrying places. Then he left his canoe upside down where it turned to stone [near Castine]. It may be seen there yet."[69]

In another legend, Gluskap beached his canoe on the eastern shore of Penobscot Bay and chased a moose up into the woods for a great distance.

> On the beach at the point mentioned is a rock about twenty-five feet long, shaped like an overturned canoe. The rocks leading from it bear footprints of Gluskap, which reappear frequently in the interior of the country according to some of the Indians who claim to have seen them. At another place farther down he killed the moose and cast its entrails across the water. There they still appear as streaks of white rock on the bottom of the bay at Cape Rosier. After cooking the moose he left his cooking pot overturned on the shore of Moosehead Lake and it is now to be seen as Kineo mountain on the eastern margin. . . . When the Indians find stones possessing natural shapes, resembling a face or a person, they sometimes keep them [saying]: "It looks like Gluskap, I guess he left his picture on it."[70]

NATIVE CARTOGRAPHY

Although there are no indications that the Wabanakis kept permanent cartographic collections, there is evidence that they made maps for temporary needs. If, for instance, a local scout encountered enemy tribesmen secretly roaming in the area, he would illustrate this for his kinsmen by scratching on a piece of bark a picture of the place, indicating the streams, points, and other landmarks. Sometimes, he would leave incisions in the bark of a tree near a stream, where his friends would follow by canoe, or place sticks on a trail, indicating that a message in picture writing, known as a *wikhegan*, was hidden nearby.[71]

Commenting on the use of such *wikhegan* among the Wabanakis inhabiting the Kennebec River area, a French missionary reported: "There [one of the tribesmen] took the bark of a tree, upon which with coal he drew [a picture of] the English around me, and one of them cutting off my head. (This is all the writing the Indians have, and they communicate among themselves by these sorts of drawings as understandingly as we do by our letters). He then put this kind of letter around a stick which he planted on the bank of the river, to give news to those passing by of what had happened to me" (see fig. 1.6).[72]

Wikhegan also served to depict regional maps. "They have much ingenuity in drawing upon bark a kind of map which marks exactly all the rivers and streams of a country of which they wish to make a representation. They mark all the places thereon exactly and so well that they make use of them successfully, and an Indian who possesses one makes long voyages without going astray" (see figs. 1.7 and 1.8).[73]

At certain points on the travel routes of the Wabanakis, tribespeople marked messages on rock ledges, which may have served as information centers. Traditionally such *wikhegan* could be found on the ledges of Hampden Narrows, which was therefore known as *Edalawikekhadimuk* (place where are markings). These marks probably indicated "the exact number of canoes going

1.6 *Wikhegan* map on birch bark (ca. 1840) by Gabrien Acquin, a Maliseet describing his hunting trip. The *wikhegan* was left for his friend, who had gone down the river. From Mallery, "Picture-Writing of the American Indians," 336.

1.7 *Wikhegan* map on birch bark (ca. 1800) by Chief Selmo Soctomah, a Passamaquoddy Chief from Pleasant Point describing a moose hunt. From Mallery, "Picture-Writing of the American Indians," 339.

up and down the river."[74] Such markings also existed at Fort Point in Stockton Springs, a place the Wabanakis knew as *Aguahassidek* (stepping ashore). One of the traditional Penobscot tribal leaders recounted that "on their annual trip to salt water for the purpose of fishing," his ancestors "gave names to a number of places along the bay and river." Landing on the west bank of the river where it flows into Penobscot Bay, "they only stopped long enough to make the sign

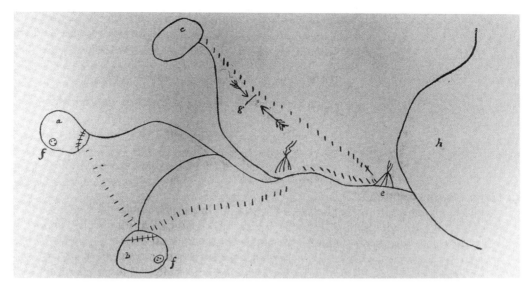

1.8 *Wikhegan* map on birch bark (ca. 1885) by Nicholas Francis, an old Penobscot hunter (from Old Town), representing a beaver trapping district near Moosehead Lake. From Mallery, "Picture-Writing of the American Indians," 338.

of their visit, showing which direction they were going, the number of their party and canoes, etc. On account of its being a marking place no one was ever allowed to mar or deface its outline by using it for a camping ground."[75]

Today, remarkable petroglyphs with canoes, birds, moose, humans, and other designs remain visible on a ledge at the west bank of the upper Kennebec River (Embden). Similar glyphs can still be seen on coastal rocks at Machias Bay (Birch Point). One mark at Machias appears to represent a native woman with sea-fowl on her head. One local Passamaquoddy hunter interpreted this symbol to mean "that squaw had smashed canoe, saved beaver-skin, walked on-half moon all over alone toward east, just same as heron wading alongshore." The hunter also noted that the three lines hammered out below the figure together resembled a bird track, or a trident, and represented the three rivers — the East, West, and Middle rivers of Machias — that merge not far above Birch Point (fig. 1.9).[76]

WENOOCH: WHO ARE THESE STRANGERS?

Thinking themselves to be the easternmost people on earth, the Wabanakis were unaware of Europeans until they sighted the first sailing ships in the early sixteenth century. Initially amazed to see bearded strangers landing on their shores, they "could not get over their wonder as they gazed at our customs, our clothing, our arms, our equipment," reported one of the early French visitors to the area.[77] Their original surprise is reflected in the Wabanaki name for the alien-looking invaders from across the ocean: *wenooch* (stranger), derived from their word for "who is that?" Other telling names, used by neighboring tribes, include "boat-men" (*mistek-oushou*), "coat-men" (*wautaconauog*), and "sword-men" or "knife-men" (*chauquaquock*).[78] New technologies, in particular steel knives, hatchets, copper kettles, glass beads, awls, mirrors,

1.9 Petroglyphs at Birch Point, Machias Bay. From Mallery, "Picture-Writing of the American Indians," 1893, plate 12.

woolen cloth, and eventually firearms, were especially appreciated by the Wabanakis and could be had in exchange for wild animal pelts.

Despite their sometimes high regard for European innovations, the Wabanakis typically regarded the strangers "as physically inferior" and "found them ugly, especially because of their excessive hairiness."[79] According to one early European who lived among the Wabanakis: "[They] regard themselves as much richer than we are . . . Also they consider themselves more ingenious, [and] they conclude generally that they are superior to all Christians."[80] An eastern Wabanaki (Micmac) tribesman may have revealed the natives' typical attitude toward the Europeans who landed on their shores when he said: "You deceive yourself greatly if you think to persuade us that your country is better than ours. For if France, as you say, is a little terrestrial paradise, are you sensible to leave it?"[81]

Although no early Wabanaki maps on birch bark or other material are believed to have survived, some documentary records indicate native cartographic skills. A wonderful piece of evidence concerning native mapmaking skill is a reference in Captain Bartholomew Gosnold's account of his voyage to the Maine coast in 1602. Referring to a surprise encounter with a party of Souriquois traders at Cape Neddick, he reported, "One that seemed to be their commander . . . with a piece of chalk described the coast thereabouts, and could name Placentia [Plaisance] of the Newfoundland."[82]

Other early European records comment on the guiding skills of Wabanaki tribesmen living in the Pemaquid coastal region. Sir Ferdinando Gorges, for example, a well-known English entrepreneur who acquired colonial title over parts of Maine as its "Lord Proprietor," wrote that he understood the natives themselves to be "exact pilots for that coast [between Cape Cod and Cape Breton], having been accustomed to frequent the same, both as fishermen, and in passing along the shore to seek their enemies."[83]

During the same period, the French navigator Samuel de Champlain ran into some native mariners off Cape Ann, who offered him an accurate description of the region ahead. "I made them understand, as best as I could, that they should show me how the coast lay. After having depicted for them, with a piece of charcoal, the bay and the Island Cape, where we were, they represented for me, with the same crayon, another [Massachusetts] bay, which they showed as very large. They put six pebbles at equal distances, thus giving me to understand that each of these stood for as many chiefs and tribes. Then they represented within this bay a river [Merrimac] which we had passed, which extends very far."[84]

But, given the strategic potential of geographic intelligence, it is understandable that Wabanaki tribesmen became increasingly reluctant informants when strangers came to their lands requesting vital geographic information, such as the location of lakes, rivers, mountains, and other marking points in the landscape. This resentment became clear when an English surveyor requested their help on an expedition to the upper Penobscot and Moosehead Lake region in the 1760s. "The Indians are so jealous of their countrey being exposed by this survey," he wrote, "as made it impracticable for us to perform this work with acqurice."[85] When finally a few tribesmen were induced to serve as guides, they did so on condition that the foreigners take no notes and make no maps.[86]

Their request was not heeded. Soon, an abstract grid of meridians and parallels clamped the wilderness. Forced to yield to analytical cartographic representation, Ketakamigwa was no longer terra incognita to the strangers. Powerless to shield their homeland from European intruders, the Wabanakis may have recalled what their divine hero Gluskap told them as he climbed on the back of a giant whale to travel to an unknown island in the western seas: "I shall leave you and shall hearken no more to your calling, but shall wait the calling of the Great Spirit. Strange things shall happen, but those who bring about the changes will tell you all about them so you may understand them."[87] Indeed, the Wabanakis have come to understand the changes, and all too well. Yet, as Gluskap's children, they endure and "look for the end of their oppressions and troubles when he comes back."[88]

NOTES

I thank Arthur Spiess and Emerson Baker, for their comments on an earlier draft of this paper, and especially my wife, Bunny McBride, for her skilful editorial hand.

1. Sebastian Rasle, "A Dictionary of the Abenaki Language in North America, [1690–1722]," in John Pickering, ed., *Memoirs of the American Academy of Arts and Sciences*, n.s., 1 (1833): 533. In Rasle's dictionary, the word is spelled *ketakamig8*. According to the orthographic system used by Dr. Frank Siebert of Old Town, Maine, the "correct" Penobscot, eastern Abenaki form is *ktahkamik* —(big land). Siebert notes that the Penobscots used the term to refer to the mainland (Siebert, personal communication).

2. George Popham, Letter to King James I, December 13, 1607, *Collections of the Maine Historical Society* 5 (1857): 359–60. For the notion that the native peoples in New England thought of their land as part of a larger island, see among others Handrick Aupamut, *History of the Muhheadkunnuk Indians* (1790), in *Massachusetts Historical Society Collections* 9 (1804): 101; William Wood, *New England's Prospect* (Boston: Publications of the Prince Society, 1865), 2; Edward Winslow, "Winslow's Relation" (1624), in *Massachusetts Historical Society Collections*, 2d set., 9 (1832): 99.

3. Rasle, "Dictionary," 434; Frank G. Speck, "Penobscot Tales and Religious Beliefs," *Journal of American Folklore* 48 (1935); 4, 18–19. Dr. Frank Siebert suggests that the term *ketchiniweskwe* (great spirit) was invented by Roman Catholic missionaries. In Abenaki, the element *ni-wes* refers to dry seed (of corn), metaphorically expressing the idea of "spirit of life" (Siebert, personal communication).

4. Among others, see Joseph Laurent, *New Familiar Abenakis and English Dialogues, the First Ever Published on the Grammatical System by Jos. Laurent, Abenakies Chief* (Quebec: L. Brosseau, 1884), 46–47.

5. Nicolar, *Life and Traditions*, 7. Note that there are various spellings of the name Gluskap, including *Gloosk-ob*, *Koluskap*, and *Slooscap*.

6. There is no agreement on the precise etymology or meaning of the name Gluskap. See among others Nicolar, *Life and Traditions*, 12.

7. Frank G. Speck, "Aboriginal Conservators," *Bird-Lore* 40 (1938): 259.

8. Not surprisingly, a limited geographic understanding of territories beyond the immediate region is typical. Compare what Edmund Carpenter observed among the Inuit: "Aivilik men are keen geographers when describing their immediate surroundings. But once they venture to tell of the outer world, geography gives way to cosmography." Edmund Carpenter, Frederick Varley, and Roberty Flaherty, *Eskimo* (Toronto: University of Toronto Press, 1959), n.p.

9. For a brief review of Paleo-Indian remains in the region, see among others Arthur E. Spiess and Deborah B. Wilson, *Michaud: A Paleoindian Site in the New England-Maritimes Region*, Occasional Publications in Maine Archaeology 6 (Augusta, Maine Historical Preservation Commission and the Maine Archeological Society, 1987), 129–55.

10. David Sanger, *Discovering Maine's Archaeological Heritage* (Augusta: Maine Historical Preservation Commission, 1979), 20; Sanger, "Maritime Adaptations in the Gulf of Maine," *Archaeology of Eastern North America* 18 (1988): 84; and William Cronon, *Changes in the Land: Indians, Colonists, and the Ecology of New England* (New York: Hill and Wang, 1983), 27.

11. "The Description of the Country of Mawooshen," in Samuel Purchas, *Hakluytus Posthumus or Purchas His Pilgrimes, Contayning a History of the World, in Dea Voyages, and Lande-Travells, by Englishmen and Others*, 20 vols. (Glasgow: James MacLehose and Songs, 1906), 19:400. Perhaps forest burning also occurred among the eastern Wabanakis inhabiting Acadia (in particular Nova Scotia and New Brunswick); see Nicolas Denys, *The Description and Natural History of the Coasts of North America (Acadia)*, ed. and trans. William F. Ganong (Toronto: Champlain Society, 1908), 377. For evidence of this practice in Massachusetts, see Wood, *New England's Prospect*, 17; see also Cronon, *Changes*, 48–52, 181–82, and Thomas Morton, *The New English Canaan, or New Canaan: Containing an Abstract of New England Composed in Three Books* (Boston: Prince Society, 1883).

12. The precontact population estimates remain subject to debate. Pierre Biard, a French Jesuit missionary active among the eastern Wabakakis (1611–13), noted in his 1616 treatise *Relation de la Nouvelle France . . .* that natives informed him "that in the region of the great river [St. Lawrence], from Newfoundland to Choeacoet [Saco], there cannot be more than nine or ten thousand people." He added, "I believe it is the highest number" (Thwaires, *Jesuit Relations* 3:109–11). In this context it is important to note that Dean R. Snow, in *The Archaeology of New England* (New York: Academic Press, 1980), 33–34 (reiterated in Dean Snow and Kim M. Lansphear, "European Contact and Indian Depopulation in the Northeast: The Timing of the First Epidemics," *Ethnohistory* 35, [1988]: 22–2), erroneously assumes that these figures are "post-epidemic" with respect to Wabanakis in northern New England. Indeed, Biard's earlier estimates were even lower by about half (Thwaires, *Jesuit Relations* 2:73). The number of 30,000 presented here is nothing but an educated guess and is relatively low in comparison with other recent estimates for the region. For instance, Dean Snow calculated that there were about 10,000 western Wabanakis (including Penacooks), 11,900 Wabanakis from Saco to the Penobscot (Armouchiquois and Etchemins), and another 7,600 eastern Wabanakis (Etchemins) in the St. Croix and St. John river areas. Farther east, he estimated the pre-epidemic number of Micmacs in the Maritimes at about 13,000 (Snow, *Archaeology*, 33–34). Snow's total population estimate for the groups here identified at eastern and western Wabanakis is 42,500. In this context, it is of interest to note that Snow's estimate for the Micmacs is substantially lower than the 35,000 recently suggested by Virginia Miller (who concluded that this was "not an unlikely minimum figure") in her article "Aboriginal Micmac Population: A Review of the Evidence," *Ethnohistory* 23(1976): 117–27. If Miller's figure had been taken into account, the total population for northern New England and the Maritimes would have been nearly 75,000.

13. The issue of ethnicity is problematical. For a more detailed discussion of Wabanaki ethnicity, see Harald Prins, *Tribulations of a Border Tribe: The Case of the Aroostook Band of Micmacs in Maine* (Ann Arbor: University Microfilms International, 1988), 152–202.

14. Biard, in Thwaites, *Jesuit Relations* 2:73.

15. "Description of the Country of Mawooshen," in Purchase, *Hakluytus Posthumus* 19:402–3. The orthography of Wabanaki names presents us with difficulties. For instance, Mentaurmet's name (as spelled by the English) was written as *Meteourmite* in Biard's 1612 letter (in Thwaites, *Jesuit Relations* 2:41).

16. Biard, in Thwaites, *Jesuit Relations* 3:89.

17. I am not suggesting that tribal territoriality among the Wabanaki ethnic groups conformed to what has been termed the "riverine model." See also Harald E.L. Prins, "Micmacs and Maliseets in the St. Lawrence River Valley," in W. Cowan ed., *Actes du 17e Congres des Algonquinistes* (Ottawa: Carleton University, 1986), 264–78; Prins, *Tribulations*, 274–76.

18. This section on material culture draws on a variety of sources, including accounts by Biard, Morton, Wood, and Denys. Other important sources include Samuel de Champlain, *The Works of Samuel de Champlain*,

ed. H.P. Biggar, 6 vols. (Toronto: Champlain Society, 1922–36); James Rosier, "A True Relation of the Most Prosperous Voyage Made This Present Yeare 1605, by Captain G. Weymouth, in the Discovery of the Land Virginia," in Henry D. Burrage, ed., *Rosier's Relation of Weymouth's Voyage to the Coast of Maine, 1605* (Portland: Gorges Society, 1887), 38–75; Marc Lescarbot, *The History of New France*, 3 vols. (Toronto: Champlain Society, 1907–14); John Josselyn, "An Account of Two Voyages to New England," *Massachusetts Historical Society Collections*, 2d ser., 3 (1833): 211–396.

19. Sebastien Rasle, Letter from Norridgewock (October 12, 1723), *Collections and Proceedings of the Maine Historical Society* 4 (1893): 267. According to Champlain (*Works* 2:15), "From Saco along the whole coast as far as Tadoussac [these birch bark canoes] are all alike." These Wabanaki hunting canoes, often no more than ten feet long, usually carries only about four to six individuals. Larger ocean-going canoes could measure more than twenty feet, carrying a fairly large number of people. Also note that Champlain (*Works* 1:338) observed that the wooden dugouts, not reported among the Wabanaki, were used south of Cape Ann, in Massachusetts and beyond.

20. Denys, *Description and Natural History*, 422; Morton, *New English Canaan*, 186.

21. Josselyn, "Account of Two Voyages," 297–98.

22. Rasle, Letter from Norridgewock, 266; Charles G. Willoughby, "Homes and Gardens of New England Indians," *American Anthropologist* 8 (1906); 116. The quote is from Biard, in Thwaites, *Jesuit Relations* 2:41.

23. Josselyn, "Account of Two Voyages," 307.

24. See among others Jesse D. Jennings, *Prehistory of North American* (Mountain View, Calif.: Mayfield Publishing Co., 1989), 258–60.

25. For general overview, see K.M. Bennett, "The Food Economy of the New England Indians," *Journal of Political Economy* 63 (1955): 269–97. See also Harald Prins, "Cornplanters at Meductic: Ethnic and Territorial Reconfigurations in Colonial Acadia," *Man in the Northeast* no. 44(1992): 55–72.

26. Biard, in Thwaites, *Jesuit Relations* 2:73.

27. Denys, *Description and Natural History*, 349.

28. Lescarbot, in Thwaites, *Jesuit Relations* 2:185. See also Rosier, who wrote that Wabanaki tribesmen on the central Maine coast hunted whales "with a multitude of their boats" (Rosier, "True Relations," 158).

29. Denys, *Description and Natural History*, 359, 171; see also Wood, *New England's Prospect*, 40, 75, 108.

30. Morton, *New English Canaan*, 39, 107, 226.

31. Denys, *Description and Natural History*, 435–37.

32. Ibid., 380, 381; Wood, *New England's Prospect*, 75; for wild rice gathering, see also Frank G. Speck, *Penobscot Man: The Life History of a Forest Tribe in Maine* (Philadelphia: University of Pennsylvania Press, 1940), 92. Frank G. Speck, "Medicine Practices on the North-eastern Algonquians," *International Congress of Americanists Proceedings* 19 (1915): 303–21.

33. Biard, in Thwaites, *Jesuit Relations* 2:77.

34. Thwaites, *Jesuit Relations* 2:49, 167, 249, 3:225. *Kenduskead* is sometimes also referred to as *Kedesquit*. See also Thwaites, *Jesuit Relations* 2:49, 3:225, and Snow, *Archaeology*, 33–47.

35. Based on Louis Paul (personal communication, 1985). Earlier, a Canadian missionary, J.A. Maurault, in *Histoire des Abenakis, depuis 1605 jusqu'à nos jours* (Sorel, Québec, Canada: L'Atelier Typographique de la Gazette de Sorel, 1866), suggested that the term referred to "land of the little dogs." See also Prins, *Tribulations*, 162.

36. Peter Thomas, "Contrastive Subsistence Strategies and Land Use as Factors for Understanding Indian-White Relations in New England," *Enthohistory* 23, (1976): 6–13, quotation on page 13; Howard S. Russell, *Indian New England before the Mayflower* (Hanover, N.H.: University Press of New England, 1980), 150–51; James Petersen (personal communication, 1989).

37. See among others Champlain, *Works* 1:327–30, 3:374–75; Lescarbot, *History of New France* 1:195; Wood, *New England's Prospect*, 106; Rasle, Letter from Norridgewock, 269; Morton, *New English Canaan*, 160; Russell, *Indian New England*, 168.

38. Wood, *New England's Prospect*, 75–77, quotation on page 75; Morton, *New English Canaan*, 205–21; Denys, *Description and Natural History*, 356–57.

39. Samuel de Champlain, *Voyages of Samuel de Champlain, 1604–1618*, ed. W.L. Grant (New York: Charles Scribner's Sons, 1907), 61–63.

40. Wood, *New England's Prospect*, 102.

41. Lescarbot, *History of New France* 2:324.

42. Wood, *New England's Prospect*, 69 (quotation), 79; Morton, *New English Canaan*, 201; B.F. De Costa, *Ancient Norumbega, or the Voyages of Simon Ferdinando and John Walker to the Perobscot River, 1579–1580* (Albany, N.Y.: Joel Munsell's Sons, 1890), 7. Regarding the intertribal trade in moose hides, it should be noted that similar

networks existed in the St. Lawrence River valley, for example, where horticultural Hurons acquired hides from Montagnais hunters in exchange for surplus corn.

43. In Thwaites, *Jesuit Relations* 2:73, 3:75. For a good overview, see also Charles G. Willoughby, "Dress and Ornament of the New England Indians," *American Anthropologist* 7 (1905): 499–508.

44. Wood, *New England's Prospect*, 70.

45. Biard, in Thwaites, *Jesuit Relations* 3:117.

46. Ibid., 75.

47. For a good overview, see also Ruth H. Whitehead, "Every Thing They Make and Wear," unpublished manuscript, n.d., Provincial Museum of Nova Scotia, Halifax.

48. Lescarbot, *History of New France* 3:133–34.

49. Champlain, *Works* 1:444–45; generally, according to Lescarbot (*History of New France* 3:133), eastern Wabanaki groups such as the Micmacs did not fancy these decorative elements. However, when Jacques Cartier encountered tribespeople (who could have been Micmacs) in the Gulf of St. Lawrence in 1532, he described them as having topknots in which they wove "a few bird's feathers." In H.P. Biggar, *The Voyages of Jacques Cartier* (Ottawa: Public Archives of Canada, 1924), 22–23.

50. Denys, *Description and Natural History*, 414.

51. Champlain, *Voyages* (New York: Charles Scribner's Sons, 1907), 61–63; Lescarbot, *History of New France* 3:135.

52. John Breaton, "A Briefe and True Relation of the Discoverie of the North Part of Virginia . . . Made This Present Yeere 1602," in L.B. Wright, ed., *The Elizabethan's America: A Collection of Early Reports by Englishmen on the New World* (Cambridge: Harvard University Press, 1965), 143; Daniel Gookin, *Historical Collection of the Indians in New England*, in *Massachusetts Historical Society Collections*, 1st set., 1 (1806): 153; Wood, *New England's Prospect*, 71–72. The Wampanoags in southern Massachusetts were described as wearing "on their heads long hair to the shoulders, only cut before [and] some trussed up before with a feather, broad-wise, like a fan; another fox tail hanging out." William Bradford, cited in H.C. Porter, *The Inconsistent Savage: England and the North American Indian, 1500–1660* (London Duckworth, 1979), 429.

53. Morton, *New English Canaan*, 197; Wood, *New England's Prospect*, 31, 74. The Micmac chieftain Membertou was described as "bearded like a Frenchman" (Thwaites, *Jesuit Relations*, 2:23; see also Lescarbot, *History of New France* 3:140). Elsewhere, tribesmen were described a "thin-bearded," and some even sported false beards fashioned "of the hair of beasts" (Breton, in Forter, *Inconsistant Savage*, 414).

54. Denys, *Description and Natural History*, 414.

55. Wood, *New England's Prospect*, 84; see also Denys, *Description and Natural History* 414; J.P. Baxter, ed., *Documentary History of the State of Maine*, col. 10 (Portland: Maine Historical Society, 1920), 463.

56. Wood, *New England's Prospect*, 95.

57. Rosier, in Porter, *Inconsistant Savage*, 270; see also Josselyn, "Account of two Voyages," 297–98.

58. Breton, in Wright, *Elizabethan's America*, 137–38.

59. Abbe S. Maillard, *An Account of the Customs and Manners of the Micmakis and Maricheets Savage Nations, New Dependent on the Government of Cape Breton* (London: S. Hooper and A. Morley, 1758), 55; Sieur N. de Dièreville, *Relation of the Voyage to Port Royal in Acadia or New France*, ed. J.C. Webster (Toronto: Champlain Society, 1933), 169–70. The quote is from Wood, *New England's Prospect*, 74.

60. The quotations are from Denys, *Descriptions and Natural History*, 407, 411; Biard, in Thwaites, *Jesuit Relations* 3:75; see also Wood, *New England's Prospect*, 101.

61. Rosier, "True Relation," 121. This red copper may have been mined locally, since the eastern Wabanakis were familiar with various mines on the coast of the Bay of Fundy. Early French explorers, including Champlain, refer to these mines (see also Thwaites, *Jesuit Relations* 3:296); a leather belt found at Merriconeag Sound, Maine, included some four hundred red copper pieces of varied size, attached to each other with soft leather strings (in *History Magazine* [1969]), 247.

62. Denys, *Description and Natural History*, 411; see also Wood, *New England's Prospect*, 108; Morton, *New English Canaan*, 201.

63. Denys, *Description and Natural History*, 370, 407, 411, 413; Wood, *New England's Prospect*, 73, 108; Morton, *New English Canaan*, 201, 207, 209, 210; see also Biard, in Thwaites, *Jesuit Relations* 3:75.

64. For the etymology of native place-names in Maine, see especially Fanny H. Eckstorm, *Indian Place Names of the Penobscot Valley and the Maine Coast* (1941; reprint, Orono: University of Maine at Orono Press, 1978).

65. Cronon, *Changes*, 65.

66. The meaning of *Mawooshen* remains unclear. Frank Siebert (personal communication, 1988) suggests that it refers to the Mousam River. In this context, it is of interest to note that Eckstorm (*Indian Place Names*, 101)

"Discovered that many place names which Peboscot Indians could not translate were easily interpreted by Passamaquoddy and Micmac Indians." Recently, a Maliseet speaker, Louis Paul of Woodstock Reserve, New Brunswick, suggested that *mawooshen* refers to "a bunch of people walking or acting together"— *mawe* referring to a "coming together" of more than two people.

67. Captain George Popham, Letter to King James I (written from Fort St. George, December 13, 1607), in *Collections of the Maine Historical Society* 5(1857): 359–60. Samuel Purchas, *Purchas, His Pilgrimage, or Relations of the World and the Religions Observed in All Ages and Places Discovered, from the Creation unto This Present*, 3rd ed. (London: Printed by William Stansby for H. Fetherstone, 1617), 939–41.

68. Nicolar, *Life and Traditions*, 5.

69. Frank G. Speck, "Penobscot Tales," 42.

70. Speck, "Penobscot Tales," 42–45; see also Eckstorm, *Indian Place Names*, 200–201.

71. Among others, see Garrick Mallery, "Petroglyphs in North America," *Tenth Annual Report of the Bureau of Ethnology to the Secretary of the Smithsonian Institution, 1888–1889* (Washington, D.C.: Government Printing Office, 1893).

72. Rasle, Letter from Norridgewock, 300.

73. Chrestien Le Clercq, *New Relation of Gaspesia, with the Customs and Religion of the Gaspesian Indians*, trans. and ed. William F. Ganong (Toronto: Champlain Society, 1910), 136; see also Wilson D. Wallis and Ruth S. Wallis, *The Micmac Indians and Eastern Canada* (Minneapolis: University of Minnesota Press, 1955), 54–56.

74. See among others Mark Hedden, "Form of the Cosmos in the Body of the Chaman," *Maine Archaeology Society Bulletin 27* (Spring 1987): ii–iv; Marc Hedden, "Prehistoric Maine Petroglyphs" (a video-script), *Maine Archeological Society Bulletin* 28(1988). The quotation is by Father Michael C.H. O'Brien, in Eckstorm, *Indian Place Names*, 66.

75. Joseph Nicolar, alias "Young Sebatis," in the *Old Town Herald* (1887?), reprinted in Eckstorm, *Indian Place Names*, 239–41, see also 65–66. Note that this place-name was originally spelled *Arquar-har-see-dek* by Nicolar.

76. In Malley, "Petroglyphs," 83. (Note than Birch Point is also referred to as Clarks Point.)

77. Lescarbot, *History of New France* 3:21.

78. *Wenooch*, also spelled *Waunnuxuh* or *a8enn8tsak*, is derived from *awaun-ewo* (who is that?) (plural *tsk*): Rasle, "Dictionary" 458; Trumbull, note 1 in Morton, "New English Canaan," 254; Roger William, *Key into the Language of the Indians of New England (1643)*, in *Massachusetts Historical Society Collections*, 1st ser., 3(1794): 89. When the eastern Wabanakis became more familiar with early Europeans on their coasts, they learned to communicate in pidgin with the strangers, referring to English as "Ingres," to the French generally as "Normans," to those from St. Malo as "Samaricois," and the Basques as "Bascua" (Biard, in Thwaites, *Jesuit Relations* 1:163).

79. Cornelius Jaenen, "Amerindian Views of French Culture in the Seventeenth Century," *Canadian Historical Review* 60 (1974): 271, 272; see also Biard, in Thwaites, *Jesuit Relations* 3:22, 75.

80. Biard, in Thwaites, *Jesuit Relations* 1:175; Francois Du Creux, *The History of Canada or New France*, ed. J.B. Conacher, 2 vols. (Toronto: Champlain Society, 1962), 1:160.

81. Cited in LeClerq, *New Relations*, 104.

82. Gabriel Archer, in *Massachusetts Historical Society Collections*, 3d ser., 8 (1843): 73–74.

83. Ferdinando Gorges, *A Briefe Narration of the Originall Undertakings of the Advancement of Plantations into the Parts of America, Especially Shewing the Beginning, Progress and Continuance of That of New England* (Boston: Publications of the Prince Society, 1890), 2:10.

84. [Samuel de Champlain], *The Voyages and Explorations of Samuel de Champlain, 1604–1616, Narrated by Himself, together with the Voyage of 1603*, trans. Annie N. Bourne, ed. Edward G. Bourne, 2 vols. (New York: Allerton Book Co., 1922), 1:106, 110.

85. Joseph Chadwick, "Survey of Routes to Canada, from Fort Pownal on the Penobscot to Quebec," manuscript, 1764, State Archives, Massachusetts State Library, Boston. Segments of this manuscript are cited in Eva L. Butler and Wendell D. Hadlock, "A Preliminary Survey of the Munsungan-Allagash Waterways," *Robert Abbe Museum Bulletin* 8 (1962): 17. Colonel Montresor, in *Maine Historical Society Collections 1* (1931): 354.

86. According to Butler and Hadlock, "[Chadwick] was allowed to keep no books and make no maps at the time, but later made a fairly accurate map and well documented account of his trip despite the difficulties he encountered" ("Preliminary Survey," 17).

87. Nicolar, *Life and Traditions*, 64.

88. Silas T. Rand, *Legends of the Micmacs* (1894; reprint, New York and London: Johnson Reprint Corp., 1971), 156.

Article Two

The French Presence in Huronia: The Structure of Franco–Huron Relations in the First Half of the Seventeenth Century

Bruce G. Trigger

Few studies of Canadian history in the first half of the seventeenth century credit sufficiently the decisive role played at that time by the country's Native peoples. The success of European colonizers, traders, and missionaries depended to a greater degree than most of them cared to admit on their ability to understand and accommodate themselves not only to Native customs but also to a network of political and economic relationships that was not of their own making. Traders and missionaries often were forced to treat Algonkians and Iroquoians as their equals and sometimes they had to acknowledge that the Indians had the upper hand. If the Europeans were astonished and revolted by many of the customs of these Indians (often, however, no more barbarous than their own), they also admired their political and economic sagacity.[1] Indeed, one Jesuit was of the opinion that the Huron were more intelligent than the rural inhabitants of his own country.[2] If the missionary or fur trader felt compelled to understand the customs of the Indians, the modern historian should feel no less obliged to do so.

In order to appreciate the role that the Indians played in the history of Canada in the first half of the seventeenth century, it is necessary to study their customs and behaviour and the things they valued. Because their way of life differed from that of the Europeans, the fur traders and missionaries who interacted with them frequently became amateur anthropologists, and some of them became very good ones. For some tribes the documentation amassed by these early contacts is extensive and of high quality. For no tribe is this truer than for the Huron.[3] From the detailed picture of Huronia that emerges from these studies, it is possible to ascertain the motives that prompted the behaviour of particular Indians, or groups of Indians, in a manner no less detailed than our explanations of those which governed the behaviour of their European contemporaries. I might add, parenthetically, that historians are not alone to blame for the failure to utilize anthropological insights in the study of early Canadian history. Iroquoian ethnologists and archaeologists have tended to avoid historical or historiographic problems. Only a few individuals, such as George T. Hunt, have attempted to work in the no man's land between history and anthropology.

Two explanations have been used by anthropologists and historians to justify the existing cleavage between their respective studies. One of these maintains that when the Europeans arrived in eastern North America, the Native tribes were engaged in a struggle, the origins and significance of which are lost in the mists of time and therefore wholly the concern of ethnohistorians. Because of this, there is no reason for the historian to try to work out in detail the causes of the conflicts and alliances that existed at that time.[4] Very often, however, the struggle between different groups is painted in crude, almost racist, terms (and in complete contradiction to the facts) as one between Algonkian- and Iroquoian-speaking peoples, the former being an indigenous population, mainly hunters, the latter a series of invading tribes

Source: "The French Presence in Huronia: The Structure of Franco–Huron Relations in the First Half of the Seventeenth Century," *Canadian Historical Review* 49 (1968): 107–41. Reprinted by permission of University of Toronto Press Incorporated (www.utpjournals.com).

growing corn and living in large villages. It should be noted that such a simplistic explanation of European history, even for the earliest periods, would now be laughed out of court by any competent historian. The alternative hypothesis suggests that European contact altered the life of the Indian, and above all the relationships among the different tribes, so quickly and completely that a knowledge of Aboriginal conditions is not necessary to understand events after 1600.[5] From an *a priori* point of view, this theory seems most unlikely. Old relationships have a habit of influencing events, even when economic and political conditions are being rapidly altered. Future studies must describe in detail how Aboriginal cultures were disrupted or altered by their contact with the Europeans, rather than assume that interaction between Indians and Europeans can be explained as a set of relationships that has little or no reference to the Native culture.

We will begin by considering developments in Huronia prior to the start of the fur trade.

THE HURON

When the Huron tribes were described for the first time in 1615,[6] they were living in the Penetanguishene Peninsula and the part of Simcoe County that runs along Matchedash Bay between Wasaga Beach and Lake Simcoe. The Huron probably numbered twenty to thirty thousand, and, according to the most reliable of the descriptions from the Jesuit missionaries,[7] they were divided into four tribes that formed a confederacy similar in its structure to the league of the Iroquois.[8] The Attignaouantan or Bear tribe, which included about half of the people in the confederacy, lived on the western extremity of Huronia. Next to them lived the Attingueenougnahak, or Cord tribe, and the Tahontaenrat or Deer tribe. Farthest east, near Lake Simcoe, were the Ahrendarrhonon or Rock nation. The Tionnontate, or Petun, who spoke the same language as the Huron and were very similar to them, inhabited the country west of Huronia near the Blue Mountain. The Petun, however, were not members of the Huron confederacy and prior to the arrival of the French, they and the Huron had been at war. Another Iroquoian confederacy, the Neutral, lived farther south between the Grand River and the Niagara frontier. Except for a few Algonkian bands that lived west of the Petun, there do not appear to have been any other Indians living in southern Ontario, except in the Ottawa Valley. The uninhabited portions of the province were the hunting territories of the Huron, Neutral, and Petun and also served as a buffer zone between these tribes and the Iroquois who lived south of Lake Ontario.

The Huron, like other Iroquoian tribes, grew corn, beans, and squash. These crops were planted and looked after by the women, who also gathered the firewood used for cooking and heating the houses. Contrary to popular notions, the men also made an important contribution to the tribal economy, inasmuch as it was they who cleared the fields for planting (no small task when only stone axes were available) and who caught the fish which were an important source of nutrition. Because of the high population density, the areas close to Huronia appear to have been depleted of game, and expeditions in search of deer had to travel far to the south and east.[9] In general, hunting appears to have been of little economic importance among the Huron.

Huron villages had up to several thousand inhabitants and the main ones were protected by palisades made of posts woven together with smaller branches. Inside large villages there were 50 or more longhouses, often 100 feet or more in length, made of bark attached to a light wooden frame. These houses were inhabited by eight to ten very closely related families. Families that traced themselves back to a common female ancestor formed a clan, which was a political unit having its own civil chief and war leader. Each tribe in turn was made up of a number of such clans and the clan leaders served on the tribal and confederal councils.[10]

The events that led to the formation of the Huron confederacy are not well understood. The Huron themselves said that it began around A.D. 1400, with the union of the Bear and Cord tribes, and grew thereafter through the addition of further lineages and tribes. Archaeologically it appears that, although one or more of the Huron tribes was indigenous to Simcoe County, other groups moved into historic Huronia from as far away as the Trent Valley, the Toronto region, and Huron and Grey counties to the west.[11] Two tribes, the Rock and the Deer, had been admitted to the confederacy not long before the arrival of the French.

Historians frequently have asserted that it was fear of the Iroquois that prompted the Huron to seek refuge in this remote and sheltered portion of Ontario.[12] While this may be why some groups moved into Huronia, it is clear that in prehistoric times the Huron outnumbered the Iroquois and probably were not at any military disadvantage. For this reason ethnologists have begun to seek other explanations to account for the heavy concentration of population in Huronia in historic times. An abundance of light, easily workable soil may be part of the answer. Since the Huron lacked the tools to work heavier soils, this advantage may have outweighed the tendency toward drought and the absence of certain trace minerals in the soil which now trouble farmers in that area.[13] Huronia also lay at the south end of the main canoe route that ran along the shores of Georgian Bay. North of there the soil was poor and the growing season short, so that none of the tribes depended on agriculture. They engaged mainly in hunting and fishing, and tribes from at least as far away as Lake Nipissing traded surplus skins, dried fish, and meat with the Huron in return for corn, which they ate in the winter when other food was scarce.[14]

As early as 1615 the French noted that Huronia was the centre of a well-developed system of trade. Hunt, however, seems to have seriously overestimated both the extent of this network and the degree to which the Huron were dependent on it.[15] The main trade appears to have been with the hunting peoples to the north, who happened to be Algonkian-speaking. The other Iroquoian tribes had economies similar to that of the Huron, so that with the exception of a few items, such as black squirrel skins, which came from the Neutral country, and tobacco from the Petun, trade with the other Iroquoian tribes was of little importance. Trade with the north, however, brought in supplies of dried meat, fish, skins, clothing, native copper, and "luxury items" such as charms, which were obtained in exchange for corn, tobacco, fishing nets, Indian hemp, wampum, and squirrel skins.[16] Although manufactured goods, as well as natural products, flowed in both directions, the most important item the Huron had for export undoubtedly was corn. In 1635 Father Le Jeune described Huronia as the "granary of most of the Algonkians."[17]

Whole bands of northerners spent the winters living outside Huron villages, trading furs and dried meat with their hosts in return for corn. The Huron assumed a dominant position in these trading relationships and the Jesuits record that when the Algonkians had dealings with them, they did so in the Huron language since the latter did not bother to learn Algonkian.[18] The social implications of such linguistic behaviour cannot be lost on anyone living in present-day Quebec. In the French accounts the Algonkians appear to have been better friends of the Rock tribe than they were of the Bear.[19]

Considerable quantities of European trade goods that are believed to date between 1550 and 1575 have been found in Seneca sites in New York State.[20] Since both archaeological and historical evidence suggests that there was contact between the Huron and the tribes that lived along the St. Lawrence River in the sixteenth century,[21] it is possible that trade goods were arriving in Huronia in limited quantities at this time as well. In any such trade the Algonkin [the Algonkian-speaking peoples of the Ottawa Valley] tribes along the Ottawa River would almost certainly have been intermediaries. It is thus necessary to consider the possibility that trade between the Huron and the northern Algonkians originally developed as a result of the Huron desire to obtain European trade goods.

There are a number of reasons for doubting that trade with the northern tribes had a recent origin. For one thing, the rules governing trade were exceedingly elaborate. A particular trade route was recognized as the property of the Huron tribe or family that had pioneered it, and other people were authorized to trade along this route only if they had obtained permission from the group to which it belonged.[22] Thus, since the Rock were the first Huron tribe to establish relations with the French on the St. Lawrence, they alone were entitled by Huron law to trade with them.[23] Because of the importance of this trade, however, the Rock soon "shared" it with the more numerous and influential Bear, and with the other tribes of Huronia.[24] The control of trade was vested in a small number of chiefs, and other men had to have their permission before they were allowed to engage in it.[25] An even more important indication of the antiquity of Huron contact with the north is the archaeological evidence of the Huron influence on the Native cultures of that region, which can be dated as early as A.D. 900 and is especially evident in pottery styles.[26] Taken together, these two lines of evidence provide considerable support for the hypothesis of an early trade.

In the historic period the Huron men left their villages to visit other tribes in the summers, while their women were working in the fields. Profit was not the only reason for undertaking long voyages. The Jesuits report that many travelled into distant regions to gamble or to see new sights — in short, for adventure. Trading expeditions, like war, were a challenge for young men.[27] Trading between different tribes was not always a safe and uncomplicated business and, for all they had to gain from trade during the historic period, the Huron frequently were hesitant to initiate trade with tribes of whom they had only slight acquaintance.

The dangers that beset intertribal contacts were largely products of another institution, as old, if not older than trade — the blood feud. If a man was slain by someone who was not his kinsman, his family, clan, or tribe (depending on how far removed the murderer was) felt obliged to avenge his death by slaying the killer or one of the killer's relatives. Such action could be averted only by reparations in the form of gifts paid by the group to which the murderer belonged to that of the murdered man. When an act of blood revenge actually was carried out, the injured group usually regarded it as a fresh injury; thus any killing, even an accidental one, might generate feuds that would go on for generations. This was especially true of intertribal feuds.[28]

The Huron and Five Nations had both suppressed blood feuds within their respective confederacies, but only with great difficulty. When quarrels arose between individuals from tribes not so united, they frequently gave rise to bloodshed and war. The chances of war were also increased because skill in raiding was a source of prestige for young men who therefore desired to pursue this activity.[29] If it were possible, prisoners captured in war were taken back to their captors' villages to be tortured to death, partly as an act of revenge, but also as a sacrifice to the sun or "god of war."[30] These three motives — revenge, individual prestige, and sacrifice — were common to all the Iroquoian-speaking peoples of the northeast and to many of their neighbours, and generated and sustained intertribal wars over long periods of time. Indeed, where no close political ties existed, such as those within the Huron confederacy, and where there were no mutually profitable trading relationships, war between tribes appears to have been the rule. The Huron were almost invariably at war with one or more of the Five Nations, and prior to the development of the fur trade (when they started to carry French goods to the south and west) they appear to have been at war with the Neutral and Petun as well.[31]

On the other hand, when a trading relationship developed between the Huron and some neighbouring tribe, every effort was made to control feuds that might lead to war between them. The payment that was made to settle a blood feud with the Algonkians was greater than that made to settle a feud inside the confederacy,[32] and the dearest payment on record was made to the French in 1648 to compensate them for a Jesuit *donné* murdered by some Huron chiefs.[33]

A second method of promoting stable relations between tribes that wished to be trading partners appears to have been the exchange of a few people both as a token of friendship and to assure each group that the other intended to behave properly. Very often, these hostages appear to have been children. Although this custom is never explicitly described by the early French writers, the evidence for its existence is clear-cut. A Huron, whose sons or nephews (sister's sons and therefore close relatives) were sent to the Jesuit seminary in Quebec, boasted that they were relatives of the French and for this reason hoped for preferential treatment when they went to trade on the St. Lawrence.[34] Others said they had "relatives" among the Neutral and Petun, and one man is reported as leaving his daughter with these relatives.[35] The priests and lay visitors who came to Huronia in early times were treated as kinsmen by the Huron, and families and individuals were anxious to have them live with them,[36] no doubt because the Huron regarded these visitors as pledges of good faith whose association with a particular family would establish good relations between that family and the French officials and traders downriver. The presentation of young children to Jacques Cartier at a number of villages along the St. Lawrence suggests, moreover, that this custom may have been an old one.[37]

The Huron thus not only traded with other tribes prior to the start of the fur trade, but also, in common with other tribes in the northeast, had developed a code or set of conventions that governed the manner in which this trade was conducted. Being a product of Indian culture, this code was designed to deal with specifically Indian problems. We will now turn to the French attempts to adapt themselves to the Native trading patterns after Champlain's first encounter with the Indians in 1608.

EARLY FRANCO–HURON RELATIONS

In 1608, the year Champlain established a trading post at Quebec, he was visited by the representatives of some Algonkin tribes from the Ottawa Valley, and, in order to win their respect for him as a warrior and to secure their goodwill, he agreed to accompany them the following year on a raid against their chief enemy, the Iroquois.[38] The regions to the north gave promise of more pelts and ones of better quality than did the Iroquois country to the south, and fighting with a tribe alongside its enemies was an effective way of confirming an alliance.[39] Thus Champlain's actions seem to have been almost inevitable. At the same time he probably also hoped to drive Iroquois raiders from the St. Lawrence Valley and to open the river as a valuable trade artery.[40]

When the Ottawa River Algonkin returned the next year, they were accompanied by a party of Huron warriors from the Rock tribe. In later times the Huron informed the Jesuits that they had first heard of the French from the Algonkians early in the seventeenth century, and as a result of this had decided to go downriver to meet these newcomers for themselves.[41] Very likely, Champlain's account and the Huron one refer to the same event. Some of the Ottawa River Algonkin, who were already probably in the habit of wintering in Huronia, may have tried to recruit Huron warriors for their forthcoming expedition against the Iroquois, and the Huron, prompted by curiosity and a desire for adventure, may have agreed to accompany them to Quebec.

Champlain was keenly interested at this time both in exploring the interior and in making contacts with the people who lived there. Learning the size of the Huron confederacy and their good relations with the hunting (and potentially trapping) peoples to the north, Champlain realized their importance for the development of the fur trade and set out to win their friendship. The Huron, on the contrary, were at first extremely hesitant in their dealings with the French,[42] in part because they had no treaty with them and also because they regarded the

French as allies of the Algonkin, who might become hostile if they saw the Hurons trying to establish an independent relationship with them.

The ambiguity of the Huron position can be seen in the exchange of children that was arranged in 1610. At that time the Huron gave Champlain custody of a boy, who was to go to France with him, and in exchange they received a young Frenchman. When the Huron departed, however, the French boy (probably Étienne Brûlé) did not leave with them, but stayed with Iroquet, an Algonkin chief from the lower Ottawa.[43] Iroquet, however, seems to have been one of the Algonkin who was in the habit of wintering in Huronia. Thus a three-sided exchange seems to have been arranged in which the Huron laid the basis for a friendly relationship with the French, but one that was subordinate to, and dependent upon, their relationship with the Algonkin.

As trade with the French increased, the Huron began to appreciate French goods and to want more of them. Metal awls and needles were superior to Native bone ones, and iron arrowheads could penetrate the traditional shields and body armour of their enemies. Metal kettles were easier to cook in than clay pots and metal knives were much more efficient than stone ones. Clearing fields and cutting wood was easier when stone axes were replaced by iron hatchets. Luxury items, such as cloth and European beads, were soon sought after as well.[44]

The growing demand for these products in a population that numbered between twenty and thirty thousand no doubt made the Huron anxious to establish closer relations with the French, without, if possible, having to recognize the Ottawa River Algonkin as middlemen or to pay them tolls to pass through their lands.[45] Since the principal item that the French wanted was beaver pelts,[46] the Huron probably also began to expand their trade with the north at this time in order to secure these furs in larger quantities. In return for these furs, they carried not only corn and tobacco but also French trade goods to their northern trading partners. The tribes north of Lake Huron seem to have continued to trade exclusively with the Huron rather than seeking to obtain goods from the French. No doubt this was in part because Huronia was nearby and reaching it did not require a long and hazardous journey down the Ottawa River. Such a journey would have been time-consuming, if not impossible, for a small tribe. More importantly, however, they wanted corn for winter consumption, which the Huron, but not the French, were able to provide. Although there is no documentary evidence to support this suggestion, it seems likely that increasing supplies of corn permitted these hunters to devote more time to trapping and relieved them of some of their day-to-day worries about survival.[47] Thus the growth of the fur trade may have led the northern groups to concentrate on trapping and the Huron to devote more of their energy to producing agricultural surpluses to trade with the north.[48] On at least one occasion, the Huron were providing even the French at Quebec with needed supplies of food.[49] In the 1640s their close friends and trading partners, the Nipissing, were travelling as far north as James Bay each year in order to collect the furs which they passed on to the Huron.[50]

In spite of the Huron desire for French goods and their ability to gather furs from the interior, the development of direct trade between Huronia and the St. Lawrence required the formation of a partnership that was expressed in terms the Indian could understand. Without continual assurances of goodwill passing between Huron and French leaders and without the exchange of gifts and people, no Huron would have travelled to Quebec without fear and trepidation. Even after many years of trade, Hurons going to Quebec felt safer if they were travelling with a Frenchman whom they knew and who could be trusted to protect their interests while they were trading.[51] Champlain understood clearly that treaties of friendship were necessary for successful trading partnerships with the Indians. For this reason he had been willing to support the Algonkin and Montagnais in their wars with the Mohawk and, since it was impossible to be friendly with both sides, had maintained his alliance with these northern tribes in spite of Iroquois overtures for peace.[52] The cementing of a treaty with the various Huron tribes was clearly the main reason he visited Huronia in 1615, a visit made in the face of considerable opposition from the Ottawa River Algonkin.[53]

Quite properly in Huron eyes, Champlain spent most of his time in Huronia with the Rock tribe. This had been the first of the Huron tribes to contact him on the St. Lawrence and therefore had a special relationship with the French according to Huron law. When he accompanied a Huron war party on a traditional, and what appeared to him as an ill-fated, raid against the central Iroquois, Champlain was resorting to a now-familiar technique for winning the friendship of particular tribes.[54] What Champlain apparently still did not realize was that the aim of these expeditions was adventure and taking prisoners, rather than the destruction of enemy villages.[55] The Huron were undoubtedly far more pleased with the results of the expedition than Champlain was.

From 1615 on, a number of Frenchmen were living in Huronia; their main purpose in being there was to encourage the Huron to trade.[56] Many of these young men, like the coureurs de bois of later times, enjoyed their life among the Indians and, to the horror of the Catholic clergy, made love to Huron women and probably married them according to local custom. The rough and tumble ways of individuals like Étienne Brûlé endeared them to their Huron hosts and this, in turn, allowed them to inspire confidence in the Indians who came to trade. It has been suggested that the main reason these men remained in Huronia was to persuade the Huron to trade in New France rather than to take their furs south to the Dutch who had begun to trade in the Hudson Valley after 1609.[57] This explanation seems unlikely, however. Until 1629 most of the Dutch trade appears to have been confined to the Mahican.[58] Although the Dutch were apparently anxious to trade with the "French Indians" as early as 1633, the Mohawk were not willing to allow them to do so unless they were in some way able to profit from the trade themselves.[59] This the Huron, who had a long-standing feud with the Iroquois, were unwilling to let them do.

The main job of the early coureurs de bois appears to have been to live in Huronia as visible evidence of French goodwill and as exchanges for the Huron youths who were sent to live with the French.[60] In this capacity they were able to encourage the Indians to engage in trade. Each year some of them travelled downriver with the Huron to see that the Algonkin did not prevent the passage of their canoes or scare the Huron off with stories of disasters or plots against them in Quebec.[61] They also acted as interpreters for the Huron and aided them in their dealings with the traders.[62] Except for the years when the Mohawk blockaded the Ottawa River, the Huron sent an annual "fleet" or series of fleets to Quebec bearing the furs they had collected.[63] It is unfortunate that the records do not supply more information on these fleets, particularly about who organized them and what was their tribal composition. The fleets left Huronia in the spring and returned several months later. When the St. Lawrence was blocked by the Iroquois, the Hurons made their way to Quebec over the smaller waterways that led through the Laurentians.[64]

The Recollet and Jesuit missionaries who worked in Huronia between 1615 and 1629 were accepted by the Huron as part of the Franco–Huron trading alliance and as individuals whose goodwill was potentially advantageous in dealing with the traders and authorities in Quebec. That they lacked interest except as shamans is evident from Gabriel Sagard's statement that it was hard to work among any tribe that was not engaged in trade (i.e., bound by the Franco–Huron alliance).[65] The priests appear to have restricted their missionary activities to caring for the needs of the French traders in Huronia and trying to make some converts among the Indians. Their preaching, as far as it was understood, did not appear to present a challenge or affront to the Huron way of life, although the customs of the priests were strange to the Indians, who found these men austere and far less appealing than the easy-going coureurs de bois.[66] For obvious reasons, relations between the priests and local traders were not good and Sagard claims that among other things the latter often refused to help the missionaries learn Native languages.[67] The most serious charge that the priests levelled at these traders was that their behaviour sowed confusion and doubt among the Huron and impeded the spread of the Christian faith among them.[68] These early experiences convinced the Jesuits that to run a mission in Huronia properly the priests must control those Europeans who were allowed to enter the country.

In the early part of the seventeenth century the colony of New France was nothing more than a trading post and its day-to-day existence depended upon securing an annual supply of furs.[69] Not understanding the long-standing hostility between the Huron and the Iroquois, the French were apprehensive of any move that seemed likely to divert furs from the St. Lawrence to the Hudson Valley. The French made peace with the Mohawk in 1624 and French traders did business with them, an arrangement that no doubt pleased the Mohawk as it made them for a time less dependent on the Dutch and therefore gave them more bargaining power in their dealings with Albany.[70] Nevertheless, the French became extremely alarmed about a peace treaty that the Huron negotiated with the Seneca in 1623. This appears to have been one of the periodic treaties that the Huron and Iroquois negotiated in order to get back members of their respective tribes who had been taken prisoner, but not yet killed, by the enemy.[71] As such, it was probably perfectly harmless to French interests. Nevertheless the situation was judged sufficiently serious for a delegation of eleven Frenchmen, including three clerics, to be sent to the Huron country.[72] Various writers have followed Jean Charlevoix in saying that this delegation was instructed to disrupt the new treaty. Charlevoix, however, wrote long after the event took place and is not an unbiased witness.[73] It seems more likely that the expedition had as its main purpose simply the reaffirming of the alliances made between Champlain and the various Huron chiefs in 1615. In actual fact the Huron probably had no thought of trading with the Iroquois at this time. To the chagrin of the Dutch, the Mohawk were firm in their refusal to allow the northern tribes to pass through their country to trade on the Hudson. The Huron undoubtedly felt that direct trade with the French, even if they were farther from Huronia than the Dutch,[74] was preferable to trade via the Mohawk with the Europeans in New York State.

The very great importance that the Huron attached to their trade with the French even at this time is shown by their efforts to prevent potential rivals, such as the Petun or Neutral, from concluding any sort of formal alliance with the French. Neither group seems to have constituted much of a threat, since the Petun had to pass through Huron territory in order to paddle north along the shore of Georgian Bay[75] and the Neutral, who do not seem to have had adequate boats, would have had to travel down the St. Lawrence River to Quebec — en route the Mohawk would have either stolen their furs or forced them to divert most of the trade to the south.[76] The Huron do not seem to have minded well-known coureurs de bois occasionally visiting the Neutral or other tribes with whom they traded, but when, on his visit to the Neutral in 1626, Father de La Roche Daillon proposed an alliance between them and the French, the Huron spread rumours about the French that brought an end to the proposed treaty.[77] The ease with which the Huron did this, and repeated the manoeuvre in 1640–41,[78] is an indication both of the insecurity that tribes felt in the absence of a proper treaty with foreigners and of the importance that the Huron placed on their privileged relationship with the French. These observations reinforce our conclusion that coureurs de bois did not live in Huronia simply to dissuade the Huron from going to trade with either the Mohawk or the Dutch, but instead were a vital link in the Franco–Huron alliance and necessary intermediaries between the Huron and the French fur traders in Quebec. Such were the services for which Brûlé received a hundred pistoles each year from his employers.[79]

Franco–Huron trade increased in the years prior to 1629. Undoubtedly the Huron were growing increasingly reliant on European goods, but it is unlikely that they were ever completely dependent on trade during this period. There is no evidence that the British occupation of Quebec led them to trade with New Holland or with the Iroquois. Several renegade Frenchmen, including Brûlé, remained in Huronia and probably encouraged the Huron to trade with the British.[80] It was during this period that Brûlé was murdered by the Huron living in Toanché. Since he was given a proper burial it is unlikely that he was tortured to death and eaten as Sagard reports.[81] More likely, he was killed in a brawl with the Huron among whom he lived. That he was killed during the British occupation of New France does not, however, seem to be without significance. Until the French withdrawal he had been protected not only by his popularity but more importantly by the Franco–Huron alliance. Once the French had departed, he was on his own.

THE JESUITS TAKE CONTROL

The Compagnie des Cent-Associés, which took effective control of the affairs of New France after the colony was retroceded to France in 1632, was different from earlier trading companies in that its members were more interested in missionary work than their predecessors had been. At this time the Society of Jesus also managed to obtain the de facto monopoly over missionary activities in New France that it was to hold for many years.[82] The Jesuits brought about a number of changes in policy with regard to Huronia. In particular, they were much more anxious to evangelize the Huron *as a people* than the Recollets had been.[83] As their prime goal they sought to lead the entire confederacy toward the Christian religion, rather than to convert individuals. Moreover, as a result of the strong influence they wielded at the French court, they were in a better position to command the support of officials and fur traders.[84] For the first while after they returned to the Huron country, the Jesuits continued many of the mission practices that had been current prior to 1629, such as sending Indian children to their seminary at Quebec.[85] As their knowledge of the Huron language and of the country improved (in both cases as a result of systematic study), they gradually began to modify their work along lines that were more in keeping with their general policy.[86]

A major bête noire of the missionaries prior to 1629 was the French traders who lived in Huronia and set a bad example for the Natives. In order to assure unity of purpose for their work, the duties that formerly had been carried out by these coureurs de bois were taken over by lay brothers, workmen, and *donnés* directly subject to Jesuit supervision.[87] Later accusations that the Jesuits were engaged in the fur trade seem to have sprung largely from this action. The oft-repeated claim that priests were vital to the fur trade in Huronia is obviously without foundation. The coureurs de bois, who had lived in Huronia for many years, not only had functioned effectively during this period without missionary support but also appear to have been substantially more popular and more effective in their dealings with the Huron than the priests had been. The Jesuits wished to be rid of this group principally to assure that the French living in Huronia would not be working at cross-purposes. The trading companies apparently were willing to allow the Jesuits to have their own way in this matter, but in return it was necessary that the laymen attached to the Jesuit mission discharge at least the most vital functions of organizing the annual trade which the coureurs de bois had done heretofore.[88] The reasons that the Jesuits had for wanting to be rid of the coureurs de bois were clearly religious, not economic.

The Jesuits' connections with the fur trade did not arise, however, simply from their desire to be rid of the coureurs de bois; they also depended on it not only to get into Huronia but also for their personal safety so long as they remained there. The Huron were obviously not at all interested in what the Jesuits had to teach, and on several occasions after 1634 they made it clear that they preferred the former coureurs de bois to the Jesuits and their assistants.[89] In 1633, and again in 1634, they offered a whole series of excuses, including the hostility of the Algonkin from Allumette Island, as reasons for not taking the Jesuits home with them.[90] Moreover, fearing revenge for the death of Brûlé, they were unwilling to allow their children to remain as seminarians at Quebec.[91] In 1634 Champlain made the official French position clear when he informed the Huron that he regarded the Jesuits' presence in their country as a vital part of a renewed Franco–Huron alliance, at the same time expressing the hope that they would someday agree to become Christians.[92] Since the Huron wanted to renew their former trading relationship with the French, they agreed to accept the priests as a token of this alliance. Henceforth they were bound by treaty to allow the Jesuits to live among them and to protect the priests from harm. The thought of having these individuals who were so respected by the French in Huronia and under their control must also have given the Huron confidence in their dealings with the French who remained in Quebec.

Although the Jesuits travelled to Huronia in 1635 in canoes that belonged to members of the Cord and Rock tribes, they were put ashore rather unceremoniously in the territory of the Bear tribe, where Brébeuf had worked previously and where Brûlé had been murdered.[93] It is not clear whether the Jesuits had wanted to go to this region or were left there by their Rock and Cord hosts who did not want to take them to their own villages. It is possible that the Bear, who were the most powerful of the Huron tribes, exerted their influence to have the Jesuits left among them. In this regard it is perhaps not without meaning that the Jesuits previously had discussed with the Indians the possibility of their settling in Ossossané, the chief town of the Bear nation.[94] Brébeuf was welcomed by the villagers of Ihonitiria, among whom he had lived before, and the Jesuits decided to settle in that village both because it was close to the canoe route to New France and also in order to persuade the villagers that they bore them no ill will for having murdered Brûlé. The latter, the Jesuits said, was regarded by the French as a traitor and debauched renegade.[95] Nevertheless, his murder haunted the Huron, and even some neighbouring tribes,[96] who feared that it might lead to war with the French. Such fears may have been responsible for the dispute that the Jesuits observed between certain villages of the Bear tribe shortly after their arrival in Huronia.[97]

It would appear that according to Native custom the Jesuits coming to Huronia had a right to expect they would receive free food and lodgings. This would have been in return for similar care given by the French to the young seminarists in Quebec.[98] In Huron eyes the latter had been exchanged as tokens of good faith in return for the Jesuits and their assistants.[99] In fact, the Huron provided food and shelter for the Jesuits only rarely. The missionaries had to purchase or provide these things for themselves and found the Huron demanding payment of some sort for most of their services.[100]

For a time after their return to Huronia the Jesuits were the objects of friendly public interest and their presence and goodwill were sought after, in part because individual Hurons sought to obtain favours in Quebec through their commendation, in part because the services people performed for the Jesuits, and even attendance at religious instruction, were rewarded with presents of trade goods and tobacco. The latter, although a Native product, was scarce in Huronia at the time.[101] Since all of the priests (except perhaps Brébeuf) were struggling to learn the Huron language, most of the missionary activities during the first few years were confined to the Bear country. Only a few trips were made into more distant areas of Huronia.[102]

THE EPIDEMICS OF 1635 TO 1640

The first serious trial for the Jesuits, and for the Franco–Huron alliance, occurred between the years 1635 and 1640. An unspecified disease, either measles or smallpox, was present in Quebec the year the Jesuits returned to Huronia, and it followed the Huron fleet upriver. This was the beginning of a series of epidemics that swept away more than half the Huron population in the next six years.[103] These new maladies were especially fatal to children and old people. Because they were fatal to the latter group, many of the most skillful Huron leaders and craftsmen, as well as the people most familiar with Native religious lore, perished.[104] The loss of children may well have meant that the proportion of men of fighting age in the Huron population was below normal by the end of the next decade.

The Jesuits, who wished to save the souls of dying children, frequently baptized them, both with and without their parents' permission. The Huron, being unclear about the Jesuits' intention in doing this, observed that children tended to die soon after baptism and came to suspect that the Jesuits were practising a deadly form of witchcraft.[105] The rumour revived that the Jesuits had been sent to Huronia to seek revenge for Brûlé's murder,[106] a rumour which gained credence from pictures of the torments of hell that the Jesuits displayed in their chapel and from the ritual of the mass (which the Huron understood had something to do with eating a corpse).[107] According to Huron law, sorcerers could be killed without a trial, and in times of crisis extensive pogroms appear to have been unleashed against persons suspected of this crime.[108] Nevertheless, while individuals threatened to murder the Jesuits and on one occasion a council of the confederacy met to try the Jesuits on a charge of witchcraft,[109] none of the Frenchmen in Huronia was killed.

Although the majority of the people were frightened of the Jesuits and believed that they were working to destroy the country, their leaders repeatedly stressed that they could not afford to rupture the Franco–Huron alliance by killing the French priests.[110] One well-placed chief said that if the Huron did not go downriver to trade with the French for even two years, they would be lucky if they found themselves as well off as the [despised] Algonkians.[111] While this statement was a bit of rhetoric, it stresses the importance of the fur trade to the Huron at this time and their growing reliance on French trade goods. During the entire course of the epidemics only one village, apparently a small one, was willing to give up the use of trade goods, and hence presumably to sever relations with the French.[112] Instead, the Huron resorted to indirect means to persuade the Jesuits to leave Huronia *voluntarily*. Children were encouraged to annoy them, their religious objects were befouled, and occasionally they were personally threatened or mistreated.[113] The Jesuits noted, rather significantly, that these persecutions diminished before the annual trip downriver or after the return of a successful fleet.[114] The French officials in Quebec were aware of the dangerous situation in which the Jesuits found themselves, but as long as feelings ran high in Huronia, these authorities could do no more than to try to spare them from the worst excesses of Huron anger. They did this by threatening to cut off trade if the Jesuits were killed.

By 1640 the serious epidemics in Huronia were over. That summer, the new governor of Canada, Charles Huault de Montmagny, took action to "punish" the Huron who came to Quebec for their bad treatment of the Jesuits.[115] It is not clear what form this punishment took, but it appears that in the course of his dealings with them he made it clear that he considered their bad treatment of the Jesuits had terminated the existing alliance. At the same time he offered to renew the alliance, but only on the clear understanding that the Jesuits would continue to live in Huronia and work there unmolested. This is the first time, to our knowledge, that French officials had injected a positive element of threat into their dealings with the Huron. Presumably, the great losses in manpower and skills that the Huron had suffered and their consequent increasing dependence on trade and French support made such action possible. The Huron were in good health and expecting an abundant harvest; hence, many of the anxieties that had plagued them in recent years were dispelled. Because of this they were once more in a good mood and, hence, under the protection of a renewed Franco–Huron alliance the Jesuits found themselves free not only to continue the mission work among them but also to intensify their efforts.[116]

Already during the final crisis of 1639, the Jesuits had decided to establish a permanent centre for their missionary work in the Huron area. This centre was foreseen as serving various functions. Not only would it provide a refuge in time of danger (such as they lacked in 1639), but it also would allow them to put up buildings of European design. It had not been economical to construct these in the Huron villages, which shifted their location about once every decade. The Jesuits' centre was thus designed to be a further example of European culture in the heart of Huronia, a focus from which new ideas could diffuse to the local population. Gradually, pigs, fowl, and young cattle were brought upriver from Quebec and European crops were grown in the fields nearby.[117] The residence of Ste Marie acquired a hospital and a burial ground and became a place where Christian Indians could come for spiritual retreats and assembly on feast days.[118] Being located apart from any one village, and near the geographical centre of the confederacy, it was better able, both from a political and a geographical point of view, to serve as a mission centre for all Huronia. (During the worst years of the epidemics the Jesuits had remained for the most part in the northwest corner of Huronia.) In 1639 the Jesuits also made a survey and census of the country prior to setting up a system of missions that would carry the Christian message to all of the Huron tribes and, as far as possible, to other tribes as well.[119]

The Jesuits had thus weathered a difficult period. It is clear that they had been allowed to enter Huronia and to continue there only because of the Franco–Huron alliance. That they were not killed or expelled from Huronia at the height of the epidemics is an indication of how dependent the Hurons were becoming on the fur trade and how much the alliance with the French meant to them. It also indicates that the Huron leaders were able to restrain their unruly followers in order to preserve good relations with New France.[120] Evidence of lingering malice towards the priests can be seen in the events that came to light on the visit of Fathers Brébeuf and Chaumonot to the Neutral country in the winter of 1640–41. There the priests learned that the Huron had offered the Neutral rich presents, if they would kill the missionaries.[121] In this way the Huron hoped to destroy two of the "sorcerers" who had been tormenting their nation, without endangering the French alliance. They also had other motives, however. The proposed murder, so long as it was not traced back to the Huron, would put the Neutral in a bad light and would prevent Brébeuf from pursuing any dealings with the Seneca. Although there is no evidence that Brébeuf planned to visit the Seneca, a rumour had spread that having failed to kill the Huron with witchcraft he now was seeking to turn their enemies loose upon them.[122]

A CRISIS IN HURON–IROQUOIS RELATIONS

If the year 1640 marked the end of the persecution of the Jesuits in Huronia, unknown to them and to their Huron hosts, it also marked the beginning of a crisis that was to destroy Huronia. Beaver had become rare in the Huron country and most of the skins they traded with the French came from neighbouring tribes to the north.[123] A similar decline in the beaver population of New York State seems to have reached a point of crisis by 1640. That year the number of pelts traded at Fort Orange is reported to have dropped sharply.[124] While it is possible that at least part of the decline was the result of clandestine traders cutting into official trade, most commentators agree that it was basically related to the exhaustion of the supply of beaver in the Iroquois' home territory.[125]

While this hypothesis is not well enough documented that it can be regarded as certain, it seems a useful one for explaining Iroquois behaviour during the next few years. There is little doubt that after 1640 the Iroquois were preoccupied with securing new sources of pelts. The main controversy concerning their relations with their neighbours during this period centres on whether they were seeking to obtain furs by forcing the Huron to share their trade with them[126] or were attacking their neighbours in order to secure new hunting territories. Although Trelease[127] supports the latter theory, the data he uses apply for the most part to a later period and come mainly from sources in New York State and New England. Contemporary Canadian evidence definitely seems to rule out his claims; indeed if his hypothesis were true, the events leading to the destruction of Huronia would make little sense at all.

Trelease's theory finds its main support in claims made by the Iroquois in the early part of the eighteenth century that they had conquered Ontario and adjacent regions as beaver hunting grounds. In the treaty of 1701, in which the Iroquois placed their "Beaver ground" under the protection of the King of England, the Iroquois said explicitly that they had driven the indigenous tribes from this area in order to hunt there.[128] Trelease errs, however, in assuming that the reasons the Iroquois gave for conquering this territory in 1701 were the same as those they actually had for doing so half a century earlier. There is no doubt that in 1701 the Iroquois (mainly the Seneca) were hunting beaver in Ontario, but since the Huron country was reported in the 1630s to be as hunted out as their own it is illogical to assume that they attacked this region in 1649 in order to secure more hunting territory. The Huron beaver supplies they sought to capture were those coming by trade from the north. Only after their attacks failed to capture the western fur trade and after Ontario was deserted for a time allowing the restoration of the local beaver population did the Iroquois begin to hunt there. Since they lacked historical records, it is not surprising that by 1701 the Iroquois believed the use that they were making of Ontario at the present time was the same reason they had for attacking the tribes there long before. The attacks the Iroquois launched against the Petun and Neutral, following their attack on the Huron, offer no opposition to this theory. Although these groups had not participated in the fur trade prior to 1649, there was considerable danger that with the Huron gone they would attempt to do so. Hence, their dispersal was also necessary.

Trelease's theory thus fails to provide an acceptable explanation of events in Canada in the middle of the seventeenth century. It seems much more likely that the Iroquois, and mainly the Mohawk, began by trying to force the Huron to trade with them and that only latterly, when their efforts in this direction were unsuccessful, did they decide to destroy the Huron (and their neighbours) as an intermediary group.

The Mohawk began to intimidate the Huron by harassing those travelling along the Ottawa River — a tactic that had the additional advantage of providing a supply of captured furs. In 1642 Iroquois raiders spread fear and terror throughout all of the Huron villages,[129] and in 1644 they succeeded in preventing contact between Quebec and Huronia.[130] The increasing number of guns that the Iroquois were acquiring from the Dutch, English, and Swedish colonies along the Atlantic seaboard gradually gave them military superiority over the Huron, among whom the French had limited and controlled the sale of guns.[131] In 1644 the French despatched more than twenty soldiers to Huronia to protect the Huron over the winter and assure the arrival of their furs in Quebec the next spring.[132] The Mohawk were also harassing the French in the St. Lawrence Valley, who were moved the next spring to discuss peace, both to assure their own safety and to reopen the river to trade. Although the subsequent treaty of 1645 was with the French, the Mohawk seem to have interpreted it as involving a commitment that in the future the Huron would trade with them as well as with the French.[133] The Huron, however, had no intention of doing this, and the French, who may not have perceived clearly what the Mohawk wanted, did not want to encourage them to divert trade. The main French reason for the treaty with the Mohawk was the short-term one of opening the river. The French had little to offer the Iroquois in return and refused to sell them guns, the one item they wanted.[134] When it became clear to the Mohawk that the Huron did not intend to trade with them, they renewed their attack on Huronia and on the Huron fleet.

THE DEVELOPMENT OF A CHRISTIAN FACTION

While this dangerous crisis in intertribal relations was boiling up, a situation was developing in Huronia that put a new strain on the Franco–Huron alliance.

Prior to 1640, most Christian converts were Hurons on the point of death, many of whom knew nothing about Christian theology but hoped that baptism would save their lives.[135] At one point during the epidemics a Huron version of the rite of baptism became part of a Native healing cult that was said to be inspired by a Native deity who had revealed himself as the real Jesus.[136] In these rites the sick were sprinkled with water as part of an orgiastic ceremony typical of traditional Huron healing rituals. After 1640, however, the Jesuits began to convert increasing numbers of people who were in good health. Many were men of importance, whose conversions made that of their families, friends, and tribesmen easier.[137] In order to prevent backsliding, the Jesuits at first made it a policy to baptize (except in cases of extreme ill health) only adults who had provided substantial proof of their devotion to Christianity and whose family life seemed to be stable.[138]

Many factors seem to have induced people to convert: some admired the bravery of the Jesuits, others wished to be able to follow a Christian friend to heaven, still others noted in their names a theological term that the Jesuits were using.[139]

Although economic motives were not the only ones involved in conversion, it is noteworthy that at least a few Huron became Christians to avoid participation in pagan feasts, which required them to give away considerable amounts of property in the form of presents and entertainment.[140] A far larger number of people hoped through conversion to receive preferential treatment in their dealings with traders and officials in New France.[141] In 1648, when only 15 percent of the Huron were Christian, half of the men in the Huron fleet were either converts or were preparing for baptism.[142] Those who traded with the French in Quebec not only were more exposed to French culture and to Christianity than were those who remained at home but also had more to gain from good relations with the French. Commercial considerations may also explain why the Jesuits generally found it easier to convert men than women.

While stressing the practical economic motives that certainly motivated many conversions, personal and cultural factors should not be ignored. The Huron were increasingly dependent on French culture and in the eyes of many, but (as we shall see) certainly not all, of the Huron the priest was coming to replace the Native sorcerer as an object of awe and respect. This did not, however, lead the Huron to lose faith in themselves or in their culture, as it did in many other tribes.[143] Supported by the respect shown by the Jesuits for the Huron people and for much of their culture, many Huron converts appear to have been imbued with a sincere zeal to change and reform their own culture. No doubt the size of the Huron confederacy and its isolation from unsupervised contact with the Europeans did much to prevent the deterioration in self-confidence that is obvious among many weaker tribes. Had other circumstances not been adverse, I think it would have been possible for the Jesuits to have transformed Huronia successfully into a nation that was both Christian and Indian.

For a time the growing number of Huron converts posed no serious problems for the rest of society, although individual converts were frequently taunted and sometimes expelled from their longhouses with much resulting personal hardship.[144] (A woman who had been a member of a pagan healing society was threatened with death when after conversion she refused to perform in the society.[145]) Threats and assassination no doubt were the fate of other converts. The Jesuits and their assistants, however, were no longer attacked or molested in any way.[146] It appears that at least some headmen surrendered their political office on becoming Christians, since they felt that the obligation to participate in Huron festivals which these offices entailed was contrary to their new faith.[147] In this and in other ways the nascent Christian community avoided for a time the possibility of an open clash with the large pagan majority.

Gradually, however, a rift began. Some Christians refused, for example, to be buried in their tribal ossuaries, which in effect was to deny membership in their village or tribe.[148] They also refused to fight alongside pagans in the war parties but instead formed their own detachments, no doubt because of the religious implications of traditional Iroquoian warfare.[149] As the number of converts grew, men retained their political offices after conversion, but appointed deputies to handle the religious functions traditionally associated with them.[150] As the number of Christians who held these important offices continued to grow, the split between pagans and Christians became increasingly a political issue.

The Jesuits, for their part, now set as their immediate goal the Christianizing of an entire village.[151] Significantly the most promising town was Ossossané, where the Jesuits had been working for a long time. This town, belonging to the Bear tribe, was also the political centre of the Huron confederacy.[152] In 1648 they achieved their objective. By then the majority of people in Ossossané were converts. And that winter the chiefs of the village refused to allow the people who remained pagan to celebrate the traditional festivals, and they appointed a Jesuit as the chief headman of the village, with the right to act as a censor of public morals.[153]

THE PAGAN REACTION AND THE DESTRUCTION OF HURONIA

Although in 1645 such social revolutions were still several years in the future, many of the pagans had already begun to fear for the survival of their traditional customs and beliefs.[154] Undoubtedly a large number of these people were genuinely attached to the old ways and for this reason alone resented the growth of Christianity. It is also possible that many chiefs who wished to remain pagan began to fear a decline in their own influence as Christians began to play a stronger role in the life of the country. They probably resented the closer contacts that Christian chiefs had with the French and feared that these contacts would be used as a source of power. As a result of these fears and rivalries, pagan and Christian factions began to develop within the various tribes and villages throughout Huronia.[155]

Although the documentation in the Jesuit *Relations* is scanty, there appears to have been a considerable variation in attitude toward the Jesuits and Christianity among the different Huron tribes. The Bear, among whom the Jesuits had lived for the longest time and whose main town, Ossossané, had a large and rapidly growing Christian community, seem to have been the most pro-Christian and pro-French.[156] The Cord probably had much the same sort of attitude.[157] The Rock and Deer tribes, however, seem to have been considerably less friendly. The Jesuits report that the former tribe, being the easternmost, had suffered most from the attacks of the Iroquois and was therefore the most inclined to seek peace with their traditional enemies. The Rock were also described, however, as a tribe with a strong aversion to the faith, who never had been converted.[158] The Deer had a reputation among the Jesuits for being sorcerers,[159] and one assumes from this that they gave the missionaries a bad time. Both of these tribes joined the Iroquois of their own free will after the break-up of Huronia in 1649.[160] Despite this variation, however, there were people in all the Huron tribes who were starting to have misgivings about the future of Huronia and who resented the changes that the French alliance was bringing about.

After 1645 these sentiments seem to have led to the formation of a sizable anti-French party, which apparently found a certain amount of support everywhere in Huronia, except perhaps in Ossossané. This marked a new development in French–Huron relations, all previous opposition having been to the priests resident in Huronia rather than to the French in general. Supporters of this party seem to have reasoned that Christianity was a threat to Huronia, that Christianity flourished because the Jesuits were able to work there under the terms of the Franco–Huron alliance, and that the best way to save the country (and enhance the power of the pagan chiefs at the expense of their Christian rivals) was therefore to expel the Jesuits, break off the alliance, and begin trading with the Iroquois. In this way, not only would the traditional culture of Huronia be saved, but the attacks of the Iroquois, which had been growing in intensity,[161] could be brought to an end. Thus for the first time a respectable body of opinion in Huronia came to believe that an alliance with enemies who shared similar beliefs and culture was preferable to one with strangers seeking to change the Huron way of life. The threat that was facing the traditionalists made the thought of trading with their old enemies and rivals seem much less unpleasant than it had been a few years previously.

The first plan for a rapprochement with the Iroquois was well conceived and sought to exploit internal differences within the Iroquois confederacy for the Hurons' own advantage. Since the treaty of 1645 had failed to obtain the furs they wanted, the Mohawk were likely to be suspicious of, if not hostile to, further Huron blandishments. The Seneca likewise were unfriendly because of recent Huron attacks on them.[162] The Onondaga, however, had long enjoyed the position of being the chief tribe in the confederacy and were increasingly jealous of the Mohawk, who were exploiting their close contacts with the Dutch and the English in an effort to dominate the league.[163] It is therefore no surprise that it was through the Onondaga that the Huron attempted to make peace with the Iroquois.

The Jesuits did not record, and may not have known, the exact nature of the treaty that the Huron were trying to negotiate. The presence of a clause promising that the Huron would trade furs with the Iroquois is suggested by a remark, attributed to the Andaste or Susquehannock (who were allies of the Huron and sent ambassadors to the Onondaga to argue on their behalf), that such a treaty would promote the trade of all these tribes with one another.[164] It is also significant that among the Huron the Bear tribe was the one most opposed to this treaty.[165] The Jesuits said this was because the Bear had suffered less from Iroquois raids than had the other Huron tribes, but a second reason could be that the Christians, who were more numerous in this tribe than in the others, saw in these negotiations a clear threat to the Franco–Huron alliance and to their own power and well-being. Negotiations continued for some time, but were terminated in January 1648, when a party of Mohawk warriors slew a Huron embassy on its way to the chief Onondaga town to arrange the final terms of the treaty.[166] A distinguished Onondaga chief, who had remained in Huronia as a hostage, committed suicide when he learned what the Mohawk had done.[167]

There seems little reason to doubt the honesty of the Onondaga in these negotiations. The Mohawk probably attacked the Huron embassy because they were angry that negotiations were being conducted with the Onondaga rather than with them. The Mohawk may also have believed that the Huron were trying to deceive the Onondaga and that the only way of dealing with the Huron confederacy was to destroy it. In any case, the Mohawk managed to bring the first major political offensive of the anti-French faction in Huronia to an ignominious conclusion.

Even though this first effort had failed, at least some Huron apparently believed that a rap-prochement with the Iroquois still was possible. Indeed, either because they were totally con-vinced of the necessity of appeasing the Iroquois or because of their extreme hatred of the Christians, a minority seems to have become convinced that a break with the French was a precondition for further negotiation. The group responsible for the next move was led by six, apparently distinguished, chiefs from three villages.[168] Unfortunately, these villages are unnamed. The chiefs decided to make a public issue of the question of a continued Franco–Huron alliance through the simple expedient of killing a Frenchman. They do not appear to have designated any particular victim, and their henchmen slew Jacques Douart, a *donné* whom they encountered not far from Ste Marie. Once Douart was slain, the conspirators issued a proclamation calling for the banishment from Huronia of the French and all of the Huron who insisted on remaining Christian.[169] An emergency council was convened (apparently from all over the country) and for several days these proposals were debated. On the one side were the Christians and those pagans who felt that the Franco–Huron alliance should continue; on the other the traditionalists who had stirred up the trouble and no doubt some other Hurons who hated neither Christianity nor the French, but who felt that a peace treaty with the Iroquois was important enough to be worth the termination of the French alliance. Among the latter must have been many refugees from the Rock tribe, which had been forced to abandon its vil-lages as a result of Iroquois attacks only a short time before.[170] The pro-French party finally won the debate and the Jesuits in turn agreed to accept the traditional Huron compensation for a murder, in this case one hundred beaver skins.[171] The ritual presentation of this settle-ment made clear that it was designed to reaffirm and protect the Franco–Huron alliance, which the unprecedented actions of these chiefs had endangered. Thus ended what appears to have been the last attempt to rupture the Franco–Huron alliance.

During the summer of 1648 the Seneca attacked and destroyed the large town of St. Joseph. As the situation grew more serious, the Huron turned increasingly to the French for help and the number of conversions increased sharply.[172] As in 1644, a few French soldiers were sent to winter in Huronia. These soldiers, so long as they remained in Huronia, were believed sufficient to hold off the Iroquois, but they had been instructed to return to Quebec with the Huron fleet in the spring.[173] As the military situation in Huronia grew more des-perate, the French in Quebec became increasingly anxious to profit as much as possible while they still could. In the summer of 1649, a party of over 30 coureurs de bois made a flying trip to Huronia and returned to Quebec bringing with them 5000 pounds of beaver.[174]

In the spring of 1649 the Iroquois unleashed the attack that resulted in the death of Fathers Lalemant and Brébeuf and brought about the dispersal of the Huron confederacy. Many factors contributed to the Iroquois victory, but their superior number of guns was undoubtedly the most important.[175] Hunt has suggested that the Huron were so given over to trading by 1649 that virtually all of their food was imported from the Neutral and Petun tribes and that the main factor in their defeat was therefore the cutting of their supply routes.[176] This sugges-tion is entirely without foundation. Agriculture was a woman's occupation and little affected by increasing trade. While men may have spent more time trading, the importation of iron axes made it easier to cut trees and hence there was no problem clearing the forests for agriculture. There are frequent references to the Huron as engaged in agricultural activities in the years prior to 1649, and one of the reasons the Iroquois returned to Huronia in the spring of 1650 was to prevent the planting of crops.[177] Driven from their homes and deprived of food, the Hurons scattered, and their trading monopoly came to an end. It is interesting that large num-bers of Huron, particularly from the Rock and Deer tribes, migrated to the Iroquois country and settled there. The latter tribe settled en masse among the Seneca, where they lived in their own village and retained their separate customs for a long time.[178] Their tribal affiliations suggest that these refugees were for the most part traditionalists and probably among them were many of the people who had been the most hostile to the French during the last years of the Jesuit mission. This hostility explains how these groups were so easily adopted by the people who had destroyed their homeland.

For the Jesuits the destruction of Huronia was the end of their first dream of leading a nation to Christianity in the heart of the Canadian forest. At least once in the Relations they mentioned the work their colleagues were accomplishing in Paraguay and compared this work with their own.[179] The chance had been lost of converting a people to Christianity while allowing them to retain their language and those institutions and customs that were not incompatible with their new faith. Because they were writing for a patriotic French audience, the Jesuits have little to say about the constitutional status of the Huronia they wished to create. Nevertheless, it seems clear that what they aimed at was not so much a French colony as an Indian state, which under Jesuit leadership could blend the good things of Europe with those already in the Native culture. A Catholic Huronia would of necessity have been allied with France, the only Catholic power in eastern North America. Years later Louis de Buade de Frontenac probably came closer to a basic truth than he realized when he accused the Jesuits at Quebec of disloyalty because they kept the Indians apart from the French and taught them in their own language.[180]

The fur trade was the one means by which the Jesuits could gain admittance to Huronia and the only protection they had while working there. Ties with fur traders and government officials in Quebec were thus vital for the success of the Huron mission, but these ties do not seem to have prevented the Jesuits from seeking to serve the best interests of their Huron converts and Huronia at large — as they perceived these interests. To reverse the equation and say that the Jesuits were in Huronia mainly *for the purpose* of serving either the fur trade or the French government does not accord with anything we know about their activities.

In the short run the destruction of Huronia was a serious setback for New France. For a time the fur trade, on which the well-being of the colony depended, was cut to practically nothing. The Iroquois, on the other hand, seem to have achieved less than they hoped for from the destruction of Huronia. The western tribes soon became involved in a protracted war with the Erie,[181] and tribal jealousies rent the confederacy. As a result of these jealousies the four western tribes began to trade with the French to avoid travelling through Mohawk towns to reach the Dutch.[182] By 1654 the French were starting to put together the rudiments of a new trading network north of the Great Lakes.[183] The remnants of the Huron and Petun who had remained in this area, and more importantly the Ottawa, an Algonkian tribe, played a major role in pushing this trading network to the west in the years that followed.[184] As the population of New France increased, the young men of the colony, with or without official permission, joined in this trade. Thus the destruction of Huronia was neither a total nor a permanent disaster for New France and certainly it did not help to save North America for Protestantism and the Anglo-Saxons, as at least one eminent historian has suggested.[185]

A more serious question is what would have happened had the anti-French party in Huronia been successful. Had they been able to organize an effective resistance to the Huron Christians and conclude a treaty with the Iroquois, the trade from the north might have been diverted permanently from the St. Lawrence into the Hudson Valley. Had that happened (and as Sagard and Le Clercq indicate the people in Quebec knew it well[186]) the chances of the infant French colony surviving even for a short time would have been slim. Instead of the destruction of Huronia tipping the balance of power in favour of the English, its survival might well have led to a Huron–Iroquois alliance that would have resulted in the destruction of New France and the end of the French presence in North America.

NOTES

1. See, e.g., Samuel de Champlain's comment on the sagacity of the Indians in trade (H.P. Biggar, ed., *The Works of Samuel de Champlain* [6 vols.; Toronto, 1922–36], 2: 171), and Jean de Brébeuf, Gabriel Lalemant, and Francesco Bressani on the efficacy of Huron law (R.G. Thwaites, ed., *The Jesuit Relations and Allied Documents* [73 vols.; Cleveland, 1896–1901], 10: 215; 28: 49–51; 38: 277).

2. Thwaites, ed., *Relations* 18: 21. A similar statement is made by Paul Ragueneau (29: 281).

3. Invariably, however, these early witnesses of Indian culture were interested in rather limited aspects of Indian life and tended to interpret Indian culture in terms of their own. Because of this, a valid assessment of these early records requires a comparative knowledge of Indian culture in later times. The groundwork for our understanding of seventeenth-century Huron culture is thus the work of several generations of ethnologists and ethnohistorians in Canada and the United States. The best résumé of Huron culture is Elisabeth Tooker, *An Ethnography of the Huron Indians, 1615–1649* (Washington, 1964). For a shorter and less complete synopsis see W.V. Kinietz, *The Indians of the Western Great Lakes, 1615–1760* (Ann Arbor, 1940).

4. F. Parkman, *The Jesuits in North America in the Seventeenth Century* (Centenary Edition, Boston, 1927), 3, 4, 435, 436; G.E. Ellis, "Indians of North America," in J. Winsor, ed., *Narrative and Critical History of America* (8 vols.; Boston and New York, 1884–89), 1: 283.

5. G.T. Hunt, *The Wars of the Iroquois: A Study in Intertribal Relations* (Madison, 1940), 4, 19.

6. Biggar, ed., *Works of Champlain* 3: 49–51; 4: 238–44.

7. Thwaites, ed., *Relations* 16: 227.

8. L.H. Morgan, *League of the Ho-de-no-sau-nee, or Iroquois* (Rochester, 1851; reprinted New Haven, 1954). For a briefer description, see Morgan's *Houses and House-life of the Indian Aborigines* (Washington, 1881; reprinted with original pagination Chicago, 1965), 23–41.

9. Meat remained largely a festive dish, commonest in winter and spring (G.M. Wrong, ed., *Sagard's Long Journey to the Country of the Hurons* [Toronto, 1939], 82; Thwaites, ed., *Relations* 17: 141–43).

10. Thwaites, ed., *Relations* 16: 227–29. See also Elisabeth Tooker, "The Iroquois Defeat of the Huron: A Review of Causes," *Pennsylvania Archaeologist* 33 (1963): 115–23, especially 119, 120.

11. J.V. Wright, *The Ontario Iroquois Tradition* (Ottawa, 1966), 68–83. For information concerning the movements from the west I am indebted to a personal communication from Dr. Wright.

12. See, for example, D. Jenness, *The Indians of Canada* (5th ed.; Ottawa, 1960), 280.

13. B.G. Trigger, "The Historic Location of the Hurons," *Ontario History* 54 (1962): 137–48. For physiographic conditions, see L.J. Chapman and D.F. Putnam, *The Physiography of Southern Ontario* (2nd ed.; Toronto, 1966), 299–312.

14. Biggar, ed., *Works of Champlain* 3: 52, 53. On the importance of corn meal among the northern hunters see Wrong, ed., *Sagard's Long Journey*, 268.

15. Hunt, *Wars of the Iroquois*, 53–65.

16. For the reference to squirrel skins see Thwaites, ed., *Relations* 7: 13; to nets, 6: 309.

17. Thwaites, ed., *Relations* 8: 15.

18. Wrong, ed., *Sagard's Long Journey*, 86.

19. For a hostile statement about the Bear by the Algonkins, see Thwaites, ed., *Relations* 10: 145.

20. C.F. Wray and H.L. Schoff, "A Preliminary Report on the Seneca Sequence in Western New York State, 1550–1687," *Pennsylvania Archaeologist* 23 (1953): 53–63.

21. Colonel James F. Pendergast (personal communication) reports finding considerable evidence of Huron influence in late Iroquoian sites along the St. Lawrence River. These probably date from the sixteenth century or only a little earlier. For the historical evidence of contacts between the St. Lawrence Iroquoians and the interior of Ontario, see H.P. Biggar, ed., *The Voyages of Jacques Cartier* (Ottawa, 1924), 170–71, 200–202.

22. Thwaites, ed., *Relations* 10: 225.

23. Thwaites, ed., *Relations* 20: 19.

24. Thwaites, ed., *Relations* 20: 19. In 1640 Lalemant reported that the Rock still considered themselves the special allies of the French and were inclined to protect them. This attitude changed after the Jesuits became more active in the interior of Huronia.

25. Wrong, ed., *Sagard's Long Journey*, 99. Sagard says that a special council decided each year the number of men who could go out from each village. For more on the control of trade by old and influential men, see Thwaites, ed., *Relations* 14: 39.

26. J.V. Wright, "A Regional Examination of Ojibwa Culture History," *Anthropologica* N.S. 7 (1965): 189–227.

27. Thwaites, ed., *Relations* 5: 241.

28. The Huron claimed that their feud with the Iroquois had been going on 50 years prior to 1615 (Biggar, ed., *Works of Champlain* 5: 78).

29. Thwaites, ed., *Relations* 23: 91.

30. Wrong, ed., *Sagard's Long Journey*, 159–61. For comparative discussions of Iroquoian warfare see Nathaniel Knowles, "The Torture of Captives by the Indians of Eastern North America," *Proceedings of the American Philosophical Society* 82 (1940): 151–225; R.L. Rands and C.L. Riley, "Diffusion and Discontinuous Distribution," *American Anthropologist* 58 (1958): 274–97.

31. For the wars with the Petun, see Thwaites, ed., *Relations* 20: 43. Even at the time of Sagard's visit, there was a threat of war with the Neutral (Wrong, ed., *Sagard's Long Journey*, 151, 156, 157).

32. Thwaites, ed., *Relations* 33: 243.

33. Thwaites, ed., *Relations* 33: 239–49.

34. Thwaites, ed., *Relations* 13: 125. The Bear Tribe wanted the French to participate in their Feast of the Dead so that they could thereby claim them as relatives (10: 311).

35. Thwaites, ed., *Relations* 27: 25; 20: 59.

36. Chrétien Le Clercq, *First Establishment of the Faith in New France*, trans. J.G. Shea, 2 vols. (New York, 1881), 1: 97; Wrong, ed., *Sagard's Long Journey*, 71.

37. Biggar, ed., *Voyages of Cartier*, 132–3, 143. The custom of giving children to Cartier may have arisen, on the other hand, as a result of the Indians observing Cartier's predilection for kidnapping Indians. In 1534 he had seized the two sons of Donnaconna, the chief of Stadacona.

38. The fact that the Huron and Algonkians both were at war with the Five Nations naturally pitted the French against these latter tribes. Presumably Champlain's decision to side with the Huron and Algonkians was based on his conviction that it was impossible to maintain satisfactory relations with both sides, as well as on the economic factors mentioned in the text. For a discussion of the origins of the hostility between the Algonkians and Five Nations, see B.G. Trigger, "Trade and Tribal Warfare on the St. Lawrence in the Sixteenth Century," *Ethnohistory* 9 (1962): 240–56.

39. For Champlain's own comment on Indian expectations in this regard, see Biggar, ed., *Works of Champlain* 2: 70, 71, 110.

40. H.A. Innis, *The Fur Trade in Canada* (2nd ed.; Toronto, 1956), 23–26.

41. Thwaites, ed., *Relations* 15: 229. The first Huron chief to have dealings with the French was Atironta of the Rock tribe.

42. Biggar, ed., *Works of Champlain* 2: 188, 189, 193. For a more general reference see 2: 254.

43. Biggar, ed., *Works of Champlain* 2: 141; 4: 118, 119. This interpretation is reinforced by Champlain's statement that the boy was brought back by 200 Huron on June 13, 1611 (2: 186; 4: 136).

44. For comments on the Indians' desire for European manufactured goods, see Innis, *Fur Trade*, 16–19; Hunt, *Wars of the Iroquois*, 4, 5.

45. For examples of Algonkin harassment of Huron trade along the Ottawa River and various Algonkin attempts to imperil Franco–Huron relations (particularly by the Algonkin from Allumette Island) see Biggar, ed., *Works of Champlain* 5: 102; Wrong, ed., *Sagard's Long Journey*, 262; Thwaites, ed., *Relations* 5: 239; 7: 213; 8: 83, 99; 9: 271; 10: 77; 14: 53. The Montagnais also tried to intimidate the Huron, mainly to get free corn (Wrong, ed., *Sagard's Long Journey*, 265–68).

46. Innis, *Fur Trade*, 3–6, 11–15.

47. This is essentially the kind of relationship that existed between trading companies and Indian trappers in the north in more recent times.

48. Champlain reports that the Huron produced large food surpluses which he says were meant to carry them over years of poor crops (Biggar, ed., *Works of Champlain* 3: 155–56). At least a part of these surpluses was used for trade.

49. Le Clercq, *Establishment* 1: 298.

50. Thwaites, ed., *Relations* 35: 201. There is good evidence, however, that the Nipissing were travelling north even earlier (Biggar, ed., *Works of Champlain* 2: 255–56).

51. Le Clercq, *Establishment* 1: 211; Wrong, ed., *Sagard's Long Journey*, 244.

52. Biggar, ed., *Works of Champlain* 5: 73–80; Hunt, *Wars of the Iroquois*, 69.

53. The Huron had invited Champlain to visit their country as early as 1609 (Biggar, ed., *Works of Champlain* 2: 105). His attempt to travel up the Ottawa River in 1613 was brought to an end by the opposition of the Algonkin, among other things. Marcel Trudel (*Histoire de la Nouvelle-France*, vol. 2, *Le Comptoir, 1604–1627* [Montréal, 1966], 198–201) may be correct when he suggests that the Algonkin stirred up trouble between Champlain and Vignau in order to protect their trading interests in the interior.

54. Although Champlain visited all the major Huron villages, he returned repeatedly to Cahiague, a Rock village. He also spent more time there than anywhere else. Lalemant reports that in 1640 his reputation was still very much alive among the Rock (Thwaites, ed., *Relations* 20: 19).

55. Biggar, ed., *Works of Champlain* 3: 66, 69, 73; 4: 254–66; also Hunt, *Wars of the Iroquois*, 20.

56. Since most of the available data about this period was recorded by priests, we have little information about these men, and practically none from a friendly source. For what there is see, Biggar, ed., *Works of Champlain* 5: 101, 108, 129, 131, 132, 207; Le Clercq, *Establishment* 1: 205; Wrong, ed., *Sagard's Long Journey*, 194–95; Thwaites, ed., *Relations* 5: 133; 6: 83; 14: 17, 19; 18: 45; 20: 19; 25: 85.

57. A.W. Trelease, *Indian Affairs in Colonial New York: The Seventeenth Century* (Ithaca, 1960), 30.

58. Trelease, *Indian Affairs*, 46. Intermittent hostilities between the Mahican and Mohawk kept the latter from Fort Orange prior to the stunning defeat of the Mahican in 1628 or 1629 (48).

59. Trelease, *Indian Affairs*, 52–54; Thwaites, ed., *Relations* 8: 59–61; Hunt, *Wars of the Iroquois*, 34. In 1638 the Huron told the Jesuits that "Englishmen" had come as far as Montreal telling the Indians that the Jesuits were the cause of sickness in Huronia (and no doubt attempting to trade with them or divert trade to the south) (Thwaites, ed., *Relations* 15: 31.)

60. See, e.g., Biggar, ed., *Works of Champlain* 5: 101, 207.

61. Biggar, ed., *Works of Champlain* 5: 108. On the usefulness of having Frenchmen accompany the fleet see Wrong, ed., *Sagard's Long Journey*, 262. Sagard reports that in the 1620s the Iroquois refrained from attacking Huron flotillas when they knew Frenchmen were travelling with the Indians (261).

62. These were at least the functions that the Huron expected Frenchmen who had lived in Huronia would perform. The coureurs de bois are frequently referred to as interpreters (Biggar, ed., *Works of Champlain* 3: 168–72).

63. Wrong, ed., *Sagard's Long Journey*, 249–56.

64. This route apparently had been used in prehistoric times as well (Biggar, ed., *Voyages of Cartier*, 200–201, as interpreted by Innis, *Fur Trade*, 22).

65. Edwin Tross, ed., *Histoire du Canada et voyages que les Frères mineurs Recollets y ont faicts pour la conversion des infidèles depuis l'an 1615 . . .* , by G. Sagard (4 vols.; Paris, 1866), 1: 42. This statement refers to the visit Le Caron made with Champlain. On the Huron desire to have the priests act as go-betweens in their trade with the French, see Wrong, ed., *Sagard's Long Journey*, 244; Le Clercq, *Establishment* 1: 211.

66. The Indians often were reluctant to take missionaries back to Huronia with them (Thwaites, ed., *Relations* 4: 221). Some priests, however, became personally popular with the Huron. The popularity of Father Brébeuf during his initial stay in Huronia is evident from the welcome he received when he returned in 1634.

67. This claim appears in the *Dictionary of Canadian Biography*, vol. 1, *1000 to 1700* (Toronto, 1966), 133. It appears to be based on Sagard's comments on the behaviour of an interpreter named Nicolas Marsolet. Although Marsolet refused to teach the Montagnais language to the Recollets, he later agreed to instruct the Jesuits (Tross, ed., *Histoire du Canada* 2: 333).

68. It is perhaps significant that the main complaint was about the sexual behaviour of these men rather than the sale of alcohol to the Indians (cf. André Vachon, "L'Eau-de-vie dans la société indienne," Canadian Historical Association, *Report*, 1960, 22–32). Alcohol does not appear to have been a serious problem in Huronia, no doubt because the Huron did not at this time feel their culture threatened by European contacts. The Jesuits' distaste for these men is reiterated in the Jesuit Relations, particularly when they are compared with the *donnés* and other men who served in Huronia under Jesuit supervision after 1634. See Thwaites, ed., *Relations* 6: 83; 14: 19; 15: 85; 17: 45.

69. Trudel, *Histoire de la Nouvelle-France* 2: 405–34.

70. Trelease, *Indian Affairs*, 52; Hunt, *Wars of the Iroquois*, 69–70.

71. Thwaites, ed., *Relations* 33: 121.

72. Le Clercq, *Establishment* 1: 204; Tross, ed., *Histoire du Canada*.

73. There is nothing in Sagard or Le Clercq that implies that the priests were instructed to disrupt this treaty, as Hunt implies. Trudel (*Histoire de la Nouvelle-France* 2: 370) says that it was necessary to send Father Le Caron and the other Frenchmen to Huronia to prevent a commercial treaty between the Huron and the Iroquois. It is my opinion that the prospect of this treaty was a figment of the imagination of the French in Quebec and never a real possibility (see text below).

74. On the Mohawk refusal to let the French Indians pass through their country to trade with the Dutch see Trelease, *Indian Affairs*, 52–53; Hunt, *Wars of the Iroquois*, 34. Trudel's (*Histoire de la Nouvelle-France* 2: 364–66) suggestion that the Huron were about to trade with the Dutch and that the French who stayed in Huronia did so to prevent this seems unlikely in view of the traditional enmity between the Huron and the Iroquois. To reach Albany the latter would have had to travel through the tribal territory of the three eastern

Iroquois tribes. Mohawk opposition to this seems to have effectively discouraged the Huron from attempting such trade.

75. Sagard says that the Huron did not permit other tribes to pass through their territory without special permission (Wrong, ed., *Sagard's Long Journey*, 99). The Jesuits say categorically that the Huron did not permit the Petun to trade with the French (Thwaites, ed., *Relations* 21: 177).

76. For a reference about canoes see Hunt, *Wars of the Iroquois*, 51.

77. Le Clercq, *Establishment* 1: 267. The Huron spread evil rumours about the Jesuits among the Petun when the Jesuits tried to do mission work there in 1640 (Thwaites, ed., *Relations* 20: 47–51).

78. Thwaites, ed., *Relations* 21: 207–15. At first the priests pretended to be traders. This pretence, however, failed.

79. Biggar, ed., *Works of Champlain* 5: 131.

80. The French later describe him as a traitor (Thwaites, ed., *Relations* 5: 241).

81. Tross, ed., *Histoire du Canada* 2: 431. For a description of his proposed reburial see Thwaites, ed., *Relations* 10: 307–309.

82. G. Lanctot, *A History of Canada*, vol. 1 (Toronto, 1963), 148–49.

83. It appears that one reason the Recollets received little support from the trading companies was that their policy of settling migratory Indians and of wanting Huron converts to settle in Quebec conflicted with the traders' own interests (Le Clercq, *Establishment* 1: 111).

84. The support of Governor Montmagny appears to have been particularly effective (Thwaites, ed., *Relations* 21: 143; 22: 309, 311).

85. Thwaites, ed., *Relations* 10: 33; 11: 97, 109, 111, 113; 13: 9; 14: 125 161, 231, 235, 255. On the discontinuation of the seminary, see 24: 103. During the first two years the Jesuits were back in Huronia they were struggling to orient themselves and to understand the nature of Huron society better. At first they tended to be rather patronizing. They gave advice on military matters (10: 53) and, failing to understand the nature of Huron politics, felt that their intervention was needed to mediate disputes among the different tribes (9: 273; 14: 17, 21). Later, when they realized how the Huron did things and that intervention was unnecessary, these efforts ceased.

86. One example is the decision to seek to baptize older men — and especially influential ones (Thwaites, ed., *Relations* 15: 109).

87. For Jesuit policy regarding lay assistants in Huronia, see Thwaites, ed., *Relations* 21: 293–303. See also 6: 81, 83; 15: 157; 17: 45; 20: 99; 25: 85; 27: 91.

88. Parkman, *Jesuits in North America*, 465–67. Concerning early charges of Jesuit participation in the fur trade and a declaration by the directors of the Company of New France concerning their innocence, see Thwaites, ed., *Relations* 25: 75.

89. Thwaites, ed., *Relations* 14: 17–19. For a clear statement that the Jesuits were aware that their presence in Huronia depended on the traders' ability to coerce the Huron to let them stay, see 34: 205. Soon after the Jesuits returned to Huronia, Brébeuf wrote that they won the esteem of the Indians by giving them arrowheads and helping them to defend their forts (34: 53). He hoped that the confidence won by these actions would permit the Jesuits eventually to "advance the glory of God."

90. The main reason seems to have been that the French had detained a Huron who was implicated in killing a Frenchman in Huronia (Thwaites, ed., *Relations* 6: 19). It is interesting to note that the Huron also made it clear they wanted Frenchmen with guns instead of, or at least alongside, the priests (7: 217).

91. Thwaites, ed., *Relations* 9: 287.

92. Thwaites, ed., *Relations* 7: 47. The officials in Quebec continued to exhort the Huron to become Christians (17: 171).

93. Thwaites, ed., *Relations* 8: 71, 91, 99.

94. That was in July 1633 (Thwaites, ed., *Relations* 5: 259). The people of Ossossané continued to press the Jesuits to move there.

95. Thwaites, ed., *Relations* 8: 99, 103–105. They also stayed at Ihonitiria because they felt it better to start work in a small village rather than a large and important one (8: 103). Ossossané was also unsatisfactory as its inhabitants were planning to relocate the village the next spring (8: 101).

96. Thwaites, ed., *Relations* 5: 239; 8: 99; 10: 309; 14: 99–103.

97. For an account of this dispute and the Jesuits' attempts to resolve it, see Thwaites, ed., *Relations* 10: 279–81, 307; 14: 21. No mention is made of the dispute after 1637, so presumably it was patched up. Brébeuf mentions elsewhere that, as a result of Brûlé's murder, other Huron were threatening the people of Toanché (the village where he was killed) with death (8: 99). The bad relations between Ossossané and the village of Ihonitiria (which was inhabited by Toanchéans) were exacerbated in 1633 when the latter became angry at the efforts of the chiefs of Ossossané to persuade all the Jesuits to settle in their village (5: 263).

98. Presents were also given to the Huron both as tokens of goodwill and to ensure the good treatment of the Jesuits.

99. For a discussion of the financial help the Jesuits expected to receive from the trading company see Thwaites, ed., *Relations* 6: 81–83. The financial support of the mission is discussed in Parkman, *Jesuits in North America*, 465–67.

100. Thwaites, ed., *Relations* 10: 249; 13: 141; 17: 95; 18: 19, 97.

101. Thwaites, ed., *Relations* 10: 301.

102. One of these trips was to visit the father of a young convert named Amantacha who lived at St. Joseph (Thwaites, ed., *Relations* 8: 139). A careful tabulation by [the author's research assistant] Miss [A. Elaine] Clark of the places the Jesuits mention visiting each year and the amount of attention given to each village in Huronia shows clearly that prior to 1640 their activities were confined to the Bear nation and particularly to the Penetang Peninsula. After that time their mission work spread into all parts of Huronia.

103. To less than twelve thousand.

104. Thwaites, ed., *Relations* 19: 123, 127; 8: 145–47. The high mortality rate among children is an overall impression gained from reading the Relations of the years 1636–40. It also corresponds with what is known about similar epidemics among other Indian groups.

105. Thwaites, ed., *Relations* 19: 223.

106. Thwaites, ed., *Relations* 14: 17, 53, 99–103.

107. Thwaites, ed., *Relations* 39: 129.

108. Thwaites, ed., *Relations* 19: 179.

109. Thwaites, ed., *Relations* 15: 59–67.

110. At all times the Huron leaders appear to have been convinced that killing a priest or one of their assistants would terminate the Franco–Huron alliance.

111. Thwaites, ed., *Relations* 13: 215, 217. For a French statement emphasizing the Huron dependence on trade goods see 32: 179 (1647–48).

112. Thwaites, ed., *Relations* 15: 21.

113. Thwaites, ed., *Relations* 15: 51.

114. Thwaites, ed., *Relations* 15: 55; 17: 115.

115. Thwaites, ed., *Relations* 21: 143; 22: 310.

116. Thwaites, ed., *Relations* 21: 131.

117. One heifer and a small cannon arrived in 1648 (Thwaites, ed., *Relations* 32: 99).

118. Thwaites, ed., *Relations* 26: 201.

119. Concerning the establishment of Ste Marie and the mission system see Thwaites, ed., *Relations* 19: 123–65.

120. There is a considerable amount of other evidence concerning the coercive power of Huron chiefs. See B.G. Trigger, "Order and Freedom in Huron Society," *Anthropologica* N.S. 5 (1963): 151–69.

121. Thwaites, ed., *Relations* 21: 213. About the same time the Huron were spreading bad reports concerning the Jesuits among the Petun (20: 54), with whom they had recently made a new treaty of friendship (20: 43). These rumours were spread by Huron traders.

122. Thwaites, ed., *Relations* 30: 75–77. So bitter was the Huron opposition to Brébeuf after he returned to Huronia that the Huron mission was compelled to send him down to Quebec until the situation quieted down (23: 35).

123. The Jesuit Relation of 1635 records that the beaver was already totally extinct in the Huron country and that all the skins they traded with the French were obtained elsewhere (Thwaites, ed., *Relations* 8: 57).

124. Trelease, *Indian Affairs*, 118–20; Hunt, *Wars of the Iroquois*, 32–34. For a later source see Jean Talon cited in Hunt, *Wars of the Iroquois*, 137.

125. Hunt, *Wars of the Iroquois*, 32–34; Trelease, *Indian Affairs*, 118.

126. This theory was first advanced by C.H. McIlwain in 1915. It was taken up in Innis, *Fur Trade*, 34–36, and Hunt, *Wars of the Iroquois*, 32–37, 74.

127. Trelease, *Indian Affairs*, 120.

128. E.B. O'Callaghan, ed., *Documents Relative to the Colonial History of the State of New York* . . . (15 vols.; Albany, 1853–87), 4: 908.

129. Thwaites, ed., *Relations* 23: 105.

130. Hunt, *Wars of the Iroquois*, 76.

131. Tooker, "Defeat of the Huron," 117–18.

132. Thwaites, ed., *Relations* 26: 71; 27: 89, 277. Brébeuf returned to Huronia at this time.

133. Hunt, *Wars of the Iroquois*, 77–78.

134. For the Iroquois desire to obtain French guns, see the evidence presented in Hunt, *Wars of the Iroquois*, 74.
135. Thwaites, ed., *Relations* 10: 13; 13: 171.
136. Thwaites, ed., *Relations* 20: 27–31.
137. Thwaites, ed., *Relations* 20: 225; 26: 275.
138. Thwaites, ed., *Relations* 15: 109. For the later relaxation of these requirements see 33: 145–47.
139. Thwaites, ed., *Relations* 19: 191.
140. Thwaites, ed., *Relations* 17: 111; 23: 129.
141. Concerning this preferential treatment see Thwaites, ed., *Relations* 20: 225, 227.
142. Thwaites, ed., *Relations* 32: 179.
143. Vachon, "L'Eau-de-vie."
144. Thwaites, ed., *Relations* 23: 67, 127; 26: 229. Pagan women also attempted to seduce Christian men to persuade them to give up their faith (30: 33). The Relation of 1643 mentions that some converts lived for six months at Quebec to avoid facing temptation in their homeland (24: 121).
145. Thwaites, ed., *Relations* 30: 23.
146. Thwaites, ed., *Relations* 21: 131.
147. Thwaites, ed., *Relations* 23: 185.
148. Thwaites, ed., *Relations* 23: 31.
149. For another reference to the Huron–pagan rift see Thwaites, ed., *Relations* 23: 267.
150. Thwaites, ed., *Relations* 28: 89. For other acts of Christian assertiveness around this time see 29: 263–69; 30: 63.
151. Thwaites, ed., *Relations* 25: 85.
152. Tross, ed., *Histoire du Canada* 1: 200; Thwaites, ed., *Relations* 5: 259.
153. Thwaites, ed., *Relations* 34: 105, 217.
154. For one incident see Thwaites, ed., *Relations* 30: 61–63. Various cults also arose that appear to have been aimed at organizing ideological resistance to Christianity. One was the cult of a forest monster (30: 27); the second was more explicitly anti-Christian (30: 29–31).
155. As one Huron put it, "I am more attached to the church than to my country or relatives" (Thwaites, ed., *Relations* 23: 137). The Jesuits also observed that it was hard to be a good Christian and a good Huron (28: 53).
156. Thwaites, ed., *Relations* 26: 217. The Jesuits had noted the special inclination of the Bear tribe to receive Christianity as early as 1636 (10: 31).
157. After the destruction of Huronia the Cord were very loyal to the French. They were the only Huron tribe that refused to leave Quebec to go and live with the Iroquois (Thwaites, ed., *Relations* 43: 191). Prior to 1640, the Cord were not at all friendly with the Jesuits (17: 59); their change in attitude seems to have come about soon after (21: 285; 23: 151; 26: 265).
158. Thwaites, ed., *Relations* 42: 73. Concerning their early desire for peace with the Iroquois see 33: 119–121.
159. Thwaites, ed., *Relations* 17: 89.
160. Thwaites, ed., *Relations* 36: 179. The Deer lived among the Seneca in their own village and on good terms with their hosts (44: 21). Many Rock people, including the Indians of Contarea, lived among the Onondaga (42: 73).
161. For evidence of incipient deterioration in morale and the beginning of the abandonment of Huronia in the face of Iroquois attack, see Thwaites, ed., *Relations* 30: 87; 33: 83–89.
162. Thwaites, ed., *Relations* 33: 125. Hunt (*Wars of the Iroquois*, 72) notes that in 1637 the Huron had broken a peace treaty with the Seneca.
163. Thwaites, ed., *Relations* 33: 71, 123.
164. Thwaites, ed., *Relations* 33: 131.
165. Thwaites, ed., *Relations* 33: 119–21.
166. Thwaites, ed., *Relations* 33: 125.
167. Thwaites, ed., *Relations* 33: 125–27. He probably did this through anger at his allies and to show the innocence of the Onondaga. He might also have committed suicide to avoid Huron vengeance directed against his person, but this would have been construed as an act of cowardice. It is unlikely that the Onondaga would have exposed an important chief to almost certain death had they not been negotiating in good faith.
168. Thwaites, ed., *Relations* 33: 229.
169. Thwaites, ed., *Relations* 33: 231.
170. Thwaites, ed., *Relations* 33: 81.

171. Thwaites, ed., *Relations* 33: 233–49.
172. Thwaites, ed., *Relations* 34: 227.
173. Thwaites, ed., *Relations* 34: 83.
174. Lanctot, *History of Canada* 1: 194, based on Thwaites, ed., *Relations* 34: 59–61.
175. Tooker, "Defeat of the Hurons," 117–18; Innis, *Fur Trade*, 35–36. For the effective use of firearms by the Iroquois see Thwaites, ed., *Relations* 22: 307. The Jesuits saw the danger of growing Iroquois firepower as early as 1642 (22: 307) but the French officials in Quebec never developed a policy to counteract it. The restiveness of the Huron pagans may be one reason why the French did not want too many guns in Huron hands, even if they were being sold only to Christians.
176. Hunt, *Wars of the Iroquois*, 59.
177. Thwaites, ed., *Relations* 35: 191.
178. Thwaites, ed., *Relations* 36: 179; 44: 21; 45: 243. Many of the Rock nation, particularly from Contarea, were later found living with the Onondaga (42: 73).
179. Thwaites, ed., *Relations* 12: 221. The work in Paraguay is also mentioned in 15: 127.
180. G. Lanctot, *A History of Canada* (Toronto, 1964), 1: 63.
181. Hunt, *Wars of the Iroquois*, 100–102.
182. Thwaites, ed., *Relations* 41: 201–203, and 44: 151; Hunt, *Wars of the Iroquois*, 99, 100.
183. Thwaites, ed., *Relations* 40: 215; Lanctot, *History of Canada* 1: 212–13. On the lack of furs in Montreal in 1652–53 see Thwaites, ed., *Relations* 40: 211.
184. Hunt, *Wars of the Iroquois*, 102–103.
185. Parkman, *Jesuits in North America*, 550–53.
186. Tross, ed., *Histoire du Canada* 3: 811; Le Clercq, *Establishment* 1: 204.

Article Three

To See Ourselves as the Other's Other: Nlaka'pamux Contact Narratives

Wendy C. Wickwire

The quincentenary of the 'discovery' of the Americas by Christopher Columbus has stimulated wide debate on the history of European contact. In December 1991 a chartered trawler carrying twelve Native people from British Columbia sailed out to meet the Spanish government-sponsored replicas of the *Nina, Pinta,* and *Santa Maria,* bound for San Juan, Puerto Rico, to commemorate Columbus's initial landing. The Natives' objective was to persuade the excursion's leader, Santiago Bolivar, a direct descendent of Columbus, to make a public apology on behalf of the Spanish government for the wrongs committed against them. The protesters estimated that 100 million or more deaths were inflicted on Native peoples from diseases introduced by Columbus and subsequent explorers.[1] In this encounter, something very basic was at stake: the history of colonial encounters from the point-of-view of First Nations' peoples.

This article examines accounts of the first meetings between Nlaka'pamux[2] and European explorers in the Fraser River canyon of south-central British Columbia in June 1808. Simon Fraser was the first non-Native to explore the area along the river that now bears his name. The leader of the North West Company crew consisting of nineteen voyageurs, two Indians,

Source: Wendy C. Wickwire, "To See Ourselves as the Other's Other: Nlaka'pamux Contact Narratives," *Canadian Historical Review,* 75:3, (1994): 1–20. University of Toronto Press Incorporated. Reprinted by permission of University of Toronto Press Incorporated (www.utpjournals.com).

and two clerks, Fraser kept a journal to record his journey — to survey, as it were, the people he met and the terrain along the way. Fraser's journal has become the primary lens through which to view the initial interaction between the Nlaka'pamux and the first white explorers.

While Fraser recorded in writing his impressions of the 'Hacamaugh' (Nlaka'pamux) at 'Camchin'[3] (present-day Lytton) on 19 and 20 June, the Nlaka'pamux recorded their impressions of him. Unlike Fraser, however, the Nlaka'pamux transmitted their impressions orally, and the stories passed from one generation to the next. Anthropologist James Teit recorded some of these accounts almost a century ago. Still others survive as living oral accounts among contemporary Native elders. This article examines these early and more recent accounts in light of what they reveal about the Native oral/historical viewpoint.

THE PROBLEM OF 'HISTORY'

In the early years of this century, British Columbia was a haven for ethnographic research. Many of the names of those who worked here are well known — Franz Boas, Edward Sapir, Thomas McIlwraith, John Swanton, Marius Barbeau, Diamond Jenness, Charles Hill-Tout, James Teit. This was the era of 'total ethnography'— the assembling of complete descriptions of other societies or cultures.[4] Anthropologists believed that by recording everything and anything imaginable, from religious worldview to pictography, they could reconstruct an image of the pure and untarnished traditional culture. One of the essentials was 'folklore.' Hundreds of traditional stories were collected for publication in the early editions of the *Journal of American Folk-Lore* and the *Jesup Expedition* monographs.

Until recently, many readers have accepted these early texts at face value. Today, however, many are reading them with serious concerns about translation and representation. Critical theorist David Murray, in a recent study of speech, writing, and representation in North American Indian texts,[5] for example, asks what was recorded and why? What language was used in the recording? Who were the 'informants'? Why did they tell what they told? Most important to Murray is the position of the 'mediator' or 'interpreter.' He suggests that we look to this individual in order to better understand the 'stories' collected.

These are key questions in British Columbia where Franz Boas played a major role. Not only did Boas collect a mass of Native texts in British Columbia himself, but he also supervised the collection of hundreds of texts by others, among them James Teit. Between 1898 and 1917 Teit recorded oral narratives in south-central British Columbia. He sent these to Boas, who edited them in preparation for publication. Boas highlighted those that he believed to be the ancient ancestral stories and he downplayed stories about current events, personal experiences, and nineteenth-century epidemics, explorers, technology, and religious ideas. This bias in the early published ethnographic record is striking when one listens to Nlaka'pamux storytellers today and learns that stories about nineteenth-century events are well known.

Although this living history has been relatively ignored in British Columbia, it has been the focus of attention in other areas. In South and Central America, for example, anthropologists have been studying the history of contact as articulated by indigenous peoples with very positive results. Jonathon D. Hill has found that by shifting the focus away from 'what *really* happened' to the Natives' *own* historical consciousness (indeed, diversity thereof), he has come to appreciate other issues, such as 'how indigenous societies have experienced history, and the ongoing means by which they struggle to make sense out of complex, contradictory historical processes.'[6] Anthropologist Terence Turner has studied the interplay between myth and history which he finds 'complementary and mutually informing.'[7] This approach, explains Turner, tends to produce new images of Westerners and Western society —'images formed by others during the process of Western expansion.' It also turns traditional anthropology on its head by placing ourselves, for a change, in the position of the 'other.'[8]

SIMON FRASER'S ACCOUNT, 1808

Fraser was much impressed with the inhabitants of Camchin and vicinity. At one village of 'about four hundred souls,' he observed that the people 'live among mountains, and enjoy pure air, seem cleanly inclined, and make use of wholesome food.' At his next stop, he was led to a camp where twelve hundred people were sitting in rows, waiting to see him and to shake his hand. The Indians fed the newcomers generously with 'salmon, berries, oil and roots in abundance,' as well as with the meat of six dogs.[9]

Fraser observed that people of Camchin attached some religious significance to his appearance. At the large ceremonial gathering there, for example, he noted that 'the Great Chief made a long harangue, in [the] course of which he pointed to the sun, to the four quarters of the world and then to us, and then he introduced his father, who was old and blind, [and who] . . . with some emotion often stretched out both his hands in order to feel ours.' After this event, Fraser noted that the Indians sang and danced all night long, while his crew-members watched with amusement. On his departure from Camchin, the Natives presented Fraser with 'berries, roots and oil in abundance.' He guessed that such gestures 'proceed[ed], perhaps, from an idea that we are superior beings, who are not to be overcome.'[10]

Fraser in turn presented one chief who had been particularly good to him with a gift: 'The Chief of [the] Camshins [sic] . . . is the greatest chief we have seen; he behaved towards us uncommonly well. I made him a present of a large silver broach which he immediately fixed on his head, and he was exceedingly well pleased with our attention.'[11] Fraser noted in his journal the Natives at Camchin had several 'European articles among them, a copper Tea Kettle, a brass camp kettle, and a strip of a common blanket, and cloathing such as the Cree women wear.'[12] These, he thought, came from settlements east of the Rockies.

On his return trip a month later, Fraser stopped again at Camchin but found the atmosphere there much changed. Not only did he feel ignored by the chief who had been so friendly towards him a month earlier, but he 'could perceive something unpleasant in their demeanour.' There was 'a disagreeable gloom' perhaps related to the fact that 'most of the children were really afflicted with some serious disorder which reduced them to skeletons.'[13]

NLAKA'PAMUX ACCOUNTS OF FRASER, CIRCA 1900

Much of what we know about the Nlaka'pamux comes from the writings of an early anthropologist, James Teit. Teit was an unusual man.[14] He had emigrated to Canada from the Shetland Islands in 1884, at the age of nineteen. When Franz Boas met him at Spence's Bridge, British Columbia, ten years later, he was living with his Nlaka'pamux wife, Lucy Antko, and was on very good terms with her people. Boas was so impressed with Teit's knowledge of the Nlaka'pamux language and culture that he engaged him right away to undertake ethnographic work. This marked the beginning of a life-long collaboration between the two men that led to the compilation of major ethnographies, collections of narratives and monographs on various subjects, including basketry and ethnobotany, much of which was edited by Boas.

Unlike many other anthropologists of the day, who entered Native communities as outsiders and who worked with one or two willing informants, Teit was an insider who consulted with a large number of individuals who were long-time friends, associates, and relatives through marriage. While he conducted his anthropological work, he simultaneously pursued other activities such as hunting and guiding, often in the company of Native people. From 1908 until his death in 1922, he played major roles in three native political organizations, The Interior Tribes of British Columbia, the Indian Rights Association, and The Allied Tribes of British Columbia.

Fortunately, Teit was interested in issues of the day as well as in issues of the past. Scattered throughout his collections of traditional folklore, for instance, are European legends, Bible stories, war stories, and accounts of noteworthy events of the 1800s.[15] In this latter category, there are also stories about the arrival of the first white explorers.

NATIVE PROPHECIES TELL OF STRANGE WHITE PEOPLE TO COME

According to Teit, there were among the Nlaka'pamux certain individuals, both male and female, who could predict the future. These prophets were much revered and travelled widely, telling people of things to come. Wherever they went, large numbers of people gathered to dance and sing, and especially to hear their messages. Although the dancing died out in 1858, the prophets lived on. Writing in 1900, Teit noted that 'in the last fifteen years, three prophets . . . have appeared among the tribe. One was a Fraser Valley prophet who travelled as far as Lytton; another was a woman from the Nicola Valley . . . and the last was an Okanagan woman who appeared in 1891.'[16] Stories of these and other prophets were still in circulation in 1915. Chief John Tetlenitsa of Spence's Bridge described a prophet who had lived in his community many years earlier. 'Present-day people,' he explained, 'believe his spirit really went over to France and that he foretold the advent of the Whites at an early date.'[17]

Teit described in detail the ritual associated with prophets' ceremonies,[18] and he recorded texts of several prophets' songs. These provide some insight into the Native perspective on initial encounters with whites. One prophet's song was said to have originated with a Spence's Bridge man named Kwalos. According to Tetlenitsa, Kwalos had been a dance chief, dreamer, and prophet who, 'before the first white people came to the county, had a series of dreams or visions which impressed him very much.' He had gathered the people together and told them about his dreams:

> He told how his spirit left his body and passed rapidly to the shores of a great lake in the far east where the clouds always hung low along the edge of the water. Here his spirit left the land and rolled along the clouds until it came to a land on the other side of the great lake. Here there were many strange people who spoke a language very different in sound from Indian languages. (He imitated the speaking of these people and what he said sounded very much like French.) [JAT] These people were very different from Indians and had many beautiful and wonderful things the Indians knew nothing of. They had light skins and different colours of hair and eyes and many kinds of fine clothes and ornaments. Both the men and women dressed differently from Indians and their clothes were of peculiar patterns and materials. The women especially had very striking and beautiful dresses. These people were very numerous and did many strange things. They lived in many high houses made of stone. They had fires inside of stones (prob. stoves), and much smoke could be seen coming out of the stones (prob. chimneys). Their houses had mouths and eyes (prob. doors and windows) and around them were many open grassy lands and plots where there were many kinds of beautiful flowers and plants and grasses, some of which they used as food (prob. fields of grain, vegetables, etc. and flower gardens). Surrounding some of the houses were gorgeous flowers. Outside the houses were many rabbits (don't know what he meant by rabbits) and many goats (prob. sheep) from which the people obtained wool for clothes. Also there were animals somewhat like buffalo (prob. cattle) from which they drew milk, and the flesh of which they ate, and there were

other animals somewhat like moose or deer (prob. horses) but without horns. All these animals were tame like dogs and mixed with the people. These white people had much music and singing, were very rich and seemed to be happy. In the dances, Kwalos prayed that the people he had seen would come over and enlighten the Indians and make them powerful, wise, rich and happy like themselves. He further stated that he believed these people would come to the Indians some time soon and then great changes would take place among the Indians — Kwalos used this song when he held dances in connection with his visions of the white man's land.[19]

Teit also recorded the prophecies of NokanekautkEn, alias Nelkwax, a dance chief of the Lytton division. Along with TcexawatEn of Ashcroft, NokanekautkEn had had visions in which he 'saw many things belonging to the whites . . . which none of the Indians had yet seen.'[20]

When one considers that European material goods had made their way to Camchin prior to Fraser's arrival, it is not surprising that stories and dreams of strange people east of the mountains also travelled to Camchin and other Native villages in British Columbia's southern interior prior to 1808.

The Sun Arrives

Teit recorded five Nlaka'pamux stories of first encounters with whites.[21] Two of these are especially interesting, because, unlike most stories, which are anonymous, the names of the storytellers are given. One was told by SEmalitsa, a woman from Styne Creek[22] near Lytton; and another was told by Waxtko, a woman from Spence's Bridge.[23] Names of the tellers of the remaining three stories are not mentioned.[24]

SEmalitsa's account of Fraser's arrival was based on a story her grandmother had told her about an event she had witnessed as a child:

My grandmother told me that when she was a young girl she was playing one day in the summer-time (about the time the service-berries get ripe) near the river-beach at the village of Strain,[25] when she saw two canoes, with red flags hoisted, come downstream. She ran and told her mother, and the people gathered to see the strange sight. Seeing so many people gathered, the canoes put ashore and several men came ashore. Each canoe carried a number of men (perhaps six or seven in each), and many of them wore strange dresses, and everything about them was strange. Some of the men looked like Indians, and others looked like what we call white men. Among them was a Shuswap chief who acted as interpreter. Our people were not afraid of the strangers, nor were they hostile to them. The strangers produced a large pipe, and had a ceremonial smoke with some of our men. After distributing a few presents, they boarded their canoes and went on to Lytton. They remained one or two days at Lytton, where they were presented with food of various kinds, and gave in exchange tobacco, beads, and knives. Runners from the river had come down about a day ahead of them along the east side of the Fraser River to Lytton. The Lytton chief ImentcutEn went up the east bank of the Fraser, and met them two or three miles above Lytton, and conducted them to his place with considerable ceremony. All the Lytton people were assembled to meet them, and before they left there they had many talks and smokes with the Indians. Next day a number of people who camped at Botani Valley came down to see them; and the news having reached up the Thompson as far as Spence's Bridge, some of the men from there also came down — those having horses, on horseback; and those having none, on foot. The Spence's Bridge chief ran on foot all the way, and arrived in time to see the strangers and to deliver a great speech, but some of his people arrived too late to see them. The Lytton chief at this time was also a great orator. The Spence's Bridge chief was presented with some kind of a metal or brass badge, and a hat worn by the leader of the strangers whom the Indians called 'the Sun.' He was called this because of some kind of shining emblem he wore on his hat or cap, which resembled the symbol of the Sun. The Indians applied names to most of the strangers, all taken from some feature of their appearance or from certain marks or emblems on their clothing.[26]

SEmalitsa's story was the only one to make reference to Fraser's second appearance at Lytton: 'Many people saw them again on their return journey, as they were again assembling on the rivers for salmon-fishing. Probably more people saw them when they came back than when they went down.'[27]

Teit published Waxtko's version of the Fraser story in 1917. Although Waxtko lived at Spence's Bridge, about twenty miles upstream from SEmalitsa's home, her story is very similar to SEmalitsa's:

> When Kwolina'u.l[28] came to Lytton . . . [i]t was in midsummer. The berries were just ripe in the river-valley; and many of the tribe were assembled at Botani, digging roots and playing games. Some Thompson men, who had been up at La Fontaine on horseback, came back quickly with the news of the approach of these people. Tcexe'x was at Botani with others from Spence's Bridge. He hurried down to Lytton, and was there when the whites arrived. The chief of the latter we called 'Sun.' We did not know his name. Several chiefs made speeches to him, but Tcexe'x made the greatest speech.[29]

According to Waxtko, Tcexex's was her own relative. She described him as 'a prominent chief and a great orator . . . [and] an elderly man at the time when these whites came to Lytton.' Like SEmalitsa, Waxtko was told that Fraser had presented Tcexe'x with a silver broach:

> This chief so pleased Sun, that he gave him a present of a large silver broach, or some other similar ornament, which he had on his person. On several occasions Tcexe'x used this attached to his hair in front, or on the front of his head. When I was a girl, I saw it worn by his sons. One of his sons inherited it; on his death his brother obtained it: and it was probably buried with the third brother who had it, as it disappeared about the time of his death. The last-named chief died at Lytton as an elderly man.[30]

Of the three remaining Simon Fraser stories, Teit noted that they were the 'mythological version[s]' of the capsizing of Fraser's canoe in Fraser River. In these three versions, Fraser and his crew are depicted as mythological figures who have returned. As the first teller noted:

> Many years ago, but at a time long after Coyote had finished arranging things on earth, he appeared on Fraser River in company with Sun, Moon, Morning-Star, Kokwela, nmuipEm ('diver') and SkwiaxEnEmux ('arrow-armed person,' 'person with arrow arms or shoulders. . . .') This is the only time Coyote has appeared since the end of the mythological age.[31]

'Sun' here, as in both SEmalitsa's and Waxtko's accounts, is probably Fraser. In the second account, three heavenly bodies are mentioned — Sun, Moon, and Morning-Star, each of whom appeared briefly after the capsizing, but all of whom disappeared forever during the night. According to a third version, there were two canoes, one of which carried seven heavenly bodies (sun, moon, morning-star, and others said to be stars); and the other carried seven Transformers — Coyote, NLikisEntem, Kokwela, Old-One, Ntcemka, SkwiaxEnEmux, and nmuipEm.

The first story describes in detail the canoe's capsizing:

> Continuing their journey, and when in the middle of the river, a short distance below Lytton, the Moon, who was steersman of the canoe, disappeared with it under water. The others came out of the water and sat down on a rock close above the river. Then Skwia'x'EnEmux ['arrow-armed person'] fired many lightning arrows,[32] and nmu'ipEm ['diver'] dived many times into the river.[33] The Sun sat still and smoked;[34] while Coyote, Kokwe'la, and Morning-Star danced. Coyote said, 'Moon will never come up again with the canoe;' but Sun said, 'Yes, in

the evening he will appear.' Just after sunset, Moon appeared holding the canoe, and came ashore. All of them embarked, and, going down the river, were never seen again.[35]

In her account, SEmalitsa included a fragment of the capsizing which is very similar: 'After leaving Lytton, at some place close to Siska, one of their canoes was swamped in a rapid, and some of the men were saved with difficulty, after having been some time in the water.' She also commented on the merger of these explanations of the newcomers:

> Very many people thought they were the beings spoken of in tales of the mythological period, who had taken a notion to travel again over the earth; and they often wondered what object they had in view, and what results would follow. They believed their appearance foreboded some great change or events of prime importance to the Indians, but in what way they did not know.[36]

Accounts Compared

There are many common threads running through these early Native accounts. Most prominent is a figure called Sun, who appears with a crew of twelve to fourteen men from upstream in one or two birch-bark canoes. The two women's accounts coincide on the time of the newcomers' arrival, as well as the large ceremonial gathering held in Fraser's honour. Both also mention Fraser's gift of a metal broach to one of the chiefs, who accepted it with much pleasure. The capsizing of one or two canoes just downstream from Lytton is described in four of the five stories.

None of these Native accounts mentions hostility towards the newcomers. On the contrary, they depict a situation of warm exchange. Neither afraid or hostile, the Nlaka'pamux shared their food supplies liberally, smoked, and welcomed the newcomers with pomp and ceremony.

These early Native accounts also share points in common with Fraser's journal — for example, Fraser's arrival at Camchin in June; the silver broach which he gave to the Chief of the Camchins; the exchange of food for 'knife, awl and trinkets'; and the fact that Fraser's crew included 'Whites' as well as Indians. There is a particularly strong parallel between Fraser's and the Native accounts on the subject of the capsizing.

NLAKA'PAMUX ACCOUNTS OF FIRST NATIVE–WHITE ENCOUNTERS, 1981–91

Over the last several years, I have talked with Native elders in Spuzzum and Lytton about the portrayal in their accounts of the first encounters with whites. In Lytton, Louis Philips explained that his ancestors had been forewarned about the arrival of the whites:

> That old man at the Stein, they call him Lytton Dick. His Indian name is N-TEEH-low,[37] and he tell something that's going to happen maybe tomorrow or maybe next day. Long before it happens . . . He used to tell the people, he'd tell the people, 'Not very long from now these peoples that's coming in here, from their country into our country . . . [they're] going to look different from what we are now and who we are. It's going to look different when those white people come here. Say they just look like us, only they're white . . . That old man, he's ahead of himself to tell all what's going to happen before it happens. . . .[38]

Louis's father had been told another story about the first whites to arrive at Lytton:

> [At the] Stein, there was a bunch of womens, old womens, young womens, out there picking 'CHA-kum,' and, hot day, they got sweating, and they go down to the river to take a bath in the river, and they see these boats coming, and the womens didn't know they were 'SHA-ma' or anything. They stay there on the beach taking a cold bath. This boat come and land.

Simon Fraser had one of them old-fashioned shirts, starch in the front, and starch in the back, and that shine. Sunny day like this. And those women thought they seen Jesus Christ in person. And they all sit there naked. Never think, well, they pretty near naked all the time. And this white man come off the boat, and he look at the women sitting down on the beach. Looked at them. And they all thought they seen Jesus Christ. That starch, they shine. They thought they seen right through him. And he turn around the other way and the starch on his back shines. They thought they seen through him. They thought they seen Jesus Christ alive. He look at them all, sized them all up. And the young lady there, lift 'em up, stand 'em up, and rub 'em, and hug 'em. And after he got through, he got in a boat and he drift down. And these old womens, they all kneel down and pray, pray to the young woman that Shu-sha-klee[39] pick on. They thought, they tell this young woman, 'Ah, you must be a good woman. Jesus Christ come and rub you up and hug you. And us, we sit there and watch you.' Say, 'You must be a good woman.' They pray to this woman that Simon Fraser hug. They thought he was Jesus Christ. Old Yen-a-ma-ken. He's an old man at the Stein. I used to go there. My father was partly raised in the Stein, and he was one of them . . . Yen-a-ma-ken is my father's uncle. He used to tell that story when Simon Fraser first come through there. And that time, I was too small. I didn't know nothing.[40]

Phillips's story even contains details of an incident not reported in the earlier accounts which he would have been told (orally), but which the Jesup expedition and Teit did not hear and record. His account suggests that prophecies and stories of first encounters with whites may have been informed by long-distance travel.

There was one guy, he used to disappear. Once time, three or four years before he come back. He goes way down south. He just go and keep on going. How far we went, he says there's no winter-time there. He said you could lay under a tree and sleep, wake up and go. He said the people around there are friendly just like our peoples here. They see a stranger, bring 'em in the house and feed you, bed you. And in the morning you go. He was the first one that seen it come true. I don't know how far he went. I don't how if he went to Mexico or where he went. But when he came back, he tell the others, he said, 'What he was telling us about, about what changes we're going to have,' he said, 'I seen some of it . . . 'And when he comes back, maybe three or four years, as soon as they see him, they call up, maybe Boston Bar and Spence's Bridge, and Lytton. And get together and talk about it, what this man seen when he was away . . . There was some Indians they used to take off three or four years. They used to go a long ways. Never hear them talk about the north. They hear them talk about the south. No road, no trail. You just go through the brush. You just go by the shade of the tree. That's all the clock he's got. And he go so far and he come back. They say, 'How long you stay in one place?' 'Oh,' he says, 'I camp. They feed me, bed me. Look after me good. They look after me better than I look after myself, because I am a stranger' . . . He says, 'It's just like we do when we get a stranger here,' he says. We get a stranger here, always try to look after him. Indians is like that all over. Look after a stranger good. It's like that yet . . . White man is not like that. Some is like that, but some you got to give 'em money first before they do anything. That time when the white man came here, buckskin or dry fish was the biggest thing they can give.[41]

Nlaka'pamux elder Annie York of Spuzzum explained that her grandparents had told her that old chief Sh-PEENT-lum and his wife of Lytton had predicted the arrival of whites prior to their actual arrival:

When Simon Fraser came down, the Lytton Indians were the first ones that knew them. They seen this man, the Lytton Indians seen this man coming down in the canoe with his party and Chief Sh-PEENT-lum soon spot it and he says, 'That's what my wife foretold. That man is coming to this area.' So he said to the Indians, 'You Indians must never touch him. You must never hurt him. See that white, what he got on his head?' He had a white handkerchief that tied around as a band. And he's the head man in the canoe. And when this Indian spotted him, Sh-PEENT-lum's servant, he camped down there somewhere on the other side of Siska. And that's where he forgot his axe, his little hatchet. But Sh-PEENT-lum said to his servants, 'You boys must make it. You must run after that canoe and you must catch up and give him his axe.'[42] And so they did. They caught up to him and gave him his axe. Sh-PEENT-lum told his men, these two boys, 'You must keep on going to Spuzzum. And send the word down there. But you must never hurt that man. That's the man of the sun. He's the son of the sun.'

So these Indians came along and they came to Spuzzum and they spread the news all around. But our grandmother, our own grandmother, she was ten years old and they lived down there, on the other side of Spuzzum Creek, right at the mouth and there were several others. And Paul Yowla was there, and several others. And a special man came in a canoe. And when they see him, they knew who he was. That was the man that was foretold to come. They welcomed him.[43]

Like Louis's account, Annie's adds a whole level of detail not found in the earlier recorded accounts. This detail she learned orally from the account as it was told to her by those who had had it passed on to them by those who retold certain aspects that others did not. Annie continued:

And when he came, this Indian came with dog, a little dog. And the Indians had fish boiled by their summer campfire, because it was in springtime. And they were boiling the fish. They offered him the fish, but he didn't want the fish. He kept pointing at the dog. And the Indians couldn't understand why he kept pointing at the dog. So they gave him the dog. What do you think they did? They killed the dog and ate it. That's what he had for his supper. The Indians didn't like that very much but the next morning they cooked the fish for them. And the chief came and then they had their pipe, the pipe that was always used. He flew his flag and he ordered all his tribe, 'You must meet this new man.' Because that was their traditional way of living. Pelok, he ordered all these people, 'You must never hurt this man. You must welcome him.' And so they did. And they stayed for a few days. And down there by the Cottonwood tree, there's a big cottonwood tree down there by Spuzzum Creek and that's where they camped, and our great grandmother was there and our grandmother was ten years old. She told us this story. There was a special woman, she's a relation of our grandmother, she was an entertainer, a singer. And she was asked to sing this special song when Simon Fraser was leaving. So they have a sort of special prayer that he must be safe in his voyage drifting down the Fraser River. Warned him . . . that's one of the waters that's very fierce . . . These people that was with Simon Fraser, they understand. When they was leaving, this woman sang this special song. And Simon Fraser, he was feeling so sad he has tears in his eyes when he was drifting away.[44]

Annie explained that Fraser's captain had forewarned the people not to touch any of the newcomers:

Funny thing about that Simon Fraser's captain. The captain of Simon Fraser at Lytton warned these people not to touch them. 'If you do it, you're going to get some kind of disease, and it's going to clean you out.' And it did. Isn't that funny? . . . Sh-PEENT-lum says, 'That man come from the sun. That's God's child to send here to be supervise us.' So he came to Spuzzum and he warned the people not to do it [touch him]. 'You're going to get sick if you do it.' It seems like this man used to get in trance and he can see everything, the way my grandaunt told it. I seen it today and I keep on seeing it.[45]

Sam Mitchell of Fountain (thirty miles upriver from Lytton) relayed another account of Fraser's encounter with some Lillooet Indians. This is, said Mitchell, a 'true story' about some people who came down the river 'a long time ago.' He had heard the story many times. This one had been told to Mitchell's father by an old Indian, 'Piyell,' who was two years old when this incident took place.

Some 'drifters,' Mitchell was told, beached their boat at a place well known for its rapids and asked some Indians there to help them carry it. The Indians helped with the portage.

Although there were some who wanted to go after these 'white men' and steal their possessions, their leader told them, 'Don't bother them; they might be able to help us one day!' According to this version of the story, the leader of the drifters was a white man who had a tattoo of the sun on his forehead and a tattoo of the moon on his chest.[46]

ACCOUNTS COMPARED

There are many common threads in these stories. Fraser is strongly associated with the sun. For example, he is the 'man of the sun, son of sun' (Annie York) and he wears a tattoo of the sun on his forehead (Sam Mitchell). Although the shining metal broach of the turn of the century is absent in these contemporary stories, there is strong brightness or whiteness associated with Fraser that is similar to that of the shining broach — for example, the white handkerchief tied around the head (Annie York), and the white starched shirt which looked very bright in the summer sun (Louis Phillips). Just as the earlier Nlaka'pamux accounts attached religious significance to the appearance of newcomers, so too do the present-day accounts. In Phillips's account, Fraser was Jesus Christ; and in Annie York's account he was the son of the sun, God's son. The present-day stories, like their turn-of-the-century counterparts, also suggest that Fraser's arrival was no real surprise. Prophets and long-distance travellers had forewarned the people about strange people with guns who would come one day. At least two of the present-day accounts suggest that the chiefs advocated a policy of behaving peacefully towards Fraser and his crew.

The similarities between these oral accounts and Fraser's 1808 journal are also striking — for example, loss and return of what Fraser calls 'a piece of Iron.' York mentions this incident in her story, noting that the item returned was an axe (the current oral account here having the great degree of precision). Just as Fraser noted in his journal that at Spuzzum he was hospitably entertained 'with salmon, boiled and roasted,' Annie York mentions that when Fraser arrived there, the Indians were boiling salmon and that he was entertained by one of the women who sang for him. Fraser's observation that he was being treated as a 'superior being'[47] is confirmed in the contemporary accounts (York was told he was 'son of the sun' or the 'sun's son'; and Louis Phillips was told he was 'Jesus Christ'). Just as one Native account makes an association between the newcomers and disease (Annie York), Fraser's account suggests a link between the Natives' cold reception at Camchin on his return trip and disease among the children there.

One point of difference between the Native and non-Native accounts is the encounter between Fraser and a young woman at the mouth of the Stein River near Lytton. Fraser's journal (not surprisingly) makes no reference to such an incident.

SO WHAT DO THESE ACCOUNTS TELL US?

Contact history is largely a history based on written records by white explorers. In the flurry of ethnographic reporting that took place at the turn of the century in British Columbia under Franz Boas and others, the prehistoric past was given precedence over all else. Because of this emphasis, many Native people became known as people with a deep past but without a more recent past. As this article shows, however, prevailing ideas on this subject may well be more a reflection of non-Native preoccupations and interests than of the Native experience. Even my preliminary research suggests that Nlaka'pamux accounts of their initial encounters with whites *are* an important and reliable historical record. Not only is there a remarkable consistency with Fraser's account, but, on some points, such as Fraser's interaction with the Natives at the mouth of the Stein (Louis Phillips) and Spuzzum (Annie York), there is more detail in the Native accounts than in Fraser's journal.

These indigenous stories also reveal other important features of Native historiography. The naming of sources is important. For example, SEmalitsa attributed her story to her grandmother, who had witnessed the arrival of the first whites on her soil. Waxtko also named various individuals from her community who had seen and interacted with the first whites. Annie York attributed her story to her great-grandmother who, like, SEmalitsa's grandmother, had witnessed the arrival of Fraser at Spuzzum. Louis Phillips explained that old Yenamaken, his father's uncle, who lived at the Stein, had told his father the story of Fraser's arrival there. Sam Mitchell explained that he heard the story from his father, who had heard it told by an Indian named Piyell who was two years old when Fraser appeared. This 'oral footnoting' is richly contextual — in many ways far richer than our formal written accounts.

Foreknowledge is also an important component of the Native historical consciousness. According to many of these accounts, both past and present, Native people had heard about the first whites before they actually saw them via stories conveyed by long-distance travellers and via their prophets. There is even some suggestion that they knew how these strangers would look and behave. In some instances, many knew fairly precisely who the strangers were. What concerned them more than the precise identity of these people, however, were the changes they would bring with them.

These accounts have evolved over the course of almost two centuries of tellings. In doing so, they temper, and, today, they give us an open window on Fraser's often partial observations — for example, his comment that 'however kind savages may appear, I know that it is not in their nature to be sincere in their professions to strangers.'[48] Given the Native accounts, Fraser's view is distinctly one-sided. Despite the prophecies and the pervasive concern and uncertainty, nowhere was there evidence of malicious intent. Generosity and hospitality prevailed with all strangers; Simon Fraser was fêted as a God.

In fact, the society that is portrayed here is one in which there is no hostility, no stealing, a liberal sharing of food, and generous assistance provided along the difficult river. This confirms the ethnographic findings of James Teit almost a century later, that these were non-aggressive and friendly peoples.[49]

These Native accounts also provide a rare glimpse of how the first whites appeared to the Indians, from their style of dress to the organization of the canoe crews. Metal ornaments were a source of fascination — in particular, the metal broach Fraser wore on his head.

It is also revealing to contrast Fraser's 'factual' account with the Native 'contextual' account. To some Natives, Fraser and his crew could be explained according to their mythology. Fraser was not just another human being; he was the 'Sun' who had come from the east and was travelling to the west. Members of his crew included 'Moon,' 'Coyote,' and 'Old One,' among others. These 'people' had taken to travelling around again, as they had done in early times. Similar religious associations are present in current accounts. In York's account, Fraser was 'the son of the sun, God's sun'; in Phillips's, 'Jesus Christ.' In Mitchell's account he was someone who could one day help the people.

Finally, there are events chronicled in these Native historical accounts that are missing in Fraser's journal — for example, the story about a woman who is fondled by Fraser at the mouth of the Stein. Also new is the fear that the Indians would be 'cleaned out' by disease simply by touching the strangers.

In light of this Native history, perhaps the big question is what, ultimately, we are to make of the non-Native historical record based on the observations of a single male operating in an official capacity with a reputation at stake. In contrast, the Native accounts draw on a vastly larger tapestry of people that spans several generations. The story survives in oral memory to this day in Phillips's and in many others' minds. Here we have surely a wider, deeper 'history,' a history that does not rely on dead documents many steps removed, but on a collective memory traced directly to the many who were there. Here it is the written that is the more limited and problematic; the oral is the history that lives and is alive.

NOTES

This paper is dedicated to Annie York and Louis Phillips, two Nlaka'pamux elders who were both extremely knowledgeable local historians. Annie died on 19 August 1991 and Louis died on 2 June 1993.

1. Scott Simpson, *Vancouver Sun*, 10 Dec. 1991
2. 'Nlaka'pamux' is the general term of identification used by the Native people of south-central British Columbia who speak a common language and who live in communities along the Fraser and Thompson rivers between Yale and Lillooet, between Lytton and Ashcroft, along the Nicola Valley between Spence's Bridge and Merritt, in the Nicola Valley to Quilchena, and in the lower reaches of the Coldwater Valley. Outsiders have called them by a variety of names, and it is these, more than their own terms of identification, by which they have become known. Simon Fraser, in 1808, called them the 'Hacamaugh' Indians. The Hudson's Bay traders called them 'Couteau' or Knife Indians. Later, in written records, they were referred to as the Thompson River Indians, after the major river in their territory. This latter term was eventually shortened to 'the Thompsons,' even though many of the people known as such lived nowhere near the Thompson River. Today, both within and outside the community, there is a revival of 'Nlaka'pamux,' their original term of self-identification.
3. W. Kaye Lamb, ed., *The Letters and Journals of Simon Fraser, 1806–1808* (Toronto 1960), 87–8
4. George E. Marcus and Dick Cushman, 'Ethnographies as Texts,' *Annual Review of Anthropology* 1982, 35
5. *Forked Tongues: Speech, Writing and Representation in North American Indian Texts* (Bloomington 1991)
6. 'Myth and History,' in Jonathan D. Hill, ed., *Rethinking History and Myth: Indigenous South American Perspectives on the Past* (Urbana 1988), 3
7. Terence Turner, 'Ethno-Ethnohistory,' in *Rethinking History and Myth*, 237
8. Ibid., 238. The title of this paper was drawn from a similar phrase used by Turner in his article, 'Ethno-Ethnohistory.'
9. Lamb, ed., *The Letters and Journals of Simon Fraser*, 86–7
10. Ibid., 87–8
11. Ibid., 95
12. Ibid., 86–7
13. Ibid., 119
14. For more on the life and works of James Teit see Wendy Wickwire, 'Women in Ethnography: The Research of James A. Teit,' *Ethnohistory*, in press.
15. Folklore scholar Jarold Ramsey, who has studied North American Native narratives in some depth, notes that Bible-derived texts in print are best represented by the Salish-speaking peoples 'thanks to the tireless and open-minded transcribing of James Teit . . . at the turn-of-the-century.' *Reading the Fire: Essays in the Traditional Indian Literatures of the Far West* (Lincoln, 1983), 168
16. James A. Teit, 'The Thompson Indians of British Columbia,' *Memoirs of the American Museum of Natural History*, vol. 1, pt 4 (New York 1900), 365–6
17. Teit unpublished notes on 'Religious or praying dance song,' Catalogue no. VI.M. 51, Archives of the Canadian Museum of Civilization (CMC), Hull, Quebec
18. Teit, 'The Thompson Indians,' 365–6
19. Teit unpublished notes on song no. VI.M.51, CMC
20. Teit, 'Religious or praying dance songs,' no. VI.M.102
21. J.A. Teit, 'Mythology of the Thompson Indians,' *Memoirs of the American Museum of Natural History*, vol. 12, pt 2, (New York 1912), 414–16; James A. Teit et al., 'Folk-Tales of Salishan and Sahaptin Tribes,' *Memoirs of the American Folk-Lore Society*, vol. 11 (Lancaster, Penn. 1917), 64
22. This is another spelling, used on several occasions by Teit. Today it is spelled 'Stein.' It is the name of the river that empties into the Fraser just above Lytton.

23. It is unusual in collections from this period to have the individual storytellers named. In the case of Waxtko, Teit noted that she was born around 1830 and died in 1912. Teit, 'Folk-Tales,' 64

24. The absence of names, dates, and locations in the published collections stands in contrast to Teit's raw field-notes.

25. The more common spelling of this river today is 'Stein.'

26. Teit, 'Mythology of the Thompson Indians,' 415

27. Ibid.

28. In a footnote, Teit notes that this word means 'birch-bark canoe,' and that it was a common name for Simon Fraser's party. Teit et al., 'Folk-Tales of Salishan and Sahaptin Tribes,' 64

29. Ibid.

30. Ibid.

31. Teit, 'Mythology of the Thompson Indians,' 416

32. This name may be related to the use of a gun. Fraser noted in his journal that at one place near Lytton, 'We fired several shots to shew the Indians the use of our guns. Some of them, through fear, dropped down at the report.' Lamb, ed., *The Letters and Journals of Simon Fraser*, 95

33. The events of this story are similarly described in Fraser's journal. Ibid., 89–92. One of Fraser's canoes capsized shortly after leaving Lytton. Two men leapt off and got to shore. Meanwhile D'Alaire was swept three miles downstream to a point where he was able to crawl onto some rocks.

34. This fact in the Native account coincides closely with Fraser's comment in his journal that he was writing in his tent when the capsizing took place. Ibid., 90

35. Teit, 'Mythology of the Thompson Indians,' 416

36. Ibid., 415

37. This transcription of Nlaka'pamux word and others throughout this paper are approximations only.

38. Excerpt from an audiotaped interview conducted by Wendy Wickwire with Louis Phillips in Lytton, 10 March 1991

39. This is a common Native term used for Jesus Christ. Teit noted it also, spelling it as 'Suskule' and 'Susakre.' 'Mythology of the Thompson Indians,' 404

40. Interview with Phillips

41. Ibid.

42. This segment of Annie York's story is corroborated by Fraser's journal: 'Two Indians from our last encampment overtook us with a piece of Iron which we had forgotten there. We considered this as an extraordinary degree of honesty and attention.' *The Letters and Journals*, 39

43. Segment of an audiotaped interview conducted by Imbert Orchard with Annie York in Spuzzum, BC, 1865. Copy given to Wendy Wickwire by Annie York, August 1981

44. Ibid.

45. Segment of an audiotaped interview conducted by Wendy Wickwire with Annie York in Vancouver, 31 May 1985

46. Randy Bouchard and Dorothy Kennedy, eds., 'Lillooet Stories,' *Sound Heritage*, 6, 1 (1977): 42–3

47. Lamb, ed., *The Letter and Journals of Simon Fraser*, 88

48. Ibid.

49. Teit, 'Thompson Indians,' 180–1

Topic Two
Acadia

Acadians saltmarsh haying in the early 1700s. The reconstruction is by Azor Vienneau.

During the 15th century, Europe entered an age of expansion, marked by the development of overseas commerce and the establishment of colonies. The English, Portuguese, Basques, and French were among the earliest Europeans to harvest the rich Newfoundland fishery, and to travel to northeastern North America. They established a number of seasonal settlements on the Atlantic coast to prepare and dry their fish. The Basques, from what is now the border country on the Bay of Biscay between Spain and France, arrived in the 1520s and 1530s.

The French established their first permanent settlement on the Atlantic coast in 1604, naming it Acadia (later to become Nova Scotia). Its strategic location near the Gulf of St. Lawrence meant that England and France fought continually for its possession. The region changed hands frequently until 1713, when France ceded Acadia to England in the Treaty of Utrecht. For the next half-century, Britain ruled over the colony with its predominantly French-speaking and Roman Catholic population.

The Acadians sought to remain neutral in conflicts between England and France. Initially this was possible, but with the revival of hostility between France and England in 1755, Charles Lawrence, Nova Scotia's lieutenant governor, and his council at Halifax insisted that the Acadians take an unconditional oath of allegiance to the British Crown. When they refused, Lawrence expelled approximately 10 000 French Acadians. In "The Golden Age: Acadian Life, 1713–1748," Naomi Griffiths reviews Acadian society before the expulsion. Why were they so prosperous under the first four decades of British rule?

In her essay "Imperial Transitions," Elizabeth Mancke reviews British rule over the Acadians in the four decades from 1713 to the expulsion in 1755. How did England initially adjust to the presence of a dominant French Catholic population in the settled areas of Nova Scotia? Why did the English ultimately decide to expel the Acadians from Nova Scotia?

For an overview of European exploration in the North Atlantic, consult Samuel Eliot Morison, *The European Discovery of America: The Northern Voyages*, A.D. *500–1600* (New York: Oxford University Press, 1971), and Robert McGhee, *Canada Rediscovered* (Ottawa: Canadian Museum of Civilization, 1991). An illustrated account of the Norse and their arrival in northeastern North America is *The Vikings and Their Predecessors*, by Kate Gordon, with a contribution by Robert McGhee (Ottawa: National Museum of Man, 1981). Harold E.L. Prins reviews the history of the Mi'kmaq in *The Mi'kmaq: Resistance, Accommodation, and Cultural Survival* (Fort Worth, TX: Harcourt Brace, 1996). Ralph Pastore provides a good overview of the First Nations in "The Sixteenth Century: Aboriginal Peoples and European Contact," in *The Atlantic Region to Confederation: A History*, eds. Phillip A. Buckner and John Reid (Toronto: University of Toronto Press, 1994), pp. 22–39.

An abundant literature exists on the Acadians; in fact, by the end of the 19th century, 200 books and pamphlets had been written on the subject of the Acadian expulsion alone, many of them of a controversial and partisan nature. For an overview of the literature, see Jean Daigle, ed., *Acadia of the Maritimes: Thematic Studies from the Beginning to the Present* (Moncton: Université de Moncton Press, 1995). A short review of the historical debate appears in Thomas Garde Barnes's "Historiography of the Acadians' *Grand Dérangement* (1755)," *Québec Studies* 7 (1988): 74–86. Good introductions to Acadian society include Naomi Griffiths's *The Acadians: Creation of a People* (Toronto: McGraw-Hill Ryerson, 1973), her *The Contexts of Acadian History, 1686–1784* (Montreal/Kingston: McGill-Queen's University Press, 1992), and her recent study, *From Migrant to Acadian: A North American Border People, 1604–1755* (Montreal: McGill-Queen's, 2005). See as well J.B. Brebner's earlier *New England's Outpost: Acadia before the British Conquest of Canada* (New York: Columbia University Press, 1927); and Andrew H. Clark's *Acadia: The Geography of Early Nova Scotia to 1760* (Madison: University of Wisconsin Press, 1968).

For an account of life at Louisbourg, consult Christopher Moore's award-winning *Louisbourg Portraits: Five Dramatic True Tales of People Who Lived in an Eighteenth-Century Garrison Town* (Toronto: Macmillan, 1982). A.J.B. Johnston has written two books on the important French port: *Life and Religion at Louisbourg, 1713–1758* (Montreal/Kingston: McGill-Queen's University Press, 1996) and *Control and Order in French Colonial Louisbourg, 1713–1758* (East Lansing: Michigan State University Press, 2001). Terry Crowley provides a short history of this important port in *Louisbourg: Atlantic Fortress and Seaport*, Canadian Historical Association, Historical Booklet no. 48 (Ottawa: CHA, 1990).

Valuable maps of early Atlantic Canada appear in the *Historical Atlas of Canada*, vol. 1, *From the Beginning to 1800*, R. Cole Harris, ed. (Toronto: University of Toronto Press, 1987). For an overview of the 17th and 18th centuries, see Philip A. Buckner and John G. Reid, eds., *The Atlantic Region to Confederation: A History* (Toronto: University of Toronto Press, 1994).

WEBLINKS

Champlain Society
http://link.library.utoronto.ca/champlain/search.cfm?lang=eng

For primary sources on Acadia from the Champlain Society, browse the database by subject and select "Acadia."

Nova Scotia: 1749–1759
http://www.canadiana.org/citm/themes/constitution/constitution4_e.html

A collection of documents relating to the governing of Nova Scotia in the mid-18th century.

Maritime First Nation Treaties in Historical Perspective
http://www.ainc-inac.gc.ca/pr/trts/hti/Marit/index_e.html

A report by W.E. Daugherty assessing historical First Nation treaties in the Maritimes from 1686 to 1779.

Joseph Robineau de Villebon
http://www.ourroots.ca/e/toc.asp?id=6151

A digitized copy of a 1934 book containing letters, journals, and memoirs of Joseph Robineau de Villebon, a commandant in Acadia, 1690–1700.

The Acadians
http://www.cbc.ca/acadian/index.html

This CBC website describes the Acadian people, their history, and their position today.

Acadian Historical Village
http://www.virtualmuseum.ca/Exhibitions/Acadie/index_e.html

An online exhibit presenting the experience of life in a historical Acadian village.

Acadia Documents
http://www.canadiana.org/citm/themes/pioneers/pioneers2_e.html#acadia

A collection of documents relating to Acadians, including a 19th-century account of their expulsion.

Article Four

The Golden Age: Acadian Life, 1713–1748

Naomi Griffiths

Until the 1950s Acadian history was most frequently written either as epic or as case study — as the drama of a people or as an example of the political and diplomatic struggles between great powers. The tragic nature of the deportation in 1755 seemed the obvious and fundamental starting point for all that the Acadians experienced since, and equally the culmination of everything that had occurred in their previous history. In the last 30 years, however, an ever-increasing number of scholarly works have been devoted to the examination of Acadian history from much more complex perspectives. These include attempts to analyze not merely 1755 as an event of major importance in the war between English and French for North America, but also works centred on Acadian language,[1] folklore,[2] geography,[3] sociology,[4] as well as on Acadian history as the history of a developing community.

Acadian studies have, in fact, come to an impressive maturity over the past 30 years. This maturity is magnificently documented in the work edited by Jean Daigle, *Les Acadiens des Maritimes*, where some twenty scholars present complex essays outlining the problems, the work done, and the work to be done in every area of Acadian studies from history to folklore, from political science to material culture.[5] The result of all this publication is, of course, the temptation, if not the necessity, for present scholars to look at past syntheses of Acadian history, to discover where the new information demands new theories, and to build, if not entirely new interpretations of the Acadian past, at least interpretations which are more richly decorated and more densely structured.

This challenge is as dangerous as it is irresistible, for the amount of material is considerable indeed. As a result, this paper is a cautious one. Its main aim is to paint Acadian life between 1713 and 1748 in such a way that the reader may sense the complex nature of the Acadian community during these years. This was the period to be remembered by the community in exile after 1755. All those over the age of ten or eleven in 1755 would have had some knowledge of these years. It was the time that would be recalled in exile and the time which would form the basis for the stories of past life as the Acadians once more established themselves in the Maritimes. It spanned the decades from the Treaty of Utrecht to that of Aix-la-Chapelle, during which years the lands on which the Acadians lived turned from being the border between two empires to the frontier between enemies.

The political geography of "Nova Scotia or Acadia," as the lands were called in the contemporary international treaties, had meant turmoil for its inhabitants from the outset of European colonization. As J.B. Brebner wrote, these lands were "the eastern outpost and flank for both French and English in North America." They made, in his words, a "continental cornice." Throughout the seventeenth century this cornice frequently changed hands between English and French. It became a true border for[,] whatever name it was given and whatever limits were claimed, it lay "inside the angle between the St. Lawrence route to French Canada and the northern route to New England which branched off from it south of Newfoundland."[6] Those who settled there in the seventeenth century would quickly find their situation akin to that of such people as the Basques, caught between France and Spain; the Alsatians, moulded

Source: Naomi Griffiths, "The Golden Age: Acadian Life, 1713–1748," *Histoire Sociale/Social History* 17, 33 (May 1984): 21–34. Reprinted by permission.

by French and German designs; and those who lived on the borders between England and Scotland or England and Wales.

It was the French who began the first permanent settlement in the area in 1604. Whatever the international designation of the colony over the next century, its non-Indian people would be called the Acadians. While predominantly French-speaking and Catholic, they were nevertheless a people who also absorbed English-speaking migrants such as the Melansons[7] and the Caisseys.[8] They also had a considerable knowledge of the Protestant religion, and it is very probable that some of the families who joined them from near Loudun in the 1630s were of the reform church.[9] By the end of the century the Acadians had known one lengthy and legitimate period of English rule, 1654–1668, as well as a number of much shorter periods of English control as a result of raids out of Massachusetts. By 1700 the Acadians were, as the detailed work of Professors Daigle and Reid has shown,[10] almost as accustomed to dealing with the officials of England as those of France. Thus the defeat of Subercase in 1710 and the subsequent transfer of the colony once more to English control by the Treaty of Utrecht was for the Acadians yet one more step in a complicated ritual, an exchange of control over them from France to England, something which had happened before and would most probably be reversed in the not too distant future.

This fundamental belief in the mutability of power, this dominant sense of the probability of alternate French and English control of the colony, became the cornerstone of Acadian politics during the years 1713 to 1748. It was the basis for the Acadian action over requests made by the English officials that they swear an oath of allegiance to the King of England. From the Acadian viewpoint, it would have been folly indeed to engage in any action which would bind them irrevocably to one Great Power when the other was still not only obviously in the neighbourhood, but even more obviously still interested in the future status of the colony and its inhabitants. Thus the Acadians built a policy compounded of delay and compromise. The oath to George I was first rejected outright; among other reasons they presented for the refusal, the Acadians of Minas remarked that "pendant que nos ancêtres ont étés sous la domination angloise on ne leur a jamais exigé de pareille Sermente."[11] [Editor's translation: While our ancestors were under English rule they were never required to make a similar oath.] Later on, oaths were taken to George II, but in such circumstances as to enable the Acadians to believe that they had been granted the right to remain neutral. In fact, as Brebner pointed out, the practice of both English and French of referring to them from 1730 on as either "les français neutres" or "the Neutral French" indicates that this accommodation was generally tolerated, if not accepted, by those in power during these years.[12]

However it might have looked to outsiders, the question of neutrality was serious enough to the Acadians. It was in fact a consistent policy that was first enunciated in 1717 by the Acadians of Annapolis Royal and later adhered to by them, and others in time of war. On being asked for an oath of allegiance to George I, the Annapolis Royal Acadians refused, the reasons given being that matters of religious freedom were not yet clarified and danger from Indians, who were bound to disapprove friendship between Acadian and English, led to fears for Acadian security. Nevertheless, the response continued, "we are ready to take an oath that we will take up arms neither against his Britannic Majesty, nor against France, nor against any of their subjects or allies."[13] In 1744 when hostilities broke out between English and French in North America, Mascerene, then the lieutenant governor of the colony, wrote to his masters in London: "These latter [i.e., the French inhabitants] have given me assurances of their resolutions to keep in their fidelity to his Majesty."[14] Mascerene was convinced that had the Acadians not remained neutral during the hostilities, the colony would have fallen to the French.[15] Certainly there is more than enough evidence to show the Acadian dislike of the war, including a most strongly worded letter from those of Grand-Pré to the French, pointing out forcibly that the village preferred peace to war, tranquillity and food to soldiers fighting across their farmlands.[16]

There is no doubt that between 1713 and 1748 the majority of the Acadians strove to live on their land truly as neutrals, giving loyalty to neither French nor English. This policy procured for their communities nearly 35 years of peace, but its final failure in 1755 has overshadowed its earlier success. It is worth emphasizing that it was a policy, not merely a series of inconsistent, unconnected reactions to the demands made by English and French. It was transmitted by delegates from the several Acadian communities to the English officials on a number of separate occasions and, as has been suggested, adhered to during a time of considerable pressure in the 1740s. It was a policy that produced peace and quiet for the Acadian communities, however catastrophic it finally proved to be. Its evolution and development gave the Acadians a knowledge of political action and a sense of their independent reality that would prove invaluable to them when they confronted the vicissitudes of the deportation.[17] Above all, it was the framework for the expansion and development of the Acadian communities between 1713 and 1748.

The demographic expansion of the Acadians during these years is commonplace in one sense; in another it is something acknowledged rather than fully understood. As Gysa Hynes wrote in 1973, "the rapid natural increase of the population of the Acadians during the period from 1650 to 1750 . . . has long been recognised, but no historian has explored the demography of Acadia before the Dispersion."[18] As a result, while it is generally agreed that the Acadian population probably doubled every twenty years between 1713 and the early 1750s without the aid of any considerable immigration, there has been little real analysis of this development.[19] Gisa Hynes's excellent article was a pioneer study relating above all to Port Royal/Annapolis Royal and has not been followed by much else. Enough raw material does exist, however, to outline the tantalizing landscape waiting to be fully explored, a demographic territory which differs significantly from contemporary Europe and also, in some considerable measure, from that of other colonial settlements in North America.

It is a debatable point whether the longevity of the Acadians or their fertility should receive most comment. At a time when only 50 percent of the population reached the age of 21 in France, 75 percent reached adulthood in Port Royal.[20] Further, while mortality did take its toll during the middle years, death coming through accident and injury rather than epidemic, old age was a common enough phenomenon. In fact at the time of the Treaty of Utrecht, when the French were making every effort to withdraw the Acadians from land ceded to the English and to establish them on Isle Royal (Cape Breton), one of the priests noted that the Acadians refused to go because

> It would be to expose us manifestly [they say] to die of hunger burthened as we are with large families, to quit the dwelling places and clearances from which we derive our usual subsistence, without any other resource, to take rough, new lands, from which the standing wood must be removed. One fourth of our population consists of aged persons, unfit for the labour of breaking up new lands, and who, with great exertion, are able to cultivate the cleared ground which supplied subsistence for them and their families.[21]

The presence of an older generation in the community meant a rich heritage of memories of past politics. Any Acadian over 42 in 1713 would have been born when the colony was controlled by the English, for the terms of the Treaty of Breda were not honoured by Temple until 10 January 1671. Any Acadian over 25 would have personal memories of the stormy raids by New Englanders on their villages and of the French countermeasures. The reality of life on a border would be a commonplace for Acadian reminiscences in a community whose people lived long enough to remember.

If Acadians could see relatively long life as a possibility, they could also see life itself as abundant. From the travelling French surgeon-poet Dièreville to the almost equally travelling English official, Governor Philipps, the observations were the same. In 1699 the Frenchman wrote that "the swarming of Brats is a sight to behold."[22] The Englishman commented in 1730 on the Acadians' ability to increase and spread "themselves over the face of the province . . . like Noah's progeny."[23] Present-day research has confirmed the accuracy of these impressions. Gisa Hynes discovered in her analysis of Port Royal that four out of five marriages were complete, that is, "were not disrupted by the death of husband or wife before the onset of menopause."[24] In these marriages, if the women were under 20 on their wedding day, they had some ten or eleven children; those wedded between 20 and 24, nine children; and those married in their late 20s, seven or eight children.[25] For the population as a whole, it is probable that the average family in the colony had six or seven children.[26]

These bare statistical bones of Acadian family life can now be covered first with the skin of individual family genealogy and then clothed with the fabric of community life. As an example of the first, there is the life of Claude Landry, born in 1663, the youngest of some ten children of René Landry of Port Royal, who himself had arrived in the colony sometime in the 1640s from Loudun.[27] When he was about eighteen, Claude married Catherine Thibodeau, whose father had been an associate of Emmanuel LeBorgne and come to the colony from around Poitiers in the 1650s.[28] She was the fifth child in a family of sixteen, eleven of whom reached adulthood.[29] Catherine was apparently fifteen when married and bore her first child within the year. She had some ten children in all, eight of whom lived to maturity.

The young couple moved very early in their marriage to Grand-Pré, where they brought up their family and watched their children's children flourish. When Claude Landry died in 1747, aged 86, his grandchildren through the male line numbered 46 and his great-grandchildren, also through the male line, eleven. Claude's last child, a son, had been born in 1708; his first grandson was born in 1710. Between 1717 and 1747 there was only one year in which no birth is recorded for his sons, and it is not unlikely that one of Claude's two daughters might have had a child that year. The year 1735 saw the birth of the first great-grandchild within the male line.[30]

The growth of such extended families was supported by a healthy mixed economy, based upon farming, hunting, and fishing with enough trade, both legal and illegal, to make life interesting. In Grand-Pré the Landry family was part of the flourishing development which Mascerene had described in 1730 as "a platt of Meadow, which stretches near four leagues, part of which is damn'd [sic] in from the tide, and produced very good wheat and pease."[31] Westward this great marsh is edged by the massive presence of Cape Blomidon; the tides of the Bay of Fundy curve across its northern shore, and wooded uplands circumscribe its other boundaries. Between 1710, when the first grandson was born, and 1747, when Claude died, the population of the area grew from well under a thousand to something more than four thousand.[32] The community lived in houses scattered across the landscape, not grouped close together in a village. Charles Morris, who was commissioned by Governor Shirley of Massachusetts to make a survey of the Bay of Fundy area in 1747, reported that the dwellings were "low Houses fram'd of timber and their Chimney framed with the Building of wood and lined with Clay except the fireplace below."[33] Very often the houses sheltered a mixture of families, and the sheer work required to provide them necessities of life must have been considerable.[34]

The daily life of both men and women would be governed by the seasons, for the frame of the economy was what was grown and raised for food and clothing. Fishing, hunting, and trade could and did provide important additions to this base, but the standard of living of the majority of the Acadians depended on the produce of their landholdings. At the very least a household would possess a garden, and from the seventeenth century on travellers had noticed the variety and abundance of vegetables grown. Dièreville, whose evidence is of the close of the seventeenth century, remarked upon the wealth of cabbages and turnips,[35] and another report of the same period lists the gardens as including "choux, betteraves, oignons, carottes, cives, eschalottes, navets, panets et touttes sortes de salades."[36] Most families would have also an amount of land varying in size between that of a smallholding and a farm, depending on where the community was in the colony and what level of resources the family in question could command. A.H. Clark considered that the households of Grand-Pré and the surrounding area usually had five to ten acres of dyked and tilled farmland within the marsh, supplemented with an orchard situated on the upland slopes. Morris reported the marshlands to be "Naturally of a Fertile Soil . . . and . . . of so strong and lasting a Nature that their Crops are not Diminished in ten or twenty years Constant Tillage."[37] The crops sown included most of the grain crops common to western Europe: wheat, oats, rye, and barley, as well as peas, hemp, and flax. Writing in 1757, another traveller remarked on the abundance of fruit trees, apples, pears, "cherry and plumb trees," and noted that "finer flavoured apples and greater variety, cannot in any other country be produced."[38]

Working with the land, whether garden or farm, did not only imply digging and ploughing, weeding and gathering. There was also the care of livestock. Poultry was everywhere about, as much for feathers as for the eggs and meat. Down-filled mattresses and coverlets were a noted Acadian possession, and the export of feathers to Louisbourg a common item of trade.[39] Pigs rooting around the houses were so common that few surveyors interested in estimating Acadian wealth even bothered to count them. A number of observers, however, remarked on the Acadian liking for fat-back (*le lard*), which could be cooked with cabbage or fried and added to whatever vegetables were available.[40] Sheep were also numerous, raised for wool rather than for meat. Most households would also possess cows and a horse. The estimation of the total livestock in the colony varies widely since the Acadians, like most peasant populations, had no great wish to inform any official of the true extent of their possessions. Life must have been sustained at considerably more than bare subsistence, however, since extant records show that in the 1740s the Acadians, particularly those of Grand-Pré and of the Minas basin in general, were able to export cattle, sheep, pigs, and poultry to Louisbourg.[41] While the authorities at Annapolis Royal thundered against such trade, they also admitted that the Acadians were no worse than others, noting that "there is so great an illicit Trade carried on by the People of Massachusetts Bay and New Hampshire."[42] As has been suggested, the trade that existed was enough to make life for the Acadians interesting, and the goods imported included not only necessities such as "Spanish Iron, French Linnens, Sail Cloth Wollen cloths," but also "Rum, Molasses, Wine and Brandy."[43]

The sum of this evidence suggests an excellent standard of living among the Acadians, something which showed, of course, in the population increase of the first half of the eighteenth century. While there is little evidence of luxury, there is less of poverty. The staples of life, food, shelter, and clothing were abundant, even if the abundance was available only after hard work. Further, the absence of conspicuous consumption and the lack of development of towns and industry in no way meant an absence of specie. It is clear from the records of the deportation itself that Acadians took coinage with them into exile.[44] The Acadian community did not have the rate of economic growth that the New Englanders possessed, but it provided amply for the totality of individuals. Fishing and hunting added to the resources of the households. Charles Morris remarked that the population around Grand-Pré "had some shallops, in which they employed themselves in the catching of Fish just upon their Harbours, being out but a few days at a Time; This was rather for their Home Consumption than the foreign Market."[45] Clark remarked that the Acadians were "particularly interested in salmon, shad, gaspereau, and the like during their spring runs up the rivers and creeks."[46] As for hunting, it was less the meat that was immediately valued than the furs. Game was sought in order to sell it in Annapolis Royal,[47] but "avec les fourrures d'ours, de castor, de renard, de loutre, et de martre" [*Editor's translation*: with the bear, beaver, fox, weasel, and marten furs], they had material which gave them "non seulement le comfort, mais bien souvent de jolis vêtements"[48] [not only comfortable, but often attractive clothing]. Dièreville had also commented on the way in which the Acadians made shoes from sealskin and the hides of moose.[49]

Given the considerable work necessary to turn the resources of their environment into food and clothing for the family, it is extraordinary that the Acadians should have been criticized for being idle.[50] The tools they worked with were scarcely labour-saving devices and were basically of their own manufacture. Clark has listed the main implements available to them as "pickaxes, axes, hoes, sickles, scythes, flails, and wooden forks and rakes," as well, of course, as spades, essential for dike-building.[51] They were known as competent carpenters and joiners, and the census made by the French during the seventeenth century reported the existence of blacksmiths, locksmiths, and nailmakers among them.[52] Working basically in wood, the Acadians built their own houses, barns, and the occasional church, made their own furniture, including enclosed beds which must have provided considerable privacy in the crowded households, tables, chairs, chests, kegs, and barrels, as well as looms and spinning wheels.[53] There was a remarkably fluid, though not entirely egalitarian social structure. Considerable importance was attached to the actual possession of land, and the recognition of proper boundaries.[54]

Specie did not serve as a major regulator of the internal economy. The available evidence shows that it was rare indeed for Acadian communities to pay one another, except in kind, for goods and services rendered. The gold gained through trade, or through wages from French and English officials, was kept for trade and most reluctantly handed over for any other purposes, especially rents and taxes.[55] Labour relations among the Acadians tended to be either barter-based (perhaps two days' digging or ploughing in exchange for some quantity of seed grain), cooperative (three or four people engaged in quilt-making or fishing, the resultant produce being divided equitably), or communal (several households joined together to build another dwelling and ready to be reconvened for such a purpose whenever the occasion warranted). The social ambiance produced by such labour relations encouraged the development of a community where family connections were as important as the particular attainments of an individual. Marriage would be seen as the connection between kin rather than the limited engagement of two individuals of particular social status. As Dièreville remarked, to his considerable surprise social barriers seemed to have no part to play in the regulation of marriage.[56]

In sum, Acadian life between 1713 and 1748 centred around the demands and rewards of family and land, although this did not mean isolation from a wider environment. During these decades the care and nurture of children must have been the dominating factor in the lives of most Acadians, male or female. A child born every two or three years on average in individual families meant the arrival of a child almost every year in multi-family households. Even with the importation of some yard goods, the provision of clothes and coverings for the children demanded continuous thought and activity. Records emphasize the extent to which the Acadians were self-sufficient in this area. Dièreville remarked on the way in which they made their own outfits, including caps and stockings.[57] Raynal, writing for Diderot's *Encyclopaedia* with information supplemented by the memorials of those Acadians exiled to France, asserted that they depended for their daily clothing on "leur lin, leur chanvre, la toison de leurs brebis"[58] [*Editor's translation*: their flax, hemp, and fleece from their sheep]. From diapers to shawls, from shirts to shifts, with considerable liking for mixing black with red for ornament, and binding their skirts with ribbons,[59] the Acadians spun, wove, knitted, and sewed their garments. Even with every economy between one generation and the next, even with children fully accustomed to hand-me-downs, the sheer number of bonnets and mittens, stockings and shoes, cloaks, coats, and trousers, shirts, blouses, and jackets that would be needed is difficult to envisage.

Organizing the clothing was probably as much a year-round occupation for the women as the provision of meals was their daily chore. Grains were usually ground at grist-mills rather than within each household, although there is a tradition that most families possessed pestles and mortars capable of making coarse flour for porridge.[60] Bread would be baked in each household and was considered by Isaac Deschamps to have been the staple of Acadian diets.[61] Linguistic studies by Massignon show that doughnuts and pancakes were also common. She discovered references to documents dated 1744 referring to *croxignoles*, a form of doughnut, as part of the Acadian diet.[62] It is also probable that those who came to the community from Normandy and Ile-et-Vilaine brought with them a taste for buckwheat pancakes, something that was certainly common among Acadians in northern New Brunswick at the close of the eighteenth century.[63] There is a strange debate about whether the Acadians grew potatoes before 1755, since a number of popular guides such as the *Guide Bleu de Bretagne* refer to them introducing the vegetable to France.[64] Again, it is certainly true that the potato was a staple of Acadian diets by the opening of the nineteenth century,[65] but more evidence is needed before one can accept that it was a common food for the Acadians 50 years earlier. Milk was abundant[66] and the Acadians found in exile that they had been particularly fortunate in this respect.[67] Its plenteousness must have been a great help in coping with what was known as the *pourginés d'enfants*.[68]

This charming word for a numerous family invites consideration of the emotional climate in which families grew and developed. The evidence here is, at present, somewhat sketchy. The extent to which the Acadians cared for one another during their exile, seeking news of brothers and sisters as well as advertising for husbands and wives, suggests the importance of family relations.[69] As to the actual treatment of children during these decades, one has very few concrete details. It is possible that the reputation the Acadians had for long and faithful marriages was not coupled with a bitterness against those whose lives followed other patterns. One of the few cases relating to children that reached the English officials at Annapolis Royal between 1720 and 1739 was one where grandparents fought for the privilege of raising an illegitimate child.[70] The folklore research of Jean-Claude Dupont reveals a considerable amount about children's toys and games current in the nineteenth century, and it is probable that some of these, at least, were also part of Acadian life during the eighteenth century. Certainly the early mobile-rattle, a dried pig's bladder filled with peas and hung so an infant could bat it about and watch it swing, listening to its noise, which Dupont has reported for the nineteenth century, would have been a useful toy to have in the house in the eighteenth century.[71]

There were, of course, the usual arguments and quarrels among the Acadians, the kinds of disputes common to any group of people. The court records of Annapolis show not only debates over landholdings and boundaries, but also slander actions, particularly between women, and at least one appeal for aid to control a nagging wife.[72] But the tenor of life was undoubtedly rendered easier by the ready supply of necessities, a supply which might depend on continuous hard work but one that was available. There was no major shortage of food for the Acadians between 1713 and 1748; shelter was readily available; clothing was adequate; and, above all, there were no major epidemics. Even when plague did reach the colony, its ravages were confined, both in 1709 and 1751, almost exclusively to the garrisons.[73]

Quite how the Acadians escaped the general epidemics of the eighteenth century has yet to be fully determined. It is obvious from the mortality rates they suffered during the early years of exile that during the first half of the eighteenth century they had acquired no community levels of immunity to smallpox, yellow fever, or typhoid. When those diseases struck as the exiles reached Boston, Philadelphia, South Carolina, or the British seaports, a third or more of the Acadians died.[74] Yet the idea that this vulnerability developed because of the more or less complete isolation of the communities from outside contact is a theory which demands a great deal more examination. The Acadian tradition of trading-cum-smuggling which was established in the seventeenth century took at least some of the men regularly enough to Boston and probably to points south.[75] In the eighteenth century this activity was continued and Acadian connections with Louisbourg were also developed. The fact that between 1713 and 1748 no large body of immigrants came to the area has tended to overshadow both the trickle of newcomers to the settlements and the continuous nature of the relationships between this "continental cornice" and the wider world. The parish records of Grand-Pré examined by Clark show that of the 174 marriages for which detailed information is available almost exactly one-third involved partners either from elsewhere in the colony or from abroad, sixteen coming from France, eight from Quebec, and three from Cape Breton.[76] As for travellers, most of the settlements encountered them in the form of soldiers and traders as well as government and church officials. Given the normal rate of the spread of infections during these decades, it is extraordinary that no epidemics seem to have come to the settlements via contact with Boston or Quebec, Annapolis Royal, or Louisbourg.

If the life of the Acadian settlements was much more open to outside influences than has been generally thought, it was also much less controlled by religious devotion than has been generally supposed. There is no question that the Acadians cherished the Catholic faith. There is also no doubt that they were as much trouble to their priests as any other group of humanity might be. The immense political importance of the Catholic religion to the community has overshadowed questions about its social importance. Acadians' delight in litigation was not their only cross-grained trait. Quarrels that sprung up through their drinking were also matters that concerned their pastors. A report of the archdiocese of Quebec of 1742, which drew particular attention to this flaw, also inferred that bars (*cabarets*) were kept open not only on Sundays and feast-days, but also during the celebration of Mass.[77] This same report went on to condemn some of the Acadian communities that allowed men and women not only to dance together after sunset but even to sing "des chansons lascives [lewd songs]." The lack of detail in the report is frustrating: was the alcohol spruce beer? Cider? Rum? Were the cabarets found in the front room of the local smuggler, or did Grand-Pré have something close to a village hostelry? Was the dancing anything more than square-dancing? Was the music played on flutes, whistles, and triangles only? Or were there also violins? And the songs — which of the currently known folklore airs might they have been: "Le petit Capucin"? "Le chevalier de la Tour ronde"?

Considerably more work needs to be done in the relevant archives before the nature of Acadian beliefs before 1755 can be fully described. The document just cited suggests only that the Acadian interpretation of Catholicism before 1755 owed very little to Jansenism. This would be scarcely surprising. There is little indication, even with the present evidence, that the Acadians indulged in major projects of ostensible devotion, either public or private. There are no stone churches built by them before 1755 nor are there any records of vocations among them before that date, either to the priesthood or to the religious life. Religion among the Acadians seems to have been a matter of necessity but not a question of sainthood, an important and vital ingredient in life but not the sole shaping force of the social and cultural life of their communities.[78]

For, in sum, the life of the Acadians between 1713 and 1755 was above all the life of a people in fortunate circumstances, the very real foundation for the later myth of a "Golden Age." The ravages of the Four Horsemen of the Apocalypse were remarkably absent, for famine, disease, and war barely touched the Acadians during these years. There was sufficient food for the growing families and apparently enough land for the growing population. One's nearest and dearest might have been as aggravating as one's kin can often be, but circumstances not only did not add the burdens of scarcity to emotional life but in fact provided a fair abundance of the necessities. Certainly the daily round for both men and women must have been exhaustingly busy; but work did have its obvious rewards and, for both sexes, it would be varied enough and carried out with companionship and sociability. While the season would often have imposed harsh demands for immediate labour, for seeds must be sown, crops gathered, fish caught and fuel cut as and when the weather dictates, the year's turning would also have brought its own festivities and holidays. Massignon's work suggests that the Acadians kept the twelve days of Christmas, the customs of Candlemas as well as the celebrations common to Easter.[79] The long winter evenings knew card-playing, dancing, and pipe-smoking, as well as storytelling and singsongs. The spring and summer months would see the celebrations of weddings and the most frequent new-births. Quarrels, scandals, politics, the visits of priests, the presence of Indians, people whose children occasionally married with the Acadians and who instructed the settlers in the use of local foods,[80] the presence of the English, now and again also marrying with the Acadians[81]—there is no doubt that Acadian life before 1755 was neither crisis-ridden nor lapped in the tranquillity of a backwater. It was instead a life of considerable distinctiveness. It was a life rich enough to provide the sustenance for a continuing Acadian identity, based not only upon a complex social and cultural life, but also upon the development of a coherent political stance, maintained throughout the settlements over a considerable period of years. It is not surprising that, fragmented in exile, the Acadians remembered these years and that this remembrance would be built into their future lives.

NOTES

1. For example, Geneviève Massignon, *Les Parlers français d'Acadie*, 2 vols. (Paris: C. Klincksieck, n.d.).
2. For example, Antonine Maillet, *Rabelais et les traditions populaires en Acadie* (Québec: Presses de l'université Laval, 1971); Anselme Chiasson, *Chéticamp, histoire et traditions acadiennes* (Moncton: Éditions des Aboiteaux, 1962); Catherine Jolicoeur, *Les plus belles légendes acadiennes* (Montréal: Stanké, 1981).
3. A.H. Clark, *Acadia: The Geography of Early Nova Scotia to 1760* (Madison: University of Wisconsin Press, 1968), and J.C. Vernex, *Les Acadiens* (Paris: Éditions Entente, 1979).
4. Jean-Paul Hautecoeur, *L'Acadie du Discours* (Québec: Presses de l'université Laval, 1976).
5. Jean Daigle, ed., *Les Acadians des Maritimes: Études thématiques* (Moncton: Centre d'Études Acadiennes, 1980). See my review in *Histoire sociale/Social History* 16 (May 1983): 192–94.
6. J.B. Brebner, *New England's Outpost* (New York: Columbia University Press, 1927), 15–16.
7. While there has been considerable debate about whether this family had anglophone roots (for example, see Clark, *Acadia*, 101), there now seems no doubt of their origins. For details of their ancestry as recorded in declarations made by their descendants in Belle-Île-en-Mer after the deportation, see M.P. and N.P. Rieder, *The Acadians in France*, 3 vols. (Metairie, LA: M.P. & N. Rieder, 1972), 2, passim.
8. Bona Arsenault, *Histoire et Généalogie des Acadiens*, 2 vols. (Québec: Le Conseil de la vie française en Amérique, 1965), 2: 550.
9. This is suggested, in particular, in the reports of discussions with the second Mme La Tour, in Candide de Nantes, *Pages glorieuses de l'épopée Canadienne: une mission capucine en Acadie* (Montréal: Le Devoir, 1927), 150f.
10. Jean Daigle, "Nos amis les ennemis: Relations commerciales de l'Acadie avec le Massachusetts, 1670–1711" (Ph.D. dissertation, University of Maine, 1975); and John Reid, *Acadia, Maine and New Scotland: Marginal Colonies in the Seventeenth Century* (Toronto: University of Toronto Press, 1981).
11. This document, headed "answer of several French inhabitants, 10 February 1717," is printed in the *Collection de documents inédits sur le Canada et l'Amérique publiés par le Canada français*, 3 vols. (Québec: Le Canada français, 1888–90), 2: 171. The collection was published anonymously, but its editor is known to be the abbé Casgrain. The original of the document is in the Public Records Office, London (hereafter PRO), CO/NS 2, as part of the Nova Scotia government documents.
12. Brebner, *New England's Outpost*, 97.
13. T.B. Akins, ed., *Selections from the Public Documents of the Province of Nova Scotia* (Halifax, 1869), 15–16.

14. Mascerene to the Lords of Trade, 9 June 1744, printed in *Collection de Documents inédits* 2: 80.

15. This was also the opinion of the French officer in charge of the attack on Grand-Pré, Duvivier. He defended himself at his court-martial on the charge of failure, by protesting that Acadian neutrality had rendered his task impossible. Robert Rumilly, *Histoire des Acadiens*, 2 vols. (Montréal: Fides, 1955), 1: 304.

16. Letter from the inhabitants of Minas, Rivière aux Canards, and Piziquid to Duvivier and de Gannes, 13 October 1744, printed in Rumilly, *Histoire des Acadiens* 1: 304–5.

17. The full story of the Acadian years in exile remains to be told, but some indication of the strength of the community is given in Naomi Griffiths, "Acadians in Exile: The Experience of the Acadians in the British Seaports," *Acadiensis* 4 (Autumn 1974): 67–84.

18. Gisa I. Hynes, "Some Aspects of the Demography of Port Royal, 1650–1755," *Acadiensis* 3 (Autumn 1973): 7–8.

19. For a good overview of what is available, see Muriel K. Roy, "Peuplement et croissance démographique en Acadie," in Daigle, *Acadiens des Maritimes*, 135–208.

20. Hynes, "Demography of Port Royal," 10–11. In recent years scholarship about demography has been prolific. One of the most readable accounts of the French reality during the late seventeenth century is that of Pierre Goubert: "In 1969 the average expectation of life is something over seventy years. In 1661 it was probably under twenty-five. . . . Out of every hundred children born, twenty-five died before they were one year old, another twenty-five never reached twenty and a further twenty-five perished between the ages of twenty and forty-five. Only about ten ever made their sixties." Pierre Goubert, *Louis XIV and Twenty Million Frenchmen* (New York Random House, 1972), 21. On the demography of New England, see esp. James H. Cassedy, *Demography in Early America: Beginnings of the Statistical Mind, 1600–1800* (Cambridge, MA: Harvard University Press, 1969). Cassedy points out that the demographic scale was at first weighted toward mortality, but at a different time for each colony, "this precarious balance righted itself." The incidence of disease, malnutrition, and frontier warfare was demonstrably greater for New England than it was for Acadia. The conditions of life along the St. Lawrence were much closer to those along the Bay of Fundy. In the eighteenth century the population of Canada doubled every 30 years. In Acadia, however, the increase was even higher: it doubled every fifteen years between 1671 and 1714, and every twenty years between 1714 and 1755. Furthermore, migration was a minimal factor in Acadian demography after 1740. On Canada, see Jacques Henripin, *La population canadienne au début du XVIIIe siècle* (Paris: Institut national d'études démographiques, 1954); on Acadia, see Roy, "Peuplement," 152.

21. Father Felix Pain to the governor of Isle Royale, September 1713, printed in Clark, *Acadia*, 187.

22. Sieur de Dièreville, *Relation of the Voyage to Port Royal in Acadia or New France*, ed. J.C. Webster (Toronto: Champlain Society, 1933), 93.

23. Public Archives of Canada (hereafter PAC), MG 11, CO 217, vol. 5, Phillipps to the Board of Trade, 2 September 1730 (PAC reel C-9120).

24. Hynes, "Demography of Port Royal," 10.

25. Hynes, "Demography of Port Royal," 10–11.

26. Clark, *Acadia*, 200f, arrived at somewhat different statistics, concluding that the average family size was closer to four or five.

27. Massignon, *Parlers français* 1: 45; Arsenault, *Généalogie* 1: 432, 433; 2: 666.

28. Arsenault, *Généologie* 1: 518.

29. This calculation rests partly upon the assumption that the Acadians followed a common contemporary practice of using the name of a child that died for the next-born of the same sex.

30. Arsenault, *Généalogie* 1: 518; 2: 666, 667f.

31. PAC, MG 11, CO 217, vol. 2 (PAC reel C-9119).

32. These figures are my own estimations, based upon the work of Clark, *Acadia*, 216, and the overview by Roy, "Peuplement," 134–207.

33. "A Brief Survey of Nova Scotia" (MS in Library of the Royal Artillery Regiment, Woolwich, n.d.), 2: 25–26, cited in Clark, *Acadia*, 217.

34. There is considerable debate about the kin system of these households. Grandparents can only have lived in one home, and there is still debate on how siblings linked housekeeping arrangements.

35. Dièreville, *Relation*, 256.

36. PAC, MG 1, Series C 11 D, 3: 199–203, Villebon to the Minister, 27 October 1694.

37. Cited in Clark, *Acadia*, 237.

38. Captain John Knox, *An Historical Journal of the Campaigns in North America for the Years 1757, 1758, 1759 and 1760*, ed. A.B. Doughty, 3 vols. (Toronto, 1914–18), 1: 105.

39. PAC, AC 2B, 12, "Supplied from Acadia entering Louisbourg, 1740," printed in Clark, *Acadia*, 259.

40. L.U. Fontaine, *Voyage de Sieur de Dièreville en Acadia* (Québec, 1885), 56.

41. "Supplies from Acadia," in Clark, *Acadia*, 259; and "Report of custom collector Newton" (PAC, AC, NSA-26, 29–33), printed in A. Shortt, V.K. Johnston and F. Lanctot, eds. *Currency, Exchange and Finance in Nova Scotia, with Prefatory Documents, 1675–1758* (Ottawa, 1933), 223–24.

42. PAC, AC, NSA-26, 52, cited in Clark, *Acadia*, 258. See also the chart of Louisbourg trade on pp. 324–25.

43. PAC, AC, NSA-26, 51, cited in Clark, *Acadia*, 258.

44. For example, the Acadians sent to Maryland and South Carolina were able to purchase ships. See PAC, NS A/60, "Circular to the governors on the continent, July 1st, 1756, Halifax."

45. Morris, "A Brief Survey," 2: 4, quoted in Clark, *Acadia*, 244.

46. Quoted in Clark, *Acadia*, 246.

47. Fontaine, *Voyage*, 56.

48. Observations made by Moise de Les Derniers shortly after 1755 and printed in Casgrain, *Un pèlerinage au pays d'Évangéline* (Paris, 1889), App. III, 115.

49. Dièreville, *Relation*, 96.

50. It was Perrot who first commented upon this in 1686 (PAC, AC, C11D-2[1], 119, mémoires généraux); and many later observers, such as Dièreville and Phillipps, insinuated similar flaws.

51. Clark, *Acadia*, 232.

52. PAC, MG1, series C11D, 2: 96-106, report on Menneval, 10 September 1688.

53. R. Hale, "Journal of a Voyage to Nova Scotia Made in 1731 by Robert Hale of Beverley," *The Essex Institute Historical Collections* 42 (July 1906): 233.

54. Comments on the litigious nature of the Acadians span all regimes. See Clark, *Acadia*, 198, and Brebner, *New England Outpost*, 140.

55. In particular, note the trouble that Subercase faced collecting taxes, in Shortt et al., *Currency*, 16.

56. Dièreville, *Relation*, 93.

57. Dièreville, *Relation*, 96.

58. Guillaume Thomas François Raynal, *Histoire philosophique et politique des établissements et du commerce des Européens dans les deux Indes* (Paris, 1778), 6: 309.

59. Moise de les Derniers, cited in Casgrain, *Un pèlerinage*, 155.

60. Massignon, *Parlers français* 2: 548, 1316. The *bûche à pilon* is illustrated in Paul Doucèt, *Vie de nos ancêtres en Acadie—l'alimentation* (Moncton: Éditions d'Acadie, 1980), 17.

61. Deschamps, cited in Clark, *Acadia*, 237.

62. Massignon, *Parlers français* 2: 550, 1320.

63. Massignon, *Parlers français* 2: 551, 1322; Ph.F. Bourgeois, *Vie de l'abbé François-Xavier LaFrance* (Montréal, 1925), 83.

64. *Les Guides Bleus de Bretagne* (Paris, 1967), 662.

65. Bourgeois, *Vie de l'abbé LaFrance*, 83.

66. Dièreville, *Relation*, 266, 110.

67. Records of the complaints of Acadians exiled to Brittany, described by Naomi Griffiths, "Petitions of Acadian Exiles, 1755–1785: A Neglected Source," *Histoire sociale—Social History* 11 (May 1978): 215–23.

68. Massignon, *Parlers français* 2: 648, 1702.

69. Griffiths, "Petitions of Acadian Exile," 218f.

70. A.M. MacMechan, ed., *Nova Scotia Archives*, vol. 3, *Original Minutes of H.M. Council at Annapolis Royal, 1720–1739* (Halifax, 1908), 112, 122.

71. Jean-Claude Dupont, *Héritage d'Acadie* (Québec: Leméac, 1977), 172, and *Histoire populaire de l'Acadie* (Montréal: Leméac, 1979).

72. MacMechan, *Nova Scotia Archives* 3: 3, 17.

73. W.P. Bell, *The "Foreign Protestants" and the Settlement of Nova Scotia: The History of a Piece of Arrested British Colonial Policy in the Eighteenth Century* (Toronto: University of Toronto Press, 1961), 44–45, 64–85, 328–35.

74. Griffiths, "Petitions of Acadian Exiles," 216f.

75. Jean Daigle, "Les Relations commerciales de l'Acadie avec le Massachusetts: le cas de Charles-Amador de Saint-Étienne de la Tour, 1695–1697," *Revue de l'Université de Moncton* 9 (1976): 353–61.

76. Clark, *Acadia*, 203–4.

77. Têtu et Gagnon, *Mandements, lettres pastorales et circulaires des évêques de Quebec, 1888*, 15–16, reprinted in E. de Grace, G. Desjardins, R.-A. Mallet, *Histoire d'Acadie par les Textes*, 4 fascicules (Fredericton: Ministère de l'éducation du Nouveau-Brunswick, 1976), 1 (1604–1760): 19.

78. A most interesting question which needs further investigation and which reinforces the theory of Acadian respect for, but not subservience to, the Catholic church, is the matter of dispensations for marriage between second cousins accorded at Annapolis Royal between 1727 and 1755, the usual reason for such dispensations being premarital pregnancy. Cf. Clark, *Acadia*, 203–4, passim.

79. Massignon, *Parlers français* 2: 691–99.
80. Not only fiddleheads but also *titines de souris (salicornia Europaia)* and *passe-pierre (saxifraga Virginiensis)*. See Massignon, *Parlers français* 1: 183.
81. Knox, *Historical Journal* 1: 94–96, quoted in A.G. Doughty, *The Acadian Exiles* (Toronto: Glasgow, Brook and Company, 1916), 40.

Article Five

Imperial Transitions

Elizabeth Mancke

In 1713 Louis XIV, ostensibly at the request of the British government, released French Protestants who had been imprisoned on naval galleys. To match this French show of benevolence, Queen Anne sent a letter to Francis Nicholson, governor of Nova Scotia, informing him that Acadians who were 'willing to Continue our Subjects [were] to retain and Enjoy their said Lands and Tenements without any Lett or Molestation.' Those who chose to relocate into French territory could sell their property. Beyond showing herself to be as magnanimous a monarch as Louis XIV, Queen Anne's letter was a personal gesture to her new 'subjects' that symbolized Britain's sovereignty over Nova Scotia.[1]

Such displays of royal benevolence anticipated a complementary show of fealty from the recipients, in the case of the Acadians an oath of allegiance. As is well known, they demurred. By declining, Acadians implicitly, though whether willfully is unclear, challenged British sovereignty in Nova Scotia. The internationally negotiated transfer of Acadia from French to British sovereignty needed acceptance and legitimation on the ground by the Acadians, if not the natives as well. The absence of clear acceptance and legitimation raised a number of problems. If Acadians did not swear an oath of allegiance, could they still own their property as Queen Anne had promised, and practise Catholicism as stipulated in the Treaty of Utrecht? Were they entitled to the crown's protection? Did the refusal to swear the oath mean that Acadians did not acknowledge the territorial transfer of Acadia from France to Britain? How was the crown's responsibility to establish civilian government to be expressed if the local population refused the crown's sovereignty? Technically not subjects or denizens, were the Acadians to be treated as friendly aliens or enemy aliens? In short, how was civilian government to be established in Nova Scotia, and what kind of government would it be?

No colony in British America offered clear precedents. In all earlier British colonial ventures, the settlement of large numbers of English subjects meant that governmental authority and sovereignty were negotiated and legitimated within a common cultural matrix that included notions about law, property holding, governmental authority, the appropriate relations between the governed and their governors, and who was friend and who foe.[2] As well, these colonies developed creole colonial elites defined not just by their social and economic power, but also by political power. Even the conquered colonies of Jamaica and New York (with New Jersey carved off the latter) did not offer precedents. After the English conquest of

Source: Elizabeth Mancke, "Imperial Transitions," in *The 'Conquest' of Acadia, 1710. Imperial, Colonial, and Aboriginal Constructions*, eds. John G. Reid, Maurice Basque, Elizabeth Mancke, Barry Moody, Geoffrey Planke, William Wicken (Toronto: University of Toronto Press, 2004): 178–202, 255–260. Reprinted with permission of the publisher.

Jamaica in 1655, most Spanish residents fled the island for Spanish territory, thereby obviating the problem of incorporating Spanish-speaking, Catholic residents into the English world.[3] In New York, conquered in 1664, most of the Dutch residents of the former colony of New Netherland had stayed; predominantly Protestants, most were naturalized by legislation or allowed resident status by executive patents.[4] In both Jamaica and New York, the arrival of English settlers soon consolidated English control.

In neither Jamaica nor New York did colonial officials suffer chronic fear that the Spanish or the Dutch would try to retake their former colonies. While Spain had other large colonies near Jamaica, in particular Cuba and Hispaniola, neither posed a threat of the magnitude that the French presence in Île Royale and Canada posed for Nova Scotia. New Netherland had been the only Dutch colony on mainland North America. After its loss, the Dutch evinced no serious interest in temperate climate colonies, concentrating their expansionist energies on colonies in tropical zones. Jamaica had no remaining native peoples, though it had a large maroon population living in the island's interior who challenged British control of the island through the eighteenth century.[5] New York had large numbers of natives, in particular the Houdenasaunee (Iroquois), and the English built on the trade and military alliances the Dutch had established. Nova Scotia's native peoples, by contrast, asserted their autonomy, intermittently resisted the British, and maintained diplomatic relations with the French.[6]

In Nova Scotia, none of the above characteristics existed. Political elites, as represented by metropolitan officials, had few ties to social and economic elites among the Acadians.[7] The dominant residential populations were Acadian and native. Acadians were Catholic and the natives at least nominally so, thus perpetuating ties to New France through the ministrations of French priests. While the British acknowledged native groups as self-governing, Acadians were to be within the pale of day-to-day British government. Yet under the English Test Act of 1673, their Catholicism made them ineligible to hold public office or sit on juries, even if they did swear an oath of allegiance. How was Nova Scotia to be governed when, by law, the majority of the European population could not participate in government? And if Acadians could not participate, who would? The near-absence of Protestant settlers in Nova Scotia before 1749 meant that under existing laws there were not enough people to establish the full apparatus of British government that had become conventional in other colonies: an assembly that would vote taxes to run the colony, county and/or town government for local administration, a land office and registry of deeds, and a judicial system.

New legislation on naval stores further complicated the recruitment of settlers for Nova Scotia, as well as reflected a piecemeal interest by the metropolitan government in the potential of new colonial resources. During the War of the Spanish Succession (1702–13), the Board of Trade persuaded Parliament to pass the Naval Stores Act (1705) to encourage the North American colonies to produce tar, pitch, rosin, turpentine, hemp, masts, yards, and bowsprits for use by the Royal Navy. To reserve the woods for naval stores, the legislation prohibited the cutting of 'Pitch, Pine, or Tar Trees,' under twelve inches in diameter on ungranted land, a clause which applied to land from New Jersey north. The 1691 charter of Massachusetts had already reserved trees over twenty-four inches in diameter for use as masts for the navy. Both the 1705 legislation and the Massachusetts charter were interpreted to extend to Nova Scotia, and thus land could not be granted to new settlers without being surveyed for naval stores. As written, the legislation implicitly required colonies to bear the cost of the surveys, and in Nova Scotia there simply was no money for such expenses.[8]

With its garrisoned, English-speaking, Protestant officials, and its dispersed native and French Catholic communities, Nova Scotia was not representative of early-eighteenth century British America. However, officials who governed Nova Scotia had the untenable charge 'to establish a form of Government consonant to that of the other Plantations in America.'[9] For nearly half a century, they struggled unsuccessfully to find the combination and sequence of conditions, short of deporting the Acadians, to pull the colony within the normative range of colonial governance. Their failure to craft and legitimate a new definition of colonial subject and an appropriate system of government that was acceptable in both Nova Scotia and Britain is testimony both to the profoundly English political and constitutional legacy of seventeenth-century colonial development and to how wrenching would be the accommodation of a more ethnically and constitutionally polyglot empire in the eighteenth century.[10]

In this sense, Nova Scotia's history is central to understanding the constitutional and political reconfiguration and redefinition of the British empire over the eighteenth century. The Acadians' refusal to swear an oath of allegiance after the Treaty of Utrecht made variable what had become normative and interdependent elements of British colonial governments. The maintenance of colonies depended on populations that acknowledged themselves subject to the British monarch, that staffed the civilian governments established on an English model, and that voted taxes to pay the expenses of running a colony. The absence of these three critical elements of colonial governments — a natural-born or naturalized subject population, a civilian government, and locally generated financial resources — stymied the men sent to govern Nova Scotia. Unable to act within established conventions, officials articulated a wide range of values about the fundamentals of colonial governance in order to explain why they were obliged to govern outside those norms. Their quandary makes the official record of post-conquest Nova Scotia an extended discussion about the nature of British colonial government.

Ironically, the severe limitations of Nova Scotia laid bare the skeleton of colonial governance that the success of other colonies obscured. Using the official record from 1710 to 1749, this chapter analyses what the political history of Nova Scotia can tell us about the nature of British colonial government in the early modern era. The chapter is divided into four sections: the first deals with the establishment of civilian government; the second considers the necessity of a civilian population of subjects; the third examines the problem of financing colonies; and the final section assesses the impact of shifting metropolitan policies after 1748. Within this analysis there are three important chronological periods. The first period, from 1710, the year of the conquest, to 1720, when Governor Richard Philipps arrived in the colony, was characterized by enormous ambiguity over the long-term status of the colony and its Acadian and native residents. The second period, 1720–30, saw the establishment of an executive council as the institutional cornerstone for the colony's civilian government. But as Philipps soon discovered, until the Acadians swore an oath of allegiance, the government would lack civilian subjects and thus the personnel to establish collateral institutions. In the late 1720s the Acadians swore qualified oaths of allegiance, giving the colony a civilian population of subjects, albeit Catholic and of suspect loyalty. In the third period, 1730–48, the colony's government began the process of surveying and registering Acadian lands and collecting quitrents, but it still could not call an assembly that could vote the taxes so necessary for financing colonies. The colony's financial straits ended in 1748 when Parliament appropriated monies to build Halifax as a north Atlantic naval port and new capital of Nova Scotia. Suddenly the colony had abundant financial resources, unprecedented both in the history of Nova Scotia and the history of British America, a shift, as it were, from colonial to imperial government.

Richard Philipps, appointed governor general of Nova Scotia in 1717, found upon his arrival in the colony in April 1720 that there 'has been hitherto no more than a Mock Government,' He recognized that without the Acadians swearing an oath of allegiance 'the British Government canot [sic] be said to be Established,' unless the government supplied resources to coax or coerce the Acadians into fidelity or to settle 'Natural born Subjects' in the colony.[11] The Acadians' unwillingness to swear an oath of allegiance compelled him to tell the Board of Trade that the effective extension of British sovereignty to Nova Scotia depended not just on the conquest and the subsequent Treaty of Utrecht, but also on the ongoing appearance and substance of a British presence in the colony. Quite simply, 'it is necessary that the Government at home exert itself a little and be at some extraordinary expence.' So appalled was Philipps at the state of the colony and the lack of resources for governing that he argued it would be better to give the territory back to the French than to 'be contented with the name only of Government.'[12]

Philipps's frustration, a decade after the 1710 conquest, is indicative of how incomprehensible conditions in Nova Scotia were from the perspective of the metropole. Much of the two years between the issuing of his original commission in 1717 and his arrival in Nova Scotia Philipps had spent in London negotiating with officials for instruction and powers that fitted the known problems of the colony. Since the conquest, metropolitan policy for governing this new acquisition was ill-defined. A garrison command under successive governors or their deputies had nominally governed the colony, and many of the concerns they communicated back to Britain dealt with the abysmal state of the finances for maintaining troops stationed at Annapolis Royal and the financial and psychological wounds sustained by everyone in the open antagonism that developed among the officers, especially between Francis Nicholson and Samuel Vetch.[13]

Various of Philipps's predecessors who had found themselves responsible for the colony had made hesitant moves to separate military and civilian governance, but like efforts to resolve other problems, their efforts fell victim to metropolitan indifference and internal squabbling. The winter after the conquest, four British army officers and two Acadians convened a court to adjudicate disputes.[14] After the Treaty of Utrecht, Thomas Caulfeild, lieutenant-governor under Nicholson and then Vetch, tried to establish courts suitable to the Acadians and the British, but Nicholson challenged his authority to do so. In reporting the incident to the Board of Trade, Caulfeild said that he had told Nicholson that as the highest civilian officer resident in the colony, he 'Should always endeavour to Cultivate as good an Understanding amongst the People as possible believing the same Essential for his Majesties Service.' Given the choice of establishing a court without a commission or holding 'myselfe blamable to Suffer Injustice to be done before Me without taking Notice thereof,' he chose the former.[15]

The decision of the French to build Louisbourg, combined with the death of Caulfeild in 1717, forced even indifferent metropolitan officials to acknowledge the colony's needs. The British crown formed a new regiment of foot, under the command of Colonel Richard Philipps, as a permanent part of His Majesty's land forces. Philipps was also appointed governor general of Nova Scotia, and his military commission would pay his gubernatorial salary. Philipps quickly recognized that his military commission did not include sufficient powers or instructions to manage Nova Scotia's known problems, much less its unknown ones. In particular, he was concerned that he have the authority to establish a civilian government. Staying in London until 1719, he negotiated with the Board of Trade and Board of Ordnance for more resources, power, and a new commission, without realizing how utterly inadequate these preparations would still be.[16]

The royal instructions to Philipps in 1719, and subsequent instructions drafted until 1749, included the injunction that until Nova Scotia's government was established the governor would receive 'a copy of the instructions given by his Majesty to the governor of Virginia, by which you will conduct yourself till his Majesty's further pleasure shall be known.'[17] John Bartlet Brebner labelled this government by analogy, which it was, but he overdrew the comparison to Virginia and underestimated the larger colonial context.[18] Since the Restoration, the Privy Council had slowly been regularizing and routinizing basic communications with colonies, and dispatches to one colony were often used as the template for instructions to other colonies.[19]

Similarities among colonies had emerged less from metropolitan design than from an English commitment to 'such devices as trial by jury, habeas corpus, due process of law, and representative government.'[20] An increasingly integrated British Atlantic economy depended on shared legal protections of property, thus encouraging compatible judicial systems throughout British America. Colonial charters, and then instructions to governors after many colonies were royalized, emphasized that no laws were to be passed that were inconsistent with English law. The Treasury expected colonies to be self-financing, and throughout the Americas this financial imperative encouraged the establishment of colonial assemblies, based on the model of the House of Commons and the principle that elected representatives should determine taxation.

By the end of the seventeenth century, from an imperial perspective, the problem with colonial governments lay not so much in their weaknesses, but stemmed rather from too much unchecked and undisciplined vitality and autonomy. Little in the 106 years between the founding of Virginia (1607) and the French cession of Acadia (1713) would lead metropolitan officials to believe that Nova Scotia would not develop a similarly vital government. And because much of metropolitan practice for governing far-flung territories had developed reactively rather than proactively, there was no bureaucratic practice of designing a colonial government.[21]

From within the colony, however, it was blindingly and frustratingly obvious that configuring Nova Scotia's government to the colonial standard would be a daunting, if not impossible, task. As Philipps noted, without people willing to acknowledge themselves subject to the British crown, the home government had to spend money to make manifest British sovereignty among a non-British people. If the merits of British government were not culturally internalized, as with natural-born subjects, or consciously accepted, as with naturalized subjects, then they had to be intentionally externalized, displayed, and made tangibly attractive. The presence of the governor general and the establishment of civilian government were two such manifestations. Philipps believed, perhaps arrogantly, that the Acadians were surprised to find that he, and not just a deputy, had come to Nova Scotia. Gauging the symbolism of leadership, the Acadians had concluded, he believed, that if the British did not send a high-ranking official to the colony, then they did not consider it important and they might well return the colony to the French.[22]

Philipps promptly set about to establish the foundation for a civilian government. He issued a proclamation to the Acadians reminding them of their duty to swear an oath of allegiance that would protect their rights to 'le libre Excercise de leur Religion,' as well as allow them 'de Droits et Privileges Civils comme S'ils estroint Anglois.'[23] On 25 April, his fifth day at Annapolis Royal, he convened a civilian council. Lacking a full complement of twelve Protestant civilians who could serve on the Council, he chose by rank three military officers.[24] A year later, on 11 April 1721, Philipps also constituted the Council as a 'Court of Judicature,' despite the absence of conditions necessary to establish courts 'according to the Lawes of Great Britain.' The Virginia instructions, however, did allow the governor and Council to sit as a court of justice, and given the large number of 'Memorialls, Petition[s], and Complaints' submitted to Philipps for his assessment, he thought it best to have them decided by the Council sitting in a judicial capacity.[25] Initially the Council planned court days for the first Tuesdays in May, August, November, and February, but in practice it heard cases throughout the year as they occurred. The Council secretaries never wrote separate minutes for executive and judicial business, and in many sittings the Council shifted back and forth between its two roles. Only by reading the text of the minutes can one discern distinctions in the Council's exercise of its two functions.

The seeming blending of executive and judicial functions was largely a consequence of limited personnel rather than a disregard of appropriate judicial procedure. In an analysis of Nova Scotia's justice system circa 1710–50, Thomas Barnes has argued persuasively that over time 'the council became less summary and more procedure-bound,' particularly after 1730, when the number of cases heard by the council increased. Lawrence Armstrong, who served as lieutenant-governor during most of the 1730s, and Paul Mascarene, who became Council president upon Armstrong's death in 1739, were staunch advocates of due process.[26] The rising number of civil cases in the 1730s prompted Armstrong to issue a memo to the Acadians that emphasized the injustice of attempts at 'Hurried' and 'Impatient' litigation that did not give people 'Due time to prepare and make Answer to Such Complaints & Petitions as have been often Lodged & Exhibited against them.' Haste also resulted in 'many frivolous and undigested Complaints' being brought to the Council. To curb the problems, Armstrong reinstated four terms in which the Council would sit as a court.[27]

The other major component of civilian government in early Nova Scotia was the system of Acadian deputies. On 29 April 1720 the Council, working beyond the letter of its instructions, voted to authorize the French inhabitants in the settlements on the Annapolis River to choose six deputies to represent their interests to the governor and Council. Within a few weeks the communities at Minas and Cobequid had also elected deputies.[28] While the system of deputies remained until the deportation of the Acadians beginning in 1755, their role in the government of Nova Scotia shifted considerably, especially after the oath taking in the late 1720s and 1730.[29]

In the early 1720s, the deputies had quasi-diplomatic functions. They were the spokespeople when the Acadians declined to swear an oath of allegiance in 1720. The Council consulted them for witnesses or evidence in both criminal and civil cases. During the hostilities between the natives and the British from 1722 until the signing of the peace treaty in 1725, the deputies were consulted about the presence of natives in their communities. Once peace obviated their quasi-diplomatic role, the importance of deputies temporarily declined. The Council contacted them very few times between 1725 and 1729 and their selection, or non-selection, became haphazard. On 21 November 1729, one day after arriving back in Annapolis Royal after an eight-year absence, Philipps notified the Council that he had appointed new deputies for the Annapolis River settlements and had increased their number from four to eight.[30] Philipps's unilateral decision to appoint deputies is indicative of how irregular their selection had become and how infrequently the Council had consulted them in the previous years. In 1732, after Philipps had returned to Britain and Lawrence Armstrong was the chief governing officer, the deputies complained that Philipps had appointed them rather than letting them be elected by the people they represented.[31]

One of the primary reasons for Philipps's 1729 return to Nova Scotia was to get the Acadians to swear an oath of allegiance, a new push that had been started in 1726 by Lawrence Armstrong after a five-year hiatus on the issue during which the peace had been negotiated with the natives. In Philipps's oath-taking negotiations with the Acadians, he promised them in the name of George II that their religious and property rights would be honoured, provided they surveyed and registered claims to the latter.[32] As he explained to the Board of Trade, the collection of quitrents would 'contribute towards the Support of Government.'[33] Informing the council on December 7, 1730, that he had obtained oaths from all the Acadians, he also noted that he had appointed Alexander Bourg, former procurator general under the French regime, as collector of rents. Philipps instructed him to report on 'what Homage and Duties they paid to the [French] Crown,' as the basis for establishing quitrents, one of the few instances of the British harkening back to practices of the French regime.[34]

The decision to survey and register Acadian lands and to charge quitrents generated a whole new set of administrative tasks that reinvigorated the role of the deputies, created new offices such as the farmers of rents, and fostered disputes over land boundaries that sent dozens of litigants to the Council for dispute resolution. It became common for deputies to ascertain the nature of land disagreements, to order inhabitants to make property lines, and to organize inhabitants to clear roads and keep dikes in good repair.[35] The enhanced importance of deputies to the administration of local government also brought about the regularization of their election. On 11 September 1732, the council decided, in consultation with lieutenant-governor Armstrong and the Annapolis River deputies, that annual elections for deputies would be held on 11 October, provided it was not a Sunday and 'then it Shall be on the Munday following.' Significantly, the chosen date commemorated the reduction of Port Royal.[36]

After Paul Mascarene became president of the council after the death of Armstrong in 1739, he wrote a memorial that codified the role of the deputies. They were to be men of property and good sense who had the interest of the community at heart. They had the power to consult among themselves and to convene meetings of the residents they represented. They were to monitor the maintenance of fences and the control of livestock, oversee the upkeep of bridges and roads, and find people to farm the king's rents.[37] In addition to the responsibilities of the deputies after 1730, the rent farmers were to record all land transactions, as well as wills and testaments, tasks associated with registrars of deeds and probate in other British colonies.

Administratively, most of the functions of local government common in British colonies had been institutionalized in Nova Scotia during the 1730s, largely through the office of the deputies, and they would remain critical to local administration until the deportation. Mascarene, in particular, described the nature of local government in Nova Scotia to the Board of Trade, noting that the needs of government were great enough to warrant allowing the Acadians to hold local offices.[38] Operational within the colony, the deputies had no legal standing under British law, which prohibited Catholics from holding public office, and virtually no acknowledgement outside the colony. Significantly, when the Acadians were deported, beginning in 1755, deputies who had faithfully served the British government were treated no differently from Acadians who had supported the French.

What is striking about Nova Scotia's early-eighteenth century record is how assiduously officials worked to create and maintain a government that honoured 'the rights of Englishmen,' including the minimization of military rule. The first four decades of British governance in Nova Scotia, despite the preponderance of members of the government with military commissions, is testimony to Jack Greene's argument that the single most defining characteristic of English, and then British, identity in the early modern Atlantic world was a commitment to English liberty.[39] If any place in seventeenth- or eighteenth-century British America had a government run on military principles, it would have been Nova Scotia, as some people at the time, and some historians, believed was true.[40] The chief pieces of evidence for this contention were the military officers and a government that deviated from other British colonial governments. Neither individually nor together do they make the case.[41]

First, we cannot assume that all men in the British army eschewed the English commitment to liberty. When outsiders charged that the officers stationed at Annapolis Royal were attempting to create a military government, ten of them protested that they served merely 'for want of other Brittish Subjects.' They acted 'with a due regard to the Liberty and Property of the Subject and the Peace and well being of his Majesty's Province,' and had 'never had any advantage or Salary.'[42] Men inclined to abuse their military power were likely to be checked, either by a superior officer or the council. After the death of lieutenant-governor Armstrong in 1739, the relationship between the civilian Council and the garrison command became a matter of contention. Alexander Cosby, lieutenant-colonel of the 40th regiment and Paul Mascarene's superior officer in the army, questioned the property of Mascarene, rather than he, serving as Council president. A Board of Trade ruling, however, had stated that in the absence of both the governor and lieutenant-governor, the most senior councillor would serve as council president, not the most senior military officer. Cosby tried to remove Mascarene from Annapolis Royal by ordering him to Canso to serve in the garrison there, but Mascarene refused to go. He reported to the Board of Trade that 'I am firmly persuaded if I had remov'd from hence, the Civil Government would have been of no use, and disorder would naturally have issued.' Despite endless slights from Cosby, Mascarene believed that he had preserved 'the good effects of the Civil Government administred . . . over the French Inhabitants of this Province.'[43]

In the settlement of Canso, inhabited largely by New Englanders engaged in the fishery, Governor Philipps had first appointed justices of the peace in 1720. In 1729, during his brief sojourn there, four residents petitioned Philipps to appoint a 'Civil Magistracy' that could sit in Canso and adjudicate 'the many Petty Differences & Cases which Daily Arise in this Fishery that Call for a determination too tedious & Triball to trouble Your Excellency with,' which he did.[44] In 1732 Edward How, one of Canso's justices of the peace, complained to Armstrong that Captain Christopher Aldridge, the highest-commanding officer at Canso, divested the 'Justices of the Peace and Civil Magistrates of all Authority.' Armstrong sent Aldridge a strong reprimand for having 'taken upon your Self the entire Management of the Civil as well as the Military affairs.' Apparently, Aldridge had told the angry JPs that he arrogated no more power than Philipps or Armstrong had as the chief authority in Annapolis. Armstrong corrected Aldridge's claim, noting that 'you assume a much Greater power than Either his Excellency or my self Ever pretended to and in making Either of us your precedent in such Respects; I must say . . . that you do us injustice.' Aldridge was not to conflate his military authority as the highest-ranking officer at Canso with his civilian authority as the president of the Council there, in which latter capacity he had to heed the advice and decisions of all civilian officers.[45]

Armstrong's strong defence of civilian government against usurpation by military men is ironic when framed against his pay. In 1728 or 1729, Armstrong petitioned the Board of Trade to receive a portion of Philipps's salary, based on the Virginia proviso that if the governor was not resident in the colony then the lieutenant-governor should receive a portion of the governor's salary. Armstrong pointed out that he, and not Philipps, had been serving as governor in Nova Scotia. The Board of Trade referred Armstrong's petition to the entire Privy Council, which concluded that it had no discretion over Philipps's salary. Virginia, which paid its governor from an export duty of two shillings per hogshead of tobacco, was the only mainland colony with a permanent revenue for the governor's salary, or the lieutenant-governor's in the former's absence. Philipps's salary, like the governors' salaries in Bermuda and South Carolina, came from the captaincy of an independent company of foot, and it was 'Founded on the Establishment of Your Majesty's Land Forces . . . and not within the Jurisdiction of Your Majesty's Privy Councill.'[46] Without an assembly to raise taxes for the governor or lieutenant-governor's salary, the men who served in Nova Scotia were entirely dependent on their military pay. Armstrong received some justice when in 1731 the British government ordered him to return to Nova Scotia with orders for Philipps's recall to answer charges that he had not paid the officers in his company. Upon resuming control of the government as lieutenant-governor, Armstrong would receive the governor's salary.[47]

The problem of how to pay officials of the crown serving in the colonies indicates that the appointment of men with military commissions to overseas postings had less to do with a desire to militarize the empire than a desire to run the empire parsimoniously. Commissioned officers had a salaried, bureaucratic relationship to the metropolitan government, whether they were stationed in London, Hanover, Gibraltar, or Annapolis Royal. Given the lack of Protestant subjects to serve in an assembly and vote taxes to pay a governor, and given an absence of metropolitan monies to pay a civilian to be governor, a British colonial government in early-eighteenth-century Nova Scotia would have been inconceivable without men who were also military officers. The ideological and pecuniary biases in favour of Protestant and self-financing overseas dependencies exaggerated the role of military men in Nova Scotia, and the men appointed to govern the colony understood the negative prejudice of that bias. Philipps,

Armstrong, and Mascarene were all acutely aware that the perception that 'martial law prevails here' discouraged settlers from moving to the colony. Despite the hardships of a shortage of subjects, a monetary deficit, and some military officers who would have abused their power had they not been checked, the government of Nova Scotia from 1720 to 1749 was more civilian than military in its ethos and execution.[48]

The problems engendered by the Acadians' refusal to swear an oath of allegiance have generally been interpreted as ones of security; they were 'Snakes in [our] Bosoms,' to use Lawrence Armstrong's graphic phrase.[49] The problem was, however, more fundamental. The lack of subjects impeded the day-to-day governing of the colony, and in the minds of most British officials, civil governance was a symbiotic and dialectical relationship between the governed and their governors. So long as Acadians did not swear an oath of allegiance, and so long as they remained on Nova Scotian soil that could not be granted to Protestant settlers, a 'proper' civilian government with officials drawn from the local population could not be established. Land could not be granted or deeded. Taxes could not be assessed, except for minimal charges. The Navigation Acts made Acadian trade illegal. And, as Philipps noted, the presence of subjects in a colony legitimated claims of sovereignty in ways that treaties and soldiers could not.

The question was, who might become these Nova Scotian subjects? And how might they be cajoled or, if need be, coerced into this role? In the minds of British officials, two different groups were possible. The Acadians could swear an oath of allegiance, which, as noted above, did make possible the deeding of land. Legally they could not hold public office, but extra-legally, given the exigencies of the colony, they did. Protestants, either British or foreign, were preferable, because there were no legal bars on their participation in government. But they needed to be persuaded to move to the colony, and the legal and financial constraints on land grants needed to be removed. The Mi'kmaq and Wulstukwiuk were never mentioned as possible subjects for the purposes of establishing English-style civilian government. In the first instance, the British wished to achieve amity, in lieu of the open enmity, with them, with occasional and unresolved discussion about whether they were 'Friends or Subjects.'[50]

The terms of the Treaty of Utrecht, followed by Queen Anne's letter to Nicholson, obliged the British government to look first to the Acadians as potential subjects. Since the signing of the terms of capitulation in 1710, the British had made intermittent attempts to persuade the Acadians to swear an oath of allegiance. The Acadians, for their part, became adept equivocators, supported in some measure by the terms of the capitulation, their treaty rights, Queen Anne's letter, the weakness of colonial government, and the volatile geopolitics of the northeast. The first systematic attempt to persuade the Acadians to swear an oath of allegiance began in 1717, when John Doucett, the new lieutenant-governor under Richard Philipps, arrived in Nova Scotia. Doucett soon heard the range of Acadian explanations for why they would not swear an oath of allegiance. The foremost plea was that they were still considering relocating. Some Acadians thought they could move across the Bay of Fundy to the Passamaquoddy area 'where they Fancy themselves secure and that there no notice would be taken of them, tho it is still in his Majesty's Dominions.' Doucett, like other officials, looked on these protestations about moving with a jaundiced eye, noting that 'this has been their declaration every Winter for Five or Six Years Past so that wee do not give much Creditt to it.'[51]

Acadians also argued that if they swore an oath of allegiance to the British monarch, they would invite the wrath of the natives. This excuse elicited little sympathy; Doucett noted that if an Indian acts 'insolent in their Houses,' they do not hesitate to throw out the person. Doucett did not know of cases of Mi'kmaq taking revenge on Acadians.[52] On this matter, his scepticism was probably unfounded, given the ongoing tensions between the natives and the British that would not slacken until the mid-1720s. The British believed that the natives were tools of the French, and resisted understanding natives as agents independent of the French and negotiating their own issues. The Acadian response probably does represent their recognition of native autonomy, from the French government and from themselves, despite a long history of trade relations, intermarriage, and at times military alliances.

Rumours, reputedly started by the French priests, provided new rationales for procrastination. After the accession of George I in 1714, a priest working in Nova Scotia reputedly received a letter from France claiming that the 'Pretender was Again Landed in Scotland.' In response to the threat George I had 'sent for Ten thousand French' troops to drive back the Stuart pretender. Upon landing in England, the French troops 'all declared for the Pretender [and] . . . Establisht him on the Throne of Great Brittain.' In gratitude, he 'intended to give to the French, all they should ask,' which presumably included Acadia. Doucett rebutted this rumour, telling Peter Mellanson of Minas that 'King George . . . is, God be Praise'd, as firm & fixt in the Throne of Great Brittain as Ever Lewis the 14th was in the French Throne.'[53]

In recounting this story to the Board of Trade, Doucett hoped it would not find him 'impertinent,' but wanted to use the incident to ask it to find 'Some Method to Convince these People that their Priests are Fallible.' The story was not entirely far-fetched. Queen Anne had died in 1714, and there had been some uncertainty over her successor. But it was far-fetched that George I, a German prince, would ask the French for military support against the Stuart pretender they had been sheltering since the flight of James II in 1688.[54] A more plausible rumour was that the Acadian right to worship as Catholics and have French priests was a ploy by the British. Their priests reminded them that the British in Ireland did not allow Catholic priests and also dispossessed Catholic landowners of their real property. This rumour cast doubt on the promise of Queen Anne that the Catholic Acadians could continue to practise their religion and retain their property.

Both sides, Acadian and British, played a waiting game. For the Acadians, if the past were any measure, British governance might well be fleeting. In the first decade after the conquest, governors tried coercion, backed not by force, but by inflated rhetoric and a willingness to let British residents suffer a penalty worse than the one they meted on the Acadians. Nicholson, in his frustration with Acadian obstinacy, banned trade with them, which caused serious deprivation among the troops, who had few alternative sources for most food supplies.[55] Meanwhile the Acadians ate well and smuggled their surpluses to the French in Cape Breton. In the fall of 1717, Doucett, appealing to the Navigation Acts, banned Annapolis River Acadians from trading and fishing. He calculated that by spring and the start of the fishing season, these Acadians would abandon their obdurate position and would swear the oath of allegiance. They did not weaken. These threats depended on some ability to enforce them. With no government vessels to patrol the waters near Annapolis Royal, much less up the Bay of Fundy to Minas Basin or Cobequid, Doucett's pronouncements to the Acadians that it was 'Dangerous . . . to Triffle with so Great a Monarch [as George I],' were little more than bluster, and the Acadians surely understood as much.[56]

Richard Philipps's decision, pursuant to his arrival in April 1720, to have the Acadians elect deputies was to give him representatives with whom he could negotiate taking the oath of allegiance. By September, the Acadians had proved 'insolent' rather than compliant, obliging the Council to address the problem 'of the most effectuall way of setling this his Majestys Province.' It recommended telling the metropolitan government that 'more regular forces [be] sent over here to curb the Insolency's of the present french Inhabitants, and Indians,' a vain request until 1749. More reasonably and immediately, it decided that the five communities of Acadians be allowed to continue to elect deputies who would report to the governor and Council.[57]

Governor Philipps and the Council wrote the King on 27 September 1720 asking for guidance on how to proceed with the problem of making the Acadians subjects, noting that the

French priests had told them that their allegiance to France was 'indissoluble,' an interpretation of the bonds of allegiance that was not inconsistent with some legal thought. After rehearsing the impunity with which the Acadians acted, largely because the King's authority scarcely extended beyond firing range of the fort, the governor and council asked for additional troops and matériel, as well as naval vessels for service in Nova Scotian waters.[58]

This letter, in the minds of the governor and council, shifted the responsibility for determining how to proceed in getting the Acadians to become British subjects to the King and his ministers. The following spring (1721) the Acadians living on the Annapolis River petitioned Philipps for permission to sow their fields or leave for Cape Breton. Philipps responded that he was extending the time allowed for them to submit to the British King, that he had written him, and until he had an answer the issue of the oath of allegiance was deferred. This deferral, unless he heard otherwise, protected their property rights.[59] In February 1723, after Philipps had returned to England, the Acadian deputies from Annapolis River presented Doucett with a memorial, along with Philipps's 1721 letter to them, requesting permission to plant their fields. Doucett and the Council determined that until they had further notice Philipps's decision stood, and they too would await a royal response.[60]

For the next three years, the issue of the Acadians swearing an oath of allegiance or leaving the colony was moot. The Board of Trade did not respond to Philipps's and the Council's 1720 letter. Peace in Europe, and especially amity with the French, had made the King's ministers complacent about colonial affairs. Relocating the Acadians posed as much of a problem for the British as it did a solution. After the signing of the Treaty of Utrecht, the French began resettling fishers from Placentia, Newfoundland, to Cape Breton. In 1717 they began the building of Louisbourg as a major administrative centre, commercial entrepôt, and naval base. The British recognized that the departure of seasoned French settlers to Cape Breton would be a gift to the French, who had a difficult time recruiting people to go to the colonies. Nova Scotian officials were also concerned that if the Acadians left the colony their lands would have to be quickly resettled and the dikes maintained so that the sea not reclaim its due.

Ongoing tensions with the natives also made peace the most pressing need in the colony, and the governor and Council dealt with little else in the early 1720s. Consequently, concern about an Acadian oath of allegiance receded. Only after 1725 did the question of establishing a civilian population of subjects re-emerge as a regular policy issue for the governor and Council, although by that time the reality of long-term Anglo-French peace muted the immediate security concerns that the Acadians had earlier posed. A new campaign to persuade them to swear an oath of allegiance began in 1725 with the appointment of Lawrence Armstrong as lieutenant-governor, who more generally attempted to implement policies that would bring the colony into greater conformity with practices of British colonial governance elsewhere.[61]

When Armstrong arrived back in Annapolis Royal, he began his efforts at getting the Acadians to swear an oath of allegiance with the people living along the Annapolis River. In the 1710s, the Acadians' two main concerns about swearing a British oath of allegiance had been whether they would relocate out of the colony and whether they would invite the retaliation of the natives; both issues had receded by 1726. Their new and persisting concern would be whether they would have to bear arms in future conflicts with the French or natives. Armstrong told them that as Catholics they were prohibited by law from military service so that the issue was irrelevant.[62] But the concern with military service was not so easily dismissed. Armstrong and the Council tried to circumvent the issue by having the Annapolis River Acadians swear an oath of allegiance with the exemption from military service noted in the margin of the French translation, neither part of the oath nor a formal addendum. The governor and council decided on this allowance as a device 'to gett them over by Degrees.'[63]

To administer an oath to the Acadians outside the Annapolis area, Armstrong commissioned Captain Joseph Bennett and Ensign Erasmus James Philipps to undertake the task. They reported back in the spring of 1727 that the Acadians had refused to swear the oath of allegiance. A priest, Joseph Ignace, told Philipps that the French and English were at peace and that 'the English Ought not to Trouble and Importune a Parcel of Inhabitants that would live quietly and pay the Taxes Justly required without takeing any Oath.' One Acadian, Baptist Veco, told Philipps that the people at Annapolis River were treated worse than before they had taken the oath, 'their Oxen being worked on the Kings Account Without being paid for them.'[64] The governor and council decided to write 'a Civil Letter' inviting 'them once more' to swear the oath of allegiance. When the Acadians declined the invitation to become subjects of the King of England, the governor and Council decided to bar trade up the bay, though the Annapolis River Acadians were exempted because of the oath they had sworn the previous fall.[65]

The death of George I and the accession of George II precipitated a second attempt in September 1727 to elicit an oath. Armstrong sent orders to the Annapolis River deputies to meet with him to consult on the matter. He discovered that the concessions he had made the previous year had not succeeded in winning them 'over by Degrees.' Rather they requested not just an exemption from military service but more priests besides, a presumption which briefly landed four deputies in jail and which prompted an extension of the trade ban to include them.[66] Armstrong and the Council hired a vessel for £100 and sent Ensign Robert Wroth and a detachment up the Bay of Fundy to proclaim the new king and ask the Acadians and natives to swear an oath of allegiance.[67] The Acadians found Wroth an obliging negotiator, who acceded in writing to their request for an exemption from military service. When he reported back to the Council, it found his concessions 'unwarrantable and dishonourable to His Majestys authority and Government and Consequently Null and Void.' At the same meeting, the Council voted that the Acadians' acknowledgement of George II's 'Title and Authority to and over this Province,' their qualifications notwithstanding, made them eligible for 'the Libertys and Privileges of English Subjects.' In particular, the trade ban that Armstrong had imposed on the Acadians would be lifted and trade between the Acadians and British was once again legal. It was yet another illustration of how difficult it was for the government to sustain any form of coercion.[68]

When Richard Philipps returned to Nova Scotia in 1729, he turned his hand to persuading the Acadians to swear an oath of allegiance that was not prejudiced by concessions. In May 1730 he informed the Council of the 'Submission of the Inhabitants of this Province,' save for 'about Seventeen of those of Chignictou who persist in their obstinacy in refusing to Conform to his Majestys Orders.'[69] Philipps might have made concessions to the Acadians to persuade them to swear an oath of allegiance, but there is no written record if he did. As governor he did not have to report in detail to the council, as had Robert Wroth, Joseph Bennett, and Erasmus James Philipps. The Acadians claimed he had made an oral promise that they would not have to bear arms, a contention that became a serious disagreement after 1749 with the establishment of Halifax and the appointment of a new colonial government.[70] During the 1730s and 1740s, however, officials in Nova Scotia treated the oaths as sufficient for beginning a more systematic, although still unconventional, development of British civilian government.

The lack of an oath had precluded much taxation of the Acadians, leaving the skeletal staff of British officials without funds to run the colony. From the conquest in 1710 to Parliament's 1748 decision to fund the building of Halifax, Nova Scotia's officials pleaded with London to finance the most basic needs of colonial government. The lack of a vessel to survey the coast, communicate with other communities, regulate trade, and protect the fishery meant that 'a Governor can be accountable for no more then [sic] the spott he happens to reside on.'[71]

By the mid-1720s the ramparts at the fort at Annapolis Royal lay 'level with the Ground in Breaches sufficiently wide for fifty men to enter a breast.'[72] Without an assembly to vote taxes there was no way to raise money in an emergency 'tho' it were but a Shilling and its safety depended on it.'[73] The metropolitan government wanted British settlers in Nova Scotia, but before a governor could grant land the woods had to be surveyed 'for the Preservation of the Woods, which are necessary for the Service of the Royal Navy.'[74] Board of Trade missives that impressed upon Nova Scotia officials the need to preserve naval stores and to settle British subjects elicited responses that stated the obvious: without money to pay a surveyor, the land would remain unused by the navy and ungranted to British settlers.[75]

The unwillingness of the metropolitan government to fund the Nova Scotia government lent urgency to the swearing of an oath by the Acadians. Acadian acceptance of British subjecthood would allow some taxation and hopefully greater Acadian participation in government. Lawrence Armstrong recommended in 1728 that plans for persuading the Acadians to swear an oath of allegiance include posting a garrison on the isthmus. It would allow some oversight of communications between natives in the eastern and western portions of the colony and allow the regulation of the trade throughout the Bay of Fundy. A small garrison, Armstrong reckoned, would not cost more than £1000, 'which those Inhabitants (when subjected) are rich enough to make good.'[76] This infrastructure, however, required an initial investment by the metropolitan government, without which the revenues from the Acadians could not be collected.

Governor Philipps and his lieutenant-governors repeatedly enjoined the Board of Trade to invest in the colony's infrastructure, arguing that the enhanced collection of trade revenues would justify the expense. Among Philipps's initial critiques of Nova Scotia in 1720 was that New Englanders nearly monopolized the trade, but paid no impost towards the maintenance of the government. Upon returning to Nova Scotia in 1729, he recommended fortifying Canso and levying duties on the fish trade, which, he predicted, would generate a colonial revenue second only to the duties collected on the export of tobacco from Virginia, and would exceed the expense of fortifying Canso. The safety of the province, he reminded the Board of Trade, depended on continued peace with France, without which Annapolis Royal and Canso were extremely vulnerable. To recover those settlements if lost would be far more than the outlay for proper regulation and taxing of the fish trade.[77] Colonial officials cautioned the Board of Trade against putting too much emphasis on the collection of quitrents and not on the collection of duties from trade. Quitrents, they believed, would only generate limited revenues; rents collected in the 1730s produced between £10 and £15 annually.[78] Armstrong told the Board of Trade that a quitrent of a penny per acre per annum was too high for the quality of the land, particularly in comparison with neighbouring colonies, and would discourage British or foreign Protestant settlers from moving into the colony.[79]

Reports to Whitehall also emphasized how the financial weaknesses of Nova Scotia's government encouraged the violation of the crown's normal prerogative, particularly by New Englanders. In 1720, Philipps reported that New Englanders regularly took coal from the upper part of the Bay of Fundy, and he was powerless to regulate it in any way.[80] New England traders were frequently cited as agitators among the Acadians. Armstrong reported that William Gamble of Boston, formerly a lieutenant in the army, had told the Acadians not to take the oath of allegiance. In this instance, the issue seemed to have been a power struggle between Alexander Cosby and Armstrong, with Gamble telling the Acadians that Cosby would soon replace Armstrong as lieutenant-governor.[81] As Armstrong tried to explain to the Board of Trade, 'if His Majesty's British Subjects are Suffered to treat his Council with such Indignity and Contempt what can we expect from the French?'[82] The lack of financial resources meant that New Englanders, Acadians, and natives could flout with impunity the authority of the royal government sitting in Annapolis Royal.

Colonial officials believed that the underfunding of government kept the Acadians from swearing an oath of allegiance. Armstrong noted that the 'Lenity' of government encouraged Acadians to stall. Under his commission, he could inflict few penalties. He could prohibit them from fishing, but the Acadians were willing to bear the losses 'in hopes of some Speedy Revolution or Change of Government.'[83] In July 1727 Armstrong barred trade up the Bay of Fundy, on the basis that the Acadians were not subjects and therefore any trade with them was in violation of the Navigation Acts. His proclamation prohibited 'English' subjects from trading with the 'French,' which incensed New Englanders. Thomas Lechmere, Britain's surveyor general for North America, wrote the Board of Trade complaining about the prohibition and asking it to override Armstrong and reopen the trade.[84]

Lack of funds also jeopardized attempts to stabilize relations with natives. Beginning in the 1710s, officials in Nova Scotia repeatedly told the Board of Trade that gift-giving in negotiations with natives was not discretionary. John Doucett informed the Board of Trade in 1718 that gifts were necessary if the natives were to remain friends of the English. He believed that 'the Generality of the Indians would be Sway'd more by the benefitts they receive in this World then trust to all Benefitts their Priests can tell them they will receive in the [next].'[85] Philipps, in contrast, was 'convinced that a hundred thousand [pounds] will not buy them from the French Interest while their priests are among them.' Nevertheless, gift-giving could not be avoided and Philipps had spent £150 on sundry presents that he had distributed in his negotiations with the natives in 1720.[86] When finalizing treaties with the Natives in the mid-1720s, Doucett spent £300 of his own money on gifts.[87] Despite abundant evidence that could demonstrate that regular gift-giving was both important and cost-effective in establishing British–Native relations, it never became routinely funded.

From the perspective of Nova Scotia, Parliament's 1748 decision to fund the building of a northern American naval port on Chebucto Bay was almost too much government and too much money too late. The establishment of Halifax was only tangentially related to the colony's internal needs. Rather it spatially represented the convergence of a number of structural stresses in the empire that had been building over the eighteenth century and metropolitan strategies for handling them. The longstanding problems of Nova Scotia were subsumed under new imperial-level policy, but that meant that the solutions were not necessarily tailored to specific colony-level needs. At the end of the War of the Austrian Succession, Britain faced the problem of how to address the circumstances that had produced its desultory military performance in the war. Both the Ministry and Parliament believed that the Treaty of Aix-la-Chapelle (1748) had created a hiatus in fighting, rather than long-term peace, and it would be but a few years before unresolved problems in both Europe and the extra-European world would produce armed conflict. The British were already planning that in the next war territorial objectives would assume an importance that they had not had in the War of the Austrian Succession (1740–8) when commercial objectives had been paramount. Nova Scotia was just one of many points of territorial tension with other imperial powers: Canada, Rupert's Land, the trans-Appalachian West, Florida, the Caribbean, and Central America were all sites of actual or potential conflict. The building of Halifax was to prepare for hemisphere-wide conflict, a northern expansion of naval bases that stretched from Jamaica to Antigua to Bermuda to Nova Scotia.[88]

For nearly four decades, British officials in Nova Scotia had attempted to make the Board of Trade understand that the poor articulation between metropolitan policy and colonial conditions posed serious long-term problems and had to be rectified. Within the colony, officials recognized that resolving local problems would also resolve imperial problems. A better infrastructure would have allowed for the generation of more revenue and allowed a more systematic surveying of the land for both naval stores and grants to settlers. More government presence might have convinced the Acadians that the British were serious about keeping the colony. As well, it might have made Nova Scotia more attractive for British settlers. Colonial officials knew that the undetermined boundaries between France and British territory, whether on the west side of the Bay of Fundy or along the Canso Strait, would eventually become volatile if not addressed in peacetime. But as Richard Philipps told the Board of Trade in a 1730 communique, 'I am only the Watchman to call and Point out the danger, tis with Your Lordships to get it prevented.'[89]

The building of Halifax did not resolve the problem of the articulation between colonial needs and metropolitan policy, but in an immediate sense made the situation worse, particularly for the Acadians and natives. The escalation of Anglo-French competition privileged imperial needs at the expense of colonial needs. By shifting the seat of the government from Annapolis Royal to Halifax and appointing a new cohort of colonial officials, the metropolitan government eliminated, albeit unwittingly, the internal articulation between British officials, Acadians, and natives, both Mi'kmaq and Wulstukwiuk, that the old regime had crafted over the decades. In so doing, it destroyed an ambiguous but nonetheless shared past, and thus exacerbated the conflict between British officials, Acadians, and natives over the relationship between the past, present, and the future of Nova Scotia and their respective places in it.

The persistent endeavours by the French government to press its interest in Nova Scotia accelerated after 1748. Capitalizing on the ambiguity of the boundary between Nova Scotia and Canada, the French built Fort Beauséjour on the Isthmus of Chignecto. They encouraged — or forced, in some cases — Acadians to move across the Missaguash River, which the French had asserted was their eastern boundary. To resolve the dispute state-to-state the French and British convened a commission to determine the boundary, while in North America, British officials in Nova Scotia built Fort Lawrence just east of the Missaguash and stepped up their presence on the Acadians to swear an unqualified oath of allegiance. In the meantime, the Mi'kmaq protested the British decision to establish settlements and forts without consulting the people whose land it was. They attempted to resolve their differences through both face-to-face meetings with British officials and with attacks on new settlements in Chebucto Bay, Mahone Bay, and Minas Basin. British officials in Nova Scotia had little intention of negotiating with native people whom they deemed to be subjects in rebellion against the crown rather than autonomous nations. Instead, the governor accelerated tensions by authorizing attacks on the Mi'kmaq and offering bounties for their scalps.[90]

In 1755, British troops attacked and seized Fort Beauséjour and in its aftermath began deporting the Acadians, a policy that would continue until 1762. With an unprecedented deployment of soldiers and sailors, the British took Louisbourg in 1758 before moving down the St Lawrence River to defeat the French at Quebec (1759) and Montreal (1760). With the deportation of the Acadians and the defeat of the French at Louisbourg, British officials again recruited Protestant settlers for Nova Scotia. In October 1758, the governor of Nova Scotia, Charles Lawrence, issued a proclamation inviting New Englanders to move to the colony, a decision that further provoked the Mi'kmaq on whose lands these new settlers would plant themselves. When New England agents visited potential town sites they found themselves confronted by militant Mi'kmaq, whose objections delayed the arrival of settlers from 1759 to 1760 and forced the British into another round of treaty negotiations that allowed for settlements on the west side of peninsular Nova Scotia.

With the end of the Seven Years' War and the Treaty of Paris in 1763, the Anglo-French imperial struggle in North America came to an end. The problems of the British empire, however, did not. To some extent, the tortuous process of accommodation that had characterized Nova Scotia since the conquest of Port Royal had left a legacy of newly crafted methods for adapting to the multiethnic empire that now existed on an even larger scale and demanded constitutional accommodation.[91] This was seen in such specific contexts as the adoption of the exact wording of Philipps's 1719 instructions regarding British–native relations — hitherto unique to Nova Scotia, and renewed in instructions to all subsequent Nova Scotia governors until 1773 — to the new Province of Quebec. Quebec governors (and those of East Florida, West Florida, and, with alterations, Grenada) were now enjoined to maintain with native inhabitants 'a strict friendship and good correspondence, so that they may be induced by degrees not only to be good neighbors to our subjects but likewise themselves to become good subjects to us.'[92] More generally, the metropolitan government realized that in its new colonies it could not pretend that they would soon have a natural subject population, English institutions of government, and locally generated financial resources to fund the government. Rather, resources had to be provided to facilitate the transition to a more accommodating form of British government, a logic that eventually found explicit parliamentary expression in the Quebec Act of 1774.

Yet, in other contexts, the problem of weak articulation between metropolitan policy and North American conditions persisted. Again, this administrative disjunction was specifically seen in such situations as General Jeffery Amherst's ill-judged decision in 1760 to eliminate further gift-giving to First Nations, contributing directly to Pontiac's insurgency in 1763. More generally, this same disjunction led frustrated British officials in the Thirteen Colonies to attempt to use coercion to resolve problems. Civil war was the result, and it is well known that the second Treaty of Paris in 1783 left British North America a much smaller place. The experience of Nova Scotia during the four decades following the conquest of Port Royal was not enough to equip contemporaries to salvage very much of the First British Empire. In enabling historians to delineate the empire's difficulties more than two centuries too late, however, the Nova Scotia experience is just the right diagnostic.

NOTES

1. Queen Anne to Francis Nicholson, 1713, PRO, CO217/1, f. 95; and Brebner, *New England's Outpost*, 64–5.
2. Greene, 'Negotiated Authorities.'
3. Dunn, *Sugar and Slaves*, 152–3. A handful of Spaniards fled into the mountains and resisted the English conquest for five years before being driven out.
4. In the English system, the crown, or in the colonies the governor, could endenize aliens with a patent. Only Parliament could naturalize subjects; the rights of colonial assemblies to naturalize subjects was contested. See Salmond, 'Citizenship and Allegiance,' 270–82; and Kettner, *The Development of American Citizenship*, 3–6, 30, 65–105.
5. Patterson, 'Slavery and Slave Revolts.'
6. See William Wicken, chapter 5 in *Essays in the History of Canadian Law*, vol. 5, ed. by Jim Phillips.
7. Maurice Basque, chapter 8 in *Essays in the History of Canadian Law*, vol. 5, ed. by Jim Phillips. Note exceptions, such as de Goutin.
8. Malone, *Pine Trees and Politics*, 10–27.
9. Paul Mascarene to Board of Trade, 16 August 1740, PRO, CO217/8 f. 72.
10. On the development of a distinctly English definition of seventeenth-century colonies in the Americas, see Canny, 'The Origins of Empire: An Introduction'; compare Griffiths, *The Contexts of Acadian History*, 39. For studies dealing with the increasingly polyglot nature of the empire, see Marshall, 'Empire and Authority in the Later Eighteenth Century'; Mancke, 'Another British America'; and Bowen, 'British Conceptions of Global Empire.'
11. Philipps to Board of Trade, 15 May 1727, PRO, CO217/4, ff. 373–4; Maxwell Sutherland, 'Richard Philipps,' DCB, III, 515–18.
12. Philipps to Board of Trade [1720], PRO, CO217/3, f. 104.
13. Bruce T. McCully, 'Francis Nicholson,' DCB, II, 96–8; and G.M. Waller, 'Samuel Vetch,' DCB, II, 650–2.
14. Brebner, *New England's Outpost*, 61.

15. Caulfeild to Board of Trade, 16 May 1716, in MacMechan, ed., *A Calendar of Two Letter-Books and One Commission-Book*, 38–9; Charles Bruce Fergusson, 'Thomas Caulfeild,' DCB, II, 122–3.

16. Maxwell Sutherland, 'Richard Philipps,' DCB, III, 515–18; *Journals of the House of Commons 1715–1751*, XVIII, 342, 483, 636; XIX, 11, 17, XXVI, 16.

17. 'Nova Scotia Governor to Follow Virginia Instructions,' in Labaree, ed., *Royal Instructions to British Colonial Governors*, I, 85.

18. Brebner, *New England's Outpost*, 73, 134, 138, 239. For an assessment see Barnes, '"The Dayly Cry for Justice,"' 14–16.

19. Labaree, ed., *Royal Instructions to British Colonial Governors*, vii–xvii.

20. Greene, 'Empire and Identity from the Glorious Revolution to the American Revolution,' 209.

21. Braddic, 'The English Government, War, Trade, and Settlement.'

22. Here, the English and French terms might have created some confusion, though one that Philipps worked to the best advantage he could with the Acadians and the Board of Trade. The governor general in New France was the top military official and resident of Quebec. Under him were governors in Trois-Rivières, Montreal, Île Royale, and Louisiana. The civilian counterpart to the governor general of New France was the intendant, with subordinates under him in each jurisdiction. In the British American colonies, each royal colony had a governor, with a lieutenant-governor who, in the absence of the governor, served in his stead. Only in some British colonies was there a governor general, that is, a military officer with a military command in addition to his civil commission as governor. André Vachon, 'The Administration of New France.'

23. Proclamation, 20 April 1720, PRO, CO217/3, f. 40. Author's translations: 'the free exercise of their religion;' and 'civil rights and privileges as if they were English.'

24. The highest-ranking civilian official in Nova Scotia, whether the governor, lieutenant-governor, or president of the Council, always had to justify the appointment of military officers to the Council. See, for example, Philipps to Board of Trade, 3 January 1729, PRO, CO217/5, ff. 190–6; Armstrong to Board of Trade, ibid., ff. 39–44; Mascarene to Board of Trade, 16 August 1740, PRO, CO217/8, f. 72; Mascarene to Board of Trade, 28 October 1742, ibid., ff. 177–8.

25. Council Minutes, 12 April 1721, in MacMechan, ed., *Original Minutes of His Majesty's Council at Annapolis Royal, 1720–1739*, 28–9.

26. Barnes, 'The Dayly Cry for Justice,' 18.

27. Armstrong, 'Proclamation to the Inhabitants of Nova Scotia,' in MacMechan, ed., *A Calendar of Two Letter-Books and One Commission-Book*, 177–8.

28. MacMechan, ed., *Original Minutes of His Majesty's Council at Annapolis Royal, 1720–1739*, 4; Philipps to Craggs, 26 May 1720, in MacMechan, ed., *A Calendar of Two Letter-Books and One Commission-Book*, 60.

29. The system of deputies is surprisingly underresearched. The standard scholarship treats the system as largely unchanging over the period c. 1710–55, which it was not. See Brebner, *New England's Outpost*, 149–52; and Griffiths, *The Contexts of Acadian History*, 41–5.

30. MacMechan, ed., *Original Minutes of His Majesty's Council at Annapolis Royal, 1720–1739*, 170.

31. Armstrong, 'Order for Choosing New Deputies,' 26 August 1732, in MacMechan, ed., *A Calendar of Two Letter-Books and One Commission-Book*, 190.

32. Minutes, 7 December 1730, in MacMechan, ed., *Original Minutes of His Majesty's Council at Annapolis Royal, 1720–1739*, 172–3; Minutes, August 1731, ibid., 188–9.

33. Philipps to Board of Trade, 25 November 1729, PRO, CO217/5, ff. 176–8.

34. Minutes, 7 December 1730, in MacMechan, ed., *Original Minutes of His Majesty's Council at Annapolis Royal, 1720–1739*, 173.

35. On the changing responsibilities of deputies from 1731 to 1740 see MacMechan, ed., *A Calendar of Two Letter-Books and One Commission-Book*, 187–247. On the appointment of rent farmers see ibid., 197, 212–13, 216–19, 226. On the increasing number of litigants, see Barnes, '"The Dayly Cry for Justice,"' 18–19.

36. Minutes, 11 September 1732, in MacMechan, ed., *Original Minutes of His Majesty's Council at Annapolis Royal, 1720–1739*, 255; and 'Order for the Election of Deputies,' 30 August 1733, 12 September 1734, and 14 September 1735, in MacMechan, ed., *A Calendar of Two Letter-Books and One Commission-Book*, 196, 200, 207–8. For whatever reason, the chosen date for commemorating the conquest did not conform to the actual anniversary.

37. Mémoire pour Monsieur [illegible], from Paul Mascarene, 27 May 1740, ibid., 241–2.

38. Mascarene to Board of Trade, 16 August 1740, PRO, CO217/8, f. 72.

39. Greene, 'Empire and Identity.'

40. Brebner, *New England's Outpost*, 137; Griffiths, *The Contexts of Acadian History*, 41; Barnes, '"Twelve Apostles" or a Dozen Traitors?'

41. See chapter 7 in *Essays in the History of Canadian Law*, vol. 5, ed. by Jim Phillips.

42. Council to Philipps, 10 June 1738, in MacMechan, ed., *A Calendar of Two Letter-Books and One Commission-Book*, 120–1.

43. Mascarene to Board of Trade, 28 October 1742, PRO, CO217/8, ff. 177–8; Maxwell Sutherland, 'Paul Mascarene,' DCB, III, 435–9.

44. MacMechan, ed., *A Calendar of Two Letter-Books and One Commission-Book*, 169; Petition of Joshua Peirce, Stephen Perkins, Elias Davis, and Thomas Kilby to Richard Philipps, 19 August 1729, PRO, CO217/5, f. 183.

45. Armstrong to Aldridge, 15 November 1732, PRO, CO217/7, ff. 6–6d; Armstrong to the Justices of the Peace at Canso, 15 November 1732, ibid., ff. 62–3.

46. Armstrong to Board of Trade, 24 November 1726, PRO, CO217/5, ff. 1–2; Extract of Instructions to Virginia, PRO, CO217/8, f. 184d; Court at St James, 10 March 1730, PRO, CO217/6, ff. 35–6; Labaree, *Royal Government in America*, 312–72; and Greene, *The Quest for Power*, 129–47.

47. MacMechan, ed., *A Calendar of Two Letter-Books and One Commission-Book*,173–4.

48. Philipps to Secretary of State, 1721, ibid., 76; Armstrong to Aldridge, 15 November 1732, PRO, CO217/7, ff. 6–6d; and Mascarene to Board of Trade, 28 October 1742, PRO, CO217/8, ff. 177–8.

49. Armstrong to Board of Trade, 2 December 1725, PRO, CO217/4, f. 314.

50. Duke of Bedford to Board of Trade, 20 July 1749, PRO, CO217/9, f. 63.

51. Doucett to Board of Trade, 6 November 1717, PRO, CO217/2, ff. 175–6. For earlier attempts to have Acadians swear an oath of allegiance, see Brebner, *New England's Outpost*, 64, 75–6.

52. Doucett to Board of Trade, 6 November 1717, PRO, CO217/2, f. 175

53. Doucett to Peter Mellanson, 5 December 1717, ibid., f. 197.

54. Doucett to Board of Trade, 6 November 1717, ibid., f. 176.

55. Caulfeild to Board of Trade, 1 November 1715, in MacMechan, ed., *A Calendar of Two Letter-Books and One Commission-Book*, 27; Caulfeild to Vetch [1715], ibid., 29.

56. Doucett to Board of Trade, 6 November 1717, PRO, CO217/2, f. 175.

57. Council Minutes, 24 September 1720, in MacMechan, ed., *Original Minutes of His Majesty's Council at Annapolis Royal, 1720–1739*, 15.

58. Philipps and Council to the King, 27 April 1720, PRO, CO217/3, f. 104; and MacMechan, ed., *A Calendar of Two Letter-Books and One Commission-Book*, 66–7.

59. Philipps to the Inhabitants at Annapolis River, 10 April 1721, ibid., 74.

60. Council Minutes, 11 February 1723, in MacMechan, ed., *Original Minutes of His Majesty's Council at Annapolis Royal, 1720–1739*, 43–4.

61. Maxwell Sutherland, 'Lawrence Armstrong,' DCB, II, 21–4.

62. Brebner, *New England's Outpost*, 88–9.

63. Minutes, 25 September 1726, in MacMechan, ed., *Original Minutes of His Majesty's Council at Annapolis Royal, 1720–1739*, 129–30.

64. Report of Erasmus James Philipps to Armstrong, 1727, PRO, CO217/5, ff. 31–2; Minutes, 23 May 1727, in MacMechan, ed., *Original Minutes of His Majesty's Council at Annapolis Royal, 1720–1739*, 144.

65. Minutes, 1 June 1727, ibid., 146; Minutes, 25 July 1727, ibid., 149–50.

66. Brebner, *New England's Outpost*, 89–91; and Sutherland, 'Lawrence Armstrong,' DCB, II, 23.

67. Minutes, 26–7 September 1727, in MacMechan, ed., *Original Minutes of His Majesty's Council at Annapolis Royal, 1720–1739*, 161–4; Instructions of Armstrong to Robert Wroth, PRO, CO217/5, ff. 49–50.

68. Minutes, 13 November 1727, in MacMechan, eds., *Original Minutes of His Majesty's Council at Annapolis Royal, 1720–1739*, 168.

69. Minutes, 16 May 1730, ibid., 171.

70. Brebner, *New England's Outpost*, 166–202.

71. Philipps to Board of Trade, 15 May 1727, PRO, CO217/4, ff. 373–4. For similar sentiments, see Report of Colonel Philipps on Newfoundland and Nova Scotia, 1718, PRO, CO217/2, ff. 171–2; Philipps to Board of Trade, 3 January 1719, PRO, CO217/3, f. 21; 'The State and Condition of His Majestys Province of Nova Scotia truely Represented,' 8 May 1728, PRO, CO217/5, ff. 17–18; David Dunbar to Board of Trade, PRO, CO217/8, ff. 107–8.

72. Philipps to Board of Trade, 15 May 1727, PRO, CO217/4, ff. 373–4.

73. 'The State and Condition of His Majestys province of Nova Scotia truely Represented,' 8 May 1728, PRO, CO217/5, ff. 17–18.

74. Report of Privy Council Committee, 15 February 1726, PRO, CO217/4, f. 324.

75. Philipps to Board of Trade, 3 January 1719, PRO, CO217/3, f. 21.

76. The State and Condition of His Majestys province of Nova Scotia truely Represented, 8 May 1728, PRO, CO217/5, ff. 17–18.
77. Philipps to Board of Trade, 2 October 1729, ibid., ff. 170–1; Philipps to Board of Trade, 2 September 1730, ibid., ff. 225–9.
78. Paul Mascarene to Board of Trade, 16 August 1740, PRO, CO217/8, f. 72. See also, 'Representation of the State of His Majesties Province of Nova Scotia,' 8 November 1745, in Fergusson, ed., *Minutes of His Majesty's Council at Annapolis Royal, 1736–1749*, 83.
79. Armstrong to Board of Trade, 20 November 1733, PRO, CO217/7 ff. 49–50.
80. Philipps to Board of Trade [1720], PRO, CO217/3, f. 104.
81. Armstrong to Board of Trade, 30 April 1727, PRO, CO217/5, ff. 28–30.
82. Armstrong to Board of Trade, 17 November 1727, ibid., f. 41.
83. Armstrong to Board of Trade, 9 July 1728, ibid., ff. 116–17.
84. Proclamation of Lt. Gov. Lawrence Armstrong, 29 July 1727, ibid., f. 71; and Thomas Lechmere to Board of Trade, 20 September 1727, ibid., f. 76.
85. Doucett to Board of Trade, 10 February 1718, PRO, CO217/2, f. 194.
86. Philipps to Board of Trade [1720], PRO, CO217/3, f. 119.
87. Doucett to Board of Trade, 16 August 1726, PRO, CO217/4, ff. 316–18.
88. Greene, '"A Posture of Hostility"'; Mancke, 'Negotiating an Empire.'
89. Philipps to Board of Trade, 2 September 1730, PRO, CO217/5, ff. 225–9.
90. Upton, *Micmacs and Colonists*, 48–60; and Paul, *We Were Not the Savages*, 86–148.
91. In recent years scholars have increasingly emphasized the multiethnic character of the North American colonies, particularly Pennsylvania, New York, New Jersey, and Delaware. But, as noted earlier, the cultural diversity in these colonies did not require serious political and constitutional adjustments on the scale of those required in early-eighteenth-century Nova Scotia and post-conquest Quebec. Indeed legal decisions have recognized that the Proclamation of 1763 and the Quebec Act of 1774 granted constitutional rights to *Canadiens* and First Nations in ways that are unparalleled in the constitutional history of the United States.
92. Labaree, ed., *Royal Instructions to British Colonial Governors*, II, 469, 478–9.

Topic Three

The Conquest and its Aftermath

This engraving by Antoine Benoist, *A view of the Bishop's House with the Ruins, as they appear in Going up the Hill from the Lower to the Upper Town,* shows a view of Quebec after the British bombardment of 1759. It is based on a sketch by Richard Short.

Contrary to popular opinion New France did not fall as a result of its defeat in the Battle of the Plains of Abraham. The conquest of New France remained incomplete at the end of 1759, with the French in control of the St. Lawrence Valley apart from the area immediately around Quebec. Only in September 1760 did the French capitulate at Montreal. As W.J. Eccles points out in his provocative essay, "The Battle of Quebec: A Reappraisal," the fall of Quebec was in no respect inevitable. Why then did the British emerge victorious?

The Treaty of 1763 that ended the Seven Years' War confirmed the cession of New France to England. The British now faced again — as they had in Acadia from 1713 to 1755 — the difficult task of formulating a policy to govern a colony whose population differed in language, culture, and religion from their own. That policy, as outlined in the Proclamation of 1763, limited New France, now renamed the Province of Quebec, to the St. Lawrence Valley. It also aimed to transform the French colony into a British one through the establishment of British institutions and laws aimed at assimilating the French-Canadian population.

The policy failed, however. Very few English-speaking immigrants came to Quebec, preferring to settle in the warmer, more fertile Ohio Valley, amidst a familiar English-speaking population. Furthermore, James Murray and Guy Carleton, the first two governors of Quebec, sided with the French-speaking seigneurs against the aggressive, English-speaking merchants in the colony. Realizing that the colony was unlikely to become anglicized, Governor Carleton recommended reinstating French civil law, the seigneurial system of landholding, and the right of the Roman Catholic Church to collect the tithe. London accepted his proposals and, in the Quebec Act of 1774, reversed its earlier policy of 1763.

By that time, however, the basic economic structure of the colony had changed. The few English-speaking colonists who had settled in Quebec had taken a prominent role in the economic life of the colony. Although small in number, this Anglo-American commercial class had gained enormous influence — enough to secure the recall of James Murray, the first governor, in 1766. In terms of economic power, this group also commanded a majority of the investments in the fur trade by 1777. How had this tiny English-speaking group prospered so? Was it because of the return to France of the commercial class of New France, the superior abilities of the English-speaking merchants, or the favouritism practised by the British administrators? In "A Change in Climate: The Conquest and the Marchands of Montreal," José Igartua examines the rise of the English-speaking merchants in the fur trade. In "The Fall of New France," the epilogue to *The People of New France*, Allan Greer assesses the impact of the Conquest on Acadia, Canada, and the interior. What was the impact of the Conquest on the general population?

For a thorough discussion of the various interpretations of the Conquest, see Ramsay Cook's "The Historian and Nationalism," in *Canada and the French-Canadian Question* (Toronto: Macmillan, 1966), pp. 119–42, and his essay "Conquêtisme," in *The Maple Leaf Forever* (Toronto: Macmillan, 1971), pp. 99–113. Also of value is S. Dale Standen's "The Debate on the Social and Economic Consequences of the Conquest: A Summary," in R. Douglas Francis and Donald B. Smith, *Readings in Canadian History: Pre-Confederation*, 6th ed. (Toronto: Nelson Thomson Learning, 2002), pp. 203–210. For a short bibliography on the final years of the struggle for New France, 1759 and 1760, see the bibliography for Topic Five.

For an overview of the immediate post-Conquest period, see A.L. Burt's *The Old Province of Quebec*, 2 vols. (Toronto: McClelland and Stewart, 1968 [1933]); Pierre Tousignant's "The Integration of the Province of Quebec into the British Empire, 1763–91, Part 1: From the Royal Proclamation to the Quebec Act," in *Dictionary of Canadian Biography*, vol. 4, *1771–1800*, pp. ii–xlix; Hilda Neatby's *Quebec: The Revolutionary Age, 1760–1791* (Toronto: McClelland and Stewart, 1966); and Philip Lawson's *The Imperial Challenge: Quebec and Britain in the Age of the American Revolution* (Montreal/Kingston: McGill-Queen's University Press,

1989). Fernand Ouellet's *Histoire économique et sociale du Québec, 1760–1850* (Montréal: Fides, 1966), translated as *Economic and Social History of Quebec, 1760–1850* (Toronto: Macmillan, 1980), is an important study. A number of Ouellet's essays, edited and translated by Jacques A. Barbier, were published in the collection *Economy, Class, and Nation in Quebec: Interpretive Essays* (Toronto: Copp Clark Pitman, 1991). Michel Brunet presents an alternative view to Ouellet's in *Les Canadiens après la Conquête, 1759–1775* (Montréal: Fides, 1969).

Dale Miquelon's *Society and Conquest* (Toronto: Copp Clark, 1977) is a valuable collection on the effect of the Conquest on French-Canadian society; see also his *The First Canada: To 1791* (Toronto: McGraw-Hill Ryerson, 1994). An important local study is Allan Greer, *Peasant, Lord, and Merchant: Rural Society in Three Quebec Parishes, 1740–1840* (Toronto: University of Toronto Press, 1985). On the history of the early English-speaking population in the province of Quebec, see Ronald Rudin's *The Forgotten Quebecers: A History of English-Speaking Quebec, 1759–1980* (Québec: Institut québécois de la recherche sur la culture, 1985).

WEBLINKS

The Battle of the Plains of Abraham
http://www.champlain2004.org/html/11/14_e.html

Digitized primary-source documents relating to the Battle of the Plains of Abraham.

Rear-Admiral Charles Holmes
http://www.lib.uwaterloo.ca/discipline/SpecColl/archives/holmes/holmes.html#letter

A digitized copy of a letter written by Rear-Admiral Charles Holmes, third-in-command under Major-General James Wolfe, five days after the Battle of the Plains of Abraham.

Tactical Positions
http://www.masshist.org/maps/2739_Atlas_16/2739_Atlas_16.html#

A digitized, interactive version of a tactical map drawn in 1759 depicting British and French forces in the St. Lawrence River at the time of the Battle of the Plains of Abraham.

Louisbourg Grenadiers
http://www.militaryheritage.com/quebec1.htm

The transcribed account of a sergeant major in James Wolfe's forces, describing the months leading up to the Battle of the Plains of Abraham, the battle, and the days after it.

Wolfe & Montcalm
http://www.biographi.ca/EN/ShowBio.asp?BioId=35842
http://www.biographi.ca/EN/ShowBio.asp?BioId=35664

Biographies of Wolfe and Montcalm, leaders at the Battle of the Plains of Abraham, from the *Dictionary of Canadian Biography Online*.

The Treaty of Paris, 1763
http://www.canadiana.org/citm/_textpopups/constitution/doc26_e.html

A summary and digitized copy of the Treaty of Paris, 1763.

Article Six

The Battle of Quebec: A Reappraisal

W.J. Eccles

More nonsense has been written over the years about this momentous battle — the battle that changed the course of North American and European history — than about any other event in Canadian history. One has only to imagine what would likely have been the ultimate course of events had the French destroyed Wolfe's army on that day in mid-September 1759 to appreciate how significant an event it was.

The paper here reprinted was written to be read at a meeting of the French Colonial Historical Society. Having only twenty minutes allotted time, I had to make it brief. Nothing that further research has uncovered since it was written, however, has caused me to alter my interpretation of the event one iota. A considerably extended study of the battle will appear in a forthcoming work. This paper contains the gist of it.

The battle that took place on the Plains of Abraham on 13 September 1759 continues to exercise fascination for historians and romantics alike. Hardly a year goes by without another work appearing on some aspect of the epic struggle. Field Marshall Viscount Montgomery described it as 'one of the great battles of the world.'[1] He was right about that, but about little else concerning this particular event. General Douglas MacArthur is reputed to have stated that his famous 'end run' in Korea, effecting a landing far in the enemy's rear, was modelled on Wolfe's tactics. He obviously had not studied the terrain at Quebec or Wolfe's actual disposition of his army.

A common feature of most of the works on the battle is the bland acceptance of the stated, or unstated, premise that the outcome was a foregone conclusion. Yet with one notable exception the main actors in the 1759 drama, on both sides, did not regard an eventual British victory as assured; quite the contrary. In May, when an English assault on Quebec was anticipated, Captain Montgay of the Béarn regiment, the comte de Malartic, and the chevaliers de Lévis and de Montreuil, all expressed optimism that it would be beaten off.[2] In the second week of September the French were confident that the campaign was over, and that they had ended it with glory. The recent movements in the English camp were interpreted as preparations for their departure,[3] as indeed to some extent they were.[4]

After the event James Murray remarked in a letter to Amherst, 'the Fact is we were surprised into a victory which cost the Conquered very little indeed'.[5] And at Louisbourg, Thomas Ainslie wrote to his friend and mentor, Murray, 'I now congratulate you on your success at Quebec, a thing little expected by any here, and posterity will hardly give credit to it that such a handful of Men should carry so great a point against such numbers, and with such advantages, thank God you have escaped, it is a miracle that you have.'[6]

Wolfe himself admitted in a dispatch dated 2 September that he was not at all sanguine of success.[7] The defences of Quebec were far more formidable than he had anticipated. His attempts to take the city had failed, his assaults on the French lines had been beaten back with heavy losses. Much has been made of the desperate conditions in Quebec, then in ruins, and the shortage of supplies. On the English side, however, conditions were far worse. Their supply line extended down the treacherous St Lawrence to Halifax and then across the Atlantic to

Source: W.J. Eccles, "The Battle of Quebec: A Reappraisal," in W.J. Eccles, *Essays on New France* (Toronto: Oxford University Press, 1987): 125–133, 207–209. Reprinted by permission of Oxford University Press.

Portsmouth. By the end of August over a thousand men were in hospital, suffering from wounds, dysentery, and scurvy. In the hot weather the camps — plagued with flies, mosquitoes, and inadequate latrines — stank to high heaven.[8] Wolfe was not the only one to be taken ill.

Of the 8,500 troops who had left Louisbourg, nearly half were unfit for duty by the end of August. On the opposing side Montcalm had some fifteen to sixteen thousand men, less than four thousand of them regulars,[9] but the Canadian militia had shown that they were a fearsome adversary when properly used. In addition there were a thousand to twelve hundred Indian warriors in the French camp.[10] They were a psychological weapon of no small account. Desertion increased in the British ranks as the campaign dragged on. The reports of these deserters to their interrogators kept the French well informed of conditions in the enemy's camp. They also raised their confidence. The intendant Bigot remarked after one such interrogation, 'those types make everything look rosy.'[11] And Montcalm informed Lévis that several of these deserters had stated that the British now despaired of taking Quebec unless Amherst's army arrived to support them.[12]

The French, however, knew that Amherst would not appear before Quebec during the present campaign. The Abenaki of Saint-François had captured two British officers, with their Mohawk guides, bearing dispatches from Amherst to Wolfe informing him that he was waiting for word of the taking of Quebec before advancing, with his habitual speed of a glacier, farther north than Fort Saint-Frédéric on Lake Champlain.[13] In fact Amherst was manifestly convinced that Quebec would not fall. He devoted the entire summer to the construction, at enormous expense, of a massive fortification at Crown Point. That structure could patently serve no useful purpose were Quebec to be taken. Its function could only be to bar the Lake Champlain route to an army ascending the lake from Canada for an invasion of New York.

It was, therefore, in desperation that Wolfe ordered the devastation of the countryside around Quebec, some four thousand farms being put to the torch.[14] The bombardment of the city continued until only a handful of buildings were habitable.[15] Wolfe had decided that if Quebec could not be taken, then the usefulness of the colony to the enemy would be reduced to the minimum.[16] It made no sense whatsoever to destroy what it was intended to occupy and subsequently put to one's own use, particularly with winter fast approaching. This too gave the French rueful cause to be confident of the final outcome of the campaign.

The one person in the French camp who was convinced that the city would eventually fall to the British was, ironically, the commander in chief, the Marquis de Montcalm. All through the war he had been a chronic defeatist. Before the opening of each campaign he had declared vociferously that it would end badly and he sought to ensure that the blame would fall elsewhere than on him. On 24 February 1759 he wrote to Lévis, 'The colony is lost unless peace comes. I can see nothing that can save it.'[17] And on 9 August he wrote to the Chevalier Bourlamaque, 'I maintain that the colony is lost.'[18] He made his plans accordingly and what ensued was a self-fulfilling prophecy.

Montcalm's tactics stipulated that what remained of the French and Canadian regular troops after the inevitable debacle, but before the ensuring capitulation of the colony, would withdraw to Louisiana in a fleet of canoes by way of the Ottawa River, the Great Lakes, and the Mississippi. This move, he assured the minister in a mémoire sent to the court with Bougainville in 1758, would prevent the loss of a sizeable body of men and preserve the honour of French arms by a feat rivalling the retreat of the Ten Thousand that had immortalized the Greeks.[19] It was likely for this reason, later seen to have been a disastrous mistake, that he established his main supply base at Batiscan, 50 miles above Quebec.[20] On strategic grounds this made no sense, since it left Quebec vulnerable to an enemy landing across that vital supply line. On the other hand were the town to fall, as Montcalm anticipated, then the supplies would be there ready for a withdrawal to Montreal and the epic retreat to Louisiana.

When the British were known to be ascending the river, Montcalm drafted the terms to be submitted to them for the capitulation of Quebec and gave a copy to the town commandment, the Sieur de Ramezay.[21] He made careful preparations for defeat, but he conspicuously failed to prepare the town's outer defences. Relying on the opinion of his self-serving engineering officer, Major Pontleroy, who informed him that an enemy landing above Quebec could not hope to succeed and that the range across the river from Pointe Lévis was too far for cannon fire to be effective,[22] he did not fortify that vital point and made only the feeblest of attempts to dislodge the British when they landed and began constructing their batteries.

The British objective all through the campaign was to take Quebec, it being rightly assumed that once Quebec fell the French would be forced to surrender the entire colony. Attempts to take the town by manoeuvre on the left flank of the French lines had conspicuously failed, with heavy losses. Massive bombardment of the town had accomplished nothing except destruction of eighty per cent of the buildings. Attempts to cut the French supply line upriver had been beaten off. The only way the objective could be gained was somehow to force Montcalm to come out from behind his fortified lines to give battle in the open and then destroy his army. Wolfe admitted that he could not stay in the river beyond the end of September.[23] Vice-Admiral Saunders dared not risk a quarter of the Royal Navy's being caught in such dangerous waters by the onset of winter. On 5 September, Saunders wrote in a dispatch to the Admiralty, 'I shall very soon send home the great ships.'[24] By early September a protracted siege was out of the question. All that the French had to do was hold the enemy off for a matter of days.

Wolfe, frustrated at every turn, felt that he had to make one last desperate attempt to take Quebec before admitting defeat, abandoning the campaign, and sailing ignominiously back to England. He proposed another assault on the Beauport lines, but when he submitted his plans to his brigadiers they curtly rejected them. They pointed out that even were Montcalm to be defeated in an action there, he could still withdraw his army either into Quebec, or upriver to his supply depot then westward to Montreal, thereby necessitating another campaign the following year.[25] They proposed instead a landing well above Quebec, between the town and Montcalm's supply base at Batiscan. This, they pointed out, would force him to come out and give battle, and if defeated, then not only Quebec but the entire colony would have to capitulate.

Wolfe accepted the brigadiers' plan in principal, but made a change that nullified its main strategic aim and placed the British army in grave jeopardy. The road from Batiscan to Quebec forked some fifteen miles above the town. The northern branch road went through Ancienne-Lorette, five miles north of the Saint Lawrence, then proceeded across the Saint Charles river to join the Quebec-Charlesbourg road. Instead of landing above the fork, thereby severing all communication between Quebec and Batiscan, which was the essential feature of the brigadiers' plan, Wolfe chose to land at the Anse au Foulon, thereby leaving the vital northern road open. It was this road that the French army was to use, after the debacle, to make good its withdrawal to Saint Augustin and later to Montreal.

Much ink has been spilled over Montcalm's failure to strengthen his right flank, and the colossal good luck that allowed the British to scale the heights, virtually unopposed, and assemble their army on the Plains of Abraham. Blame for the event has been duly apportioned to certain individuals with varying degrees of regard for the evidence,[26] it being assumed that once Wolfe had gained that position what ensued was inevitable. C. P. Stacey has stated that since Wolfe was astride Quebec's supply line, which he clearly was not,[27] 'Nothing was left but for Montcalm to take the chance of a desperate stroke against an army far better than his own.'[28] Stacey also opines that no matter how Montcalm had reacted to Wolfe's surprise landing, the French were doomed to defeat, 'so serious was the difference in military quality between the opposing forces.'[29] This assertion begs the question why it was that 3,500 troops of that same French army had been able to inflict such a crushing defeat on 15,000 British and American troops at Carillon the preceding year. Or why the chevalier de Lévis, again with that selfsame army, was able to defeat resoundingly the British under Murray on those same Plains of Abraham just seven months later.

What we have here is a classic case of the argument that because something happened, it *ipso facto* had to happen, was in fact virtually preordained. As the American novelist Mary McCarthy remarked about other battles in another war, 'a successful action is never examined in terms of what caused it, the result is seen as the cause.'[30] Anglophone historians are particularly prone to take this view since what the consequences of a French victory would have been are too mind-boggling to contemplate. Toronto, for example, might then today be a French-speaking city; and the Americans would have had to postpone their bid for independence.

If we strip ourselves of hindsight and examine closely the position of the British and French forces on the morning of 13 September, what do we actually find? Wolfe's army, numbering at most 4,500 men, extended in two lines from the edge of the cliff overlooking the Saint Lawrence to the wooded escarpment overlooking the Saint Charles river. To cover that front of some 1,300 yards the ranks had to be stretched thin. The files were over three feet apart, with a forty-yard interval between each of the battalions.[31] The soldiers had spent the previous day on the ships manoeuvring upriver or preparing to embark. At nine o'clock at night they had begun embarking in the landing craft. Five hours later the first of the three waves began slipping downstream with the tide towards the Anse au Foulon. They made their first landing in the final hours of darkness. The boats then returned to embark the next wave. By eight the entire force was on the heights, having had little or no sleep for the past twenty-four hours. They carried the usual hard rations and the only water they had was in their canteens. They had no tents or blankets, their only ammunition was that in their pouches. Two light field guns were brought up, but for one of them they had the wrong ammunition. They apparently had no doctors or surgeons with them.* This small army was ready for battle, provided it were to be fought within a few hours. Manoeuvre in that confined area, or a protracted assault on the town's fortifications, was out of the question. Time was not on their side.

One vital element that Wolfe had achieved, however, was surprise. Everything therefore depended on how Montcalm would react. Although he had been informed at dawn that the British had effected a landing, he refused to believe it. It was not until six-thirty, after receiving further frantic reports that the British were massed on the Plains, that he rode off to see for himself, then gave orders for the troops in the Beauport lines to be brought up at the double.[32]

The significance of this three-hour interval between Wolfe's arrival on the heights and Montcalm's appearance is that Wolfe was thereby afforded ample time, undisturbed, to survey the terrain and make his dispositions accordingly. The position that he chose and its relation to his objective, the destruction of the French army and the occupation of Quebec, therefore deserves critical examination.

It was axiomatic that an army, in the presence of an enemy, should seek to occupy the high ground. In this particular instance one would have expected Wolfe to occupy the heights of the Plains of Abraham, the broken ridge known as the Buttes à Neveu, which would have given him a clear view of the town. Provided he could hold that commanding site, he could have brought up his heavy guns to batter a breach in Quebec's fortifications prior to an assault. Montcalm would not necessarily have brought his army out to give battle. He would still have

---

*When Vaudreuil learned that Wolfe had been wounded he wrote to Bougainville that he believed M. de Ramezay, commander of the Quebec garrison, had already sent two surgeons to the English general. Arthur G. Doughty and G. W. Parmalee, eds., *The Siege of Quebec and the Battle of the Plains of Abraham*, 6 vols., Quebec, 1901, vol. IV, 127; Vaudreuil à Bougainville, 13 Sept. 1759.

had the option of keeping his main forces behind the town walls, relying on his own guns to disrupt the enemy's artillery emplacements[33] and using the Canadians—in conjunction with Bougainville's elite force ten miles upriver—to harass the British rear, with its precarious supply line. The obvious move for Wolfe to make under the circumstances was to occupy the commanding heights no matter how Montcalm reacted.

The astonishing thing is that Wolfe did *not* occupy those heights, despite the fact that nothing stood in his way. Inexplicably he drew up his little army on the low reverse slope, some six hundred paces from the crest of the ridge. From that position he could not see the walls of Quebec, or any part of the town.[34] Had he managed to bring up every gun in his massive armoury, not one of them could have ranged in on the walls of Quebec. If the French *quartier général* had racked their brains to devise a disposition of the enemy's forces best suited to their own purpose, they would have been hard pressed to come up with anything better than that position. If they had lured Wolfe into it, they could have expected plaudits from the shade of the Maréchal de Saxe. There Wolfe waited for Montcalm to come to him, while the Canadian militia spread along the brush-covered slopes on both his flanks and began inflicting casualties. In front of him, but out of sight, was the fortified town and the main French force. Ten miles to his rear was Bougainville with an elite force of 3,000 regulars and militia with some light cannon.[35] They could be expected to arrive on the scene at any moment. They would then have been across the British communication route and line of retreat to the Anse au Foulon. Wolfe had no reserves. Were he to fail to gain a crushing victory, retreat would have been extremely difficult, if not impossible. His army would have had to fight its way through Bougainville's force, then withdraw down the steep path to the beach and there wait for the tide to allow the boats to come in from the fleet to take them off. This would have been a lengthy operation, since it would have required three trips. It could hardly have been expected that the French would allow this withdrawal to go unharassed. Even if the first wave of boats managed to get away unscathed, the troops remaining on the beach would have been rendered all the more vulnerable. It is difficult to see how such a hastily improvised operation could have resulted in anything but surrender or slaughter. Wolfe and his men must have been aware of this as they stood there, waiting. Montcalm had that British army at his mercy.

All through the summer Montcalm had fought a defensive campaign, forcing Wolfe to come to him only to be beaten back with heavy losses. He had passed up obvious opportunities to launch limited attacks on the enemy's vulnerable position at Montmorency, and both officers and men had been sharply critical of his timidity.[36] He is reputed, on one occasion, to have rejected Lévis's urging to attack with the sage comment, 'Drive them thence and they will give us more trouble. So long as they stay there they cannot hurt us. Let them amuse themselves.'[37] All that Montcalm now had to do was to continue to employ that same Fabian strategy: seize the vacant high ground, bring up his guns, and wait for Wolfe to make a move. The longer he could delay an action the stronger became his position.

His contemporary defenders, and some historians, have sought to excuse his fatal decision to attack precipitately on the grounds that to have waited would have allowed the British to entrench themselves, thereby rendering an attack on their lines hopeless. Yet the British could have built the most formidable of entrenchments with the material available, logs and earth, and it would have availed them nothing. They would have dominated nothing more than the six hundred paces of terrain facing them. Guns on the commanding ridge would quickly have rent any such entrenchments asunder. Moreover, the British could sustain themselves on that site only for a matter of days, and only provided that they kept their supply line open. Water would have been a major problem. The Canadians and Indians, not to mention the French gunners, could have seen to it that they got precious little sleep. Moreover, the logs of the

British ships state that on the 16th the weather broke. For the ensuing three days there were gale-force winds and heavy rain.[38]

There is just one point that needs to be made concerning the actual battle. Everyone remarks on Wolfe's thin red line of two ranks. What was really significant was that Montcalm chose not to advance in line but to attack in column. Captain John Knox, in his journal, states that the French attacked in three columns, two inclining to the right, opening fire obliquely as they advanced, at the extremities of the British line from 130 yards' distance.[39] Major Patrick MacKellar stated that when the French were within a hundred yards of the British line, 'it mov'd up regularly with a steady fire, and when within 20 or 30 yards of closing gave a General One,' which caused the French to turn and flee.[40] The British centre had not come under fire and it was its volleys, according to Knox, that broke the French charge.

In French military circles at this time a debate raged over the relative effectiveness of attack in column and attack in line. Eventually the proponents of attack in line gained the ascendancy. It came to be accepted that the column should be used to bring the army as close as possible to the enemy without coming under serious fire, then deeply into line by a variety of complex parade-ground manoeuvres ready for the attack. This allowed every man in the ranks to bring his musket to bear on the opposing force. To attack in column meant that only the front ranks could fire; those in the rear could merely take the places of those before them who fell, or else the columns had to change direction oblique to the enemy line, but even then only the outside file of one side of the column could use their muskets effectively. This is what occurred in Montcalm's attack, and with predictable results.

Some military thinkers in France, however, maintained that the shock effect of a charging column would break the line. It was also held that training and discipline were so poor in the French army that the line formation was too difficult to execute on the battlefield and maintain under fire. Moreover, it was believed that the French temperament, with its reckless but mercurial bravery, made attack in column something that only exceptionally well-trained and disciplined troops could withstand.[41]

The battle at Quebec on 13 September 1759 proved all the above points. The battle fought on the same ground the following year, between the same two armies, and again of equal numbers,[42] added further proof. This time it was the British commander, Brigadier-General James Murray, who obliged the enemy and marched out of the fortified town to give battle in the open. He massed his troops on the Buttes à Neveu, the same ground that Wolfe had allowed Montcalm to occupy undisputed. As C. P. Stacey succinctly puts it, 'This rise was an admirable position for a defensive battle, and with his numerous guns disposed in the intervals between his battalions Murray could expect to inflict a severe reverse on Lévis if the latter had the temerity to attack him'[43] Exactly the same, of course, had held true for Montcalm. Murray, however, repeated Montcalm's mistake. Fearing that Lévis would construct redoubts and be difficult to dislodge, he abandoned the high ground and launched an assault, hoping to strike them before they could form to receive the charge. In this he failed. Lévis got his battalions into line, repelled the British attack, then counter-attacked their flanks. The left flank was turned. A bayonet charge then broke the British line. They turned and fled, abandoning their guns. Murray came dangerously close to having his army destroyed.[44]

There was one signal difference between this battle and the previous one. This time both generals survived, which was perfectly normal for eighteenth-century warfare. The odd fact that in the 1759 battle both Wolfe and Montcalm received mortal wounds is a sure indication that there was something seriously wrong with the tactics they employed on that day. Yet regardless of how haphazard it all was, the outcome caused the history of North America to take a drastic turn with consequences that still plague us today. It gives one to think that perhaps the most overlooked determining factor in history has been stupidity.

NOTES

1. Field-Marshal Viscount Montgomery of Alamein, *A History of Warfare*, (London, 1968), 320.
2. Archives du Ministère de la Guerre, Vincennes. Series A1, vol. 3540, ff. 136–7, M. de Montgay à . . . Mtl., 17 mai 1759; ibid., f. 39, Malartic à . . . Mtl., 9 avril 1759; ibid., ff. 138–9; Lévis à . . . Mtl., 17 mai 1759; ibid., f. 115, Montreuil à Mgr . . . Mtl., 6 mai 1759.
3. Archives du Séminaire de Québec, Séminaire 7, no. 72C, Journal de l'Abbé Richer, 22 aoust.
4. Archives du Ministère de la Guerre, Vincennes, Series A1, vol. 3540, no. 103, Bigot au Ministre de la Guerre, Mtl., 15 oct 1759.
5. Public Archives of Canada, Murray papers, MG23, GII-1, vol. 1, 30, Murray to Amherst, Que., 19 May 1760.
6. Ibid., 8–9, Thos. Ainslie to James Murray, Louisbourg, 28 Oct. 1759.
7. C.P. Stacey, *Quebec 1759. The Siege and the Battle*, (Toronto, 1959), 184–91. The dispatch is here printed *in toto*.
8. Christopher Hibbert, *Wolfe at Quebec* (London, 1959), 104.
9. Archives du Ministère de la Guerre, Vincennes. Series A1, vol. 3540, f. 128, Journal de M. Malartic 1758–9; ibid., 149, Situation des huit Bataillons d'Infanterie françaises servant en Canada d'Après la Revue qui en a été faitte en Mai; *Rapport de l'Archiviste de la Province de Québec 1920–21*, 155, Journal du Siège de Québec, du 10 mai au 18 septembre 1759; Archives Nationales, Paris, Colonies, Series F3, Moreau de St Méry, vol. 15, f. 334, Bigot au Ministre, Qué., 15 oct. 1759.
10. Ibid.; H.-R. Casgrain, ed., *Collection des manuscripts du Maréchal de Lévis*, vol. VI, 214.
11. Ibid., vol. IX, 48–9.
12. Ibid., vol. VI, 183.
13. Archives Nationales, Paris, Colonies, Series C11A, vol. 104, f. 193, 1759 Journal tenu à l'armée; Casgrain, op. cit., vol. V, 41-2.
14. Archives du Ministère de la Guerre, Vincennes. Series A1, vol. 3574, f. 112, Evenemens du Canada depuis le Mois d'Octobre 1759 Jusqu'au mois de Septembre 1760; Casgrain, op. cit., vol. IX, 56.
15. Journal de M. Malartic 1758–9, loc. cit.; Casgrain, op. cit., vol. V, 349.
16. Public Archives of Canada, MG 23, GII-1, series 2–7, P. MacKellar's Short Account of the Expedition against Quebec, 20.
17. Casgrain, op. cit., vol. VI, 163.
18. Ibid., vol. V, 343.
19. Archives du Ministère de la Guerre, Vincennes. Series A1, vol. 3405, no. 217.
20. 1759 Journal tenu a l'armée, op. cit., f. 187.
21. Archives Nationales, Paris, Colonies. Series C11A, vol. 104, f. 332, Mémoire du Sieur de Ramezay.
22. Casgrain, op. cit., vol. IV, 96.
23. Stacey, op. cit., 102.
24. Sir Julian S. Corbett, *England in the Seven Years' War*, (London 1918), vol. I, 454, n. 1; Hibbert, op. cit., 126.
25. Stacey, op. cit., 97–8.
26. See in particular Stacey, op. cit., 162–78, 'Generalship at Quebec'.
27. Ibid., 154.
28. Ibid., 137.
29. Ibid., 154.
30. *New York Review of Books*, 25 Jan. 1973.
31. Capt. John Knox, *An Historical Journal of the Campaigns in North America*, (Champlain Society edition, Toronto, 1914–16), 99–101.
32. Stacey, op. cit., 135; Archives Nationales, Paris. Series F3, Moreau de St Méry, vol. 15, ff, 286–8, Vaudreuil au Ministre, Mtl., 5 oct. 1759; Archives du Ministère de la Guerre, Vincennes. Series A1, vol. 3540, no. 103, Bigot au Ministre, Mtl., 15 oct. 1759.
33. A great deal has been written on the weakness of the Quebec fortifications. Montcalm was scathing in his comments, but he always sought to make his situation appear far worse than it actually was. The engineering officer Pontleroy was equally critical, but he was not disinterested; he sought the post of chief engineer for the colony, claiming that such an appointment was needed since all the colony's forts would have to be rebuilt and he was the obvious man to do it. According to this, and Montcalm's rubric a fortified place that the French held was indefensible, but the moment the enemy occupied it, it became, *ipso facto*, impregnable. The other serving engineering officer in Canada, Desandrouins, a competent man of integrity, submitted a *mémoire* in 1778 on what forces would be required were the French to send an expedition to retake Quebec. He gave a good description of the fortifications, stated that they mounted 180 large guns, plus a large number of mortars, and made it plain that the fortifications of Quebec were indeed formidable. See Casgrain, op. cit., vol. IV, 322–4.

34. Francis Parkman, who went over the battlefield in 1879, noted in his *Montcalm and Wolfe* that, from the British line Quebec was hidden from sight by the Buttes à Neveu. He failed, however, to appreciate the military significance of the fact. Since his day the ridge has been reduced in height and levelled by the construction of buildings and, on the St Lawrence side, of a covered reservoir under what is today the battlefield park.

35. Archives Nationales, Paris, Colonies, Series F3, Moreau de St Méry, vol. 15, ff. 284–5, Vaudreuil au Ministre, Qué., 5 oct. 1759; ibid., ff. 337–40, Bigot au Ministre, Mtl., 15 oct. 1759.

36. Ibid., Series CIIA, vol. 104, ff. 168, 175–6, 179–80, 196, Journal tenu à l'Armée.

37. Corbett, op. cit., vol. I, 431.

38. William Charles Henry Wood ed., *The Logs of the Conquest of Canada*, (Champlain Society edition, Toronto, 1909), 315–16.

39. Knox Journal, op. cit., 99–101.

40. P. MacKellar, op. cit., 34.

41. Robert S. Quimby, *The Background to Napoleonic Warfare: The Theory of Military Tactics in Eighteenth Century France*, (New York, 1957).

42. G.F.G. Stanley, *New France, The Last Phase 1744–1760*, (Toronto, 1968), 248.

43. Stacey, op. cit., 164.

44. Stacey, op. cit., 245–9.

Article Seven

A Change in Climate: The Conquest and the *Marchands* of Montreal

José Igartua

When the British government issued the Royal Proclamation of 1763, it assumed that the promised establishment of "British institutions" in the "Province of Quebec" would be sufficient to entice American settlers to move north and overwhelm the indigenous French-speaking and Papist population. These were naive hopes. Until the outbreak of the American Revolution, British newcomers merely trickled into Quebec, leading Governor Carleton to prophesy in 1767 that "barring a catastrophe shocking to think of, this Country must, to the end of Time, be peopled by the Canadian Race."[1] But the British newcomers, few though they were, had to be reckoned with. By 1765 they were powerful enough to have Governor Murray recalled and by 1777 they would be strong enough to command the majority of investments in the fur trade.[2] Did their success stem from superior abilities? Did the British take advantage of the situation of submission and dependence into which the Canadians had been driven by the Conquest? Did the newcomers gain their predominance from previous experience with the sort of political and economic conditions created in post-Conquest Quebec?

Historians of Quebec have chosen various ways to answer these questions. Francis Parkman was fond of exhibiting the superiority of the Anglo-Saxon race over the "French Celt."[3] More recently the studies of W.S. Wallace, E.E. Rich, and D.G. Creighton took similar, if less overt, positions.[4] One of the best students of the North West fur trade, Wayne E. Stevens, concluded: "The British merchants . . . were men of great enterprise and ability and they began gradually to crowd out the French traders who had been their predecessors in the field."[5]

The French-Canadian historian Fernand Ouellet attributed the rise of the British merchants to the weaknesses of the Canadian trading bourgeoisie: "Son attachement à la petite

Source: José Igartua, "A Change in Climate: The Conquest and the *Marchands* of Montreal," *Historical Papers* (1974): 115–34. Reprinted by permission of the author and the Canadian Historical Association.

entreprise individuelle, sa réponse à la concentration, son goût du luxe de même que son attrait irrésistible pour les placements assurés étaient des principaux handicaps" [*Editor's translation:* their attachment to small personal business, their response to concentration, their love of luxury, as well as their irresistible attraction to safe investments were the main drawbacks]. No evidence is given for this characterization and the author hastens to concede that before 1775 "le problème de la concentration ne se pose pas avec acuité" [*Editor's translation:* the problem of concentration was not acute], but for him it is clear that the economic displacement of the Canadians resulted from their conservative, "ancien régime" frame of mind, bred into them by the clergy and the nobility.[6] Ouellet painted British merchants in a more flattering light as the agents of economic progress.[7]

Michel Brunet has depicted the commercial competition between the British newcomers and the Canadian merchants as an uneven contest between two national groups, one of which had been deprived of the nourishing blood of its metropolis while the other was being assidu-ously nurtured. For Brunet the normal and natural outcome of that inequality was the domi-nation of the conqueror, a situation which he sees as prevailing to the present day.[8]

Dale B. Miquelon's study of one merchant family, the Babys, shed new light on the ques-tion of British penetration of Canadian trade. It outlined the growth of British investments in the fur trade and the increasing concentration of British capital. The author concluded:

> The French Canadians dominated the Canadian fur trade until the upheaval of the American Revolution. At that time they were overwhelmed by an influx of capital and trading per-sonnel. English investment in the top ranks of investors jumped by 679% and was never sig-nificantly to decline. Even without explanations involving the difference between the French and English commercial mentalities, it is difficult to believe that any body of merchants could recover from an inundation of such size and swiftness.[9]

This conclusion had the obvious merit of staying out of the murky waters of psychological inter-pretations. But Miquelon's own evidence suggests that the "flood theory" is not sufficient to account for the Canadians' effacement; even before the inundation of 1775–83, British invest-ment in the fur trade was growing more rapidly than Canadian. By 1772, to quote Miquelon, the "English [had] made more impressive increases in the size of their investments than [had] the French, and for the first time [had] larger average investments in all categories."[10]

It is difficult not to note the ascendancy of the British in the fur trade of Canada even before the American Revolution. The success of the British merchants, therefore, was rooted in something more than mere numbers. It was not simply the outcome of an ethnic struggle between two nationalities of a similar nature; it was not only the natural consequence of the Canadians' conservative frame of mind. It arose out of a more complex series of causes, some of them a product of the animosities between Canadians and British, others inherent to the dif-ferences in the socioeconomic structures of the French and British empires; together, they amounted to a radical transformation of the societal climate of the colony.

The aim of this paper is to gauge the impact of the Conquest upon a well-defined segment of that elusive group called the "bourgeoisie" of New France. It focuses on Montreal and its Canadian merchants. Montreal was the centre of the fur trade and its merchants managed it. Historians of New France have traditionally seen the fur trade as the most dynamic sector of the colony's economy; by implication it is generally believed that the fur trade provided the like-liest opportunities for getting rich quickly and maintaining a "bourgeois" standard of living.[11] It is not yet possible to evaluate the validity of this notion with any precision, for too little is known about other sectors of the economy which, in the eighteenth century at least, may have generated as much or more profit. Research on the merchants of Quebec should provide new information on the wealth to be made from the fisheries, from wholesale merchandising, and from trade with Louisbourg and the West Indies. But if one is concerned with the fate of Canadian merchants after the Conquest, one should examine the fate of men involved in the sector of the economy of Quebec which was the most dynamic *after* the Conquest, the fur trade. The paper examines the impact of the arrival of (relatively) large numbers of merchants on the Montreal mercantile community, the attitude of British officials towards the Canadians, and the changing political climate of the colony. It is suggested that it was the simultaneous conjunction of these changes to the "world" of the Montreal merchants, rather than the effect of any one of them, which doomed the Canadian merchants of Montreal.[12]

THE MONTREAL MERCHANTS AT THE END OF THE FRENCH REGIME

In 1752 a French Royal engineer passing through Montreal remarked that "la plupart des habitants y sont adonnés au commerce principalement à celui connu sous le nom des pays d'en haut"[13] [*Editor's translation:* the majority of the inhabitants involved in commerce were active principally in the upper part of the region—the back country (west and north of Montreal)]. It was only a slight exaggeration. By the last year of the French regime one could count over one hundred négociants, merchants, outfitters, traders, and shopkeepers in Montreal. The overwhelming majority of them had been in business for some years and would remain in business after the Conquest. Over half were outfitters for the fur trade at some time or other between 1750 and 1775; these men comprised the body of the merchant community of Montreal. Above them in wealth and stature stood a handful of import merchants who did a comfortable business of importing merchandise from France and selling it in Montreal to other merchants or directly to customers in their retail stores. Below the outfitters a motley group of independent fur traders, shopkeepers, and artisans managed to subsist without leaving more than a trace of their existence for posterity.[14]

The fur trade, as it was conducted by the merchants of Montreal before 1760, had little to do with the glamorous picture it sometimes calls to mind. For the outfitter who remained in Montreal, it was not physically a risky occupation; its management was fairly simple and the profits which it produced quite meagre. For the last years of the French regime the fur trade followed a three-tier system. Fort Frontenac (present-day Kingston) and Fort Niagara were King's posts; they were not lucrative and had to be subsidized to meet English competition. The trade of Detroit and Michilimackinac, as well as that of the posts to the southwest, was open to licencees whose numbers were limited. Some coureurs de bois (traders without a licence) also roamed in the area. The richest posts, Green Bay and the posts to the northwest past Sault Sainte-Marie, were monopolies leased by the Crown to merchants or military officers.[15] The export of beaver was undertaken by the French Compagnie des Indes, which had the monopoly of beaver sales on the home market. Other furs were on the open market.

The system worked tolerably well in peace time: there was a stable supply of furs, prices paid to the Indians had been set by custom, the prices paid by the Compagnie des Indes were regulated by the Crown, and the prices of trade goods imported from France were fairly steady. There was competition from the Americans at Albany and from the English on the Hudson Bay, to be sure, but it appeared to be a competition heavily influenced by military considerations and compliance with Indian customs.[16]

The system faltered in war time. Beaver shipments to France and the importation of trade goods became risky because of British naval power. Shipping and insurance costs raised the Canadian traders' overhead, but the Indians refused to have the increase passed on to them. This was the most obvious effect of war, but it also produced general economic and administrative dislocations which led H.A. Innis to conclude that it "seriously weakened the position of the French in the fur trade and contributed to the downfall of the French *régime* in Canada."[17]

Nevertheless, outside of wartime crises, the fur trade of New France was conducted with a fair dose of traditionalism. This traditionalism resulted from two concurrent impulses: Indian attitudes towards trade, which were untouched by the mechanism of supply and demand and by distinctions between commercial, military, political, or religious activities; and the mercantilist policies of France, which tried to control the supply of furs by limiting the number of traders and regulating beaver prices on the French market. While the fur trade structure of New France had an inherent tendency towards geographic expansion, as Innis argued, it also had to be oligopolistic in nature, if investments in Indian alliances, explorations, and military support were to be maximized. Open competition could not be allowed because it would lead to the collapse of the structure.[18]

It is not surprising, therefore, that most outfitters dabbled in the fur trade only occasionally. On the average, between 1750 and 1775, the Canadian merchants of Montreal invested in the trade only four times and signed up about eleven engagés each time, not quite enough to man two canoes. Few merchants outfitted fur trade ventures with any regularity and only six men hired an average of twelve or more engagés, more than twice before 1761 (see Table 7.1). Three of these were unquestionably wealthy: Louis Saint-Ange Charly, an import merchant who, unlike his colleagues, had a large stake in the fur trade, realized 100 000 livres on his land holdings alone when he left the colony for France in 1764; Thomas-Ignace Trotier Desauniers "Dufy," who in a will drawn up in 1760 bequeathed 28 000 livres to the Sulpicians; the illiterate Dominique Godet, who in a similar document of 1768 mentioned 5000 livres in cash in hand, land in three parishes in the vicinity of Montreal, "Batiment & Bateaux qui en dependent," around 5000 livres in active debts, and two black slaves.[19] Two other large outfitters left relatively few belongings at the time of their death: Alexis Lemoine Monière left less than 1000 livres, all of it in household goods, and François L'Huillier Chevalier just slightly more.[20] Little is known about the sixth man, Jean Léchelle.

If the fur trade made few wealthy men among those who invested heavily in it, it would be hard to argue that less considerable investors were more successful. It is not unreasonable to conclude that the fur trade was not very profitable for the overwhelming majority of outfitters and that it sustained only a very limited number of them each year. Yet the French had reduced costly competition to a minimum and had few worries about price fluctuations. How would Canadian outfitters fare under a different system?

Table 7.1   Largest Canadian Fur Trade Outfitters in Montreal, 1750–1760

Name	Total No. of Years	Total No. of Hirings	Yearly Average
Charly, Louis Saint-Ange	6	85	14.1
Godet, Dominique	5	85	17.0
Léchelle, Jean	4	130	32.5
Lemoine Monière, Alexis	7	300	42.8
L'Huillier Chevalier, François	7	90	12.6
Trotier Desauniers, Thomas-Ignace "Dufy"	5	129	25.8

Source: "Répertoire des engagements pour l'ouest conservés dans les Archives judiciaires de Montréal," *Rapport de l'Archiviste de la province de Québec* (1930–31): 353–453; (1931–32): 242–365; (1932–33): 245–304.

THE ADVENT OF THE BRITISH MERCHANTS

With the arrival in Montreal of British traders, the workings of the fur trade were disrupted. At first, the licensing system was maintained and some areas were left to the exclusive trade of particular traders.[21] But from the very beginning the trade was said to be open to all who wanted to secure a licence, and the result could only be price competition. With individual traders going into the fur trade, the organization of the trade regressed. The previous division of labour between the Compagnie des Indes, the import merchants and outfitters, the traders, the voyageurs, and the engagés was abandoned and during the first years of British rule the individual trader filled all of the functions previously spread among many "specialists."

The story of Alexander Henry, one of the first British merchants to venture into the upper country, illustrates the new pattern of trade. A young man from New Jersey, Alexander Henry came to Canada in 1760 with General Amherst's troops.[22] With the fall of Montreal Henry saw the opening of a "new market" and became acquainted with the prospects of the fur trade. The following year, he set out for Michilimackinac with a Montreal outfitter, Étienne Campion, whom he called his "assistant," and who took charge of the routine aspects of the trip.[23] Henry wintered at Michilimackinac. There he was urged by the local inhabitants to go back to Detroit as soon as possible for they claimed to fear for his safety. Their fears were not without foundation, but Henry stayed on. His partner Campion reassured him: "the Canadian inhabitants of the fort were more hostile than the Indians, as being jealous of British traders, who . . . were penetrating into the country."[24] At least some of the Canadians resented the British traders from the outset and a few tried to use the Indians to frighten them away.[25]

Henry proceeded to Sault Sainte-Marie the following year. In the spring of 1763, he returned to Michilimackinac and witnessed the massacre of the British garrison during Pontiac's revolt.[26] He was eventually captured by the Indians and adopted into an Indian family with whom he lived, in the Indian style, until late June 1764. Undaunted, Henry set out for the fur trade again, exploring the Lake Superior area. He was on the Saskatchewan River in 1776, tapping fur resources which the French had seldom reached.[27] Finally he settled down in Montreal in 1781, and while he did join the North West Company after its formation, he seldom returned to the upper country himself.[28]

Henry was not the first British merchant to reach the upper country. Henry Bostwick had obtained a licence from General Gage before him in 1761,[29] and the traders Goddard and Solomons had followed Henry into Michilimackinac in 1761. By early 1763 there were at least two more British merchants in the area.[30] In Montreal alone there were close to 50 new merchants by 1765. Governor Murray's list of the Protestants in the district of Montreal gives the names, the origins, and the "former callings" of 45.[31] Over half of them came from England and Scotland and 20 percent were from Ireland. Only 13 percent came from the American colonies and an equal number came from various countries (Switzerland, Germany, France, Guernsey). In the proportion of more than three to one, the newcomers had been merchants in their "former calling." The others had been soldiers and clerks. Many of the newcomers were men of experience and enterprise. Among them were Isaac Todd, Thomas Walker, Lawrence Ermatinger, Richard Dobie, Edward Chinn, John Porteous, William Grant, Benjamin Frobisher, James Finlay, Alexander Paterson, Forrest Oakes, and the Jewish merchants Ezekiel and Levy Solomons, all of whom became substantial traders.[32]

The arrival of so many merchants could only mean one thing: strenuous competition in the fur trade. Competition ruthlessly drove out those with less secure financial resources or with no taste for sharp practices. Among the British as among the French, few resisted the pressures. The story of the trader Hamback is not untypical. Out on the Miami River in 1766 and 1767, he found that competition left him with few returns to make to his creditor William Edgar of

Detroit. "I live the life of a downright exile," he complained, "no company but a Barrel of drunken infamous fugitives, and no other Comfort of Life."[33]

The Canadian merchants of Montreal had competition not only from British merchants in their town, but also from American merchants moving into Detroit and Michilimackinac. William Edgar, a New York merchant, was at Niagara in late 1761.[34] In 1763 he was established at Detroit, where he conducted a brisk trade supplying individual traders at Michilimackinac and in the southwest district.[35] From Schenectady, the partnership of Phyn and Ellice also carried on a profitable supply trade for the fur traders of the interior.[36]

Competition also came from the French on the Mississippi, who were trading in the Illinois country and the Lake Superior region. These French traders could all too easily link up with French-speaking traders from Canada, whose help, it was feared, they could enlist in subverting the Indians against British rule.[37] This always troubled Sir William Johnson, the Superintendent for Indian Affairs, who refused to abandon his suspicions of the French-speaking traders from Canada.

This many-sided competition produced a climate to which the Canadian merchants were not accustomed. The increased numbers of fur traders led to frictions with the Indians, smaller returns for some of the traders, and unsavoury trade practices.[38] Even the retail trade was affected. Merchants from England flooded the market at Quebec "with their manufactures, so much so that they are daily sold here at Vendue Twenty per Cent below prime Cost."[39] In 1760 alone, the first year of British occupation, £60000 worth of trade goods had been brought into Canada.[40] From 1765 to 1768 the pages of the *Quebec Gazette* were filled with notices of auctions by merchants returning to England and disposing of their wares after unsuccessful attempts to establish themselves in the trade of the colony.[41]

By 1768 some thought the Canadians still had the advantage in the fur trade, even though there was "Competition" and a "strong jealousy" between Canadian and English. The Canadians' "long Connections with those Indians," wrote General Gage, "and their better Knowledge of their Language and Customs, must naturaly for a long time give the Canadians an Advantage over the English."[42] Sir William Johnson had expressed a similar opinion the previous year and had deplored the British merchants' tactics: "The English were compelled to make use of Low, Selfish Agents, French, or English as Factors, who at the Expence of honesty and sound policy, took care of themselves whatever became of their employers."[43]

Another observer, the Hudson's Bay Company trader at Moose Factory, complained of "Interlopers who will be more Destructive to our trade than the French was." The French had conducted a less aggressive trade: they "were in a manner Settled, their Trade fixed, their Standards moderate and Themselves under particular regulations and restrictions, which I doubt is not the Case now."[44] Competition was forcing the British merchants in Montreal into ruthless tactics, a development which upset the Hudson's Bay Company man and which would unsettle the Canadians.

The pattern of British domination of the fur trade began to emerge as early as 1767. Trading ventures out of Michilimackinac into the northwest were conducted by Canadians, but British merchants supplied the financial backing. The northwest expeditions demanded the lengthiest periods of capital outlay, lasting two or three years. British merchants, it seems, had better resources. Of the fifteen outfitters at Michilimackinac who sent canoes to the northwest in 1767, nine were British and six were Canadian; the total value of canoes outfitted by the British came to £10812.17 while the Canadians' canoes were worth only £3061.10. The British outfitters — most notably Alexander Henry, Isaac Todd, James McGill, Benjamin Frobisher, Forrest Oakes — invested on the average £1351.12 and the Canadians only £510.5. The average value of goods invested in each canoe stood at £415.17 for the British and £278.6 for the Canadians.[45] The Canadians' investment per canoe was only two-thirds that of the British and the Canadians were already outnumbered as outfitters in what would become the most important region of the fur trade.[46]

Open competition was not conducive to the expansion of the fur trade and an oligopolistic structure reminiscent of the French system soon reappeared as the only solution.[47] This led to the formation of the North West Company in the 1780s but already in 1775, those Montreal merchants who had extended their operations as far as the Saskatchewan felt the need for collaboration rather than competition. Again developments in the more remote frontiers of the fur trade foretold of events to occur later in the whole of the trade: the traders on the Saskatchewan were almost all of British origin.[48] The fur trade was returning to the structures developed by the French, but during the period of competition which followed the Conquest the Canadians were gradually crowded out. There was some irony in that. Why had the Canadians fared so badly?

THE ATTITUDE OF GOVERNMENT OFFICIALS

Much has been made of the natural sympathies of Murray and Carleton towards the Canadians and their antipathies towards the traders of their own nation. Yet for all their ideological inclinations there is no evidence that the governors turned their sentiments into policies of benevolence for Canadians in trade matters. Rather, it is easier to discover, among the lesser officials and some of the more important ones as well, an understandable patronizing of British rather than Canadian merchants. Colonial administrators may not have set a deliberate pattern of preference in favour of British merchants. But the Canadian merchants of Montreal, who put great store by official patronage, cared not whether the policy was deliberate or accidental; the result was the same.

Official preferences played against the Canadian traders in many ways. First, the lucrative trade of supplying the military posts was given to British and American merchants as a matter of course, and this occasion for profit was lost to the Canadians. Under the French regime some of the Montreal merchants, notably the Monières and the Gamelins, had profited from that trade.[49] Now it fell out of Canadian hands. This advantage did not shift to the sole favour of the British merchants of Quebec. New York and Pennsylvania traders were also awarded their share of the trade. The firms of Phyn, Ellice of Schenectady and Baynton, Wharton, and Morgan of Philadelphia received the lion's share of that business while the upper country was under the jurisdiction of Sir William Johnson.[50] But this was of little comfort to the Canadians.

Less tangible by-products of the British occupation of the former fur trading areas of New France are more difficult to assess than the loss of the supply trade; they were, however, quite real. One was the British military's attitude towards Canadians. The military were wary of French-speaking traders in Illinois and on the Mississippi. Although the French from Canada had been vanquished, French traders in the interior could still deal with France through New Orleans. No regulations, no boundaries could restrain French traders operating out of Louisiana from dealing with the Indians, and the Canadians who were confined to the posts protested against the advantage held by the French traders.[51] But who were these French traders? Did they not include Canadian coureurs de bois and wintering merchants? How could one really tell a French-speaking trader from Canada from a French-speaking trader out of New Orleans? Were not all of them suspect of exciting the Indians against the British, promising and perhaps hoping for France's return to America?[52] As late as 1768, when Indian discontent in the west threatened another uprising, General Gage failed to see any difference between French-speaking Canadians and the French from New Orleans:

> There is the greatest reason to suspect that the French are Endeavoring to engross the Trade, and that the Indians have acted thro' their Instigation, in the Murders they have committed, and the Resolutions we are told they have taken, to suffer no Englishman to trade with them. And in this they have rather been Assisted by the English Traders, who having no Consideration but that of a present gain, have thro' fear of exposing their own Persons, or hopes of obtaining greater influence with the Indians, continually employed French Commissarys or Agents, whom they have trusted with Goods for them to Sell at an Advanced price in the Indian Villages.[53]

Gage's suspicions of the French traders were nurtured by Sir William Johnson, who had to keep the Indians on peaceful terms with one another and with the British. It was part of Johnson's function, of course, to worry about possible uprisings and about subversive individuals. His job would be made easier if he could confine all traders to military posts where they could be kept under surveillance. But the traders had little concern for Sir William's preoccupations. If British traders were irresponsible in their desires of "present gain," the Canadian traders' vices were compounded by the uncertainty of their allegiance to the British Crown:

> Since the Reduction of that Country [Canada], we have seen so many Instances of their [the Canadian traders'] Perfidy false Stories & Ca. Interested Views in Trade that prudence forbids us to suffer them or any others to range at Will without being under the Inspection of the proper Officers agreeable to His Majesty's Appointment.[54]

Johnson's attitude spread to the officers under him, even though Carleton had found nothing reprehensible in the Canadians' behaviour.[55] Johnson's deputy, George Croghan, believed there was collusion between the French from Canada and the French from Louisiana.[56] In 1763 the commandant at Michilimackinac, Major Etherington, had displayed a similar mistrust of the Canadians.[57] Major Robert Rogers, a later commandant at Michilimackinac, checked the Canadians by trading on his own account.[58]

The British military's mistrust of the French traders from Canada was understandable. Before 1760, one of the major reasons for the American colonials' antagonism towards New France had been the French ability to press the Indians into their service to terrorize the western fringes of American settlement. Thus there was a historical as well as a tactical basis for the military's attitude towards the Canadians. But British officers failed to recognize that not all Canadian traders were potential troublemakers and that there was indeed very little tangible evidence, as Carleton had reminded Johnson, of any mischief on their part. The military's attitude was directed as much by ethnic prejudice as by military necessity.

The Canadian traders could not fail to perceive this prejudice, and it dampened their spirits. Perhaps the military's attitude, as much as competition, forced the Canadians into partnerships with British merchants. (The express purpose of the bonds required for the fur trade was to ensure loyal conduct; what better token of loyalty could there be for a Canadian trader than a bond taken out in his name by a British partner?) The military's mistrust of the Canadian traders did not lessen with time. The advantage which this prejudice gave British traders would continue for some twenty years after the Conquest, as the American Revolution rekindled the military's fears of treasonable conduct by the Canadians.

Other patronage relationships between British military officials and British traders also deprived the Canadians of an equal chance in the competition for furs. It is hard to evaluate precisely the effect of such patronage; only glimpses of it may be caught. Late in 1763 a Philadelphia merchant who had lost heavily because of Pontiac's uprising wrote to William

Edgar in Detroit that Croghan was in England where he was to "represent the Case of the Traders to his Majesty" and that General Amherst had "given us his faithful promise that he will do everything in his power in our behalf."[59] In 1765 Alexander Henry was granted the exclusive trade of Lake Superior by Major Howard, the military commandant at Michilimackinac. Nine years later Henry received the support of such patrons as the Duke of Gloucester, the consul of the Empress of Russia in England, and of Sir William Johnson in an ill-fated attempt to mine the iron ore of the Lake Superior area.[60]

These were obvious examples of patronage; other forms of cooperation were less visible. Another correspondent of William Edgar, Thomas Shipboy, asked Edgar to represent him in settling the affairs of a correspondent at Detroit and at Michilimackinac where, he added, "if you find any Difficulty in procuring his effects I dare say the Commanding officer will be of Service to you if you inform him in [sic] whose behalf you are acting."[61] Benjamin Frobisher also asked Edgar to "use your Interest with Capt. Robinson" to put a shipment of corn aboard the government vessel which sailed from Detroit to Michilimackinac.[62] Such shipping space was scarce and was only available through the courtesy of military officers or the ships' captains. Here again British traders put their social connections to good use. A last resort was sheer military force. Out on the Miami River, the trader Hamback saw "little hope of getting any thing from [Fort] St. Joseph at all, if I don't get protected, by the Commanding Officer, who might easily get those [Canadian] rascals fetch'd down to Detroit if He would."[63]

None of this patronage appears to have been available to Canadians. It is impossible to ascertain the degree to which military suspicions and patronage lessened the Canadians' chances in the fur trade. But more important, perhaps, than the actual loss of opportunities was the psychological handicap imposed upon the Canadians. What heart could they put in the game when the dice were so obviously loaded?

THE MERCHANTS' POLITICAL ACTIVITIES

The enmity between British merchants and the military, the merchants' growing agitation in favour of "British liberties," and their sentiments of political self-importance have been ably told by others and need not be retold here.[64] What needs to be underlined is that political agitation was unfamiliar to the Canadians. They had had no experience in these matters under French rule. Only on rare occasions during the pre-Conquest years had the Canadian merchants engaged in collective political representations; such representations were elicited by the governor or the intendant to obtain the merchants' advice on specific issues.[65] As French subjects, the Canadian merchants of Montreal had lacked the power to foster their economic interests through collective political action.

After 1760, the Canadian merchants would gradually lose their political innocence under the influence of the British merchants. During the 30 years which followed the Conquest they would make "l'apprentissage des libertés anglaises" and in 1792 they would take their place in the newly created legislative assembly more cognizant of the workings of the British constitution than the British had expected.[66] But that is beyond the concern here. In the years preceding the American Revolution the Montreal merchants were still looking for bearings. They showed their growing political awareness by following in the *Quebec Gazette* the political and constitutional debates which were rocking the British Empire. The merchants also began to voice their concerns in petitions and memorials to the authorities in the colony and in London.

The *Quebec Gazette* was the province's official gazette and its only newspaper before 1778. The paper published public notices for the Montreal district and occasional advertisements sent in by Montrealers as well as matters of concern to Quebec residents. It also made an effort to publish Canadian news of a general character. It closely followed the debates raging across the Atlantic over the *Stamp Act* and the general issues of colonial taxation. It reported on changes in the Imperial government and on contemporary political issues in England, notably the Wilkes affair.[67]

The pages of the *Gazette* also served on occasion as a forum for political discussion. In September 1765 a "Civis Canadiensis" declared his puzzlement at all the talk of "British liberties" and asked for enlightenment. The following year, a Quebec resident wrote a series of letters arguing that the colony should not be taxed.[68] In 1767, a debate arose on the British laws relating to bankruptcy and their applicability in Quebec.[69] Because of the pressures of Governor Carleton the *Gazette* stifled its reporting of controversial issues after 1770 and thereafter had little to print about American affairs.[70] In 1775 the *Gazette*'s political outpourings were directed against the American rebels and towards securing the loyalty of those Canadians who might be seduced by revolutionary propaganda.[71] The paper had become more conservative in its selection of the news but those Canadians who read the *Gazette* had been made familiar with the concepts of personal liberty, of "no taxation without representation," of the limited powers of the sovereign, and of the rights of the people. The *Gazette*'s readers most probably included the leading merchants of Montreal.

The *Gazette* was not the only instrument for the learning of British liberties. Anxious to give the appearance of a unanimous disposition among all merchants in Montreal, the British merchants often called on their Canadian confrères to add their names to various memorials and petitions dealing with the political and the economic state of the colony. The Canadian merchants who signed these petitions and memorials represented the top layer of the Canadian mercantile group in Montreal. Those who signed most often were the import merchants and the busy outfitters.

These Canadian merchants followed the political leadership of the British merchants. From 1763 to 1772 their petitions were either literal translations or paraphrased equivalents of petitions drafted by British merchants. It was only in December 1773 that they asserted views different from those of their British counterparts.[72] They petitioned the King that their "ancient laws, privileges, and customs" be restored, that the province be extended to its "former boundaries," that some Canadians be taken into the King's service, and that "the rights and privileges of citizens of England" be granted to all.[73]

The Canadians were becoming aware of their own position and were seeking to consolidate it against the attacks of the British element. The demand for the maintenance of the "ancient laws" was designed to counter British demands for British laws and representative institutions. The Canadians opposed the latter since, in their view, the colony was "not as yet in a condition to defray the expences of its own civil government, and consequently not in a condition to admit of a general assembly."[74] The demand for "a share of the civil and military employments under his majesty's government" came naturally to those who had lived under the French system of patronage. The Canadians had been accustomed to seek official patronage as the main avenue of upward mobility. The prospect of being denied such patronage was "frightful" to them, since they had little familiarity with alternate patterns of social promotion.[75]

In style as well as in content the Canadian merchants' petitions and memorials revealed differences in attitudes between Canadians and British. British memorials and petitions were rarely prefaced by more than the customary "Humbly showeth" and went directly to the point. In their own memorials and petitions, the Canadians first took "the liberty to prostrate themselves at the foot" of the royal throne and surrendered themselves to the "paternal care" of their sovereign. They often appealed to the wisdom, justice, and magnanimity of the king.[76] Their formal posture of meekness contrasted sharply with the self-assertion of the British. The Canadians'

"Habits of Respect and Submission," as one British official put it,[77] may well have endeared them to Murray and Carleton, but those habits constituted a psychological obstacle against their making full use of their newfound "British liberties" to foster their own economic interest.

CONCLUSION

With the fall of Montreal to British arms in September 1760 something was irrevocably lost to the Canadian merchants of that city. More than the evil effects of the war or the postwar commercial readjustments, the most unsettling consequence of the Conquest was the disappearance of a familiar business climate. As New France passed into the British Empire, the Montreal outfitters were thrown into a new system of business competition, brought about by the very numbers of newly arrived merchants, unloading goods in the conquered French colony and going after its enticing fur trade. In opening up the trade of the colony to competition, the British presence transformed Canadian commercial practices. The change negated the Canadian merchants' initial advantage of experience in the fur trade and created a novel business climate around them.

Competition in trade, the new political regime, the Canadian merchants' inability to obtain the favours of the military, all these created a mood of uncertainty and pessimism among the Montreal merchants. The merchants could only conclude from what was happening around them that the new business climate of the post-Conquest period favoured British traders at their expense. They can be understood if they were not eager to adapt their ways to the new situation.

It may be argued, of course, that the changes which produced the new situation are subsumed under the notion of "Conquest" and that the previous pages only make more explicit the "decapitation" interpretation advanced by the historians of the "Montreal school."[78] It is true enough that the new business climate described here may not have been created after the Seven Years' War had Canada remained a French possession. But there is no guarantee that other changes would not have affected the Montreal merchants. During the last years of the French regime they had reaped few profits from the fur trade. After the Conquest they continued in the fur trade much on the same scale as before. The Montreal merchants were not "decapitated" by the Conquest; rather, they were faced in very short succession with a series of transformations in the socioeconomic structure of the colony to which they might have been able to adapt had these transformations been spread over a longer period of time.

This paper has attempted to show that the fate of the Canadian merchants of Montreal after the Conquest followed from the nature of trade before the Conquest and from the rate at which new circumstances required the merchants to alter their business behaviour. But it should be remembered that the decapitation hypothesis still remains to be tested in the area of the colony's economy which was most heavily dependent upon the control of the metropolis, the import-export trade of the Quebec merchants. Only a detailed examination of the role and the activities of the Quebec merchants, both before and after the Conquest, will fully put the decapitation hypothesis to the test.

NOTES

1. Public Archives of Canada [hereafter PAC], C.O. 42, vol. 27, f. 66, Carleton to Shelburne, Quebec, 25 November 1767; quoted in A.L. Burt, *The Old Province of Quebec*, 2 vols. (Toronto, 1968), 1:142.
2. See Burt, *Old Province*, vol. 1, ch. 6; Dale B. Miquelon, "The Baby Family in the Trade of Canada, 1750–1820" (Unpublished Master's thesis, Carleton University, 1966), 145–46.

3. Francis Parkman, *The Old Regime in Canada*, 27th ed. (Boston, 1892), ch. 21, especially 397–98.

4. W. Stewart Wallace, ed., *Documents Relating to the North West Company* (Toronto, 1934); Wallace, *The Pedlars from Quebec and Other Papers on the Nor'Westers* (Toronto, 1954); E.E. Rich, *The Fur Trade and the Northwest to 1857* (Toronto, 1967); Rich, *The History of the Hudson's Bay Company*, vol. 2 (London, 1959); D.G. Creighton, *The Empire of the St. Lawrence* (Toronto, 1956).

5. Wayne E. Stevens, *The Northwest Fur Trade, 1763–1800* (Urbana, IL, 1928), 25.

6. Fernand Ouellet, *Histoire économique et sociale du Québec, 1760–1850* (Montreal, 1966), 77.

7. Ouellet, *Histoire économique*, 104–6.

8. Michel Brunet, *Les Canadiens après la Conquête, 1759–1775* (Montreal, 1969), 173–74, 177–80.

9. Miquelon, "The Baby Family," 158.

10. Miquelon, "The Baby Family," 142.

11. The implication is unwarranted. A given economic sector can be dynamic and even produce the largest share of marketable commodities and still provide individual entrepreneurs with meagre profits. The macroeconomic level of analysis should not be confused with the microeconomic level. Jean Hamelin showed that only around 28 percent of the profits from the beaver trade remained in Canada. Since the Canadians had an assured market for beaver, one can wonder how much more profitable it was for them to deal in other peltries. See Hamelin, *Économie et Société en Nouvelle-France* (Quebec, 1960), 54–56.

12. The obvious economic explanation for the downfall of the Canadian merchants after the Conquest has to be dismissed. The liquidation of Canadian paper money by France hurt most of all those British merchants who bought it from Canadians for speculation. Canadian merchants had already compensated in part for the anticipated liquidation by raising prices during the last years of the Seven Years' War. Those Montreal merchants who had the greatest quantity of French paper were not driven out of business; on the contrary, the most prominent merchants were able to open accounts with British suppliers soon after the Conquest without too much difficulty. See José E. Igartua, "The Merchants and *Négociants* of Montreal, 1750–1775: A Study in Socio-Economic History" (Unpublished Ph.D. thesis, Michigan State University, 1974), ch. 6.

13. Franquet, *Voyages et mémoires sur le Canada en 1752–1753* (Toronto, 1968), 56.

14. For a more elaborate description of the size and the socioeconomic characteristics of the Montreal merchant community at this time, see Igartua, "The Merchants and *Négociants* of Montreal," ch. 2.

15. See H.A. Innis, *The Fur Trade in Canada*, rev. ed. (Toronto, 1956), 107–13.

16. See Abraham Rotstein, "Fur Trade and Empire: An Institutional Analysis" (Unpublished Ph.D. thesis, University of Toronto, 1967), 72.

17. Innis, *Fur Trade*, 117. For his discussion of the impact of war on the fur trade and on New France, see 114–18.

18. In theory, the French licensing system set up to restrict the trade remained in operation from its reestablishment in 1728 to the end of the French regime; only 25 *congés* were to be sold each year. In practice, military officers in the upper country could also acquire for a modest fee exclusive trade privileges for their particular area. With some care, concluded one author, they could make an easy fortune. See Émile Salone, *La Colonisation de la Nouvelle-France* (Trois-Rivières, 1970), 390, 392–93. No clear official description of the licensing system was found for the period from 1750 to 1760, but the precise way in which the fur trade was restricted matters less than the fact of restriction.

19. On Charly see PAC, RG 4 B58, vol. 15, 19 September 1764, pass by Governor Murray to "Monsr. Louis Saint-Ange Charly [and his family] to London, in their way to France agreeable to the Treaty of Peace"; Archives Nationales du Québec à Montréal [formerly Archives judiciaires de Montréal; hereafter ANQ-M], Greffe de Pierre Panet, 16 août 1764, no. 2190. Trotier Desauniers "Dufy's" will is in ANQ-M, 29 juillet 1760, no. 1168, and Godet's will is in ANQ-M, 28 décembre 1768, no. 3140.

20. The inventory of Monière's estate is in ANQ-M, 28 décembre 1768, no. 3141; that of L'Huillier Chevalier's in ANQ-M, 15 [?] juin 1772, no. 3867.

21. See Alexander Henry, *Travels and Adventures in Canada* (Ann Arbor, University Microfilms, 1966), 191–92.

22. W. S. Wallace, *Documents Relating to the North West Company*, Appendix A ("A Biographical Dictionary of the Nor'Westers"), 456.

23. See Henry, *Travels*, 1–11, 34.

24. Henry, *Travels*, 39.

25. Henry, *Travels*, 50. Cf. the rosier picture by Creighton, *The Empire of the St. Lawrence*, 33.

26. Henry, *Travels*, 77–84. The Indians killed the British soldiers but ransomed the British traders, giving to each according to his profession.

27. Henry, *Travels*, 264–92.

28. See Wallace, *Documents*, 456; Milo M. Quaife, ed., *Alexander Henry's Travels and Adventures in the Years 1760–1776* (Chicago, 1921), xvi–xvii.

29. Henry, *Travels*, 11; Quaife, *Henry's Travels*, 12 n. 6.

30. Rich, *History of the Hudson's Bay Company*, 2: 9.

31. See PAC, C.O. 42, vol. 5, ff. 30–31, Murray's "List of Protestants in the District of Montreal," dated Quebec, 7 November 1765.

32. See Miquelon, "The Baby Family," 181–87.

33. PAC, MG 19 A1, 1, William Edgar Papers, 1: 97, F. Hamback to W. Edgar, 2 November 1766. See also 1: 95, Hamback to D. Edgar, 29 October 1766, and 1: 104–106, same to Edgar, 23 March 1767.

34. William Edgar Papers, 1: 12.

35. See William Edgar Papers, vols. 1 and 2.

36. R.H. Fleming, "Phyn, Ellice and Company of Schenectady," *Contributions to Canadian Economics* 4 (1932): 7–41.

37. See Marjorie G. Jackson, "The Beginnings of British Trade at Michilimackinac," *Minnesota History* 11 (September 1930): 252; C.W. Alvord and C.E. Carter, eds., *The New Regime, 1765–1767* (Collections of the Illinois State Historical Library, vol. 11), 300–301; Alvord and Carter, eds., *Trade and Politics, 1767–1769* (Collections of the Illinois State Historical Library, vol. 16), 382–453.

38. See "Extract of a Letter from Michilimackinac, to a Gentleman in this City, dated 30th June," in *Quebec Gazette*, 18 August 1768; see also Rich, *History of the Hudson's Bay Company* 2: 26: "The suspicions between the Pedlars [from Quebec], and their encouragements of the Indians to trick and defraud their trade rivals, especially by defaulting on payments of debt, were widespread and continuous."

39. *Quebec Gazette*, 7 January 1768.

40. Burt, *Old Province*, 1: 92.

41. The flooding of the Quebec market by British merchants was part of a larger invasion of the colonial trade in North America. See Mark Egnal and Joseph A. Ernst, "An Economic Interpretation of the American Revolution," *William and Mary Quarterly*, 3rd series, 29 (1972): 3–32.

42. Quoted in Alvord and Carter, eds., *Trade and Politics*, 288.

43. Alvord and Carter, eds., *Trade and Politics*, 38.

44. Quoted in E.E. Rich, *Montreal and the Fur Trade* (Montreal, 1966), 44.

45. These figures are somewhat distorted by the inclusion of a single large British investor, Alexander Henry, who outfitted seven canoes worth £3400 in all. See Charles E. Lart, ed., "Fur-Trade Returns, 1767," *Canadian Historical Review* 3 (December 1922): 351–58. The definition of the northwest as including Lake Huron, Lake Superior, and "the northwest by way of Lake Superior" given in Rich, *Montreal and the Fur Trade*, 36–37, was used in making these compilations. The French traders were "Deriviere," "Chenville," St. Clair, Laselle, "Guillaid [Guillet]," and "Outlass [Houtelas]."

46. See Rich, *Montreal and the Fur Trade*, 36–37.

47. Jackson, *Minnesota History*, 11: 268–69.

48. Rich, *History of the Hudson's Bay Company* 2: 68.

49. On the Monières, see Igartua, "The Merchants and *Négociants* of Montreal," ch. 2. On the Gamelins, see Antoine Champagne, *Les La Vérendrye et les postes de l'ouest* (Québec, 1968), passim.

50. See R.H. Fleming, *Contributions to Canadian Economics* 4: 13; on Baynton, Wharton and Morgan, see *The Papers of Sir William Johnson* [hereafter *Johnson Papers*], 14 vols. (Albany, 1921–1965), vols. 5, 6, 12, passim.

51. PAC, C.O. 42, vol. 2, ff. 277–80, petition of the "Merchants and Traders of Montreal" to Murray and the Council, Montreal, 20 February 1765; *Johnson Papers* 5: 807–15, memorial and petition of Detroit traders to Johnson, 22 November 1767; 12: 409–14, 1768 trade regulations with the merchants' objections.

52. See Alvord and Carter, eds., *The New Regime*, 118–19, and *Trade and Politics*, 39, 287; see also Stevens, *The Northwest Fur Trade*, 44.

53. *Johnson Papers*, 12: 517, Thomas Gage to Guy Johnson, New York, 29 May 1768.

54. *Johnson Papers* 5: 481. See also Alvord and Carter, eds., *The New Regime*, 118–19; *Johnson Papers* 5: 362; Alvord and Carter, eds., *Trade and Politics*, 39; *Johnson Papers* 5: 762–64; 12: 486–87; Stevens, *The Northwest Fur Trade*, 28.

55. PAC, C.O. 42, vol. 27, ff. 81–85, Carleton to Johnson, Quebec, 27 March 1767.

56. *Johnson Papers* 12: 372–75, Croghan to Johnson, 18 October 1767.

57. Henry, *Travels*, 71–72.

58. See PAC, C.O. 42, vol. 26, f. 13, Court of St. James, Conway [Secretary of State] to the Commandants of Detroit and Michilimackinac, 27 March 1766. See also Alvord and Carter, eds., *Trade and Politics*, 207–8, Gage to Shelburne, 12 March 1768; 239, Johnson to Gage, 8 April 1768; 375, Gage to Johnson, 14 August 1768; 378, Gage to Hillsborough, 17 August 1768; 384, Johnson to Gage, 24 August 1768; 599, Gage to Hillsborough, 9 September 1769. More than trading on his own account, Rogers was suspected of setting up an independent Illinois territory. He was eventually cleared. See "Robert Rogers," *Dictionary of American Biography*, vol. 16 (New York, 1935), 108–9, and *Johnson Papers*, vols. 5, 6, 12, 13, passim.

59. PAC, William Edgar Papers, 1: 43–44, Callender to Edgar n.p., 31 December 1763.

60. Henry, *Travels*, 191–92, 235.

61. PAC, William Edgar Papers, 1: 90, Thos. Shipboy to Rankin and Edgar, Albany, 21 August 1766.

62. William Edgar Papers, 1: 201, Benjamin Frobisher to Rankin and Edgar, Michilimackinac, 23 June 1769.

63. William Edgar Papers, 1: 104–106, F. Hamback to Edgar, 23 March 1767.

64. The most detailed account is given in Burt, *Old Province*, vol. 1, chs. 6 and 7. See also Creighton, *Empire of the St. Lawrence*, 40–48.

65. See for instance E.-Z. Massicotte, "La Bourse de Montréal sous le régime français," *The Canadian Antiquarian and Numismatic Journal*, 3rd series, 12 (1915): 26–32.

66. See Pierre Tousignant, "La Genèse et l'avènement de la Constitution de 1791" (Unpublished Ph.D. thesis, Université de Montréal, 1971).

67. See *Quebec Gazette*, 15 September 1766 and the issues from June to September 1768.

68. See *Quebec Gazette*, 26 September 1765. Tousignant, "La Genèse," pp. 21–39, points out the political significance of this letter.

69. See texts by "A MERCHANT" in the 10 and 17 December 1767 issues, and rebuttals in the 24 and 31 December 1767 and 7 and 21 January 1768 issues.

70. Tousignant, "La Genèse," 39.

71. See issues of 13 and 27 July, and 5 October 1775.

72. Canadian notables of Quebec broke with the "Old Subjects" earlier: a petition, thought to date from 1770 and signed by leading Canadians of that city, asked for the restoration of Canadian institutions. See Adam Shortt and Arthur G. Doughty, *Documents Relating to the Constitutional History of Canada*, 2nd. ed. (Ottawa, 1918) [hereafter *Docs. Const. Hist. Can.*], 1: 419–21.

73. The petition and the memorial are reproduced in *Docs. Const. Hist. Can.* 1:504–6, 508–10.

74. *Docs. Const. Hist. Can.* 1: 511. The British merchants of Montreal signed a counter-petition in January 1774, requesting the introduction of an assembly and of the laws of England. See 1: 501–502.

75. Recent historians have highlighted the influence of the military and civil administrations as sources of economic and social betterment in New France. See Guy Frégault, *Le XVIIIe siècle canadien* (Montréal, 1968), 382–84; W.J. Eccles, "The Social, Economic, and Political Significance of the Military Establishment in New France," *Canadian Historical Review* 52 (March 1971): 17–19; and Cameron Nish, *Les Bourgeois-Gentilshommes de la Nouvelle-France* (Montréal, 1968), passim.

76. See PAC, C.O. 42, vol. 24. ff. 72–73v.; ff. 95–95v; vol. 3, f. 262; *Docs. Const. Hist. Can.* 1: 504–508.

77. See *Docs. Const. Hist. Can.* 1: 504.

78. Maurice Séguin, of the History Department of the Université de Montréal, was the first to present a systematic interpretation of the Conquest as societal decapitation. His book, *L'Idée d'indépendance au Québec: Genèse et historique* (Trois-Rivières, 1968), which contains a summary of his thought, was published twenty years after its author first sketched out his thesis. Guy Frégault's *Histoire de la Nouvelle-France*, vol. 9, *La guerre de la Conquête, 1754–1760* (Montréal, 1955) is a masterful rendition of that conflict, cast as the *affrontement* of two civilizations. Michel Brunet, the most voluble of the "Montreal school" historians, has assumed the task of popularizing Séguin's thought. See Brunet, "La Conquête anglaise et la déchéance de la bourgeoisie canadienne (1760–1793)," in his *La Présence anglaise et les Canadiens* (Montréal, 1964), 48–112. Brunet developed the point further in *Les Canadiens après la Conquête*, vol. 1, *1759–1775* (Montréal, 1969). An abridged version of Brunet's position is provided in his *French Canada and the Early Decades of British Rule, 1760–1791* (Ottawa, 1963). For a review of French-Canadian historiography on the Conquest up to 1966, see Ramsay Cook, "Some French-Canadian Interpretations of the British Conquest: Une quatrième dominante de la pensée canadienne-française," Canadian Historical Association, *Historical Papers* (1966): 70–83.

Article Eight

The Fall of New France

Allan Greer

Built over the course of a century and a half, the French empire in North America suddenly collapsed between 1758 and 1760. The French had begun the Seven Years' War (on this continent, 1754–60) with a string of victories, coupled with devastating frontier raids mounted by Natives and French Canadians. But eventually Britain, urged on by the beleaguered Thirteen Colonies, decided on an all-out effort to crush French power in Canada. Though the conflict centred primarily on Europe (there it did actually last seven years, 1756–63) and involved clashes around the globe, Prime Minister William Pitt resolved to make the North American theatre a top priority. By the summer of 1758, some 42 000 British and colonial troops had been assembled, poised for the attack on New France. Just as significant, about one-quarter of the formidable British navy was deployed in the area, dominating the northwestern Atlantic so completely that supplies and reinforcements from France were effectively cut off. France and England had been squabbling in North America inconclusively for six decades, but now, quite suddenly, the balance of forces shifted dramatically against the French and, for the first time, the British could realistically aim, not simply at territorial gains and strategic advantages, but at total victory.

The naval blockade strangling trade into the St. Lawrence was devastating in its effects on both Canada and the *pays d'en haut*. In the Laurentian colony, its effects combined with an unfortunate series of short harvests to produce a shortage of almost all vital commodities, above all, food. At the same time, an unprecedented military build-up and the voracious appetite for supplies that it accompanied placed impossible demands on colonial supplies. Urban civilians were particularly hard hit and, in the winter of 1758–59 starvation became a serious threat. In Quebec City, it was said, "workers and artisans, ravaged by hunger, can no longer work; they are so weak they can hardly stand up." In an effort to relieve the cities and ensure supplies to the military, squadrons of soldiers were sent into the countryside to requisition grain at the point of a gun. Meanwhile, in the *pays d'en haut*, post commanders lacked the gifts and trade goods needed to play the role of a proper "father." Moreover, the French, under the pressures of intensifying war, had been taking a high-handed approach with the Indian nations of the Great Lakes and the Ohio country, effectively abandoning the cultural compromises underpinning the "middle ground," and alienating their allies. Thus, when the British appeared on the horizon with substantial forces, most Native groups made peace with the invaders, in part in order to rid the country of the now-hated French. These defections opened the way to the British, who soon captured Detroit and the other western posts.

Meanwhile, Canada was under attack by two major armies of invasion, one of them making its laborious way up the heavily defended corridor leading north via Lake Champlain to Montreal, the other taking a seaborne route by way of the Gulf of St. Lawrence. This latter, amphibious, assault entailed a costly but successful siege of Louisbourg in 1758, followed by the siege of the hitherto impregnable defences of Quebec. Week after week in the summer of 1759, British batteries bombarded the capital without mercy, while raiding parties burned villages all up and down the St. Lawrence in defiance of then-current rules of civilized warfare. Finally, a

Source: Allan Greer, "The Fall of New France," *The People of New France* (Toronto: University of Toronto Press, 1997), pp. 109–21. Reprinted by permission of the publisher.

decisive engagement on the Plains of Abraham delivered Quebec to the English. This battle, so widely known today because of its dramatic qualities, was really only one episode in a much larger campaign. Historians have pointed out that it was, in fact, a very near thing, which, with a little luck on their side, the French might well have won. But even so, would a different outcome on the Plains of Abraham have kept Canada French? Not likely. The British investment in the reduction of New France was simply overwhelming. Not one, but three armies were pressing into the colony, from the west and the south, as well as the east, and in the summer of 1760 they all bore down on the last French stronghold of Montreal. Its fate more or less sealed two years earlier, Canada was, on 9 September, finally surrendered to the invaders.

England was definitely on a winning streak in the later part of the Seven Years' War. Its European ally, Prussia, emerged victorious in central Europe, and Britain itself captured French possessions around the world: slaving stations on the coast of Africa, colonial establishments in India, and precious sugar islands in the West Indies. Then Spain entered the war on France's side, and the English promptly took Havana and Manila. In the complicated diplomatic arrangements which concluded the war (1763), Britain acquired title strictly within the realm of European imperial pretensions, of course—to most of North America. France retained fishing rights on the coast of Newfoundland, but Île Royale was annexed to Nova Scotia, and Canada was recognized as a British province. Louisiana, which had been largely untouched by the fighting, was divided: the western part, including New Orleans, went to Spain, while Britain acquired the eastern part along with formerly Spanish Florida.

And where are the people of New France in this geopolitical story of conquest and defeat? Did the social configurations sketched out in earlier sections of this book [*The People of New France*] play any part in provoking war? Nineteenth-century historians sometimes suggested that a fight to the finish between the French and the English in North America was somehow the product of essential differences in the two nationalities which led to the formation of fundamentally incompatible colonial societies, and vestiges of that view can still be found in modern interpretations. Equally influential — and just as misleading, in my opinion — is the notion that New France was doomed to be a loser in the inevitable struggle because of some sort of basic fatal flaw.

Certainly there were important differences distinguishing the French and English colonial societies in North America: differences in language, religion, political institutions, and relations between Natives and European colonists. But there was also great diversity within each of the two camps. Within the broadly delineated New France of the eighteenth century could be found the comparatively Europeanized society of Canada, with its military aristocracy; its seigneurial agrarian life; and its towns, with their diverse assortment of merchants, artisans, priests, nuns, soldiers, and officials. Île Royale, on the other hand, displayed a much more capitalist character, with fishing and trading to the fore and little trace of any feudal elements, whereas Acadia had been dominated by its free peasantry. Slavery and plantation agriculture were prominent features of life in Louisiana. And in the backcountry claimed by Louisiana, as well as Canada's *pays d'en haut*, various Aboriginal modes of existence prevailed, and the handful of French who frequented these regions had to adapt to that reality. French North America, like English North America, was not a homogeneous whole. In searching out the causes of all-out war, one might just as well point to affinities linking neighbouring sections of the rival empires Louisiana and South Carolina, Canada and New York, Île Royale and Massachusetts as an attempt to find some essential cultural dichotomy.

The fact is that, through most of the colonial period, New France and English America were at peace, and when they did come to blows, it was seldom over genuinely colonial issues. Aboriginal nations such as the Mi'kmaq had basic and enduring motives for hostility toward the colonizing powers, and since the English usually posed a greater threat, they often ended up allying themselves with the French. But French Canadians had little cause, obedience to their monarch apart, for fighting New Englanders. There was always a certain amount of border skirmishing in peripheral regions of uncertain ownership, such as Newfoundland and Hudson Bay, but, by and large, the two nations colonized separate regions and had few points of friction. Historians used to believe that competition over the western fur trade drove the English and French colonizers into mortal combat, but recent research indicates that international fur trade rivalries were more a result than a cause of international hostilities; the two powers used the fur trade in an attempt to attract Native nations into their respective commercial-diplomatic orbits. Indeed, it seems quite likely that, if left to their own devices, French Canadians and Anglo-Americans would have shared the continent just as the Spanish and Portuguese shared South America, not always in peace perhaps, but without harbouring plans to destroy each other's settlements utterly.

In colonial North America, war — that is, war between English and French, though not war between colonizers and Natives — was largely a European import. Canada went to war because France went to war. Men from the Iroquoian communities of St. Lawrence, along with *troupes de la marine* and French-Canadian militia, as well as allied Natives from the *pays d'en haut*, relied mainly on guerrilla raids to harass the designated enemy to the south. As long as war was conducted mainly by North Americans, New France more than held its own; even though it was vastly outnumbered by the Anglo-Americans, authoritarian French Canada was organized for war and, more important, it could rely on Native support. Thus, the idea that defects in French colonial society preordained the defeat of 1760 are hard to credit, since Canada's military record suggests strength rather than weakness through most of the period. In a sense, that very strength itself led to the downfall, in that early French successes in the Seven Years' War helped to galvanize England and British North America into an extraordinary mobilization of forces. What sealed the doom of New France was the sudden Europeanization of the conflict in 1758. When Britain poured men, ships, and equipment into the fray, the mode of fighting changed abruptly, as did the balance of forces, and Canada's brand of frontier raiding was now of little account. In sum, New France's involvement in major war, and also its ultimate defeat, were mainly the result of European intervention; they were not determined by the shape of its colonial society.

And what of the consequences of the Conquest? Generations of Canadians, English- as well as French-speaking, have come to view this event as the central cataclysm in their country's history, a humiliating defeat which lies at the root of Quebec nationalism, and a heavy blow to the social development of French Canada which left it backward and impoverished for centuries to come. Of course, the Conquest did ultimately have far-reaching effects for Canada; without it there would never have been an English Canada, nor would there have been a binational federal state. But was French Canada humiliated by the Conquest and did it then enter a period of social disarray?

That is certainly not the way it appeared to most contemporaries in the 1760s. Then it seemed clear that England had beaten France in a war and had taken Canada as its prize. French Canadians had no reason to feel like a defeated and humbled people, and there is little indication that they did feel that way in the decades following the Conquest. There may have been some apprehension that property would be threatened, that the Catholic religion would be persecuted, or even that residents would be deported as the Acadians and the people of Île Royale had been only a few years earlier. These concerns proved groundless, however, for, with the war now at an end, Britain had no need and no desire to depopulate the colony. There were, indeed, some troublesome issues surrounding the legal system, the status of the Church, and the admission of French Canadians to public office. Moreover, some residents — mostly government officials, merchants, and military officers — quit the colony as soon as it passed into Britain's empire, though it is an exaggeration to refer to this exodus as a social "decapitation," particularly when many of the emigrants were metropolitan French who would likely have left Canada even if it had remained under the rule of France. As a colony, New France had always been dominated by European intendants, bishops, and, to a large extent, judges and merchants. After 1760 it would be ruled by a different set of outsiders who happened to be British. This did not seem remarkable to most contemporaries, for nationalism — the belief that government and governed should have the same ethnic and linguistic identity — was not then a powerful force anywhere in the world.

The idea that French Canada was a conquered nation rather than a ceded colony was the product of a very different epoch, one that began almost a century after the conclusion of the Seven Years' War. Between the Conquest and the emergence of the Myth of the Conquest stretched a long and eventful period of history filled with momentous developments in Canada and around the Atlantic world. The American Revolution, the Haitian Revolution, and the Latin American wars of independence brought European imperial rule to an end throughout most of the western hemisphere. With the French Revolution and the wars of Napoleon, *anciens régimes* crumbled and the "principle of nationality" gained adherents across Europe. French Canada felt the force of these global developments. One result was the nationalist-democratic Rebellion of 1837–38, a revolt against British rule inspired by a republican vision of national independence (not, as some have suggested, by any sort of desire to return to Bourbon rule). Only after the defeat of this insurrection, and after the predominantly French portion of Canada (Lower Canada) had been yoked politically to English-speaking parts of British North America, did chastened and more conservative elements of the French-Canadian elite begin to speak longingly of the glories of New France. Along with the idealization of the supposedly conservative and Catholic French regime went a view of French–English conflict as inveterate, enduring, and unchanging. This idea that "the English" were the enemy and that the Conquest had been a social disaster that ruined French Canada's development began to enjoy wide appeal in the second half of the nineteenth century; this was when the French were losing political influence to a rapidly expanding English Canada, and when ordinary French Canadians found their lives disrupted by a capitalism that seemed to speak only English and to benefit only anglophones. The Myth of the Conquest, the belief that the cession constituted an epoch-making tragedy with social as well as political dimensions, was a product of French Canada's social stresses in the 1860s, not the 1760s. And, as the political economy of Canadian capitalism continued to develop to the disadvantage of French Quebec, the Myth of the Conquest continued to hold sway throughout the twentieth century.

Canada in the immediate wake of the Conquest was certainly a traumatized society, but the trauma it suffered had been caused much more by the war itself than by the cession to Britain. Especially in Quebec City and its region, the physical destruction had been immense, not to mention the economic dislocation occasioned by the blockade and famine. To make matters worse, the French government's partial renunciation of its debts wrecked many colonial fortunes. Rebuilding took years. But the Conquest as such — the transfer of New France from one empire to another — struck at French-Canadian society only in limited and selective ways.

For most people, and in most aspects of existence, the advent of British rule made little difference. The habitants — which is to say, the great majority of French Canadians — continued their agrarian way of life, colonizing ever-expanding territories on the edges of the St. Lawrence valley. Basic family self-sufficiency remained central, but increasingly habitants lucky enough to possess prime wheat-growing lands grew substantial surpluses for sale overseas. Access to British imperial markets helped stimulate this development, but the trend toward export agriculture had been set long before the Conquest. Tithes and seigneurial exactions continued more or less as before, though some of the seigneurs were now English merchants and officers who had purchased seigneuries from emigrating French seigneurs. Over the decades, seigneurial rents tended to bear down more heavily on the peasantry as land became more scarce and agriculture more lucrative, but, again, the tendency under the British regime was the culmination of developments begun under the French regime; the Conquest was largely incidental.

At the top levels of French-Canadian society, the change in imperial masters posed serious problems. The clergy were no longer subsidized, nor were they integrated into the state, now officially Protestant. However, the Catholic Church weathered the storm quite nicely, quietly developing a working relationship with a succession of British governors and discovering, for the rest, the benefits of ecclesiastical independence beyond the reach of their Most Catholic Majesties of France. The *noblesse* was damaged badly by the elimination of the colonial military force and of the officers' careers it had come to depend on. The rising value of seigneurial incomes helped to cushion the blow, but nobles could no longer look to government for preferment as they had in the past. Canadian merchants were also damaged by the Conquest. Traders from Britain and the Thirteen Colonies swarmed into the St. Lawrence Valley hard on the heels of the conquering armies, bringing low-priced merchandise that undercut resident merchants. Business connections with Britain and contacts with the occupying army were at a premium now that Canada's commerce had to be redirected into a different imperial system, and so French-Canadian importers and exporters were immediately placed at a disadvantage. The fur traders of Montreal held out for a time, but, within twenty years, anglophone capitalists dominated even that branch of commerce.

Was the Conquest good or bad for women? In most essential respects, it seems to have left power relations between the sexes unchanged. French-Canadian civil law, including the rules defining marital property rights and inheritance, remained in place after an initial period of uncertainty following the cession. Visitors from overseas — British now, rather than French — still remarked on the independent and domineering character of the Canadian ladies. There were certainly major realignments of gender ideology in the nineteenth century, as public life was, with increasing insistence, declared off limits to women. This occurred long after the Conquest, however, and the change clearly mirrored widespread international trends, discernible in France itself, as well as in England and English-speaking North America.

The Iroquois, Huron, and other Natives resident in the St. Lawrence colony certainly suffered as a result of the Conquest; or, to put it more accurately, the conclusion of French–English conflict reduced the Natives' value as military auxiliaries and gave them less bargaining power and room to manoeuvre. Officials under the British regime wished to retain the allegiance of the local Aboriginal population, particularly as war once again loomed: against the United States and France. After the 1820s, peace seemed more assured and Iroquois assistance less necessary, and subsidies meant to reward allegiance were phased out. Encroachment on their land base at Kahnawaké and Oka undermined the Natives' agrarian economy, just at a time when government tribute was disappearing. Many men sought external income working in the northwest fur trade and the forest industry, but impoverishment was the fate of these Native communities in the post-Conquest era.

In the *pays d'en haut*, war's end brought a painful transition as options suddenly closed down for the Aboriginal nations of the west. The Seven Years' War had kept American settlers and land speculators at bay, but soon they were pouring over the Appalachians in spite of Britain's efforts to reserve the territory to Amerindians. Moreover, the British military, after dislodging the French from Detroit and other posts in the region, settled in as an army of occupation in spite of Native protests. They also cut off "presents," the tribute previously offered as a token of alliance. The overall refusal of the British to play the role of a good alliance "father" provoked the reconstitution of an anti-British alliance of many western tribes which, under Pontiac's leadership, came close to driving the British out of the region. One enduring legacy of the period of French ascendancy in the *pays d'en haut* was the tradition of Pan-Indian alliances. Creating unity out of these culturally diverse and politically fragmented groups was exceedingly difficult, but, from Pontiac's time until the early nineteenth century, a series of concerted efforts did help slow the Anglo-American onslaught. The fact that the British, now embroiled in conflict with their colonists, were prevailed on to take up aspects of Onontio's role was certainly a factor, but the impulse to resist came largely from the Natives themselves.

New France did indeed disappear, both in its narrow "Canadian" sense and in its wider, continental meaning, encompassing the *pays d'en haut* and the scattered enclaves of French settlement. After the Conquest, the Maritime region took on a distinctly British character. The residents of Île Royale were all deported, though with less brutality than the Acadian removal a few years earlier. Soon Yankee settlers from New England spread through the region, followed by British immigrants and Loyalist refugees; when Acadians began to straggle back years later, they found themselves geographically, culturally, and politically marginalized. In Louisiana, the French and African elements of colonial society, along with the institution of slavery, persisted under Spain's rule. The arrival of Acadian refugees to colonize the bayous of the lower Mississippi only reinforced the French quality of the colony. Under Napoleon, France repossessed Louisiana, then promptly sold it to the young American republic. Society was thoroughly Americanized in the nineteenth century, though French and Creole ways subsisted as picturesque folkloric vestiges.

If we were to seek for the legacy of New France, we might find it, at the most superficial level, in the French place-names — Coeur d'Alene, Terre Haute, Port Mouton — strewn across North America and regularly mispronounced by the current inhabitants. It might also be found in the various pockets in Canada and the United States where French is still spoken. More significantly, of course, the Canadian settlement along the banks of the St. Lawrence established frameworks — language, customs, law — for the development of modern Quebec (not that one would wish to portray French Quebec as a mere survival left over from the French regime; contemporary Quebec has been shaped by its colonial past no more and no less than Connecticut or Ontario). There is a third aspect to the legacy of New France, broader in scope and more profound in its implications than the other two mentioned so far: that is its role as a critical part of the colonial history of North America generally.

The thrust of this book [*The People of New France*] has been to present the people of New France as participants in a momentous and multidimensional process of colonization, one in which mere "Frenchness" is only part of the story. In the seventeenth and eighteenth centuries, Catholic immigrants from France, working often in close relations with Natives, blacks, and Protestants, reconstituted a version of European society on the banks of the St. Lawrence. The settler society of "Canada" spawned smaller French colonies, none of them homogeneously French, in the Great Lakes, the Mississippi, and the Maritimes. Through the process of expansion, the French collided with, traded with, fought, wooed, and allied themselves with dozens of Aboriginal peoples, from the Arctic to the Gulf of Mexico. This was one element, though a crucially important one, of the broad process of colonization which also involved other Natives of North America, as well as English, Spanish, and Dutch settlers, and enslaved Africans. In that it constituted, not simply a community of transplanted Europeans, but a complicated pattern of Native–European interaction over a vast terrain, New France shaped the destinies of a continent.

Topic Four

Upper Canada and the War of 1812

POLICE.

WHEREAS authentic intelligence has been received that the Government of the United States of America did, on the 18th instant, declare War against the United Kingdom of Great Britain and Ireland and its dependencies, Notice is hereby given, that all Subjects or Citizens of the said United States, and all persons claiming American Citizenship, are ordered to quit the City of Quebec, on or before TWELVE o'clock at Noon, on WEDNESDAY next, and the District of Quebec on or before 12 o'clock at noon on FRIDAY next, on pain of arrest.　　　ROSS CUTHBERT, C. Q. S. & Inspector of Police.

The Constables of the City of Quebec are ordered to assemble in the Police Office at 10 o'clock to-morrow morning, to receive instructions.

Quebec, 29th June, 1812.

FROM A WALL POSTER.

Notice published in Quebec City, 29 June 1812, ordering all persons of American citizenship to leave the city immediately, or face arrest.

With the *Constitutional Act* of 1791, Upper Canada emerged as a new British colony, composed largely of Loyalists escaping from the newly independent Thirteen Colonies. The Loyalists, however, dropped in three decades from a majority to minority status. On account of the large-scale American (non-Loyalist) migration, the Americans by 1812 outnumbered the Loyalists and recent British immigrants by four to one in the colony's population of roughly 75 000. The War of 1812 pressured the American immigrants to choose sides. Not all Upper Canadians were prepared to support Britain, as Jane Errington points out in "Reluctant Warriors: British North Americans and the War of 1812." With such initial indifference to the British cause, how did England ultimately successfully defend the colony?

Women played a role in the Upper Canadian theatre of war, the most famous being Laura Secord. But has the role of Secord been exaggerated in later accounts? In her essay, "'Of Slender Frame and Delicate Appearance': The Placing of Laura Secord in the Narratives of Canadian Loyalist History," Cecilia Morgan examines Secord's image in the literature of the late 19th and early 20th centuries. She concludes that Canadian historians transformed her into a larger-than-life figure by focusing on her loyalty and patriotism.

Although a growing literature now exists on Upper Canada, the best introductory text remains Gerald M. Craig's *Upper Canada: The Formative Years, 1784–1841* (Toronto: McClelland and Stewart, 1963). Important sources on the Loyalists who settled in the new colony include Bruce Wilson, *As She Began: An Illustrated Introduction to Loyalist Ontario* (Toronto: Dundurn Press, 1981); James J. Talman, ed., *Loyalist Narratives from Upper Canada* (Toronto: Champlain Society, 1946); and Janice Potter-MacKinnon, *While the Women Only Wept: Loyalist Refugee Women in Eastern Ontario* (Montreal/Kingston: McGill-Queen's University Press, 1993). Mrs. Simcoe's diary is an invaluable primary text for the early social history of the province; John Ross Robertson's fully annotated edition of the diary appeared under the title *The Diary of Mrs. John Graves Simcoe, Wife of the First Lieutenant-Governor of the Province of Upper Canada, 1792–6* (Toronto: Coles Publishing, 1973 [1911]). Mary Quayle Innis edited an abridged version, entitled *Mrs. Simcoe's Diary* (Toronto: Macmillan, 1965).

Currently, a great deal is being published on the economic and political history of Upper Canada. Economic issues are introduced in Chapter 6 ("Upper Canada") of Kenneth Norrie and Douglas Owram's *A History of the Canadian Economy*, 2nd ed. (Toronto: Harcourt Brace, 1996), pp. 115–45, and, in greater depth, in Douglas McCalla's "The 'Loyalist' Economy of Upper Canada," *Histoire Sociale/Social History* 16, 32 (November 1983): 279–304, as well as in his *Planting the Province: The Economic History of Upper Canada, 1784–1870*, Ontario Historical Studies Series (Toronto: University of Toronto Press, 1993). For the early history of the ideology of Upper Canada politics, see Jane Errington, *The Lion, the Eagle and Upper Canada: A Developing Colonial Ideology* (Montreal/Kingston: McGill-Queen's University Press, 1987), and David Mills, *The Idea of Loyalty in Upper Canada, 1784–1850* (Montreal/Kingston: McGill-Queen's University Press, 1988).

For background on the response of the First Nations in Upper Canada to the war of 1812, consult Charles M. Johnston, ed., *The Valley of the Six Nations: A Collection of Documents on the Indian Lands of the Grand River* (Toronto: Champlain Society, 1964); Peter Schmaltz, *The Ojibwa of Southern Ontario* (Toronto: University of Toronto Press, 1991); Janet Chute, *The Legacy of Shingwakanse: A Century of Native Leadership* (Toronto: University of Toronto Press, 1998); and Donald B. Smith, *Sacred Feathers: The Reverend Peter Jones (Kahkewaquonaby) and the Mississauga Indians* (Toronto: University of Toronto Press, 1987). The First Nations played a vital role in defending Upper Canada for the British in the war of 1812. Daniel G. Hill's *The Freedom-Seekers: Blacks in Early Canada* (Agincourt, ON: Book Society of Canada, 1981) is a popular summary of the history of African Canadians in Upper Canada and in British North America in general.

Pierre Berton has written two popular accounts of the War of 1812: *The Invasion of Canada, 1812–1813* (Toronto: McClelland and Stewart, 1980), and *Flames across the Border, 1813–1814* (Toronto: McClelland and Stewart, 1981). A more recent study is Wesley B. Turner's *The War of 1812: The War That Both Sides Won* (2nd ed., Toronto: Dundurn Press, 2000). A more detailed treatment is Victor Suthren, *The War of 1812* (Toronto: McClelland and Stewart, 1999). George F.G. Stanley's *The War of 1812: Land Operations* (Toronto: Macmillan, 1983) provides the best review of the war's military history. In *The Iroquois in the War of 1812* (Toronto: University of Toronto Press, 1998), Carl Benn looks at the Six Nations' involvement. The best biography of one of the greatest First Nations leaders of all times is John Sugden's *Tecumseh: A Life* (New York: Henry Holt and Company, 1997). George Sheppard examines the social fabric of Upper Canadian society at the time of the War of 1812 in *Plunder, Profit and Paroles: A Social History of the War of 1812 in Upper Canada* (Montreal/Kingston: McGill-Queen's University Press, 1994). David S. Heidler and Jeanne T. Heidler have edited *Encyclopedia of the War of 1812* (Santa Barbara, CA: ABC-CLIO, 1997).

Alison Prentice et al., *Canadian Women: A History*, 2nd ed. (Toronto: Harcourt Brace, 1996) examines changes in the lives of British North American women in the late 18th and early 19th centuries. See as well Jane Errington, *Wives and Mothers, School Mistresses and Scullery Maids: Working Women in Upper Canada, 1790–1840* (Montreal/Kingston: McGill-Queen's University Press, 1995); and Cecilia Morgan, *Public Men and Virtuous Women: The Gendered Languages of Religion and Politics in Upper Canada, 1791–1850* (Toronto: University of Toronto Press, 1996). Colin M. Coates and Cecilia Morgan's *Heroines and History: Madeline de Verchères and Laura Secord* (Toronto: University of Toronto Press, 2001) compares the images of these two "heroines" in early Canadian historical writing.

WEBLINKS

The War of 1812
http://www.archives.gov.on.ca/english/exhibits/1812/index.html

A virtual exhibit on the War of 1812 by the Government of Ontario. Contains details on participants, battlegrounds, and many digitized primary source documents.

The Treaty of Ghent
http://www.dfait-maeci.gc.ca/department/history/keydocs/keydocs_details-en.asp?intDocumentId=3

The 1814 peace Treaty of Ghent, which ended the War of 1812 between Great Britain and the United States.

Context of the War of 1812
http://www.galafilm.com/1812/e/index.html

This website contains many documents and images concerning the participants in the War of 1812.

Peace and Conflict: The War of 1812
http://www.histori.ca/peace/page.do?pageID=336

Journal entries, speeches, images, and maps relating to the participants in the War of 1812.

War of 1812 Articles
http://www.warof1812.ca/1812art.htm

Many articles containing excerpts from journals and letters of participants in the War of 1812. The site also contains battle reports and biographies.

Negotiations
http://www.galafilm.com/1812/e/people/iroq_negos.html

The account of John Norton, or Teyoninhokarawen, of negotiations between Iroquois in both Canada and the United States during, and after, the War of 1812. Norton's full account is available in the Champlain Society database.

Article Nine

Reluctant Warriors: British North Americans and the War of 1812

E. Jane Errington

Come all ye bold Canadians,
I'd have you lend an ear,
Unto a short ditty
Which will your spirits cheer.
Concerning an engagement
We had at Detroit town,
The pride of those Yankee boys,
So bravely we took down.[1]

So began one of the few Canadian ballads from the War of 1812. It tells the story of the glorious Canadian victory at Detroit, of how "our brave commander, Sir Isaac Brock" together with a handful of eager, undaunted Canadian boys forced the Yankees to surrender.

Those Yankee hearts began to ache,
Their blood it did run cold,
To see us marching forward
So courageous and so bold.
Their general sent a flag to us,
For quarter he did call,
Saying "Stay your hand, brave British boys,"
"I fear you'll slay us all."

Source: E. Jane Errington, "Reluctant Warriors: British North Americans and the War of 1812," in *The Sixty Years' War for the Great Lakes, 1754–1814*, ed. David Curtis Skaggs and Larry L. Nelson (East Lansing: Michigan State University Press, 2001): 325–336.

The ballad, like many others of its kind, extolled the glorious victory of a heroic and patriotic people. And the sentiments expressed in this particular campfire song have become, if only unconsciously, part of the Canadian legacy of the War of 1812. In popular culture, the War of 1812 is often characterized as the first real test of the new peoples and of their earlier decision to remain loyal to the Empire and the British King during the first American civil war, or what is more commonly termed the Revolution. In 1812, the story goes, Canadians, and particularly Upper Canadians, gallantly fought for their homes, their communities, their colony, and their King. They fought for peace, and to preserve a way of life that was inherently more "civilized" than that of the enemy from the south. The Canadian victory, first at Detroit and then of the war itself, both confirmed the justness of their cause and illustrated that Upper Canadians were willing and eager combatants who had remained true to their loyalist heritage.

But as we know, how governments and popular culture remember and extol a conflict often bears little resemblance to the nature of the war itself or the attitudes of its participants. In the case in point here, all that fought in the War of 1812 claimed and continue to claim victory. For U.S. songwriters, veterans and their families, politicians, and even historians, the War of 1812 was the second War of Independence. It confirmed the righteousness of the Revolution and illustrated the ability of the new republic and its people to defend themselves against all odds. For Upper Canadians in 1815 and throughout the nineteenth and into the early twentieth centuries, the war represented the beginning of nationhood. It illustrated the strength of a nation in arms and the innate patriotism and loyalty of the Canadian people. And for the British of course, the War of 1812, if ever mentioned, was a minor, if regrettable, campaign in their contest with Napoleon.

Yet when Stephen Miles, editor of the Kingston *Gazette*, reported in late June 1812 that the United States and Great Britain and, thus, its British colonies in North America were now officially at war, his readers, although not particularly surprised, were nonetheless dismayed.[2] Since before the turn of the century, many Upper Canadians had lived in fear that they would be forced to take up arms against friends, family, and neighbors to the south. And, for twenty years, local residents had done all they could to avoid what most considered would be an "unnatural" conflict. But it had been to no avail. Miles' announcement, and General Isaac Brock's call to arms and hasty march to Detroit brought an end to years of speculation and trepidation. Upper Canadians in 1812 did not want war. Those who in the post war period came to be characterized as "brave Canadian boys" were, in 1812, very reluctant warriors. Few, if any, were willing, as the ballad related to "go along with Brock . . . without further adieu." Indeed, throughout the three years of war, as had been the case since the colony had been created, colonial leaders lived with the knowledge that some, if not most, Upper Canadians were not only reluctant, but would refuse to fight at all. Even worse it was feared, some would join the invading forces or welcome them with open arms.

The roots of this reluctance, or what one historian has characterized as wide spread indifference, can be traced back to the time before the creation of the colony.[3] The American Revolution, it is frequently asserted, created not one nation but two. In 1783–84, as Americans debated how best to govern themselves, approximately ten thousand former residents of the old thirteen colonies began to make their way north to the British colony of Quebec.[4] This heterogeneous group of "Loyalists" was bitter and felt betrayed. They were the losers in that momentous civil war over the future of their homes; and, harassed and persecuted by neighbors and republican officials, they were now political refugees — forced to leave their homes and most of their possessions and seek asylum, as one loyalist later remembered "in the howling wilderness."[5] For some at least, their flight north across the St. Lawrence or lower Great Lakes was a confirmation of their continued allegiance to the king and to a way of life that ensured order, stability and personal liberty, (not licentiousness as they believed was now being encouraged in the new republic).[6] Yet these British loyalists were, by birth and inclination, also Americans. Although they were still British subjects, "home" was North America; and it was with this land and these people, not with the rolling hills of the British Isles, with whom they identified.

It is therefore not surprising, as one commentator noted, that, soon after the Revolution, "passions mutually subsided" on both sides of the border.[7] In 1792, local officials of the newly formed colony of Upper Canada invited American settlers to cross the border and take up land and establish businesses. With reportedly little or no "attachment to the King of Great Britain" or consciousness of the international border, thousands of restless pioneers came north, as many of their neighbors went west, to find land, to find employment, and generally to grasp new opportunities for themselves and their children.[8] By 1810, it is estimated that "loyalist element was scarcely noticeable amongst the diversity of people" who had flooded into the colony after about 1792.[9] Just before the War of 1812, Upper Canada was, demographically at least, an American colony.[10]

The geographic realities, which facilitated the movement of American pioneer farmers north, also encouraged Upper Canadians to look and travel south. Although poor and in many cases nonexistent roads and other means of communication isolated individual Upper Canadian communities from each other, the St. Lawrence River and the lower Great Lakes provided easy access north and south. Until well into the 1830s, residents of New York and the New England states were Upper Canadians' closest and most accessible neighbors. Visitors, mail, news, and information from Europe, from the United States, and even from the most eastern sections of British North America traveled fastest and most efficiently to and from Upper Canada by way of New York, Boston, or Philadelphia.[11]

The bonds forged by geography were strengthened in the early years by strong personal and professional ties, north and south. Despite the turmoil and, for some loyalists, the legacy of bitterness left by the Revolution, Upper Canadians and Americans "were still interesting objects to each other."[12] For almost all Upper Canadians before the War of 1812, the United States was their former home and remained the home of relatives and friends. A French traveler, La Rochefoucault-Liancourt noted as early as 1795, that though some "American Loyalists . . . still harbour enmity and hatred against their native land and countrymen . . . these sentiments [were] daily decreasing" and were "not shared by the far greater number of emigrants who arrive from the United States, Nova Scotia and New Brunswick."[13] Within a short time, it was reported that "the most social harmony" existed between "gentleman on the American side and those on the British side" of the border.[14] Leading loyalists like Richard Cartwright of Kingston regularly visited their old homes in the United States; merchants, traders, and farmers engaged in lucrative economic relations with associates across the border; Upper Canadians entertained American visitors in their homes; a growing number attended camp meetings and met at quarterly sessions led by itinerant American preachers; some Upper Canadian children went south to school; and a few residents, taking advantage of the regular ferry services, which by 1800 linked Kingston and Niagara and their closest American communities, crossed the border to shop or take a cure.[15] Being a resident of this British colony did not mean that even the most loyal subjects rejected their close association with their old homes. Indeed, throughout the first twenty-five years of colonial development, most Upper Canadians considered themselves part of a North American community, which spanned the border.

Upper Canada was officially and administratively a British colony, however. To gain land and vote, settlers had to swear an oath of allegiance to the British crown and, twice annually, adult men had to muster for militia training. Moreover, there is no question that for colonial leaders, including British office holders sent by London, like Lieutenant Governors Simcoe and Gore and General Sir Isaac Brock, and members of the indigenous elite, like Richard Cartwright of Kingston, allegiance to the Empire and to the principles enshrined in the British Constitution also helped to define who and what they were.

Some historians have suggested that for these men, being Upper Canadian meant being anti-American; and that throughout the first generation of colonial development, these Upper Canadians rejected all things emanating from south of the Great Lakes. Thus, it is implied, Upper Canadians in 1812 were willing and, in fact, eager to defend their place in the Empire. Certainly, many leading Upper Canadians, like the Reverend John Strachan of York, were scornful of the republic and its lack of order and justice. And in 1812, many went out of their way to express their willingness to take up arms in defense of their homes. However, even the most conservative and patriotic Upper Canadians could not and did not try to deny the importance of geography and shared interests with neighbors to the south.

As they began to lay the political and economic foundations of the new British colony, the Upper Canadian elite could not help but be conscious of how similar the colony was to communities south of the frontier. Upper Canadians and Americans, particularly in New York and New England, shared not only a land and people, they also shared many common concerns of settlement and of future development. Most Upper Canadians were pioneer farmers and their daily struggle for survival — clearing the bush, building homes, planting and harvesting — was a re-creation of events being pursued south of the border. As a number of commentators noted, there was little to distinguish the backwoods of Upper Canada from the frontier of the United States.[16] Upper Canadians of all economic and political stripes drew frequently on American models when considering, for example, how to build roads, till the soil, establish banks, or foster local markets. Although Upper Canada was a British province, many consciously acknowledged that the United States had much to offer residents in the new colony.

Even in political affairs, colonial leaders did not reject all things American. Although they feared the insidious influence of republicanism and democracy and often predicted the political disintegration of the United States, men like John Strachan and Richard Cartwright believed that many Americans shared their concerns. In particular, they applauded the Federalists of New England and New York for their stance in support of order against unbridled democracy. And Upper Canadians recognized that, like themselves, the Federalists wanted to maintain and increase commerce and contact across the border. Between 1800 and 1812, and indeed, throughout the years of war, leading Upper Canadians made fine distinctions between those they viewed as "good" American citizens and the policies of the American government; and they were sympathetic to the plight of those Americans who, like themselves, were suffering under the policies of rapacious republicanism.[17]

Thus, for most Upper Canadians, allegiance to Great Britain usually did not automatically conflict with their continuing sense of being part of a North American community. There were times, however, when Upper Canadians were forced to recognize the apparent contradiction of their position. The colony had been created, after all, not by amicable cooperation but out of bitter confrontation between Great Britain and the United States. Moreover, although geographic proximity encouraged a sense of community that spanned the lakes, it also provided the continuing potential for local tensions, as well as the possibility that the Great Lakes–St. Lawrence basin might once again be the theater of armed conflict between the two nations.

Between 1791 and 1812, Upper Canadians worked hard to re-establish and cement amicable relations along what was still a largely unmarked and porous border. Both prudence and personal inclination encouraged this. Most Upper Canadians lived, it must be remembered, within a few miles of the expanding and dynamic republic. More importantly, close personal and economic associations with friends and family members south of the Great Lakes would be harmed and perhaps irrevocably severed if the two governments were at odds.

It was not surprising, therefore, that just before the turn of the century, one settler in Niagara suggested that residents of the area gather together for various sporting events, to supplement the already existing "intercourse of economic, friendship and sociability between the people of the province and those in the neighbouring part of the United States."[18] Upper Canadians applauded when the American garrison showed the colony's flag and played the "British Grenadiers" on the occasion of the king's birthday. "Such acts of civility" should be encouraged, many Upper Canadians believed.[19] Upper Canadians, too, should show "a spirit of mutually liberality, candour and forbearance," for only "by preserving harmony and promoting good neighbourhood" could "friends of both nations . . . respectively increase their national prosperity."[20]

Colonial leaders also pointedly condemned those counterfeiters, smugglers, criminals, and deserting British soldiers who used the border to avoid apprehension. "National difficulties," as one commentator terms it, erupted frequently as a result of "the mutual incursions and acts of jurisdiction and other interferences of the subject of one government within the known and acknowledged limits of the other."[21] Such acts were to be "deprecated" and Upper Canadians were cautioned to avoid "becoming habituated to mutual prejudices, jealousies, reflections, reproaches and all that process of national alienation which had, in the progress of ages, rendered the British and the French so inveterate in their hostility as to call each other natural enemies."[22]

At the same time, it is clear that many Upper Canadians never really recognized that a border existed at all — and they not only traveled back and forth at will, but after 1800 when customs duties were established, regularly avoided paying duties on trade goods. Smuggling seems to have been one of the most lucrative and accepted (if not respectable) means of doing business and it was eagerly supported on both sides of the border.[23] In the summer, "crafts of all sorts and sizes crowded the River St. Lawrence."[24] In the winter, ice conditions permitting, sleighs laden with goods made the journey. One U.S. customs officer at Sackets Harbor reported in 1809, at the height of the Embargo, "all the force I can raise is not sufficient to stop them." The smugglers "appear determined to evade the law at the risk of their lives." Indeed, he concluded, fearfully, "my life and the lives of my deputies are threatened daily; what will be the fate of us God only knows."[25]

Many Upper Canadians and Americans obviously benefited from smuggling; the embargo of 1808 and the War of 1812 only enhanced their profits. For officials on both sides of the border, however, the extensive smuggling threatened to disrupt peaceful relations between their governments. Therefore, some in the colony (a number of whom were undoubtedly losing business to the smugglers) called on Upper Canadians to stop evading the law. In the fall of 1810, for example, residents of Kingston and officials on the south shore of Lake Ontario organized a cooperative effort to apprehend smugglers. "Such instances of the reciprocation of acts of justices and liberality," one contributor to the Kingston *Gazette* remarked with approval, "were much more conducive to mutual prosperity than a state of legislative counteraction and hostility."[26] Everyone, it was believed, had a responsibility to encourage "the preservation of peace" between Upper Canada and the United States.[27]

The periodic problems that erupted along the border were, for the most part, local concerns. And various individual attempts to encourage civility and goodwill in the years before the War of 1812 seemed to be successful. Yet, it was always evident that harmony on the Great Lakes frontier did not ensure peace between the governments of the United States and Great Britain. For, although open warfare between Great Britain and the United States had ended in 1784, the Treaty of Paris had not stopped the two nations from jockeying for position on the western frontier.

In July 1794, Upper Canadians read excerpts from an Albany paper that the United States intended a "total conquest" of the west and "a reduction of the interior posts of the Upper Provinces."[28] First, American officials began to stop all boats and goods from entering Upper Canada from the south. Then, General "Mad" Anthony Wayne and a contingent of troops began to advance on British forts inside the young republic. What had sparked these actions was the U.S. government's belief that British officials were actively encouraging the Native nations of the northwest to raid American frontier settlements. Moreover, Great Britain was refusing to relinquish forts in the west. Upper Canadians watched apprehensively as imperial officials responded and most expected that war would be declared immediately. It was with considerable relief that leading colonists learned of the success of John Jay's mission to London.[29]

It was soon evident that the resolution of this controversy in 1795 did not really resolve the differences between the two governments. Between 1796 and 1800, Upper Canadians watched with interest and some concern as American neutrality was buffeted by the combined pressure of war in Europe and internal political divisions. Thomas Jefferson's victory in 1800 brought renewed fears that the United States would join France in its campaign against Great Britain. And, although those fears appeared for a time to be unfounded, the *Chesapeake* Affair in 1807 threatened once again to bring war to the Great Lakes frontier. Despite calls by Upper Canadians and Federalists in the United States for restraint, the American government sounded the alarm and made preparations for war. Upper Canadian leaders had little alternative but to call the colony to arms.

The most pressing concern of colonial leaders in 1807 and 1808, as it would be in 1812, was that the majority of Upper Canadians would be at best, reluctant combatants. Indeed, it was feared that many might refuse to fight at all. Most residents had no political or emotional attachment to the king or the British Empire. Moreover, most had only recently arrived from the United States.

Colonial leaders did what they could to cope with the situation. In a speech to the local militia in December 1807, Richard Cartwright explained to assembled men that it was the American government, and the Republicans, "that blind and misguided party," who were threatening to plunge the continent into war. The "most enlightened and patriotic citizens" of the United States realized that war would harm American commerce and "ultimately the existence of their independence." By defending themselves, Cartwright intimated, Upper Canadians were defending not only their homes, but also the interests of many of their friends and neighbors in the United States. As the official government gazette, the *Upper Canada Gazette* reported, "one congressman had even written to the present that 'we are doing no good. I fear we are about to plunge the nation into the most dreadful calamities, unnecessarily and wantonly.'"[30]

For the next four years, the Upper Canadian elites waged a pointed and increasingly assertive propaganda campaign to try to convince their readers that, if and when war broke out, settlers could and should defend their new homes against the forces of tyranny (and republicanism). By doing so, it was explicitly stated, they would be remaining true to their old homes and beliefs. Most Upper Canadians appear to have ignored such entreaties. And although international tensions continued to threaten local peace, residents continued to move back and forth across the border, and till their fields and trade.

Even in January and February 1812, when General Isaac Brock, the president of the colony, warned that although "we wish and hope for peace" war was probably at no great distance and "it was our duty to be prepared"[31] most turned a deaf ear. The members of the House of Assembly refused to pass measures to require militiamen to forswear allegiance to any foreign country; and Brock's request to suspend the writ of habeas corpus was denied. As George Sheppard has commented in his groundbreaking work, *Plunder, Profits and Paroles*, "The colonists were firm in their belief that they were not responsible for the deteriorating relationship between Britain and the United States."[32] And one colonist suggested, in a letter in a provincial newspaper that "if your [the United States] quarrel is with Britain, go and avenge yourselves on her own shores."[33]

Colonial leaders and Imperial officials were, not surprisingly, alarmed. For the next four months, the propaganda campaign to convince Upper Canadians to take up arms if need be, intensified. But, when editor Stephen Miles of Kingston announced that war had been declared in June 1812, life continued as usual for most Upper Canadians; individuals, goods, and news continued to flow across the border. More to the point, most settlers resisted calls to muster and train. Even when Brock instituted changes to the Militia Act that granted volunteers exemptions from statute labor, jury duty and personal arrest for small debts, militia quotas were rarely met. It is clear in June and July 1812, that most Upper Canadians were still reluctant to go to war. And Brock and others feared that "the great mass of people" would either flee back to their old homes or "join the American government" and work for the overthrow of the British in North America.[34]

Even once actual fighting began, the war seemed to have little direct impact on the lives of most Upper Canadians. It was only in the western portions of the colony that residents suffered property damage, men were injured and died of their wounds or disease, and families were left bereft. And although many of the militiamen in the Niagara region called out in late June and early July seemed to be willing to defend their own homes and businesses, the incident of desertion was high. Moreover, Brock predicted that "most would leave anyway once the harvest began."[35] As George Sheppard has observed, colonists' indifference to the war was striking and it was not restricted to only the "recent arrivals from the United States."[36] Both Loyalists and late Loyalists, farmers, craftsmen, and politicians tried to avoid service.

As the war dragged on, many Upper Canadians even began to resist providing supplies and support to the British cause. Although there is no question that some Upper Canadians directly benefited from the war, many others did not. Militia duty took men away from the fields and their shops; the prices of goods and services increased dramatically; and the British forces often confiscated livestock, grain and other goods when they could not purchase them. In parts of the province, Upper Canadians watched, seemingly helpless, as their farms were razed to the ground by enemy forces; war widows were often frustrated when they turned to colonial officials for financial assistance.

For most Upper Canadians, the actual conflict did little to break down their reluctance to take up arms. And for many, being thrust into the maelstrom of battle only served to foster a resentment of their own government as well as that of the enemy. As Sheppard has concluded, "while a few colonists assisted the British forces, the majority resorted to desertion or paroles to avoid serving."[37]

> Come all ye bold Canadians,
> Enlisted in the cause,
> To defend your country,
> And to maintain your laws,
> Being all united,
> This is the song we'll sing;
> Success unto Great Britain,
> And God save the King.

It seems more than questionable that these words were truly sung by Canadians during the first months of the War of 1812. In June and July 1812, as had been the case for the previous twenty-five or so years, Upper Canadians did all they could to avoid war. Geography, personal incli-nation, commerce, and, to some degree, politics all encouraged these British colonists to consider themselves part of a community, which spanned the Great Lakes and the St. Lawrence basin. To find that, despite all their best efforts, war was being thrust upon them, was daunting and many, no doubt, resented this intrusion onto their lives. It is not surprising that Upper Canadians were reluctant warriors in 1812. It was only after the war was over and that memory had dimmed that these reluctant warriors could become "bold Canadians."

NOTES

1. "The Bold Canadian: A Ballad of the War of 1812," taken from Morris Zaslow, ed., *The Defended Border* (Toronto: Macmillan Co. of Canada, 1964), 303–4.
2. Kingston *Gazette*, 30 June 1812, taken from the *Albany Gazette*. Miles began, "it is pretty clearly ascertained that war with the United States is no longer to be avoided."
3. George Sheppard, *Plunder, Profits and Paroles: A Social History of the War of 1812 in Upper Canada* (Montreal and Kingston: McGill–Queen's University Press, 1994).
4. Certainly, estimates vary from 6,000 to 10,000.
5. [Richard Cartwright], *Letters from an American Loyalist in Upper-Canada*, Letter X, (Halifax, Nova Scotia: 1810).
6. See among others, Janice Potter, *The Liberty We Seek: Loyalist Ideology in Colonial New York and Massachusetts* (Cambridge, Mass: Harvard University Press, 1983) for a detailed discussion of loyalist ideology.
7. Francóis-Aléxandre-Fréderic, duc de La Rochefoucault-Liancourt, *Travels in Canada* (1795; Reprint, Toronto: William Renwick Riddell, 1917), 44.
8. Ibid., 36. See also John Maud, *Visit to the Falls of Niagara in 1800* (London: Longmans, Rees, Orme, Brown and Green, 1826), 60.
9. Michael Smith, *A Geographical View of British Possessions in North America* (Philadelphia: P. Mauro, 1813), 82.
10. See among others, Smith, *A Geographical View*, 61, for estimates of population in the colony in 1810.
11. See Stephen Roberts, "Imperial Policy, Provincial Administration and Defences of Canada" (Ph.D. thesis, Oxford University, 1975); John Lambert, *Travels Through Canada and the United States* (London: C. Cradock and W. Joy, 1814); John Melish, *Travels Through the United States of America* (Belfast: Jos. Smyth, 1818).
12. Robert Gourlay, *General Introduction to Statistical Account of Upper Canada* (London: Simpkin and Marshall, 1822), 115.
13. Ibid., 74.
14. D'Arcy Boulton, *A Sketch of His Majesty's Province of Upper Canada* (London, 1805; Reprint, Toronto: Baxter, 1961), 32.
15. See travelers' accounts already cited and numerous references in the local papers, including *Upper Canada Gazette*, 19 April 1797; 25 September 1817; 10 February 1820; 23 June 1825. It is known that Richard Cartwright, a prominent resident of Kingston, regularly made trips south after 1800. See Cartwright, see among others, Smith, *A Geographical View*, 61, for estimates of population in the colony in 1810. Papers, Q.U.A. So too did Joel Stone, Solomon Jones Papers, Q.U.A. and Robert Hamilton (Bruce Wilson, *The Enterprises of Robert Hamilton* [Ottawa: Carleton University Press, 1984]) to name only a few.
16. Ralph Brown, *Mirror for Americans* (New York: American Geographical Society, 1903) and travel accounts previously noted.
17. I have developed these ideas extensively in *The Lion, The Eagle and Upper Canada: A Developing Colonial Ideology* (Kingston and Montreal: McGill–Queen's University Press, 1987, 1995).
18. *Upper Canada Gazette*, 31 May 1799.
19. Ibid., 27 January 1798.
20. Kingston *Gazette*, 25 September 1810.
21. Ibid., 11 October 1810.
22. Ibid., 25 September 1810.
23. In addition to numerous references in the local newspapers, for the most part condemning the practice, and in travel accounts, governments on both sides of the border were forced to try to cope with the issue.

See A.L. Burt, *The United States, Great Britain and British North America* (New York: Russell and Russell, 1961); Alexander C. Flick, ed., *The History of the State of New York*, 10 vols. (New York: Columbia University Press, 1933–37).

24. Matilda Ridout, Lady Edgar, *General Brock* (Toronto: Oxford University Press, 1926), 109.
25. Report of Hart Massey, 14 March 1809, quoted in Flick, *The History of the State of New York*, 5:199.
26. Kingston *Gazette*, 2 October 1810; 6 November 1810.
27. Ibid., 6 November 1810; 11 October 1810.
28. *Upper Canada Gazette*, 10 July 1794.
29. See Burt, *The United States*, for discussion of the rising tensions before the war; and Errington, *Lion and the Eagle*, chapter 4 for a more complete discussion of Upper Canadian reaction to this.
30. *Upper Canada Gazette*, 15 October 1808.
31. Reported in the Kingston *Gazette*, 28 January 1812.
32. Sheppard, *Plunder*, 37.
33. Quoted in ibid., 36.
34. Melish, *Travels*, 485. See also discussion in Errington, *Lion and the Eagle*, chapter 4, and Sheppard, *Plunder*.
35. Sheppard, *Plunder*, 47.
36. Ibid., 74.
37. Ibid., 98.

Article Ten

"Of Slender Frame and Delicate Appearance": The Placing of Laura Secord in the Narratives of Canadian Loyalist History

Cecilia Morgan

To most present-day Canadians, Laura Secord is best known as the figurehead of a candy company, her image that of a young, attractive woman wearing a low-cut ruffled white gown.[1] Some may even harbour a vague memory from their high-school courses in Canadian history of her walk in 1813 from Queenston to Beaver Dams, to warn British troops of an impending American attack. From the mid-nineteenth century, the story of that walk has been told by a number of Canadian historians of the War of 1812 in Upper Canada. Its military implications in assisting the British during the War of 1812 have been the subject of some rather heated debate. Did Laura Secord actually make a valuable contribution to the war? Did her news arrive in time and was it acted upon? However, another and as yet little-discussed issue is the way in which late-nineteenth- and early-twentieth-century historians attempted to transform Secord into a heroine, a symbol of female loyalty and patriotism in this period's narratives of Loyalist history.

As historian Benedict Anderson argues, the formation of modern national identities has involved more than the delineation of geographically defined boundaries and narrow political definitions of citizenship. Nations, Anderson tells us, are "imagined political communities," created by their citizens through a number of political and cultural institutions and practices: shared languages, newspapers, museums, and the census. Furthermore, as Anderson (and

Source: Cecilia Morgan, "'Of Slender Frame and Delicate Appearance': The Placing of Laura Secord in the Narratives of Canadian Loyalist History," *Journal of the Canadian Historical Association*, New Series, vol. 5 (1994): 195–212.

others) have emphasized, it is also within narratives of "the nation's" history that these imagined communities are formed and national identities are created.[2] To the promoters of late-nineteenth-century Canadian nationalism and imperialism, such narratives were of critical importance in understanding Canada's link to Britain and British political, social, and cultural traditions. As Carl Berger argues in *The Sense of Power*, "history in its broadest cultural sense was the medium in which [these traditions were] expressed and history was the final and ultimate argument for imperial unity."[3] Those who wrote these historical narratives also worked diligently to create national heroes who symbolized loyalty and the preservation of the imperial link. Historians interested in early-nineteenth-century Ontario history found that a cast of such figures lay conveniently close to hand: Major-General Sir Isaac Brock and the Upper Canadian militia, the colony's saviours during the American invasion of 1812.

But Brock and the militia were not the only significant figures to be commemorated and celebrated, for it was during this period that Laura Secord became one of the most significant female symbols of Canadian nationalism. As feminist historians have pointed out, the formation of imagined national communities has been frequently, if not inevitably, differentiated by gender. While Anderson's work has been extremely influential on historian's understanding of national identities, he fails to recognize "that women and men may imagine such communities, identify with nationalist movements, and participate in state formations in very different ways."[4] And, in their use of iconography, monuments, or written narratives of the nation's history, proponents of nationalism have frequently relied on gender-specific symbols and imagery.[5] Yet in these textual and visual representations of nationalities, gender as an analytic category has also varied according to its context and has been influenced by other categories and relationships, particularly those of race, class, religion, and sexuality. By looking at the process whereby Secord became a national heroine and at the narratives that were written about Secord's walk, we can further our understanding of the links between gender, race, and imperialism in late-nineteenth-century Canadian nationalism and feminism.[6]

Secord became part of the narratives of Loyalist self-sacrifice and duty to country and Crown primarily — although not solely — because of the attempts of women historians and writers who, from the 1880s on, strove to incorporate women into Canadian history and to dislodge the masculine emphasis of the nineteenth-century Loyalist myths of suffering and sacrifice. Women such as Sarah Curzon, the feminist writer, historian, and temperance advocate, insisted that white Canadian women, past and present, had something of value to offer the nation and empire and that their contribution as women to the record of Canadian history be acknowledged and valued. Secord, she (and others like her) argued, was not outside the narrative of Canadian history and she (and other women) therefore had a place in shaping the "imagined communities" of Canadian nationalist and imperialist discourse. Unlike that of other, potentially unruly and disruptive, women in Canadian history, Laura Secord's image could be more easily domesticated to accord with late-Victorian notions of white, middle-class femininity.[7] It could also be moulded by feminists to argue for a greater recognition of the importance of such femininity to Canadian society. Moreover, Laura Secord was not an isolated figure. Ranged behind and about her was a whole gallery of women in Canadian history, from Madeleine de Verchères of New France to the anonymous, archetypal pioneer woman of the backwoods of Upper Canada; women, these "amateur" historians insisted, who were historical figures as worthy of study as their male contemporaries.[8]

Before discussing the writing of Laura Secord into Loyalist history, however, it is crucial to outline the gendered nature of the nineteenth-century narratives of the War of 1812. Historians who have studied Upper Canadian politics have duly noted that assertions of loyalty and sacrifice during the war became the basis for many claims on the Upper Canadian state, in the competition for land and patronage appointments and for compensation for war losses.[9] Donald

Akenson, for example, has pointed to the way in which claims to loyal duty during the war were used in attempts to justify the access of some residents to certain material benefits. Such claims were also made to legitimate the exclusion of others from such rewards.[10] Yet what has not been included in these historians' analysis of sacrifice in the war as a bargaining chip in the struggle for material gains in Upper Canada is the gendered nature of the narratives that were used. In Upper Canadians' commemorations of the War of 1812, the important sacrifices for Country and monarch were made by Upper Canadian men, frequently in their capacity as members of the militia who risked life and limb to protect women and children, homes and hearths, from the brutal rampages of hordes of bloodthirsty Americans. During the war, and in its aftermath, women's contributions to the defence of the colony were either downplayed or ignored, in favour of the image of the helpless Upper Canadian wife and mother who entrusted her own and her children's safety to the gallant militia and British troops.[11]

Personifying the whole, of course, was the masculine figure of Isaac Brock, the British commander who made the ultimate sacrifice for the colony when he died at the Battle at Queenston Heights in 1812. Brock provided those who shaped the history of the war with a dualistic image of nationalism, one that managed to celebrate both Upper Canadian identity and colonial loyalty to Britain. He was also a Christ-like figure, a man who had given both his troops and the colony beneficent paternal guidance and wisdom but who had not spared himself from the physical dangers of war — physical dangers that really only threatened men in the military. Those who contributed to the glorification of Brock claimed that he had provided an invaluable means whereby the colonists might resist the enemy's encroachments. Brock had inspired Upper Canadian men, who might emulate his deed of manly patriotism, and he had reassured Upper Canadian women that, come what may, they could look to their husbands, fathers, sons, and brothers for protection.[12]

This kind of narrative, which emphasized masculine suffering, sacrifice, and achievements, was not unique to that of the War of 1812. As Janice Potter-MacKinnon argues, the history of Upper Canadian Loyalism focused on male military service and the political identification of male Loyalists with the British Crown and constitution:

> Well into the twentieth century, loyalty was a male concept in that it was associated with political decision-making — a sphere from which women were excluded. The same can be said of the idea that the Loyalists bequeathed conservative values and British institutions to later generations of Canadians: women have had no role in fashioning political values and institutions. The notion that the Loyalists were the founders of a nation had obvious and unequivocal gender implications. The amateur historian William Caniff was right when he equated the "founders" with the "fathers."[13]

Admittedly there was no automatic and essential connection between military activities and masculinity in Canadian history for, as Colin Coates has pointed out, the woman warrior tradition was not unknown to nineteenth-century Canada.[14] But specific female images (or images of femininity in general) as symbols of loyalty and patriotism in Upper Canada are almost completely lacking in the discourses of the period, and they display a general reluctance to admit that women could have contributed to the war effort as civilians.[15] This silence about women and the feminine — except as helpless victims to which the masculine bravery of Upper Canadian men was inextricably linked — was quite the opposite of the discourses of the French Revolution, with their glorification of Marianne; the American Patriot's figure of the republican mother; or even the more conservative use of the British figure of Britannia.[16]

The earliest efforts to call attention to Secord's contribution to the war were made by her husband James, by her son, and by Laura herself. In a petition written February 25, 1820, and addressed to Lieutenant Governor Sir Peregrine Maitland, James Secord requested a licence to

quarry stone in the Queenston military reserve. After mentioning his own wartime service —
he had served as a captain in the militia — his wounds, and the plundering of his home by
American troops, Secord claimed that "his wife embraced an opportunity of rendering some
service, at the risk of her own life, in going thru the Enemies' Lines to communicate information to a Detachment of His Majesty's Troops at the Beaver Dam in the month of June 1813."[17]
A second, similar petition was turned down in 1827 but Maitland did propose that Laura apply
for the job of looking after Brock's monument. It is not clear whether Maitland was aware of
the gendered and nationalist symbolism of a Canadian woman caretaking the memory of a
British general; he did, however, have "a favourable opinion of the character and claims of
Mr. Secord and his wife."[18] However, Maitland's successor, Sir John Colborne, was apparently
not as well-disposed toward the family and the job went to Theresa Nichol, the widow of
militia Colonel Robert Nichol.[19]

When James died in 1841, Laura submitted two petitions to Governor Sydenham: one that
asked that her son be given his father's post as customs' collector and another that asked for a
pension. Both cited her poverty, her lack of support since her husband's death, and her need to
support her daughters and grandchildren. While her petitions used the language of female
dependency noted by Potter-MacKinnon in Loyalist women's submissions, they also featured
her service to her country in 1813 and her new position as the head of a household.[20] Her son
Charles's article, published in an 1845 edition of the Anglican paper, *The Church*, publicized
her walk, calling attention to his mother's service to her country and the British Crown.[21]
Eight years later Laura Secord wrote her own account of her trek to warn the British Lieutenant
James Fitzgibbon, in a piece that appeared in the *Anglo American Magazine* as part of a larger
narrative of the war. While this article would be used and cited by others from the 1880s on,
it was written in a straightforward manner, with few of the rhetorical flourishes or personal
details that would characterize later accounts. And, while Secord concluded her story with the
observation that she now wondered "how I could have gone through so much fatigue, with the
fortitude to accomplish it," she did not stress her need to overcome physical frailty in reaching
Fitzgibbon.[22]

Secord achieved some success in her campaign for some financial recognition on the part
of the state in 1860, when she presented her story to the Prince of Wales during his tour of
British North America. She was also the only woman whose name appeared on an address presented by the surviving veterans of the Battle of Queenston Heights to the Prince, in a ceremony attended by five hundred visitors and at which a memorial stone was laid on the site
where Brock fell. Her "patriotic services," claimed the *Niagara Mail* in 1861, were "handsomely
rewarded" by the prince with an award of £100.[23] One of her more recent biographies argues
that the prince "provided the magic touch that transformed the 'widow of the late James
Secord' into the heroine, Laura Secord."[24]

However, Secord did not become a heroine overnight. Her own efforts to draw attention
to the service she had rendered to her country should not be seen as attempts to create a cult
for herself, but rather as part of the Upper Canadian patronage game, in which loyal service to
Crown and country was the way to obtain material rewards.[25] Furthermore, she died in 1868,
almost twenty years before her popularity began to spread. Still, references to Secord had begun
to appear in a few mid-nineteenth-century accounts of the War of 1812. For example, the
American historian Benson J. Lossing's *The Pictorial Field-Book of the War of 1812* devoted a
page to Secord and the Battle of Beaver Dams. The page's caption read "British Troops saved
by a Heroine," and Laura's own written account was the voice that supplied Lossing with his
information.[26] The Canadian historian and government official, William F. Coffin, elaborated
on her story by adding the cow — which, he claimed, she had milked in order to convince the
American sentry to let her pass. While some regard Coffin's account as yet another example of

a romantically inclined nineteenth-century historian playing fast and loose with the facts, his placing of Secord in a context of pioneer domesticity foreshadowed subsequent stories appearing two decades later.[27] Secord thus was not rescued from complete obscurity by Curzon and others in the 1880s and '90s; she was, however, given a much more prominent place in their narratives of the war and Upper Canadian loyalty.

Sarah A. Curzon has become known in Canadian women's history as a British-born suffrage activist and a founding member of the Toronto Women's Literary Society (which would later become the Canadian Woman's Suffrage Association) and the editor of a women's page in the prohibition paper, the *Canada Citizen*. But she was also an avid promoter of Canadian history and was one of the co-founders of the Women's Canadian Historical Society of Toronto (WCHS) in 1885, along with Mary Agnes Fitzgibbon, a granddaughter of Lieutenant James Fitzgibbon. Furthermore, Curzon and Fitzgibbon were supporters of Canada's "imperial connection" to Britain, a link which they believed would benefit Canada both economically and culturally.[28] Emma Currie was another major contributor to the campaign to memorialize Secord. Indeed, her book, *The Story of Laura Secord and Canadian Reminiscences*, was published in 1900 as a fundraiser for a monument to the "heroine" of Upper Canada. Currie lived in St. Catharines, helped found the Woman's Literary Club in that city in 1892, and would later join the Imperial Order of the Daughters of the Empire (IODE). She too was a supporter of the Women's Christian Temperance Union and women's suffrage.[29]

But these women were not alone in their crusade to win recognition for Secord. Other Canadian nationalist writers like Charles Mair, Agnes Maule Machar, and William Kirby praised Secord's bravery in their poetry and prose,[30] while local historical societies and those who purported to be "national" historians, such as Ernest Cruikshank, also published papers that focused on the Battle of Beaver Dams and acknowledged Secord's role in it.[31] Much of their work, as well as that of Curzon and Currie, was part of late-Victorian Canadian imperialist discourse, which perceived the past as the repository of those principles (loyalty to Britain, respect for law and order, and the capacity for democratic government) that would guide the nation into the twentieth century.[32] As Berger has argued, the local history societies that spread in the 1880s and 1890s were part of this "conservative frame of mind" in which loyalism, nationalism, and history were inextricably linked.[33]

Tributes in ink comprised the bulk of this material but they were not the only efforts to memoralize Secord. As Currie's book indicates, printed material might be used to raise funds and spread awareness in order to create more long-lasting, substantive reminders, such as monuments and statues. On June 6, 1887, W. Fenwick, a grammar school principal in Drummondville, wrote to the *Toronto World and Mail* asking for better care for the Lundy's Lane graveyard, a national monument to be erected to honour those who had died there, and a separate monument to Laura Secord. Curzon joined in a letter-writing campaign, calling for the women of Canada to take up the matter, and petitions were presented to the Ontario legislature. When these were unsuccessful, the Lundy's Lane and Ontario Historical Societies mounted fundraising drives for the monument, sending out circulars asking Canadian women and children to contribute 10¢ and 1¢ respectively to the cause.[34] A competition for the sculpture was held and won by a Miss Mildred Peel, an artist and sculptor who also would paint the portrait of Secord hung in 1905 in the Ontario legislature.[35] After fourteen years of campaigning, the monument was unveiled June 22, 1901, at Lundy's Lane. In 1911, the Women's Institute of Queenston and St. David's felt that the village of Queenston (site of the Secord home during the War of 1812) had not done enough to honour Secord's memory and built a Memorial Hall as part of Laura Secord school. The gesture that ensconced her name in popular culture came in 1913, when Frank O'Connor chose Secord as the emblem for his new chain of candy stores.[36]

While it was not suggested that celebrating Secord's contribution was the sole responsibility of Canadian womanhood, many aspects of this campaign were shaped by deeply gendered notions and assumptions about both past and present. The idea that women might have a special interest in supporting the subscription drive, for example, or petitioning the legislature, linked perceptions of both womanhood and nationalism, drawing on the underlying assumptions of self-sacrifice and unselfishness that lay at the heart of both identities.[37] Groups such as the WCHS, with their "unselfish patriotism," were exactly what the country needed, Kirby told Mary Agnes Fitzgibbon upon being made an honorary member of the society, adding "let the women be right and the country will be might!"[38] Moreover, while male writers and historians certainly expressed an interest in Secord, it is important not to overlook the significance of the participation of Anglo-Celtic, middle- and upper-middle-class women in the writing of Canadian history, a task they frequently undertook as members of local historical societies. Such women scrutinized historical records in order to find their foremothers (in both the literal and metaphorical sense).[39] However, they also were fascinated with the entire "pioneer" period of Canadian history, both French and English, and with both male and female figures in this context. For the most part, women members of historical societies researched and presented papers on as many generals and male explorers as they did "heroines."[40]

There was, however, a difference in their treatment of the latter. They insisted that Canadian women's contributions to nation building be valued, even though they had not achieved the fame and recognition of their male counterparts. To be sure, they did not offer alternative narratives of early Canadian history and tended to place political and military developments at its centre. Nevertheless, they sought to widen the parameters of male historians' definitions of these events in order to demonstrate their far-reaching effects on all Canadian society. In the meetings of organizations such as Canadian Women's Historical Societies of Toronto and Ottawa, papers were given on topics such as "Early British Canadian Heroines" or "Reminiscences" of pioneer women.[41] Women such as Harriet Prudis, who was active in the London and Middlesex Historical Society during this period, believed that while the history of the pioneer women of the London area

> records no daring deed . . . nor historic tramp, like that of Laura Secord, yet every life is a record of such patient endurance of privations, such brave battling with danger, such a wonderful gift for resourceful adaptability, that the simplest story of the old days must bear, within itself, the sterling elements of romance. While they took no part in the national or political happenings of the day, it may be interesting to us, and to those who come after us, to hear from their own lips how these public events affected their simple lives.[42]

Their efforts were shared by male novelists and historians who not only glorified Secord but also wished to rescue other Canadian women of her era and ilk from obscurity.[43] However, as more than one honorary member of the WCHS told Fitzgibbon, Canadian women should have a special desire to preserve records of their past. According to Mair, "the sacred domestic instincts of Canadian womanhood will not suffer in the least degree, but will rather be refreshed and strengthened" by the Society's "rescuing from destruction the scattered and perishable records of Ontario's old, and, in many respects, romantic home life."[44] The collection of material concerning this latter area, Mair and others felt, should be the special work of Canadian women.[45]

The extent to which this relegation of the "social" realm to women historians sets a precedent for future developments, whereby "romantic home life" was perceived as both the preserve of women and the realm of the trivial and anecdotal is not entirely clear.[46] Certainly it does not appear to have been Mair's intention that these areas be perceived as trivial or unworthy of male historians' attention, while women such as Mary Agnes Fitzgibbon were as eager to research battles and collect military memorabilia as they were concerned with "primitive clothing, food cookery, amusements, and observances of festivals attending births and wedlock or the Charivari."[47] Yet it was probably no coincidence that the first historian to seriously challenge the military value of Secord's walk was the male academic W.S. Wallace, who in 1930 raised a furor among public supporters of Secord with questions concerning the use of historical evidence in documenting her walk.[48]

This, then, was the context in which Laura Secord became an increasingly popular symbol of Canadian patriotism: one of feminism, history, patriotism, and imperialism. While many of these histories were, as Berger has pointed out, local and might seem incredibly parochial in their scope, their authors saw locally based stories as having a much wider emotional and moral significance in the narratives of the nation.[49] Hence, narratives of Secord's contribution to the War of 1812 and to the colonial link with the British Empire were marked by the interplay of locality, nationality, and gender. First, Laura and James Secord's backgrounds were explored and their genealogies traced, in order to place them within the Loyalist tradition of suffering and sacrifice. For those writers who were concerned with strict historical accuracy, such a task was considerably easier for the Secords than for Laura's family, the Ingersolls. James's male ancestors had fought in the Revolutionary War for the British Crown and the many military ranks occupied by the Secord men were duly listed and acclaimed. Moreover, the Secords could claim a history of both allegiance to the British Crown and a desire for the protection of the British constitution; they were descended from Huguenots who arrived in New York from LaRochelle in the late seventeenth century.[50]

But it was not only the Secord men who had served their country and suffered hardships. The Loyalist legacy inherited by both Laura and James had, it was pointed out, been marked by gender differences. As Curzon told her audiences, James Secord's arrival in Canada had been as a three-year-old refugee, part of his mother's "flight through the wilderness, with four other homeless women and many children, to escape the fury of a band of ruffians who called themselves the "sons of Liberty." After enduring frightful hardships for nearly a month, they finally arrived at Fort Niagara almost naked and starving." Curzon went on to comment that these were by no means "uncommon experiences." Frequently, she pointed out, Loyalist men had to flee "for their lives" and leave their women and children behind (as well as their "goods, chattels, estates, and money"). Their loved ones were then left to endure the terrors of the wilderness

> unprotected and unsupported, save by that deep faith in God and love to King and country which, with their personal devotion to their husbands, made of them heroines whose story of unparalleled devotion, hardships patiently borne, motherhood honourably sustained, industry and thrift perseveringly followed, enterprise successfully prosecuted, principle unwaveringly upheld, and tenderness never surpassed, has yet to be written, and whose share in the making of this nation remains to be equally honored with that of the men who bled and fought for its liberties.[51]

Unfortunately for Laura's popularizers, the Ingersoll family did not fit as neatly into the Loyalist tradition. Her father, Thomas, had fought against the British in 1776 and had seen his 1793 land grant cancelled as a result of British efforts to curb large-scale immigration of American settlers into Upper Canada.[52] As J.H. Ingersoll observed in 1926, Laura's inability to claim the United Empire Loyalist pedigree "has been commented upon." However, some historians argued that Thomas Ingersoll came to Upper Canada at Lieutenant Governor Simcoe's request.[53] For those poets and novelists who felt free to create Laura's loyalism in a more imaginative manner, her patriotism was traced to a long-standing childhood attachment to Britain. They insisted that she chose Canada freely and was not forced to come to the country as a refugee.[54] Moreover, despite these historians' fascination with lines of blood and birth, they were equally determined to demonstrate that the former could be transcended by environment and force of personality. The loyal society of Upper Canada and the strength of Laura's own commitment to Britain were important reminders to the Canadian public that a sense of imperial duty could overcome other relationships and flourish in the colonial context.[55]

Accordingly, these historians argued, it should come as no surprise that both Laura and her husband felt obliged to perform their patriotic duty when American officers were overheard planning an attack on the British forces of Lieutenant Fitzgibbon.[56] However, James was still suffering from wounds sustained at the Battle of Queenston Heights and it therefore fell to Laura — over her husband's objections and concern for her safety — to walk the twenty miles from Queenston to warn the British troops at Beaver Dams. (Here the linear chronology of the narratives was frequently interrupted to explain out that Laura had come to his aid after the battle when, finding him badly wounded and in danger of being beaten to death by "common" American soldiers, she had attempted to shield him with her own body from their rifle butts — further evidence that Laura was no stranger to wifely and patriotic duty.[57])

Laura's journey took on wider dimensions and greater significance in the hands of her commemorators. It was no longer just a walk to warn the British but, with its elements of venturing into the unknown, physical sacrifice, and devotion to the British values of order and democracy, came to symbolize the entire "pioneer womanish experience in Canadian history."[58] Leaving the cozy domesticity and safety of her home, the company of her wounded husband and children, Secord had ventured out into the Upper Canadian wilderness with its swamps and underbrush in which threatening creatures, such as rattlesnakes, bears, and wolves, might lurk.[59] And even when Sarah Curzon's 1887 play permitted Laura to deliver several monologues on the loveliness of the June woodland, the tranquillity of the forest was disrupted by the howling of wolves.[60]

But most serious of all, in the majority of accounts, was the threat of the "Indians" she might meet on the way. If Secord's commitment to Canada and Britain had previously been presented in cultural terms, ones that could be encouraged by the colonial tie and that might transcend race, it was at this point that her significance as a symbol of white Canadian womanhood was clearest. While her feminine fragility had been the subject of comment throughout the stories, and while her racial background might have been the underlying subtext for this fragility, it was in the discussions of the threat of Native warriors that her gender became most clearly racialized.[61] Unlike the contemporary racist and cultural stereotypes of threatening Black male sexuality used in American lynching campaigns, however, her fears were not of sexual violence by Native men — at least not explicitly — but of the tactics supposedly used by Native men in warfare, scalping being the most obvious.[62]

To be sure, some stories mentioned that Secord had had to stay clear of open roads and paths "for fear of Indians *and* white marauders" (emphasis mine).[63] But even those who downplayed her fear of a chance encounter with an "Indian" during her journey were scrupulous in their description of her fright upon encountering Mohawks outside the British camp. Secord herself had stated that she had stumbled across the Mohawks' camp and that they had shouted "woman" at her, making her "tremble" and giving her an "awful feeling." It was only with difficulty, she said, that she convinced them to take her to Fitzgibbon.[64] As this meeting with the Natives was retold, they became more menacing and inspired even greater fear in Secord. In these accounts, at this penultimate stage in her journey she stepped on a twig that snapped and startled an Indian encampment. Quite suddenly Secord was surrounded by them, "the chief throws up his tomahawk to strike, regarding the intruder as a spy."[65] In some narratives, he shouted at her "woman! What does woman want!" "Only by her courage in springing to his arm is the woman saved, and an opportunity snatched to assure him of her loyalty."[66]

Moved by pity and admiration, the chief gave her a guide, and at length she reached Fitzgibbon, delivered and verified her message —"and *faints*."[67] Fitzgibbon then went off to fight the Battle of Beaver Dams, armed with the knowledge that Secord had brought him and managed to successfully rout the American forces. In a number of narratives, this victory was frequently achieved by using the threat of unleashed Indian savagery when the Americans were reluctant to surrender.[68] While the battle was being fought, Secord was moved to a nearby house, where she slept off her walk, and then returned to the safety of her home and family. She told her family about her achievement but, motivated by fear for their security (as American troops continued to occupy the Niagara area) as well as by her own modesty and self-denial, she did not look for any recognition or reward. Such honours came first to Fitzgibbon.[69]

Women such as Curzon and Currie might see Secord's contribution as natural and unsurprising (given her devotion to her country) but they also were keenly aware that their mission of commemoration necessitated that their work appeal to a popular audience. These narratives were imbued with their authors' concerns with the relations of gender, class, and race and the way in which they perceived these identities to structure both Canadian society and history. For one, Secord's "natural" feminine fragility was a major theme of their writings. As a white woman of good birth and descent, she was not physically suited to undertake the hardships involved in her walk (although, paradoxically, as a typical "pioneer woman" she was able to undertake the hardships of raising a family and looking after a household in a recently settled area.) Her delicacy and slight build, first mentioned by Fitzgibbon in his own testimony of her walk, was frequently stressed by those who commemorated her.[70] Her physical frailty could be contrasted with the manly size and strength of soldiers such as Fitzgibbon and Brock.[71] Nevertheless, the seeming physical immutability of gender was not an insurmountable barrier to her patriotic duty to country and empire. The claims of the latter transcended corporeal limitations. Even her maternal duties, understood by both conservatives and many feminists in late-nineteenth-century Canada to be the core of womanly identity, could be put aside or even reformulated in order to answer her country's needs.[72] While her supporters did not make explicit their motives in stressing her frailty, it is possible to see it as a subtext to counter medical and scientific arguments about female physical deficiencies that made women, particularly white, middle-class woman, unfit for political participation and higher education.[73]

Furthermore, there were other ways to make Secord both appealing and a reflection of their own conceptions of "Canadian womanhood," and many historians treated her as an icon of respectable white heterosexual femininity. Anecdotes supposedly told by her family were often added to the end of the narratives of her walk — especially those written by women — and these emphasized her love of children, her kindness and charity toward the elderly, and her very feminine love of finery and gaiety (making her daughters' satin slippers, for example, and her participation as a young woman in balls given by the Secords at Newark). Indeed, they went so far as to discuss the clothing that she wore on her walk. Her daughter Harriet told Currie that she and her sisters saw their mother leave that morning wearing "a flowered print gown, I think it was brown with orange flowers, at least a yellow tint."[74] Elizabeth Thompson, who was active within the Ontario Historical Society and was also a member of the IODE, also wrote that Secord wore a print dress, adding a "cottage bonnet tied under her chin . . . balbriggan stockings, with red silk clocks on the sides, and low shoes with buckles"— both of which were lost during the walk.[75]

For her most active supporters, the walk of Laura Secord meant that certain women could be written into the record of loyalty and patriotic duty in Canadian history, and female heroines could gain recognition for the deed they had committed. In the eyes of these historians, such recognition had heretofore been withheld simply because of these figures' gender, for in every other significant feature — their racial and ethnic identities, for example — they were no different than their male counterparts. But such additions to the narrative were intended to be just that: additions, not serious disruptions of the story's focus on the ultimate triumph of British institutions and the imperial tie in Canada. Like her walk, Secord herself was constructed in many ways as the archetypical "British" pioneer woman of Loyalist history, remembered for her willingness to struggle, sacrifice, and thus contribute to "nation building." These historians also suggested that patriotic duties and loyalty to the state did not automatically constitute a major threat to late-nineteenth-century concepts of masculinity and femininity. Secord could undertake such duties, but still had to be defined by her relations to husband and children, home and family. She did not, it was clear, take up arms herself, nor did she use her contribution to win recognition for her own gain.

In the context of late-nineteenth- and early-twentieth-century debates about gender relations in Canadian society, Secord was a persuasive symbol of how certain women might breach the division between "private" and "public," the family and the state, and do so for entirely unselfish and patriotic reasons. The narratives of Laura Secord's walk helped shape an image of Canadian womanhood in the past that provided additional justification and inspiration for turn-of-the-century Canadian feminists. These women could invoke memory and tradition when calling for their own inclusion in the "imagined community" of the Canadian nation of the late nineteenth century.[76] Furthermore, for those such as Curzon who were eager to widen their frame of national reference, Secord's legacy could be part of an imperialist discourse, linking gender, race, nation, and empire in both the past and the present.

NOTES

Much of the research and writing of this paper was conducted with the financial assistance of Canada Employment. I would also like to thank Colin Coates, Marian Valverde, and the *Journal*'s anonymous readers for their much-appreciated suggestions and encouragement. The members of the gender, history, and national identities study group have provided invaluable comments and support: Lykke de la Cour, Paul Deslandes, Stephen Heathorn, Maureen McCarthy, and Tori Smith.

1. A Dorian Gray–like image that, as the company has enjoyed pointing out, becomes younger with the passage of time. See the advertisement, "There must be something in the chocolate," *The Globe and Mail*, November 25, 1992, A14.
2. This term has been an invaluable methodological tool in thinking about the narratives of Secord. See Benedict Anderson, *Imagined Communities: Reflections on the Origin and Spread of Nationalism*, rev. ed. (London and New York, 1991). See also Eric Hobsbawm and Terence Ranger, eds., *The Invention of Tradition* (New York, 1983). Like Anderson's work, however, this collection does not address the complex relationships of gender, nationalism, and the "invented traditions" it analyzes.
3. Carl Berger, *The Sense of Power: Studies in the Ideas of Canadian Imperialism 1867–1914* (Toronto, 1970), 78.
4. Catherine Hall, Jane Lewis, Keith McClelland, and Jane Rendall, "Introduction," *Gender and History: Special Issue on Gender, Nationalisms, and National Identities* 5, 2 (Summer 1993): 159–64.
5. Recent work by historians of Indian nationalism explores the use of female images, particularly that of the nation as mother. See, for example, Samita Sen, "Motherhood and Mother Craft: Gender and Nationalism in Bengal," *Gender and History: Special Issue on Gender, Nationalisms and National Identities*, 231–43. See also the essays in *History Workshop Journal Special Issue: Colonial and Post-Colonial History* 36 (Autumn 1993), and Mrinalini Sinha, "Reading *Mother India*: Empire, Nation, and the Female Voice," *Journal of Women's History* 6, 2 (Summer 1994): 6–44.
6. One of the few Canadian historians to point to these connections has been George Ingram, in "The Story of Laura Secord Revisited," *Ontario History* 57, 2 (June 1965): 85–97. Other works tackling these questions have looked at such areas as social reform. See Angus McLaren, *Our Own Master Race: Eugenics in Canada, 1885–1945* (Toronto, 1990), and Mariana Valverde, *The Age of Light, Soap, and Water: Moral Reform in English Canada 1885–1925* (Toronto, 1991).

7. For a heroine who was not so easily domesticated, see Colin M. Coates, "Commemorating the Woman Warrior of New France: Madeleine de Verchères, 1696–1930," paper presented to the 72nd Annual Conference of the Canadian Historical Association, Ottawa, June 1993; also Marina Warner, *Joan of Arc: The Image of Female Heroism* (London, 1981).

8. See, for example, the *Transactions* of both the Women's Canadian Historical Society of Ottawa and those of the Women's Canadian Historical Society of Toronto, from the 1890s to the 1920s.

9. David Mills, *The Idea of Loyalty in Upper Canada, 1784–1850* (Montreal and Kingston, 1988).

10. Donald H. Akenson, *The Irish in Ontario: A Study in Rural History* (Montreal and Kingston, 1984), 134.

11. See Cecilia Morgan, "Languages of Gender in Upper Canadian Politics and Religion, 1791–1850" (Ph.D. thesis, University of Toronto, 1993), ch. II. It is interesting that, while the militia myth has been challenged by many historians, its gendered nature has received very little attention. See, for example, the most recent study of the War of 1812, George Sheppard's *Plunder, Profit, and Paroles: A Social History of the War of 1812 in Upper Canada* (Montreal and Kingston, 1994).

12. Morgan, 56–60; see also Keith Walden, "Isaac Brock: Man and Myth: A Study of the Militia Myth of the War of 1812 in Upper Canada 1812–1912" (M.A. thesis, Queen's University, 1971).

13. Janice Potter-Mackinnon, *While the Women Only Wept: Loyalist Refugee Women in Eastern Ontario* (Montreal and Kingston, 1993), 158.

14. Coates, "Commemorating the Heroine of New France."

15. Morgan, ch. II.

16. On the French Revolution, see Maurice Agulhon, *Marianne into Battle: Republican Imagery and Symbolism in France, 1789–1880*, trans. Janet Lloyd (Cambridge, 1981). For republican motherhood, see Linda Kerber, "The Republican Mother: Female Political Imagination in the Early Republic," in *Women of the Republic: Intellect and Ideology in Revolutionary America* (Chapter Hill, 1980); for Britannia, see Madge Dresser, "Britannia," in Raphael Samuel (ed.), *Patriotism, the Making and Unmaking of British National Identity*, vol. 3; *National Fictions*, ed. Raphael Samuel (London, 1989), 26–49.

17. The petition is reprinted in Ruth McKenzie's *Laura Secord: The Legend and the Lady* (Toronto, 1971), 74–5. To date, McKenzie's book is the most thorough and best-researched popular account of the development of the Secord legend.

18. Ibid., 76.

19. Ibid., 76–77; also Sheppard, 221.

20. McKenzie, 84–85.

21. Ibid., 49ff.

22. Ibid., 91–92; also in Benson J. Lossing, *The Pictorial Field-Book of the War of 1812* (New York, 1869), 621.

23. McKenzie, 102.

24. Ibid., 103–4.

25. For an analysis of patronage in nineteenth-century Ontario, see S.J.R. Noel, *Patrons, Clients, Brokers: Ontario Society and Politics 1791–1896* (Toronto, 1990).

26. Lossing, 621.

27. William F. Coffin, *1812: The War, and Its Moral: A Canadian Chronicle* (Montreal, 1864), 148.

28. See Sarah A. Curzon, *Laura Secord, the Heroine of 1812: A Drama and Other Poems* (Toronto, 1887). For biographical sketches of Curzon and Fitzgibbon, see Henry James Morgan, *The Canadian Men and Women of the Time: A Hand-Book of Canadian Biography* (Toronto, 1898 and 1912), 235–36 and 400. Curzon's work is briefly discussed in Carol Bacchi's *Liberation Deferred? The Ideas of the English-Canadian Suffragists, 1877–1918* (Toronto, 1981), 26–27 and 44, but Bacchi's frame of reference does not take in Curzon's (or other suffragists') interest in history as an important cultural aspect of their maternal feminism and imperialism.

29. Morgan, 1912, 288–89; see also Mrs. G.M. Armstrong, *The First Eight Years of the Women's Literary Club of St. Catharines, 1892–1972* (n.p., 1972); Emma A. Currie, *The Story of Laura Secord and Canadian Reminiscences* (St. Catharines, 1913).

30. Charles Mair, "A Ballad for Brave Women," in *Tecumseh: A Drama and Canadian Poems* (Toronto, 1901), 147; William Kirby, *Annals of Niagara*, ed. and intro. by Lorne Pierce (Toronto, 1927 [1896]), 209–10. Kirby had been Currie's childhood tutor in Niagara and both she and Curzon continued to look to him for advice, support, and recognition (Archives of Ontario [AO]), MS 542, William Kirby Correspondence, Reel 1, Curzon and Currie to Kirby, 1887–1906). Kirby and Mair were made honorary members of the WCHS (AO, MU 7837-7838, Series A, WCHS papers, Correspondence File 1, William Kirby to Mary Agnes Fitzgibbon, April 11, 1896, Charles Mair to Fitzgibbon, May 8, 1896). For Machar, see "Laura Secord," in her *Lays of the True North and Other Poems* (Toronto, 1887), 35. See also Ruth Compton Brouwer, "Moral Nationalism in Victorian Canada: The Case of Agnes Machar," *Journal of Canadian Studies* 20, 1 (Spring 1985): 90–108.

31. See, for example, "The Heroine of the Beaver Dams," *Canadian Antiquarian and Numismatic Journal* 8 (Montreal, 1879): 135–36. Many thanks to Colin Coates for this reference. See also Ernest Cruikshank, *The Fight in the Beechwoods* (Drummondville: Lundy's Lane Historical Society, 1889), 1, 13–14, 19.

32. Berger, 89–90.

33. Ibid., 95–96.

34. Janet Carnochan, "Laura Secord Monument at Lundy's Lane," *Transactions of the Niagara Historical Society* (Niagara, 1913), 11–18.

35. Carnochan, 13.

36. McKenzie, 118–19.

37. Marilyn Lake has made a similar argument about Australian nationalist discourse during World War One. See her "Mission Impossible: How Men Gave Birth to the Australian Nation — Nationalism, Gender and Other Seminal Acts," *Gender and History. Special Issue on Motherhood, Race and the State in the Twentieth Century* 4, 3 (Autumn 1992): 305–22, particularly 307. For the theme of self-sacrifice in Canadian nationalism, see Berger, 217. The links between the discourses of late-Victorian, white, bourgeois femininity and that of Canadian racial policy have been explored by Valverde in *The Age of Light, Soap, and Water*, in the contexts of moral reform, the white slavery panic, and immigration policies. See also Bacchi, *Liberation Deferred?*, ch. 7. For gender and imperialism in the British and American contexts, see Vron Ware, *Beyond the Pale: White Women, Racism and History* (London and New York, 1992). The seminal article on imperialism and British womanhood is Anna Davin, "Imperialism and Motherhood," *History Workshop Journal* 5 (Spring 1978): 9–65.

38. WCHS papers, MU 7837-7838, Series A, Correspondence File 1, Kirby to Fitzgibbon, April 14, 1896.

39. See, for example, Mrs. J.R. Hill, "Early British Canadian Heroines," *Women's Canadian Historical Society of Ottawa Transactions*, 10 (1928): 93–98; Harriet Prudis, "Reminiscences of Mrs. Gilbert Ponte," *London and Middlesex Historical Society Transactions* (1902, pub. 1907): 62–64.

40. Harriet Prudis, "The 100th Regiment," *L & M H S Transactions*, V (1912–1913), n.p.; Agnes Dunbar Chamberlin, "The Colored Citizens of Toronto," *WCHS of Toronto Transactions*, 8 (1908): 9–15; also the biography of Brock by Lady Edgar, one of the first presidents of the WCHS [*Life of General Brock* (Toronto, 1904)].

41. See note 37 above.

42. Prudis, 62.

43. See Ernest Green, "Some Canadian Women of 1812–14," *WCHS of Ottawa Transactions* 9 (1925): 98–109.

44. WCHS papers, MU 7837-7838, Series A, Correspondence File 1, Mair to Fitzgibbon, May 8, 1896.

45. Ibid.; see also WCHS papers, MU 7837-7838, Series A, Correspondence File 1, John H. to Fitzgibbon, May 6, 1896.

46. As Linda Kerber argues, it was precisely this relegation that women's historians of the 1960s and '70s had to confront in their attempts to lift women's lives from the "realm of the trivial and anecdotal." See her "Separate Spheres, Female Worlds, Woman's Place: The Rhetoric of Women's History," *The Journal of American History* 75, 1 (June 1988): 9–39, esp. 37.

47. Mair to Fitzgibbon, May 8, 1896.

48. W.S. Wallace, *The Story of Laura Secord* (Toronto, 1932). For a response to Wallace, see "What Laura Secord Did," *Dunnville Weekly Chronicle*, 35 (1932), reprinted from Toronto *Saturday Night*, June 22, 1932.

49. Berger, 96. As M. Brook Taylor has pointed out about the work of nineteenth-century writers such as John Charles Dent, Francis Hincks, and Charles Lindsey, "National historians were essentially Upper Canadian historians in masquerade." See his *Promoters, Patriots, and Partisans: Historiography in Nineteenth-Century Canada* (Toronto, 1989), 231.

50. Currie, 21–33.

51. Curzon, *The Story of Laura Secord, 1813* (Lundy's Lane Historical Society, July 25, 1891), 6–7.

52. See Gerald M. Craig, *Upper Canada: The Formative Years 1784–1841* (Toronto, 1963), 49, for a discussion of this shift in policy. McKenzie also argues that Ingersoll did not fulfill his settlement obligations (29). See also Currie, 38–39.

53. J.H. Ingersoll, "The Ancestry of Laura Secord," *Ontario Historical Society* (1926): 361–63. See also Elizabeth Thompson, "Laura Ingersoll Secord," 1. Others argued that Ingersoll was urged by Joseph Brant to come to Upper Canada (Ingersoll, 363). The Brant connection was developed most fully and romantically by John Price-Brown in *Laura the Undaunted: A Canadian Historical Romance* (Toronto, 1930). It has also been pointed out that Price-Brown picked up the story, "invented out of whole cloth" by Curzon, that Tecumseh had fallen in love with one of Secord's daughters. See Dennis Duffy, *Gardens, Covenants, Exiles: Loyalism in the Literature of Upper Canada/Ontario* (Toronto, 1982), 61. In Price-Brown's account, Tecumseh proposes just before he is killed; Laura, however, disapproves of the match (259–69).

54. Price-Brown, 16–17, 180–82.

55. Just as French Canadians could overcome other ties (see Berger, 138–39).

56. Thompson, 2; Currie, 48; Ingersoll, 362.

57. Price-Brown's "fictional" account is the most colourful, since one of the American officers who did not intervene to save the Secords was a former suitor of Laura's, whom she had rejected in favour of James and Canada (252–55). See also Currrie, 53–54.

58. Norman Knowles, in his study of late-nineteenth-century Ontario commemorations of Loyalism, argues that pioneer and rural myths subsumed those of Loyalism ("Inventing the Loyalists: The Ontario Loyalist Tradition and the Creation of a Usable Past, 1784–1924," Ph.D. thesis, York University 1990). To date, my research on women commemorators indicates that, for them, both Loyalism (particularly people, places, and artifacts having to do with 1812) and the "pioneer past" were closely intertwined; both were of great significance and inspirational power in their interpretations of the past. See Elizabeth Thompson, *The Pioneer Woman: A Canadian Character Type* (Montreal and Kingston, 1991) for a study of this archetype in the fiction of Canadian authors Catherine Parr Trail, Sara Jeanette Duncan, Ralph Connor, and Margaret Laurence.

59. The most extensive description is in Curzon's *The Story of Laura Secord*, 11–12.

60. Curzon, *Laura Secord: The Heroine of the War of 1812*, 39–47.

61. While examining a very different period and genre of writing, I have found Carroll Smith-Rosenberg's "Captured Subjects/Savage Others: Violently Engendering the New American" to be extremely helpful in understanding the construction of white womanhood in the North American context. See *Gender and History* 5, 2 (Summer 1993): 177–95. See also Vron Ware, "Moments of Danger: Race, Gender, and Memories of Empire," *History and Theory* (1992): 116–37.

62. See Ware, "To Make the Facts Known," in *Beyond the Pale* for a discussion of lynching and the feminist campaign against it. Smith-Rosenberg points to a similar treatment of Native men in Mary Rowlandson's seventeenth-century captivity narrative (183–84). While the two examples should not be conflated, this issue does call for further analysis.

63. Cruikshank, 13.

64. Secord in Thompson, 4–5.

65. See, for example, Blanche Hume, *Laura Secord* (Toronto, 1928), 1. This book was part of a Ryerson Canadian History Readers series, endorsed by the IODE and the provincial Department of Education.

66. Ibid., 15.

67. Curzon, *The Story of Laura Secord*, 13.

68. See, for example, Cruikshank, 18.

69. Currie, 52–53. Fitzgibbon supposedly took full credit for the victory, ignoring both Secord's and the Caughnawaga Mohawks' roles (McKenzie, 66–67). He later became a colonel in the York militia and was rewarded for his role in putting down the 1837 rebellion with a £1000 grant (89–90).

70. Fitzgibbon in Thompson, 6.

71. Hume, 4.

72. For example, in Curzon's play Secord is asked by her sister-in-law, the Widow Secord, if her children will not "blame" her should she come to harm. She replies that "children can see the right at one quick glance," suggesting that their mother's maternal care and authority is bound to her patriotism and loyalty (34).

73. See Wendy Mitchinson, *The Nature of Their Bodies: Women and Their Doctors in Victorian Canada* (Toronto, 1991), esp. "The Frailty of Women."

74. Currie, 71.

75. Thompson, 3. Balbriggan was a type of fine, unbleached, knitted cotton hosiery material.

76. See Hobsbawm and Ranger, "Introduction: Inventing Tradition," particularly their argument that invented traditions are often shaped and deployed by those who wish to either legitimate particular institutions or relations of authority or to inculcate certain beliefs or values (9). In this case I would argue that the Secord tradition served very similar purposes, although it was used both to legitimate and, for certain groups of women, to subvert.

Topic Five

Rupert's Land and the Red River Colony

An ox pulls a Red River cart through a prairie community in this mid-19th-century painting by W.G.R. Hind.

By the mid-19th century, a new and distinct society emerged in the Red River Colony at the junction of the Red and the Assiniboine rivers in Rupert's Land, the vast area of the North American continent controlled by the Hudson's Bay Company. In particular, a distinct society had formed at the junction of the Red and Assiniboine rivers, known as the Red River colony. By 1850, the colony had a population of more than 5000 mixed-bloods and several hundred non-Native settlers. Of the mixed-blood population, roughly half were English-speaking Métis, or "Country-born," the descendants of the British fur traders and their First Nations wives. The other half were French-speaking Métis, the descendants of the early French fur traders and their First Nations wives.

Did these two groups create a cohesive society, or did they coexist in a state of friction? In "The Flock Divided: Factions and Feuds at Red River," Frits Pannekoek argues that religion split the colony into two hostile factions. Fellow historian Irene Spry reaches the opposite conclusion in "The Métis and Mixed-Bloods of Rupert's Land before 1870." She argues that the two groups of mixed-bloods were united by their common Aboriginal heritage. Any division that existed was class-based, relating to the occupational differences between the farmers and the hunters or plains traders. In "The Michif Language of the Métis," linguist Peter Bakker explores "Michif," the unique language the French-speaking Métis developed. Essentially half-Cree and half-French, it provides another example of the new culture born of the meeting of two different peoples. Although the English-speaking mixed-bloods could not speak Michif, Bakker points out both groups could use Cree as a common language to communicate.

The early chapters of Gerald Friesen's *The Canadian Prairies: A History* (Toronto: University of Toronto Press, 1984) offer a good overview of the history of Rupert's Land. Sarah Carter's *Aboriginal People and Colonizers of Western Canada to 1900* (Toronto: University of Toronto Press, 1999) is also very useful. A valuable new collection of essays is Theodore Binema, Gerhard J. Ens, and R.C. Macleod, eds., *From Rupert's Land to Canada* (Edmonton: University of Alberta Press, 2001).

D.N. Sprague looks at the Red River Colony in the mid-19th century in his introduction to *The Genealogy of the First Métis Nation: The Development and Dispersal of the Red River Settlement, 1820–1900* (Winnipeg: Pemmican Publishers, 1983), compiled by D.N. Sprague and R.P. Frye. Frits Pannekoek provides a full study of Red River society in *A Snug Little Flock: The Social Origins of the Riel Resistance, 1869–70* (Winnipeg: Watson and Dwyer, 1991). J.R. Miller reviews the secondary literature on the Red River Colony in "From Riel to the Métis," *Canadian Historical Review* 69 (1988): 1–20. This study complements Frits Pannekoek's "The Historiography of the Red River Settlement, 1830–1868," *Prairie Forum* 6 (1981): 75–85. Important essays on the Métis appear in Jennifer S. Brown and Jacqueline Peterson, eds., *The New Peoples: Being and Becoming Métis in North America* (Winnipeg: University of Manitoba Press, 1985). Gerhard Ens provides an interesting insight into Red River society in "Dispossession or Adaptation? Migration and Persistence of the Red River Métis, 1835–1890," *Historical Papers*, Canadian Historical Association (1988): 120–44; and in his book, *Homeland to Hinterland: The Changing Worlds of the Red River Métis in the Nineteenth Century* (Toronto: University of Toronto Press, 1996). A recent local study is Robert J. Coutts, *The Road to the Rapids: Nineteenth Century Church and Society at St. Andrew's Parish, Red River* (Calgary: University of Calgary Press, 2000). J. Barkwell Lawrence, Leah Dorion, and Darren R. Prefontaine have edited an interesting collection of papers on the Métis, entitled *Métis Legacy* (Winnipeg: Pemmican Publications, 2001).

Excellent maps of the Red River and all of Rupert's Land appear in Richard Ruggles's *A Country So Interesting: The Hudson's Bay Company and Two Centuries of Mapping, 1670–1870* (Montreal/Kingston: McGill-Queen's University Press, 1991).

Dale R. Russell provides a detailed review of the location of First Nations groups on the territory that is now the Prairie provinces in *Eighteenth-Century Western Cree and Their Neighbours* (Hull, PQ: Canadian Museum of Civilization, 1991). As a supplement to this monograph, see James G.E. Smith's "The Western Woods Cree: Anthropological Myth and Historical Reality," *American Ethnologist* 14 (1987): 434–48. Interesting excerpts from early travellers' accounts of what is now western Canada appear in Germaine Warkentin's edited work *Canadian Exploration Literature: An Anthology* (Toronto: Oxford University Press, 1993). Hugh A. Dempsey's two biographies, *Crowfoot* (Edmonton: Hurtig, 1972) and *Big Bear* (Vancouver: Douglas and McIntyre, 1984), introduce the Plains Indians in the mid-19th century; see also his *The Amazing Death of Calf Shirt and Other Blackfoot Stories: Three Hundred Years of Blackfoot History* (Saskatoon: Fifth House, 1994). A recent study of Big Bear's First Nation is John S. Milloy's *The Plains Cree: Trade, Diplomacy and War, 1790 to 1870* (Winnipeg: University of Manitoba Press, 1989). The Blackfoot experience is reviewed by John Ewers in *The Blackfeet: Raiders in the Northwestern Plains* (Norman, OK: University of Oklahoma Press, 1958). Laura Peers looks at the Western Ojibwa in *The Ojibwa of Western Canada: 1780–1870* (Winnipeg: University of Manitoba Press, 1994).

A comparative description of two 19th-century families, one from the Red River Colony and one from Prince Edward Island, is provided by J.M. Bumsted and Wendy Owen in "The Victorian Family in Canada in Historical Perspective: The Ross Family of Red River and the Jarvis Family of Prince Edward Island," *Manitoba History* 13 (1987): 12–18.

WEBLINKS

Champlain Society
http://link.library.utoronto.ca/champlain/search.cfm?lang=eng

The digital collections of the Champlain Society contain several important European accounts of Rupert's Land and the Red River Colony. Browse the database by subject, and select for example, "Manitoba — History," "Northwest, Canadian — History — Sources," or "Selkirk, Thomas Douglas, Earl of, 1771–1820 — Diaries."

Red River Settlement Papers
http://www.nosracines.ca/e/toc.asp?id=1180

Digitized collection of published letters, dispatches, and other documents from the early Red River Settlement, published in 1819.

Red River Journal
http://www.canadiana.org/ECO/ItemRecord/41912?id=a2008919b6c6abaa

A digitized journal depicting life at the Red River Colony during the years 1820–1823.

Red River Settlement Council Minutes
http://www.mhs.mb.ca/docs/pageant/24/minutes1837.shtml

Recorded minutes of a Council meeting held at Fort Garry, Red River Settlement, on 16 June 1837.

The Red River
http://www.ccge.org/ccge/english/Resources/rivers/tr_rivers_redRiver.asp

A website by the Canadian Council for Geographic Education about the Red River.

Article Eleven

The Flock Divided: Factions and Feuds at Red River

Frits Pannekoek

The settlement of Red River changed in the late 1850s and early 1860s. From a relatively quiet backwater, it became the confluence of the northward frontier of the American Republic and the western frontier of the Canadian colonies. In 1858 there were only a few buildings outside Upper Fort Garry at the forks of the Red and Assiniboine, but within ten years there was a drugstore, grist mill, gun shop, harness shop, bookstore, butcher shop, tinsmith, photography studio, carriage shop, two saloons, and a newspaper office. Steamboats, the *Anson Northup* (1859) and the *International* (1862), even attempted, although without great success, to navigate between Moorhead in Dakota and Red River.

Much of this change was due to a major influx of Canadian and American immigrants. Even before the immigration, however, Red River was changing of its own accord. During the six years before 1849, 1232 new people were added to the colony. This growth was internal, rather than the result of immigration, since only 28 families arrived in Red River between 1849 and 1856. This increase placed a substantial burden on the means of livelihood: the river lot and the hunt. Because the family lands could no longer be divided indefinitely among the numerous sons, as had been the tradition, many moved to the plains along the Assiniboine River. Others moved to the United States or into the western interior along the Saskatchewan River at places such as Victoria in what is now Alberta and Prince Albert in present-day Saskatchewan.

There were four major groups in the Red River settlement. The most significant were those of mixed-blood heritage. In 1871 the total population was 11 400. Of these, 5740 were Métis or Catholic French/Cree-speaking mixed-bloods. These lived in the parishes south and immediately west of the junctions of the Red and Assiniboine rivers. The 4080 Protestant and English-speaking mixed-bloods lived in the parishes largely north of the junction of the two rivers and after 1854 around Portage la Prairie. It has been argued by some that the Indian blood tied these two groups together as one family. While that would seem commonsense, in fact there was little unity between the two groups during the Riel Resistance. Indeed, the English-speaking Protestant mixed-bloods, who proudly called themselves Halfbreeds, were at odds with Riel. Why? It would seem that the two groups should be of single mind. When the events in the decade preceding the resistance are examined closely, the influence of the Reverend Griffiths Owen Corbett in creating a split between the Halfbreeds and Métis is evident. This bizarre clergyman with his petty politics and religious bigotry managed to effectively divide the mixed-blood community into its Protestant and Catholic halves. Coincidentally he reinforced the Halfbreeds' anti-Hudson's Bay Company and pro-imperial sentiments. When Riel attempted to appeal to the mixed bloods for unity in 1869 he would fail. Corbett had been too effective. The Canadians, with their anti-Catholicism and imperial bombast, would find supporters in the Halfbreed parishes of Red River.

In the 1850s, at the same time that there were significant demographic and social changes in Red River, both Canada and Great Britain began to show a peculiar interest in the future of Rupert's Land. Red River, of course, chased every rumour of change and there were as many

Source: This article, taken from Frits Pannekoek's *A Snug Little Flock: The Social Origins of the Riel Resistance, 1869–70* (Winnipeg: Watson and Dwyer, 1991), pp. 143–70; originally appeared in *The Beaver* 70, 6 (December 1990–January 1991). Reprinted by permission.

factions as there were alternatives. In the early 1860s Crown Colony status seemed most likely. The Duke of Newcastle, colonial secretary from 1859 to 1864, favoured the creation of a Crown Colony in Rupert's Land as a connecting link between Canada and British Columbia, all of which would eventually comprise a British North American federation. He was supported in his stand by substantial Canadian and British railroad and financial interests. But Red River was only vaguely aware of what was happening in the Colonial Office and at Hudson's Bay House, London. As rumour increased of imperial support for the Crown Colony status after 1859, it seemed apparent to Red River that change of some sort was inevitable. The settlement hoped that it would be immediate. No firm plan was offered, however, by either the Canadian government, the imperial government, or the Company. Confusion remained the only political certainty.

The agitation for change in Red River's political status started in 1856–57 in Canada and filtered through to Red River via the *Globe*, the Toronto newspaper read by many of the informed and literate. James Ross, Halfbreed son of Alexander Ross, historian and former sheriff, expressed the prevailing sentiments:

> We ought to have a flood of immigration to infuse new life, new ideas, and destroy all our old associations with the past, *i.e.*, in so far as it hinders our progress for the future — regular transformation will sharpen our intellects, fill our minds with new projects and give life and vigour to all our thoughts, words and actions.

The first petition for change came in June of 1856 from the Protestant clergy. Their demands were moderate, including only restrictions on the importing of alcohol and the introduction of the elective principle in the Council of Assiniboia. They did not wish the removal of the Councillors, only that vacancies be filled by election, and that the settlement be divided for that purpose into districts.

No serious pro-Canadian agitation developed until a few months later. On 26 February, William Dawson of the Dawson-Hind expedition, sent by the Canadian government to assess the fertility of the Assiniboine-Saskatchewan country, gave a lecture, "Canada Past and Present." Interest was high and the governor, the clergy, and some of the Company's active and retired gentlemen attended. There was, however, no open political movement at the parish level. Interest turned into open agitation only when William Kennedy returned to Red River on 7 February 1857 after a number of years of anti-Company agitation in Upper Canada. Like his relative Alexander Kennedy Isbister, who had been instrumental in the presentation of the 1847 petition to the imperial parliament, he was an embittered ex–Hudson's Bay Company employee.

From March to May, a number of meetings organized by Kennedy were held in the Kildonan school house and in the neighbouring Halfbreed parishes. An elder of the Presbyterian Church, Kennedy ingratiated himself with the Kildonan settlers, especially Donald Gunn, one of its leading members, and Rev. John Black, who had strong Canadian sympathies. The Company was severely criticized and annexation to Canada advocated. When Governor F.G. Johnson, who had succeeded Adam Thom as recorder, attended one of the first March meetings, he was requested to leave. As a result of the meetings the younger settlers displayed their open sympathy with Kennedy and signed his petition for union with Canada. The older settlers, still believing that a certain deference was due the Company, hesitated to make a decision.

In May, Kennedy convinced some in Red River — the exact parishes cannot now be known, but probably they were those between the Upper and Lower Forts — to elect five members, including himself and Isbister, to serve in the provincial legislature of Canada. Kennedy for his part had allowed reports to spread that he was a representative of Canada. While he publicly denied these reports, he left the vague impression that he had to do so because he was a secret agent. The five members were actually sent off, but Kennedy had second thoughts about the legality of the proceedings. He chose to recall the delegates when he heard that Captain John Palliser was arriving at the head of the British expedition to the North-West and that he might have some concrete instructions for Red River's future.

This spelled the effective end of Kennedy's agitation. By the winter of 1858–59, the semblance of unity that momentarily had existed in Red River disintegrated under the force of new pressures. Rev. G.O. Corbett, arriving in the spring of 1858, was the cause.

Corbett, of the Church of England, was a contentious and difficult individual, spending much of his life quarrelling with his bishops, the Hudson's Bay Company, his fellow clergymen, and the Colonial and Continental Church Society, which sponsored him. While not a charismatic leader, he was something of a gadfly with strong convictions about the rights of Englishmen, and even stronger convictions that these rights were being denied to the Halfbreeds by the tyranny of the Hudson's Bay Company and the Church of Rome. A popular and effective speaker, his views fell on the fertile ground of the political and social unrest in the late 1850s and early 1860s. Corbett aroused the Halfbreeds and directed their energies against both the Company and the Catholics, convincing them that their future lay within a Protestant Crown Colony firmly affixed to the British Empire. Crown Colony status seemed to guarantee an extension of the full rights and privileges of the British constitution and offered a fellowship of English-speaking people, under the loose British nationalism with which the empire had always anointed its subjects.

When in 1862 Corbett found himself the centre of an unsavoury scandal and defended himself by identifying it as a Company plot to discredit him and his movement for Crown Colony status, feelings grew so intense that Red River split into two factions. The pro-Company group, who believed Corbett guilty, included strangely enough the Métis, who disliked his anti-Catholicism. The anti-Company group, who were the most fervent Crown Colony advocates, believed him innocent, and were composed principally of the Protestant English-speaking Halfbreeds. In the end the two groups verged on open war.

Rev. G.O. Corbett despised the Catholics, considered them barbarians, and used the newspaper to propagandize his sentiments. In a community torn by dissent and rife with status tensions, Corbett's anti-Catholicism was absorbed as eagerly as his anti-Company rhetoric. He taught the Halfbreeds that because they were Protestant they were superior to the Catholic Métis of Red River.

Corbett felt that the British liberties of Red River, a Protestant colony of a Protestant queen, were succumbing to the tyranny of the Church of Rome. Corbett, seeing, as he imagined, too many examples of the growing power of the papal "anti-Christ," felt it his duty to warn of the dangerous consequences. His greatest concern was William Mactavish, the governor of Assiniboia. Mactavish had married a Catholic daughter of Andrew McDermot in Saint-Boniface cathedral, and in the following years baptized his children into the Catholic faith. All of Protestant Red River had considered the marriage an insult to Bishop Anderson of the Church of England, who had apparently expected to conduct the ceremony. Corbett was convinced that, with the governor a virtual Catholic, and with seven Catholics against seven Protestants on the Council of Assiniboia, "the balance of power [was] with the Pope of Rome."

When an official report of the legislative proceedings of the Council of Assiniboia referred to the Catholic bishop as "Lord Bishop," Corbett had what he considered proof. Legally only Bishop Anderson, who wanted no part in the controversy and who unsuccessfully cautioned Corbett to moderate his stand, was entitled to the title. Only Anderson had been appointed by "Her Most Gracious Sovereign the Queen." Corbett considered use of the title for Bishop Taché both "insidious" and "unconstitutional." When the Council of Assiniboia continued its folly by passing a law forbidding all government activity on Catholic holidays, there was no longer any doubt in Corbett's mind — Red River had fallen to the pope.

These religious tensions that had split the society asunder tended to centre on the settlement along the Assiniboine River, but their impact was felt throughout the whole of Red River. The *Nor'Wester* newspaper was particularly effective in ensuring that the controversies of the 1860s would continue to exacerbate social, religious, and racial divisions. Every imagined slight was well publicized and exaggerated. In 1860, for example, a heated battle waged between Henry Cook, a Halfbreed Anglican schoolmaster, and François Bruneau, one of the principal Métis, over the quality of Protestant and Catholic education. So virulent did Protestant sentiment become that James Ross, rather moderate in his anti-Catholicism and at times a restraining influence on Corbett, fearing a loss of Protestant business, refused on first request to publish an obituary and eulogy for Sister Valade, one of the first and most venerated sisters at Saint-Boniface. When in August 1861 Ross dared to publish an article suggesting that the Halfbreeds were superior to the Métis, the elder Riel visited Ross and "il lui a chanté une chanson, la chanson du juge Thom." In other words Riel threatened Ross's life, just as he had done years earlier to Adam Thom, the first recorder of Rupert's Land, who had voiced similar bigotries.

An understanding of these religious divisions is critical to the understanding of the crises which faced Red River as Corbett commenced his agitation for Crown Colony status in 1858. In December of 1858 Corbett and his cohort, Reverend John Chapman of St. Andrew's parish, the Company's chaplain, circulated their first petition advocating Crown Colony status. Corbett believed that annexation to Canada would place Red River "altogether in the hands of a subordinate power." He felt that if Red River were a Crown Colony, it would become the civil and commercial hub of the west, with its own elected assembly — a feature that was central to all of Corbett's arguments. He believed that "whatever advantages Canada enjoys, apart from her natural position, she derives these from her connection with England as Crown Colony." He damned the Company for its alleged inability to maintain law and order and its obstruction of material progress. Both would be remedied, he believed, when Rupert's Land assumed its rightful place in the empire as a Crown Colony.

Donald Gunn, William Kennedy, and James Ross, the leaders of the Canadian party, vigorously opposed Corbett and circulated a counter-petition advocating annexation to Canada. At this point, William Kennedy and James Ross, both Halfbreeds with strong British-Canadian connections, still felt Canada offered the best future — and Crown Colony status would offer continued domination by the Company. Both petitions were sent to the House of Lords, where they were ignored.

Corbett's agitation for political change assumed an even wider and more popular basis in the early 1860s. On 30 October 1862 the Council of Assiniboia petitioned the British government for troops in the face of a rumoured Sioux attack, a feared American invasion, and the growing local disaffection. The Council's petition made the rounds of Kildonan, Headingley, and St. Paul's parishes, gathering some 1183 signatures. As the petition was circulating, Rev. G.O. Corbett; Rev. John Chapman, the former Company chaplain; and James Ross, who joined Corbett's party when it became apparent that Canada was no longer interested in annexation, circulated a counter-petition condemning the Council of Assiniboia and the Company, and requesting Crown Colony status. Ross also refused to publish the Council's petition in his newspaper, the *Nor'Wester*. The counter-petitioners claimed that troops were not so much needed as a more efficient government. There was considerable confusion as to who supported which petition, since many attempted to delete their signatures from the Council's petition in order to support the counter-petition. The Company, as a disciplinary action, deprived Ross of his public offices of sheriff, governor of the gaol, and postmaster. Both petitions were ultimately sent to the Colonial office, where they too were ignored.

The Council's petition was seen by the aroused Halfbreeds as a plot to crush their efforts to throw off the yoke of the Hudson's Bay Company. Consequently, when the lurid details of Corbett's presumed attempts to induce the miscarriage of his illegitimate child by Maria Thomas struck like a thunderbolt from nowhere, his protested innocence and his accusations of a Company conspiracy appeared completely credible to the Halfbreeds. After all, earlier that winter Maria had been persuaded in front of a magistrate to deny the rumours of an affair. The denial had been acceptable, but when Corbett was jailed on the abortion charges and refused bail, in spite of precedent for granting such a request, the Halfbreeds were certain that the Company had resurrected a charge which had no substance and which had already been dismissed. Many were convinced that Maria Thomas's father, having pressed the charges, and Thomas Sinclair, the magistrate, were in the Company's pay. In effect, the question became not one of Corbett's guilt or innocence, but rather one of support for, or opposition to, the Company's supposed tyranny.

Corbett was charged with violation of 24 and 25 Victoria ch. 100, passed in 1861. It states that:

> Whosoever, with intent to procure the miscarriage of any woman, whether she be, or not be with child, shall unlawfully administer to her or cause to be taken by her, any poison or noxious thing, or shall unlawfully use an instrument or other means whatsoever with the like intent, shall be guilty of felony, and, being convicted thereof, shall be liable at the discretion of the Court to be kept in penal servitude for life, or for any term not less than three years, or to be imprisoned for any term not exceeding two years, with or without hard labour, and with or without solitary confinement.

In his charge to the jury on the ninth day of the Corbett trial, which was published on 12 May 1863 in the *Nor'Wester*, Recorder Black felt that he ought to elaborate on the law:

> I may state that the law regarding this crime has within the last 35 years, undergone various changes. At one time the law made a distinction between acts in which the attempt was made on a woman quick with child and one not quick with child. Previous to the passing of the statute under which the prisoner is indicted that which regulates this offence made it material whether or not the woman was pregnant. By a subsequent statute 7 Wm. IV, and Vic. ch. 85, that distinction was done away with, and there were some slight differences and alterations, which were embodied in the statute under which the prisoner is indicted.

The outcome of the case was not the result of this new "mass" concern with abortion that swept America and Great Britain in the 1850s through to the 1880s. Prior to the 1850s and 1860s life was construed to begin with "quickening" or "stirring in the womb," and abortion before "quickening" was not a felony. Corbett attempted to abort Maria Thomas's and his alleged child after the fourth month. The scurrilous *Nor'Wester* indicated that Corbett, whom they supported, had been unjustly accused of "murder." Nevertheless the abortion was not successful, and despite Maria Thomas's explicit testimony, Corbett was jailed for six months, an extremely light sentence given the damning evidence.

The trial commenced on Thursday, 19 February 1863, continued for nine days, and heard 61 witnesses. Rev. John Chapman described the shocking trial to the secretaries of the Church Missionary Society:

> What a spectacle . . . Mr. Corbett in one box & Maria Thomas a young girl of 16 years in the witness box, with her babe in her arms which she declares is Mr. Corbett's and whose embryo life he is charged with attempting to destroy by means of medicine, instruments &c.

The Bishop appointed Archdeacon James Hunter to conduct an independent church investigation and, before the court made its own decision, he pronounced Corbett guilty as charged. The court then followed suit. Corbett refused to recognize the jurisdiction of the Court of Assiniboia, or to accept its decision, and continued his accusations of a conspiracy on the part of the Company and the Church of England. For the rest of his life, he insisted upon his innocence and he was supported in his view by many in Red River. Some indeed were prepared to resort to arms.

The first incident occurred at nine o'clock on the morning of Saturday, 6 December 1862. In response to the denial of bail for Corbett, 150 to 200 persons, principally from Headingley but with groups from St. James, St. John's, St. Paul's, and St. Andrew's, arrived at Fort Garry. Governor Alexander Grant Dallas, Simpson's unpopular successor from the Pacific coast, favoured a hard line, but when riot was threatened he allowed Corbett to address the crowd. Corbett, for his part, encouraged all to continue their fight for justice. Finally James Ross and ten to twelve of the more respected members of the crowd persuaded Dallas that he would have to allow bail or suffer the consequences.

The second instance of mob rule occurred during the third month of Corbett's six-month sentence. On 14 April the Halfbreeds submitted a petition signed by 552 of their number, requesting a pardon for Corbett. Six days later, after Dallas had refused to consider their pleas, Corbett was freed by force. The governor responded by arresting James Stewart, the mixed-blood schoolmaster of St. James parish school and a ringleader in the agitation.

Governor Dallas, suspecting a plot to free Stewart, called upon 25 Métis and 25 Halfbreeds to defend the prison. Only five of the Halfbreeds would serve; the Métis, who had no use for "Corps Bête" as they called the anti-Catholic Corbett, appeared in full force. At ten o'clock on the morning of 22 April, 27 protesters, headed by William Hallett and James Ross, demanded an interview with Dallas. When Dallas refused to meet the insurgents, Ross sent a petition demanding the liberation of Stewart, the cessation of all discussion over the Corbett affair, and the removal of Sheriff McKenney, a supporter of the Company, who had replaced Ross. Dallas again refused, and Ross rode into the prison compound and liberated Stewart. It is evident that had Dallas not forbidden a violent confrontation, the Métis would have used force to stop Ross, which in turn would have triggered *une guerre civile* between Protestant and Catholic Red River. Fortunately, most of the 25 Métis were from Saint-Boniface and under the control of the moderate François Bruneau. Had *les hivernants*, the Métis boatmen and tripmen living at Cheval Blanc and Saint-Norbert, been involved, as had been initially intended, blood would most certainly have been shed. The "winterers" were hardly as charitable as their brethren at Saint-Boniface and after a long season of winter confinement would have been ready to flex their muscles in a Red River spring in order to teach the insolent Protestants a lesson. Consequently nothing was done to recapture Stewart.

The situation had deteriorated to such an extent that late in May, one month after the Corbett escape, John Bourke, who had been involved in all three acts of defiance, and James Stewart went so far as to attempt the organization of a "provisional government." It is probable that Corbett himself was involved. Stewart suggested that Headingley, St. James, and Portage la Prairie should secede from Red River and form an independent colony subordinate only to the Crown. Ultimately the proposal failed to gain sufficient support, and the conspirators, who lacked apparent organizational ability, gave up the plan.

Within the colony generally the jail breaks were followed by an increased questioning of Red River's traditional leaders. Even after suspension by both the bishop and the Colonial and Continental Church Society, Corbett returned to Headingley, where he assumed his clerical duties. The bishop sent replacements, including William Henry Taylor from the neighbouring parish, but the congregation locked the church doors and refused admittance to any clergyman save Corbett. In a ludicrous climax to the issue, John Chapman, formerly Corbett's ally, finally forced the door and preached to an empty church. The bishop then ordered Corbett to leave

Rupert's Land by 1 September 1863, but even in this he was defied and Corbett remained in the settlement until the following June.

In the neighbouring parish of St. James the persecution of the pro-Corbett group was equally vigorous if somewhat less successful. While James Stewart was allowed to teach for two months following his escape, Rev. William Henry Taylor, on poor terms with Stewart because of an earlier dispute over the location of the school, hired a replacement with the bishop's approval. Stewart then opened a private school where the great majority sent their children, forcing Taylor to close his. Taylor never regained his popularity.

The parishes along the Red River were also affected by the upheaval. Not only did many refuse to attend church services, but Archdeacon James Hunter was attacked for his investigations into the Corbett case. John Tait, a carpenter and miller from St. Andrew's parish, circulated a number of vicious rumours against Hunter to prove that any untruth could find support in Red River. Consequently, he reasoned, Corbett was probably just as easily innocent as guilty. Bishop Anderson urged Hunter to sue but a court case was avoided when Tait signed an apology that was read from St. Andrew's pulpit, and paid Hunter £100. Hunter announced that he would distribute the sum among Tait's daughters and when he failed to do so, Tait sued but lost.

As a result of the gossip and ill-feeling generated by the Corbett and related affairs, both Bishop Anderson and Archdeacon Hunter, his presumed successor, resigned their positions. Hunter commented that "the storm is pitiless, *a systematic blackening of the characters of all*. No one can live in this land with this adversary, and my prophecy is that in two years there will not be four clergymen on the two rivers."

His prediction possessed a degree of truth and by 1867 all of the most prominent clergymen had left Red River: Anderson in 1864, Hunter in 1865, and Chapman and Taylor in 1867. Their numbers were further reduced by William Cockran's death in 1864.

By 1865, then, the Halfbreeds had achieved a degree of confidence about their own identity, largely through Corbett's influence. They were to liberate Red River from the two tyrannies of the Hudson's Bay Company and the Roman Church. With Red River a Crown Colony, they would then follow Corbett, a thoroughly Protestant Englishman. They would have the balance of power. In the first decades of the history of the settlement, identity had been based on race, and rank in the Company. With Corbett's agitation acting as a catalyst, racial ties were weakened. They did not see themselves as English-speaking Protestant versions of the Métis. They did not identify with the Métis Nation. They were not petty settlers in a squalid little Company settlement in the isolated and frigid heart of British North America. They were not poverty-stricken coloured parishioners of the white-missionary–dominated Church of England. They were Protestant subjects of Her Most Britannic Majesty's Empire, an empire upon which the sun never set.

Article Twelve

The Métis and Mixed-Bloods of Rupert's Land before 1870

Irene M. Spry

Were the English-speaking mixed-bloods and French-speaking métis of what is now western Canada separate and mutually hostile groups? Or were they friendly and closely linked with each other? Frits Pannekoek contends that the *country-born* (as he terms the English-speaking mixed-bloods)[1] and the métis of Red River Settlement "were at odds years before the [Riel] resistance, and the origins of that hatred lay in the nature of Red River society." He concludes: "In fact, upon closer examination of the origins of Métis–Country-born hatred, it becomes apparent that the first Riel resistance was in part caused and certainly exacerbated not by racial and religious antagonisms introduced by the Canadians, but rather by a sectarian and racial conflict with roots deep in Red River's past."[2]

This view of the divisions within Red River Settlement is directly contrary to what a métis, Louis Goulet, remembered. Writing of 1867, when his family returned to Red River from the far western plains, he recollected:

> Something was missing in the Red River Colony: There wasn't the same feeling of unity and friendship that had always been felt among those people of different races and religions. And he [his father] wasn't the only one unhappy with the way things were going.
>
> The old-timers seemed to feel a strange mood in the air. Newcomers, especially the ones from Ontario, were eagerly sowing racial and religious conflict, banding together to fan the flames of discord between different groups in the Red River Settlement. These émigrés from Ontario, all of them Orangemen, looked as if their one dream in life was to make war on the Hudson's Bay Company, the Catholic Church and anyone who spoke French. . . . The latest arrivals were looking to be masters of everything, everywhere.[3]

Continuing tradition among twentieth-century English-speaking descendants of the Selkirk settlers supports Louis Goulet. As Miss Janet Bannerman of Old Kildonan recalled, "The relations between the French-speaking families and the rest of us in Red River were always of friendliness and goodwill. In the very earliest and hardest days of the settlement that friendship was established upon a lasting foundation by the French-Canadians and the métis who showed warmhearted kindness to the poor Scottish people when the lack of food at the Forks compelled them to go down to the buffalo hunters' headquarters at the mouth of the Pembina river in the winter time."[4] This, in turn, is consistent with Miss Anne Henderson's memories of walks, when she was a child early in this century, with her grandfather, who introduced her to all the friends he met, many of whom were French-speaking.[5] Similarly, George Sanderson, Jr., writing of his boyhood in Portage la Prairie, mentioned among his chums the "Pochas" [Poitras] and "Demers" [Desmarais] boys.[6]

Very little evidence of conflict, let alone "hatred," has come to light except in the clerical sources on which Pannekoek's conclusion seems in large measure to be based. Such sources, it is submitted, must be used with great reserve. Independent evidence is needed to test the

Source: Irene M. Spry, "The Métis and Mixed-Bloods of Rupert's Land before 1870," *The New Peoples: Being and Becoming Métis in North America*, eds. Jacqueline Peterson and Jennifer S.H. Brown (Winnipeg: University of Manitoba Press, 1985). Reprinted by permission.

testimony of writers who were concerned to convert the adherents of rival dogmas and to protect their own flocks from counter-conversion. Hostility between Catholic and Protestant divines was a byword in Rupert's Land.[7] Such antagonism as there may have been between French- and English-speaking communities was, indeed, largely sectarian, but it does not seem to have been racial in origin.

A preliminary survey of such nonclerical evidence as is available concerning the nature of the relationships of the natives of the country of Indian and French and Indian and other white descent[8] suggests that, far from being mutually hostile, métis and mixed-bloods were, as W.L. Morton put it, linked by "ties of blood and of long association on hunt and trip."[9]

Alexander Ross's celebrated statement may, perhaps, be taken with a pinch or two of salt, but it must at least be considered:

> We have now seen all the different classes of which this infant colony was composed brought together. The better to advance each other's interest, as well as for mutual support, all sects and creeds associated together indiscriminately, and were united like members of the same family, in peace, charity, and good fellowship. This state of things lasted till the Churchmen began to feel uneasy, and the Catholics grew jealous; so that projects were set on foot to separate the tares from the wheat. . . .
>
> Party spirit and political strife has been gaining ground ever since. The Canadians became jealous of the Scotch, the half-breeds of both; and their separate interests as agriculturalists, voyageurs, or hunters, had little tendency to unite them. At length, indeed, the Canadians and half-breeds came to a good understanding with each other; leaving then but two parties, the Scotch and the French. Between these, although there is, and always has been, a fair show of mutual good feeling, anything like cordiality in a common sentiment seemed impossible; and they remain, till this day, politically divided.[10]

Significantly, Ross said nothing about the mixed-bloods as a separate group, except as he described where each community lived; on the contrary, in his book *The Red River Settlement*, he noted a number of apparent affinities among and cooperation between métis and mixed-bloods. Thus, in his account of talk among Rupert's Landers, Ross mentioned their "narrations." These were "made up of an almost unintelligible jargon of the English, French and Indian languages."[11] This suggests at least some mingling of the English- and French-speaking elements in the population of mixed descent, an impression borne out by a traveller's observation concerning a cart train south of Red River Settlement: "In the 'polyglot jabber'" of the métis drivers "he heard 'fine broad Scotch,' a scattering of Gaelic and Irish brogue, and a plentiful mixture of 'rapidly uttered French *patois*.'"[12] Another traveller in the Red River Valley in 1864 joined a cart train under the command of Antoine Gingras, who "knew English" as well as French, though his drivers spoke only Indian and French.[13] J.G. Kohl in the 1850s recorded a bilingual statement by a métis: "Où je reste? Je ne peux pas te le dire. Je suis Voyageur — je suis Chicot, monsieur. Je reste partout. Mon grand-père était Voyageur: il est mort en voyage. Mon père était Voyageur: il est mort en voyage. Je mourrai aussi en voyage, et un autre Chicot prendra ma place. Such is our course of life."[14]

Louis Goulet, in describing the Frog Lake massacre, mentioned that he and his friends, André Nault and Dolphis Nolin, conversed in English mixed with a little French when they were held by the Cree.[15] He noted, too, that a French-speaking métis of Scottish descent, Johnny Pritchard, was interpreter to Tom Quinn. Presumably this meant that he could speak English.[16] A granddaughter of Norbert Welsh (an Irish-French métis), in enumerating the languages that her grandfather had at his command, ended the list with "and, of course, English."[17]

Similarly, some mixed-bloods spoke French — people such as Charles Thomas, who was in charge of the Hudson's Bay Company post at Reindeer Lake when Father Taché visited it in

1847.[18] "Big Jim" McKay, later to become the Honourable James McKay of Deer Lodge, whose father came from Sutherlandshire, spoke French,[19] as did members of another family of McKays, the "Little Bearskin" McKays, William McKay, his brother John ("Jerry") McNab Ballenden McKay, and his son Thomas.[20] Joseph Finlayson, one of the Roderick Finlayson family, also wrote and spoke French fluently.[21] It would appear, therefore, that many métis and mixed-bloods, at least among the elite, spoke both French and English, as well as one or more of the Indian languages, in which tongues those who did not speak both French and English could and did communicate. The English-speaking pioneer settlers of Portage la Prairie, for instance, were fluent in Cree, which "enabled them to associate freely with the French Half-breeds" of White Horse Plain, among whom most of them could claim cousins.[22]

No doubt the métis and mixed-bloods of Rupert's Land spoke this diversity of languages at least in part because they were the descendants of a rich diversity of ancestors. Their maternal forebears included Cree, Ojibwa, and Chipewyan, as well as French Canadians and Scots; their paternal ancestry included not only French and English, but also Orcadian, Scots, Irish, Shetland, and other European strains, notably the Danish ancestry of the numerous progeny of Peter Erasmus, Sr.[23] Baptiste Bruce, for instance, the guide with Dr. John Rae's Arctic expedition of 1848–49, claimed Highland and French as well as Indian descent.[24] Alick Fisher's mother was a métis.[25] Baptiste Robillard, a former guide with the Cumberland boat brigade, was accompanied out on the plains by a son-in-law, John Simpson, said to be the natural son of Thomas Simpson, the ill-fated Arctic explorer.[26] A long roster of names like Baptiste Kennedy attests to the complex mixture of origins among the métis. Among the mixed-bloods, similarly, there were many with French ancestry. "Big Jim" McKay had French antecedents through his mother, who was a Gladu(e).[27] Joe McKay, a "Little Bearskin," married one of the Poitras girls.[28] George Sanderson had two French grandmothers and a niece named Desmarais.[29]

It would be interesting to have a count of all mixed marriages, both *à la façon du pays* (according to the custom of the country) and those solemnized by the clergy. The fragmentary nature of the documentary record makes this impossible, but, even without such comprehensive information, it is evident that many marriages spanned the alleged gulf between the mixed-blood and métis groups. Among the marriages recorded in the Protestant parishes of Red River Settlement, a number involved couples with French and non-French names. It cannot, of course, be assumed that having a Scottish name meant that an individual was a mixed-blood, nor that all métis had French names. Some whose fathers came from Scotland or the Orkneys grew up speaking French and were assimilated to the culture of a French-speaking, Catholic métis mother, as in the case of the Bruce and Dease families.[30] In other cases, seemingly non-French marriages had in them a strong French element, as in the case of James McKay's marriage to Margaret Rowand[31] and Jeanette [Janet] Tate's marriage to Alex Birston.[32] Moreover, dominance in a family of French, Catholic culture did not necessarily exclude non-French influences any more than a dominant non-French culture excluded French or Catholic influences.

A further complication in an attempt to analyze marriages listed in the parish registers is that not all the apparently French–non-French marriages were between métis and mixed-bloods of whatever descent. At least a dozen Swiss–Swiss and a half-dozen French–French (or, more likely, Canadien–Canadienne) unions have been identified. Further, an apparently métis–mixed-blood marriage may turn out to be a Canadian–Scottish marriage. This adds uncertainty to the relevance of seeming cross-marriages to the question of métis–mixed-blood relationships. Norman Kittson, for example, who came from Quebec, married a daughter of Narcisse Marion, also from Quebec.[33]

Unfortunately, it has not been possible to analyze marriages in the Indian settlement, although some of the settlers there, such as Joseph Cook and his children,[34] were of mixed origin. Nor has it been possible to include data from the French-Catholic parishes. The fire that destroyed St. Boniface cathedral in 1860 destroyed most of the early formal records. There is, however, a list in the Provincial Archives of British Columbia of men married by the Catholic missionaries from the time of their arrival in 1818 to February 15, 1831.[35] Among the almost three hundred names listed, nearly twenty are non-French: mostly McDonnells, McLeods, and the like. Undoubtedly, some of their descendants had been assimilated to the culture of métis mothers, though the wives' names are not given.

Other scattered records that survive show that non-French names were, in some instances, changed to a spelling better suited to French pronunciation than the original spelling was. For example, "Sayer" became "Serre"[36] and "McKay" became "Macaille."[37] Similarly, French spelling was sometimes anglicized. Thus, the descendants of Michel Reine (Rayne and other variants), from Strasbourg, became "Wren."[38]

Despite all these gaps and ambiguities, the records in the Hudson's Bay Company and church registers of what appear to be cross-marriages between métis and mixed-bloods in the Protestant parishes of Red River Settlement from 1820 to 1841[39] are of considerable interest (see Table 12.1).

The spelling of names in these records varies from one to another and even from index to entry. It is, moreover, phonetic in character, and in many cases difficult to make out. Some marriage entries in the parish registers differ from those in the company registers and some either do not appear in the latter or are illegible. The usage adopted by the Provincial Archives of Manitoba in its index has therefore been followed.

Some of the men whose names appear in this list may have come from Europe. Certainly men from the Orkneys, Scotland, England, and elsewhere married women of mixed Indian–French ancestry, such as Hugh Gibson from the Orkneys, who married Angélique Chalifoux; Francis Heron and Henry Hallet, Sr., from England, who married Isabella Chalifoux and Catherine Dansee, respectively; meanwhile, Louis Gagnon from France married Jane McKay. John Wasuloski, probably a de Meuron, married Justine Fournier. George Saunderson (Sr.), from Scotland, married Lisset Lagimonère (Lagimodière), both of whose parents came from Quebec. There are other uncertainties in the list, but, imperfect as it is, it suggests that some 30 marriages among a total of 450, probably 5 percent or more, were marriages of men and women with French names to men and women with non-French names. This surely indicates that the métis and mixed-blood communities cannot have been rigidly isolated from each other. Indeed, the Reverend William Cockran bears witness to a French element in the mixture of origins among his parishioners at St. Andrews: In 92 families there were 39 European males and one female. The rest were "Orkney, English, Scotch, French, Welsh, Norwegian, Negro, and Jewish half-breeds."[40]

The Company's register of marriages for 1841 to 1851[41] shows proportionately fewer apparent cross-marriages, only some nine or ten out of a total of more than four hundred, but even this must have meant that there was a certain amount of going and coming between the métis and mixed-blood groups.

Further, marriages recorded in the parish registers were only those formally solemnized by the clergy. Unregistered marriages, à la façon du pays, may well have involved a greater proportion of cross-marriages, since the clergy were not, in general, sympathetic to members of their own congregation marrying into a rival sect. Fragmentary evidence of marriages which do not appear to be listed in the official registers has come to light. A paper on James McKay mentions two such cross-marriages: John Rowand to Julie Demarais; Angus McKay to Virginia Boulette.[42] John Moar married Matilda Morrisseau at Lac Seul in 1859.[43] Angus Harper married Peggy La Pierre at Oxford House in 1830,[44] and Joseph Everette married Nancy McKay in 1846.[45] The financial records for Red River Settlement mention one Louise McLeod, widow of Baptiste Larocque.[46] Nancy McKenzie, the discarded country wife of Chief Factor J.G. McTavish, married Pierre Leblanc.[47] One of the Carrière sisters of St. Boniface married Roger Marion (son of Narcisse Marion), while the other became Mrs. Henry Donald Macdonald.[48]

That Protestant anglophones and Catholic francophones did, indeed, associate with each other is made still more clear by reminiscences recorded in W.J. Healy's *Women of Red River*. Father Louis-François Laflèche used to visit the Sinclair house to play the piano there and to exchange music with the Sinclair girls. Everybody in the Settlement seems to have gone to St. Boniface cathedral to hear Sister Lagrave play the organ built by Dr. Duncan, medical officer of the Sixth Regiment of Foot[49] and "Christmas midnight mass at St. Boniface cathedral was always attended by many parties from across the river."[50]

On the St. Boniface side of the river, the Narcisse Marion home was a centre of hospitality that included English-speaking Protestants. Mrs. Henry Donald Macdonald (née Angélique Carrière) related that it was a "great house for dances. . . . Many of the Kildonan people and the other people across the river used to come to our parties, and we went to theirs. We knew them all."[51] Indeed, it was Narcisse Marion who hospitably received the Reverend John Black when he arrived to become the first Presbyterian minister in the Colony, and arranged for him to be taken across the river to the home of the leading Presbyterian, Sheriff Alexander Ross.[52]

Not only did colonists from the different parishes go to each other's parties, but also their children mixed with each other at school. Miss Janet Bannerman recalled that there were several children from well-to-do French-speaking families at her first school, St. John's parochial school. Among them she remembered Joseph and Marguerite Leclair, Emile Bouvette, Ambroise Fisher, Henri Laronde, and Baptiste Beauchemin.[53] By the same token, some anglophone children went to school in St. Boniface, notably James McKay's three children.[54]

Mrs. W.R. Black, granddaughter of Kate and Alexander Sutherland of Kildonan, rounded off her recollections in this way: "I have said so much about the Riels and the Lagimodières because they and the other French-speaking families who were our neighbours are associated with my earliest memories almost as much as the English-speaking families of Red River." Her father, John Sutherland, built a new house across the river after the flood of 1852 swept away the original Sutherland house at Point Douglas. The whole family spoke French as well as English and John Sutherland became a confidant of his French-speaking neighbours and a link between them and the Kildonan settlers.[55]

Business transactions also linked the French- and English-speaking communities: grain from the Carrières' farm at St. Boniface was taken to Robert Tait's mill to be ground;[56] Moise Goulet, a noted plains trader, when illness forced him to retire, sold his whole outfit to A.G.B. Bannatyne;[57] Norbert Welsh, another prominent trader of Irish and Quebec descent, after a disillusioning transaction with "Bobbie" (Robert) Tait, took charge of Bannatyne's cart trains en route to St. Paul and, when he set up in business for himself, dealt with Bannatyne.[58] On January 1, 1846, Peter Garrioch went to see his friend Pascal Berlan[d], about getting some buffalo for him, in company with Peter Pruden and two others.[59] Frederick Bird was apprenticed to a Catholic blacksmith named Bovette.[60]

Although the evidence is scanty, it would appear that métis and mixed-bloods joined together in the great Red River buffalo hunt. Alexander Ross records that in 1840 the captain of the hunt was one Jean-Baptiste Wilkie, "an English half-breed brought up among the French," while one of Wilkie's captains was a member of the Hallett family.[61] Ross himself travelled with the hunt that year; the late Miss Sybil Inkster once spoke to me of her relatives going to the buffalo hunt; and Henry Erasmus "accompanied the buffalo hunters on trips to the prairies after meat," of which he got a full share, even though he did not actually take part in the hunt itself.[62] The Reverend John Smithurst wrote in June 1840 that most of his parishioners (all Anglicans)

Table 12.1   Apparent Marriages between Métis and Mixed-Bloods

Entry Number	Cross-Marriage, with Date and Reference Number
13	Michael Lambere to Peggy (January 25, 1821 SJM[a] 1820–1835)
18	George Saunderson to Lisset Lajimonierè (March 30, 1821 SJM 1820–1835)
23	William Dickson to Justine Pacquette (June 9, 1821 SJM 1820–1835)
36	John Warring to Lydia Fournier (November 11, 1821 SJM 1820–1835)
37	Martin Norte to Catherine Treathey (November 11, 1821 SJM 1820–1835)
58	Joshua Halero to Françoise Laurain (November 18, 1823 SJM 1820–1835)
82	Henry Hallet, Jr., to Catherine Parenteau (October 18, 1824 SJM 1820–1835)
83	David Sandison to Louisa Giboche (October 19, 1824 SJM 1820–1835)
111	John Anderson to Mary (Murray?) [Desmarais] (January 31, 1826 SJM 1820–1835)
122	William Mackay to Julia Chalifoux (August 13, 1826 SJM 1820–1835)
124	James Swain to Margaret Racette (October 3, 1826 SJM 1820–1835)
125	William Birston to Hazelique Marchand (December 8, 1826 SJM 1820–1835)
129	William Bruce to Frances Andre (1827 SJM 1820–1835)
134	Andrew Spence to Susette L'Eunay (October 30, 1827 SJM 1820–1835)
167	George Kipling to Isabella Landrie (November 19, 1828 SJM 1820–1835)
176	Peter Pruden to Josette (Susette) Gothvier (May 7, 1829 SJM 1820–1835)
177	James Monkman to Nancy Shaboyee (May 12, 1829 SJM 1820–1835)

Table 12.1   (*Continued*)

Entry Number	Cross-Marriage, with Date and Reference Number
194	Pierre St. Pierre to Susannah Short (February 8, 1830 SJM 1820–1835)
202	Francis Desmarais to Harriet Spence (date and reference number missing)
212	John Batish Shurdan to Mary Lewis (January 6, 1831 SJM 1820–1835)
215	Aimable Hogue to Margarette Taylor (March 24, 1831 SJM 1820–1835)
221	Hugh Cameron to Mary Jordan (October 26, 1831 SJM 1820–1835)
236	John Aimable McKay to Lizette La Vallee (March 12, 1832 SJM 1820–1835)
253	Charles Desmarais to Harriet Favel (February 7, 1833 SJM 1820–1835)
272	William Spence to Loraine Truche (March 6, 1834 SJM 1820–1835)
287	James Swain to Josette Couteau (January 7, 1835 SJM 1820–1835)
289	William Sutherland to Suzette Truche (December 26, 1834 SJM 1835–1854)
308	James McNab to Sarah Michael (January 21, 1836 SJM 1835–1854)
331	John Swain to Mary Alerie (January 18, 1837 SJM 1835–1854)
332	Baptiste De Champ to Margaret Johnston (January 19, 1837 SAM[b] 1835–1860)
376	Baptist DeMarais to Sophia Erasmus (December 28, 1837 SJM 1835–1860)
390	Andrew Dennet to Mary Martinois (September 25, 1838 SAM 1835–1860)
434	Peter Warren Dease to Elizabeth Chouinard (August 3, 1840 SAM 1835–1860)

Source: Provincial Archives of Manitoba; HBCA, E.4/1b; parish registers for St. John's and St. Andrew's (Church of England Index to Parish Registers, 1820–1900).

[a] sjm — St. John's Marriages

[b] sam — St. Andrew's Marriages

had gone either on the buffalo hunt or with the boat brigades.[63] In June 1845, Peter Garrioch was with the buffalo hunt, which certainly numbered métis families among those in the one hundred tents. Of these, Garrioch mentioned Francis Lauze [Lauzon] and Morin.[64] George Sa[u]nderson, Jr., gives a lively description of the way in which francophone boys were trained to hunt buffalo. He appears to have watched these proceedings. He states explicitly that the "Pochas" [Poitras] family were on one hunt in which his family took part.[65]

Besides the buffalo hunt, the major occupation of the mixed-bloods and métis was freighting, in boat brigades to York Factory and up the Saskatchewan; in the Red River cart trains to the south, to St. Peter's and St. Paul, and west by the Carlton Trail and other traditional overland routes; and in winter with dog trains carrying the winter packet or other urgent freight.

Scattered data about the personnel of boat brigades suggest a mixture of racial origins. In the Hudson's Bay Company's account books the names of some of the tripmen who received advances are listed, especially in the case of advances made at York Factory. The record of advances at York in the summers of 1826 and 1830, for example, gives a mingle-mangle of French and non-French names: In 1826, ten men with French names and four with non-French names received advances. Five others with French names and one uncertain did not have accounts.[66] In 1830, ten French names appear, with four names that originated in the United Kingdom, two mixed names (François Whitford and François Bruce), and one Indian name.[67] It is possible, though not documented, that the crew of each boat was separated on the basis of French or non-French origin.

Information about the personnel of the cart brigades is also limited, but suggests a similar mixture. The *Daily Minnesotan* for July 22, 1854, stated that "Messrs. Kittson, Rolette, Caviller, Grant and others had arrived at Traverse des Sioux with nearly two hundred carts." The same journal published a letter on September 13, 1858, stating that the Sioux had killed two men on the plains, "Busquer" [Louis Bosquet], in charge of Henry Fisher's carts, and John Beads.[68] *The St. Paul Daily Pioneer* reported on July 12, 1870, that the *St. Cloud Times* had recorded 70 arrivals of Red River carts since July 9. They belonged to Gingras and Bannatyne.[69] The voyageurs' signatures to a Hudson's Bay Company contract to make the journey from Fort Garry to St. Peter's in 1850 included nine French names and seven Orcadian and other non-French names.[70]

Only one document has been found containing information about mixed personnel travelling in winter with dog trains. The party left from Île-à-la-Crosse, not from Red River, but it may be significant: Samuel McKenzie, writing on January 15, 1867, noted that "Peter Linklater and Michel Bouvier go with the North Packet to Carlton accompanied by Baptiste Payette and James Wilson."[71] A party was sent from Red River Settlement in 1832 to bring back a herd of sheep from the United States. It too was mixed, having had in it, besides Scots, a French Canadian, and an Irishman, two French half-breeds and two young English half-breeds.[72]

Some information is available about the voyageurs and hunters who accompanied the increasingly numerous expeditions engaged in exploration, surveying, and other official missions in the nineteenth century, to say nothing of pleasure parties travelling on the western plains in "search of adventure and heavy game."[73] John Rae's Arctic searching expedition of 1848–49, for example, included, besides Canadians and Shetlanders, Baptiste Bruce, the guide already mentioned, Baptiste Emelin [Hamelin], Baptiste Fredrique, Xavier Laplante [Antoine Plante], William Sabiston, and Edmund Stevenson, all natives of the country, and so, presumably, of mixed-blood or métis origin. The natives in his team in 1850–51 were John Fidler, John Hébert dit Fabien (not from Red River), Charles Kennedy, Alexandre Laliberté dit Lachouette, Peter Linklater, Baptiste Marcellais, Baptiste Peltier, and Samuel Sinclair, who was probably a native of the country. However, none of the Rupert's Landers with Rae's 1853–54 expedition had a French name. They were Jacob Beads; John Beads, Jr.; Henry Fidler; and James Johnstone.[74]

Palliser's expedition set out from Red River in 1856 with the following men, besides James Beads, the expedition's servant: John Ferguson, first guide; Henry Hallet[t], second guide; Pierre Beauchamp; Samuel Ballenden[dine]; George Daniel; Baptiste Degrace; Perre Falcon; Amable Hogue; Donald Matheson; [Antoine] Morin; John Foulds; George Morrison; Charles Racette; John Ross; John Simpson; Thomas Sinclair; Robert Sutherland; George Taylor; Joseph Vermette; and Pascal.[75] At least some of Palliser's "Red River contingent" in 1858 were of French origin: among the Red River men who stayed with him at Fort Edmonton during the winter of 1858–59 were Pierre Beauchamp and Baptiste La Graisse, while Chief Factor W.J. Christie, who, on behalf of Palliser, paid off those who returned to Red River, called out *"assez"* to each man when he had taken all the trade goods to which his wage entitled him. Others, such as Todd and Ballenden, were of at least partly non-French origin.[76] In the fall of 1858, James Beads returned from Edmonton to Red River, on hearing that his brother had been killed by the Sioux. When Beads came back in the spring of 1859 he brought with him the redoubtable hunter Jean-Baptiste Vital[le].[77]

When Henry Youle Hind set off in 1858 for the western plains, his party included "six Cree half-breeds, a native of Red River of Scotch descent [John Ferguson?], one Blackfoot half-breed, one Ojibway half-breed, and one French Canadian." It is noticeable that, with one exception, he did not consider the European derivation of the "half-breeds" of sufficient importance to be mentioned.[78]

The Boundary Survey of 1872–76 recruited a troop of native scouts styled "the 49th Rangers," under the command of William Hallett. The deputy commander's name was McDonald, and the names of the three sub-leaders were Gosselin, Lafournais, and Gaddy. The rank and file, too, included men of both French and Scottish or other descent.[79]

Records of sportsmen travelling in the west for pleasure do not always give the names of their voyageurs and hunters, but Hudson's Bay Company accounts show that the Comte de la Guiche had in his employment John Ferguson, Alexis Goulait, and Goulait's son,[80] in June 1851, when he left Red River on a trip to the Rocky Mountains. Lord Dunmore's party set out on August 22, 1862, with Jim McKay (spelled Mackay by Dunmore) as hunter-in-chief, Baptiste Valet as hunter, James Whitford, Pierre (?) and (?) De Charme as buffalo hunters and drivers, and Joe Macdonald as hunter, cook, and driver.[81]

None of this suggests any sharp segregation between Red River mixed-bloods and métis. Indeed, Palliser, describing the expedition's great buffalo hunt in 1858 in the neighbourhood of modern Irricana, Alberta, commented: "The run was magnificent, and there was considerable emulation between my Saskatchewan and my Red River men,"[82] a comment that indicates some solidarity of the group from Red River, regardless of descent, vis-à-vis the group from Lac Ste. Anne; elsewhere, however, Palliser commented on what seemed to him a remarkable difference in energy and progressiveness between the Canadian and French and the Scottish "half-breeds."[83]

Other mixed ventures include the party of emigrants from Red River to the Columbia River, which in 1841 made the extraordinary journey across the plains and through the mountains under James Sinclair's leadership. Its members numbered among them an almost equal balance of men with names suggesting French and non-French origin, all of them speaking either French or English. Table 12.2 shows the list of men in the original agreement between the emigrants and the Company. Cash advances were made to all but three of these men and to two not listed in the agreement: David Flett and Pierre Larocque, Jr.[84] John Flett is not in either list, but other evidence makes it clear that he was with the party.[85]

In contrast, none (or, at most, one)[86] of the second group of Red River emigrants to the Columbia, who, again under James Sinclair's leadership, went in 1854 to Walla Walla (Washington), seems to have had a French name, at least according to the list given by John V. Campbell, Sinclair's brother-in-law, who, as a lad, was a member of the party.[87]

Table 12.2   Emigrants from Red River Settlement to the Columbia River, in the James Sinclair Party, 1841

François Jacques	James Birston
Julien Bernier	John Cunningham
Baptiste Oreille or Rhelle	Alexander Birston
Pierre Larocque	Archibald Spence
Louis Larocque	François Gagnon
Pierre St. Germain	Joseph Klyne
John Spence	James Flett
Henry Buxton	John Tate
Gonzaque Zastre	Horatio Nelson Calder
William Flett	Toussaint Joyal
Charles McKay	[David Flett]

Source: HBCA, B.235/d/82, p. 56; A.12/7, fo. 392d (agreement between emigrants to the Columbia River and Hudson's Bay Company, dated 31 May 1841); William J. Betts, "From Red River to the Columbia," *The Beaver* (Spring 1971): 50–55.

Of greater importance than evidence of mixed parties freighting, travelling, and emigrating from Red River Settlement is the story of the joint mixed-blood–métis struggle against the claim of the Hudson's Bay Company to the exclusive right to trade in furs in Rupert's Land and, until the License to Trade lapsed in 1859, in the Indian territories beyond. W.L. Morton tells this story admirably in his introduction to *Eden Colvile's Letters, 1849–52*.[88] With a brief lull, while the Sixth Regiment of Foot were stationed at Red River from 1846 to 1848, the mixed-blood–métis population of Red River Settlement agitated throughout the 1840s for recognition of their "rights," as natives of the country, to take part in the fur trade and for redress of other grievances. The Sayer trial in 1849 established that, in practice, the joyful shout of the métis, "Le commerce est libre," was justified, but the natives of Rupert's Land still wanted a voice in the government of the colony.

Evidence in Peter Garrioch's diary of métis–mixed-blood friendship and fraternization has already been cited. Garrioch also makes it clear that the men who banded together in 1845 to resist the imposition by the Council of Assiniboia of an import duty on goods brought in from American territory were of diverse origins: Canadian, Irish, métis, and mixed-blood. Besides Peter Garrioch, they were Peter Hayden, Alexis Goulet, St. Germain (which Garrioch spelled Chagerma), Dominique Ducharme, Henry Cook, and Charles Laroque.[89]

On August 29, 1845, a larger group of mixed-blood and métis traders submitted a list of questions to Governor and Chief Factor Alexander Christie concerning their rights (see Table 12.3).[90] In another version of this list of signatures, given by Alexander Begg in his *History of the North-West*, four of these names are omitted: Pierre Laverdure, Edward Harmon [or Harman], James Monkman, and Edward [Antoine] Desjarlais, Sr.[91] Two others were added: Adal Trottier and Charles Hole [possible Houle]. Again, this is a not uneven mixture of métis and mixed-bloods.

In 1846, two parallel petitions, one in French and one in English, were drafted at a meeting held on February 26 in Andrew McDermot's house. The petitions contained demands for free trade and representative government. James Sinclair carried both of them to England, where Alexander K. Isbister submitted them to the imperial government.[92] As W.L. Morton noted: "The settlement was an Anglo-French colony, a European-Indian community, and the métis, excluded from public office like the English half-breeds, were only demanding that the

Table 12.3 Signatories to the Letter to Governor C.F. Alexander Christie, dated 29 August 1845

James Sinclair	Peter Garrioch
Baptiste Laroque	Jack Spence
Thomas Logan	Alexis Goulait [Goulet]
Pierre Laverdure	Antoine Morin
Joseph Monkman	William McMillan
Baptiste Wilkie	Louis Letendre [dit Batoche]
Baptiste Farman (Famian)	Robert Montour
Edward Harman	Jack Anderson
John Dease	James Monkman
Henry Cook	Antoine Desjarlais, Snr.
William Bird	Thomas McDermot
John Vincent	

Source: HBCA, D.5/15, fos. 139a–139b; PAM MGZ 135, "Red River Correspondence"; Alexander Begg, *History of the North-West*, 3 vols. (Toronto: Hunter, Rose and Co., 1894–95), 1: 261–62. Begg omits Montour but adds Adel Trottier and Charles Hole.

institutions of the Colony should reflect its ethnic composition. In so doing they spoke for the English half-breeds as well as for themselves, as they were to do again in 1869."[93] As well, "English half-breeds" such as James Sinclair spoke for their métis associates — as, for instance, in the Sayer trial, at which Sinclair represented the four métis defendants and their armed colleagues who had surrounded the court house.[94]

The younger generation of mixed-bloods and métis was frustrated and restless. The demand for representation on the council and for a free trade in furs was a demand for an outlet for ambition, energy, and enterprise.[95]

The métis organized a "council of the nation" and pressed upon Sir George Simpson still another petition when he arrived in the Settlement in June 1849. Sent with a covering letter from Sinclair, dated June 14, 1849, this petition was signed by William McMalen [McMillan], Louis Rielle [Riel Sr.], Pascal Berland, Baptiste Fairjeu, Baptiste Laroque, Antoine Morein, Louis Letendre, Solomon Amelin, and Urbain Delorme.[96] A letter presented to Simpson when he was again in Red River Settlement in the summer of 1850 was signed by William McMillan, Solomon Amelin, Louis Riel, and eighteen others. They demanded that Recorder Thom should go and that they should have representation on the Council "chosen from our nation by ourselves."[97]

Yet another petition in 1851 reached the Company via the Aborigines' Protection Society and the Colonial Office asking "that Red River be granted British liberty, a Governor appointed by the Crown, a judge similarly appointed and able to speak English and French, power in the Governor to appoint Councillors in an emergency, the dismissal of Councillors who had forfeited public confidence or been subservient to the Company, and the removal of Thom to some other British colony." The 540 signatures were attested by five leading métis.[98]

These data, fragmentary and incomplete as they are, cannot be conclusive, but, as far as they go, they do suggest an intermingling of mixed-bloods and métis, fellow feeling and cooperation between the two groups, not separation or hostility. This impression is strengthened by yet another petition sent in 1857 to the Legislature of Canada "from Donald McBeath and others[,] inhabitants and Natives of the Settlement situated on the Red River, in the Assiniboine Country. . . ."[99]

This petition was promulgated by a mixed-blood, "Captain" William Kennedy, of Arctic fame, who visited Red River in 1857 as an emissary of Canadian commercial interests. It bore the signatures of 119 men with French names or known to be French-speaking, as well as fourteen more who may have been of French origin, and two with mixed names, out of a total of 511, including a number with Indian or probably Indian names. Though not all the apparently French signatures were those of métis — that of Narcisse Marion, for example — the francophone roster is considerable. This is surprising, since, according to Alvin C. Gluek, Jr., the Catholic clergy had discouraged their parishioners from signing the petition.[100]

As late as 1869–70, a contemporary observer, Walter Traill, commented: "The natives [of Red River Settlement], both English and French, though not resenting the newcomers from the newly formed Dominion, wonder why it is that they . . . should be slighted by Canadians who are coming to rule them." And again: "If the Canadian Government . . . had recognized the natives, both English and French, both would have given their loyal support."[101]

"Hostility" reported by rival clerics, if it existed, may well have reflected deference to the missionaries' wishes and pressures. However, at least one missionary, that turbulent priest Father G.-A. Belcourt, cooperated closely with Sinclair and Isbister. Besides Sinclair, Thomas McDermot, John Anderson, and Peter Garrioch attended the meeting on February 26, 1846, at which Belcourt presided, speaking in French. It appears that they were the only English-speaking people at this meeting.[102]

An observation made by Eugene Bourgeau, botanical collector with the Palliser expedition, is further evidence of mutual métis–mixed-blood friendship. A compatriot, Ernest St. C. Cosson, the eminent French botanist, said of Bourgeau: "Par l'influence que lui donnait sa double qualité de Français et de catholique, il se concilia l'amitié de ces peuplades [the natives of the West], qui ont gardé le souvenir de notre domination, comprennent notre langue, et sont restées fidèles aux principaux dogmes de notre religion."[103] [*Editor's translation*: Because of the influence he has as both a Frenchman and a Catholic, he has won the friendship of these natives of the west, who remember our rule, understand our language, and have remained loyal to the principal beliefs of our religion.] This was the man whose account of the Sunday services held by Palliser (a staunch Protestant) led Charles Gay to write in *Le Tour du Monde*: "Touchant accord que celui de ces croyances si diverses, ailleurs si fécondes en antagonismes et en rivalités, se confondant, au pied des montagnes rocheuses, dans une même bonne foi et dans une commune simplicité!"[104] [*Editor's translation*: Religious beliefs, so full of divergences leading to conflicts and rivalries, came together at the foot of the Rocky Mountains, into a common good faith and simplicity.]

Palliser, too, noted this harmony. The métis Catholics from Lac Ste. Anne asked leave "to attend Divine worship," despite the fact that the prayers read for the Red River men, who "belonged to the Church of England," were from that Church's service. Palliser, therefore, through an interpreter, "conducted the lessons and half the prayers in Cree." He mentioned "this circumstance to show the respectful tendency and absence of bigotry of these men, in their appreciation of Divine service."[105]

If, then, even religious differences did not go very deep, were there important cleavages in Red River society? The answer must surely be yes. There were two fundamental divisions,[106] but these were not divisions between métis and mixed-blood.

The first was a division between the well-educated and well-to-do gentry, the officers and retired officers of the Hudson's Bay Company and those of their progeny who had achieved respectability, the clergy, and the prosperous merchants, in contrast to the mass of unlettered, unpropertied natives of the country — the "engagés" of the Hudson's Bay Company and of the Nor'Westers before them and their descendants. James Sinclair, for example, was recognized as a "gentleman"; he was a close friend of his British-born son-in-law, Dr. William Cowan, an officer of the Hudson's Bay Company, as well as of his brother, Chief Factor William Sinclair II, and even of Sir George Simpson, despite his battles with the Company.[107] This set him apart from the ordinary tripmen, whom he employed on his freighting ventures. The gap was one occasioned by ambition, affluence, education, and social status as against poverty and the inferior status of employees or, at best, of hunters, petty traders, or small farmers.

The second was the division between the professional farmer and the hunter and plains trader, between the sedentary population and those to whom the freedom of a wandering life out on the plains was more important than economic security and material comfort. This was the irreconcilable cleavage, so convincingly analyzed in George F.G. Stanley's classic, *The Birth of Western Canada*,[108] and described in Goulet's, Welsh's, and Sanderson's reminiscences.

As Jennifer Brown concludes in *Strangers in Blood*, the "half-breed" descendants of the men of both the North West and Hudson's Bay Companies "combined to define and defend common interests and finally to take military action in the Rebellions of 1869 and 1885."[109] Western Canada, as we know it today, was indeed born of conflict, conflict not between métis and mixed-blood, but between a wandering, free life and settlement; a conflict between agriculturalists, especially the flood of newcomers in search of landed property and wealth, and the old way of life that both métis and mixed-bloods had had in common with their Indian cousins, a way of life based on adjustment to the natural environment and the shared use of the free gifts of nature. That way of life was doomed with the coming of surveyors, fences, police, organized government, settlers, and private rights of property in real estate and natural resources.[110] With it went the prosperity and independence of all but a small elite of métis and mixed-bloods alike.

NOTES

1. Here the term *mixed-blood* is used (in spite of its biological ineptitude) instead of Pannekoek's term *country-born* to denote anglophone Rupert's Landers of hybrid Indian and white ancestry. After all, the children of Jean-Baptiste and Julie Lagimodière and those of Kate and Alexander Sutherland and other Selkirk settlers were country-born even though they had no Indian ancestry. A possible alternative might be to use *métis* with a qualifying adjective, as Alexander Morris did: "The *Metis* who were present at the [North West] Angle [of the Lake of the Woods] and who, with one accord, whether of French or English origin." (*The Treaties of Canada with the Indians of Manitoba and the North-West Territories* [Toronto: Belfords, Clarke and Co., 1880], 51). Similarly, Isaac Cowie wrote of one man being an Irish and another a French Métis in his book, *The Company of Adventurers: A Narrative of Seven Years in the Service of the Hudson's Bay Company* (Toronto: William Briggs, 1913), 191, and George F.G. Stanley of "English Métis" in "Indian Raid at Lac la Biche," *Alberta History* 24 (Summer 1976) 3: 25. It seems simpler, however, to use *mixed-blood* for the anglophones of mixed ancestry as a reasonably close equivalent of *métis* for the francophones of mixed descent.
2. Frits Pannekoek, "The Rev. Griffiths Owen Corbett and the Red River Civil War of 1869–70," *Canadian Historical Review* 57 (June 1976) 2: 134.
3. Guillaume Charette, *Vanishing Spaces: Memoirs of Louis Goulet* (Winnipeg: Éditions Bois-Brûlés, 1980; translated by Ray Ellenwood, from the original French edition, *L'Espace de Louis Goulet*, 1976), 59.
4. W.J. Healy, *Women of Red River* (Winnipeg: Russell, Lang and Co. Ltd., 1923), 88.
5. Personal conversation, Winnipeg, May 22, 1973.
6. George William Sanderson, "'Through Memories [sic] Windows' as Told to Mary Sophia Desmarais, by her Uncle, George William Sanderson (1846–1936)," 2, Provincial Archives of Manitoba (hereinafter cited as PAM) MGI/A107.
7. John Palliser wrote from Edmonton of "the black looks of the hostile divines. I understand that sometimes hostilities have proceeded further than mere looks." (HBCA, D.5/49, 1859 [2], fos. 245–46). I am grateful to the Hudson's Bay Company for kind permission to use material in its archives. The Rev. John Smithurst wrote in his journal: "We see the eagle of Rome watching to seize as its prey these precious souls." (PAC, MG19, E6, vol. 2, June 12, 1841). Father A.G. Morice, in his *Histoire de l'Église catholique dans l'Ouest canadien* (St. Boniface et Montréal: Granger Frères, 1915), 1:216, commented on the arrival of the Methodist missionaries that they "allaient se mesurer plutôt avec les enseignements de la Robe Noire et les pratiques religieuses que ses néophytes tenaient d'elles, qu'avec les ténèbres épaisses et l'immoralité révoltante dans lesquelles croupissaient

encore plusieurs des nations barbares du Canada central" (i.e., western Canada). There are many similar passages throughout the work.

8. Since the European origins of mixed-bloods included Highland and Lowland Scottish, Orcadian, Shetland, Swiss, Danish, and other strains, as well as French, the commonly used description, *English*, scarcely seems appropriate.

9. W.L. Morton, ed., *Alexander Begg's Red River Journal and Other Papers Relative to the Red River Resistance of 1869–1870* (Toronto: Champlain Society, 1956), 12.

10. Alexander Ross, *The Red River Settlement* (London: Smith, Elder and Co., 1856; reprinted Edmonton: Hurtig, 1972), 80–81. References are to the Hurtig reprint.

11. Ibid., 79.

12. Cited in Rhoda R. Gilman, Carolyn Gilman, and Deborah M. Stultz, *The Red River Trails: Oxcart Routes between St. Paul and the Selkirk Settlement, 1820–1870* (St. Paul: Minnesota Historical Society, 1979), 14. This "polyglot jabber" was, no doubt, Bungay, which the late Mrs. J.L. Doupe told me was widely used when she was a child in Winnipeg.

13. J.A. Gilfillan, "A Trip through the Red River Valley in 1864," *North Dakota Historical Quarterly* 1 (October 1926 to July 1927) 4: 37–40.

14. J.G. Kohl, *Kitchi-Gami: Wanderings round Lake Superior*, trans. Lascelles Wraxall (London: Chapman and Hall, 1860; reprinted Minneapolis: Ross and Haines, 1956), 260. I am indebted to Jacqueline Peterson for this reference.

15. Charette, *Vanishing Spaces*, 119.

16. Ibid., 116.

17. Television broadcast, Ontario TV, 1981. "The Last Buffalo Hunter," featuring Norbert Welsh.

18. Barbara Benoit, "The Mission at Île-à-la-Crosse," *The Beaver* (Winter 1980): 46.

19. Inkster papers, typescript account of the career of "The Honourable James McKay — Deer Lodge," 1 and 5, PAM. See also Allan Turner, "James McKay," *Dictionary of Canadian Biography*, ed. Francess G. Halpenny and Jean Hamlin, 11 vols. (Toronto: University of Toronto Press, 1972) 10: 473–75; N. Jaye Goossen, "A Wearer of Moccasins: The Honourable James McKay of Deer Lodge," annotated typescript published in substance in *The Beaver* (Autumn 1978): 44–53; and Mary McCarthy Ferguson, *The Honourable James McKay of Deer Lodge* (Winnipeg: published by the author, 1972).

20. Cowie, *Company of Adventurers*, 191–92.

21. Ibid., 192.

22. A.C. Garrioch, *The Correction Line* (Winnipeg: Stovel Co. Ltd., 1933), 200–1. I am indebted to Mr. Brian Gallagher for this reference.

23. Irene M. Spry, "A Note on Peter Erasmus's Family Background" and "Family Tree," in Peter Erasmus, *Buffalo Days and Nights* (Calgary: Glenbow-Alberta Institute, 1976), 303–5, 324–28, and end papers.

24. E.E. Rich, ed., *John Rae's Correspondence with the Hudson's Bay Company on Arctic Exploration, 1844–1855* (London: Hudson's Bay Record Society [HBRS], 1953), 353–54.

25. Cowie, *Company of Adventurers*, 220.

26. Ibid., 348. It is possible that Cowie was mistaken; Sir George Simpson also had a son called John.

27. Inkster Papers, "James McKay," 1, PAM.

28. Mary Weekes, *The Last Buffalo Hunter, As Told by Norbert Welsh* (New York: Thomas Nelson and Sons, 1939; Toronto: Macmillan of Canada, 1945), 23.

29. Sanderson, "Memories," title and p. 8, and list of marriages, Table 1, p. 101, PAM, MGI/A107.

30. Lionel Dorge, "The Métis and Canadian Councillors of Assiniboia," *The Beaver* (Summer, Autumn, and Winter 1974), especially Part 3, 56–57. Douglas N. Sprague, in his research on Sir John A. Macdonald and the métis, has analyzed cross-marriages on the basis of the 1870 census, from which he has been able to trace all marriages back for three generations.

31. Goossen, "James McKay," 47.

32. Charles A. Throssell wrote the following note on January 20, 1966: "John Tate — Who's [*sic*] only daughter, Jeanette, married Alex Burston about 1830. . . . They were both of French Canadian descent." This note was sent by Alex Burston's daughter, Mrs. Mary Burston Throssell, to Mr. William J. Betts of Bremerton, Washington. He very kindly sent me a copy on November 14, 1971. An entry in St. John's parish register states that Alex Burston [Birston] married Janet Tate on June 28, 1832, No. 237, St. John's Marriage Register, 1820–1835.

33. W.L. Morton, Introduction in E.E. Rich, ed., *London Correspondence inward from Eden Colvile, 1849–1852* (London: HBRS, 1956), xiv, l, 246.

34. HBCA, E.4/1b, also recorded in PAM, Parish records. Some cross-marriages are recorded in the Indian church register of marriages, such as that of Sally Erasmus to Antoine Kennedy, December 23, 1847 (no. 57d), HBCA E.4/2.

35. Provincial Archives of British Columbia (hereinafter cited as PABC), Add Mss 345, File 135.
36. Les Archives de la Société historique de St. Boniface has the record of the marriage of "Guillaume Serre," alias William Sayer. I am indebted to Lionel Dorge for a copy of this record.
37. Dorge, "Métis and Canadian Councillors," Part 3, 57.
38. PABC, Wren Family papers; Spry, "Note on Family Background," in Erasmus, *Buffalo Days and Nights.*
39. HBCA, E.4/1b and 2, and PAM microfilm of parish registers. There are some discrepancies between these two sets of records. Marriages of Barbara Gibson and Isabella Spence to James Louis have been omitted because James Louis was the son of a mulatto from New England, not, as might be supposed, of French extraction. A record of the marriage of Margaret Louis [or Lewis] is omitted for the same reason (HBCA, E.4/1b, fo. 221, and A.38/8, fo. 36). I am indebted to the keeper of the Hudson's Bay Company Archives for this information. Nancy Budd's marriage to Michel Reine is also omitted because he was from Strasbourg.
40. John E. Foster, "Missionaries, Mixed-bloods and the Fur Trade: Four Letters of the Rev. William Cockran, Red River Settlement, 1830–1833," *Western Canadian Journal of Anthropology* 3 (1972) 1: 110 and 112.
41. HBCA, E.4/2.
42. Goossen, "James McKay," 48.
43. The marriage contract is reproduced in Sylvia Van Kirk, *"Many Tender Ties": Women in Fur-Trade Society, 1670–1870* (Winnipeg: Watson and Dwyer Publishing Ltd., 1980), 118.
44. Ibid., 117–19.
45. HBCA, B.239/Z/39, fo. 22.
46. HBCA, B.235/c/1, fo. 248d.
47. Van Kirk, *"Many Tender Ties,"* 188.
48. Healy, *Women of Red River,* 119.
49. Ibid., 34–35.
50. Ibid., 208.
51. Ibid., 119.
52. Ibid., 68.
53. Ibid., 87.
54. Ferguson, *James McKay,* 60.
55. Healy, *Women of Red River,* 59 and 61.
56. Ibid., 119.
57. Charette, *Vanishing Spaces,* 70.
58. Weekes, *Last Buffalo Hunter,* 35–45, 57, 60–72, and 201–2.
59. Garrioch Journal, January 1, 1846, PAM.
60. Sanderson, "Memories," 12, PAM, MGI/A107.
61. Ross, *Red River Settlement,* 248 and 271.
62. Erasmus, *Buffalo Days and Nights,* 6.
63. PAC, MG19 E6, vol. 2, journal entry for June 21, 1840.
64. Garrioch Journal, June 10 and 16, October 1 and 2, 1845, PAM.
65. Sanderson, "Memories," 3, PAM, MG9/A107.
66. HBCA, B.235/d/26, fo. 2d, 1826.

John Ashburn	Louis Lapierre dit Brilliant
J. Bts [sic] Boisvert (no account)	François Laframboise (no account)
Alexis Bonamis dit Lesperence	William Malcolm
Rennes Cardinal (no account)	Simon Martin (no account)
Antoine Deschamps (no account)	Pierre Papin
Antoine Dagenais	Medard Poitras
Leon Dupuis	David Scott
Toussaint Joyal	Jacques St. Denis
Louis La Rive	David Sandison
Jacques Le'Tang (no account)	Louis Thyfault [sic]

67. HBCA, B.235/d/44, 1830.

François Savoyard	Henry House [Howse?]
Carriole Lagrasse	Joseph Savoyard
Pierre Savoyard	Richd Favel
James Birston	Bte Boyer
Antoine Lambert	George Kipling
Alex Carrier	Charles Larocque

François Whitford   Amable Lafort
François Bruce   Joseph Delorme
Matouche

Cowie wrote that Baptiste Kennedy was a guide in a brigade with steersmen from Red River Settlement named Cameron, Spence, Cunningham, and William Prince, an Indian (*Company of Adventurers*, 117).

68. Minnesota Historical Society, St. Paul.

69. St. Paul Public Library, Minnesota.

70. PABC, Add Mss 345, vol. 2, file 70.

71. HBCA, B.27/c/1, fo. 20.

72. Robert Campbell, "A Journey to Kentucky for Sheep: From the Journal of Robert Campbell, 1832–1833," *North Dakota Historical Quarterly* 1 (October 1926 to July 1927) 1: 36.

73. A phrase used by Palliser of the two friends who joined him on his expedition, Captain Arthur Brisco and William Roland Mitchell (Irene M. Spry, ed., *The Papers of the Palliser Expedition* [Toronto: Champlain Society, 1968], 338–39).

74. Rich, ed., *John Rae's Correspondence*, 350–78.

75. Spry, ed., *Palliser Papers*, 37 n.1.

76. Ibid., 340–41.

77. Ibid., 403.

78. *North-West Territory: Report on the Assiniboine and Saskatchewan Exploring Expedition* (Toronto: John Lovell, 1859), 39.

79. John E. Parsons, *West on the 49th Parallel* (New York: William Morrow and Co., 1963), 53.

80. HBCA, B.235/a/15, Upper Fort Garry Journal, June 16, 1851.

81. "Log of the Wanderers on the Prairies in Search of Buffalo Bear Deer &c in 1862," ms. in the possession of Lord Dunmore.

82. Spry, ed., *Palliser Papers*, 258.

83. Ibid., 169.

84. HBCA, A.12/7, fo. 392d. Agreement between emigrants to the Columbia River and Hudson's Bay Company, dated May 31, 1841, and HBCA, B.235/d/82, fo. 30. 56. cash paid to emigrants. Whether there were two Pierre Larocques is not clear. The accounts list Pierre Larocque Jr., the agreement simply Pierre Larocque.

85. William J. Betts, "From Red River to the Columbia," *The Beaver* (Spring 1971): 50–55, reproduces John Flett's own account of the journey.

86. Toussaint Joyal may have been with the second group of emigrants.

87. John V. Campbell, "The Sinclair Party — An Emigration Overland along the Old Hudson's Bay Company Route from Manitoba to the Spokane Country in 1854," *Washington Historical Quarterly* 8 (July 1916): 187–201.

88. See also Irene M. Spry, "Free Men and Free Trade," unpublished paper submitted to the Canadian Historical Association meeting held in Saskatoon in 1979, and "The 'Private Adventurers' of Rupert's Land," in John E. Foster, ed., *The Developing West: Essays on Canadian History in Honor of Lewis H. Thomas* (Edmonton: University of Alberta Press, 1983), 49–70.

89. Garrioch Journal, March 1 and 9, 1845, PAM. See also E.H. Oliver, *The Canadian North-West: Its Early Development and Legislative Records*, vol. 1 (Ottawa: Government Printing Bureau, 1914), 315, which lists Charles Laurance, Dominique Ducharme, Peter Garrioch, Henry Cook, Peter Hayden, and Alexis Goulait as petitioners to the Council. It does not include St. Germain.

90. Christie to Simpson, September 5, 1845, enclosing the letter from Sinclair et al. dated August 29, 1845, HBCA, D.5/15, fos. 139a, 139b. Sinclair's letter is reproduced in Lewis G. Thomas, ed., *The Prairie West to 1905* (Toronto: Oxford University Press, 1975), 56–57, with Christie's reply, 58–59. No source is given and the spelling of some of the names is different from that in the copy enclosed by Christie. Another copy of the letter is in PAM, RRS/RRC, 1845–47.

91. Alexander Begg, *History of the North-West*, 3 vols. (Toronto: Hunter, Rose, 1894–95), 261–62.

92. Correspondence Relating to the Red River Settlement and The Hudson's Bay Company, *British Parliamentary Papers*, vol. 18, 1849, Colonies, Canada (Shannon: Irish Universities Press, 1969).

93. Morton, Introduction in Rich, ed., *Eden Colvile's Letters*, lxxxix.

94. A good account of the trial and of the role of Sinclair and Garrioch is given in Morton, Introduction in Rich, ed., *Eden Colvile's Letters*, lxxxii–lxxxvi, and another in Roy St. George Stubbs, *Four Recorders of Rupert's Land* (Winnipeg: Peguis Publishers, 1967), 26–29.

95. Morton, Introduction in Rich, ed., *Eden Colvile's Letters*, lxxxix.

96. Ibid., citing HBCA, D.5/25, June 2, 1849, enclosed in Sinclair to Simpson, June 14, 1849.

97. Ibid., p.c., citing HBCA, D.5/28, June 1, 1850; HBCA, A.13/4, fos. 519–20; and A.12/5, Simpson, July 5, 1850.

98. Ibid., pp. cvii–cviii, citing HBCA, A.13/5, enclosure in a letter from F. Peel, C.O., to Pelly, dated December 30, 1851. Attempts to find the signatures in HBCA, the Public Record Office, London, England, and the Archives of the Aborigines' Protection Society, Rhodes House, Oxford, England, have failed, so it has not been possible to discover the origins of the signatories.

99. The original petition with all the signatures is in PAC, RG 14-C-I, vol. 64, petition no. 1176, received and filed May 22, 1857. Oddly, the signature of Roderick Kennedy is not among the 511 signatures attached to the petition, though he presented it to the Legislature, and his name is the only one given in the Select Committee version. It was printed in *The Toronto Globe* for June 12, 1857, and as Appendix 15 of the *Report of the Select Committee of the House of Commons on the Hudson's Bay Company, 1857.*

100. Alvin C. Gluek, Jr., *Minnesota and the Manifest Destiny of the Canadian Northwest* (Toronto: University of Toronto Press, 1965), 123–25.

101. Mae Atwood, ed., *In Rupert's Land: Memoirs of the Walter Traill* (Toronto: McClelland and Stewart, 1970), 204 and 208. Sanderson wrote of the Rising when he was captured by Riel's men, when he was with the Portage party: "I was not afraid of the French half-breeds . . . I knew Riel and many of his adherents, in fact I was related to some of his leaders" (PAM, MG9/A107, Part 2, 1).

102. Garrioch Journal, February 26, 1846, PAM.

103. *Bulletin de la Société botanique de France* vol. 13, 1866, liv, cited in Spry, ed., *Palliser Papers*, xxviii n. 5. The number of the volume is given incorrectly in this citation.

104. "Le Capitaine Palliser et l'Exploration des Montagnes Rocheuses, 1857–1859," *Le Tour du Monde: Nouveau Journal des Voyages* (Paris: 1861), 287, cited in Spry, ed., *Palliser Papers*, xxviii.

105. Spry, ed., *Palliser Papers*, 238 n.5.

106. A third cleavage might be identified, namely, the generation gap between the children and grandchildren of the well-established Principal Settlers of the colony and their aging precursors. See Morton, Introduction in Rich, ed., *Eden Colvile's Letters*, 1xxxix.

107. This impression is derived from a wide range of material by and concerning both James Sinclair and William Sinclair II, including Journal of Dr. William Cowan, PAC, MG19 E8.

108. George F.G. Stanley, *The Birth of Western Canada* (Toronto: University of Toronto Press, 1960; 1963; reprinted from the original edition, Longmans, Green and Co. Ltd., 1936).

109. Jennifer S.H. Brown, *Strangers in Blood: Fur Trade Company Families in Indian Country* (Vancouver and London: University of British Columbia Press, 1980), 173.

110. Irene M. Spry, "The Tragedy of the Loss of the Commons in Western Canada," in *As Long as the Sun Shines and Water Flows: A Reader in Canadian Native Studies*, ed. Ian A.L. Getty and Antoine S. Lussier (Vancouver: University of British Columbia Press, 1983), 203–28.

Article Thirteen

The Michif Language of the Métis

Peter Bakker

Michif[1] is an unusual language in a number of respects. First, it is syncretic, in that it is not classifiable as belonging to a single language family. Michif is just as much an Algonquian as an Indo-European language, so it can be said to belong to two language families at the same time. Michif has grammatical[2] and lexical[3] features from the two languages in roughly equal numbers, which may very well make it unique among the languages of the world. It is certainly

Source: Peter Bakker, "The Michif Language of the Métis," in *Metis Legacy: A Metis Historiography and Annotated Bibliography*, ed. by Lawrence J. Barkwell et al. (Winnipeg: Pemmican, 2001), pp. 177–9.

distinctive in its distribution of the elements of the two source languages: no mixed language shows nouns from one language and verbs from another.

Second, Michif appears to be unlike all other languages arising from the Aboriginal-European contact phenomena. In particular, Michif is not a trade language, a Pidgin, a Creole, an interlanguage, a case of code mixing, nor a case of second language acquisition.

Third, concerning the social circumstances under which Michif arose, only one suggestion makes sense: the fact that its speakers, having double ancestry, form a fairly atypical group. It is possible that the mixed nature of Michif is associated with the mixed nature of the people who speak it.

Fourth, the only linguistic phenomena to which Michif shows vague similarities are code mixing and relexified languages, both of which are cases of language mixture by bilinguals. Code mixing is a spontaneous, ad hoc mixture, and relexified languages are mother tongues. However, with Michif, there are so many important differences so that neither of these theses provides obvious clues to the genesis of this strange mixed language.

The Michif language is half Cree (an Algonquian language) and half French (an Indo-European language). It is a mixed language, drawing its verbs and associated grammar from Cree and its nouns and associated grammar from Michif-French. The Saulteaux language contributes some verbs, sounds and nouns to the mixture.

The historical continuum of the French language contribution to Michif is: European French → Québécois French → Acadian French → Western Canadian French → Métis French → the French component of Michif. The nouns, numerals, articles, almost all adjectives, most conjunctions, and most prepositions in Michif are of French derivation.

The historical continuum of the Cree language contribution to Michif is: Algonquian languages → Western Swampy Cree → Southern Plains Cree (Southeastern Downstream People) → the Cree component of Michif.

The verbs, question words, demonstratives, personal pronouns and postpositions in Michif are Cree. Michif nouns that are not English or French are often Saulteaux (Ojibway) rather than Cree. Plains-Ojibway has had a lexical and phonological[4] influence on the French part of the Michif language.

Métis people also refer to the Michif-French language as Michif. This Métis-French differs considerably from European French and is a source language for Michif-Cree French as noted above. It is closest to Prairie Canadian French. Métis French and Louisiana Cajun French are the most divergent dialects of standard French in North America.

Michif-French differs lexically from other French dialects and many of the Métis words of French origin have meanings that are different from other French dialects. Michif French also uses some Ojibway and Cree words. As in Cree and Ojibway, there are no gender differences in personal pronouns when referring to persons in Michif-French. Numerals are placed before articles and nouns instead of between them as in standard French. There are unique elisions and many other differences in the spoken language.

It is beyond doubt that the Métis as a people were a product of the fur trade. The quest for furs brought French and British entrepreneurs and adventurers into contact with the existing Indian tribes. The Métis speak a mixture of the languages of their paternal and maternal ancestors. The Métis are the only speakers of the Michif language. The existence of these people, who constitute an ethnic group with their own culture and history and who recognize their double ancestry, seems to be related to the existence of a language with a double genetic origin.[5]

There is a strong Ojibway influence on both the Michif language and Métis mythology. There was a high frequency of Ojibway marriage partners for French Canadians and Métis around 1800. There are three reasons for this. First, the *voyageurs* probably spoke Ojibway, as well as French, since their canoe routes went through Ojibway territory and it is known that they spoke Indian languages well. Second, the Métis from the Great Lakes who settled in the Red River settlement probably spoke Ojibway or perhaps even a mixture of Ojibway and French. Third, the Indian women whom the French men married in the Red River settlement were mostly Ojibway. These women undoubtedly also spoke Cree, and different Ojibway dialects may have been involved, certainly Saulteaux, the language of the Plains Ojibway women. As a result, Ojibway has had a lexical, morphological[6], and phonological influence on the Cree part of Michif, and possibly also a phonological and lexical influence on the French part. One can safely say that there is an Ojibway substrate in the Cree part of Michif, elements that one would expect when many Ojibway speakers speak Cree as their second language. Given all of this, one must question why Michif is not a mixture of Ojibway and French. The reason is the following: Plains Cree was the lingua franca[7] of the Plains, where the Métis bison hunters spent much of their time between the 1820s and the 1840s.

It is not only important to know which languages were spoken as mother tongues but also which languages were spoken in intertribal contacts. Some languages were widely used as a second language by different Native peoples. Plains Cree, the Amerindian part of Michif, is among these contact languages, which are also called lingua francas. A lingua franca is a language commonly used between people who have different mother tongues. English, in the modern world, can be seen as a lingua franca in many situations which involve people who do not speak each other's language. Indeed, today English is the lingua franca among Aboriginal peoples in North America, rather than a Native language.

Plains Cree was the lingua franca on the northern Plains. This is, of course, important since Plains Cree is one of the source languages of Michif. This language was also used as a lingua franca between Métis and English-speaking "half-breeds" and possibly White people in the Red River Settlement in the 1860s: "Thus a man whose usual language is English, and one who speaks French alone, are enabled to render themselves mutually intelligible by means of Cree, their Indian mother tongue, though each is totally ignorant of the civilized language used by the other" [Joseph James Hargrave, *Red River* (Montreal: Lovell, 1871: 181)]. It is also clear that in all tribes adjacent to Plains Cree territory, there were people who spoke the Plains Cree language. This is relevant to the origin of Michif in that the Amerindian ancestors of the Métis need not have been Plains Cree Indians: they could have originated from any of the groups who spoke Plains Cree as a second language.

It is a paradoxical fact that Michif is a language usually associated with the fur trade, which took place in the woodlands, whereas Michif contains mostly elements of the Cree language of the Plains, where the role of the fur trade was less significant. The solution for this is found in the historical circumstances of the early Red River settlement. Michif is the language the Métis used in the bison hunt and the wintering camps which were built in the parklands immediately adjacent. The Métis bison hunters of Saint François Xavier and Baie Saint Paul used their land in the Red River settlement just as a base. The mainstay of their lives was their travels south and west into the prairies in search of bison. They were joined by groups of Indians in this hunting, but they were the largest ethnic group there.

Since the Métis trace their ancestry to the Saulteaux (Ojibway), Cree and Assiniboine nations, all speakers of Plains Cree, it is among these tribes that one finds the ancestors of the speakers of Michif. All four of these groups (Cree, Assiniboine, Ojibway and Métis), spoke Cree as a first or second language and regularly met at the bison hunt and the winter camps in the parklands.

Most of the Métis spoke Ojibway, Cree and French, whereas the Indians all spoke Cree, as well as Assiniboine or Ojibway. It is then only natural that Cree would be the contact language between the Métis and these Indians; it was the language that all the people involved had in common. Because of the growing importance of the bison hunt after 1821, there was increasing Métis contact with the Cree-speaking Indians and Ojibway became less important. Thus within the mixed marriages resulting in bilingual children, it was within the hunting camps where Cree was the lingua franca that the mixture of languages became a fixed code and took the form of Cree verbs and French nouns.

Michif was used only as an in-group language of the Métis. It was not used with outsiders, so that its existence remained largely unknown to the outside world until a few decades ago. It was probably only after the massive dispersal of the Métis after the 1860s onward that their knowledge of French, Cree and/or Ojibway was lost, so that Michif became the only language spoken by several thousands of people much later.

This scenario explains a number of factors that have remained enigmatic until now. It explains why the Cree dialect in Michif is Plains Cree. It accounts for an Ojibway substrate in the Cree part of Michif. It explains why the Plains Cree dialect is somewhat more simplified than other Cree dialects and why the Cree part of Michif is slightly more simplified than Plains Cree: after all it was learned by many as a second language. It explains why Michif today is spoken in locations associated with the early Métis wintering camps on the plains. It indicates why the sources of the 1800s about the Red River settlement mention mostly Ojibway as a language spoken by the Métis and not Cree. It also explains why Cree was more and more mentioned as a language of the Métis after the 1840s. It also suggests why only the descendants of the Métis bison hunters, freighters and itinerant prairie traders speak Michif and not the descendants of the more stationary Métis farmers and fishermen.

The Métis speak a mixed language because they have a mixed identity. They do not feel that they belong to either of the groups whose languages they speak. They are a new ethnic group, born out of the meeting of two very different peoples: French-Canadian fur traders and Amerindian women. Their traditional culture combines elements from both ancestries, but it also shows numerous innovations unique to the Métis as well.

In similar circumstances elsewhere in the world, comparable events have occurred: a new ethnic group arose whose members speak a new language. Such new languages are typically mixed, through a process that I call language intertwining. The first generation of children born of these mixed-language marriages is typically bilingual, speaking the languages of both the mother and the father. Since the fathers come from a different area and the mothers speak an Indigenous language, these children have more opportunity to speak the language of the mothers than of the fathers. In addition, the mothers (and/or other women who speak the same language) probably raised these children, providing more language input in the maternal language than in the paternal one. So there are several reasons why these first-generation children speak the language of their mothers better than the language of their fathers. In the case of first-generation Métis, they must have spoken better Cree than French.

In general, when there are many mixed couples with bilingual children, they can start to speak a mixed language. When the mothers of the first generation speak a language different from the fathers, the new mixed languages of their descendants, if they are a considerable group, appear to combine the grammatical system of the mothers' language and the lexicon of the father's. They intertwine the vocabulary of the father's language into the grammatical framework of the mother's language. In fact, in Michif the same thing occurred, but because of the typological features of Cree, the process led to the atypical result of a language with French nouns and Cree verbs. It can be argued that Michif has a Cree grammatical system, which includes verbs, and a French lexicon, which is mostly nominal. In Cree verbs it is impossible to separate the affixes (endings) from the stem. In fact the whole verb consists only of affixes and should therefore be considered part of the grammatical system of the language. The result of this process is a language with Cree verbs, demonstratives, personal pronouns, and question words and French articles, nouns and prepositions. The French nouns can have Cree affixes.

Michif is a unique language in many respects. It is unclassifiable genetically and therefore comparable with the duck-billed platypus or the panda in biology. It is a matter of deep regret that human languages that are threatened with extinction—especially those as unique as Michif—do not receive as much attention as animals in the same situation.

NOTES

1. This chapter is based on Peter Bakker's book, *A Language of Our Own: The Genesis of Michif, the Mixed Cree-French Language of the Canadian Métis*. New York: Oxford University Press, 1997.
2. Grammar is the system of rules for speaking and writing a language, e.g. word order, and word endings.
3. A lexicon is the stock of words.
4. Phonography relates to the sounds of speech. Phonology refers to the system of speech sounds. Michif is mixed in all respects except one — its phonological system. Its phonology consists of two separate systems, one for the Cree part and one for the French part. These systems do not influence each other at all. English elements are phonologically adjusted toward the French component, never toward the Cree.
5. The Scottish "half-breeds" or "country born," many of whom were retired Hudson's Bay Company employees and their families, lived at Red River north of the forks. These Gaelic-speaking people also spoke Bungee, a mixed language which consisted of Cree, Ojibway, Gaelic and English. Gourneau (1980) refers to *Les Michif Anglais* at Turtle Mountain spoken by the Scottish-English Michifs.
6. Morphology is the study and description of the word-forming elements and processes of a language (such as inflection, derivation and compounding).
7. Lingua franca literally means "language of the Franks." This was originally the name of the mixture of French, Provençal, Spanish, Italian, Arabic, and other languages that was used by the sailors and the soldiers of the Mediterranean, at least from the late Middle Ages.

Topic Six

The Pacific Coast

These men were members of the first elected assembly of the colony of Vancouver Island, which met in 1856.

In the early 19th century, North West Company traders, operating out of Montreal, reached the Fraser and Columbia River basins. Subsequently, the Hudson's Bay Company, after its union with the North West Company in 1821, extended fur-trading operations from Fort Vancouver on the Columbia (opposite present-day Portland, Oregon) all along the north Pacific coast, including the area of the present-day American states of Washington and Oregon. The extension of the boundary between present-day Canada and the United States along the 49th parallel to the Pacific coast in 1846, however, forced the Hudson's Bay Company to leave Fort Vancouver. It established its new commercial headquarters at Victoria, on Vancouver Island. This new society was initially a cultural mix of First Nations and Europeans before it became predominantly non-Native. Sylvia Van Kirk looks at five interracial families in "Tracing the Fortunes of Five Founding Families of Victoria," an article that complements her essay in Topic Two on Indian women in fur trade society. Why did female descendants of prominent fur trade families adjust more successfully to the new British American society than their male counterparts?

In 1858, the discovery of gold on the Fraser River opened up the mainland. Britain organized the separate colony of British Columbia that same year, to secure British control. James Douglas, the governor of Vancouver Island, became governor of the new mainland colony as well, establishing British institutions and making New Westminster the new capital. In 1866, the two colonies were united to become the colony of British Columbia. In "Hardy Backwoodsmen, Wholesome Women, and Steady Families: Immigration and the Construction of a White Society in Colonial British Columbia, 1849–1871," Adele Parry describes the ideal immigrants sought for the new settler society of British Columbia. Why did the attempt to establish the desired "stable settler society of the imperialists' dreams," fail to materialize?

The maritime fur trade is reviewed in Robin Fisher's *Contact and Conflict: Indian–European Relations in British Columbia, 1774–1890*, 2nd ed. (Vancouver: University of British Columbia Press, 1992), and James R. Gibson's *Otter Skins, Boston Ships, and China Goods: The Maritime Fur Trade of the Northwest Coast, 1785–1841* (Montreal/Kingston: McGill-Queen's University Press, 1992). R. Cole Harris's *The Resettlement of British Columbia* (Vancouver: University of British Columbia Press, 1996) reviews First Nations and newcomer interchanges. The impact of disease is examined in Robert Boyd, *The Coming of the Spirit of Pestilence: Introduced Infectious Diseases and Population Decline among Northwest Coast Indians 1774–1874* (Vancouver: University of British Columbia Press, 1999). A *Stol:lo Coast Salish Historical Atlas*, ed. Keith Thor Carlson (Vancouver: Douglas & McIntyre, 2001) provides an extraordinary review of the history of the Stol:lo people of the lower Fraser River in southwestern British Columbia, and northwestern Washington. For the early history of the Hudson's Bay Company on the Columbia, and along the Pacific Coast, see Dorothy Nafus Morrison's *Outpost: John McLoughlin and the Far Northwest* (Portland, Oregon: Oregon Historical Society Press, 1999, 2004).

Margaret A. Ormsby has written a valuable introduction to *Fort Victoria Letters, 1846–51* (Winnipeg: Hudson's Bay Record Society, 1979), edited by Hartwell Bowsfield. *The Fort Langley Journals, 1827–30*, ed. Morag MacLachlan (Vancouver: University of British Columbia Press, 1998) contain rich ethnographic information. In "The Colonization of Vancouver Island, 1849–1858," *B.C. Studies* 96 (Winter 1992–93): 3–40, Richard Mackie reviews the colony's first decade, and in *Trading beyond the Mountains: The British Fur Trade on the Pacific, 1793–1843* (Vancouver: University of British Columbia Press, 1996), he examines the precolonial period. Clarence G. Karr looks at James Douglas, the early governor, in "James Douglas: The Gold Governor in the Context of His Times," in *The Company on the Coast*, ed.

E. Blanche Norcross (Nanaimo: Nanaimo Historical Society, 1983): 56–78. Very valuable for an understanding of the lives of both James and Amelia Douglas is their joint biography by John Adams, *Old Square-Toes and His Lady* (Victoria, BC: Horsdal & Schubart Publishers Limited, 2001). On the history of coal mining in the early settlement period, see Lynne Bowen's *Three Dollar Dreams* (Lantzville, BC: Oolichan Books, 1987) and John Douglas Belshaw's "Mining Technique and Social Division on Vancouver Island, 1848–1900," *British Journal of Canadian Studies* 1 (1986): 45–65. Tina Loo recounts the history of law and order in British Columbia in *Making Law, Order, and Authority in British Columbia, 1821–1871* (Toronto: University of Toronto Press, 1994). Adele Perry expands upon the themes of her article in *On the Edge of Empire: Gender, Race and the Making of British Columbia 1849–1871* (Toronto: University of Toronto Press, 2001).

The standard, but now rather dated, history of the area is Margaret Ormsby's *British Columbia: A History* (Toronto: Macmillan, 1958). It should be supplemented by Jean Barman, *The West beyond the West: A History of British Columbia*, rev. ed. (Toronto: University of Toronto Press, 1996) and Hugh J.M. Johnston, ed., *The Pacific Province: A History of British Columbia* (Vancouver: Douglas and McIntyre, 1996). *British Columbia: Historical Readings*, eds. W. Peter Ward and Robert A.J. McDonald (Vancouver: Douglas and McIntyre, 1981) contains several valuable essays on early British Columbia history. A valuable well-illustrated account of the province's entire history is Patricia E. Roy and John Herd Thompson's *British Columbia: Land of Promises* (Don Mills, ON: Oxford University Press, 2005).

WEBLINKS

Pacific Explorations
http://www.library.ubc.ca/prdla/explore.html

A database of primary-source records of early voyages of exploration of the Pacific Coast.

The Colonization of Vancouver Island
http://www.canadiana.org/ECO/mtq?id=7a8668f9e0&doc=61818

A digitized copy of correspondence from the chair of the Hudson's Bay Company with regard to the colonization of Vancouver Island.

The Oregon Treaty, 1846
http://www.ccrh.org/comm/river/docs/ortreaty.htm

Text of the Oregon Treaty of 1846 between the United States and the United Kingdom.

1862 Smallpox Epidemic in Victoria
http://web.uvic.ca/vv/student/smallpox

This site details the historical events of the 1862 smallpox epidemic in Victoria, and the reactions of people with religious, medical, and governmental backgrounds to it.

Historical Censuses of Vancouver Island
http://history.mala.bc.ca

Personal directories, property registries, and censuses for communities on Vancouver Island from about the time of Confederation to several decades afterwards.

Queen Victoria's Victoria
http://web.uvic.ca/vv/

This website describes with vivid pictures and detail daily life in the city of Victoria, during the reign of its namesake.

British Columbia Landscapes
http://www.royalbcmuseum.bc.ca/exhibits/journeys/english/index.html

An interactive site detailing the widely varying environments of the province of British Columbia. Such challenging physical geography had great influence on settling patterns.

Article Fourteen

Tracing the Fortunes of Five Founding Families of Victoria

Sylvia Van Kirk

A recent popular history of Victoria is entitled *More English Than the English*.[1] While this might symbolize the ethnic aspiration of this city, it obscures the actual mixed-race origins of many of its founding families. Only recently has there been much pride or interest in the fact that among the most prominent of Victoria's founders were families who were also of First Nations origin. This article explores why this was so by looking at the processes of colonization experienced by five Hudson's Bay Company/Native families who were comprised of some of the earliest principal settlers of Victoria. A look at a map of the settlement in 1858 (Map 14.1) illustrates the dominant position of the family properties of James Douglas, William H. McNeill, John Work, John Tod, and Charles Ross. These men had all been officers of the Hudson's Bay Company (HBC): all had Native wives, but of different First Nations origin. Although all these officers had toyed with the idea of retiring to Britain or eastern Canada, they chose to settle at Fort Victoria, the heart of the new Crown Colony of Vancouver Island (created in 1849). Coming from the elite of the fur trade hierarchy, these men had the wherewithal to purchase the expensive estates made available by the HBC. In Victoria, they hoped to maintain their social and economic standing by becoming part of the landed gentry, the elite class in the Wakefieldian colonization scheme that aimed to replicate an essentially British social hierarchy.[2]

For these men, Victoria offered the prospect of settling their families in "civilized" yet geographically familiar surroundings, where it was hoped that they would secure a place as part of the colonial elite. Being of mixed race, however, these families confronted particular challenges in adapting to this cultural frontier. Recent studies of prevailing colonial discourses reveal that the new settler society was intent on reproducing White British "civilization"—a project in which miscegenation was increasingly feared and denigrated. According to one commentator, the progeny of mixed unions were "a bad lot," being weak both "morally and intellectually."[3] With Aboriginal ancestry quickly becoming a source of shame, Native mothers and children

Source: *BC Studies* 115/116 (Autumn/Winter 1997/98): 149–79.

Map 14.1   Victoria, 1858 (drawn from Official District Map)

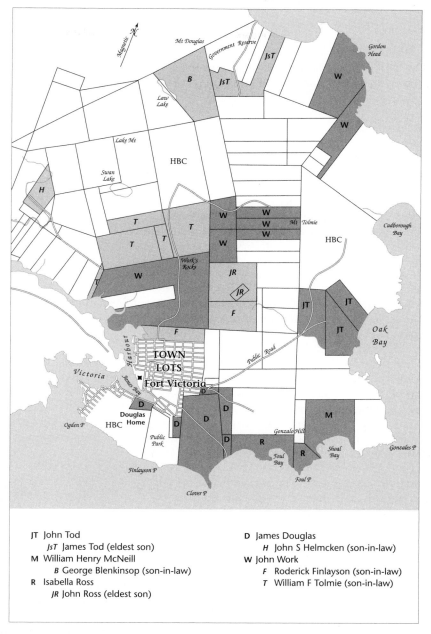

JT   John Tod
  JsT   James Tod (eldest son)
M   William Henry McNeill
  B   George Blenkinsop (son-in-law)
R   Isabella Ross
  JR   John Ross (eldest son)

D   James Douglas
  H   John S Helmcken (son-in-law)
W   John Work
  F   Roderick Finlayson (son-in-law)
  T   William F Tolmie (son-in-law)

were subject to growing pressure to acculturate to the fathers' British heritage. Assimilation can be seen as a strategy adopted by these families in an effort to maintain class status, which could be undermined by the racist attitudes of incoming colonists. Especially for the second generation, there was little room for a middle ground; these children could not build an identity that acknowledged the duality of their heritage.

Little attention has been paid to the fact that this process of acculturation was gendered and that it entailed different role expectations for sons and daughters, respectively. In examining the fortunes of the second generation in these five families, it appears that a complex interaction of gender and class dynamics, coupled with the particular demographics of early Victoria, enabled the girls to transcend the racist climate of the colony more successfully than the boys. The sons had considerable difficulty in securing the status of gentlemen; none enhanced, and most failed to maintain, the families' fortunes. Racial stereotypes helped to blight the sons' prospects, as did deficiencies in colonial schooling and the vagaries of pioneer agriculture. If they married, and quite a few did not, it was (with one exception) to Métis or Indian women. Both occupationally and socially, the mixed-blood sons, even in these elite families, could not really compete with the influx of aspiring young Englishmen. Many of the daughters, however, were well secured within the colonial elite. Paradoxically, although the daughters' options were restricted to marriage, the second generation was highly successful in fulfilling that role. Unlike their brothers, colonial demographics worked to the advantage of the daughters; in the early decades there were few marriageable immigrant women who could compete with the acculturated daughters of former HBC officers. All the daughters of the second generation married: almost all married White men. Their marriage patterns evolved from marrying promising young HBC officers to marrying colonial officials and incoming White settlers. Newcomers to the colony were soon aware of the influence of what was dubbed the "Family Company Compact" and the advantage that could accrue from marrying "*a big wigs daughter.*"[4]

A fascinating window on the experiences of these families and the process of acculturation is provided by the rich collection of portraits in the British Columbia Archives and Records Service (now BC Archives). As several commentators have observed, photographs are, themselves, valuable historical documents that have not received enough serious study from historians.[5] In these families, photos convey in ways that words cannot the process of acculturation, especially as experienced by the Native wives. Most of the photos have come to the archives as part of family albums and collections. Whether the originals were small *cartes de visite* or cabinet portraits, they illuminate social networks and family aspirations. In the second generation, the scarcity of sons' portraits may in itself be a significant indicator of social failure, while the numerous portraits of the daughters underscore their successful assimilation to British material culture.

In order to appreciate the social challenges faced by these families, it is necessary to sketch their fur trade background.[6] Most of the husbands had spent the better part of their careers at various posts in the Columbia Department (Map 14.2). They had initially married according to the fur trade "custom of the country" and produced large families. Family size varied between seven and thirteen children, with the sex ratio weighted heavily in favour of daughters.

Most significant to the social hierarchy of this new British colony was the fact that the governor, James Douglas, was an HBC officer who had a part-Cree wife, Amelia (Plates 14.1 and 14.2). As the daughter of Chief Factor William Connolly and Miyo Nipiy, her marriage at Fort St. James in 1828 was typical of the pattern of young officers marrying the daughters of their superiors.

Plate 14.1 BC Archives, A-2833

Map 14.2   Select Posts of the Columbia District of the HBC

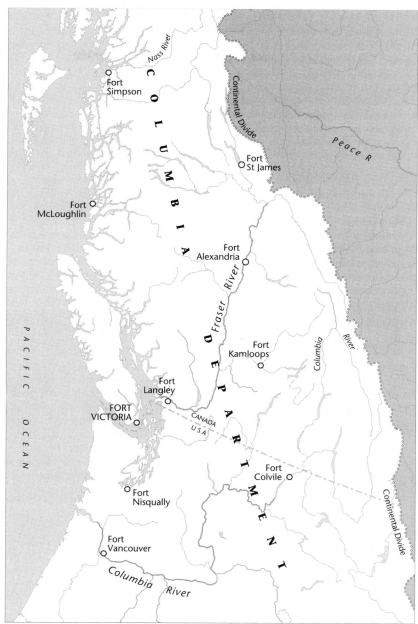

The Douglases soon moved to Fort Vancouver, where most of their thirteen children were born. Unlike the other families, the mortality rate in the Douglas family was high. When they moved to Fort Victoria in 1849, there were only four surviving daughters, two boys and five girls having died very young. Another son and daughter born in the early 1850s completed the family. Douglas bought up several hundred acres of choice land in Victoria, which he parlayed into considerable wealth, and he was among the first to build a substantial home outside the fort. In 1863, when he was knighted for his services to the colony, his wife became Lady Douglas.

One of Douglas's colleagues who had high hopes for the opportunities Victoria promised his large family was Chief Factor John Work. His Métis wife, Josette Legacé, the daughter of a French-Canadian father and a Spokane mother, had grown up at posts on the Columbia River. Married in 1826, the Works spent many years much farther north at Fort Simpson before retiring to Victoria in 1850 with a family of three boys and eight girls. John Work became the largest landowner in early Victoria, his Hillside Farm encompassing over 1000 acres. Although he died in 1861, his wife survived him by 35 years (Plate 14.3).

The untimely death of a father could seriously affect the fortunes of an HBC family. Charles Ross only lived long enough to see Fort Victoria built in 1844, but he left his widow able to buy her own estate of 145 acres on Ross Bay. Like Josette Work, Isabella Ross (Plate 14.4) was the daughter of a French-Canadian engagé but, like Amelia Douglas, she was born far from Victoria. Her mother was Ojibway; Isabella had grown up in the Great Lakes region and was married at Rainy Lake in 1822. Most of her children, six boys and four girls, were born west of the Rockies and all lived to adulthood.

Although often referred to as "Indian," the wives of these men were all of mixed descent. Although these marriages cut across class and ethnicity, they are, nonetheless, representative of fur trade endogamy. The wives' fathers were connected to the HBC, and the women themselves grew up within or near various fur trade posts. All these marriages were long-lasting monogamous unions, the country marriages eventually being confirmed by church rites whenever clergymen became available. The Douglases and the Rosses had church marriages at Fort Vancouver in 1838, and the Works had one upon their arrival at Fort Victoria in 1849.

Plate 14.2 Portrait of Amelia, Lady Douglas. This plate and Plate 14.1 show Lady Douglas's acculturation to the role of governor's wife over a decade, c. 1858 to 1872. BC Archives A-01679

Plate 14.3 Mrs. John Work and her two youngest children. Original: *Carte de visite*. Photographer: S.A. Spencer. BC Archives, A-01825

In the other two families, the McNeills and the Tods, the marriages harkened back to the long-established pattern of officers contracting alliances with high-ranking First Nations women whose connections were useful to advancing their husbands' respective commercial positions. Captain William H. McNeill was a Bostonian who first entered the Pacific coast trade in competition with the HBC. His first wife, known as Mathilda, was a Kaigani Haida chief, an alliance which undoubtedly helped to make him such a successful trader that the HBC went to some lengths to lure him into its service in the early 1830s. This union produced twelve children, with seven girls and three boys surviving to adulthood. Mathilda died in 1850, shortly after the birth of the youngest children (twin girls), and McNeill soon settled his motherless family in Victoria. Upon his later retirement in 1863, he brought a second wife, a high-ranking

Nishga woman named Neshaki, to live on his 200-acre estate, which encompassed much of south Oak Bay.

Chief Trader John Tod had a more checkered marital experience than did most of his contemporaries. By his first short-lived country marriage to a mixed-blood woman, Tod had a son (James) who eventually settled in Victoria. Through an ill-fated marriage to an English woman in the late 1830s, he had a daughter, but his second wife, having gone mad, was placed in an asylum in England. Tod then returned to the Columbia District, where he took his last country wife around 1843. Sophia Lolo was the daughter of a prominent chief at Fort Kamloops (Jean-Baptiste Lolo dit St. Paul) and his Shuswap wife (Plate 14.5). In 1850, Tod settled with Sophia and a growing family, ultimately five boys and two girls, on a 100-acre estate in Oak Bay.

In these families, the patriarchal role exercised by the British fathers was greater than usual because of their own cultural bias. In fur trade society, Native wives brought their husbands valuable knowledge with regard to trade and even survival. There is also ample evidence that they were devoted mothers and exercised a strong influence within the family circle. When McNeill's Haida wife died in 1850, he took the unusual step of lamenting his loss to Governor Simpson: "My poor Wife . . . had been a good and faithful partner to me for twenty years and we had twelve children together ... the deceased was a most kind mother to her children, and *no* Woman could have done her duty better, although an Indian."[7] Moving though it is, this quotation underscores McNeill's ambivalence toward his wife's Native background. Like the other patriarchs in this study, he was to be an active agent in the colonization of his own family.

HBC officers never seem to have questioned the desirability of acculturating their families to British norms and customs. Though their private correspondence is filled with paternal concern for the welfare of their children, this was posited in terms of negating the latter's Indianness. It was never suggested that the children's First Nations heritage should be actively incorporated into their upbringing. At the fur trade posts, fathers sought to Anglicize their wives and children, introducing them to the basics of English literacy and to Christian observances such as Bible reading and prayers. Material acculturation also started at the posts, as is illustrated in Plate 14.6, a fascinating 1865 portrait of Sophia Lolo's parents and two younger sisters. Here the traditional costume of the mother is contrasted to the partially anglicized dress of the daughters. Tartan dresses and shawls, worn with First Nations leggings and moccasins, became the typical costume for women at the HBC forts in the early nineteenth century.[8]

Plate 14.4 Isabella Ross in her widow's weeds. Photographer: probably S.A. Spencer. BC Archives, 7029A-1280

Plate 14.5 Sophia Lolo, wife of John Tod. Photograph may have been taken on the occasion of the Tod's church marriage in 1863. Photographer: S.A. Spencer. BC Archives A-01483

Plate 14.6 Jean-Baptiste Lolo dit St. Paul, his wife and two daughters. Taken by Charles Gentile in 1865 at Fort Kamloops. BC Archives, 2007 A-950

Fathers worried about their children growing up at isolated posts without "proper education or example." In 1834, John Work wrote to his retired colleague Edward Ermatinger: "I have now here four fine little girls, had I them a little brushed up with education, and a little knowledge of the world, they would scarcely be known to be Indians."[9] Thus fur trade officers were eager to place their children at the first school established at Fort Vancouver in the 1830s; after that venture failed, Douglas and Work both placed their daughters with American missionaries in the Willamette Valley.[10] To provide the requisite education for enabling sons to secure a position in the HBC or to take up some other profession was a problem. To send sons (or daughters) away to eastern Canada or Great Britain was a risky and expensive business, even if they were entrusted to the care of relatives or friends.

These concerns much occupied Charles Ross, who had kept his large family under his wing until he received a promotion upon moving to Fort Victoria. In the fall of 1843 he sent his three teenaged children (two sons and a daughter) off to England for an education. Colleagues were aghast at the expense, but Ross had hopes that his offspring would do well with his nephew in London. A touching letter written to his "honoured Father" by eighteen-year-old Walter indicates that he had found a good placement as a wool merchant's clerk and that his brother and sister were "much improved in their learning." Ross never received this letter, however, having died the previous year, and relatives were soon expressing their dissatisfaction with his children, whom they found "extremely indocile and addicted to habits incompatible with a residence in this country."[11] The three children were sent back to their mother in Victoria in the fall of 1845. Further light is shed on father–son relationships and on the difficulties of educating sons by looking at the efforts of Edward Ermatinger who, after retiring to St. Thomas (Ontario), acted as a "surrogate father" for sons of colleagues such as John Tod. In 1841, Tod sent James, his eldest son, east to Ermatinger where, in spite of social conflict, James gained agricultural skills that helped him to manage his own property later in Victoria.[12]

In colonial Victoria, where the norms of their husbands' culture were dominant, the role of Native mothers in socializing their children was circumscribed. The fathers' prescriptions were now supported by new agents of colonization: the church and the school. All these families adhered to the Church of England, which helped to affirm their elite status. Their marriages were sanctioned by church rite, and the wives and children were baptized and became active members of the Anglican congregation that formed around the Reverend Edward Cridge after his arrival in 1855.[13] Christian education was deemed of the utmost importance, and schooling specifically for the children of the elite was set up with the arrival of the first Anglican missionaries, Robert and Emma Staines. The five families in question dominated the Fort Victoria school register in the early 1850s; out of 30 pupils listed, there were four Douglases, five Works, three McNeills, three Rosses, and two Tods.[14] Boarding children at this school was expensive (fifteen pounds per annum), so it was frustrating to fathers subscribing to this school when their hopes, especially for their boys, were disappointed. By all accounts Mrs. Staines and her successors were much more successful with the girls' education than was her husband with the boys' education. The girls were being groomed for marriage; their education emphasized dress, deportment, and ladylike accomplishments such as music, singing, drawing, and languages.[15] The boys, on the other hand, did not really get the more demanding education, either practical or classical, that their role expectations demanded. Staines was evidently not up to the job and attempted to control his teenage charges by meting out severe corporal punishment.[16] Life at this school stood in painful contrast to the more carefree and close familial life most of these children had previously known. Although the boys' school had improved considerably by the early 1860s, the differential impact of this early colonial education appears to have been a significant factor in shaping the next generation.

In colonial Victoria racism intensified, generating invidious comparisons. It irked some incoming settlers that Native families should rank so high in the social hierarchy. Visitors and even working-class British immigrants pronounced society in the new colony deficient because some of its leading officials were married to Native women. Shortly after her arrival from England in 1854, Annie Deans wrote home disparagingly of Douglas: a man who had spent his life among North American Indians and got one for a wife could scarcely know anything about governing an English colony.[17] While there is ample evidence that the daughters of these HBC families featured in the early society of Victoria, they could be subject to unflattering evaluation. Charles Wilson, a British army officer, recounting the round of balls and other social activities he attended in the early 1860s, observed: "Most of the young ladies are half breeds & have quite as many of the propensities of the savage as of the civilized being."[18] Among these families, such remarks increased attempts to hide Native backgrounds and to adopt all the trappings of British fashion and mores.

These social tensions were poignantly revealed in the Douglas family which, because of its position, was subject to particular scrutiny. Initially, Amelia Douglas kept in the social background, partly because she did not speak English very well. The social calendar was kept by her daughters and a Douglas niece from Britain, but as the contrasting portraits indicate (compare Plate 14.1 and 14.2), Lady Douglas became increasingly comfortable in her role as the governor's wife. Douglas wrote proudly of his wife after a New Year's levee in the early 1870s: "Darling good Mamma was nicely got up and won all hearts with her kindness and geniality."[19] When Lady Franklin visited Victoria in 1861, she was curious to meet the "Indian" wife of the governor. She found Amelia to have "a gentle, simple & kindly manner" and was fascinated that her Native features were less pronounced than were those in some of her daughters.[20]

Plate 14.7, the earliest known picture of the Douglas daughters, shows them in completely Anglicized, if modest, daytime apparel; other portraits reveal that their costumes soon reflected the latest European styles. The weddings of the four Douglas daughters, which occurred between 1852 and 1862, became increasingly elaborate affairs. When Agnes married Arthur Bushby, a well-born young British civil servant, a guest observed that it was a gorgeous wedding, "the ladies coming out in style."[21] But nothing in early Victoria capped the wedding of the youngest daughter, Martha, who, after being "finished in England," married another colonial official, Dennis Harris, in 1878. Plate 14.8 features the bride and numerous attendants in elaborate imported gowns; many of Victoria's notables are among the guests. The now-widowed Lady Douglas is prominent at the right edge of the

Plate 14.7 An early 1850's photograph of the Miss Douglases. Left to right are Agnes, Jane and Alice. Taken outside at Fort Victoria. BC Archives, A-02836

Plate 14.8 The Wedding of Martha Douglas to Dennis Harris, 1878. Taken on the veranda of the Douglas home by Hannah Maynard. BC Archives A-01236. On the next page, detail of wedding party. BC Archives, A-01236

photo, while the Douglas heir, James Jr., is cavalierly reclining at his sister's feet.

In the mid-1860s Governor Douglas had decided to send his teenaged son to England for further education (Plate 14.9). Douglas's ensuing correspondence provides detailed insight into his aspirations for his son:

> I had one main object in sending [James] to England which was, to give him a sound and good education, that he might . . . be qualified, through his own exertions to occupy a respectable position in society, and perhaps take a distinguished part, in the legislation of his Native country . . . he was to come here, and assist in the management of my property which with his political avocations, would furnish employment enough, and emolument greater than any other profession he might engage in.[22]

But young James was to cause his father much anguish from disappointment when he displayed little intellectual progress to mortification when he appeared about to fall into bad company and pawned the farewell gifts from his parents. James Jr. eventually returned to the colony to do his father's bidding, and in 1878 he married a White woman, Mary Elliott, daughter of a colonial politician. But contemporary observers emphasized that young Douglas was not a patch on his father.[23] Whatever promise he had was cut short by his death in 1883 at the age of 32. Family affairs in the second generation of the Douglas family were largely managed by the prominent White sons-in-law, especially Dr. J.S. Helmcken, who had married the eldest daughter, Cecilia.

Among the most socially successful families in early Victoria were the Works. Hillside House (Plate 14.10), renowned for its hospitality, was much frequented by military officers and prominent settlers. Charles Wilson's description of a New Year's celebration in 1861 appears to have been typical: "There were about 30 at dinner—such a display of fish, flesh and fowl and pastry as is seldom seen. We danced until 12 & then all hands sat down to a sumptuous supper and then set to work

Plate 14.9 A formal portrait of the governor's son, James Douglas, Jr. BC Archives A-01240

dancing again until a very late hour." "The Works," this young officer enthused, "are about the kindest people I ever came across."[24] Mrs. Work seems to have been very much part of this scene and earned the admiration of all who met her. Even the American historian Hubert H. Bancroft acknowledged that "the Indian wife, in body and mind, was strong and elastic as steel."[25] By the time Bancroft met her in 1878, Josette had been a widow for over fifteen years, but as her portrait (Plate 14.11) indicates, she had become the epitome of the Victorian matron. At a glance, she could be taken for Queen Victoria herself! When she died at an advanced age in 1896, she was eulogized for "her usefulness in pioneer work and many good deeds."[26]

Plate 14.10 The Work family home, Hillside house, built in the HBC style of the early 1850s. Note Mrs. Work, now widowed, is in the centre of the family group. BC Archives A-05578

In no family were the fortunes of sons and daughters so sharply contrasted as they were in the Work family. John Tod, who was much interested in the welfare of his colleague's family, observed in 1864: "It is rather remarkable that so numerous a family of daughters should have turned out so well, their exemplary good conduct having gained the universal esteem and respect of their neighbours, and the only two Sons, who survived their father, should have displayed characters the very reverse!"[27] At the time of their father's death in 1861, most of the daughters had already married, the two eldest long since to HBC officers Roderick Finlayson and W.F. Tolmie, respectively, both of whom were to number among Victoria's most prominent citizens. The sons, however, were still young. At age 22, John Jr. proved quite incapable of taking on the role of head of household; friends worried that he would bring ruin on the family with his intemperate and extravagant habits.[28] Whatever his faults, his mother was prepared to overlook her

Plate 14.11 Josette Work as "Queen Victoria." Cabinet Portrait. Photographer S.A. Spencer. BC Archives A-01836

son's failings and he lived out his life with her, helping to manage a diminished Hillside Farm. David, the younger son (Plate 14.3), eventually secured employment as a clerk in the HBC store in Victoria, but for some reason Tod thought him a despicable character. Neither David

Plate 14.12 "Rock Bay," the home of Roderick and Sarah (Work) Finlayson. BC Archives, 31163 B-2262

nor John Jr. married, dying at the ages of 49 and 32, respectively. Again leadership in this family passed to the British sons-in-law. The opulent lifestyle enjoyed by several of the Work daughters in the late nineteenth century is seen in Plate 14.12. In building his mansion at Rock Bay, Roderick Finlayson was the first person to import California redwood; his wife Sarah developed an active interest in gardening, becoming renowned for her Oriental poppies.[29]

It is interesting to speculate what would have happened to the Ross family had the father lived to preside over the Victoria years. Charles Ross's eldest sons had come of age before the settlement period, and he had sought to prepare them for placement in the HBC. Governor Simpson had apparently assisted in securing a position for John, the eldest son. After his father's death, John continued in the HBC service at Fort Victoria, and tried to assume the role of head of the family. His brothers, who had been returned from England, were taken into the HBC's farming operations at Fort Nisqually, leaving the younger sons to continue their education in Victoria and to help their mother develop her estate. In 1858 John Ross had expanded the family holdings in Victoria by purchasing a 200-acre farm called Oaklands, but with his premature death several years later this asset was quickly liquidated.[30] By this time, unfortunately, the younger sons had gained a reputation as "bad boys," running into debt and being in trouble with the law for disorderly conduct.[31]

Family problems were compounded when the widow herself married again in 1863 to a young fortune hunter from Canada, Lucius Simon O'Brien.[32] The new stepfather was soon at odds with the sons, going so far as to charge Alexander several times with assault. Ross was never convicted, but relations deteriorated so badly that his mother wanted to separate from her new husband. While O'Brien had been prepared to overlook race in marrying the landed widow, once his plans went awry, he played to racist stereotypes in a vicious manner, publishing the following notice in the Victoria *Daily Chronicle* in April 1864:

> Whereas My Wife, Isabella, has left my bed and board because I will not support her drunken sons, nor allow her to keep drunk herself, and have a lot of drunken squaws about her, this is to forbid all persons, harbouring her, or trusting her on my account, as I will pay no debts she may contract.[33]

A few days later, the youngest son, William, attempted to come to his mother's defence and charged that O'Brien was trying to swindle the family:

> His every act since his marriage has been to try to get everything from my mother, and turn us (the children) out of the house; selling all he could lay his hands on, and by his conduct, turn my mother out of her own house. Will you do me and my mother the simple justice to publish this, as such a statement as O'Brien has made is calculated to injure her and myself.[34]

When the family then began proceedings against O'Brien to prove that he was actually a bigamist, he apparently decided to seek his fortune up-island, where he came to an untimely end a few years later.[35]

This was not the end of Ross family trials, however. In 1866, after numerous brushes with the law, sons Francis and William were convicted of robbing a Chinese man and were sentenced to five years at hard labour. This harsh fate aroused public sympathy and a widely supported petition to the governor asked for their release, claiming that their health was suffering. Sir James Douglas testified that he had known their "most respectable parents" and that these young men were not the blackguards they were made out to be.[36] After serving about two years, the Ross boys were released on condition of their banishment from the colony.

Although the younger Ross daughters attended the balls given by the officers of the British navy in the 1850s, they never attained the status they desired. Thomas Hankin observed that although they were very fine-looking girls, "they had a great deal of Indian blood in them and were supposed to be only on the edge of society."[37] Of all the daughters in the five families under discussion, the Ross daughters were the only ones who married mixed-bloods. The eldest married Charles Wren, a Métis who had emigrated from Red River to Oregon; after her death in 1859, he married her younger sister.[38] Flora, the youngest Ross daughter, married Paul K. Hubbs in 1859, an American settler who was described as "a white Indian," but within a decade this marriage had dissolved.[39] Flora Ross went on to become the only woman in this study to have her own occupation, becoming Matron of the Asylum at New Westminister. Plate 14.13, a portrait of Flora Ross taken in the 1890s, makes a statement about the social respectability she had achieved in her own right.

By the early 1870s, the Victoria Rosses had had to sell off a good deal of their property. The remaining son, Alexander, settled down and married in 1868 but was reduced to being a labourer on the neighbouring Pemberton estate where he died suddenly of a heart attack in 1876.[40] The widow Ross, until her death in 1885, was maintained by her daughter Flora in a small house on the grounds of the convent of the Sisters of St. Ann.[41] A desire for respectability and a disavowal of any Native heritage is manifest in Plate 14.14, an astonishing family portrait of the one surviving Ross son who, after some years in Victoria, settled in Washington State. While this picture strikes contemporary viewers as amusing, this was not its intent. It symbolizes Charles Jr.'s ethnic identification with his Highland Scots father. The

Plate 14.13 Flora, the youngest daughter of Charles and Isabella Ross. Taken in New Westminister in 1896. Note the 1890's fashions. BC Archives, 7052 A-022445

poignancy of this picture becomes apparent when one knows the family history and realizes that Charles Jr.'s wife, Catherine Toma, was a Nisqually from the Puget Sound Region.[42]

Scottish affectations are also evident in the McNeill family. Like his contemporaries, the elder McNeill tried to place his sons in the HBC, but the 1850s were a time of hardening attitudes toward taking sons into junior officer ranks. One son, Harry, was apparently an efficient trader at Fort Simpson but resented not being given the rank of clerk. He went on to disobey his father over a romantic entanglement with a Native woman and quit the service, joining his brothers in Victoria in the mid-1850s.[43] While the younger McNeill boys did not gain the notoriety of the Rosses, they did seem to have trouble settling down in Victoria, appearing in police records as having been charged with disorderly conduct. Sons Harry and Alfred apparently sought better prospects on the mainland. Harry was an effective overseer of Native work crews that were clearing the way for the Collins Overland Telegraph in the mid-1860s, but he returned to Victoria where he died in 1872 at the age of 38.[44] Alfred is listed as a farmer in the Yale District in the 1881 census, but, curiously, he is omitted from his father's will of 1876. Only Captain McNeill's eldest son and namesake seems to have given him any satisfaction.

Plate 14.15, one of the few portraits of second-generation males that has survived, conveys the younger McNeill's gentlemanly aspirations. His wedding in June 1853 to Mary Macauley, the mixed-blood daughter of the bailiff of one of the HBC farms, underscores this couple's ethnic orientation. It was a "proper and grand wedding," which included a procession around the village led by a piper in full Scottish regalia.[45] The younger McNeill had been employed as master of the mail boat (which ran a regular route between Victoria and the Puget Sound in the 1840s) and as part of several exploratory expeditions to the mainland before he settled down to farm his father's estate. He died in 1889 at the age of 57 as a result of injuries suffered in a buggy accident.[46]

Although he maintained a certain respectability, it appears that William Jr. did not

Plate 14.14 A Highland chieftain? Charles Ross Jr. with his Native wife and family. The origin of this picture is not known, but it was given to the BC Archives by a descendant. Note the fur rug on the floor. BC Archives, 97185 H-4646

Plate 14.15 William Henry McNeill Jr., eldest son of Captain McNeill and his Haida wife, known as Mathilda. Note velvet lapels on his coat and plaid tie. BC Archives, G-03236

achieve the social status of his sisters. Plate 14.16 is most intriguing, for it reflects the surviving McNeill sisters' acculturation and also makes a significant statement about kin ties. All the sisters are dressed in elaborate but sombre Victorian gowns, which indicates that this photo may have been taken around the time of their father's death in 1875. Standing at the back are the youngest and still-unmarried twins Rebecca and Harriet; dominant on the right is the matriarchal eldest sister Lucy. Her marriage to HBC officer Hamilton Moffat in 1856 underscored the social networking among the women in these families, for her bridesmaids were Jane Douglas and Mary Work.[47] The other McNeill sisters were all considered to have married well. In 1864, Fanny married bank clerk James Judson Young, who became provincial secretary. Both the twins married Englishmen; in 1879 Rebecca married Thomas Elwyn, who had served as gold commissioner, and in 1889 Harriet married John Jane, who had been a Royal Engineer.

Of all members of these five families, the record is most sparse with regard to John Tod's Shuswap wife and their children. Apart

Plate 14.16 Five surviving daughters of Captain W.H. McNeill and his Haida wife, c. 1875. Standing are the twins, Rebecca (l) and Harriet(r); seated (l to r) are Fanny, Mathilda (holding a family photograph album now in the BC Archives), and Lucy. Photographer: Hannah Maynard. BC Archives, F-09960

from vital statistics, Plate 14.5 is the most informative surviving clue about Sophia Lola and how she adapted to life in Victoria. This picture, which may have been taken at the time of her church marriage in 1863, invites various readings, but it seems to indicate an ambivalence about the constraints of Victorian dress and customs. Unlike their mother, the Tod daughters mixed with other fur traders' families in Victoria society. Mary, the eldest, married American settler J.S. Bowker in 1864, while the younger sister married a successful merchant, J.S. Drummond.[48]

The Tod sons did not find suitable wives, and the 1881 census finds all five, ranging in ages from 24 to 36, still under the family roof working the farm. The eldest son and namesake, John Jr., failed to secure the family estate; after an ill-fated venture as a saloon-keeper, he left for the States. The second son, Alexander, showed promise as a farmer and stock raiser but died of consumption in 1889, as had a younger brother before him. A good deal of the Tod estate passed into the hands of the Bowker son-in-law, but by the 1890s the original family house had been purchased by strangers. Only James, Tod's eldest son by his first marriage, enjoyed any real success as a farmer. Tod had bought James his own farm when he arrived from the east; reputedly a man of prodigious strength, the younger Tod developed an extensive property known as Spring Bank Farm, which he passed on to two of his sons.[49] In 1857 James married one of the Macauley daughters, making him a brother-in-law of William McNeill Jr.

The wives and children in these elite HBC/Native families were subject to a process of acculturation designated to negate their Native heritage. To a considerable degree this was successful. Generally, the Native wives adapted remarkably well to being mistresses of substantial colonial households. The second generation, having the benefits of considerable education, was far removed from its Aboriginal roots. Yet there was no guarantee that the stigma of Native blood could truly be transcended. Indeed, racist attitudes intensified in the late nineteenth century, and miscegenation was held to be undesirable. These attitudes are painfully underscored in the public denunciation of some of Victoria's founding families by the American historian, Hubert Howe Bancroft.

In the late spring of 1878, Bancroft spent a month in Victoria collecting reminiscences and records for his mammoth history of the Pacific northwest. Anxious to meet the retired HBC officers who had played such an important role in the development of the region, he was gratified by the hospitality and generous assistance of former traders and/or their descendants.[50] One can only imagine, then, the dismay that these families must have felt to find their Native heritage so excoriated in the pages of the awaited *History of the Northwest Coast* when it appeared in 1886. In a highly personal passage, in which some of Victoria's leading citizens were named, Bancroft ruminates on "the fur trader's curse":

> It has always seemed to me that the heaviest penalty the servants of the Hudson's Bay Company were obliged to pay for the wealth and authority advancement gave them, was the wives they were expected to marry and the progeny they should rear . . . I could never understand how such men as John McLoughlin, *James Douglas*, Ogden, *Finlayson*, *Work* and *Tolmie* and the rest could endure the thought of having their name and honors descend to a degenerate posterity. Surely they were possessed of sufficient intelligence to know that by giving their children Indian or half-breed mothers, their own old Scotch, Irish or English blood would in them be greatly debased, and hence they were doing all concerned a great wrong. Perish all the Hudson's Bay Company thrice over, I would say, . . . sooner than bring into being offspring subject to such a curse.[51]

Bancroft's lament was implicitly gendered. He was decrying the sons: those who had failed to carry on the family name with any success. But, as we have seen, miscegenation was not the problem—the differing experience of sons and daughters gives the lie to Bancroft's assertion. The dynamics of class and race, it should be emphasized, have a gendered impact. Males were required to move in a more public occupational and social world than were their female counterparts, and racial stereotyping, which emphasized deficiencies as inherent, worked strongly against them. Among the boys, what might have passed as rowdy youthful behaviour among other elite males was associated with dissolute Native character and resulted in their being subjected to harsh discipline. Many were not well trained to play the roles that their fathers had hoped for them. Indeed, their fathers themselves may have colluded in racist stereotyping, expressing doubts about their sons' ability to succeed and favouring White suitors for their daughters.[52] Given the gender demographics of colonial Victoria, the sons in these families were soon outnumbered by well-educated, ambitious young Englishmen with whom they had to compete both occupationally and socially. In early Victoria, these sons are conspicuous by their almost complete absence from the social record. They must have resented the competition from the young British gentlemen who monopolized the affections of their sisters. Significantly, in the second generation there was no intermarriage among these families.

Unlike their brothers, whose success and failures would be judged in the public sphere, the daughters' success and failures would occur in the private sphere of marriage. Here colonial demographics worked to the advantage of the daughters; in the early decades there were few marriageable immigrant women who could compete with these elite "daughters of the country." For the most part, the fathers' wealth and position and the daughters' personal success in equipping themselves to play the roles expected of British middle-class wives and mothers were sufficient to overcome racial prejudice. This fact accounts for the astonishing

Plate 14.17 Tolmie family group, taken in front of their veranda at Cloverdale in 1878. Mother and father are seated, flanked by three sons, standing, and enclosing the youngest children, symbolizing family solidarity. (Man seated apart is a family friend.) BC Archives, G-4990

marriage rate of 100 percent for the daughters of the second generation. Their marriages to incoming White colonists served, of course, to dilute Native ancestry even further.[53]

The spread of attitudes such as Bancroft's contributed to the process of distancing and denial experienced by many descendants of the five founding families of Victoria. Family narratives and obituaries increasingly highlighted the pioneering role of these fathers; if the mothers were mentioned at all, there was no reference to their being Native. When Simon Fraser Tolmie, who became premier of the province, fondly reminisced about growing up at Cloverdale (Plate 14.17), the family estate, he hardly mentioned his mother and omitted all reference to his remarkable Work grandmother.[54] In his family narrative of 1924, Donald H. McNeill was at pains to emphasize that his grandfather had been the first White settler of south Oak Bay but did not acknowledge that he was descended from high-ranking Haida and Tongass women.[55] Popular writers also ignored the Native heritage of these families. A 1928 volume about the early women of Vancouver Island includes a whole chapter entitled "The Wives of the First Landowners"; although it focuses on the Work women, the reader would be hard pressed to know that they were of Native descent.[56]

And so the Native origin of some of Victoria's founding families was obscured for decades. The reclamation of this part of these family histories not only adds to the richness of the city's history, but also illuminates the complex intersection of the dynamics of race, class, and gender.

NOTES

This article originated as a presentation to an invited symposium on cultural borderlands at Princeton University in March 1995. I benefited greatly from the comments of participants, especially Natalie Zemon Davis. Revisions of this work were stimulated by the responses to versions given at First Nations House at the University of Toronto, my seminar on Aboriginal/non-Aboriginal relations, and several conferences. My research assistant in Victoria, Christopher Hanna, has been an invaluable aid, and I am grateful to Adele Perry, Ted Chamberlin, Jean Barman, John Adams, Charlene Porsild, Bettina Bradbury, Jack Gregg, Jennifer Brown, and Shirley Wishart for their interest and comments. The staff of the British Columbia Archives were ever helpful, especially Kathryn Bridge, with her expertise in photographs. Many thanks also to Cole Harris for his careful, thoughtful editing and to Eric Leinberger for drawing the maps. All the photographs are published with the permission of the BC Archives.

1. Terry Reksten, *"More English Than the English": A Very Social History of Victoria* (Victoria: Orca, 1986).

2. For an excellent discussion of the ideology behind the colonization scheme for Vancouver Island, see Richard Mackie, "The Colonization of Vancouver Island, 1849–58," *BC Studies* 96 (Winter 1992–93): 3–40. According to Mackie, "the rank structures of the company and the colony merged. The Family Company Compact made the transition from a fur trade elite to a colonial elite through its control of land and political power" (31–32).

3. BC Archives, E/B/A1 5.2, Alexander Allan, "Cariboo & the Mines of British Columbia" (1878); see also Adele Perry, "'The Prevailing Vice': Mixed-Race Relationships and Colonial Discourse in British Columbia, 1858–1871" (Ph.D. thesis, Department of History, York University, 1977), ch. 3. For a more general study of the growing fear of miscegenation in the nineteenth-century Anglo-American context, see Robert Young, *Colonial Desire: Hybridity in Theory, Culture and Race* (London: Routledge 1995).

4. Margaret Ormsby, ed., *Fort Victoria Letters, 1846–1851* (Winnipeg: Hudson's Bay Records Society, 1979), vol. 32, LX.

5. For a useful discussion of the importance of photographs as historical documents and the challenges involved in reading them, see J. Robert Davison, "Turning a Blind Eye: The Historian's Use of Photographs," *BC Studies* 52 (Winter 1981–82): 16–38; Elizabeth Heyert, *The Glass-House Years: Victorian Portrait Photography, 1839–70* (London: George Prior, 1978); and Alan Thomas, *The Expanding Eye: Photography and the Nineteenth-Century Mind* (London: Croom Helm, 1978).

6. The following synopsis of the origins of these five families is derived mainly from Sylvia Van Kirk, *"Many Tender Ties": Women in Fur Trade Society in Western Canada, 1670–1870* (Winnipeg: Watson and Dwyer, 1980).

7. Hudson's Bay Company Archives (hereafter HBCA), D.5/30, Simpson Correspondence Inward, McNeill to Simpson, 5 March 1851.

8. BC Archives, Edward Ermatinger Correspondence, John Work to Ermatinger, Fort Simpson, 13 December 1834. See also "Five Letters of Charles Ross, 1842–844," *British Columbia Historical Quarterly* 7 (April 1943): 109.

9. For a discussion of Native women's evolving fashions at the fur trade posts, see Van Kirk, *"Many Tender Ties,"* 99–103.

10. For the difficulties with the school at Fort Vancouver, see Thomas Jessett, ed., *Reports and Letters of Herbert Beaver, 1836–38* (Portland: Champoeg Press, 1959).

11. BC Archives, Charles Ross Clipping File, Walter to Father, 1 March 1845; HBCA, A.10/19 and 20, Walter P. Ross and Mary Tait to HBC Secretary, 13 June and 7 August 1845.

12. Jennifer Brown, *Strangers in Blood: Fur Trade Company Families in Indian Country* (Vancouver: UBC Press, 1980), 185–90.

13. BC Archives, Reminiscences of Bishop Edward Cridge. In 1875, most of the old HBC families followed Cridge to his Reformed Episcopal Church, formed after his break with Bishop George Hills.

14. BC Archives, ADD. MSS. 1774, School Register, Fort Victoria, 1850–52.

15. Dorothy Blakey Smith, ed., *The Reminiscences of Doctor John Sebastian Helmcken* (Vancouver: UBC Press, 1975), 120; Dorothy B. Smith, ed., *Lady Franklin Visits the Pacific Northwest* (Victoria: Provincial Archives of British Columbia, 1974), II, 34–35.

16. BC Archives, ADD. MSS. 1912, *Memoirs of James Anderson*, vol. 9, 158–76.

17. BC Archives, E/B/D343, Annie Deans Correspondence, 29 February 1854.

18. George Stanley, ed., *Mapping the Frontier; Charles Wilson's Diary of the Survey of the 49th Parallel, 1858–1862* (Toronto: Macmillan, 1970), 28, 45, 87–88.

19. Marion B. Smith, "The Lady Nobody Knows," *British Columbia: A Centennial Anthology* (Toronto: McClelland and Stewart, 1958), 479.

20. Smith, *Lady Franklin Visits*, 12, 22–23.

21. Wilson, *Mapping the Frontier*, 175.

22. BC Archives, B/40/2A, Douglas Private Letter-Book, 1867–79, to A.G. Dallas, 23 July 1867.

23. Hubert Howe Bancroft, *Literary Industries* (San Francisco: History Co., 1890), 534.

24. Wilson, *Mapping the Frontier*, 135.

25. Bancroft, *Literary Industries*, 534.

26. Nellie de Bertrand Lugrin, *The Pioneer Women of Vancouver Island, 1843–1866* (Victoria: Women's Canadian Club of Victoria, 1928), 64.

27. BC Archives, Ermatinger Correspondence, John Tod to Ermatinger, 1 June 1864.

28. Ibid., 15 March 1864 and 12 November 1868.

29. Reksten, *"More English Than the English,"* 82–84.

30. *British Colonist*, 14 December 1863 and 8 February 1864.

31. *British Colonist*, 30 April 1859, 2 and 20, and 21 May 1862, 3. See also several entries in the charge books of the Victoria Police Department from 1858 to 1860 in BC Archives.

32. BC Archives, Records of Christ Church Cathedral, Marriage Register, 29 June 1863. O'Brien is identified as the eldest son of Dr. Lucius O'Brien of Quebec, C.E.

33. *Daily Chronicle*, 30 April 1864. See also *British Colonist*, 26 August 1863, 3; 1 September 1863, 3; 27 September 1864, 3; and *Daily Chronicle*, 1 September 1863.

34. *Daily Chronicle*, 4 May 1864.

35. BC Archives, Vancouver Island, Supreme Court, Cause Books, 616–17; Colonial Correspondence, John Morley, file 1,170, Inquest into the Death of Lucius O'Brien, 1866.

36. BC Archives, Colonial Correspondence, file 1,352, petitions (1866).

37. BC Archives, Philip Hankin Reminiscences, 166.

38. BC Archives, Wren Family Papers, Will of Charles Wren, 6 February 1864.

39. BC Archives, Christ Church Cathedral, Marriage Register, 6 December 1859; Gordon Keith, ed., *The James Francis Tullock Diary, 1876–1910* (Portland: Binford and Mort, 1978), 16.

40. *British Colonist*, 23 September 1876, 3.

41. *Daily Chronicle*, 24 April 1885; BC Archives, Wren Family Papers, Carrie to Isabella, 17 August 1880.

42. BC Archives, Charles Ross Clipping File, Biographical Notes. For further discussion on the Ross family in Washington State, see Cecelia Svinth Carpenter, *Fort Nisqually: A Documented History of Indian and British Interaction*. (Tacoma: Tahoma Research Service, 1986). Carpenter is a descendant of Charles and Catherine Ross.

43. BC Archives, McNeill Letterbook, 18 October 1855; Helen Meilleur, *A Pour of Rain: Stories from a West Coast Fort* (Victoria: Sono Nis, 1980), 207.

44. Meilleur, *A Pour of Rain*, 208; British Columbia, Division of Vital Statistics, Death Certificate of Henry McNeill.

45. Smith, *Helmcken Reminiscences*, 153–54.

46. BC Archives, Donald McNeill, Personal Record, 1924; *British Colonist*, 31 October 1889.

47. BC Archives, Lucy Moffat Clipping File.

48. James K. Nesbitt, "The Diary of Martha Cheney Ella, 1853–56," *British Columbia Historical Quarterly* 13, Pt. 1 (April 1949): 91–112; and Part 2 (July–October 1949): passim.

49. For biographical information on the Tod family, see Robert Belyk, *John Tod: Rebel in the Ranks* (Victoria: Horsdal & Schubart, 1995).

50. Bancroft, *Literary Industries*, 530–39.

51. Hubert Howe Bancroft, *History of the Northwest Coast* (San Francisco: History Co., 1886), vol. 2, 650–51. I have italicized all the officers who settled in Victoria. My attention was first drawn to this quote when reading Janet Campbell Hale's fascinating autobiography, *Bloodlines: Odyssey of a Native Daughter* (New York: Random House, 1993). Bancroft's thoughts on miscegenation reflect the growing prejudice in the United States, especially after the American Civil War, as discussed in Young, *Colonial Desire*.

52. For further discussion of fathers' ruminations on the failings of their mixed-blood sons, see Brown, *Strangers in Blood*, 188–89: John Tod wrote to Ermatinger, "Well have you observed that all attempts to make gentlemen of them have hitherto proved a failure. The fact is there is something radically wrong about them all."

53. Although a detailed analysis of the third generation of these families is beyond the scope of this study, it should be observed that the sharply divergent patterns of the second generation do not hold into the third generation. Sons in the female lines of such families as the Helmckens, the Finlaysons, and the Tolmies did distinguish themselves in various branches of Victoria's professional and political life in the later nineteenth century. However, by this time, both in terms of blood and socialization, there was little of their Native ancestry left. On the other hand, the marriage rate of the daughters was not nearly as high as it was during the previous generation—a trend that requires further investigation.

54. See. S.F. Tolmie, "My Father: William Fraser Tolmie, 1812–1886," *British Columbia Historical Quarterly* 1 (October 1937): 227–40.

55. Ibid. 46, Donald McNeill, Personal Record, 1924.

56. Lugrin, *Pioneer Women of Vancouver Island*, ch. 5.

Article Fifteen

Hardy Backwoodsmen, Wholesome Women, and Steady Families: Immigration and the Construction of a White Society in Colonial British Columbia, 1849–1871

Adele Perry

Who was in and who was out? One of the primary ways which mid-nineteenth-century British Columbians negotiated inclusions and exclusions was through the practice and discourse of immigration. Immigration derived its social and political significance from its double ability to dispossess local peoples and establish a settler-society in their stead. The settler society this process sought to build was explicitly racialized and deeply gendered. In seeking "hardy backwoodsmen", colonial promoters encouraged men committed to hard work, steadiness, and rural life; in demanding "wholesome women", they sought women who would simultaneously serve as beacons of imperial society and constrain the excesses of white men; in courting "steady families", they pursued stable units that would exemplify the virtues of the same-race, nuclear family. Together, "hardy backwoodsmen, wholesome women and steady families" were constructed as the immigrants able to transform British Columbia into the stable settler society of imperialists' dreams.

Studies of the flow of people between Europe and the Americas in the "Great Migration Era" have tended to leave a blind spot, namely their disinterest in interrogating the politicized character of nineteenth-century "new world" migration.[1] When people left Europe for the Americas or Australia, they did not simply move into large, empty spaces. Instead, they participated in a process of colonization in which Aboriginal dispossession and settler migration were irreparably linked. As Daiva Staisulis and Nira Yuval-Davis argue, migration is one of the chief ways in which settler societies constitute themselves.[2] For individuals and families, migration was probably motivated primarily by straightforward social and economic needs, but the overarching structure of imperialism transformed these needs into imperial acts.[3] Immigration sometimes

Source: "Hardy Backwoodsmen, Wholesome Women, and Steady Families: Immigration and the Construction of a White Society in Colonial British Columbia, 1849–1871," by Adele Perry, *Histoire sociale/Social History* 33 (November 2000): 343–360. Reprinted by permission.

troubled and sometimes nourished the politics of empire. In either case, it cannot be separated from them.

A better acknowledgement of the connections between migration and imperialism necessitates a return to an older phase in the writing of Canadian history, albeit with newly critical eyes. The past two decades have witnessed an increasing emphasis on the social experience of immigrant peoples to Canada. Historians have rejected earlier studies in which "immigration was acknowledged as a key ingredient in transcontinental nation-building but the immigrants were largely ignored or relegated to cameo appearances".[4] They have embraced the vantage point of the immigrant instead of the policy-maker and analysed how these people, like women and the working class, were active agents who shaped their own history. This historiographic shift is premised on a needed critique of histories that artificially isolate the powerful from both the cause and effect of their authority. An unintended and less useful consequence of changing historiographic imperatives has been to detach the process of migration from its larger political context. Instead of treating the political and social history of immigration as distinct processes, historians need to reckon with the profound ties that connect the politician with the peasant and the policy-maker with the people.

Acknowledging these ties is crucial to understanding white settler colonies like British Columbia. The significance of immigration in colonial contexts derives from its central position in the very business of imperialism. Settler societies aim simultaneously to dispossess Aboriginal peoples and to replace them with relatively homogeneous settler populations, and immigration is one of the tools that has allowed them to do so. Colonies of settlement are distinguished from other kinds of colonies chiefly by their reproductive and gendered character. That colonizers *settle* implies more than residence. It denotes a reproductive regime dependent on the presence of settler women who literally reproduce the colony. Immigration must therefore provide more than non-Aboriginal bodies. Ideally, it must provide the right kind of bodies, those suited to building a white settler colony.

These connections between immigration, empire, and gender came together in mid-nineteenth-century British Columbia in an especially revealing way. Its society was the product of three sometimes conflicting imperial intentions: the fur trade, the gold rush, and the British tradition of settler colonies. North America's northern Pacific coast and the Columbia Plateau were densely populated by linguistically, culturally, and politically diverse First Nations people reliant on foraging, hunting, and fishing. The Hudson's Bay Company (HBC) began trading with local peoples in the late eighteenth century, and formal colonial authority was established in 1849 when Vancouver Island was made a British colony.

The discovery of gold on the mainland's Fraser River in 1858 precipitated the creation of a mainland colony called British Columbia. It was, according to imperial opinion, destined to be a major colony of settlement. "[N]ever did a colony in its infancy present a more satisfactory appearance," remarked one Anglican cleric. By 1866 and 1867, however, "those who once entertained most extravagant expectations began to despond."[5] Imperial downsizing followed despondency. In 1866 the two colonies were merged, retaining the name of British Columbia, and in July 1871 British Columbia joined Canada as a province, bringing the colonial period to a close.

These shifts in political form reflected widespread disappointment in British Columbia's performance as a settler colony. "The high tide of immigration expected never reached the Colony" explained Governor Frederick Seymour, "and the ebb proved much stronger than anticipated."[6] To be sure, the population expanded: there were fewer than 1,000 settlers in 1855 and over 10,000 in 1871. But the settler population never rivalled the Aboriginal one, which, despite massive depopulation wrought by smallpox, likely hovered around the 45,000 mark in the early 1870s.[7]

Settler British Columbia did not grow as quickly as imperial observers hoped it would, nor did it grow in the way they had hoped. The periphery, like the metropole, defied pretences of ethnic and racial homogeneity.[8] For a supposed white settler colony, British Columbia was not very white: Chinese, African-American, Latino, and Kanaka (Hawaiian) settlers were a significant presence. Jews and continental Europeans pressed operative definitions of whiteness, and Americans unsettled the colony's claims to Britishness. In 1861 the local official for Douglas, a small gold-rush town on the mainland, enumerated 97 Chinese, 40 Americans, 20 Mexicans, 17 Europeans, and 6 "coloured" people. They dwelled amongst "About 700 Natives".[9] It would have been difficult to find in one place a greater mixture of different nationalities," wrote German mathematician Carl Friesach after visiting Yale, another small mining town. "Americans were undoubtably [sic] in the majority—California, especially had sent a large contingent. Then followed Germans, French, and Chinese. Next came Italians, Spaniards, Poles, etc.," he noted.[10]

The special plurality that characterized resource towns helped shape the entire colony. American missionary Matthew Macfie found Victoria, the capital city, a small and alarmingly cosmopolitan place in the early 1860s:

> Though containing at present an average of only 5,000 or 6,000 inhabitants, one cannot pass along the principal thoroughfares without meeting representatives of almost every tribe and nationality under heaven. Within a limited space may be seen—of Europeans, Russians, Austrians, Poles, Hungarians, Italians, Danes, Swedes, French, Germans, Spaniards, Swiss, Scotch, English and Irish; of Africans, Negroes from the United States and the West Indies; of Asiatics, Lascars and Chinamen; of Americans, Indians, Mexicans, Chilanoes, and citizens of the North American Republic; and of Polynesians, Malays from the Sandwich Islands [Hawaii].[11]

Macfie's fevered attempt to classify this population perhaps speaks more to his own discomfort with the mutability of racial boundaries, but it is not surprising that this discomfort was triggered in British Columbia. The diversity fostered by the gold rushes of the early colonial days diminished but never disappeared. When British Columbia entered Canadian confederation in 1871, its settler society was constituted, according to one probably conservative count, by 8,576 whites, 1,548 Chinese, and 462 Africans.[12]

That British Columbia's settlers were overwhelmingly male further suggested its failure to fit the norms of a white settler colony. While the female proportion ebbed and flowed over the colonial period, it never exceeded a high of 35 per cent of the white society and reached lows of 5 per cent.[13] Imperial discourse that accorded white women a special role as harbingers of empire rendered this demographic problem a political one. A popular emigration guide by "A Returned Digger", like so many others, despaired of what to do with a society so lacking in women. "The great curse of the colony", he explained, "is the absence of women. I doubt if there was one women to a hundred men twelve months ago. I am quite sure that now, when I am writing, there must be at least two hundred men to every woman."[14] In colonial discourse, the continuing demographic dominance of First Nations people, the plurality of settler society, and its prevailing masculinity became irreparably intertwined, a three-part symbol of British Columbia's departure from dominant social norms and expectations.

Colonial promoters—a term I apply to a loose collection of journalists, politicians, officials, missionaries, and self-appointed do-gooders—looked to immigration to address the smallness, diversity, and masculinity of settler British Columbia and to render it a prosperous and respectable settler colony. They attributed the colony's lamentable imperial performance to the sparseness of its settler society. The *British Columbian* newspaper argued that the colony's poor showing stemmed from its underpopulation, "because we have only a mere handful of population, a few thousand people living upon one another".[15] The colony lacked white population of nearly every description. The Victoria press noted,

> If we enter our churches, they want worshippers; our school houses want scholars; our streets and highways want pedestrians and vehicles; our merchants want trade; our traders want customers; our steamboats want passengers and freight; our workshops want workmen; our fertile valleys want farmers; our gold and silver mines want miners; in short, the two Colonies want population.[16]

While the colony had resources, wrote the *Cariboo Sentinel*, "without a population a country may remain forever a barren wilderness, dotted here and there with a few fisherman's huts and a few miners' and lumberman's cabins, and known only to the world as an inhospitable and poverty-stricken place."[17]

If colonial promoters suggested that British Columbia's ills stemmed from the sparseness of the white population, they had a related and almost boundless faith in the political potential of white bodies to make it a successful colonial enterprise. Even the most shameless boosters, however, recognized that British Columbia's distance from centres of white population meant that active state intervention was required for mass immigration to occur. If they wanted a white population, they would have to work for it, bidding it to come hither, assisting its passage, and supporting it on arrival. "To have our country filled up we must not only assist people to reach our shores, but we must show them the way to earn a living after they get here," wrote the *Colonist* in 1866.[18] The intervention of both the local and colonial state was required. "What right has the most remote of the British Colonies to expect immigration without even *asking for it*," agreed the New Westminster press, "to say nothing of *assisting* it?"[19]

Colonial promoters' demands for immigration were part and parcel of a programme of asserting white supremacy in British Columbia. Himani Bannerji has recently dubbed immigration a "euphemistic expression for racist labour and citizenship policies".[20] In colonial British Columbia the process worked to exclude First Nations migrants and to minimize non-white settlers. It was difficult, although hardly impossible, to argue for the removal of First Nations with local and obvious territorial claims. Those from distant territories were easy targets for settlers committed to visions of racial segregation. The city of Victoria worked hard to control and limit the presence of the so-called Northern Tribes—people from the coastal societies of the Nisga'a, Hieltsuk, Nexalk, Kwakwaka'wakw, Tlingit, and especially the wealthy and powerful Haida and Tsimshian—who made annual spring visits to Victoria for trade, wage work, and festivity. In 1859 a police constable found 2,235 Northern peoples, the bulk of them probably Haida and Tsimshian, living on the outskirts of Victoria.[21] As annually as they arrived, local burghers demanded their eviction. The language they used to stigmatize Northern peoples invoked the overlapping discourses of morality, criminality, and gender that have often been used to identify and marginalize immigrant groups. "Vagrancy, filth, disease, drunkenness, larceny, maiming, murder, prostitution, in a multiplied form, are the invariable results of an annual visit from the Northern Tribes," raged the *Colonist*. "We unhesitantly declare for stopping the immigration."[22]

Those who defended the rights of Northern peoples to visit Victoria—and, by implication, their status as legitimate immigrants and thus colonial citizens—relied on another staple of immigration discourse, namely the argument that the Northern peoples' presence, however unpalatable, was sweetened by their cheap labour. When settlers demanded that Northern peoples be forcibly evicted, missionary William Duncan argued that "the driving-away policy is contrary to the interests of our Colony, which needs at least the labor of the Indians". He referred to those who doubted the local need for Aboriginal labour to "the kitchens and nurseries, the fields and gardens around Victoria".[23] Governor James Douglas proposed schemes of moral and social regulation as an alternative to eviction, arguing that Northern peoples' willingness to serve as a colonial labour force made them valuable to whites. "[I]t is hardly creditable to the civilization of the nineteenth century, that so especial an element of health, as labour of the cheapest description, should be, in a manner, banished from the Colony," he explained.[24]

The sweat and toil of the Northern peoples ultimately failed to buy them a legitimate role in settler Victoria. Those who wanted racial segregation of colonial space were bolstered and legitimated by the apocalyptic smallpox epidemic of 1862, when Northern peoples were repeatedly and forcibly evicted from Victoria, a process later condoned and organized by public health legislation.[25] A brand of settler imperialism premised on the removal and containment of local peoples ultimately won out over the version that positioned them as subservient labourers for the ruling minority. Historians need to broaden our understanding of migration to account for the plurality and movement of the so-called old world and to make room for the migrations of Aboriginal North America. Doing so complicates our analysis of migration and lays bare the extent to which immigration functioned as a mechanism of inclusion and exclusion.

That this process worked to include whites and exclude others is confirmed by the experience of settlers of Asian and African extraction. Douglas—himself an archetypal hybrid figure, hailing from a "creole" mother and a Scottish father and having married the half-Cree Amelia Connolly—encouraged the migration of mainly middle-class African Americans associated with the Pioneer Society of San Francisco in 1858. Other settlers did not share his enthusiasm. Despite the African Americans' apparent fit with the colony's putative values of hard work, Protestantism, and respectability, their sizable presence in Victoria was regarded by many white people as a problem. Whether Victoria would replicate or challenge American-style segregation in her churches, theatres, and saloons was a significant item of debate until the black population began to disperse in the mid-1860s.[26]

It was Chinese immigration that created the most ambivalence among British Columbia's white commentators. Representations of Chinese men celebrated industriousness and sometimes located them on the colonists' side of the local imperial divide. The Grand Jury of Cayoosh (later Lillooet) told the Governor in 1860 that Chinese settlers were a benefit to white traders and the government alike. The jury further requested that the state acknowledge the Chinese as settlers, asking that they "afford them every due protection to prevent their being driven away, wither by attacks from Indians or otherwise".[27]

More often Chinese men were positioned as undesirable immigrants who would imperil rather than bolster colonialism. The *Cariboo Sentinel* argued that Chinese men should not be colonists for a variety of reasons, all indicating their fundamental difference and many invoking explicitly gendered images. The Chinese, the newspaper argued, were "aliens not merely in nationality, but in habits, religion"; they never became "good citizens" or served on juries or fire companies; they never married or settled outside China and were "more apt to create immorality than otherwise"; they dealt "entirely with their own countrymen"; they hoarded their money and evaded taxes; and, lastly, they were, ironically for immigrants, "inimical to immigration".[28] No restrictions were imposed on Chinese immigration, although colonists debated ways—prominent among them being a miner's licence fee levied on Chinese men alone—designed to regulate their place within settler society."[29] Such discussions anticipated the highly organized, pervasive, and vociferous attacks on Chinese people that began later in the nineteenth century and continue to shape contemporary life and politics.[30]

The role of immigration to colonial British Columbia was thus an explicitly racial one. The "'bone, muscle, and intellect,' that is required here", explained the Victoria press plainly, "differs materially from the Indian or the African. It is Caucasian—Anglo-Saxon bone, muscle, and intellect we want."[31] Class, and the politics of respectability that so often went with it, also helped determine who would be included and who excluded. Not all white people were created equal. British Columbia's colonial promoters did not want convicts, although one, tellingly, was willing to tolerate juvenile offenders as long as they were placed on First Nations settlements.[32] When the Colonial Office inquired about the emigration of distressed Lancashire mill operatives, local officials were similarly unreceptive. Douglas replied that "this Colony offers but a poor field for destitute immigrants", warning that "instead of improving their condition, it is to be feared, that by emigrating in great numbers to this Colony, they would only be involved in a more hopeless state of distress and poverty".[33] British Columbia's officials were ultimately as fearful of organized immigration's class implications—of the shov-elling out of paupers—as were others in British North America.

Immigration to this settler colony was an issue of race and class, and also very much one of gender. British Columbia's colonial failure was linked, in critics' minds, not only to the smallness and diversity of the settler society but also to the failure of increasingly hegemonic gender norms to take root there. British Columbia was home to a small, highly mobile handful of settler men living amongst a large Aboriginal society. This particular demography fostered a rough, vibrant homosocial culture created by and for young men and the widespread practice of white-Aboriginal domestic and conjugal relationships. Immigration was sought as a correc-tive for both. When promoters called for immigration, they called for a process that would address the society's perceived gendered deficiencies as well as its racial peculiarities.

Three gendered images dominated discussions of immigration. First, the hardy backwoodsman—a steady, hard-working man willing to meet the difficulties of colonial life and permanently settle in British Columbia—shaped discussions of men and migration. The hypothetical hardy backwoodsman was constructed in contrast to the rough gold miners who so pervaded the colony. British Columbia had two major gold rushes—the Fraser River Gold Rush of 1858 and the Cariboo Gold Rush of 1862–1863—and a host of smaller ones. Waves of young, footloose men disillusioned with the false promises of capitalist, industrial society were attracted by each strike of gold. Prevailing discourse understood these men as wandering, immoral, and anti-social. George Grant, secretary of a surveying party, argued that the gold rushes brought "not an emigration of sober, steady householders, whose aim was to establish homes, and live by their own industry, but of fever-hearted adventurers from all parts of the world,—men without a country and without a home".[34]

Miners' inadequacies as colonists became axiomatic in popular colonial discourse. "It must be admitted that a very considerable section of our population is composed of adventurers, who, having been attracted to our shores by our gold, feel little or no interest in the permanent success of the Colony," wrote the *British Columbian*.[35] For British Columbia to fulfil its impe-rial potential, hardy backwoodsmen would have to replace the wandering miners. In 1859 Douglas told the Colonial Office, "The mining population are proverbially migratory and unsettled in their habits, seldom engaging in any other than their own absorbing pursuits, and therefore, it is he who tills the soil, the industrious farmer, who must clear the forest, bring the land into cultivation, and build up the permanent interests and prosperity of the Colony."[36]

The hardy backwoodsman stood in contrast not only to the wandering miner but to another masculine drain on the colonial enterprise, the "croaker". This term, along with grum-bler, was applied to men deemed unable to weather the difficulties of colonial lie. Whether an erstwhile son of wealth or an urban loafer, the croaker was flummoxed by the realities of pio-neering and proceeded to complain instead of work. Gilbert Malcolm Sproat, a sawmill owner, magistrate, amateur anthropologist, and promoter of immigration, described the croakers:

> [C]ertain persons came into the country who had a strong desire to make a living without taking off their coats—a desire which could not be gratified. The friends of these persons at home sent them money, which they put into silly investments. They rode to the diggings, and road [sic] back again. They hung, like mendicants, round the doors of the Government offices. They croaked in the streets, spent their time idly in bar-rooms, and finally disappeared.[37]

Here, the language of class is put to work in the service of gender and race: the croaker is idle and delicate, bearing the mark of both femininity and bourgeois laxity. The local press argued a similar position. Some settlers, one paper argued, "only remain to croak and whine for a season, and eventually, like sickly lambs or untimely fruit, unequal to the task of combatting [sic] and overcoming the hardships and privations incident to all new countries, drop off to their native land".[38] The test of manliness these "sickly lambs" fail is thus generated by the specificities of the colonial context.

This was a test that the hardy backwoodsman passed. Just as they repelled the weak, colonies were thought to attract the most manly of British men who stood in contrast not only to their less rugged fellows, but to the indigenous men they alternately feminized or feared.[39] "As a rule," commented the local press, "it is the most energetic, hardy, manly, self reliant of her sons who first people her Colonies."[40] Ideal male immigrants were hard-working, disciplined, and predisposed to rural life. The new colony, argued a supporter in 1860, "does not want the idle, the profligate, and sickly".[41] The hardy backwoodsman embraced diligent labour, especially agricultural labour, just as the gold miner rejected it. His single state meant that he was able to devote himself fully to labour, to define himself as an entirely economic being. One much-reprinted emigration guide advised, "A family is a burden till a man is established."[42]

The discourse of the hardy backwoodsman both reflected and masked single men's economic significance to a colony materially tied to resource extraction. Despite the significance of Aboriginal people to British Columbia's wage-labour force, employers persisted in seeking non-Native miners and farmers and believed, in keeping with the Anglo-American world, that only men could fulfil these roles. That a work force of single men was literally reproduced elsewhere spared the colony the costs of maintaining and creating labour in the next generation.[43] Labour-force politics reinforced the prevailing gendered patterns of immigration and ensured that single men formed the overwhelming majority of independent immigrants. They also comprised a surprising percentage of assisted ones. Between 1849 and 1852 the HBC imported over 400 people, 250 of whom were adult men mainly destined to labour on Island farms.[44] The search for hardy backwoodsmen persisted throughout the colonial period. A proposed 1864 Vancouver Island scheme put "farm labourers" alongside "unmarried female domestic servants" and "married couples" as people whose passages should be subsidized.[45]

Yet single men, hardy or otherwise, constituted an ambivalent force for colonial promoters. Sproat thought that their tendency to wander made them a waste of public funds.[46] More fundamentally, imperial regimes were consistently troubled by the large numbers of working-class men assigned responsibility for practically enforcing them [the rules of the colony].[47] White soldiers, miners, and farmers frequently failed to meet standards of racial distance and superiority set by imperial masters. Racial concerns about young, footloose men in colonial contexts were also gendered concerns. Colonial promoters were disturbed by how regularly white men formed relationships and families with local women. Settler men who opted to remain single were also a worry. Increasingly in the mid-nineteenth century the domestic family was constructed as a necessary component of adult life. To be rendered a responsible colonial citizen who was appropriately distanced from local peoples, the hardy backwoodsman needed a wholesome woman.

The scarcity of white women in British Columbia became, along with the smallness of the settler population, axiomatic for the colony's condition. As I have argued elsewhere, white women were constructed as "fair ones of a purer caste"[48] with three related roles in the local colonial project. White women would first compel white men to reject the rough homosocial culture of the backwoods in favour of normative standards of masculinity, respectability, and permanence. "Women! women! women! are the great want," wrote aristocrat Harry Verney from London. "The normal state is man with a help meet for him, and if something is not soon done, either by the Imperial or Colonial Government, or by some philanthropists at home, I know not what will become of us. Poor man goes sadly down hill if he remains long without the supporting influence of women."[49] White women were considered to be men's collective better half, as the only force capable of ensuring their proper behaviour. Such a discourse accorded them a role, albeit a limited one, as agents in both imperialism and immigration.

White women would secondly address shortages in the local labour market and relieve overpopulation in Britain. That the supposed need for domestic servants and wives in British Columbia neatly matched fears of "surplus women" in Britain gave calls for female immigration a special efficacy. A female immigration to British Columbia, wrote one observer, "would be as great a boon to the colony as I am sure it would be to many of the underpaid, under-fed, and over-worked women who drag out a weary existence in the dismal back streets and alleys of the metropolis".[50] Immigration was thus invoked as a mechanism for simultaneously resolving the different crises of gender that troubled the metropole and the periphery.

White women's third service to the colonial project was the explicitly racial one of dis-couraging mixed-race sexual, domestic, and conjugal relationships. As white men's "natural" objects of desire, they would draw men away from the temptations of Aboriginal women and, in doing so, shore up the colonial project as a whole. "That many of the native women are cleanly, industrious, and faithful, we do not pretend to deny," wrote New Westminster's *Mainland Guardian*, "but, we regret to to [sic] say, they are the exceptions. With the increase of our white female population, we look for new life in our agricultural pursuits and we hope that every inducement will be offered to healthy industrious women, who are desirous of finding good husbands and comfortable homes, in this province, to come out to us."[51] This discourse was premised on the construction of white women as uplifting and on the representation of First Nations women as base and threatening that circulated throughout colonial British Columbia.

In these ways, the discourse of wholesome women emphasized the political utility of ordi-nary, working-class women above those who held an official role in the colonial project like missionaries' or officials' wives. Their contribution lay not in independent action, but rather in their ability to transform plebeian men. Such a discourse imbued women migrants with an agency less often acknowledged in historiography. At any rate, the sheer ideological weight of the conviction that a society lacking white women could not be a moral or even adequate one provided the motivation necessary to orchestrate immigration schemes in 1862, 1863, and 1870. Organized as joint efforts of the local elite, missionaries, and British feminists, these immigration campaigns are remembered in popular lore as the "brideships", as colony- (and, later, nation-) building enterprises. Together, the *Tynemouth*, *Robert Lowe*, and *Alpha* carried roughly a hundred women, largely teenagers from working-class and sometimes indigent back-grounds. They were putatively destined to be domestic servants, but popular discourse ensured that their real destiny lay in the marriage market. As wives of miners and farmers, colonial promoters hoped, these wholesome women would render British Columbia's fragile colonial project a stable one.[52]

The young working-class women produced by these female immigration schemes ulti-mately unsettled the colonial project rather than securing it. Instead of behaving as beacons of imperial rectitude, the immigrants acted like the young, working-class women that they were. Colonial promoters were deeply disappointed. By the close of the colonial period, their faith in the political usefulness of white female migration was profoundly shaken. In 1872 Sproat looked back on his experience with three separate female immigration efforts, commenting, "How to send single women to Victoria safely across the continent, and through San Francisco, is a problem which I cheerfully hand over for solution to those who are more experienced in the management of that sex than I am."[53] The fundamental problem with white female migration, he argued, was that *single* women were necessarily a moral problem. "The very delicate and difficult question of introducing single unmarried women into British Columbia might be partly solved by sending out a few, in charge of the heads of families—the women being from the same district as the families, and thus having an addition[al] guard for their self-respect," he argued.[54]

Wholesome women, much like hardy backwoodsmen, challenged the colonial project at the same time as they bolstered it. The enthusiasm for white female migration was always tempered and eventually overwhelmed by the conviction that single women, like men, were a dangerous population that could only be properly contained by families. After the disasters of the assisted female migration efforts of 1862 and 1863, the "steady family" gained a special cachet in pro-immigration discourse that would only increase after the 20 servant-women transported on the *Alpha* in 1870 proved, like their predecessors, a disappointment to those who so sought their importation. The Female Immigration Board that oversaw this scheme recommended that the colonial government abandon the project of female immigration and shift its monies and attentions to the "assisted passages of Families, and relatives of Farmers, Mechanics, and others settled in this Colony".[55] In pledging their support for the importation of families, and not single women, members of the board endorsed the stable family as the best kind of immigration for the colony.

They were not alone in suggesting that same-race domestic families would be the best base for a settler society and thus the best immigrants. Families simultaneously constrained young women and encouraged men to be permanent and diligent settlers. The *Victoria Press* argued, "The very class which we want above all others is the married agriculturist—the man whose social circumstances will bring him to the soil, and make him a permanent as well as productive inhabitant."[56] Sproat agreed, writing that "the married farmer with modest means, and accustomed to work in the fields, is the best kind of immigrant for British Columbia".[57] The HBC supported family migration when it imported 36 married colliers to work Nanaimo's coalfields.[58] That the Colonial Office shared this familial ideal is suggested by its willingness to pay for the passage of the wives and families of the Royal Engineers, the soldier-settlers sent to enforce British claims to the mainland.[59] On rare occasions the colonial government subsidized the migration of individual families,[60] but more often used land law to buttress domestic family formation. In Vancouver Island, nuclear family formation was encouraged by laws that gave white men an additional 50 acres of free land if they were married and 10 more acres for each child under the age of 10.[61]

The overlap between immigration discourse and immigration practice was usually indirect. These demands for hardy backwoodsmen, wholesome women, and steady families were rarely parlayed into concrete action. Immigration was what colonial pundits always wanted and never got. In referring to immigrants as "mythical beings", politician John Sebastian Helmcken astutely recognized the somewhat hypnotic role immigration played in colonial discourse.[62] The mythic rather than actual character of immigration to colonial British Columbia was not for lack of heated rhetoric or wild scheming. Colonial promoters held mass meetings, struck committees, wrote passionate letters, and developed plans for using immigration to secure their imperial fortunes.[63] With the exception of the 20 servant women carried on the *Alpha* in 1870, however, the colonial government's immigration efforts were largely confined to the cheap and discursive: they subsidized mail, explored territory, printed essays, and hired lecturers to regale the masses of various urban centres. In 1861, for instance, British Columbia created an exhibit for the World's Fair designed to prove to "struggling, hard worked Englishmen how easily a livelihood may be earned here".[64]

The modesty of these efforts deeply disappointed those who considered immigration key to imperial success. They complained bitterly about the local government's apparent inability to organize immigration. In 1864 the mainland press commented that, excepting "fifty pounds paid to a parson at Lillooet for an Essay," the colony had "not yet expended a single dollar" on immigration.[65] Five years later, the same newspaper despaired that there was not one person responsible for immigration "[a]mongst the army of officials who absorb the revenue of the Colony."[66]

If British Columbia's local government was unable, its imperial masters were unwilling. The Colonial Office argued that, given its location, British Columbia could only reasonably expect emigrants from the Australasian colonies, not from Britain, and repeatedly announced that it had no intention of ever assisting emigration to the colony.[67] When pestered to subsidize steam communication, Colonial Office staff made it clear that they lacked the requisite political will. "When this Country was supposed to be overpeopled, there was the appearance of a domestic object in schemes for using the proceeds of English taxes to encourage emigration. But that state of things has long ceased to exist," one noted.[68] Domestic issues like overpopulation fuelled the various assisted emigration schemes of the 1830s and 1840s and would again motivate major emigration schemes in the *fin de siècle*. These efforts ground to a near halt when popular economic fortunes bettered and events like New Zealand's Maori Wars and the Indian Rebellion of 1857 challenged British faith in the imperial project.

Whether in London, Victoria, or New Westminster, many doubted British Columbia's ability to attract settlers, but only a few challenged its need for a large white population. In 1861 the *Victoria Press* argued that mass immigration was an impractical goal cooked up by those unaccustomed to colonial labour, race politics, and labour relations. "It may suit a number of lackadaisical beings who are entirely unfitted for Colonial, or in fact any practical useful life, to be enabled to obtain, by a superabundant supply of immigrants, civilized *servants* at the same price they now pay for Indians," the press wrote.[69] Yet those who questioned the merits of feasibility of mass white immigration never captured the mainstream of public discourse. Ultimately, British Columbia's apparent inability to attract white and especially British immigrants served not as a reason for challenging the viability of colonialism, but rather as a rationale for the colony's entry into Canadian confederation.[70] If British Columbia could not use immigration to become a stable settler colony in its own right, it would try to do so as a Canadian province. That British Columbia finally registered a white majority in the first census taken after confederation suggests that this strategy was effective. With continuing depopulation of First Nations and the arrival of the transcontinental railroad in 1866—that tangible technology of both capital and nation and conveyor of migrants *par excellence*—British Columbia would begin to look increasingly like a textbook white settler colony, but it would continue to be haunted by a spectre of hybridity that was, in the final analysis, more nurtured by immigration than vanquished by it.

British Columbia's colonial pundits spilled much ink on the topic of immigration. They did so because immigration was central to their effort to transform British Columbia into a white settler colony. For them, immigration was a mechanism of inclusion and exclusion, one that would marginalize First Nations people, minimize non-white settlers, and nurture white migration. It would do so in explicitly gendered ways that reflected the importance of gender to the construction of a settler society. In newspapers, government reports, and colonial circles, they called for the immigration of white, preferably British immigrants who would fit into three gendered models: the hardy backwoodsman, the wholesome woman, and the steady family. This discourse reflected a minority's aspirations rather than a society's social experience. However constant and blustery the pro-immigration discourse, British Columbia's settler society would continue to be small, dominated by men, and relatively diverse until the Canadian Pacific Railroad integrated the province into more continental patterns of demography and settlement. Immigration was indeed a tool for negotiating exclusions and inclusions, but not always in predictable ways.

NOTES

This article is drawn from her *On the Edge of Empire: Gender, Race, and the Making of British-Columbia, 1849–1871* (Toronto: University of Toronto Press, 2000). She would like to thank the organizers of the conference "Recasting European and Canadian History" for their contributions to this paper.

1. See, for instance, Bernard Bailyn, *The Peopling of British North America: An Introduction* (New York: Knopf, 1986). For a revealing example, see the explicit definition of Ontario's Leeds and Landsdowne townships as "empty" in Donald Harman Akenson, *The Irish in Ontario: A Study in Rural History* (Montreal and Kingston: McGill-Queen's University Press, 1984), p. 55.
2. Daiva Staisulis and Nira Yuval-Davis, "Introduction: Beyond Dichotomies—Gender, Race, Ethnicity and Class in Settler Societies", in Staisulis and Yuval-Davis, eds., *Unsettling Settler Societies: Articulations of Gender, Race, Ethnicity and Class* (London: Sage, 1995).
3. On this point in a later period, see Stephen Constantine, "Introduction: Empire Migration and Imperial Harmony", in Constantine, ed., *Emigrants and Empire: British Settlement in the Dominions Between the Wars* (Manchester: Manchester University Press, 1990). See also Rita S. Kranidis, ed., *Imperial Objects: Essays on Victorian Women's Emigration and the Unauthorized Imperial Experience* (New York: Twanye, 1998).
4. On this shift, see Franca Iacovetta, "Manly Militants, Cohesive Communities, and Defiant Domestics: Writing About Immigrants in Canadian Historical Scholarship", *Labour/Le Travail*, vol. 36 (Fall 1995), p. 221. Also see Iacovetta with Paula Draper and Robert Vantresca, "Preface", in Iacovetta, Draper, and Vantresca, eds., *A Nation of Immigrants: Women, Workers, and Communities in Canadian History, 1840s–1960s* (Toronto: University of Toronto Press, 1998).
5. Henry Wright, *Nineteenth Annual Report of the Missions of the Church of England in British Columbia for the Year 1877* (London: Rivingtons, 1878), pp. 16–17.
6. British Columbia Archives (hereafter BCA), GR 1486, mflm B–1442, Great Britain, Colonial Office, British Columbia Original Correspondence (hereafter CO 60), CO 60/32, Frederick Seymour to Duke of Buckingham and Chandos, March 17, 1868.
7. All population figures from colonial British Columbia are at best guesses. These are from British Columbia, *Report of the Hon. H. L. Langevin, C.B., Minister of Public Works* (Ottawa: I. B. Taylor, 1872), p. 22; and Edward Mallandaine, *First Victoria Directory, Third [Fourth] Issues, and British Columbia Guide* (Victoria: Mallandaine, 1871), pp. 94–95. Also see R. Cole Harris and John Warkentin, *Canada Before Confederation: A Study in Historical Geography* (Ottawa: Carleton University Press, 1991), chap. 7.
8. Antoinette Burton, *At the Heart of Empire: Indians and the Colonial Encounter in Late-Victorian Britain* (Berkeley: University of California Press, 1998).
9. BCA, "Colonial Correspondence", GR 1372, mflm B–1330, file 620/16, John Bowles Gaggin to W. A. G. Young, April 3, 1861.
10. Carl Friesach, "Extracts from *Ein Ausflug nach Britisch-Columbien im Jahre 1858*", in E. E. Delavault and Isabel McInnes, trans., "Two Narratives of the Fraser River Gold Rush", *British Columbia Historical Quarterly*, vol. 1 (July 1941), p. 227.
11. Matthew Macfie, *Vancouver Island and British Columbia: Their History, Resources and Prospects* (London: Longman, Green, Longman, Roberts & Green, 1865), pp. 378–379.
12. British Columbia, *Report of the Hon. H. L. Langevin*, p. 22.
13. On this, see Adele Perry, *On the Edge of Empire: Gender, Race, and the Making of British Columbia, 1849–1871* (Toronto: University of Toronto Press, 2000), chap. 1.
14. A Returned Digger, *The Newly Discovered Gold Fields of British Columbia* (London: Darton and Hodge, 1862, 8th ed.), p. 7.
15. "Our Great Want", *British Columbian*, January 9, 1869.
16. "Our Wants", *British Colonist*, June 5, 1861.
17. "Emigration", *Cariboo Sentinel*, June 18, 1868.
18. "Assisted Immigration", *British Colonist*, December 11, 1866.
19. "Population, Population", *British Columbian*, May 29, 1869.
20. Himani Bannerji, *On the Dark Side of the Nation: Essays on Multiculturalism, Nationalism and Gender* (Toronto: Canadian Scholars' Press, 2000), p. 4.
21. "Our Indian Population", *Weekly Victoria Gazette*, April 28, 1859.
22. "Invasion of the Northern Indians", *British Colonist*, April 18, 1861.

23. William Duncan, "The Indian Question", *British Colonist*, July 4, 1861. On Aboriginal wage labour, see John Lutz, "After the Fur Trade: Aboriginal Wage Labour in Nineteenth-Century British Columbia", *Journal of the Canadian Historical Association* (1992), pp. 69–94.

24. National Archives of Canada (hereafter NAC), Great Britain, Colonial Office Correspondence, Vancouver Island (hereafter CO 305), CO 305/10, mflm B–238, James Douglas to Sir Edward Bulwer Lytton, May 25, 1859.

25. See Perry, *On the Edge*, chap. 5.

26. For an argument for black migration to Vancouver Island, see Mary A. Shadd, *A Plea for Emigration; or, Notes of Canada West, in its Moral, Social, and Political Aspect With Suggestions Respecting Mexico, West Indies, and Vancouver's Island, for the Information of Colored Emigrants* [Detroit: George W. Pattison, 1842), pp. 43–44. On black people in Victoria society, see Irene Genevieve Marie Zaffaroni, "The Great Chain of Being: Racism and Imperialism in Colonial Victoria, 1858–1871" (MA thesis, University of Victoria, 1987), chap. 4; Crawford Killian, *Go Do Some Great Thing: The Black Pioneers of British Columbia* (Vancouver: Douglas and McIntyre, 1978).

27. NAC, CO 60/8, MG 11, mflm B–83, "Address of the Grand Jury at Cayoosh to Governor Douglas", in James Douglas to Duke of Newcastle, October 9, 1860.

28. "Our Chinese Population", *Cariboo Sentinel*, May 16, 1867.

29. See, for an explanation of why they were impracticable, NAC, CO 63/3, mflm B–1489, "Speech of His Honor the Officer Administering the Government at the Opening of the Legislative Council", *British Columbia Government Gazette*.

30. On this, see Kay Anderson, *Vancouver Chinatown: Racial Discourse in Canada, 1875–1980* (Montreal and Kingston: McGill-Queen's University Press, 1991); Patricia E. Roy, *A White Man's Province: British Columbia Politicians and Chinese and Japanese Immigrants, 1858–1914* (Vancouver: University of British Columbia Press, 1989).

31. "Indian vs. White Labor", *British Colonist*, February 19, 1861.

32. "Convict Labor", *British Columbian*, January 11, 1865; "Juvenile Offenders—Colonization", *British Columbian*, May 30, 1869.

33. NAC, CO 305/20, MG 11, mflm B–244, and CO 60/16, MG 11, mflm B–89, James Douglas to the Duke of Newcastle, July 14, 1863.

34. George M. Grant, *Ocean to Ocean: Sandford Fleming's Expedition Through Canada in 1872* (Toronto: James Campbell & Son, 1873), p. 308. Also see Adele Perry, "Bachelors in the Backwoods: White Man and Homosocial Culture in Up-Country British Columbia, 1858–1871", in R. W. Sandwell, ed., *Beyond City Limits: Rural History in British Columbia* (Vancouver: University of British Columbia Press, 1998).

35. "Arterial Highways", *British Columbian*, January 2, 1862.

36. NAC, CO 60/4, MG 11, mflm B–80, James Douglas to Edward Bulwer Lytton, July 11, 1859.

37. Gilbert Malcolm Sproat, *British Columbia: Information for Emigrants* (London: Agent General for the Province, 1873), p. 4.

38. "The Soil of British Columbia", *British Columbian*, February 3, 1863.

39. On masculinity and colonization, see Mrinalini Sinha, *Colonial Masculinity: The "Manly Englishman" and the "Effeminate Bengali" in the Late Nineteenth Century* (Manchester: Manchester University Press, 1995); Elizabeth Vibert, *Traders' Tales: Narratives of Cultural Encounters on the Plateau, 1807–1846* (Norman: University of Oklahoma Press, 1997).

40. "The Colonial Policy of Great Britain", *British Colonist*, May 2, 1863.

41. "Testimonial to D. G. F. MacDonald, Esq., C.E.", *Weekly Victoria Gazette*, January 30, 1860.

42. A Returned Digger, *The Newly Discovered Gold Fields*, p. 8.

43. This is dealt with, to some extent, in Alicja Muszynski, *Cheap Wage Labour: Race and Gender in the Fisheries of British Columbia* (Montreal and Kingston: McGill-Queen's University Press, 1996). Muszynski, however, discusses the economics of the single male immigrant as unique to Chinese men, when in fact most non-Natives lacked co-resident families.

44. University of British Columbia Library (hereafter UBCL), CO 305/3, mflm R288, A. Colville to John Packington, November 24, 1852, p. 1.

45. British Library, BS 72/1, "England, Emigration Commissioners", *Colonization Circular*, no. 25, 1866 (London: Groombridge and Sons), p. 8.

46. BCA, Add Mss 257, file 3, Gilbert Malcolm Sproat to Lieutenant Governor, "Memo re European Immigration into B.C.", November 3, 1871.

47. See, for instance, Kenneth Ballhatchet, *Race, Sex and Class under the Raj: Imperial Attitudes and Policies and their Critics, 1783–1905* (London: Werdenfeld and Nicholson, 1980), chap. 5.

48. One of the Disappointed, untitled piece in the *British Columbian*, June 7, 1862, Adele Perry, "Fair Ones of a Purer Caste: White Women and Colonialism in Nineteenth-Century British Columbia", *Feminist Studies*, vol. 23, no. 3 (Fall 1997), pp. 501–524.

49. "Sir Harry Verney Upon British Columbia", *British Columbian*, August 20, 1862.

50. A. D. G., "British Columbia: To the Editor of the Times", *London Times*, January 1, 1862.

51. "Immigration", *Mainland Guardian*, February 9, 1871.

52. See Perry, *On the Edge*, chaps. 6–7, for an analysis of female immigration to British Columbia.

53. BCA, GR 419, box 10, file 1872/1, British Columbia, Attorney General, "Documents", G. M. S., "Memorandum on Immigration, Oct. 1972", pp. 95–96.

54. BCA, GR 419, box 10, file 1872/1, "Attorney General Documents", G. M. Sproat, "Memorandum of a few Suggestions for opening the business of emigration to British Columbia, referred to as Memo C, in a letter of G. M. Sproat to the Honourable the Provincial Secretary, dated 29th August 1972", pp. 4–5.

55. BCA, GR 1372, mflm B–1314, file 995/23, "Colonial Correspondence", Wm. Pearse, John Robson, W. J. MacDonald to Colonial Secretary, July 12, 1870; E. G. A. "The Immigration Board", *British Colonist*, June 24, 1870.

56. "The Overland Route", *Victoria Press*, March 16, 1862.

57. BCA, GR 419, box 10, file 1872/1, British Columbia, "Papers Related to Immigration, 1972", G. M. S., "Memorandum on Immigration, Oct. 1872".

58. BCA, add mss E/BM91A, Andrew Muir, "Private Diary", November 9, 1848–August 5, 1850 [transcript]; Add Mss A/C/20.1/N15, James Douglas—Joseph William McKay, "Nanaimo Correspondence, August 1852–September 1853" [transcript].

59. NAC, MG 11, CO 609/9, mflm B–83, G. C. Lewis to James Douglas, August 11, 1860, draft reply, in James Douglas to the Duke of Newcastle, May 12, 1860.

60. See, for instance, James E. Hendrickson, ed., *Journals of the Colonial Legislatures of the Colonies of Vancouver Island and British Columbia, 1851–1871*, vol. 1: *Journals of the Council Executive Council, and Legislative Council of Vancouver Island, 1851–1866* (Victoria: Provincial Archives of British Columbia, 1980), pp. 133–134.

61. "The New Land proclamation for Vancouver Island", *British Colonist*, March 8, 1861; "Salt Spring Island", *Victoria Press*, November 10, 1861; Macfie, *Vancouver Island and British Columbia*, p. 205.

62. "Legislative Council", *British Colonist*, February 4, 1869.

63. See examples in Hendrickson, ed., *Journals of the Colonial Legislatures*, vol. 2: *Journals of the House of Assembly, Vancouver Island, 1856–1863*, vol. 3: *Journals of the House of Assembly, Vancouver Island, 1863–1866*, and vol. 4: *Journals of the Executive Council, 1864–1871, and of the Legislative Council, 1864–1866, of British Columbia*.

64. "Industrial Exhibition Circular", *British Columbian*, May 30, 1861.

65. "Emigration", *British Columbian*, June 15, 1864.

66. "What Shall We Do With Them?", *British Columbian*, June 4, 1869.

67. NAC, MG 11, CO 60/5, mflm B–81, T. W. C. Murdoch and Frederic Rogers to Herman Merivale, April 28, 1859; mflm 69.303, Great Britain, House of Commons, Parliamentary Papers, vol. 38 (1863), no. 403, "Emigration: Number of Emigrants who left the United Kingdom for the *United States, British North America, the several colonies of Australia, South Africa*, and other Places respectively: distinguishing, as far as practicable, the Native Country of the Emigrants, 1860–1863", mflm 69.303, p. 7.

68. NAC, MG 11, CO 60/14, mflm B–87, H. M. [Herman Merivale], April 8, note *en verso* in T. W. C. Murdoch to Frederic Rogers, March 31, 1862.

69. "The Immigration Bubble", *Victoria Press*, July 27, 1861.

70. BCA, GR 1486, CO 60/29, mflm B–1440, Frederick Seymour to Duke of Buckingham and Chandos, September 24, 1867.

Topic Seven

Confederation

LA CONFEDERATION!!!

This political cartoon was drawn in 1864 for *La Scie* by Quebec cartoonist Jean-Baptiste Côté. Côté portrays Quebec as a lamb about to be swallowed. Upper Canada Reform leader George Brown is riding the seven-headed Confederation monster, and Lower Canada Conservative leader George-Étienne Cartier is one of the two men wafting incense. Both men supported Confederation.

English-Canadian historians, writing within the national school of Canadian historiography in the interwar years, looked upon Confederation as a great nation-building event in Canada's evolution from colony to nation. They saw the union of the three colonies of the United Canadas, Nova Scotia, and New Brunswick in 1867 as the political nucleus around which the great transcontinental nation of Canada, rivaling that of the United States, was destined to evolve. These historians, in effect, focused largely on the great political figures that brought about Confederation and had the vision of its potential.

Since the 1960s, revisionist historians have taken issue with this interpretation of Confederation. The following three readings reflect this new historical trend. In "The Case Against Canadian Confederation," Ged Martin challenges both the "inevitability" of Confederation and the noble vision of the Fathers of Confederation. He argues that "an atmosphere of crises" in the 1860s, rather than the unfolding of a nation's destiny, made Confederation acceptable to a majority of the Fathers of Confederation. Furthermore, he argues that, once convinced of the necessity of Confederation, the actions of the Fathers of Confederation perhaps were not as high-minded as previous English-Canadian historians inferred. Martin contends that a study of the opponents of Confederation reveals how the supporters manipulated the situation. They did so to create the illusion of a crisis that only Confederation could resolve, and that they were the only ones capable of resolving it.

Writing in the context of the divisive Canadian constitutional debate of the 1980s and 1990s, John A. Rohr, an American observer, focuses on the differing opinions among the Fathers of Confederation on such issues as a legislative versus a federal union, imperial ratification of the constitution as opposed to the people's consent, the inclusion or exclusion of the Intercolonial Railway in the British North America (BNA) Act, and the need for close or distant relations with the United States. In "Current Canadian Constitutionalism and the 1865 Confederation Debates," Rohr argues that Confederation was not inevitable. As well, by contrasting the ideas and actions of the Canadian Fathers of Confederation with the American founding fathers, Rohr notes important differences in the Canadian and American political traditions.

Paul Romney also uses the divisive constitutional debate of the 1990s as the basis for raising questions about the intentions of the Fathers of Confederation and the fundamental principles of the BNA Act. He focuses on what we now believe to be one of the fundamental principles of the constitution and intentions of the Fathers of Confederation, namely to create a democratic country. He argues that the majority of the Fathers of Confederation distrusted American-style democracy and championed instead representative government: rule by an elite rather than by the people.

What were the arguments against Confederation put forward by the anti-Confederates? What were the opposing views of the Fathers of Confederation with regards to the nature of the union, the basis of consent to its ratification, and relations with the United States? What were the views of the Fathers of Confederation concerning democracy? All three readings deal with the question of the ideas of the Fathers of Confederation but come to quite different conclusions regarding their ideas. What accounts for these differing conclusions?

A traditional English-Canadian nationalist perspective on Confederation can be found in the following three general texts: Donald Creighton, *The Road to Confederation: The Emergence of Canada, 1863–1867* (Toronto: Macmillan, 1964); W.L. Morton, *The Critical Years: The Union of British North America, 1857–1873* (Toronto: McClelland and Stewart, 1964); and P.B. Waite, *The Life and Times of Confederation, 1864–1867: Politics, Newspapers, and the Union of British North America* (Toronto: University of Toronto Press, 1962). Christopher Moore takes a more recent look at the topic of Confederation in the context of the current constitutional debate in *1867: How the Fathers Made a Deal* (Toronto: McClelland & Stewart, 1997). For a more extensive look at Paul Romney's views on Confederation, see his *Getting It Wrong: How Canadians Forgot the Past and Imperiled Confederation* (Toronto: University of Toronto Press, 1999). A good primary source is P.B. Waite, ed., *The Confederation Debates in the Province of Canada, 1865* (Toronto: McClelland & Stewart, 1963). Janet Ajzenstat, et al., *Canada's Founding Debates* (Don Mills, ON: Stoddart Publishing, 1999), is also an important work. *Confederation*, edited by Ramsay Cook (Toronto: University of Toronto Press, 1967), contains important articles on the subject, including the essay on New Brunswick by Alfred G. Bailey entitled "The Basis and Persistence of Opposition to Confederation in New Brunswick" and George F.G. Stanley's "Act or Pact: Another Look at Confederation." Ged Martin has edited an interesting collection, *The Causes of Canadian Confederation* (Fredericton: Acadiensis Press, 1990), which includes his essay for this topic. J.M.S. Careless's *Brown of the Globe*, vol. 2 (Toronto: Macmillan, 1963), and Donald Creighton's *John A. Macdonald*, vol. 1, *The Young Politician* (Toronto: Macmillan, 1952), review the ideas and the important role of these leading figures in the Confederation movement.

For an account of Canada East's response, see A.I. Silver, *The French-Canadian Idea of Confederation, 1864–1900*, 2nd ed. (Toronto: University of Toronto Press, 1997), and Marcel Bellavance, *Le Québec et la Confédération: Un choix libre? Le clergé et la constitution de 1867* (Sillery, PQ: Septentrion, 1992). An older treatment of the same subject is Jean-Charles Bonenfant, *The French Canadians and the Birth of Confederation*, Canadian Historical Association, Historical Booklet no. 21 (Ottawa: CHA, 1966).

On the Maritime provinces and Confederation, see Phillip A. Buckner, "The 1860s: An End and a Beginning," in Phillip A. Buckner and John G. Reid eds., *The Atlantic Region to Confederation: A History* (Toronto: University of Toronto Press,1994), pp. 360–86. See as well, Phillip Buckner, with P.B. Waite and William M. Baker, "CHR Dialogue: The Maritimes and Confederation: A Reassessment," *Canadian Historical Review*, 71, 1 (March 1990): 1–45.

On the American influence on Confederation consult Robin Winks, *Canada and the United States: The Civil War Years* (Montreal: Harvest House, 1971 [1960]), and Greg Marquis, *In Armageddon's Shadow: The Civil War and Canada's Maritime Provinces* (Montreal/Kingston: McGill-Queen's University Press, 1998). Studies of Britain's influence include C.P. Stacey, *Canada and the British Army, 1841–1871*, rev. ed. (Toronto: University of Toronto Press, 1963 [1936]) and Ged Martin, *Britain and the Origins of Canadian Federation, 1837–67* (Vancouver: University of British Columbia Press, 1995).

WEBLINKS

Approaching Confederation
http://www.canadiana.org/citm/themes/constitution/constitution12_e.html

A collection of documents from 1850 to 1867, detailing the letters and early resolutions that were precursors to the successful union of British North America.

Confederation: Quebec
http://www.collectionscanada.ca/confederation/023001-2140-e.html

This site richly describes the historical context of the province of Quebec at the time of Confederation.

Confederation Rejected: Newfoundland
http://www.heritage.nf.ca/law/debate.html

An account of the debate and ultimate rejection of Confederation in Newfoundland.

Joseph Howe

http://www.gov.ns.ca/legislature/Facts/Howebio.html

A biography of Joseph Howe. Includes digitized letters by Howe, among other resources.

Quebec Resolutions, 1864

http://www.archives.gov.on.ca/english/centennial/12_quebec_resolutions.htm

A digitized page of the Quebec Resolutions, 1864. Adopted at the Quebec Conference in October 1864.

Confederation Documents

http://www.collectionscanada.ca/confederation/023001-2600-e.html

Dozens of digitized documents that demonstrate the unique issues faced by all provinces and territories that entered Confederation.

British North America Act

http://www.ola.bc.ca/online/cf/documents/constitution1867.html

The full text of the British North America Act of 1867.

Article Sixteen

The Case Against Canadian Confederation

Ged Martin

The men who met at Charlottetown and Quebec in 1864 to design the Dominion of Canada live in legend as the "Fathers of Confederation". They gaze at us, from sombre photographs and dignified portraits, with a grave demeanour which makes it hard to believe that any of them could ever have called an opponent a liar or promised to build a bridge to win an election. We need not begrudge them their mythic status in Canadian history, for our real difficulty lies in reconciling the claim for their far-sighted wisdom with the equally patriotic efforts of Canada's historians, who have related the saga of the coming of Confederation as if it were the inevitable outcome of the problems of the 1860s.[1] "Only a general union, balanced with all the care and precision of a cantilever, was practical in 1864", wrote W.L. Morton a century later. If Confederation was indeed the inescapable solution in 1864, how can we attribute such superior wisdom to the Fathers? Surely they were no more than the unconscious instruments of historical inevitability? Morton implicitly confronted the issue by describing the cabinet headed by John Sandfield Macdonald, which immediately preceded the Confederation Coalition in the province of Canada, as "provincial politicians who had failed to sense the new currents which had begun to flow in Canadian politics since 1857".[2] Confederation, then, was inevitable, but perspicacity and vision were needed to grasp this evident fact. By implication, those who failed to see the necessity for Confederation got it wrong.

Such an approach can hardly encourage an unprejudiced analysis of the arguments advanced between 1864 and 1867 by those who opposed the new constitutional system.[3] The

Source: Ged Martin, ed., "The Case Against Canadian Confederation," from *The Causes of Canadian Confederation*, (Frederiction: Acadiensis Press, 1990), pp. 19–49.

scheme drawn up at Quebec in 1864 was rejected by the voters in New Brunswick in 1865, would probably have been decisively rejected had there been an election in Nova Scotia, and might even have failed to win a majority in Lower Canada. Indeed, it is at least possible that Confederation was ultimately accepted in spite of the case against it rather than because of the arguments in its favour. Consideration of the objections raised by opponents may enable us to decide whether Confederation really was the logical deduction from interlocking circumstances, or whether we should look to other explanations for its adoption. Perhaps Confederation was not a logical deduction from the circumstances of 1864 at all, but a panic response to what C. P. Stacey has called "[t]he atmosphere of crisis" in the closing phases of the American Civil War, something which was simply not susceptible to logical refutation, however detailed and effectively argued.[4] Or was Confederation, on the other hand, something which had long been seen as the ultimate destiny of the British provinces in North America, an idea whose time had come in 1864?[5] This interpretation would help to explain why the provinces should have turned to a *federal* scheme in 1864. After all, it is hard to believe that it was possible to deduce from the circumstances of the time — given the bloody war of secession to the south — that a federal system was in itself the ideal political structure. The pre-existence of a mental "blueprint" for the union of the provinces would also help explain inconsistencies in the pro-Confederation case: for instance, why a scheme intended to contribute to a long-term continental balance of power should abruptly be put forward as part of an immediate defence package against the United States, or why the Intercolonial Railway, which could not be constructed overnight, should be embraced as a device to deter or resist an American invasion which might come within weeks or months. Some colour is lent this line of interpretation by the fact that while some politicians debated whether or not Confederation was an entirely new idea,[6] others concentrated not on whether it was a desirable outcome in itself, but on proving that it was premature. The arguments against Confederation, then, may give us a mirror-image of the reasons why it was actually adopted.

There is a second, longer-term reason for examining the arguments of the critics of Confederation. When the Confederate States were overwhelmed in 1865, the Southern fire-eater Edmund Ruffin wrapped himself in the Stars and Bars and blew his brains out. By contrast, the critics of Canadian Confederation proved to be embarrassingly good losers. Sandfield Macdonald became Sir John A.'s Ontario lieutenant in 1867; Joseph Howe joined his cabinet in 1868; Christopher Dunkin followed the next year. This may prove only that they were hypocritical in their opposition to the new system, but it is probably fairer to conclude that in coming aboard, they helped in practice to shape it to meet their concerns. In contrast to countries in which major constitutional change left a long-lasting legacy of bitterness, the distinction between those who had argued for or against Confederation quickly blurred. In the 1870s, the admittedly unimpressive cabinet of Alexander Mackenzie was largely composed of anti-Confederates. In the 1880s, the provincial campaign to roll back the frontiers of central control was led by Oliver Mowat, himself a Father of Confederation, while Wilfrid Laurier, a spirited and scornful opponent of Confederation, was to be prime minister of Canada from 1896 to 1911. Only rarely did the old bitterness surface. "I am an Anti Confederate. I cannot forget the manner in which Nova Scotia was forced into the union", W.S. Fielding wrote in 1886, the year in which he campaigned for a secessionist mandate in the provincial "Repeal" election.[7] Yet he ended his political career as finance minister under Mackenzie King. In the longer term, the "Antis" were to prove as much the Fathers of the Canada that we know today as the pro-Confederates.

There are basic difficulties in assessing the validity of the debates and petitions on Confederation. How far were they designed to convince, and how far merely to mobilise? The historian seizes on the thousand pages of the published *Confederation Debates* of 1865 in the

Canadian provincial parliament in the spirit in which historians operate — that of logical discussion.[8] Yet this approach may not be faithful to the spirit of the original. 1867 was the year not only of the British North America Act, but of Britain's Second Reform Act, which Maurice Cowling portrays as a classic exercise in "high politics"— the exploitation of a major issue not on its own terms, but as part of the manoeuvrings for alliances and offices among a key group of political leaders.[9] Confederation is more than susceptible to a similar analysis. Viewed from the patriotic point of view of Canadian nation-building, George Brown's coalition with Macdonald and Cartier in June 1864 was a remarkably magnanimous departure from old feuds. Seen through the less rosy spectacles of factional politics, Confederation offered a sufficiently lofty reason for old enemies to get into bed — and, more important, office. On what other issue could Brownite Reformers have coalesced with Macdonald Conservatives and Bleus?[10] The problem with putting together a majority on such an overarching issue was that too rapid a delivery of the goods would remove its unifying purpose: the Cartier-Macdonald government had used the aim of federation to win Galt in 1858–59,[11] and could hope to repeat the exercise in 1864. Two years later, minus Brown but still backed by a significant slice of his former followers, the Canadian cabinet showed itself so lacking in zeal to get to Britain and tie the knot with the Maritimes that the governor-general hinted at resignation.[12] In other provinces, a similar case can be made. Arthur Gordon, lieutenant-governor of New Brunswick, can be dismissed as a sardonic observer, but he may well have been right in reporting in December 1864 that there was "an indisposition to believe that the change is seriously mediated and an indication to regard the plan rather as intended to produce by its agitation some immediate effect on the condition of political parties than as designed to inaugurate a new Constitutional system".[13] From Newfoundland, Ambrose Shea assured Galt that "the question will break up our local parties", adding "if even for no other reason I should hail its introduction on this account".[14] Shea certainly used the Confederation issue to form a new political alliance, as did Adams G. Archibald in Nova Scotia and William McDougall in Upper Canada. It remains possible to suspect that personal rivalry between Howe and "the d —— d Tupper" played a part in the former's disavowal of his earlier sentiments in favour of British North American union.[15]

A "high politics" view of Confederation would lead us to question the value of the actual arguments put forward against Confederation, since the root reason for opposition in many cases could be suspected to be resentment at not being taken aboard. At the very least, the prospect of loaves and fishes could soften the opposition of some critics of Confederation. Members of Albert J. Smith's New Brunswick ministry were prepared to take up the question in 1866, despite having been elected in 1865 to oppose it.[16] In Nova Scotia, the spectacular bolt to change sides in April 1866 was alleged to have been touched off by the suspicious decision of two anti-Confederates that others would rat first, and "we . . . had better get into line or we should be left out in the cold and lose all chance of obtaining good positions".[17]

The two major sources on which this paper is based are the *Confederation Debates* of 1865 in the province of Canada, and the Nova Scotia petitions of 1866 in the *British Parliamentary Papers*. The Canadian parliament had not previously printed its debates, and we may echo the lament of Dr. Joseph Blanchet, four weeks and 545 pages after discussion began on 3 February 1865, that the decision "to have the speeches of this House printed in official form certainly did no good service to the country". Yet vast as was the eventual volume, it does not necessarily do justice to the opposition case. In the early phases of the debate, there was a tendency to demand further information, for the Quebec plan required much fleshing-out of practical details on which the ministers were unforthcoming — and it was tempting to debunk the visionary orations of Macdonald and McGee by trumpeting that there was no case to answer. Luther Holton replied to the first great onslaught of explanations with the flourish that if the government's speeches "contain all that can be said in favour of this scheme, we have no fear of letting them go unanswered". As the Canadian debate was getting into its stride, so news arrived of Tilley's defeat in New Brunswick which, A-A. Dorion claimed, caused the issue "to lose much of its interest".[18] Much of the debate was taken up with members taunting each other with inconsistency, which often provoked elaborate apologetics. Some speeches were intended to drag matters out while petitions were circulated:[19] Cartier embarrassed Eric Dorion, by reading into the record a circular letter he had sent to supporters requesting them to have anti-Confederation petitions "signed as soon as possible by men, women and children".[20] Similar devices were used to produce petitions in Nova Scotia, as the governor-general, Lord Monck, and a former lieutenant-governor, the Marquess of Normanby, assured the House of Lords in 1867.[21] It is certainly hard to believe that the 210 inhabitants of the district of Port Medway who signed their names to a massive, two thousand word petition against Confederation were entirely unprompted,[22] and it may be doubted if any of the petitions emerged from the sober atmosphere of a political science seminar. At Yarmouth, Joseph Howe preceded a two hour assault on Confederation with "an eloquent eulogy on the character of Her Majesty Queen Victoria, as a child, a wife and mother, a queen and a widow" which was much cheered.[23] It is not surprising that in Nova Scotia opposition to Confederation became what modern American politics would term a "motherhood" issue.

There are other difficulties in accommodating the available material to the logical approach of the historian. A sound historical analysis would seek to balance arguments for and arguments against, coming to a fair and reasonable conclusion. The arguments *for* Confederation, which we normally equate with the reasons for its adoption, are clear enough and capable of neat presentation. The arguments *against* offend our sense of order. Cartier was able to have fun playing off opposites: the Montreal *Witness* warned that Protestantism in Lower Canada would be doomed by Confederation, while its deadly rival, the *True Witness*, saw it as leading to the destruction of French Canada.[24] The easy but fallacious assumption behind such debating devices is that the two strands of argument cancel each other out, whereas in reality one or the other — perhaps even both, but for different reasons — might well be entirely valid. Perhaps the real task of explanation is not to explain *why* Confederation was accepted, but *how* it managed to seize the central ground and divide the opposition to right and left.

"I do not know of any one opposed to union in the abstract", said New Brunswick's Timothy Warren Anglin. "But my impression is that the time has not arrived for any kind of union, and I will oppose it to the last".[25] This was a common theme among the critics: intercolonial union in principle, union one day, but not this union, not now.[26] As Edward Whelan put it, the critics accepted the principle of ploughing the field, but objected to destroying the daisies and field mice.[27] How sincere were these protestations — by some, but by no means all the critics of Confederation — in favour of an eventual British North American union? Perhaps they were gestures of open-mindedness merely to win over waverers. David Reesor found it "extraordinary" that so many members of the Canadian Legislative Council spoke "strongly and emphatically against many of the resolutions: while declaring their reluctant intention to vote for the package.[28] Yet even A-A. Dorion, who went to some lengths to clear his name of the slander of having ever spoken favourably of the idea, could leave open a faint and distant possibility: "Population may extend over the wilderness that now lies between the Maritime Provinces and ourselves, and commercial intercourse may increase sufficiently to render Confederation desirable".[29] As late as August 1864, admittedly at a social occasion, Joseph Howe proclaimed: "I have always been in favour of uniting any two, three, four, or the whole five of the provinces".[30] It is not necessary to follow McGee in the full flight of his oratory, but he may have been right in thinking of the idea of Confederation as an autonomous cause of its own happening. "If we have dreamed a dream of union . . . it is at least worth while remarking that a dream which has been dreamed by such wise and good men, may, for aught we know or you know, have been a sort of vision — a vision foreshadowing forthcoming natural events in a clear intelligence".[31]

If some of the opponents subscribed to the idea of an eventual intercolonial union, most of the critics in the province of Canada argued that Confederation was not a solution to present difficulties, and it would itself require a far greater degree of political wisdom than was necessary to rescue the existing system. Henry Joly felt that the various provinces would meet in a confederated parliament "as on a field of battle". Christopher Dunkin referred to the airy dismissals of such warnings by ministerial supporters: "Oh! there won't be any trouble; men are in the main sensible, and won't try to make trouble". If public men were so reasonable as to be able to work the new system, why then had the province of Canada had "four crises in two years"? In any case, even if it were accepted that Upper and Lower Canada were not living together in harmony, the answer was surely for them to work out a new system of government and not to claim that only through a wider union could they get along. Dunkin noted that in the five years between the lapsing of Galt's federation initiative in 1859 and the formation of the Grand Coalition of June 1864, "we quarrelled and fought about almost everything, but did not waste a thought or a word upon this gigantic question of the Confederation of these provinces". "Surely", Thomas Scatcherd argued, "if parties could unite as they did in June last, they could have united to prevent the difficulty complained of . . . without entering upon a scheme to subvert the Constitution".[32]

While some critics of Confederation admitted that the Canadian Union had its problems, others felt them to have been exaggerated. Henri Joly contrasted Taché's claim that "the country was bordering on civil strife" with the ministry's throne speech, which thanked "a beneficent Providence for the general contentment of the people of this province".[33] Joseph Perrault asked "have we not reason to be proud of our growth since 1840, and of the fact that within the past twenty-five years, our progress, both social and material, has kept pace with that of the first nations in the world"?[34] For French Canadians, a crucial issue was whether they could indeed maintain the equal representation which the two sections of the province of Canada had in the Assembly. In 1858, Joseph Cauchon had believed that Lower Canada had enough allies in the upper province to stand firmly on its rights. By 1865, those allies were becoming fewer; the minority English-speaking representatives from Lower Canada now held the balance of power between French Canadians and an upper province increasingly united in its demand for representation by population. The entrenchment of equal representation in the imperial act of 1840, which required a two-thirds vote to change the balance of representation, had been repealed in 1854 — and replaced by a simple majority, thus opening the way to the carrying of "rep. by pop." through the sudden defection of the Lower Canadian English. From that perspective, Confederation — a negotiated scheme which gave French Canadians their own legislature — was preferable to swamping within the existing structure.[35] However, other French Canadian politicians took the threat of "rep. by pop." less seriously, dismissing it — in Joly's words — as "one of those political clap-traps which ambitious men, who can catch them no other way, set to catch the heedless multitude". Joly argued that hypocrisy was proved by the alacrity with which Upper Canada Reformers had entered the Macdonald-Sicotte administration of 1862, which agreed not to press the issue — proof that "Upper Canada is much more indifferent, and its leaders much less sincere touching this question of the representation, than they would have us believe".

Perrault went much further. In a speech presumably aimed at stoking every French Canadian fear of assimilation — it ranged from the Acadian deportation, via the history of Mauritius, to the francophobia of Lord Durham's Report — Perrault denied that Upper Canada had more people than Lower Canada at all. The "true total" of the population of Upper Canada had been "greatly exaggerated" in the census of 1861, a fraud revealed by the fact that

the census figure for population under the age of one year exceeded the live births of the previous twelve months by eight thousand. Perrault also claimed that the census had under-
counted the population of Lower Canada, for "our farmers have always stood in dread of the
census, because they have a suspicion that it is taken with the sole object of imposing some tax,
or of making some draft of men for the defence of the country". Yet, confusingly, he contended
that even if Upper Canada's population did exceed that of Lower Canada, it was no more than
a temporary blip, caused by Irish famine migration, which had now ceased. So too had the outward flow of French Canadians to New England, with the result that within ten years, the higher
birth rate of Lower Canada would bring the two provinces back to equality of population.[36]

   The core of the case against Confederation was that there was no crisis sufficient to justify so large a change. Consequently, critics largely refused to enter the trap of offering alternative solutions. "We are asked, 'what are you going to do? You must do something. Are you
going to fall back to our old state of dead-lock?'", Dunkin reported, adding that whenever he
heard the argument "that something must be done, I suspect that there is a plan on foot to get
something very bad done". Henri Joly took the same line. "I am asked: 'If you have nothing to
do with Confederation, what will you have?' I answer, we would remain as we are".[37] "Now my
proposition is very simple", Joseph Howe told the people of Nova Scotia. "It is to let well
enough alone".[38] Not surprisingly, the opponents of Confederation indignantly rejected the
argument that they were — wittingly or otherwise — working for annexation to the United
States. They replied that the campaign for Confederation itself contained the germ of an
annexationist threat. Matthew Cameron, one of the few prominent Upper Canada
Conservatives to oppose the scheme, warned that the delusive arguments of material gain from
Confederation with the tiny Maritimes "are arguments ten-fold stronger in favour of union
with the United States".[39] Nor did the danger lie simply in encouraging hopes of greater prosperity, as was shown when a moderate Lower Canadian journal could proclaim "qu'à tous les
points de vue, nos institutions, notre langue, et nos lois seront mieux protégés avec la confédération américaine qu'avec le projet de confédération de l'Amérique Britannique du
Nord".[40] "Once destroy public confidence in our institutions", warned T.C. Wallbridge, "and it
is impossible to predict what extremes may be resorted to".[41] Joseph Howe similarly predicted
that the imposition of Confederation on unwilling provinces would lead to "undying hatreds
and ultimate annexation".[42]

   At first sight, it might seem surprising that the opponents of Confederation were able to
escape the tactical trap of offering alternative solutions to intercolonial problems. Christopher
Dunkin and Joseph Howe were on insecure ground in putting forward the far more ambitious
idea of imperial federation,[43] while Tupper found that Maritime Union had no friends at all
when he attempted the ploy of reviving it in 1865.[44] In the province of Canada, the demand
for an alternative would have been dangerous for the cause of Confederation after its defeat in
the New Brunswick election of 1865. The teleological and celebratory accounts of the textbooks stress that the Great Coalition of June 1864 was pledged "in the most earnest manner,
to the negotiation for a confederation of all the British North American provinces". Less
noticed is the fact that the agreement contained a fall-back position, that "failing a successful
issue to such negotiations, they are prepared to pledge themselves to legislation during the next
session of Parliament for the purpose of remedying existing difficulties by introducing the federal principle for Canada alone", with provision for future expansion. Minutes before the celebrated coalition deal was struck at the St Louis Hotel, Brown had still been insisting that
"the Canadian federation should be constituted first". In March 1865, after the setback in New
Brunswick, the coalition came close to breaking up over Brown's insistence on invoking
the fall-back position. Brown pressed the issue again in the negotiations for the succession to
Taché in August 1865, and forced John A. Macdonald to give formal endorsement, in the name

of the new premier, Sir Narcisse Belleau, to his interpretation of the coalition deal. Brown, leader of the majority party in the majority section, could afford to be philosophical about the defeat of Confederation after the New Brunswick election: "If it fails after all legitimate means have been used, we will go on with our scheme for Canada alone".[45] For John A. Macdonald, such a solution could offer little comfort: as a Conservative, he had been dependent since 1857 on Bleu support for his periods of office. Anything which strengthened Upper Canada and its Reform party against Lower Canada was likely to mean problems for the Conservative party. Once it seemed that New Brunswick had dropped out, Brown and his Upper Canada Reform colleagues were under pressure to deliver the small print of the coalition bargain. "The Administration could not give a pledge that they would carry the Confederation of all the provinces", A-A. Dorion reminded his former allies, "but they could pledge and did pledge themselves to bring in, in the event of the failure of that scheme, a measure for the federation of Upper and Lower Canada".[46] Far from heading a triumphant march to nationhood, Macdonald and his allies were walking a desperately narrow tightrope.

Consequently, supporters of Confederation could not afford to admit that rival schemes might be possible. Rather they were obliged to present the Quebec scheme as an immutable package, a balanced intercolonial treaty — thus denying themselves any room for manoeuvre to win over those Maritimers who objected to the terms rather than the aim of Confederation. Critics objected to being faced with the resolutions as a package. "What is the use of considering them if we cannot come to our conclusions and give them effect in the shape of amendments?", asked one Upper Canadian critic. At Quebec, Dunkin pointed out, twenty three men had sat for seventeen working days to produce "a scheme of a Constitution which they vaunt as being altogether better than that of the model republic of the United States, and even than that of the model kingdom of Great Britain".[47] William Annand of Nova Scotia thought that a scheme "matured in a few weeks, amid exhaustive festivities" could not be the best constitution possible.[48] Joseph Howe noted that the inflexibility of the Quebec scheme would be carried forward to the future: "No means are provided by which the people, should it be found defective, can improve it from time to time. Whenever a change is required they must come back to the Imperial Parliament".[49] Indeed, the Canadian people were to continue coming back to Westminster until 1982.

Coupled with resentment at the rejection of any possibility of amendment was anger at the total refusal of a popular vote on so major a constitutional change. An exasperated Hamilton paper exclaimed that if there was to be no general election on Confederation, the polling booths "may as well be turned into pig-pens, and the voters lists cut up into pipe-lighters".[50] In Nova Scotia, where petition after petition dwelt on the province's long tradition of representative and responsible government, the people of Shelburne put the issue in more fundamental and sober terms: "whilst Your Majesty's petitioners freely admit the right of their representatives in Provincial Parliament to legislate for them within reasonable limits, they cannot admit the right of such representatives to effect sudden changes, amounting to an entire subversion of the constitution, without the deliberate sanction of the people expressed at the polls". As Joseph Howe put it in more succinct and homely terms, the local legislature had "no right to violate a trust only reposed in them for four years, or in fact to sell the fee simple of a mansion of which they have but a limited lease". Even if the scheme were beneficial, which the people of Queen's County flatly doubted, "the means employed to force it upon the country without an appeal to the people, and with full knowledge of their intense dislike of the measure" were enough to discredit it.[51]

Both in Canada and the Atlantic provinces, opponents of Confederation attached the scheme as "very costly, for the money is scattered on all sides in handfuls".[52] Simply listing the promised commitments left critics breathless with horror. Joseph Howe recounted that with a debt of $75 million, "the public men of Canada propose to purchase the territories of the Hudson's Bay Company, larger than half Europe", take over British Columbia and Vancouver Island, "provinces divided from them by an interminable wilderness", as well as absorb the Atlantic provinces, "countries severally as large as Switzerland, Sardinia, Greece, and Great Britain".[53] Dunkin similarly warned that with "a promise of everything for everybody", the scheme could only "be ambiguous, unsubstantial and unreal".[54] Others feared not disappointment but jobbery. "The proposed Constitution framed by arch jobbers is so devised as to provide for the very maximum of jobbing and corruption", Arthur Gordon assured Gladstone.[55] Unfortunately, responses to the threat of corruption depended on assessments by individuals of whether they would be victims or gainers from it. "Are the people of Nova Scotia prepared to yield up their flourishing customs revenue to a federal treasury in Canada, there to be squandered in jobbery and corruption?", asked the Yarmouth *Tribune*.[56] The people might indeed balk at the idea, but their elected representatives were perhaps open to persuasion: as Joseph Howe lamented, when John A. Macdonald "opened his confederation mousetrap he did not bait it with toasted cheese".[57] A scheme of government launched in this way could hardly bode well for the future. Christopher Dunkin warned that the representatives of each province would seek popularity back home by inching up federal subsidies or by taking special arrangements for one province as a benchmark and precedent for comparable concessions. They would prove to be "pretty good daughters of the horse-leech, and their cry will be found to be pretty often and pretty successfully —'Give, give give!'".[58] His warning can hardly be dismissed as inaccurate.

Related to the general question of cost were various predictions about the effect of Confederation on tariffs. James Currie predicted that Canada's tariff would have to rise by fifty percent to produce the necessary revenue to pay for Confederation. Other Canadian critics recognised that the province's existing tariff, which leaned towards protectionism, would have to be cut in order to meet the free-trading Maritimers half-way. This would reduce revenue at a time when more, not less, money was needed to meet increased costs. Letellier de St. Just predicted that "the deficit which that reduction of our revenue will produce will have to be filled up by the agriculture and industry of Canada" and Dunkin thought it "rather strange" that a government should propose to cut its tariff income and "at the same time, so to change our whole system as to involve ourselves in the enormous extravagances here contemplated". Dunkin felt that no plan of direct taxation could possibly meet the cost, and that the only alternative was a reckless policy of borrowing, except that "we cannot even borrow to any large amount unless under false pretences".[59] The argument that Confederation would create a larger credit base and make it easier to attract investment evidently did not convince everybody.

If Canadian critics feared the consequences of lowering the tariff at the dictation of the lower provinces, Maritimers feared even the compromise increase that Confederation seemed to imply. "Unless Canada consents to economize and curtail its expenses to a very considerable degree, which is not likely to happen", explained the Fredericton *Headquarters*, "the Lower provinces will have to raise their tariffs to that standard, as they will require a greater revenue to meet the expenses of government under the new confederation".[60] Whereas the Canadian tariff was intended to protect industry, Nova Scotia's commercial policy was aimed at fostering the province's worldwide carrying trade.[61] Thus raising the tariff would destroy trade rather than increase revenue — pointing to direct taxation which, Ambrose Shea warned, was "a point on which it is easy to alarm the masses everywhere". It certainly had that effect on Prince Edward Island, where the despairing Edward Whelan reported that it scared "the asses of country people, who can't see an inch beyond their noses".[62] A British journalist who visited Charlottetown in 1865 reported that taxation was regarded as "an evil which not only the

Prince Edward Islanders, but the British colonies generally throughout North America, seem to consider as the greatest which can befall a community".[63] Historians have not been notably more sympathetic. When George Coles stated at Quebec that if Prince Edward Island surrendered control over customs and excise "she would have no revenues left with which to carry on the business of the Province", he was surely not adopting "the obstructionist tactics which were destined to characterize the Island's attitude" at the conference, but rather stating a simple fact. The province of Canada derived one third of its revenue from customs and would dominate the new political structure. Prince Edward Island raised three-quarters of its income from customs duties, and the Islanders would be a tiny minority in a British American union.[64]

Textbook explanations of the coming of Confederation assume that it was necessary for the construction of the Intercolonial Railway, and that the Intercolonial was necessary both for defence and to give Canada a winter outlet, freeing its trade from the twin strangleholds of a frozen St Lawrence and a capriciously hostile United States. Opponents accepted neither argument and indeed found much to object to in the whole scheme. First, to reassure Maritimers who had not forgotten the Canadian bad faith of 1862, the railway project was actually written into the Quebec Resolutions, and would thus form part of the British legislation and the constitution of the Confederation —"novelty, perhaps, that might not be found in the constitution of any country".[65] It certainly gave an unusual status to a mere railway line, the more so as its route had yet to be agreed. Arthur Gordon argued forcefully that to include such a provision in an Act of the British parliament would "be either unnecessary or unjust"— unnecessary if, as everyone assumed, the federal legislature proceeded with the scheme and "unjust if it were to have the effect of forcing on the people of British America the execution of a work which their representatives in Parliament may consider it inexpedient to undertake". In any case, such a provision "would be impossible to enforce, as no penalty could be inflicted after the passage of the Act, in the event of the subsequent neglect of its provisions by the Federal Government and Legislature".[66]

Canadian critics were less concerned by the constitutional impropriety of giving a railway the same status as peace, order and good government as by the fact that the Intercolonial would gain an advantage over their own preferred projects, especially hopes for improved communications to the Red River.[67] Suspicions were further fuelled by ministerial reluctance to say where the Intercolonial would run or how much it would cost, thus prompting the prediction that "it will be a piece of corruption from the time of the turning of the first shovelful of earth".[68] It was widely appreciated that the reason for vagueness lay in the local politics of New Brunswick, where military security pointed to a route along the thinly populated North Shore, but political expediency required a vote-pulling line up the Saint John valley, never far from the American border. Tilley attempted to offer all routes to all men, prompting the only durable piece of doggerel from the Confederation controversy: "Mr. Tilley, will you stop your puffing and blowing / And tell us which way the railway is going?"[69] The question of the cost of the Intercolonial was a sore point to Upper Canada critics of Confederation. In 1862, the Sandfield Macdonald-Sicotte ministry had withdrawn, abruptly and in an unedifying manner, from an interprovincial agreement backed by an imperial loan guarantee, by which the province of Canada undertook to pay five-twelfths of the cost of the line — which, as Henri Joly pointed out, meant that the railway could be built if required without an accompanying political union. Now Canada, with three-quarters of the population, was accepting a *pro rata* obligation to shoulder double the share envisaged in 1862. "This will involve five to seven millions of dollars of an expense more than we had any occasion for incurring", complained David Reesor, "for the other provinces were all [sic] willing to have been responsible for the rest, and there is very good reason why they should".[70] Indeed, Galt had assured Maritimers at a banquet in Halifax in September 1864, "you will get the best of the bargain". Yet, ironically, Canada's sudden outburst of generosity aroused counter-suspicions. In New Brunswick, Albert J. Smith hinted darkly that Canada must have some hidden motive for increasing the very offer it had so recently dishonoured.[71]

Fundamentally, opponents argued that the Intercolonial was no more attractive a project in 1865 than it had been when rejected in 1862. "I have not heard any reason why we should pledge our credit and resources to the construction of the Intercolonial Railway, even previous to any estimate of its cost being made, that was not urged in 1862 when the question was before the country", A-A. Dorion asserted. William McMaster, a leading Toronto merchant, challenged the argument that the Intercolonial was "an indispensable necessity in order to secure an independent outlet to the seaboard". Rather than use the existing railways to American ports, Upper Canada merchants and millers preferred to pay warehousing, insurance and interest charges to keep wheat and flour in store through the winter months, "until the opening of the navigation". They were even less likely to use a railway to Halifax, which would be double the distance to the American winter ports. Henri Joly also doubted whether the Intercolonial could be used to send flour to the Maritimes, for "the cost of transport over five hundred miles of railway would be too great".[72]

The critics did not simply doubt whether trade could profitably flow along the Intercolonial; they also wondered whether Canada and the Maritimes were likely to have any trade at all. "Let us not . . . be lulled with fallacies of the great commercial advantages we shall derive from a Confederation of these provinces", intoned Eric Dorion. "We have wood, they produce it; we produce potash, and so do they".[73] "With regard to timber", said Henri Joly, "the Gulf Provinces have no more need of ours than we of there". Canada imported its coal direct from Britain, as ballast on returning timber ships. If that supply should ever fail, "Upper Canada will probably get its coal from the Pennsylvania mines, which are in direct communication with Lake Erie".[74] Yet, at the same time, Canadian critics could argue that free trade with the Maritimes could be achieved without "this mock Federal union", just as the provinces had enjoyed a decade of closer economic relations with the United States through the Reciprocity Treaty.[75] Not everyone shared these doubts: it was alleged that some Halifax merchants opposed Confederation precisely because they feared the competition it would bring, and it has indeed been contended that by 1874 "Central Canadian business owed its prosperity to its successful conquest of the market in the Maritimes".[76] Nonetheless, the belief that there was a prospect of major trading gains and the assumption that these would be dependent upon a political union were not held by everyone.

The critics were no more convinced by the argument that the Intercolonial was necessary for the defence of the provinces. A-A. Dorion argued that "a railway lying in some places not more than fifteen or twenty miles from the frontier, will be of no use whatever. . . . An enemy could destroy miles of it before it would be possible to resist him, and in time of difficulty it would be a mere trap for the troops passing along it, unless we had almost an army to keep it open". However far the Intercolonial snaked away from the American border, there was an existing stretch of the Grand Trunk "at places within twenty-six miles of the boundary of Maine", and thus easily vulnerable to American attack. Far from transporting large numbers of troops, the Intercolonial would need large forces simply to guard it. "Unless with a strong force to defend it, in a military point of view, it would be of just no use at all". In summary, the Intercolonial, centrepiece of so many textbook explanations of the causes of Confederation, was comprehensively dismissed by James L. Biggar: "Looking at it from a military point of view, it is well known that part of the proposed line would run within twenty-six miles of the American frontier, and that communication could be cut off at any moment by an American army; and that as a commercial undertaking it could never compete with the water route during the season of navigation; and in winter it would be comparatively useless on account of the depth of snow".[77]

The opponents of Confederation were unconvinced that the political union of the provinces would strengthen their defences in any way. "We do not need Confederation to give us that unity which is indispensable in all military operations — unity of headship. A commander-in-chief will direct the defence of all our provinces", argued Henri Joly. Defence had remained outside the orbit of colonial self-government until very recent times, and Canada's record on militia reform was hardly impressive. Consequently, the argument that unity meant strength is one which appeals more to the twentieth century observer than it did to contemporaries, especially when the unity proposed involved such tiny provinces. John S. Sanborn was simply bewildered. "How the people of New Brunswick could be expected to come up to Canada to defend us, and leave their own frontier unprotected, he could not comprehend". Conversely, Matthew Cameron asked why Canada should be taxed to build fortifications in the Maritimes: "Fortifications in St. John, New Brunswick, would not protect us from the foe, if the foe were to come here". Sanborn argued that if there were indeed a war with the United States, each province would be attacked from a neighbouring state. "Under these circumstances, each section of the Confederation would have enough to do to attend to its own affairs". Except, contended A.-A. Dorion, that New Brunswick could not defend itself, since the province's population of a quarter of a million was only one-third that of the adjoining state of Maine: "Those 250,000 Canada will have to defend, and it will have to pledge its resources for the purpose of providing means of defence along that extended line".[78]

In the Atlantic colonies, the arguments were inverted. Petitioners from Nova Scotia's Digby County were ready to rally to "the defence of their country and their flag" but were "not disposed to adopt, as a means of ensuring their more efficient defence, a union with a Province which in 1862 refused to sanction a measure involving increased outlay for the better and more elaborate organisation of their mlitia".[79] Joseph Howe deftly alluded to Canadian complicity in border raids by Southern sympathizers, and the resulting threats of Northern retaliation, proclaiming: "let those who provoke these controversies fight them out".[80] He objected to a system under which Nova Scotia's militia "may be ordered away to any point of the Canadian frontier".[81] Prince Edward Islanders feared that they would be "marched away to the frontiers of Upper Canada" or, as John Hamilton Gray put it with vivid bitterness, "drafted for slaughter".[82] In Newfoundland, the outspoken Charles Fox Bennett spoke of the island's young men "leaving their bones to bleach in a foreign land", a phrase which he was to refine in the 1869 election into the celebrated references to "the desert sands of Canada".[83]

In three of the four Atlantic provinces, insularity was a physical as well as a mental factor. "We are surrounded by the sea", proclaimed Joseph Howe and — what was more to the point — "within ten days' sail of the fleets and armies of England".[84] J.C. Pope of Prince Edward Island echoed Canadian critics in predicting that an American attack would make it "necessary to retain all available strength in each of the provinces for the defence of their respective territories". His emphasis differed in his confidence that local efforts would be powerfully seconded by the British navy and army.[85] Many critics argued that Confederation would actually make the defence of British North America more difficult. Henri Joly argued that there was "no need" of political union to warn "our neighbours" not to pick on a single province. The Americans were "sufficiently sharp-witted to discover, without being told it, that if they content themselves with attacking us at a single point at a time, of course they will have to meet all our strength". Perhaps, he added sarcastically, they could be persuaded to "enter into a contract, binding them to attack us at a single point only at one time — say Quebec". More seriously, L.A. Olivier warned that if Confederation was thrust upon an unwilling population, they could not be expected to rally to the defence of their homeland with the full enthusiasm shown in earlier conflicts. Joseph Howe similarly warned that if the rights of Nova Scotians were "overridden by an arbitrary Act of Parliament, very few of them will march to defend Canada".[86]

"With Confederation, neither the number of men in the several provinces, nor the pecuniary resources now at their disposal, will be increased". The kernel of the Canadian opposition case on defence was that Confederation involved too much territory and no additional manpower. "Can you alter the geographical position of the country?", asked Benjamin Symour. "Will you have any more people or means?" "If nature were to make the necessary effort and move their territory up alongside of us, and thus make a compact mass of people, I would at once agree that it would strengthen us in a military point of view", Philip Moore ironically conceded. In reality, however, Confederation "will weaken instead of strengthen us", since "the union will give an extension of territory far greater in proportion to the number of the population than [sic] now exists in Canada". The planned massive extension into empty and inaccessible territory westward to the Pacific struck A-A. Dorion as "a burlesque" in terms of defence. In short, critics found the defence argument literally laughable: "If we could attach the territory possessed by the moon to these provinces, and obtain the assistance for our joint defence of the man who is popularly supposed to inhabit that luminary, we might derive strength from Confederation".[87]

Critics were equally unimpressed by ringing talk of a "new nationality" in British North America. "I cannot see that the Federation of these provinces has anything of a national phase in it", commented Thomas Scatcherd. "When you speak of national existence, you speak of independence; and so long as we are colonists of Great Britain we can have no national existence".[88] Some Nova Scotian petitions protested that British North America was "incapable of forming a new nationality",[89] but the loyal people of Barrington township had an each-way bet in wanting no part of "new nationalities too feeble to stand alone, yet difficult to be controlled".[90] Their governor, Sir Richard MacDonnell, was

> unable to see in what way England would be less vulnerable through Canada or Canada less vulnerable through England when a confederated Parliament meets at Ottawa than now. There is not a foot of territory in all these hundreds of thousands of square miles which would thereby become less English than now, so long as the Queen's Representative is head of the Federation; nor is there any obligation in regard to these Provinces which now devolves upon Britain that would be diminished by their being thus huddled into one heterogeneous assemblage.[91]

In fact, critics feared that Confederation would actually provoke Americans into hostilities. Howe warned: "let this guy of 'new nationality' be set up . . . and every young fellow who has had a taste of the license of camp life in the United States will be tempted to have a fling at it".[92] Christopher Dunkin even expressed alarm at the tone of the Confederation debates, asking "how is the temper of the United States going to be affected . . . by the policy here urged on us, of what I may call hostile independent effort — effort made on our part, with the avowed object of setting ourselves up as a formidable power against them[?]". The Northern States, A-A. Dorion pointed out, had put into the field an army of 2,300,000, "as many armed men as we have men, women and children in the two Canadas". Military expenditure on any large scale would be useless and "we are not bound to ruin ourselves in anticipation of a supposed invasion which we could not repel". Public opinion should force the Canadian press to cease its anti-American outbursts: "The best thing that Canada can do is to keep quiet, and to give no cause for war".[93] Joseph Howe agreed that British North America could never stand alone militarily against the United States, but he took the argument a stage further. "Inevitably it must succumb to the growing power of the republic. A treaty offensive and defensive with the United States, involving ultimate participation in a war with England, would be the hard terms of its recognition as a separate but not independent state".[94]

Given their overwhelming rejection of the case for Confederation as a defence measure, it is hardly surprising that this aspect of the scheme produced some of the most colourful imagery among critics. Joining with the Maritimes, said James Currie, "was like tying a small twine at the end of a long rope and saying it strengthened the whole line". Incorporating the vast Hudson's Bay Territories, said Henri Joly, would create "the outward form of a giant, but with the strength of a child".[95] John Macdonald, member for Toronto West, thought "the casting of the burden of defence upon this country is like investing a sovereign with all the outward semblance of royalty, and giving him a dollar per day to keep up the dignity of his court". Macdonald has been overshadowed by his namesake to the point of invisibility, but he had a homely touch in his comments, telling the legislators as they met for the last year in Quebec City that Confederation was like taking the engine from the Lévis ferry and using it "to propel the *Great Eastern* across the Atlantic".[96] In a far smaller town, an angry young Rouge editor denounced Confederation in less whimsical imagery. As a defence against the United States it was like being "armed with an egg-shell to stop a bullet . . . a wisp of straw in the way of a giant".[97] The writer's name was Wilfrid Laurier.

Studies of the opposition to Confederation within the individual provinces have tended to concentrate on the risks and disadvantages of Confederation to each community — an approach which by its nature portrays the critics as "parochial".[98] However, while the objections made on behalf of each province were naturally contradictory, they fell into a common pattern. John Simpson denied that seventeen additional MPs would be of any use to Upper Canada, while Matthew Cameron argued that if the eighty-two Upper Canadians proposed to develop the North-West, they would be outvoted by "sixty-five members from Lower Canada and forty-seven from the Lower Provinces, whose interests will be united against us".[99] By contrast, Joseph Howe warned that New Brunswick and Nova Scotia "must be prey to the spoiler" for "having but forty-seven representatives, all told, it is apparent that the Government of the confederacy will always rest upon the overwhelming majority of 147, and that, even when close divisions and ministerial crises occur, the minority can easily be split up and played off against each other for purely Canadian purposes".[100] French Canadians challenged that assumption of a unity of purpose, doubting that "all the members from Lower Canada would make common cause on any question". Although the province was guaranteed sixty-five MPs in perpetuity, they would not all be francophones: "we shall have forty-eight members in the Federal Parliament against one hundred and forty of English origin; in other words, we shall be in a proportion of one to four. What could so weak a minority do to obtain justice"?[101] Joseph Howe evidently felt that French Canadians possessed a greater measure of political skill than Maritimers, for he warned that "as the English will split and divide, as they always do, the French members will in nine cases out of ten, be masters of the situation".[102] A-A. Dorion agreed that they "would go as a body to the Legislature, voting as one man, and caring for nothing else but the protection of their beloved institutions and law, and making government all but impossible", but he felt this a "deplorable state of things".[103]

There was little direct contact between Canada and the Maritimes prior to Confederation: during a visit to Montreal in 1860, T. Heath Haviland of Prince Edward Island had encountered "the utmost difficulty" in finding "so much as a newspaper from the Lower Provinces".[104] It is therefore surprising to discover the extent of their mutual antipathy. The "plain meaning" of the Canadian ministry's desire to force through the Quebec Resolutions without amendment was "that the Lower Provinces have made out a Constitution for us and we are to adopt it", said A-A. Dorion. Voting at the Quebec Conference had been by provinces, which "made Prince Edward Island equal to Upper Canada". Dorion complained of "the humiliation of seeing the Government going on its knees and begging the little island of Prince Edward to come into this union".[105] Only by appreciating the existence of this sentiment of disdain for the Maritimes among Canadian critics can we understand why Macdonald and his colleagues had no alternative but to outface and outmanoeuvre opposition in Nova Scotia and New Brunswick.

Maritimers returned the hostility. James Dingwell of Prince Edward Island thought "Canadians had not been able to manage the business of their country as we have been to manage ours; and why should we trust the management of our own affairs to people who have never been able to manage their own with satisfaction?"[106] With colourful exaggeration, Joseph Howe claimed that Canadians were "always in trouble of some sort, and two or three times in open rebellion".[107]

Despite Howe's suspicions that Lower Canadian solidarity in the federal parliament would entrench French power, hostility to Confederation in the Atlantic colonies seems to have been directed against the whole of what later became the monster of "central Canada" and was relatively free of explicit francophobia. There was a hint of it an open letter to the British Colonial Secretary in January 1867, when a recitation of Nova Scotia's loyal service to the Empire in wars against France was followed by the waspish comment: "We are now asked to surrender it to Monsieur Cartier".[108] Although francophobia was so endemic that it was not necessary to articulate it, inter-communal flashpoints in the mid-nineteenth century were more likely to concern sectarian schooling than the politics of language. Memories of their homeland's forced unification with Britain led many Irish Catholics to oppose Confederation. If anti-Confederates had warned of the danger of French power, Irish Catholics might have concluded that Confederation could bring benefits for their Church. In any case, Acadians were as suspicious of Confederation as their anglophone neighbours, and it suited Howe to portray them as one of the contented minorities — along with Micmacs and Blacks — who had flourished under the benign institutions of an autonomous Nova Scotia.[109]

In each province, critics argued that their constituents had got the worst of the bargain. That their arguments were contradictory did not much matter, since by definition they were intended for purely local consumption, directed at those whose "mental vision"— as an impatient Halifax newspaper put it —"is bounded by Dartmouth on the one side, and Citadel Hill on the other".[110] However, claims in each province of a bad deal provoked supporters of Confederation into refutations which were seized upon by critics elsewhere as confirmation of their fears. One of the earliest public expositions of the Quebec scheme came in a major speech by Galt at Sherbrooke in November 1864. Tupper admired it, but mildly complained that it was "a little too much from the Canadian point of view to suit this meridian". From Prince Edward Island, Edward Whelan similarly warned that "in the Lower Provinces a view of the Confederation question with a very decided Canadian colouring is apt to lessen confidence in it as we barbarians down in these lower regions are terribly doubtful and suspicious of Canadian intentions".[111] Within a few months, hard-pressed Confederates in the Maritimes had given similar hostages to the scheme's critics in the province of Canada. David Reesor read into the record extracts from Tilley's election speeches to show that politicians in the Maritimes "see the great advantage they have gained over Canada, and are not slow to set them [sic] before the people". Dorion similarly quoted Tilley and Whelan, and pictured them "chuckling over the good bargains they have made at the expense of Canada".[112]

Behind these mutual suspicions, there surely lay something deeper than the cussedness which we normally dismiss as parochialism. Even in the super-heated provincial politics of the mid-nineteenth century, it seems exaggerated that Cartier could have been accused of "la lâchéte la plus insigne dans la trahison la plus noire", merely for forming a coalition with George Brown, or that Prince Edward Island representatives at the Charlottetown conference were pointed out in the street as "the men who would sell their country".[113] The fact that such remarks were made suggests that the different provinces felt themselves to possess distinct social and political cultures. This was most obvious in predominantly French-speaking and Catholic Lower Canada: "Confederation is in fact a Legislative union, because upon the Federal Government is conferred the right of legislating upon those subjects which Lower Canada holds most dear".[114] The complication in Lower Canada was the existence of a minority-within-a-minority, equally suspicious of those aspects of the new constitution which guaranteed provincial autonomy under a local francophone majority. Principal Dawson of McGill thought that "scarcely anyone among the English of Lower Canada desires Confederation, except perhaps as an alternative to simple dissolution of the Union".[115] This was a case where clashing objections had a reinforcing effect, for every reassurance offered to the Lower Canada English was a confirmation of French Canadian fears.[116]

The separate identity of French Canadian society on an Anglo-Saxon continent was obvious enough. What may be less obvious is that in the Maritimes — and especially in Nova Scotia — there was as great a sense of being different from the province of Canada as modern Canadians would today feel separates themselves from their neighbours in the United States. True, Joseph Howe could welcome a party of Canadian visitors to Halifax in August 1864 with the sentiment: "I am not one of those who thank God that I am a Nova Scotian merely, for I am a Canadian as well".[117] Yet the picture which emerges from his subsequent anti-Confederation campaign is of a province not simply resentful of losing its autonomy, but fearful of being subordinated to the capricious and unattractive values of "those who live above the tide", "the administration of strangers".[118] A recurrent theme of Nova Scotian opposition was loss of its historic self-government. Behind the issue of high principle, there lay practical and local fears. The petitioners of Digby County pointed out that "while that portion of this county which borders on the sea is thickly inhabited and rapidly increasing in population and wealth, there are still considerable districts but lately reclaimed from the primaeval forest", which required grants of public money for the development of roads and bridges. They regarded "with dismay" the transfer of control over public expenditure "to a Government by which they would necessarily all be expended for widely different purposes".[119] Canada was associated with inflationary paper money and high interest rates. "Every post-master and every way office keeper is to be appointed and controlled by the Canadians".[120] Canada was as distant from Nova Scotia as Austria from Britain.[121] "You cannot . . . invest a village on the Ottawa with the historic interest and associations that cluster around London", wrote Joseph Howe — and he emphatically preferred "London under the dominion of John Bull to Ottawa under the domination of Jack Frost".[122] To the modern mind, Joseph Howe was descending to the darkest depths of petty parochialism when he proclaimed that travellers "can scarcely ride five miles in Upper Canada without being stopped by a toll bar or a toll bridge. There are but two toll-bridges in Nova Scotia and all the roads are free".[123] Yet Howe's complaint was really little different in spirit from modern Canadian concern to defend welfare and regional programmes against American allegations of unfair wage subsidies.[124]

Another theme common to the critics, whatever their regional loyalty, was rejection of both the proposed provincial governments and the confederate upper house as safeguards for their rights. "Ce n'est donc pas une confédération qui nous est proposée, mais tout simplement une Union Législative déguisée sous le nom de confédération", argued A-A. Dorion.[125] George Coles predicted that under Confederation, the legislature of Prince Edward Island "would be the laughing stock of the world", left "to legislate about dog taxes, and the running at large of swine".[126] While some critics concluded that the whole plan of union should be abandoned, others argued from similar premises that the union should be strengthened. The Halifax *Citizen* agreed that the Quebec scheme "has given these local legislatures very little to do", and predicted that they would occupy themselves in mischief, preserving local loyalties which would prevent "the fusion of the British American population in one actual individual nationality".[127] "One of the worst features of the Union plan proposed by Canada is, that it will leave our local legislature still in existence", lamented the Saint John *Globe*, which would have preferred to see outright unification.[128] Even the fervent anti-Confederation. T. W. Anglin, writing in the rival *Freeman*, agreed that if they had to have Confederation, "it would be better to abolish the local Legislatures at once in appearance as well as in reality".[129]

The critics were not reassured by the fact that both lieutenant-governors and members of the upper house were to be appointed by the central government. The prospect of lieutenant-governors drawn from provincial politics aroused little enthusiasm. "Let any one of our dozen or twenty most prominent Canadian politicians be named Lieutenant-Governor of Upper or of Lower Canada, would not a large and powerful class of the community . . . be very likely to resent the nomination as an insult?", asked Christopher Dunkin.[130] In Canada, where the legislative Council had become elective in 1856 — with life members retaining their seats — there was resentment at the reintroduction of nomination, "because the Maritime Provinces are opposed to an elective Chamber, and hence we in Canada — the largest community and the most influential — must give way to them".[131] There was also resentment at the provision in the Quebec Resolutions by which the first Confederate legislative councillors would be appointed from the existing Legislative Councils (except in Prince Edward Island) — a transparent bribe to curb the opposition in the upper houses. Worse still, the first Confederate upper house was to be appointed for life, on the nomination of the existing provincial governments — with the central government not even possessing a veto. A-A. Dorion's objection was not to the principle but to the unlucky fact that most British North American governments were Conservative. "For all time to come, as far as this generation and the next are concerned, you will find the Legislative Council controlled by the influence of the present government".[132] Future appointment by the central government aroused no more enthusiasm, since as Dunkin suggested, a government might be formed in which an entire province "either is not represented, or is represented otherwise than it would wish to be". How would such a province, "out in the cold", be served when vacancies in the upper house came to be filled?[133] Macdonald and McGee may strike posterity as the visionaries of the time, but it was the dry-as-dust Dunkin who foresaw the position of Alberta in the later Trudeau years, or Quebec under Joe Clark.

The arguments of the critics of Confederation must be conceded to have been at least plausible. Why then did they fail to prevent the passage of the British North America Act in 1867? First, of course, their arguments did not pass unchallenged. Just as conventional studies of the causes of Confederation tend to underplay the opposition case, so a study of the critics necessarily distorts the debate in their favour. Indeed, arguments which high-minded posterity may find irrefutable could perhaps have produced diametrically opposite responses among contemporaries: Upper Canadian critics, in damning the Intercolonial as an irresponsible waste of money, might have convinced some Lower Canadians of its pork-barrel value.[134] Even if the opposition case against the Intercolonial Railway had been overwhelming, Confederation might still have been supported on general grounds as the most practicable solution to a range of problems. The Confederation package mattered more than the interlocking detail, and not everybody bothered with those details. Bishop Laflèche did not allow ignorance of the latter to inhibit him from pronouncing on the former: "Le projet de Confédération est tellement vaste et complexe en lui-même et dans ses details qu'il est bien difficile de l'aborder sans en avoir auparavant faire une etude spéciale; et c'est que je n'ai point fait". What Laflèche saw was a province in which the legislative process was paralysed, where political opponents confronted each other almost like enemy camps, a state of affairs which could only end disastrously for Lower Canadians — either in "la guerre civile ou la domination du Haut-Canada dans l'Union Législative".[135] The bishop was probably wrong — at least in his fears of civil war — but could anyone be sure? In any case, even if the argument were won inside the provinces, there remained that "atmosphere of crisis" over the North American continent. "Look around you to the valley of Virginia", McGee challenged those who wanted to know why Confederation was necessary, "look around you to the mountains of Georgia, and you will find reasons as thick as blackberries".[136] Perhaps the fundamental mistake of the opponents of Confederation was to ask people to react logically to the activities of Macdonald and Cartier in the conference chamber rather than to the operations of Grant and Sherman on the battlefield. The question for explanation then becomes why it should have been intercolonial union — rather than, say, neutrality or annexation — which met the psychological need for a dramatic response to continental crisis. One explanation may be that the idea had been around for a long time, an answer looking for a question. "Everybody admits that Union must take place sometime", said John A. Macdonald, "I saw now is the time".[137] In seeking to account for the adoption of so vast a scheme as Canadian Confederation, historians have naturally turned to the arguments of its supporters, and have been tempted to conclude that the arguments put forward *for* Canadian Confederation equal the reasons *why* Canadian Confederation came about. Certainly hindsight finds it easy to draw neat lines of causation linking argument to outcome: the lines may be straight, but the process itself is circular, since it identifies the winners of history as — in Morton's terms — those who sensed the currents of events. Yet we should not forget that the case against Confederation was argued as tenaciously, as eloquently and — we must assume — as sincerely as the arguments in its favour. However much historians may admire the "Fathers of Confederation", only by recognising not just the strength of opposition to Confederation but also the plausibility of some of the arguments put forward, can we begin to see that the outcome was by no means inevitable. Of course, some historians believe that posterity is not entitled to second-guess past controversies, that a century later we cannot award points to individual arguments, for or against, since we cannot make ourselves fully part of the atmosphere of the time. Yet such an attitude is tantamount to an uncritical abdication of our own judgement to each and every claim made by those who were on the winning side perhaps for reasons other than the simply intellectual. "La raison du plus fort, c'est toujours la meuilleure", is not the most appropriate explanatory strategy for the historian to adopt. Hindsight may yet conclude that while the Antis lost the battle, they won at least some of the arguments.

NOTES

1. The major accounts of the coming of Confederation remain D. G. Creighton, *The Road to Confederation: The Emergence of Canada 1863–1867* (Toronto, 1964); W. L. Morton, *The Critical Year: The Union of British North America 1857–1873* (Toronto, 1964) and P. B. White, *The Life and Times of Confederation 1864–1867: Newspapers, and the Union of British North America* (Toronto, 1962). My debt to Waite's study of press sources is obvious from the footnotes below, in which the book is cited as *Life and Times*.

2. W. L. Morton, *The Kingdom of Canada: A General History from Earliest Times* (2nd ed., Toronto, 1969), pp. 317, 314–15.

3. Paradoxically, given the relative lack of general overviews, opposition to Confederation in individual provinces and sections had been widely studied, conveying the impression that parochialism predominated. For bibliographies, see D. A. Muise, ed., *A Reader's Guide to Canadian History: I, Beginnings to Confederation* (Toronto, 1982), pp. 237–48 and *Life and Times*, pp. 342–52.

4. C. P. Stacey, "Confederation: The Atmosphere of Crisis" in Edith G. Firth, ed., *Profiles of a Province: Studies in the History of Ontario* (Toronto, 1967), pp. 73–79.

5. Cf. Ged Martin, "An Imperial Idea and Its Friends: Canadian Confederation and the British", in G. Martel, ed., *Studies in British Imperial History: Essays in Honour of A. P. Thornton* (London, 1986), pp. 49–94.

6. Critics argued that the idea of British North America union had barely been a public issue in recent years; supporters that they had "forgotten that the question of Confederation was discussed both in Parliament and in the country in 1859, and that since then the Legislature and the press have occupied themselves with it often enough". Compare Joseph Armand (p. 209) and Dr. Joseph Blanchet (p. 545) with Philip H. Moore (p. 226) and Christopher Dunkin (p. 484) in *Parliamentary Debates on the Subject of the Confederation of the British North American Provinces* (3rd Session, 8th Provincial Parliament of Canada, Quebec 1865) [hereafter cited as *CD*].

7. Fielding to Blake, 8 January 1886, quoted in Colin Howell, "W. S. Fielding and the Repeal Elections of 1886 and 1887 in Nova Scotia", in P. A. Buckner and D. Frank, eds, *Atlantic Canada after Confederation: The Acadiensis Reader Volume Two* (Fredericton, 1985), p. 101.

8. The published debates began on 3 February 1865 and ended at 4:15 a.m. on 11 March. The atmosphere is well described by P. B. Waite in his introduction to the abridged version, *The Confederation Debates in the Province of Canada 1865* (Toronto, 1963), pp. i–xviii.

9. Maurice Cowling, *1867: Disraeli, Gladstone and Revolution* (Cambridge, 1967).

10. J. M. S. Careless, *Brown of the Globe: II, The Statesman of Confederation 1860–1880* (Toronto, 1963), chs 3–6. The process of using the Confederation issue to forge unlikely alliance continued after 1867, e.g., in Sir John A. Macdonald's selection of Sandfield Macdonald as his Ontario lieutenant.

11. Morton, *Critical Years*, ch. 4; Creighton, *Macdonald The Young Politician*, ch. 11; O. D. Skelton, *Life and Times of Sir Alexander Tilloch Galt* (ed. G. MacLean, Toronto, 1966), chs 7, 8.

12. Memorandum by Monck, 6 June 1866, printed in J. Pope, *Memoirs of the Right Honourable Sir John Alexander Macdonald* (Toronto, 1894), pp. 710–11, and Monck to Macdonald, confidential, 21 June 1866, *ibid.*, pp. 316–18.

13. London, Public Record Office [cited as PRO], CO 188/141, Gordon to Cardwell, no. 93, 5 December 1864, fos 395–96. For his attitude to Confederation, see J. K. Chapman, *The Career of Arthur Hamilton Gordon: First Lord Stanmore 1829–1912* (Toronto, 1964), ch. 2 and his "Arthur Gordon and Confederation", *Canadian Historical Review*, XXXVII (1956), pp. 142–57.

14. Shea to Galt, 15 December 1864, in W. G. Ormsby, "Letters to Galt Concerning the Maritime Provinces and Confederation", *Canadian Historical Review*, XXXIV (1953), pp. 167–68.

15. Quoted in E. M. Saunders, *Three Premiers of Nova Scotia* (Toronto, 1909), p. 371.

16. Cf. A. G. Bailey, "The Basis and Persistence of Opposition to Confederation in New Brunswick", *Canadian Historical Review*, XXIII (1942), pp. 367–83 and Carl Wallace, "Albert Smith, Confederation and Reaction in New Brunswick, 1852–1882", *ibid.*, XLIV (1963), pp. 285–312.

17. G. Patterson, "An Unexplained Incident of Confederation in Nova Scotia", *Dalhousie Review*, VII (1927), pp. 442–46.

18. *CD*, pp. 545 (Blanchet); 147 (Holton); 682 (Dorion).

19. *Life and Times*, p. 154.

20. Not reported in *CD*, but see Waite, ed., *Confederation Debates*, pp. xv–xvi.

21. *Hansard's Parliamentary Debates* (3rd series), CLXXXC, 19 February 1867, cols. 579–80, 577.

22. *British Parliamentary Papers* [cited as BPP], 1867, XLVIII, *Correspondence Respecting the Proposed Union of the British North American Provinces*, pp. 75–77.

23. *Ibid.*, p. 68. Howe's tour is described in J. M. Beck, *Joseph Howe: II, The Briton Becomes Canadian 1848–1873* (Kingston, 1983), p. 201.

24. *CD*, p. 61.

25. Speech of 7 April 1866, quoted in William M. Baker, *Timothy Warren Anglin 1822–1896: Irish Catholic Canadian* (Toronto, 1977), p. 103, and see also p. 58. Anglin was editor of the Saint John *Morning Freeman*. According to Creighton, Anglin was "an unsubdued ex-rebel" who "flung the full force of his abusive and mendacious journalism against Confederation" (*Road to Confederation*, p. 251, and see also p. 247). It is unlikely that Anglin took part in the Irish rising of 1848 and there is no reason to think that his journalism was unusually abusive or mendacious by contemporary standards, which were admittedly low. Thus have critics of Confederation been dismissed.

26. Similar views were expressed in the Canadian Legislative Council by James G. Currie, Bill Flint and David Reesor and in the Assembly by Christopher Dunkin, Joseph Perrault, Thomas Scatcherd and T. C. Wallbridge, *CD*, pp. 46, 164, 319, 483, 585, 759, 660.

27. Charlottetown *Examiner*, 30 January 1865, quoted in *Life and Times*, p. 186.

28. *CD*, p. 328.

29. *CD*, p. 248. In May 1860, Dorion had said that he regarded a federation of the two Canadas as "le noyau de la grande confédération des provinces de l'Amérique du nord que j'appelle de mes voeux". Quoted in Joseph Cauchon, *L'Union des Provinces de l'Amérique Britannique du Nord* (Quebec, 1865), p. 7.

30. Speech in Halifax, 13 August 1864, in J. A. Chisholm, ed., *The Speeches and Public Letters of Joseph Howe* (2 vols., Halifax, 1909), II, p. 433.

31. *CD*, p. 126.

32. *CD*, pp. 352 (Joly); 508, 485 (Dunkin); 747 (Scatcherd).

33. *CD*, p. 357.

34. *CD*, p. 586.

35. *CD*, p. 357 (Joly) and cf p. 591 (Perrault).

36. *CD*, pp. 593–95, 625–26.

37. *CD*, pp. 543 (Dunkin); 356–57 (Joly).

38. Open letter, 10 April 1866, in Chisholm, ed., *Speeches and Public Letters of Joseph Howe*, II, p. 463.

39. *CD*, p. 456.

40. *L'Ordre*, 7 June 1865, quoted in *Life and Times*, p. 147.

41. *CD*, p. 659.

42. Howe to Isaac Buchanan, 20 June 1866, in Chisholm, ed., *op. cit.*, p. 464. In his 1866 pamphlet, *Confederation Considered in Relation to the Interests of the Empire*, Howe complained that in the New Brunswick election that year, "one half of an entirely loyal population were taught to brand the other half as disloyal". Quoted in *ibid.*, II, p. 484.

43. Dunkin spoke about imperial federation in *CD*, p. 545, and was criticised by Frederick Haultain, MPP for Peterborough, p. 646. Howe's long-standing enthusiasm culminated in his 1866 pamphlet, *The Organisation of the Empire*, quoted in Chisholm, ed., *op. cit.*, II, pp. 492–506. Tupper savagely exploited the logical contradictions in Howe's position: within an imperial federation, Nova Scotians would be in a far more insignificant minority than within Confederation, liable to fight in bloody wars in all corners of the world, a scheme "as useless as it would be unjust and repressive". Letter in Halifax *British Colonist*, 13 December 1866, in E. M. Saunders, ed., *Life and Letters of Sir Charles Tupper* (2 vols, London, 1916), I, pp. 139–40.

44. Creighton, *Road to Confederation*, pp. 266–67.

45. Pope, ed., *op. cit.*, p. 684, and quoted by Dorion, *CD*, p. 654. See also *CD*, p. 248 (and cf. p. 657) for the negotiations after the death of Taché, Pope, ed., *op. cit.*, pp. 700–706. George Brown's letter to his wife of 8 March 1865 is quoted in Careless, *op. cit.*, II, p. 190.

46. *CD*, p. 657.

47. *CD*, pp. 155, 158 (James Aikens, MLC); 487 (Dunkin).

48. Halifax *Morning Chronicle*, 24 January 1866, quoted in *Life and Times*, p. 221. Annand used the argument not to reject Confederation, but as a device to suggest an alternative approach. The allusion to "festivities" may have been a coded reference to a campaign of denigration directed against John A. Macdonald's intermittent bouts of drunkenness.

49. *BPP*, 1867, XLVII, Howe, Annand and McDonald to Carnarvon, 19 January 1867, p. 13.

50. Hamilton *Times*, November 1864, quoted in *Life and Times*, p. 122. See also Bruce W. Hodgins, "Democracy and the Ontario Fathers of Confederation", in Bruce Hodgins and Robert Page, eds, *Canadian History Since Confederation: Essays and Interpretations* (2nd ed., Georgetown, Ontario, 1979), pp. 19–28.

51. *BPP*, 1867, XLVIII, *Correspondence*, pp. 70, 75; Howe *et al.* to Carnarvon, 19 January 1867, p. 18.

52. *CD*, p. 179 (L. A. Olivier, MLC for the Lanaudière).

53. Quoted in Chisholm, ed., *op. cit.*, II, p. 473.

54. *CD*, p. 490.

55. Gordon to Gladstone, private, 27 February 1865, in Paul Knaplund, ed., *Gladstone-Gordon Correspondence, 1851–1896* (Transactions of the American Philosophical Society, n.s., LI, pt 4, 1961), p. 46.

56. Yarmouth *Tribune*, 9 November 1864, quoted in *Life and Times*, p. 202.

57. Speech at Dartmouth, NS, 22 May 1867, quoted in Chisholm, ed., *op. cit.*, II, p. 514.

58. *CD*, p. 520.

59. *CD*, pp. 50 (Currie); 188 (Letellier); 524 (Dunkin).

60. Fredericton *Headquarters*, 19 October 1864, quoted in Bailey, "Basis and Persistence", p. 375.

61. "We have the trade of the world now open to us on nearly equal terms, and why should we allow Canada to hamper us?", Yarmouth *Herald*, 15 December 1864, quoted in *Life and Times*, p. 202.

62. Shea to Galt, 15 December 1864 and Whelan to Galt, 17 December 1864, in Ormsby, "Letters to Galt", pp. 167, 168.

63. Charles Mackay, "A Week in Prince Edward Island", *Fortnightly Review*, V (1865), p. 147.

64. Bolger, *Prince Edward Island and Confederation*, p. 68. In 1863, while the province of Canada derived 35.95 percent of its revenue from customs, New Brunswick derived 66.12 percent, Nova Scotia 81.09 percent, Prince Edward Island 74.66 percent and Newfoundland 86.08 percent. However, in per capita yield, Canadians paid roughly double Maritimers. The figures for 1863 customs revenues (with year of population in parentheses) were: Canada (1865) £1.04; New Brunswick (1861) £0.36; Nova Scotia (1861) £0.52; Prince Edward Island (1863) £0.35; Newfoundland (1857) £0.79. (Calculated from *BPP*, 1866, LXXIII, Colonial Trade Statistics, pp. 126, 148–49, 160–61, 168, 174.) Estimated wages rates (*ibid.*, pp. 159, 173, 181) for tradesmen in 1863 were between £0.3 and £0.4 per diem in Newfoundland, and £0.25 and £0.4 in New Brunswick, but the

Prince Edward Island figure (£40 per annum) suggests that tradesmen were employed for only 100 to 160 days each year. Thus for a tradesmen on Prince Edward Island supporting a wife and four children, a rise in per capita tariff yield to Canadian levels would have cost over £4 a year, or about five weeks' wages.

65. *CD*, p. 17 (Holton).

66. PRO, CO 188/143, Gordon to Cardwell, no. 23, 27 February 1865, fos 181–85, printed in *BPP*, 1867, XLVIII, *Correspondence*, pp. 88–89.

67. Article 69 of the Quebec Resolutions offered only that improved communications to the Red River "shall be prosecuted at the earliest possible period that the state of the Finances will permit". According to T. C. Wallbridge, this meant "that the North-West is hermetically sealed". *CD*, p. 453 and cd. Matthew Cameron, pp. 452–53.

68. *CD*, p. 759 (Scatcherd).

69. Fredericton *Headquarters*, 1 February 1865, quoted in Bailey, "Basis and Persistence", p. 379.

70. *CD*, pp. 356 (Joly); 164 (Reesor). The 1862 agreement involved only the two provinces of New Brunswick and Nova Scotia.

71. Wallace, "Albert Smith", p. 289. The Nova Scotia deputation to London in 1867 could "scarcely bring themselves to discuss" the Intercolonial, "so selfish and unfair at all times has been the conduct of the public men of Canada in regard to it". *BPP*, 1867, XLVIII, Howe *et al.* to Carnarvon, 19 January 1867, p. 8. For Galt's Halifax speech, see Edward Whelan, comp., *The Union of the British Provinces* (Charlottetown, 1865), p. 48.

72. *CD*, pp. 263 (Dorion); 230 (McMaster); 356 (Joly).

73. *CD*, p. 863, Canada took 1.11 percent of its imports from the other British North American territories, and sent them 2.2 percent of its exports. New Brunswick took 2.3 percent of its imports from Canada, to which it sent 0.87 percent of its exports. Prince Edward Island took 2.1 percent of its imports from Canada, to which it sent 0.6 percent of its exports. Newfoundland took 3.9 percent of its imports from Canada, to which it sent 0.68 percent of its exports. (Calculated from *BPP*, 1866, LXIII, *Colonial Trade Statistics*, pp. 132, 152, 170, 177.) Nova Scotia figures are less helpful, but in 1866 the province took 5.5 percent of its imports from Canada, and sent 7.15 percent of its exports (1865 figures being 3.5 percent and 4.96 percent). (Calculated from *BPP*, 1867–68, LXXI, *Colonial Trade Statistics*, p. 144.)

74. *CD*, p. 355.

75. *CD*, pp. 356 (Joly) and 528 (Dorion).

76. Halifax *Evening Reporter*, 10 December 1864, quoted in *Life and Times*, p. 208; Peter B. Waite, *Canada 1874–1896: Arduous Destiny* (Toronto, 1971), p. 76. This "conquest" of Maritime markets could not have been the result of the Intercolonial, which was not completed until 1876. In 1875, Senator A. W. McLelan of Nova Scotia described Canadian goods and produce arriving "by steamer and sail on the Gulf and by the Grand Trunk via Portland", *ibid.*, pp. 76–77.

77. *CD*, pp. 257 (Dorion); 750 (Scatcherd); 521 (Dorion); 883 (Biggar).

78. *CD*, pp. 355 (Joly); 123 (Sanborn); 456 (Cameron); 124 (Sanborn); 256 (Dorion).

79. *BPP*, 1867, XLVIII, *Correspondence*, pp. 69–70.

80. Halifax *Morning Chronicle*, 11 January 1865, quoted in Chisholm, ed., *op. cit.*, II, p. 435 (the first of the celebrated "Botheration Scheme" letters).

81. Speech at Dartmouth, 22 May 1867, quoted in *ibid.*, II, p. 512.

82. *Islander*, 6 January 1865 and J. H. Gray to Tupper, 7 January 1865, quoted in *Life and Times*, pp. 186, 183.

83. *Newfoundlander*, 12 January 1865, quoted in *Life and Times*, p. 167. It was alleged that in the 1869 election, Newfoundlanders were told "that their young children would be rammed into guns" by Canadians. James Hiller, "Confederation Defeated: The Newfoundland Election of 1869" in J. Hiller and P. Neary, eds, *Newfoundland in the Nineteenth and Twentieth Centuries: Essays in Reinterpretation* (Toronto, 1980), p. 83.

84. Quoted in Chisholm, ed., *op. cit.*, II, pp. 435–36.

85. Quoted in Bolger, ed., *Canada's Smallest Province*, pp. 175–76.

86. *CD*, pp. 354 (Joly); 180 (Olivier); *BPP*, 1867, XLVIII, Howe *et al.* to Carnarvon, 19 January 1867, p. 7.

87. *CD*, pp. 176 (Olivier); 203 (Seymour); 229 (Moore); 263 (Dorion); 234 (John Simpson, MLC for Queen's). The Halifax *Citizen* alleged that Tupper was perfectly capable of campaigning for federation with the Moon if he thought it would divert public attention. Quoted in *Life and Times*, p. 200.

88. *CD*, p. 758. Critics dismissed appeals to Italian and German unity as proving that the spirit of the times pointed to wider unions. Henri Joly gave a list of federations which had failed (*CD*, pp. 346–48), while the imperially minded Howe likened Confederation to a handful of small states withdrawing from the North German Confederation, or "a few offshoots from Italian unity" attempting to form "an inferior confederation". *BPP*, 1867, XLVIII, Howe *et al.* to Carnarvon, 19 January 1867, p. 21.

89. E.g. Petition from King's, *BPP*, 1867, XLVIII, *Correspondence*, p. 67.

90. *Ibid.*, p. 71.

91. PRO, CO 217/235, MacDonnell to Cardwell, 22 November 1865, fos 187–212.

92. Quoted in Chisholm, ed., *op. cit.*, II, p. 487.

93. *CD*, pp. 529 (Dunkin); 257 (Brome).

94. Quoted in Chisholm, ed., *op. cit.*, II, p. 489.

95. *CD*, pp. 46 (Currie); 353 (Joly). Henri Joly doubted comparisons between the Hudson's Bay Territories and European Russia, doubting that the West could ever support a large population. It may be noted that he ended his public career by serving as lieutenant-governor of British Columbia, 1900–1906. John A. Macdonald believed in 1865 that the prairies were "of no present value to Canada" which had "unoccupied land enough to absorb the immigration for many years". To open Saskatchewan would be to "drain away our youth and strength". Macdonald to E. W. Watkin, 27 March 1865, in Pope, *Memoirs*, pp. 397–98.

96. *CD*, p. 753.

97. Quoted in J. Schull, *Laurier: The First Canadian* (Toronto, 1966), p. 57.

98. Localism could also be harnessed to Confederation, influencing the kind of scheme which emerged. Elwood H. Jones, "Localism and Federalism in Upper Canada in 1865", in Bruce W. Hodgins, D. Wright and W. H. Heick, eds, *Federalism in Canada and Australia: The Early Years* (Waterloo, Ont., 1978), pp. 19–41.

99. *CD*, pp. 232 (Simpson); 452–53 (Cameron).

100. Quoted in Chisholm, ed., *op. cit.*, II, p. 490.

101. *CD*, pp. 191 (J. Bureau, Rouge MLC for De Lorimier); 624 (Perrault). McGee argued that in addition up to seven members from the Lower Provinces would represent largely francophone ridings. *CD*, p. 137.

102. Halifax *Morning Chronicle*, 13 January 1865, quoted in *Life and Times*, p. 212.

103. *CD*, p. 264.

104. Speech at Montreal, 28 October 1864, in Whelan, comp., *Union*, p. 115.

105. *CD*, pp. 252, 47, 656.

106. Quoted in Bolger, ed., *Canada's Smallest Province*, II, p. 177.

107. Howe to Earl Russell, 19 January 1865, quoted in Chisholm, ed., *op. cit.*, II, p. 437.

108. *BPP*, 1867, XLVIII, Howe *et al.* to Carnarvon, 19 January 1867, p. 16. See also *ibid.*, p. 12 for an unsubtle reference to the Hundred Years War.

109. *Ibid.*, p. 17. Cf. Leon Thériault, "L'Acadie, 1763–1978: Synthèse Historique" in Jean Daigle, éd., *Les Acadiens des Maritimes: Etudes Thématiques* (Moncton, 1980), pp. 63–68.

110. *Morning Chronicle*, 23 December 1864, quoted in *Life and Times*, p. 208.

111. Tupper to Galt, 13 December 1864, and Whelan to Galt, 17 December 1864, in Ormsby, "Letters", pp. 166, 168.

112. *CD*, pp. 329 (Reesor); 261 (Dorion).

113. *Le Pays*, 27 June 1864, quoted in Creighton, *Road to Confederation*, p. 78, and *bid.*, p. 122.

114. *CD*, p. 174, and cf. pp. 192 (Bureau) and 350 (Joly). An emotive example cited was central control of divorce proceedings.

115. Dawson to Howe, 15 November 1866, quoted in *Life and Times*, p. 135.

116. *CD*, p. 351 (Joly).

117. Speech, 13 August 1864, in Chisholm, ed., *op. cit.*, II, p. 433. Howe rose to speak at ten minutes to midnight. "Who ever heard of a public man being bound by a speech on such an occasion as that?", he asked three years later. Beck, *op. cit.*, II, p. 182. In fact, Howe spoke before the Charlottetown conference.

118. Speech at Dartmouth, 22 May 1867, in Chisholm, ed., *op. cit.*, II, p. 511.

119. *BPP*, 1867, XLVIII, *Correspondence*, pp. 69–70.

120. Dartmouth speech, Chisholm, ed., *op. cit.*, II, pp. 512, 511.

121. Port Medway petition, *BPP*, 1867, XLVIII, *Correspondence*, p. 76; Howe *et al.* to Carnarvon, 19 January 1867, p. 7.

122. *BPP*, 1867, XLVIII, Howe *et al.* to Carnarvon, 19 January 1867, p. 15. J. W. Longley, *Joseph Howe* (Toronto, 1906), p. 202, and cf. Beck, *op. cit.*, II, p. 202. The reference to "a village" was, of course, unfair, but Dunkin was concerned that the federal capital was to remain "within the jurisdiction of a subordinate province". *CD*, p. 507.

123. *BPP*, 1867, XLVIII, Howe *et al.* to Carnarvon, 19 January 1867, p. 17 and cf. Dartmouth speech, 22 May 1867, in Chisholm, ed., *op. cit.*, II, p. 517.

124. The Nova Scotia press, it was alleged, emphasised the less attractive aspects of Canadian life, just as modern Canadians often reflect a cataclysmic view of the United States. "Not a fight occurs, not a train runs off the track and kills one or two persons in that Province but it is blazoned forth in that press". Speech by

Dr. Hamilton, *Debates and Proceedings of the House of Assembly of Nova Scotia 1865*, pp. 264–65. I am grateful to Dr. James Sturgis for this reference.

125. Dorion's anti-Confederation manifesto was widely published in 1864. Quoted in *Life and Times*, p. 142. His objection may partly have originated in an element of mistranslation: "Confederation" in English had come to be a shorthand term for a reasonably centralised form of intercolonial union, while its French equivalent continued to mean a loose alliance.

126. Quoted in Bolger, ed., *op. cit.*, p. 174.

127. Halifax *Citizen*, 19 November 1864, quoted in *Life and Times*, p. 203. The lieutenant-governor, Sir Richard MacDonnell, used the same argument a few days later in a despatch: "I do not believe that so long as the boundaries of the different Provinces are maintained and Local Legislatures and petty politics fostered, the Confederation can rise to that status, and that dignity of national feeling, which creates and maintains a national military spirit and self-reliance". PRO, CO 217/235, MacDonnell to Cardwell, 22 November 1864, fos 187–212.

128. Saint John *Daily Evening Globe*, 17 October 1864, quoted in *Life and Times*, p. 136.

129. Saint John *Freeman*, 3 November 1864, quoted in Baker, *Anglin*, p. 65. Joseph Howe also condemned the duplication of legislatures as "cumbrous and expensive". Howe to Earl Russell, 19 January 1865, in Chisholm, ed., *op. cit.*, II, p. 437.

130. *CD*, p. 504. Perrault alleged that some politicians were influenced by hopes of "being governor of one of the Federated Provinces", as did Letellier, who subsequently became a lieutenant-governor himself. *CD*, pp. 626, 188.

131. *CD*, p. 157 (James Aikins).

132. *CD*, p. 253. Dorion chose to overlook the provision in Article 14 of the Quebec Resolutions that "in such nomination due regard shall be had to the claims of the Members of Legislative Council in Opposition in each Province, so that all political parties may as nearly as possible be fairly represented".

133. *CD*, pp. 494–95. The fear was a real one for French Canadians. Cf. *CD*, p. 174 (Olivier).

134. Support for the Intercolonial might not translate into support for Confederation, as in the case of J. B. Pouliot, MPP for Témiscouata.

135. Laflèche to Boucher de Niverville, 2 March 1864, quoted in Walter Ullman, "The Quebec Bishops and Confederation", *Canadian Historical Review*, XLIII (1963), p. 218.

136. Speech at Montreal, 29 October 1864, in Whelan, comp., *op. cit.*, pp. 122–23.

137. Speech at Halifax, 12 September 1864, in *ibid.*, p. 46.

Article Seventeen

Current Canadian Constitutionalism and the 1865 Confederation Debates

John A. Rohr

Tantae molis erat
Romanam condere gentem.

Aeneid: I, 33

The purpose of this article is to examine the Confederation debates of 1865 in the hope of illuminating some dark corners of the exhausting constitutional quarrels that have dominated Canadian politics for the past two decades. By the "Confederation debates of 1865," I mean the debates of the 8th Provincial Parliament of Canada, which were held during February and March of 1865 in Quebec City. These debates focused on a set of resolutions adopted by delegates from Canada, New Brunswick, Newfoundland, Nova Scotia, and Prince Edward Island at

Source: John A. Rohr, "Current Canadian Constitutionalism and the 1865 Confederation Debates," *American Review of Canadian Studies*, 28,4 (Winter 1988): 413–444.

a conference also held in Quebec City during the previous October. These resolutions led eventually to the British North America (BNA) Act of 1867.

The reader might wonder why I turn — of all places — to the Confederation debates for enlightenment on a contemporary crisis. Having read all 1,032 pages of these debates, I harbour the suspicion that I belong to a very exclusive club of North American academic eccentrics and, as an American, I expect that mine is a very small subset of this club. My most recent work has analyzed contemporary problems in terms of certain themes evident in the founding periods of the United States and of the Fifth French Republic.[1] Following the lead of Hannah Arendt, I believe that, for many western nations, founding periods are normative and that those who study such periods often discover events, arguments, and principles that illuminate a nation's subsequent development.[2]

To apply this idea to Canada presents a problem I did not encounter in studying the United States or the Fifth Republic. Despite the importance of the Declaration of Independence in American history, it is the drafting of the Constitution of the United States in 1787 and the subsequent debates over its ratification that define the founding of the present American Republic. Although the origins of France itself trail off into some dim and distant past, there can be no doubt that the Fifth Republic was founded in 1958. In studying the founding of the present regimes in France and the United Stares, I knew at once where to turn. With Canada, it was not as simple. The Proclamation Act, the Quebec Act, and the Act of Union present worthy challenges to Confederation as the founding period of Canada and, even if these challengers are ultimately exposed as impostors, the Confederation period itself harbors enough important events — most notably, the crucial meeting in Quebec City in October 1864 — to make the Confederation debates something less than the sole contender for serious study of Canada's founding.[3] Despite these methodological problems, I shall focus exclusively on the Confederation debates of 1865.[4] I do so because no other event from the Confederation period has records as complete as these and, more importantly, because these records reveal a sustained level of serious — and at times profound — public argument which, I believe, is unequalled in Canadian constitutional history.

In the months preceding the 1995 Quebec Referendum, considerable attention was lavished upon the precise wording of the text to be submitted to the people. At first, the debate focused on the speculative question of what it would be and, once this was known, what it should have been.[5] Federalists argued that their opponents had deliberately muddied the waters, misleading Quebeckers into thinking that they could live in a sovereign Quebec that somehow remained part of Canada. The federalist strategy was to reduce the question to a stark dichotomy: either you are in or you are out — a formulation sovereigntists wisely ignored. Both sides invoked such powerful symbols as Canadian passports and currency to support their respective positions. Post-election analysis revealed that substantial numbers of Yes voters thought that a sovereign Quebec would in some way or other remain part of Canada, despite the scoldings they received from stern federalists for being so illogical. Although no end to the crisis is in sight, I cannot help thinking that when the end comes, it will appear — much to the chagrin of ideologues of all stripes — in some hopelessly illogical compromise, whose sole merit will be that it works. If so, the Confederation debates on Canadian federalism offer an illuminating precedent. Perhaps Justice Holmes had it right when he said that a page of history is worth a volume of logic. Following the texts of the debates, this article has four substantive sections: the distribution of powers in Canadian federalism; the need for popular consent to constitutional change; the central role of public administration; and the image of the United States throughout the Confederation debates. The paper concludes with some brief unsolicited advice for my neighbors to the north, the musings of one who has thought long and often on these foundational matters.

CANADIAN FEDERALISM AND THE DISTRIBUTION OF POWERS

Americans who study Canadian constitutional history feel right at home when they get around to examining the regulation of commerce, because both countries impose an interprovincial or interstate limitation on the regulatory powers of their respective federal governments. Thus, in principle, neither Ottawa nor Washington may regulate commercial affairs that are strictly intraprovincial or intrastate. Despite this similarity in principle, Washington's writ, in fact, runs much further and deeper into the economic life of the United States than does Ottawa's in Canada. Noting this difference, a widely used textbook on Canadian constitutional law states that "ironically, the express restrictions in the American constitution have proved to be far less of a barrier to the development of national economic policies than have the judicially created restrictions in Canada."[6] This is "ironic" because the Constitution of the United States explicitly limits its federal government's regulatory power to "commerce among the states," whereas article 91 of the BNA Act of 1867 imposes no such limitation. Among the explicitly enumerated powers entrusted to "the exclusive Legislative Authority of the Parliament of Canada," one finds quite simply "the Regulation of Trade and Commerce." The "judicially created restrictions" mentioned in the text quoted above refer primarily to a series of late-nineteenth and early-twentieth century decisions by the Judicial Committee of the Privy Council (JCPC) — the British institution which, despite the creation of the Supreme Court of Canada in 1875, *de facto* exercised the ultimate judicial authority in Canadian affairs until 1949.

In the late 1920s and early 1930s, Canadian constitutional scholars who favored a more active role for their federal government subjected the JCPC decisions limiting Ottawa's power over commerce to a withering attack. The gist of their argument was neatly captured in a pithy and oft-quoted sentence written by the distinguished jurist William Kennedy: "Seldom have statesmen more deliberately striven to write their purposes into law, and seldom have these more signally failed before the judicial technique of statutory interpretation."[7] Kennedy's complaint finds considerable support in the unadorned text of the BNA Act, which the JCPC had construed quite narrowly. Article 91 confers upon Parliament a sweeping power "to make Laws for the Peace, Order and good Government of Canada in relation to all Matters not coming within the Classes of Subjects by this Act assigned exclusively to the Legislatures of the Provinces." Then, for good measure, it specifies a long list of explicit federal powers that are added "for greater Certainty, but not so as to restrict the Generality of the foregoing Terms of this Section"— that is, of the peace, order, and good government or "POGG" clause, as it came to be known. Among these enumerated powers one finds "the Regulation of Trade and Commerce." Jurisprudentialists of a federalist persuasion held that POGG was the sole grant of power to the federal government and the specific enumerations were merely concrete examples of the broader, more comprehensive power. The practical point of their position was that the federal government enjoyed plenary power to regulate trade and commerce.

The JCPC had interpreted the text differently, finding in the exclusive grant to the provinces in article 92 of a power to "make laws in relation to . . . Property and civil Rights in the Province" an impressive limitation on the federal government's power over trade and commerce. Much of the jurisprudence of the late-nineteenth and early-twentieth centuries centered on JCPC's effort to find the right balance between these texts, with most of the decisions favoring the provinces.[8] This line of reasoning culminated in a series of opinions authored by Lord Haldane which restricted POGG to an "exceptional" power to be used only in an "emergency" or in the face of "sudden danger to the social order" or in "special circumstances such as a great war."[9]

Canadian nationalists, like William Kennedy, seem to be on target when they find JCPC's interpretation of the BNA Act crabbed and strained. Although the Quebec Resolutions, the text debated in 1865, differed somewhat from the BNA Act of 1867, it was close enough to provide evidence suggesting that a good number of the delegates favored expansive powers for the federal government.[10] The 29th Resolution, anticipating what would eventually emerge as the POGG clause in the BNA Act, provided: "The General Parliament shall have power to make Laws for the peace, welfare, and good government of the Federated Provinces (saving the Sovereignty of England) and especially laws respecting the following subjects." It then went on to enumerate a long list of specific powers, most of which reappeared in the BNA Act. Among them was the "Regulation of Trade and Commerce."

During the Confederation debates, support for a broad interpretation of federal power came first and foremost from John A. Macdonald. Warming to one of his favorite topics — how to avoid the fatal flaws in the Constitution of the United States — Macdonald celebrated the superior wisdom of the Quebec Resolutions as follows:

> [The Americans] commenced, in fact, at the wrong end. They declared by their Constitution that each state was a sovereignty in itself, and that all the powers incident to a sovereignty belonged to each state, except those powers which, by the Constitution, were conferred upon the General Government and Congress. Here we have adopted a different system. We have strengthened the General Government. We have given the General Legislature all the great subjects of legislation. We have conferred on them, not only specifically and in detail, all the powers which are incident to sovereignty, but we have expressly declared that all subjects of general interest not distinctly and exclusively conferred upon the local governments and local legislatures, shall be conferred upon the General Government and Legislature.[11]

Variations on this theme can he found throughout the debates. Following Macdonald's lead, Isaac Bowman contrasts the Quebec Resolutions favorably with the Constitution of the United States, and then goes on to assert: "In the scheme submitted to us, I am happy to observe, that the principal and supreme power is placed in the hands of the General Government, and that the powers deputed to local governments are of a limited character."[12]

David Jones sees in the American doctrine of states' rights "the cause of the bloodshed and civil war" that has ravaged that unhappy land for the last four years." He then points out that "our case is exactly the reverse," in that instead of having the provinces delegate powers to the proposed central government, the central government "gives to these provinces just as much or as little as it chooses." He then quotes in full the centralizing language of Quebec Resolution 45: "In regard to all subjects over which jurisdiction belongs to both the General and Local Legislatures, the laws of the General Parliament shall control and supersede those made by the Local Legislature, and the latter shall be void so far as they are repugnant to, or inconsistent with, the former."[13] Richard Cartwright is pleased to report that "every reasonable precaution seems to have been taken against leaving behind us any reversionary legacies of sovereign state rights to stir up strife and discord among our children."[14] Finally, John Scoble advises his colleagues that a "careful analysis of the scheme convinces me that the powers conferred on the General or Central Government secure it all the attributes of sovereignty, and the veto power which its executive will possess and to which all local legislation will be subject, will prevent a conflict of laws and jurisdictions in all matters of importance, so that I believe in its working it will be found, if not in form yet in fact and practically, a legislative union."[15]

Scoble's reference to a "legislative union" is particularly significant because throughout the debates many delegates from Canada West who supported the Quebec Resolutions added that their only disappointment lay in the federal character of the proposed union. They would have preferred a legislative union — that is, an even more centralized regime than the one they were approving. Nevertheless, they would support the Quebec Resolutions because they bid fair to bring about a unified structure close enough to the legislative union they really desired.[16] Such statements, combined with those cited above, go a long way toward supporting William Kennedy's remark that "seldom have statesmen more deliberately striven to write their purposes into law" and that these purposes included an extremely vigorous federal government.

Upon closer examination, however, the federalist case is not as strong as it might at first appear. The friends of Confederation from Canada East seemed at times to be reading a text quite different from the strongly centralized document revealed in the passages we have just quoted. Take, for example, the following comments from four of the most prominent members of the Quebec delegation supporting Confederation:

> Etienne Pascal Taché: ". . . for all questions of a general nature would be reserved for the General Government, and those of a local character to the local governments, who would have the power to manage their domestic affairs as they deemed best."[17]

> George Cartier: "Questions of commerce, of international communication, and all matters of general interest, would be discussed and determined in the General Legislature."[18]

> Hector-Louis Langevin: "All local interests will be submitted and left to the decision of the local legislatures."[19]

> Joseph Cauchon: "But if no mention was made of divorce in the Constitution, if it was not assigned to the Federal Parliament, it would of necessity belong to the local parliaments as it belongs to our Legislature now, although there is not one word respecting it in the Union Act."[20]

What these remarks have in common is an exceedingly broad interpretation of provincial power under the Quebec Resolutions and one that finds little support in the text. Their argument seems to rely inordinately upon clause 18 of Resolution 43, which gives the provincial legislatures power to make laws respecting "generally all matters of a private or local nature, not assigned to the General Parliament." This passage is no match for the sweeping power of the General Parliament "to make laws for the peace, welfare, and good government of the Federated Provinces."[21] As noted above, this sweeping power was supplemented with the power to legislate "especially" in a long list of substantive areas which concludes with the power to legislate "generally respecting all matters of a general character, not specially and exclusively reserved for Local Government and Legislatures." The distinction drawn by the Quebec delegates between general and local matters was too neat and simple. They seemed to assume that the distinction between the two spheres was almost self-evident. Such an assumption is at odds with the language of the Quebec Resolutions. As we saw above, Resolution 45 anticipated that there would be jurisdictional conflicts between general and local legislation and that they should be resolved in favor of the federal government.[22]

The highly centralized character of the proposed confederation did not escape its opponents from Quebec. Unlike Taché, Cartier, et al., anticonfederationists, like the Dorions (Antoine-Aimé and Jean Baptiste Eric), Joseph Perrault, and L.A. Olivier, agreed entirely with John A. Macdonald's strongly federalist interpretation of the proposed constitution and for that very reason voted against it. Consider the following:

> J.B.E. Dorion: "I am opposed to this scheme of Confederation, because we are offered local parliaments which will be simply nonentities, with a mere semblance of power on questions of minor importance."[23]

> Joseph Perrault: "Local governments . . . will be nothing more than municipal councils, vested with small and absurd powers, unworthy of a free people, which allow us at most the control of our roads, our schools, and our lands."[24]

A.A. Dorion: "I find that the powers assigned to the General Parliament enable it to legislate on all subjects whatsoever. It is an error to imagine that these powers are defined and limited, by the 29th clause of the resolutions. Were it desirous of legislating on subjects placed under the jurisdiction of the local legislatures, there is not a word in these resolutions which can he construed to prevent it, and if the local legislatures complain, Parliament may turn away and refuse to hear their complaints, because all the sovereignty is vested in the General Government, and there is no authority to define its functions and attributes and those of the local governments."[25]

If we look only at the *Franco-Français* debate on the Resolutions, it seems clear that the opponents of Confederation read the text more accurately but the Quebec supporters read it more wisely. It is inconceivable that men as sophisticated as Taché, Cartier, and Langevin did not understand the meaning of the text before them. They understood it only too well, but imposed a strained interpretation upon it that would sufficiently obfuscate its clear meaning so as to make it politically possible for Quebec to enter the Confederation. Further, their point of view prevailed when, some years later, the JCPC found in the tiny acorn of provincial power over property and civil rights the origins of what eventually became the mighty oak of decentralization that overshadowed POGG and the rest of Macdonald's carefully laid plans. Events proved that there was too little political support, not just in Quebec but in all of Canada for Macdonald's grand vision ever to become a reality. The Quebec Confederationists were poor exegetes but great statesmen. They knew that at times confusion is the friend of compromise. Perhaps there is a lesson in all this for the contemporary and possibly salutary confusion over the meaning of sovereignty.

CONSENT OF THE GOVERNED

Peter H. Russell begins his widely read *Constitutional Odyssey* by recalling what he describes as "perhaps the most haunting lines in Canadian history." He refers to a letter written in 1858 by three prominent fathers of Confederation, George-Etienne Cartier, Alexander Galt, and John Ross, to Sir Edward Bulwer-Lytton, the British colonial secretary at that time. The "haunting lines" are as follows: "It will be observed that the basis of Confederation now proposed differs from that of the United States in several important particulars. It does not profess to be derived from the people but would be the constitution provided by the imperial parliament, thus remedying any defect."[26]

Russell then contrasts this statement with a comment by Newfoundland premier Clyde Wells in 1990: "The Constitution belongs to the *people* of Canada — the ultimate source of sovereignty in the nation." Russell assures his reader that "between the two passages quoted lies much more than the gulf of years."[27] Indeed, the "constitutional odyssey" on which he embarks is the fascinating story of how Canadians made their way from the first statement to the second.

Although the Confederation debates provide many passages echoing the sentiments of the authors of the letter to Bulwer-Lytton, they also provide, however illogically, many passages anticipating Clyde Wells's statement as well. Despite the nearly universal support among the delegates for the monarchy and the no less universal rejection of both republicanism and democracy, the issue of whether the Quebec Resolutions should somehow be ratified by the people of Canada revealed a curious commitment to the notion that the legitimacy of a major constitutional change requires some sort of popular consent.

Naturally, the opponents of the Quebec Resolutions pressed this argument ceaselessly. They hoped that some sort of referendum, or even a new election, focused exclusively on confederation, would open the proposed text to a careful public scrutiny, which its most controversial measures could not withstand. They knew, for instance, that the confederation document was exceedingly vulnerable on the grounds that it called for a legislative council — later to be renamed the Senate — whose members were to be appointed for life by the Crown and whose number could not be increased. This measure was a concession to the Maritime provinces and enjoyed little support in Canada where, as of 1865, the members of the upper house of Parliament, the "legislative council," were elected. The opponents of Confederation knew that if they could rivet the attention of the people on the appointive senate and other unpopular measures, the supporters of the constitution might have to accept some amendments to the proposed Quebec Resolutions. This, they surmised, would set off a chain reaction in the Maritime provinces, which would demand further changes and thereby unravel the whole scheme. Thus the question of the need for recourse to the people was of considerable strategic importance throughout the debates. It was a point on which the friends of Confederation could not yield an inch. The interesting point for our purposes is to review the arguments both sides made in support of their respective positions.

The argument of the anticonfederationists was straightforward. Consider the following:

James O'Halloran: "I remarked at the outset, that I must deny to this House the right to impose on this country this or any other Constitution, without first obtaining the consent of the people. Who sent you here to frame a Constitution? You were sent here to administer the Constitution as you find it."[28]

J.B.E. Dorion: "I am opposed to the scheme of Confederation, because I deny that this House has the power to change the political constitution of the country, as it is now proposed to do, without appealing to the people and obtaining their views on a matter of such importance."[29]

Matthew Cameron: "Sir, I cannot conceive it to be possible that any body of men sent here by the people under the constitution will make changes in that Constitution which were not contemplated by those who sent them here, without submitting those changes first to the people."[30]

One could hardly ask for clearer statements affirming the principle that constitutions derive their just powers from the consent of the governed. Similar statements abound throughout the debates.[31]

The friends of Confederation were clearly embarrassed by this call for a recourse to the people. Their determination to reject it was thoroughly justified strategically, as the almost disastrous results of an election in New Brunswick, held as the Canadian Confederation debates were in progress, amply demonstrated.[32] The problem for the Confederationists was that their objections were merely strategic. They struggled in vain to find a principled response to the demand that the people of the two Canadas approve the proposed massive constitutional revision. The best they could do was to make tradition do the work of principle by arguing that recourse to the people was not the British way of doing things. Typical of this approach was the following comment from John Ross, one of the authors of Peter Russell's "haunting lines": "I will add that this mode of appealing to the people is not British but American, as under the British system the representatives of the people in Parliament are presumed to be competent to decide all the public questions submitted to them."[33] The problem with this argument was that it was easily defeated by recalling that there were ample precedents for Canadians and other colonists adapting British practices to local circumstances. Recourse to the people, like Confederation itself, would be such an adaptation.[34]

Throughout the debates, the Confederationists were reluctant to challenge directly the call for recourse to the people, preferring instead to dismiss it on procedural grounds. For example, when James Currie, an articulate anticonfederationist, introduced a resolution that the Legislative Council should not make a decision on the Quebec Resolutions "without further manifestation of the public will than has yet been declared," he met a host of procedural objections.[35] Alexander Campbell queried him on just how this "further manifestation of the public will" would come about. Transforming Currie's resolution into a man of straw, he dismissed as absurd the notion — a notion never proposed by Currie — that "the nearly four millions of people who comprise the provinces to be affected by the union should meet together *en masse.*"[36] He also rejected the possibility of a special election on Confederation because such an election would require that Parliament first be dissolved, an impossible precondition since a majority of the members in both houses supported the government's commitment to Confederation and, therefore, there was no basis for dissolution. "Receiving the support of more than two-thirds of the representatives of the people as the present Government does," Campbell asked, "how is it possible that Parliament could be dissolved to suit the views of a small minority?"[37]

Timing was another procedural roadblock the Confederationists placed in the path of recourse to the people. On the very first day of the debates, 3 February 1865, Confederationist Fergusson Blair said that submitting the plan to the electors at that time "would involve a delay which could not be compensated for by any benefit proposed to be derived from such a course." He allowed, however, that "the subject would present a different aspect" in the event that at a later date there should be "numerous petitions in favor of an appeal to the people."[38]

As the debates drew to a close, however, the Confederationists changed their position on timing. On Saturday, 11 March 1865, the Legislative Assembly finally voted to approve the Quebec Resolutions. When the same body reconvened the following Monday, John Cameron, a supporter of the text, surprised his colleagues by offering a resolution requesting the Governor General to "be pleased to direct that a constitutional appeal shall be made to the people" before the text is dispatched to London for "the consideration of the Imperial Parliament."[39] Thomas Parker, who, like Cameron, had voted for the Resolutions on the previous Saturday, opposed the Monday morning resolution to submit the text to the people before it went to London. Timing was his principal concern. "If the resolutions were to be referred to the people at all," he said, "it should have been before they received the sanction of the House." He asked rhetorically, "Are we to turn round today and reverse what we did on Saturday last?" He would have favored recourse to the people earlier, "but not now, after their [the Resolutions'] deliberate sanction by the House; to do so would stultify the Legislature."[40] Thus Parker opposed recourse to the people at the end of the debates because it was too late, whereas his fellow Confederationist, Fergusson Blair, opposed it at their beginning because it was too early.

The Confederationists' reluctance to answer directly the argument for consulting the people was underscored in their determination to expand the variety of procedural considerations they relied upon to sidestep the intrinsic merits of the issue. These additional procedural matters included: efforts to have resolutions calling for consultation ruled out of order; complaints about the expense such consultations would involve; and, most importantly, a constantly recurring theme that there was no need to consult the people in a formal referendum or an election because they had already been consulted in countless informal ways that made their overwhelming support for Confederation abundantly clear.[41]

Throughout the debates the participants frequently went out of their way to proclaim their loyalty to the British monarchy and their widespread contempt for republicanism and democracy, especially in their American incarnations. Despite these commitments, both sides in the Confederation debates revealed a surprising acceptance of the liberal principle demanding popular consent for major constitutional change. Political strategy governs the manner in which this acceptance becomes manifest. The anticonfederationists shout it from the rooftops, while their opponents grumble discreetly about the practical problems of implementing in deed the doctrine they will not condemn in principle.

THE CENTRALITY OF PUBLIC ADMINISTRATION

Americans following recent constitutional vagaries in Canada were surprised to learn that less than a month after the 1995 Quebec Referendum, Prime Minister Chrétien delivered himself of the opinion that "the real problems in Canada are economic growth and the creation of jobs and good solid administration."[42] That the Prime Minister of Canada would mention "good solid administration" as one of the nation's three "real" problems in the immediate aftermath of a referendum that nearly destroyed his country must surely have struck interested Americans as extraordinary and perhaps even as bizarre. Public administration is not prestigious activity in the United States. It is inconceivable that an American president in the midst of a great constitutional crisis would turn to administration — good and solid or otherwise — as the path to political salvation. Not so in Canada. Chrétien's remark was part of a national chorus that evoked the muse of administration to inspire politicians to achieve the high statesmanship needed to bind up the nation's wounds. Constitutional debates over the very survival of the regime moved effortlessly into detailed discussions of such classic administrative themes as environmental management, immigration policy, public finance, civil service pensions, education, manpower and training, unemployment benefits, control of natural resources, and, of course, that hardy perennial of Canadian Federalism, equalization of payments. Federalists were not alone in enlisting administration to support their cause. Quebec sovereigntists, most notably Premier Lucien Bouchard, frequently tempered the high rhetoric of sovereignty with the mundane details of education, employment, health care, civil service reform, and financial management that would make it all possible and worthwhile.[43]

The striking variation in the value Canadians and Americans assign to public administration marks an important difference in the political cultures of the two countries. Some have traced it back to the American Revolution, arguing that refugee Loyalists brought to their new country an affection for government that was quite literally alien to their erstwhile rebellious neighbors to the south.[44] This affection, so the argument goes, was reinforced by the warm welcome they found in what remained of British North America. Whatever the explanation, the phenomenon itself is clear enough today among both federalists and sovereigntists. It was also true in 1865 when both friends and foes of the Quebec Resolutions enlisted detailed questions of administration as weapons in defending their respective positions. The Confederation debates reveal a host of administrative questions that absorbed the attention of the delegates. The topics ranged from broad generalizations on the hopes for improved administration that Confederation was expected to provide, to more focused attention to public works, and, finally, to very specific discussions on canals and schools.[45] Woven into the fabric of these arguments was a curious debate over the provision in Resolution 64 that the "General Parliament" would make "an annual grant in aid" to each province "equal to eighty cents per head of the population, as established by the census of 1861." Subsequent resolutions provided special benefits for New Brunswick, Newfoundland, and Prince Edward Island. These provisions triggered debates foreshadowing later controversies over the equalization payments that would play so important a role in the administration of Canadian federalism.[46]

Among the many administrative questions debated in 1865, however, none can match the importance of the Intercolonial Railway. In rehearsing the debates over this immensely controversial innovation, I have no intention of weighing the merits of the issue. I examine the railroad question, which was to dominate the early development of Canadian administration, only to give a very specific example of the salience of administration in the debates. I do this to establish a link between past and present, thereby suggesting that when contemporary Canadians link mundane questions of administration to the high statesmanship of saving a great nation, they echo sentiments harking back to the beginnings of Confederation.

Quebec Resolution 68 proposed an "Intercolonial Railway" to extend "from Rivière du Loup, through New Brunswick, to Truro in Nova Scotia." Its importance in the debates for friend and foe alike of the resolutions is textually demonstrable. Speaking before the Legislative Council, William Macmaster, an opponent of Confederation, denounced the proposed railroad as "a very questionable part of the project" and then elevated its importance by adding "indeed to my mind it is the most objectionable of the whole."[47] Echoing these sentiments, anticonfederationist Matthew Cameron saw the railroad as nothing less than the "leading feature" of the proposed constitutional change and one of the main reasons why it should be rejected."[48]

Not to be outdone, the friends of Confederation were no less outspoken in supporting the railroad than their adversaries were in condemning it. For Antoine Harwood, "the building of the Intercolonial Railway" was "the most important consideration of all for everyone, and one which would of itself be sufficient to make us desire the union of the provinces."[49] Raising his sights beyond the railway proposed in the text before him, Colonel Arthur Rankin proclaimed it but the first step toward "that still more important and magnificent project, the Atlantic and Pacific Railway." Seeing the embryo of this grander project in the proposed Intercolonial Railway, Rankin assured his colleagues that "it would be impossible to overestimate the advantages which any country must derive from being possessed of a line of communication destined to become the highway from Europe to Asia."[50]

With such strong statements both in its favor and against it, the Intercolonial Railway became, of course, the subject of considerable controversy. At the very outset of the debates in the Legislative Assembly, Luther Holton, a prominent anticonfederationist, went to the heart of the matter when he registered his surprise at finding in a constitutional text a proposal to build a railway. He ridiculed this provision as "a novelty that, perhaps might not be found in the constitution of any country."[51] To this John A. Macdonald replied: "The railroad was not, as stated by Mr. Holton, a portion of the Constitution, but was one of the conditions on which the Lower Provinces agreed to enter into the constitutional agreement with us."[52]

Macdonald's distinction between "a portion of the Constitution" and a "condition" for accepting the constitution was no shallow legalism. It produced an immediate and most unwelcome reaction in New Brunswick where the friends of Confederation were facing an imminent election that focused on the Quebec Resolutions. For Samuel Tilley, the leading New Brunswick Confederationist, the Intercolonial Railway was absolutely essential. It was, as Donald Creighton puts it, "Tilley's biggest political asset."[53] Albert J. Smith, Tilley's principal opponent, seized on Macdonald's unfortunate comment that the railway was not a "portion of the Constitution" to argue that the commitments in the Quebec Resolutions most favorable to New Brunswick, above all the Intercolonial Railway, meant nothing at all. Frantically, Macdonald sent a telegram to Tilley assuring him that the provision for the Railway — regardless of its status as part of the constitution — would appear in the text of the imperial act which was the ultimate goal of the Quebec Resolutions. His remarks helped to reassure the "terrified Unionists" in New Brunswick, but mistrust and hard feelings remained.[54]

The prominent place given to the railway provision in the proposed constitution brought a technical dimension to the Confederation debates conspicuously absent from the comparable debates in the United States in 1787 or in France in 1958. The railroad clause prompted extremely lengthy and detailed discussions of what we might call today financial management.

The wearisome detail in the two excerpts that follow capture nicely the technical flavor of much of the debate over the railroad:

> Hon. Mr. RYAN —[speaking in favor of the resolutions on 20 February] . . . I want to shew by this [a lengthy discussion he had just finished on the economics of transporting a barrel of flour] that the carrying of flour over the Intercolonial Railway will not be so difficult of accomplishment as people who have not gone into the calculation closely may be disposed to imagine. (Hear, hear.) I have here, too, a statement of the imports of flour into New Brunswick, Nova Scotia, and Newfoundland. It is as follows:

Imports of Flour	Barrels
New Brunswick	243,000
Nova Scotia	328,000
Newfoundland	226,000
[Total]	797,000

> Mr. A. MACKENZIE —[speaking against the resolutions on 23 February] . . . Major Robinson estimates the cost of the road at about £7,000 Pounds per mile, or about £2,800,000 altogether. I do not think, judging from the statement he gives of the grades in the road, the bridges to be built, and the material to be found along the line, that it is a fair inference that the cost would equal the amount he sets down. The character of the ground over which the road will pass is very similar to the railways of Canada. It is represented to be very much of the nature of the country through which the Great Western runs westward of Hamilton over a great portion of the line. The best portion of the line is equal to the worst portions of the Great Western. Even at the cost of £7,000 per mile the expense of constructing the entire road would be a little over fifteen millions of dollars.[55]

Statements of this nature abound throughout the Confederation debates.[56] As noted above, there is nothing like them in the French or American debates. Luther Holton was right. To insert a clause about a specifically named railroad into a constitution was an innovation, but it underscores a blending of administration and constitutionalism in a distinctively Canadian way.

Before concluding our study of the railroad as an example of administration in the Confederation debates, we should note the theme of technology driving constitutional reform. Speaking in favor of the resolutions, John Ross invoked Lord Durham's famous (or infamous) *Report* of 1839 in which he argued that a railroad "between Halifax and Quebec would, in fact, produce relations between these provinces that would render a general union absolutely necessary."[57] This same passage is cited by Anselme Paquet, an opponent of Confederation, as a reason for rejecting the Quebec Resolutions.[58] The curious fact that the same author is cited verbatim, first for Confederation and then against it, is explained by the diametrically opposed memories of Lord Durham in the two Canadas as of 1865. Generally loved and admired in Ontario, in Quebec he was, quite simply, despised.[59] What is interesting for our purposes, however, is that both friends and foes of Lord Durham agree with his prediction that an Intercolonial Railway would be a particularly apt means for achieving political unity. Logically enough, Ross and Paquet cite Lord Durham's argument, each to his own end of bringing about Confederation (for Ross) or of stopping it (for Paquet.) For the latter the railroad should be opposed because it would lead to political union as the *mal-aimé* Durham had correctly surmised. For the former, the railroad should be supported for precisely the same reason. For our study of the administrative-constitutional link, however, the important point is that Lord Durham had the wit to foresee technological innovation as a sure path to constitutional reform and that men on both sides of the 1865 debate recognized that he was right.

The Confederation fathers of 1865 had no need of promptings from Lord Durham to see the connection between the Intercolonial Railway and Confederation. Thus, anticonfederationist

James Currie, noting that "some leading men in Halifax had said 'the Railway first, and Confederation next,'" argues that the simplest way to defeat Confederation would be to reject the railway proposal. He was satisfied that "if the Intercolonial Railway project were taken out of the scheme [that is, the proposed constitution], we would not hear much about it afterwards."[60] Although Currie, like Lord Durham, saw a close connection between the railway and Confederation, he did not fear the railway as simply a means to Confederation. His argument was that the Confederationists in the Maritime provinces cared only about the railway but would cynically embrace Confederation as a necessary evil. This position was expanded by A.A. Dorion who attributed to Samuel Tilley, the prominent New Brunswick Confederationist, the sentiment "no railway, no Confederation." Indeed, A.A. Dorion went on to denounce the entire Confederation plan as nothing but an elaborate scheme to rescue the financially troubled Grand Trunk Railroad.[61]

Confederationist Hector-Louis Langevin candidly acknowledges that his cause would be doomed without the Intercolonial Railway, "for it is almost impossible that so great an enterprise [as the Intercolonial Railway] should succeed unless it is in the hands of a great central power."[62] Thus Langevin joins his opponents Currie and Dorion in acknowledging, albeit for very different reasons, the close link between the proposed railroad and Confederation itself. In the passage just cited, however, Langevin seems to reverse Lord Durham's timetable because he envisions Confederation ("a great central power") preceding the railroad. Langevin's priorities differ sharply from those of his fellow Confederationist A.M. Smith who, rather surprisingly, concedes that "as a commercial undertaking, the Intercolonial Railway presents no attraction." He then adds, however, that "for the establishing of those intimate social and commercial relations indispensable to political unity between ourselves and the sister provinces, the railway is a necessity."[63]

Although there are many variations on the theme, the theme itself is clear and unambiguous.[64] Regardless of how they might differ on the merits of the Quebec Resolutions, the men of 1865 were at one in seeing a close connection between Confederation and the great public enterprise of the Intercolonial Railway. That is, they found in railroads, the "high tech" of their day, a path to meaningful compromise that created a great nation. Today there is no dearth of technological innovation; it is the hallmark of our time. Perhaps some bright statesmen in Quebec City or Ottawa will seize upon it to restore that nation.

THE IMAGE OF THE UNITED STATES IN THE CONFEDERATION DEBATES

The United States has played a muted role throughout the present constitutional crisis of its neighbor to the north. The official position of the U.S. government has been to encourage Canadians of all stripes to patch up their differences, while it maintains a low profile to avoid aggravating a situation that is already volatile enough. Some attention has been given to the likely impact of an independent Quebec upon the North American Free Trade Agreement, but this question tends to be readily subsumed under the larger question of the economic viability of Quebec as a nation in its own right. Howard Galganov, an outspoken defender of Anglophone rights in Quebec, had little to show for his ill-advised trip to Wall Street to discourage American investment in his province because of its language policies. Traditional trade disputes between Canada and the United States continue apace, but this is simply business as usual with little relevance to Quebec's claims of sovereignty.

This subdued role contrasts sharply with the dark shadow cast by the United States upon the Confederation debates of 1865 which took place during the closing months of the American Civil War. One of the major arguments for Confederation was the need to prepare for a possible attack from the United States once the war was over. Canadian statesmen of all persuasions knew that the government of the United States was greatly displeased with the sympathetic position of the British Empire toward the southern states throughout the war. Several minor but exceedingly unpleasant border skirmishes had not escaped the attention of thoughtful Canadians. The record of the debates reveals a serious concern that the victorious Union armies might soon invade Canada to settle some scores with the British Empire and even to annex certain sections of British North America.

American influence on the Confederation debates was not limited to the fear of armed invasion. American ideas and institutions made their mark as well. Although the Confederation fathers outbid one another in condemning American republicanism, the republican Constitution of the United States fared better at their hands, playing, as it were, to mixed reviews, while top billing was reserved for the framers of the American Constitution. Let us examine more closely how the Confederation fathers regarded these three crucial elements of the American founding: republicanism, the constitutional text, and the authors of that text.

We have already had occasion to note the pervasive commitment to monarchy among the participants in the Confederation debates. Consequently, their pejorative references to American republicanism come as no surprise, being simply the opposite side of the monarchist coin. Thus Benjamin Seymour can refer to "all the wild republican theories of our neighbor," while Philip Moore rejects the proposed constitution because "the engrafting of this system of government upon the British Constitution has a tendency to at least introduce the republican system."[65] Alexander Vidal, one of the few Confederationists who favored referring the proposed text to the people, warned his fellow Confederationists that "I am not to be deterred from expressing my views by the taunt of republicanism."[66] J.O. Bureau, an opponent of Confederation, professed to detect "republican sentiments" among members of the government who had introduced the Quebec Resolutions, whereas Colonel Frederick Haultain, a staunch Confederationist, suspected some of his opponents of being "men with annexation tendencies . . . who are inclined toward republican institutions."[67] Thus, both friends and foes of Confederation used republicanism as a club to beat their opponents. At times American republicanism was identified with democracy, as when David Macpherson predicted that failure to approve the Confederation plan would put Canada on an inclined plane leading inevitably to its incorporation into the American union. Canadians would find themselves "plunged into a malstrom [sic] of debt, democracy and demagogism." To which his listeners shouted "Hear, Hear."[68]

The American Constitution itself fared better at the hands of the Confederation fathers than the republican principles that underlay it. For every John Sanborn labeling it as "that horror of our constitution-makers," there was a David Christie ready to celebrate "the wonderful fabric of the American constitution."[69] As noted above, John A. Macdonald took the lead in singling out the decision to leave residual power with the states as the great flaw in the constitution of the United States. Learning from this American mistake, the Confederationists proposed to confer on the "General Parliament" the sweeping power "to make Laws for the peace, welfare and good government of the Federated Provinces"—the forerunner of the POGG clause of the BNA Act. Although Macdonald was unrelenting in condemning this fundamental flaw in the American Constitution, he also found in it much to admire. At the very outset of the Confederation debates, he made it clear that he would not follow "the fashion to enlarge on the defects of the Constitution of the United States," adding that he was "not one of those who look upon it as a failure." On the contrary, he considered it "one of the most skillful works which human intelligence ever created" and "one of the most perfect organizations that ever governed a free people." To recognize "that it has some defects is but to say that it is not the work of Omniscience, but of human intellects." Canadians are "happily situated in having had the opportunity of watching its operation, seeing its working from its infancy till now." Consequently, "we can now take advantage of the experience of the last seventy-eight years, during which that Constitution has existed, and I am strongly of the belief that we have, in a great measure, avoided in this system which we propose for the adoption of the people of Canada, the defects which time and events have shown to exist in the American Constitution."[70] This is a rather generous assessment, coming as it did near the end of the fourth year of the dreadful civil war fought to preserve the Constitution of the United States.

Not everyone agreed with Macdonald's analysis that the tragic flaw in the American Constitution lay in its defective federalism, which failed to give adequate power to the national government. Leonidas Burwell found no fault with American federalism. Indeed, he thought that "as a principle of free government it has been successful" and he doubted "whether history records a like example, under ordinary circumstances, of such great success and prosperity." For Burwell, the failure to come to terms with slavery was the great American tragedy. Slavery "was the cause of the war. It was opposed to the spirit of the age and had to be eradicated."[71] David Christie echoed Burwell's sentiments. The American Constitution "has stood many rude tests and but for the existence . . . of an element in direct antagonism to the whole genius of their system — negro slavery — the Constitution would have continued to withstand — yes, and after the extinction of that element, will continue to withstand — all the artillery which their own or foreign depotism can array against it."[72]

For the most part, references to the Constitution of the United States came in general statements on its spirit and institutions with little attention to specific textual provisions. There were some interesting exceptions, however. The partial veto of the American president over acts of Congress struck anticonfederationist Philip Moore as an attractive alternative to Parliament's power of disallowance over provincial legislation.[73] J.B.E. Dorion praised the complex procedure Americans required for constitutional change and contrasted it pointedly with the willingness of the Confederationists to adopt the Quebec Resolutions by a simple act of the Canadian Parliament with no recourse to the people.[74] John A. Macdonald cited the proposal in the Quebec Resolutions to subject criminal offenses to federal jurisdiction as a marked improvement over the American constitutional practice of leaving such matters to the states.[75] On the other hand, in a somewhat confused reference to the contracts clause — that is, the clause in the American Constitution which forbids states from impairing the obligation of contracts — John Sanborn lauded the Americans for providing greater protection for property against state governments than the Quebec Resolutions offered against provincial governments.[76]

Despite its republican foundations, the Constitution of the United States received, on balance, rather high marks from the monarchist Canadian Parliamentarians of 1865. The rave reviews, however, were saved for the framers of the American Constitution and appeared in such statements as Joseph Cachon's reference to "the illustrious founders of the Union" and Isaac Bowman's salute to the American founding fathers as "some of the wisest and ablest statesmen."[77] Even when George-Etienne Cartier condemns George Washington's "insidious offer" to Quebeckers to join the American Revolution, the context makes clear that the target of his contempt is the offer itself but not the man from whom it issued.[78] The most remarkable encomium, however, came from John Ross, who suggested that opponents of Confederation might overcome their narrow provincialism if they would take the trouble to "read the debates which preceded the establishment of the American Constitution." He singled out the debates in Virginia, "which at that time, by reason of its wealth and population, bore a similar relation to the other colonies to that which Canada now bears to the Lower Provinces." By reading the great speeches of "the Madisons, the Marshalls, the Randolphs, the Henrys, the Lees and others," opponents of Confederation would see that "those great patriots," setting aside the small-village feelings and animosities tending to embarrass and to destroy harmony, "acted like great men, true and noble men as they were, and applied themselves to their task with the purpose of bringing it to a successful issue."[79]

In view of the high esteem in which the Confederation fathers held the framers of the American Constitution, it seems fitting that we examine the extent to which they used ideas, strategies, and arguments similar to those employed by their American predecessors. Here we meet at once an embarrassment of riches. The founding fathers in both countries:

- insisted that the time for constitutional reform was "now or never," with the Americans threatening the grim spectre of civil war or foreign invasion and the Canadians the inevitable slide down the inclined plane leading to annexation to or conquest by the United States;[80]
- maintained that the new constitution would provide better public administration;[81]
- congratulated their fellow citizens on having the rare opportunity to choose their destiny freely;[82]
- answered arguments from their opponents to the effect that enhanced military readiness would provoke attacks from potential enemies;[83]
- endured severe attacks from their opponents on alleged procedural irregularities and out-right illegalities in their innovations;[84] and
- weighed the merits of invoking divine intervention on behalf of their efforts.[85]

Although the topics from which to choose are many and varied, I shall develop only one of them here: the constructive use of ambition by statesmen. Perhaps the most famous line in American political science appears in *Federalist 51*, where James Madison looks to the ambition of statesmen to safeguard the cardinal constitutional principle of separation of powers. Although the Canadian Confederation is not grounded in the principle of separation of powers, the broader implications of the creative possibilities of political ambition were not lost on the Confederation fathers. In his opening address to the Legislative Assembly, John A. Macdonald suggested that Confederation would enhance the prestige of Canada to such an extent that the representative of Queen Victoria in Canada would always be a man of the highest quality, perhaps even "one of her own family, a Royal Prince." Although Canadians could put no restrictions on Her Majesty's prerogative to appoint whomever she wished, he added that once Confederation is in place, "it will be an object worthy of the ambition of the statesmen of England to be charged with presiding over our destinies."[86]

Canadian statesmen would also feel the attraction of ambition once they have a broader political field for their actions. Lord Durham had anticipated this development when he wrote that the union he envisioned in 1839 "would elevate and gratify the hopes of able and aspiring men. They would no longer look with envy and wonder at the great arena of the bordering Federation, but see the means of satisfying every legitimate ambition in the high office of the judicature and executive government of their own union."[87] Charles Alleyn echoed Lord Durham's sentiments when he predicted that with Confederation a "worthy field will be opened for the ambition of our young men and our politicians will have a future before them, and may fairly aspire to the standing and rewards of statesmen. (Cheers.)"[88]

The release of creative energy occasioned by Confederation was felt as far away as British Columbia. Although British Columbia was not a party to the Quebec Resolutions, many people in that part of British North America felt — correctly as it turned out — that the proposed Confederation would soon include them as well. Hector-Louis Langevin read aloud an edito-rial from a British Columbia newspaper, which included the following consideration among the advantages of Confederation:

> Instead of seeing the talent of our statesmen fettered, harassed and restrained within the narrow limits of local politics, we shall find its scope extended to a whole continent, while a more vast and more natural field will be thrown open to the active and enterprising spirit of the North American Provinces.[89]

Participants in the Confederation debates felt that the seriousness of the topic under consideration was bringing out the best in them. Colonel Arthur Rankin allowed that "it is to me a matter of congratulation to observe that, at last, something has arisen which has given a higher tone to the debates in this House, and to the utterances of our public men." He attributed this improvement "to the fact that we are discussing a question of greater importance than has ever before been brought under our consideration." Finally, he added, the Legislative Assembly has turned its attention "to something worthy of the consideration of gentlemen who aspire to establish for themselves the reputation of statesmen."[90]

In a remarkably eloquent address, Thomas D'Arcy McGee celebrated the capacity of the Confederation question to elevate the tone of public life throughout British North America. "The provincial mind, it would seem, under the inspiration of a great question, leaped at a single bound out of the slough of mere mercenary struggle for office, and took post on the high and honorable ground from which alone this great subject can be taken in all its dimensions." He congratulated the "various authors and writers" on Confederation because they seem "to be speaking or writing as if in the visible presence of all the colonies." No longer are such public men merely "hole-and-corner celebrities." They now write and speak as though "their words will be scanned and weighed afar off as well as at home." He was pleased to observe that "many men now speak with a dignity and carefulness which formerly did not characterize them, when they were watched only by their own narrow and struggling section, and weighed only according to a stunted local standard." He hoped that the proposed Confederation would "supply to all our public men just ground for uniting in nobler and more profitable contests than those which have signalized the past."[91] Thomas D'Arcy McGee's high-minded sentiments challenge serious statesmen on both sides of today's Quebec separation issue to maintain a level of public argument worthy of their subject. The subject itself merits the best efforts of ambitious men and women, for on one side there is the creative exhilaration of founding a new nation and on the other the patriotic duty of saving an old one.

CONCLUSION

To conclude this article, I shall revisit John Ross's extraordinary advice to his fellow legislative councilors that they read the Virginia debates on the ratification of the Constitution of the United States. He mentioned specifically James Madison, John Marshall, Edmund Randolph, Patrick Henry, and Richard Henry Lee. Anyone who followed Ross's advice might have been surprised to discover that two of these five men, Henry and Lee, opposed ratification of the Constitution and a third, Edmund Randolph, somewhat characteristically, straddled the issue by refusing to sign it as a delegate to the Constitutional Convention in Philadelphia and then reluctantly supporting it during the crucial debates in Richmond. Henry, Lee, and, to a lesser extent, Randolph were "Anti-Federalists"; that is, they formed part of the broad, articulate, and very able opposition to the proposed constitution. Like most backers of losing causes, the Anti-Federalists were not treated kindly by history.[92] This began to change, however, as Americans prepared to celebrate the bicentennial of their constitution in 1987. Thanks to the prodigious scholarly efforts of Herbert J. Storing, the writings and speeches of the Anti-Federalists were compiled in a seven-volume work entitled *The Complete Anti-Federalist*.[93] Storing made a powerful argument that the Anti-Federalists should be included among the founding fathers of the Republic even though they opposed the Constitution that still governs that Republic. His reason was that they contributed substantially to "the dialogue of the American founding." That is, the Constitution of the United States was a product of a great public argument, as befits the origins of a free society, and the Anti-Federalists formed an essential, though ultimately unsuccessful, part of that founding argument. Today American constitutional scholars take the Anti-Federalists far more seriously than they did just two decades ago, crediting them with initiating the movement for the Bill of Rights and for pointing out serious flaws in the Constitution that are still with us today. Contemporary Americans familiar with the Anti-Federalist literature bring a much richer understanding to their country's constitutional problems than those unfamiliar with it.

I am not prepared to repeat Ross's advice today; but, in the spirit of his comments, I shall take the liberty of urging contemporary Canadians to familiarize themselves not with the Virginia statesmen of 1788, but with their own Canadian statesmen of 1865, including those who opposed Confederation — the Canadian version of the American Anti-Federalists. Etienne Taché urged those "honorable members" of the Legislative Council "who objected to any particular measure" to make their objections part of the record "and so secure the advantage of placing their views before the country."[94] The "honorable members" were not bashful about airing their dissenting views nor were the members of the Legislative Assembly. Perceptive contemporary statesmen may find in these anticonfederationist arguments considerable insight into the flaws of Canadian federalism. The same holds for the arguments of many of those Quebeckers who supported Confederation but did so with a far more guarded interpretation of the extent of federal power over the provinces than a literal reading of the Confederation text would suggest. Here they will find Canadian public argument at its best.[95]

Robert Vipond surely had it right when he said that the Confederation debates of 1865 lack the depth of the American debates of 1787–88. Events did not force the Canadians of 1865 to examine "first political principles" as they did for the Americans who had recently emerged from a revolution that had made a definitive "self-conscious break with the past."[96] Consequently, when compared with their American counterparts, the Canadian debates may seem forbidding, burdened as they are with admittedly tedious discussions on how to finance railroads, canals, and other public works. But in this very tedium, with its meticulous attention to exquisite administrative detail, contemporary Canadians may learn something about themselves and what their history tells them of how they go about solving their problems, even problems of the highest questions of state such as those that Quebec asks today.

NOTES

The research for this article was made possible through generous support from the Canadian Studies Research Grant Program of the Canadian Embassy in Washington. I am particularly grateful to Ms. Judy Meyer, Chief Librarian at the Embassy, and her competent staff for their gracious help and encouragement.

1. John A. Rohr, *To Run a Constitution: The Legitimacy of the Administrative State* (Lawrence, KS: University Press of Kansas, 1986); John A. Rohr, *Founding Republics in France and America: A Study in Constitutional Governance* (Lawrence, KS: University Press of Kansas, 1995).
2. Hannah Arendt, *On Revolution* (New York: Viking Press, 1963), 214.
3. Unfortunately, the records of the Quebec Conference of October 1864 are fragmentary at best. See A.G. Doughty, "Notes on the Quebec Conference, 1864," *Canadian Historical Review* (March 1926): 26–47. For informative accounts of what is known about this conference, see Donald Creighton, *The Road to Confederation: The Emergence of Canada, 1863–1867* (Toronto: Macmillan, 1964), chapters 5–6; W.L. Morton, *The Critical Years: The Union of British North America, 1857–1873* (Toronto: McClelland and Stewart, 1964), 155–162; Robert Rumilly, *Histoire de la Province de Quebec*, 2 vols. (Montreal: Editions Bernard Valiquette, 1940), 22–26; P.B. Waite, *The Life & Times of Confederation 1864–1867* (Toronto: University of Toronto Press, 1962), chapter 7.
4. *Parliamentary Debates on the Subject of the Confederation of the British North American Provinces*, 3d Session, 8th Provincial Parliament of Canada (Quebec: Hunter, Rose & Co., 1865). Hereafter *Debates*. In referencing

the *Debates*, I will give the page or pages and, where appropriate, I will also insert parenthetically the numbers 1 or 2 and the letters a, b, and c to indicate the column from which the citation was taken and its position within the column. Thus (2c) means the text cited can be found in the lowest third of the second column; (1a) means the top third of the first column; (1b) the middle third of the first column, etc.

5. The wording of the referendum text was a new economic and political partnership within the scope of the Bill respecting the future of Quebec and of the agreement signed on June 12, 1995?"

6. Peter H. Russell, Rainer Knopff, and Ted Morton, *Federalism and the Charter: Leading Constitutional Decisions* (Ottawa: Carleton University Press, 1993), 38. The statement remains true today despite the recent decision of the Supreme Court of the United States in *U.S. v. Lopez* 115 S. Ct. 1624 (1995).

7. Richard Risk, "The Scholars and the Constitution: P.O.G.G. and the Privy Council," *Manitoba Law Journal* 23 (1996): 509.

8. The story is told with admirable clarity in Robert P. Vipond, *Liberty and Community: Canadian Federalism and the Failure of the Constitution* (Albany: SUNY Press, 1991), chapter 2.

9. Risk, 500–501, citing *Board of Commerce Reference* [1922] 1 A.C. 191 at 197–8 and *Fort Frances Pulp and Power v. Manitoba Free Press* [1923] A.C. 696 at 703 and 704.

10. The differences between the two texts can be traced to a conference in London where certain changes were introduced into the text approved in the colonies to meet objections from the mother country. See Donald Creighton, *The Road to Confederation*, chapter 14.

11. *Debates*, 33(2b.) For further development of this theme by John A. Macdonald, see pages 40(1c)–42(2c).

12. Ibid., 807(2b).

13. Ibid., 818(1c).

14. Ibid., 823(1b).

15. Ibid., 911(2a).

16. For examples of statements supporting legislative union, see ibid., 75(2); 425(1a); 465(1a); 749(2c); 806(2c); 818(2c); 918(1a); 976(2).

17. Ibid., 9(2c).

18. Ibid., 55(1b).

19. Ibid., 373(1a).

20. Ibid., 702(2b).

21. Resolution 29.

22. For a discussion of the Confederationists' studied efforts to avoid clarifying jurisdictional questions, see Vipond, chapter 2.

23. *Debates*, 859(2a).

24. Ibid., 623(2b).

25. Ibid., 689(2c). For similar statements, see 690 and 176(1c–2b).

26. Peter H. Russell, *Constitutional Odyssey: Can Canadians Become a Sovereign People?* 2nd ed. (Toronto: Univ. of Toronto Press, 1993), 1.

27. Ibid., 2.

28. *Debates*, 797(2b).

29. Ibid., 864(1a).

30. Ibid, 985 (1b).

31. See, for example, 12(2c); 120(1b); 277(2b); 733(2a); 883(1b); 894(2c); 934(1b).

32. See Creighton, 246–252.

33. *Debates*, 77(2c.) For similar statements, see 471(2)–472(1); 579(2c); and 1004.

34. *Debates*, 330(1b).

35. Ibid., 269(1b).

36. Ibid., 292(2c).

37. Ibid., 295(1c–2a). Currie's proposal was received favorably by some supporters of the Quebec Resolutions. See the remarks of Alexander Vidal and Walter Dickson, *Debates*, 284–290 and 301–309.

38. Ibid., 11(2c). For another statement anticipating a later appeal to the people, see *Debates*, 840(2b).

39. Ibid., 962(2c).

40. Ibid., 1019(2b).

41. Ibid., 327(2b,) 769–770, 990(1b,) 110–115 *passim*, 432(1c), 765(2a), 809(1 c), 888(1), 891(2c), 995(2b).

42. "PM Eyes Way to Improve Federation," *Toronto Star* (22 November 1995), reprinted in NEWSCAN of 24 November 1995.

43. See especially Premier Bouchard's remarks of 6 December 1995 at Laval in what *L'Actualité* called "*un veritable discours du trône.*" Michel Vestel, "Bouchard l'énigme," *L'Actualité* 21 (février 1996): 17–25 at 20. See also

"A l'écoute du Quebec," *L'Actualité* 21 (1er mars 1996): 13; Jean Pare, "Le Grand theatre de Quebec," *L'Actualité* 21 (1er mai 1996): 8; Jean Chartier, "Plan O: l'opération secrète de Parizeau," *L'Actualité* 21 (1er juin 1996): 11–12; Michel Vastel, "Le Bilan de Fernand Dumont," *L'Actualité* 21 (15 septembre 1996): 86–96; "Lucien Bouchard and the Weekend Psychodrama," *The Globe and Mail* (28 November 1996), reprinted in NEWSCAN of 29 November 1996.)

44. David V.J. Bell, "The Loyalist Tradition in Canada," *Journal of Canadian Studies* 5 (1970): 22–33.

45. For the general statements, see Debates, 30(1c) and 131(2c); on public works, see 366(1a) and 920(1b); on education, see 95(1) and 411 (1b–2b). The discussion of canals was pervasive throughout the debates. To sample some of the main arguments, see 79(1c), 639(1b–2c), 680(2c).

46. Ibid., 69(2), 93(2h), 377(1c)–379, 158(2c)–159, 178(1a), 258(2c)–259, 280(2b), 758(1b), 861(2a), 945(2b)–947(2b).

47. Ibid., 229(2c).

48. Ibid., 979(2a).

49. Ibid., 832(2c).

50. Ibid., 920(2b).

51. Ibid., 17(2h).

52. Ibid., 18(1c).

53. Creighton, 250.

54. Ibid., 250–251.

55. *Debates*, 336(1c) and 430(2c)–431(1a).

56. Ibid., 109(1c), 201(2a), 377–379, 386(2b), 415(2c)–416, 467–469, 512(1b–c), 553, 677(2), 681(2), 693(2)–694(1), 702(1h), 703(1a), 751–757, 762(1c), 791, 812–814, 901(1a).

57. Debates, 77(1 a).

58. Ibid., 790(1h).

59. French Canadians have tended to look upon Durham as an unmitigated racist with nothing but contempt for the French way of life in British North America. For a convincing statement of a more generous interpretation, see Janet Ajzenstat, *The Political Thought of Lord Durham* (Montreal/Kingston: McGill-Queen's University Press, 1988). For examples of French Canadian resentment of Lord Durham, see 789, 844(1h), 850(2b)–852(2b); for a defense of Lord Durham, see 908(1c)–910(1a).

60. *Debates*, 52(1b).

61. Ibid., 251(2a).

62. Ibid., 356(2a).

63. Ibid., 901(2c).

64. For other statements linking railroads to confederation, see 896(1a), 227(1a), 132(2a), 297(1b).

65. Ibid., 205(1b) and 228(2c).

66. Ibid., 304(1b).

67. Ibid., 190(1a) and 636(1a).

68. Ibid., 152(1b). The "inclined plane" metaphor was originally introduced by Etienne Taché at the very beginning of the debate in the Legislative Council and became a standard rhetorical weapon of the confederationists throughout the debates. See *Debates*, 6(1c), 343(1a), 82(2b), 152(2b), 155(2a), 206(2a), 325(1c), 326(1c), 332, 342(2c), 741(2c), 746(2b), 826(1a). The metaphor was rejected as inappropriate at 46(1b) and 60(1c). For examples of antirepublican statements in addition to those provided in the text, see 129(2b), 143(1b), 189(2c), 209(2b), 241(2c)–242(1a), 288(1a).

69. Ibid., 122(2b) and 219(2c).

70. Ibid., 32(2c). Macdonald's assessment of the constitution was echoed by Thomas D'Arcy McGee; see *Debates*, 145(1b).

71. Ibid., 446(2a–b).

72. Ibid., 212(1c).

73. Ibid., 238(2c).

74. Ibid., 228(2c)–229(1a). Dorion does not have the American system for amending the constitution quite right, but his description is close enough to support the point he was making when he introduced it into the debates.

75. Ibid., 41(1).

76. Ibid., 123(1c). Sanborn correctly refers to "the celebrated Dartmouth College decision in which Webster so distinguished himself." He mistakenly states that the case turned on a clause in the Constitution of the United States "provides that no law could be passed which would affect the rights of property." The case actually involved the clause in the tenth section of the first article, which prohibits the states from passing laws "impairing the Obligation of Contracts."

77. Ibid., 565(2b) and 804(2b).
78. Ibid., 57(2c).
79. Ibid., 74(1b).
80. For the origins of the inclined Plane metaphor, see the remarks of Etienne Taché at 152 (1h). For examples of the use of the "now or never" argument at the time of the founding of the American Republic, see Rohr, *Founding Republics*, 184–189.
81. *Debates*, 30(1c) and 131(2c); for the American position on this point, see Rohr, *To Run a Constitution*, 1–3.
82. *Debates*, 363(1c); Federalist 1.
83. *Debates*, 621(2a); John A. Rohr, "Constitutional Foundations of the United States Navy: Text and Context," *Naval War College Review* 45 (1992): 68–83.
84. *Debates*, 704(16), 705(1b), 857(1b); Forrest MacDonald, *Novus Ordo Seclorum: The Intellectual Origins of the Constitution* (Lawrence, KS: University Press of Kansas, 1985), 279–284.
85. *Debates*, 648(1a); on Benjamin Franklin's call for prayer at the convention, see Max Farrand, ed., *The Records of the Federal Convention of 1787*, 4 vols. (New Haven: Yale University Press, 1966), 1, 450–452.
86. *Debates*, 34(2a).
87. Ibid., 790(2a), where Lord Durham's *Report* was quoted.
88. Ibid., 672(1a).
89. Ibid., 381(lc).
90. Ibid., 913(1a).
91. Ibid., 128.
92. Lee and Henry are, of course, revered for their outstanding contribution to the Revolution, but few Americans are aware of their opposition to the Constitution.
93. Herbert J. Storing, ed., *The Complete Anti-Federalist*, 7 vols. (Chicago: University of Chicago Press, 1981). See also Jackson Turner Main, *The Anti-Federalists: Critics of the Constitution 1781–1788* (New York: Norton, 1961).
94. *Debates*, 83(1c–2a).
95. If there is any merit in my suggestion, the first practical step toward implementing it might well be to bring the Confederation debates back into print. At present, it is very difficult to purchase a copy of the complete text either in English or in French.
96. Vipond, 20.

Article Eighteen

Was Canada Meant to Be a Democracy?

Paul Romney

Canadian law does not permit a province to secede unilaterally, even with the clearest mandate from the province's voters. That was the Supreme Court's conclusion in the *Quebec Secession Reference* of 1998. In reply to a federal government query, posed in the wake of the 1995 sovereignty referendum, the court decided that Quebec's secession would amount to an amendment of the Canadian constitution and would therefore require the agreement of Ottawa and the other provinces.

The Canadian constitution says nothing about a province's right to secede, so the court had to base its decision on the fundamental principles of the constitution. But this was not as easy as you might think. What are those principles? Since its amendment in 1982, the constitution has declared that "Canada is founded upon principles that recognize the supremacy of

Source: Paul Romney, "Was Canada Meant to Be a Democracy?" *The Beaver* (April/May 2000): 6–7. By permission of the author.

God and the rule of law." But it doesn't say outright what those principles are, though you can infer them from the Charter of Rights and Freedoms. That, though, is a modern document. Canada's original charter (the British North America Act, which some now call the Constitution Act, 1867) is even more reticent. It merely notes the desire of the colonies concerned to be "federally united . . . with a constitution similar in principle to that of the United Kingdom."

Accordingly, the court based its decision on four unwritten constitutional principles, which it detected in the history of Canada and its founding. They were federalism, democracy, respect for minority rights, and, finally, "constitutionalism and the rule of law." Though unwritten, except for those vague allusions in the British North America Act, "it would be impossible to conceive of our constitutional structure without them."

Few Canadians today would deny the fundamental importance of these principles. But are they as deeply entrenched in Canada's past as the Supreme Court says? In some respects, the judges' opinion is surprising, to say the least.

Take what they say about democracy. "The principle of democracy has always informed the design of our constitutional structure," they tell us. It "can best be understood as a sort of baseline against which the framers of our Constitution, and subsequently, our elected representatives under it, have always operated. It is perhaps for this reason that the principle was not explicitly identified in the text of the Constitution Act, 1867 itself. To have done so might have appeared redundant, even silly, to the framers."

Well, there is no need for the Supreme Court or anyone else to speculate on the framers' failure to identify democracy as a fundamental principle. Leading founders had plenty to say about democracy, in the legislature and elsewhere, and it's clear that they simply didn't like it. It stood for everything that they abhorred about the United States and were trying to avoid in designing their own federation. As George-Étienne Cartier, the leading French-Canadian advocate of Confederation, put it, in the U.S. "the ruling power was the will of the mob, the rule of the populace." Universal suffrage had caused mob rule to supplant legitimate authority, resulting in anarchy and civil war. Cartier promised that Confederation would not repeat the American error. Its object was to perpetuate constitutional monarchy, and the British values it stood for, in North America.

John A. Macdonald dwelt on one virtue of the British system in particular: "In all countries the rights of the majority take care of themselves, but it is only in countries like England, enjoying constitutional liberty, and safe from the tyranny of a single despot or an unbridled democracy, that the rights of minorities are regarded." Richard John Cartwright, scion of a leading Loyalist family from Macdonald's hometown of Kingston, saw democracy as the chief peril to liberty in North America: "Our chiefest care must be to train the majority to respect the rights of the minority, to prevent the claims of the few from being trampled under foot by the caprice or passion of the many. For myself, sir, I own frankly that I prefer British liberty to American equality. I had rather uphold the majesty of the law than the majesty of Judge Lynch."

Fear of the majority inspired several features of the scheme of union. It was invoked to justify an appointed rather than an elected senate. It lay behind the various safeguards for minority languages and educational institutions — safeguards that, in the 1870s, were reproduced in the Manitoba Act and the North-West Territories Act. In a sense, it underlay Confederation itself. Macdonald could not deny French Canadians' concern to reestablish Lower Canada — their ancestral homeland — as an institutional bulwark against the growing anglophone majority. That was one reason why the British North American union had to be federal, with political authority divided between a central government and individual provinces, despite the discredit brought on federalism by the American Civil War. And (as Macdonald also noted) the Atlantic provinces, fearful of life as tiny minorities alongside the Canadian leviathan, also insisted on federal union, although Charles Tupper and some other leading Nova Scotians preferred a completely centralized union.

But when Macdonald and Cartwright extolled the virtues of "British" or "constitutional" liberty, they almost certainly had a different sort of minority in mind. As Macdonald told the Quebec Conference of 1864, which laid the basis of union, "the rights of the minority ought to be protected, and the rich are always fewer in number than the poor."

In the British tradition, *liberty* meant, first and foremost, freedom from arbitrary imprisonment or confiscation by the Crown. By the 1860s, though, the propertied classes controlled the state. They no longer feared the Crown but the people. In Britain itself, property was protected from the people by means of a strong executive, a hereditary House of Lords, and a voting system that disqualified "the poor." But the North American colonies had no hereditary aristocracy and a broader franchise. "British liberty" Canadian-style meant limiting the role of this broader electorate. It would elect representatives to the lower house of the legislature, but the upper house would be appointed by the Crown. There was no question of American-style referendum and recall, or of electing judges.

But fear of the majority did not mean that democracy had *no* place in the constitution. When British American politicians denounced it, they were usually speaking of it as a dominant principle, as in the United States. Macdonald juxtaposed "constitutional liberty" to *unbridled* democracy. Cartier condemned the U.S. system as one of *purely* democratic institutions marred by universal suffrage. A Lower Canadian legislator, Thomas Ryan, quoted a new book on representative government by the British radical thinker John Stuart Mill, who advised "that there should be in every polity a centre of resistance to the predominant power in the constitution — and in a democratic constitution, therefore, a nucleus of resistance to the democracy." That was why the upper house had to be appointed and not elected.

No British North American, however conservative, could deny democracy a place in the political order. True, universal suffrage was not the rule. Nova Scotia had universal male suffrage between 1854 and 1863, and Prince Edward Island also had it virtually, though not explicitly, but women were disqualified either by custom or by law, and there was normally a property qualification in the British style. In North America, though, the property qualification was much less exclusive than in Britain, because the distribution of wealth was much less uneven. Most small farmers had the vote, and many ordinary townspeople too. (Among voters in the Toronto election of 1836, the largest single occupational group was "labourer.")

The fact is that democracy didn't necessarily mean universal suffrage and certainly not female suffrage — women didn't normally vote in the United States either. Democracy means "rule by the people," and in mainly rural societies, like those of British North America in the 1860s, a system that enfranchised most farm owners and small businessmen was at least partly democratic, though admittedly it was a patriarchal sort of democracy.

Indeed, Reformers — self-styled friends of the people who had organized in reaction to Tory domination — tended to see universal suffrage as an antidemocratic institution, which diluted the power of the people. Rapid immigration was inundating British North America with newcomers, most of them impoverished and nearly all of them ignorant of the struggles by which the people of the various colonies were trying to assert their right to control colonial politics. To most Reformers, these newcomers were not part of "the people" — though British, they were aliens. Their poverty made them easily bribable by the embattled colonial elites (as in Britain, voting was done in public, not by secret ballot), and their ignorance rendered them susceptible to demagogic denunciations of the Reformers themselves as "disloyal." In Canada in the 1830s and 1840s, hyper-loyalist Irish Protestants organized in Orange lodges lustily opposed the campaign for Responsible Government. In Nova Scotia it was a Conservative government that introduced manhood suffrage and a Reform government that abolished it nine years later.

So democracy did not mean in 1860s everything it does today, but such as it was it had a place in British American politics, and Canada's founders undoubtedly expected it to have a place in the politics of the new Dominion. It was not, however, as the Supreme Court calls it, a principle that "informed the design of our constitutional structure." To men like Cartier and Macdonald, Cartwright and Ryan, in fact, it was not a principle at all. The informing principle was *representative government*, about which the founding charter had plenty to say. Democracy was merely a condition — a necessary condition of representative government in the egalitarian societies of North America. It was not a good but an unavoidable evil, and they did what they could to keep it in its place.

Topic Eight

The North-West Rebellion of 1885

Louis Riel addresses the jury during his trial in Regina in July 1885.

Few issues in Canadian history have generated more heated debate than the North-West Rebellion of 1885. For a long time, the debate centred on the main protagonist, Louis Riel, the ill-fated leader of both the Métis resistance of 1869/70 and the rebellion of 1885. To what extent was he alone responsible for the North-West Rebellion of 1885? Should he be seen as a rebel leader or as a mere victim of circumstances? Did he represent cultural, linguistic, or regional interests?

More recently, Canadian historians have shifted their focus from Riel to his followers. Moving away from the "Great Man Theory of History," these historians have been more interested in ascertaining why certain Métis and a small number of First Nations individuals followed Riel while others did not than in explaining why Riel led them into rebellion. They also try to discover whether Riel's followers represented particular interest groups in their respective communities.

The following two articles reflect this new historiographical trend. In "The Métis Militant Rebels of 1885," David Lee examines the cultural background of the most radical of the Métis participants in the rebellion. He shows that a correlation existed between the militancy of these individuals and their livelihood, language, age, and social outlook. A. Blair Stonechild presents a First Nations' view of the rebellion in "The Indian View of the 1885 Uprising." He emphasizes the difficulty in reconstructing a First Nations' perspective on account of the lack of traditional written sources. What Stonechild uses instead are oral histories and stories to present a refreshingly new, Native-oriented explanation for why some First Nations communities joined the rebellion while the majority did not. He maintains that to a large extent the First Nations were forced into the conflict as a result of misunderstanding on the part of Métis leaders in the region, prejudice on the part of the white settlers and military leaders, and the sinister intent of the Canadian government.

The literature on Riel and the Métis is extensive. For a concise overview of the history and culture of the Métis, see D.B. Sealey and A.S. Lussier's *The Métis: Canada's Forgotten People* (Winnipeg: Métis Federation Press, 1975). A growing literature exists on Louis Riel and the Métis in 1869–70 and 1885. The five-volume *Collected Writings of Louis Riel/Les Écrits complets de Louis Riel* (Edmonton: University of Alberta Press, 1985), under the general editorship of George F.G. Stanley, is currently available. Secondary studies include G.F.G. Stanley's *The Birth of Western Canada: A History of the Riel Rebellion* (Toronto: University of Toronto Press, 1961 [1936]); Thomas Flanagan's *Louis "David" Riel: "Prophet of the New World,"* rev. ed. (Toronto: University of Toronto Press, 1996); H. Bowsfield's *Louis Riel: The Rebel and the Hero* (Toronto: Oxford University Press, 1971) and his edited collection, *Louis Riel: Selected Readings* (Toronto: Copp Clark, 1987); Joseph Kinsey Howard's *Strange Empire* (New York: William Morrow, 1952); and B. Beal and R. Macleod's *Prairie Fire: A History of the 1885 Rebellion* (Edmonton: Hurtig, 1984). Hugh Dempsey presents one First Nations leader's response in *Big Bear* (Vancouver: Douglas and McIntyre, 1984). For a critical view of the Métis position, see T. Flanagan, *Riel and the Rebellion: 1885 Reconsidered* (Saskatoon: Western Producer Books, 1983). An opposite viewpoint is presented in D.N. Sprague, *Canada and the Métis, 1869–1885* (Waterloo: Wilfrid Laurier University Press, 1988).

George F.G. Stanley reviews the various interpretations of Riel in "The Last Word on Louis Riel — The Man of Several Faces," in *1885 and After*, eds. F. Laurie Barron and James B. Waldram (Regina: Canadian Plains Research Centre, 1986), pp. 3–22. A good historiographical article is J.R. Miller's "From Riel to the Métis," *Canadian Historical Review* 69 (March 1988): 1–20. Diane Payment's *"The Free People — Otipemiswak": Batoche, Saskatchewan, 1870–1930* (Ottawa: Canadian Parks Service/National Historic Parks and Sites, 1990) is an in-depth study of the important Métis community of Batoche. In *Views from Fort Battleford: Constructed Visions of an*

Anglo-Canadian West (Regina: Canadian Plains Research Centre, University of Regina, 1994), Walter Hildebrandt discusses aspects of the conflict between the First Nations and the Anglo-Canadians on the Prairies. His *The Battle of Batoche: British Small Warfare and the Entrenched Métis* (Ottawa: National Historic Parks and Sites, Parks Canada, 1985) discusses the military engagement at Batoche. Ramon Hathorn and Patrick Holland have compiled an interesting anthology entitled *Images of Louis Riel in Canadian Culture* (Lewiston, NY: E. Mellen Press, 1992). George Melnyk's *Radical Regionalism* (Edmonton: NeWest Press, 1981) and his edited collection *Riel to Reform: A History of Protest in Western Canada* (Saskatoon: Fifth House Publishers, 1992) examine the roots of Western protest, and its relationship to regional identity. An important study of the Native involvement in the North-West Rebellion is Blair Stonechild and Bill Waiser, *Loyal till Death: Indians and the North-West Rebellion* (Calgary: Fifth House, 1997). For a discussion of the role that women played in the rebellion and in mythologizing white women in the context of the North-West Rebellion, see Sarah Carter, *Capturing Women: The Manipulation of Cultural Imagery in Canada's Prairie West* (Montreal/Kingston: McGill-Queen's University Press, 1997). Hugh Dempsey explains the participation of Big Bear's band in the North-West Rebellion in *Big Bear: The End of Freedom* (Vancouver: Douglas and McIntyre, 1984), as does J.R. Miller in *Big Bear (Mistahimusqua)* (Toronto: ECW Press, 1996).

WEBLINKS

North West Canada Medal

http://www.vac-acc.gc.ca/remembers/sub.cfm?source=collections/cmdp/mainmenu/group03/nwc

The North West Canada Medal was awarded to participants on the side of the Government of Canada in the suppression of the North-West Rebellion.

Virtual Museum of Métis History and Culture

http://www.metismuseum.ca/main.php

This site contains a large number of resources and documents relating to the culture and history of the Métis, including the times of the North West Rebellion.

La Presse

http://www.histori.ca/peace/page.do?subclassName=Document&pageID=295

The response of the Montreal newspaper La Presse in 1885 upon the news of the hanging of Louis Riel. Debates in the House of Commons regarding Riel and the rebellion are also available at this site.

Rethinking Louis Riel

http://archives.cbc.ca/IDD-1-73-1482/politics_economy/louis_riel/

A collection of CBC radio and video footage regarding the controversial status of Louis Riel in contemporary times.

Battle of Fish Creek

http://www.collectionscanada.ca/canadian-west/052920/05292030_e.html

A letter by Thomas Bull, participant in the Battle of Fish Creek, to his father regarding the battle. This document is the first in a series regarding the North-West Rebellion.

Department of Indian Affairs Annual Reports
http://www.collectionscanada.ca/indianaffairs/020010-101.01-e.php

A database of annual reports of the Department of Indian Affairs, covering the years 1864 to 1990.

Article Nineteen

The Métis Militant Rebels of 1885

David Lee

A great avalanche of writing on the North-West Rebellion or "resistance" of 1885 appeared in the decade preceding the centenary of that dramatic event.[1] These studies pursue a variety of themes, theories, and preoccupations, some conflicting with others. Still, the writers generally agreed on the larger picture. They viewed the rebellion of 1885 as a response by the Métis of the Northwest Territories to the trauma of an abrupt and perceivedly baneful change in circumstances. These people, of mixed Indian and French ancestry, futilely attempted (with the assistance of a few Indians) to resist the notion of change by taking up arms. The indicators of change were numerous and inescapable: the disappearance of the buffalo; decline of the fur trade; the supplanting of cart and canoe freighting by rail and steamboat; the prospect of having to live a sedentary, agricultural life; an increasingly interventionist yet dilatory government bureaucracy, slow to act on land entitlements and surveys; and the influx of aggressive immigrants who knew how to use government authority to serve their own interest. Feeling that they were about to lose control over their destiny, the Métis reacted by establishing their own provisional government on the South Saskatchewan River and by taking violent action against agents of the Canadian government.

However, despite the depth and breadth of the avalanche, some parts of the story still remain relatively unexamined. Little has been done, for example, to examine the range of opinion in the Métis community regarding the notion of rebellion, to gauge the degree of support for that course of action, to identify those Métis most militantly committed to taking up arms, or to inquire into their backgrounds.

Thomas Flanagan has written that "probably a strong majority" of the community "accepted" the notion of insurrection.[2] Walter Hildebrandt lists Gabriel Dumont and ten others as the "hardcore" of Louis Riel's followers.[3] However, Louis Schmidt, a Métis who was present during the uprising but did not fight, put the number of highly committed combatants much higher. In his memoirs, he estimated that one-quarter to one-third of the Métis fought "vaillamment" (ardently); the remainder, he recalled, participated only "mollement" (lukewarmly) or not at all, either due to a lack of ammunition or because the idea of "révolte . . . les rend timides."[4] George Woodcock has opined that it was "the wilder" of the Métis who were the most "discontented" and committed to armed insurrection; he estimated the militants to number "at most a few dozen men."[5] Discussion of commitment among the rebels, then, has been rather limited.

Source: "The Métis Militant Rebels of 1885," *Canadian Ethnic Studies* 21, 3 (1989): 1–19. Reprinted by permission.

The study which follows will examine the people of mixed Indian and European ancestry living on the South Saskatchewan River in 1885 and, more specifically, the men who fought in the battles of Duck Lake, Fish Creek, and Batoche in the spring of that year. The study will show that there was a fairly wide spectrum of both political opinion and cultural background within the Métis community. More significantly, it will be seen that the two spectra were almost congruent with one another. It will also show that, while the most militant men in the community were chiefly older and less acculturated, the insurrectionary movement was quite deeply based.

MÉTIS COMMUNITY

As might be expected, the South Saskatchewan Métis were not a fully homogeneous group but rather a community with a variety of internal divisions and tensions, both political and cultural. At one end of the cultural spectrum were a small number of Métis who, through education or perhaps solely ambition, were well on their way to acculturation; that is, they were adjusting their lifestyles to meet the demands of an increasingly intrusive Euro-Canadian society. Some of these people were active in commerce while a few held salaried, government positions. At the other end of this spectrum were Métis who (though they considered themselves distinct from, and sometimes even superior to, Indians) were, in many ways, close to the Plains Cree and Saulteaux in culture; these people were not receptive to the ways of the powerful newcomers. They were unable or unwilling to abruptly take up such new endeavours as agriculture, animal husbandry, technical crafts, or retail trade, for example. The reasons could have been lack of confidence, incentive, capital, aptitude, or education, but may also have included satisfaction and pride in their traditional lifeways. These more conservative, or "more Indian," Métis would, for example, have been far more at ease in a tent on the Plains than in a house at Prince Albert or Saskatoon. As will be seen, they were often not much different from many so-called "Treaty Indians" living on nearby reserves. With regard to the community's political attitudes, i.e., its feelings regarding the notion of insurrection, the spectrum ranged from militancy through moderation to opposition. More significantly, it will be seen that the most militant proponents of rebellion can be largely characterized as conservatives while opponents were among the most acculturated in the community.

The evidence presented in this study involves a consideration of the background, age, livelihood, religion, social structure, and language of the South Saskatchewan River Métis. The evidence is scattered, fragmented, and usually nonquantifiable, but it is nevertheless revealing in the aggregate. Before proceeding any further, two questions, both of definition, must be resolved.

The most obvious question is, if the Métis exhibited such a wide diversity of culture, how can they be identified? The problem is readily resolved, however, if (as Joe Sawchuk has suggested) one employs a concept of ethnicity (rather than of culture or biology), especially the ascriptive approach advanced by the anthropologist Fredrik Barth.[6] By ascription, anyone could be a member of the Métis ethnic group who identified himself as such and who was considered as such by others, both inside and outside the group. By this means, then, the word "Métis" can encompass wide variations in culture, such as language, degree of acculturation, and expectations for the future. It even allows for "ethnic boundaries" (as Barth calls them) to be crossed; as will be seen, in the 1880s it was not uncommon on the South Saskatchewan for people to move back and forth between Indian and Métis groups (though there was little or no interchange with the European group). Indeed, there were people in each group who were culturally quite similar, sharing, for example, the same language, the same territorial claims, historical experiences, expectations for the future, and often even religion and a common, mixed ancestry. Marcel Giraud has observed that some Métis felt inferior in the presence of whites,[7] but, nevertheless, there is no doubt that they took pride in their ethnic identification. They were especially proud of their record of individualism, self-regulating independence, equestrianism, and survival as a group. Developing in the relative isolation of the northwest, this ethnic pride had grown into a feeling of separate nationhood.

A second question which must be answered involves the meaning of the word "Indian." As will be seen later, many residents of the northwest who were considered Métis spoke only native languages while, on the other hand, many who were considered Indian were themselves of mixed ancestry and had already undergone some acculturation, for example, conversion to Christianity. For the purposes of this study, an Indian will be anyone who in the 1870s and 1880s sought official Indian status and was granted that status by the Canadian government. This is an artificial, administrative identification but it was consciously taken. These people chose to "take treaty," an act which entitled them to an annuity and other benefits from the Department of Indian Affairs; most of them lived on reserves set aside for their bands.

The territory under consideration in this study embraced two distinct Métis settlements on the South Saskatchewan River, one small, one larger. The first was the tiny community of Prairie-Ronde, located near Dundurn, a little south of Saskatoon. Initially used as a wintering camp for buffalo hunters in the 1850s, Prairie-Ronde had become a year-round Métis settlement by 1885. The population was probably less than 100, most of them members of one extended family—the Trottiers. The people of Prairie-Ronde had recently established links with White Cap's band of Sioux Indians, who had recently moved onto a reserve nearby. The community had no church or resident priest but missionaries visited frequently from Batoche, 100 kilometres to the north (downstream).[8]

The second, larger settlement consisted of a triangle of land, encompassing both sides of the South Saskatchewan River, stretching from St-Louis-de-Langevin in the north to Duck Lake on the west and Fish Creek on the south; the missions of St-Laurent-de-Grandin, Sacré-Coeur (Duck Lake), and St-Antoine-de-Padoue (Batoche) lay within this ambit. In the 1880s this triangle, 50 kilometres long at most, was often generally referred to as the South Branch settlement. Some observers have viewed the triangle as the home territory and even the final refuge of the Northwest Métis.[9] However, even this circumscribed area was not exclusively theirs; by 1885 a number of Europeans had moved in and more were expected. Living within the area were at least fifteen Anglo-Canadian families, a half-dozen or so French-Canadian households, as well as three or four French Oblate Catholic priests.[10] Just outside the triangle lay several Cree Indian reserves, including those of Beardy and Okemasis near Duck Lake, and that of One Arrow, which abutted the village of Batoche. And only 30 kilometres north of St-Louis was the fast-growing town of Prince Albert. The majority of the inhabitants in this area were Anglo-Canadian but it also included a strong component of people of mixed British and Indian ancestry, usually identified as "Halfbreeds" rather than Métis; most of this group was English-speaking and Protestant.

It was in the early 1870s that a number of Métis first decided to build permanent homes on the South Branch; many of these original settlers were people who had lived most of their lives on the Plains. Although they intended to plant gardens, good soil was not a major consideration in their choice of land; they were more interested in a spot close to productive hay-lands, good wood lots, and reliable supplies of water. In succeeding years, the area attracted two further migrations of Métis (1877–78 and 1882–83). Most of these later migrants came from Manitoba, where their most recent experience was in small-scale farming and stock raising, practices which they hoped to continue on the South Branch.[11]

For those who were serious about pursuing an agricultural life, the early years on the Saskatchewan were disappointing. Seed and equipment were expensive, local demand for their produce was weak, and, in the two years before the rebellion, unseasonable weather curtailed production. A few Métis (such as the Tourond family) did enjoy some success in agriculture, but they were not numerous. More than one outside observer felt that the Métis were not fully committed to farming as a livelihood. In 1884 Lawrence Clarke, Chief Factor for the Hudson's Bay Co. at Prince Albert, claimed that "these men are not farmers [but] merely cultivating small patches of land little larger than kitchen gardens. They live by hunting and freighting." These pursuits, he said, were in decline, so the Métis were "getting poorer by the year."[12] The Dominion Lands Agent at Prince Albert felt similarly; he concluded that most of the Métis who were pressing land claims before him were more interested in hunting than farming.[13] Many of those who applied for land in 1884 called themselves farmers but, as Diane Payment has noted: "Poussés à se déclarer agriculteurs, il est probable que plusieurs hesitent, ou négligent de dire qu'il font encore la chasse."[14] At Prairie-Ronde the population was even less involved in agriculture, as the story of Charles Trottier indicates. Although the settlement was dispersed after the rebellion, the people returned to the area in the early years of the twentieth century; Trottier, leader of the settlement (almost an Indian band chief, in fact) applied for land there on his return in 1903. In his application, he swore that "I took up this land as far back as 1855 when I was with my parents hunting the buffaloes in the plains." He said that on the eve of the rebellion he had a house and stable there and had broken fifteen acres of soil; but he admitted that he had not got around to sowing it before fleeing to the United States "on account of the rebellion."[15]

In effect most Métis on the South Saskatchewan in the mid-1880s sought their livelihood as hunters, gatherers, freighters, trappers, and farmers in varying degrees of precedence. Hunting remained important. For example, when applying for land in the years following the rebellion, some men who had taken part in that conflict still listed their occupation as "Hunter, freighter & farmer"— in that order.[16] The days of the great buffalo hunts were over, however. The last organized hunt from the Saskatchewan, led by Gabriel Dumont in 1880, had ridden as far south as the Cypress Hills and even into the United States in search of buffalo.[17] With the disappearance of the buffalo there was hunger on the Plains, it is true. But there was still other game around, even in later decades. One of the people whose family later returned to Prairie-Ronde has recalled that, while the Métis who resettled there "weren't no farmers," they were still able to hunt deer (and this was the twentieth century).[18] Augustin Laframboise, one of the fighters killed at the Battle of Duck Lake, is known to have been in the Cypress Hills — undoubtedly hunting — as late as 1882,[19] and there must have been others from the South Branch also hunting there in the years immediately preceding the rebellion. Small game, such as prairie chickens and ducks, were also still fairly plentiful on the Plains. Gathering, as a pursuit, included the traditional Métis and Cree practices of collecting duck eggs, picking berries, and digging roots — particularly Indian turnips (*Psoralea lanceolata*) — as dietary supplements. Wood was also cut and hauled for sale in Prince Albert and Saskatoon.[20]

Freighting had long been important, especially as payment was made in cash and as it provided the Métis the chance to satisfy their love of travelling the Plains. The use of Red River carts to transport freight declined with the arrival of regular steamboat service on the Saskatchewan River and the building of the Canadian Pacific Railway across the southern Plains in the 1880s. Demand for freighters rose again for awhile, however, when Fort Carlton was made a distribution point for the Hudson's Bay Co. in 1884.[21] Lastly, some Métis found they were able to shift from hunting buffalo to trapping fur-bearing animals in the parklands and woodlands north of the Saskatchewan River. Again, in addition to the economic inducement, it may have been their traditional love of travel which drew the Métis to trapping. In any case, there seems no doubt that, because they pursued other means of livelihood — hunting, gathering, freighting, and trapping — the Métis were absent for long periods from whatever crops or livestock they may have been trying to raise, and their agricultural effectiveness suffered significantly.

By mid-1884 the Métis population of the South Branch was estimated to be 1300 people. Adding the 100 or so at Prairie-Ronde, the South Saskatchewan Métis numbered no more than 1400 men, women, and children. About 1100 were originally from Manitoba.[22] The remaining 300 had been born in what, in 1870, had become the Northwest Territories. As will be seen, it was from this small group, combined with a number of men who had been born in Manitoba but had lived most of their lives on the Plains, that most of the militantly committed rebels of 1885 came.

In their fight with the Canadian authorities, the Métis had to rely almost exclusively on this small population base. Few outsiders came to join the fighting. Messages were sent to solicit assistance from Prince Albert, as well as from Métis communities at Qu'Appelle and Battleford, but the response was disappointing. A Militia Roll, drawn up after the Battle of Duck Lake, shows a fighting force of 18.5 companies, each consisting of a captain and ten soldiers — over 200 names in all.[23] This number is incomplete, however. A list provided by Philippe Garnot to Bishop Taché after the rebellion notes the names of about 280 men who were present (though not necessarily active combatants) at the Battle of Batoche.[24] The Militia Roll and the Garnot list cover the adult male population of the two South Saskatchewan communities involved and, as such, include a handful of people of mixed British and Indian ancestry who lived in the area. (A significant number of reserve Indians also joined in the fighting; their participation will be examined later.) The number of men who could take an active part in the actual fighting was limited by the supply of arms available. One report notes an initial stock of 253 guns, of which 48 were inoperative.[25] By the end of the hostilities this stock had been reduced — through loss, damage, and lack of ammunition — to only 60 or 70 guns.[26] The best estimate of the number of Métis who had any involvement in the hostilities of March, April, and May 1885 would be about 250. Not all were combatants; many served auxiliary roles — guarding prisoners, carrying messages, caring for livestock and horses, scrounging for supplies, performing reconnaissance.

MILITANT MÉTIS

An estimate of those Métis who could be considered the most militantly committed to the notion of rebellion is also difficult to compute. Upon first consideration one might think that membership in the "Exovedate" would help identify the militants. This body was the council or provisional government which Louis Riel set up to handle the administrative and military (and even theological) affairs of the community during the insurrection. Over twenty men were appointed to the council but two — J-B. Boyer and C. Nolin — were unsympathetic to the rebellion and left town. The council also included three non-Métis — White Cap, the Sioux chief from Saskatoon, and two French Canadians, conscripted for their literacy, who served for short periods as secretary. A second indicator of militancy might be appointment as captain of one of the nineteen militia companies.[27] Among these men, however, was one — W. Boyer — who refused to take up arms and quietly left town. The exceptions show that mere appointment to these two bodies is not necessarily an accurate guide to insurrectionary ardour; some men were evidently appointed in ignorance of their opinions. A third consideration in determining militancy might be the secret oath drawn up by Louis Riel on 5 March 1885, to which ten Métis affixed their marks; in it, the men swore to take up arms, if necessary, to save their country from a wicked government.[28] As will be seen, however, it would be too restrictive to limit militancy to only ten men.

Instead, this study will use two other criteria to identify the most ardent rebels. First, it will include all those who fled to the United States after the Battle of Batoche. In effect, these men identified themselves as highly implicated in rebellion. After all, removing themselves from the heartland of the Métis nation and (often) their families was a serious step; their flight will be taken as evidence that their involvement in the insurrection was so deep that they expected particularly severe treatment from the victorious Canadian authorities. Flight cannot be considered mere cowardice, for the fugitives included many men of undoubted courage. Most of the participants chose not to flee, however, and these included some of the most ardent proponents of rebellion. Canadian authorities charged many of them with the crime of treason felony. Eighteen were found guilty and sentenced to prison terms of one, three, or seven years. The second indicator of militancy, then, will be those whose involvement in rebellion was judged by the courts to deserve the severest sentence.[29] As Table 19.1 shows, at least 28 Métis rebels are known to have fled to the United States and nine more were sentenced to seven-year prison terms. The table includes most, but not all, of those who signed the secret oath and of those appointed to the Exovedate and as militia captains. Louis Riel is covered by none of the criteria, nor was he a member of the Exovedate or a combatant; in some ways he was an outsider and not part of the South Branch community. For these reasons, he and men such as William H. Jackson will be excluded from those considered in this study as militants.

Some weaknesses are apparent in employing the above criteria to identify the most militantly committed rebels. First, there quite possibly may have been more than 28 men who fled the country in May 1885; this figure is simply the total so far uncovered in various documentary sources. Second, there were doubtless some Métis among the nineteen killed at Duck Lake, Fish Creek, and Batoche who were as deeply committed to the uprising as those noted in Table 19.1. Death in battle is no certain indication of ardour but, undoubtedly, a number of the men, had they lived, would either have felt compelled to flee the country or have received long prison sentences for their activities during the rebellion. For example, three of the dead had signed the secret oath to take up arms if necessary. For this reason, Table 19.2, noting the men who died in the fighting, has been drawn up. Inclusion on this list can be considered as at least a secondary indicator of militancy.

A third weakness of the criteria is that the courts may have erred in determining which men were the most deeply implicated rebels. Albert Monkman, for example, was undoubtedly one of the most militant rebels throughout most of the uprising (he was accused of forcing others to fight) and received a seven-year court sentence. By the end, however, he had aroused Riel's suspicions (perhaps for not delivering the support of the Protestant Halfbreeds of Prince Albert) and Riel had him arrested before the Battle of Batoche.[30] Sixteen trials were held at Battleford and Regina in the summer of 1885 for crimes arising out of the rebellion. The accused were generally grouped by ethnicity and locality. The largest group was the 30 residents of the South Saskatchewan who, after pleading guilty to treason felony, received their sentences at Regina on 14 August. One witness complained that, through negligence, some important rebels had never been arrested but he gave no names. All members of the Exovedate who were not dead or had not fled were charged; one received a suspended sentence, two were given three years in prison, while five received seven-year terms. Appointment as a militia captain was not considered important — seven captains were not even charged, though the three who were, received seven-year sentences. Still, the court's conclusions were not manifestly capricious. The deciding factors by which it assessed the degree of involvement in rebellion was the testimony given in affidavits by anglophone settlers whom the rebels had held as prisoners, by local priests, and by a few Métis who had taken no part in the uprising. Thus, although not foolproof, a seven-year sentence is, on the whole, not an unreasonable guide to the degree of insurrectionary involvement.[31]

Table 19.1   Fugitive and Imprisoned Militants

Name	Age	Fug./Sentence	Years in NWT	Remarks
J-Bte. Boucher Sr.	47	fugitive	since 1882	Exovede
Josué Breland		fugitive		
Ambroise Champagne		fugitive	Plains Métis*	militia captain
Norbert Delorme	48	fugitive	since 1874	Exovede
Maxime Dubois	36	7 years		
Michel Dumas	36	fugitive	since 1880	Public Servant
Edouard Dumont	45	fugitive	born in NWT	militia captain
Elie Dumont	39	fugitive	Plains Métis*	
Gabriel Dumont	47	fugitive	Plains Métis*	Exovede/took oath
Jean Dumont	52	fugitive	Plains Métis*	cousin of above three
Philippe Gariépy	48	7 years	since 1872	militia captain/oath
Pierre Henry	40	7 years	since 1882	Exovede
Antoine Lafontaine	36	fugitive		militia captain
Calixte Lafontaine	39	fugitive		militia captain/oath
Louis Lafontaine		fugitive	by at least 1876	
Pierre Laverdure	66	fugitive	by at least 1870	
Maxime Lépine	49	7 years	since 1882	Exovede/took oath
William Letendre		fugitive	Plains Métis*	
Albert Monkman	29	7 years		Protestant Halfbreed
Abraham Montour Sr.	53	fugitive	born in NWT	took secret oath
Jonas Moreau		fugitive		militia captain
Napoléon Nault	27	fugitive	since 1878	took secret oath
Julien Ouellette	36	fugitive	since 1868	
J-Bte. Parenteau	55	fugitive	since 1858	
Pierre Parenteau	72	7 years	since 1882	Exovedate Pres./oath/ famed buffalo hunter
John Ross Jr.	28	fugitive	born in NWT	took secret oath
Pierre Sansregret	44	fugitive	by at least 1866	
James Short	50	7 years	born in NWT	
André Trottier	25	fugitive	Plains Métis*	nephew of Charles Sr.
Charles Trottier Sr.	49	fugitive	Plains Métis*	Exovede
Isidore Trottier	22	fugitive	Plains Métis*	son of Charles Sr.
J-Bte. Trottier	20	fugitive	Plains Métis*	son of Charles Sr.
Johny Trottier	22	fugitive	Plains Métis*	nephew of Charles Sr.
Rémi Trottier	24	fugitive	Plains Métis*	son of Charles Sr.
J-Bte. Vandal	54	7 years	born in NWT	militia captain
Pierre Vandal	39	7 years	since 1872	sought Big Bear's support
James Ward	34	fugitive	born in NWT	

*Plains Métis: Permanent, long-time resident of what became the Northwest Territories (1870), even though perhaps born in what became the province of Manitoba (1870) and occasionally trading there.

Sources: Census, Prince Albert, Wood Mountain, and Cypress Hills, 1881, NAC, MG31, Microfilm C 13285. (Unfortunately, the pages are often illegible so the census data are not fully available.) Clarence Kipling Collection, NAC, MG 25, G 62. Dumont family genealogy in NAC, MG 17, A 17, no. 88, pp. 724–29. G.F.G. Stanley et al. (eds.), *The Collected Writings of Louis Riel* (Edmonton, 1985), vol. 5, Biographical Index. Affidavit of Père André, Canada, Parlement, *Documents de la Session, 1886*, no. 52, pp. 389–94. William Pearce Report, Canada, Parlement, *Documents de la Session, 1886*, no. 86, pp. 1–18. Diane Payment, "Monsieur Batoche," *Saskatchewan History* (Autumn 1979): 81–103. For references regarding fugitives, see note 29.

Table 19.2   Men Killed in Battle

Name	Age	Battle	Years in NWT	Remarks
François Boyer	28	Fish Cr.		
Isidore Boyer	60	Batoche		
Damase Carrière	34	Batoche		Exovede
Michel Desjarlais	30	Fish Cr.		
Isidore Dumont Jr.	55	Duck L.	born in NWT	militia captain; took secret oath
Ambroise Jobin	35		born in NWT	Exovede; died of wounds, 23 May
Augustin Laframboise	46	Duck L.	Plains Métis	militia captain; took secret oath
André Letendre	48	Batoche	Plains Métis	bro. of F-X. Letendre
J-Bte. Montour		Duck L.	Plains Métis	
Joseph Montour		Duck L.		
Joseph Ouellette Sr.	93	Batoche	Plains Métis	took secret oath
St. Pierre Parenteau	25	Fish Cr.	since 1882	
Donald Ross	63	Batoche		Exovede
John Swan (Swain)	56	Batoche		
Calixte Tourond		Batoche	since 1882	
Elzéar Tourond		Batoche	since 1882	
Michel Trottier Sr.	64	Batoche	Plains Métis	uncle of Charles Trottier Sr.
Joseph Vandal	75	Batoche		
Joseph Vermette	56	Fish Cr.		

Sources: Census, Prince Albert, Wood Mountain, and Cypress Hills, 1881, NAC, MG 31. Stanley et al., *Collected Writings*, vol. 5, Biographical Index. Registre de la paroisse St-Antoine-de-Padoue (Batoche, Sask.), sépultures. A. Ouimet, B.A.T. de Montigny (eds.), *La vérité sur la question Métisse au Nord-Ouest* (Montréal, 1889), p. 138. William Pearce Report, Canada, Parlement, *Documents de la Session*, 1886, no. 8, pp. 1–18. Payment, "Monsieur Batoche." NAC, RG 15, D II, 1, Commission on Rebellion Losses, vol. 914, f. 892,789, no. 21.

At the other end of the political spectrum from the most militant rebels were a smaller number of men who opposed taking up arms. Their feelings may not have been known at the beginning of the uprising and, as a result, some of them were named to positions in the militia or the Exovedate. For several reasons, the support of these men would have brought important benefits to the insurrectionary cause. They were generally younger than the militants. Some were educated and had useful skills to offer; others were merchants with valuable stocks of provisions and ammunition. Their nomination may also have been made in a (vain) hope of uniting all sectors of the community. Table 19.3 lists ten Métis now known to have opposed the notion of rebellion and who made sure they were absent from the scene of action. When hostilities began, the merchants F-X. Letendre (also known as Batoche), for whom the village was named, and Salomon Venne were away and refused to return; Letendre's store was looted for its supplies. The other eight men fled the South Branch, taking refuge at either Prince Albert or Qu'Appelle. Louis Marion was threatened with death for treason before escaping. Charles Nolin initially supported the insurrection but, for reasons which remain unclear, reversed his position; arrested by the rebels, he feigned submission and then fled. Of course, besides these known examples, there may have been other men who left quietly to avoid enlistment into the cause.[32]

Table 19.3   Métis Who Opposed Rebellion

Name	Age	Occupation	Remarks
C-E. Boucher	20	store clerk	father a fugitive in the U.S.
J-Bte. Boucher	23	store clerk	father a fugitive in the U.S.; initially named a militia captain
J-Bte. Boyer	40	merchant	initially named to Exovedate
William Boyer	34		initially named a militia captain
Georges Fisher		merchant	
Roger Goulet		farmer	initially named a militia soldier
F-X. Letendre	44	merchant	wealthiest Métis on South Branch
Louis Marion		Pub. Servant	instructor at Beardy Indian reserve
Charles Nolin	48	entrepreneur	member of Manitoba Assembly, 1874/79; initially named to Exovedate
Salomon Venne	48	merchant	

Sources: RG 15, D II, 1, Commission on Rebellion Losses, claim of J-Bte. Boucher, vol. 915, f. 892,789, no. 64. D. Payment, "Monsieur Batoche." D. Payment, *Batoche, 1870–1910*, p. 103. MG 26, G, (Laurier Papers), vol. 2, A. Fisher to Laurier, 14 Mar. 1888, pp. 676–91. Stanley et al., *Collected Writings*, vol. 5, Biographical Index. Walter Hildebrandt, *The Battle of Batoche* (Ottawa, 1985), p. 20.

The vast majority of Métis on the South Saskatchewan can probably be said to have occupied neither end of the political spectrum — they were neither militantly committed to rebellion nor opposed to it. Some of them, initially indifferent or undecided, were undoubtedly coerced into participating. At the treason felony trial of August 1885, a number of witnesses testified that some Métis had been threatened with destruction of property and even death if they did not show proper devotion to the insurrectionary cause. The enforcers singled out were, of course, the militants; care was taken, however, to implicate only those who could not be hurt further — men such as Joseph Vandal and Damase Carrière (both killed at Batoche), or Napoléon Nault, Norbert Delorme, and Gabriel and Jean Dumont (all safely in the United States).[33] Despite the intimidation, however, morale was not a problem among the less committed, even after the first men were killed in action at Duck Lake. When Mrs. Louis Marion arrived in Prince Albert to join her husband, who had fled there, she reported on the situation at Batoche; though obviously not sympathetic to the rebel cause, she insisted that there had been no tears shed at the funerals and that the people were as determined as ever to resist.[34]

It is evident that the Métis who were on the end of the political spectrum which opposed rebellion (Table 19.3) were those who had found some success in adapting to the new circumstances of life in the Northwest Territories. They all seem to have had some formal education; seven of them were involved in trade while one held a government position. Most were related to one another.[35] These men comprised nearly all the incipient acculturates among the South Saskatchewan Métis. The only known exceptions — the only men with similar backgrounds who supported the notion of rebellion — were Emmanuel Champagne, Michel Dumas, and Maxime Lépine. The first was a successful farmer and fur trader who was charged with treason felony but received a suspended sentence (probably for age and health reasons). Dumas, although a farm instructor at the One Arrow Indian reserve, was a militant proponent of rebellion who fled to the United States. Lépine, a small-scale businessman and farmer, was also a militant rebel; he received a seven-year prison sentence.

The militants, for their part, were almost entirely made up of long-time freighters and buffalo hunters; they were middle-aged men who had found it difficult to adjust to a sedentary, agricultural life. Thus, it can be seen that the political and cultural spectra of the community closely corresponded. As Table 19.1 shows, seventeen were what will be referred to hereafter as Plains Métis (Marcel Giraud called them "métis de l'Ouest");[36] that is, they were men who had spent much of their lives in what, in 1870, had become the Northwest Territories, or had been born there. Some, it is true, had been born in American territory or in what had become the province of Manitoba; many traded in Manitoba regularly and a few had even received the land or scrip to which they were entitled by the Manitoba Act. Many of the Dumonts and Trottiers had this background, but there can be no doubt that they were Métis of the Plains. Another example is Jean-Baptiste Parenteau, rebel and fugitive in 1885, who was born at Red River about 1830; in 1900, in an affidavit supporting his son's application for land, he swore that

> I was married at Winnipeg 42 years ago (1858) to Pélagie Dumont [sister of Gabriel] and since that time I have always lived in the North-west Territories & until about twenty five years ago I was a Buffalo hunter and at the time of the Red River Rebellion [1869] I was living . . . near Fish Creek where the Traders & Hunters used to winter. I never had a house in . . . Manitoba since I was married and I only went there in the Spring of each year to sell furs, returning in the fall. When I was out hunting the whole family used to follow me. My son Alexandre was born on the third day after we arrived in Winnipeg in the spring twenty five years ago and about fifteen days after his birth we started out on our journey back.[37]

Most of the militants seem to have been among the original Métis settlers of the South Saskatchewan, i.e., those who had arrived in the early 1870s; few were among the more agriculture-oriented settlers who had come after 1877. Of the militants whose age is known (Table 19.1), the average was 41 years old. A few of the militants were young, but it is revealing to learn that at least four children of fugitive militants, though living in the area and old enough to fight, took no part at all in the insurrection.[38] The evidence in Table 19.2 listing the Métis killed in action also supports a conclusion that the militants were largely made up of older (average age 51) Plains Métis, representatives of the Plains buffalo-hunting tradition. And, as will be seen, many of these men were, in various ways, close to the Plains Indians in culture.

Many Métis undoubtedly considered themselves distinct from, and superior to, Indians. Others, however, though they called themselves Métis, were not reluctant to point out the similarities between the two groups, especially the Plains Métis, who had long followed lifeways similar to their kin the Plains Cree and Saulteaux — a migratory life based on the hunt. In 1877 a number of Plains Métis petitioned the government for relaxation of the game laws and for assistance in establishing themselves on farms. They described themselves as leading "an entirely nomadic life, as the Indians on the plains."[39] Among the petitioners were at least three Métis who participated in the rebellion on the South Saskatchewan, and one, James Ward, is classified as a militant in Table 19.1. Another interesting document is a recently discovered petition forwarded by Inspector James Walsh of the North-West Mounted Police from the Cypress Hills in 1876.[40] The petitioners describe themselves as "half-breeds of the Cree and Saulteaux Tribes" who "have lived from childhood upon the prairies and adopted the customs of the Indians." They ask to be admitted into Treaty No. 4 as a group and elect their own chief. Again, among those affixing their marks to the petition were two or three Métis who later participated in the South Saskatchewan conflict. Two years later, another petition was circulated in the Cypress Hills among Métis who described themselves as having been long "in the habit of roaming over the prairies of the North-West for the purposes of hunting." They asked for a "special reserve" of land "to the exclusion of all whites" except government officials. Signing the petition were fourteen men who are listed among the militants or the dead in Tables 19.1 and 19.2.[41]

While some of those petitioners who, in the 1870s, called themselves Métis or Halfbreeds continued to identify with that group, many others ended up on reserves as Treaty Indians. Government officials early recognized that it was difficult to determine an Indian by ancestry alone;[42] people of mixed Indian and European ancestry who wished to identify themselves as Indians were permitted to "take Treaty." Many did so to take advantage of Treaty benefits — an annuity, land on a reserve, agricultural assistance and instruction, and so forth. By the mid-1880s, however, many Treaty Indians had become dissatisfied with reserve life and some of those with mixed ancestry then decided to withdraw from Treaty. Withdrawals accelerated when the government finally acted on the demand of the Northwest Métis that they, like their kin in Manitoba, should be compensated for the extinguishment of their territorial claims. The land question had long rankled the Métis, and government inaction culminated in rebellion in March 1885. The North-West Half Breed Commission established later offered the Métis compensation in the form of land or scrip.[43] This concession prompted a large number of people, who for a decade had identified themselves as Indians, to leave the reserves. In 1886 over half the Métis who were granted scrip by the Commission were mixed bloods who had withdrawn from Treaty.[44] Within a few years, some, however, were asking to be readmitted to Treaty.[45]

Thus, in the 1870s and 1880s, many people moved back and forth across the ethnic boundaries between Indian and Métis groups, for not only did the Métis retain many elements of their Indian heritage, but Indians were assimilating European traits at the same time as well. To cross the Métis ethnic boundary, it appears one had only to have mixed ancestry, profess Christianity, and identify oneself as Métis. With these characteristics, it seems that one was readily accepted as Métis and, as well, was acknowledged by outsiders as such. Mixed ancestry was essential, however; no whites are known to have been considered as Métis. One Indian, Kitwayo or Alexandre Cadieux — "une sauvage pur sang," as he was described — did live among the South Branch Métis; but, despite the French name, he was always identified as an Indian because of his unmixed parentage.[46]

Inter-ethnic movements were particularly easy on the South Saskatchewan River. In the Duck Lake area, for example, even those people who had chosen to live on reserves as Indians were almost entirely of mixed ancestry.[47] In addition, a large number of the reserve Indians had been baptized and regarded themselves Christian.[48] Indeed, the first person killed in the 1885 uprising was a Christian Cree (from the Beardy reserve) shot at the Battle of Duck Lake.[49] The Métis group may have been more orthodoxly and homogeneously Christian but still the Christianity which some of them practised included elements of Indian origin such as healing rituals, precognition, and seeing at a distance.[50]

While the Plains Métis retained traces of Indian religion, their social structures also remained remarkably similar to those of the Cree. Following the individualistic traditions of their Indian ancestors, each Métis was a generalist; that is, there was little specialization of work beyond age or sex — although there was considerable sharing within the community, each family made its own cart, dwelling, clothing and so on. On the South Saskatchewan the only exceptions were a few Métis merchants and traders. (The handful of priests and teachers living in the area were all outsiders.) Also, like the Cree, the Métis had no strong social or political hierarchy; strict obedience to leaders was common only in the buffalo hunt and in war.[51] Indeed, the organization of the Métis militia in 1885 strongly resembled Indian custom. Commanding the militia was Gabriel Dumont, whose authority was, in many ways, similar to that of a Plains Indian chief. Louis Riel wrote Sir John A. Macdonald, pointing out that, while the government had recognized even the "most insignificant" chiefs in treaties, "Gabriel Dumont was altogether ignored." This indignity, Riel claimed, "has always been rankling in his mind."[52]

When the time came for armed action, Dumont naturally expected assistance from Indians throughout the northwest. He was only partly successful. Big Bear, Poundmaker, and other Cree chiefs living up the North Saskatchewan River also rose in rebellion in the spring of 1885; Dumont sent messengers requesting their help on the South Branch but none arrived before the final defeat at Batoche on 12 May.[53] Aid was also requested from reserves to the south but the only Indians who came from that direction were White Cap and about twenty of his men from Moose Woods near Saskatoon. Surprisingly, these were Sioux with whom the Métis traditionally had few ties; there is some reason to believe that the aggressive Trottier family of nearby Prairie-Ronde coerced them to travel to Batoche. Four Sioux died in the fighting. The most important support came from Indians in the South Branch area. Scores of men arrived from the One Arrow, Beardy, Okemasis, Chakastapaysin, and Petaquakey reserves; only one was killed in the fighting, but a chief, One Arrow, was subsequently sentenced to three years in prison.[54]

Dumont and the other militants had every reason to count on support from neighbouring reserves because of the strong ties between the Métis and those Indians. Indeed, at least six Métis who participated in the rebellion had themselves been on the paylists (i.e., for annuities) of neighbouring reserves as recently as 1884.[55] Another combatant, Charles Trottier Jr., was still a Treaty Indian (Beardy's reserve) at the time of the uprising. A nephew of Charles Trottier Sr., leader of the Prairie-Ronde clan, he was married to the daughter of Okemasis, chief of a South Branch band. He fought at Duck Lake and seems to have fled the country; but, as he was a Treaty Indian, he is excluded from Table 19.1.[56]

It is not surprising that there was frequent inter-marriage between South Branch Métis and reserve Indians; Diane Payment affirms that there are numerous cases mentioned in local church registers.[57] Although the couples may not have resided full-time on the reserves, the spouse was able to collect an annuity. Several combatants of 1885 had Treaty Indian wives. One was Augustin Laframboise, Métis militia captain killed at Duck Lake; his wife was on the paylist of Petaquakey reserve.[58] Another was Michel Trottier, a Métis killed at Batoche; married to an Indian of Duck Lake Agency, he was the brother of Charles Trottier Sr.[59]

Gabriel Dumont himself had close kin on reserves, including that of One Arrow, which was only a short distance from his residence. There, his first cousin, Vital Dumont (also known as Cayol), son of his uncle Jean-Baptiste, had chosen to live as a Treaty Indian (even though both his parents were of mixed ancestry). In 1885 Vital Dumont and his two adult sons, Louis and Francis, answered Gabriel's call to arms. The three of them subsequently felt so deeply implicated in the rebellion that they fled to the United States.[60] As Treaty Indians, however, they too will be excluded from Table 19.1.

Language was another cultural trait which many Métis shared with the Plains Indians. Because most Métis had French ancestors and bore French names, they were labelled as French. Many, however, also had Indian names and, perhaps not surprisingly (given their strong kinship ties with local Indians), many of them were, in fact, unilingual Cree-speakers. This linguistic persistence was particularly evident among the Plains Métis and, indeed, among the militant supporters of the 1885 rebellion. For years Roman Catholic missionaries on the South

Saskatchewan had lamented their parishioners' preference for Cree. It is known that, at religious services in the 1880s, hymns were sometimes sung in Cree. In education, however, the policy of the Church was to try to downgrade native language and encourage the use of European languages, especially French. The efforts were not always successful. As late as 1897 it was reported that most Métis school children at Batoche could understand neither French nor English![61] For many years the use of Cree remained vigorous among people of mixed ancestry living in scattered parts of the northwest. By the twentieth century, certainly, some groups had incorporated elements of European languages into their speech, thus developing a tongue known popularly as "Michif." Linguists studying Michif have discovered that, while its noun phrases are usually French in origin, syntax and verb structures are mainly Cree. As one linguist has said, "Michif is best viewed as a dialect of Cree."[62]

In August 1885 the 30 South Saskatchewan Métis charged with the crime of treason felony went on trial at Regina. At the outset, all but one requested that the court proceedings be translated into Cree and the judge complied with their wish. Even so, the lawyer for the accused remarked that his clients were still not clear about the meaning of their charge, "the interpreter not being able to translate into their language the words of the law."[63] In the end, the only Métis who did not understand Cree was given a conditional discharge while, of those who preferred Cree, eighteen were sentenced to prison, including, of course, the eleven militants listed in Table 19.1 who received seven-year terms. It can be said, then, that of all the Métis whose linguistic preference is known, the most militant proponents of insurrection in 1885 were men who were most at ease speaking the language of the Plains Indians.

Less is known of the language spoken by the other Métis listed in Tables 19.1 and 19.2. However, some impression can be gained by examining the preferences of their children. In the months after the rebellion, the Half Breed Commission visited the South Branch area offering scrip to the Métis. Few people accepted the offer in 1885, though many did in ensuing years. Naturally, those who had participated in the uprising were reluctant to apply, but two adult children whose fathers were fugitives and two whose fathers had been killed in the fighting did dare to request scrip. The Commission's procedure that year provided for an explanation of one's rights in a choice of languages. Of the four, all of whose fathers appear in Tables 19.1 and 19.2, one requested an explanation in French, two in Cree, and one in both languages.[64] This number, though small, would again suggest that, in the houses of the most militant rebels, it was the language of the Plains Cree which was spoken.

It is quite possible that the language spoken by the Métis accused of treason felony and those whose children applied for scrip after the rebellion included a degree of French in addition to Cree; that is, they probably spoke a form of incipient Michif. Even so, however, their stated preference for Cree once again indicates that most of the militant supporters of insurrection in 1885 were culturally close to Plains Indians.

From the foregoing examination of their background, age, livelihood, religion, social structure, and language, it can be seen that the Métis who were the most militantly involved in the 1885 rebellion were the most conservative, most Indian-like in the community. The militants were, with only a few exceptions, men of an older generation, former buffalo hunters and freighters only marginally involved in agriculture; they were Métis of the Plains tradition who were unable or unwilling to adjust their lives to the rapidly changing conditions of the new northwest. In contrast, the Métis who opposed taking up arms were, with no apparent exceptions, younger men who had enjoyed some success in fields which held promise in the new order of things. While there was a fair measure of diversity in both the political spectrum and the cultural spectrum of the South Saskatchewan community, the two spectra were almost congruent.

CONCLUSION

A number of implications may be seen to arise from these conclusions. For example, although both contemporaries and more recent observers commonly speak of French Métis, Scottish mixed bloods, and English Halfbreeds, this is a labelling often based only on their names. However, it is evident that in the 1880s (and even later) there was a substantial group of people of mixed ancestry outside Manitoba who spoke only native languages or whose best facility was in a native language. (Not only Cree was used; Métis beyond the Saskatchewan even today speak a number of Dene tongues.) For these people, a linguistic characterization is meaningless. Thus, insofar as one is concerned with their European traits, it may be more useful to categorize them as either Roman Catholic or Protestant mixed bloods, for they were virtually all one or the other.

The persistence of Plains hunting traditions among many Métis can have other implications — for example, in their decision in 1885 to take up arms. It should not be surprising that these people should have reacted violently when confronted with a faceless, seemingly immovable government bureaucracy which appeared to be totally indifferent to their customs, anxieties, and needs. Numerous petitions had been sent to the government, whose response was usually long in coming, if it came at all. The complicated statutes and regulations of the Department of the Interior were unfathomable to this non-literate people, and the length of time it took to obtain a decision from Ottawa became intolerable.

The Plains Métis were men of action, unaccustomed to standing passively by as their situation deteriorated. They had much honour to lose if they did not take action; and, also, as the least acculturated in the community, generally had the least property to lose if they did. The missionaries tried to talk them out of insurrection but, again as the least acculturated, their respect for the authority of the Church was perhaps not as strong as, for example, that of the men listed in Table 19.3. And when it came to military planning, the leading insurrectionists totally miscalculated the power behind the government's authority. Accustomed only to fighting Indians, the Plains Métis did not expect the soldiers to come in such great numbers; nor were they aware that, unlike Indians, the new enemy, after suffering losses at Duck Lake and Fish Creek, would be more determined to fight, not less.

The sizable number of militants which has been identified above indicates that, apart from the few, more acculturated people in the community, the insurrectionary movement on the South Saskatchewan was quite deeply based. This finding would contradict the views of some contemporary observers as well as more recent commentators. At the treason felony trial of August 1885 the missionary fathers, André and Fourmond, testified that the militant proponents of rebellion were very few — essentially just Riel and three others: Gabriel Dumont and Napoléon Nault (both fugitives in the United States) and Damase Carrière (killed at Batoche). Using tricks, threats, and lies, this handful of men were said to have seduced a large but weakly committed group of gullible Métis into taking up arms.[65] However, by resting the blame entirely on Riel and those who were conveniently beyond reach of the law, it is likely that the priests were seeking to minimize their parishioners' role in the uprising and thus mitigate the court's punishment. Similarly, the arguments of two recent historians have also diminished the importance of free will in the actions of the rebels: Thomas Flanagan and Donald McLean contend that the Métis were manipulated into rebellion either by Louis Riel, or by Sir John A. Macdonald and Lawrence Clarke, each for his own purpose.[66] By the findings of this study, however, it would appear that the rebellion was a popular movement. The militants may have tricked or coerced some Métis into participating, but those militants were a sizable group in themselves.

NOTES

1. See, for example, F.L. Barron, J.B. Waldram (eds.), *1885 and After: Native Society in Transition* (Regina, 1986); Bob Beal, Roderick Macleod, *Prairie Fire: The 1885 North-West Rebellion* (Edmonton, 1984); Thomas Flanagan, *Louis "David" Riel: "Prophet of the New World"* (Toronto, 1979); Thomas Flanagan, *Riel and the Rebellion: 1885 Reconsidered* (Saskatoon, 1983); Julia Harrison, *Métis: People between Two Worlds* (Vancouver, Toronto, 1985); Walter Hildebrandt, *The Battle of Batoche: British Small Warfare and the Entrenched Métis* (Ottawa, 1985); A.S. Lussier (ed.), *Riel and the Métis: Riel Mini-Conference Papers* (Winnipeg, 1979); Gilles Martel, *Le messianisme de Louis Riel* (Waterloo, 1984); Donald McLean, *1885: Métis Rebellion or Government Conspiracy?* (Winnipeg, 1985); Diane Payment, *Batoche (1870–1910)* (St-Boniface, 1983); J. Peterson, J.S.H. Brown (eds.), *The New Peoples: Being and Becoming Métis in North America* (Winnipeg, 1985); G.F.G. Stanley et al. (eds.), *The Collected Writings of Louis Riel*, 5 vols. (Edmonton, 1985); George Woodcock, *Gabriel Dumont: The Métis Chief and His Lost World* (Edmonton, 1975).

2. Flanagan, *Louis "David" Riel*, p. 148.

3. Hildebrandt, *Battle of Batoche*, p. 21. The ten men were D. Carrière, I. Dumont, D. Ross, N. Delorme, N. Nault, M. Dumas, M. Lépine, Ph. Cariépy, P. Garnot, and J-B. Boucher.

4. Journal of Louis Schmidt, National Archives of Canada (NAC), MG 17, A 17, no. 37.

5. Woodcock, *Gabriel Dumont*, pp. 120, 156.

6. Fredrik Barth, *Ethnic Groups and Boundaries* (Boston, 1969), pp. 9–15. See also Joe Sawchuk, The *Métis of Manitoba* (Toronto, 1978), pp. 8–10, 39.

7. Marcel Giraud, *Le Métis Canadien* (Paris, 1945; St-Boniface, 1984), p. 1190.

8. Rita Schilling, *Gabriel's Children* (Saskatoon, 1983). Norbert Walsh, *The Last Buffalo Hunter* (Mary Weekes, ed.), (Toronto, 1945), passim.

9. Beal, Macleod, *Prairie Fire*, p. 228. Diane Payment, "The Métis Homeland: Batoche in 1885," *NeWest Review* 10 (May 1985): 11, 12.

10. Report of William Pearce on South Branch land claimants, Canada, Parlement, *Documents de la Session*, 1886, no. 8b, pp. 10–18.

11. Diane Payment, "Batoche after 1885: A Society in Transition," in Barron, Waldram, *1885 and After*, pp. 174, 182. P.R. Mailhot, D.N. Sprague, "Persistent Settlers: The Dispersal and Resettlement of the Red River Métis, 1870–1885," *Canadian Ethnic Studies* 17, 2 (1985): 8.

12. NAC, MG 26A, Sir John A. Macdonald Papers, Clarke to J.A. Grahame, 20 May 1884, vol. 105, pp. 42244–50.

13. E.A. Mitchener, "The North Saskatchewan River Settlement Claims, 1883–84," in Lewis Thomas (ed.), *Essays in Western History* (Edmonton, 1976), pp. 134–35.

14. Payment, *Batoche (1870–1910)*, pp. 14–15, 34 (n. 24).

15. Saskatchewan Archives Board, homestead records, Charles Trottier affidavit, 17 December 1903.

16. NAC, RG 15, D II, 8(b), North West Half Breed land applications, A. Letendre, vol. 1329, no. 1301, and J-B. Parenteau fils, vol. 1362, no. 953.

17. Giraud, *Le Métis Canadien*, p. 1164.

18. Schilling, *Gabriel's Children*, p. 115.

19. NAC, RG 15, D II, 8(c), land applications, vol. 1353, no. 319.

20. Diane Payment, "Structural and Settlement History of Batoche Village," Parks Canada, *Manuscript Report Series*, no. 248 (1977), pp. 73–75. D.M. Loveridge, B. Potyondi, "From Wood Mountain to the Whitemud," ibid., no. 237 (1977), p. 95.

21. G.F.G. Stanley, *The Birth of Western Canada* (Toronto, 1936), p. 185. Mailhot, Sprague, "Persistent Settlers," p. 8. Giraud, *Le Métis Canadien*, p. 1171.

22. Mailhot, Sprague, "Persistent Settlers," p. 12.

23. Canada, Parliament, *Sessional Papers*, 1886, no. 43h, pp. 16–18.

24. Archives de l'Archévêché de St-Boniface (Manitoba), T, fonds Taché, lettres reçues, Garnot to Taché, 28 juillet 1885.

25. NAC, MG 17, A 17, no. 38, Cloutier report, "Effectifs."

26. Hildebrandt, *Battle of Batoche*, p. 74. NAC, MG 17, A 17, journal of Père Végreville, 16 mai 1885.

27. Listed in Canada, Parliament, *Sessional Papers*, 1886, no. 43h, pp. 16–18.

28. See text in Stanley, *Birth of Western Canada*, pp. 442–43 (n. 67).

29. For sentencing, see Canada, Parlement, *Documents de la Session*, 1886, no. 52, p. 308. References to fugitives are numerous; all are at NAC. RG 10, Dept. of Indian Affairs, Report of Sgt. Paterson, NWMP, 3 Oct. 1885, vol. 3722, file 24, 125; Insp. A.R. Cuthbert to Supt. A.B. Perry, 20 Jan. 1886, vol. 3585, file 1130-8. MG 27, I C4, Edgar Dewdney Papers, Report of J. Anderson, 29 Nov. 1885, 8 Dec. and 18 Dec. 1885, pp. 1524–26, 1531,

1536: McKay Report, 8 Jan. 1886, p. 1263; Report of O. Pichette, 1 Feb. 1886, pp. 1274–79; Report on half-breeds, 30 Mar. 1886, pp. 611–12; Nichol Report, May 1886, pp. 1290–97; Report of Cpl. Bossange, 22 April 1888, pp. 1337–39. RG 13, Dept. of Justice, B2, North-West Rebellion records, vol. 816, pp. 2398–2404, 2409–12; vol. 818, pp. 2780–86; vol. 821, pp. 3474–3518.

30. Jackson and Sanderson affidavits, Canada, Parlement, *Documents de la Session*, 1886, no. 52, pp. 399, 416. William Pearce Report, ibid., 1886, no. 8b, p. 12.

31. Affidavits and proceedings of the trial published in Canada, Parlement, *Documents de la Session*, 1886, no. 52, pp. 375–416.

32. Diane Payment, "Monsieur Batoche," *Saskatchewan History* (Autumn 1979): 95–96, 102 (n. 60). NAC, RG 13, Dept. of Justice, vol. 817, Marion testimony, pp. 2787–90. Hildebrandt, Battle of Batoche, p. 20.

33. Canada, Parlement, *Documents de la Session*, 1886, no. 52, pp. 389–416. NAC, RG 15, Dept. of the Interior, vol. 914, file 892,789, rebellion losses claim of Josephte Tourond, no. 21. NAC, RG 13, Dept. of Justice, B2, vol. 817, C. Nolin statement, pp. 2780–86.

34. NAC, MG 17, A 17, no. 37, André to Grandin, 31 mars 1885.

35. Payment, "The Métis Homeland," pp. 11, 12.

36. Giraud, *Le Métis Canadien*, p. 1148 *et passim*.

37. NAC, RG 15, vol. 1362, no. 667.

38. In addition to J-B. Boucher's sons cited in Table 6.3, the sons of Ambroise Champagne and Pierre Sansregret also avoided any involvement in the uprising. NAC, RG 15, Dept. of the Interior, vol. 1326, scrip claim no. 1555, and vol. 1331, claim no. 1504; vol. 915, rebellion losses claim, file 892,789, no. 64.

39. Canada, Parliament, *Sessional Papers*, 1886, no. 45a, pp. 4–5.

40. NAC, RG 10, vol. 3637, file 7089, petition 6 Sept. 1876.

41. N. Delorme, A. Lafontaine, L. Lafontaine, P. Laverdure, Jul. Ouellette, A. Trottier, C. Trottier, I. Trottier, J-B. Trottier, J. Trottier, J. Trottier, I. Dumont, A. Laframboise, Jos. Ouellette, M. Trottier in Canada, Parliament, *Sessional Papers*, 1886, no. 45, pp. 10–16.

42. Alexander Morris, *The Indian Treaties of Canada* (Toronto, 1880), pp. 293–95. John L. Taylor, "The Development of an Indian Policy for the Canadian North-West, 1869–1879," Ph.D. thesis, Queen's University, 1975, pp. 228–31.

43. Ken Hatt, "The North-West Rebellion Scrip Commissions, 1885–1889," in Barron, Waldram, *1885 and After*, pp. 189–204.

44. Dept. of Interior, Annual Report, 1886, in Canada, Parliament, *Sessional Papers*, 1887, no. 7, Part I, p. 76.

45. Giraud, *Le Métis Canadien*, pp. 1217–18.

46. Canada, Parlement, *Documents de la Session*, 1886, no. 52a, p. 393.

47. David Mandelbaum, *The Plains Cree* (Regina, 1979), p. 10.

48. Canada, Indian Affairs Branch, *Annual Report*, 1892, pp. 318–19.

49. NAC, MG 17, A 17, no. 37, André to Grandin, 31 mars 1885.

50. Payment, "The Métis Homeland," p. 12. Guillaume Charette, *Vanishing Spaces: Memoirs of Louis Goulet* (Winnipeg, 1980), p. 146.

51. Mandelbaum, *Plains Cree*, p. 115.

52. NAC, MG 26, A, p. 42529, Riel to Macdonald, 17 July 1885.

53. Adolphe Ouimet, B-A-T. de Montigny (eds.), *La Vérité sur la question Métisse au Nord-Ouest* (Montréal, 1889), p. 130.

54. Canada, Parliament, *Sessional Papers*, 1886, no. 52, pp. 22, 49–50. NAC, RG 10, vol. 3584, file 1130, list of reserves, 1885.

55. RC 10, Paylists, vol. 9417, pp. 70, 85: J. Parisien, B. Deschamps, J. Vandal; vol. 9419, p. 137: J. Trottier, J. Flammant. RG 15, vol. 1369, scrip no. 1124: A. Trottier. Canada, Parliament, Sessional Papers, 1886, no. 43h, pp. 16–18, 44.

56. RG 10, Paylists, vol. 9421, p. 155. RG 15, vol. 1369, no. 1722 & no. 2108.

57. Payment, *Batoche (1870–1910)*, p. 121.

58. RG 10, vol. 9419, pp. 115–18.

59. RG 15, vol. 1369, no. 73.

60. RG 10, Paylists, vol. 9423, p. 304. RG 15, vol. 1345, no. 1251; vol. 1346, no. 148. Dumont genealogy in MG 17, A 17, no. 88, p. 727.

61. J. Brian Dawson, "The Relationship of the Catholic Clergy to Métis Society in the Canadian North-West, 1845–1885, With Particular Reference to the South Saskatchewan District," Parks Canada, *Manuscript Report Series*, no. 376 (1979), p. 255. Payment, *Batoche (1870–1910)*, pp. 44, 55, 63 (n. 6). Giraud, *Le Métis Canadien*,

p. 1042. J.E. Foster, "The Métis: The People and the Term," in Lussier, *Riel and the Métis*, p. 90. Among the militants known to have Indian names were N. Delorme, C. Lafontaine, and C. Trottier Sr.

62. John C. Crawford, "What Is Michif?" in Peterson, Brown, *The New Peoples*, p. 238.
63. Canada, Parlement, *Documents de la Session*, 1886, no. 52, pp. 374, 377–78.
64. RG 15, vol. 1326, no. 1555: N. Champagne; vol. 1327, no. 1292: J. Dumont; vol. 1329, no. 1301: A. Letendre; vol. 1331, no. 1504: P. Sansregret.
65. Canada, Parlement, *Documents de la Session*, 1886, no. 52, pp. 389–94, 403–05.
66. Flanagan, *Riel and the Rebellion*; McLean, *1885: Métis Rebellion or Government Conspiracy?*

Article Twenty

The Indian View of the 1885 Uprising

A. Blair Stonechild

THE INDIAN VERSION OF THE REBELLION: AN UNTOLD STORY

Although there is no shortage of written material on the North-West Rebellion of 1885, Indian Elders have said that the full story of the Indian involvement has yet to be told.

As one Elder put it, "This story was told only at night and at bedtime. And not the whole story. No way. They did not want to tell on anyone who were [*sic*] involved. It is like when something is covered with a blanket and held down on the ground on all four sides. They talked about it in parts only. And they got nervous telling it. They were afraid of another uprising and more trouble. And they were also afraid of getting the young people into trouble."[1]

Some Elders did not like to tell the stories simply because it made them sad. Other Elders did not tell their stories to any white person, even priests, as they were afraid that these stories would be used for the profit of others.

Most historians have used only written documents and official interpretations in their research. After the rebellion the Indian people did not have the freedom or luxury of doing their own research and putting forward their own views. As a result, contemporary interpretations of the Indian role have remained very biased.

HOW THE REBELLION STARTED

The first Indian involvement in the rebellion is said to have been at the Duck Lake fight on 26 March 1885. A few Indians were among Gabriel Dumont's group of about 30 men; but then, considering that the fight itself occurred on Beardy's Reserve, it should not be so surprising that Indians were present at all. One of the least understood aspects of the Duck Lake fight is why one of Chief Beardy's Headmen (Assiyiwin) was shot during the purported parley preceding the fight. How did an old, half-blind, unarmed Headman of the Band become involved in the fracas?

What does Indian oral history have to say about this? The following story is told by Harry Michael of Beardy's Reserve. Harry Michael's grandfather was the nephew of Assiyiwin:

> Assiyiwin had gone to town, to Duck Lake to visit a friend, a half-breed by the name of Wolfe.
> Over there he heard that there was going to be some trouble. Something very bad was going

Source: "The Indian View of the 1885 Uprising," in *1885 and After: Native Society in Transition*, ed. F. Laurie Barron and James B. Waldram (Regina: University of Regina, 1986), pp. 155–70. Reprinted by permission of the author.

to happen. He had gone to town on horseback and he bought some goods from the store in Duck Lake which he tied on his saddle. He then started walking home. The town of Duck Lake was not too far from the camp.

The old man had very poor eyesight — he was almost blind. And as he was approaching the reserve and the camp he noticed something. He heard a lot of voices, a lot of talking. But he could not see anything until he came near the people.

It was then a half-breed spoke to him — called in Cree and said, "Stop! Don't you know what is going to happen?"

Assiyiwin said, "I am blind. Exactly what is it?"

The half-breed answered, "There is going to be a battle. Didn't you hear about it?"

Assiyiwin answered, "Yes, I heard about it."

The half-breed replied, "You have walked right into it. Turn back where you came from."

Assiyiwin answered, "Ha! I cannot turn back. I'm going home. This is my reserve land. If you are going to have a battle, if you are going to spill blood, you cannot do it on our reserve land." And he remained standing there with his horse.

The half-breed said, "Go back where you came from."

Assiyiwin replied, "No, I am going home."

This half-breed threw his coat to Assiyiwin. His name was Joe McKay. He said, "Step over my coat . . . I'll shoot you."

That was the time when Assiyiwin heard someone saying while he was standing there, "Don't shoot each other. Don't shoot." It was said in Cree. It was a half-breed. He must have been very brave, coming into the centre of the two sides of the people on horseback, half-breeds and Indians on one side and the Northwest [sic] Mounted Police on the other side. He was trying to tell the people not to shoot each other. He came running from the half-breed side. He did not know the name of this man. He was waving his hands shouting, "Don't shoot each other! People are trying to find a way on how they can get along better. Don't try and kill each other." He got as far as their location.

It was then Assiyiwin stepped over and passed the coat of McKay and said, "I am going home."

Assiyiwin witnessed the days of intertribal [sic] battles with the Blackfeet. Assiyiwin performed some brave acts when he had the strength and power in his legs. He had some scalps in a wooden box. He had fought and killed in battles and scalped. This was a brave man. That is why he did not back out from Joe McKay's orders. He refused Joe McKay and stepped over past the coat and said he was going to go on home. He was not about to get frightened. His bravery must have returned to him in spite [of the fact] that he was an old man.

The gun went off and fired. McKay shot the old man Assiyiwin down, hitting him in the stomach. Then there were blasts of gunfire coming from all directions.

They came later after the old man. He didn't die right away that night. He died at sunrise the following morning. He was the first Cree Indian killed. That's how my grandfather told this story.[2]

The official interpretation of the event at Duck Lake was that Beardy's Band had joined the rebellion. The story of Assiyiwin, however, presents an entirely different view. An older man, with poor eyesight, Assiyiwin was hardly likely to be associating with young fighters. Moreover, as one of Beardy's Headmen, he probably shared Beardy's disassociation from Riel's activities, and Beardy's dislike of intruders on their Indian reserve land.

It appears that Assiyiwin's mistake was being in the wrong place at the wrong time, and being too bold in asserting his indignation at what was occurring. Gabriel Dumont did not see his brother Isidore or Assiyiwin approach Crozier and McKay. What was probably not so much a parley as an effort to defuse a tense situation turned into a senseless slaughter when Joe McKay pulled his trigger.

It later became clear that Chief Beardy had not ordered his men to support the rebellion, yet through the incident at Duck Lake the Indian people were fully implicated.

INDIAN TREATIES WERE A COMMITMENT TO PEACE

In order to more clearly understand the Indian attitude at the time of the rebellion, one has to look back to the period prior to the signing of the treaties. Indian Nations waged tremendous battles against each other as a result of inter-tribal conflicts created by the expansion of the fur trade. In some battles between the Cree and the Blackfoot, such as that on the Oldman River in 1870, several hundred warriors were killed. An even greater killer — the epidemics — wiped out over half of the tribes in some outbreaks. The result of all this was the drastic depopulation of the Indian Nations, and an increasing awareness among Indian leaders that their Nations had to come to grips with a very fundamental and real issue — that of survival.

Because of these experiences a strong peace movement began to develop among the Indian Nations. One famous peacemaker was the Cree Chief Maskipitoon, who strove to mend relations between the Cree and the Blackfoot during the 1860s. He eventually fell victim to a misguided warrior's bullet. The adoption of the Cree Poundmaker by the Blackfoot Chief Crowfoot was another important development in the cementing of peaceful relations between the two Nations.

It was because of this sentiment for peace that Indian leaders were receptive to the signing of treaties in the 1870s. Not only had Indians never been at war with whites in the northwest, but they also sought to prevent such a thing from ever happening. Treaty Six stated, "they will maintain peace and good order between each other, and also between themselves and others of Her Majesty's subjects."[3] To Indian Nations, that was one of the most important principles of the treaty.

For Indians, the signing of treaties was far more than a political act — it was also a sacred act. By the ceremony of smoking the Sacred Pipe, the Indian people pledged before the Creator that they would uphold the treaties. As Senator John Tootoosis puts it, "We signed an agreement with the Crown, with the Queen not to fight any more. We were to live in peace. We had to live up to this Treaty. We promised in the name of the Creator to keep the Treaty. The Indian people feared offending the Creator."[4] If the treaty was ever broken, it would not be the Indian people who broke it first.

Around the time of the rebellion, white people did not fully appreciate the commitment of the Indian people. They had the perception that Indian people were no more than hunters and warriors. When the Marquis of Lorne, Queen Victoria's son-in-law, met Poundmaker in 1881, he expected to hear many war stories, and was surprised that instead he heard mainly about the spiritual and political ideas of the Indian people.

THE SOLUTIONS TO TREATY PROBLEMS WOULD BE POLITICAL

The Indian leadership was aware that there were serious shortcomings in the implementation of the treaties. In the councils of the political leaders the focus of attention was on the dissatisfaction being experienced by those Indians settling on reserves. During those days of "The Time of the Great Hunger," Indians were seeing few of the benefits promised them under the treaty. The meager rations provided to them did little to stop the loss of life. Between 1880 and 1885 the Indian population dropped from 32 549 to 20 170 — a death rate of nearly 10 percent per year.[5]

At the Duck Lake Council, held in early August of 1884, Indian leaders presented a list of eighteen specific treaty grievances including complaints about untamed horses and cows, inadequate rations, poor implements, lack of schools and medical assistance and general dissatisfaction with government measures. The report on their presentation stated "that requests for redress of their grievances have been again and again made without effect. They are glad that the young men have not resorted to violent measures to gain it. That it is almost too hard for them to bear the treatment received at the hands of the government after its 'sweet promises' made in order to get their country from them. They now fear that they are going to be cheated. They will wait until next summer to see if this council has the desired effect, failing which they will take measures to get what they desire. (The proposed 'measures' could not be elicited, but a suggestion of the idea of war was repudiated.)"[6]

One measure being proposed by the Chiefs was a meeting of the Grand Council to be held on Little Pine's Reserve in 1885. The Blackfoot would be invited to attend. Once a united position was agreed upon, a delegation of Chiefs would travel to Ottawa where it was believed someone with sufficient authority could make some changes.

Thus, the Indian people were charting their own course of action to deal with Indian problems. It was a plan which called for concerted political action, and under it any outbreak of violence would be viewed as an undesirable course of events.

THE SPREAD OF THE REBELLION TESTS INDIAN LOYALTIES

Following the outbreak of hostilities at Duck Lake, Riel, attempting to spark a Territory-wide insurrection, sent messengers to many reserves urging the Indians to join him. The response of most Indian leaders was to send messages to government authorities reaffirming their loyalty.

On 28 March 1885, a delegation of Touchwood Chiefs sent a message expressing "to his Excellency the Lieutenant-Governor and through him to the Governor-General, their loyalty to their Great Mother the Queen, and further wish to express their disapproval of the course of action pursued by those at the head of the present struggle."[7]

At a meeting called by Riel's messengers at the Crooked Lakes Reserves, the Indians decided to remain loyal. Chief Kahkewistahaw made the following statement: "Agent, you remember the time I promised I would go to my reserve. I also said that I and my young men's fighting days were over. I stick to those words no matter what may be done up north, we will remain on our reserves and attend to our work."[8]

Chief Piapot, the main Cree leader in the South, wrote: "It is eleven years since I gave up fighting. When I took the government Treaty I touched the pen not to interfere with the whiteman and the whiteman not to interfere with me."[9]

Also on 28 March, Indian Agent Rae visited old Chief Mosquito on his reserve a few miles south of Battleford and received the Chief's assurances that the band would remain loyal. At about the same time, Riel's messengers were visiting both Mosquito's and Red Pheasant's Reserves.

On Mosquito's Reserve a band member named Itka had been grieving over the death of his daughter, which he blamed on Farm Instructor Payne. A few days before her death, Payne had physically thrown the frail girl out of his house. Itka decided the time was opportune for revenge, went to the Farm Instructor's home and shot him dead. Relatives of Itka, convinced that Canadian authorities would conduct an American-style retaliation against them, decided that their best alternative would be to seek refuge. They went to the house of Barney Tremont, a local farmer, demanding horses. When Tremont refused, he was shot and killed.

While these events were occurring on the Mosquito Reserve, Chiefs Poundmaker and Little Pine, concerned about the outbreak at Duck Lake, decided to travel to Battleford to express their loyalty to the Queen. Poundmaker also decided that at the same time he would take the opportunity to attempt to gain government concessions for food and other treaty provisions. Hearing this, most of the band members decided to accompany their Chiefs in the hope that they would be present for the distributions.

The two Chiefs and their followers met with Chief Young Sweetgrass on 28 March at the Sweetgrass Reserve, about ten miles west of Battleford. Farm Instructors Jefferson and Craig debated whether or not they should accompany the Indians to Battleford, but decided against it for fear of disapproval by their superiors, who wanted Indians to remain on their reserves.

Also present was Peter Ballantyne, who was operating as a spy for Edgar Dewdney. He checked on the Indians' plans and came to the conclusion that their intentions were peaceful.

Meanwhile in Battleford, rumours were rampant that Poundmaker was approaching to attack the town.

BATTLEFORD—THE SIEGE THAT NEVER OCCURRED

When Poundmaker and his followers reached Battleford on the morning of 30 March, they were surprised to find the town deserted. The residents had taken refuge in the North-West Mounted Police Barracks on the other side of the river.

Poundmaker sent a message to the fort stating his peaceful intentions and requesting a meeting with Indian Agent Rae. Rae refused to leave the fort, but Peter Ballantyne and Hudson's Bay Company Factor McKay came out to meet Poundmaker. McKay agreed to release food to the Indians from the Hudson's Bay Company store.

Governor Dewdney was sent a telegram stating, "Indians willing to go back to reserves tomorrow if their demands for clothing are met. Strongly urge you to deal with them as we are not in a position at present to begin an Indian war."[10] Dewdney later replied, although too late, that he would meet with Poundmaker.

There were other groups who had arrived at Battleford — some of the Stoneys from Mosquito's Reserve, and Riel's agitators from Duck Lake. As Ballantyne and McKay were returning to the fort after failing to arrange talks with Rae, some of the Métis took shots at them. Later that day, some of the Stoneys began to break into stores and loot. Poundmaker and Little Pine tried to restrain their followers from looting, but with only limited success.

By the next morning, Poundmaker and most of his followers were on their way home. The strain of the troubles was too great for Little Pine, who had been suffering from temporary blindness and other symptoms of starvation. He died on 31 March 1885, a few miles before reaching his reserve. Little Pine's death, and that of old Chief Red Pheasant a few days earlier, meant that Poundmaker had become the main Indian leader in the Battleford area.

Accounts of the siege were blown well out of proportion. The telegraph line had not been tampered with, allowing the Battleford residents to send out daily messages of alarm. During the 25 days before relief troops arrived, the 500 settlers barricaded in the fort were even able to obtain water safely from their only source a mile outside of the barracks. According to one observer, "one solitary individual — the cook — had the temerity to continue in residence at the old government house. He had many visitors that day, gave them to eat, when they departed without harming him."[11]

Interestingly enough, another observer reported, "They [the Indians] had been too hurried to take much; the principal looting was the work of white men. As soon as the coast was clear in the morning they came over in detachments and finished what the Indians had begun. They made a clean sweep."[12]

Not the least of these raiders was Farm Instructor Craig, who "devoted his time and attention to looting the stores and houses that had been broken into by the Indians, but his enterprise was frustrated by persistent robbing of his tent whenever he left it."[13]

Several observers were of the opinion that looting would never have taken place had the townspeople not deserted their houses and stores. By and large, the "siege" was a fabricated event.

BIG BEAR'S MISFORTUNE PEAKS AT FROG LAKE

Big Bear had become the principal leader of the northern Plains Cree in 1877, following the death of Chief Sweetgrass. Unfortunately, he had a poor relationship with the government. One of the tactics used by the government during treaty negotiations had been to fail to send notification of the meetings to Indian leaders who were considered difficult to deal with. Such was the reason for Big Bear's arrival at Fort Pitt a day after Treaty Six had been signed.

During a speech objecting to the lack of consultation with the several bands he was representing, Big Bear said:

> I have come off to speak for the different bands that are out on the Plains. It is no small matter we were to consult about. I expected the Chiefs here would have waited until I arrived. . . . I heard the Governor was to come and I said I shall see him; when I see him I will request that he will save me from that which I most dread, that is: the rope to be about my neck, it was not given to us by the Great Spirit that the red man or the white man should shed each other's blood.[14]

The official treaty interpreter had already left and Reverend McKay, whose mastery of Cree was far from perfect, misinterpreted Big Bear's words to mean a fear of hanging (*ayhahkotit*). Big Bear was actually saying that he did not wish to lose his freedom, like an animal with a rope around its neck (*aysakapaykinit*).[15] Nevertheless, the impression created of Big Bear was that he was evil and cowardly, an image which would haunt him up to his final days.

Steadfast in his belief that he could get a revision of Treaty Six, similar to those of Treaties One and Two, Big Bear held out from signing Treaty Six longer than any other Chief. He was forced to sign six years later, when it became clear that his Band members would starve unless they obtained government rations.

In 1884, after years of urging, Big Bear agreed to choose a reserve next to Poundmaker's. Deputy Superintendent-General of Indian Affairs Lawrence Vankoughnet, a man who disliked Big Bear, vetoed the plan, suggesting that it would not be a good idea to have too many "idle Indians" in one area. Instead, Vankoughnet warned Big Bear to take a reserve already set aside near Fort Pitt — a location which Big Bear had already rejected — or face a cut-off of rations during the winter of 1884–85. Big Bear refused to comply.

An unhealthy blend of ingredients was being mixed. Many members of Big Bear's band, including his son Imases and the War Chief Wandering Spirit, were becoming frustrated with the state of affairs. Compounding the problem was the presence of Indian Agent Quinn, a man known to have been abusive to Indians, and Farm Instructor Delaney, who had been accused of violating Indian women. The government was aware of the unpopularity of these men with the Indians, and had been planning to relocate them.

News of the Duck Lake fight did not reach Agent Quinn until late on 31 March 1885. The next day, 1 April or "Big Lie Day," as the Indians called it, Quinn summoned Big Bear's band members to inform them of the incident. Imases, speaking on behalf of Big Bear, who was out hunting for food for the band, replied:

> They have already risen; we knew about it before you. They have beaten the soldiers in the first fight, killing many. We do not wish to join the half-breeds, but we are afraid. We wish to stay here and prove ourselves the friends of the white man.[16]

Imases then asked Quinn to provide rations to the band. Quinn refused, saying he would have to speak to Big Bear first.

Later that day Big Bear returned empty-handed from hunting and led a delegation to request rations from Quinn. Big Bear was upset at his refusal. Imases, hoping to win a compromise, suggested that Quinn give the Indians food for a feast as a gift to the band, and he would not then have to call it rations. Quinn, however, had decided to give them nothing.

That night, unknown to Big Bear, Wandering Spirit and several members of the Rattler's Warrior Society held a dance in secret. As dawn broke some twenty armed warriors came to the Frog Lake community, waking up the residents and herding them to Quinn's house.

That morning, when asked for food and other supplies, Quinn was willing to comply, and various Indians were allowed to have goods from the stores.

That day was Holy Thursday, and two priests who had come for the occasion asked permission to hold church services. The hostages were all allowed to attend church. By this time Big Bear had learned of the trouble and had joined the whites in the church to ensure that nothing worse occurred.

As the church service progressed, the noise outside increased. The warriors had broken into the stores and had found wine, spirits, and painkillers. As these were consumed the shouting and yelling of the warriors grew louder, and they eventually began to enter the church and disrupt the service.[17]

Big Bear decided to leave the church and begin warning the other residents of the community, who were in their houses, to leave in case trouble broke out. He was at Mrs. Simpson's house when he heard shots. The church service had been cut short.

Wandering Spirit, the War Chief, ordered the whites to go to the Indian camp, a short distance away. Quinn refused to move, and after repeated warnings Wandering Spirit shot him dead.

Big Bear ran outside, yelling at the warriors to stop it, but it was too late. Urged on by the prompting of Wandering Spirit, the warriors soon killed eight white men.

Perhaps the violence would have been averted had Quinn simply given food to the starving band the day before. It did not appear that the band was thinking seriously of any sort of insurrection at that time. Even on the following day, had Quinn been liberal with Indian requests for food and simply complied with the warriors' orders, it is possible that bloodshed could have been averted entirely. The presence of alcohol and painkillers can be the only explanation for the gruesomeness of the murders. In Indian thinking, it was considered dishonourable and cowardly to kill an unarmed man for no reason at all.

Big Bear's hopes of peaceful dealings with government had all but vanished, yet he distinguished himself by protecting the lives of the remaining white captives, and by preventing greater bloodshed at Fort Pitt.

The warriors moved to seize the provisions at Fort Pitt on 14 April. Big Bear, no longer in control of the band, argued for an attempt to arrange a peaceful surrender of the Fort. He held the warriors back for one night, and the next day persuaded 44 civilians to surrender to the band. With this achieved, the North West Mounted Police detachment had little reason to stay, and was allowed to escape down the river by boat. Big Bear's vigilance was an important factor in preventing any deaths among them.

THE UNPROVOKED ATTACK ON CUTKNIFE HILL

Although Poundmaker had been forced to relinquish power to the warrior society, he was influential in maintaining calm among the Indians camped at Cutknife Hill following the so-called siege of Battleford.

Lieutenant-Colonel Otter arrived at Battleford on 24 April 1885 with close to 550 troops. Also, part of his arsenal was a Gatling gun sent for demonstration by the United States Army.

Otter's troops were sorely disappointed at not seeing action on arrival at Battleford. Otter had been ordered by Middleton to stay at Battleford and guard the townspeople. Sensing the unrest of his troops, and seeing the opportunity to gain personal glory, Otter wired Dewdney, "I proposed taking part of my force at once to punish Poundmaker leaving 100 men to garrison Battleford. Great depredations committed. Immediate decisive action necessary. Do you approve?"[18]

Dewdney, probably after consulting the Prime Minister, wired Otter with approval.

Otter planned to surprise Poundmaker and force him to surrender. On the evening of 28 April, he left Battleford for Cutknife Hill. Otter's timing was good, and he arrived at the foot of Cutknife Hill at 5:15 the following morning. Fortunately for Poundmaker's camp, an old man, Jacob With the Long Hair, was awake and heard the sounds of the approaching soldiers. He ran through the camp shouting warnings.

At that point Otter ordered his guns to open fire on the sleeping camp. The barrage knocked over some tipis, but all of the occupants managed to scramble to safety.

Some of the Indian warriors ran out to confront the troops while others began shooting from nearby coulees. According to Robert Jefferson, an eyewitness, "Not more than 50 [Indians] altogether, had taken part in the battle. This was excusable since few were armed."[19] As the battle continued throughout the morning, Otter realized that his troops were in a vulnerable position and were slowly being surrounded. Just before noon, he ordered his men to retreat.

The warriors wanted to pursue Otter. Knowing the land like the backs of their hands and gaining the advantage of nightfall, the warriors could have inflicted heavy casualties on the tiring soldiers. Poundmaker refused to agree, maintaining that while the Indians were right in defending themselves on their land, it would be wrong to go on the offensive.

There had been a split among the people at Cutknife Hill. On the one side was the pro-Riel faction consisting of the Métis agitators and the Stoney warriors. On the other side were those led by Poundmaker who wanted to have as little as possible to do with the rebellion. Poundmaker had tried to lead his followers west toward the hilly country around Devil's Lake, with plans to eventually take refuge near Crowfoot, but the warriors and Métis prevented them from leaving.

Poundmaker was essentially being used as a spokesman by the belligerent faction. An example of this was a letter to Riel dictated by Riel's sympathizers but bearing the "signatures" of Poundmaker and several other Indians. Poundmaker's lack of verbal or written knowledge of either French or English put him at a great disadvantage. The fact was that Poundmaker was not in control, and the insinuation of support for Riel contained in the letter was out of character with his actions. That letter later became the main piece of evidence used in convicting Poundmaker.

Following the Battle of Cutknife Hill, it was decided that it was no longer safe to remain on the reserve. When the pro-Riel faction decided to join Riel at Batoche, Poundmaker attempted to lead his followers west, away from trouble. The dispute nearly led to bloodshed, but Poundmaker's poorly armed followers relented. Poundmaker's lack of cooperation and additional efforts to break away from the camp slowed the Indians' progress to Batoche by several days.

Poundmaker's stalling tactics saved many Indian lives, for as they neared Batoche on 14 May, they received news that Middleton's army had just defeated the Métis. After some discussion, Poundmaker sought terms of surrender from Middleton; when refused, he surrendered unconditionally at Battleford on 26 May 1885.

Poundmaker's plan to abandon his reserve and seek refuge by moving to an isolated area was not unique. A significant number of band members, from reserves such as Mosquito's, Red Pheasant's, One Arrow's and Thunderchild's, went north to avoid any involvement in the troubles.

During this period, Sir John A. Macdonald was attempting to exploit tribal differences by inquiring about sending Indian patrols against Poundmaker and Big Bear. He wrote Dewdney on 29 March 1885, "I understand that the Crees dread the Blackfeet like the devil. Now a corps of scouts under Crowfoot might be formed."[20] Because of the relationship between Crowfoot and Poundmaker this plan never succeeded, despite repeated requests from the Prime Minister.

AT BATOCHE AGAINST THEIR WILL

Part of the strategy of Riel's provisional government was based on the belief that they held influence over the Indians. In a note to the English half-breeds on 22 March 1885, they wrote, "We are sure that if the English and French half-breeds unite well in this time of crisis, not only can we control the Indians, but we will also have their weight on our side."[21] With Indians outnumbering both Métis and whites in the northwest, their support in a conflict could be critical, but the presumption of Indian involvement was made without consultation with any of the Indian leaders.

On 18 March 1885, one day before Riel's proclamation of his provisional government, that process of "controlling" Indians began. About 40 Riel supporters arrived at One Arrow's Reserve, approximately two miles east of Batoche, taking the Indian agent and farm instructor prisoner. The next day, One Arrow and fifteen of his men came to Batoche. As One Arrow testified at his trial,

> I am an old man now. . . . I was taken to the place, Batoche's, to join Riel by Gabriel. I did not take myself to the place. They took me there. I could not say how many there were of them that took me there, but there was quite a number of them. . . . so when I went there and got there I was taken prisoner.[22]

Witnesses testified that One Arrow was seen in the area during both the Duck Lake fight and the Battle of Batoche. In his defence, One Arrow testified that,

> All that was said against me was thrown upon me falsely. I did not take up my gun with the intention to shoot at any man. I was on the brink of the hill the whole day, and I had my gun there, but, of course, not with the intention to use the gun against any man, and when I saw the whitemen coming down, I ran down the hill too, and ran off.[23]

On 10 April 1885, around twenty Riel supporters arrived at Whitecap's Reserve, a few miles south of Saskatoon. Whitecap, the Chief of a band of refugee American Dakota, had resisted Riel's overtures two weeks previous. Before the Métis began forcing Whitecap and twenty of his men toward Batoche, Whitecap managed to send a message to a white friend in Saskatoon, Gerald Willoughby, asking him for assistance. When the group reached Saskatoon, a group of nine citizens tried to persuade the Métis to allow Whitecap to return to his reserve. Outnumbered, they were unsuccessful.

When Whitecap arrived at Batoche, he was appointed the only Indian member of Riel's council on internal matters, but because he understood neither French nor Cree, he attended only one meeting.

Whitecap's men were seen at the battles of Fish Creek and Batoche. Testimony provided by the main prosecution witnesses showed that Whitecap could not be positively identified as having been among the several old Indian men at Batoche, but it was mainly because of the evidence showing that Whitecap had been coerced to fight that all charges against him were dropped.[24]

THE INDIAN TRIALS: UNWARRANTED PUNISHMENT

Poundmaker, despite evidence of his efforts to maintain peace, was convicted of treason-felony on the basis of the letter to Riel bearing his name. Speaking after hearing the guilty verdict, Poundmaker categorically denied any wrongdoing, saying, "Everything that is bad has been laid against me this summer, there is nothing of it true."[25] On hearing that he was sentenced to three years at Stony Mountain, Poundmaker declared, "I would prefer to be hung at once than to be in that place."[26] Poundmaker was released in the spring of 1886, largely because of public sympathy, but he died in June after making a trek on foot to visit his adoptive father, Crowfoot.

Although the evidence was strongly in favour of Big Bear, it appeared that the outcome of his trial was predetermined, and he was sentenced to the same three-year term as Poundmaker. There was less public sympathy for Big Bear, and he was not released until 3 February 1887, after a medical report confirmed his badly deteriorating health. He had no band to return to, as it had been dispersed by the government. Most of his family he would never see, as they were fugitives in the United States. With his heart broken and no cause to live for, he died on 18 January 1888.

When Chief One Arrow heard the charges of treason-felony translated to him, it came out in Cree as "knocking off the Queen's bonnet and stabbing her in the behind with a sword."[27] This moved One Arrow to ask the interpreter if he was drunk. The conviction of One Arrow was based on his presence at the battle sites, and his account of how he came to be there was ignored.

One Arrow was not so fortunate as to make it back to his own reserve. He was released from Stony Mountain Prison on 21 April 1886, and died four days later at Archbishop Taché's residence in St. Boniface. He was baptized just before his death and lies in St. Boniface cemetery in an unmarked grave.

In order to save money, a decision was made not to hold all of the rebellion trials at Regina. Several of them were held in Battleford instead. The atmosphere in Battleford was not hospitable toward Indians, as an editorial in the *Saskatchewan Herald* on 23 April 1885 shows:

> The petted Indians are the bad ones. The Stonies have been treated as being of a superior race, and are the first to shed the blood of their benefactors. Poundmaker has been petted and feted, and stands in the front rank as a raider. Little Pine, bribed to come north and kept in comfort, hastens to the carnage. Big Bear, who has for years enjoyed the privilege of eating of the bread of idleness, shows his gratitude by killing his priests and his best friends in cold blood. Little Poplar, a non-treaty Indian, has been liberally supplied with provisions and other necessaries and thus enabled to spend all his time in travelling up and down the land plotting mischief and preparing for this season's carnival of ruin. The petted Indians have proved the bad ones, and this gives weight to the old adage that the only good Indians are the dead ones.[28]

Judge Rouleau, who would pass the judgements, had narrowly missed being murdered along with Farm Instructor Payne, and was also bitter about the burning of his mansion at Battleford. He was known before the trials to advocate harsh punishment as a deterrent to future rebellious acts by Indians.

The eight Indians eventually hanged were at a disadvantage. They knew nothing of the legal system and had no legal counsel or other advice. No effective defence of any sort was mounted which might have created sympathy for the defendants — for example, the reality of their starvation under Indian Affairs administration, or the excesses brought on by alcohol and drugs at the Frog Lake massacre.

Several Indian Elders are certain that at least one of the Indians, Man-Without-Blood, was wrongly hanged for the shooting of Farm Instructor Payne. They claim it was done by the other Stoney, Man-With-a-Black-Blanket. According to one story,

> The two of the Stoney young men were arrested also. They were accused of killing the farm instructor and they were both arrested. And at that time people were very respectable. There was a lot of respect for the older people. Now the one who did not kill the Indian Agent, he was the one who was accused by his partner. So the one who was accused of killing the farm instructor, when he went to trial, the officer asked him, "Is it true what you did? Or is it not true?" He replied, "Maybe it is true, and maybe it is not." And he really had nothing to do with it, he didn't shoot the Indian Agent. So when he said, "Maybe they are telling the truth," that was accepted as his plea, as telling the truth. So he got the blame for the death of the farm instructor. So he was one of them that got hanged. They weren't going to sympathize with him or feel sorry for him.[29]

According to another story, "It's him who killed the ration feeder. And the one who followed him shot the dog. He was the one who got hung instead, said my father, the one who shot the dog. He did not want to report his partner."[30]

No clear evidence of committing murder was shown against Iron Body and Little Bear, two of the six Indians tried for their role in the Frog Lake massacre. They were hanged on the basis that, by aiding and abetting the others, they were equally guilty.

Four Sky Thunder received a sentence of fourteen years for burning down the Frog Lake church. Another Indian, whose only wrongdoing was having been seen with Big Bear, was sentenced to six years in prison.[31]

Several Indians were never brought to justice. Among them was Man-Who-Speaks-Our-Language, who nearly caused the outbreak of fighting with the North West Mounted Police on Poundmaker's Reserve in 1884, and was responsible for some of the killings at Frog Lake.

The hangings at Battleford took place on 27 November 1885. Indians from several reserves were there to witness the event.

A new section was built at Stony Mountain Penitentiary to accommodate the 25 Indians and eighteen Métis sentenced to prison. Several of the Indians never returned to their reserves, and are buried in the St. Boniface cemetery.

THE AFTERMATH: SUPPRESSION OF INDIANS

The government saw the rebellion as an opportunity to achieve a goal which had eluded it since 1870, that of gaining total control over Indians. In July of 1885, Assistant Commissioner Hayter Reed drew up a list of fifteen recommendations on actions to be taken following the rebellion. Among these were the following:

> The leaders of the Teton Sioux who fought against the troops should be hanged and the rest be sent out of the country;
>
> Big Bear's band should either be broken up and scattered among other bands or be given a reserve adjacent to that at Onion Lake;

One Arrow's band should be joined with that of Beardy and Okemasis and their reserve surrendered;

No annuity money should be now paid any bands that rebelled, or to any individuals that joined the insurgents;

The tribal system should be abolished in so far as is compatible with the Treaty;

All half-breeds, members of rebel bands, although not shown to have taken any active part in the rebellion, should have their names erased from the paysheets;

No rebel Indians should be allowed off the Reserves without a pass signed by an Indian Department official; and

All Indians who have not during the late troubles been disloyal or troublesome should be treated as heretofore.[32]

Reed had also prepared a list of every Indian band in the northwest and had identified 28 disloyal bands. In his enthusiasm he erroneously included several reserves, such as Sweetgrass and Thunderchild, which had been very loyal. Most of the others had actually been loyal, with only the odd individual implicated in the rebellion. Of all the bands identified as disloyal in the rebellion, it is clear that none of the Chiefs, whether Big Bear, Poundmaker, Mosquito, Red Pheasant, Little Pine, Beardy, One Arrow or Whitecap, politically supported the rebellion. All were drawn into the conflict by circumstances beyond their personal control. In all, less than five percent of the Indian population of the northwest was involved.

The original proposal to disallow rebel Indians from leaving their reserves without a pass soon became a measure to be applied to all Indians. In approving this plan, Sir John A. Macdonald was aware that he was contravening the treaties. He noted:

Mr. Dewdney thinks that the pass system can be generally introduced in July. If so, it is in the highest degree desirable. As to the disloyal Bands, this should be carried out as the consequence of their disloyalty. The system should be introduced in the loyal Bands as well and the advantage of the change pressed upon them. But no punishment for breaking bounds could be inflicted and in the case of resistance on the grounds of Treaty rights should not be insisted on.[33]

The measures taken against Indians, in particular those restricting them to reserves, were measures which would have a profound effect on subsequent Indian developments. What little influence Indian people had over their own lives was removed, and Indian people became vulnerable to government whim, manipulation and mismanagement.

It was regrettable that Sir John A. Macdonald, who was Superintendent General of Indian Affairs and Prime Minister, never once bothered to visit the people over whom he had charge during the eight critical years he held office, from 1879 to 1887.

Had the Indian people been able to retain their freedom of movement, things might have turned out much differently. Big Bear and other Indian leaders might have met Sir John A. Macdonald in 1885. Nationally, efforts to form the League of Indians of Canada in the 1920s and the North American Indian Brotherhood in the 1940s would have been more successful and probably would have received the bulk of their strength from the prairies. Indian political development in Canada was probably put back by two generations.

The rebellion has left a legacy of a century of suspicions about Indian political abilities and loyalties, and misconceptions about the validity of Indian treaties.

In concluding, I would say that a clear understanding of the Indian view of the 1885 Uprising is the least that can be done to right the blunders of the past.

NOTES

1. Florence Paul, interview by Wilfred Tootoosis, One Arrow Indian Reserve, 15 March 1985.
2. Harry Michael, interview by Wilfred Tootoosis, Beardy's Indian Reserve, 14 March 1985.
3. Canada, *Treaty Number Six Between Her Majesty the Queen and the Plain and Wood Cree Indians and other Tribes of Indians* (Ottawa: Queen's Printer, 1964), 5.
4. John B. Tootoosis, interview by Wilfred Tootoosis, Poundmaker Indian Reserve, 30 November 1984.
5. Canada, *Sessional Papers*, 1886, No. 36, 2.
6. Public Archives of Canada (hereafter PAC), RG 10, Vol. 3697, File 15,423, MacRae to Dewdney, 25 August 1884.
7. PAC, RG 10, Vol. 3584, File 1130, Pt. 3A, McBeath to Macdonald, 28 March 1885.
8. PAC, RG 10, Vol. 3584, File 1130, Pt. 3A, Macdonald to Indian Commissioner, 8 April 1885.
9. PAC, RG 10, Vol. 3584, File 1130, Pt. 3A, Piapot to Macdonald, 30 April 1885.
10. Dewdney Papers, Vol. 5, 1879–1880, Rae to Dewdney, 30 March 1885.
11. Robert Jefferson, *Fifty Years on the Saskatchewan* (Battleford: Canadian Northwest Historical Society, 1929), 127.
12. Ibid., 128.
13. Ibid., 126.
14. Alexander Morris, *Treaties of Canada With the Indians of Manitoba and the North-West Territories* (Toronto: Coles Publishing Limited, 1971), 239.
15. Hugh Dempsey, *Big Bear — The End of Freedom* (Vancouver: Douglas and McIntyre, 1984), 74.
16. W.B. Cameron, *Blood Red the Sun* (Edmonton: Hurtig Publishers, 1977), 33.
17. Dempsey, *Big Bear*, 155.
18. Dewdney Papers, Vol. 5, p. 1806, Otter to Dewdney, 26 April 1885.
19. Jefferson, *Fifty Years*, 146.
20. PAC, MG 26A, Vol. 526, p. 1404, Macdonald to Dewdney, 29 March 1885.
21. Bob Beal and Rod Macleod, *Prairie Fire: The 1885 North-West Rebellion* (Edmonton: Hurtig Publishers, 1984), 148.
22. Canada, *Sessional Papers*, 1886, No. 52, 33.
23. Ibid., 32.
24. Ibid., 13.
25. Ibid., 336.
26. Ibid., 337.
27. Beal and Macleod, *Prairie Fire*, 309.
28. *Saskatchewan Herald* (Battleford), 23 April 1885.
29. Lawrence Lonesinger, interview by Wilfred Tootoosis, Sweetgrass Indian Reserve, 13 March 1985.
30. Alex Sapp, interview by Wilfred Tootoosis, Little Pine Indian Reserve, date not available.
31. S.E. Bingaman, "The North-West Rebellion Trials, 1885" (Master's thesis, University of Regina, 1971), 133.
32. PAC, RG 10, Vol. 3710, File 19, 550–3, Reed to Dewdney, 20 July 1885.
33. PAC, RG 10, Vol. 3710, File 19, 550–3, Vankoughnet to Superintendent General, 17 August 1885.

Topic Nine

Racism and Nationalism

The priests, nuns, and teachers of the Fort Qu'Appelle Industrial School stand behind the school's Native students in this 1899 photo.

In the past, Canadian historians were reluctant to admit to racism in their history, believing that it would detract from an image of Canada as a united and harmonious nation. If reference to ethnic groups arose, it was usually in terms of their positive contribution to the settlement of the West. If a negative perspective arose, it was in reference to ethnic radicals and insurrections, especially with regards to the Winnipeg General Strike. But shortly after the Second World War, ethnic history emerged as a sub-field of Canadian social history. Ethnic historians were interested in looking beyond the history of ethnic immigration to study their experiences as minority groups within the country. What obstacles stood in the way of their being accepted and integrated into Canadian society? What were the attitudes of the host society towards these newcomers? Although First Nations' people were not recent immigrants, they too experienced racism.

The following three articles deal with racism in the late 19th and the early 20th centuries. This proved to be a period of transition for First Nations under the federal government's aggressive policy of assimilation into Canadian society. In "Taming Aboriginal Sexuality: Gender, Power, and Race in British Columbia, 1850–1900," historian Jean Barman examines attitudes toward First Nations peoples in British Columbia. She argues that the dominant male society viewed First Nations women as sexually independent, and hence "wild" and "untamed." Such attitudes fitted into the prevailing Social Darwinist views of racial hierarchy. Social Darwinist attitudes, Barman shows, were also evident on issues of housing, the potlatch, and child care.

Historian Howard Palmer examines attitudes of assimilation toward non-British and non-French immigrants in the late 19th to the middle of the 20th centuries. He identifies three assimilation theories. The first he describes as anglo-conformity, which predominated from the 1880s to 1945. This was followed in the post-World War II period by the "melting pot" theory. Then beginning in the 1960s, a theory of "cultural pluralism" took hold, reflected in the federal government's policy of "multiculturalism." All three policies, he argues, ultimately shared an acceptance of the need for assimilation. Such attitudes, Palmer points out, challenged two Canadian myths: first, that Canadians have throughout their history been tolerant of minority groups, and, second, that Canadians have adopted a "mosaic" approach to ethnic groups that encourages ethnic differences, unlike the American "melting-pot" approach that demands conformity.

Racism reached new levels in Canada during times of war. Historian James W. St.G. Walker examines the factor of racism in the recruiting of visible minorities for the Canadian Expeditionary Force during World War I. He emphasizes that Canada was not alone in applying racist attitudes, that the other Dominions as well as the European countries in the Western world shared the same ideology of "race." They held to a common belief that this was "a white man's war." In the early years of the war when the supply of volunteers exceeded demand, "race" was a factor for rejecting certain volunteers. Only when casualties at the front eroded the number of soldiers available, and as recruitment died off, did the army recruit visible minorities; even then, they were often given lesser duties or allowed to belong to "special" segregated units only. These actions discouraged minorities from enlisting. Those who did enlist did so on the belief that if they fought for their country, their country would grant them the rights of Canadian citizenship. For many, these hopes remained unfulfilled after the war's end.

What were the common assumptions about "race" that lay behind discrimination against First Nations women in British Columbia in the settlement period, ethnic groups on the Prairies during a similar settlement period, and visible minorities in World War I? How was racism linked to nationalism? Has racism lessened over time, or simply taken a new form and been expressed in a different way today?

Brian Titley reviews the policy of the Canadian government toward First Nations in *A Narrow Vision: Duncan Campbell Scott and the Administration of Indian Affairs in Canada* (Vancouver: University of British Columbia Press, 1987). On First Nations–newcomer relations, see J.R. Miller, *Skyscrapers Hide the Heavens: A History of Indian-White Relations in Canada*, 3rd ed. (Toronto: University of Toronto Press, 2000). A valuable article is John L. Tobias, "Canada's Subjugation of the Plains Cree, 1879–1885," *Canadian Historical Review*, 64, 4 (December 1983): 519–548. On the role of residential schools as seedbeds of racism, see J.R. Miller, *Shingwauk's Vision: A History of Native Residential Schools* (Toronto: University of Toronto Press, 1996); and John S. Milloy, *A National Crime: The Canadian Government and the Residential School System 1879–1986* (Winnipeg: The University of Manitoba Press, 1999). With regards to the Canadian government's prejudicial attitudes toward Natives in the context of farming on the reserves, see Sarah Carter, *Lost Harvests: Prairie Indian Reserve Farmers and Government Policy* (Montreal/Kingston: McGill-Queen's University Press, 1990); and Helen Buckley, *From Wooden Ploughs to Welfare: Why Indian Policy Failed in the Prairie Provinces* (Montreal/Kingston: McGill-Queen's University Press, 1992).

Howard Palmer explores racism in Alberta's history in greater depth in *Patterns of Prejudice: A History of Nativism in Alberta* (Toronto: McClelland & Stewart, 1982). On racism and European immigrants, see Donald Avery, *Reluctant Host: Canada's Response to Immigrant Workers, 1896–1994* (Toronto: McClelland and Stewart, 1979). Prejudice from the immigrant experience can be examined in R.F. Harney and H. Troper, *Immigrants: A Portrait of the Urban Experience, 1890–1930* (Toronto: Van Nostrand Reinhold, 1975); Arnold Itwaru, *The Invention of Canada* (Toronto: Tsar Publications, 1990); and from John Marlyn's novel, *Under the Ribs of Death* (Toronto: McClelland & Stewart, 1957).

On discrimination against Asians in British Columbia, see W. Peter Ward, *White Canada Forever: Popular Attitudes and Public Policies towards Orientals in British Columbia* (Montreal/Kingston: McGill-Queen's University Press, 1978). For an alternative view, see Patricia Roy's "British Columbia's Fear of Asians, 1900–1950," *Histoire sociale/Social History* 13 (May 1980): 161–72, and her book, *A White Man's Province: British Columbia Politicians and Chinese and Japanese Immigrants, 1858–1914* (Vancouver: University of British Columbia Press, 1989). See as well, Patricia Roy, "'The wholesome sea is at her gates/Her gates both east and west': Canada's Selective and Restrictive Immigration Policies in the First Half of the Twentieth Century," in *Canada, 1900–1950: A Country Comes of Age*, eds. Serge Bernier and John MacFarlane (Ottawa: Organization for the History of Canada, 2003), pp. 33–49.

On ethnic relations during wartime, see John Herd Thompson, *Ethnic Minorities During Two World Wars* (Ottawa: Canadian Historical Association, 1991). On the only African-Canadian battalion see John G. Armstrong, "The Unwelcome Sacrifice: A Black Unit in the Canadian Expeditionary Force," in *Ethnic Armies: Polyethnic Armed Forces from the Time of the Hapsburg to the Age of the Superpowers*, ed. N.F. Dreisziger (Waterloo, ON: Wilfrid Laurier University Press, 1990), pp. 178–97; and Calvin Ruck, *The Black Battalion, 1916–1920: Canada's Best Kept Military Secret* (Halifax: Nimbus, 1987). On First Nations soldiers see Fred Gaffen, *Forgotten Soldiers* (Penticton, BC: Theytus Books, 1985); and James Dempsey, *Warriors of the King: Prairie Indians in World War I* (Regina: Canadian Plains Research Center, 1999).

For a discussion of discrimination toward Japanese Canadians during World War II, see W. Peter Ward, "British Columbia and the Japanese Evacuation," *Canadian Historical Review*, 57, 3 (September 1976): 289–309, and the relevant section of *White Canada Forever* (cited earlier). See as well, Patricia Roy et al., *Mutual Hostages: Canadians and Japanese during the Second World War* (Toronto: University of Toronto Press, 1990), and J.L. Granatstein and Gregory Johnson, "The Evacuation of the Japanese Canadians, 1942: A Realist Critique of the Received

Version," in *On Guard for Thee: War, Ethnicity, and the Canadian State, 1939–1945*, eds. N. Hillmer et al. (Ottawa: Canadian Committee for the History of the Second World War, 1988) pp. 101–129. Ann Gomer Sunahara's *The Politics of Racism: The Uprooting of Japanese Canadians during the Second World War* (Toronto: Lorimer, 1981) is a carefully documented study of this same issue; it should be read in conjunction with Ward's study.

WEBLINKS

Open Hearts, Closed Doors
http://www.virtualmuseum.ca/Exhibitions/orphans/english/themes/immigration/page1.html

Documents regarding Canada's immigration policies from the late 19th century to today.

Immigration Report of 1887
http://www.dcs.uwaterloo.ca/~marj/genealogy/reports/report1887west.html

Extracts from a federal immigration report from 1887.

Chinese Immigration Act
http://www.canadiana.org/ECO/PageView/9_02345/0019

Complete text of the 1885 Chinese Immigration Act, which includes among other requirements the initial "head tax" of $50 per Chinese immigrant.

Residential Schools
http://www.ainc-inac.gc.ca/ch/rcap/sg/sgm10_e.html

A chapter from the Royal Commission on Aboriginal Peoples regarding residential schools. For more information on residential schools see

http://archives.cbc.ca/IDD-1-70-692/disasters_tragedies/residential_schools.

Wartime Elections Act
http://www.canadiana.org/ECO/ItemRecord/9_07190

A digitized copy of the 1917 Wartime Elections Act. The act allowed some Canadian women to vote, but also denied the right to vote to some naturalized Canadians from overseas.

Aboriginal Soldiers
http://www.vac-acc.gc.ca/general/sub.cfm?source=history/other/native

Detailed descriptions of the contributions made to the Canadian military by aboriginal soldiers from World War I to the present.

Article Twenty-One

Taming Aboriginal Sexuality: Gender, Power, and Race in British Columbia, 1850–1900[1]

Jean Barman

In July 1996 I listened in a Vancouver court room as Catholic Bishop Hubert O'Conner defended himself against charges of having raped or indecently assaulted four young Aboriginal women three decades earlier. His assertion of ignorance when asked what one of the complainants had been wearing on the grounds that, "as you know, I'm a celibate man" encapsulated his certainty that he had done nothing wrong.[2] He admitted to sexual relations with two of the women, but the inference was clear: they had made him do it. They had dragged him down and led him astray. The temptation exercised by their sexuality was too great for any mere man, even a priest and residential school principal, to resist.

I returned home from that day, and subsequent days in the court room, deeply troubled. I might have been reading any of hundreds of similar accounts written over the past century and more about Aboriginal women in British Columbia. This essay represents my first attempt to come to terms with Bishop O'Conner and his predecessors, made more necessary on reading the National Parole Board's decision of March 1997. The Board denied Bishop O'Conner parole, subsequent to his conviction on two of the charges, because "your recent psychological assessment indicates that you hold your victims in contempt," and "at your hearing today . . . you maintain that . . . you in fact were seduced."[3] If I earlier considered that my response to my days in the courtroom might have been exaggerated, I no longer did so. My interest is not in Bishop O'Conner's guilt or innocence in a court of law, but, rather, in tracing the lineage of his attitudes in the history of British Columbia.

The more I have thought about Bishop O'Conner, the more I realize that those of us who dabble at the edges of Aboriginal history have ourselves been seduced. However much we pretend to read our sources "against the grain," to borrow from the cultural theorist Walter Benjamin, we have become entrapped in a partial world that represents itself as the whole world. Records almost wholly male in impetus have been used by mostly male scholars to write about Aboriginal men as if they make up the entirety of Aboriginal people.[4] The assumption that men and male perspectives equate with all persons and perspectives is so accepted that it does even not have to be declared.[5] Thus, an American researcher wanting to find out about her Aboriginal counterparts discovered that "indigenous communities had been described and dissected by white men — explorers, traders, missionaries, and scholars — whose observations sometimes revealed more about their own cultural biases than about Native people. Misperceptions of Indian women were rampant because they were held up to the patriarchal model."[6]

So what happens when we turn the past on its head and make our reference point Aboriginal women instead of Aboriginal men? We come face to face with Aboriginal sexuality or, more accurately, with male perceptions of Aboriginal sexuality. The term 'sexuality' is used here in its sociological sense as "the personal and interpersonal expression of those socially constructed qualities, desires, roles and identities which have to do with sexual behaviour and activity," the underlying contention being "the social and cultural relativity of norms surrounding sexual behaviour and the sociohistorical construction of sexual identities and

Source: Jean Barman, "Taming Aboriginal Sexuality: Gender, Power, and Race in British Columbia, 1850–1950," BC Studies, No. 115/116 (Autumn/Winter 1997/98): 237–66.

roles."[7] In a useful summary of recent scholarship, English sociologist Gail Hawkes tells us that the word sexuality "appeared first in the nineteenth century," reflecting "the focus of concerns about the social consequences of sexual desire in the context of modernity." Christian dogma defined sexual desire "as an unreasoned force differentially possessed by women, which threatened the reason of man" and the "inherent moral supremacy of men." According to Hawkes, "the backbone of Victorian sexuality was the successful promotion of a version of women's sexuality, an ideal of purity and sexual innocence well fitted to the separation of spheres that underpinned the patriarchal power of the new ruling class."[8] Sexuality, as Hawkes contextualizes the term, helps us better to understand the critical years in British Columbia, 1850–1900, when newcomers and Aboriginal peoples came into sustained contact.

Everywhere around the world Indigenous women presented an enormous dilemma to colonizers, at the heart of which lay their sexuality.[9] Initially solutions were simple and straightforward. During conquest local women were used for sexual gratification as a matter of course, just as had been (and still are) female victims of war across the centuries. If unspoken and for the most part unwritten, it was generally accepted that, so long as colonial women were absent, Indigenous women could be used to satisfy what were perceived to be natural needs.[10] No scruples existed over what the pioneering scholar on race Philip Mason has termed "the casual use of a social inferior for sexual pleasure."[11] The growth of settler colonies changed the 'rules of the game.' As anthropologist and historian Ann Laura Stoler astutely observes, drawing from her research on colonial Asia, "while the colonies were marketed by colonial elites as a domain where colonizing men could indulge their sexual fantasies, these same elites were intent to mark the boundaries of a colonizing population, to prevent these men from 'going native,' to curb a proliferating mixed-race population that compromised their claims to superiority and thus the legitimacy of white rule."[12]

In British Columbia gender, power, and race came together in a manner that made it possible for men in power to condemn Aboriginal sexuality and at the same time, if they so chose, to use for their own gratification the very women they had turned into sexual objects. While much of what occurred mirrored events elsewhere, some aspects were distinctive.[13] Colonizers never viewed Aboriginal men as sexual threats,[14] whereas attitudes toward women acquired a particular self-righteousness and fervor. The assumptions newcomers brought with them shaped attitudes, which then informed actions. By the mid-nineteenth century Europeans perceived all female sexual autonomy to be illicit, especially if it occurred in the public sphere, considered exclusively male. Aboriginal women in British Columbia not only dared to exercise agency but often did so publicly, convincing men in power that their sexuality was out of control. To the extent that women persisted in managing their own sexual behaviour, they were wilded into the 'savages' that many newcomers, in any case, considered all Indigenous peoples to be.[15] That is, until Aboriginal women acceded to men in power by having their sexuality tamed according to their precepts, they were for the taking, an equation of agency with sexuality that encourages Aboriginal women's portrayal, even today, as the keepers of tradition. As noted about American anthropological writing, "Native women are pictured as unchanging — clinging to a traditional way of life that exists outside the vicissitudes of history."[16] To avoid the image that men like Bishop O'Conner continue to project on them, Aboriginal women have had to be stripped of their agency past and present.

PROSTITUTION

Indigenous sexuality struck at the very heart of the colonial project. British historian Catherine Hall has noted, in reference to Victorian England, that "sex was a necessary obligation owed to men and not one which women were permitted to talk or think about as owed to themselves."[17]

Sexual independence, or circumstances where that possibility existed, was the ultimate threat to the patriarchal family. Children were considered to belong to their father, who had to have the assurance that they were indeed his biological heirs. As succinctly summed up by George Stocking in his history of Victorian anthropology, "if the ideal wife and mother was 'so pure-hearted as to be utterly ignorant of and averse to any sensual indulgence,' the alternate cultural image of the 'fallen woman' conveys a hint of an underlying preoccupation with the threat of uncontrolled female sexuality." By the time Victoria came to the throne in 1837, "the basic structure of taboos was already defined: the renunciation of all sexual activity save the procreative intercourse of Christian marriage; the education of both sexes in chastity and continence; the secrecy and cultivated ignorance surrounding sex; the bowdlerization of literature and euphemistic degradation of language; the general suppression of bodily functions and all the 'coarser' aspects of life — in short, the whole repressive pattern of purity, prudery, and propriety that was to condition sexual behavior for decades to come." Counterpoised to this stereotype were "savages," who were by definition "unrestrained by any sense of delicacy from a copartnery in sexual enjoyments."[18]

Any interpretation of events in British Columbia must adopt the language of colonialism as it was applied to Indigenous women's sexual independence. Around the colonized world the charge of prostitution, engaging in a sexual act for remuneration, was used by those who sought to meddle in Indigenous lives. Sexuality was not to be talked about openly, but prostitution and all that it implied could be publicly condemned. In other words, sexuality had to be wilded into prostitution or possibly concubinage, cohabitation outside of marriage, in order for it to be tamable. Hawkes traces the fervor over prostitution back to Christianity, which both gave it prominence and held out promise for "the redemption of the prostitute, the personification of polluting and uncontrolled women's sexuality." Moving to the nineteenth century, "Victorian sexual morality was focused on, and expressed through, the 'social evil' of prostitution. Prostitution was discussed in such diverse venues as popular journalism, serious weekly reviews, medical tracts and publications from evangelical organizations devoted to the rescue of fallen women . . . prostitution provided a forum within which to express, covertly, anxieties about, and fascination with, the characteristics of women's sexuality."[19]

No question exists but that Aboriginal people in British Columbia viewed their sexuality differently than did colonizers. It is difficult, if not impossible, to reconstruct gender relations prior to newcomers' arrival, nor is it necessary to do so in order to appreciate the enormity of contact. The scholarship is virtually unanimous in concluding that, traditionally, marriages were arranged, with goods passing to the woman's family.[20] Intrusions of European disease, work patterns, and economic relations unbalanced Aboriginal societies and tended to atomize gender relations. Women possessed opportunities for adaptation not available to their male counterparts.[21] Many of the taboos normalized and universalized by Europeans simply did not exist in Aboriginal societies. If for Europeans sexuality had to be strictly controlled in the interests of assuring paternity, the link may have been less critical for Aboriginal people in that the group, rather than the immediate biological family, was the principal social unit.

To grasp the rapidity with which Aboriginal women became sexualized as prostitutes in colonial British Columbia, it is instructive to go back in time to another bishop, George Hills, first Anglican bishop of Vancouver Island. Arriving in Victoria in January 1860, he encountered a figurative tinder box, a fur-trade village which in just twenty months had been turned upside-down by the gold rush, bringing with it thousands of newcomers from around the world, almost all of them men. Bishop Hills was almost immediately condemning "the profligate condition of the population." "The Road to Esquimalt on Sunday is lined with the poor Indian women offering to sell themselves to the white men passing by —& instances are to be seen of open bargaining."[22] Bishop Hills's Methodist counterpart Thomas Crosby, who arrived in the spring of 1862, was similarly struck by "the awful condition of the Indian women in the streets and lanes of Victoria."[23]

What newcomers constructed as prostitution did become widespread during the gold rush, just as it had existed to some extent during the fur trade. The evidence may be largely anecdotal, but it is consistent and, for some times and places, overwhelming.[24] Virtually all of the descriptions come from a colonial male perspective, but they are so graphic and diverse as to leave little doubt as to the circumstances. The most visible sites were seasonal dance halls where for a price miners could while away "the long winter evenings" by interacting socially with Aboriginal women.[25] A New Westminster resident evoked its "Squaw Dance-House" frequented by miners "hastening to throw away their hardly earned gold." Her description is graphic: "As soon as eight or half-past struck, the music of a fiddle or two and the tramp of many feet began. Later on the shouts of drunken men and the screams of squaws in like condition made night hideous. Each man paid fifty cents for a dance, and had to 'stand drinks' at the bar for himself and his dusky partner after each."[26] Bishop Hills described "houses where girls of no more than 12 are taken in at night & turned out in the morning — like cattle."[27] Even while acknowledging dance halls' contribution to urban economies, the press repeatedly denounced the Aboriginal women whose presence made them possible, as in an 1861 editorial charging that "prostitution and kindred vices, in all their hideous deformity, and disease in every form, lurk there." In their San Francisco counterparts "the females were at least civilized," but "here we have all the savagery of the ancient Ojibbeways [sic], with all the vice of a reckless civilization."[28] If the decline of the gold rush from the mid-1860s put an end to dance halls' excesses and dampened down excitement over prostitution,[29] the wildness associated with Aboriginal sexuality had permeated settler consciousness.

FEMALE AGENCY

Turned on their head, contemporary portrayals of Aboriginal women during the gold rush affirm their agency. Agency is by its very nature relational and interactive. Just as occurred during the fur trade[30] and in traditional societies,[31] Aboriginal women both initiated and responded to change. They scooted around, they dared, they were uppity in ways that were completely at odds with Victorian views of gender, power, and race. Some likely soon realized that, however much they tried to mimic newcomers' ways, they would never be accepted and so might as well act as they pleased.[32] An Aboriginal woman "dragged" the friend of a man who had assaulted her to a nearby police station "to be locked up as a witness," only to have him seek "the protection of the police, which was granted" until she left.[33] The jury in a court case against a Victoria policeman accused of "having attempted to ravish the person of an Indian squaw" was told that the verdict hinged on whether "you believe the simple evidence of the three Indian women" and, "after consulting together about one moment, [the jury] returned a verdict of 'Not guilty.'"[34] In some cases Aboriginal women were encouraged or forced by the men in their lives. References abound to fathers selling their daughters "for a few blankets or a little gold, into a slavery which was worse than death,"[35] exchanges likely viewed by some as only continuing traditional marital practices. Yet even missionary accounts hint at female agency, as with Bishop Hills's comment after unsuccessfully remonstrating with "a woman making up a dress" for the dance house that night: "Poor creatures they know these things are wrong — but the temptations are too strong."[36]

Perhaps the most telling evidence of Aboriginal women's management of their sexual behaviour are the numbers who chose to live, at least for a time, with non-Aboriginal men.

The nature of some decisions is suggested by Crosby's account of a twelve-year-old girl who, having "refused at first to follow a life of sin," "was visited by a great rough fellow who, with his hand full of money and with promises of fine clothes and trinkets and sweets, coaxed her and finally prevailed upon her to come and live with him."[37] Although referring to a later point in time, Emily Carr's observations in her fictionalized memoirs are particularly evocative, as in a conversation between two Aboriginal women whom she almost certainly knew personally. "We got a house with three looms, and a sink and kitchen tap. Jacob and Paul go to school with white children. Too bad you not got white man for husband, Susan."[38] Aboriginal women caught in the tumultuous world that was the gold rush sometimes had to make hard decisions, whether for material goods or personal safety. In such circumstances a lonely miner's entreaties could be persuasive.

Non-Aboriginal men had their own reasons for entering into relationships. During the heady years of the gold rush, at least 30,000 White men and several thousand Chinese and Blacks sought their fortunes in British Columbia. Most soon departed, for the difficulties of getting to the gold fields were horrendous, but however long they stayed, their utter loneliness in a sea of men cannot be discounted. The most fundamental characteristic of non-Aboriginal women in gold-rush British Columbia was their paucity.[39] A Welsh miner reported back to his local cleric how "considerable value is placed on a good woman in this country"[40] An Englishman who had already tried his hand in Australia lamented: "The great curse of the colony so far, as it must always be the curse of any colony in which such a want exists, is the absence of women . . . there must be at least two hundred men to every woman. . . . I never saw diggers so desirous of marrying as those of British Columbia." "If it is one thing more than another a miner sighs for after a hard day's work, it is to see either his tent, or his log hut, brightened up by the smiles of a woman, and tidied up by a woman's hand. . . . The miner is not very particular—'plain, fat, and 50' even would not be objected to, while good-looking girls would be the nuggets, and prized accordingly."[41] When a non-Aboriginal man saw an Aboriginal woman, what he may have perceived was not so much her Aboriginality as her gender and, certainly, her sexuality.

Structural factors specific to British Columbia encouraged couplings. At the level of everyday life Aboriginal people were not nearly so alien as sometimes portrayed, or as they became in the American Pacific Northwest.[42] Relations were generally peaceful, and many miners and settlers survived only because of local largesse. A German visiting the gold fields in 1858 reported that "many Indians lived in the neighborhood, who on the whole are on friendly footing with the Whites."[43] A guide to prospective settlers published a quarter of a century later asserted: "The intending settler may depend on finding the Indians peaceable, intelligent, eager to learn and industrious, to a degree unknown elsewhere among the aborigines of America."[44] Another factor was ease of communication through common knowledge of the Chinook trading jargon. Containing about 600 words and a large variety of non-verbal additions, Chinook facilitated conversations across the races. People could talk to each other on an ongoing basis, and sometimes they did more than just talk.

Although some of the relationships spawned by the gold rush extended through the couple's lifetime, many were fairly transient, two persons cohabiting for a time until one or the other decided to move on.[45] In most cases it was the man who did so, and, as one Aboriginal woman recalled,

> Oh, it was hard on Indian wives, I guess,
> But they always managed
> To raise their children
> Even if their husbands finished with them.[46]

Women might end relationships, as in the gold-rush town of Lytton in 1868 where a man "lately left by his Indian wife who had had two children by him . . . confesses having sown the seed he has reaped."[47] Other women simply ensured that their husbands knew that they could leave if they wished to do so. An early novel depicted a saloon keeper with a "squaw wife" named Desdemona whose independent character drew on the author's many years in British Columbia.

> All who know the habits of the squaws married to white men, especially if they lived in one of the towns, will remember the overmastering desire they occasionally developed for a return to their tribe, and a resumption of their old life for at least a time. To fish all night from a light cedar canoe, with no thoughts of the white man's scorn, to pick berries, cut and dry fish till their garments were saturated with the odour of salmon, gather roots, herbs, and the bark of trees for baskets, the rushes also for klis-klis or mats. To extract the beautiful and durable reds and blues from certain plants and berries, and generally to revel in God's great temple of nature.

So it was with Desdemona. "One of these calls from the wild had taken Desdemona, and when her tenase tecoup man (small white man) came in one night, the house was dark, and she and the children gone." She had "stepped into a canoe, paddled across the wide [Fraser] river, and up the salmon stream," and only when it suited her fancy did she return home to her husband.[48]

The various data from personal accounts, church records, and the manuscript censuses suggest that, in those areas of British Columbia opened up to Europeans during the gold-rush years, about one in ten Aboriginal women cohabited at some point in her life with a non-Aboriginal man.[49] The prevalence of such unions even caused the first session of the new provincial legislature, following entry into Confederation in 1871, to pass a bill, subsequently disallowed by the federal government, to legitimize children of unions between Aboriginal women and non-Aboriginal men whose parents wed subsequent to their birth.[50]

TAMING ABORIGINAL SEXUALITY

By the time British Columbia became a Canadian province in 1871 Aboriginal women had been almost wholly sexualized.[51] The perception of widespread prostitution, and if not prostitution then concubinage, gave men in power the freedom to speak openly about matters that otherwise would have been only whispered.[52] Newcomers took for granted the fall as depicted in the Bible. Human nature was weak, and the biological man could easily be tempted to evil by his female counterpart, just as Bishop O'Conner considers himself to have been a century later. It was woman's place to be docile and subservient so as not to provoke man. For all those seeking to control Aboriginal peoples, women who exercised sexual autonomy had to be subdued. Conversion to Christianity held the key, for "woman was always the slave or burden-bearer until the Gospel came and lifted her into her true social position," which was essentially as man's handmaiden.[53] Whether missionaries, government officials, or Aboriginal men, the common perception was that the only good Aboriginal woman was the woman who stayed home within the bosom of her family. So an informal alliance developed between these three groups to refashion Aboriginal women.

This tripartite alliance, wherein men in power buttressed and comforted each other, was grounded in mutual expediency and, to some extent, in mutual male admiration. With entry into Confederation, responsibility for Aboriginal people shifted to the federal government under the terms of the British North America Act, and it did not take long for newly appointed officials to realize the enormous benefit to be had from establishing cordial relations with missionaries, who were already at work across much of the sprawling province. Officially, missionaries had no status, but unofficially they became the government's foot soldiers, and its eyes and ears. Aboriginal policy, as it developed in British Columbia, was to minimize official involvement in everyday affairs, which effectively meant letting missionaries have a free hand.[54] If disagreeing in many areas, including Aboriginal people's right to an adequate land base, government officials repeatedly commended missionaries for having "taught, above all, the female portion of the community to behave themselves in a modest and virtuous manner."[55] The other prong of the alliance crossed racial boundaries in the interests of gender solidarity and mutual self-interest. Members of the Indian Reserve Commission active across British Columbia in the mid-1870s left an extensive paper trail and repeatedly expressed approval of Aboriginal "manliness" and of "the industry of the men."[56] Similarly, in missionary accounts it is almost wholly Aboriginal men who are given individuality and personality.[57] Men, particularly those who emulated colonial ways, needed to have suitable spouses, and for this reason too Aboriginal women had to have their sexuality tamed.

As for Aboriginal men, they were likely motivated by a shortage of women and also, some of them, by a desire to please their colonial mentors. Reports of a shortage are sufficiently widespread to be convincing. As early as 1866 Bishop Hills observed "a scarcity of wives" among the northern Tsimshian, many of whose members camped in Victoria on a seasonal basis.[58] The Indian Reserve Commission's census of a decade later counted 1,919 Aboriginal persons in the area extending from Burrard Inlet north to Jervis Inlet, across to Comox, and down through the Saanich peninsula, including the Gulf Islands; of these, 979 were adult males compared with 919 adult females, and 94 male youth compared with 84 female youth.[59] The enumerator of the Southern Interior, extending from Lytton through the Nicola Valley, counted 884 adult males compared with 803 adult females and lamented "the absence of females both adults and youths — those who should have been the future mothers of the tribe."[60] Some Aboriginal men, in effect, made deals to behave in accordance with missionary aspirations for them in exchange for getting wives.[61] Crosby described a visit to a Queen Charlottes village in about 1885, where local men promised him: "Sir, if you will come and give us a teacher, we will stop going to Victoria. Victoria has been the place of death and destruction to our people, as you see we have no children left to us. All our young women are gone; some of our young men can't find wives any more; and we wish that you could help them to get wives among the Tsimpshean people."[62]

The tripartite campaign to tame the wild represented by Aboriginal sexuality had two principal goals. The first was to return Aboriginal women home. The second was to desexualize Aboriginal everyday life, in effect to cleanse it so that the home to which women returned would emulate its colonial counterpart.

RETURNING ABORIGINAL WOMEN HOME

Marriage lay at the heart of newcomers' morality and, as anthropologist George Stocking concludes, "it is perfectly clear that 'marriage proper' meant proper Victorian marriage" whose "purpose was to control human (and especially female) sexuality, so that there might be 'certainty of male parentage.'"[63] As summed up by historians Leonore Davidoff and Catherine Hall for England between the late eighteenth and mid-nineteenth centuries, "marriage was the economic and social building block for the middle class." "Marriage became both symbol and institution of women's containment. It was marriage which would safely domesticate the burgeoning garden flower into an indoor pot plant; the beautiful object potentially open to all men's gaze became the possession of one man when kept within the house like a picture fixed to the wall."[64]

In theory, two marital strategies could have tamed Aboriginal sexuality. One was to encourage non-Aboriginal men to wed their Aboriginal partners, the other to return Aboriginal women home to wed Aboriginal men. Either would have satisfied Victorian notions of marriage, but the alliance of interests that existed among men in power combined with growing racism to ensure that the second option would be favoured. As early as 1873 an agitated provincial official pointed to the federal government's responsibility for "the care and protection of the native race in this Province, [and] so long as this shameful condition of things is suffered to continue unchecked, the character of that race in the social scale is practically a delusion."[65] Reserve commissioners reported on conversations with chiefs at Nanaimo, where "the evil of concubinage of their young women with the white men around were specially pointed out."[66] By 1884 an Indian agent with an Aboriginal wife and grown daughters felt able to argue, perhaps with a touch of self-interest, that "with the present state of civilization in the country and the abundance of white and educated half breed women — such a practice should be put a stop to in future."[67] Aboriginal women were needed at home to service their menfolk.

For men in power, gender and race neatly dovetailed. Within the mix of pseudo-scientific ideas associated with Social Darwinism, newcomers accepted, as seemingly demonstrated by the triumph of colonialism and technological advances, that mankind had evolved into a hierarchy with Whites on the top and Aboriginal people near the bottom.[68] Persons of mixed race ranked even lower, for, to quote a colonial visitor, "half-breeds, as a rule, inherit, I am afraid, the vices of both races."[69] Concerns grew over "a class of half-breed children . . . who, under the bond of illegitimacy, and deprived of all incentives in every respect, will in course of time become dangerous members of the community."[70] During the late 1870s such fears were exacerbated by a murderous rampage by the young sons of a Hudson's Bay trader and Aboriginal woman,[71] and given a sexual edge by female-mixed race students at a public boarding school becoming pregnant by their male counterparts.[72] While some encouragement was given to non-Aboriginal men to marry Aboriginal women with whom they were cohabiting, this was, for the most part, done somewhat grudgingly.[73] Petitions became a favoured means to compel Aboriginal women back home. The tripartite alliance developed a dynamic whereby Aboriginal men signed petitions orchestrated by missionaries who then dispatched them to government officials to justify their taking action.[74] Both Catholic and Protestant missionaries participated, as did Aboriginal men across much of the province and numerous officials at various levels of government.

In 1885 Oblates missionaries stage-managed two identical petitions to the Governor General that were affirmed with their marks by 962 Aboriginal men, including at least eighteen chiefs, from across the Cariboo and south through the Lower Fraser Valley. In the best English prose the petitions "beg[ed] to lay before your Excellency" that a "great evil is springing up amongst our people" whereas "on a dispute between a married couple, the wife leaves her husband and goes off the Reservation, and takes up with a bad white man, China man, or other Indian, and [they] live together in an unlawful state." The men sought permission to "bring back the erring ones by force if necessary."[75] Caught up in the rhetoric to tame Aboriginal sexuality, the Ministry of Justice drafted an even broader regulation for consideration by the chiefs, one which made it possible to "bring back to the reserve any Indian woman who has left the reserve and is living immorally with any person off the reserve." The proposal was only derailed by the Ministry of Justice's suggestion, made almost in passing, that the Department of Indian Affairs should "consider before it is passed whether or not the putting of it in force will lead to riots and difficulties between the Indians and the white people and others with whom the Indian women are said to be living immorally."[76] Three of the four Indian agents consulted considered that this might well happen were chiefs given such authority. One of them acknowledged female agency in his observation that, "while in some cases the Indian woman might be brought back without trouble, it would be impossible to keep her on a reserve against her will."[77] The project was shelved, even though the Catholic Bishop at New Westminster intervened directly at the federal ministerial level in an attempt to bypass the bureaucrats.[78]

The campaign to tame Aboriginal sexuality was not to be thwarted, and the Oblates were almost certainly behind a bolder petition dispatched in 1890 to the Governor General. The chiefs of fifty-eight bands, again extending from the Cariboo through the Fraser Valley, indicated by their marks that they were "much aggrieved and annoyed at the fact that our wives, sisters and daughters are frequently decoyed away from our Reserves by ill designing persons." No means existed to return "these erring women," but, even were this possible, "in most cases these women are induced to return again to their seducers." Fearing that "some of our young men who are sufferers will certainly take the law into their own hands and revenge themselves on the offending parties," the petition sought "a law authorising the infliction of corporal punishment by the lash."[79] The advisability of "legislation, making it an offence for a white man to have sexual intercourse with an Indian woman or girl without Christian marriage," was referred to the Ministry of Justice,[80] which in this case pulled the plug. The Ministry considered the legislation unnecessary, since "the laws relating to the protection of females and for the punishment of persons who seduce or abduct them, apply to Indian women as well as to white women."[81] Yet the campaign persisted, and later in 1890 the Indian agent at Lillooet urged, on behalf of "the Chiefs of the numerous Bands around here," that "a severe penalty should be imposed upon any person, not an Indian, who, harbouring an Indian woman, does not deliver her up to the Chief of the Reserve."[82]

At this point the enthusiasts may have stumbled. Acting largely independently of civil authority, the Oblates had allied themselves across much of the Interior with local Aboriginal men in order to effect control over everyday life.[83] As one Indian agent noted in the early 1890s, although the "flogging habit has been abandoned for some years past" and fines are not so common as they once were, "considerable sums of money are annually collected by the chiefs and their watchmen for the benefit of the churches whose functionaries attend to their spiritual welfare."[84] In the spring of 1892 the Oblate missionary at Lillooet, the chief, and four other Aboriginal men were brought before the local magistrate, convicted, and given jail sentences for "flogging a young girl . . . on the report only of a fourth party" for some unspecified sexual activity. "Without investigation he [priest] ordered 15 lashes. His plea was 1st ancient customs of the Indians & 2nd necessity for such punishment in order to suppress immorality." The Indian agent who made the report considered both that the "ancient customs" were not as portrayed by the missionary and that the local men should not have been punished so severely, since they "believed the Priest to be their Commander in all Church matters — and that consequently they were obliged to obey him."[85] The incident appears to have cooled the alliance between the Oblates and local men, who "were astonished at the extent of the jurisdiction of the Courts of law, when even the dictates of a Priest should be upset and the Priest himself held accountable."[86]

The Protestants could be just as enthusiastic as the Catholics in allying themselves with local men to keep women at home and then calling on federal officials to enforce what they could not effect by their own devices. In 1889 the Indian agent at Alert Bay, acting in concert with the local Anglican missionary, stopped a group of women from boarding a steamer to Victoria. His justification was that they "went with the avowed purpose of prostituting themselves" and he "had previously been requested by numbers of young men to prevent if possible their wives and sisters from going to Victoria."[87] Reflecting the tripartite alliance's perspective, the Indian agent considered that "nearly all the young women, whenever they leave their homes, whether ostensibly for working at the canneries or at the Hop Fields, do so with the ultimate idea of making more money by prostitution."[88] The steamboat company vigorously protested and the provincial Indian superintendent was lukewarm to the action, astutely observing that "the Indian women and their friends come to Victoria, and other places, in their canoes," making their restriction practically impossible.[89] Nonetheless, the Indian agent and Anglican missionary did such a successful end run to federal officials as to persuade them to propose legislation to keep at home, by force if necessary, "Indian women from the West Coast of British Columbia, who are in the habit of leaving their Villages and Reserves by steamers and by other mode of transport with the object of visiting the Cities and Towns of that Province for immoral purposes."[90]

The proposed legislation hit a snag only after the federal Minister of Justice indicated "that there is not at present sufficient material on hand to permit of the drawing up of a Bill fully dealing with the question."[91] The Minister requested the provincial superintendent to circularize Indian agents around the province. Even though the agents would likely have found it far easier to acquiesce to expectations than to dispute them, they were all, apart from those at Alert Bay and Babine in the Northern Interior, remarkably sanguine. On the west of Vancouver Island, "I do not know of a single instance on this Coast where a young girl has been taken to Victoria or elsewhere for the purposes of prostitution."[92] His neighbour was "not aware of any Indian women belonging to the Cowichan Agency who leave their Reservations for immoral purposes."[93] In the Fraser Valley and Lower Mainland, "there are very few immoral women."[94] As for the Central Interior, "the practice of Indian women leaving their Reserves for the purpose of leading immoral lives is not common in this Agency."[95] The Southern Interior agent offered a general observation: "Indians are in their nature, in consequence of their training, habits and surroundings, far less virtuous than the average whites. Their morality should not therefore be judged by the standards of the white people. The Indian woman, although, as above stated, inclined to be worse in her morals, is naturally modest."[96] The North Coast agent considered that the "Indians have learned from sad experience the effects of immorality in the cities and are rapidly improving their conduct."[97] Summarizing the responses, the provincial superintendent concluded that "the few Indian women who may be found living an immoral life in our towns and Cities are less in number as a rule than of their white sisters."[98]

Nonetheless, the depiction of Aboriginal sexuality as out of control was too attractive an explanation for missionary and government failings to be abandoned. Just three years later, in 1895, a petition signed by thirty-four men from central Vancouver Island, all but one with their marks, demanded legislation to prevent "our wives and daughters and sisters" from being "carried to Victoria for illegitimate purposes."[99] The British Columbia senator to whom the petition was addressed took its claims at face value and demanded that steps be taken to "prevent the deportation of Indian women," seeing that "Indians are wards of the government under tutelage and not qualified to manage their own affairs wisely." The senator, who simply assumed that Aboriginal women's sole role was to service their menfolk, emphasized that an "increase, instead of a decrease, is much to be desired" in the Aboriginal population.[100] The federal response is interesting because, rather than quoting from the Indian agents' reports in their files, officials emphasized the difficulties of securing legislation. In doing so, they revealed, perhaps inadvertently, that women were de facto having their travel restricted by local Indian agents "when requested by the husband or brother or anyone having proper authority, to stop a woman from going away, and so the men have the prevention of that of which they complain almost entirely in their own hands."[101] The sexualization of Aboriginal women had far less to do with reality than with the needs, and desires, of men in power. So long as settler society perceived a need to tame Aboriginal sexuality, men in power could reorder Aboriginal society with impunity.

REORDERING ABORIGINAL SOCIETY

Over time virtually every aspect of Aboriginal everyday life acquired a sexual dimension, thereby justifying its reordering. Aboriginal sexuality, or perhaps more accurately the fear of Aboriginal women's agency, became a lens through which traditional preferences in housing, social institutions, and child care were critiqued and found wanting.

The rhetoric condemning the 'big houses' inhabited by Coastal peoples made explicit Victorian fears of the body and of human sexuality. It also reflected Social Darwinian notions of the hierarchy of species, at the top of which lay Western societies premised on the monogamous conjugal family. The very existence of sites where more than a single family lived together was equated with immorality. No doubt existed but that, given the opportunity, men and women would act on their impulses. Davidoff and Hall have linked the subordination of women to the private home: "Woman had been created for man, indeed for one man, and there was a necessary inference from this that *home* was 'the proper scene of woman's action and influence.' . . . The idea of a privatized home, separated from the world, had a powerful moral force and if women, with their special aptitude for faith, could be contained within that home, then a space would be created for true family religion."[102] So also in British Columbia, the single family home came to be seen as a necessary prelude to Christian conversion.

Men in power repeatedly lauded the single-family house, as in side notes on the Reserve commission's census of Aboriginal people. At Burrard Inlet: "The houses at this place have a pleasing appearance when viewed from the sea. They are mostly of the cottage style, white washed and kept cleaner in this than is usual with most Indians." In contrast, along the Fraser River: "Most of the houses of this tribe are of the primitive style. There are however several cottages kept and fitted up in a neat manner." At Cowichan on Vancouver Island: "There are a few tidy cottages—what they require is a desire and encouragement.[103] Missionaries like Crosby were even more fervent and repeatedly linked housing to sexuality. "The old heathen house, from its very character, was the hot-bed of vice. Fancy a great barn-like building, . . . occupied by as many as a dozen families, only separated from each other by low partitions." The interior seemed made for naughty deeds. "Picture such a building, with no floor other than the ground, no entrance for light except the door, when open, and the cracks in the walls and the roof. Around the inside of such a building were ranged the beds, built up on rude platforms." "Is it any wonder that disease and vice flourished under such favorable surroundings?"[104] In sharp contrast stood "the Christian home." Crosby considered that "the only way to win the savage from his lazy habits, sin and misery" was to "be able and willing to show how to build a nice little home, from the foundation to the last shingle on the roof."[105]

Fear of Aboriginal sexuality became frenzied in the rhetoric around the institution of the potlatch. Missionaries led the campaign against this social activity practiced across most of the province, garnering support from government officials and over time from some converted Aboriginal men. Initially arguments focused on the event itself as being "demoralizing," leading to "debauchery."[106] Federal legislation banning the potlatch took effect at the beginning of 1885, but did not bring about wholesale conversion to Christianity. Missionaries soon sought both allies in Aboriginal men in search of wives and reasons, apart from themselves, to explain their failure to live up to their expectations for themselves.[107] The ethnographer Marius Barbeau concluded in 1921, after examining federal files on the potlatch, that, "as the Church has not succeeded in making converts to any material extent . . . there must be found a scapegoat, and as the potlatch already had a bad name, it was blamed."[108]

The sexualization of the potlatch had a number of components, but centred on the supposed sale of Aboriginal women as wives or prostitutes to get the money to potlatch.[109] In 1893 a Toronto newspaper reported that a group of missionaries had witnessed "blankets for potlatch procured at the expense of the virtue of women," an event which the local Indian agent determined was sensationalized. [110] By the end of the century the press was convinced that "the potlatch is the inciting cause of three-fourths of the immorality that exists among Indian women."[111] Writing shortly thereafter, the Indian agent at Alert Bay asserted the that younger generation of Aboriginal men supported his attempt to persuade his superiors in Ottawa to act against potlatching: "It looks cruel to me to see a child 13 or 14 years of age put up & sold just like sheep or a nanny goat, to a bleary eyed siwash old enough to be her grand-father, for a pile of dirty blankets, which will in turn be Potlatched to the rest of the band, and all to make the proud Father, a big Injun," rather than "let her marry a young man whom I am sure she wanted."[112] The Indian agent quoted a longtime missionary to make his point that "the girls die off and the young men for the most part cannot get wives because as a rule they have no blankets or money unless they are sons of chiefs and the others cannot get wives until they are able to command a certain sum which is so difficult as they have to compete with the older men who hold the property."[113]

The unwillingness to tolerate Aboriginal women's agency was a major factor in the determination to replace familial child care with residential schools operated by missionaries under loose government oversight. As attested by the scholarship, schools sought total control over pupils' sexuality, particularly that of girls.[114] The twinned concepts of Christian marriage and the Christian home depended on young women remaining sufficiently unblemished so that they could become good wives according to Victorian standards of behaviour. The attitudes and actions of Thomas Crosby and his wife Emma are instructive. Crosby considered that parents, "though kind and indulgent to their children, are not capable of teaching and controlling them properly" and "something must be done to save and protect the young girls . . . from being sold into the vilest of slavery."[115] "On account of the prevalence of this traffic in Indian girls, many of the early missionaries were led to establish 'Girls' Homes' for the rescue and further protection of these poor victims of this awful system."[116] The taming that went on in the Crosbys' girls' home, as in residential schools across the province, left no doubt as to Aboriginal agency. As remembered by a Crosby school matron in the early 1880s, the girls required "a great deal of Grace, Patience and determination, they were so obstinate and disobedient."[117]

The wildness associated with Aboriginal sexuality explains attitudes toward a girl's transition from pupil to wife. Reflecting the assumptions of the day, the superintendent of the Children's Aid Society in Vancouver expressed relief that "the savage was so thin and washed out" of two young women of mixed race, that they were able to find happiness with their White lovers. Yet this represented "only a glimmer of light in the darkness."[118] According to Crosby's biographer, "girls stayed at the Home until they were married, at which time a new girl would be admitted."[119] The full extent of missionaries' distrust of their charges is evident in the musings of another Crosby matron regarding the potential marriage of a fourteen-year-old student: "It would seem sinful to allow such things to be mentioned if they were white girls, but here they are safer when married young."[120]

Again, the informal alliance operated. Schools measured their success by numbers of girls who "have married Christian Indians, have helped to build up Christian homes, to civilize the people generally and to aid in developing their own neighborhood." "Instead of a young man with his friends going with property and buying a wife, as was done formerly, many of our brightest young men tried to make the acquaintance of the girls in the Home." Women might no longer be sold by their fathers, but they were no less commodities when it came to marriage. The Crosbys, like other missionaries, put a romantic spin around what was, in effect, a good being made available to a handful of men considered suitably Christian. "There was no doubt in our minds that real, true love again and again developed between the young people who thus became acquainted. This acquaintance finally resulted in their marriage and the happy life that followed."[121]

CONSEQUENCES

By the end of the nineteenth century settler society took for granted the interpretation that men in power put on Aboriginal women's agency. The ongoing frenzy over the potlatch is indicative. The press became ever more determined to expose its supposed basis in Aboriginal sexuality. "Indian girl sold for 1,000 blankets" hit Vancouver streets in 1906.[122] The story makes clear that the supposed revelation about "the awful Indian practice of potlatch" originated with an Anglican missionary who was disgruntled because a pupil had married someone other than the man she had selected for her. Later in the year both Vancouver and Ottawa newspapers trumpeted "Five Indian Girls Sold,"[123] a report that, on investigation, proved to be groundless.[124] A Vancouver paper headlined a year later, "Squaw sold for $400.00 at Alert Bay to a grizzled Chief from Queen Charlottes."[125] It turned out that, while two marriages had occurred, neither involved "a grizzled chief," and the local Indian agent considered the article to be "very misleading."[126] The press coverage prompted a host of women's voluntary associations across the country to demand legislation to "put an end to this great blot on the Civilization and Christianity of Canada."[127] Writing in 1921, a barrister who was the son of the former Indian agent at Alert Bay, and who represented Aboriginal people opposed to the potlatch ban, considered that "the strongest reason for enforcing the law against the Potlatch is the question of Indian marriages. . . . It is also contended that women are bought and sold, [but] this is not true."[128] Had the potlatch not been so successfully sexualized, it is doubtful that opponents could have maintained its illegality into the mid-twentieth century. The taming of Aboriginal sexuality had become a means to an end, as well of course as an end in itself, but the effects were no less detrimental to Aboriginal women.

For Aboriginal women, the consequences of the ceaseless rhetoric of scorn heaped on them in the interests of men in power were enormous. Some women acquiesced and returned or remained at home,[129] and the Crosbys delighted "in visiting around among the villages, to pick out these Christian mothers who had the privilege of the 'Home' life and training."[130] In a broad sense, Aboriginal societies did come to mimic their colonial counterparts, which is not unexpected given federal policies and the material advantages to be got from doing so. An Aboriginal informant explained in 1950 how "converts were sometimes termed 'made white men', as they used different types of houses and they dressed in white men's clothes, while their heathen brothers . . . indulged in all of the old rituals."[131] Some women had the decision taken out of their hands. As more marriageable White women became available and attitudes hardened, numerous non-Aboriginal men shed their Aboriginal partners. The manuscript censuses for the late nineteenth century indicate that, while some of these women did return home and enter into new unions with Aboriginal men, others scraped along at the edges of settler society.

Other women continued to dare.[132] Many inter-racial unions survived the campaign to tame Aboriginal sexuality, in some cases by the partners legally marrying or retreating outward into the frontier, or by simply standing their ground.[133] The encouragement that missionaries and government officials gave to Aboriginal men may have caused some women to disengage from their home communities in search of more satisfying life opportunities. To the extent that traditional patterns of gender relations gave way to male mimicry of European practices, so the social distance between the sexes may have widened. Women still married out, as indicated by the 1901 manuscript census[134] and evoked in a Carr vignette about a woman who had "married white" and "both loved her husband and gloried in his name," for "it was infinitely finer to be 'Mrs Jenny Smith' than to have her name hitched to an Indian man's and be 'Jenny Joe' or 'Jenny Tom.'"[135]

Most important, the campaign to tame Aboriginal sexuality so profoundly sexualized Aboriginal women that they were rarely permitted any other form of identity. Not just Aboriginal women but Aboriginal women's agency was sexualized. In the extreme case their every act became perceived as a sexual act and, because of the unceasing portrayal of their sexuality as wild and out of control, as an act of provocation. By default, Aboriginal women were prostitutes or, at best, potential concubines. Their actions were imbued with the intent that men in power had so assiduously ascribed to them, thus vitiating any responsibility for their or other men's actions toward them. Sexualization of Aboriginal women's agency occurred within a context in which they were already doubly inferior by virtue of their gender and race, thus virtually ensuring that any Aboriginal woman who dared would become colonialism's plaything. Again, the stories are legion, be it the Okanagan Valley in the 1880s, Vancouver Island in the 1920s, the North Coast in the 1960s, or Bishop O'Conner. Sometimes the accounts embody a strong element of bravado, in other cases the wish fulfillment of lonely men, but in yet others a strong dose of action, as with O'Conner.

A young Englishman who arrived in the Okanagan Valley shortly after the completion of the transcontinental railroad in 1886 exemplified a generation of newcomers who took for granted Aboriginal women's sexualization. "Most of these girls were graceful, some even pretty; clear, light bronze skins with just a touch of color in the cheeks, even teeth and glossy jet black hair, that had almost a tinge of blue in it; their black eyes would be modestly cast down in the presence of white men. And sometimes a shy upward glance of coquetry — but not if there were any bucks in sight." He recalled a contemporary who, "fed up with batching, had disturbed the monastic peace of the community by taking unto himself a dusky mistress." The sexualization of Aboriginal women's agency removed any sense of responsibility. Even as his friends were deciding whether to be jealous, "he and his lady had a bad row, and realizing that his little romance was ended he fired her out, and as none of the rest of the old boys were gallant enough to take a chance on her, the lady returned to the bosom of her tribe, and once more there was peace on earth in the little community."[136]

Even persons who supported Aboriginal people, as did the lawyer representing them in the 1920s against the potlatch ban, persisted in seeing women in sexual terms, considering that "contact between Indians and loggers has always been fraught with dire results — particularly to the Indian women." This assessment was in sharp contrast to his view of Aboriginal men: "The Indian man in his own environment is a man of dignity, big and venerable."[137]

In a generally sympathetic account of a summer sojourn in 1966 at Telegraph Creek on the North Coast, a young American made clear that Aboriginal women's agency remained sexualized. "More than they would have in the old days, I'm sure, they make fun of the Indians to me . . . [for] their limber-limbed promiscuity." A friend "eats supper with me, chatting about the morals of the Indian girls ('No morals at all if you scratch their stomachs a minute')." Their every action became a sexual action, thus his vignette relating how "earlier in the spring a girl appeared in the store, sent by her parents, and took up the broom' and began to sweep, after the historical fashion of a squaw proposing to a white man." For this young man, the wild which was Aboriginal sexuality remained mythic. Noting that "in New York to dream of woman is an unremarkable event" but "here it invests the whole night with sexual urgency," he repeatedly found himself tempted, as after "I've had a day hearing stories of . . . Indian women being mounted and screwed." He resisted, but precisely because he did accept the equation of Aboriginal female agency with sexuality: "Of course these Indian girls are too vulnerable to fool with, so I have only the past to keep me company in bed."[138]

Hence we come full circle to Bishop O'Conner who at virtually the same time that this young American was fantasizing acted on his impulses. Like so many men before him, he still considers himself to have been "seduced" and, a full generation later, remains in his heart "a celibate man." I have no doubt that O'Conner feels himself to be sincere, just as I now have no doubt of the importance of newcomers' construction of Aboriginal women's sexuality for understanding events during that critical half century, 1850–1900, when your, my, and Bishop O'Conner's British Columbia came into being.

NOTES

1. Earlier versions of this essay were presented at the BC Studies Conference in May 1997 and, thanks to Elizabeth Jameson and Susan Armitage, at the Western Historical Association in October 1997. I am grateful to everyone who has commented on the essay, especially to Robin Fisher at BCS, Elizabeth Jameson at WHA, and the two anonymous reviewers for *BC Studies*. The Social Sciences and Humanities Research Council generously funded the research from which the essay draws.

2. This statement by Bishop O'Conner was taken up forcefully in Reasons for Judgment, Vancouver Registry, no. CC9 206 17, 25 July 1996.

3. National Parole Board, Decision Registry, file 905044C, 21 March 1997.

4. The three best books for understanding Aboriginal people in British Columbia are, in my view, Robin Fisher, *Contact and Conflict: Indian-European Relations in British Columbia, 1774–1890* (Vancouver: UBC Press, 1970 and 1992); Paul Tennant, *Aboriginal Peoples and Politics: The Indian Land Question in British Columbia, 1849–1989* (Vancouver: UBC Press, 1990); and Cole Harris, *The Resettlement of British Columbia: Essays on Colonialism and Geographical Change* (Vancouver: UBC Press, 1997), each of which is driven by a male perspective as to sources, authorship, subjects, and interpretation. Much the same observation might be made about the bulk of the ethnographic literature; a recent summary of the historiography (Wayne Suttles and Aldona Jonaitis, "History of Research in Ethnology," in Wayne Suttles, ed., *Northwest Coast*, vol. 7 of William C. Sturtevant, ed., *Handbook of North American Indians* [Washington, DC: Smithsonian Institution, 1990], 84–86) does not even include private life or women, much less sexuality, as topics.

5. This general point is made by, among other authors, Sandra Harding in *The Science Question in Feminism* (Milton Keynes: Open University Press, 1986); Catherine Hall in *White, Male, and Middle- Class: Explorations in Feminism and History* (New York: Routledge, 1988); and Vron Ware in *Beyond the Pale: White Women, Racism and History* (London: Verso, 1992). A handful of exceptions by Canadian scholars are principally concerned with an earlier time period, as with Karen Anderson, *Chain Her By One Foot: The Subjugation of Native Women in Seventeenth-Century New France* (New York: Routledge, 1991); Sylvia Van Kirk, *"Many Tender Ties": Women in Fur Trade Society, 1670–1870* (Norman: University of Oklahoma press, 1980); and Ron Bourgeault, "Race, Class and Gender: Colonial Domination of Indian Women," *Socialist Studies* 5 (1989), 87–115. The two principal analyses of perceptions of Aboriginal people consider women, if at all, as extensions of their menfolk; see Robert F. Berkhofer, Jr., *The White Man's Indian: Images of the American Indian from Columbus to the Present* (New York: Vintage, 1979), and Daniel Francis, *The Imaginary Indian: The Image of the Indian in Canadian Culture* (Vancouver: Arsenal Pulp Press, 1992).

6. Jane Katz, ed., *Messengers of the Wind: Native American Women Tell Their Life Stories* (New York: Ballentine Books, 1995), 5.

7. David Jary and Julia Jary, *Collins Dictionary of Sociology*, 2nd ed. (Glasgow: HarperCollins, 1995), 590–1. It was 1914 before the Oxford English Dictionary got to the letter 's.' All of its quotes were from the nineteenth century and, while the first definition of sexuality was "the quality of being sexual or having sex," the second and third were the "possession of sexual powers or capability of sexual feelings" and "recognition of or preoccupation with what is sexual." See Sir James A.H. Murray, ed., *A New English Dictionary on Historical Principles*, vol. 8 (Oxford: Clarendon Press, 1914), 582. Interest in the concept of sexuality, and more generally in regulation of the body, mushroomed with the publication of Michel Foucault's *History of Sexuality* in 1978 (Harmondsworth: Penguin, esp. vol. 1) and Peter Gay's *The Bourgeois Experience* in 1986 (Oxford: Oxford University Press, 2 vols.). Particularly helpful for interpreting Foucault is Ann Laura Stoler's *Race and the Education of Desire: Foucault's History of Sexuality and the Colonial Order of Things* (Durham: Duke University Press, 1995).

8. Gail Hawkes, *A Sociology of Sex and Sexuality* (Buckingham and Philadelphia: Open University Press, 1996), 8, 14, 42.

9. This point underlies Ronald Hyam, *Empire and Sexuality: The British Experience* (Manchester: University of Manchester Press, 1990); and Margaret Strobel, *Gender, Sex, and Empire* (Washington: American Historical Association, 1993), which critiques Hyam's contention that empire enhanced men's sexual opportunities.

10. Among the more perceptive recent examinations of aspects of this topic are Margaret Jolly and Martha MacIntyre, ed., *Family and Gender in the Pacific: Domestic contradictions and the colonial impact* (Cambridge: Cambridge University Press, 1989); Strobel, *Gender, Sex, and Empire*; Robert Young, *Colonial Desire: Hybridity in Theory, Culture and Race* (London: Routledge, 1995); Stoler, *Race and the Education of Desire*; and Frederick Cooper and Ann Laura Stoler, ed., *Tensions of Empire: Colonial Cultures in a Bourgeois World* (Berkeley: University of California Press, 1997).

11. Philip Mason, *Patterns of Dominance* (London: Oxford University Press for the Institute of Race Relations, 1970), 88.

12. Ann Laura Stoler and Frederick Cooper, "Between Metropole and Colony: Rethinking a Research Agenda," in Cooper and Stoler, ed., *Tensions of Empire*, 5. Although Stoler and Cooper co-wrote this introductory essay, the insight is clearly Stoler's, since it is her research on colonial Asia that is cited.

13. As diverse examples of a similar sequence, if not necessarily interpretation, of events, see Albert L. Hurtado, *Indian Survival on the California Frontier* (New Haven: Yale University Press, 1988), 169–92; and Caroline Ralston, "Changes in the Lives of Ordinary Women in Early Post-Contact Hawaii," in Jolly and MacIntyre, ed., *Family and Gender*, 45–82. In *Capturing Women: The Manipulation of Cultural Imagery in Canada's Prairie West* (Montreal and Kingston: McGill-Queen's University Press, 1997), Sarah Carter links the sexualization of Aboriginal women on the Canadian prairies to their participation in the 1885 uprising (esp. 8–10, 161, 183, 187, 189).

14. In *Allegories of Empire: The Figure of the Woman in the Colonial Text* (Minneapolis: University of Minnesota Press, 1993), Jenny Sharpe argues that, after rebellions in India in the 1850s, raped colonial women provided the basis for racializing Indigenous peoples as inferior.

15. The concept of wildness is examined in Sharon "Tiffany and Kathleen Adams, *The Myth of the Wild Woman* (Cambridge: Schenken, 1985).

16. Patricia C. Albers, "From Illusion to Illumination: Anthropological Studies of American Indian Women," in Sandra Morgan, ed., *Gender and Anthropology: Critical Reviews for Research and Teaching* (Washington: American Anthropological Association, 1989), 132. Carol Devens appears to accept this perspective in "Separate Confrontations: Gender as a Factor in Indian Adaptation to European Colonization in New France," *American Quarterly* 38, 3 (1986), 461–80; and in her *Countering Colonization: Native American Women and Great Lakes Missions, 1630–1900* (Berkeley: University of California Press, 1992). The identification of Aboriginal women's conversion to Christianity with their desire to maintain traditional values underlies much of the special *Ethnohistory* issue (43. 4, Fall 1996), "Native American Women's Responses to Christianity, edited by Michael Harkin and Sergei Kan, esp. 563–66, 574–75. 614, 629–30, 655, 675–76. Others authors sidestep issues of sexuality altogether, as with most of the essays in Laura F. Klein and Lillian A. Ackerman, ed., *Women and Power in Native North America* (Norman: University of Oklahoma Press, 1995); and Nancy Shoemaker, ed., *Negotiators of Change: Historical Perspectives on Native American Women* (New York: Routledge, 1995).

17. Hall in *White, Male, and Middle-Class*, 61–62.

18. George W. Stocking, Jr., *Victorian Anthropology* (New York: Free Press, 1987), 199–200, 202.

19. Hawkes, *Sociology of Sex*, 14–15, 42.

20. Despite its male perspective, a good basic source, although limited to Coastal peoples, remains Suttles, ed., *Northwest Coast*.

21. Especially useful is Carol Cooper, "Native Women of the Northern Pacific Coast: An Historical Perspective, 1830–1900," *Journal of Canadian Studies* 27, 4 (Winter 1992–93), 44–75, which points out that what new-comers labeled prostitution sometimes simply continued traditional social structures wherein some persons were deprived of their autonomy as "slaves" (58) and traces the seasonal migrations of North Coast women to Victoria with their families.

22. 24 September 1860 entry, Bishop George Hills, Diary, in Anglican Church, Ecclesiastical Province of British Columbia, Archives; also letter to the editor from C.T.W. in *Victoria Gazette*, 22 September 1860; and Matthew MacFie, *Vancouver Island and British Columbia* (London: Longman, Green, Longman, Roberts, & Green, 1865), 471.

23. Thomas Crosby, *Up and Down the North Pacific Coast by Canoe and Mission Ship* (Toronto: Missionary Society of the Methodist Church, 1904), 17. On the relevance of missionary accounts, see Jean and John Comaroff, *Of Revelation and Revolution: Christianity, Colonialism and Consciousness in South Africa* (Chicago: University of Chicago Press, 1991).

24. This contention is supported by Chris Hanna's extensive research on colonial Victoria, and I thank him for sharing his findings with me.

25. "Can such things be?" *Victoria Daily Chronicle*, 16 November 1862.

26. Francis E. Herring, *In the Pathless West With Soldiers, Pioneers, Miners, and Savages* (London: T. Fisher Unwin, 1904), 173–75.

27. 21 April 1860 entry, Hills, Diary; also 12 August and 24 September 1860, 31 January 1862 entries.

28. "The Dance Houses," *British Colonist*, 20 December 1861. For events in California, see Alfred Hurtado, "When Strangers Meet: Sex and Gender on Three Frontiers," in Elizabeth Jameson and Susan Armitage, ed.,

Writing the Range: Race, Class, and Culture in the Women's West (Norman: University of Oklahoma Press, 1997), 134–7.

29. In *During My Time: Florence Edenshaw Davidson, a Haida Woman* (Vancouver and Seattle: Douglas & McIntyre and University of Washington Press, 1982), 44–45, Margaret Blackman links the decline to the smallpox epidemic of 1862–63, but newspaper coverage suggests that the principal cause was fewer lone men.

30. On the maritime fur trade, see Lorraine Littlefield, "Women Traders in the Maritime Fur Trade," in Bruce Alden Cox, ed., *Native People, Native Lands: Canadian Indians, Inuit and Metis* (Ottawa: Carleton University Press, 1991), 173–85; and on the land-based trade Van Kirk, *"Many Tender Ties."* Devens probes "native women as autonomous, sexual active females" in seventeenth-century New France in *Countering Colonization*, 25 and passim.

31. For a case study, see Jo-Anne Fiske, "Fishing is Women's Business: Changing Economic Roles of Carrier Women and Men," in Cox, cd., *Native People, Native Lands*, 186–98.

32. On the concept of mimicry, see Homi Bhabha, "Of Mimicry and Man: The Ambivalence of Colonial Discourse," in Cooper and Stoler, ed., *Tensions of Empire*, 152–60.

33. "A Squaw Arrests a White Man," *British Colonist*, 17 January 1862.

34. "Attempted rape," *British Colonist*, 17 August 1860.

35. Thomas Crosby, *Among the An-ko-me-nums, Or Flathead Tribes of Indians of the Pacific Coast* (Toronto: William Briggs, 1907), 62.

36. 1 February 1862 entry, Hills, Diary.

37. Crosby, *Among the An-ko-me-nums*, 63.

38. Emily Carr, *The Heart of a Peacock* (Toronto: Irwin, 1986), 96.

39. Adele Perry admirably tackles this and related topics in "'Oh I'm just sick of the faces of men': Gender Imbalance, Race, Sexuality and Sociability in Nineteenth-Century British Columbia," *BC Studies* 105–06 (Spring/Summer 1995), 27–43.

40. Letter of Morgan Lewis to Rev. D.R. Lewis, New Westminster, 29 October 1862, printed in *Seren Cymru*, 23 January 1863, quoted in Alan Conway, "Welsh Gold Miners in British Columbia During the 1860's," *Cylchgrawn I Iyfrgell Genedlaethol Cymru: The National Library of Wales Journal* 10, 4 (Winter 1958), 383–84.

41. *Cariboo, the Newly Discovered Gold Fields of British Columbia* (Fairfield, WA: Ye Galleon Press, 1975), 7–8, 19–20.

42. See Jean Barman, "What a Difference a Border Makes: Aboriginal Racial Intermixture in the Pacific Northwest," *Journal of the West*, forthcoming.

43. Carl Friesach, *Ein Ausflug nach Britisch-Columbien in Jahre 1858* (Gratz: Philosophical Society, 1875), reprinted in *British Columbia Historical Quarterly* 5 (1941), 227.

44. *The West Shore*, September 1884, 275, cited in Patricia E. Roy, "*The West Shore's* View of British Columbia, 1884," *Journal of the West* 22, 4 (October 1984), 28.

45. For a case study, see Jean Barman, "Lost Okanagan: In Search of the First Settler Families," *Okanagan History* 60 (1996), 8–20.

46. Mary Augusta Tappage, "Changes," in Jeane E. Speare, *The Days of Augusta* (Vancouver: J.J. Douglas, 1973), 71.

47. 27 May 1868 entry, Hills, Diary.

48. Francis E. I Herring, "Pretty Mrs. Weldon" in her *Nan And Other Pioneer Women of the West* (London: Francis Griffiths, 1913), 122, 1 24–25.

49. The base used is the greatly diminished Aboriginal population of about 25–30,000 following the devastating smallpox epidemic of the early 1860s. Another measure is the number of children resulting from the relation-ships, as indicated in the "Supplementary Report" to British Columbia, Department of Education, *First Annual Report on the Public Schools in the Province of British Columbia*, 1872, 38.

50. David R. Williams, . . . *The Man for a New Country: Sir Matthew Baillie Begbie* (Sidney: Gray's Publishing, 1977), 106–07.

51. The age-linked, equally essentializing counterpart was, of course, an absence of sexuality. Aboriginal woman as drudge is discussed in, among other sources, Elizabeth Vibert, *Traders' Tales: Narratives of Cultural Encounters in the Columbia Plateau, 1807–1846* (Norman: University of Oklahoma Press, 1997), 127–31, 136, and 233–39.

52. In referring to men in power, I do not mean to suggest that non-Aboriginal women were completely absent from the discourse but I do contend that, at least in British Columbia, their voices were muted compared to those of men; for a brief introduction to this literature, see Strobel, *Gender, Sex, and Empire*. Myra Rutherdale, "Revisiting Colonization to Gender: Anglican Missionary Women in the Pacific Northwest and Arctic, 1860–1945," *BC Studies* 104 (Winter 1994–95), 3–23, discusses the priorities of female missionaries but without reference to sexuality.

53. Crosby, *Among the An-ko-me-nums*, 96.

54. See, for example, private memorandum of Gilbert Malcolm Sproat, Indian Reserve Commissioner, Okanagan Lake, 27 October 1877, in DIA, RG 10, vol. 3656, file 90063, C-10115.

55. Remarks enclosed with George Blenkinsop, secretary and census taker to Indian Reserve Commission, to Sproat, Douglas Lake, 20 September 1878, in DIA, RG 10, vol. 3667, file 10,330.

56. Private memorandum of Sproat, 27 October 1877; and Alex C Anderson and Archibald McKinlay, Report of the proceedings of the Joint Commission for the settlement of the Indian Reserves in the Province of British Columbia, Victoria, 21 March 1877, in DIA, RG 10, vol. 3645, file 7936, C-10113.

57. Crosby, *Among the An-ko-me-nums*, esp. 206–32 and passim; and Crosby, *Up and Down*, passim.

58. 24 May 1866 entry, Hills, Diary.

59. Census data included with Anderson and McKinlay, Report, 21 March 1877.

60. Remarks enclosed with Blenkinsop to Sproat, 20 September 1878.

61. Such a contention is not inconsistent with Devens's view that Aboriginal men in the Great Lakes region more easily accommodated to missionaries' aspirations for them than did women; see her *Countering Colonization*.

62. Crosby, *Up and Down*, 270–71.

63. Stocking, *Victorian Anthropolopy*, 202.

64. Leonore Davidoff and Catherine Hall. *Family Fortunes: Men and women of the English middle class, 1780–1850* (London: Hutchinson, 1987), 322, 451.

65. Alex C. Anderson, J.P. to Sir Francis Hincks, MP for Vancouver District, Victoria, 26 August 1873, excerpted in undated memorandum of Anderson in DIA, RG 10, vol. 3658, file 9404, C-10115.

66. Anderson and McKinlay, Report, 21 March 1877.

67. William Laing Meason, Indian Agent of Williams Lake Agency, to I.W. Powell, Superintendent of Indian Affairs, Lillooet, 25 March 1884, in DIA, RG 10, vol. 3658, file 9404, C-10115.

68. This topic is examined in Berkhofer, Jr., *White Man's Indian*, esp. 50–61; Brian W. Dippie, *The Vanishing American: White Attitudes & U.S. Indian Policy* (Lawrence: University Press of Kansas, 1982), *passim*; Robert E. Bieder, "Scientific Attitudes Toward Indian Mixed-Bloods in Early Nineteenth Century America," *Journal of Ethnic Studies* 8 (1980), 17–30; and Robert Miles, *Racism* (London: Routledge, 1989).

69. R.C. Mayne, *Four Years in British Columbia and Vancouver Island* (London: John Murray, 1862), 277.

70. Anderson to John Ash, Provincial Secretary, of British Columbia, 16 April 1873, excerpted in undated memorandum of Anderson, in DIA, RG 10, vol. 3658, file 9404, C-10115

71. The fullest account of the events occurring in 1879 is by a descendent: Mel Rothenburger, *The Wild McLeans* (Victoria: Orca, 1993).

72. The sequence of events at Cache Creek School in 1877 was followed closely in the Victoria press.

73. Drawing on Stoler, Carter suggests that, on the prairies, opposition grew out of fears of mixed-race children becoming heirs; see *Capturing Women*, xvi, 14–15, 191–92.

74. The constructed nature of all Aboriginal petitions is indicated by the alacrity with which missionaries and others warned federal officials about upcoming petitions "purporting to come from the Indians," but which were in fact being organized by an opposing religious group or others not to their liking, as with Alfred Hall, Anglican missionary, to Superintendent of Indian Affairs, Alert Bay, 5 October 1889, in RG 10, vol. 38 16, file 57,045-1, C-10193.

75. Petitions of the Lillooet tribe of Indians and from Lower Fraser Indians, s.d. [summer and late fall 1885], and s.d. [summer 1885] in RG 10, vol. 3842, file 71,799, C-10148. On the Oblates' role see memo from Bishop Louis d'Herbomez, OMI, to the Governor General, s.d. [1887], in same.

76. George N. Burbidge, Deputy Minister of Justice, to L. Vankoughnet, Deputy Superintendent General of Indian Affairs, Ottawa, 3 February 1886, and enclosure, in RG to, vol. 3842, file 71-799, C-10148.

77. W.H. Lomas, Indian Agent of Cowichan Agency, to Powell, Quamichan, 20 May 1886; also draft of Vankoughnet to Powell, 13 February 1886; P McTiernan, Indian Agent at New Westminster, to Powell, New Westminster, 9 April 1886; Meason to Powell, Little Dog Creek, 25 March 1886; J.W. Mackay, Indian Agent of Kamloops-Okanagan Agency, to Powell, Sooyoos [Osoyoos], 2 May 1886; and Powell to Superintendent of Indian Affairs, Victoria, 21 June 1886, in RG 10, vol. 3842, file 71,799, C-10148.

78. Memo from d'Herbomez, [1887]; and Hector Langevin, Minister of Public Works, to John Macdonald, Superintendent of Indian Affairs, Ottawa, 25 April 1887, in RG 10, vol. 3842, file 71,799, C-10148.

79. Petition, New Westminster, 1 September 1890, in RG 10, vol. 3842, file 71,799, C-10148.

80. Draft from Department of Indian Affairs to Deputy Minister of Justice, 17 December 1890, in RG 10, vol. 3842, file 71-799, C-10148.

81. Draft of letter from Department of Indian Affairs to A. W. Vowell, Indian Superintendent, Ottawa, 26 December 1890, in RG 10, vol. 3842, file 71,799, C-10148.

82. Meason to Vowell, Lillooet, 4 August 1890, in RG 10, vol. 3816, file 57,045-1, C-10193.

83. For the Cariboo, see Margaret Whitehead, *The Cariboo Mission: A History of the Oblates* (Victoria: Sono Nis, 1981).

84. Mackay to Vowell, Kamloops, 24 May 1892, in RG 10, vol. 3875, file 90,667-2 C-10193.

85. Meason to Vowell, Lillooet, 14 May 189 2, in RG 10, vol. 3875, file 90,667-2, C-10193. The incident, its impetus in Oblate policy, and its aftermath are summarized in Whitehead, *Cariboo Mission*, 96–7. At the behest of Catholic authorities, the Governor General remitted the sentences.

86. Mackay to Vowell, 24 May 1892.

87. R.H. Pidcock, Indian Agent of Kwawkwelth Agency, to Powell, Alert Bay 3 April 1889, in DIA, RG 10, vol. 3816, file 57045, C-10193.

88. Pidcock to Vowell, n.d., in RG 10, vol. 38 16, file 57,045-1, C-10193.

89. Vowell to Deputy Superintendent of Indian Affairs, Victoria, 25 March 1890, in RG 10, vol. 3816, file 57,045-1, C-10193.

90. Memorandum of Superintendent General of Indian Affairs to Privy Council of Canada, Ottawa, 20 February 1890, in DIA, RG 10, vol. 3816, file 57045-1, C-10193.

91. John S.D. Thompson, Minister of Justice, to Governor General in Council, 1890, in RG 10, vol. 3816, file 57,045-1, C-10193.

92. Henry Guillod, Indian Agent of West Coast Agency, to Vowell, Ucluelet, 22 August 1890, in RG 10, vol. 3816, file 57,045-1, C-10193.

93. Lomas to Vowell, Quamichan, 22 November 1890, in RG 10, vol. 3816, file 57,045-1, C-10193.

94. McTiernan to Vowell, New Westminster, 23 June 1890, in RG 10, vol. 3816, file 57,045-1, C-10193.

95. Meason to Vowell, Lillooet, 4 August 1890, in RG 10, vol. 3816, file 57,045-1, C-10193.

96. Mackay to Vowell, Kamloops, 4 July 1890, in RG 10, vol. 3816, file 57,045-1, C-10193.

97. C. Todd, Acting Indian Agent of North West Coast Agency, to Vowell, Metlakatla, 8 October 1890, in RG 10, vol. 3816, file 57,045-1, C-10193.

98. Vowell to Vankoughnet, Victoria, 25 February 1891, in RG 10, vol. 3816, file 57,045-1, C-10193.

99. Petition to Pidcock, Fort Rupert, 8 March 1895, in RG 10, vol. 38 16, file 57,045-1, C-10193.

100. Senator W.J. Macdonald to Minister of the Interior, Ottawa, 6 May 1895, in RG 10, vol. 3816, file 57,045-1, C-10193.

101. Deputy Superintendent General of Indian Affairs to Vowell, Ottawa, 20 May 1895, in RG 10, vol. 3816, file 57,045-1, C-10193.

102. Davidoff and Hall, *Family Fortunes*, 115.

103. Census data included with Anderson and McKinlay, Report, 21 March 1877.

104. Crosby, *Among the An-ko-me-nums*, 49–50. On the related issue of domestic hygiene, see Michael Harkin, "Engendering Discipline: Discourse and Counterdiscourse in the Methodist-Heiltsuk Dialogue," *Ethnohistory* 43, 4 (Fall 1996), 647–48.

105. Crosby, *Up and Down*, 74.

106. For example, Cornelius Bryant, Methodist missionary, to Lomas, Nanaimo, 30 January 1884; G. Donckel, Catholic missionary, to Lomas, Maple Bay, 2 February 1884; Lomas to Powell, Maple Bay, 5 February 1884; and Powell to Superintendent General of Indian Affairs, Victoria, 27 February 1884, in DIA, RG 10, vol. 3628, file 6244-1, C-10110.

107. This point is supported by DIA to Powell, 6 June 1884, in DIA, RG 10, vol. 3628, file 6244-1, C-10110; and stated explicitly in E.K. DeBeck, "The Potlatch and Section 149 of the Indian Act," Ottawa, 11 May 1921, in DIA, RG 10, vol. 3628, file 6244-X, C-10110; and in C.M. Barbeau, "The Potlatch among the B.C. Indians and Section 149 of the Indian Act," 1921, in DIA, RG 10, vol. 3628, file 6244-X C-10111.

108. Confidential memo to C.M.B., 17 February 1921, in Barbeau, "The Potlatch."

109. Douglas Cole and Ira Chaikin, *An Iron Hand Upon the People: The Law Against the Potlatch on the Northwest Coast* (Vancouver and Seattle: Douglas & McIntyre and University of Washington Press, 1990), 75–83; and Douglas Cole, "The History of the Kwakiutl Potlatch," in Aldona Jonaitis, ed., *Chiefly Feasts: The Enduring Kwakiutl Potlatch* (Vancouver and New York: Douglas & McIntyre and American Museum of Natural History, 1991), 150–52, discuss sexual and marriage practices of the Kwakiutl as linked to the potlatch from a perspective which, while very informative and reliable, more or less accepts at face value the critiques of men in power. In *Severing the Ties that Bind: Government Repression of Indigenous Religious Ceremonies on the Prairies* (Winnipeg: University of Manitoba Press, 1994), Katherine Pettipas essentially equates the perspective of

males with the entirety of perspectives in reference both to the potlatch (90–6) and to the sundance. With a single exception noted only in passing (62), Joseph Masco does much the same in "'It Is a Strict Law That Bids Us Dance': Cosmologies, Colonialism, Death, and Ritual Authority in the Kwakwa'wakw Potlatch, 1849 to 1922," *Comparative Studies in Society and History* 37, 1 (January 1995), 41–75.

110. *Empire* (Toronto), received 9 February 1893, and letter from Pidcock, 16 March 1893, in Barbeau, "The Potlatch."

111. Crosby, *Up and Down*, 316.

112. G.W. DeBeck, Indian Agent of Kwawkwelth Agency, to Vowell, Alert Bay, 29 December 1902, and E.A. Bird, teacher at Gwayasdurus, to DeBeck, Alert Bay, 23 June 1902, in DIA, RG 10, vol. 6816, file 486-2-5, C-8538. The meaning of "child marriage" is explored in Harkin, "Engendering Discipline," 646–47.

113. Bird to DeBeck, 23 June 1902.

114. Most recently, J.R. Miller, *Shingwauk's Vision: A History of Native Residential Schools* (Toronto: University of Toronto Press, 1996).

115. Letter from Thomas Crosby, *Missionary Outlook* 9 (1989), 100, cited in Bolt, *Thomas Crosby*, 64; and Crosby, *Up and Down*, 85.

116. Crosby, *Among the An-ko-me-nums*, 63.

117. Kate Hendry to sister Maggie, 26 December 1882, Kate Hendry Letterbook, British Columbia Archives, EC/H38.

118. C.J. South, Superintendent, Children's Protection Act, to Secretary, Department of Indian Affairs, Vancouver, 20 September 1905, in RG 10, vol. 3816, file 57,045-1, C-10193.

119. Bolt, *Thomas Crosby*, 64.

120. October 1886 entry in Agnes Knight, Journal, 1885–87, British Columbia Archives, F7/W 15.

121. Crosby, *Up and Down*, 89, 92–3.

122. "Indian girl sold for 1,000 blankets,' *World* (Vancouver), 2 January 1906.

123. "Five Little Girls Sold at Alert Bay Potlatch," *World*, 4 April 1906; and "Five Indian Girls Sold, Vancouver, B.C., April 6," *Journal* (Ottawa), 9 April 1906.

124. Letter of Vowell, 16 April 1906, in Barbeau, "The Potlatch."

125. "Squaw sold for $400.00 at Alert Bay to a grizzled Chief from Queen Charlottes," *Daily News Advertiser* (Vancouver), 6 April 1907.

126. Letter of William Halliday, 9 July 1907, in Barbeau, "The Potlatch."

127. The quotes are from Emily Cummings, Corresponding Secretary, National Council of Women, to Minister of Indian Affairs, Toronto, 19 February 1910, in RG 10, vol. 38 16, file 57,045-1, C-10193, which contains the many letters, often virtually identical in language, from the different associations.

128. DeBeck, "The Potlatch and Section 149."

129. Margaret Whitehead emphasizes this point in "'A Useful Christian Woman': First Nations' Women and Protestant Missionary Work in British Columbia," *Atlantis* 18, 1–2 (1992–93), 142–66.

130. Crosby, *Up and Down*, 92.

131. John Tate (Salaben), Gispaxloats, informant, recorded by William Beynon in 1950, in George F. MacDonald and John J. Cove, ed., *Tsimshian Narratives*, collected by Marius Barbeau and William Beynon. Vol. 2: *Trade and Warfare* (Ottawa: Canadian Museum of Civilization, 1987), 207.

132. A fascinating question beyond the scope of this essay, which grows out of Foucault's work on power, concerns the extent to which some Aboriginal women internalized the assertions being made about them and considered that, yes, they must be prostitutes simply because they had been so informed so many times.

133. This topic is explored in Jean Barman, "Invisible Women: Aboriginal Mothers and Mixed-Race Daughters in Rural Pioneer British Columbia," in R.W. Sandwell, ed., *Negotiating Rural: Essays from British Columbia* (Vancouver: UBC Press, 1998).

134. The 1901 manuscript census indicates persons' "colour" and mixed-race origins, making it possible to determine the character of individual households.

135. Carr, *Heart of a Peacock*, 110–1.

136. C.W. Holliday, *The Valley of Youth* (Caldwell, ID: Caxton, 1948), 155, 226.

137. DeBeck, "The Potlatch and Section 149."

138. 16, 17, and 25 June and 26 July 1966 entries in Edward Ho agland, *Notes From the Century Before: A Journal from British Columbia* (New York: Ballantine, 1969), 92, 96, 101, 141, 186, 250.

Article Twenty-Two

Reluctant Hosts: Anglo-Canadian Views of Multiculturalism in the Twentieth Century

Howard Palmer

INTRODUCTION

The way in which Anglo-Canadians have reacted to immigration during the twentieth century has not simply been a function of the numbers of immigrants or the state of the nation's economy. The immigration of significant numbers of non-British and non-French people raised fundamental questions about the type of society which would emerge in English-speaking Canada; hence, considerable public debate has always surrounded the issue of immigration in Canada. The questions which have repeatedly been raised include the following: Were the values and institutions of Anglo-Canadian society modelled exclusively on a British mould and should immigrants be compelled to conform to that mould? Or, would a distinctive identity emerge from the biological and cultural mingling of Anglo-Canadians with new immigrant groups? Would cultural pluralism itself give English-speaking Canada a distinctive identity? These three questions reflect the three theories of assimilation which have dominated the twentieth-century debate over immigrant adjustment.

The assimilation theory which achieved early public acceptance was anglo-conformity. This view demanded that immigrants renounce their ancestral culture and traditions in favor of the behaviour and values of Anglo-Canadians. Although predominant prior to World War II, anglo-conformity fell into disrepute and was replaced in the popular mind by the "melting pot" theory of assimilation. This view envisaged a biological merging of settled communities with new immigrant groups and a blending of their cultures into a new Canadian type. Currently, a third theory of assimilation —"cultural pluralism" or "multiculturalism"— is vying for public acceptance. This view postulates the preservation of some aspects of immigrant culture and communal life within the context of Canadian citizenship and political and economic integration into Canadian society.[1]

There has been a recent burgeoning of historical and sociological research on Anglo-Canadian attitudes toward ethnic minorities. Much of this research contradicts the view which has been advanced by some Anglo-Canadian historians[2] and politicians that Anglo-Canadians have always adopted the "mosaic" as opposed to the American "melting pot" approach. Much of this rhetoric has simply been wishful thinking. Perhaps immigrant groups did not "melt" as much in Canada as in the United States, but this is not because Anglo-Canadians were more anxious to encourage the cultural survival of ethnic minorities. There has been a long history of racism and discrimination against ethnic minorities in English-speaking Canada, along with strong pressures for conformity to Anglo-Canadian ways.

Source: Howard Palmer, "Reluctant Hosts: Anglo-Canadian Views of Multiculturalism in the Twentieth Century," adapted from *Multiculturalism as State Policy*, 1976 Canadian Consultative Council of Multiculturalism, Department of Canadian Heritage. Reproduced with the permission of Public Works and Government Services Canada, 2005.

#1

THE "SETTLEMENT" PERIOD AND THE PREDOMINANCE OF ANGLO-CONFORMITY: 1867–1920

Among the several objectives of the architects of the Canadian confederation in 1867, none was more important than the effort to accommodate the needs of the two main cultural communities. There was virtually no recognition of ethnic diversity aside from the British–French duality. This is, of course, somewhat understandable since at the time of Confederation, only 8 percent of the population of 3.5 million were of non-British[3] or non-French ethnic origin. There were, however, significant numbers of people of German and Dutch origin, well-established black and Jewish communities, as well as a few adventurers and entrepreneurs from most European ethnic groups now in Canada.

The proportion of people of other than British, French, or Native origin in Canada remained small until nearly the turn of the twentieth century; the United States proved more attractive for most European emigrants. In fact it was attractive for many Canadians as well, and the Dominion barely maintained its population. But with the closing of the American frontier, which coincided with improving economic conditions in Canada and an active immigration promotion campaign by Wilfrid Laurier's Liberal government, many immigrants began to come to the newly opened land of western Canada in the late 1890s.[4] Immigration policy gave preference to farmers, and most non-British immigrants came to farm in western Canada. However, some immigrants ended up working in mines, laying railway track, or drifting into the urban working class.[5] During this first main wave of immigration between 1896 and 1914, three million immigrants, including large numbers of British labourers, American farmers, and eastern European peasants, came to Canada. Within the period of 1901 to 1911, Canada's population rocketed by 43 percent and the percentage of immigrants in the country as a whole topped 22 percent. In 1911, people of non-British and non-French origin formed 34 percent of the population of Manitoba, 40 percent of the population of Saskatchewan, and 33 percent of the population of Alberta.

Throughout the period of this first large influx of non-British, non-French immigrants (indeed up until World War II), anglo-conformity was the predominant ideology of assimilation in English-speaking Canada.[6] For better or for worse, there were few proponents of either the melting pot or cultural pluralism. Proponents of anglo-conformity argued that it was the obligation of new arrivals to conform to the values and institutions of Canadian society — which were already fixed. During this period when scarcely anyone questioned the verities of God, King, and country, there was virtually no thought given to the possibility that "WASP" values might not be the apex of civilization which all men should strive for.

Since at this time the British Empire was at its height, and the belief in "progress" and Anglo-Saxon and white superiority was taken for granted throughout the English-speaking world, a group's desirability as potential immigrants varied almost directly with its members' physical and cultural distance from London (England), and the degree to which their skin pigmentation conformed to Anglo-Saxon white. Anglo-Canadians regarded British and American immigrants as the most desirable.[7] Next came northern and western Europeans who were regarded as culturally similar and hence assimilable. They were followed by central and eastern Europeans, who in the eyes of Clifford Sifton and immigration agents, had a slight edge on Jews and southern Europeans, because they were more inclined to go to and remain on the land. These groups were followed in the ethnic pecking order by the "strange" religious sects, the Hutterites, Mennonites, and Doukhobors, who were invariably lumped together by public officials and the general public despite significant religious and cultural differences between them. Last, but not least (certainly not least in the eyes of those British Columbians and their sympathizers elsewhere in the country who worried about the "Asiatic" hordes), were the Asian immigrants — the Chinese, Japanese, and East Indians (the latter of whom were dubbed "Hindoos," despite the fact that most were Sikhs). Running somewhere close to last were black immigrants, who did not really arise as an issue because of the lack of aspiring candidates, except in 1911, when American blacks were turned back at the border by immigration officials because they allegedly could not adapt to the cold winters in Canada — a curious about-face for a department which was reassuring other American immigrants that Canadian winters were relatively mild.[8] *Prejudice reigned*

As might be expected, prevailing assumptions about the relative assimilability of these different groups were quickly transformed into public debate over whether immigrants whose assimilability was problematic should be allowed into the country. During this first wave of immigration, considerable opposition developed to the entry of central, southern, and eastern European immigrants, Orientals, and to the three pacifist sects. Opposition to these groups came from a variety of sources, for a variety of reasons. But one of the most pervasive fears of opinion leaders was that central, southern, and eastern Europeans, and Orientals would wash away Anglo-Saxon traditions of self-government in a sea of illiteracy and inexperience with "free institutions."[9] Many English-Canadian intellectuals, like many American writers at the time, thought that North America's greatness was ensured so long as its Anglo-Saxon character was preserved. Writers emphasized an Anglo-Saxon tradition of political freedom and self-government and the "white man's" mission to spread Anglo-Saxon blessings.[10] Many intellectuals and some politicians viewed Orientals and central, southern, and eastern European immigrants as a threat to this tradition and concluded that since they could not be assimilated they would have to be excluded. The introduction in Canada of a head tax on Chinese immigrants, a "gentlemen's agreement" with Japan which restricted the number of Japanese immigrants, the passing of orders-in-council which restricted immigration from India, the gradual introduction of restrictive immigration laws in 1906, 1910, and 1919 relative to European immigration, and the tightening of naturalization laws were based in considerable part on the assumptions of anglo-conformity — immigrants who were culturally or racially inferior and incapable of being assimilated either culturally or biologically would have to be excluded.[11] Those who rose to the immigrants' defence argued almost entirely from economic grounds: immigration from non-British sources was needed to aid in economic development, not because it might add anything to Canada's social or cultural life.

Although the trend toward restrictionism during the early 1900s seemed to indicate a government trend toward anglo-conformity in response to public pressure, for the most part between 1867 and 1945, there was no explicit federal government policy with regard to the role of non-British and non-French ethnic groups in Canadian society. It was generally assumed, however, that immigrants would eventually be assimilated into either English-Canadian or French-Canadian society. A recent careful study of Clifford Sifton's attitudes toward immigrant groups in Canadian society concludes Sifton assumed that central and eastern Europeans "would be 'nationalized' in the long run through their experience on the land."[12] The federal government's concern was tied to the economic consequences of immigration, while schools, the primary agents of assimilation, were under provincial jurisdiction. The federal government had encouraged Mennonites and Icelanders to settle in blocks in Manitoba during the 1870s and had given them special concessions (including local autonomy for both and military exemptions for the Mennonites) to entice them to stay in Canada rather than move to the United States.[13] But this was not because of any conscious desire to make Canada a cultural mosaic, nor was it out of any belief in the value of cultural diversity. Block settlements, by providing social and economic stability, were simply a way of getting immigrants to settle in the west and remain there.[14] The government policy was pragmatic and concerned primarily with economic growth and "nation building"; there was little rhetoric in immigration propaganda picturing Canada as a home for oppressed minorities who would be able to pursue their identities in Canada.

Provincial governments were faced with the problems of assimilation more directly than the federal government since the provinces maintained jurisdiction over the educational systems. The whole question of the varying attitudes of provincial authorities toward assimilation is much too complex to outline in this article; suffice it to say that with some notable exceptions (like the bilingual school system in Manitoba between 1896 and 1916, and the school system which was established for Hutterites in Alberta), anglo-conformity was the predominant aim of the public school system and was an underlying theme in the textbooks.

Anglo-conformity was most pronounced during World War I as nationalism precipitated insistent hostility to "hyphenated Canadianism" and demanded an unswerving loyalty. For many Anglo-Canadians during the war, loyalty and cultural and linguistic uniformity were synonymous. During the war, western provincial governments acted to abolish the bilingual schools which had previously been allowed.[15] The formation of the Union government of Conservatives and Liberals during the First World War was an attempt to create an Anglo-Saxon party, dedicated to "unhyphenated Canadianism" and the winning of the war; even if this meant trampling on the rights of immigrants through press censorship and the imposition of the War Time Elections Act, which disfranchised "enemy aliens" who had become Canadian citizens after March 21, 1902.[16] Various voluntary associations like the YMCA, IODE, National Council of Women, Canadian Girls in Training, Girl Guides, Big Brothers and Big Sisters Organizations, and Frontier College, as well as the major Protestant denominations, also intensified their efforts to "Canadianize" the immigrants, particularly at the close of the war when immigrant support for radical organizations brought on anti-radical nativist fears of the "menace of the alien."[17] The pressures for conformity were certainly real, even if English-Canadians could not always agree completely on the exact nature of the norm to which immigrants were to be assimilated.

All the major books on immigration prior to 1920, including J.S. Woodsworth's *Strangers within Our Gates*, J.T.M. Anderson's *The Education of the New Canadian*, Ralph Connor's *The Foreigner*, Alfred Fitzpatrick's *Handbook for New Canadians*, C.A. Magrath's *Canada's Growth and Some Problems Affecting It*, C.B. Sissons' *Bilingual Schools in Canada*, and W.G. Smith's *A Study in Canadian Immigration*, were based on the assumptions of anglo-conformity. To lump all these books together is of course to oversimplify since they approached the question of immigration with varying degrees of nativism (or anti-foreign sentiment) and humanitarianism. Nor were all of the voluntary organizations' attempted "Canadianization" work among immigrants motivated solely by the fear that immigrants would undermine the cultural homogeneity of English-speaking Canada. Many of these writers and organizations saw their work with the immigrants as a means of fighting social problems and helping immigrants achieve a basic level of political, social, and economic integration into Canadian society. But it cannot be denied that their basic assumption was that of anglo-conformity. Cultural diversity was either positively dangerous, or was something that would and should disappear with time, and with the help of Anglo-Canadians.

Perhaps it should be emphasized that the individuals advocating anglo-conformity were not just the reactionaries of their day. Protestant Social Gospellers (including J.S. Woodsworth, later one of the founders of the CCF), who played such a prominent role in virtually all the reform movements of the pre–World War I period (including women's rights, temperance, and labour, farm, and penal reform), believed that immigrants needed to be assimilated to Anglo-Canadian Protestant values as part of the effort to establish a truly Christian society in English-speaking Canada.[18] Women's groups pushing for the franchise argued that certainly they deserved the vote if "ignorant foreigners" had it, and joined in the campaign to Canadianize the immigrants who "must be educated to high standards or our whole national life will be lowered by their presence among us."[19]

But there was a central contradiction in Anglo-Canadian attitudes toward ethnic minorities. Non–Anglo-Saxon immigrants were needed to open the west and to do the heavy jobs of industry. This meant not only the introduction of culturally distinctive groups, but groups which would occupy the lower rungs of the socioeconomic system. The pre-1920 period was the period of the formation of, and the most acute expression of, what was later called the "vertical mosaic." Anglo-Canadians were not used to the idea of cultural diversity, nor the degree of class stratification which developed during this period of rapid settlement and industrialization. The answer to all the problems of social diversity which the immigrants posed was assimilation. The difficulty, however, with achieving this goal of assimilation was not only the large numbers of immigrants, or the fact that not all (or even a majority) of them wanted to be assimilated. One of the major factors preventing assimilation was discrimination by the Anglo-Canadian majority.

The basic contradiction, then, of Anglo-Canadian attitudes as expressed through the "Canadianization" drives was the tension between the twin motives of humanitarianism and nativism — between the desire to include non-British immigrants within a community and eliminate cultural differences and the desire to stay as far away from them as possible because of their presumed "undesirability." This contradiction was graphically revealed at the national conference of the IODE in 1919. The women passed one resolution advocating a "Canadianization campaign" to "propagate British ideals and institutions," to "banish old world points of view, old world prejudices, old world rivalries and suspicion" and to make new Canadians "100 percent British in language, thought, feeling, and impulse." Yet they also passed another resolution protesting "foreigners" taking British names.[20]

It does not appear that this was simply a case of the Anglo-Canadian majority being divided between those who wanted to pursue a strategy of assimilation and those who wanted to pursue a strategy of subordination and segregation. Certainly there was some division along these lines, but as suggested by the IODE resolutions, discrimination and anglo-conformity were often simply two different sides of the same coin — the coin being the assumption of the inferiority of non–Anglo-Saxons.

What developed throughout English-speaking Canada during this period was a vicious circle of discrimination. Non–Anglo-Saxons were discriminated against because they were not assimilated, either culturally or socially, but one of the reasons they were not assimilated was because of discrimination against them. As one researcher noted in a 1917 report on "Social Conditions in Rural Communities in the Prairie Provinces," the group "clannishness" of immigrants which was so widely deplored by the public was caused as much by the prejudice of the "English" as it was by the groups' desire to remain different.[21]

There is no need to catalogue here the extensive patterns of social, economic, and political discrimination which developed against non–Anglo-Saxons.[22] Patterns of discrimination parallelled preferences of immigrant sources, with northern and western Europeans encountering relatively little discrimination, central and southern Europeans and Jews encountering more discrimination, and non-whites encountering an all-pervasive pattern of discrimination which extended to almost all aspects of their lives. Discrimination was one of the main factors which led to the transference (with only a few exceptions) of the same ethnic "pecking order" which existed in immigration policy to the place each group occupied in the "vertical mosaic," with the British (especially the Scots) on top, and so on down to the Chinese and blacks who occupied the most menial jobs.[23] Non-British and non-French groups not only had very little economic power; they also would not even significantly occupy the middle echelons of politics, education, or the civil service until after World War II.

The ethnic stereotypes which developed for eastern European and Oriental groups empha-sized their peasant origins. These stereotypes played a role in determining the job opportuni-ties for new immigrants and functioned to disparage those who would climb out of their place. Opprobrious names such as "Wops," "Bohunks," and especially "foreigner" indicated class as well as ethnic origin and these terms were used as weapons in the struggle for status. The very word "ethnic" carried, for many people, such an aura of opprobrium that even recently there have been attempts to expurgate the use of the word. Ethnic food and folklore were regarded by most Anglo-Canadians as not only "foreign," but "backward" and lower class. Folklorist Carole Henderson has aptly described the views of Anglo-Canadians toward folklore (views which continue to the present day): "Except for members of some delimited regional, and usu-ally ethnic, subcultures such as Newfoundlanders or Nova Scotian Scots, most Anglo-Canadians simply fail to identify folklore with themselves, and tend to consider such materials to be the . . . unimportant possessions of the strange, foreign, or 'backward people in their midst.'"[24]

＃2 THE 1920s AND THE EMERGENCE OF "MELTING POT" IDEAS

The 1920s brought the second main wave of non-British and non-French immigrants to Canada and saw the emergence of the second ideology of assimilation, the "melting pot." During the early 1920s both Canada and the United States had acted to further restrict immi-gration from southern, central, and eastern Europe and from the Orient. Chinese were virtu-ally excluded from Canada, and central, southern, and eastern Europeans were classified among the "non-preferred" and restricted category of immigrants. But by the mid-1920s several pow-erful sectors of Canadian society, including transportation companies, boards of trade, newspa-pers, and politicians of various political persuasions, as well as ethnic groups, applied pressure on the King government to open the immigration doors.[25] These groups believed that only a limited immigration could be expected from the "preferred" countries and that probably only central and eastern Europeans would do the rugged work of clearing marginal land. The rail-ways continued to seek immigrants to guarantee revenue for their steamship lines, traffic for their railways, and settlers for their land. With improving economic conditions in the mid-twenties, the federal government responded to this pressure and changed its policy with respect to immigrants from central and eastern Europe.

While continuing to emphasize its efforts to secure British immigrants, in September 1925 the Liberal government of Mackenzie King entered into the "Railways Agreement" with the CPR and CNR, which brought an increased number of central and eastern Europeans. The government authorized the railways to encourage potential immigrants of the "non-preferred" countries to emigrate to Canada and to settle as "agriculturalists, agricultural workers, and domestic servants."[26]

Through this agreement, the railways brought to Canada 165 000 central and eastern Europeans and 20 000 Mennonites. They represented a variety of ethnic groups and a diversity of reasons for emigrating. Most of the Ukrainian immigrants were political refugees. Poles, Slovaks, and Hungarians were escaping poor economic conditions. German-Russians and Mennonites were fleeing civil war, economic disaster, and the spectre of cultural annihilation in Russia.[27] Often they chose Canada since they could no longer get into the United States because of its quota system and the Canadian route was the only way they could get to North America. With this new wave of immigration, the proportion of the Canadian population that was not of British, French, or native origin rose to more than 18 percent by 1931.

In responding to this new wave of immigration, many opinion leaders held to an earlier belief that Canada should be patterned exclusively on the British model, and continued to advocate anglo-conformity. In national periodicals and newspapers during the 1920s, the emphasis which was placed on the need to attract British immigrants was related to this assumption that anglo-conformity was essential to the successful development of Canadian society. "Foreign" immigrants had to be assimilated and there needed to be enough Britishers to maintain "Anglo-Saxon" traditions.[28] R.B. Bennett, later to become the Conservative prime minister during the early 1930s, attacked melting pot ideas in the House of Commons and argued "These people [continental Europeans] have made excellent settlers: . . . but it cannot be that we must draw upon them to shape our civilization. We must still maintain that measure of British civilization which will enable us to assimilate these people to British institutions, rather than assimilate our civilization to theirs."[29]

The influx of new immigrants from central and eastern Europe during the mid- and late twenties also aroused protests from a number of nativist organizations, such as the Ku Klux Klan, The Native Sons of Canada, and The Orange Order, who were convinced that Canada should "remain Anglo-Saxon."[30] Nativist sentiment in western Canada was most pronounced in Saskatchewan, where one of its leading spokesmen was George Exton Lloyd, an Anglican bishop and one of the founders of the Barr colony at Lloydminster.

In a torrent of newspaper articles and speeches, Lloyd repeated the warning that Canada was in danger of becoming a "mongrel" nation: "The essential question before Canadians today is this: Shall Canada develop as a British nation within the empire, or will she drift apart by the introduction of so much alien blood that her British instincts will be paralyzed?"[31] According to Lloyd, Canada had but two alternatives: it could either be a homogeneous nation or a heterogeneous one. The heterogeneous or "melting pot" idea had not worked in the United States (as evidenced by large numbers of unassimilated immigrants at the outbreak of World War I), and could not, he argued, work in Canada. With Lloyd, as with other individuals and organizations promoting anglo-conformity at this time, one gets the distinctive feeling that they were on the defensive. Like other English-speaking Canadians who had a strong attachment to Britain and the Empire, Lloyd saw a threat to Canada's "British" identity, not only in the increasing numbers of "continental" immigrants, but also in the declining status of things British as Canadians moved toward a North-American–based nationalism which did not include loyalty to the British Empire as its primary article of faith.[32]

During the late 1920s, a new view of assimilation, the melting pot, developed greater prominence. This view of assimilation, which arose partly as a means of defending immigrants against nativist attacks from people like Lloyd, envisioned a biological merging of Anglo-Canadians with immigrants and a blending of their cultures into a new Canadian type. Whereas Lloyd and other nativists argued that since immigrants could not conform to Anglo-Canadian ideals they should be excluded, a new generation of writers argued that assimilation was indeed occurring, but to a new Canadian type.[33] Since assimilation was occurring, nativist fears were unwarranted. Indeed, immigrants would make some valuable cultural contributions to Canada during the process of assimilation. Although these writers did not all use the "melting pot" symbol when discussing their view of assimilation, one can lump their ideas together under the rubric of the "melting pot" because they did envisage the emergence of a new society which would contain "contributions" from the various immigrant groups.

Most of these writers who defended "continental" European immigration did not seriously question the desirability of assimilation. Robert England, a writer and educator who worked for the CNR, had read widely enough in anthropological sources to be influenced by the cultural relativism of Franz Boas and other anthropologists and did in his writing question the desirability of assimilation.[34] But most of these writers were concerned primarily with attempting to promote tolerance toward ethnic minorities by encouraging their assimilation, and many became involved in programs to facilitate this assimilation.

Advocates of anglo-conformity and the melting pot both believed that uniformity was ultimately necessary for unity, but they differed on what should provide the basis of that uniformity. Advocates of the melting pot, unlike the promoters of anglo-conformity, saw assimilation as a relatively slow process, and saw some cultural advantages in the mixing that would occur.

There was not, however, always a clear distinction between anglo-conformity and the melting pot. Rhetoric indicating that immigrants might have something more to offer Canada than their physical labour was sometimes only a thinly veiled version of anglo-conformity; the melting pot often turned out to be an Anglo-Saxon melting pot. For example, John Blue, a prominent Edmonton promoter and historian, wrote in his history of Alberta in 1924 that the fears about foreign immigration destroying Canadian laws and institutions had proved groundless. "There is enough Anglo-Saxon blood in Alberta to dilute the foreign blood and complete the process of assimilation to the mutual advantage of both elements."[35]

There were a variety of reasons for the development of melting pot ideas during the 1920s.[36] The growth during the 1920s of an autonomous Canadian nationalism helped the spread of melting pot ideas. Some English-Canadian opinion leaders began to discuss the need for conformity to an exclusively Canadian norm rather than a "British" norm. One of the arguments that John W. Dafoe, the influential editor of the *Winnipeg Free Press*, and J.S. Ewart, a constitutional lawyer, used in support of their view of Canadian nationalism was that non-British immigrants could not be expected to feel loyalty to the British Empire.[37]

Melting pot advocates tended to be people who had some personal experience with immigrants, and recognized both the intense pride that immigrants had in their cultural backgrounds as well as the rich cultural sources of those traditions. But they also lived in a time when recognition of ethnicity meant mostly Anglo-Canadian use of ethnicity as a basis of discrimination or exploitation. It was also a time when some ethnic groups were still close enough to their rural peasant roots that ethnic solidarity was often not conducive to upward mobility. The view of most melting pot advocates that the disappearance of ethnicity as a basis of social organization would increase the mobility opportunities of the second generation was based on a sound grasp of the realities of the day. The lifelong campaign of John Diefenbaker for "unhyphenated Canadianism" and "one Canada" grew out of this experience with ethnicity as something that could be used to hinder opportunities, and was consistent with his emphasis on human rights, rather than group rights.[38]

THE 1930s

Although immigration was severely cut back during the depression of the 1930s, the role of ethnic minorities in English-speaking Canada continued to be a major public concern. Paradoxically, although the depression witnessed the high point of discrimination against non–Anglo-Saxons, it was also during the 1930s that the first major advocates of cultural pluralism in English-speaking Canada began to be heard.

The depression affected non–Anglo-Saxon immigrants more than most other groups in the society. These immigrants, because of their language problems and lack of specialized skills, were concentrated in the most insecure and therefore most vulnerable segments of the economy. Since immigrants were the last hired and the first fired, a large proportion were forced onto relief. Government officials were gravely concerned about the way immigrants seemed to complicate the relief problem. Calls by some officials for deportation as the solution to the relief problem were heeded by the federal government; sections 40 and 41 of the Immigration Act (still essentially the same act as the one which existed in 1919) provided for deportation of non-Canadian citizens on relief, and government officials took advantage of the law to reduce their relief rolls.

While there was some continuing concern over the assimilation of non-British and non-French immigrants during the 1930s, most Anglo-Canadians were more concerned about protecting their jobs.[39]

Prior to the depression, most Anglo-Saxons were content to have the "foreigners" do all the heavy work of construction, and the dirty work of the janitors and street sweepers. But as the economy slowed down, these jobs became attractive. Whereas the pre-depression attitude was "let the foreigners do the dirty work," the depression attitude became "how come these foreigners have all of our jobs?" The 1930s also saw the high point of anti-Semitism in English-speaking Canada as the patterns of discrimination which had hindered the desires of second generation Jews for entry into the professions were extended into a vicious and virulent anti-Semitism by fascist groups.[40]

Barry Broadfoot's book *Ten Lost Years* also makes it very clear that discrimination and prejudice flourished during the depression. In the transcripts of his interviews with the "survivors" of the depression, one is struck by the all-pervasiveness of derogatory ethnic epithets in interviewees' recollections of their contact with immigrants. One does not read of Italians, Chinese, or Poles. One reads of "Dagos," "Wops," "Chinks," "Polacks," "Hunyaks."[41] One "survivor" of the depression, waxing philosophical, gives explicit expression to the prevailing attitudes of the time. He compares how the depression affected people from R.B. Bennett down to "the lowest of the low," "some bohunk smelling of garlic and not knowing a word of English."[42] Another "survivor" recalls that her boy had great difficulty finding work during the depression, and went berserk because of the blow to his self-esteem when the only job he could find was "working with a bunch of Chinks."[43]

The vicious circle of discrimination became perhaps even more vicious during the 1930s as non–Anglo-Saxons' political response to the depression further poisoned attitudes toward them. The discrimination and unemployment which non–Anglo-Saxons faced was an important factor in promoting the support of many for radical political solutions to the depression, in either communist or fascist movements. Indeed the vast majority of the support for the communists throughout Canada, and for the fascists in western Canada, came from non–Anglo-Saxons.[44] Ethnic support for these two movements, and the conflict between left and right within most central and eastern European groups and the Finns was seen as further evidence of the undesirability of non–Anglo-Saxons. The existence of fascist and communist movements in Canada was not of course due simply to the presence of immigrants bringing "old world" ideas. The leaders in both movements were predominantly of British origin,[45] and their "ethnic" support came more from immigrants reacting to depression conditions than from immigrants bringing to Canada "old world" ideas. But the depression gave further support to the notion of non–Anglo-Saxons being unstable politically; one more proof along with immigrant drinking, garlic eating, and the legendary violence at Slavic weddings, that non–Anglo-Saxons were in dire need of baptism by assimilation. Deporting immigrant radicals was seen as one alternative to assimilation and the federal government did not hesitate to use this weapon.[46]

The relationship in the public mind between ethnicity, lower social class origins, and political "unsoundness" explains why during the late 1920s so many second generation non–Anglo-Saxons who were anxious to improve their lot economically made deliberate attempts to hide their ethnic background, such as changing their names. Ethnic ties were clearly disadvantageous for those non–Anglo-Saxons seeking economic security or social acceptance. The experience of the second generation in English-speaking Canada was similar to the second-generation experience as described by a historian writing about ethnic groups in the United States. "Culturally estranged from their parents by their American education, and wanting nothing so much as to become and to be accepted as Americans, many second generation immigrants made deliberate efforts to rid themselves of their heritage. The adoption of American clothes, speech, and interests, often accompanied by the shedding of an exotic surname, were all part of a process whereby antecedents were repudiated as a means of improving status."[47]

Despite the continuing dominance of the old stereotypes concerning non–Anglo-Saxons and the continuing dominance of assimilationist assumptions, the 1930s also saw the emergence of the first full-blown pluralist ideas in somewhat ambiguous form in John Murray Gibbon's book, *The Canadian Mosaic*, and in the writings of Watson Kirkconnell, then an English professor at the University of Manitoba. These writers were much more familiar than earlier writers with the historical backgrounds of the ethnic groups coming to Canada, and they were influenced by a liberalism which rejected the assumptions of Anglo-Saxon superiority. Gibbon, a publicity agent for the Canadian Pacific Railway, wrote his book as an expansion of a series of CBC radio talks on the different ethnic groups of Canada. He traced the history of each group and related their "contributions" to Canadian society. Although he was concerned with the preservation of folk arts and music, he also went out of his way to alleviate fears of unassimilability by discussing individuals' assimilation as well as the "cement" of common institutions which bound the Canadian mosaic together. Although Gibbon was not the first writer to use the mosaic symbol, he was the first to attempt to explore its meaning in any significant way.

Kirkconnell was an essayist, poet, and prolific translator of European verse from a number of European languages. His writing on ethnic groups was based on a different approach than Gibbon's. He tried to promote tolerance toward "European Canadians" by sympathetically portraying the cultural background of the countries where the immigrants originated and by demonstrating the cultural creativity of European immigrants in Canada through translating and publishing their creative writing.[48] In his writing he attacked the assumptions of anglo-conformity, and advocated a multicultural society which would allow immigrants to maintain pride in their past:

> It would be tragic if there should be a clumsy stripping-away of all those spiritual associations with the past that help to give depth and beauty to life. . . . If . . . we accept with Wilhelm von Humboldt "the absolute and essential importance of human development in its richest diversity," then we shall welcome every opportunity to save for our country every previous element of individuality that is available.[49]

Kirkconnell was not advocating complete separation of ethnic groups so that they might be preserved. He believed that assimilation needed to occur in the realm of political and economic values and institutions but he hoped that some of the conservative values and folk culture of immigrants could be preserved.

Kirkconnell did not ignore the political differences within ethnic groups. Indeed, with the outbreak of World War II he wrote a book in which he attempted to expose and combat both fascist and communist elements in different ethnic groups.[50] But he was also active in attempts to bring various other factions of eastern European groups together in order to alleviate public criticism of divisions within ethnic groups.[51]

These advocates of pluralism believed that ethnic diversity was not incompatible with national unity. Unity need not mean uniformity. They believed that recognition of the cultural contributions of non–Anglo-Saxon groups would heighten the groups' feeling that they belonged to Canada and thus strengthen Canadian unity. But Gibbon and Kirkconnell were voices crying in the wilderness — a wilderness of discrimination and racism.

#3 AFTER WORLD WAR II: THE EMERGENCE OF MULTICULTURALISM

The war period and early postwar period was a transitional time with respect to attitudes toward immigration and ethnicity. Although the war brought renewed hostility toward enemy aliens, a number of developments during the war eventually worked to undermine ethnic prejudice. During the arrival of the third wave of immigration in the late 1940s and 1950s, many pre-war prejudices lingered, and ethnic minorities encountered considerable pressures for conformity. But for a variety of intellectual, social, and demographic reasons, the ideology of cultural pluralism has been increasingly accepted in the post–World War II period. The postwar decline of racism and the growing influence of theories about cultural relativism opened the way for the emergence of pluralist ideas. The arrival of many intellectuals among the postwar political refugees from eastern Europe and the growth in the number of upwardly mobile second- and third-generation non–Anglo-Canadians, some of whom felt that they were not being fully accepted into Canadian society, increased the political pressures at both federal and provincial levels for greater recognition of Canada's ethnic diversity. Some suggested that this could be achieved through the appointment of senators of a particular ethnic origin, or through the introduction into the school curriculum of ethnic content and of ethnic languages as courses (and sometimes as languages of instruction).[52]

These demands for greater government recognition of "other ethnic groups" increased during the 1960s in response to the French-Canadian assertion of equal rights and the Pearson government's measures to assess and ensure the status of the French language and culture. In 1963 the Royal Commission on Bilingualism and Biculturalism was appointed to "inquire into and report upon the existing state of bilingualism and biculturalism in Canada and to recommend what steps should be taken to develop the Canadian Confederation on the basis of an equal partnership between the two founding races, taking into account the contribution made by the other ethnic groups to the cultural enrichment of Canada." Many non-British, non-French groups, but particularly Ukrainians, opposed the view that Canada was bicultural. By 1961, 26 percent of the Canadian population was of other than British or French ethnic origin; over two hundred newspapers were being published in languages other than French and English; there were fairly well-defined Italian, Jewish, Slavic, and Chinese neighbourhoods in large Canadian cities, and there were visible rural concentrations of Ukrainians, Doukhobors, Hutterites, and Mennonites scattered across the western provinces: thus, how was it possible for a royal commission to speak of Canada as a *bicultural* country?

This feeling that biculturalism relegated all ethnic groups who were other than British or French to the status of second-class citizens helps explain the resistance some of these groups expressed to the policies and programs that were introduced to secure the status of the French language in Canada. The place of the so-called "other" ethnic groups in a bicultural society became a vexing question for federal politicians, who had originally hoped that steps to ensure French-Canadian rights would go a long way toward improving inter-ethnic relations in Canada. The partial resolution of this dilemma was the assertion in October 1971 by Prime Minister Trudeau that, in fact, Canada is a *multi*cultural country and that steps would be taken by the federal government to give public recognition to ethnic diversity through the introduction of a policy of multiculturalism. Several provinces with large numbers of non–Anglo-Canadians have also initiated their own policies of multiculturalism.

Although most political leaders in English-speaking Canada have accepted and proclaimed the desirability of Canada's ethnic diversity, the Canadian public has not given unanimous support to pluralism. The debate over the place of ethnic groups in Canadian life continues, focusing on such questions as: Does the encouragement of pluralism only serve to perpetuate the vertical mosaic, in which class lines coincide with ethnic lines, or does it help break down class barriers by promoting acceptance of the legitimacy of cultural differences? Are the goals of current government policy — cultural pluralism and equality of opportunity — mutually compatible? Does the encouragement of ethnic group solidarity threaten the freedom of individuals in these groups, or can ethnic groups provide a liberating, rather than a restricting, context for identity? Does the encouragement of cultural diversity serve to perpetuate old-world rivalries, or will the recognition of the contributions of Canada's ethnic groups heighten their feeling that they belong in Canada and thus strengthen Canadian unity? Is government talk of multiculturalism just a way to attract the "ethnic vote," or is positive action necessary to preserve cultural pluralism when cultural diversity throughout the world is being eroded by the impact of industrial technology, mass communication, and urbanization? Does the encouragement of multiculturalism simply heighten the visibility of the growing numbers of non-whites in the country and hinder their chances of full acceptance as individuals into Canadian life, or is a public policy of multiculturalism essential to an effective campaign against racism? The nature of these arguments suggests that the prevailing assumptions about immigration and ethnicity have changed over time in English-speaking Canada. They also suggest that the discussion about the role of immigration and ethnic groups in Canadian life is still an important, and unfinished, debate.

NOTES

1. For a discussion of these three ideologies of assimilation in the United States, see Milton Gordon, *Assimilation in American Life* (New York, 1964).
2. L.G. Thomas, "The Umbrella and the Mosaic: The French–English Presence and the Settlement of the Canadian Prairie West," in J.A. Carroll, ed., *Reflections of Western Historians* (Tucson, Arizona, 1969), 135–52; Allan Smith, "Metaphor and Nationality in North America," *Canadian Historical Review* 51, 3 (September 1970).
3. The Canadian census has consistently classed the Irish as part of the "British" group.
4. Howard Palmer, *Land of the Second Chance: A History of Ethnic Groups in Southern Alberta* (Lethbridge, 1972); Norman Macdonald, *Canada Immigration and Colonization, 1841–1903* (Toronto, 1967); Harold Troper, *Only Farmers Need Apply* (Toronto, 1972).
5. Donald Avery, "Canadian Immigration Policy and the Foreign Navy," Canadian Historical Association, *Report* (1972); Edmund Bradwin, *Bunkhouse Man* (New York, 1928); H. Troper and R. Harney, *Immigrants* (Toronto, 1975).
6. Donald Avery, "Canadian Immigration Policy, 1896–1919: The Anglo-Canadian Perspective" (unpublished Ph.D. thesis, University of Western Ontario, 1973); Cornelius Jaenen, "Federal Policy Vis-à-Vis Ethnic Groups" (unpublished paper, Ottawa, 1971); Howard Palmer, "Nativism and Ethnic Tolerance in Alberta, 1880–1920" (unpublished M.A. thesis, University of Alberta, 1971); Palmer, "Nativism and Ethnic Tolerance in Alberta, 1920–1972" (unpublished Ph.D. thesis, York University, 1973).
7. H. Palmer, "Nativism and Ethnic Tolerance in Alberta, 1880–1920" (unpublished M.A. thesis, University of Alberta, 1971), ch. 1 and 2; H. Troper, *Only Farmers Need Apply* (Toronto, 1972); D.J. Hall, "Clifford Sifton: Immigration and Settlement Policy, 1896–1905," in H. Palmer, ed., *The Settlement of the West* (Calgary, 1977), 60–85.
8. H. Troper, "The Creek Negroes of Oklahoma and Canadian Immigration, 1909–11," *Canadian Historical Review* (September 1972), 272–88.
9. Rev. George Bruce, "Past and Future of Our Race," *Proceedings*, Canadian Club of Toronto, 1911, pp. 6–7; C.A. Magrath, *Canada's Growth and Problems Affecting It* (Ottawa, 1910); Goldwin Smith in *Weekly Sun*, Feb. 1,

1899, Sept. 17, 1902, Sept. 23, 1903, May 18, 1904, Aug. 16, 1905; W.A. Griesbach, *I Remember* (Toronto, 1946), 214–17, 220–21.

10. Carl Berger, *Sense of Power* (Toronto, 1970), 117–88.

11. Morton, *In a Sea of Sterile Mountains* (Vancouver, 1974); W.P. Ward, "The Oriental Immigrant and Canada's Protestant Clergy, 1858–1925," *B.C. Studies* (Summer 1974), 40–55; Ted Ferguson, *A White Man's Country* (Toronto, 1975).

12. D.J. Hall, "Clifford Sifton: Immigration and Settlement Policy: 1896–1905," in H. Palmer, ed., *The Settlement of the West* (Calgary, 1977), 79–80.

13. W.L. Morton, *Manitoba: A History* (Toronto, 1957), 161, 162.

14. J.B. Hedges, *Building the Canadian West* (New York, 1939); Frank Epp, *Mennonites in Canada, 1786–1920* (Toronto, 1974).

15. Cornelius J. Jaenen, "Ruthenian Schools in Western Canada, 1897–1919," *Paedagogica Historica: International Journal of the History of Education* 10, 3 (1970): 517–41. Donald Avery, "Canadian Immigration Policy," 374–420.

16. Avery, "Canadian Immigration Policy," 408.

17. Kate Foster, *Our Canadian Mosaic* (Toronto, 1926); J.T.M. Anderson, *The Education of the New Canadian* (Toronto, 1918); C.B. Sissons, *Bi-Lingual Schools in Canada* (Toronto, 1917); W.G. Smith, *Building the Nation* (Toronto, 1922). For a discussion of some of the concrete activities involved in these "Canadianization" programs, see R. Harney and H. Troper, *Immigrants*, ch. 4.

18. J.S. Woodsworth, *Strangers within Our Gates* (Winnipeg, 1909); Marilyn Barber, "Nationalism, Nativism and the Social Gospel: The Protestant Church Response to Foreign Immigrants in Western Canada, 1897–1914," in Richard Allen, ed., *The Social Gospel in Canada* (Ottawa, 1975), 186–226.

19. Quoted in Barbara Nicholson, "Feminism in the Prairie Provinces to 1916" (unpublished M.A. thesis, University of Calgary, 1974), 71. For the views of womens' groups on immigration and the role of immigrants in Canadian society, see pp. 83–85, 86, 114, 121, 133, 165–69, 186–87.

20. Reported in *Lethbridge Herald*, May 29, 1919.

21. J.S. Woodsworth, "Social Conditions in Rural Communities in the Prairie Provinces" (Winnipeg, 1917), 38.

22. For a fairly extensive chronicling of patterns of discrimination against a number of minority groups, see Morris Davis and J.F. Krauter, *The Other Canadians* (Toronto, 1971).

23. For an analysis of the various causes of ethnic stratification (settlement patterns, time of arrival, immigrant and ethnic occupations, ethnic values, language barriers, and discrimination and exploitation) see Book 4, *Report of the Royal Commission on Bilingualism and Biculturalism* (Ottawa, 1969), ch. 2.

24. Carole Henderson, "The Ethnicity Factor in Anglo-Canadian Folkloristics," *Canadian Ethnic Studies* 7, 2 (1975), 7–18.

25. *Canadian Annual Review* (1923), 264–65; (1924–25), 190–92.

26. *Canada Year Book* (1941), 733.

27. Olha Woycenko, *The Ukrainians in Canada* (Winnipeg, 1967); Victor Turek, *Poles in Manitoba* (Toronto, 1967), 43; J.M. Kirschbaum, *Slovaks in Canada* (Toronto, 1967), 101; Edmund Heier, "A Study of German Lutheran and Catholic Immigrants in Canada formerly residing in Czarist and Soviet Russia" (unpublished M.A. thesis, University of British Columbia, 1955), ch. 3.

28. R.B. Bennett, House of Commons *Debates*, June 7, 1929, pp. 3925–27.

29. Bennett, House of Commons *Debates*, 3925–27.

30. H. Palmer, "Nativism in Alberta, 1925–1930," Canadian Historical Association, *Report* (1974), 191–99.

31. G.E. Lloyd, "National Building," *Banff Crag and Canyon*, Aug. 17, 1928.

32. A.R.M. Lower, *Canadians in the Making* (Don Mills, Ontario, 1958), ch. 22, 27.

33. J.S. Woodsworth, "Nation Building," *University Magazine* (1917), 85–99. F.W. Baumgartner, "Central European Immigration," *Queen's Quarterly* (Winter 1930), 183–92; Walter Murray, "Continental Europeans in Western Canada," *Queen's Quarterly* (1931); P.M. Bryce, *The Value of the Continental Immigrant to Canada* (Ottawa, 1928); E.L. Chicanot, "Homesteading the Citizen: Canadian Festivals Promote Cultural Exchange," *Commonwealth* (May 1929), 94–95; E.K. Chicanot, "Moulding a Nation," *Dalhousie Review* (July 1929), 232–37. J.H. Haslam, "Canadianization of the Immigrant Settler," *Annals* (May 1923), 45–49; E.H. Oliver, "The Settlement of Saskatchewan to 1914," *Transactions of the Royal Society* (1926), 63–87; Agnes Laut, "Comparing the Canadian and American Melting Pots," *Current Opinion* 70 (April 1921), 458–62; Kate Foster, *Our Canadian Mosaic* (Toronto, 1926). Robert England, "Continental Europeans in Western Canada," *Queen's Quarterly* (1931).

34. Robert England, *The Central European Immigrant in Canada* (Toronto, 1929).

35. John Blue, *Alberta Past and Present* (Chicago, 1924), 210.

36. There were some advocates of the melting pot prior to 1920, but it did not gain widespread acceptance until the 1920s. See H. Palmer, "Nativism in Alberta, 1880–1920," ch. 1; Marilyn Barber, "Nationalism, Nativism, and the Social Gospel."

37. Douglas Cole, "John S. Ewart and Canadian Nationalism," *Canadian Historical Association, Report* (1969), 66.

38. John Diefenbaker, *One Canada* (Toronto, 1975), 140, 141, 218–19, 274.

39. H. Palmer, "Nativism in Alberta, 1920–1972," ch. 3.

40. James Gray, *The Roar of the Twenties* (Toronto, 1975), ch. 11; Lita-Rose Betcherman, *The Swastika and the Maple Leaf* (Don Mills, Ontario, 1975).

41. Barry Broadfoot, *Ten Lost Years*, 25, 70, 76, 132, 156–64, 186, 279.

42. Broadfoot, *Ten Lost Years*, 132.

43. Broadfoot, *Ten Lost Years*, 186.

44. Ivan Avakumovic, *The Communist Party in Canada: A History* (Toronto, 1975), 66–67; Lita-Rose Betcherman, *The Swastika and the Maple Leaf*, ch. 5.

45. See note 44 above.

46. H. Palmer, "Nativism in Alberta, 1920–1972," ch. 3.

47. M.A. Jones, *American Immigration* (Chicago, 1960), 298. For fictional treatments of the second generation's repudiation of the ethnic past in an attempt to become accepted, see John Marlyn, *Under the Ribs of Death* (Toronto, 1971) and Magdalena Eggleston, *Mountain Shadows* (New York, 1955), 122. See also *Change of Name* (Toronto: Canadian Institute of Cultural Research, 1965).

48. Watson Kirkconnell, *The European Heritage: A Synopsis of European Cultural Achievement* (London, 1930) and *Canadian Overtones* (Winnipeg, 1935). For a complete listing of Kirkconnell's work, see the list in his memoirs, *A Slice of Canada* (Toronto, 1967), 374–75. For an assessment of his work, see J.R.C. Perkin, ed., *The Undoing of Babel* (Toronto, 1975).

49. W. Kirkconnell, trans., *Canadian Overtones*, preface.

50. Watson Kirkconnell, *Canada, Europe, and Hitler* (Toronto, 1939).

51. W. Kirkconnell, *A Slice of Canada*.

52. For documentary evidence of changing ethnic attitudes in the post-war era and the emergence of multiculturalism as an idea and as a governmental policy, see H. Palmer, *Immigration and the Rise of Multiculturalism* (Toronto, 1975), ch. 3.

Article Twenty-Three

Race and Recruitment in World War I: Enlistment of Visible Minorities in the Canadian Expeditionary Force

James W. St.G. Walker

Contemporaries called it 'the war to end all wars' and 'the war to make the world safe for democracy.' During it, women throughout the North Atlantic world stepped forcefully into public affairs; subject populations in central Europe emerged into national self-determination; the proletariat triumphed beyond the Eastern front. But if World War I has thus been deemed 'progressive,' whatever its horrible cost, it was not intended as a liberal social instrument. For example, the relations between categories of people termed 'races' were regarded as immutable, and therefore expected to emerge from the war intact. Science and public opinion accepted

Source: James W. St.G. Walker, "Race and Recruitment in World War I: Enlistment of Visible Minorities in the Canadian Expeditionary Force" *Canadian Historical Review*, 70:1 (March 1989): 1–26. © University of Toronto Press 1989. All Rights Reserved. Reprinted by permission of University of Toronto Press Incorporated (www.utpjournals.com).

that certain identifiable groups lacked the valour, discipline, and intelligence to fight a modern war. Since those same groups were also the subjects of the European overseas empires, prudence warned that a taste of killing white men might serve as an appetizer should they be listed against a European enemy. The obvious conclusion was that this must be 'a white man's war.'

This decision was reached by virtually all the protagonists, but it was modified by an admission that since the subject races would clearly benefit from the victory of their own masters, they might be allowed to do their bit for the cause as appropriate to their own perceived abilities. Early in the war, when they constituted the empire's largest reserve of trained men, British Indian troops from the 'martial races' of the subcontinent were committed to France. But when the nature of the conflict became evident, and British forces available, it was discovered that Indian combat troops were unsuitable for Europe. Most were diverted to the Middle Eastern campaigns, where their targets were non-Europeans, though thousands of Indian labourers remained in Europe. Similarly New Zealand sent a Maori labour unit to Gallipoli, and a Maori labour unit to Belgium and France. Even sensitive South Africa agreed, when labour shortages were most pressing in 1916, to enlist blacks for non-combat duties in Europe. China's contribution as an ally was to provide 50,000 'coolies' to labour behind the lines in France. Typically contrary, France itself began the war using its 'force noire' only at Gallipoli and as garrison troops in the French colonies, but the huge losses of men on the Western Front overcame the doubts of the high command and in 1916 African troops appeared in the European trenches. When the Americans entered the war in 1917, black volunteers were at first rejected. Though later recruited and conscripted in large numbers, fewer than 10 per cent ever fired a rifle in the direction of a German; the overwhelming majority were consigned to non-combat service battalions.[1]

Canada shared the Western ideology of 'race,' and Canadian wartime practice generally was in step with the allies: until manpower needs at the front surmounted the obvious objections, killing Germans was the privilege of white troops. Even when called upon, members of Canada's 'visible' minorities were accompanied overseas by a set of presumptions about their abilities which dictated the role they were to play and which limited the rewards they were to derive.[2] An examination of policy towards them and of their participation in the war offers a temporary opening in the curtain which typically covers Canadian racism, revealing some details from the set of stereotypes applied to certain minorities. The curtain also lifts upon the determination and self-confidence of Canadian minorities, and their struggle to be accorded equal responsibilities as well as equal opportunities. The struggle is further revealed, in many instances, as a community effort: communities encouraged, organized, and financed the enlistment of their young men, and those men volunteered in order to gain group recognition and to further the rights of whole communities.

In August 1914 a surge of patriotism, assisted by severe unemployment, prompted the enlistment of more than the 25,000 volunteers initially required for the first CEF contingent. For over a year, in fact, the supply of men exceeded demand: recruiting officers could afford to be selective, and one of the selection criteria was the 'race' of the applicant. Under the terms of the minister of militia's 'call to arms,' existing militia units enrolled volunteers directly, and the local militia officers had complete discretion over whom to accept.[3] There was one exception, however: within days of the first shots in Europe, the Militia Council forbade the enlistment of native Indians on the reasoning that 'Germans might refuse to extend to them the privileges of civilized warfare.' This directive was not, however, made public, and some recruiting officers remained ignorant of it. Indian youth, like their white counterparts, were anxious to participate and presented themselves to their local units. Many were enlisted only to be turned away when their Indian status was discovered. Some were able to slip through undetected, with or without the collusion of their commanders, so that the early contingents did contain some native soldiers despite the official policy.[4]

Members of the other 'visible' groups were less successful. Individual unit discretion appears to have kept East Indians entirely outside the Canadian forces, and in British Columbia, where most of them lived, Japanese were rejected completely. The fate of Chinese Canadians is less clear, but if any were accepted in the early years of the war their numbers must have been extremely small.[5] In a memo of November 1914 responding to a query on 'coloured enlistment,' the militia would only refer to the established policy that personnel selection was a matter for each commanding officer, though the chief of general staff offered the prevailing opinion: 'Would Canadian Negroes make good fighting men? I do not think so.'[6] One Cape Breton black volunteer, who decided that 'It's a job that I'll like killing germans,' was told he was ineligible to join any white unit; a group of about fifty blacks from Sydney, who went to enlist together, were advised: 'This is not for you fellows, this is a white man's war.'[7]

The Canadian volunteers rejected by this policy were not content to accept either their exclusion or the reasoning that went with it. They sought enlistment in large numbers, and insisted on knowing why their offer was not accepted. As early as November 1914 the black community of North Buxton was complaining to Ottawa and seeking corrective action; from Hamilton blacks came the charge that it was 'beneath the dignity of the Government to make racial or color distinction in an issue of this kind'; blacks in Saint John condemned recruitment discrimination and added for the record an account of the discrimination they met daily in their home city.[8] Saint John MP William Pugsley, at the request of Ontario and New Brunswick black representatives, raised the issue in the House of Commons. The government insisted that 'there is no Dominion legislation authorizing discrimination against coloured people,' and the militia was able to state that 'no regulations or restrictions' prevented 'enrollment of coloured men who possess the necessary qualifications,' but no remedies were offered or comment made upon clear evidence of exclusion for 'racial' reasons.[9] And yet the urge to enlist persisted. A group of Cape Croker Indians applied to four different recruitment centres and were rejected from each one; Japanese in British Columbia made repeated attempts to enlist; blacks in Nova Scotia travelled from one unit to another hoping to find acceptance.[10] To some extent this persistence must have been prompted by young men's sense of adventure and patriotism, but they were moved as well by a consciousness that a contribution to the war effort could help to overcome the disadvantages faced by their communities. The Japanese believed that war participation would earn them the franchise, a hope that was shared by some Indian groups. Blacks maintained that war for justice must have an impact on 'the progress of our race' in Canada.[11]

White intransigence was not overcome by these efforts, but a compromise seemed possible: if whites and non-whites could not stand shoulder to shoulder in defence of the empire, perhaps they could stand separately. 'Coloured candidates are becoming insistent,' a Vancouver recruiter complained, and his superior advised that 'as white men will not serve in the same ranks with negros or coloured persons,' the only solution was to create a separate unit.[12] Because of the numerous black applications in Nova Scotia, several similar suggestions were made, and one commanding officer, though rejecting individual blacks, agreed to accept an entire platoon if one were formed.[13] On the 'reliable information' that 10,000 blacks inhabited Edmonton region from whom 1000 could easily be recruited, Alberta district commander Cruikshank, with the support of the lieutenant governor, offered to create a black battalion since a racially integrated Alberta regiment 'would not be advisable.' On the same principle General Cruikshank proposed that a 'Half-Breed Battalion' be recruited in Alberta.[14] More insistent and widespread were suggestions to raise distinct regiments of native Indians. Every province from Ontario west produced proposals to enlist natives in segregated units where, under careful supervision of white officers, their 'natural' talents as fighters and marksmen could best be utilized.[15] Some of these suggestions were enthusiastically endorsed by the affected groups, believing that as a recognizable unit they could gain more attention for their communal cause,[16] but none were more energetic than the Japanese. In August 1915 the Canadian Japanese Association of Vancouver offered to raise an exclusively Japanese unit. Receiving a polite reply, the association began to enlist volunteers, eventually 227 of them, who were supported at Japanese community expense and practised their drill under British veteran and militia captain R.S. Colquhoun. With one company thus trained, the association made a formal offer to the government in March 1916 of a full battalion.[17]

The Japanese offer, like every other proposal to create a racially defined battalion, was rejected by Militia Headquarters. Officials doubted that enough volunteers from any group could be found to create and maintain a unit as large as a battalion, and furthermore its members could not be used as reinforcements in other battalions, as was frequently required in trench warfare, if integration should prove difficult. Privately, the combat abilities of blacks and Indians were considered questionable, and although Japanese were regarded as 'desirable soldiers,' their enlistment was feared as a step towards enfranchisement. Individual 'half-breeds,' blacks, and Japanese were theoretically admissible into all militia units. 'There is no colour line,' insisted the adjutant general, but commanding officers were free to accept or reject any volunteer for any reason.[18] One incident more than any other provoked this statement. In November 1915 twenty black volunteers from Saint John were sent to Camp Sussex, where they were told to go instead to Ontario where a 'Coloured Corps' was being formed. Protesting that this action was 'shameful and insulting to the Race,' the Saint John blacks pressed their case with the government general and militia minister Sir Sam Hughes. Apparently outraged, Hughes ordered a full investigation into the incident and promised that there would be no racial barriers and no segregated units in his army. When the Sussex commanding officer complained that it was not 'fair' to expect white troops 'to mingle with negroes,' a sentiment supported by all the commanding officers in the Maritime district, militia officials quickly explained that local commanders retained their discretionary powers: 'it is not thought desirable, either in the interests of such men themselves or of the Canadian Forces, that Commanding Officers should be forced to take them.'[19] Whatever Hughes's intentions, the statement reinforced the status quo. It remained a white man's war.

At the outbreak of the war a surplus of volunteers had afforded considerable latitude in selecting recruits. By the spring of 1915, when the second Canadian Contingent sailed, trench warfare had eroded all hopes for a short and glorious war, and casualty rates were horrifying. Domestic production competed with the armed services for manpower, just as more and more men were required for the trenches. Selectivity became less rigid, as height, medical, and marital requirements were relaxed, and the recruitment method itself came under scrutiny. In the fall of 1915 a new policy was substituted, enabling any patriotic person or group to form a battalion. This 'patriotic phase,' distinguished from the earlier 'militia phase,' led to the proliferation of new units and to rivalries among them for the available manpower. Since the fighting regiments were not being reinforced directly by new recruitment, the 'patriotic' policy also meant that the units thus raised almost inevitably had to be broken up on arrival in Europe to be used to fill the gaps caused by casualties in the existing regiments. The entire situation was compounded by Prime Minister Borden's announcement that, as of 1 January 1916, Canada would pledge 500,000 troops to Europe. With prevailing casualty rates, it would require 300,000 new recruits per year to maintain this figure in the field.[20]

All these developments — the scramble for men, the raising of special regiments, and their use as reinforcements for fighting overseas — had implications for recruiting 'visible' minorities. First to fall was the restriction against Indian enlistment. Certain regiments had been discreetly recruiting Indians since 1914, but when Ontario's new 114th Battalion was being formed in November 1915 its commander hoped to enlist four companies of Brantford and region Indians. His superior, the Toronto district commander, lent support to the plan on the understanding that all Indians recruited in his division would be transferred to the 114th. It was apparently this limited plan, consistent with the 'special units' policy, that was at first approved by the militia minister; Indians already in other regiments were invited to transfer to the 114th, and the new battalion was permitted to recruit Indians outside its own geographical territory.[21] The memo that went out to commanding officers, however, stated that Indian enlistment was henceforth authorized 'in the various Units for Overseas Service,' and this impression was reinforced in individual letters to commanders permitting Indian enlistment. The confusion amongst recruiting officers was shared by the chief of general staff, Willoughby Gwatkin, who confessed that he did not know whether open enlistment was now the rule or whether Indian battalions were to be formed.[22] Meanwhile, the 114th was advertising itself, even in the public press, as *the* Indian unit, and at least a dozen regiments transferred their Indian recruits to the 114th.[23] In the event, pressure from other battalion commanders convinced divisional headquarters to cease transferring Indians to the 114th, which was therefore unable to fill more than two Indian companies. The result was a concentration of Indians in the 114th, but others were scattered individually throughout the battalions willing to accept them.[24]

It was perhaps this reigning confusion over special units, coupled with the pressure to find a half million men, that led to one of the war's most discouraging episodes for black Canadians. In November 1915 J.R.B. Whitney, editor of a Toronto black newspaper, the *Canadian Observer*, wrote to Hughes asking if the minister would accept a platoon of 150 black men provided it would be maintained at that strength throughout the war. Hughes warmly replied that 'these people can form a platoon in any Battalion, now. There is nothing in the world to stop them.'[25] On this basis Whitney began to advertise through the *Observer*, and enlisted volunteers in the projected platoon. Early in January 1916 he was able to report to Hughes that he had enlisted a number of Toronto recruits, adding a request to second a black enlisted man for a recruitment tour of southwestern Ontario. Hughes passed this on to the adjutant general, W.E. Hodgins, for action, and this latter official was forced to return to Whitney for an explanation of what was meant by all this. In the process Hodgins discovered that no arrangement had been made with any battalion commander to receive a black platoon. In fact, advised Toronto's General Logie, it was doubtful if any commander would accept 'a coloured platoon' into 'a white man's Battalion,' Hodgins therefore decided that permission to recruit a black unit could not be granted, and he asked Toronto division so to inform Mr Whitney. On 15 March Whitney received a blunt letter from the Toronto recruiting officer stating that as no commanding officer was willing to enlist them, the plan must be abandoned.[26]

A very hurt Whitney asked for a reconsideration; he had already gathered forty volunteers and could not now tell them to disband. An embarrassed Hodgins begged Logie to find some unit prepared to admit Whitney's platoon, and Logie diligently conducted a canvas of his district. The responses from battalion commanders dramatically revealed the prevailing feelings among the military leadership in 1916. Most rejected the idea without explanation, stating simply their unwillingness to accept blacks. Several acknowledged that white recruitment would be discouraged, and dissatisfaction aroused amongst men already enlisted. Some confirmed that they had already rejected numbers of black volunteers. The most ambiguous answer came from the 48th Highlanders, whose adjutant stated that 'we have, being a kilted regiment, always drawn the line at taking coloured men.' No one apologized or offered any positive suggestions. No one seemed to think his prejudices would not be understood, and shared, in headquarters. Logie replied to Hodgins that the situation was obviously hopeless. Whitney's personal appeal to Hughes provoked sympathy and some furious cables, but the result could not be changed. Even with a half million soldiers to find, Ontario's military establishment could not 'stoop' to the recruitment of blacks.[27]

But Ottawa desks had been shaken, and General Gwatkin was ordered to write a report on 'the enlistment of negroes in the Canadian Expeditionary Force.' Besides Whitney's experience, overtures from black Nova Scotians had become more difficult to ignore, since they were supported by several influential Conservative politicians.[28] Gwatkin's memorandum was scarcely complimentary, but it did offer an opportunity for blacks to join the war. 'Nothing is to be gained by blinking facts,' Gwatkin began:

> The civilized negro is vain and imitative; in Canada he is not being impelled to enlist by a high sense of duty; in the trenches he is not likely to make a good fighter; and the average white man will not associate with him on terms of equality. Not a single commanding officer in Military District No. 2 is willing to accept a coloured platoon as part of his battalion; and it would be humiliating to the coloured men themselves to serve in a battalion where they were not wanted.
>
> In France, in the firing line, there would be no place for a black battalion, CEF. It would be eyed askance; it would crowd out a white battalion; it would be difficult to reinforce.
>
> Nor could it be left in England and used as a draft-giving depot; for there would be trouble if negroes were sent to the front for the purpose of reinforcing white battalions; and, if they are good men at all, they would resent being kept in Canada for the purpose of finding guards &c.

Gwatkin concluded with the recommendation that blacks could be enlisted, as at present, in any battalion willing to accept them, and that a labour battalion could additionally be formed exclusively for them.[29] On 19 April 1916, with Prime Minister Borden presiding, the Militia Council decided to form a black labour battalion headquartered in Nova Scotia, provided the British command would agree. This approval was received three weeks later.[30]

'It is a somewhat peculiar command,' admitted Adjutant General Hodgins, after some difficulty was experienced in finding a qualified officer willing to head a black battalion. But Prime Minister Borden, himself a Halifax politician, took a personal interest in the new project and suggested the name of a potential commander, Daniel H. Sutherland. On 5 July, the day after Sutherland's acceptance, the Nova Scotia No 2 Construction Battalion (Coloured) was formally announced. Officered by whites, the unit was authorized to recruit blacks from all across Canada.[31] The black community in Nova Scotia heartily welcomed the formation of the No 2. 'Considerable joy and happiness' erupted, particularly among the young men, for the No 2 seemed to recognize that 'they were men the same as everybody else.' The African Baptist Association, at its 1916 annual meeting, expressed the view that through the No 2 'the African race was making history,' and pledged to do all in its power to encourage enlistment.[32] Although the all-white No 1 Construction Battalion complained bitterly about its name, fearing association with 'work which might be done by the negro race,'[33] no doubts seem to have been uttered by black representatives at the nature of the work or the fact of segregation.

By the summer of 1916 Canadian blacks, Indians, and Japanese were all being actively recruited into the services. Following the rejection of the Canadian Japanese Association's offer to form a full battalion, militia authorities encouraged other battalions to accept their volunteers who had already received basic training through their private efforts. The association itself promoted this policy, appealing to Alberta's General Cruikshank to permit Japanese to enlist in his district, since BC commanders remained adamantly opposed. On his return trip to Vancouver from Ottawa, where he had gone to present the case for a Japanese battalion, association president Yasuchi Yamazaki met with Cruikshank in Calgary, and the general immediately wrote to battalion commanders with the offer of up to 200 Japanese recruits.[34] The response was overwhelmingly positive. The 192nd Battalion offered to receive all 200, and the 191st asked for 250, but this was vetoed from headquarters as 'there is no objection to the enlistment of odd men, but large numbers are not to be enlisted,' Advertisements from Alberta recruiters appeared in Vancouver's Japanese language press, and temporary recruiting offices were established in British Columbia, though this latter practice was contrary to regulations. Battalions from other provinces, too, sought Japanese recruits. Eventually 185 served overseas in eleven different battalions, mainly in the 10th, 50th, and 52nd infantry battalions. It was undoubtedly at this time that individual Chinese were being enlisted by under-strength battalions.[35]

The rivalry to recruit Japanese was being reflected in the much larger campaign to enlist native Indians. The 114th began with the advantage of being identified as an Indian battalion, and confusion continued for several months over whether all Indians, recruited before or since December 1915, were to be transferred to it. Some Indians who had enlisted in other regiments applied to transfer to the 114th; others asked not to be transferred because they preferred not to serve with 'Mohawks.'[36] The Department of Indian Affairs lent its official support to the 114th recruitment drive, and seconded Charles Cooke to the regiment with the honorary rank of lieutenant. Described as 'the only male Indian employed in the Service at Ottawa,' Cooke toured the Ontario reserves on behalf of the 114th, sometimes in the company of an Indian commissioned officer, stressing the pride and the opportunity derived from serving in an identifiably Indian unit. Although by this time it had been determined that only two companies, that is half the battalion, would in fact consist of Indians, the 114th stressed its Indian connection. The regimental badge contained two crossed tomahawks, and its band, composed mostly of Brantford reserve Iroquois, gave concerts which included Indian war dances.[37]

Other battalions were not slow to enter the recruitment race. Hodgin's attempt to settle the 114th's jurisdiction, by giving it authority to recruit Indians beyond its regimental territory but not *exclusive* authority, seems merely to have stimulated rivalries. Other commanding officers sought to entice Charles Cooke into their service; one battalion allegedly was offering a $5 recruitment bonus to Indians plus a free trip to Europe in case the war ended before they went overseas; others were reportedly recruiting young boys from the residential schools. In July 1916, when Colonel Mewburn called for a report on Indians enlisted in Military District 2, headquartered in Toronto, the 114th had 348, including five officers, and 211 others were arrayed across fifteen different units. This did not include the 107th battalion, raised in Winnipeg and commanded by G.L. Campbell, a senior Indian Affairs official. At first intended as an all-Indian battalion, the 107th shared the experience of Ontario's 114th and eventually enlisted approximately one-half its membership among Indians.[38]

Although these numbers were all recruited, at least ostensibly, into infantry battalions, there were parallel efforts to enlist Indians in non-combatant labour and construction units, particularly for forestry. Duncan Campbell Scott, the senior Indian Affairs official, urged this movement through Indian agents across Canada. When white officers and recruits in forestry units, primarily on the west coast, objected to working amongst 'Indians and Half-breeds,' authority was granted to establish separate native companies and platoons.[39] One of the construction units to recruit amongst Indians was none other than the No 2, from Nova Scotia. Five Indians joined the No 2 at Windsor, Ontario, allegedly on the promise of becoming non-commissioned officers. Once enlisted they claimed to be disgusted by the fighting, gambling, and drinking going on in the No 2 camp, and they called for a transfer. When Colonel Sutherland's response was slow, Chief Thunderwater of the Great Council of the Tribes took up the Indians' case, claiming 'a natural dislike of association with negroes on the part of Indians.' The adjutant general in Ottawa and General Logie in Toronto had to become involved before this entanglement could be settled and the Indians moved to the 256th Railway Construction Battalion, which had a large Indian component. Chief Thunderwater admonished the adjutant general 'that you so arrange that Indians and negroes are kept from the same Battalion.'[40]

The reason the No 2 was in Windsor, Ontario, was that Sutherland had been given authority to recruit nationally, though this clearly meant that he could recruit blacks, for whom there was no inter-regimental competition. Information was sent to every commanding officer in the country authorizing 'any of the coloured men in Canada, now serving in units of the C.E.F., to transfer to the No 2 Construction Battalion, should they so wish.' Several black volunteers did transfer from other units, at least some with the overt encouragement of their officers.[41] Within Nova Scotia a regimental band was organized, holding recruiting concerts in churches and halls wherever a black audience might be attracted. In the larger black communities, Citizens Recruiting Committees were formed to encourage enlistment, the Rev. W.A. White of the African Baptist Church in Truro gave 'stirring' speeches, and black church elders lent moral support.[42] Early recruiting reports were satisfying, but by November 1916 Sutherland felt it necessary to undertake a more active campaign outside Nova Scotia. His request to recruit in the West Indies was turned down, but funds were authorized in January 1917 to take the band on a tour to Montreal and Toronto, and black centres in southwestern Ontario. After a decline between October and December, recruitment picked up again in January, most of it in Windsor, Ontario, where many American blacks joined the Canadian unit.[43] In western Canada Captain Gayfer established a recruiting office in Edmonton, from which he too conducted tours and spoke in black churches. He later moved his headquarters to Winnipeg, leaving a black enlisted man in charge of the Edmonton office while a lieutenant visited British Columbia. All across Canada young black men were being advised that 'the need of the day' was for pioneers and construction workers whose contribution to the movement forward to victory was vital.[44]

Two years into the war, recruitment policy towards 'visible' minorities had been reversed completely. But during those two years, the ardour to join their white brethren in the defence of Canadian democracy had been somewhat dampened among the minority youth. Japanese recruitment never remotely approached the thousand men projected by Yamazaki, perhaps because they were not allowed to serve in recognizable units as they believed was essential to win rights for their community. Native Indians did have the opportunity to enlist in concentrated units, but where such units existed they never recruited up to their authorized strength. The fact was that the invitation to serve was coming too late, and after a discouraging demonstration of majority attitudes towards their potential contribution. The Six Nations, who had offered their assistance as allies to the king in 1914, now opposed recruiters on the ground that they were an independent people and would enlist only upon the personal appeal of the governor general and recognition of their special status.[45] Other Indian groups complained that 'We are not citizens and have no votes, as free men'; anti-recruiters followed recruiters around the reserves, speaking out against Indian enlistment during 'Patriotic' meetings, reminding Indians of their grievances and the many government promises made to them which had been broken throughout history.[46] Other factors interfered as well. There was resentment against recruitment methods, including reports of intimidating tactics and the enrolment of underage boys. Indignation followed a rumour that overseas the Indians would be discussed as Italians, thus preventing any recognition for their accomplishments. Complaints from Indians already enlisted, alleging racial discrimination and inferior treatment in the forces, filtered back to the reserves. Other letters from Indians at the front described 'the awfulness of war' and 'openly advised the Indians not to think of enlisting.'[47]

Nor did black Canadians fail to register scepticism at the recruitment campaign. In Nova Scotia, where black community leadership was won over, many individuals 'were feeling keenly that their Loyal offers of service were refused in so many instances,' and were reluctant now to join the No 2. Blacks in the west told recruiters the same thing.[48] Resentment at previous insult was reinforced by continued insult: in Winnipeg black recruits were derided and called 'nigger' by medical staff assigned to examine them. When Colonel Sutherland decided to move his headquarters from Pictou to Truro, he rented a suitable building and had begun furnishing it when the owner suddenly cancelled the contract. The same thing happened to Captain Gayfer when the other of his recruiting office cancelled the contract 'on account of color of recruits.' Eventually established in Truro, black recruits met segregation in the local theatre. Rumours percolated through the black communities as well, for example that they were to be used only as trench diggers in France.[49] Although several prominent whites, notably Nova Scotian MPs Fleming McCurdy and John Stanfield and businessman H. Falconer McLean, assisted in the formation and recruitment of the No 2, the military hierarchy itself was less than enthusiastic, perhaps feeling that the black battalion had been imposed on them for political reasons. The chief of general staff regarded the unit as 'troublesome.' It took Sutherland two months to gain approval for his tour beyond Nova Scotia, and then only with the strictest admonitions to economize. Western recruiter Gayfer was denied office supplies, had his transport warrants delayed, and received no rations or barrack accommodation for his recruits.[50] And yet Sutherland received constant memos and cables asking him when his unit would be ready for overseas service. The first target was three months; after seven months, Sutherland was told to prepare the men already recruited for sailing, and new recruits could follow later; eventually it was in March 1917, nine months after recruitment began, that the No 2 embarked for England, and with only 603 men enlisted of an authorized strength of 1033 other ranks.[51] Because it arrived in Britain below battalion strength, the No 2 was converted to a labour company of 500 men, and Sutherland was reduced in rank to major.[52]

It was not only 'visible' minority youth who had developed a reluctance to volunteer. In July 1916 recruitment in general plummeted, from monthly peaks near 30,000 earlier in the year to fewer than 8000, and continued to fall to around 3000 a month. Not a single battalion raised after July 1916 reached its full strength, from any part of Canada. Employment in domestic war production, and increasing awareness of the carnage at the front, caused the virtual collapse of the voluntary system just at the time when the push was being made to enlist 'visible' minorities. In May 1917, when casualty rates in Europe were more than double new recruitment, Prime Minister Borden announced his intention to introduce conscription with the cry that 'the battle for Canadian liberty and autonomy is being fought today on the plains of France and Belgium.' The Military Service Act, when effected later that year, was less than a popular success among those liable to its call. Over 90 per cent of them applied for exemption.[53]

Canada's Indians were immediate and outspoken in denying the legality of their conscription. 'Indians refuse to report,' cabled one anxious Indian agent. More sophisticated responses referred to the fact that Indians were 'wards of the government,' legally 'minors' and treated as children: surely children were not being called to defend the empire? Since they had no vote, and no voice in the conduct of the war or of the councils of state, it was unfair to expect them to participate now in the war. 'We cannot say that we are fighting for our liberty, freedom and other privileges dear to all nations, for we have none,' stated an Ontario Indian declaration. BC Indians considered 'that the government attitude towards us in respect to our land troubles and in refusing to extend to us the position of citizens of Canada are unreasonable, and until we receive just treatment . . . we should not be subject to conscription.' Still others quoted the treaties made in the 1870s, and the negotiations surrounding those treaties, during which Indians were assured that they would never be called to war. Petitions flowed to Ottawa, and even to the king: if they were not to have the rights of citizens, they must not be forced to perform a citizen's duty.[54] Similar petitions came from BC Japanese, pointing out that although they were naturalized Canadians they lacked the franchise and other citizenship privileges, and they claimed exemption from obligatory military service.[55] In these objections to conscription there was a scarcely submerged articulation of the 'war aims' of Canadian minorities: if it was to be their war, it must result in the extension of equality to their people.

The government hesitated. Indians were first granted an extension of the time required to register; then they were advised officially to seek exemption under some existing regulation, such as agricultural employment.[56] Finally, on 17 January 1918, an order in council exempted Indians and Japanese, on the grounds of their limited citizenship rights and, for the former, the treaty promises. The order also referred to the War Time Elections Act which had deprived certain naturalized Canadians of the franchise and at the same time relieved them of military service. In March the regulations were amended so that any British subject disqualified from voting at a federal election was exempted from conscription. Despite the fact that they would already have been covered by this regulation, East Indians were granted a special exemption order three months later.[57]

This did not of course apply to black Canadians, who already enjoyed the franchise and therefore remained liable to conscription. The No 2, still smarting from its demotion to a labour company, immediately requested that all blacks conscripted across Canada be sent to it, so that it could be restored to battalion status. The No 2 proposal was promoted by Nova Scotian MP Fleming McCurdy, among others, and was received sympathetically by the new militia minister, General Mewburn, who confessed that 'The whole problem of knowing how to handle coloured troops has been a big one for some years back.' A collection depot was established in London, Ontario, where No 2 reinforcements could be made ready for overseas, and orders were sent to commanding officers to transfer all 'coloured men' to the London depot. The wording of the order did not appear to leave the commanders with any choice in keeping black conscripts in their own units.[58] In March, when it began to seem that black numbers were lower than anticipated, No 2 recruiters travelled to Detroit to attract black Canadians living there, but this was squelched by Ottawa on the grounds that 'we are not hunting for coloured recruits but merely making a place for them as they come in under the Military Service Act.' Again, when the British-Canadian Recruiting Mission in New York announced that 'about two thousand colored British subjects have registered,' some or all of whom could be sent to reinforce the No 2, Ottawa's answer was a terse 'none required.'[59] Deciding that the number of black conscripts coming in, directly or by transfer, was not worth the effort, Ottawa ordered the abandonment of the London reception centre in May. Sutherland was informed that his company would not be restored to battalion strength after all.[60]

There was one more try. The Rev. William White, chaplain to the No 2 and as an honorary captain 'the only coloured officer in our forces,' wrote an impassioned letter to the prime minister. 'The coloured people are proud that they have at least one definite Unit representing them in France,' he stated, requesting that the conscripted blacks be sent to strengthen the No 2.[61] As a consequence Major Bristol, secretary to the Canadian overseas militia minister in London, was asked to make a report. In a response labelled 'personal,' Bristol admitted that 'these Niggers do well in a Forestry Corps and other Labour units,' but since numbers were so limited 'the prospects of maintaining a battalion are not very bright.' Following a survey of district commanders, it appeared that scarcely more than 100 identified black conscripts were already enlisted, and 'on this showing it would hardly be possible to carry out the suggestion made' to use them to enhance the No 2. The plan was dropped once and for all.[62] Fifty-five black conscripts already gathered in Halifax were trained in Canada as infantrymen, together with white conscripts, but on arrival in England they were placed in a segregated labour unit. Eventually assigned to the 85th Battalion, the Armistice intervened before they could leave Britain.[63]

The ambivalence and the frankly racist confusion surrounding their recruitment was reflected in the overseas experiences of the enlisted minorities. The Japanese, it appears, were consistently used as combat troops, which was their purpose in volunteering.[64] The Indians had a mixed reception. The 114th, recruited with such pride as an Indian unit, was broken up on arrival in England and the men assigned to different battalions, many for labour duties. The 107th, also recruited with an Indian identity and as a fighting unit, was converted to a pioneer battalion in France, where the men dug trenches and built roads and muletracks under direct enemy fire, with heavy casualties. Some Indians did go to the front as combatants, but a sizeable contingent served in forestry work, chiefly within Britain itself.[65] Those blacks who served individually in combat regiments, since their admission had been entirely voluntary on the part of their officers, apparently met few problems. When the 106th Battalion was broken up, for example, its black members went to the Royal Canadian Regiment as reinforcements on the front lines, where they were welcomed. Undoubtedly there were many more where blacks served without incident.[66] But the No 2 itself, as a separate unit with its own administration and records, leaves a different trail. To avoid 'offending the susceptibility of other troops,' it was suggested that the black battalion be sent overseas in a separate transport ship, without escort. Since their sailing occurred during the war's worst period for German submarine attacks, it is fortunate that this suggestion was rejected by the Royal Navy.[67] The battalion arrived in England under strength, and the decision was made not to absorb the men into different units, where whites might object, but to keep them together as a labour company attached to the Forestry Corps in French territory. Working as loggers and in lumber mills, and performing related construction and shipping work, the men of the No 2 were established near La Joux, in the Jura region of France, with smaller detachments at Cartigny and Alençon. Although they laboured side by side with white units, the black soldiers were segregated in their non-working activities. Remote from any means of amusement, they had to await the creation of a separate 'coloured' YMCA for their evenings' entertainment. When ill, they were treated in a separate 'Coloured Wing' of the La Joux hospital. Those who strayed from military discipline were similarly confined in a segregated punishment compound. An extra Protestant chaplain had to be sent into Jura district 'as the Negro Chaplain is not acceptable to the White Units.' Always regarded as a problem and never seriously appreciated, the No 2 was disbanded with almost unseemly haste soon after the Armistice was announced, though the demand for forestry products remained high, and they were among the earliest Canadian units to leave France.[68]

The treatment received by 'visible' Canadians did not originate with the military; recruitment policy and overseas employment were entirely consistent with domestic stereotypes of 'race' characteristics and with general social practice in Canada. And Canadian attitudes themselves were merely a reflection of accepted and respected Western thought in the early twentieth century. Racial perceptions were derived, not from personal experience, but from the example of Canada's great mentors, Britain and the United States, supported by scientific explanations.[69] In these circumstances it is notable that the Canadian military, while by no means avoiding the influence of prevailing ideology, at least had the independence to be less restricting than most of the allies. For example, General Headquarters advised the Forestry Corps to reorganize the No 2 to conform to imperial standards, as were applied to South African, Chinese, and Egyptian 'coloured labour' units. This would have affected their pay and privileges, and for black non-commissioned officers it would mean a reduction to private. Colonel J.B. White, Forestry's La Joux commander rejected this directive because 'the men of this Unit are engaged in exactly the same work as the white labour with whom they are employed . . . and it is recommended that no change be made,' Headquarters withdrew the order and the men of the No 2 continued to be treated as other Canadian forestry units.[70] One reason for assigning the No 2 to French territory was to avoid contact and comparison with other British 'coloured labour' units 'who are kept in compounds, and not permitted the customary liberties of white troops.'[71] Black American troops in France were completely segregated, forbidden to leave their bases without supervision, and barred from cafés and other public places. Friendly relations with French civilians led to the strictest measures, including the arrest of blacks who conversed with white women, and to an official American request to the French military beseeching the co-operation in keeping the races separate. British East Indian troops were restricted in their off-base activities and were liable to a dozen lashes for 'seeking romance' from white women. Senior army officials objected to East Indian sick and wounded being treated by white nurses. South African black labourers were kept in guarded compounds. Throughout the ranks of the Allies, with the partial exception of the French, non-white soldiers and workers were humiliated, restricted, and exploited. It was simply not their war.[72]

Generally speaking, the efforts of 'visible' enlisted men did not gain recognition for themselves or for their communities at home. Postwar race riots in the United States generated the worst violence experienced by black Americans since slavery. Attempts by Punjabi veterans to gain moderate political reforms led to the infamous Amritsar Massacre in April 1919, where 379 peaceful demonstrators were killed and 1208 wounded while trapped in a box-like park. French use of African troops to occupy defeated Germany led to condemnation by the Allies and to international censure for subjecting white Germans to the horrors of black authority.[73] Respect, evidently, had not been won by four years in defence of Western ideals. There was even a Canadian incident to illustrate this situation: on 7 January 1919 at Kinmel Park Camp in Britain, white Canadian soldiers rioted and attacked the No 2 ranks on parade after a black sergeant arrested a white man and placed him in charge of a 'coloured' escort.[74] Far from expressing gratitude for their services, the militia minister in 1919 seemed unaware that the No 2 had even existed.[75] It is true that individual Japanese veterans were granted the franchise, belatedly and grudgingly in 1931 by a one-vote margin in the BC legislature, and native Indians actually serving in the forces were enfranchised by the War Time Elections Act and its successors, but their families and other members of their communities remained as only partial Canadian citizens.[76] Especially indicative of their failure to attain genuine acceptance was the fact that at the outset of World War II, 'visible' volunteers would again be rejected altogether or directed towards support and service functions consistent with their peacetime stereotypes.[77]

During World War I about 3500 Indians, over 1000 blacks, and several hundred Chinese and Japanese enlisted in the Canadian forces. To their number must be added the many who tried to enlist and were rejected. Though there was an understandable resistance to later attempts to recruit and conscript them, still the numbers in uniform were impressive, a demonstration of loyalty and a confidence that accepting equal responsibilities would win the advantages of Canadian citizenship. Individual exceptions occurred, but as a group they were denied that equal opportunity to defend their country and empire. Stereotypes which at first excluded them continued to restrict their military role, and even survived the war. In 1919 respect and equality remained beyond reach. Lessons which could and should have been learned in the first war had to be taught all over again in a second global conflict.

The experience of 'visible' minorities in World War I illustrates the nature of Canadian race sentiment early in this century. Most abruptly, it demonstrates that white Canadians participated in the Western ideology of racism. This was true not only in the general sense of accepting white superiority, but in the particular image assigned to certain peoples which labelled them as militarily incompetent. Canadian history itself should have suggested the contrary — blacks and Indians, for example, had a proud record of military service prior to Confederation — but the stereotypes derived from Britain and the United States were more powerful than domestic experience. Some degree of cynicism is discernable in the rejection of 'visible' volunteers, for example, the fear that military duty would enable them to demand political equality, yet it is not possible to read the entire record without concluding that most white Canadians, including the military hierarchy, were convinced by the international stereotypes and their supporting scientific explanations. This was carried to the point where Canada's war effort was impeded by prejudices for which there were no Canadian foundations.

Equally interesting is what the World War I experience reveals about the minorities themselves. Their persistence in volunteering, their insistence upon the 'right' to serve, their urgent demand to know the reasons for their rejection, all suggest that 'visible' Canadians had not been defeated by the racism of white society, had not accepted its rationalizations, and were not prepared quietly to accept inferior status. They retained a confidence in themselves, most obviously that they could achieve a glorious war record if given the opportunity. While recognizing the restrictions imposed on themselves and their communities, they were convinced that by their own efforts and the good will of white Canada they could remove those restrictions. Their appeals to parliament and the crown reveal as well that they had not lost faith in British/Canadian justice. The minority campaigns during World War I, for recruitment and later against conscription, were only possible for persons convinced that they were equal and could achieve recognition of their equality. Their loyalty to Canada and the empire included loyalty to an ideal which the dominant majority had forgotten.

NOTES

This article was presented at the Canadian Ethnic Studies Conference, Halifax, in October 1987. I am grateful to the Social Sciences and Humanities Research Council for financial assistance, and to the following for their critical comments: John Armstrong, Norman Buchignani, Michael Craton, Thamis Gale, Roy Ito, Desmond Morton, Palmer Patterson, John Stubbs, Stephanie Walker, and Glenn Wright.

1. For example, see Jeffrey Greenhut, 'The Imperial Reserve: The Indian Corps on the Western Front, 1914–15,' *Journal of Imperial and Commonwealth History* 11 (1983): 54–73, and 'Sahib and Sepoy: An Inquiry into the Relationship between the British Officers and Native Soldiers of the British Indian Army,' *Military Affairs* 48 (1984): 15–18; Keith L. Nelson, 'The Black Horror on the Rhine: Race as a Factor in Post-World War I Diplomacy,' *Journal of Modern History* 62 (1970): 606–8; Fred Gaffen, *Forgotten Soldiers* (Penticton, BC 1985), 24, 74–5; B.P. Willan, 'The South African Native Labour Contingent, 1916–1918,' *Journal of African History* 19 (1978): 61–86; C.J. Balesi, *From Adversaries to Comrades in Arms: West Africa and the French Military, 1885–1918* (Waltham, Mass. 1979), 112–13, 120–1; C.M. Andrew and A.S. Kanya-Forstner, 'France, Africa, and the First World War,' *Journal of African History* 19 (1978): 11–23; A.E. Barbeau and F. Henri, *The Unknown Soldiers: Black American Troops in World War II* (Philadelphia 1974); J.D. Foner, *Blacks and the Military in American History: A New Perspective* (New York 1974), 109–32. Black combat troops remained an American embarrassment. The all-black 93rd Division, for example, was first offered to the British army, and upon refusal was eventually attached to the French army for its combat service. The Chinese 'coolies' were shipped across Canada, en route to and from France, in sealed railway carriages. There are voluminous files on this episode in the Directorate of History, Department of National Defence (DND), Ottawa, and in RG 24 at the National Archives of Canada (NA).

2. A small but growing literature is available on the subject of minority Canadian participation in the world wars. Pioneering chapters on black Nova Scotians in M. Stuart Hunt, *Nova Scotia's Part in the Great War* (Halifax 1920), 148–53, and Ontario blacks and Indians in Barbara M. Wilson, *Ontario and the First World War, 1914–1918: A Collection of Documents* (Toronto 1977), cviii–cxiv, 166–75, are being supplemented with more detailed studies. Gaffen's *Forgotten Soldiers* is a colourful description of native Indian soldiers in both world wars, a welcome addition to James Dempsey's brief account, 'The Indians and World War I,' *Alberta History* 31 (1983): 1–8, and a useful corrective to Duncan Campbell Scott, 'The Canadian Indian and the Great World War,' in *Canada and the Great World War* (Toronto 1919), III, 285–328. Calvin W. Ruck, *Canada's Black Battalion: No. 2 Construction 1916–1920* (Halifax 1986), is anecdotal and illustrative, with portraits and quotations from several of the black veterans themselves. The first scholarly treatment of the No 2 is Major John G. Armstrong's 'The Unwelcome Sacrifice: A Black Unit in the Canadian Expeditionary Force, 1917–1919,' unpublished paper

presented at RMC Military History Symposium, March 1986. Roy Ito, *We Went to War: The Story of the Japanese Canadians who Served During the First and Second World Wars* (Stittsville, Ont. 1984), is a valuable combination of scholarship and reminiscence, though most of the attention is paid to the second war. Further detail on World War II can be found in Patricia Roy, 'The Soldiers Canada Didn't Want: Her Chinese and Japanese Citizens,' *Canadian Historical Review* (CHR) 59 (1978): 341–58.

3. Robert Craig Brown and Donald Loveridge, 'Unrequited Faith: Recruiting the CEF 1914–1918,' *Revue internationale d'histoire militaire* 51 (1982): 56; Desmond Morton, *A Military History of Canada* (Edmonton 1985), 130; G.W.L. Nicholson, *Canadian Expeditionary Force, 1914–1919* (Ottawa 1962), 18, 19, 212, 213

4. NA, RG 24, vol. 1221, file 593–1–7, vol. 1, telegram, 8 Aug. 1914, Scott to Hughes, 16 June 1915, and reply, 23 June, Nethercott to Hughes, 11 Oct. 1915, Armstrong to Hughes, 10 Oct. 1915, and replies, 18 Oct., Brown to Hodgins, 9 Oct. 1915, and reply, 22 Oct. Gaffen, *Forgotten Soldiers*, 20, points out correctly that since 'race' was not recorded on recruitment documents, it is not possible to give precise numbers on Indian volunteers. The same caveat should apply to the other minority groups discussed here as well.

5. After the war, the minister of militia and defence, Hugh Guthrie, told the House of Commons that the CEF had enlisted 'something like twelve' Chinese and no East Indians; *Debates*, 29 April 1920, 1812. Several sources refer to larger numbers of Chinese veterans in postwar Canada, for example, Jin Tan and Patricia Roy, *The Chinese in Canada* (Ottawa 1985), 15, Edgar Wickberg et al., *From China to Canada: A History of the Chinese Community in Canada* (Toronto 1982), 200, and Carol F. Lee, 'The Road to Enfranchisement: Chinese and Japanese in British Columbia,' IBC *Studies* 30 (1976): 57–8. A search of the records in the National Archives of Canada and the Directorate of History, Department of National Defence, failed to identify these men. Some could have served as British 'coolies' rather than as Canadian soldiers. Guthrie's comment does suggest that a small number were enlisted as regular soldiers, an impression confirmed by Professors Graham Johnson and Edgar Wickberg who report in a personal communication, 31 Oct. 1987, having seen photographs of Chinese in the uniform of the CEF. A separate Sikh regiment had been suggested as early as 1911, apparently with favourable comment from Sam Hughes, but no action was ever taken; Norman Buchignani, personal communication, 14 Oct. 1987. On British Columbia's rejection of all Japanese volunteers see NA, RG 24, vol. 4740, file 448–14–262, vol. 1, Cruikshank, circular letter, 26 April 1916.

6. NA, RG 24, vol. 1206, file 297–1–21, memo, 13 Nov. 1914, Gwatkin to Christie, 30 Sept. 1915

7. NA, RG 24, vol. 4562, file 133–17–1, Bramah to Rutherford, 4 Oct. 1915, and reply, 6 Oct.; Ruck, *Black Battalion*, 58, quoting interview with Robert Shepard. Despite these obstacles, some Nova Scotia blacks are reported to have been in the first contingent which left Canada in October 1914. Ibid., 11

8. NA, RG 24, vol. 1206, file 297–1–21, Alexander to Hughes, 13 Nov. 1914, Morton to Hughes, 7 Sept. 1915, Richards to Duke of Connaught, 4 Oct. 1915, Hamilton to Duke of Connaught, 29 Dec. 1915

9. House of Commons, *Debates*, 24 March 1916, 2114–15; NA, RG 24, vol. 1206, file 297–1–21, Edwards to Stanton, 31 Jan. 1916, Hodgins to Stewart, 16 Oct. 1915

10. NA, RG 24, vol. 1221, file 593–1–7, Duncan to Scott, 19 Nov. 1915; RG 24, vol. 1860, file 54; RG 24, vol. 4740, file 448–14–262, vol. 1; RG 24, vol. 4562, file 133–17–1, Bramah to Rutherford, 4 Oct. 1915

11. Ito, *We Went to War* 8ff; NA, RG 10, vol. 2640, file 129690–3, Jacobs, circular letter, 17 Aug. 1917; RG 24, vol. 1206, file 297–1–21, *Canadian Observer*, 8 Jan. 1916

12. NA, RG 24, vol. 1206, file 297–1–21, Henshaw to Ogilvie, 7 Dec. 1915, Ogilvie to Hodgins, 9 Dec. 1915

13. Ibid., Tupper to Hughes, 11 Nov. 1915, Allen to Rutherford, 14 Dec.; NA, RG 24, vol. 4562, file 133–17–1, Langford to Rutherford, 23 Sept. 1915, Borden to Rutherford, 23 March 1916

14. NA, RG 24, vol. 4739, file 448–14–259, McLeod to Cruikshank, 25 Nov. 1915 and 20 Jan. 1916, Munton to Cruikshank, received 11 March 1916, Cruikshank to Hodgins, 11 March 1916, Brett to Cruikshank, 13 March 1916, Martin to Cruikshank, 17 March 1916; RG 24, vol. 4739, file 448–14–256, 'Half Breed Battalion,' 1915

15. NA, RG 24, vol. 1221, file 593–1–7, vol. 1, inspector of Indian agencies, Vancouver, to Fiset, 23 Dec. 1915, Jackson to Ruttan, 20 Dec. 1915, McKay to Hodgins, 3 Jan. 1916, Rendle to Department of Indian Affairs, 17 Feb. 1916, Henderson to Hughes, 18 March 1916

16. For example, see *Canadian Observer*, 8 and 15 Jan. 1916; NA, RG 24, vol. 1221, file 593–1–7, vol. 1, Chief Thunderwater, on behalf of the Council of the Tribes, to Hodgins, 29 May 1916; RG 24, vol. 1469, file 600–10–35, White to McCurdy, nd; RG 24, vol. 4662, file 99–256, resolution, BC Indian Peoples, 1 Feb. 1916

17. NA, RG 24, vol. 1860, file 54, 'Recruiting — Special Units and Aliens,' numerous letters and telegrams, Jan.–April 1916; Roy Ito, personal communication, 18 Nov. 1987. An overseas battalion in the CEF consisted of approximately 1000 men grouped in four companies each with two platoons.

18. NA, RG 24, vol. 1860, file 54, Gwatkin to Yamazaki, 21 April 1916; RG 24, vol. 1206, file 297–1–21, Gwatkin to Christie, 30 Sept. 1915, Hodgins to Tupper, 11 Nov. 1915, Hodgins to Armstrong, 19 Nov. 1915, Gwatkin to

Hodgins, 22 Dec. 1915, Hodgins to Ogilvie, 23 Dec. 1915, Hodgins to Gwatkin, 21 March 1916, MacInnes to Hodgins, 25 March 1916; RG 24, vol. 1221, file 593–1–7, vol. 1, Fiset to inspector of Indian agencies, Vancouver, 29 Dec. 1915, Hodgins to McKay, 3 Jan. 1916, Gwatkin, memo, 12 Feb. 1916, Ogilvie to Hodgins, 23 March 1916; RG 24, vol. 4599, file 133–17–1, Hodgins to Rutherford, 29 Oct. 1915; RG 24, vol. 4739, file 448–14–256, Hodgins to Campbell, 15 July 1915, Hodgins to Cruikshank, 20 Nov. 1915; file 448–14–259, Hodgins to Cruikshank, 9 Dec. 1915 and 23 March 1916, Cruikshank to Martin, 27 March 1916; Ito, *We Went to War*, 25

19. RG 24, vol. 1206, file 297–1–21, Richards to governor general, 20 Nov. 1915, *Saint John Standard*, 20 Nov. 1915, Hughes to Richards, 25 Nov. 1915, Fowler to GOC Halifax, 25 Nov. 1915, Hodgins to GOC, Halifax, 29 Nov. 1915, reply, 10 Dec., Hodgins to GOC Halifax, 22 Dec. 1915, Gwatkin to Hodgins, 22 Dec. 1915, MacInnes to Hodgins, 25 March 1916. Interestingly, at least one commanding officer interpreted the minister's statement as a direct instruction. Lt Col W.H. Allen of the 106th Battalion, Halifax, accepted sixteen black Nova Scotians into his unit, though he reported that it discouraged white volunteers, since 'word has come from Ottawa that there is to be no distinction of colour for enlistments,' Allen to GOC Halifax, 14 Dec. 1915

20. Brown and Loveridge, 'Unrequited Faith,' 59, 60; Morton, *History*, 135–41, 147; Nicholson, *Canadian Expeditionary Force*, 212–15, 223; J.L. Granatstein and J.M. Hitsman, *Broken Promises: A History of Conscription in Canada* (Toronto 1977), 22–59

21. NA, RG 14, vol. 1221, file 593–1–7, Logie to Hodgins, 23 Nov. 1915, and reply, 26 Nov., Logie to Hodgins, 27 Nov. 1915, and replies, 6 Dec. and 10 Dec.; RG 24, vol. 4383, file 34–7–109, transfer order, 11 Dec. 1915

22. NA, RG 24, vol. 1221, file 593–1–7, Hughes to Donaldson, 4 Dec. 1915, Hodgins to McLean, 9 Dec. 1915, Hodgins, circular letter, 10 Dec. 1915, Gwatkin to Hodgins, 6 Jan. and 4 May 1916

23. NA, RG 24, vol. 4383, file 34–7–109, 'Enlistment of Indians in CEF,' numerous reports, OC 44th Regiment to Logie, 17 Jan. 1916, Scott to Logie, 19 Jan. 1916, and reply, 21 Jan., OC 114th Battalion to Logie, 27 Jan. 1916

24. Ibid., Logie to OC 114th Battalion, 22 Jan. and 28 Jan. 1916, Hodgins to Logie, 31 Jan. 1916, Hodgins to Baxter, 8 Feb. 1916

25. NA, RG 24, vol. 1206, file 297–1–21, Whitney to Hughes, 24 Nov. 1915, and reply, 3 Dec. A platoon would contain about 125 men in a standard CEF overseas battalion.

26. Ibid., *Canadian Observer*, 8 and 15 Jan. 1916, Whitney to Hughes, 19 Jan. 1916, and reply, 26 Jan., Hodgins to Logie, 3 Feb., 8 and 13 March 1916, Logie to Hodgins, 4 and 10 March 1916, Trump to Whitney, 15 March 1916

27. Ibid., Whitney to Logie, 24 March 1916, to Kemp, 29 March 1916, Hodgins to Logie, 31 March 1916, Logie to commanding officers, 3 April 1916, Logie to Hodgins, 10 April 1916, Whitney to Hughes, 18 April 1916, Hughes to Logie, 3 May 1916, and reply, 4 May. Battalion replies to Logie's appeal of 3 April 1916 are found in NA, RG 24, vol. 4387, file 34–7–141, as are copies of much of the correspondence cited from file 297–1–21.

28. NA, RG 24, vol. 1206, file 297–1–21, Christie to Gwatkin, 29 Sept. 1915, Allen to GOC Halifax, 14 Dec. 1915; RG 24, vol. 4562, file 133–17–1, Langford to Rutherford, 23 Sept. 1915; RG 9, III, vol. 71, file 10–99–40, McCurdy to Harrington, 16 July 1919

29. NA, RG 24, vol. 1206, file 297–1–21, 'Memorandum on the enlistment of negroes in Canadian Expeditionary Force,' 13 April 1916

30. Ibid., Militia Council minutes, 19 April 1916, cable to War Office, 19 April 1916, and reply, 11 May

31. Ibid., Militia Council, memo, 2 June 1916; RG 24, vol. 1469, file 600–10–35, Hodgins to Gwatkin, 5 June 1916, and reply, 11 June, Hodgins to Sutherland, 13 June 1916, and reply, 4 July

32. Ruck, *Canada's Black Battalion*, 27, quoting interview with Mrs. Mabel Saunders; African Baptist Association, annual meeting, minutes, 1916

33. NA, RG 24, vol. 1469, file 600–10–35, Ripley to Hodgins, 7 and 15 July 1916, Hodgins to Ripley, 10, 19, and 21 July 1916

34. NA, RG 24, vol. 1860, file 54, 'Recruiting — Special Units and Aliens'; RG 24, vol. 4740, file 448–14–262, Ityama to Cruikshank, 24 April 1916, Cruikshank, circular letter, 26 April 1916

35. Ibid., OC 192nd Battalion to Cruikshank, 28 April, 19 May, 4 Aug. 1916, Cruickshank to OC 192nd Battalion, 16 and 20 May and 1 Aug. 1916, Cruikshank to Hodgins, cable, 4 May 1916, and reply, same date, Cruikshank to Yamazaki, 5 May 1916; Ito, *We Went to War*, 34, 70 and App. III, and personal communication, 18 Nov 1987. RG 24, vol. 1860, file 54, gives the number of Japanese Canadians enlisted as 166, while the militia minister reported 194 Japanese enlistments; House of Commons, *Debates*, 29 April 1920, 1812. On Chinese recruits see note 5, above.

36. NA, RG 14, vol. 1221, file 593–1–7, vol. 1, Chief Thunderwater to Hodgins, 29 May and 20 June 1916; RG 24, vol. 4383, file 34–7–109, Mewburn to OC 119th Battalion, 26 April 1916, OC 227th Battalion to Mewburn, 4 May 1916. Although the adjutant general directed in February that Indian transfers should thereafter be carried

out only when 'special circumstances exist, as in the case of brothers,' Colonel Mewburn was still writing in April demanding the transfer of Indians to the 114th. See Hodgins to Baxter, 8 Feb. 1916.

37. NA, RG 24, vol. 1221, file 597–1–7, vol. 1, Cooke to minister of militia, 15 Dec. 1916; RG 24, vol. 4383, file 34–7–109, Hodgins to Logie, 31 Jan. 1916, Baxter to Hodgins, 2 Feb. 1916, Scott to Logie, 22 Jan. 1916, Logie to Hodgins, 22 Feb. 1916, Thompson to Mewburn, 13 April 1916; Gaffen, *Forgotten Soldiers*, 23

38. NA, RG 24, vol. 4383, file 34–7–109, Hodgins to Logie, 22 Feb. 1916, Thompson to OIC Divisional Recruiting, 1 March 1916, Thompson to Mewburn, 20 April 1916, Mewburn to OC 227th Battalion, 10 April 1916, and reply, 26 April, various regimental reports to Mewburn, July 1916; Gaffen, *Forgotten Soldiers*, 23

39. NA, RG 10, vol. 6766, file 452–13, Scott to Renison, 15 Jan. 1917, cables to Indian agents, 15 Jan. 1917, Militia Department to Tyson, 5 April 1917; RG 24, vol. 1221, file 597–1–7, vol. 1, Scott to Fiset, 15 Jan. 1917, vol. 2, Ogilvie to Hodgins, cable, 22 March 1917; RG 24, vol. 4662, file 99–256, Ogilvie to Hodgins, 23 March 1916, Reynolds to Ogilvie, 20 March 1917, Tyson to Scott, 21 March 1917, Ogilvie to Hodgins, 22 March 1917

40. NA, RG 24, vol. 1221, file 593–1–7, vol. 1, Chief Thunderwater to Hodgins, 30 Dec. 1916, 2 Jan. 1917, Hodgins to Logie, 8 Jan. 1917, vol. 2, John to Thunderwater, 19 Feb. 1917, Mrs. Maracle to Thunderwater, 17 Feb. 1917, Thunderwater to Hodgins, 23 Feb. 1917, Hodgins to Logie, 9 and 22 March 1917, Logie to Hodgins, 15 and 24 March 1917. Colonel Thompson of the 114th Battalion had rejected the offer of Whitney's Toronto black volunteers by explaining 'The introduction of a coloured platoon into our Battalion would undoubtedly cause serious friction and discontent.' RG 24, vol. 4387, file 34–7–141, Thompson to Logie, 4 April 1916

41. Ibid., Wright to Logie, 4 April 1916; RG 24, vol. 4680, file 18–25–2. Adjutant General's Office to district commanding officers, circular letter, 16 August 1916; RG 24, vol. 4486, file 47–8–1, transfer order, 28 Aug. 1916

42. NA, RG 24, vol. 1469, file 600–10–35, Sutherland to McCurdy, 7 August 1916, Hodgins to Sutherland, 8 Aug. 1916; RG 24, vol. 1550, file 683–124–2, Sutherland to Hodgins, 27 Nov. 1916, to McCurdy, same date

43. NA, RG 24, vol. 1469, file 600–10–35, Sutherland to Hodgins, 25 Aug. 1916, Elliott to Hodgins, 19 Oct. 1916, Hodgins to Sutherland, 1 Dec. 1916; RG 24, vol. 1550, file 683–124–2, Sutherland to Hodgins, 27 Nov. 1916 and 4 Jan. 1917, memorandum, Minister's Office, 5 Jan. 1917, adjutant general to GOC Halifax, 23 Jan. 1917; RG 24, vol. 4486, file 47–8–1, Morrison, memo, 31 Aug. 1916. The Sailing List of the No 2 Construction Battalion, 28 March 1917, contains information on the birth place, recruitment place and date for each man, so that monthly and regional totals can be compiled.

44. NA, RG 24, vol. 4739, file 448–14–259, Duclos to Cruikshank, 8 Sept. 1916, Gayfer to Cruikshank, 6 and 18 Sept. 1916, 9 and 15 Oct. 1916; No 2 Recruitment Poster, Ruck, *Canada's Black Battalion*, Appendix, 126

45. NA, RG 10, vol. 6765, file 452–7, Cooke to Scott, 12 Feb. and 4 March 1916; minutes of the Six Nations Council, 15 Sept. 1914, in Wilson, *Ontario and the First World War*, 174

46. NA, RG 24, vol. 1221, file 593–1–7, vol. 1, Chief George Fisher to Gray, 19 Feb. 1916; RG 24, vol. 4383, file 34–7–109, Baxter to Williams, 18 Dec. 1915, Whitelaw to Baxter, 31 Dec. 1915; RG 10, vol. 6765, file 452–7, Cooke to Scott, 4 April 1916

47. NA, RG 24, vol. 1221, file 593–1–7, vol. 1, Chief Thunderwater to Hodgins, 20 June and 29 Nov. 1916, Indian Mothers from Saugeen Reserve to Sir Robert Borden, 12 Oct. 1916, Smith to Scott, 1 Oct. 1916; RG 10, vol. 6765, file 452–7, Cooke to Scott, 28 Feb. 1916

48. NA, RG 24, vol. 1469, file 600–10–35, Sutherland to Hodgins, 18 Dec. 1916; RG 24, vol. 4599, file 20–10–52, Gayfer to Gray, 22 Nov. 1916; RG 9 III, vol. 81, file 10–9–40, Sutherland to Perley, 27 April 1917

49. NA, RG 24, vol. 4599, file 20–10–52, Gayfer to GOC Winnipeg, 23 Oct. 1916, to Gray, 22 Nov. 1916; RG 24, vol. 1469, file 600–10–35. Stackford to McCurdy, 7 Sept. 1916, Sutherland to Hodgins, 17 Jan. 1917, to Kemp, 18 Jan. 1917; RG 24, vol. 4558, file 132–11–1, GOC Halifax to Sutherland, 5, 8, and 10 Sept. 1916; Ruck, *Canada's Black Battalion*, 24, and Appendix interviews

50. NA, RG 24, vol. 1469, file 600–10–35, Gwatkin to Hodgins, 18 Sept. 1916; RG 24, vol. 1550, file 683–124–2, Militia Ottawa to GOC Halifax, 23 Jan. 1917; RG 24, vol. 4739, file 448–14–259, Gayfer to Cruikshank, 6 Sept., 18 Sept., 4 Oct., and 7 Nov. 1916, and replies, 9 Sept., 19 Sept., 10 Oct., Cruikshank to Grant, 6 Nov. 1916, Aitken to Cruikshank, 9 Nov. 1916

51. NA, RG24, vol. 4558, file 132–11–1, Hodgins to GC Halifax, 31 July 1916, to Sutherland, 22 Dec. 1916. Sailing List, No 2 Construction Battalion, 28 March 1917. Of the 603 enlisted men and non-commissioned officers (not including white officers), 342 were Canadian-born, 72 were West Indian, 169 American, and 20 of various other nationalities. Nova Scotia supplied 296, Ontario 207, and the west 33.

52. NA, RG 9 III, vol. 81, file 10–9–40, Sutherland to Perley, 27 April 1917, McCurdy to Perley, 1 Oct. 1917, and reply, 1 Nov., White to Stanfield, 18 Oct. 1917

53. Brown and Loveridge, 'Unrequited Faith,' 55–6, 60–4, 67, App. D, 76; Nicholson, *Canadian Expeditionary Force*, 344, 347, 350, App. C, 546; Morton, *History*, 153, 156–8; Granatstein and Hitsman, *Broken Promises*, 60–104; A.M. Williams, 'Conscription 1917: A Brief for the Defence,' CHR 37 (1956): 338–51

54. NA, RG 10, vol. 6768, file 452–20, Mississauga of New Credit to Scott, 22 Oct. 1917, Nishga to prime minister, Nov. 1917, Chief Peter Angus to the King, 13 Nov. 1917, Committee of Allied Tribes to prime minister, 17 Nov. 1917, BC Indian agent to department, 26 Nov. 1917, Chief John Prince to Scott, 27 Nov. 1917, Garden River Reserve to governor general, 4 Dec. 1917, Katzelash band to Department of Indian Affairs, 4 Dec. 1917, Kitzumkalwee band to department, 4 Dec. 1917, Michipocoten band to department, 5 Dec. 1917, Edmundston, NB, Reserve to department, 15 Dec. 1917, Manitoba Rapids Reserve to department, 24 Dec. 1917, Hurons of Lorette to government general, 10 Jan. 1918; RG 24, vol. 11221, file 593–1–7, vol. 2, Military Sub-committee to Chisholm, 28 Nov. 1917, and reply, 29 Nov.

55. DND, DHist, minister of justice to Governor General in Council, 31 Dec. 1917

56. NA, RG 10, vol. 6788, file 452–20, Scott to Ditchburn, 1 Dec. 1917, to Anaham Reserve, 14 Dec. 1917.

57. PC III, 17 Jan. 1918; Military Service Regulations, Sections 12 and 16 as amended, 2 March 1918; PC 1459, 12 June 1918

58. NA, RG 24, vol. 1469, file 600–10–35, McLean to McCurdy, 10 Oct. 1917, McCurdy to Perley, 14 Nov. 1917, White to McCurdy, nd, Gwatkin to adjutant general, 21 Oct. 1917, Shannon to adjutant general, 16 Jan. 1918, McCurdy to Mewburn, 17 Jan. 1918, and reply, 21 Jan., adjutant general to Shannon, 5 Feb. 1918, Shannon to adjutant general, 13 and 21 Feb. 1918, adjutant general, circular letter to commanding officers, Feb. 1918, White to Sir Robert Borden, 11 Aug. 1918

59. Ibid., Young to Milligan, 13 March 1918, Shannon to adjutant general, 19 April 1918, adjutant general to Shannon, 24 and 30 April 1918, British-Canadian Recruiting Mission, New York, to adjutant general, 1 May 1918, and reply, 2 May

60. Ibid., adjutant general to Brown, 8 May 1918, to Sutherland, 22 May 1918

61. Ibid., White to Sir Robert Borden, 11 Aug. 1918

62. Ibid., Bristol to Creighton, personal, 26 Aug. 1918, Creighton to AG Mobilization, 14 Sept. 1918, cable to commanding officers, 17 Sept. 1918, and replies, Creighton to Bristol, personal, 28 Sept. 1918. The record of black conscripts provided by commanding officers showed London, Ont. 23, Toronto 10, Kingston 4, Halifax 55, Saint John 13. The Military Service Council asserted, however, that it had 'no record of coloured men who are liable to draft, as all men are shown according to Nationality regardless of colour,' Ibid., Captain Newcombe, memo, 25 Sept. 1918.

63. Ruck, *Canada's Black Battalion*, 37–9, and interview with Isaac Phills, 57

64. Ito, *We Went to War*, 70 and App. III. Of 185 volunteers, 54 were killed and 119 wounded.

65. NA, RG 9 III, vol. 5010, War Diaries, 107th Pioneer Battalion. In 1918 the 107th was disbanded and the men absorbed into an engineering brigade. See also Gaffen, *Forgotten Soldiers*, passim.

66. Ruck, *Canada's Black Battalion*, 65, interview with Sydney Jones of the 106th. At a black veterans' reunion in 1982, reference was made to eight different units, besides the No 2, in which the survivors had enlisted; ibid., chap. 6, Reunion and Recognition Banquet. Mr. Thamis Gale of Montreal, himself a World War II veteran and whose father was in the No 2, has been assiduously tracking down every black to serve in the CEF. From his as-yet unpublished results it appears that there may have been more than 1200 blacks in the CEF, which would mean over 600 distributed in various units outside the No 2; personal communications, 16 and 24 June 1986 and 14 Feb. 1988

67. NA, RG 24, vol. 1469, file 600–10–35, Mobilization to Gwatkin, 19 Feb. 1917, and reply, nd, memo to naval secretary, 21 Feb. 1917 and reply, 23 Feb.; Hunt, *Nova Scotia's Part*, 149–50

68. NA, RG 24, vol. 1469, file 600–10–35, Morrison to Bristol, 20 Dec. 1917; RG 9 III, vol. 1608, file E–186–9, director of forestry to YMCA, 9 June 1917, OC No 12 District to Timber Operations, 17 Jan. 1918, OC No 9 District to Timber Operations, 19 Aug. 1918, director of timber operations to General Headquarters, 28 Nov. 1918, and signal, 30 Nov. 1918; RG 9 III, vol. 4616, file c-B–8, assistant director to director, Chaplain Services, 20 Feb. 1918; RG 9 III, vol. 4645, folder 747, War Diaries, 2nd Canadian Construction Coy (Colored), vol. 11–10, 13, and 22 March 1918, vol. 12–14 and 17 April 1918, vol. 13–8 and 12 May 1918

69. There is of course a huge literature on the nature and extent of Western racist thought, and it is not considered necessary to recount its features here. Studies which explicitly set Canadian developments within a broader context, usually imperial or continental, include Carol Bacchi, 'Race Regeneration and Social Purity: A Study of the Social Attitudes of Canada's English-Speaking Suffragists,' *Histoire Sociale/Social History* 11 (1978): 460–74; Carl Berger, *The Sense of Power: Studies in the Ideas of Canadian Imperialism, 1867–1914* (Toronto 1970), and *Science, God, and Nature in Victorian Canada* (Toronto 1983); Douglas Cole, 'The Origins of Canadian

Anthropology, 1850–1910,' *Journal of Canadian Studies* 8 (1973): 33–45; Terry Cook, 'George R. Parkin and the Concept of Britannic Idealism,' *Journal of Canadian Studies* 10 (1975): 15–31; Robert A. Huttenback, *Racism and Empire: White Settlers and Colored Immigrants in the British Self-Governing Colonies, 1830–1910* (Ithaca and London 1976); and Howard Palmer, 'Mosaic Versus Melting Pot? Immigration and Ethnicity in Canada and the United States,' *International Journal* 31 (1976): 488–528.

70. NA, RG 9 III, vol. 1608, file E–186–9, Provisional Mobilization Store Table for a Labour Company, White to GHQ, 10 Jan. 1918, and reply, 14 Jan.

71. NA, RG 9 III, vol. 81, file 10–9–40, Morrison to Bristol, 20 Dec. 1917

72. DND, DHist, 'Secret Information Concerning Black American Troops'; Foner, *Blacks and the Military*, 121–2; Balesi, 'From Adversaries to Comrades,' 112–13; Jeffrey Greenhut, 'Race, Sex and War: The Impact of Race and Sex on Morale and Health Services for the Indian Corps on the Western Front, 1914,' *Military Affairs* 45 (1981): 72–3; Willan, 'South African,' 71–3.

73. Nelson, 'Black Horror,' passim; Robert C. Reinders, 'Radicalism on the Left. E.D. Morel and the Black Horror on the Rhine,' *International Review of Social History* 13 (1968): 1–28; John C. Cairns, 'A Nation of Shopkeepers in Search of a Suitable France,' *American Historical Review* 79 (1974): 718; Bernard Shaw, *What I Really Wrote About the War* (New York 1932), 32–3; Robert A. Huttenback, *The British Imperial Experience* (New York, 1966), 175–89

74. NA, RG 9, III, vol. 1709, file D–3–13, Collier to OC Canadian Troops, 10 Jan. 1919; Ruck, *Canada's Black Battalion*, 58–60, interviews with Robert Shepard and A. Benjamin Elms. See also Desmond Morton, 'Kicking and Complaining: Demobilization Riots in the Canadian Expeditionary Force, 1918–19,' CHR 61 (1980): 341, 343, 356

75. House of Commons, *Debates*, 20 June 1919, 3741

76. Ito, *We Went to War*, 73; Roy, 'Soldiers,' 343; Provincial Elections Act Amendment Act, *Statutes of British Columbia*, 1931, C 21; War Time Elections Act, *Statutes Canada*, 1917, C 39

77. See, for example, NA, RG 24, vol. 2765, file 6615–4-A, vol. 6, secret memorandum no 1, to all chairmen and divisional registrars, 20 Nov. 1941, and order from adjutant general to all district commanders, 12 July 1943; RG 27, vol. 130, file 601-3-4, 'Conscription of East Indians for Canadian Army'; DND DHist, 'Sorting out Coloured Soldiers' and 'Organization and Administration: Enlistment of Chinese'; *The Kings Regulations and Orders for the Royal Canadian Air Force*, 1924, amended 1943; *Regulations and Instructions for the Royal Canadian Navy*, amended by PC 4950, 30 June 1944. Ito and Roy give considerable detail on Chinese- and Japanese-Canadian efforts to enlist during World War II.

Topic Ten
The Impact of Industrialization

Workers in a textile factory around 1908.

The emergence of Canadian social history shifted the focus of Canadian history from political events and economic trends to social change. Social historians have been especially interested in the transformation of Canada from an agricultural and commercial to an industrial economy. A number of them have examined the impact of the shift from rural to urban living on the "average" Canadians living in industrial cities — the working class and the urban poor. Many Canadian families had to adjust to living in slum areas of a city, and to having at least one parent, and, in many cases, both parents, as well as older children, working outside the home. Such changes affected the composition, social dynamics, and even decision-making process within the family. For working-class males, industrial life meant insecurity of work with the constant threat of layoffs for extended periods of time, low wages, and monotonous jobs that afforded them little or no sense of self worth or pride in their work. They sought out places where they could meet other workers and develop a sense of camaraderie.

The following two readings examine the impact of industrialization on family life and on working-class males in Montreal in the late nineteenth century — the period when the transition to industrialization first occurred. In her article, "Gender at Work at Home: Family Decisions, the Labour Market, and Girls' Contributions to the Family Economy," historian Bettina Bradbury examines how a division of labour along sexual lines in the workplace had already been shaped by decisions in the family based on gender as to who should work outside the home. Such family decisions were based as much on the family economy as on the economy of the workplace. Using predominantly census data for two working-class wards in Montreal, Bradbury shows that there was a trend as to whether sons or daughters went out to work based on family structure, attitudes of patriarchy, and the dynamics of a capitalist economy.

Historian Peter DeLottinville explains how Joe Beef's Canteen, a tavern in downtown Montreal, assisted sailors and longshoremen, and cultivated a working-class culture in the late nineteenth century, through a sketch of the owner, Charles McKieran, a re-creation of the atmosphere of the pub, and an examination of a cross-section of the patrons. He then goes on to explain the demise of the tavern in the 1880s as a result of changing work patterns, the rise of the Knights of Labor, and new attitudes toward leisure and urban conditions.

What were the factors that affected the decision in working-class families as to whether to send sons or daughters out to work? What were the cultural dynamics in working-class Montreal in the period from 1869 to 1889 that Joe Beef's Canteen both contributed to and benefited from? Both Bradbury and DeLottinville study working-class culture in Montreal in the same time period, but from different perspectives. In what ways are their perspectives and conclusions similar and different?

On the subject of women who work outside the home, see the relevant sections in Alison Prentice et al., *Canadian Women: A History*, 2nd ed. (Toronto: Harcourt Brace, 1996); Marjorie Griffin Cohen, *Women's Work, Markets, and Economic Development in Nineteenth-Century Ontario* (Toronto: University of Toronto Press, 1988); and Graham S. Lowe, *Women in the Administrative Revolution: The Feminization of Clerical Work* (Toronto: University of Toronto Press, 1987). Mary Kinnear, ed., *First Days, Fighting Days: Women in Manitoba History* (Regina: Canadian Plains Research Centre, 1987) contains several essays on women workers. See also *Women at Work: Ontario, 1850–1930*, eds. Janice Acton et al. (Toronto: Women's Educational Press, 1974), and Wayne Roberts, *Honest Womanhood: Feminism, Femininity and Class Consciousness among Toronto Working Women, 1893 to 1914* (Toronto: New Hogtown Press, 1976). A comparative study of men and women workers in the Ontario towns of Paris and Hanover is provided by Joy Parr in *The Gender of Breadwinners: Women, Men, and Change in Two Industrial Towns, 1880–1950* (Toronto: University of Toronto Press, 1990). For an interpretative article, see Ruth A. Frager, "Labour History and the Interlocking Hierarchies of Class, Ethnicity, and Gender: A Canadian Perspective," *International Review of Social History*, 44 (1999): 197–215. On the impact of industrialization on women and/or the family, see Bettina Bradbury's *Working Families: Age, Gender and Daily Survival in Industrializing Montreal* (Toronto: McClelland and Stewart, 1993) and the essays in Section 4 of her *Canadian Family History: Selected Readings* (Toronto: Copp Clark Pitman, 1992), as well as Peter Gossage, *Families in Transition: Industry and Population in Nineteenth-Century Saint-Hyacinthe* (Montreal/Kingston: McGill-Queen's University Press, 1999), and R. Marvin McInnis's "Women, Work and Childbearing: Ontario in the Second Half of the Nineteenth Century," *Histoire sociale/Social History* 24, 48 (November 1991): 237–62.

Three excellent primary sources on the impact of industrial growth in Canada at the turn of the century are *The Royal Commission on the Relations of Labour and Capital, 1889*. An abridged version has been published under the title *Canada Investigates Industrialism*, edited and with an introduction by Greg Kealey (Toronto: University of Toronto Press, 1973); and the two collections, *The Workingman in the Nineteenth Century*, ed. M.S. Cross (Toronto: Oxford University Press, 1974), and *The Canadian Worker in the Twentieth Century*, eds. I. Abella and D. Millar (Toronto: Oxford University Press, 1978). Three worthwhile collections are *Canadian Working Class History: Selected Readings*, eds. Laurel Sefton MacDowell and Ian Radforth (Toronto: McClelland and Stewart, 1992); *Essays on Canadian Working Class History*, eds. G. Kealey and P. Warrian (Toronto: McClelland and Stewart, 1976); and *Canadian Labour History: Selected Readings*, eds. D.J. Bercuson and David Bright (Toronto: Copp Clark, 1994). Terry Copp provides an in-depth study of working-class life in Montreal in his *The Anatomy of Poverty: The Conditions of the Working Class in Montreal, 1897–1929* (Toronto: McClelland and Stewart, 1974). A similar study for Toronto is Greg Kealey's *Toronto Workers Respond to Industrial Capitalism, 1867–1892* (Toronto: University of Toronto Press, 1980). A second valuable study on Toronto is Michael Piva's *The Conditions of the Working Class in Toronto, 1900–1921* (Ottawa: University of Ottawa Press, 1979). For Ontario in general, see Paul Craven, ed., *Labouring Lives: Work and Workers in Nineteenth-Century Ontario* (Toronto: University of Toronto Press, 1995). On Atlantic Canada, see Daniel Samson, ed., *Contested Countryside: Rural Workers and Modern Society in Atlantic Canada, 1800–1950* (Fredericton: Acadiensis Press, 1994). David Bright looks at the history of the labour movement in Calgary in his *The Limits of Labour: Class Formation and the Labour Movement in Calgary, 1883–1929* (Vancouver: University of British Columbia Press, 1998).

For a discussion of working-class culture, see Bryan Palmer's *A Culture in Conflict: Skilled Workers and Industrial Capitalism in Hamilton, Ontario, 1860–1914* (Montreal/Kingston: McGill-Queen's University Press, 1979), and his *Working-Class Experience: The Rise and Reconstitution of Canadian Labour, 1800–1991*, 2nd ed. (Toronto: McClelland and Stewart, 1993). On the importance of Labour Day parades as a cultural phenomenon, see Craig Heron and Steve Penfold, "The Craftmen's Spectacle: Labour Day Parades, The Early Years," *Social History/Histoire sociale*, 29, 58 (November 1996): 357–389.

WEBLINKS

Canadian Labour History
http://www.civilization.ca/hist/labour/lab02e.html

An account of early unions in Canada, with historical interviews from workers.

Industrialization in Newfoundland and Labrador
http://www.heritage.nf.ca/society/industry.html

A detailed description of the changes that industrialization and diversification brought to the economies of Newfoundland and Labrador.

Industrial Architecture of Montreal
http://digital.library.mcgill.ca/industrial/showbuilding.php?id=IN139

Interior illustrations of a Montreal factory in 1891. This site is part of a larger database of images relating to Montreal's industrial architecture.

Article Twenty-Four

Gender at Work at Home: Family Decisions, the Labour Market, and Girls' Contributions to the Family Economy

Bettina Bradbury

INTRODUCTION

"Gender at work" can be read in two ways. In the first, work is a noun, and the central question is "How do definitions of skill, of appropriate work for men and women, get negotiated within the workplace by men and women, workers and capital?" Recent discussions of the sexual division of labour in diverse industries, of "gender at work," of the social construction of skill, and of the role of unions in perpetuating women's unequal position in the workforce have made major contributions to our understanding of the complexities of the relationships between gender and class, between patriarchy and capitalism. Historical research in this field is rich and fascinating, and is reshaping both women's history and working-class history in Canada as elsewhere.[1]

"Gender at work" can also be read, if my grammar is correct, as a verb. Here the question posed would be "How does gender work as a process in society which means that men and women end up with different work and life experiences?" To answer this question involves consideration of factors other than those found in the workplace. In this paper I would like to argue that while workplace-centred approaches go a long way toward explaining sex segregation within specific trades, they ignore different levels of decision making and other institutions that have already gendered the workforce before it arrives at the factory gate.[2] Equally, while approaches stressing the strength of patriarchal ideology or the importance of domestic labour help explain why married women remained out of the workplace, they fail to grasp the complex interactions between patriarchy and capitalism. Furthermore they are more difficult to apply when dealing with the work of daughters rather than their mothers.

Within families, decisions were made about who should stay home to look after children and do housework and who should earn wages which had wide-reaching impact on the composition of the workforce. Such decisions were never made in an ideological or economic

Source: *Canadian and Australian Labour History*, ed. Gregory S. Kealey and Greg Patmore (Sydney: Australian Society for the Study of Labour History and the Committee on Canadian Labour History, 1990), pp. 119–40. Reprinted by permission.

vacuum; they represented a complex and often unconscious balance between basic need, existing ideology and practice regarding gender roles, the structure of the economy, and the particular economic conjuncture. Schools taught specific skills and implanted tenacious ideas about future roles. At its broadest level this paper represents a simple plea to those looking at divisions of labour in the workplace to also consider the work done by historians of the family and education. In Canada such work offers some clues about this broader process, although little research systematically examines the question.[3] To the extent that historians interested in how gender is worked out within the workplace and in the unions ignore what happens prior to men's and women's arrival at work, their explanations will fail to consider the wider and deeper sexual division of labour, which not only relegated women to jobs defined as less skilled in workplaces shared with men and to feminine ghettos, but also determined that large numbers would simply not enter the workforce or would do so only sporadically.

More specifically, the paper focuses on one aspect of the question, namely, how family decisions in interaction with the nature of local labour markets influenced sons' and, in particular, daughters' contributions to the family economy.[4] The paper concentrates on the micro-level, examining what I have been able to deduce about family decision-making processes regarding which family members should seek wage labour in two Montreal working-class wards between the 1860s and 1890s. A brief description of the major sectors employing males in Montreal is followed by an assessment of the importance of additional wage earners to working-class families. The respective work of sons and daughters within the family economy is evaluated.

I argue that the sexual division of labour within the family, and the need for additional domestic workers as well as extra wage labourers, meant that the context, timing, and contours of boys' and girls' participation in wage labour were different. By looking at the role of girls in the family economy and not just in the labour market,[5] we can better see how the major changes accompanying the emergence of industrial capitalism in Montreal did not modify the dominant sexual division of labour.

MONTREAL FAMILIES AND WAGE LABOUR, 1860–1890

The years 1860 to 1890 were characterized by the growing dominance of industrial capital in the economic structure of Montreal and the increasing dependence on wage labour of a major proportion of its population. Canada's first and largest industrial city, "the workshop" of Canada, had a wide and complex array of industries. Most important were those relating to rail and water transportation, shoemaking, clothing, and food and beverages. The metallurgy sector, dominated by production for the railroads, provided jobs for skilled immigrants from Great Britain, and some French Canadians with a long tradition of working in metal. In shoemaking and dressmaking, as in numerous other smaller trades, artisanal production was rapidly, if unevenly, giving way to production in large factories. Minute divisions of labour accompanied the utilization of new types of machinery throughout the period, drawing immigrants and French Canadians new to the city into the myriad of largely unskilled jobs that were being created. Broadly speaking, the male workforce was divided into four groups. Best paid and most secure were the relatively skilled workers involved in the new trades that emerged with the industrial revolution — the engineers, machinists, moulders, and others who worked in the foundries and new factories. More subject to seasonal and conjunctural unemployment were skilled workers in the construction trades. A third group comprised those workers in trades undergoing rapid deskilling and reorganization; most important among these were the shoemakers. General unskilled labourers made up the other major subgroup within the working class. About 25 cents a day separated the average wage of each of these groups, setting the stage for potential differences in their standard of living and their family economy.[6] Women and girls worked largely in separate sectors of the economy, particularly as domestic servants and dressmakers and in specific kinds of factory work. In virtually every sector, their wages were half those of males or less.[7]

THE IMPORTANCE OF ADDITIONAL EARNERS IN THE FAMILY WAGE ECONOMY

These disparities of approximately 25 cents a day had the potential to separate the working class into identifiable fractions, each capable of achieving a different standard of living in good times, and each vulnerable in diverse ways to the impact of winter, cyclical depressions, and job restructuring. Throughout most of the period, the most skilled had more flexibility in their budget and a greater chance of affording to eat and live at a level that may also have helped to ward off the diseases that spread only too quickly through the poorly constructed sewers and houses of the city. This greater margin of manoeuvre which higher daily wages, greater job security, and the possession of skills that were scarce and usually in demand gave to the skilled was not constant. It was particularly likely to be eroded in times of economic depression or of rapid transformations in the organization of work.

While some skilled workers organized successfully during this period, the major element of flexibility in the family income, for skilled and unskilled alike, lay not so much in the gains that organization could offer, but in the ability to call on additional family members to earn wages, to gain or save money in other ways, or to limit the necessity of spending cash. Decisions about who additional family workers would be were therefore crucial in determining the contours of the family economy and of the labour force. An examination of the importance of secondary wage earners and of who they were in terms of their age and sex allows a better grasp of the interaction between family labour deployment decisions, the "gendering" of the workforce, and the structure of the economy. This section therefore assesses the importance of additional wage earners in families headed by men in different types of occupations.[8] The following section then attempts to determine who such workers were.

The average number of workers reported by the families of the two working-class areas studied here, Ste. Anne and St. Jacques wards, fluctuated over the family life cycle. Among young couples who had not yet borne children, the wife would occasionally report an occupation, and sometimes another relative lived with the couple, contributing to the number of workers in the household, so that until 1881 families averaged just over one worker at this first stage of a couple's married life. Most families then passed through a long period of relative deprivation as children were born, grew, and required more food, clothing, and larger living premises. Between the time when the first baby was born and some children reached twelve or thirteen, the families of Ste. Anne and St. Jacques continued to have only slightly more than one worker. Then children's contribution began to make up for the difficult years. In 1861, families where half the children were still under fifteen averaged 1.34 workers; once half were fifteen or more they averaged 1.97. In subsequent decades the expansion of wage labour made children's contribution even more important. Whereas in 1861 the average family with children over the age of eleven had only 0.48 of them at work, in 1881 it had 1.16. By 1871 the average family with offspring aged fifteen or more had nearly as many children living at home and working as there had been total number of workers a decade earlier. From 0.85 children at work, the number reported increased to 1.85. The total number of family workers increased from an average of under two at this stage in 1861 to nearly three a decade later. Children's wages became more and more important as children came to constitute a wage-earning family's major source of security.

The prosperity that this number of workers could have secured was temporary. It depended largely on the ability of parents to keep their wage-earning children in the household. As older sons or daughters began to leave home to work or marry, the average dropped down again. If both members of a couple survived they would find themselves struggling again in their old age on a single wage, or no wage at all. For aged working-class widows and widowers, the situation was particularly bleak if there were no children able to help.[9]

Over these years the patterns of the working-class and non-working-class families diverged. In 1861 the non-working class, particularly in St. Jacques, included a high proportion of artisans and shopkeepers, men whose family economy required not the wages, but the work of wives and children. As a result, the average number of workers and of children at work in their families was higher than in all other groups except the unskilled. Over the next two decades, artisans became less and less common. Family labour was increasingly limited to enterprises like small corner groceries. Professionals and some white-collar workers became more important among the non-working-class populations. After 1871, the reporting of jobs by children was least likely among this group.

It was within the working-class family economy that the most dramatic changes occurred over this period, although there were significant and changing differences between the skilled, the unskilled, and those in the indentured trades. The inadequacy of the $1.00 a day or less that a labourer could earn remained a constant throughout this period. As a result, unskilled families consistently relied on additional workers when they were able to. In 1861 they averaged 1.45 workers, compared to 1.27 among the skilled. Over the next two decades the growing number of jobs available allowed them to increase the average number of family workers to 1.62, then 1.66. Among those with working-age offspring, the average number at work increased by 123 percent, from 0.60 in 1861 to 1.34 two decades later.

For these unskilled workers, the period before children were old enough to work was the most difficult. It is worth examining how some such families managed at the critical stage of the family life cycle and later, as children matured. Olive Godaire, wife of labourer Pierre, worked, probably at home as a dressmaker, in 1861, to help support their three children, aged two to eight. Ten years later, it was her eighteen-year-old daughter who was taking in sewing, while a ten-year-old boy was apprenticed to be a tinsmith.[10] In the case of labourer John Harrington's family, the period when the father was the only earner within the nuclear family lasted for at least eighteen years. When John and Sarah's children were under ten, they took in boarders and had John's 50-year-old father, also a labourer, living in the household. Whatever money these extra family and household members contributed would have helped compensate for John's low wages or irregular work, and they continued to take in boarders over the next ten years. Their oldest son, Timothy, was still going to school in 1871, and the family was cramped in a rear dwelling where rent was minimal. Somewhere between 1871 and 1881, the boys joined their father in seeking general labouring jobs. For the first time, the family lived alone, without additional household members. With three wage earners — indeed, three labourers — they must have enjoyed a standard of living that was relatively high compared to the previous year.

The degradation of work conditions and lower wages that typified trades like shoemaking appear to have been counteracted by families' sending growing numbers of their members to seek steady work. In 1861, families in such trades had only 1.08 workers — fewer than any other group. By 1881, they averaged 1.62 workers. Most dramatic was the increased importance of the contribution of children resident at home. Among families with children of working age, the average number of children reporting a job nearly tripled over the two decades, from 0.55 to 1.51. At that date, a few families, like that of Angeline and Alexis Larivière, had four workers. Their two daughters, 22-year-old Josephine and sixteen-year-old Marie-Louise, worked as general labourers. The twenty-year-old son, Charles, was a stone-cutter.[11]

The relative superiority of the wages of skilled workers seems clear in 1861, when they appear to have been able to manage with fewer workers than other groups — averaging only 1.27. A decade later, with 1.5 workers, they still needed fewer than the rest of the working class. The depression that hit in 1874, however, appears to have eroded much of the superiority of the skilled workers. In 1881, after seven years of major depression, which was only just lifting and which must have left many a family heavily indebted, the pattern of family labour deployment was similar to that of the unskilled and those in the indentured trades.

This convergence of experiences within the working class over this period is not surprising, given the impact of the depression, combined with the degeneration of work conditions in some skilled trades. In the metal-working trades, for example, trade was said to be dead in the winter of 1878. Half the local unionized workers were said to be "working at any kind of labouring work." Two years earlier, a moulder drew attention to the desperate condition of Montreal mechanics, "working on a canal at 60 cents per day, men who have served years in securing a trade, the wages they receive being only a mockery of their misery."[12]

Families clearly attempted to shape their own economies by adjusting the numbers of wage earners to fit their expenses when they were able to do so. Additional wage earners were not only needed, but were used by all fractions of the working class, with differences stemming from the economic conjuncture, the nature of the labour market, and their own life cycle and earning power. In this way, working-class families influenced the city's labour pool and enhanced their own survival. The increasing availability of wage labour in the factories, workshops, and construction sites of Montreal meant that even in times of depression more and more sons and daughters could and did find work. The reliance of employers in certain sectors on women and youths resident at home depressed male wages generally, while offering families the opportunity to counter a father's low earnings.

Economic transformation thus interacted dialectically with family needs, reshaping the labour market, the family economy, and the life course of children. This interaction is clearest in the case of workers in those sectors undergoing the most dramatic transformation. The continued reorganization of production in trades like shoemaking was reflected not only in the greater increase in the number of their children seeking waged work over the period, but also in a tendency to delay marriage and reduce family size. In the labour market in general, children living at home became a much more significant proportion of workers.[13] In the sewing trades, for example, one-quarter of the workers had been co-resident children in 1861; by 1881, 55 percent were.

AGE, GENDER, AND ADDITIONAL FAMILY EARNERS

To try to grasp the decision-making processes behind these patterns of change in the average numbers of family members reporting work over this period, it is necessary to determine who the family workers were in terms of age and gender, and to examine the families from which they came.

Older sons still living at home were the most usual second earners in a family. The number of really young children or married women reporting a job was insignificant beside the importance of children in their late teens or twenties, despite the attention focused on such young workers by contemporaries.[14] Once sons, in particular, reached fifteen or sixteen, they were expected to work. "In our culture," reported Alice Lacasse, the daughter of a French-Canadian immigrant to New Hampshire, "the oldest children always went to work."[15] Wage labour for boys over fifteen became the norm in this period, as more and more were drawn into the labour force. Growing numbers of girls did report a job, but the proportion of boys at work remained consistently higher than that for girls in all age groups. And the pattern of involvement over a girl's life course continued to be completely different from a boy's.

By the age of fifteen or sixteen, 30 percent of the boys who lived at home in these two wards were reporting a job in 1861. Others no doubt sought casual labour on the streets, working from time to time, at other times roaming together in the gangs of youths that dismayed middle-class contemporaries, and filled up the local police courts. In 1871, when times were good, and industrial capitalism more entrenched, nearly 46 percent of boys this age could find a job, while in the depression of the 1870s and early 1880s, the percentage dropped back to 37 percent. After the age of sixteen, and increasingly over the period, boys' involvement with wage labour or other work would grow steadily as they aged. At ages seventeen to eighteen, 50 percent reported a job in 1861, nearly 68 percent two decades later. By age 21 nearly 90 percent of boys listed a job at the end of the period.

Among the girls of Ste. Anne and St. Jacques wards, the work found and the pattern of job reporting over their lives was very different from that of the boys. Once boys passed their early teens, they found work in a wide variety of jobs in all sectors and workplaces of Montreal. Girls, in contrast, remained concentrated within specific jobs and sectors. For girls as for boys, the chances of finding work clearly expanded with the growth of Montreal industry. At ages fifteen to sixteen, for instance, only 13 percent reported a job in 1861, compared to 30 percent in 1881. At the peak age at which girls reported working, nineteen to twenty, 25 percent worked in 1861, nearly 38 percent in 1871, and 35 percent in 1881. Even then, however, the visible participation rate of girls was only half that of boys.[16] After age twenty, the experiences of boys and girls diverged quickly and dramatically, as most, but never all, women withdrew from the formal labour market while most men found themselves obliged to seek work for the rest of their lives.

For those girls who did earn wages, then, paid labour was apparently undertaken for a brief period of their lives prior to marriage. At any one time, most girls aged fifteen or more who remained at home with their parents in these wards reported no job at all. Joan Scott and Louise Tilly have suggested that within the "industrial mode of production" "single women are best able to work, since they have few other claims on their time."[17] The discrepancy in the formal wage labour participation rates for boys and girls in these two Montreal wards suggests to me that single women did, in fact, have other claims on their time. In particular, the heavy and time-consuming nature of nineteenth-century housework, the prevalence of disease, the wide age spread among children in most families, and the myriad of other largely invisible pursuits and strategies necessary to survival for the working-class family meant that many of these girls were needed by their mothers to help with work at home. Their role in the division of labour within the family is highlighted on one census return where members' roles were explicitly described. Louis Coutur, a carter who was 50 in 1861, reported that his 21-year-old son was a shoemaker and that his wife's job was "housework."[18] It seems fair to assume, making allowance for the under-enumeration of steady labour and casual work among daughters, that most of the girls who listed no job or school attendance worked periodically, if not continually, at domestic labour as mother's helpers in and around the home. It is thus in the light of family decisions about the allocation of labour power at home, as well as in the structure of jobs available in the marketplace, that the patterns of children's wage labour as well as of their schooling must be interpreted.

At home, girls served an apprenticeship in the reproduction of labour power — in babysitting, cleaning, mending, sewing, cooking, and shopping and, by the end of the century, in nursing and hygiene.[19] Religious leaders were explicit about the need for mothers to educate their daughters in their future roles. "Apply yourselves especially to the task of training your daughters in the functions they will have to perform for a husband and family, without neglecting your other children," wrote Père Mailloux in a manual for Christian parents that was republished several times between the middle and end of the nineteenth century.[20] When girls attended school, the subjects learned were not very different. Education for females, except in a few expensive academies out of reach of the working class, taught only the most basic and general of subjects and housekeeping-type skills. Whereas boys' schools offered bookkeeping and geography, girls' schools offered music, needlework, and sewing.[21] Curriculums aimed to prepare girls for their future role as housekeeper, wife, and mother.[22] The minister of education was explicit. He feared that too many young women were being educated above their station in life, and suggested that bookkeeping and domestic economy constituted the best basis of female education.[23]

Girls, then, were increasingly likely to become secondary wage earners within the working-class family economy during this period, but remained less likely to report a job than were boys. The importance of their contribution to domestic labour, the lower wages they could make in the formal labour market, or an ideological repulsion to girls' labour either within the working class or among capitalists constitute partial explanations for their lower rate of participation. In the absence of interviews or written memoirs, it is important to examine the work patterns of specific families more closely to see what reasons can be deduced from the evidence.[24]

Even among the families apparently in greatest need, sons seem to have been sent out to work in preference to daughters. If any families needed to draw on as many workers as possible, it should have been those headed by the labourers or shoemakers of these wards. In such families, food costs alone for a family with several growing children rapidly outstripped a man's incoming wages. Yet even these families appear to have avoided sending girls out to work, if possible. Among labourers' families in Ste. Anne in 1881, for example, 66 percent of those who had boys over ten reported having a son at work, while only 28 percent of those with girls the same age did so. If older brothers were working, girls generally did not. Girls of age twenty or more would stay at home while a teenage son worked. Their respective roles seem clearly defined. Twenty-six-year-old Ellen Mullin, for example, reported no occupation. Two brothers, aged nineteen and 23, worked as carters. Ellen's role was to help her mother with the domestic labour for the three wage earners and her fourteen-year-old younger brother.[25]

In Ste. Anne, even families without sons, or with young sons only, seem to have been either unwilling to send girls to work or unable to find work that was seen as suitable in the neighbourhood. Forty-two-year-old Octave Ethier must surely have had trouble supporting his four daughters, aged one to seventeen, and his wife on his labourer's wages. Yet neither seventeen-year-old Philomène nor fifteen-year-old Emma reported having a job.[26]

The girls in labourers' families who did report an occupation fell into two categories. Half were the oldest child, either with no brothers or only brothers who were much younger than they were. Nineteen-year-old Sarah Anne Labor, for instance, was the oldest in a family of six children. The closest brother was only seven. She worked as a soap maker. Her wages, and the fact that the family shared the household with several other families, must have helped make ends meet.[27]

The second group of girl workers in Ste. Anne and St. Jacques came from labourers' families that sent almost all their children to work regardless of gender. Catherine Harrigan, for instance, was fourteen. She worked as a servant. Her two brothers, aged fifteen and twenty, were labourers like their father. In the family of St. Jacques labourer Damase Racette, four girls, aged seventeen to 25, were all dressmakers, as was his wife, Rachel. A 27-year-old son was a cigar maker.[28] This latter group of families appears the most desperate, perhaps because of recurrent illness or the habitual drunkenness of a parent. When Commissioners Lukas and Blackeby were examining the work of children in Canadian mills and factories in 1882, they reported finding too many cases in the cities and factory districts where parents with "idle habits" lived "on the earnings of the children, this being confirmed" in their eyes by one instance where three children were at work, having a father as above described.[29] Yet, such a family could simply have been taking advantage of the fact of having more children of working age to make up for years of deprivation on the inadequate wages most family heads could make. Two years later, reports made to the Ontario Bureau of Industries stressed the inadequate wages of family heads as the major cause of children's working, while mentioning that dissipation of the husband or father was less often a cause.[30] When a father was chronically ill or a habitual drunkard, the wages of several children would indeed have been necessary to support a family. The use of daughters and of children aged ten to twelve to earn wages in this minority of labourers' families contrasts with the absence of such workers in other labourers' families, high-lighting the relative infrequency of a daughter's work, even among those in greatest need.

Was it in part working-class ideology that kept girls at home if at all possible, seeing the workplace as unfit for them, or was it rather a pragmatic response to the fact that boys' wages rapidly outstripped those of girls? Pragmatism, made necessary by the exigencies of daily life, must certainly have played an important part. It made good sense to have boys earn wages rather than girls, for while young children of each sex might earn a similar wage, once they reached fifteen or sixteen, girls' wages were generally half those of young men. On the other hand, when there was work available that girls could do, more were likely to report a job. Thus, the labourers of St. Jacques were more likely to have daughters at work than those of Ste. Anne. St. Jacques labourers' families with children aged eleven or over had an equal percentage of girls and boys at work. The fact that nearly 80 percent of these girls worked in some branch of the sewing industry shows how families took advantage of the availability of this kind of work in the neighbourhood.

Family labour deployment decisions, then, were forged in the context of their own needs, invariably arising partly from the size, age, and gender configurations of the family, as well as from the kind of work the family head could find. They were realized in relationship with the structure of the local labour market, of job possibilities, and of local wage rates for men and women, boys and girls. And they were influenced by perceptions, ideologies, and gut reactions about what was appropriate for sons and daughters. Thus, it was not just the fact that sewing was available in St. Jacques ward that made this such a popular choice for daughters living in that ward, for putting out could theoretically operate anywhere in the city or the surrounding coun-tryside. It was, I suspect, the very fact that it could be done at home that was crucial. For, while domestic service no doubt took some young women from families in these wards away from their own families and into the homes of others, sewing usually kept daughters working at home.[31]

Home-work offered parents, and mothers in particular, several advantages. First, they could oversee their daughters' work and behaviour, avoiding the individualism that working in a factory might encourage and skirting the dangers and moral pitfalls that at least some con-temporaries associated with factory work for young, unmarried women.[32] More important, girls sewing at home, like their mothers, could combine stitching and housework, take care of younger children, run odd errands, or carry water as needed, because they were right there and were always paid by the piece.

The clustering of two to five family members, all seamstresses, commonly found in the census returns for St. Jacques ward suggests very strongly that here was a centre of the home-work that was crucial to Montreal's sewing and shoemaking industries during this period. It was not uncommon to find three to four sisters, ranging in age from eleven to 28, all working, presumably together, as sewing girls. In the Mosian family of St. Jacques ward, for instance, four daughters worked as seamstresses in 1871. The father was a labourer, and although the wife reported no occupation, she probably also did some sewing at home at times.[33] In 1881, the family of Marie and Michel Guigère had reached a relatively secure stage in their family life cycle. With nine children at home, aged two to 23, this joiner's family reported seven workers. Four of the girls, aged thirteen to 23, were seamstresses; one son worked as a labourer; and the thirteen-year-old son was an apprentice. The girls could combine sewing with helping their mother keep house for other workers, care for the younger children, shop, cook, clean, and also look after her husband's 70-year-old father, who lived with them. Marie too probably helped sporadically with sewing.[34]

Some parents with the liberty to choose must have been reluctant to expose their daughters to the long hours, continual supervision, exhausting work, and brutal forms of discipline that existed in some of Montreal's workshops and factories. Work at home could counteract such factors of "repulsion"[35] in some of the sectors employing girls. Cigar-making factories provided jobs for girls and boys in Ste. Anne and St. Jacques alike. While some manufacturers appear to have been decent men, neither fining nor beating their employees, others, in an apparently desperate attempt to control their youthful workforce, resorted to physical violence, heavy fines, even locking up children, as they strove to mould this young generation of workers to industrial work. Children, like adults, in these factories worked from six or seven in the morning until six at night, and sometimes later.[36] Unlike adult males, they were subject to a vast array of disciplinary measures aimed at making them more productive and more responsible as workers. One child reported:

> If a child did anything, that is, if he looked on one side or other, or spoke, he would say: I'm going to make you pay 10 cents fine, and if the same were repeated three or four times, he would seize a stick or a plank, and beat him with it.[37]

Mr. Fortier's cigar-making factory was described as a "theatre of lewdness." There was said to be "no such infamous factory as M. Fortier's . . . nowhere else as bad in Montreal." There, one cigar maker described apprentices as being "treated more or less as slaves."[38] It was the evidence of the treatment of one eighteen-year-old girl that really shocked both the public and the commissioners examining the relations between labour and capital in 1888. Georgina Loiselle described how Mr. Fortier beat her with a mould cover because she would not make the 100 cigars as he demanded.

> I was sitting, and he took hold of me by the arm, and tried to throw me on the ground. He did throw me on the ground and beat me with the mould cover.
> Q. Did he beat you when you were down?
> A. Yes, I tried to rise and he kept me down on the floor.[39]

The case of Mr. Fortier's cigar factory was not typical. It created a sensation when the evidence was heard. At least some of the mothers of girls working there got together, perhaps encouraged by Mr. Fortier, to give evidence to counteract the impact of such bad publicity. "I am the mother of a family and if I had seen anything improper I would not have stayed there," explained a Mrs. Levoise. "I have my girl working there."[40]

While conditions in other Montreal factories were not as extreme, there was sufficient evidence of beatings, other draconian forms of discipline, and heavy fines to explain why many girls and their parents may have wished to avoid factory labour. In cotton factories there was some evidence of boys and girls being beaten. Furthermore, fines in at least one Montreal cotton factory could reduce pay packages by between $1.00 and $12.00 in two weeks. Work there began at 6:25 a.m. and finished at 6:15 p.m. When extra work was required, employees had to stay until 9 p.m., often without time off for supper.[41] There were some perks to working in the textile industry. Nineteen-year-old Adèle Lavoie explained that the girls were accustomed to "take cotton to make our aprons." Apparently this was usually allowed, but on at least one occasion she was accused by the foreman of having taken 40 to 50 yards. When a search of her house produced no results, she reported that the foreman returned to the factory to insult and harass her sister. When she did not produce the cotton, "he stooped at this time and raising the skirt of my sister's dress, he said she had it under her skirt."[42]

Airless, hot, dusty factories, such sexual abuse by foremen, work conditions, and the long hours were all factors that may have discouraged parents from sending girls into factory work. More significant were the wages they earned. For children under fourteen or so, wages varied little by sex. After that, male and female differentials hardened. Girl apprentices in dressmaking, mantlemaking, and millinery sometimes earned nothing for several years until they learned the trade; then they received around $4.00 a week only. "Girls" in shoe manufactories received $3.00 to $4.00, compared to the $7.00 or $8.00 earned by men. A girl bookbinder made between $1.50 and $6.00 weekly, compared to an average of $11.00 for male journeymen. Even on piece-work, girls and women generally received less than men. In general, wage rates for women were approximately half those of men.[43]

Over this period, more and more working-class boys would have reached manhood accustomed to wage labour. Because of duties at home and low wages, however, their sisters, whether they worked in or outside the home, were much more likely to move backwards and forwards between paid work and housework in response to the family's economic needs and their position in the household. Once boys, and particularly those who had been fortunate enough to acquire a skill in demand in the marketplace, reached their late teens, their earning power might rival that of their father. Wage labour offered such children potential freedom from their family in a way that had not been possible in family economies based on shared work and the inheritance of property. Such freedom was seldom possible for girls, unless they were willing to complement wage labour with prostitution.

AGE, GENDER, AND CHANGING PATTERNS OF RESIDENCE, SCHOOLING, AND DOMESTIC LABOUR

Yet, boys in general do not appear to have taken dramatic advantage of such potential freedom. Nor did girls.[44] In 1861, living with others was still an important stage in the lives of some young people of both sexes. Among the seventeen-year-old girls residing in Ste. Anne and St. Jacques, 35 percent were boarding with other families, living with relatives, or working and living in as a servant. Twenty years later, only 12 percent of girls that age were not living with their parents, and half of these were already married. Among boys aged eighteen, 34 percent were not living with their parents in 1861, compared to only 17 percent two decades later. Living longer at home with their parents was a fundamental change in the life cycle of boys and girls alike during this period of industrial expansion.[45]

Behind the percentages of children living with their parents or elsewhere lies a complex history of tension between family needs and individual desires, of children balancing off the advantages of the services offered at home against the relative independence that living with strangers, or even relatives, might offer.[46] For all families who had passed through at least fifteen years of budget stretching, house sharing, and debt building while their children were young, the relative prosperity that several workers could offer was to be jealously guarded.

It was precisely "because young adults could find jobs" that it "was in the interest of parents to keep their children at home as long as possible."[47] The patterns of residence of children suggest that, whatever conflicts there were overall, in these two wards of Montreal between 1861 and 1881, it was increasingly the parents who were the winners.

The motives behind individual decisions, the weight of traditions of family work, are difficult to grasp in the absence of written records. The factors constraining or encouraging one choice or another are clearer. Most children would have left home once they had a job only if their wages were adequate to pay for lodgings and they felt no commitment to contributing to the family income.[48] Clearly, more older boys earned enough to pay for room and board than did girls. Thus, in 1871, when work was readily available, 29 percent of the 23-year-old males living in these wards were boarding or with relatives, 39 percent were living with their parents, and 32 percent had married. Among girls the same age, the low wages they could make severely limited their options. Only 15 percent were boarding, 41 percent were still with their parents, and 44 percent were already married. The contraction of work and the lower wages that accompanied the depression that hit in 1874 limited the possibility of leaving home to lodge with others or to marry. In 1881, the percentage of 23-year-old boys married had dropped to 25 percent; only 10 percent were boarding or living with relatives. Sixty-five percent remained at home with their parents, presumably pooling resources to survive the difficult times. The depression appears to have hastened the decline of this stage of semi-autonomy. What occurred in subsequent years remains to be determined.

The different roles of boys and girls in the family economy are confirmed in the different patterns of school attendance by age and sex. In general, school and work appear to have been complementary rather than in competition. Some children began school at four years old. By age seven, approximately 60 percent of boys and girls were receiving some education. In 1881, this percentage rose to a peak of 78 percent for eight- and nine-year-old boys, and around 80 percent for girls aged nine to twelve, then fell off rapidly once both sexes reached thirteen. The proportion of children receiving some schooling increased, but not dramatically, between 1861 and 1881. Age, gender, and the economic conjuncture created variations within this overall trend. Most important was the more erratic pattern in the attendance of boys that hints at relationships between age, gender, schooling, and wage labour that require further investigation. Overall, the percentage of ten- to fourteen-year-old girls at school increased slowly but steadily, from 57 percent in 1861 to 68 percent in 1881.[49] The increase was greater in St. Jacques than Ste. Anne, but the pattern was similar. Among boys in each ward, in contrast, the proportion at school was lower in 1871 than any other year, and the proportion of ten- to nineteen-year-olds at work increased. In Ste. Anne, in particular, the factories, workshops, and general labouring jobs attracted growing numbers of these youths. The percentage of fifteen- to nineteen-year-old boys reporting working in that ward increased from 38 in 1861 to 64 a decade later. While a certain number of families appear to have taken advantage of boom periods to draw their sons, in particular, out of school, the majority of families appear to have got the best of both worlds. Most working-class boys went to school for varying lengths of time before they reached thirteen or so, and then sought wage labour.

These figures confirm the greater importance of a son's wage contribution to the family economy. Girls' role is clear in the high proportion that continued to report neither a job nor school attendance. Transformations of the economy and the passage of time were slow to modify this gender difference in the relationship between girls' and boys' schooling and their roles in the family economy. A study conducted in Quebec in 1942, just before school was finally made compulsory in that province, found that among children quitting school before the age of sixteen, 61 percent of girls gave as their reason, "Maman avait besoin de moi," while 50 percent of boys stated, "Ma famille avait besoin d'argent." Only 10 percent of girls gave that reason.[50] The centrality of girls' domestic labour in a different Canadian city, Toronto, is corroborated by evidence showing that potential foster parents in that city at the turn of the century were four times more likely to seek girls than boys, specifically for their usefulness as domestics and nursemaids.[51]

CONCLUSION

Gender was clearly at work in both senses of the word in nineteenth-century Montreal. On the one hand, the labour market was characterized by a sexual division of labour which, despite the rapid and dramatic changes occurring in the period, limited the numbers of jobs where capitalists considered employing women. This was not immutable, as the cases where "girls" were used as strikebreakers made clear. Montreal's labour market included major sectors, particularly sewing and shoemaking, that employed large numbers of girls and women. Yet, the figures of labour-force participation rates for the two wards studied here suggest strongly that girls and women seldom entered the workforce in proportions equivalent to their brothers or boys the same age, and that over their life courses their participation was totally different.

The reasons why lie at least partially within the workings of the family-wage economy. Working-class families in Montreal clearly both needed and used additional family workers to counteract low wages, and to improve their standard of living. The number of extra workers varied with the skill of the family head and the worth of that skill in the labour market. Thus, while skilled workers managed, in good times, with fewer family workers than the unskilled or those in indentured trades, economic depression eroded such superiority. Yet in whatever complex and probably tension-loaded decisions were made about who would seek what kind of work, boys were much more likely to be the auxiliary wage earners than girls.

To explain why brings us, in a sense, to the heart of the debate about the relative importance of patriarchy and capitalism in explaining women's oppression.[52] That the domestic labour of wives has been crucial both to family survival and to women's inequality has long been recognized both empirically and theoretically. But where do daughters fit in? Fathers, one could argue, by keeping girls at home along with their mothers to serve their daily need for replenishment, ensured that the work of all women was viewed as intermittent and secondary to that of the major wage earners.[53] Alternatively, the accent can be put on the nature of specific industries, or more generally on the capitalist labour market, which, by setting women's wage rates at half those of men, made it logical to send boys to work rather than girls.[54] Unequal access to work on the same terms as men thus not only perpetuated women's position in the home, but tragically disadvantaged those single women and widows who alone, or supporting children or elderly parents, had to live on such wages.

Clearly a dialectic is at work here. Neither empirically nor theoretically can the workings of patriarchy or capitalism be neatly separated from each other.[55] The nature of the interaction between the two and the weight of one over the other will vary historically and geographically. Among Montreal families, decisions were made in part in relation to existing jobs and wage rates, and such decisions perpetuated and reified the idea that women's work was temporary, performed before marriage or in moments of family crisis.[56] Admitting the dialectic adds complexity to the explanation but remains, I suspect, insufficient, because the emphasis remains on the formal, wage-earning labour market. Domestic labour in the nineteenth century was fundamental to family survival, to the transformation of wages into a reasonable standard of living, and to the reproduction of the working class. Historians have recognized the importance of this job for the working-class wife and mother; the role of daughters has been examined less explicitly.[57] Yet, for nineteenth-century mothers whose children were widely spaced in age and in whose homes technology had made virtually no inroads to lighten their labour, the help of daughters was invaluable. Housewives had no control over the amount of wages the husband earned, and little over how much was turned over to them. Housework was labour intensive and time consuming. One of the only ways in which wives could control the content and intensity of their work was to get children to help. Wherever possible, once girls reached an age where they could be of use to the mother, they were used to babysit, to run errands, to clean, sew, and cook. If this could be combined with wage-earning activities, as in the case of homework in the sewing industry, then such girls did work more formally. If there were no brothers of an age to earn, daughters might work in factories, offices, or shops, or as domestics. But the need of mothers for at least one helper at home would mean that the rate of formal labour-force participation for girls would generally be lower than that for boys.[58] Patriarchal ideas within the working class, elements of male pride and self-interest, economic pragmatism, and the daily needs of mothers and housewives thus interacted, creating a situation in which most girls served an apprenticeship in domestic labour prior to, or in conjunction with, entering the workforce.[59] In cities and towns where the labour market was completely different, where whole families or women were explicitly sought by employers, this division of labour, indeed, the very institutions of marriage and the family, could be modified. The question of how to ensure that the necessary domestic labour was performed, however, would remain fundamental.[60] The working out of roles by gender at home would continue to influence the configurations of gender at work.

NOTES

1. Heidi Hartmann, "Capitalism, Patriarchy, and Job Segregation by Sex," *Signs* 1 (Spring 1976): 137–69; Judy Lown, "Not So Much a Factory, More a Form of Patriarchy: Gender and Class during Industrialisation," in E. Garmarnikow et al., *Gender, Class, and Work* (London, 1983); Sonya O. Rose, "Gender at Work: Sex, Class, and Industrial Capitalism," *History Workshop Journal* 21 (Spring 1986): 113–31; Nancy Grey Osterud, "Gender Divisions and the Organization of Work in the Leicester Hosiery Industry," in Angela V. John, *Unequal Opportunities: Women's Employment in England, 1800–1918* (Oxford: Basil Blackwell, 1986), 45–70; Sylvia Walby, *Patriarchy at Work: Patriarchal and Capitalist Relations in Employment* (Minneapolis: University of Minnesota Press, 1986); Ruth Milkman, *Gender at Work: The Dynamics of Job Segregation by Sex during World War II* (Urbana: University of Illinois Press, 1987). For Canadian articles touching on the question, see Gail Cuthbert Brandt, "The Transformation of Women's Work in the Quebec Cotton Industry, 1920–1950," in *The Character of Class Struggle: Essays in Canadian Working Class History, 1840–1985*, ed. Bryan D. Palmer (Toronto: McClelland and Stewart, 1986) pp. 115–134; Mercedes Steedman, "Skill and Gender in the Canadian Clothing Industry, 1890–1940," in *On the Job: Confronting the Labour Process in Canada*, ed. Craig Heron and Robert Storey (Montreal: McGill-Queen's University Press, 1986), 152–76; Marta Danylewycz and Alison Prentice, "The Evolution of the Sexual Division of Labour in Teaching: A Nineteenth-Century Ontario and Quebec Case Study," *Histoire sociale/Social History* 6 (1983): 81–109; Marta Danylewycz and Alison Prentice, "Teachers, Gender, and Bureaucratising School Systems in Nineteenth-Century Montreal and Toronto," *History of Education Quarterly* 24 (1984): 75–100; Jacques Ferland, "Syndicalisme parcellaire et syndicalisme collectif: Une interpretation socio-technique des conflits ouvriers dans deux industries québécoises, 1880–1914," *Labour/Le Travail* 19 (Spring 1987): 49–88.
2. This argument is obviously not mine alone. It is fundamental to much of the discussion of the workings of patriarchy and to the domestic labour debate, where too often it remains at an abstract theoretical level or based on cursory historical data. It is worth making here because much theoretical work places too much emphasis on either capitalist relations or reproduction and patriarchy, simplifying the complexity of relations between the two, while historical literature on the workplace or the family tends to treat the relation between the two simplistically.
3. Joy Parr's recent articles offer the first major sustained analysis in which decisions and conditions in the home and in the workplace and the relationship between the two are constantly and systematically examined. See especially "Rethinking Work and Kinship in a Canadian Hosiery Town, 1910–1950," *Feminist Studies* 13, 1

(Spring 1987): 137–62; and also "The Skilled Emigrant and Her Kin: Gender, Culture, and Labour Recruitment," *Canadian Historical Review* 68, 4 (Dec. 1987): 520–57, reprinted in *Rethinking Canada: The Promise of Women's History*, 2nd ed., ed. Veronica Strong-Boag and Anita Clair Fellman (Toronto: Copp Clark Pitman, 1991), 33–55. Gail Cuthbert-Brandt does so in a different sense in "Weaving It Together: Life Cycle and the Industrial Experience of Female Cotton Workers in Quebec, 1910–1950," *Labour/Le Travailleur* 7 (Spring 1981). Mark Rosenfeld's recent article "'It Was a Hard Life': Class and Gender in the Work and Family Rhythms of a Railway Town, 1920–1950," *Historical Papers* (1988), and reprinted in this volume [i.e., *Canadian and Australian Labour History*], carefully unravels how the rhythms of work in the running trades structured the family economy and gender roles in Barrie, Ontario, a railway town.

4. No Canadian work directly confronts this question either in the econometric sense in which Claudia Goldin poses it in "Family Strategies and the Family Economy in the Late Nineteenth Century: The Role of Secondary Workers," in *Philadelphia: Work, Space, Family and Group Experience in the Nineteenth Century*, ed. Theodore Hershberg (New York: Oxford University Press, 1981), 277–310, or in the more feminist and qualitative way that Lynn Jamieson poses it in "Limited Resources and Limiting Conventions: Working-Class Mothers and Daughters in Urban Scotland c. 1890–1925," in *Labour and Love: Women's Experience of Home and Family, 1850–1940*, ed. Jane Lewis (Oxford: Basil Blackwell, 1986), 49–69.

5. Marjorie Cohen makes a similar argument without elaborating on its implications for daughters in stating that "the supply of female labour was limited by the labour requirements of the home." *Women's Work, Markets, and Economic Development in Nineteenth-Century Ontario* (Toronto: University of Toronto Press, 1988), 139. Her insistence on the importance of domestic production and women's work in the home for rural and urban families alike and for an understanding of the wider economy represents an important contribution to economic history as well as to the history of women and the family in Canada.

6. On the average, in the early 1880s, for example, a labourer earned around $1.00 a day, a shoemaker $1.25, a carpenter $1.50, and various more highly skilled workers anything from $1.75 (blacksmith) up. See Bettina Bradbury, "The Working-Class Family Economy, Montreal, 1861–1881" (Ph.D. diss., Concordia University, 1984), 18; Canada, Parliament, *Sessional Papers*, 1882, Paper No. 4, Appendix 3, Annual Report of the Immigration Agent, 110–11, lists wages in a variety of trades.

7. In this, Montreal and Canada were little different from other cities and countries, nor has much of the discrepancy been eliminated today.

8. The figures used in this paper are derived from research done for my Ph.D. thesis, currently under revision for publication. A 10 percent random sample was taken of households enumerated by the census takers in Ste. Anne and St. Jacques in 1861, 1871, and 1881. This resulted in a total sample of 10 967 people over the three decades. They resided in 1851 households and 2278 families as defined by the census takers.

9. For a brief and preliminary examination of how widows of all ages survived, see my "Surviving as a Widow in Nineteenth-Century Montreal," *Urban History Review* 17, 3 (1989): 148–60, reprinted in *Rethinking Canada*, 2nd ed., ed. Strong-Boag and Fellman.

10. These life histories were re-created by tracing families between the censuses of 1861, 1871, and 1881.

11. Mss. Census, St. Jacques, 1881, 17, p. 110.

12. *Iron Moulders Journal*, Jan. and June, 1878, Report of Local 21; *Iron Moulders Journal*, Jan. 1876, Report of Local 21 and open letter from Local 21 to the editor, cited in Peter Bischoff, "La formation des traditions de solidarité ouvrière chez les mouleurs Montréalais: la longue marche vers le syndicalisme, 1859–1881," *Labour/Le Travail* 21 (Spring 1988): 22. Bischoff suggests, sensibly, that among moulders the homogenizing experience of these years of depression left them more open to the idea of including less skilled workers in their union in the 1880s. The widespread appeal of the Knights of Labour could be seen in the same light.

13. In 1861, for example, only 16 percent of those reporting jobs in these two wards were children residing at home; twenty years later nearly one-third of all reported workers were offspring living with their parents. Peter Bischoff found a similar trend among moulders. The percentage of moulders for the entire city of Montreal that were sons living with their parents rose from 25 percent in 1861 to nearly 40 percent in 1881. Peter Bischoff, "Les ouvriers mouleurs à Montréal, 1859–1881" (M.A. thesis, Université de Québec à Montréal, 1986), 108.

14. There is no doubt that the wage labour both of young children and married women was under-enumerated. However, as no labour laws existed in Quebec until 1885, and education was not compulsory until 1943, it is unlikely that fear of repercussions would have inhibited parents from responding as it might have elsewhere. It seems fair to assume that the under-reporting of children's jobs, and probably married women's, would have been no greater in Montreal than in other cities of Canada, England, or America, and probably less.

15. Tamara K. Hareven and Randolph Langenbach, *Amoskeag: Life and Work in an American Factory City* (New York: Pantheon Books, 1978), 262.

16. Caution has to be exercised when using reported jobs for women and children. There is a tendency now in some of the literature on the subject to suggest that gender differentials in workforce participation are largely a result of women's work not being adequately enumerated. While I am sure that some under-enumeration of women's work occurred in Montreal, as elsewhere, I don't think that under-enumeration can explain away the differential. Nor is the phenomenon easy to measure. More important, I think, was the nature of women's work, which, because of its lack of regularity, its more informal nature, was less likely to be reported. On the problem of under-reporting, see, in particular, Sally Alexander, "Women's Work in Nineteenth-Century London: A Study of the Years 1820–1850," in *The Rights and Wrongs of Women*, ed. Juliett Mitchell and Ann Oakley (London: Penguin Books, 1976), 63–66; Karen Oppenheim Mason, Maris Vinovskis, and Tamara K. Hareven, "Women's Work and the Life Course in Essex County, Massachusetts, 1880," in Tamara K. Hareven, *Transitions: The Family and the Life Course in Historical Perspective* (New York: Academic Press, 1979), 191; Margo A. Conk, "Accuracy, Efficiency and Bias: The Interpretation of Women's Work in the U.S. Census of Occupations, 1890–1940," *Historical Methods* 14, 2 (Spring 1981): 65–72; Edward Higgs, "Women, Occupations, and Work in the Nineteenth-Century Censuses," *History Workshop* 23 (Spring 1987).

17. Joan Scott and Louise Tilly, *Women, Work, and Family* (New York: Holt, Rinehart and Winston, 1979), 231.

18. Mss. Census, 1861, St. Jacques, 11, p. 7750.

19. By the end of the century the need for this kind of education of daughters was being explicitly preached by Montreal doctors and by church representatives, and was formalized in Quebec with the creation of *écoles ménagères* after the 1880s. Carole Dion, "La femme et la santé de la famille au Québec, 1890–1940" (M.A. thesis, Université de Montréal, 1984).

20. A. (Père) Mailloux, *Le manuel des parents Chrétiens* (Quebec, 1851, 1910), cited in Carole Dion, "La femme et la santé de la famille," 60–65.

21. L.A. Huguet-Latour, *L'Annuaire de Ville Marie: Origine, utilité, et progrès des institutions catholiques de Montréal* (Montreal, 1877), 165–70.

22. Marie-Paule Malouin, "Les rapports entre l'école privée et l'école publique: L'Académie Marie-Rose au 19e siècle," in *Maîtresses de maison, maîtresses d'école*, ed. Nadia Fahmy-Eid and Micheline Dumont (Montreal: Boreal Express, 1983), 90.

23. Québec, *Documents de la Session*, 1874, "Rapport du Ministre de l'instruction publique," vii.

24. In Lynn Jamieson's study of working-class mothers and daughters in Scotland, which is based on interviews, she makes it clear that mothers made different demands upon boys and girls in terms of the contributions they should make to the family economy. Mothers "pre-occupied with their housekeeping responsibilities" were much more likely to keep girls home from school to help with housework than to encourage boys to go out and earn. If a father died, for example, daughters or sons might enter full-time paid employment, but if a mother died "only daughters left school early to become full-time housekeepers." "Working-Class Mothers and Daughters in Scotland," in *Labour and Love*, 54, 65.

25. Mss. Census, Ste. Anne, 1881, 5, p. 1.

26. Mss. Census, Ste. Anne, 1881, 5, p. 1.

27. Mss. Census, Ste. Anne, 1881, 9, p. 208.

28. Mss. Census, St. Jacques, 1881, 17, p. 340.

29. "Report of the Commissioners Appointed to Enquire into the Working of the Mills and Factories of the Dominion and the Labour Employed Therein," Canada, Parliament, *Sessional Papers*, 1882, Paper No. 42, p. 2.

30. Annual Report of the Ontario Bureau of Industries, 1884, cited in Cohen, *Women's Work*, 128.

31. The fact that domestic service was Montreal's leading employment for girls, and that it usually involved living in, complicates this analysis of the work of children. Girls could work away from home as domestics and contribute their pay to their parents; they would not, however, figure among the average number of workers found in census families, nor would their experience be captured in the proportion of girls having a job. On the other hand, neither is that of any boys who left to find work in construction shanties, lumbering camps, railroad work, etc. The figures given in the text are always the percentages of those living in the ward, and with their parents, who reported a job. Those who lived and worked elsewhere are thus always removed from both the numerator and the denominator.

32. On the commissioners' concerns about this, see Susan Mann Trofimenkoff, "One Hundred and One Muffled Voices," in *The Neglected Majority: Essays in Canadian Women's History*, ed. Susan Mann Trofimenkoff and Alison Prentice (Toronto: McClelland and Stewart, 1977). How the working class viewed these morality issues requires examination.

33. Mss. Census, St. Jacques, 1871, 6, p. 137.

34. Mss. Census, St. Jacques, 1881, 12, p. 101.

35. Sydney Pollard, *The Genesis of Modern Management: A Study of the Industrial Revolution* (London: Edward Arnold, 1965), 162.

36. Royal Commission on the Relations of Capital and Labour (RCRCL), *Quebec Evidence*, evidence of Wm. C. McDonald, tobacco manufacturer, p. 529.

37. RCRCL, *Quebec Evidence*, anonymous evidence, p. 42.

38. RCRCL, *Quebec Evidence*, pp. 44–47.

39. RCRCL, *Quebec Evidence*, p. 91.

40. RCRCL, *Quebec Evidence*, evidence of Mrs. Levoise.

41. RCRCL, *Quebec Evidence*, evidence of a machinist, Hudon factory, Hochelaga, pp. 273–74.

42. RCRCL, *Quebec Evidence*, evidence of Adèle Lavoie, pp. 280–82.

43. RCRCL, *Quebec Evidence*, evidence of Patrick Ryan, cigar maker, p. 37; machinist, Hudon Mills, p. 271; Samuel Carsley, dry goods merchant, p. 15; Oliver Benoit, boot and shoemaker, p. 365; Henry Morton, printer, p. 297; F. Stanley, foreman at the Star, p. 331.

44. Here I am referring to the percentage of children at home as opposed to boarding, living with relatives, or living in someone else's house as a servant. The samples taken in each census do not allow me to follow children over time and identify those who actually left home.

45. The same process occurred in Hamilton, and in other cities that have been studied. See Michael Katz, *The People of Hamilton*, 257, 261; Mary P. Ryan, *The Cradle of the Middle Class: The Family in Oneida County, New York, 1790–1865* (New York: Cambridge University Press, 1981), 168–69; Richard Wall, "The Age at Leaving Home," *Journal of Family History* 8 (Fall 1983): 238.

46. For a careful analysis of the relationship between women's wages, costs of board, and decisions about where to live, see Gary Cross and Peter Shergold, "The Family Economy and the Market: Wages and Residence of Pennsylvania Women in the 1890s," *Journal of Family History* 11, 3 (1986): 245–66.

47. Paul Spagnoli, "Industrialization, Proletarianization and Marriage," *Journal of Family History* 8 (Fall 1983): 238.

48. Michael Anderson's careful analysis of which children left home shows that boys in Preston, Lancashire, were more likely to do so than girls. He believes children made "a conscious calculation of the advantages and disadvantages, in terms of the standard of living which they could enjoy," based on the wages they could make, their father's wage, and the amount they were required to hand over to their parents. *Family Structure*, 67, 127–29.

49. A similar, but greater, increase in girls' school attendance is described for Hamilton by Michael B. Katz and Ian E. Davey in "Youth and Early Industrialization," in *Turning Points: Historical and Sociological Essays on the Family*, ed. John Demos and Sarane Spence Boocock, pp. 81–119.

50. "Le problème des jeunes qui ne fréquent plus l'école," *École Sociale Populaire* 351 (April 1941), 26, cited by Dominique Jean, "Les familles québécois et trois politiques sociales touchant les enfants, de 1940 à 1960: Obligation scolaire, allocations familiales et loi controlant le travail juvenile" (Ph.D. diss., Université de Montréal, 1988).

51. "First Report of Work Under the Children's Protection Act," p. 26; "Third Report of Work Under the Children's Protection Act," p. 10, cited in John Bullen, "J.J. Kelso and the 'New' Child-Savers: The Genesis of the Children's Aid Movement in Ontario" (Paper presented to the CHA Annual Meeting, Windsor, Ont., June 1988), 35–38.

52. The usefulness of taking a category of women other than wives and mothers to test the soundness of contemporary feminist theory on this question is clear in the article of Danielle Juteau and Nicole Frenette, who start with an examination of the role of nuns in late-nineteenth- and early-twentieth-century Quebec, and use their insights to critique much contemporary feminist theory. "L'évolution des formes de l'appropriation des femmes: Des religieuses aux 'mères porteuses,'" *Canadian Review of Sociology and Anthropology* 25, 2 (1988).

53. One of the great advantages of the domestic labour debate was its recognition of the importance of housework and reproduction of labour power to capitalism. Less clear in much of the writing was the failure of most writers to acknowledge the interest of men in the perpetuation of domestic labour. For an elaboration of this critique, see Walby, *Patriarchy at Work*, 18–19.

54. Ruth Milkman criticizes labour-segmentation theory, early Marxist-feminist writing, and Hartmann's description of patriarchy for paying insufficient attention to the effect of industrial structure on the sexual division of labour and struggles over "woman's place" in the labour market. Looking much more concretely than theorists have done at specific industries, she argues that "an industry's pattern of employment by sex reflects the economic, political, and social constraints that are operative when that industry's labour market initially forms." *Gender at Work*, 7.

55. Herein lies the problem of the "dual systems" approach of Hartmann and others. Heidi Hartmann, "Capitalism, Patriarchy and Job Segregation by Sex," *Signs* (1977); Varda Burstyn, "Masculine Dominance and the State,"

in Varda Burstyn and Dorothy Smith, *Women, Class, Family, and the State* (Toronto: Garamond Press, 1985), pp. 45–89; Sylvia Walby succeeds better than others in drawing out the links between the two, but insists on their relative autonomy in *Patriarchy at Work*.

56. Canadian historians, whether in women's history or working-class history, are only just beginning to unravel this complex, dialectical relationship between the structure of the economy and the needs of the family, in interaction with both capital's and labour's definitions of gender roles. It is an unravelling that must continue if we are to understand how gender was at work and continues to work outside the workplace as well as within it.

57. Some of the problems faced by feminist theoreticians grappling with the relationship between women's oppression by males within marriage, their subordination in the labour market, and the wider forces of patriarchy stem from the assumption that only wives perform domestic labour. This seems to me a profoundly ahistorical view, and one that downplays the importance of the family as a place of socialization and training.

58. Here would be an example of mothers making choices that made their lives easier, but that in the long run perpetuated, even exaggerated, men's more privileged position in the marketplace. On this, see Gerder Lerner, *The Creation of Patriarchy* (Oxford: Oxford University Press, 1986), cited in Bonnie Fox, "Conceptualizing Patriarchy," *Canadian Review of Sociology and Anthropology* 25, 2 (1988): 165.

59. Psychological, Freudian theories about gender identity seem less important here than the practical day-to-day experience in the home and the role model of the mother. Nancy Chodorow, *The Reproduction of Mothering* (Berkeley: University of California Press, 1978).

60. For a superb description of the complex ways in which women in Paris, Ontario — a knitting town where job opportunities for women were much greater than for men — dealt with domestic labour, see Joy Parr, "Rethinking Work and Kinship in a Canadian Hosiery Town, 1910–1950," *Feminist Studies* 13, 1 (Spring 1987): 137–62.

Article Twenty-Five

Joe Beef of Montreal: Working-Class Culture and the Tavern, 1869–1889

Peter DeLottinville

Montreal was a city of contrasts. The casual tourist, following the advice of his *Strangers' Guide to Montreal*,[1] would spend days viewing florid Gothic and ornate Italian church architecture, the engineering marvel of Robert Stevenson's Victoria Bridge, and the various monuments to commercial power. This faithful *cicerone*, however, would not give the tourist the total picture of a nineteenth-century urban landscape. The official face of Canada's first city consisted of monuments to individual industry, public morality, and social harmony. Absent from the official guide were the inhabitants of the narrower streets — the factory workers, the frequenters of taverns, the waterfront street gangs, or the crowds of longshoremen outside the Allen Line office waiting for work. What the tourist needed to see was a monument to Montreal's working class. Had he accidentally wandered into Joe Beef's Canteen, the tourist might have found it, where the rules and procedures of official Montreal had little value.

During the late nineteenth century, Joe Beef's Canteen was a notorious part of that underworld which existed in the Victorian city.[2] Located in the centre of the waterfront district, the Canteen was the haunt of sailors and longshoremen, unemployed men and petty thieves. Middle-class Montreal saw this tavern as a moral hazard to all who entered and a threat to

Source: "Joe Beef of Montreal: Working-Class Culture and the Tavern, 1869–1889," *Labour/Le Travailleur* 8/9 (1981/1982): 9–40. © Canadian Committee on Labour History.

social peace. Yet if critics called the Canteen's owner, Charles McKiernan, the "wickedest man" of the city, working-class residents along the waterfront claimed McKiernan as their champion. His tavern was a popular drinking spot, but also a source of aid in times of unemployment, sickness, and hunger. For its patrons, Joe Beef's Canteen was a stronghold for working-class values and a culture which protected them from harsh economic times.

Primarily, this essay describes the working-class culture which grew around Joe Beef's Canteen and analyzes that culture in terms of the community which supported it. The efforts of middle-class organizations to improve the conditions of the waterfront labourers are examined in the light of this culture. Finally, by placing this culture within the major developments influencing Montreal during the 1880s, the decline of Joe Beef's Canteen can be understood. Through this process a clearer understanding of the relationship between cultural change and historic development can be reached.

As the recent lively debate bears witness,[3] the concept of working-class culture in historical analysis is both fruitful and problematic, and before entering into a detailed discussion of the working-class tavern, it is necessary to define this concept and establish the limitations of its application. Working-class culture covers a wide range of recreational, social, and job-related activities from labour day parades and trade union picnics to charivaris and the secret ceremonies of the Knights of Labor. While each form of culture can only be understood within its specific time and place, there was a common thread which made particular cultures working-class cultures. As Raymond Williams has stated, working-class culture embodies "a basic collective idea and the institutions, manners, habits of thought and intentions which proceed from this."[4] By assuming an "active mutual responsibility"[5] between workingmen, working-class culture offered an alternative to the individualist, competitive philosophy of the nineteenth-century middle class. Nothing was as common as a tavern in nineteenth-century Montreal, and because of this, working-class taverns probably represented one of the most basic forums of public discussion. Drawing their customers from the neighbouring streets, such meeting places were the first to sense a change in mood, or experience the return of economic prosperity. Joe Beef's Canteen, while attracting a wider clientele than most taverns, was essentially the same type of focal point for the dockyard workers. The uncommon aspect of the Canteen was the remarkable ability of Charles McKiernan, the tavern's owner, to transform this rather commonplace forum into a dynamic force for the working class of Montreal.

The depression which accompanied the 1870s had a great impact on those who, like the patrons of Joe Beef's Canteen, were at the bottom end of the economic scale. Gareth Stedman Jones, in his study of casual labour and unemployment, *Outcast London*, demonstrated that middle-class London saw the casual labourers of East London as unregenerated workers who had yet to accept the industrious habits of their fellow workingmen of the factories.[6] These "dangerous classes," much like the patrons of the Canteen, were perceived as a threat to social order. While Montreal's waterfront could not compare to the horrors of East London, Montreal's middle classes were concerned about a "dangerous class" united by a forceful, if eccentric, spokesman who articulated labourers' frustrations and demands. Joe Beef would have been taken much less seriously had his success not coincided with the increasing number of factory workers, both skilled and unskilled, who appeared on the streets of Montreal. Municipal authorities, encouraged by middle-class reformers, paid more attention to questions of public order and morality in the face of such a mass of new residents. Drunkenness, blood sports, and street brawls associated with the waterfront taverns could not be permitted to flourish if all workers were to adopt the disciplined virtues of the new industrial society.

Charles McKiernan was born on 4 December 1835, into a Catholic family in Cavan County, Ireland. At a young age, he entered the British Army and, after training at the Woolwich gunnery school, was assigned to the 10th Brigade of the Royal Artillery. In the

Crimean War, McKiernan's talent for providing food and shelter earned him the nickname of "Joe Beef," which would stay with him for the rest of his life. In 1864, McKiernan's Brigade was sent to Canada to reinforce the British forces at Quebec. By then a sergeant, McKiernan was put in charge of the military canteens at the Quebec barracks and later on St. Helen's Island. If army life had seemed an alternative to his Irish future, then McKiernan saw better opportunities in North America. In 1868, McKiernan bought his discharge from the Army and with his wife and children settled in Montreal, opening the Crown and Sceptre Tavern on St. Claude Street.[7]

By settling in Montreal, McKiernan joined an established Irish community which accounted for 20 percent of the total population. Centred in Griffintown, the largely working-class Irish had their own churches, national and charitable societies, political leaders, and businessmen.[8] And as a tavern owner, McKiernan entered a popular profession in a city with a liquor licence for every 150 inhabitants.[9] The increasing number of taverns caused one temperance advocate to lament that if trends continued Montreal was destined to become "the most drunken city on the continent."[10] The Crown and Sceptre, commonly known as "Joe Beef's Canteen," had a central location, with Griffintown and the Lachine Canal to the east and the extensive dockyards stretching out on either side. Business was good for Charles McKiernan.

In spite of the large numbers of taverns, Joe Beef's Canteen had an atmosphere, and a reputation, which was unique. Located in the waterfront warehouse district and at night identified only by a dim light outside the door, the Canteen housed a fantastic assortment of the exotic and the commonplace. One visitor described it as "a museum, a saw mill and a gin mill jumbled together by an earthquake; all was in confusion."[11] The barroom was crudely furnished with wooden tables and chairs, sawdust covering the floor to make cleaning easier. At one end of the bar, great piles of bread, cheese, and beef supplied the customers with a simple meal. Behind the bar a large mirror reflected a general assortment of bottles, cigar boxes, and curios. One bottle preserved for public display a bit of beef which lodged — fatally — in the windpipe of an unfortunate diner. The quick-witted McKiernan served his patrons with an easy manner. An imposing figure with a military bearing and fierce temper, the owner had few problems with rowdyism.[12]

Joe Beef's Canteen had a special type of patron, and McKiernan aptly referred to his establishment as the "Great House of Vulgar People." His clientele was mostly working class. Canal labourers, longshoremen, sailors, and ex-army men like McKiernan himself were the mainstays of the business. Along with these waterfront workers, Joe Beef's Canteen attracted the floating population along the Atlantic coast. W.H. Davies, in his *Autobiography of a Super-Tramp*, remarked that, "not a tramp throughout the length and breadth of the North American continent . . . had not heard of [Joe Beef's Canteen] and a goodly number had at one time or another patronized his establishment."[13] McKiernan's tavern was also a well-known rendezvous for the "sun-fish" or "wharf-rats" of the harbour who lived a life of casual employment and poverty. Newspaper reporters often dropped into the tavern to check on petty criminals who mingled with the crowd. Unemployed labourers visited the Canteen in the early morning to look for a day's labour and often remained there throughout the day in the hope of something turning up. In all it was not a respectable crowd[14] and, no doubt, was shunned by the more self-respecting artisans of the neighbourhood.

For working-class Montreal, the tavern held attractions beyond the simple comforts of food and drink. With no public parks in the immediate area, and only occasional celebrations by national societies and church groups, their daily recreational activities were centred around places like Joe Beef's Canteen. McKiernan's tavern was exceptionally rich in popular recreations. A menagerie of monkeys, parrots, and wild cats of various kinds were from time to time exhibited in the Canteen, but it was McKiernan's bears which brought in the crowds. Joe Beef's first bear, named Jenny and billed as the "sole captive" of the "courageous" 1869 expedition to the North West, never retired sober during the last three years of her life. One of her cubs inherited the family weakness. Tom, who had a daily consumption of twenty pints of beer, was often as "drunk as a coal heaver" by closing. Indeed, Tom was one of the regulars, usually sitting on his hind quarters and taking his pint between his paws, downing it without spilling a drop. Local temperance men had always pointed out that drink turned men into animals, but in observing Tom's habits Joe Beef could point out this curious reversal of behaviour which the Canteen produced.[15] Other bears were kept in the tavern's cellar and viewed by customers through a trap door in the barroom floor. Occasionally, McKiernan brought up the bears to fight with some of his dogs or play a game of billiards with the proprietor.

The tavern was not an ideal place for animals and one observer remarked on the mangy, dirty, and listless character of the bears.[16] Beatings were often used to rouse the animals into their "naturally" ferocious state. Sometimes McKiernan was mauled during these demonstrations and once a buffalo on exhibit sent him to hospital for a number of days.[17] A Deputy Clerk of the Peace, inspecting the tavern to renew its licence, was bitten by one of Joe Beef's dogs.[18] There was little public outcry over these conditions. Montreal's Royal Society for the Prevention of Cruelty to Animals was still a fledgling organization in the 1870s which spent its time regulating butchers' practices and prosecuting carters for mistreatment of their horses. As long as they presented no public danger, McKiernan's menagerie was left undisturbed.

Although lacking formal education, Charles McKiernan considered himself a man of learning and regularly read the *New York Journal*, the *Irish American*, the *Irish World*, and local newspapers. He employed a musician (which was illegal under the terms of his licence) to entertain his customers. Regular patrons played the piano in the tavern. McKiernan, however, led much of the entertainment. Drawing on personal experience and varied readings, McKiernan eagerly debated topics of the day, or amused patrons with humorous poems of his own composition. He had a remarkable ability to ramble on for hours in rhyming couplets. Sometimes to achieve this end, he distorted the accepted English pronunciation beyond recognition. This disgusted some middle-class visitors to the Canteen, but regular customers clearly enjoyed these feats of rhetoric.[19] Behind the bar, two skeletons were hung from the wall and served as props for McKiernan's tales. From time to time, the skeletons represented the mortal remains of McKiernan's first wife, his relatives in Ireland, or the last of an unfortunate temperance lecturer who mistakenly strayed into Joe Beef's Canteen one night.

From the occasional poetry which McKiernan printed in the newspapers, the style and subjects of these evenings can be seen. Concentrating on the figures of authority in the workingman's life, the employer, the Recorder, the landlord, or the local minister, McKiernan's humour allowed his patrons a temporary mastery over the forces which dominated their lives outside the Canteen doors. Inside the Canteen, the rights of the common man always triumphed. On local issues, McKiernan complained about the lack of municipal services for the waterfront community. He demanded,

> Fair play for Sammy, Johnny and Pat as
> well as the Beaver Hall Bogus Aristocrat![20]

Legal authority, most familiar to his patrons through the Recorder's Court, was also denounced, but feared. An engraving of the Recorder looked down on the patrons from above the bar, and wedged into the frame were a number of dollar bills and notes which served as a reserve fund. McKiernan used this fund to pay fines imposed upon his regular customers.[21] Since most depended upon day labour, even a short jail term could spell disaster for the labourers' families. Imprisonment in lieu of fines was a very contentious issue, as the vehemence of the following poem illustrates.

> They have taken me from my father,
> They have taken me from my mother,
> They have taken me from my sister,
> They have taken me from my brothers,
> In this wintry season of woe
> And for the sake of *one* paltry, lousy *Dollar*,
> Down to jail, for to die, like a Dog, amongst *Bugs* and *Vermin*, I had to go.
> I died amongst howling and laughter,
> I died howling for a drink of water
> But you living *Tyrants*, and *Two Legged Monsters* take warning and remember that cold,
> cold Saturday Morning!!!
> For man's vengeance is swift, though God's vengeance is with some, rather slow.[22]

McKiernan himself was no stranger to the Recorder's Court. In July 1867, the tavern keeper faced charges from a disgruntled patron who had been roughly thrown into the street for rowdyism. On different occasions, McKiernan's musician and a former servant complained of beatings they had received for drunkenness on the job.[23] Along with the violations of his liquor licence, such incidents illustrated that Joe Beef's legal opinions were grounded in experience.

Another prominent subject in Joe Beef's Canteen was the economic depression which hovered over Montreal for much of the 1870s. As casual labourers, the Canteen's patrons were severely affected by commercial slumps. In "Joe Beef's Advice to Biddy, the Washerwoman," McKiernan wrote,

> I must tell you that Kingston is dead, Quebec is
> Dying and out of Montreal, Ottawa and Toronto hundreds are flying
> In the country parts unless you can
> Parlez-vous, There is nothing for you to do
> And in John's office it is all the cry
> No Union printers for work need apply
> And if the landlord his rent you cannot
> Pay your sewing machine he will take
> Away. So in the fall God help the
> Poor of Montreal.[24]

The unwillingness of the private and public authorities to provide adequate relief systems also attracted Joe Beef's notice. In a parody of the economic theories of industrialists, McKiernan professed,

> Joe Beef of Montreal, the Son of the People,
> He cares not for the Pope, Priest, Parson or King
> William of the Boyne; all Joe wants is the Coin.
> He trusts in God in the summer time to keep him
> from all harm; when he sees the first frost and
> snow poor old Joe trusts to the Almighty Dollar
> and good maple wood to keep his belly warm.[25]

These were problems which his patrons had little difficulty in understanding.

Central to all of McKiernan's pronouncements was the belief that the common problems of casual labourers and the poor of Montreal should overcome the religious and national differences which separated them. Joe Beef did "not give a damn Whether he is an Indian a Nigger a Cripple a Billy or a Mich"[26] when attempting to help the unemployed. What the unemployed and casual labourer lacked, in McKiernan's opinion, was a common voice. Since no one else was likely to assume that role, Joe Beef became the self-appointed champion of the waterfront workers. His success was remarkable as he gained the confidence of his neighbours and attracted the attention of many residents who were unaware of the poor conditions on their doorstep. He made friends with both English and French journalists, and Joe Beef's Canteen and the waterfront community appeared regularly in the press. While such publicity was good for the Canteen, few accused McKiernan of self-interest. "Joe Beef" became so well known that few knew precisely who Charles McKiernan was. And despite his Irish background, Joe Beef had considerable appeal to French-Canadian workers as well, if one can judge popularity from the coverage Joe Beef received in the French-language press.

The recreational aspects of Joe Beef's Canteen covered only a narrow spectrum of the interaction between the tavern owner and his patrons. As the focal point of social activities, Joe Beef's Canteen also provided the initiative for a number of social services which were a logical outgrowth of the close relationship between McKiernan and his neighbourhood. His role in alleviating problems of housing, job hunting, health care, and labour unrest indicated the possibility of a collective response to the common problems among casual labourers of Montreal's waterfront.

The most visible service which Joe Beef's Canteen offered was a cheap place to stay for transient and single workers. In the Crown and Sceptre, the barroom was situated next to a dining room and sleeping quarters. The sleeping area contained about 40 wooden sofas which served as beds. At eleven o'clock, boarders deposited ten cents at the bar and were handed a blanket. The men then spread a mattress over the wooden sofa, stripped off all their clothes, and went to sleep. McKiernan insisted that all his boarders sleep naked as a matter of cleanliness. Those found dirty were ordered upstairs to use one of the wash tubs. Each boarder also had to have his hair cut short, and those failing to meet the standards were sent to Joe Beef's "inspector of health," or barber, to comply. No conversation was permitted after eleven o'clock and everyone was roused out of bed at seven sharp. These rules were enforced personally by McKiernan in his best British Army sergeant's manner. Three-quarters of the tavern's boarders were boys between the ages of twelve and fourteen who earned their living selling newspapers. For twenty cents a day, they received their food and lodging and, although the conditions set down by Joe Beef might be draconian, they were clearly preferred to similar facilities offered by church organizations. Indeed, the Crown and Sceptre proved such a popular place that one of the prime reasons for moving to Common Street in 1876 was the lack of space. His waterfront location had room for 200 men.[27]

Fees for room and board were often waived for those without the means to pay such modest sums. McKiernan's tavern was also close to the sources of casual employment, which was an important consideration when a day's work might depend on arriving early on the job site. McKiernan often loaned shovels to men engaged in snow shovelling and other jobs. And as the natural resting place for all types of labourers on the docks, Joe Beef's Canteen was an ideal location to learn who might be hiring in the future. In this way, the tavern allowed transient workers to familiarize themselves with the local labour market and to make a decision whether to stay in Montreal or move on.[28]

Other social services grew informally as local residents turned to McKiernan for assistance in times of trouble. When a Lachine Canal labourer was injured during a blasting operation, fellow workers brought him to Joe Beef's to recuperate. After two men got into a drunken brawl and the loser stripped naked in the street, the crowd brought the man to Joe Beef's for care. A young immigrant who collapsed on the docks also ended up in the tavern for convalescence. While Joe Beef's served as a neighbourhood clinic, McKiernan's folk cures left much to be desired. The young immigrant was treated with a vinegar-soaked towel bound tightly around his head. McKiernan also professed faith in cayenne pepper and whiskey to cure cramps and Canadian cholera. All this in twenty minutes.[29] Still, many people in the nineteenth century attributed medicinal powers to alcohol, and McKiernan did state an intention to take courses at the Montreal General Hospital to improve his knowledge of basic medicine.

These experiences led the tavern owner to lobby established medical institutions to improve health care services for waterfront residents. In December 1879, he set up a collection box in his tavern for the Montreal General Hospital and invited his customers to contribute. Donating one-tenth of his receipts from all his dinners and a similar share of his boarding house income, McKiernan hoped to raise $500 a year. In the following years, McKiernan offered $100 to the Montreal General if they would provide a doctor to attend the poor in their homes. The hospital declined the offer. Unsuccessful in a more formal improvement of health care services, McKiernan continued to provide emergency relief. When the body of a suicide was buried in August 1883, the tavern keeper provided a tombstone.[30]

The question of class allegiance was most clearly defined by the incidents of labour unrest which periodically disrupted the city. In December 1877, over 1000 labourers working on the enlargement of the Lachine Canal abandoned their picks and shovels after a reduction in wages. The Irish and French workers paraded behind a tricolour flag along the canal banks and drove off those who refused to participate in the strike. Following a riot at the offices of canal contractor William Davis, during which the strike leader was shot, the Prince of Wales Rifles were called out to protect the canal and those workers who continued to work at reduced wages.[31] The strikers demanded a wage increase to a dollar a day, a nine-hour day, regular fort-nightly payments, and an end to the "truck system" of payment.[32] Among the Montreal citizens, there appeared to be some sympathy with the poor working conditions of the labourers, notably from the *Montreal Witness* and local MP Bernard Devlin,[33] but the militant behaviour of the strikers was generally condemned.

Strongest support for the strikers came from the waterfront community. Practical in all things, McKiernan realized that strikers, like the army, travel on their stomachs. On the morning of 20 December, he sent 300 loaves of bread, 36 gallons of tea, and a similar quantity of soup. These supplies required two wagons to be delivered. In addition to feeding the strikers, McKiernan took in as many as the Canteen could hold. One night 300 people found shelter under his roof. Throughout the strike McKiernan was observed "carting loaves and making good, rich soup in mammoth boilers, as if he were a commissary-general with the resources of an army at his back."[34] No doubt his military training was put to the test in maintaining order in his kitchen. That background also made the tavern keeper aware of the awkward position of the Prince of Wales Rifles who had been hastily summoned to guard the canal. To ensure that the soldier ate as well as a striker, McKiernan despatched a wagon of bread to the men on duty. The soldiers saw the humour in Joe Beef's assistance and gave most of the bread away to the crowd.[35] Some of the tension between striker and soldier was successfully released.

McKiernan, of course, was not popular with the canal contractors for his whole-hearted support of the labourers. William Davis, pointing suspiciously to the fourteen taverns in the immediate area, wrote that the strike was caused by outside trouble makers. Another con-tractor was more direct in his accusations. "All of the trouble which we have had on the canal this winter has been caused mostly by men that never worked a day on the canal and have been started in a low Brothel kept by one *Joe Beef* who seems to be at the head of it all."[36] Despite this claim, McKiernan had only a supporting role in the labourers' actions, but such comments indicated the success of McKiernan's efforts to aid the strike.

Besides using his Canteen to take care of the strikers' physical needs, McKiernan also used his skills as an orator to attract public attention to the strikers' demands. By 1877, Joe Beef was a figure of some notoriety in Montreal and the local press found that his exploits made good copy. His support of the strike was reported extensively in Montreal and even in one Ottawa newspaper. The strikers' first meeting took place outside Joe Beef's Canteen and the tavern owner was asked to say a few words. Those nightly discussions in the tavern had given McKiernan a remarkable ease with language, and his talent for speaking in rhyming couplets was not wasted. Most of his speech to the crowd was in rhyming form, which so impressed the *Montreal Witness* reporter that he apologized for only reporting the substance of the speech and not its form as well. McKiernan explained his actions in the following terms.

> I have been brought up among you as one of yourselves since I was a boy running about barefooted. When I heard of the strike on the Lachine Canal, I thought I would try to help you, for I knew that men employed there had much to put up with. So I sent you bread to help you hold out. I could not send you whiskey, because you might get drunk, and commit yourselves. In this way you might have injured your cause, and perhaps made the volunteers fire on you. (Laughter) . . . The greatest philanthropists in the world are in Montreal, and the public here will sympathize with you. They will not see you tyrannized over. But if you are riotous, depend upon it, as sure as you are men before me, the law will take it in hand and crush you. I have nothing against the contractors and you will succeed by speaking rightly to them. You will get your $1 a day for nine hours, or perhaps for eight hours (cheers) or perhaps more (loud cheers). But keep orderly; mind your committee.[37]

The speech was received with "deafening" cheers.

These mass meetings organized by the strike committee were an important part of their efforts to secure better working conditions. Since the canal enlargement was a federal project, Alexander Mackenzie's government was anxious to have it completed before the next election. Failure to live up to this previous election promise would cost the Liberals votes in Montreal.[38] By rallying public support for their cause, the strikers hoped that Ottawa would intervene on their behalf and compel the contractors to make concessions. As the strike continued, the size of the mass meetings grew. In Chaboillez Square 2000 people assembled to hear McKiernan and other speakers. Joe Beef lectured on the theme of the "Almighty Dollar."

> My friends, I have come here tonight to address you on "the Almighty Dollar." The very door bells of Montreal ring with the "Almighty Dollar." The wooden-headed bobbies nail you, and you have to sleep on the hard floor provided by the City Fathers, and the next morning the fat Recorder tells you: "Give me the 'Almighty Dollar,' or down you go for eight days." The big-bugs all have their eyes on the "Almighty Dollar," from the Bishop down, and if you die in the hospital, they want the almighty dollar to shave you and keep you from the students. No one can blame you for demanding the "Almighty Dollar" a day. The man who promises 90¢ a day and pays only 80¢ is no man at all. The labourer has his rights.[39]

Public support for the strikers did not alter the fact that the labourers were without income, and after eight days on strike, they returned to the canal at the old wages.[40]

The canal labourers, however, refused to admit defeat. In mid-January, a strike committee went to Ottawa with funds raised by McKiernan and others in order to plead their cause before Alexander Mackenzie. They reduced their demands to the single request that the contractors pay them every fortnight in cash.[41] Mackenzie was sympathetic but non-committal. When the committee returned to Montreal, the mass meetings became overtly political and the problems of the canal labourers were attributed to the inaction of the Liberal government.[42] Meanwhile,

Mackenzie had ordered an investigation into the Lachine situation which revealed the wide-spread use of store payment which considerably reduced the real wages of the labourers. Sensing a political disaster in the making, the government ordered the contractors to end store payments.[43] All contractors complied immediately and the labourers won a modest victory. McKiernan's efforts, while not the only factor in this outcome, did help the strikers publicize their demands and eased their physical hardships. In doing so, he demonstrated the potential strength of a waterfront community united in a common cause.

The canal labourers' strike was McKiernan's most extensive effort in aiding strikers, but not his only involvement. During a strike against the Allen line, ship labourers used the Canteen as a rallying point and the flag they used in their parades came from the tavern. In April 1880, when the Hochelaga cotton mill workers struck, Joe Beef again assumed his role as people's commissary-general by supplying the strikers with bread.[44] Such incidents illustrated how the working-class culture which centred around the tavern could be mobilized to produce benefits for the Canteen's patrons. But in doing so, McKiernan also attracted the criticism of middle-class reformers who felt that such a culture encouraged workers in a dangerous behaviour which threatened the social stability of Montreal.

During the 1870s, middle-class reformers began to enter into the waterfront community to assist the workingman in overcoming his social and economic poverty. The YMCA, the Salvation Army, as well as local employers and clergy, all found themselves confronted by an existing culture and community services centred around Joe Beef's Canteen. Their response to McKiernan's activities illustrated the immense social differences between the middle and working class of Montreal. One visitor to the city described Joe Beef's Canteen as a "den of robbers and wild beasts" over which McKiernan presided, "serving his infernal majesty in loyal style." The patrons were "unkempt, unshaven, fierce-looking specimens of humanity," and "roughs of various appearances, ready apparently, either to fight, drink, or steal, if the opportunity offered." In conclusion, this visitor wrote, "As we came away from his canteen where we felt that dirt, bestiality, and devilment held high carnival, my friend said, 'I believe Joe is worse than his bears and lower down in the scale of being than his monkeys. No monkey could ever be Joe's ancestor, though he is the father of wild beasts that prey on society.' "[45] While Montreal's middle class did not engage in the "slumming parties" which were popular in London, portrait painter Robert Harris and his companion William Brymmer visited the Canteen to satisfy their curiosity.[46] The actions of middle-class men on the waterfront revealed a fundamental misunderstanding of the nature of the working-class behaviour which they observed.

The common middle-class picture of the waterfront community was one of drunkenness, immorality, and lawlessness. Waterfront taverns like the Canteen, or French Marie's, were described by the Montreal Police Chief as "hot beds of all that is vicious" whose patrons were "always on the look out for mischief, and whose chief and most relished pastime seems to consist in attacking the police, rescuing prisoners, and spreading terror."[47] Sub-Chief Lancy reported that the only reason why police did not close down Joe Beef's Canteen was that "it is better to have all these characters kept in one place so that they might be dropped upon by the detectives."[48] Indeed, there was much truth to police complaints about public order on the waterfront, but they were less than candid in public statements about the role which men like Charles McKiernan played in the maintenance of order. The Black Horse Gang, composed of working-class youths, roamed the waterfront for years, extorting drinking money from lone pedestrians and robbing drunken sailors. Implicated in at least one death, the Black Horse Gang rarely faced prosecution because their violent reputation intimidated many witnesses from pressing charges. And the Black Horse Gang did frequent Joe Beef's Canteen, or at least until October 1876, when McKiernan threw four of its members out into the street for rowdiness. Ironically, one of the gang members attempted to lay charges against the tavern owner for injuries resulting from the incident.[49] The waterfront also harboured "Joe Beef's Gang," which in November 1878 was involved in a market square battle with local butchers.[50]

Violations of public order, however, must be distinguished from acts of criminality. Indeed, McKiernan was known to assist the police in their efforts to capture criminals. Police arrested ten men on charges of highway robbery in September 1880 following a tip from McKiernan. In minor cases, the tavern owner was called upon to give character references for waterfront residents. McKiernan's censure was enough to send a local street gang leader to two months' hard labour. When the prisoner tried to retaliate by charging Joe Beef's Canteen with violations of its liquor licence, the judge, grateful for the favour to the court, refused to admit the evidence.[51] McKiernan, like many working-class people, did not consider occasional drunkenness or acts of rowdyism sufficient cause to send men to jail, especially if imprisonment meant certain ruin for a labourer's family. The informal, if sometimes rough, justice which McKiernan enforced upon his patrons was obviously preferable to the legal penalties of the court. While not publicly admitting such an accommodation, the Montreal police found that such informal cooperation worked in their favour.

The difference between the middle-class attitude toward the police and that of the waterfront residents was illustrated by the experience of the YMCA's first venture into the area. As an alternative to the saloon, the YMCA established a reading room on Craig Street. In January 1877, eight men were arrested there for creating a disturbance, and the *Montreal Witness* accused McKiernan of offering a reward to the men who closed down the operation. The tavern owner refuted these charges by pointing out that the incident had occurred only because of the YMCA's mishandling of the situation. As McKiernan explained, "Joe Beef never called on one policeman to arrest any of those men who frequent *his* place. If those eight had only been sent to him he would have given them work and food and sent them back better behaved."[52] By using the police to settle their problems, the YMCA violated one of the unwritten rules of behaviour on the waterfront.

The influence of waterfront taverns upon sailors visiting Montreal was a constant concern among ship owners. Searches for deserting sailors often started with a visit to Joe Beef's Canteen and a quick check of its customers. As an alterative to the tavern, the Montreal Sailors Institute was established in 1869 "a stone's throw" from nine taverns. Open from May to November, the Institute had a reading room, writing desks, stationery, and sabbath services. Food, for a price, could be bought but not alcohol. In 1879, the Institute sold 4885 cups of coffee and confidently concluded that "Every cup lessen[ed] much the demand for whiskey." Encouraging sailors to sign abstinence pledges, the Institute recognized that sober sailors were dependable sailors.[53] But like the YMCA, the Institute had little understanding or sympathy for the working-class culture of the neighbourhood. The Institute manager, Robert R. Bell, described tavern patrons as "the lowest and most depraved human beings."[54] Dock workers, in particular, he found "a class much given to alcoholic liquors."[55] Bell lamented the inability to enforce the Sunday liquor laws and suggested the local policemen were in league with the tavern keepers. In his attempts to save the waterfront workers from their own culture as well as from economic hardship, Bell was typical of the middle-class professionals who came into the area. With 60 percent of the Institute's budget earmarked for the salary of Bell and his two assistants, and liberal contributions from local ship owners,[56] the motives behind such projects were viewed suspiciously by the waterfront workers.

The most ardent attempts to reform the moral and social habits of the waterfront workers came from Montreal's clergy. The importance of the church in nineteenth-century social welfare services need not be recounted here,[57] but the resources of Montreal's various churches dwarfed anything which the waterfront community could organize on its own. McKiernan's public attitude toward all denominations of clergy was openly hostile. He wrote that

"Churches, Chapels, Ranters, Preachers, Beechers and such stuff Montreal has already got enough."[58] The cartoon from *Le Canard* illustrated quite clearly that Joe Beef would look almost anywhere for salvation before turning to the church. Respectable Montreal was shocked in 1871 when McKiernan buried his first wife. On leaving the cemetery, he ordered the band to play the military tune, "The Girl I Left Behind Me." This so outraged the *Montreal Witness* that its editor only described the funeral as a "ludicrous circumstance" without going into details.[59] And, probably to his great delight, McKiernan actually convinced the census taker in 1881 that he was a practising *Baptist!*[60]

Clergy who ventured onto the waterfront, however, were sometimes pleasantly surprised at McKiernan's behaviour. John Currie, a Presbyterian minister, ventured into Joe Beef's Canteen to preach to its patrons as an "act of Faith." After some initial heckling from the tavern owner, Currie was allowed to finish his sermon. On its conclusion, McKiernan offered any man who went to Currie's services a dinner and night's lodging for free.[61] The YMCA and a "Hot Gospeller" at different times held religious services in the dining room attached to Joe Beef's Canteen. The apparent contradiction in McKiernan's public and private behaviour originated with his general distrust of a clergy which was essentially middle class. Once he viewed individual ministers at close range and found them willing to treat his patrons as their equals — at least before the eyes of God — then the tavern keeper had no objection to their work. As Joe Beef reported to the press,

> A Preacher may make as many proselytes as he chooses in my canteen, at the rate of ten cents a head. That's my price . . . for if I choose to give myself the trouble I could make them embrace any faith or none at all or become free thinkers.[62]

Not all preachers received a welcome into Joe Beef's Canteen. Mr. Hammond, a travelling revivalist whose views on tobacco and drink were at odds with McKiernan's, was invited to the Canteen for a debate. Before the evening was out, Mr. Hammond had been chased around the Canteen by a pack of Joe Beef's bears and dogs to the general amusement of the tavern's patrons.[63] When the Salvation Army first appeared in Montreal, McKiernan supported them. With their military bearing and brass-band approach to salvation, they were a natural to play outside the Canteen, and McKiernan paid them to do so. This harmonious relationship abruptly ended when an Army officer called the Canteen "a notorious *rendez-vous* of the vicious and depraved."[64] Shortly afterwards the band was arrested for disturbing the peace and McKiernan was suspected of being behind the complaint.

These clashes between the local clergy, reform groups, the police, and Joe Beef were carefully chronicled by the editor of the *Montreal Witness*, John Dougall. Dougall founded the *Witness* to instruct the general public in the Christian way of life and frequently drew upon Joe Beef for examples of modern depravity. Dougall was not unsympathetic to the economic hardships of Montreal's working class. He gave extensive coverage to the 1877 canal labourers' strike and attacked industrialists for their lack of concern over the moral implications of modern industry upon employees. But Dougall was convinced that the working-class culture which centred around taverns was a dangerous influence for all workingmen. As one contemporary described Dougall, he was "a fighter in the cause of temperance, of political purity, of public morals, of municipal righteousness, of Free Trade and of aggressive Christianity."[65] The unyielding earnestness of Dougall's public statements made him a frequent target for Joe Beef's satires. A typical verse stated,

> Bitter beer I will always drink,
> and Bitter Beer I will always draw
> and for John and his song singing
> Ranters never care a straw.[66]

When the *Witness* dismissed six of its printers for belonging to the International Typographers Union, McKiernan naturally sided with the union's efforts to have the men reinstated.[67]

Dougall characterized Joe Beef as the "hunter for the souls of men"[68] and, instead of seeing the social services which surrounded the Canteen as a positive contribution to the community, believed that these were merely clever ways of entrapping unsuspecting workers into a world of drink and sin. The death of John Kerr in April 1879 confirmed Dougall's conviction. Kerr was a regular at the Canteen who made his living doing odd jobs around the docks. One day in April, Kerr did not go out to work and by nightfall had drank himself to death. During the Coroner's inquest, McKiernan explained his policy of never calling in the police. When men got rowdy, he simply put them in a room under the bar to sleep it off. Customers, McKiernan went on, were never treated roughly and they were "all in good health. We never club them; you know you can squeeze a man to make him do what you want, without beating him."[69] Kerr, a well-behaved man and often sick, was never treated in this manner. Yet the existence of the "Black Hole" (as the jury foreman described it) caught Dougall's attention. In a scathing editorial, the *Witness* charged that McKiernan preyed on the unemployed in a merciless way.

> What an empire within an empire is this, where law is administered and Her Majesty's peace kept without expense to Her Majesty. How joyfully should Government renew the licence of this carer of the poor, who can squeeze a man even to the last cent he wants, even to go uncomplainingly to prison, or to working for him all day with the snow shovel he provides, and bringing home his earning daily and nightly to hand over the counter for the poison which is his real pay.[70]

Dougall demanded the Canteen's licence be revoked. The coroner's jury, however, did not see anything illegal in the unconventional practices of Joe Beef.

"Into Africa" was the phrase that one visitor to the waterfront used to describe his experience, and the social isolation of the middle and working classes of Montreal in the 1870s was quite remarkable. Yet these initial failures for the reformers did not stop their efforts, and throughout the coming decades they continued to establish links between the waterfront and the rest of the city. McKiernan, though suspicious, was not entirely hostile to these men addressing themselves to the obvious problems of the casual labourers. Their working-class culture was still strong enough to ensure that social assistance did not mean social control. Forces beyond the control of the waterfront community, however, were already weakening that culture.

The world of Joe Beef, which developed during the 1870s, continued to function throughout the 1880s, but its dynamic qualities appeared to be on the wane. Joe Beef's public profile certainly declined in the 1880s. The eventual disintegration of this culture cannot be attributed to any single factor either within the working-class community or from some of the larger developments of the decade. A combination of factors, including a decasualization of dockwork, the rise of the Knights of Labor, plus new attitudes toward leisure and urban conditions, made the survival of Joe Beef's Canteen beyond the death of its owner unlikely.

As a waterfront tavern, Joe Beef's Canteen depended upon the patronage of the longshoremen who unloaded and loaded the ships in the Montreal harbour. Longshoremen worked irregular hours, sometimes as long as 36 hours at a stretch. Crews were hired by stevedores who contracted with a ship's captain to unload the vessel for a fixed price and provided the necessary equipment. Longshoremen, therefore, spent long periods of time on the docks either working, or contacting stevedores about the prospects for employment. With between 1700 and 2500 men competing for work, individuals had to spend much of their time ensuring that they earned the average wage of $200 per season.[71] Given these job conditions, the attraction of a waterfront tavern where one could eat, sleep, drink, and scout around for employment cannot be underestimated.

The nature of employment on the docks began to change in the mid-1880s. H. & A. Allen Company, one of the larger shipping firms in the port, introduced a system of contract labour. Over 100 longshoremen signed contracts directly with the shipping company, which guaranteed steady employment for the season. The contract specified that each contract employee would have to pay 1 percent of his wages toward an accident insurance plan, as well as agree to have 10 percent of his total wages held back until the end of the season. Any man who left before the term of his contract forfeited claim to these wages. With a rate of 25 cents per hour, the pay of the Allen contract employees was slightly better than that of regular longshoremen, but these relinquished their traditional rights to refuse work which did not suit them.[72] Longshoremen testifying before the 1889 Royal Commission on the Relations of Capital and Labour were certainly critical of the contract system, which most felt gave the company a guaranteed labour supply without contributing greatly to the welfare of the longshoremen.[73] While the contract system accounted for only a fraction of the total labour force on the docks, the Allen Company's desire to "decasualize" their labour force was an indication of the future. Such a system made a convenient tavern unnecessary.

It was no coincidence that the Allen Company attempted to introduce the contract system among longshoremen at the same time that labour organizations appeared on the waterfront. Edmund Tart told the Royal Commission that he belonged to a "secret trades organization" which existed on the docks.[74] Possibly a local of the Knights of Labor, the union had its own benefit plan to offset the Allen Company insurance scheme. Patrick Dalton, a longshoreman for the Allen Company, testified against the contract system. Pointing to the organization of the Quebec City longshoremen, Dalton stressed that only the organization of all longshoremen could guarantee higher wages. Dalton concluded by saying that labour unions were not fundamentally concerned with wages, but with bettering "the condition of the men, socially and morally."[75]

The rise of the Knights of Labor in the mid-1880s produced profound changes in the dynamics of working-class development, and the culture surrounding Joe Beef's Canteen was shaken up by their emergence. Along with lawyers, bankers, and capitalists, the Knights of Labor banned tavern owners from their ranks. Testifying before the Royal Commission on the Liquor Traffic, Louis Z. Boudreau, president of the Montreal Trades and Labour Council, reflected this attitude toward drink when he stated that "people we meet in the Trades and Labor Council are not drinking men as a whole. They are a good class of men."[76] As skilled workers accepted the need for temperance, the unskilled waterfront labourers might also reexamine the benefits of tavern life. This did not signal an alliance between organized labour and the temperance advocates who attacked Joe Beef in the 1870s. Spokesmen for organized labour criticized most of these temperance workers for failing to realize that much of the drunkenness among workingmen resulted from economic hardship. Clearly, William Darlington, a prominent Montreal Knight of Labor, shared McKiernan's distrust of the clergy's attempt to reform the workingman. Darlington told the Liquor Commission that "the workingmen feel that the church is a religious institution without Christianity, and that the clergy is simply a profession, got up for the purpose of making money in some instances, and in others, for preaching in the interest of capital against labour. . . . They find out in reality that the Knights of Labor preach more Christianity than the churches."[77] Despite such similarities, there was no room for Joe Beef in the Knights of Labor.

Outside of the working-class neighbourhoods, other forces were emerging which shaped public attitudes toward Joe Beef's Canteen. Throughout the 1880s, Montreal's middle-class residents grew more critical of the police force's inability to enforce the liquor laws. This new mood was captured by the Law and Order League (also known as the Citizens League of Montreal) which was formed in 1886. The League's purpose was to pressure police to enforce the liquor and public morality laws by publicizing open violations. Operating in cooperation with the Royal Society for the Prevention of Cruelty to Animals, the League was able to effect a dramatic increase in the number of prosecutions against tavern owners.[78] Under such pressure, the police were less likely to work informally with Joe Beef on matters of public order.

New attitudes toward leisure activities were also coming to the fore during the 1880s. With the growth of the YMCA and the Amateur Athletic Associations, urban youths were encouraged to spend their time in organized sport and develop the socially useful traits of "teamwork, perseverance, honesty and discipline — true muscular Christianity."[79] As one YMCA lecturer told his audience, recreation had to "invigorate the mind and body, and have nothing to do with questionable company, being regulated by Christian standards."[80] While such campaigns were not designed to recruit former members of street gangs, but rather the middle-class youth and clerks from the new industrial factories, these new approaches to recreation did have an impact on general tolerance of the waterfront culture. Prize fighting, probably a favoured sport of Joe Beef's patrons, was publicly denounced as a barbaric and dangerous sport.[81] With the growing alliance between the RSPCA and the Law and Order League, the Canteen's menagerie could not have survived a public outcry. New recreational opportunities for working-class Montreal, such as the opening of Sohmer Park in the early 1890s,[82] indicated that the necessity to centre all recreational life around the tavern was diminishing.

There was also a perceptible shift in public attitudes toward poverty and the city slums. With the reformers' concentration on the physical aspects of their city — clean water, paved streets, public parks, and adequate fire protection — urban slums were no longer seen only as places for poor people to live, but as potential threats to public health. Herbert Ames, a pioneer in efforts to clean up Montreal, stated that in matters of public health a simple rule existed — "the nearer people live to each other, the shorter they live."[83] Such programs as the Fresh Air Fund, which sent mothers and children of the slums to a country retreat for temporary escape from the noise and smoke of the city, testified to the concern among middle-class reformers about the dangerous effects of an industrial city.[84] The *Montreal Star* carried a series of reports on the terrible living conditions in Montreal's slums.[85] In 1885 during a smallpox epidemic, riots broke out when health authorities tried to vaccinate working-class people against the disease.[86] The great physical dangers which the slums created for the city, let alone the social danger, forced local authorities to take a closer look at the waterfront neighbourhoods.

Many of these fears and developments seem to have been familiar to the reporter who visited the Canteen in 1887. While the bears received the familiar treatment, the reporter was quite disturbed at the new attitude among the patrons. He wrote, "Nothing is more striking than the demeanor of the poor folk who fill the room. No oaths are uttered, no coarse jests, no loud talking, and never a laugh is heard. A very quiet, not to say sombre, lot of men. One would like to see a little more animation and liveliness, to hear now and then a good hearty laugh."[87] Nor was this brooding silence unique to Joe Beef's Canteen, as the reporter found several other taverns similarly devoid of their regular good cheer. These dull vacant looks, the reporter went on, "are the kind of faces one meets in the east end of London and other similar districts; but we should hardly expect to find them here. They are here, though, you see."[88] The reporter's reference to East London was repeated a few years later by the author of *Montreal by Gaslight*, a muckraking study of the city's "underworld." For the local observer, the most frightening prospect for his city was to duplicate the urban miseries of the East End of London. In *Montreal by Gaslight*, the author warned against the social consequences of drink and crushing poverty. "Last and greatest of all, think you that the modern plague of London is not known to us? Are we not infected?"[89] Along the waterfront, the silence of the labourers was feared to be the incubation period of this great urban disease. Of its eventual outbreak, one author wrote, "It may be that some day labor will raise and demand that for which it now pleads. That demand will mean riot, strike, and even civil war."[90] *Montreal by Gaslight* was written as a warning that a solution must be found before it was too late. The general outcome of such fears was that middle-class Montreal began to pay more attention to its waterfront area just as the social and economic circumstances which gave rise to Joe Beef's Canteen were changing.

The rough life along the waterfront had its own hazards and on 15 January 1889 Charles McKiernan died of heart failure in his Canteen while only 54 years of age. His death was received with great sadness in many quarters of the city and the funeral attracted large crowds. As the *Gazette* reporter commented, "Every grade in the social scale was represented in those assembled in front of the 'Canteen.' There were well known merchants, wide awake brokers, hard working mechanics and a big contingent of the genus bum, all jostling one another for a glimpse of the coffin containing what remained of one, whatever may have been his faults, who was always the poor man's friend."[91] After a short Anglican service, McKiernan's body was carried out of the tavern and the procession started for Mount Royal Cemetery. Among those in the procession were representatives from 50 labour societies who acknowledged for the last time Joe Beef's support of the trade union movement. The exception to this general sympathy was the *Montreal Witness*, which published its own death notice.

> Joe Beef is dead. For twenty five years he has enjoyed in his own way the reputation of being for Montreal what was in former days known under the pet sobriquet of the wickedest man. His saloon, where men consorted with unclean beasts was probably the most disgustingly dirty in the country. It has been the bottom of the sink of which the Windsor bar and others like it are the receivers. The only step further was to be found murdered on the wharf or dragged out of the gutter or the river, as might happen. It was the resort of the most degraded of men. It was the bottom of the pit, a sort of *cul de sac*, in which thieves could be corralled. The police declared it valuable to them as a place where these latter could be run down. It has been actively at work over all that time for the brutalizing of youth — a work which was carried on with the utmost diligence by its, in that sense, talented proprietor.[92]

Perhaps more than any of Joe Beef's lampoons, this editorial showed the limits of the *Witness*'s Christian charity.

With McKiernan's death, Joe Beef's Canteen declined. The transient customers were the first to suffer. Thomas Irwin, a "protege" of the Canteen, was arrested a few days after McKiernan's death for stealing a piece of flannel. In explaining his crime, Irwin stated "There is no use for me trying to make my living now that poor old Joe is dead and gone. I must get a home somewhere in winter; won't you admit that? Well, I stole to get a lodging."[93] For the wharf-rats and sun-fish, Joe Beef's was closed. His bears met an ignoble end as well. In April police officers shot Joe Beef's bears on the request of McKiernan's widow. She planned to have them stuffed.[94] By 1893 the Canteen was gone. The Salvation Army bought the tavern and under the banner of "Joe Beef's Converted" continued many of the services to transient workers which McKiernan had pioneered. Masters at adapting popular culture to their religious beliefs, the Salvation Army transformed one of their most troublesome enemies into a prophet for bread and salvation.[95]

In assessing the significance of Charles McKiernan to the Montreal working class in the 1870s and 1880s, one must remember that when McKiernan arrived in 1868 he did not create the working-class culture associated with Joe Beef's Canteen. That culture, which had grown out of the daily routines of the casual labourers on the docks, already existed. What Joe Beef accomplished was to give that culture a public face and voice, a figure upon which the local press and reformers could focus. In doing so, Joe Beef saved that culture from the obscurity which generally surrounds work cultures. The material necessary for that culture was amply demonstrated by the numerous community services which grew up around the tavern. This waterfront culture possessed its own values of mutual assistance, hard work, good cheer, and a sense of manly dignity. The necessity to "act like men," which McKiernan urged upon striking canal labourers, was an important code of ethics which the tavern owner used as a measure of all things. Clergy who treated his patrons "as men" were allowed into the Canteen, but organizations which resorted to the police to settle problems deserved condemnation for such unmanly behaviour. Even McKiernan's denunciations of Montreal industrialists, the "Big Bugs," or John Dougall were denunciations of individuals and not social classes. Indeed, the tendency to personalize every problem facing the waterfront community pointed out the necessity for longshoremen to find some larger institutional framework through which they could preserve the values that their work culture generated. The Knights of Labor provided this opportunity, but the Knights built upon the traditional values preserved and strengthened by Joe Beef.

While Joe Beef's controversies with the middle-class reformers who entered into his neighbourhood were genuine, the lasting influence of such incidents appeared small. For all his bluster, Joe Beef was a limited threat to the social order of Montreal. As a spokesman for rough culture, Joe Beef satirized only the pretensions and hypocrisy which he saw in the smooth behaviour of middle-class men. He did not advocate class antagonism, but a fair deal. For a short time, Joe Beef's influence was able to reach a fair deal with municipal authorities. What frightened some observers was the possibility that the growing numbers of unskilled factory workers, that unknown quantity of industrial transformation, would adopt the working-class culture of Joe Beef, with its violence and disregard for legal and moral authority. No doubt these observers were pleased that the new factory hands followed the lead of respectable skilled workers within the Knights of Labor.

The culture represented by Joe Beef was certainly different than that of the skilled tradesmen of Montreal. Only with difficulty can one imagine an experienced typographer making regular trips to the Canteen to see the bears. Though rough and respectable cultures interacted, they were clearly separate.[96] The culture surrounding the casual labourers grew out of a physically demanding life of marginal economic benefit, obtained through the common exertion of labour. In these respects, Joe Beef's world was closer to the world of Peter Aylen and the Shiners of the Ottawa Valley than to that of the typographers in the offices of the *Montreal Witness* or of the cotton mill workers of Hochelaga.[97] The waterfront world had its own internal hierarchy as Joe Beef vigorously defended his patrons against middle-class charges of drunken violence, but then threw them into the street when they got rowdy. While McKiernan's background, as his Irish verses confirm,[98] was rural, he lived in an industrial city and had to contend with the economic and social restrictions which this implied. Realizing the growing power of the police and social reformers to define the limits of acceptable behaviour, Joe Beef attempted to convince these men of the validity of working-class culture. He was not very successful. To the very end, McKiernan was rooted in the culture of his tavern and neighbourhood. For him, the liquor business was not a means of upward mobility and the tavern owner's sons remained working class.

Joe Beef's Canteen illustrated the complex nature of working-class culture. In the narrow, traditional sense of culture as artistic creation, the satiric verses, engravings, or cartoons by McKiernan and others about Joe Beef contributed in a minor way to the nineteenth-century radical literature in Canada. Local historians of Montreal were well aware of this tradition left behind by Joe Beef.[99] In the broader sense of culture as popular culture, the tavern life of bears, debates, and songs acknowledged a recreational culture created by the working class and not for them. The coming of rational recreation would weaken this tradition, but McKiernan's death had little long-term effect on this level. Finally, Joe Beef's Canteen represented a material culture of community services relating to the employment, housing, and health of the working-class neighbourhood. This culture was the most important manifestation of the Canteen in terms of class conflict.[100] All aspects of culture surrounding Joe Beef's Canteen demonstrated the integral nature of the life of the labouring men along the waterfront who would probably not have recognized distinctions between recreation and work, between a popular and material culture.

To label Joe Beef's Canteen a "pre-industrial" fragment in an industrial world obscures the fact that working-class culture was a fluid culture borrowing from its own past and from contemporary middle-class culture. Middle-class disgust at Joe Beef's antics grew largely out of his ability to parody their most pious thoughts. While Joe Beef rejected these new industrial virtues, this hardly distinguished him from thousands of other Montreal labourers and skilled workers. In many ways, the culture of Joe Beef had reached its own limits. Successful in bargaining social questions of public conduct and order, McKiernan played only a supporting role in the economic struggles in the factories and on the docks. The attempt to form new alliances between skilled and unskilled, men and women, tradesman with tradesman, would be made not by the Joe Beefs of the nineteenth century but by the Knights of Labor.

NOTES

1. Montreal Illustrated; or The Strangers' Guide to Montreal (Montreal, 1875). For a more thematic guide to the city in the 1880s, see S.E. Dawson, Hand-Book for the City of Montreal and Its Environs (Montreal, 1883). Lovell's Historic Report of the Census of Montreal (Montreal, 1891) is a good example of how the material progress of Montreal was equated with social and moral improvements. As Lovell stated, "Peace, happiness and prosperity abound, and brotherly love forms a link that might be prized in any city. The policeman is seldom needed. Intemperance is becoming a thing of the past." (45) Lovell's private census should not be confused with the Dominion census conducted that same year. The Montreal Star, in its 16 September 1886 issue, carried special stories on the city's capitalists and their contribution to social development.

2. This underground Montreal is given a muckraker's treatment in Montreal by Gaslight (Montreal, 1889), which contains a chapter on Joe Beef's Canteen. Charles McKiernan's landlord, F.X. Beaudry, was closely connected with the local prostitution trade, as his obituary (Montreal Witness, 25 March 1885) details. On gambling dens, see Montreal Witness, 14 September 1876, and Montreal Star, 30 October 1889. The Star, 23 January 1872, carries an article on a local cockfight.

3. The most recent contributions to this debate are Kenneth McNaught, "E.P. Thompson vs. Harold Logan," Canadian Historical Review 62 (1981): 141–68; Gregory S. Kealey's "Labour and Working-Class History in Canada: Prospects in the 1980s," and David J. Bercuson's "Through the Looking Glass of Culture," both from Labour/Le Travailleur 7 (1981): 67–94, 95–112. The history of Joe Beef hopefully shows some of the merits of a cultural approach to working-class history.

4. Raymond Williams, Culture and Society (London, 1960), 327.

5. Williams, Culture and Society, 330.

6. Gareth Stedman Jones, Outcast London (Oxford, 1971). Comparisons between Montreal and London, at least on general terms, are not as tenuous as might first appear. Contemporary observers of the waterfront often compared these slums to those of East London. Herbert Ames's attempt to introduce model housing for the workingman was modelled on the efforts of Octavia Hill's plan to help the London poor (The City Below the Hill [Toronto, 1972], 114). McKiernan received his training at Woolwich, which William Booth studied before founding his Salvation Army. The Salvation Army was one of the more successful groups in the waterfront neighbourhood.

7. Montreal Star, 16 January 1889. See also Edgar A. Collard's Montreal Yesterdays (Toronto, 1962) for a good general assessment of Charles McKiernan, and the Montreal City Archives clipping file R. 3654.2 "Rues, Commune, Rue de la," for general press coverage of McKiernan by Collard and other Montreal historians.

8. Dorothy Suzanne Cross, "The Irish in Montreal, 1867–1896," (M.A. thesis, McGill University, 1969) gives a general account of the Montreal Irish community. For contemporary descriptions, see John Francis Maguire's The Irish in America (Montreal, 1868), and Nicholas Flood Davin, The Irishman in Canada (Toronto, 1877).

9. Montreal by Gaslight, 10. Other well-known taverns were Tommy Boyle's The Horseshoe, which catered to those who followed prize fighting, and the Suburban, which had a reputation for giving the poor man a helping hand (94–105).

10. *Montreal Star*, 14 February 1888. Liquor licences, which included hotels, restaurants, saloons, and groceries, increased from 723 in 1879 to 1273 in 1887. Joe Beef's Canteen had a hotel licence.
11. *Montreal Witness*, 4 April 1881.
12. *Toronto Globe*, 14 April 1876; *Halifax Herald*, 28 June 1880; *Montreal Star*, 3 October 1887.
13. W.H. Davies, *The Autobiography of a Super-Tramp* (London, 1964), 131, cited in Clayton Gray, *Le Vieux Montreal* (Montreal, 1964), 16.
14. *Montreal Witness*, 4 April 1881. In an account of Joe Beef's encounter with the census taker, the problems of tracing the transient population were made clear. Of all the one-night guests which the Canteen provided for, only ten men were found by the census taker. Two of these, an Irish musician and a Spanish cook, were probably employees of the tavern. Also listed were an English coachmaker, an Irish blacksmith, an American barber, a Scottish commercial agent, an English (Quaker) leather merchant, an Irish accountant, an English labourer, and an Irish tanner. McKiernan's fifteen-year-old son was listed as a rivet maker and was likely serving an apprenticeship. See Public Archives of Canada (hereafter PAC), RG 31, *Census of Canada*, 1881, Manuscript, Montreal, West Ward, Division 3, p. 1.
15. *Toronto Globe*, 14 April 1876.
16. *Montreal by Gaslight*, 115.
17. *Montreal Star*, 10 September 1883; 11 September 1883; 3 October 1883.
18. *Montreal Witness*, 17 March 1881; 22 March 1881.
19. *Montreal Herald*, 21 April 1880; *Montreal Witness*, 6 August 1875. Jon M. Kingsdale, "The Poor Man's Club: Social Functions of the Urban Working Class Saloon," *American Quarterly* 25 (1973): 472–89, provides an excellent background to the discussion which follows and demonstrates that many of the Canteen's services were common to nineteenth-century taverns.
20. *La Minerve*, 2 August 1873.
21. *Toronto Globe*, 14 April 1876; *Halifax Herald*, 28 June 1880; *Montreal Star*, 3 October 1887.
22. *La Minerve*, 20 January 1874.
23. *Montreal Star*, 14 July 1876; *Montreal Witness*, 22 October 1873; 12 November 1877.
24. *La Minerve*, 7 November 1873. John was John Dougall of the *Montreal Witness* who had recently dismissed some union employees. Although the Canteen was a male bastion, McKiernan was not unaware of the growing number of women workers in the Montreal labour force. For the employment of women, see Dorothy Suzanne Cross's "The Neglected Majority: The Changing Role of Women in Nineteenth Century Montreal," *Social History* 12 (1973): 202–203.
25. *Montreal Yesterdays*, 273–74.
26. *La Minerve*, 28 December 1878.
27. *Toronto Globe*, 14 April 1876.
28. The integration of transient labour into urban centres was very important and a failure to do so is described in Sydney L. Harring's "Class Conflict and the Suppression of Tramps in Buffalo, 1892–1894," *Law and Society Review* 11 (1977): 873–911. See also James M. Pitsula's "The Treatment of Tramps in Late Nineteenth-Century Toronto," *Historical Papers* (1980), 116–32.
29. *Montreal Star*, 5 February 1877; *Witness*, 2 August 1876; *Star*, 3 October 1879.
30. *Star*, 15 January 1878; 29 December 1879; 27 February 1880; 25 March 1880; 1 April 1880. H.E. MacDermot in his *History of the Montreal General Hospital* (Montreal, 1950) wrote that Joe Beef's Canteen was "a particularly staunch supporter, and entries of donations from 'Proceeds of iron box, barroom, of Joe Beef' are frequent, or from 'his own skating Rink,' as well as contributions for the care of special patients" (55). MacDermot's work was cited in Edgar Collard's "All Our Yesterdays," *Montreal Gazette*, 9 January 1960. William Fox Beakbane, who drowned at Allan's wharf on 29 July 1883, was buried in the McKiernan family plot in Mount Royal Cemetery (*Star*, 10 August 1883).
31. *Witness*, 17 December 1877; 19 December 1877. Strike leader Lucien Pacquette spent several days in hospital recovering from his wound. For contractor William Davis, this was not the first time his workers reacted violently to his labour practices. A year earlier someone tried to blow up the contractor's house and severely damaged the building (*Witness*, 20 December 1877).
32. *Witness*, 17 December 1877.
33. *Witness*, 19 December 1877, 20 December 1877. Bernard Devlin (1824–80) came to Quebec in 1844 and published the *Freeman's Journal and Commercial Advertiser*. He ran unsuccessfully for the 1867 Parliament against Thomas D'Arcy McGee, who accused Devlin of being secretly in support of the Fenians. Devlin served as a Liberal MP for Montreal West from 1875 to 1878 (DCB 10: 250).
34. *Star*, 20 December 1877; *Witness*, 24 December 1877.
35. *Star*, 19 December 1877.

36. PAC, Dept. of Public Works, RG11, B1(a), vol. 474, p. 2534, Whitney & Daly to F. Braun, 22 January 1878.

37. *Witness*, 21 December 1877.

38. *Witness*, 22 December 1877.

39. *Witness*, 21 December 1877.

40. *Witness*, 26 December 1877.

41. *Ottawa Citizen*, 18 January 1878. The Citizen carried a copy of a strikers' petition to Mackenzie which was signed by 122 people including McKiernan. Most of the signers were untraceable in local business directories, but some local grocers and dry goods merchants did support the strikers' demands and this suggests some degree of neighbourhood support. Original petition in PAC, RG11, B1(a), vol. 473, pp. 2514–20.

42. *Ottawa Citizen*, 24 January 1878. An admitted weakness of this study is the failure to document the political connections which McKiernan had with municipal politicians. Federally, McKiernan was a Conservative and this no doubt played some part in his attack on Mackenzie. During the 1872 election, McKiernan led a group of sailors into a Liberal polling station and began serenading them with a concertina. When surrounded by an angry crowd, McKiernan pulled out a pistol and fired into the air. In the tumult which followed McKiernan and his companions were beaten and had to be rescued by the police. *Montreal Witness*, 28 August 1872.

43. PAC, RG11, B1(a), vol. 473, pp. 2514–69. Not all contractors paid their workers in truck, and those who did argued that the workers benefited from the arrangement. Davis argued that monthly pay periods increased productivity. "On Public Works as a Rule, a large number of men lose time after pay day, and, thereby disarrange and retard the progress of the Works." (Davis to Braun, 21 January 1878, p. 2532). John Dougall of the *Montreal Witness*, however, published an account of the supplies given to a labourer instead of cash. For $1.75 owing in wages, the worker received whiskey, sugar, tobacco, cheese, and bread valued at $1.05. The goods were on display throughout the strike at Joe Beef's Canteen (*Witness*, 22 January 1878).

44. *Star*, 17 April 1880; *Witness*, 21 April 1880.

45. *Halifax Herald*, 28 June 1880.

46. PAC, MG28, I 126, vol. 15, *Royal Canadian Academy of Art Scrapbook*; *Montreal Gazette*, 7 February 1916, cited in Montreal Yesterdays, 271.

47. "Third Report of the Select Committee of the House of Commons respecting a Prohibitory Liquor Law," *House of Commons Journals*, 1874, Testimony of F.W. Penton, 9.

48. *Montreal Gazette*, 22 April 1880. The importance of battles between the police and working-class people is illustrated by Robert D. Storch in "The Policeman as Domestic Missionary: Urban Discipline and Popular Culture in Northern England," *Journal of Social History* 9 (1976): 481–509.

49. Star, 30 October 1876. The Black Horse Gang's activities are reported in the *Witness*, 26 May 1875; 27 May 1875; *Star*, 1 February 1876; *Witness*, 24 July 1880; 10 May 1882. Street gangs in general are discussed in the *Witness*, 31 May 1875.

50. *Witness*, 19 November 1878; 18 November 1878. The *Witness* story on the incident was protested by "Joe Beef's Gang" who turned up in the editor's office and claimed that they were "respectable mechanics and that the butchers are on the contrary not noted for their respectable behaviour."

51. *Witness*, 28 September 1880; 24 July 1879.

52. *Witness*, 8 February 1877.

53. *Annual Report of the Montreal Sailors Institute for the Year Ending January, 1870* (Montreal, 1870), 5; *Annual Report of the Montreal Sailors Institute of 1870* (Montreal, 1871), 8.

54. Royal Commission on the Liquor Traffic, *House of Commons Sessional Paper*, no. 21, 1894, 584.

55. *House of Commons Sessional Paper*, no. 21, 1894, 589.

56. *House of Commons Sessional Paper*, no. 21, 1894, 586.

57. The difference of religious sentiment was reflected in the organization of benevolent associations. Roman Catholic Montreal had its own hospitals and dispensaries, thirteen benevolent institutions caring for the aged, orphaned, and widowed. Nine Catholic charitable societies also contributed to the welfare of the impoverished citizens. Protestant Montreal, besides having its hospitals, had sixteen benevolent institutions for the same clientele as the Catholic institutions as well as homes for female immigrants and sick servant girls. Religious differences were further complicated by the national origins of Montreal residents. To aid fellow countrymen there were several national societies including the St. George, St. Andrew, St. Patrick, St. Jean Baptiste, Irish Protestant, Italian, Welsh, Scandinavian, and Swiss benevolent organizations. See Lovell's *Historic Report of the Census of Montreal* (Montreal, 1891), 62–63, 72–73. See also Janice A. Harvey's "Upper Class Reaction to Poverty in Mid-Nineteenth Century Montreal: A Protestant Example," (M.A. thesis, McGill University, 1978) for descriptions of Protestant charities.

58. *Montreal Yesterdays*, 273–74.

59. *Montreal Star*, 29 September 1871; *Montreal Yesterdays*, 272–73. McKiernan's 25-year-old wife Mary McRae and her baby died on 26 September 1871, and it is uncertain whether the contemporary accounts correctly interpreted McKiernan's actions. Interestingly enough, McKiernan's republican sentiments exhibited themselves on his wife's gravestone. Her inscription read in part,

> I leave a husband and four orphan babes
> To mouth their mother's loss
> Who will never return.
> But let that tree, which you see
> Be the tree of Liberty
> And in its stead never let the tree of [Bigotry]
> Be planted between them and me.

60. *Montreal Witness*, 4 April 1881; PAC, RG31, *Census of Canada*, 1881 Manuscript, Montreal, West Ward, Division no. 3, p. 1.
61. *Montreal Yesterdays*, 279–80.
62. *Toronto Globe*, 14 April 1876; *Montreal Star*, 31 July 1876.
63. *Halifax Herald*, 28 June 1880. For Mr. Hammond's preaching style see *Montreal Star*, 18 March 1880.
64. Edgar Collard, "Of Many Things," *Montreal Gazette*, 28 February 1976. For the legal problems of the Salvation Army, see the *Montreal Star*, 19 August 1886; 3 September 1886; 14 September 1886.
65. *Montreal Star*, 9 January 1911. See J.I. Cooper's "The Early Editorial Policy of the Montreal Witness," Canadian Historical Association, *Report* (1947), 53–62, and Dougall's obituary in the *Montreal Star*, 19 August 1886.
66. *La Minerve*, 13 March 1873.
67. *Montreal Star*, 26 November 1872; 27 November 1872; 28 November 1872.
68. *Montreal Witness*, 8 February 1877.
69. *Montreal Witness*, 4 April 1878.
70. *Montreal Witness*, 5 April 1879.
71. Royal Commission on the Relations of Capital and Labour, 1889, *Quebec Evidence*, vol. 1, pp. 150–86.
72. Royal Commission on the Relations of Capital and Labour, Testimony of R.A. Smith, 156–60; James Urquhart, 173–75.
73. Royal Commission on the Relations of Capital and Labour, Testimony of Patrick Dalton, 183–85.
74. Royal Commission on the Relations of Capital and Labour, Testimony of Edmund Tart, 175–81.
75. Royal Commission on the Relations of Capital and Labour, Testimony of Patrick Dalton, 186.
76. Royal Commission on the Liquor Traffic, 512.
77. Royal Commission on the Liquor Traffic, 583.
78. *Montreal Star*, 28 January 1886. On the Law and Order League, see *Star*, 16 August 1887; 24 January 1889; 16 February 1889, 10 March 1887.
79. Alan Metcalfe, "The Evolution of Organized Physical Recreation in Montreal, 1840–1895," *Social History* 21 (1978): 153. For the role of the YMCA in the new attitude toward leisure activities, see David Macleod, "A Live Vaccine: The YMCA and Male Adolescence in the United States and Canada, 1870–1920," *Social History* 21 (1978): 5–25. An excellent study of recreation in England is Peter Bailey, *Leisure and Class in Victorian England* (Toronto, 1978).
80. *Montreal Star*, 15 November 1873.
81. For denunciations of prize fighting see *Star*, 4 January 1887; 9 May 1887; 20 May 1887; 23 May 1887; 15 September 1887.
82. *Montreal Star*, 6 June 1893; 13 July 1893. Richard Bell of the Montreal Sailors Institute preferred that sailors drink at Sohmer Park rather than in the waterfront taverns. Royal Commission on the Liquor Traffic, 584–89.
83. Herbert B. Ames, "Why We Should Study the Municipal System of Our City," *Abstract of a Course of Ten Lectures on Municipal Administration* (Montreal, 1896), 7.
84. *Montreal Star* contains several articles promoting the Fresh Air Fund: see 11 June 1887; 18 June 1887; 25 June 1887; 6 July 1887. On the Fresh Air Home, see *Star*, 23 June 1888.
85. *Star*, 24 December 1883; 29 December 1883.
86. *Star*, 29 September 1885.
87. *Star*, 3 October 1887.
88. *Star*, 3 October 1887.
89. *Montreal by Gaslight*, 10.
90. *Montreal by Gaslight*, 35.
91. *Montreal Gazette*, 19 January 1889.

92. *Montreal by Gaslight*, 119.

93. *Star*, 24 January 1889.

94. *Star*, 29 April 1889.

95. *Star*, 26 May 1893; 27 May 1893. R.G. Moyles, in The Blood and Fire in Canada (Toronto, 1977), remarked that this was a new venture for the Salvation Army. "Whereas other men's hostels had been designed as rescue centres for ex-prisoners and for total derelicts, Joe Beef's was a hostel for transients, providing a cheap bed for the unemployed man with little money and a cheap meal for the poor city labourer" (69).

96. Peter Bailey's "Will the Real Bill Banks Please Stand Up? Towards a Role Analysis of Mid-Victorian Working-Class Respectability," *Journal of Social History* 12 (1979), offers some interesting insights into the differences between rough and respectable workingmen.

97. Michael S. Cross, "The Shiners' War: Social Violence in the Ottawa Valley in the 1830's," *Canadian Historical Review* 54 (1973): 1–26. For a description of an early Ottawa tavern see W.P. Lett, "Corkstown," Recollections of Old Bytown (Ottawa, 1979), 81–86.

98. See the attitudes reflected in "Spurn Not the Poor Man," *La Minerve*, 7 January 1874; "I am Long Past Wailing and Whining," *La Minerve*, 27 January 1874; and "The Big Beggarman," *La Minerve*, 13 January 1874. Poetic style makes it unlikely that these verses are from McKiernan's pen, but by printing them with his advertisements he demonstrated a sympathy with their author.

99. Frank W. Watt, "Radicalism in English Canadian Literature since Confederation" (Ph.D. thesis, University of Toronto, 1957). Watt does not mention McKiernan but Watt's description of a literature disillusioned with nation building and inclined to associate patriotic feelings with the motives and methods of capitalist exploitation could accommodate much of McKiernan's verse.

100. Bryan D. Palmer's *A Culture in Conflict* (Montreal, 1979) contains the fullest discussion of the importance of culture in Canadian class conflict. See also Gareth Stedman Jones, "Working-Class Culture and Working-Class Politics in London, 1870–1900," *Journal of Social History* 7 (1974): 460–508.

Topic Eleven

World War I

Members of the 29th (Vancouver) Batallion advance across "No Man's Land" at Vimy Ridge in April 1917.

In 1914, Canada participated in its first large-scale war. Over the next four years, the nation of fewer than 10 million people provided more than half a million men as soldiers, sailors, and fliers, as well as several thousand women as nursing sisters, to the Allied war effort. More than 60 000 Canadians died fighting in the struggle. English-Canadian historians have used this tremendous war effort as evidence of Canada coming of age as a nation, arguing that Canadian nationalism was born on the battlefields of Europe. But not all groups contributed equally to the war effort, and certainly not all Canadian soldiers experienced fighting as a glorious feat. Many returned maimed in both body and mind, scarred forever by their experience.

The following three articles take a more critical look at the war. The Talbot Papineau–Henri Bourassa correspondence reminds us that many French Canadians opposed Canada's involvement in the war in Europe, and especially conscription, for a war that they believed was of no interest or benefit to them. But equally, the Papineau–Bourassa correspondence reminds us that many French Canadians *did* fight in World War I despite the obstacles they faced. Canadian historians have tended to focus on the opposition among French Canadians at the expense of recognizing those who did fight. The correspondence shows that both sides had compelling reasons for the positions taken.

Today it is difficult for students to visualize the conditions of trench warfare in World War I. The horrendous experience that soldiers endured serves as a reminder of the magnitude and horrifying nature of that war. The following excerpt from Will R. Bird's war memoirs, *Ghosts Have Warm Hands*, published in 1930 but based on extensive diary entries written during the war years, gives a vivid account of life in the trenches and at the front in general. Bird's account adds the personal feelings and human tragedies of war absent from the "official" military accounts. This particular excerpt describes his experience during the battle of Vimy.

Voluntary recruitment of soldiers for the war effort passed through various phases between 1914, the advent of war, and 1917, the implementation of conscription. Historian Ronald G. Haycock examines the role that Sam Hughes, the Minister of Militia, played in the recruitment effort. Haycock maintains that Hughes failed to appreciate the difficulties of recruiting soldiers in a geographically enormous country, and one divided by the war effort. Haycock is also critical of Hughes's archaic views that winning the war required more and more soldiers, and not necessarily better-trained soldiers.

What are the arguments for and against French-Canadian enlistment put forward in both the Papineau–Bourassa correspondence and in Haycock's article? How does Will Bird's account of fighting at the front tie in with Haycock's study of Sam Hughes's views on recruitment? Primary sources are essential for good historical writing. What are the strengths (and weaknesses) of using the Papineau–Bourassa correspondence and Will Bird's memoirs as sources for World War I?

For a compelling account of the war years from the perspective of social history, see Desmond Morton and Jack Granatstein, *Marching to Armageddon: Canadians and the Great War, 1914–1919* (Toronto: Lester and Orpen Dennys, 1989); Daniel Dancocks, *Spearhead to Victory: Canada and the Great War* (Edmonton: Hurtig, 1987); and Desmond Morton, *When Your Number's Up* (Toronto: Random House, 1994). For an overview of the war years, see the relevant chapters in R.C. Brown and R. Cook's *Canada, 1896–1921: A Nation Transformed* (Toronto: McClelland and Stewart, 1974). A quick overview is found in Roger Sarty and Brereton Greenhous, "The Great War," *Horizon Canada* 85 (1986): 2017–23. A valuable collection of essays is B.D. Hunt and R.G. Haycock, eds., *Canada's Defence: Perspectives on Policy in the Twentieth Century* (Toronto: Copp Clark Pitman Ltd., 1993). A number of biographies of key politicians during World War I contain useful discussions of the war years. The most important are R.C. Brown's *Robert Laird Borden: A Biography*, vol. 3, *1914–1937* (Toronto: Macmillan, 1980); J. Schull's *Laurier: The First Canadian* (Toronto: Macmillan, 1965); Robert Rumilly's *Henri Bourassa* (Montreal: Chantecler, 1953); and R. Graham's *Arthur Meighen*, vol. 1, *The Door of Opportunity* (Toronto: Clarke, Irwin, 1960). On Canada's most important military commander in World War I, see A.M.J. Hyatt, *General Sir Arthur Currie: A Military Biography* (Toronto: University of Toronto Press, 1987). A new collection of essays on the war years is David MacKenzie, ed., *Canada and the First World War: Essays in Honour of Robert Craig Brown* (Toronto: University of Toronto Press, 2005).

John Swettenham's *To Seize the Victory* (Toronto: Ryerson, 1965) and Robert James Steel's *The Men Who Marched Away: Canada's Infantry in the First World War, 1914–1918* (St. Catharines: Vanwell, 1989) describe Canadian participation at the front, as does Sandra Gwyn's *Tapestry of War: A Private View of Canadians in the Great War* (Toronto: HarperCollins, 1992). On Canada's involvement in the Ypres Salient, see Daniel Dancocks, *Welcome to Flanders Fields: The First Canadian Battle of the Great War, Ypres, 1915* (Toronto: McClelland and Stewart, 1988). Pierre Berton tells the story of Canada's greatest battle in *Vimy* (Toronto: McClelland and Stewart, 1986). On the nature of trench warfare, see Bill Rawling, *Surviving Trench Warfare: Technology and the Canadian Corps, 1914–1918* (Toronto: University of Toronto Press, 1992); and Tim Cook, *No Place to Run: The Canadian Corps and Gas Warfare in the First World War* (Vancouver: University of British Columbia Press, 1999).

On the issue of conscription, see Elizabeth Armstrong's *The Crisis of Quebec, 1914–1918* (New York: Columbia University Press, 1937); J.L. Granatstein and J.M. Hitsman's *Broken Promises: A History of Conscription in Canada* (Toronto: Oxford University Press, 1977; new edition, 1984); Desmond Morton's "French Canada and War, 1868–1917: The Military Background to the Conscription Crisis of 1917," in *War and Society in North America*, eds. J.L. Granatstein and R. Cuff (Toronto: Nelson, 1970), pp. 84–103; Brian Cameron's "The Bonne Entente Movement, 1916–17: From Cooperation to Conscription," *Journal of Canadian Studies* 13 (Summer 1978): 1942–55; the relevant chapters in John English, *The Decline of Politics: The Conservatives and the Party System, 1901–1920* (Toronto: University of Toronto Press, 1977); and Jean Pariseau, "La participation des Canadiens français à l'effort des deux guerres mondiales: Démarche de ré-interprétation," *Canadian Defence Quarterly/ Revue canadienne de défense* 13, 2 (Autumn 1983): 43–48. Henri Bourassa's views are presented in Joseph Levitt, ed., *Henri Bourassa on Imperialism and Bi-culturalism, 1900–1918* (Toronto: Copp Clark, 1970). The Papineau–Bourassa debate over conscription is reviewed in Sandra Gwyn, *Tapestry of War: A Private View of Canadians in the Great War* (Toronto: HarperCollins, 1992).

Two novels help to re-create the atmosphere of Canada during World War I: Philip Child's *God's Sparrows*, published in 1937 and reprinted in 1978 with an introduction by Dennis Duffy (Toronto: McClelland and Stewart), and Timothy Findley's award-winning *The Wars* (Toronto: Clarke, Irwin, 1977). Grace Morris Craig's *But This Is Our War* (Toronto: University of Toronto Press, 1981) is both her own recollection of the war years at home in Ontario and a collection of letters from her two brothers at the front.

Modris Ekstein's *Rites of Spring: The Great War and the Birth of the Modern Age* (Boston: Houghton Mifflin, 1989) looks at the Great War from a broader perspective. Jonathon F. Vance's *Death So Noble: Memory, Meaning and the First World War* (Vancouver: UBC Press, 1997) is an excellent study of the image of the Great War in the popular culture of the interwar years.

WEBLINKS

Canada and World War I
http://www.collectionscanada.ca/firstworldwar/index-e.html

War diaries, letters, and other documents detailing the experiences of Canadian soldiers in World War I.

Propaganda Posters
http://www.firstworldwar.com/posters/canada.htm

A series of propaganda posters used in Canada during the time of World War I to boost recruitment and support for the Canadian forces.

Canadian Expeditionary Force Photographs
http://gateway.uvic.ca/spcoll/Digit/WOD/index.htm

A collection of photographs of the Canadian Expeditionary Force recruiting and training in Quebec prior to their departure for Britain in 1914. Photographs were taken by J.A. Miller of the *Montreal Daily Star*.

National Film Board of Canada: World War I
http://www.nfb.ca/enclasse/ww1/en/frame_index.php

Films of training and conflict in World War I documented by the National Film Board of Canada.

Canvas of War
http://www.civilization.ca/cwm/canvas/1/cwd1e.html

A series of paintings depicting events in World War I from the Canadian War Museum.

Vimy Ridge
http://www.cbc.ca/news/background/vimy/

A detailed description of the battle for Vimy Ridge, with links to related websites.

Echo in My Heart
http://ca.geocities.com/echoinmyheart@rogers.com

A series of letters between Canadians Fred Albright and Evelyn Albright spanning their marriage in 1914, Fred's enlistment in 1916, and his participation in the war until 1917.

Article Twenty-Six

An Open Letter from Capt. Talbot Papineau to Mr. Henri Bourassa

(A copy of this letter was sent to Mr. Bourassa by Mr. Andrew-R. McMaster, K.C., on July 18, 1916. It was published, on July 28, in most Montreal, Quebec, Ottawa, and Toronto papers, both English and French.)

In the Field,
France, March 21, 1916.

To Monsieur Henri Bourassa,
Editor of *Le Devoir*,
Montreal.

My dear Cousin Henri,

I was sorry before leaving Quebec in 1914 not to have had an opportunity of discussing with you the momentous issues which were raised in Canada by the outbreak of this war.

You and I have had some discussions in the past, and although we have not agreed upon all points, yet I am happy to think that our pleasant friendship, which indeed dates from the time of my birth, has hitherto continued uninjured by our differences of opinion. Nor would I be the first to make it otherwise, for however I may deplore the character of your views, I have always considered that you held them honestly and sincerely and that you were singularly free from purely selfish or personal ambitions.

Very possibly nothing that I could have said in August 1914 would have caused you to change your opinions, but I did hope that as events developed and as the great national opportunity of Canada became clearer to all her citizens, you would have been influenced to modify your views and to adopt a different attitude. In that hope I have been disappointed. Deeply involved as the honour and the very national existence of Canada has become, beautiful but terrible as her sacrifices have been, you and you alone of the leaders of Canadian thought appear to have remained unmoved, and your unhappy views unchanged.

Too occupied by immediate events in this country to formulate a protest or to frame a reasoned argument, I have nevertheless followed with intense feeling and deep regret the course of action which you have pursued. Consolation of course I have had in the fact that far from sharing in your views, the vast majority of Canadians, and even many of those who had formerly agreed with you, were now strongly and bitterly opposed to you. With this fact in mind, I would not take the time from my duties here to write you this letter did I not fear that the influence to which your talent, energy, and sincerity of purpose formerly entitled you, might still be exercised upon a small minority of your fellow countrymen, and that your attitude might still be considered by some as representative of the race to which we belong.

Nor can I altogether abandon the hope — presumptuous no doubt but friendly and well-intentioned — that I may so express myself here as to give you a new outlook and a different purpose, and perhaps even win you to the support of a principle which has been proved to be dearer to many Canadians than life itself.

I shall not consider the grounds upon which you base your opposition to Canadian participation in this more than European — in this World War. Rather I wish to begin by pointing out some reasons why on the contrary your whole-hearted support might have been expected.

Source: *Canadian Nationalism and the War*. Published in Montreal, 1916.

And the first reason is this. By the declaration of war by Great Britain upon Germany, Canada became "ipso facto" a belligerent, subject to invasion and conquest, her property at sea subject to capture, her coasts subject to bombardment or attack, her citizens in enemy territory subject to imprisonment or detention. This is not a matter of opinion — it is a matter of fact — a question of international law. No arguments of yours at least could have persuaded the Kaiser to the contrary. Whatever your views or theories may be as to future constitutional development of Canada, and in those views I believe I coincide to a large extent, the fact remains that at the time of the outbreak of war Canada was a possession of the British Empire, and as such as much involved in the war as any country in England, and from the German point of view and the point of view of International Law equally subject to all its pains and penalties. Indeed proof may no doubt be made that one of the very purposes of Germany's aggression and German military preparedness was the ambition to secure a part if not the whole of the English possessions in North America.

That being so, surely it was idle and pernicious to continue an academic discussion as to whether the situation was a just one or not, as to whether Canada should or should not have had a voice in ante bellum English diplomacy or in the actual declaration of war. Such a discussion may very properly arise upon a successful conclusion of the war, but so long as national issues are being decided in Prussian fashion, that is, by an appeal to the Power of Might, the liberties of discussion which you enjoyed by virtue of British citizenship were necessarily curtailed and any resulting decisions utterly valueless. If ever there was a time for action and not for theories it was to be found in Canada upon the outbreak of war.

Let us presume for the sake of argument that your attitude had also been adopted by the Government and people of Canada and that we had declared our intention to abstain from active participation in the war until Canada herself was actually attacked. What would have resulted? One of two things. Either the Allies would have been defeated or they would not have been defeated. In the former case Canada would have been called upon either to surrender unconditionally to German domination or to have attempted a resistance against German arms.

You, I feel sure, would have preferred resistance, but as a proper corrective to such a preference I would prescribe a moderate dose of trench bombardment. I have known my own dogmas to be seriously disturbed in the midst of a German artillery concentration. I can assure you that the further you travel from Canada and the nearer you approach the great military power of Germany, the less do you value the unaided strength of Canada. By the time you are within fifteen yards of a German army and know yourself to be holding about one yard out of a line of five hundred miles or more, you are liable to be enquiring very anxiously about the presence and power of British and French forces. Your ideas about charging to Berlin or of ending the war would also have undergone some slight moderation.

No, my dear Cousin, I think you would shortly after the defeat of the Allies have been more worried over the mastery of the German consonants than you are even now over a conflict with the Ontario Anti-bilinguists. Or I can imagine you an unhappy exile in Terra del Fuego eloquently comparing the wrongs of Quebec and Alsace.

But you will doubtless say we would have had the assistance of the Great American Republic! It is quite possible. I will admit that by the time the American fleet had been sunk and the principal buildings in New York destroyed the United States would have declared war upon Europe, but in the meantime Canada might very well have been paying tribute and learning to decline German verbs, probably the only thing German she *could* have declined.

I am, as you know, by descent even more American than I am French, and I am a sincere believer in the future of that magnificent Republic. I cannot forget that more than any other nation in the world's history — England not excepted — she has suffered war solely for the sake of some fine principle of nationality. In 1776 for the principle of national existence. In 1812 for the principle of the inviolability of American citizenship. In 1860 for the preservation of National unity and the suppression of slavery. In 1896 for the protection of her National pride and in sympathy for the wrongs of a neighbouring people.

Nor disappointed as I am at the present inactivity of the States will I ever waiver in my loyal belief that in time to come, perhaps less distant than we realize, her actions will correspond with the lofty expression of her national and international ideals.

I shall continue to anticipate the day when with a clear understanding and a mutual trust we shall by virtue of our united strength and our common purposes be prepared to defend the rights of humanity not only upon the American Continent but throughout the civilized world.

Nevertheless we are not dealing with what may occur in the future but with the actual facts of yesterday and today, and I would feign know if you still think that a power which without protest witnesses the ruthless spoliation of Belgium and Serbia, and without effective action the murder of her own citizens, would have interfered to protect the property or the liberties of Canadians. Surely you must at least admit an element of doubt, and even if such interference had been attempted, have we not the admission of the Americans themselves that it could not have been successful against the great naval and military organizations of the Central Powers?

May I be permitted to conclude that had the Allies been defeated Canada must afterwards necessarily have suffered a similar fate.

But there was the other alternative, namely, that the Allies even without the assistance of Canada would *not* have been defeated. What then? Presumably French and English would still have been the official languages of Canada. You might still have edited untrammeled your version of Duty, and Colonel Lavergne might still, publicly and without the restraining fear of death or imprisonment, have spoken seditiously (I mean from the Prussian point of view of course). In fact Canada might still have retained her liberties and might with the same freedom from external influences have continued her progress to material and political strength.

But would you have been satisfied — you who have arrogated to yourself the high term of Nationalist? What of the Soul of Canada? Can a nation's pride or patriotism be built upon the blood and suffering of others or upon the wealth garnered from the coffers of those who in anguish and with blood-sweat are fighting the battles of freedom? If we accept our liberties, our national life, from the hands of the English soldiers, if without sacrifices of our own we profit by the sacrifices of the English citizen, can we hope to ever become a nation ourselves? How could we ever acquire that Soul or create that Pride without which a nation is a dead thing and doomed to speedy decay and disappearance?

If you were truly a Nationalist — if you loved our great country and without smallness longed to see her become the home of a good and united people — surely you would have recognized this as her moment of travail and tribulation. You would have felt that in the agony of her losses in Belgium and France, Canada was suffering the birth pains of her national life. There even more than in Canada herself, her citizens are being knit together into a new existence because when men stand side by side and endure a soldier's life and face together a soldier's death, they are united in bonds almost as strong as the closest of blood-ties.

There was the great opportunity for the true Nationalist! There was the great issue, the great sacrifice, which should have appealed equally to all true citizens of Canada, and should have served to cement them with indissoluble strength — Canada was at war! Canada was attacked! What mattered then internal dissentions and questions of home importance? What mattered the why and wherefore of the war, whether we owed anything to England or not, whether we were Imperialists or not, or whether we were French or English? The one simple commending fact to govern our conduct was that Canada was at war, and Canada and Canadian liberties had to be protected.

To you as a "Nationalist" this fact should have appealed more than to any others. Englishmen, as was natural, returned to fight for England, just as Germans and Austrians and Belgians and Italians returned to fight for their native lands.

But we, Canadians, had we no call just as insistent, just as compelling to fight for Canada? Did not the *Leipzig* and the *Gneisnau* possibly menace Victoria and Vancouver, and did you not feel the patriotism to make sacrifices for the protection of British Columbia? How could you otherwise call yourself Canadian? It is true that Canada did not hear the roar of German guns nor were we visited at night by the murderous Zeppelins, but every shot that was fired in Belgium or France was aimed as much at the heart of Canada as at the bodies of our brave Allies. Could we then wait within the temporary safety of our distant shores until either the Central Powers flushed with victory should come to settle their account or until by the glorious death of millions of our fellowmen in Europe, Canada should remain in inglorious security and a shameful liberty?

I give thanks that that question has been answered not as you would have had it answered but as those Canadians who have already died or are about to die here in this gallant mother-land of France have answered it.

It may have been difficult for you at first to have realized the full significance of the situation. You were steeped in your belief that Canada owed no debt to England, was merely a vassal state and entitled to protection without payment. You were deeply imbued with the principle that we should not partake in a war in the declaration of which we had had no say. You believed very sincerely that Canadian soldiers should not be called upon to fight beyond the frontier of Canada itself, and your vision was further obscured by your indignation at the apparent injustice to a French minority in Ontario.

It is conceivable that at first on account of this long-held attitude of mind and because it seemed that Canadian aid was hardly necessary, for even we feared that the war would be over before the first Canadian regiment should land in France, you should have failed to adapt your mind to the new situation and should for a while have continued in your former views;— but now — now that Canada has pledged herself body and soul to the successful prosecution of this war — now that we know that only by the exercise of our full and united strength can we achieve a speedy and lasting victory — now that thousands of your fellow citizens have died, and alas! many more must yet be killed — how in the name of all that you hold most sacred can you still maintain your opposition? How can you refrain from using all your influence and your personal magnetism and eloquence to swell the great army of Canada and make it as representative of all classes of our citizens as possible?

Could you have been here yourself to witness in its horrible detail the cruelty of war — to have seen your comrades suddenly struck down in death and lie mangled at your side, even you could not have failed to wish to visit punishment upon those responsible. You too would now wish to see every ounce of our united strength instantly and relentlessly directed to that end. Afterwards, when that end has been accomplished, then and then only can there be honour or profit in the discussion of our domestic or imperial disputes.

And so my first reason for your support would be that you should assist in the defence of Canadian territory and Canadian liberties.

And my second would be this:—

Whatever criticism may today be properly directed against the Constitutional structure of the British Empire, we are compelled to admit that the *spiritual* union of the self-governing portions of the Empire is a most necessary and desirable thing. Surely you will concede that the degree of civilization which they represent and the standards of individual and national liberty for which they stand are the highest and noblest to which the human race has yet attained and jealously to be protected against destruction by less developed powers. All may not be perfection — grave and serious faults no doubt exist — vast progress must still be made — nevertheless that which has been achieved is good and must not be allowed to disappear. The bonds which unite us for certain great purposes and which have proved so powerful in this common struggle must not be loosened. They may indeed be readjusted, but the great communities which the British Empire has joined together must not be broken asunder. If I thought that the development of a national spirit in Canada meant antagonism to the "spirit" which unites the Empire today, I would utterly repudiate the idea of a Canadian nation and would gladly accept the most exacting of imperial organic unions.

Hitherto I have welcomed your nationalism because I thought it would only mean that you wished Canada to assume national responsibilities as well as to enjoy its privileges.

But your attitude in the present crisis will alienate and antagonize the support which you might otherwise have received. Can you not realize that if any worthy nationality is possible for Canada it must be sympathetic to and must cooperate with the fine spirit of imperial unity? That spirit was endangered by the outbreak of European war. It could only be preserved by loyal assistance from all those in whom that spirit dwelt.

And so I would also have had you support Canadian participation in the war, *not* in order to maintain a certain political organism of Empire, but to preserve and perpetuate that invaluable *spirit* which alone makes our union possible.

The third reason is this: You and I are so called French Canadians. We belong to a race that began the conquest of this country long before the days of Wolfe. That race was in its turn conquered, but their personal liberties were not restricted. They were in fact increased. Ultimately as a minority in a great English-speaking community we have preserved our racial identity, and we have had freedom to speak or to worship as we wished. I may not be, like yourself, "un pur sang," for I am by birth even more English than French, but I am proud of my French ancestors, I love the French language, and I am as determined as you are that we shall have full liberty to remain French as long as we like. But if we are to preserve this liberty we must recognize that we do not belong entirely to ourselves, but to a mixed population, we must rather seek to find points of contact and of common interest than points of friction and separation. We must make concessions and certain sacrifices of our distinct individuality if we mean to live on amicable terms with our fellow citizens or if we are to expect them to make similar concessions to us. There, in this moment of crisis, was the greatest opportunity which could ever have presented itself for us to show unity of purpose and to prove to our English fellow citizens that, whatever our respective histories may have been, we were actuated by a common love for our country and a mutual wish that in the future we should unite our distinctive talents and energies to create a proud and happy nation.

That was an opportunity which you, my cousin, have failed to grasp, and unfortunately, despite the heroic and able manner in which French-Canadian battalions have distinguished themselves here, and despite the whole-hearted support which so many leaders of French-Canadian thought have given to the cause, yet the fact remains that the French in Canada have not responded in the same proportion as have other Canadian citizens, and the unhappy impression has been created that French Canadians are not bearing their full share in this great Canadian enterprise. For this fact and this impression you will be held largely responsible. Do you fully realize what such a responsibility will mean, not so much to you personally — for that I believe you would care little — but to the principles which you have advocated, and for many of which I have but the deepest regard? You will have brought them into a disrepute from which they may never recover. Already you have made the fine term of "Nationalist" to stink in the nostrils of our English fellow citizens. Have you caused them to respect your national views?

Have you won their admiration or led them to consider with esteem, and toleration your ambitions for the French language? Have you shown yourself worthy of concessions or consideration?

After this war what influence will you enjoy — what good to your country will you be able to accomplish? Wherever you go you will stir up strife and enmity — you will bring disfavour and dishonour upon our race, so that whoever bears a French name in Canada will be an object of suspicion and possibly of hatred.

And so, in the third place, for the honour of French Canada and for the unity of our country, I would have had you favourable to our cause.

I have only two more reasons, and they but need to be mentioned, I think, to be appreciated.

Here in this little French town I hear all about me the language I love so well and which recalls so vividly my happy childhood days in Montebello. I see types and faces that are like old friends. I see farm houses like those at home. I notice that our French-Canadian soldiers have easy friendships wherever they go.

Can you make me believe that there must not always be a bond of blood relationship between the Old France and the New?

And France — more glorious than in all her history — is now in agony straining fearlessly and proudly in a struggle for life or death.

For Old France and French civilization I would have had your support.

And in the last place, all other considerations aside and even supposing Canada had been a neutral country, I would have had you decide that she should enter the struggle for no other reason than that it is a fight for the freedom of the world — a fight in the result of which like every other country she is herself vitally interested. I will not further speak of the causes of this war, but I should like to think that even if Canada had been an independent and neutral nation she of her own accord would have chosen to follow the same path of glory that she is following today.

Perhaps, my cousin, I have been overlong and tedious with my reasons, but I shall be shorter with my warning — and in closing I wish to say this to you.

Those of us in this great army, who may be so fortunate as to return to our Canada, will have faced the grimmest and sincerest issues of life and death — we will have experienced the unhappy strength of brute force — we will have seen our loved comrades die in blood and suffering. Beware lest we return with revengeful feelings, for I say to you that for those who, while we fought and suffered here, remained in safety and comfort in Canada and failed to give us encouragement and support, as well as for those who grew fat with the wealth dishonourably gained by political graft and by dishonest business methods at our expense — we shall demand a heavy day of reckoning. We shall inflict upon them the punishment they deserve — not by physical violence — for we shall have had enough of that — nor by unconstitutional or illegal means — for we are fighting to protect not to destroy justice and freedom — but by the invincible power of our moral influence.

Can you ask us then for sympathy or concession? Will any listen when you speak of pride and patriotism? I think not.

Remember too that if Canada has become a nation respected and self-respecting she owes it to her citizens who have fought and died in this distant land and not to those self-styled Nationalists who have remained at home.

Can I hope that anything I have said here may influence you to consider the situation in a different light and that it is not yet too late for me to be made proud of our relationship?

At this moment, as I write, French and English Canadians are fighting and dying side by side. Is their sacrifice to go for nothing or will it not cement a foundation for a true Canadian nation, a Canadian nation independent in thought, independent in action, independent even in its political organization — but in spirit united for high international and humane purposes to the two Motherlands of England and France?

I think that is an ideal in which we shall all equally share. Can we not all play an equal part in its realization?

I am, as long as may be possible,

Your affectionate Cousin,
TALBOT M. PAPINEAU.

MR. BOURASSA'S REPLY TO CAPT. TALBOT PAPINEAU'S LETTER

Montreal, August 2nd, 1916.

Andrew-R. McMaster, Esq., K.C.,
189 St. James St.,
City.

Dear Sir,

On my return from an absence of several weeks, I found your letter of the 18th ult., and the copy of a letter apparently written to me by your partner, Capt. Talbot Papineau, on the 21st of March.

Capt. Papineau's letter, I am informed, appeared simultaneously, Friday last, in a number of papers, in Montreal, Quebec, Ottawa, and elsewhere. You have thus turned it into a kind of political manifesto and constituted yourself its publisher. Allow me therefore to send you my reply, requesting you to have it transmitted to Capt. Papineau, granting that he is the real author of that document. I can hardly believe it. A brave and active officer as he is has seldom the time to prepare and write such long pieces of political eloquence. Then, why should Capt. Papineau, who writes and speaks French elegantly, who claims so highly his French origin and professes with such ardour his love of France, have written in English to his "*dear cousin Henri*"? How is it that a letter written on the 21st of March has reached me but four months later, through your medium? For what purpose did you keep it so long in portfolio? and why do you send me a copy, instead of the letter itself?

It is, you say, an "open letter." It was, nevertheless, meant to reach me. It opens and ends with forms of language bearing the touch of intimate relationship — more so even than could be expected from the rare intercourse which, in spite of our blood connection, had so far existed between your partner and myself. The whole thing has the appearance of a political manoeuvre executed under the name of a young and gallant officer, who has the advantage or inconvenience of being my cousin. That Capt. Papineau has put his signature at the foot of that document, it is possible; but he would certainly not have written it in cool thought, after due reflection. It not only expresses opinions radically opposed to those I heard from him before the war; it also contains inaccuracies of fact of which I believe him honourably incapable.

He mentions "some discussions in the past," "differences of opinion," which have left "uninjured" a "pleasant friendship," dating, he says, "from the time of [his] birth." From his childhood to his return from Oxford, I do not think we had ever met, and certainly never to exchange the slightest glimpse of thought or opinion. Of matters of national concern we talked but once in all my life. From that one conversation I gathered the impression that he was still more opposed than myself to any kind of imperial solidarity. He even seemed much disposed to hasten the day of the Independence of Canada. Since, I met him on two or three occasions. We talked of matters indifferent, totally foreign to the numerous questions treated with such eloquent profuseness and so little reasoning in his letter of the 21st of March.

How can he charge me with having expressed "unhappy views" "at the outstart of the war," in August 1914, and held them stubbornly "unchanged" till this day? In August 1914, I was abroad. My first pronouncement on the intervention of Canada in the war is dated September 8th, 1914. In that editorial, while repelling the principles of Imperial solidarity and their consequences, and maintaining the nationalist doctrine in which Capt. Papineau — and you as well — pretends to be still a believer, I pronounced myself in favour of the intervention of Canada, *as a nation*, for the defence of the superior interests uniting Canada with France and Britain. My "unhappy views" were thus analogous to those of your partner. It is but later, long after Capt. Papineau was gone, that my attitude was changed and brought me to condemn the participation of Canada in the war,— or rather the political inspiration of that participation and the many abuses which have resulted therefrom. The reasons of that change are well known to those who have read or heard with attention and good faith all my statements on the matter. To sum them up is now sufficient.

The free and independent participation of Canada — free for the nation and free for the individuals — I had accepted, provided it remained within reasonable bounds, in conformity with the conditions of the country. But the Government, the whole of Parliament, the press, and politicians of both parties all applied themselves systematically to obliterate the free character of Canada's intervention. "Free" enlistment is now carried on by means of blackmailing, intimidation, and threats of all sorts. Advantage has been taken of the emotion caused by the war to assert, with the utmost intensity and intolerance, the doctrine of Imperial solidarity, triumphantly opposed in the past by our statesmen and the whole Canadian people, up to the days of the infamous South African War, concocted by Chamberlain, Rhodes, and the British imperialists with the clear object of drawing the self-governing colonies into "the vortex of European militarism." That phrase of your political leader, Sir Wilfrid Laurier, is undoubtedly fresh in your mind. After having given way to the imperialistic current of 1899, Sir Wilfrid Laurier and the liberal party had come back to the nationalist doctrine. The naval scare of 1909 threw them again under the yoke of imperialism; the war has achieved their enslavement: they united with the tory-jingo-imperialists of all shades to make of the participation of Canada in the war an immense political manoeuvre and thus assure the triumph of British imperialism. You and your partner, like many others, have followed your party through its various evolutions. I have remained firmly attached to the principles I laid down at the time of the South African war and maintained unswervingly ever since.

As early as the month of March 1900, I pointed out the possibility of a conflict between Great Britain and Germany and the danger of laying down in South Africa a precedent, the fatal consequence of which would be to draw Canada into all the wars undertaken by the United Kingdom. Sir Wilfrid Laurier and the liberal leaders laughed at my apprehensions; against my warnings they quoted the childish safeguard of the "no precedent clause" inserted in the Order in Council of the 14th of October 1899. For many years after, till 1912, and 1913, they kept singing the praises of the Kaiser and extolling the peaceful virtues of Germany. They now try to regain time by denouncing vociferously the "barbarity" of the "Huns." Today, as in 1900, in 1911, and always, I believe that all the nations of Europe are the victims of their own mistakes, of the complacent servility with which they submitted to the dominance of all Imperialists and traders in human flesh, who, in England as in Germany, in France as in Russia, have brought the peoples to slaughter in order to increase their reapings of cursed gold. German Imperialism and British Imperialism, French Militarism and Russian Tsarism, I hate with equal detestation; and I believe as firmly today as in 1899 that Canada, a nation of America, has a nobler mission to fulfill than to bind herself to the fate of the nations of Europe or to any spoliating Empire — whether it be the spoliators of Belgium, Alsace, or Poland, or those of Ireland or the Transvaal, of Greece or the Balkans.

Politicians of both parties, your liberal friends as well as their conservative opponents, feign to be much scandalized at my "treasonable disloyalty." I could well afford to look upon them as a pack of knaves and hypocrites. In 1896, your liberal leaders and friends stumped the whole province of Quebec with the cry "WHY SHOULD WE FIGHT FOR ENGLAND?" From 1902 to 1911, Sir Wilfrid Laurier was acclaimed by them as the indomitable champion of Canada's autonomy against British Imperialism. His resisting attitude at the Imperial Conferences of 1902 and 1907 was praised to the skies. His famous phrase on the "vortex of European militarism," and his determination to keep Canada far from it, became the party's by-word — always in the Province of Quebec, of course. His Canadian Navy scheme was presented as a step toward the independence of Canada.

Then came the turn of the Conservatives to tread in the footsteps of the Nationalists; they soon outstripped us. A future member of the conservative Cabinet, Mr. Blondin, brought back to life an old saying of Sir Adolphe Chapleau, and suggested to pierce the Union jack with bullets in order to let pass the breeze of liberty. The tory leaders, Sir Robert Borden, Sir George Foster, the virtuous Bob Rogers, and even our national superKitchener, Sir Sam Hughes, while trumpeting the purity of their Imperialism, greeted with undisguised joy the anti-imperialist victory of Drummond-Arthabaska, and used it for all it was worth to win the general elections in 1911.

By what right should those people hold me as a "traitor," because I remain consequent with the principles that I have never ceased to uphold and which both parties have exploited alternately, as long as it suited their purpose and kept them in power or brought them to office?

Let it not be pretended that those principles are out of place, pending the war. To prevent Canada from participating in the war, then foreseen and predicted, was their very object and *raison d'être*. To throw them aside and deny them when the time of test came, would have required a lack of courage and sincerity, of which I feel totally incapable. If this is what they mean by "British loyalty" and "superior civilization," they had better hang me at once. I will never obey such dictates and will ever hold in deepest contempt the acrobats who lend themselves to all currents of blind popular passion in order to serve their personal or political ends.

This, let it be well understood, does not apply to your partner. His deeds have shown the sincerity of his political turn. Without agreeing with his new opinions, I admired his silent courage in running to the front at the first call. His verbose political manifesto — supposing he is really responsible for it — adds nothing to his merits. Still less does it enhance the dignity and moral worth of the politicians and pressmen of all kinds, who, after having denounced war and imperialism, and while taking great care not to risk their precious body, have become the apostles of war and the upholders of imperialism.

I will not undertake to answer every point of the dithyrambic plea of my gallant cousin. When he says that I am too far away from the trenches to judge of the real meaning of this war, he may be right. On the other hand, his long and diffuse piece of eloquence proves that the excitement of warfare and the distance from home have obliterated in his mind the fundamental realities of his native country. I content myself with touching upon one point, on which he unhappily lends credit to the most mischievous of the many anti-national opinions circulated by the jingo press. He takes the French Canadians to task and challenges their patriotism, because they enlist in lesser number than the other elements of the population of Canada. Much could be said upon that. It is sufficient to signalize one patent fact: the number of recruits for the European war, in the various Provinces of Canada and from each component element of the population, is in inverse ratio of the enrootment in the soil and the traditional patriotism arising therefrom. The newcomers from the British Isles have enlisted in much larger proportion than English-speaking Canadians born in this country, while these have enlisted more than the French Canadians. The Western Provinces have given more recruits than

Ontario, and Ontario more than Quebec. In each Province, the floating population of the cities, the students, the labourers and clerks, either unemployed or threatened with dismissal, have supplied more soldiers than the farmers. Does it mean that the city dwellers are more patriotic than the country people? or that the newcomers from England are better Canadians than their fellow citizens of British origin, born in Canada? No; it simply means that in Canada, as in every other country, at all times, the citizens of the oldest origin are the least disposed to be stampeded into distant ventures of no direct concern to their native land. It proves also that military service is more repugnant to the rural than the urban populations.

There is among the French Canadians a larger proportion of farmers, fathers of large families, than among any other ethnical element in Canada. Above all, the French Canadians are the only group exclusively Canadian, in its whole and by each of the individuals of which it is composed. They look upon the perturbations of Europe, even those of England or France, as foreign events. Their sympathies naturally go to France against Germany; but they do not think they have an obligation to fight for France, no more than the French of Europe would hold themselves bound to fight for Canada against the United States or Japan, or even against Germany, in case Germany should attack Canada without threatening France.

English Canada, not counting the *blokes*, contains a considerable proportion of people still in the first period of national incubation. Under the sway of imperialism, a fair number have not yet decided whether their allegiance is to Canada or to the Empire, whether the United Kingdom or the Canadian Confederacy is their country.

As to the newcomers from the United Kingdom, they are not Canadian in any sense. England or Scotland is their sole fatherland. They have enlisted for the European war as naturally as Canadians, either French or English, would take arms to defend Canada against an aggression on the American continent.

Thus it is rigourously correct to say that recruiting has gone in inverse ratio of the development of Canadian patriotism. If English-speaking Canadians have a right to blame the French Canadians for the small number of their recruits, the newcomers from the United Kingdom, who have supplied a much larger proportion of recruits than any other element of the population, would be equally justified in branding the Anglo-Canadians with disloyalty and treason. Enlistment for the European war is supposed to be absolutely free and voluntary. This has been stated right and left from beginning to end. If that statement is honest and sincere, all provocations from one part of the population against the other, and exclusive attacks against the French Canadians, should cease. Instead of reviling unjustly one-third of the Canadian people — a population so remarkably characterized by its constant loyalty to national institutions and its respect for public order,— those men who claim a right to enlighten and lead public opinion should have enough good faith and intelligence to see facts as they are and to respect the motives of those who persist in their determination to remain more Canadian than English or French.

In short, English-speaking Canadians enlist in much smaller number than the newcomers from England, because they are more Canadian; French Canadians enlist less than English Canadians because they are totally and exclusively Canadian. To claim that their abstention is due to the "baneful" influence of the Nationalists is a pure nonsense. Should I give way to the suggestion of my gallant cousin, I would be just as powerless as Sir Wilfrid Laurier to induce the French Canadians to enlist. This is implicitly acknowledged in Capt. Papineau's letter: on the one hand, he asserts that my views on the participation of Canada in the war are denied by my own friends; on the other he charges the mass of the French-Canadian population with a refusal to answer the call of duty. The simple truth is, that the abstention of the French Canadians is no more the result of the present attitude of the Nationalists than the consequence of the liberal campaign of 1896, or of the conservative appeals of 1911. It relates to deeper causes: hereditary instincts, social and economic conditions, a national tradition of three centuries. It is equally true, however, that those deep and far distant causes have been strengthened by the constant teaching of all our political and social leaders, from Lafontaine, Cartier, Macdonald, Mackenzie, to Laurier inclusively. The only virtue, or crime, of the Nationalists is to persist in believing and practising what they were taught by the men of the past, and even those of today. This is precisely what infuriates the politicians, either *blue* or *red*. To please the Imperialists, they have renounced all their traditions and undertaken to bring the French Canadians under imperial command. Unable to succeed, they try to conceal their fruitless apostasy by denouncing to the hatred of the jingos the obtrusive witnesses of their past professions of faith.

The jingo press and politicians have also undertaken to persuade their gullible followers that the Nationalists hinder the work of recruiters *because* of the persecution meted out to the French minorities in Ontario and Manitoba. This is but another nonsense. My excellent cousin, I am sorry to say,— or his inspirer — has picked it up.

The two questions are essentially distinct; this we have never ceased to assert. One is purely internal; the other affects the international status of Canada and her relations with Great Britain. To the problem of the teaching of languages we ask for a solution in conformity with the spirit of the Federal agreement, the best interests of Confederation, and the principles of pedagogy as applied in civilized countries. Our attitude on the participation of Canada in the war is inspired exclusively by the constant tradition of the country and the agreements concluded half a century ago between Canada and Great Britain. Even if the irritating bilingual question was non-existent, our views on the war would be what they are. The most that can be said is, that the backward and essentially Prussian policy of the rulers of Ontario and Manitoba gives us an additional argument against the intervention of Canada in the European conflict. To speak of fighting for the preservation of French civilization in Europe while endeavouring to destroy it in America, appears to us as an absurd piece of inconsistency. To preach Holy War for the liberties of the peoples overseas, and to oppress the national minorities in Canada, is, in our opinion, nothing but odious hypocrisy.

Is it necessary to add that, in spite of his name, Capt. Papineau is utterly unqualified to judge of the feelings of the French Canadians? For most part American, he has inherited, with a few drops of French blood, the most *denationalized* instincts of his French origin. From those he calls his compatriots he is separated by his religious belief and his maternal language. Of their traditions, he knows but what he has read in a few books. He was brought up far away from close contact with French Canadians. His higher studies he pursued in England. His elements of French culture he acquired in France. The complexity of his origin and the diversity of his training would be sufficient to explain his mental hesitations and the contradictions which appear in his letter. Under the sway of his American origin, he glories in the Revolution of 1776; he calls it a war "for the principle of national existence." In good logic, he should approve highly of the tentative rebellion of the Sinn Feiners, and suggest that Canada should rise in arms to break the yoke of Great Britain. His American forefathers, whom he admires so much, fought against England and called upon France and Spain to help them against their mother-country, for lighter motives than those of the Dublin rebels. The Imperial burden they refused to bear was infinitely less ponderous than that which weighs today upon the people of Canada.

With the threat contained in the conclusion of his letter, I need not be concerned. Supposing always that he is truly responsible for that document, I make broad allowance for the excitement and perturbation resulting from his strenuous life. He and many of his comrades will have enough to do in order to help Canada to counteract the disastrous consequences of the war venture in which she has thrown herself headlong. To propagate systematically national discord by quarrelling with all Canadians, either French or English, who hold different views as to the theory and practice of their national duty, would be a misuse of time. Moreover, it would be a singular denial of their professions of faith in favour of liberty and civilization.

As to the scoundrels and bloodsuckers "who have grown fat with the wealth dishonourably gained" in war contracts, I give them up quite willingly to their just indignation. But those worthies are not to be found in nationalist ranks: they are all recruited among the noisiest preachers of the Holy War waged for "civilization" against "barbarity," for the "protection of small nations," for the "honour" of England and the "salvation" of France.

Yours truly,
HENRI BOURASSA

P.S.— I hope this will reach you before you leave for the front: no doubt, you have been the first to respond to the pressing call of your partner.   H.B.

Article Twenty-Seven

Ghosts Have Warm Hands

Will R. Bird

He led us down a long trench, and at last we were really at the front. We had become used to the slamming roar of gunfire and now we also heard the barking of machine-guns. Bullets came singing overhead, to go swishing into the darkness. Some struck on wire and we heard the sibilant whine of ricochets. We had sandbags to fill. One man held them and the other shovelled in gruel-like mud. When twenty were filled a man jumped on top and emptied the bags as they were handed up to him. It was ticklish work, as the one emptying had to jump down when machine-guns opened on that section.

We got soaked to the skin. The cold slime ran down our wrists as we lifted the bags, and our boots sunk in the mire until our feet were numbed, sodden things. All the next day we growled at Tommy for causing us such a night. Then, at dusk, Stevenson found us. Three of us were to go at once to an emplacement used by a big mortar they called a "flying pig."

When we got there we noticed a peculiar odour. All the shapeless ruin of Neuville St. Vaast stank of decay and slime, but this new smell halted us. "Here's bags," said Stevenson. "Go in there and gather up all you can find, then we'll bury it back of the trench. Get a move on."

A "flying pig" had exploded as it left the gun and three men had been shredded to fragments. We were to pick up legs and bits of flesh from underfoot, place all in the bags and then bury them. It was a harsh breaking-in. We did not speak a word as we worked. When we were done Stevenson told us we could go, but Tommy and I lingered in a trench bay and stared over the dark, flickering, silhouetted landscape.

Over the tangle of wire in front lay the no man's land about which we had heard. Not two hundred yards away were the Germans in their trenches. A thin stalk of silver shot up as we looked, curved over in a graceful parabola and flowered into a luminous glow, pulsating and wavering, flooding the earth below with a weird, whiteness. It was a Verey light. We craned our

Source: Excerpt from Will R. Bird, *Ghosts Have Warm Hands: A Memoir of the Great War, 1916–1919*. Reprinted with permission.

necks and stared. Jumbled earth and debris, jagged wreckage: it looked as if a gigantic upheaval had destroyed all the surface and left only a festering wound. Everything was shapeless, ugly and distorted.

We went on doing working parties and gradually got acquainted with the rest of the company. There were only a few "originals," the rest were reinforcements like ourselves, mostly from the 92nd of Toronto. Back we went to Mont St. Eloi and were billeted in huts on the hillside. It was wet and freezing cold at night. After the first day of sleeping and resting the men grew garrulous, and we listened to all they said about different craters such as Patricia, Birken, Common and Vernon. Across from where we slept was a Scot who was always singing "Maggie frae Dundee" or quarrelling with Stevenson, who had charge of the hut. Next to him was a tall, clean-built man, Roy MacMillan, from the 92nd. He and I became friends and he told me his experiences on the Somme.

When we went back for a second trip in the line, the wind was raw with driving rain. Once more we were on working parties. All this time we had not got to know an officer, and when we asked who commanded the company all they grunted was "Dugout Ray." One night Tommy and I were detained by Stevenson, who had us repair a place that had caved in. We were wet and cold and hungry. Rations were very slim, six men to one loaf of bread, and only bully and hardtack to help out. The hot tea kept up the morale. We got our messtins from our bunks and went over to a corner, where a sullen-faced man dished out the dinner. We stayed in the dugout and heated tea and mulligan and though we avoided shell fire we did not envy him his lot. There was no tea for us, he announced, but at that moment Stevenson came and got his messtin full.

We stepped forward and looked in the Dixie. There was plenty more and I said so. The cook snarled back that we had better be in France more than five minutes before trying to run things. Tommy took charge. He was well built and fast with his hands. He gave the fellow one short minute to fill his tin or else. The tin was filled. Later, when we were supposed to be sleeping, I heard the "old-timers" discussing us. They agreed it would be bad policy to try to run us, and the cook received no sympathy.

It was another six-day trip, but when we went back to Mont St. Eloi we felt old soldiers, and "Maggie frae Dundee" rang out merrily. This time there was a parade. Our company commander was a genial-looking gentleman. Our platoon officer was a MacDonald and seemed a good sort. We were taken to the "baths." In an old building through which the winter wind whistled, we undressed on a floor covered with slime and in turn crouched under an icy trickle from overhead pipes, the water always failing when one had soaped himself. When we went to get dressed we found our shirts were gone and a bleary-eyed character tossed over any size garment he happened to pick up, with unmatched socks.

When we went back to the line, Stevenson told me I would be one for Vernon Crater, and from the way he said it I judged it would be something unusual. Roy MacMillan joined me and said that he was to team up with me, that Vernon was a three-sentry post, had not been held in daytime before, and was not more than sixty yards from German posts. We were to hold the place for four days.

The weather turned the coldest France had known in thirty years. All the ground was frozen like iron. We wore leather jerkins over our greatcoats, had Balaclavas under our steel helmets, and socks on our hands. The supply of gloves was only enough for the oldtimers. It was very clear weather and every sound carried, so that we moved with utmost caution and very slowly. The main trench was a long, black-shrouded ditch full of dark figures muttering to each other, and there were hissed curses when a steel helmet clanged against a rifle barrel.

We turned from the main trench and went up a low-walled reach to the post, a wide affair in three sections. The right-hand corner was like an enlarged well with a fire step. Two men were placed there. On the left was a similar post and in it were Laurie and old Dundee. MacMillan and I were in the centre, a cup-like hollow. Behind us was a roofed space about six feet square in which Corporal Sellars, in charge, stayed. He had a seat there, a flare pistol and flares, and extra bombs. A blanket was hung over the rear entrance.

MacMillan explained everything about sentry duty, and I did not duck when the first flares went up. We could hear the Germans walking in their trenches, hear them coughing, hear them turning a creaking windlass that would be hauling up chalk from a dugout under construction. At daylight we put up small periscopes on slivers stuck in the sandbagged parapet and watched through them until dark.

The next night I saw my first uncaptured German. He was only a boy, as young-looking as Mickey, and he was standing waist-high above his trench wall as one of our flares burst directly above him and placed him in dazzling light.

He did not move at first — both sides had strict orders against any movement when a flare burst — but I knew he had seen me because I was as high on our side. He waved, and some wild impulse caused me to wave back to him as I jumped down. MacMillan cursed me soundly. After midnight I stepped back to talk with Sellars and, as it was bright moonlight, pushed aside the blanket at the rear and looked toward our trench. Ping! A bullet embedded itself in the wooden post beside me. I ducked back, very frightened. There were hurried steps outside and a corporal from the trench wanted to know if anyone was hit. A new draft of men, the 132nd from New Brunswick, had come into the line and one of them had watched our post all the time, thinking it was the German front.

A light snow fell the next day and whitened the jagged wilderness between the lines. There was a wrecked cart near the German wire, and as I peered at it, it blotted out, then appeared again. A whisper alerted MacMillan, and we detected two of the enemy crawling outside their post. "If we can catch them it's leave for us," hissed MacMillan. "Strip off your gear."

We shed jerkins and greatcoats and steel helmets, and examined our rifles. Unluckily mine stood at the back of the post and water from melted snow had frozen over the muzzle. MacMillan's had the breech uncovered and it was a lump of mud and ice. We jumped for our bombs and found them blocks of frozen mud, then looked over and saw the Germans reentering their post. With first light we cleaned our rifles and bombs and made sure they would remain in good order.

Each morning a sergeant brought a rum issue just before light. I did not take mine and Laurie did not take his. A dozen or more of us in the draft never drank or smoked. This morning an officer was with the sergeant. He came in and stood beside me as MacMillan had his turn off and asked many questions while the sergeant was at the post on the right. He told me his name was Larson, that he was from Bear River, Nova Scotia, and thrilled with the front line. He wanted to know how near the Germans were.

I told him and he said it sounded unreal to him. It had become light as he talked, and when I put up the periscope it was shot away by a German sniper. "That fellow must be very near," said Larson.

"I'll take a quick look."

"Don't!" I yelled and grabbed at his coat. He stretched up in spite of my protest. The bullet entered his forehead and went out the back, breaking the strap of his helmet and carrying it to the rear of the post. I lowered the body to the trench floor and covered the face with a clean sandbag.

MacMillan was shocked. "Too much rum!" he said. The sergeant came from the other post and he was stunned. He said he would report what had happened and was hardly away when we heard a shot on the left post. The sergeant had given old Dundee two extra rum rations, mine and Laurie's, and the Scot had seized his rifle and started to clean it, saying he was going to get the sniper. The weapon went off in his hands and the bullet stuck the frozen side of the post, chipping bits from it. One struck Laurie on the foot and stung badly.

MacMillan tried to calm Dundee but he refused to listen. The rum had him wild. He raised up to aim his rifle, and the German shot. Dundee's head was turned so that the bullet took both eyes out. He tumbled down, clawing at his face and groaning.

Something had to be done and quickly. Sellars would not go for help. So I shed my equipment and crouched low as the sergeant had done. It was hard to keep that way, but when I raised ever so little a bullet burned the back of my neck like a hot iron. I reached the trench and got a stretcher bearer and stretcher. We were careful going in and arrived safely. But Dundee was in a bad state. We had to tie him on the stretcher, as he would not listen to anyone. Getting the stretcher and its load to the trench took almost half an hour. The stretcher bearer was ahead, pulling the stretcher, and I pushed from the rear. Finally it was done. Then I crawled back and sat all day beside the dead officer.

At dark we were relieved by the Princess Patricias. We went to Neuville St. Vaast again and into the cellars. Before morning a few of us were called out to form a ration party and we saw how easily a man could get a "blighty." We passed an old ruin with a long wall extending beyond it, light flickering through a small opening as flares went up. As we passed by there was a snapping of machine bullets overhead but they were disregarded, since the wall protected us. Then a man behind us yelled. A chance bullet had come through that brick-sized opening and hit him in the leg. He was bandaged and went cheerfully down the line.

When we returned with the rations I slept several hours, then was wakened and told to put on my pack and go with three other men to Mont St. Eloi. There we would meet a sergeant who would take us to a bombing school. The three of us met, had no conversation, but trudged out of the line and in due course arrived at long huts, where we found ourselves with men of the other battalions of the brigade. We were to be instructed in shooting rifle grenades and throwing Mills bombs. Our practice would be with live ones.

It was very pleasant. The hours were short and the rations plentiful. The next day at noon as we lolled in our bunks, there was a sudden shrill tearing sound and a terrific explosion just outside. Pieces of shrapnel came through the side of the hut. We leaped to the floor and raced from the building. A second shell came and there were loud cries for stretcher bearers. Four men were killed and seven wounded, but there was not a third shell.

To my delight I quickly learned the proper elevation for shooting rifle grenades, made top marks and also did well with the throwing. The battalion came to the huts at Mont St. Eloi and had it easy. When our six-day course was over I reported back to the platoon and was told I had been transferred to the battalion bombers. Tommy declared I had pulled strings to get such a shift. The weather became colder than ever, and we went into the line again and relieved the Pats.

The bombers were a grand lot, and I teamed with Sammy Sedgewick, a real gentleman. Chiefly we had to patrol the trenches. We had a good dugout and plenty of rations, and our hours were much easier than in the company, where a man did six hours on and six hours off with monotonous regularity all the time he was in the line. There you came down from your post, chilled through, dazed from lack of sleep, and pushed your way into the crowded underground to your chicken-wire bunk. You could lie and eat your rations, and consider yourself lucky if there was any lukewarm tea. The warmth of the men thawed the earth and chalk walls enough to make them ooze dampness. Rats were everywhere, podgy brutes with ghoulish eyes. They crawled over you as you lay under a blanket and tried to shiver yourself warm.

Twice in one night Sammy and I had a bomb target. A sentry stopped us and whispered as he pointed to dark blurs working at the German wire. We sent two grenades among them and a Lewis gun helped to complete the job. Later another sentry said the Germans were working at something opposite his post; he could hear thumping sounds, as if they were driving posts. We listened and heard the noise, set our rifles carefully and fired. There was the red flash of explosion and then a long drawn yell that ended in a screaming heard all along the line. The enemy sent over "darts" in reply, but none fell near us.

It was cold as ever the next night and no working parties were about. The ground was like rock. Sammy and I found a Lewis gun crew asleep, every man, and removed the gun, threw chalk and wakened them. They had a bad minute and didn't likely doze again that night. Sometimes I stopped with Mel Baillie or Mickey or Jenkins and talked with them of the home town.

The war changed men mightily. Down in dugouts where there was hardly room to breathe, men who had come from comfortable homes moved without complaint. All grousing was reserved for the "brass hats," who were supposed to be responsible for all that went wrong. The men were unselfish, each with a balance and discipline of his own. We endured much. Dugouts reeked with odours of stale perspiration and the sour, alkaline smell of clothing. There was never enough water to permit frequent washing and when we could get warm the lice tormented us. The vermin were in every dugout, millions of descendents of the originals of 1915. We seared the seams of our shirts with candles, fought them constantly but never conquered them.

The third afternoon the sergeant sent me on an errand up La Salle Avenue, a trench often strafed. Another man was walking ahead of me, and as we hurried along I heard the familiar phew-phew-phew in the air and yelled. The fellow sprinted like mad and I tried to follow suit, but my world crashed in a bang. A million bells rang in my ears. Lights danced and sparkled and I could not get my breath. Hands tugged at me. Eventually I got up, to stare at a smoking crater not ten feet from where I had fallen. The big "rum jar" had fallen between us, though the other man was twice as far from it. He was shell-shocked and taken from the line. I was sick for an hour and my head throbbed half the night but I stayed in the trenches.

The next night I stopped to talk with Fernley, a quiet fellow of the 42nd who was a real friend. He stood his rifle against the side of the trench and was pacing up and down and beating his chest with his arms in an effort to get warm. We chatted a time and then I moved on and was about ten yards from him when a German "dart" burst on the parapet several feet from where Fernley was walking. He sank to the duckboards like a wet sack. I hurried to him and spoke but he did not answer. He was dead.

There was not a mark on him. I got the sergeant and he examined Fernley, but he was mystified too. We carried him to the dressing station and they stripped him and could not find a mark of injury. I went back to the trench and looked around. Suddenly I noticed Fernley's rifle still standing there — and the top part of the bayonet gone! The mystery was soon solved. The piece had entered an armpit and pierced his heart. Not a drop of blood had issued from the wound.

We were in supports again, then back in the front trench. Seven men went out with sickness, two with foot trouble, and I found myself on a crater post doing a regular turn of six hours on. It was very cold and I was about fifteen yards from the main trench. One night I saw someone coming up the sap with no rifle. That meant he was an officer, and when he stood with me in the post and asked questions I was careful, for a time, about what I said. He asked me where I was from, what I had done before the war. I told him of taking up a homestead in Alberta, the big money I had made for a time working for an eccentric American who used the name Smith. Smith had imported four wolf hounds from Russia and purchased a pair of half-broken broncos and a buckboard. He built a large box on the back of the buckboard and put the hounds in it. The box had a door attached to a wire. When he saw a coyote we drove past it, and at the second of passing the door was flipped up and out shot the hounds, who would run the coyote down. There was a bounty of fifty cents per coyote snout. I told the officer about our hunts, about the hard work on the harvest field, and about the sugar maple trees in the hills where I was born. He stayed and stayed and brought the talk around to the battalion. How did I like the infantry? I was careful, and he knew it. He laughed at some of my answers and finally asked me if I knew who he was. I said I had no idea. He asked who commanded the 3rd Division.

"Major-General Lipsett," I said.

"Does he ever come to the front line?" was the next question. I said I did not know. We were standing shoulder to shoulder in the narrow post and he nudged me. "You're an interesting fellow, Bird," he said. "I am Lipsett!" The information was so surprising I became tongue-tied and he nudged me again. "I don't blame you in the least if you don't believe me," he said, "so I'm going to give you a snapshot I had taken in 1913. All I ask is that you will not tell your mates I did so."

He tugged the postcard-size snapshot from an inner pocket and gave it to me, shook my hand warmly and left. I still have that picture.

The sergeant came and said I was for a reconnaissance with him. We crawled out under our wire at a place where it had been raised, and moved away by inches as we wormed between Durrand and Duffield Craters. After each yard we listened, so that it was an hour before we were in a position to examine the enemy wire. When we got back to our trench we were nearly frozen. The other bombers said a raid was to be made from both our craters and from the Patricia posts. The next day the Stokes mortars pounded the German line.

The raid was on February 13 and zero hour was 9:15 a.m. The German trench was to be given a baptism of rifle grenades, so each bomber was given ten grenades. We had exactly two minutes to shoot them. It was easy to make a mistake and cause a premature burst, but no accident occurred and we got our barrage away on time. Then we went into a tunnel entrance and awaited the raiders' return. Two officers and six men were wounded. Two prisoners were taken.

That night we relieved the "Van Doos" and it was my job to guide their bombers to our dugout. There were only six of them and they had me nervous before my chore ended. They had had too much rum, they lagged all the way, talked loudly, and one man played a mouth organ. The 42nd bombers took a chance overland and we got out ahead of the company. Shortly after they took over, the Germans gave the Van Doos a housewarming in the shape of a "Minnie" bombardment. We were told they had thirty casualties in the hour.

The next day we marched and marched and marched, going through several towns, and at last arrived at Divion. After the long session in the crater line with little exercise, it was a hard grind. Three fellows dropped out. My legs were very tired but I lasted the route. We moved into a billet and a runner arrived to tell us the bombers were no more. A re-organization was taking place and we were to return to our respective platoons.

When I woke in the morning I was very stiff and sore. Someone reported me, and the battalion medical sergeant, a prince of a fellow, came and asked me about my experience with the "rum jar." He said I had undoubtedly suffered a concussion, that I was to remain in billets and go on sick parade in the morning. Our billet was a French cottage, a miner's home. Downstairs was a fair-sized room with a tall, pot-bellied stove, table and chairs. Two small bedrooms opened from it. Upstairs was one large space. There was no window and we slept on the first floor, four of us.

Article Twenty-Eight

Recruiting, 1914–1916

Ronald G. Haycock

Military records show that by the end of the Great War 619 636 Canadian men and women had served with the army. It took four years to raise such a number, and well over half enlisted while Sam Hughes was war minister. By late 1916 when he was fired from the cabinet, the army overseas had four divisions and another ready for organization. But Canadians at home had lost much of their enthusiasm for volunteering to feed the field force. However, two years earlier the opposite had been true when the majority of Canadians seemed determined to do their duty. After the first contingent left Valcartier, the prime minister authorized a second one in mid-October. The next month militia headquarters decided to maintain 30 000 men under arms in Canada. By July 1915 the overall total was 150 000 and three months later 250 000. On New Year's Day 1916, the prime minister announced that the national establishment of the Canadian Expeditionary Force (CEF) would be a half million men. It all looked so easy. But by mid-1916, the volunteer system began to falter all over the country. As the war effort stepped up, the demands of the other equally vital forces of industry and agriculture competed for the men. Enlistments slowed down. In English Canada pessimistic conscription rumours turned into open demands; and as enlistments dried up before the mounting casualties in Europe, French Canadians recoiled at the prospect of being drafted for a foreign war, which by 1916 they no longer considered much of their concern.

To avoid a national schism — perhaps even an open rebellion — the government desperately tried other solutions. By the fall of 1916 national registration to co-ordinate the wealth of the nation had come and gone. In early 1917, amid the crescendo of English-Canadian voices demanding conscription, the harried Borden administration attempted to free volunteers for the front by establishing the Canadian Defence Force for domestic duty, but it too failed. That spring, after the British authorities predicted the need for more and more troops, the prime minister finally resigned himself to military conscription. In May 1917 he announced his intention and padded the blow by promising to bring in conscription through a union government. In the next six months, the declaration split the country along French and English lines, irrespective of party, and by the general election in December 1917, Canada had both coalition government and conscripts.[1] The story of these events involves Sam Hughes, and to a large degree he, like his prime minister, must bear both praise and blame.

Sam Hughes' one-man mobilization effort in 1914 set the tone for recruiting in the next two years. Hughes gave to the recruitment effort nerve-end leadership — spirit, enthusiasm, vigour, hope, and confidence — but little order and less administration. He conceived of Canada's war contributions mainly in terms of fighting troops in a national army. But he never appeared to understand fully the modern needs of such a force. He could not see, first, that national war must have at least a semblance of consensus of the nation's people — both French and English — and second, that limits on the size of the force and the method of keeping it at established strength were problems which eventually would have to be faced. Force size was a political problem that belonged to the government as a whole but one for which Sam Hughes

Source: From *Sam Hughes: The Public Career of a Controversial Canadian, 1885–1916*, Ronald G. Haycock, Wilfrid Laurier University Press in collaboration with the Canadian War Museum, the Canadian Museum of Civilization, and the National Museums of Canada, 1986, pp. 198–224. Used with permission.

as militia minister must give sound and realistic advice to the cabinet. Maintenance of strength, however, was an administrative question that for the most part belonged to Sam Hughes. Instead of understanding these dimensions, he seemed governed solely by a desire to show Canada's martial prowess on the battlefield in a huge patriotic and volunteer army without regard for the effects of unrestrained recruiting on industry, agriculture, or the combat efficiency of the force.[2] But in 1914 and 1915 the faults of Sam Hughes's recruiting system were not immediately obvious because the demands of war were not known; and in all fairness to Hughes, few of his fellow ministers in the beginning had any more of an accurate conception of how best to respond to the crisis. For months all of them worked in the dark using dilapidated tools of state. Some found both light and better utensils; Hughes never did.

When the first contingent had sailed in October 1914, Hughes had been thankful that Borden had allowed all the volunteers to go, a sure sign that both men agreed in the limited and archaic view that the best way to pursue the war effort was with soldiers in large numbers. When Hughes returned from England early the next month he immediately plunged into the organization of the second contingent, recently announced by the prime minister. In terms of manpower, he swung back to the old decentralized recruiting arrangements that had been with the militia since Confederation. In the scheme, authority rested with the officers commanding the divisions, who in turn gave quotas to each of the militia units of their areas. The quotas were supplied by headquarters, but beyond that there was little help from Ottawa in personnel, funds, or organization. In the first three years of the war, Ottawa spent only $27 000 on recruitment, most of it in 1917. But then little help was expected.[3]

The months from August 1914 to July 1915 are best described as ones of the enlisting rather than recruiting. Nearly 60 000 had joined in 1914 alone. By February 1915 Hughes announced that a third contingent would be sent and optimistically told the Commons that "I could raise three more contingents in three weeks if necessary." As yet there was no perceived shortage of manpower in industry or agriculture. But it was the off-season for agriculture, and others presumed that the recession-induced unemployed were being conveniently siphoned off into CEF units. By June 1915 the overseas force had 100 247 officers and men. During the special session of Parliament the year before, Hughes had made it clear that as far as he was concerned this war would be one of volunteers, not conscripts. The prime minister had agreed when he told a Halifax audience in December that "there has not been, there will not be compulsion or conscription." The only technique Hughes applied during this period was to keep close watch on who got the commands of each new battalion.[4] Sometimes the divisional commanders asked that units be allowed to organize in their districts; other times — and increasingly so — Hughes made arrangements himself with specific individuals, then informed the divisional organization to expect a new unit in the area. True to his romantic view of war, the minister was convinced that in a crisis a citizen's patriotic sense of duty would be sufficient to supply all the volunteers necessary. All he had to do was constantly remind them of it. As soon as he recovered sufficiently from the illness that had put him in the hospital in late December, Hughes took to his private rail car late in January to encourage volunteering. He had to get back to Ottawa by the opening of the new session on 5 February but before that he covered seven thousand miles in two weeks and delivered over twenty-five recruiting speeches across the country.[5]

Hughes gave out the stuff that many wanted to hear: the Empire was threatened; Canada had to do its duty. Canadians could do it and would do it; it was the moment of national greatness; Canada was a principal in the war, not a colony. Hughes's battle message, mixing national pride and imperial obligation, was contagious. No wonder Castell Hopkins considered him during those early days to be the single most visible and enthusiastic recruiting agent in the country.[6] The minister's confidence, pride, and cajoling also added to the impression that manpower resources were infinite and no other government facilities except Sam Hughes's sermons were necessary in raising the country to war.

The illusion was substantially aided by patriotic citizens themselves. The fervour seemed so great that the problem was not in stirring it up but in controlling it. The various gifts of money and food sent to the Belgian Relief Fund and to the British government in the early days were ample evidence of that spirit; so were the campaigns in many communities to contribute to the well-being of the soldiers. Local councils quickly arranged for gifts of money, clothing, and the small amenities like cigarettes and socks. Many churches and women's organizations across the country did their bit as well. The Ontario government donated a half million dollars to the Imperial War Fund in Great Britain. The same special session of Parliament that brought the ominous War Measures Act into being in August 1914 also created the Canadian Patriotic Fund, of which Hughes was one of the honorary vice-presidents. This group was dedicated to raising and distributing money to soldiers' families and it expanded and carried out this function throughout the war. In fact, the general shortage of equipment produced such a spontaneous public response of private donations, like "the machine gun movement," that militia officials and Borden were so embarrassed by the summer of 1915, they refused to accept such gifts. Hughes, however, had no such pangs. His role, he knew, was to encourage the people on to new heights of patriotic effort. In fact, Robert Borden's biographer claims that this sort of decentralized war responsibility was a calculated "policy decision at the beginning of the war." Hughes's activities in recruiting, therefore, were not out of tune with the rest of the government's general view of its role in promoting active citizen participation in the war effort.[7]

However, by the spring of 1915 there were signs that these time-honoured concepts were not adequate. There were thirty-six thousand Canadians already overseas, with an entire division in the trenches after February 1915. The war had lasted longer than the predicted six months; Christmas had come and gone and there were yet no victories. Then in mid-March, the British reported thirteen thousand casualties, including one hundred Canadians, at Neuve Chapelle, and bungled the opportunity for the elusive "breakthrough" on the western front to regain the magic mobility every general sought. Even though few Canadian were victims, the twenty-five thousand lost on both sides was a terrible omen for Canadians. The CEF did not have long to wait: a few weeks later the Canadians held a bulging section of the line near Ypres in Belgium. Late in the day of 22 April, the Germans smashed into the French colonial troops to the left of the Canadians with artillery and the dreaded chlorine gas. In a ferocious defensive battle lasting nearly a week, Canada's tenacious amateurs restored the line at the terrible price of nearly six thousand men. They won the admiration of all. Their effort was quickly followed by smaller but similarly expensive defences at Festubert in May and Givenchy in June. The Germans torpedoed the supposedly unarmed British liner *Lusitania* off the coast of Ireland on 8 May. It took twelve hundred lives, one hundred of them from Ontario. This was indeed war; Canadians were stunned.[8]

Back home the successes of the CEF in these battles stirred the Canadian soul; but they also were a rude awakening to the true sacrifices. The Canadian Ross rifle, it was reported, had not worked well. Some said gunners had not had enough artillery shells to give adequate support to the Canadian infantry. But the most shocking revelations were the casualty lists. An increasing number of Canadian homes mourned the loss of loved ones; and it was not likely to stop. At the end of May the British government announced, largely as a result of the jolt to its own complacency caused by the German spring offensive, that "His Majesty's Government would accept with deep gratitude" any number of troops the Canadians could send.[9] Hughes took it as a personal signal.

But would Hughes's non-system of recruiting provide the reinforcements? Even before Ypres there were signs that the rural militia units were having trouble filling their enlistment quotas. *Globe* columnist Peter McArthur demanded that it was time the militia minister coordinate his actions with the Agriculture Department in some definite recruiting policy. Part of the flash of enthusiasm which had given nearly sixty thousand volunteers in 1914 was that most of the ranks — over 70 percent in the first contingent — were not Canadians, but British-born immigrants. Initially native Canadians had little enthusiasm to fight for king and Empire in Europe. This fact made no impression on Hughes, at least not one that he nor anyone else admitted publicly. Yet suspicions indicated something extra was needed. Other citizens began stepping into the breach with or without Sam Hughes. The same month as Neuve Chapelle, the Speakers Patriotic League, the joint brainchild of H.A. Ames, a Quebec Conservative MP, and N.F. Davidson, an Ontario Tory organizer, was created in Toronto. It was the first of many private civilian associations designed to promote all facets of the patriotic response to the war, including a more systematic recruiting organization. From this point, private recruiting leagues appeared all over English Canada. Their proliferation in Ontario was so rapid that by November 1915 they combined into a central organization — the Ontario Recruiting Association with branches throughout the province working hand in hand with local militia authorities.[10]

Hughes was all for the local organizations and a personal approach to the war effort, as he had been since he had sent out his famous 226 night telegrams mobilizing the first contingent shortly after the war started. After that he had used the existing local militia structure to funnel into the CEF whole battalions closely associated with particular areas. But he did not do it without opposition. Since September 1914, the chief of the general staff had warned Hughes that he could not keep adding such units to the overseas force. What should be done, Gwatkin had then protested, was to establish modern centrally located depots providing basic training for the unbrigaded troops before they were syphoned off as reinforcements for the veteran line units. Before the war Sir Ian Hamilton had also warned Hughes about this lack of depots. Their reasons were solid. More efficient training and use of manpower and a smaller casualty rate were three important ones. As well, authorities would have some accurate idea of available resources on hand, a fact not always present in the anachronistic and decentralized method which Hughes had followed since the outbreak of hostilities. The American Civil War, of which Hughes claimed to be a student, had pointed out the perils of constantly raising new battalions, then sending these fresh but green troops into battle. But the minister did not believe it was so; the Boer war needed no such elaborate and soulless depots to produce good fighting men, so he ignored his staff.[11]

After the spring battles of 1915, the shocking casualties and increased demands reaffirmed Hughes's resolve to secure more men. The second contingent had lingered long in Canada awaiting transport and billets in England. Hughes was anxious to get it overseas. By the middle of June it sailed, but the recruiting news at home, while gratifying, was not as spectacular as it had been. It seemed that just as the manpower demands were rising remarkably, the will to supply them was faltering. The possibilities of a substantial short-fall were obvious after it became clear at the end of June that Hughes wanted to form a Canadian corps of two divisions. The thought horrified Connaught; he secretly confided to Kitchener that the move was a ruinous one contrived by Hughes for no other reason than to satisfy his ego for a Canadian national force "possibly with a view of obtaining the command . . . himself." The Duke also suffered from his own form of exaggeration: he was afraid of an invasion by German-Americans from the still neutral United States, and even more of a revolt in the west by recent immigrants from enemy countries. Troops should therefore be kept in Canada. More accurately, Connaught worried about the disastrous effect on vital agricultural and industrial production caused by Hughes's wholesale recruiting. Connaught protested to Lord Kitchener that it was "extremely doubtful" if the Dominion could "keep an Army Corps in the field up to its proper establishment."[12]

It was not probable that Hughes had duped Borden into supporting the formation of a Canadian corps, as the governor general also imagined. The prime minister was himself determined to send more troops. Nevertheless, the governor general had put his finger on the exact point that caused the regular soldiers so much anxiety. An army corps meant at least fifty thousand troops in France. A corps was also the natural precursor of an army. Gwatkin and Deputy Minister Fiset had been greatly alarmed at the wastage of the CEF in the spring of 1915. At that time, Canada had to contend only with one division. The possibility of twice as many casualties came with the formation of a corps. An army, if it came out of that, would be impossible to maintain. Gwatkin wanted no more than a corps, and certainly not an army. In June when he told Borden that Hughes's grandiose plans were a "mistake;" it had made no impression. A few days later, in responding to an enthusiastic militia colonel, who like many of the patriots wanted many more men sent, Gwatkin bluntly stated that it was wrong "to go on adding to the number of regiments, batteries, and battalions at the front." Better, he thought, to train reinforcements and produce war material rather than to be drawn into an intolerable and exhausting war effort because of a commitment to an unrealistic combat force.[13] The true import of his and the Duke's message was that Sam Hughes's vision of a massive field effort was courting ruin, and that there were different ways to make war other than by sending warriors. Also implicit was that Hughes should advise Borden that a realistic establishment had to be determined and then adopt an efficient method of maintaining it that was in tune with national capabilities.

It was not to happen. On 8 July 1915, Robert Borden increased the CEF force to 150 000.[14] The new figure meant more recruits. While the monthly enlistments had gone up in June, they were not sufficient to allow for even normal wastage in the new national goal.

In response Hughes remained largely on the old personal course. But a few weeks earlier, he had made some small concessions in applying direct government aid for recruiting when he decided that central rather than regimental recruiting offices would be set up and that recruiting would be continuous. In August, as a further inducement for volunteers, he approved from afar a national recruiting poster campaign; one hundred thousand of them were distributed from coast to coast. After that no other national advertising went on out of the militia headquarters for over a year, and even then the minister rejected the Canadian Press Association's offer to cooperate in a national newspaper campaign to stimulate recruiting.[15]

In the summer of 1915, Hughes spent two months in England. Like the prime minister who was also there, Hughes went to the front where he saw the magnitude, the horror, and the deadlock of the war situation. When he got back to Canada in early September, what he had seen and heard only cemented his determination to step up the national effort. Canada now had a corps, but victory was not close; the British had not handled the first year at all well. What was needed was more and more troops. At the end of September, enlistment figures dipped threateningly. Hughes told reporters about his new local battalion and billeting plans. Modelled in part on Lord Derby's battalions in England, Hughes promised to house and train troops in any centre that could raise twenty-five or more district recruits. Surely, he reasoned, it would help the citizens realize the importance of the war as well as comfort men anxious about doing initial duty in a strange place. But the other aspect of the scheme had its roots in the traditional local unit structure of the non-permanent militia. Indeed, that was its very essence and the sum of Sam Hughes's forty-one years of experience in the Canadian volunteers. Hughes believed in the time-honoured technique of raising citizen-soldiers by appointing prominent politicians and businessmen as lieutenant-colonels to enlist battalions in their own local areas.[16] Sometimes these men were the minister's personal and political friends who had no particular military knowledge. Over the next year, because recruiting "was continuous" and the men were penny-packeted across the country, the training was a hit and miss affair. The first man to enlist trained most, the last man hardly at all. Often those early volunteers, in effect, immediately became recruiters themselves in the desperate rush to get other men. The local billeting made the plan costly. In some cases supervision was nearly impossible and consequently discipline was often poor. Evidently the plan also deviated from the central recruiting centres set down earlier in the summer. Implicit in Hughes's scheme was the suggestion that recruits raised from the same locality would go overseas and fight together. As it turned out, the units were broken up in England to maintain the strength of the corps in France. A.M.J. Hyatt and Desmond Morton have called Hughes's scheme variously a "confidence trick" or a hoax. Since the labels both imply deliberate intent to defraud, such charges are not fair to Hughes any more than they are to Borden who supported the methods. Yet continuous recruiting until the moment of departure made retraining in England almost a certainty. Nevertheless, these problems were not Hughes's concern; and even though they should have been, his mind could not handle those sorts of details, if he saw the flaws at all. He wanted men, and at October's end, Borden followed Hughes's lead, again raising the national commitment to 250 000.[17]

Why Borden did this is not clear. His biographer suggests the cause was rising casualties, more and more demands, poor leadership in London and Ottawa, and the lack of decisive victory. The papers of Captain Harold Daly, Hughes's assistant, explain more:

> Once toward the end of 1915, he [Hughes] decided to raise another 100 000 men. He went over to see Sir Robert Borden, got authority for it, and told me to send over and get an atlas showing the different [political] constituencies. He then dictated about a hundred telegrams to different people, one in each constituency and out of that I think we got 60 000–70 000 men. He knew everybody all over the country who was popular and who could raise men.[18]

If Daly's memory is correct, the comment epitomizes the personal improvised nature of Hughes's recruiting ideas. But more than that, Daly's observations point out the scope of political party organization; with its emphasis on patronage as the means, the party system had traditionally performed many of the social duties that, in later days, Canadians expected the state to undertake. When war was declared this party machinery geared up to help solve the country's recruitment problem.

Hughes was one of the chief supporters and users of this traditional party system. In 1914 it was at the root of his 226 night telegrams; it was present in his retention of control over military offices and later recruiting. As represented by Sam Hughes, the government provided the impulses to the party structure to secure volunteers. What was in the interest of the party was good for the country. On that October day in 1915, when he told Daly to get out the constituent map, he was really calling for a stepped-up effort by the old party system as one of the normal pieces of machinery running that portion of the war effort. The episode also illuminates the relationship and similarity of ideas between Hughes and Borden. For a short time at least, it appeared that Hughes's recruiting rationale was paying off. With the new establishment set that October, enlistments jumped by five thousand in November, and again in December.[19]

While men like Daly may have thought the minister's recruiting accomplishments "wonderful," the other powerful reasons for the success remained the loyal and hard work of the volunteer citizens, recruiting leagues, and sufficient men who were willing to join. Yet Hughes remained, with his continuous touring, speeches, and inspections, the most visible single national recruiting figure in the entire improvised scheme. The apparent success of the combination, which he believed was mostly due to his own efforts, stirred the minister to make bigger promises and more boastful claims. Already on record the previous February as claiming that he could raise three more contingents in three weeks, a little later he told a Montreal audience that he could "send a fifth [division] a sixth, a tenth or a twentieth." In Toronto in October, he declared to an enthusiastic recruiting rally: "We are coming General Kitchener, 500 000 strong." By the end of the year, Borden had translated that optimism into a half-million-man establishment for the CEF.[20]

On 30 December, when Hughes and two other cabinet colleagues, White and Reid, met with Borden, the prime minister proposed that the overseas forces' establishment should be raised to five hundred thousand. The move, Borden was convinced, would be welcomed by English Canadians who were beginning to think that the Conservative administration, except for Hughes's activities no doubt, was not fighting the war vigorously enough. He also believed that the larger the physical contribution the greater would be Canada's influence over British war policy. With the way events were going at the front, the prime minister went on to reason, surely such a force would be needed. If all three visitors were surprised by the proposal, Hughes at least expected and wanted the new commitment; and he supported it fully. By 12 January, the establishment of the CEF was put at five hundred thousand men. The question was: Could it be done?[21]

By now there were even Canadians who felt that it was too dangerous and too difficult a task; and as for others, maybe because they were Englishmen or professional soldiers or both, no one had bothered to consult General Gwatkin, the governor general, or the people at the War Office; all of them were opposed. Borden also ignored R.B. Bennett, his parliamentary secretary, who had complained earlier that December that the new figure was impossible. Evidently few other ministers were consulted before Borden's decision was made. The new goal had been an impulse supported by Hughes, by White and Reid, and indirectly endorsed by Sir George Foster in the trade department, who naively thought that if 40 percent of the population of about eight million was of military age then a five hundred thousand man CEF was not unrealistic. Ironically, Foster also thought that Hughes's recruiting methods were unrealistic and chaotic.[22]

But there was no doubt in the militia minister's mind that they could get the half million. Neither a challenge to the prime minister's judgment nor a doubt of its subsequent effect on other vital sectors of the war effort came from Hughes. Privately he told Borden, "we can easily live up to your offer, if right systems are pursued." Immediately he plunged into the new challenge by commissioning more local battalions and more local prominent citizens, friends, and businessmen. In 1915 alone, beyond the elements of the second contingent, Hughes had already approved of 141 CEF units; in 1916 the same method added 79 more; and as the local sources were no longer as fruitful, Hughes encouraged special interests, which encouraged the proliferation of Highland battalions, "Pals" and "Bantams" formations, and Irish regiments. Early in 1916 Hughes also promised that he would bring the best of the overseas officers home from the front to raise new units, a proposal which must have alarmed CEF commanders already suffering from serious shortages of reinforcements and experienced officers. As before, the minister rejected using only the regular military structure; what he sought, he said, was "strong men who have successful business or professional training . . . the best soldiers are such men as engineers, barristers, contractors, large businessmen with military training. . . . They far surpass the professional soldier."[23]

Ministerial optimism knew no bounds. In January 1916 Hughes easily convinced Borden to approve the establishment of a fourth Canadian division; the announcement sparked Max Aitken, the minister's chief overseas agent, to wire flatteringly: "Your exertions may save the Empire." Certainly the accolade spurred the militia minister on; in February he told a New York *Times* reporter that he could raise one and three-quarter million men without compulsion in a matter of a few months. In Ottawa he laid out an elaborate plan to raise nearly twenty more divisions. It was unrealistic. Toronto was to give five, Ontario four; Manitoba and Saskatchewan, Quebec, British Columbia, and the Maritimes each gave two.[24]

By then the magnitude of Hughes's plans started to frighten his cabinet colleagues. Frequently council meetings, already stormy, became even more bitter. Thomas White was now alarmed. Hughes, he complained, "wants to press recruiting regardless of other considerations." It was true. Even the prime minister was finally having doubts about his own national pledge in the hands of Sam Hughes. He asked the militia minister not to recruit so that it dislocated other national priorities or denuded some localities of their manpower. Hughes paid little heed, but continued to cajole the country into sending more of its sons. From January to March 1916 over ninety thousand Canadians joined up.[25]

But in the spring of 1916 there were pressing public arguments against unrestrained enlistments. Ironically much of the discontent came from those groups which had often been the minister's most fervent recruiting aids — the civilian recruiting leagues. Dissatisfied for some time, they all agreed that the government could no longer count on volunteering to provide the resources. Now that Canadian industry, agriculture, timber, and mining resources were beginning to feel the strains of full wartime employment, the government had to impose a centralized and integrated recruiting policy to avoid harming the effort of the home-front. Moreover, the burden had to be distributed so that all parts of the Dominion were sharing it equally; and many identified Quebec as delinquent in doing its share. To some, what was needed was a national registration of the manpower, to others, an inventory of all wealth of the nation including human, and to even others, compulsion if necessary. But they all agreed that the Borden government could no longer avoid direct involvement in recruiting and national mobilization.

Two of the most prominent critics were Lord Shaughnessy, president of the CPR, and Senator James Mason, the seventy-three-year-old former commanding officer of the 10th Royal Grenadiers. Both men had been great supporters of the war effort. But by March they were sceptical about meeting the new national pledge of half a million men. When Shaughnessy spoke out in Montreal about the goal's harmful effect on national production, Hughes scornfully dismissed the warning as a "piffle," and publicly told Shaughnessy to mind his own business. Privately Borden agreed, choosing to believe that Shaughnessy's statement was nothing more than a political conspiracy against his administration. But then James Mason laid bare for his senate colleagues the hard realities of Borden's goals and the weaknesses of Hughes's improvised recruiting. "This large number [500 000]," he told a hushed chamber, "means that we shall have to provide each month . . . at least 25 000 new men — or 300 000 a year. There can he no question that the additional 250 000 to bring our quota up to 500 000 and the 300 000 if required annually to keep it at that figure will not be obtained under the present system of enlistment."[26] To Hughes it was still "piffle."

But it was not so to others. Many of the provincial governments had organized their war effort far better than Hughes had his own department. The Canadian Manufacturers' Association followed up Shaughnessy's predictions in a memorandum critical of Hughes's unlimited and unorganized recruiting. Various patriotic and recruiting leagues called for conscription or at least creation of a national register of wealth. So did Sir John Eaton, and executives of the Nova Scotia Steel Company, Consumers Gas, and the Dominion Steel Corporation. In April the New Brunswick Legislature passed a resolution asking Borden to employ "scientific means" in recruiting to protect industry and agriculture; and many national newspaper editorials carried similar messages. The old Tory, Castell Hopkins, sadly reported to readers of his *Canadian Annual Review* that during these months "the arbitrary policy and personality of Sam Hughes sometimes worked against recruiting as his enthusiasm and efforts worked for it." There was more alarming evidence long before the year was through. By April the monthly recruiting figures started to plummet from over thirty-four thousand in March to a low of about six thousand by September 1916, where they remained for some time. However, the previous spring while the protest was rising and the enlistments falling, Borden had done little publicly to change Hughes's improvised methods. In April the prime minister refused to hear a delegation of recruiting league members who had come to him hoping that he would do something in terms of registration and compulsion. When he refused to act, as Sir George Foster confessed to the delegates the next day, it was because the cabinet was afraid of riots in Quebec. In the same month, the frustrated recruiters formed the Canadian National Service League and openly lobbied for the draft.[27]

While Hughes remained in effective control of his department through 1915 and 1916, he continued to ignore the criticisms that his method of recruiting did not work. But many of his newly minted colonels who were raising local battalions were increasingly aware that there were serious problems. Frequently Hughes had authorized several units in the same area, and the battalion commanders ended up in cutthroat competition for men. Many used any method they could to secure the quotas; and it varied from bribing to shaming the individual into enlisting. None of it encouraged the hesitant volunteer. Two examples seem typical of those who had problems. Late in 1915 the militia minister let his old friend, William Price, raise a unit, the 204th, in Quebec's Eastern Townships. After spending three months and a great deal of his time and money, and still never forming much of a battalion, Price lost his enthusiasm. His complaints to Hughes's aide in February 1916 sum up many unit commanders' frustrations and the minister's inability to give recruiting some structure:

> I can now see that there will be difficulty in raising many men in this province. The organi-
> zation is rotten and there is a complete misunderstanding of how to get French-Canadians to
> recruit. Each battalion should be given a certain district and should be forced to recruit from
> there and not allowed outside. This would force the battalions to recruit their localities thor-
> oughly; at present, they do as they like and steal from each other. The way things go I am going
> to have a hard time to raise my men. . . . You might tell Sir Sam after what I have, it is impos-
> sible with the present organization to raise twenty thousand men from the district. To do so
> requires a complete new system and some slave driver at the head with the power of sacking.[28]

This unit never completed its establishment. Further west, where recruiters did not have to contend with reluctant French Canadians, Lieutenant-Colonel W.A. Griesbach, commanding officer of the 49th (Edmonton Regiment), had much more success. But he still complained of the lack of organization and the disastrous effects of interbattalion competition.[29] One of the problems was that Hughes would not establish a centrally controlled system. The "slave driver," as Price said, also needed to be one who was willing to delegate authority and to pay close attention to routine detail.

But it was not only the home-front that suffered under Hughes's recruiting improvisations. Once in England the supposedly trained Hughes battalions were mercilessly broken up and retrained by the British, then transferred to France as drafts. Consequently, now unemployed, bitter, and increasingly vocal officers were an embarrassment to the Canadian government. Hughes ignored, then denied their existence as a problem, but the complaints continued to embarrass all. So too did the slowly emerging realization that Hughes's labyrinth of an overseas organization was starving the front of desperately needed reinforcements. One side-effect was to encourage Hughes to try to add more divisions to the Canadian corps as a simple solution. Yet the corps commander, General Alderson, knew that this was not the answer; steady and adequate reinforcement of his existing divisions was. By mid-February 1916, he actually returned to England to try to solve the reinforcement bottleneck. But with little help from Hughes's appointees there, and desperate in the expectation of huge casualties in the spring and summer fighting, the frustrated Alderson circumvented Hughes by placing his grievances directly before his old army friend, the Duke of Connaught. The facts, he told the governor general, spoke for themselves: of the 1476 officers and 25 087 men in the Canadian camp at Shorncliffe, only 75 and 2385, respectively, were trained to go to France. The problem, according to Alderson, was due not only to Hughes's multi-headed overseas administration, but also to the poor state of the recruits coming from Canada.[30]

By then Hughes was not insensitive to the reinforcement problem, but he would not let anyone else try to resolve it. In March, when Parliament was halfway through its 1916 session — and at a time when rumours of Militia Department scandals were growing steadily — Hughes decided to rush over to England to straighten out personally the problems in reinforcement and administration. In the meantime, Gwatkin, who had likely been alerted by Connaught, informed Hughes's temporary replacement, A.E. Kemp, of the dangerous reinforcement situation due to the minister's snafu in training. If Kemp had hoped to improve things during Hughes's absence, a severe political storm focusing directly on Hughes prevented it. Before he could solve anything in England, the attacks on his administration became so acute that Borden had to order him back to Canada in April. It left the situation in England and at the front unresolved. On his return Hughes commissioned General Lessard to make a confidential inspection of training depots in England. After touring the camps for several weeks in April and May, Lessard confirmed Aldersons's and Gwatkin's charges. But Hughes never made public Lessard's damning report. To do so would have been to admit the failure of the minister's local recruiting and training program. If the prime minister knew about it, there [were] also certain benefits for the government in keeping silent on Lessard's findings. Opposition attacks during the parliamentary session, which had ended in mid-May, were very heavy. Most of them were focused on the militia minister and, thereby, the entire Conservative administration. Two royal commissions also were still pending; and both were concerned with Sam Hughes's office. With the recent high casualties coming from the Battle of St. Eloi in March and April, Lessard's news would not be welcomed by the public. But whatever the motives for suppressing the report, the problems of the surplus officers and the quality and training of the troops continued for more months — the months of Mount Sorrel and the Somme.[31]

If Sam Hughes's recruiting policy caused problems in English Canada where the majority viewed the war as a national crusade, then it proved calamitous in French Canada where there was no such passion. As the war progressed, the difference in attitudes between French and English Canada became more and more obvious; and with the imposition of conscription in 1918, it led to near open rebellion that spring. During the previous three years, with a population of about two million, French Canada had given far fewer soldier to the overseas battalions than had English Canada. Soon there were charges that Quebec was not doing its duty. In response, the province became increasingly more sullen: it was a foreign war; Canada was not threatened; there were more pressing problems at home, especially when English Ontario was trying to take away the French-language school rights of her French-speaking citizens. There was also little attraction for most Quebecois in giving their lives for either Great Britain or France. Of the fourteen thousand or so French Canadians who actually joined during Hughes's tenure, many did so not because of patriotism, but for economic and other practical reasons. Yet in the end, the Quebecois in particular — for French Canadians in other parts of the Dominion had enlisted in about the same proportion as their English-speaking confrères — were more seriously divided from the rest of the nation than they had ever been since Confederation. Whose fault was it? As Desmond Morton has pointed out, since Confederation the militia had become increasingly anglicized in men, manners, and equipment. Consequently fewer French Canadians joined its ranks.[32]

Sam Hughes was an important part of the process that led to that alienation. It did not matter much in peacetime, but it did in war. The minister had always been remarkably insensitive to French Canadians. For a long time Hughes foolishly believed that his remote Huguenot ancestry and his friendship with nationalists like Armand Lavergne made him acceptable to Quebec. He was peculiarly unaware that his previous campaigns against separate schools, French priests, Canadian Papal Zouaves, French-Canadian military representation in Catholic ceremonies, and his Orange Lodge activities had overpowered the limited attractions of ancestry or friendship. Nor was he aware that his image as an imperialist, however national-istic, was not attractive to many French Canadians, who were not at all concerned about defending the Empire outside of Canada.[33]

None of it augered well for a war in 1914. It was not that Sam Hughes did not want to recruit French Canadians. He did. But he did not realize that by scrapping the Gwatkin mobi-lization scheme, which gave a balanced national representation to French Canada in the form of their own units, he scuppered separate French-Canadian battalions in the first contingent. Still he wanted Quebec's numbers. One of the first things he did was visit Cardinal Begin of Quebec in September 1914 in an attempt to secure priests for the initial force, but the Cardinal gave him little hope of obtaining any number for overseas service.[34] With this warning, the minister should have seen that Quebec was going to need special care if recruiting for a foreign war was to succeed in the province.

Yet the outbreak of the war did produce some initial sympathy in Quebec for participation; and Hughes wanted a national effort. That had been part of the rationale behind his national-istic "fiery-cross" call to arms in August. But as the response to it poured into Valcartier he allowed for no separate identity by giving privileges as well as responsibilities to members of the various French-Canadian regiments who turned out. Instead units like the Carabiniers Mont-Royal, the Chausseurs Canadiens, the Voltigeurs de Quebec, and the Carabiniers de Sherbrooke were absorbed into the 12th and 14th Battalions, both of which were English-speaking. Only the 14th went to France where it was reinforced by French Canadians from the 12th Battalion. When Liberal MP and former cabinet minister Rodolphe Lemieux requested the creation of a separate French-Canadian unit with its own officers in the first contingent, Hughes refused. Even the attestation documents were worded in such a fashion that no French-Canadian vol-unteer could record his racial origin. There were over twelve hundred French Canadians at Valcartier in 1914, sufficient to assemble one complete battalion including officers.[35]

At the beginning of the war, the militia minister had two ready-made native sons of Quebec and generals at his disposal to rally the Canadiens: François Lessard and Oscar Pelletier. Both were regular soldiers of substantial experience. But while Hughes was in office, no meaningful role was ever given them, in spite of pleas by prominent English-Canadian Tories, like Toronto MP and patronage co-ordinator Edmund Bristol, who wanted Lessard to command the second contingent. All Hughes gave him was public abuse over his Toronto mobilization trials and a bitter ministerial squabble over inspection services. As late as 1916, Hughes again refused to make him an overseas brigadier, or even use him in the disastrous Quebec recruiting drives of that year. Only after Hughes was fired did Lessard get a Quebec battalion to recruit. But by then it was too late; he secured only ninety-two men, and he had no battle experience, so was unsuitable for overseas command. As for Pelletier — the son of a Liberal senator and the man whom Hutton had chosen as commander of one of his Boer war infantry columns — in 1919 the minister could only give the major-general command of a half dozen troops guarding a wireless station on Anticosti Island — and that was all.[36]

If Sam Hughes made little use of individual French Canadians, he had not much greater concern for their units. Once the first division got into the fighting, it was this bloody experi-ence that trained many of the future officers of the subsequent divisions. Because the first con-tingent had few middle and senior level French-Canadian officers beyond the company level, there never would be enough of them to lead other units of their own culture, even if Hughes had wanted to send them. He seemed to think of Quebec with its two-million population only as a place to get numbers, not French Canadians. But the Canadiens themselves had been concerned in September 1914. Then Rodolphe Lemieux and Dr. Arthur Mignault, a wealthy Quebec pharmaceutical manufacturer, led a delegation of fifty-eight influential Liberal and Conservative Quebecois to Ottawa to make sure that at least the second contingent had an identifiable battalion. They warned Borden that if care was not taken to give Quebec representation on the national fighting force, there was a strong risk of losing its active support. Apparently with hardly more sympathy than Hughes, Borden only consented after the militia minister had sailed for England. The result was the formation of the 22nd Battalion commanded by F.M. Gaudet, which went to France with the second contingent the next spring. By then even it was having trouble: 10 percent of the number were English-speaking, and French-Canadian troops had to be transferred from two other battalions recruiting in Quebec before it could sail. In the first two contingents, then, French Canadians were represented only by one battalion and it was to remain the only official one in the Canadian Corps during the entire war.[37]

There was hardly any doubt about the potential enthusiasm for enlistment in French Canada just before and after the 22nd was announced. However, Hughes appeared unappreciative of it. In February 1915 he could only give vague answers about establishing a French-Canadian brigade when questioned in the Commons, and he even seemed unsure of the number of French Canadians who by then had enlisted. Just before the second division sailed for France in mid-1915, a French-Canadian lawyer and militia soldier, Colonel J.P. Landry, who had been given command of one of its brigades as a small conciliation to Quebec, was removed. To replace him came a Tory journalist friend of the minister, Brigadier David Watson, fresh from the First Division. It was inevitable that Landry should lose out. His fate was one of the earliest consequences of Hughes's not including French Canadians of middle and high command in the first contingent the previous year. Landry had no battle experience, and no one willingly was going to jeopardize lives and efficiency with an untested brigadier. Watson had nearly a year under his belt. Back in Canada, however, no one in Quebec would question Landry's competence. To them there was another obvious reason for his removal. The deposed brigadier's father, Conservative Senator Philippe Landry, had been a major spokesman in the defence of the Franco-Ontario's fight against their Tory government's infamous Regulation 17 denying them French-language rights; to many French Canadians Hughes, the vengeful Orangeman, had simply retaliated.[38]

After mid-1915 when Hughes was trying to recruit the Third and Fourth Divisions, to encourage Quebec enlistments he brought home some of the few French Canadians who had served with the corps overseas. But there were never enough veterans even to begin the job. Mostly he had to use the same method employed in the rest of Canada—prominent citizens and promises of local battalions.[39] From October until the summer of 1916, twelve such groups canvassed in various areas of the province. Most of them had little success. By then an unmoved or lukewarm clergy, stories of the horrors waiting on Flanders' battlefields, and the general shortcomings of the militia minister's recruiting system, all made the Canadiens stubbornly resist any foreign military service. The new munitions industries with their steady and lucrative employment represented a far safer calling. The sneers and accusations of English Canada and the relentless antiwar campaign of Henri Bourassa and his nationaliste allies were strong inducements for many Quebecois to stay away from the colours. Nevertheless Hughes pressed for the numbers.

Wealthy French Canadians were not so willing to become some of Sam Hughes's recruiting colonels as were many in English Canada. As a result, many whom Hughes chose were less than worthy and their units were often doomed. One such example was the 41st Battalion. After a scandalous record both in Canada and England, which included desertion, two murders, and many court-martials, the unit was finally broken up to feed the 22nd in France.[40] Others were little more successful. In the fall of 1915, Hughes asked Armand Lavergne to raise a unit in Montreal. The year before he might have done it, but now his response was an embarrassing public letter in the columns of Bourassa's *Le Devoir* in which he refused to accept what he said was nothing more than an interesting adventure in a foreign country. Unexpectedly, the offer was then accepted by Olivar Asselin — an ardent nationaliste. Whatever his real motives for doing it, Asselin had a little more success than many others. His energy, popularity, and discipline got recruits and better officers, but not full ranks. Only too quickly Asselin discovered that Hughes had authorized a Conservative lawyer, Tancrède Paquelo, to raise the 206th Battalion in the same area. Paquelo was a former commanding officer of the 85th militia regiment and was representative of the declining quality of French-Canadian officers brought about by increasing anglicization in the militia. While Asselin brought men into his unit by hard work and discipline, Paquelo seduced his by appealing to baser values and promises of being "le dernier regiment à parter, le premier à profiter de la victoire." Asselin was so frustrated at the cutthroat competition between the two rivals, he demanded that Hughes get rid of Paquelo's battalion. Asselin's unit was transferred to Bermuda, not France; and Paquelo's was disbanded, with the bulk of them being transferred to the distraught Asselin. When the furious Paquelo heard what was to happen, he paraded his men and told those few who had not already disappeared to desert. For this he was court-martialled, and during the trial it was found that he and some of his officers had also defrauded the unit of funds. Paquelo went to jail.[41]

On other occasions, when Hughes could not get suitable French-Canadian colonels, he chose English-Canadian ones to recruit in Quebec. William Price was one. In spite of the general popularity the Price family had had in Quebec for years, there was little attraction to serve an imperialist "English" colonel in a foreign war; and Price, already encumbered by Hughes's bad system, added his own insensitivities, and so failed. According to Price: "I tell them what no politician dare tell them, that they are away behind all the other provinces and that though they have a double duty, one to the Empire and one to France, yet they are laggards and that they should as a matter of fact furnish more than any other province."[42]

In the summer of 1916, the half dozen battalions still trying to reach their quotas were really only fragments of military units. With a lack of discipline and equipment and ranks thinned by desertion and drafts to other battalions, few were sent to England. Of those who got there, they were broken up to reinforce the 22nd in France. In all, by 1916 the possibility of having a French-Canadian brigade, native sons in senior command, or any serious encouragement for national war participation had all but disappeared under Sam Hughes. Instead the spectacle of most of those French-Canadian battalions stumbling incompetently and often dishonestly through a vain quest for full establishments caused the Quebecois to withdraw further into demoralized and sullen inaction in the province; outside of it, the show reaffirmed the belief that French Canadians were incompetent and unpatriotic.

If Hughes was a major cause of the situation, others must also share the guilt with him. During the first two years, Borden in particular had little more appreciation of cultural politics than did Sam Hughes. Since the prime minister had scant support in the province even after the 1911 election, he should have realized that Quebec would be a special case in a national crisis. Just before the war, he and Monk had parted. The prime minister's failure to respond to the Quebec delegation that wanted a French unit in the first force, his failure to find any post for Lessard, his securing the resignation of two of his three French-Canadian cabinet ministers in the fall of 1914 — all these actions held little evidence of an understanding of French Canada. His position on the imperialist side in the naval debate in 1910, and in 1913 the question of cash contributions to the Admiralty only confirmed the nationalistes' charges after 1914 that French Canada was being tossed into a foreign war. So did Borden's quick acceptance of sending more and more troops thereafter. Even after the reshuffle in 1914, his cabinet had no

French Canadians with any credibility to defend war participation. Nearly all of them had campaigned for votes in the 1911 election by attacking Laurier's naval bill as conscriptionist. After 1914, how could these same men persuade their confrères that they must participate in a British war? Similarly, Borden and his cabinet seemed to be incapable of or unwilling to support the Franco-Ontarians against the English-speaking "Boches" in the Ontario schools question.[43]

Like Hughes, Borden tried to enthuse Quebec. Early in 1916 he told Hughes that he should be sure that French Canadians who had distinguished themselves at the front were rewarded with decorations that the French government had put at his disposal. The prime minister also suggested that, if Hughes would authorize a Quebec unit for service in the French army, recruiting would be greatly encouraged. But General Gwatkin knew better and so advised against it; he recognized that French Canadians had no particular loyalty to France and that pay difference between the two forces would discourage any chance of success. No one seemed to listen to Gwatkin. Overseas Max Aitken, the government "Eye-Witness" in France, offered Hughes and Borden "a French mission . . . sent to Canada by the Jesuits or other religious orders for religious purposes but really to assist recruiting in Quebec." In all, these schemes represented the bankruptcy of Hughes's and Borden's attitudes to French Canadians. To them France was never an attraction; Canada was. But in order to gain French Canada's support of an external policy, national leaders first would have to give the minority a definite, identifiable, and responsible role and to ensure its well-being at home. Neither Hughes nor his prime minister seemed aware of this. What came from them came too little and too late.[44]

But one of the most objectionable things about Borden for French Canadians was that he would not or could not control Sam Hughes. Most of the time Hughes continued to proclaim his belief that French Canada would measure up to his expectations, or, as Mason Wade puts it, Hughes kept his honest opinion about French Canada to himself. That may be true, but from time to time he made some stupid public moves, often in themselves small but collectively lethal, concerning recruiting in Quebec. When again unsuccessful in obtaining support from Cardinal Begin in mid-1916, the minister uttered his infamous statement in Lindsay that Quebec had not done its duty. Earlier he had countered questions from an opposition MP, asking why western French Canadians were not organized into a battalion, by saying that their numbers were too small, that they would be better off in English-speaking battalions, and that the local French-Canadian officer of the proposed unit was incompetent. When the same member confronted Hughes with the 1911 census figures indicating that there were over forty thousand French Canadians in the west, Hughes replied that he would order two French-Canadian "half-breed" battalions to be raised. Perhaps the most celebrated and distorted case of Hughes's neglect of sympathetic organization in French Canada occurred in August 1916 when the minister was again out of the country. Military authorities wanted a new enlistment drive in the Montreal area to be jointly headed by two clergymen as representatives of both cultures and faiths. By that time, however, no French Canadian priest would accept the post. But the campaign proceeded anyway, headed by a Methodist clergyman, Reverend C.A. Williams. Williams was hardworking and far more tolerant of French Canada than many have given him credit for. But predictably his efforts ended in failure. The Williams affair was not as it was portrayed by extreme nationalists — an example of Hughes's anti-Catholicism. Nor was Williams a bigoted Orangeman sent by the minster to ride herd on French Canada. The entire episode represented what was tragic about the minister's methods. He could not understand that French Canada required a different approach than the rest of the population. Quebec, because it provided the basis of Laurier's power, was suspect to an old party politician like Hughes. In the past two years he had given Quebec nothing except discrimination to be enthusiastic about. Soon the province was not interested and soon Hughes and his local military officers had run out of prominent French Canadians for such duties; authorities had to use whomever they could get. So they got men like Williams. Common sense, however, should have dictated that it not be a Methodist clergyman. But by then it was a vicious circle.[45]

The militia minister showed more creative imagination in recruiting foreigners for military duty than he did French Canadians. For example, there was the minister's "American Legion" scheme. Soon after the war began, Hughes offered and had accepted for overseas service a battalion of American citizens living in Canada; the offer was a substantial mental somersault for Hughes's usual anti-Americanism. A few weeks later, he extended the project to three "corps of splendid fighters," numbering "sixty thousand," which now included Russians and Serbs.[46]

The British authorities could not co-ordinate their reaction. The Colonial Office authorities were hesitant because they said that such a force would violate the US Foreign Enlistment Act of 1818, and that they did want to keep relations as cordial as possible with the neutral republic. By the same token they did not want to tread on Canadian sensitivities, especially those in the hands of the prickly Sam Hughes. Consequently, the British referred the question back to the governor general, whom they said was free to act as he saw fit. Connaught, who had never seen the first communications between Hughes and Kitchener, and did not like being left out, was puzzled. So he enquired at militia headquarters. The deputy minister said he knew nothing about the scheme either; nor did the Militia Council, but if such a proposal had been made by Hughes, they recommended it be quickly dropped. Meanwhile Kitchener, supported by the king, Churchill, Sir Richard McBride, and Acting High Commissioner Perley gave Hughes permission to send at least one American unit, providing no recruiting went on outside of Canada.[47]

Hughes did not move on the issue until domestic volunteering started to slow down in the fall of 1915. Then he allowed the limited acceptance of American citizens resident in Canada to mushroom ultimately into plans for a full-fledged American brigade of five overseas battalions. The minister had created a special cap badge with an American flag surrounded by clusters of maple leaves. As the first of these units, designated the 97th Overseas Battalion, quickly filled up its ranks during the winter of 1915–1916, Hughes got the idea that he could recruit unlimited numbers. As a result he authorized four more by the late spring (the 211th, 212th, 213th, and the 237th) and labelled them the "American Legion." Their cap badge was a variation of the 97th and all of them wore American Legion shoulder flashes. As was the case elsewhere, none of these units had much success. The minister created each new battalion long before the others finished recruiting, and so they competed, often viciously, with each other for volunteers and none of them ever reached establishment — most of them reached less than half of it. During June 1916, 20 percent of the legion deserted. Hughes also used the typical special agent to organize the entire scheme. C.W. Bullock, who had suggested the brigade idea to the minister, was an American citizen and a Unitarian minister whose military career, as General Gwatkin scornfully commented, "is remarkable. Appointed chaplain with the honorary rank of captain in October last [1915], he is now a lieutenant-colonel commanding an overseas battalion." Whether Hughes ordered it or not is not known, but recruiting took place on American soil. Certainly the minister aided it by making a personal arrangement with customs officials to turn a blind eye to these recruits when they were brought across the border.[48]

These frequent abuses of American neutrality aggravated and embarrassed the Washington and London authorities equally. Every time Connaught confronted Hughes about the foreign recruiting, the minister denied it and then blatantly let it continue. American authorities increasingly objected to the continued use of the US flag displayed at various Canadian recruiting offices; and so there were several stiff diplomatic notes exchanged with British diplomats over Hughes's scheme. In Ottawa, Gwatkin, Fiset, and the governor general had no more success in stopping the plan. For their part, the British would not let the legion come to England until all outward connections with the United States were cut.[49]

By the mid-spring 1916, tired of the long wait, endless changes in officers, and constant haggling, the legionnaires were frustrated. Desertions and resignations mounted while enlistments nearly stopped. Like some of the other battalions Hughes had authorized, the legion had its share of scandal. The Toronto chief of police described the 97th as the "worst behaved battalion in the city." Drunkenness, fraud, embezzlement (including the decamping of the 97th's first commanding officer with all the unit funds), and incompetence plagued the force. In May Fiset said he would be pleased to send the legion overseas before "they all desert," but not until they got rid of American insignia. Connaught's constant complaints and Hughes's lack of response finally brought the prime minister into the picture.[50]

Like many others, Borden was totally surprised at what had so far taken place. Hughes had not told him much in the previous two years and precious time was now wasted while he tried to sort through the minister's mess. In the process, it involved Borden in a first-class row with the governor general, whom the prime minster felt was exerting far too much pressure in a domestic Canadian matter. By late July, when Hughes was out of the country, Borden ended the affair by consolidating the legion's five battalions into one, the 97th, and sending it overseas, shorn of all its insignia. The process only added to its further demoralization. With financial and leadership problems still festering in its ranks, in the end it was broken up to feed the corps' battalions in France.[51]

The prime minister's decision on the American Legion was part of a larger judgment on Hughes's entire domestic administration. In August 1916 he took recruiting out of Sir Sam's hands. First Borden tried a director general of recruiting to give order to the chaos and to secure the vital enlistments; then in the autumn he tried the National Service Board which was responsible to the cabinet and dedicated to the same causes. Both had little success. By the spring of 1917, large numbers of casualties and the conviction that it was essential to have a Canadian voice in imperial councils made a reluctant prime minister believe that only conscription could do it. By year's end compulsory service had arrived at the hands of the newly elected union government. The war would be pursued to bitter victory. But over a year before, Borden had got rid of Hughes, a major cause of his bad luck; and before Hughes had gone in 1916, he too had come out hotly for conscription — typically without consulting anyone and apparently oblivious to its party or national cost.[52]

By the end of 1916 there were over 250 overseas battalions. Hughes had authorized most of them while he was minister. But earlier that summer, the Canadian Corps was complete at 48 battalions. Except for some reinforcements, it remained at that level in spite of Hughes's attempts to add two more divisions before he left office. The remaining battalions either suffered collapse before they left Canada or were doomed to be broken up in England. Over the previous two years, Sam Hughes had taken the declaration of war as a personal challenge to lead a national crusade to raise as many men as possible. In doing so, he had little regard for dislocation, or for the advice of his professional staff, or for responsibility to his government. He showed no more awareness of the cultural politics of French Canada. While trying to heighten patriotism and enlistment by throwing responsibility to the citizens, he left them confused and adrift when the war demands transcended the ability of individuals, of the party structure, and of local groups to handle them on a national scale. Yet he constantly interfered even in this process because he could neither delegate the necessary authority nor apply himself to the daily routine of coordinating a national effort. Moreover, the local battalions ended up being destroyed by the same spontaneity that created them and that helped sour and alienate the two cultures, both from the government and one from the country. Certainly Hughes's prime minister must bear some of the blame. In part Borden put up with Hughes's recruiting ways because in those early years the militia minister gave the most vitality to a pale and hesitant war administration. But neither man checked each other with sound advice or firm control. That Sam Hughes demonstrated initiative, confidence, and an unrelenting energy, which helped rally many Canadians to the early war effort, cannot be doubted. But there was also overwhelming evidence that he lacked the skills of sound administration which the larger war — the one of 1916 and after — demanded. Ironically he was a major force in creating the particular size of the Canadian war effort but he could not cope with its demands. He was a spirited improviser, intolerant of criticism, jealous of power, and imbued with the philosophy of the citizen-soldier in a conflict which no longer belonged to the individual citizens. He did not see that Canada had created, with the masses of his recruits, professional demands and a professional modern army. As long as the spirit and manpower were in abundance, and the sophisticated needs few, Sam Hughes's local talents remained unchallenged. When these lagged, Hughes's regime collapsed.

NOTES

1. Desmond Morton, *Canada and War: A Military and Political History* (Toronto: Butterworth's, 1981), chap. 3.
2. *Hansard*, 1917, pp. 261, 269–70 for Hughes's own description of his recruiting methods.
3. R.C. Brown, *Robert Laird Borden, a Biography*, vol. 2, 1914–1937 (Toronto: Macmillan, 1979), 27–28; and Barbara M. Wilson, *Ontario and the First World War 1914–1918: A Collection of Documents* (Toronto: Champlain Society, 1977), xxxi.
4. *Canadian Annual Review of Public Affairs* (hereafter *CAR*), 1915, p. 188; J.L. Granatstein and J.M. Hitsman, *Broken Promises: A History of Conscription in Canada* (Toronto: Oxford University Press, 1977), 34; *Hansard*, special session, 1914, pp. 17, 95; Col. A.F. Duguid, *The Official History of the Canadian Forces in the Great War 1914–1919* (Ottawa: King's Printer, 1938), app. 55; and Address, 18 Dec. 1914, Sir Robert Laird Borden Papers, Public Archives of Canada (hereafter PAC), MG26, p. 34672.
5. *CAR*, 1915, pp. 187–88.
6. Murray Donnelly, *Dafoe of the Free Press* (Toronto: Macmillan, 1968), 76.
7. Wilson, *Ontario and the First World War*, xxi, xxix–xliii; G.N. Tucker, *The Naval Service of Canada* (Ottawa: King's Printer, 1952), chap. 13; note on Canadian Expeditionary Force, Edmund Bristol Papers, Public Archives of Ontario (hereafter PAO), 283, Armour file; *CAR*, 1915, pp. 213–14; and Brown, *Borden*, 2:68–69.
8. John Swettenham, *To Seize Victory: The Canadian Corps in World War One* (Toronto: Ryerson Press, 1965), 71–95; Wilson, *Ontario and the First World War*, xxx.
9. Perley to Borden, 29 May 1915, in Canada, Department of External Affairs, *Documents on Canada's External Relations 1909–1918*, vol. 1 (Ottawa: Queens Printer, 1967), 73–74.
10. *Globe* (Toronto), 22 Jan. 1915, 6; Wilson, *Ontario and the First World War*, xxxv–1, 6–8, B4; Duguid, *The Official History of the Canadian Forces*, app. 86; Canada, Senate, *Debates*, 1916, p. 406; Granatstein and Hitsman, *Broken Promises*, 23–24; and R. Mathew Bray, "Fighting as an Ally: The English-Canadian Patriotic Response to the Great War," *The Canadian Historical Review* 61 (2 Nov. 1980), 147–49.
11. Gwatkin to Hughes, 21 Sept. 1914, W.G. Gwatkin Papers, PAC, MG30; G13, F4; PAC, Pamphlet, no. 4039, p. 8; Gen. Charles F. Winter, *Lieutenant General the Hon. Sir Sam Hughes, K.C.B., M.P., Canada's War Minister 1911–1916* (Toronto: Macmillan, 1931), 88–89.
12. Connaught to Kitchener, 1 July 1915, Lord Kitchener Papers, Public Records Office, London, 30/57/56, FNG 43A and B.
13. Gwatkin to Mason, 3 July 1915, Gwatkin Papers, f2; and Gwatkin to Christie, 24 May 1915, Borden Papers, p. 709601.
14. Brown, *Borden*, 2:28.
15. Wilson, *Ontario and the First World War*, xxxii, 8, B5, Militia Order no. 340, 12 July 1915; Basset to Winter, 19 Aug. 1915, John Basset Papers, PAC, MG 30, E 302; *CAR*, 1915, p. 190; and P.D. Ross, *Retrospects of a Newspaper Person* (Toronto: Oxford, 1931), 206–11.
16. "Memorandum on Recruiting in England Prior to the Derby Recruiting Scheme," Borden Papers, OC313, claims Hughes's method was similar to that in Britain; an improvised, local volunteer response with little government planning. Also see G.W.L. Nicholson, *Official History of the Canadian Army in the First World War: The Canadian Expeditionary Force, 1914–1919* (Ottawa: Queen's Printer, 1962),109; and PAC, RG 24, vol. 6999, 593-1-40.

17. *Hansard*, 1916, pp. 3288–89; "Report on the work of the Department of Militia and Defence to Feb. 1, 1915," Memorandum no. 1, Gwatkin to the Prime Minister, 1 Feb. 1915, PAC, RG 24, vol. 413; Memorandum no. 3, Gwatkin to the Prime Minister, 1 Dec. 1916, PAC, RG 24, vol. 413; McCurdy to Borden, 7 Oct. 1916, Borden Papers, OC313; *Hansard*, 1917, p. 263; Canada, National Defence Headquarters, Ottawa, Directorate of History, Historical Section, *Canadian War Records*, vol. 1, *A Narrative of the Formation and Operations of the First Canadian Division, to the End of the Second Battle of Ypres*, May 4, 1915 (Ottawa: Historical Section, General Staff, King's Printer, 1920), 3; and Desmond Morton, *A Peculiar Kind of Politics: Canada's Overseas Ministry in the First World War* (Toronto: University of Toronto Press, 1982), 44.

18. "Memoire notes," Harold Mayne Daly Papers, PAC, MG 27, 111, f9, D.

19. Nicholson, *Official History of the Canadian Army in the First World War*, 213–14, 546; and John English, *The Decline of Politics: The Conservatives and the Party System, 1901–1920* (Toronto: University of Toronto Press, 1977), 95–105.

20. CAR, 1915, pp. 187–93, 222–27; and *Hansard*, 1915, p. 438.

21. Canada, Department of the Secretary of State, *Copies of Proclamations, Orders-in-Council and Documents relating to the European War* (King's Printer, 1915 and 1917), no. 556; PC 36, 12 Jan. 1916; and Brown, *Borden*, 2:32–34.

22. Bennett to Borden, 7 Dec. 1915, Sir George Perley Papers, PAC, MG27, II, D12, vol. 5; Stanton to Blount, 31 Dec. 1915, in Sir Robert Laird Borden, *Robert Laird Borden: His Memoirs*, ed. Henry Borden, vol. 1 (Toronto: Macmillan, 1938), 529; 10 Aug. 1915, Sir George Foster Diaries, PAC; Memorandum no. 3, PAC, RG 24, vol. 413; and Brown, *Borden*, 2:33–35.

23. *Hansard*, 1917, pp. 269–71; Sir Robert Laird Borden, *Private Diaries*, 18 Jan. 1916, PAC; Desmond Morton, *Canada and War* (Toronto: Butterworth's, 1981), 60; Wilson, *Ontario and the First World War*, xxxvi, xlv; *Free Press* (Winnipeg), 29 May 1916; and CAR, 1916, p. 256.

24. *Times* (New York), 27 Feb. 1916, 3; CAR, 1916, p. 303; and General Hughes, no. 2, Lord Beaverbrook Papers (BBK), The House of Lords Record Office, Westminster, Great Britain; Hughes to Aitken, 15 Jan. 1916, IP; and Aitken to Hughes, 19 Jan. 1916, IP.

25. Borden, *Private Diaries*, 18 Jan. 1916 and 5 Feb. 1916, PAC; Flavelle to W.E. Rundle, 14 June 1916, Joseph Wesley Flavelle Papers, Queen's University, Douglas Library, C25, B2, pp. 1,500–502; and *Hansard*, 1917, pp. 269–70.

26. Senate, *Debates*, 7916, pp. 127–32; Borden to Perley, 14 March 1916, Perley Papers, vol. 5; CAR, 1916, p. 319; *Hansard*, 1917, pp. 269–71; and *Daily Herald* (Calgary), 11 March 1916, 6.

27. For instance, in Ontario see Wilson, *Ontario and the First World War*, li–Iii. Also see *Hansard*, 1916, pp. 145, 440, 498–500, 3550; Nicholson, *Official History of the Canadian Army in the First World War*, 219; CAR, 1916, pp. 310–24; *Citizen* (Ottawa), 14 April 1916, 1; *Globe* (Toronto), 28 June 1916, 6; *Daily Herald* (Calgary), 29 March 1916, 6.

28. Price to Bassett, 25 Feb. 1916, Bassett Papers, vol. 5. On the recruiting methods in Ontario, see Wilson, *Ontario and the First World War*, xlii–Iiii.

29. Griesbach to Hughes, 13 May 1915, Major-General W.A. Griesbach Papers, PAC, MG30, E15, vol. 1.

30. Report of IG (Imperial) on Canadian Troops, no. 47/560/MT2, 16 June 1915, app. A, in Lessard to Hughes, May 1916, F.L. Lessard Papers, PAC, MG 30, G 47; Hughes to Lessard, 16 April 1916, F.L. Lessard Papers; Nicholson, *Official History of the Canadian Army in the First World War*, 202, 225; Duguid, *Official History of the Canadian Forces in the Great War*, app. 8; Alderson to Governor General, 17 Feb. 1916, Sir Edward Kemp Papers, PAC, MG27, II, D9, vol. 110; McCurdy to Hughes, 21 July 1916, and Hughes to Borden, 2 Aug. 1916, Borden Papers, OC318. When Hughes was fired, Perley resolved the problem of surplus officers by sending them home or letting them go to France with a lesser rank. Nicholson, *Official History of the Canadian Army in the First World War*, 223–24.

31. Gwatkin to Kemp, 1916, Kemp Papers; Hughes to Lessard, 16 April 1916, and Lessard to Hughes, May 1916, Lessard Papers; Borden to Hughes, 19 Aug. 1916, Borden Papers, OC318; and Gwatkin to Christie, 27 June 1916, Borden Papers, OC322.

32. For an overview, see Granatstein and Hitsman, *Broken Promises*, 22–34; Desmond Morton, "French Canada and the War, 1868–1917: The Military Background to the Conscription Crisis of 1917," in *War and Society in North America*, ed. J.L. Granatstein and R.D. Cuff (Toronto: Nelson, 1971), 84–103.

33. Mason Wade, *The French Canadians, 1760–1967*, vol. 2 (Toronto: Macmillan, 1968), 640–41. See ibid., 640–726 for the trials of French Canadians during the war. Also Elizabeth A. Armstrong, *The Crisis of Quebec, 1914–1918* (Toronto: McClelland and Stewart, 1974), 35–160.

34. Winter, *Lieutenant-General the Hon. Sir Sam Hughes*, 140.

35. Duguid, *Official History of the Canadian Forces in the Great War*, app. 85, "Composition of Provisional Infantry Brigades and Battalions, Valcartier Camp, Sept. 3, 1914," app. 88, "Questions to be put before attestation," and app. 86; Morton, "French Canada and the War, 1868–1917," 96; *Hansard*, 1916, p. 3283; Gwatkin to Sladen, 27 Aug. 1915, Gwatkin Papers, F2.

36. Bristol to Borden, 17 Oct. 1914, and Bristol to Hazen, 17 Oct. 1914, Bristol Papers, PAO, 285, political 1914; *Hansard*, 1916, p. 3281; Morton, "French Canada and the War, 1868–1917," 102; and Wade, *The French Canadians, 1760–1967*, 2:668, 708, 709; and Oscar Pelletier, *Memoires, Souveniers de Famille et Récits* (Quebec, 1940), 382–90.

37. Duguid, *Official History of the Canadian Forces in the Great War*, apps. 74, 711, 843; and Armstrong, *The Crisis of Quebec*, 70, 83–84.

38. Department of Militia and Defence, *The Militia Lists of the Dominion of Canada, 1875–1920*, Sept. 1914, p. 204; Henry James Morgan, ed. *The Canadian Men and Women of the Time: A Handbook of Living Characters* (Toronto: Briggs, 1912), 436, 447; Morton, "French Canada and the War, 1868–1917," 97.

39. Desmond Morton, "The Limits of Loyalty: French Canadian Officers and the First World War," in *Limits of Loyalty*, ed. Edgar Denton (Waterloo: Wilfrid Laurier University Press, 1980), 92–93.

40. Gwatkin to Sladen, 27 Aug. 1915, Gwatkin Papers, 172; and Desmond Morton, "The Short, Unhappy Life of the 41st Battalion CEF," in *Queens Quarterly* 81, 1 (1974), 70–80.

41. CAR, 1916, p. 194; *Hansard*, 1916, p. 3283; Oliver Asselin, *Pourquoi Je m'enrole* (Montreal, 1916), esp. 32; and Morton, "The Limits of Loyalty," 92–94.

42. Price to Bassett, 24 Feb. 191:6, Bassett Papers, vol. 5.

43. Granatstein and Hitsman, *Broken Promises*, 30.

44. Aitken to Borden, 17 May 1916, Beaverbrook Papers, E, 7–8; Borden to Hughes, 25 Jan. 1916, Borden Papers, OC68; Gwatkin to Kemp, spring 1916, Gwatkin Papers, Fl; and CAR, 1916, p. 258.

45. Wade, *The French Canadians, 1760–1967*, 2:727; E.M. MacDonald, *Recollections: Political and Personal* (Toronto: Ryerson Press, 1939), 335; *Current Opinion* (Sept. 1917),158; *Free Press* (London), 12 June 1916, 4; *Daily Herald* (Calgary), 18 July 1916, 6; *Hansard*, 1916, pp. 1373–74; Mason Wade, *The French Canadian Outlook* (Toronto: McClelland and Stewart, 1964), 52; Nicholson, *Official History of the Canadian Army in the First World War*, 221; and Morton, "French Canada and the War, 1868–1917," 98–99.

46. Law to Governor General, 30 Aug. 1914, and Kitchener to Hughes, 7 Sept. 1914, Borden Papers; and Duguid, *Official History of the Canadian Forces in the Great War, app.* 87, Hughes to Kitchener, 29 Aug. 1914.

47. Fiset to Sec. External Affairs, 24 Oct. 1914, and McBride to R.L. Borden, 25 Nov. 1914, Borden Papers, OC322, vol. 70. Also see W.S. Churchill memo, 5 Sept. 1914, Edwin Pye Papers, Directorate of History, National Defence Headquarters, Ottawa (hereafter DHist), Fl, f5; and Perley to Borden, 2 Dec. 1914, First Viscount Harcourt Papers, Oxford University, Box 465, p. 49.

48. Minute of Militia Council, 13 Jan. 1916, PAC, RG 24, vol. 1542, 689-1174-1; Gwatkin to Sladen, 31 July 1916, PAC, RG 24, vol. 14071, vol. 461; Gwatkin to Cliristie (HQC 1562), 18 June 1916, Connaught to Borden, 25 June 1916, and DMD memo, 4 July 1916, Borden Papers, OC322, vol. 70; J.G. Mitchell, Department of Interior to Sam Hughes, 3 Nov. 1915, Pye Papers, DHist, Fl, f5; and PAC, RG 24, vol. 1383, 593-6-1-93.

49. F? to Spring-Rice, 17 July 1916, Beaverbrook Papers, E/18, 97th Battalion; Spring-Rice to Connaught, 2 May 1916, US Department of Justice to US Secretary of State, 17 Jan. 1916, Beaverbrook Papers, RG 7, 14071, vol. 452; Spring-Rice to Governor General, 1 July 1916, Beaverbrook Papers, RG 7, 14071, vol. 455; and *Free Press* (Detroit), 19 Dec. 1915, 24 Dec. 1915, and 6 Jan. 1916, editorial.

50. "Notes by Pye," CGS to AG, 3 March 1916, Pye Papers; and Fiset to Christie, 27 March 1916, Borden Papers, OC322, vol. 70.

51. R.G. Haycock, "The American Legion in the Canadian Expeditionary Force, 1914–1917: A Study in Failure," in *Military Affairs* 43, 3 (Oct. 1979), 115–19.

52. Morton, "The Limits of Loyalty," 91; Hughes to Borden, 23 Oct. 1916, Borden Papers, OC318; and CAR, 1916, pp. 265–66. For a review of Borden's course after 1916, see Brown, *Borden, vol.* 2, chaps. 8–10. As early as August 1914, Sir Charles Ross had protested the loss of his skilled machinists in Hughes's "fiery cross" mobilization. See Ross to Hughes, 6 Aug. 1914, Sir Charles Ross Papers, PAC, MG30, A95, vol. 5.

Topic Twelve

Foreign Policy and World War II

Members of the Royal Canadian Engineers briefly pray with a chaplain immediately prior to boarding their aircraft for the D-Day invasion.

Twenty years after the Great War, Canada entered World War II (1939–1945). The causes of the two world wars differed, as did Canada's reasons for entering and the nature of its contribution. But in both cases, Canada contributed large numbers of men and women, and enormous financial, agricultural, and industrial resources to the war effort. Equally significant is the impact that both wars had on Canada. While each world war had a different impact, both wars dramatically changed the nature of Canada in domestic and foreign policy.

The following two articles look at the impact of the World War II. In "Battle Exhaustion and the Canadian Soldier in Normandy," historian J. Terry Copp examines the impact of battle exhaustion on the soldiers who fought in this important battle. Copp describes battle exhaustion as "the catch-all term used by the Army to describe stress-related neuro-psychiatric casualties" experienced by the Canadian infantry during fighting at the front. Copp explains how psychiatrists accounted for battle exhaustion, how they assessed those believed to be suffering from the disease, and what methods of treatment they used.

Historian Jack Granatstein examines Canada's shifting foreign policy during World War II in "Staring into the Abyss." He argues that although Canada had already begun to distance itself from Britain and to ally itself with the United States in World War I and in the interwar years, it was Britain's military weakness during World War II that drove Canada into the arms of the United States. He sees the signing of the Ogdensburg Agreement between Canada and the United States in August 1940 as the turning point, and argues that this Agreement should not be seen as a Canadian "sell out to the United States" but rather as an attempt to maintain Canadian autonomy.

What were the assumptions about the nature of Canada, of Canadian-British relations, and of Canadian-American relations that underlay the formulation of Canadian foreign policy during World War II? Noted Canadian analyst Harold A. Innis once described Canada's foreign policy from 1914 to 1945 as going from "colony to nation to colony." How accurate was his assessment according to Granatstein in his analysis of Canadian foreign policy during World War II? What does Terry Copp's discussion of battle exhaustion during World War II reveal about the experience of Canadian soldiers at the war front? How does the experience of soldiers in World War II compare with those of World War I as described in Will Bird's personal account in Topic Eleven?

On the impact of the war, see Desmond Morton, *Canada and War: A Military and Political History* (Toronto: Butterworths, 1981); Norman Hillmer et al., eds., *A Country of Limitations: Canada and the War in 1939* (Ottawa: Canadian Committee for the History of the Second World War, 1996); and J.L. Granatstein and Desmond Morton, *A Nation Forged in Fire: Canadians and the Second World War, 1939–1945* (Toronto: Lester & Orphen Dennys, 1989). On Canadian participation in the war, see W.A.B. Douglas and Brereton Greenhous, *Out of the Shadows: Canada in the Second World War*, rev. ed. (Toronto: Dundurn Press, 1995); David J. Bercuson, *Maple Leaf against the Axis: Canada's Second World War* (Toronto: Stoddart, 1995); Ted Barris and Alex Barris, *Days of Victory: Canadians Remember, 1939–1945* (Toronto: Macmillan, 1995); Desmond Morton and J.L. Granatstein, *Victory 1945: Canadians from War to Peace* (Toronto: HarperCollins, 1995); and Mark Zuehlke, *Ortona* (North York, ON: Stoddart Publishing, 1999). Useful collections of essays include Peter Neary and J.L. Granatstein, eds., *The Good Fight: Canada and the Second World War* (Toronto: Copp Clark Longman, 1994); and Marc Miller, ed., *Canadian Military History: Selected Readings* (Toronto: Copp Clark Pitman, 1993).

For overviews of Canadian foreign policy in the interwar years and in World War II, see C.P. Stacey, *Canada and the Age of Conflict*, vol. 2, *1921–1948: The Mackenzie King Era* (Toronto: University of Toronto Press, 1981); Richard Veatch, *Canada and the League of Nations* (Toronto: University of Toronto Press, 1975); and Norman Hillmer and J.L. Granatstein,

Empire to Umpire: Canada and the World to the 1990s (Toronto: Copp Clark Longman, 1994). On Mackenzie King's foreign and domestic policies during the war years, see J.L. Granatstein, *Canada's War: The Politics of the Mackenzie King Government, 1939–1945* (Toronto: University of Toronto Press, 1975, 1990). R.D. Cuff and J.L. Granatstein review aspects of Canadian-American relations in *Ties that Bind: Canadian-American Relations in Wartime from the Great War to the Cold War,* 2nd ed. (Toronto: Samuel Stevens Hakkert, 1977).

WEBLINKS

Declaration of War on Germany
http://www.dfait-maeci.gc.ca/department/history/keydocs/keydocs_details-en.asp?intDocumentId=18

A transcribed copy of the Government of Canada's declaration of war against Germany. Further documents regarding Canada's international affairs in this time period are available at

http://www.dfait-maeci.gc.ca/department/history/keydocs/keydocs_views-en.asp?RefValue=1900&view=4

World War II Collections
http://web.mala.bc.ca/davies/letters.images/collection.pages/WWII.htm

A diverse collection of documents and photographs of Canadian combatants and civilians in World War II.

Diaries of Prime Minister Mackenzie King
http://king.collectionscanada.ca/EN

The complete digitized diaries of Prime Minister Mackenzie King. The diaries are extensive and cover King's life from 1893 to 1950.

Canadian Newspapers and World War II
http://warmuseum.ca/cwm/newspapers/intro_e.html

A searchable database of the published content of Canadian newspapers such as *The Globe and Mail* and *Hamilton Spectator* with regard to World War II.

National Film Board of Canada: D-Day
http://www.nfb.ca/enclasse/dday/dday.html

D-Day video archives of the National Film Board of Canada.

Article Twenty-Nine

Battle Exhaustion and the Canadian Soldier in Normandy

J. Terry Copp

The fortieth anniversary of the Normandy invasion brought forth a new flood of books, each purporting to tell the real story of the battle. Strategic questions have been reassessed, the significance of Ultra brought to light and the personalities of the leading figures re-examined. There is a good deal of new information in the recent studies of the 1944 campaign but almost all of it[1] relates to questions which are quite remote from the actual experience of the young men who fought the battle in close contact with the enemy.

The purpose of this paper is to attempt to get some measure of the experience of the Canadian infantry soldier by examining the phenomenon of Battle Exhaustion, the catch-all term used by the Army to describe stress-related neuro-psychiatric casualties. But before attempting to analyze this small part of the story it seems necessary to explain some facets of the organization of the Canadian and British forces who set out to invade Normandy on 6 June 1944 and to make some comments of the nature of the campaign in Normandy.

We must first always remind ourselves that the Allied plan for the invasion of northwest Europe was dependent upon the ability of the Red Army to continue operations which occupied the energies of three-quarters of the German army. The Allies had simply not created a force large enough to confront the bulk of the German army. Indeed British (and thus Canadian) preparations for Operation Overlord were strongly affected by the overall war policy of Great Britain which was based on the desire to defeat the enemy by means other than direct conflict with substantial elements of the German army. In the spring of 1944 the British-Canadian component of the Allied forces, available for the invasion of Normandy, included a formidable tactical air force, a naval commitment of unparalleled power, and a small army which was rich in every resource except infantry.

Twenty-one Army Group which was charged with the responsibility for the invasion was to have an establishment of some 750 000 men but there were only nine infantry divisions (including two Canadian) available. Fifteen percent of the total troops were infantry,[2] but the designation "Infantry" should not be confused with actual commitment to battle in a rifle company. A standard 1944 infantry division contained 915 officers and 17 247 men, but less than half were infantry and of those only 4500 served in the thirty-six division rifle companies.[3]

The British had long since determined, as the Germans in Normandy were soon to discover, that artillery was to be the army's principal weapon and fully 18 percent of the troops in the bridgehead were artillerymen.[4] The planners also hoped that the fourteen armoured brigades allotted to 21 Army Group would play a prominent role in cracking the German defenses. It was hoped that these two Arms, together with the 2nd Tactical Air Force, would ensure that the Battle of Normandy would not become a bloody replay of the Western Front in World War I.

Viewed in hindsight the Normandy campaign went much better than the planners hoped. Not only were the Germans unable to bring substantial reinforcements from the Eastern Front

Source: J. Terry Copp, "Battle Exhaustion and the Canadian Soldier in Normandy," from the *British Army Review* 85 (April 1987), 46–54. Reprinted with permission of the author.

(the Russian summer offensive which began two weeks after D Day was to cost the Germans close to one million casualities) but the Allied deception scheme "Fortitude" kept large elements of their western forces away from Normandy until it was too late. The Tactical Air Force, naval guns, the heavy bombers, and the artillery struck the German defenders with such a weight of high explosives that it may reasonably be argued that the Germans were blasted out of Normandy acre by acre.

But, and it is a very large but, the skill and resilience of the German defenders meant that the Allied infantry were required to attack, occupy, and hold small parcels of ground under circumstances which fully paralleled the horrors of the fighting of the Western Front in the first World War.

Modern memory has a firm image of "suicide bombers" and long casuality lists in the First World War, but we are not accustomed to thinking of Normandy in these terms, perhaps because of the relatively short duration of the campaign (88 days) and the overwhelming victory which climaxed the battle. A single crude comparison will help to make the point. During a 105-day period in the summer and fall of 1917, British and Canadian soldiers fought the battle known as 3rd Ypres which included the struggle for Passchendaele. When it was over our forces had suffered 244 000 casualties[5] or 2324 a day. Normandy was to cost the Allies more than 200 000 casualties or 2325 a day and 70 percent of these casualties were suffered by the tiny minority of men who fought in infantry rifle companies.[6]

So far what we have been trying to establish is that the fighting in Normandy placed a burden of almost unbearable proportions on one small Arm of the Allied armies — the Infantry. British (and thus Canadian) planners had not, despite the lessons of Italy, been willing to prepare for this eventuality. Well before D Day Montgomery had been worried that reserves of infantry replacements were dangerously limited. The War Office had already calculated that "at least two infantry divisions and several separate brigades might have to be disbanded by the end of 1944 for lack of reinforcements."[7] By early July the character of the Normandy battle had brought this crisis to hand and infantry battalions were frequently operating well below strength. By early August the Canadians, for whom infantry casualties were running at 76 percent of the total,[8] were reporting a deficiency of 1900 general duty Infantry[9] or the equivalent of four battalions of riflemen. By the end of August shortages had reached the staggering figure of 4318.[10]

This situation, which was proportionally only slightly less serious among British divisions, forced Montgomery to cannibalize the 59th division. On 14 August he told Alanbrooke, "My infantry divisions are now so low in effective rifle strength they can no longer — repeat, no longer — fight effectively in major operations. The need for action has been present for some time, but the urgency of the battle operations forced me to delay a decision."[11]

Perhaps enough has been said to indicate something of the context within which the Infantry fought in Normandy. Let us turn to the impact which the battle had upon the men who fought it as measured by the phenomenon of Battle Exhaustion. Needless to say, Battle Exhaustion was largely an infantry-man's problem. More than 90 percent of the known cases were among infantry. The large majority of individuals diagnosed as suffering from Battle Exhaustion exhibited what the psychiatrists described as acute fear reactions and acute and chronic anxiety manifested through uncontrollable tremors, a pronounced startle reaction to war-related sounds, and a profound loss of self confidence. The second largest symptomatic category was depression with accompanying withdrawal. Conversion states such as amnesia, stupor, or loss of control over some physical function, which had made up a large component of those described as "shell shocked" in World War I, were rarely seen in World War II.[12]

In preparing for Operation Overlord the Canadian Army was able to draw upon its own experience with Battle Exhaustion in the Italian campaign as well as the much more extensive information available from British and American sources. The assumptions of Canadian military authorities in May of 1944 may be summarized quite briefly.

The most commonly used method of measuring exhaustion rates was the so-called NP ratio which measured neuropsychiatric casualties in relation to total non-fatal battle casualties. Experience in the Mediterranean among British, American, and Canadian units suggested that a NP ratio of 23 percent, more than 1 in 5 of non-fatal casualties, was normal for infantry divisions in combat.[13]

Neither the military planners, frightened by the shrinking pool of General Service infantry reinforcements, nor the psychiatrists, professionally committed to reducing the NP ratio, were happy with either the quantity or predictability of neuropsychiatric casualties. The military authorities could and did, on occasion, issue directives attempting to forbid soldiers from breaking down. The major impact of such orders was to make life difficult for the Regimental Medical Officer and to make it nearly impossible for historians to compile accurate battle exhaustion statistics. Shortly after General Burns assumed command of 1st Corps, RMOs were ordered to be strict and hold all NP cases until it was certain that they could not be returned to unit and regimental CO's were told that battle exhaustion was their responsibility and if it occurred in the coming action "it would be taken as a reflection upon the ability of these officers."[14] General Guy Simonds never went quite that far, but it is evident that he had little patience with the policies of First Canadian Army relating to battle exhaustion.[15]

The psychiatrists in the Canadian Army, fully supported by their Allied colleagues, took a different approach. If battle exhaustion was a psycho-neurosis, i.e.

> an emotional disorder in which feelings of anxiety, obsessional thoughts, compulsive acts and physical complaints, without objective evidence of disease, in various patterns, dominate the personality,

then their training indicated that the neurotic individual must have been predisposed to neurosis by childhood experiences. If enough attention was paid to screening combat units for predisposed individuals, then the NP ratio could be significantly reduced. Dr. Arthur Manning Doyle, the First Division psychiatrist (and the only Canadian psychiatrist, in May 1944, with direct experience of battle exhaustion) did admit that "stress of battle" as well as pre-disposition was a variable, but he could only offer advice on the desirability of "weeding" units to remove the pre-disposed.[16]

Doyle's careful investigation of the NP ratio in the various regiments of the 1st Division should have suggested that a more elaborate diagnosis was required. His own figures showed that the Loyal Edmonton Regiment had less than half the NP casualties of some other regiments and that the variation between regiments was very large. It was also evident that 3 Brigade continued to have a much higher NP ratio than other brigades,[17] but no conclusions were drawn or indeed questions raised about these striking differences.

For Overlord the emphasis was on "weeding" and Dr. Gregory, the 3 Division psychiatrist, rejected 150 men — including three officers and one senior NCO — in the weeks before D Day, even though the division's regiments had been repeatedly "weeded" in the long months of assault training.[18] Once in combat the division utilized one of its Field Dressing Stations as an exhaustion unit, treating 208 men in the first two weeks of combat.[19] Exhaustion soon became the "outstanding problem"[20] for the medicals and in early July, Colonel Watson, the division's ADMS, issued instructions asking units to keep what he called "physical exhaustion" cases with the left-out-of-battle personnel. True battle exhaustion cases should come to the attention of the medical services only after they had had a rest.[21]

Colonel Watson and the divisional psychiatrist became convinced that common sense was "the first quality required" in the control of battle exhaustion. The truly neurotic soldier was a "menace to the stability of the force, even during rest periods" and must be removed. But for the rest, common sense meant:

> planned rest periods on a company, unit, brigade or division basis with diversions in the form of movies, sport, etc. must be arranged. During battle this can only be done on a platoon or company basis.
>
> During these periods, even if bombing or shelling are only remotely possible, adequate protection in the form of solid buildings and numerous slit trenches should be readily available to the soldier. For psychological reasons, the soldier should not be in a position where he is constantly having to search for a place to duck in an emergency; if so, he becomes cowardly; plenty of obvious slit trenches makes him feel secure and he becomes brave and does not require to use them. Troops in rest areas, even where odd shells are falling, should sleep above ground.
>
> (d) The Divisional Psychologist (sic) should be possessed of a degree of common sense well above that of the average officer. It is an essential appointment for the right man. His duty is to discuss with the ADMS all measures which will raise the morale of the fighting soldier as they apply to each separate situation and to examine and classify all casualties which are referred to him. He should not have to make a professional show by having specially allotted Field Dressing Stations or Field Ambulances filled with cases on which he can base statistics and lengthy reports to Headquarters. In fact, if he has many patients and issues long reports, he should be removed at once for failing in his job.
>
> The 'G' staff should be alert to the fact that providing the medicals have done their job, a high incidence of exhaustion cases indicates deficient training, poor leadership with a low fighting ability of the force. Battles are won by causing exhaustion in the enemy's ranks!![22]

All of this was at least an improvement on the preoccupation with childhood neuroses, but it was quite remote from the actual experience of 3 Division rifle companies. In *Maple Leaf Route: Falaise*, Robert Vogel and I reproduced the only battalion casualty report we found that dealt frankly with the problem of Battle Exhaustion. This report by the Officer Commanding the Canadian Scottish Regiment noted that, on 28 July, the regiment (which had begun the campaign with 38 officers and 815 other ranks) had suffered 569 casualties and contained only 15 officers and 321 other ranks who had landed on D Day. Many of the survivors were, of course, not rifle-men. Of the 421 men who had been "wounded" to that date, 117 had been evacuated as Battle Exhaustion cases. Not included on the list were the "24 men sent down to Corps Rest Camp and a large number (approx. 36) withdrawn from the front line during periods of relative quiet who, in the opinion of the company commanders and Medical Officers, required twenty-four or forty-eight hours of rest."[23]

The Canadian Scottish Regiment was, by any standards, well led, well trained and was as effective a unit as the Allied armies possessed. Furthermore, unlike a number of its sister regiments, it had yet to experience[24] one of those single day disasters that had scarred units like the Royal Winnipeg Rifles, The North Nova Scotia Regiment or the Highland Light Infantry. The Canadian Scottish had, however, remained in the line continuously under fire and had taken part in some of the most difficult battles.

By late July the Canadian Scottish, like the rest of the division, had reached a dangerous state of nervous tension and Colonel Watson, the senior Medical Officer, "drew the attention of the GOC to the situation in a letter which he in turn discussed with the Brigade Commanders who strongly supported the request for a rest of seven to ten days . . ."[25] The Third Division was finally pulled out of the line.

The experiences of British 3 Division which fought alongside the Canadians in the first phase on the Normandy campaign was similar with 253 cases in June and 736 cases in July.[26] Overall the exhaustion ratio in 2 British Army rose from 9.5 percent in June to 22 percent in late July.[27] The 2 Army psychiatrist, Major A. Watterson, described the situation in these terms:

> The high optimism of the troops who landed in the assault and early build-up phases inevitably dwindles when the campaign for a few weeks appeared to have slowed down. Almost certainly the initial hopes and optimism were too high and the gradual realization that the "walk-over" to Berlin had developed into an infantry slogging match caused an unspoken but clearly recognizable fall of morale. One sign of this was the increase in the incidence of psychiatric casualties arriving in a steady stream at the Exhaustion Centres and reinforced by waves of beaten, exhausted men from each of the major battles. For every man breaking down there were certainly three or four ineffective men remaining with their units.[28]

The pattern of battle exhaustion casualties in both 3 Canadian and 3 British Division could be understood in the terms outlined by Watson and Gregory — psychiatric casualties would increase over time if units were not relieved. What disturbed Canadian Army authorities was the sudden influx of NP casualties from 2 Division in the early weeks of combat. It must be stressed that no accurate count of NP casualties is possible. Indeed, given the attitude of 2 Canadian Corps headquarters that "there will be no evacuation of psychiatric casualties in 2 Corps"[29] and the refusal to accept a divisional psychiatrist on the staff of 2 Division,[30] estimates for the 2 Division are even more difficult to arrive at than for 3 Division.

First Canadian Exhaustion unit, which had been activated with 2 Corps, dealt with 2 Division NP casualties during mid-July before divisional recovery centres were functioning. In the period 13 July to 24 July it reported approximately 300 cases from 2 Division, including 13 officers.[31] After 24 July, 4 Canadians FDS [Field Dressing Station] was used as a divisional recovery centre and, in the first seven days, it admitted 118 cases.[32] A similar number were admitted to the Corps Exhaustion unit that terrible week.[33] For the entire period, 13 July to 15 August, First Canadian Exhaustion Unit reported 576 cases from 2 Division and as many as 200 further cases were treated at Field Dressing stations; 23 officers were evacuated to hospital.[34] This indicates a NP ratio well above 30 percent and clearly demonstrates that 2 Division's first weeks in battle were even more horrific than existing accounts of the battles of Verrières Ridge suggest.

The extent of battle exhaustion casualties in 2 Division became a subject of considerable notoriety in the Canadian Army and, after the Battle of Normandy was over, Dr. Burdett McNeel who had commanded the Corps Exhaustion Centre in July and August, was asked to investigate the situation in 2 Division.[35] By eliminating the first nine days of the division's frontline experiences from consideration, McNeel was able to show that the division's exhaustion rate was not higher than 3 Division's. This did nothing to clarify the situation. However, McNeel's own War Diary and quarterly report covering the entire period do provide some insight.

The first wave of exhaustion cases from 2 Division included truckloads, complete with NCO's, of "dirty, haggard and dejected men"[36] from a regiment whose lead companies were caught by their own artillery barrage. The next day these were joined by more than one hundred cases largely from the three regiments shattered in the dying hours of Operation Goodwood on the rain-drenched and deadly slopes of Verrières Ridge.

In conversation with Dr. McNeel some forty years later,[37] it was evident that he had known nothing of the military situation which precipitated the evacuation of so many men from the 2 Division, either on 20th July or in the aftermath.

It seems quite clear that a detailed knowledge of the events of mid-July provides an adequate explanation of the extent of Battle Exhaustion in 2 Division. The Division was ordered into the Normandy battle in the final stages of an operation (Goodwood) which had already failed. The decision to commit two "green" infantry brigades to a frontal attack on a position which the Germans were steadily reinforcing was not a wise one. The results were horrific. The division suffered 1149 casualties in its first battle since Dieppe and four of its regiments were devastated. Everything was out of control and no one's morale was in very good shape after the battle.

The renewal of offensive operations on 25th July (Operation Spring) was a replay of the disasters of the 19th–20th. The Canadian army experienced a catastrophe of almost Dieppe proportions, losing 1500 men, most of them from 2 Division, in the space of 24 hours. No division could be expected to absorb these kinds of casualties in offensive operation which were clearly failures and maintain high morale. Substantial Battle Exhaustion casualties were simply inevitable.

At the time psychiatrists, wedded to their theories on pre-disposition, could only assume that 2 Division had been less carefully screened than 3 Division. The Exhaustion Units' diagnosis of cases seen in this period suggest just how committed to personality development theory the psychiatrists were. Almost half the evacuees were labelled psychopathic personalities, i.e.:

> a disorder of behaviour towards other individuals or towards society in which reality is clearly perceived except for an individual's social and moral obligations. . . .

Even a layman can be forgiven for doubting that the two harassed psychiatrists who dealt with hundreds of cases in a matter of a few days, would have accurately diagnosed 197 psychopaths! [38]

However, McNeel's report on 2 Division which was written in late September reflected his growing awareness of the nature of warfare in Northwest Europe. He spoke with both medical and line officers in 2 Division and became convinced that casualty statistics and exhaustion ratios were of doubtful value in assessing personnel or performance. He wrote:

> The source of error in the compilation of statistics and the use of such a figure as an exhaustion ratio are so numerous as to make any conclusion based on statistics alone of very doubtful value. The incidence of exhaustion in any unit is only a part of the picture of that unit's efficiency and is outweighed in a positive direction by a generally high standard of performance and in a negative direction by large numbers of AWOL, POW, and trivial illnesses. I have been told that one regiment which has a high exhaustion ratio is always reliable and has never withdrawn from an action, whereas another regiment with a low exhaustion ratio has usually withdrawn from an action whenever the stress became great . . . The exhaustion ratio will also be altered by the wholesale evacuation of trivial sick or wounded . . . For these reasons the thoughtful appraisal of a unit's overall performance by responsible officers who know all the factors is of more value than any set of statistics or ratios can ever hope to be. However the latter may be used as a lead. [39]

McNeel gave a further illustration of the problems of using battle exhaustion ratios. He had spoken with an RMO in July about the number of evacuations from his regiment and urged him to keep the men with the unit. Later he had occasion to compliment the RMO on the changed situation only to be told "Well, I don't know — we had 50 men AWOL today." [40]

McNeel's superior officer, Colonel P.H. van Nostrand, was equally dubious about the value of exhaustion ratios. The Colonel, who had been pulled out of regimental duties in 1942 when General McNaughton had become alarmed over the number of psychiatric cases in the Army overseas, assumed responsibility as the Consultant Neuropsychiatrist Canadian Army overseas. "Van," as he was universally known, brought a degree of common sense and unpretentiousness to psychiatric work that was badly needed. McNeel tells the story of a discussion on NP ratios as predictive tools in which he, McNeel, was fumbling for a statement of his own doubts when Van Nostrand calmly brought the debate to a halt with these lines:

> There was a young man named Paul
> Who had a hexagonal ball
> The square of its weight
> Plus his penis times eight
> Was two-third of three-fifths of ****-all.[41]

The conclusion of the Battle of Normandy brought an end to the battle exhaustion crisis. Cases were rare during the September pursuit and, when neuropsychiatric casualties began to accumulate again in October, there was no sudden influx of large numbers. There was now time available for more careful diagnosis and treatment.

Dr. Travis Dancey, the new Corps Exhaustion psychiatrist, wrote:

> The type of NP case seen . . . has been much different from that so frequently described in the literature and from that admitted this summer. Although recent reinforcements who break down tend to show gross demoralization characterized by conversion-hysteria or anxiety-hysteria, we are handling an increasing number of men who have carried on under considerable stress for long periods of time . . . We are not dealing with chronic psychoneurotics, or with men who could be called inadequate in any sense of the term.[42]

Dancey, who was not in France during the Normandy battle, was not yet prepared to challenge the literature or to suggest that the Normandy experience be reassessed. It was not until the battle of 1945, when a more elaborate system of diagnosing and treating NP casualties was developed, that new evidence began to accumulate.[43] Many "predisposed" neurotic personalities had functioned very well and many "normal" individuals had broken down. It further became evident that every infantry soldier who remained for any length of time in combat developed neurotic traits which, in civilian life, would have indicated serious personality disturbance. The question was, why some men became incapacitated by stress and why others (often with "weaker" personalities) did not.

William C. Menninger who served as Chief Consultant in Neuropsychiatry to the US Army provided this answer:

> The breakdown of the soldier in combat, whether it was during his first week or his fifteenth month, was related to the ability of his personality to maintain further the balance between stress and compensating support. Support was derived from various sources. The external situation which presented the necessity of killing in order not to be killed, was stimulus to keep the aggression mobilized for action. Fear, if controlled, was a factor in maintaining . . . alertness. Very significant aids in the control of this aggression were the approval and command of the leader and the identification and close association with a group of men who shared the same plight.
>
> The same psychological reinforcements which made it possible for the soldier to fight were potential causes of the development of psychiatric casualty, if they suddenly disappeared. Because of great dependence on them, the ego was left without support in their absence . . . The very occasional soldier might carry on alone . . . More often, as the tension increased, the personality tried to relieve its distress by transforming anxiety into symptoms.[44]

Canadian army psychiatrists never quite went this far, though one study of 544 cases did conclude with the following:

> Two thirds of the cases gave no apparent history of neurotic predisposition or previous instability . . . only 19% of the total could have been considered as originally unfit . . . 30% were

sensitized by long service alone (average 230 days). 23% had an added factor of being previously wounded and 18% had been previously evacuated for exhaustion . . . A further finding of interest was that of the 167 cases with long front-line service . . . 42 cases or 23% had carried on in spite of the fact that they had histories of previous nervous disorders or evident traits predisposing to neurotic breakdown . . . even a neurotic can stand a long period of battle stress when he has good drive, morale and character . . . a man can be "burnt out" due to long exposure to battle conditions even when he is considered quite normal. [45]

Here we are less interested in the education of Canadian psychiatrists than we are with the solider in Normandy so I will say no more about psychiatric reports. When Canadians and other Allied veterans assemble this June to commemorate the beginning of the campaign to liberate the peoples of Western Europe all of them will be deserving of our gratitude but perhaps it would not be unfair if we kept a special place in our hearts for the rifleman who fought "without promise of reward or relief." For no one, not even a psychiatrist or an historian "however he may talk has the remotest idea of what an ordinary infantry soldier endures."

NOTES

1. See John Ellis, *The Sharp End of War* (London, 1980), which attempts to describe combat in World War II from the point of view of the ordinary soldier. Carlo D'Este, *Decision in Normandy* (London, 1983). This contains a good discussion of infantry manpower problems.
2. The figures adjusted to include Canadian personnel are from L.F. Ellis, *Victory in the West* (London, 1962), vol. 1, HMSO, app. 4.
3. M. Hitsman, *Manpower Problems of the Canadian Army*, Report #63 Historian Section, Department of National Defense, app. L, 352.
4. Ellis, *Victory in the West*, app. 4.
5. John Terraine, *The Smoke and the Fire* (London, 1980), 46.
6. C.P. Stacey, *The Victory Campaign* (Ottawa, 1960), calculates Canadian infantry casualties as 76 percent of the total. The figure of 70 percent appears to be an accepted average for all allied casualties. See Ellis, *The Sharp End of War*, 158.
7. D'Este, *Decision in Normandy*, 252.
8. Stacey, *The Victory Campaign*, 284.
9. C.P. Stacey, *Arms, Men and Government* (Ottawa, 1970), 435.
10. Ibid. 438–39.
11. D'Estem *Decision in Normandy*, 262.
12. There does not seem to be any adequate explanation for this difference.
13. A.M. Doyle, "Report of 1 Cdn. Neuropsychiatrist, period 1 April–20 June 1944," Public Archives of Canada (hereafter PAC), Record Group (hereafter RG) 24, vol. 15, G46, p. 11.
14. W.R. Feasby, *Official History of the Canadian Medical Services 1939–45*, vol. 2 (Ottawa, 1956), 58.
15. On 29 August Simonds in a letter to his divisional commanders urged greater efforts to limit straggling, absenteeism, and battle exhaustion and suggested that the latter problem should not occur under the conditions of fighting in Normandy.
16. It should be noted that by 1945 Dr. Doyle was arguing that: the following factors are those that affect the incidence of Neuropsychiatric casualties in order of importance.
    a) Quality of Personnel
    b) Degree and severity of action
    c) Duration of Action
    d) Quality of leadership
    e) Considerations such as weather, opportunity for rest and recreation and other such items relating to the welfare of the soldier.
    Doyle's emphasis on quality of personnel was reflected in his overall conclusion that "the units which have shown consistently high neuropsychiatric ratios are those units who have had in their ranks too many

inadequate, neurotic or mentally defective personnel." This judgment was to be challenged by the end of the Northwest European campaign.

See Lt. Col. A.M. Doyle "Psychiatry with the Canadian Army in Action in the C.M.F." *The Journal of the Canadian Medical Services*, vol. 3 (January 1946), 93. I wish to thank Dr. Bill McAndrew (DHist, National Defence) for discussing this point with me and sharing his own research into battle exhaustion in Italy.

17. Doyle may well have been thinking about 3 Brigade in particular when he emphasized quality of personnel but the difficulties encountered by 3 Brigade from training through its first months in combat require a far more complex analysis than this.

18. Dr. Dick Gregory was an unusual individual. Energetic, gregarious and colourful, he won the confidence of the ADMS, Col. Watson, and of the Regimental Medical Officers. He was able to arrange for the officers of each divisional Field Ambulance to attend an American School of Psychiatry and did much to prepare both medical and non-medical personnel for battle exhaustion casualties to their unit after brief treatment at the Field Ambulance recovery centre. This "success rate" was so extraordinarily high that his fellow psychiatrists were frankly dubious. However it is clear that 3 Division, as a whole, was better prepared for dealing with psychiatric casualties than the other divisions and it may be early rest and reassurance did work well. R.A. Gregory "Psychiatric Report 3 Division," 18 March 1944, 11 April 1944, and 17 May 1944, PAC, RG 24, vol. 15 661. Interview with Dr. B.H. McNeel (3 Dec. 1982) "War Diary 1 Cdn. Exhaustion Unit," July 1944, PAC, RG 24, vol. 15 659.

19. "War Diary, ADMS 3 Cdn. Inf. Division," June 1944, PAC, RG 24, vol. 15 661.

20. "War Diary, ADMS 3 Cdn. Inf. Division," July 1944, PAC, RG 24, vol. 15 661.

21. Ibid.

22. Ibid.

23. Terry Copp and Robert Vogel, *Maple Leaf Route: Falaise* (Alma, Ont., 1983), 34.

24. The Canadian Scottish were to experience such a day on 15 August when the Regiment took 130 casualties in the space of a few hours at Pt. 168, north of Falaise. The royal Winnipeg Rifles lost 128 men on D Day, 256 on 8 June in the defence of Putôt-en-Bessin and 132 on 4 July in the attack on Carpiquet Airport. The North Nova Scotia Regiment lost more than 200 men on 7 June and a similar number on 25 July. The Highland Light Infantry were reduced to 50 percent of their strength in their first major battle 8 July at Buron.

25. "War Diary, ADMS 3 Cdn. Inf. Div.," July 1944, PAC, RG 24, vol. 15 661.

26. "Way Diary, ADMS 3 Division," July 1944, PRO, WO 177/344. There was an extraordinary variance in N.P. ratios among the regiments of the division but the overall ratio was under $10^{1}/_{2}$ for June and over $30^{1}/_{2}$ for July (app. C, August War Diary ADMS).

27. "Report by Psychiatrist attached 2nd Army" for Month of July 1944, app. AI, WO 1777/321.

28. Ibid.

29. Quoted from an interview with Dr. B. McNeel, 3 Dec., 1982.

30. Dr. John Burch had been assigned as 2 Division psychiatrist but he was quickly transferred out. No psychiatrist was appointed to 4 Division.

31. John Burch, "Quarterly Report 1 Cdn. Exhaustion Unit 1 July–30 Sept. 1944," PAC, RG 24, vol. 15 659.

32. "War Diary, 4 Cdn. Field Dressing Station," July 1944.

33. "War Diary, 1 Cdn. Exhaustion Unit," July 1944, PAC 24, vol. 15 659.

34. Burch, "Quarterly Report."

35. B. McNeel, "Report on Exhaustion Cases 2 Cdn. Inf. Division."

36. "War Diary, 1 Cdn. Exhaustion Unit."

37. McNeel Interview.

38. Burch, "Quarterly Report."

39. B.H. McNeel, "Re: Cases of Exhaustion — 2 Cdn. Inf. Div. War Diary," app. DDMS 2 Cdn. Corps Oct. 1944.

40. McNeel Interview.

41. Ibid.

42. "Quarterly Report, 1 Cdn. Exhaustion Unit, 30 Sept.–30 Dec. 1944," PAC, RG 24, vol. 15 569.

43. See, for example, B.H. McNeel and Travis Dancey, "The Personality of the Successful Soldier," *American Journal of Psychiatry* 102, 3 (Nov. 1945), 338.

44. William C. Menninger, *Psychiatry in a Troubled World* (New York, 1948), 145.

45. Quoted in J.C. Richardson, "Neuro-psychiatry with the Canadian Army in Western Europe, 6 June 1944–8 May 1945." Typescript 17 pages nd (loaned to the author by Dr. Richardson.)

COMMENT BY DIRECTOR OF ARMY PSYCHIATRY, BRITISH ARMY

It may seem easy for a well-informed historian to deride the follies of the military authorities who attempted "to forbid soldiers from breaking down" or medical commanders who maintained that the "specially allotted Field Dressing Stations or Field Ambulances filled with cases" were merely a "professional show."

They were, however, guilty of overlooking the clearly established lessons of World War I, a trap into which every new generation is in danger of falling.

Battle exhaustion, battleshock as we now call it, is simply an inseparable concomitant of the kind of ferocious warfare in which "lead companies were caught by their own artillery barrage" and friends are killed and injured on all sides: "1500 men, most of them from 2 Division, in the space of 24 hours."

But that is not the end of the story. It is unfortunate that Professor Copp fails to record crucially important figures which put the whole question in perspective. From the Exhaustion Centres in that same terrible battle for Normandy 70 percent returned to duty of whom no more than 7 percent relapsed. The exhaustion or shock need only be temporary and it is up to everyone from junior commanders to doctors to see that it is so. (See note 18.)

Article Thirty

Staring into the Abyss

Jack Granatstein

'HISTORY REPEATS ITSELF.' That is a popular view of the past, but it is not, I suspect, a view shared by most historians. The differences in personalities, in context, in subtleties and shadings usually combine to persuade historians that the crisis of one decade or century is different in class and kind from that of another. But, sometimes, history really does seem to repeat itself.

In the First World War . . . the United Kingdom's weakened financial condition led Whitehall to pressure Canada to turn to the United States to raise money. At the same time, Britain proved unable or unwilling to take all the food and munitions produced by Canada unless Ottawa picked up a greater share of the costs, and the Canadian government had little choice other than to agree. In an effort, both politically and economically inspired, to keep munitions factories working at full blast in Canada, the Imperial Munitions Board, a Canadian-operated imperial procurement and production agency, actively sought contracts from the U.S. War Department. At the same time, other arms of the Canadian government lobbied in Washington to get their share of scarce raw materials. The net effect of the First World War on Canadian-American relations was to strengthen the links across the border and to increase the number and complexity of the ties of economics, politics, and sentiment that bound the two North American nations together. The defeat of reciprocity in the 1911 election, therefore,

Source: Jack Granatstein, "Staring into the Abyss," from *How Britain's Weakness Forced Canada into the Arms of the United States* (1989): 21–40, University of Toronto Press Inc., © J.L. Granatstein 1989. Reprinted with permission of the publisher.

seemed only a temporary check, one virtually nullified by the greater necessity of wartime integration and cooperation.

It should have been no surprise, then, that Canada entered the 1920s with Conservative Prime Minister Arthur Meighen urging Britain to seek an accommodation with the United States and not to renew the Anglo-Japanese Alliance.[1] Nor was it a surprise that Canada welcomed more investment from the United States while, despite repeated efforts by the Liberal governments of Mackenzie King to enhance trade with the United Kingdom, its commerce with its neighbour continued to increase.[2] The Great Depression and the massive increases in the American tariff put in place by a protectionist Congress and then matched by Canadian governments, however, temporarily cut into Canadian-American trade.

While these restrictions led many Canadians to look overseas with renewed imperial fervour, some Britons nonetheless feared for Canada's survival as a British nation in the face of the power of the United States. One example of the first tendency was Harry Stevens, soon to be minister of trade and commerce in R.B. Bennett's government, who told the voters in 1930 that 'My ambition for Canada is that she may become a unit of the Empire and concerned not with a few petty tariff items, but with all the great problems confronting the Home Government.' No worse fate could have befallen Canadians! In contrast, Leo Amery, the dominions secretary in 1928, returned from a trip to Canada worried that 'the din and glare of the great American orchestra' might drown out Canada. His hopes were bolstered, however, by the conviction that there was 'no deeper fundamental instinct of the Canadian national character than dislike of the United States as belonging to an inferior political civilisation.'[3] For their part, officials of the United States government, as Peter Kasurak has noted, began 'from a single point of view in the area of Canadian affairs — fear that Britain was forging its Empire into an international colossus which would dominate world trade.'[4] To Washington, that fear seemed to be realized after the Ottawa Conference of 1932.[5]

But not even the Imperial Economic Conference and the imperial preferences agreed on at Ottawa could truly reverse the historic trend towards North American continentalism that had accelerated during the Great War. The two 'hermit kingdoms,' to use Charles Stacey's phrase uttered from this platform a dozen years ago,[6] had a great deal in common in an era when British trade as a percentage of world trade continued its decline and Britain's overall military power ebbed. Mackenzie King had begun the transformation of the empire into the Commonwealth during the Chanak affair of 1922 and at the Imperial Conference of 1923, where 'the decisive nature of the English defeat at Mackenzie King's hands' was nothing less than a 'surrender, which changed the course of the history of the empire.'[7] Those apocalyptic phrases were the considered judgment of Correlli Barnett, 'the Jeremiah of British historians,' or so Noel Annan has recently called him.[8] They sound very similar in tone to the words of Donald Creighton, the Jeremiah of Canadian historians, who wrote that King, 'a stocky barrel-like figure, with an audible wheeze when in full voice,' was no 'bulky St. George confronting a slavering imperial dragon.' He was 'a citizen of North America . . . determined to destroy' the Commonwealth.[9]

When Mackenzie King came back to power in the middle of the Great Depression in 1935, the Ottawa agreements had demonstrably not restored Canada's economic health. Prime Minister Bennett had seemingly recognized the failure of the imperial initiative by launching his own somewhat desultory efforts to strike a trade agreement with Washington, but his attempt at an accommodation with the United States could not come to fruition before the voters eagerly dispensed with the Tory government's services.[10] It fell to the new prime minister, choosing what he described to the United States minister in Canada as 'the American road,' to negotiate that trade agreement with the Roosevelt administration.[11] Mackenzie King reinforced it with another trade pact with the United States three years later.[12]

Simultaneously, King and his advisers in the Department of External Affairs looked with dismay at the wide-ranging rivalry between London and Washington, most pronounced in the Pacific where the two English-speaking powers jostled for economic and political dominance with each other and an aggressive Japan. Conflict between Canada's mother country and its nearest neighbour held out only the prospect of terrible divisiveness in Canada.[13] Nonetheless, the prime minister gladly accepted and immediately reciprocated President Franklin Roosevelt's assurances, delivered at Queen's University in Kingston on 18 August 1939, 'that the people of the United States will not stand idly by' if Canada were ever threatened.[14] That guarantee had to be called upon just two years later.

By 1939, as the Nazis prepared to plunge Europe into the war that was to ensure America's half century of world economic hegemony, U.S. companies and investors and the American market had already established their pre-eminence in Canada. The United States provided 60 per cent of the foreign capital invested in Canada while British sources put up only 36 per cent. In 1914 the figures had been 23 and 72 per cent, respectively. In terms of Canadian exports, shipments to the United States in 1939 exceeded those to Britain by 20 per cent; in 1914 exports to Britain had been 10 per cent higher than those to the United States. Similarly, in 1914 Canada had imported three times as much from the United States as from the United Kingdom; in 1939 Canada imported four times as much.[15] The years of the Great War had provided the impetus for Canada's shift from the British to the American economic sphere.

During the Second World War, the events of the Great War were repeated with a stunning similarity. To be sure, different men from different political parties were in charge in Canada. Mackenzie King, that most unadmired of Canadian leaders, was at the helm in Ottawa, and his attitudes and prejudices were certainly far different from those of Sir Robert Borden.

Ramsay Cook predicted almost two decades ago that King was certain to become the subject of a book of readings for students under the title 'Mackenzie King: Hero or Fink?' Cook knew that the fink side of the debate would be easy to document. He suggested that King had become the central figure in the Canadian mythology, the most convenient one of all, because he was the 'cause of all our failings,' including the decline and fall of the British Empire in Canada.[16] Cook was certainly correct in assessing the little man's place, and few have yet come forward to argue that Mackenzie King was a great Canadian hero. Charles Stacey, in the last words of his Joanne Goodman lectures in 1976, however, did say — and I expect he was only half-jesting — that he would 'not be altogether surprised if he turned up, one of these days, as the patron saint of the new nationalism.'[17]

Still, King is difficult to elevate to sainthood. Even (or especially) those who observed or worked intimately with him had scant admiration for him. Tom Blacklock, a Press Gallery member in the 1920s, complained that King was 'such a pompous ass that an orang-outang that would flatter him could choose its own reward.'[18] Leonard Brockington wrote speeches for King for a time during the early years of the Second World War, and when he quit in exasperation he told a friend that he was 'sick and tired of being mid-wife to an intellectual virgin.'[19] Senator Norman Lambert ran elections for the Liberal leader, and Mackenzie King gratefully elevated him to the Upper Chamber. Nonetheless, Lambert told Grant Dexter of the *Winnipeg Fire Press* that 'he simply can't stand the worm at close quarters — bad breath, a fetid, unhealthy, sinister atmosphere like living close to some filthy object . . . But,' the senator added, 'get off a piece and he looks better and better.'[20]

That last comment on Mackenzie King I have always thought the nearly definitive one. Up close, there was little that was admirable about the Liberal leader, much that was slippery and sleazy. But acquire some distance, get off a piece, as Lambert said, and the dumpy little laird of Kingsmere — and Canada — began to look not unlike a giant. To bring us back to Earth, I might point out that the fine Canadian novelist Hugh Hood has his main character in

The Swing in the Garden note, 'I think always of W.C. Fields when I think of Mackenzie King.'[21] That may be *the* definitive description.

I have no intention of trying to paint Mackenzie King as a superhero here, though, despite years of reading Donald Creighton and W.L. Morton, I cannot yet bring myself to see him as a filthy object or even as a fink. For me, the crucial factor in assessing the common charge that Mackenzie King sold us out to the Americans is that the prime minister during the Second World War faced similar, but greater, problems to those Sir Robert Borden had had to confront a quarter century before. But though he had more resources at his disposal than his predecessor in the Prime Minister's office, King had no greater freedom of action when British military and economic weakness forced his country into grave difficulties. When it came to directing the weak corner of the North Atlantic Triangle in its efforts to stay safe and secure in a world suddenly unstable, King, much like Borden before him, had to turn to the United States for assistance.

One major factor was different in the Second World War. In the Great War, Britain and France lost battles but they did not suffer catastrophic defeats that placed their survival as nation-states at stake. In May and June 1940, of course, Hitler's astonishingly effective armies defeated Britain and France in the Low Countries and in France, the French capitulated, and the British Army, without equipment, found its way home thanks only to a miracle at Dunkirk.

For Canada in that terrible summer of defeat and despair, the changes in the military balance of power were catastrophic. The country had gone to war with the idea that it could fight as a junior partner with 'limited liability.' The government had hoped that its war effort could be small, balanced, and relatively cheap, and Quebec and the country had been promised that there would be no conscription for overseas service. Now, the planning of late 1939 had to be scrapped. Canada, with its population of eleven million and suddenly Britain's ranking ally, was in the war to the utmost — except for conscription, which was still politically unacceptable. Moreover, a huge proportion of this country's under-equipped and partially trained air, army, and naval forces was already in the United Kingdom, and if — or when — Britain fell they were certain to be completely lost. The Royal Navy had its hands full in trying to protect home waters and block the expected Nazi invasion. The aircraft necessary to operate the centrepiece of the Canadian war effort, the British Commonwealth Air Training Plan, had been scheduled to come from Great Britain, but now would not arrive. If Britain fell and, especially, if the Royal Navy passed into German hands, Canada was likely to be subject to Nazi attack.[22] Britain's military weakness in July and August 1940 was exposed for all to see; so too was Canada's.[23]

The military weakness of the United States was also apparent, but there can be no doubt that President Franklin Roosevelt's country was the only hope of the Allies — and of Canada. Many in Canada recognized this truth in the days after Dunkirk, and they realized the new obligations this would force on the dominion. Donald Creighton, writing years later, noted that for many Canadians — and he had his despised colleague Frank Underhill in mind — the war's course 'hastened the growth' of Canada's 'new North American nationality by proving that . . . Great Britain . . . could no longer act as Canada's main defence against danger from abroad.'[24]

At the time, the bureaucratic response to the new state of affairs came from Hugh Keenleyside of the Department of External Affairs, who set out the fullest statement of the likely Canadian situation as France surrendered to Hitler. It was improbable, he wrote, that the United States would protect Canada without 'demanding a measure of active cooperation in return. It is a reasonable expectation that the United States will expect, and if necessary demand, Canadian assistance in the defence of this continent and this Hemisphere.' Canada, he noted, would feel some obligation to participate; 'thus the negotiation of a specific offensive-defensive alliance is likely to become inevitable.'[25]

President Roosevelt himself was thinking along these lines. In August, Loring Christie, the Canadian minister in Washington, reported to Mackenzie King that the president 'had been thinking of proposing to you to send to Ottawa 3 staff officers . . . to discuss defence problems . . . He had in mind their surveying [the] situation from [the] Bay of Fundy around to the Gulf of St. Lawrence. They might explore [the] question of base facilities for United States use.'[26] But on 16 August Roosevelt asked King to meet him at Ogdensburg, NY, the next day to discuss 'the matter of [the] mutual defence of our coasts on the Atlantic.'[27]

What the president wanted was the creation of a Permanent Joint Board on Defence with equal representation from each country and a mandate limited to the study of common defence problems and the making of recommendations to both governments on how to resolve them. Delighted at the prospect of forging a military alliance with the United States, King queried only Roosevelt's desire that the board be 'permanent.' 'I said I was not questioning the wisdom of it,' King noted, 'but was anxious to get what he had in mind.' According to King's diary, Roosevelt replied that he wanted 'to help secure the continent for the future.'[28] The Canadian leader sometimes suffered from 'the idea,' in the superb Australian novelist Thomas Keneally's phrase, 'that the only empire you need to suspect is the British.'[29] Mackenzie King probably ought to have asked whose empire and whose future, but in August 1940 that question was virtually impossible even to raise — when the fear was that it might be Adolf Hitler's empire and Germany's future if no action were taken.

The decision to create the PJBD was an important one. The board sprang into existence within two weeks and began surveying defences on both the Atlantic and the Pacific coasts. A Joint Canadian-United States Basic Defence Plan, produced by the board's military members, aimed to meet the situation that would arise if Britain were overrun. In that event, strategic control of Canadian forces was to pass to the United States. A second plan, produced in the spring of 1941 and called ABC-22, looked at Canadian-American cooperation in a war in which the United States was actively engaged on the side of the Allies. The Americans again sought strategic control of Canadian forces and to integrate the Canadian east and west coast regions directly into their military commands. It was one thing to agree to American military direction in a war that saw North America standing virtually alone; it was another thing entirely in a war where Britain remained unoccupied and the United States was a partner. 'The American officers,' to use Keneally again, 'listened . . . with that omnivorous American politeness . . . we poor hayseeds would come to know so well and mistrust, perhaps, not enough.'[30] Nonetheless, Canada refused to accept Washington's aims for ABC-22 and won its point, thereby demonstrating that Mackenzie King's government could and would fight for its freedom of action.[31] Whether such independence could have survived a German or Japanese invasion happily never had to be tested.

The significance of the PJBD in its context of August 1940 was that a still-neutral United States had struck an alliance with Canada, a belligerent power. 'That had to be seen as a gain for Britain — and for Canada, too. Important as that was, for the war, the true meaning of the Ogdensburg meeting was that it marked Canada's definitive move from the British military sphere to the American. The British had lost whatever capacity they might have had to defend Canada, and in August 1940 their ability even to defend the British Isles successfully was very much in doubt.[32] In the circumstances, Canada had no choice at all. Canada had to seek help where help was to be found, and that meant Washington.

Few people truly realized the significance of the Permanent Joint Board on Defence and the Ogdensburg Agreement that had created it in the summer of 1940. Some Conservatives grumbled at Mackenzie King's actions, former Prime Minister Arthur Meighen being the most caustic. He had noted that 'I lost my breakfast when I read the account this morning and gazed on the disgusting picture of these potentates'— that is, King and Roosevelt —'posing like monkeys in the very middle of the blackest crisis of this Empire.'[33] Most Tories and almost all the Canadian press showed more sense.[34]

The one critic who shook Mackenzie King, however, was Winston Churchill. The new British prime minister, in office only since 10 May 1940, had replied to King's telegram on the Ogdensburg meeting by stating 'there may be two opinions on some of the points mentioned. Supposing Mr. Hitler cannot invade us . . . all these transactions will be judged in a mood different to that prevailing while the issue still hangs in the balance.'[35] Churchill, disgustedly seeing Canada scurrying for shelter under the eagle's wing, evidently realized that a major shift had occurred. What he would have had Canada do, what he would have done differently had he been Canadian prime minister, was never stated. Certainly he failed to recognize that with its security now guaranteed by the United States, Canada could send every man and weapon possible to defend Britain, something it dutifully and willingly did.

As for me, no matter how often I try to appraise the situation, I cannot see any other option for Mackenzie King. The issue potentially was the survival of the Canadian nation in face of an apparently defeated Great Britain and a victorious Nazi Germany. King did what he had to do to secure Canada's security. The reason Mackenzie King had to strike his arrangement with Roosevelt was the military weakness of Great Britain in the summer of 1940.[36]

The immediate result of the Ogdensburg Agreement was wholly beneficial to Canada and Canadian interests. But we can see now that the long-term implications included the construction of major American installations and the presence in substantial numbers of American troops in the Canadian Northwest from 1942,[37] the 1947 military agreement with the United States that continued joint defence cooperation, the North American Air Defence Agreement of 1957–8, and eventually even Cruise missile testing and the possibility of Star Wars installations in the Canadian North.

Many Canadians may be less than happy with the way matters turned out. In his *Lament for a Nation*, George Grant wrote:

> In 1940, it was necessary for Canada to throw in her lot with continental defence. The whole of Eurasia might have fallen into the hands of Germany and Japan. The British Empire was collapsing once and for all as an international force. Canada and the United States of America had to be unequivocally united for the defence of this hemisphere. But it is surprising how little the politicians and officials seem to have realized that this new situation would have to be manipulated with great wisdom if any Canadian independence was to survive. Perhaps nothing could have been done; perhaps the collapse of nineteenth-century Europe automatically entailed the collapse of Canada. Nonetheless, it is extraordinary that King and his associates in External Affairs did not seem to recognize the perilous situation that the new circumstances entailed. In all eras, wise politicians have to play a balancing game. How little the American alliance was balanced by any defence of national independence![38]

Much of Grant's assessment is correct. Certainly, Canada had no choice in August 1940 in the situation in which it found itself. But to me, Mackenzie King's actions in August 1940 were an attempt to protect Canadian independence — and ensure Canada's survival — in a world that had been turned upside down in a few months by the defeat of Britain and France. Grant, writing a quarter century after the event, does not say what King might have done after Ogdensburg to achieve a balance to the American alliance. Nor did Churchill in 1940. In the remainder of this essay, I will try to show how King successfully struggled to preserve at least a measure of financial independence for Canada.

Those who believe, like George Grant and Donald Creighton, that the Ogdensburg Agreement and its aftermath were a virtual sell-out to the United States have an obligation to offer an alternative vision. If there was 'a forked road' in August 1940 and if Canada went in the wrong direction, where might the other road have led? What should Mackenzie King and his government have done that they did not do? I await the response.

The Ogdensburg Agreement had secured Canada's physical defences, but it had done nothing to resolve the country's economic difficulties. As in the Great War, the problem came about because Canada was caught between a strong United States and its desire to help an economically weak Great Britain. Indeed, Britain was weak. The ambassador in Washington, Lord Lothian, summed it up when he told a group of reporters: 'Boys, Britain's broke. It's your money we want.'[39] It was soon to be Canada's money that London wanted too.

Britain had begun the war in 1939 convinced that purchases had to be switched away from North America to conserve scarce dollar exchange. That laudable goal threatened Canadian tobacco, fruit, and wheat exports and provoked extraordinary outrage in Ottawa and threats that such a policy might hurt what Mackenzie King delicately' called 'our ability to render assistance.' Similarly, British munitions orders in the Phoney War months were less than expected; that too angered the King government. But the same German victories that forced Canada to seek assistance to the south also obliged London to look to Canada for more — more money, more food, more munitions, more of everything.[40]

By February 1941, therefore, the Department of Finance in Ottawa estimated that the British deficit with Canada was $795 million, an amount that had been covered by transfers of gold, debt repatriation, and a large sterling accumulation in London.[41] Ottawa also predicted that war expenditures for the year would amount to $1.4 billion and that $433 million was needed for civil expenditure. A further $400 million would be required to repatriate additional Canadian securities held in Britain, in effect a way of giving Britain additional Canadian dollars with which to pay for the goods it bought in Canada. At the same time, the mandarins in Finance estimated that the provincial and municipal governments would spend $575 million for a total governmental expenditure of almost half Canada's Gross National Income.[42] Could the country function, they asked, if half of all production were devoted to government operations?

Historically, Canada's economic position had depended on the maintenance of a 'bilateral unbalance within a balanced "North Atlantic Triangle." '[43] That meant, in effect, that our chronic trade deficit with the United States was covered by a surplus with Britain. Pounds earned in London were readily converted to American dollars, and thus the bills could be paid. But now sterling was inconvertible, and as Canada built up large balances in London, these could no longer be used to cover the trade deficit with the United States.

Compounding the problem was that as Canada strained to produce greater quantities of war material and food for Britain, more components and raw materials had to be imported from the United States. Every time, for example, that a truck, built in Canada by General Motors or Ford, went to Britain, it contained an imported engine, specialty steels, and a variety of parts brought in from south of the border. Almost a third of the value of a tank, ship, or artillery piece had to be imported. The result was a classic squeeze. Canadian goods went to Great Britain where the British could pay for them only in sterling, which was of little use to Canada outside the British Isles (though we could buy New Zealand lamb or Malayan tin, for example, with it). In effect, Canada was financing the British trade deficit. But at the same time and as a result of war production for Britain, Canadian imports from the United States were expanding rapidly, far more so than exports to the United States. The result was a huge trade deficit with the United States, one that grew worse the more Canada tried to help Britain. In April 1941 Ottawa's estimates of the deficit for that fiscal year were $478 million; by June, officials argued that imports from the United States had risen by $400 million a year while exports to the south had increased by only half that sum.[44]

Canada had been trying to grapple with this problem for some time. Efforts had been made since September 1939 to control foreign exchange, to promote Canada as a tourist mecca for

Americans ('Ski in a country at war,' the advertisements could have said), and by devaluing the dollar to 90 cents U.S. to restrict imports from and encourage export sales to the United States. Each measure had some positive results, but together they amounted to very little against the flood of components pouring over the border for an expanding war industry. Soon, Ottawa slapped stringent controls on the U.S. dollars Canadian travellers could acquire, and a wide range of import prohibitions were put in place in December 1940 on unnecessary imports. Those measures, strong enough to anger the American government and American exporters, also failed completely to reverse the steady growth in the deficit with the United States.[45]

What else remained? A loan from the United States government? O.D. Skelton, the undersecretary of state for external affairs until his death in January 1941, told Pierrepont Moffat, the very able American minister in Canada, that 'it would be disastrous to face a future of making heavy interest payments to the United States year after year in perpetuity, or alternatively having a war debt controversy.'[46] Canada was physically too close to the United States to owe debt directly to Washington, or so Skelton and his colleagues in the Ottawa mandarinate believed. What then? Could Canadian investments in the United States, estimated at $275 million to $1 billion in worth, be sold off to raise American dollars? They could, but those investments cushioned Canada from the strain of her foreign indebtedness, and there were obvious political problems in forcing private investors to sell their holdings at wartime fire-sale prices.[47] That was not a feasible route for the Mackenzie King government.

At this point, the situation altered dramatically. The United States Congress accepted President Roosevelt's proposal for Lend-Lease, a scheme to permit the United States to give the Allies war materiel effectively free of monetary cost, though there were political costs of which the British were all too aware.[48] The initial appropriation accompanying the bill was $7 billion. This was, as Churchill called it, 'the most unsordid act,' an extraordinarily generous step by the still-neutral United States. But Lend-Lease posed terrible problems for Ottawa. First, the Canadian government did not want to take charity from the United States — 'the psychological risk,' two historians noted, 'of becoming a pensioner of the United States was too great.'[49] Second, if Britain could get war materiel from the United States free of charge, what was to happen to the orders it had placed in Canada and for which it had to pay, even if only with inconvertible sterling? C.D. Howe, presiding over Canada's war production as the minister of munitions and supply, told the Cabinet War Committee that he was 'gravely concerned' that those orders might be shifted to the United States.[50] If that happened, what would the impact be on Canada's war employment and wartime prosperity? It was the spring of 1917 all over again, and history repeated itself.

The British characteristically and quickly saw the advantages offered by the situation and began to press Canada. Although junior ministers in Churchill's cabinet bemoaned what they saw as Canada's accelerating drift out of the empire,[51] the hardheaded officials at the Treasury knew what they wanted. Cut purchases of non-essential goods in the United States, Ottawa was told. Accept Lend-Lease. Sell off Canadian securities held in the United States. Such a regimen meant higher taxes and inflation for the Canadians, the British knew, but as the Treasury officials said, 'It is as much in their interests as in ours to act along these lines, seeing that our only alternative, if we are unable to pay for our orders in Canada, is to place them instead in the United States in cases in which we should be able to obtain the goods under the "Lease and Lend" Act.'[52]

Thus Canada's problem. Some way had to be found to keep the British orders, so essential for wartime prosperity, without selling the country lock, stock, and barrel to the United States. Though the Liberal government faced no immediate election, as had Borden in 1917 in similar circumstances, the retention of prosperity was every bit as much a political necessity. At the same time, and again the parallel with Sir Thomas White's refusal to borrow from the U.S.

government is clear, the King government was adamant in its refusal to take Lend-Lease. That was little better than a loan and, while relations with Franklin Roosevelt's Washington were very good, no one wanted to be quite so indebted to the great nation with which Canada shared the continent. The Americans, as Clifford Clark, deputy minister of finance, noted fearfully, might later drive a very hard bargain on tariffs.[53] Nonetheless, Canada's trade with the United States somehow had to be brought into balance.

The ideal solution, as Canadian officials came to realize in the spring of 1941, was an arrangement that would see the United States increase its purchases in Canada and, in addition, supply the components and raw materials Canada needed to produce munitions for the United Kingdom. Those components could be charged to Britain's Lend-Lease account, a clever device that could let Canada keep its war economy going at full blast without bankrupting itself in the process. In the meantime, desperate to ensure the continuation of orders in Canada, Ottawa agreed to finance the British deficit with Canada.[54] That was again a repetition of the events of 1917. Though there is no sign in the files that anyone realized this parallel, so too was the Canadian proposal to the United States.

The Hyde Park Declaration, signed by Mackenzie King and Franklin Roosevelt on 'a grand Sunday' in April, put the seal on the Canadian proposal. The United States agreed to spend $200–300 million more in Canada, largely for raw materials and aluminum. 'Why not buy from Canada as much as Canada is buying from the United States,' Mackenzie King said he had told the president,'— just balance the accounts.' Roosevelt thought this was a swell idea.[55] In addition, the president agreed that Britain's Lend-Lease account could be charged with the materials and components Canada needed to produce munitions for export.[56] That too dealt the trade deficit a mighty blow.

The declaration signed at Hyde Park was a splendid achievement for Canada. Howe told Mackenzie King that he was 'the greatest negotiator the country had or something about being the world's best negotiator,' the prime minister recorded.[57] Howe soon created War Supplies Limited, a crown corporation with E.P. Taylor as its head, to sell Canadian-manufactured war equipment and raw materials in the United States.[58]

The Hyde Park Declaration allowed Canada to do its utmost for Britain without fear of financial collapse. Most important, King had won Roosevelt's agreement without having to give up anything tangible — in the short-run. Unlike Great Britain, Canada was not obliged to sell off its investments prior to receiving U.S. aid; nor was Canada to be required to take Lend-Lease, both measures that the government sought to avoid.[59] Knowing that the desperate plight of the British had forced him to seek assistance for Canada from the United States, Mackenzie King had secured that help on the very best terms. For his part, Roosevelt could agree to King's proposals (incidentally, entirely on his own without any consultation with Congress or the State Department) because they cost the United States almost nothing, because he was friendly to Canada, and because he considered that his country's long-term interests would be best served by having an amicable and prosperous Canada on his northern border, a nation tightly linked to the United States. Undoubtedly, Roosevelt was correct. He served his country's interests well.

In retrospect, however, we can see that the inextricable linkages created or strengthened by the Second World War were the key long-term results of the 1941 agreement. The Hyde Park Declaration effectively wiped out the border for war purposes, allowing raw materials to pour south while munitions components came north. To help the war effort, to produce the goods for a desperate Great Britain, Mackenzie King's Canada tied itself to the United States for the war's duration. There is no point in complaining about this almost a half century later. The Hyde Park Declaration was one of many actions that were necessary to win the war against Hitler, and everything done to further that end was proper and right. But neither is there any point in blinking at the facts. Canada tied itself to the United States in 1941, just as it had done in 1917, because Britain was economically weak. That weakness forced Canada to look to Washington for assistance, and the Americans provided it, freely and willingly. It served Washington's interests; it served Canada's immediate interests; above all, it served the cause of victory.

The short-term results of the Hyde Park Declaration were much as the Canadian government had hoped. American purchases in Canada rose rapidly, and Canada's dollar shortage came to an end in 1942; indeed, the next year controls had to be put in place to prevent Canada's holdings of U.S. dollars from growing too large. The wartime prosperity that Hyde Park solidified was such that in 1942 Canada could offer Great Britain a gift of $1 billion, and the next year Canada created a Mutual Aid program that eventually gave Britain an additional $2 billion in munitions and foodstuffs. The total of Canadian aid to Great Britain during the war was $3.468 billion,[60]— and a billion then was really worth a billion. That was help to a valued ally and friend, of course, just as much as it was an investment in continued high employment at home. As an official in the Dominions Office in London noted, 'Per head of population the Canadian gifts will cost Canada about five times what lend lease costs the United States. Canada's income tax is already as high as ours; it may have to go higher . . . Canada is devoting as large a proportion of her national income to defence expenditure as any other country; in no other country is the proportion of defence expenditure which is given away in the form of free supplies anywhere near so high as in Canada.'[61] The war had cost Canada about $18 billion, and almost one-fifth of that staggering total was given to Britain in the form of gifts. That Canada could offer such assistance freely was the best proof possible that Mackenzie King's policy in 1941 had been correct and successful.

Still, there can be no doubt that the Hyde Park Declaration reinforced the trends that had begun to take form during the Great War. Some of those were psychological. Two bureaucrats who dealt with the United States regularly during the War had gushed fellowship in an article they published in the *Canadian Journal of Economics and Political Science* at the end of the war. 'There has been the open exchange of confidence between the Americans and Canadians, the warm welcome, the freedom from formality, the plain speaking and the all-pervading friendship,' Sydney Pierce and A.F.W. Plumptre wrote. 'This was the result of 'our common background of language and culture, and to the close trade and industrial relationship: in part it is due to the fact that our approach to problems is similar.'[62] That was all true, too.

Other trends were financial and commercial. By 1945 American investment had risen to 70 per cent of the total foreign capital invested in Canada. Exports to the United States were more than three times what they had been in 1939 and were 25 per cent greater than war-swollen Canadian exports to Britain. Imports from the United States were now ten times those from Britain.[63] The war undoubtedly had distorted Canada's trade figures, but the direction was clear and it would be confirmed by the events of the reconstruction period.

By 1945 Canada was part and parcel of the continental economy. It was a two-way North American street now, and the North Atlantic Triangle, if it still existed at all, was a casualty of the world wars. Despite this . . . the Canadian government tried desperately, if unsuccessfully, to restore the traditional balance in the postwar years.

NOTES

1. See Philip Wigley, *Canada and the Transition to Commonwealth: British-Canadian Relations 1917–1926* (Cambridge 1977), 129ff. D.C. Watt erroneously saw 'geographical or racialist factors' responsible for 'the pro-American orientation' of Canadian foreign policy, and he argued that British actions here were taken 'for the sake of keeping Canada in the Empire.' *Succeeding John Bull: America in Britain's Place 1900–1975.* (Cambridge 1984), 50, 52

2. King expressed strong support for the effort to widen imperial preferences at the Imperial Economic Conference of 1923. See R.M. Dawson, *William Lyon Mackenzie King*, vol. 1: *A Political Biography 1874–1923* (Toronto 1958), 469ff. The 1930 Liberal budget lowered the duties on 270 British goods exported to Canada and threatened countervailing duties against the United States. See H.B. Neatby, *William Lyon Mackenzie King*, vol. II: *The Lonely Heights* (Toronto 1963), 323–4. On reaction to U.S. investment in this period and after see Peter Kresl, 'Before the Deluge: Canadians on Foreign Ownership, 1920–1955,' *American Review of Canadian Studies* 6 (spring 1976), 86ff.

3. Quoted in Norman Hillmer, 'Personalities and Problems in Anglo-Canadian Economic Relations between the Two World Wars,' *Bulletin of Canadian Studies* 3 (June 1979), 5, 8

4. Peter Kasurak, 'American Foreign Policy Officials and Canada, 1927–1941: A Look Through Bureaucratic Glasses,' *International Journal* 32 (summer 1977), 548

5. The best study of the Ottawa Conference, including its origins and aftermath, is in Ian Drummond, *Imperial Economic Policy 1917–1939* (London 1974), chap. 5ff.

6. C.P. Stacey, *Mackenzie King and the North Atlantic Triangle* (Toronto 1976), chap. 2

7. Correlli Barnett, *The Collapse of British Power* (London 1972), 195. Barnett's index reference under Mackenzie King refers to this episode as 'destroys imperial alliance.' Stacey's judgment is more sensible and accurate: King 'challenged this idea of a common foreign policy and, essentially, destroyed it.' Stacey, *Mackenzie King*, 33

8. 'Gentlemen vs Players,' *New York Review of Books* (29 Sept, 1988), 63

9. Donald Creighton, "The Decline and Fall of the Empire of the St. Lawrence,' *Historical Papers 1969*, 21

10. Within a year of giving up the Conservative party leadership, Bennett left Canada to live in England. 'It's grand to be going home,' the New Brunswick-born Bennett said as he left for the mother country. That may have been the most revealing comment ever made about Canadian Conservatism prior to the Second World War. Bennett soon violated Canadian law by accepting a peerage.

11. F.D. Roosevelt Library, Roosevelt Papers, PSF, box 33, Armour to Phillips, 22 Oct. 1935

12. On the decline in British trade see Paul Kennedy, *The Rise and Fall of the Great Powers* (Toronto 1987), 316. On the Canadian-American trade agreements see J.L. Granatstein, *A A Man of Influence* (Ottawa 1981), chap. 3, and R.N. Kottman, *Reciprocity and the North Atlantic Triangle, 1932–1938* (Ithaca 1968).

13. This is the subject of Gregory Johnson's York University doctoral dissertation in progress on the relations of Canada, the United States, and the United Kingdom in the Pacific from 1935 to 1950.

14. R.F. Swanson, *Canadian-American Summit Diplomacy, 1923–1973* (Toronto 1975), 52ff. According to D.C. Watt, Mackenzie King was 'yet another channel by which disguised isolationist ideas could be fed to the president.' *Succeeding John Bull*, 78

15. M.C. Urquhart and K.A.H. Buckley, eds., *Historical Statistics of Canada* (Toronto 1965), F345–56: F.H. Leacy, ed., *Historical Statistics of Canada* (Ottawa 1983), G188–202. I have used 1939 data, though Canada's trade with the United States was higher then than throughout the rest of the decade since that was the first year that showed the impact of the 1938 trade agreement. In other words, had the Second World War not distorted trade patterns, the 1939 trends would likely have continued.

16. *Globe Magazine*, 15 Aug. 1970, quoted in Norman Hillmer, "'The Outstanding Imperialist": Mackenzie King and the British,' Part 1 of *Britain and Canada in the Age of Mackenzie King*, Canada House Lecture Series No 4 [1979], 3–4

17. Stacey, *Mackenzie King*, 68

18. National Archives of Canada (NA), Robert Borden Papers, Note by Loring Christie, nd, f 148398

19. L.L.L. Golden interview, 3 Oct. 1965

20. NA, John W. Dafoe Papers, Grant Dexter to Dafoe, 18 April 1941

21. Hugh Hood, *The Swing in the Garden* (Toronto 1975), 165

22. The fate of the Royal Navy naturally concerned the United States and involved Mackenzie King in an excruciating role between Churchill and Roosevelt. See David Reynolds, *The Creation of the Anglo-American Alliance 1937–1941* (Chapel Hill, NC 1982), 115ff, for an American historian's view.

23. Barnett nonetheless argues that the presence of a Canadian corps in England did not make up for the dispatch of British troops to the Middle and Far East. 'The nations of the empire were true "daughters" of the Mother Country in that at no time during the war did their contributions defray the cost of their own strategic keep.' Barnett, *Collapse*, 586. In his later book, *The Audit of War* (London 1986), 3, he adds that the empire produced only 10 per cent of the munitions of war supplied to British and imperial forces. So much for Canada's unstinted contribution to the war.

24. D.G. Creighton, 'The Ogdensburg Agreement and F.H. Underhill,' in C. Berger and R. Cook, eds., *The West and the Nation* (Toronto 1976), 303

25. NA, Department of External Affairs Records (EAR), vol. 781, file 394, 'An Outline Synopsis,' 17 June 1940

26. NA, W.L.M. King Papers, Black Binders, vol. 19, Christie to King, 15 Aug. 1940. Reynolds, *Creation*, 118, describes FDR'S request for the Ogdensburg meeting as being necessary to formulate 'contingency plans in case Britain lost control of the North Atlantic.' See also Reynolds, *Creation*, 132, 183.

27. J.W. Pickersgill, ed., *The Mackenzie King Record*, vol. 1: 1939–44 (Toronto 1960), 130–1

28. Ibid., 134

29. Thomas Keneally, *The Cut-Rate Kingdom* (London 1984), 125. This novel of Australia's experience with, among other things, the United States in the Second World War has some useful and suggestive parallels for the Canadian case.

30. Ibid., 14

31. J.L. Granatstein, *Canada's War: The Politics of the Mackenzie King Government, 1939–45* (Toronto 1975), 131–2

32. Gerard S. Vano has suggested that there had been a reversal of military obligation within the empire by this period. No longer was Canada under the British military shield, but 'Britain was, to a degree, falling under a Canadian shield.' *Canada: The Strategic and Military Pawn* (New York 1988), 87. Reynolds, *Creation*, 136, notes that Australia and New Zealand, as well as Canada, were forced closer to the United States by the events of the summer of 1940.

33. NA, R.B. Hanson Papers, file S-175-M-1, Meighen to Hanson, 19 Aug. 1940

34. Professor Underhill, who spoke the truth about the changed Canadian relationships produced by the war, almost lost his job at the University of Toronto as a result. See Creighton, 'Ogdensburg Agreement,' 300ff, and Douglas Francis, *F.H. Underhill: Intellectual Provocateur* (Toronto 1986), chap. 10.

35. NA, Privy Council Office Records, Cabinet War Committee Records, Documents, Churchill to King, 22 Aug. 1940

36. Even the usually shrewd observer of Canadian-American relations, Gordon Stewart, has missed this key point. He noted that in the 1940s, Canada 'participated willingly in military and defense integration . . . it is inaccurate to regard American policy as being imposed on an unwilling and unknowing country. If the United States is judged guilty of imperialism, then Canada must accept a ruling of contributory negligence.' "'A Special Contiguous Country Economic Regime": An Overview of America's Canada Policy,' *Diplomatic History* 6 (fall 1982), 354–5. True enough, but Britain aided and abetted the process. John Warnock in *Free Trade and the New Right Agenda* (Vancouver 1988), 255, notes similarly that 'The Mackenzie King government chose to conduct the war effort on a continental basis' and thus 'greatly undermined Canadian sovereignty.' Some choice in August 1940!

37. The King government was slow to recognize the dangers posed to Canadian sovereignty by the U.S. presence. But once it was alerted to the problem (by the British high commissioner to Canada!), it moved quickly to appoint a special commissioner in the northwest and, at war's end, Canada paid the United States in full for all facilities built in Canada — quite consciously in an effort to ensure that its rights were fully protected. See Department of External Affairs, Records [DEA], documents on files 52-B(s) 5221-40C, the records of the special commissioner (NA, RG 36–7), and Granatstein, *A Man of Influence*, 120ff.

38. George Grant, *Lament for a Nation* (Toronto 1965), 50

39. Cited in David Dilks, 'Appeasement Revisited,' *University of Leeds Review* 15 (May 1972), 51

40. Based on Hector Mackenzie, 'Sinews of War: Aspects of Canadian Decisions to Finance British Requirements in Canada during the Second World War,' Canadian Historical Association paper 1983, 3

41. King Papers, W.C. Clark to King, 9 April 1941, ff 288021ff

42. H.D. Hall, *North American Supply* (London 1955), 230. Later, more accurate assessments put war spending in 1941–42 at $1.45 billion, aid to the United Kingdom at $1.15 billion, and civil expenditures at $1 billion. With a national income of $5.95 billion, public expenditure amounted to 60.5 per cent. King Papers, 'Canada's War Effort,' 4 April 1941, ff 288088ff

43. The phrase is R.S. Sayers's in *Financial Policy, 1939–45* (London 1956), 322–3. The balance, however, was less than real for the British. They had large peacetime trade deficits with the United States and could pay Canada in U.S. dollars only because they received them from other parties in a pattern of multilateral settlement that ended with the outbreak of war. I am indebted to Professor Ian Drummond for this information.

44. King Papers, Clark to King, 9 April 1941, ff 288014ff. The actual figures were even worse than these estimates. See Urquhart and Buckley, eds., *Historical Statistics*, F334–47. But whether the situation was as bleak as government officials believed at the time is less certain. Although munitions exports to Britain did stimulate the growth of imports from the United States, still more came from the war effort itself, which stimulated imports directly (in the form of components) and indirectly (by increasing consumer demand and domestic investment in plant and equipment). I am again indebted to Professor Drummond.

45. Granatstein, *Canada's War*, 135–6; Granatstein, *A Man of Influence*, 94ff

46. EAR, vol. 35, 'United States Exchange Discussions,' 20 Nov. 1940
47. Urquhart and Buckley, eds., *Historical Statistics*, F164–92; King Papers, Clark to King, 9 April 1941, ff 288018ff; Queen's University Archives, Grant Dexter Papers, Memorandum, 11 March 1941
48. On the costs to the United Kingdom see Barnett, *Collapse*, 591ff. Churchill was asked if Britain would be able to repay the United States for its aid: 'I shall say, yes by all means let us have an account if we can get it reasonably accurate, but I shall have my account to put in too, and my account is for holding the baby alone for eighteen months, and it was a very rough brutal baby.' Quoted in David Dilks's introduction to Dilks, ed., *Retreat from Power*, vol. II: *After 1939* (London 1981), 14
49. Robert Bothwell and John English, 'Canadian Trade Policy in the Age of American Dominance and British Decline, 1943–1947,' *Canadian Review of American Studies* 8 (spring 1977), 54ff. A.F.W. Plumptre commented that 'Ottawa apparently believed that it is well to keep Canada as independent as possible and to avoid borrowing or begging as long as may be.' *Mobilizing Canada's Resources for War* (Toronto 1941), 80. Cf R.W. James, *Wartime Economic Cooperation* (Toronto 1949), 32
50. Cabinet War Committee Records, Minutes, 18, 26 Feb. 1941
51. Public Record Office (PRO), London, Prime Minister's Office Records, PREM4/43B/2, Cranborne to Churchill, 5 March 1941; ibid., Treasury Records, T160/1340, Amery to Kingsley Wood, lo May 1941
52. Ibid., T160/1054, 'Canadian Financial Assistance to this Country,' nd [14 March 1941]
53. Granatstein, *Canada's War*, 139
54. Cabinet War Committee Records, Minutes, 12, 13 March 1941; Sayers, *Financial Policy*, 338ff
55. Dexter Papers, Memo, 21 April 1941
56. The text of the Hyde Park Agreement is printed as an appendix to R.D. Cuff and J.L. Granatstein, *Canadian-American Relations in Wartime* (Toronto 1975), 165–6.
57. Pickersgill, ed., *Mackenzie King Record*, 1, 202
58. C.P. Stacey, *Arms, Men and Governments* (Ottawa 1970), 490; Richard Rohmer, *E.P. Taylor* (Toronto 1978), 106
59. This was seen as a virtual miracle. See *Financial Post*, 26 April 1941.
60. See J.L. Granatstein, 'Settling the Accounts: Anglo-Canadian War Finance, 1943–1945,' *Queen's Quarterly*, 83 (summer 1976), 246.
61. PRO, Dominions Office Records, DO35/1218, Minute by A.W. Snelling, 26 Jan. 1943; Sayers, *Financial Policy*, 350ff
62. S.D. Pierce and A.F.W. Plumptre, 'Canada's Relations with War-Time Agencies in Washington,' *Canadian Journal of Economics and Political Science* 11 (1945), 410–11
63. Urquhart and Buckley, eds., *Historical Statistics*, F345–56; Leacy, ed., *Historical Statistics*, G188–202

Topic Thirteen
Gender and the Consumer Society

Women shop in a Woodward's department store in Vancouver.

The history of consumerism is a growing field of study, especially when linked to gender history. Social historians have revealed how advertisers projected images of the ideal woman or man, representations they believed fit the stereotype of the age, to assist in selling consumer products. One period of interest is the 1950s, because it was a time of adjustment after a period of depression and war. Gender roles in particular were re-examined and re-defined. The 1950s were also a time of economic prosperity based on consumerism. Advertisers found sophisticated and subtle ways of selling consumer goods to a Canadian society eager to purchase them and with money to do so. But advertising was as much about selling image and identity — both gender identity and Canadian identity — as selling products.

The following two articles examine consumerism in the period from 1940 to 1960 in the context of gender analysis. In "Home Dreams: Women and the Suburban Experiment in Canada, 1945–1960," historian Veronica Strong-Boag examines the role that residential suburbs played in separating the role of men and women by looking at the economic, and, more importantly, the psychological factors that reinforced the image of residential suburbs as the "woman's domain." She shows that suburban women were deeply divided as to whether the suburban experience benefited or worked against their sense of self-identity.

In "Fatherhood, Masculinity, and the Good Life During Canada's Baby Boom, 1945–1965," historian Robert Rutherdale examines the impact that the changing view of fathers in advertising, from workers to masculine domestics, had on family life. He argues that materialism and masculinity went together, because it was the ability of fathers to provide material comfort and pleasure that was projected as a positive defining role of masculinity in this period.

What role did advertising and mass media play in constructing the image of suburban Canadian women as domestics and Canadian men as fathers and masculine domestics in the period 1945 to 1965? To what extent are Strong-Boag's and Rutherdale's studies of gendered roles during the same period complementary and/or contradictory? What contribution does the history of consumerism make to our understanding of the years 1945–1960?

A general study of the post–World War II period is Robert Bothwell, Ian Drummond, and John English, *Canada since 1945: Power, Politics, and Provincialism*, rev. ed. (Toronto: University of Toronto Press, 1989). For more of an emphasis on social history, see Alvin Finkel, *Our Lives: Canada After 1945* (Toronto: James Lorimer, 1997). Doug Owram, *Born at the Right Time: A History of the Baby-Boom Generation* (Toronto: University of Toronto Press, 1996) is most informative. Joy Parr examines consumerism in *Domestic Goods: The Material, the Moral, and the Economic in the Postwar Years* (Toronto: University of Toronto Press, 1995). Paul Rutherford looks at the role of television in this period in *When Television Was Young: Primetime Canada, 1952–1962* (Toronto: University of Toronto Press, 1990). An excellent collection on gender roles in history is Kathryn McPherson et al., *Gendered Pasts: Historical Essays in Femininity and Masculinity in Canada* (Toronto: Oxford University Press, 1999).

On women in the postwar era, see the report of the Royal Commission on the Status of Women in Canada (Ottawa: Information Canada, 1970); Micheline Dumont et al., *Quebec Women: A History* (Toronto: Women's Press, 1987); and Alison Prentice et al., *Canadian Women: A History*, 2nd ed. (Toronto: Harcourt Brace, 1996). Women in Ontario are examined in Joy Parr, ed., *A Diversity of Women: Women in Ontario since 1945* (Toronto: University of Toronto Press, 1995). Valerie Korinek studies a women's magazine in *Roughing It in the Suburbs: Reading Chatelaine Magazine in the Fifties and the Sixties* (Toronto: University of Toronto Press, 2000); see as well her article, "'Mrs. Chatelaine' vs. 'Mrs. Slob': Contestants, Correspondents and the Chatelaine Community in Action, 1961–1969," *Journal of the Canadian Historical Association*, New Series, 9 (1998): 209–223. Alexandra Palmer, *Couture and Commerce: The Transatlantic Fashion Trade in the 1950s* (Vancouver: UBC Press, 2001) discusses the world of fashion.

Studies of masculinity are limited. A valuable companion piece to that of Rutherdale's is Chris Dummitt, "Finding a Place for Father: Selling the Barbecue in Postwar Canada," *Journal of the Canadian Historical Association*, New Series, 9 (1998): 209–223.

WEBLINKS

Programming for the Modern Homemaker
http://archives.cbc.ca/IDD-1-69-1192/life_society/women_programming/

A sample of CBC programming aired in the late 1940s and in the 1950s generally intended for women.

Canadian Mail Order Catalogues
http://www.collectionscanada.ca/mailorder/h33-101.02-e.php#g

Digitized mail order catalogues spanning the 20th century including the postwar period.

Canadian War Brides
http://www.canadianwarbrides.com

Statistics and stories of many British and European women who immigrated to Canada, after marrying Canadian serviceman who were stationed overseas during World War II.

Canadian Home Journal
http://www.crcstudio.arts.ualberta.ca/canadianmagazines/viewtext.php?s=browse&tid=154&route=bytitle.php&start=12

A digitized 1945 copy of the *Canadian Home Journal*, a popular magazine in Canada at the time.

Chatelaine
http://www.crcstudio.arts.ualberta.ca/canadianmagazines/viewtext.php?s=browse&tid=73&route=bytitle.php&start=36#

A digitized 1948 copy of *Chatelaine*, a popular woman's issues magazine that continues publishing to this day.

Statistics Canada: Labour Force
http://www.statcan.ca/english/freepub/11-516-XIE/sectiond/sectiond.htm

Comparative statistics regarding the labour force in Canada generally over the time period of 1946 to 1975.

Article Thirty-One

Home Dreams: Women and the Suburban Experiment in Canada, 1945–1960

Veronica Strong-Boag

In the years after the Second World War in Canada, residential suburbs provided symbolic female counterparts, "bedrooms" as it were, to the male-dominated, market-oriented world of modern cities.[1] Tracts of new housing embodied a separation of the sexes that held women particularly responsible for home and family, and men for economic support and community leadership. Such a gendered landscape was far from new or unusual in Canada. Women and men had long moved in somewhat different worlds, presiding over residential and public space in varying degrees as dictated by custom and, sometimes, by law.[2] After 1945, however, women's, particularly wives', rising labour-force participation might have suggested that spatial segregation on the suburban frontier was ill-timed. Why and how, then, did there occur a massive increase in residential suburbs remote from opportunities for employment, lacking many community resources, and reliant on female labour? What did female residents and contemporary observers make of this investment on the suburban frontier? This article begins to answer these questions by examining the conditions that gave rise to postwar suburbs, the character of housing initiatives, and the nature and meaning of that experience for Canadian women.

Historians of the United States have associated postwar housing development not only with technological improvements, gas and oil discoveries, and a massive increase in the number of private automobiles, but also with political conservatism, racism, and domestic roles for women.[3] While scholars studying Canadian suburbs will find much that is useful in American assessments, particularly in their exploration of suburbia's gendered terrain, Paul-André Linteau's question, "Does the border make a difference?"[4] inevitably arises. Works like Michael A. Goldberg and John Mercer's *The Myth of the North American City: Continentalism Challenged* (1986) and Caroline Andrew and Beth Moore Milroy's *Life Spaces: Gender, Household, Employment* (1988) have offered the beginnings of a reply. In particular, Andrew and Milroy point to safer and more livable cities, a long tradition of resource towns, and "the particular institutional and policy framework that exists in Canada,"[5] all of which distinguish Canadian women's lives. Although comparisons with the United States remain peripheral to the study here, my reading of the Canadian suburban "script" suggests that, for all the proliferation of American influences in the years after 1945, life north of the forty-ninth did indeed differ. In particular, Canada's cities, lacking racial divisions comparable with those in the United States, never lost their attraction for citizens of all classes. And just as flight from urban dangers does not seem as influential in Canada, suburbia does not appear as homogeneous as many American commentators have suggested. Communities composed of war veterans, industrial workers, rural emigrants, newcomers to Canada, and the middle-class native- and urban-born contribute to a picture that, as the sociologist S.D. Clark convincingly demonstrated in *The Suburban Society* (1968), seems every bit as complicated as what was happening downtown. While middle-class WASPs were a major presence, they were never alone on the outskirts of

Source: Veronica Strong-Boag, "Home Dreams: Women and the Suburban Experiment in Canada, 1945–1960," *Canadian Historical Review* 72: 4 (December 1991): 471–504. © University of Toronto Press 1991. Reprinted by permission of University of Toronto Press Incorporated.

Table 31.1 Age-Specific Fertility Rates for Canadian Women, 1921–1960

Year	Age Group of Women						
	15–19	20–4	25–9	30–4	35–9	40–4	45–9
1960	59.8	233.5	224.4	146.2	84.2	28.5	2.4
1940	29.3	130.3	152.6	122.8	81.7	32.7	3.7
1921	38.0	165.4	186.0	154.6	110.0	46.7	6.6

Source: John R. Miron, *Housing in Postwar Canada* (Kingston and Montreal, 1988), from table 3, p. 35.

cities. Suburbia's meaning is further complicated by the influence of region. The background of residents and the rate of suburbanization in these years varied from one part of the country to the other, distinguishing the experience of Montreal from Toronto and from Halifax, Winnipeg, Edmonton, and Vancouver. Facing as they did a different set of contingencies, Canadian women were not mere reflections of American suburbanites. The nature of their story is set out below.

The postwar experiment with the promise of a spatial segregation that placed Canadian women in suburban homes and men in employment located elsewhere was fuelled by high rates of fertility. During the Second World War and into the 1950s, couples married at ever younger ages. First and second babies came earlier in these marriages, and increasing numbers of women gave birth to third children (see Table 31.1). Fewer women had no children. Bigger families increased women's home-based responsibilities. Not surprisingly, women were often preoccupied with their roles as wives and mothers. Housing where children could be cared for comfortably and safely was an urgent priority in many women's lives.

Whereas their parents had often had to be crowded and uncomfortable, postwar Canadians aspired to something better. Between 1945 and 1960 nearly continuous prosperity, high employment, the extension of the welfare state, and the presumption of a limitless bank of natural resources generated income and hopes for a better life, and, if possible, the lifestyle of comfortable homes and new products advertised since the 1920s in the continent's popular media.[6] Rising car ownership offered unprecedented numbers of citizens the opportunity to search for homes well beyond areas where employment opportunities were concentrated.[7] Many male breadwinners, the most likely both to drive and to control the use of cars,[8] no longer had to rely on walking or public transit to get to work. An increase in the production of oil, gas, and hydro-electric power was available to power both new cars and the central heating characteristic of new homes.[9] Residential suburbs on the periphery were the beneficiaries of these developments.

New housing that enshrined a gendered division of labour also responded to a generation's anxiety about changes in the world about them. The threat of the Cold War and the Korean War encouraged citizens to prize the private consumption and accumulation of products in the nuclear family household as proof of capitalism's success. Stable families, full-time mothers, and the benefits they produced in sound citizenship were to provide the first defence against the "Red Menace," symbolized in Canada by the Gouzenko Affair.[10] Suburban housewives at home in ever larger houses epitomized the promise that prosperity would guarantee both individual happiness and the final triumph over communism.[11]

The inclination to concentrate on private matters and to cling to the faith in women's particular talent and responsibility for family survival was fostered further in the 1940s and 1950s by the highly publicized predicament of many of the world's citizens. The statelessness of the "Displaced Persons," or "DPs," as the 165 000 who had come to Canada by 1953 were commonly known,[12] like the plight of concentration camp survivors, captured especially poignantly what it meant to lose families and homes. The arrival of 48 000 war brides added to Canadians' consciousness of how much the future depended on the establishment of new households and the persistence of marital bonds.[13] The promise of a renewed family life, secured by all the benefits of a revived capitalist economy, became in some ways the *leitmotif* of the second Elizabethan Age. As one typical enthusiast put it, "the Duke and Duchess of Edinborough [sic] are young, modern parents who, like many other young people, in an anxious and insecure world, find their deepest happiness and satisfaction in the warm circle of family life."[14] In suburban homes and families, Canadians endeavoured modestly to echo the ideals embodied in the domesticated monarchy of the youthful Elizabeth II.

The popular and academic social sciences of the day sanctioned the inclination to believe that collective happiness and well-being were most likely when women concentrated their energies on the home front. Experts' secular sermons, frequently presented in the guise of a celebration of female nature, stressed women's unique qualities. With some few exceptions, assertions of inferiority were out of fashion. As one Toronto psychiatrist observed, "Today we think of marriage as a partnership of equals."[15] To this end, modern fathers were encouraged to take on some care of children.[16] Yet, while up-to-date advisers flattered their female audiences with claims for equality, even superiority, "true" women had normally to demonstrate their authenticity by pursuing roles centred on the private rather than the public sphere. Women's ability to take on a broad range of duties, so well demonstrated during the years of depression and war, was conveniently dismissed as an aberration. In advising Canadians how to live, experts returned to opinions that were reminiscent of the 1920s.[17]

Lives that were gender-specific lay at the heart of a number of influential texts that enjoyed general circulation across Canada in the years after the Second World War. Among the earliest and most influential was Dr. Benjamin Spock's best-selling *Common Sense Book of Baby and Child Care* (1947).[18] As one Canadian from the suburb of Lachine, Quebec, recalled, "Dr Spock of course was my 'Bible.'"[19] Although most women consulted the good doctor for practical advice on treating childhood ills, his answers reinforced conventions holding women primarily responsible for the emotional and practical functioning of the household. A veteran of suburbs in Cooksville and North York, Ontario, summed up the conclusions of many of her generation: "I felt quite sure in those days that women who chose to have a family should stay home and raise them! I had worked as a social worker for the Children's Aid Society and had seen the emotional devastation in children separated from mothers."[20]

Spock was far from alone in applauding women who mothered. Ashley Montague's best seller *The Natural Superiority of Women* (1953) celebrated women both for their gentler dispositions and for their biological superiority. Not coincidentally, he concluded that "the most important of women's tasks is the making of human beings . . . [and] because mothers are closer to their children than fathers, they must of necessity play a more basic role in the growth and development of their children."[21] A self-proclaimed women's champion, Montague applied his reading of modern science to "undermine the age-old belief in feminine inferiority,"[22] but in the process he reasserted the faith that biology was destiny. The capacity for motherhood was, as with both the older anti-feminist and the maternal feminist tradition, identified as the very source of superiority.

Ashley Montague's fundamentally conservative message appeared in the same year as the publication of *Sexual Behaviour in the Human Female* (1953),[23] the second volume on human sexuality by Alfred Kinsey and his colleagues. In the forefront of the "sexology" of its day, this volume documented women's possession of a powerful libido, the physiological equivalent of male sexual response.[24] Under the influence of such scientific authority, an active sexuality became increasingly accepted as the prerequisite of satisfactory personal and marital life.[25] The result could be higher levels of intimacy and equality between the sexes, but women's erotic potential could easily be incorporated into an updated domestic ideal. Kinsey's support for the female libido and his opposition to guilt and shame about sexual acts were closely tied to marital and social stability. His early work was used to justify Canadians' youthful marriage: only then could sexuality find its proper channels.[26] Ultimately, Kinsey's pioneering studies reinforced the tendency to dedicate women to private life.

The assignment of women to roles as wives and mothers was further legitimated by the popularity of the functionalist school of sociology that dominated the discipline as it established itself throughout Canada. The work of the leading American "father" of this tradition, Talcott Parsons, drew on the "anatomy is destiny" psychiatry of Freud and his followers to argue that women and men naturally had different, albeit compatible and equal, roles within society. Women were responsible for expressive functions of mediating and nurturing; men for instrumental functions of struggle and leadership. The first responsibilities directed women to the private sphere and the second legitimated men's domination of public life. Husbands concentrated on the workplace and its values of "rationality, impersonality, self-interest," while wives guided children in the traditional family values of "love, sharing, cooperation."[27] Domestic life might no longer require long hours of hard physical labour, but the unremitting pressure of modern corporate life on men appeared to make women irreplaceable in the home as psychosexual managers.[28] The appropriate division of duties was summed up by Bell Telephone's company magazine, *The Bluebell*, which pointed to wives' appropriate role in a short story entitled "WE Were Promoted."[29] Both capitalist prosperity and humanized relationships were to be guaranteed by the functionalist division of labour. Such conclusions became the stock-in-trade of Canadian sociologists like J.R. Seeley, R.A. Sim, and E.W. Loosley, the authors of one of the foremost North American studies of suburban life, *Crestwood Heights* (1956).

Home-grown authorities like the popular gynecologist Dr. Marion Hilliard of Toronto's Women's College Hospital regularly voiced the conservative conclusions of the contemporary social sciences. Speaking to her own patients and countless others through articles in *Chatelaine*, she spread prevailing medical opinion:

> The burden of creating a happy marriage falls mainly on the wife. A man's life is much more difficult than a woman's, full of the groaning strain of responsibility and the lonely and often fruitless search for pride in himself. A cheerful and contented woman at home, even one who must often pretend gaiety, gives a man enough confidence to believe he can lick the universe. I'm certain that the woman who enriches her husband with her admiration and her ready response gets her reward on earth, from her husband.[30]

Hilliard and most other Canadian "experts" on home and family joined their American colleagues in arguing that women's most basic satisfactions came through service to others in the domestic sphere.

The verdict of professionals was repeatedly echoed in the dominion's mass media. Typical advertisements credited the housewife with "the recipe for good citizenship . . . for a woman's influence extends far beyond the horizons of housekeeping. She guards the family health by her buying standards; she shares in plans for the family welfare; hers is the opportunity of training her children . . . of promoting good character and good citizenship."[31] Companies readily championed a feminine ideal that offered them real benefits. Corporate profits and male careers alike depended on women's concentrated efforts in the private sphere, more especially in new suburban homes, where opportunities for purchases were unsurpassed.

Advertising in these years was only one part of a commercial onslaught hitting Canadians. Newspapers, magazines, radio, films, and, by the 1950s, television entered households with a distinct message about the meaning of the "good life." Radio soap operas such as *Road of Life*, *Big Sister*, *Lucy Linton*, *Life Can Be Beautiful*, and *Ma Perkins* offered women escape from isolation and loneliness in dreams of consumption, romance, and improved family life.[32] Television shows like *The Adventures of Ozzie and Harriet*, *I Love Lucy*, *The Honeymooners*, and *Father*

Knows Best made it quite clear that good wives and mothers stayed properly at home, far from the temptations of employment. Just as important, they suggested that women reaped real advantages from this division of duties. Wives may have looked a little foolish in these sitcoms, but audiences were encouraged to join in a conspiracy of good-humoured silence about the real power that they wielded. Housewives, after all, had the freedom to construct their own routines, while spouses were tied to onerous duties as breadwinners.

What the experts and the media largely ignored after World War II was a massive increase in the labour-force participation rate of married women. This increased from 4.5 percent in 1941, to 11.2 percent in 1951, to 22.0 percent in 1961. In the same years, wives rose from 12.7 percent to 30.0 percent to 49.8 percent of all women in paid employment.[33] For all this dramatic change meant in terms of disposable family income and the nature of the labour market, it appears to have done little initially to challenge women's primary identification as labourers in the domestic workplace.[34] Many postwar wives accepted periods of employment before childbirth and, sometimes, after children were in high school, as intervals in a modern life cycle that still saw them as chiefly responsible for home and family. In particular, energetic young wives could take pride in establishing families on a sound economic footing. Such was true of a "white-collar wife" in her early twenties employed by Montreal's CIL. Vivian used her salary to purchase new housing and "other rewards: electrical kitchen appliances, bedroom and living room furniture, a small English car." Her husband, David, paid other expenses. Traditional appearances were maintained when she assumed responsibility for most housework and received an allowance from David. Vivian planned to leave CIL at about the age of 25 to have between two and four children.[35] Many women hoped to do the same. The same assumption underlay the "putting hubby through school" phenomenon that first attracted public attention with the return of war veterans to university.[36] Women's work in the labour market regularly represented an investment in a more domestic future.

Incentives for female citizens to return home as soon as possible always remained considerable. Never missing were unequal opportunity and wages. Resources in support of female workers were meagre.[37] Matters at home were hardly better. Most families could afford only one car, on which the husband had first claim, and few settlements boasted adequate public transportation. Nor was that all. Working wives had to face the "double day of labour." One refugee from a clerical office explained that she had cheerfully given up a schedule that required "twelve hours or more a day, seven days a week."[38] Another clerical worker from North Toronto added:

> As a married woman for fourteen years and a working wife for less than one year . . . the two don't go together. You can't be a success at both. So I decided to quit my job to save my marriage.
>
> You simply can't look after a home and go to the office too. I don't care who you are or how well organized you are, you can't be a good wife and mother, hostess and housekeeper and also do a good job for your employer all at the same time. When you try, someone is bound to get cheated.[39]

Working wives had no right to hope for relief at home. As one writer for the *Star Weekly* insisted: "I don't see how a job gives a woman a legitimate out on housekeeping. She still has the basic responsibility to run a home for the family . . . [and] a man whittles himself down to less of a man by consistently performing woman's work."[40] In the decades after the Second World War, income tax law, the absence of daycare, formal and informal bars to female employment,[41] and school schedules combined with a commercially fuelled celebration of domesticity and maternity and the general reluctance of husbands to assume household responsibilities to confirm the wisdom of staying home, if you had a choice.

Such decisions were applauded by experts who feared the worst. In 1953 a counsellor for Toronto's Family Court and the United Church summed up prevailing opinion, arguing that "where the husband and wife are both working outside the home, very often a dangerous spirit of independence exists. Finally, it is quite impossible to do two jobs well."[42] Women who dismissed such arguments could look forward to being scapegoated for a host of society's problems, blamed for homosexual sons, juvenile delinquents, mental cripples, wandering and alcoholic husbands, and school truants.[43]

When authorities repeatedly insisted that women were needed at home, the corollary often was that men were too weak to have them anywhere else. As the Kinsey reports had documented in detail, sexual orientation was conditional; men were the more vulnerable sex. When men's physical weakness was further disclosed by experts like Ashley Montague,[44] female discontent or competition appeared enormously threatening. A wife's wages might endanger the very core of the fragile male personality.[45] By the same measure, houseworking men challenged the very basis of contemporary masculinity. The Montreal psychiatrist Dr. Alastair MacLeod plaintively summed up modern problems for *Chatelaine*'s readers:

> Father no longer has opportunities for pursuing aggressive competitive goals openly at work. Some of his basic masculine needs remain unmet. Mother no longer feels she has a real man for a husband and becomes openly aggressive and competitive herself, even moving out of the home into industry in her efforts to restore the biological balance.
>
> Faced with an increasingly discontented and dominating wife, father becomes even more passive and retiring. . . . Certain trends in modern industry are theoretically capable of disturbing the biological harmony of family organization. The resulting disharmony can lead to psychological and psychosomatic illnesses.[46]

The message was clear: domestic women guaranteed both their own femininity and their husbands' masculinity.

In the 1940s and 1950s Canadians had many reasons to believe that the gendered division of labour was the most appropriate response to their own and their nation's needs. While some citizens always challenged too narrowly defined roles, many were prepared to accept the fact that women and men had different duties in the family and in society at large. Residential suburbs that enshrined the notion of largely separate spheres for the two sexes proved attractive because most Canadians preferred women at home and out of the labour market.

The recurring housing crisis of the 1940s and 1950s provided the crucial opportunity to fix this preference in space.[47] The dominion entered the postwar years with "a large stock of aging and substandard housing, communities that lacked appropriate municipal services, rural areas that lacked electric power, and with a substantial number of households living in crowded conditions or paying shelter costs they could ill afford."[48] Families with youngsters were particularly hard hit. A boom in babies and immigrants raised the costs of even inferior accommodation.[49] The January 1946 occupation of the old Hotel Vancouver protesting the lack of housing for veterans and their families, like the later seizure of several government buildings in Ottawa by members of the Veterans' Housing League, were only the most visible symptoms of widespread dissatisfaction and rising unrest.[50] The *Star Weekly* summed up popular sentiments: "It must be remembered that the whole situation is charged with an intense emotional desire on the part of veterans and non-veterans alike to have homes of their own. The years of loneliness and being apart, the years of cramped, semi-private living, have created a desire as strong as the migrating instinct in birds to have a home."[51] Not surprisingly, crowded accommodation was regularly cited as contributing to family breakdown and social disarray.[52]

Prime Minister Mackenzie King's postwar government, already alerted by the report of the Advisory Committee on Reconstruction on housing and planning to the magnitude of the housing shortage[53] and fearful of the appeal of the Co-operative Commonwealth Federation, moved to fill the gap. The passage in 1944 of the second National Housing Act (NHA) and the creation of the Central Mortgage and Housing Corporation (CMHC) one year later confirmed the significance of housing for peacetime construction.[54] With some few exceptions, strong anti–public housing sentiments and official reluctance to interfere with the "free market" sharply limited the reclamation of urban residential cores.[55] Across the dominion, despite the substantial investment in urban infrastructure — sewers, schools, public transportation, sidewalks, churches, and the like — that cities represented, they did not become the focus of government housing initiatives. Attention focused instead on the construction of new houses in the suburbs.

Despite their neglect by governments, city neighbourhoods continued to attract middle- and working-class Canadians, but many tried to maximize dollars and improve family situations by turning to new residential communities. Not all benefited from state support. In British Columbia's Lower Mainland, poorer citizens made do with little better than squatters' quarters in Bridgeview, a marginal Surrey settlement, without sidewalks and sewers.[56] In Quebec the Montreal working class had to satisfy its land hunger in Ville Jacques Cartier. There the discomfort and distress of life in tarpaper and tin shacks on postage-sized lots bought on the installment plan helped embitter the future separatist Pierre Vallières.[57] In Newfoundland, the city of St. John's was surrounded by "fringe areas . . . characterized by very poor, substandard housing, complete lack of services (piped water and sewer facilities, garbage collection, street-lighting, etc.), poor roads and low family incomes."[58] Few residents in such locations used the provisions of the National Housing Act, since borrowers in the years after World War II had to earn steadily higher gross family incomes in order to pay rising down payments and interest rates.[59]

Atlantic Canadians, poorer on average than their contemporaries elsewhere, were particularly unlikely to receive federal mortgage help: between 1954 and 1966 only 23.4 percent of all new "dwelling units" in the Atlantic region were completed with CMHC assistance, compared to 51.9 percent in Ontario in the same period.[60] The variability of financing meant that housewives in different regions sometimes confronted dramatically different working conditions. In 1960 and the first five months of 1961, for example, 38.5 percent of new units located in Atlantic Canada lacked flush toilets and 41.9 percent furnace heating, compared with 8.7 percent and 8.2 percent, respectively, in Ontario.[61] Such distinctions helped ensure that accommodation on the urban periphery varied, often tremendously, from one part of the country to the other. In the Maritimes, suburbia would be neither as extensive nor as prosperous as in many other regions of the country.

In contrast to the plight of the poor, the housing predicament of a broad range of Canadians was addressed by federal enthusiasm for subsidizing the construction of single-family homes and the desire of private developers, contractors, and mortgage lenders to maximize profits. For those who could meet income requirements, mortgage money, at artificially low rates, was made available to build hundreds of thousands of three-bedroom "residential units."[62] While the foremost scholar of Canadian suburbs, S.D. Clark, has concluded that residents were frequently "middle class in terms of income . . . Canadian born, of British origin, and of Protestant religious affiliation,"[63] suburbs always attracted ambitious working-class and immigrant citizens as well. One daughter remembered that "as refugees from Hungary," her parents "could hardly wait to leave" downtown Toronto "for [what was], to them, the lavish splendour of the suburbs," where they settled without regret.[64] In a subdivision of owner-built houses in Cooksville, Ontario, in the 1950s, an English immigrant remembered friendly Italian neighbours whose comfortable homes were constructed by their labouring and small-contractor husbands.[65] The Yugoslav immigrant who began work as a carpenter and plasterer when he arrived after the war and went on to achieve his dream of a suburban bungalow, in his case in Winnipeg's West Kildonan, may not have been in the majority, but he had imitators from one end of the country to the other.[66] The eclectic nature of the suburban community was captured by the comment from a resident who insisted that her modest suburb west of Toronto, whose residents included Olga, Grand Duchess of Russia, was "neither purely WASP nor dull."[67]

Once families moved to suburbia, they often found themselves with people of similar income and in houses of similar price. Neighbours were "all in the same boat."[68] New communities often revealed a distinct class and ethnic character, one that was sometimes legally imposed. Until their overthrow by the Supreme Court in 1951, residential covenants that included race as criteria were commonplace. Drawing on Canadian property law, they were used by land developers to exclude "undesirables" and to set minimum house values.[69] Even after covenants had lost some of their power, homogeneity often survived, a testament to more informal support. In 1957 the new North York suburb of Don Mills, for example, attracted certain occupational groups: 32.1 percent of male homeowners were executives, 23.7 percent professionals, 19.9 percent skilled technicians, 11 percent salesmen, and 3.8 percent teachers and professors, with the remaining 9.5 percent listed as miscellaneous.[70] The hopes of many suburbanites were summed up by one observer in 1945: "It's not just a house, but a way of life that people are seeking . . . Most people wanted to be a part of a community which consisted of congenial people, equality of income — restricted house values."[71] Different suburbs could have distinctive characters, depending on the ability of different groups to afford the cost of houses in their community.

The availability of CMHC mortgages for new homes, relatively low land costs, and builders' incentives, such as that by Saracini Construction in NHA's Glen Park development in Etobicoke in the early 1950s, which gave purchasers the "option of taking a lower priced home and completing part of it at a later date,"[72] made a difference to many Canadians. Despite the continuing decline in the rural population, where ownership was most common, the number of owner-occupied houses in Canada increased from 57 percent in 1941 to 65 percent in 1951 to 66 percent in 1961.[73]

Immediately after the Second World War much new housing was constructed, either individually, often by "do-it-yourselfers," or as part of developments of a few to several hundred houses. Most early construction took place either within older suburbs like East Vancouver or East York in Toronto or in the first ring of surrounding townships or municipalities, such as British Columbia's Burnaby and Ontario's Etobicoke. By the early 1950s, however, high demand plus the enlarged scale of the development industry increasingly directed growth to more remote areas, many without existing municipal services. There, in sites like Halifax's Thornhill Park, Toronto's Don Mills, and Edmonton's Crestwood, appeared the suburban, automobile-dependent sprawl that came to characterize the last half of the twentieth century. Between 1951 and 1961 the population in metropolitan areas around city cores grew far more than that in city centres (see Table 31.2).

Table 31.2 Percentage Increases in Population for the Central Cities and Remaining Parts of the 1961 Census Metropolitan Areas, Canada and the Regions, 1951–1961

Census Metropolitan Area	Central City	Remainder of Metropolitan Area
Canada	23.8	110.7
Atlantic	11.7	70.6
Quebec	27.9	117.7
Ontario	15.5	116.3
Prairies	50.2	133.0
British Columbia	10.9	90.7

Source: Peter McGahan, *Urban Sociology in Canada* (Toronto, 1986), from table 61.

These first homes meant a great deal. Coming out of depression and war, couples struggled to become property owners. A team effort was common. As one observer noted of veteran housing: "There is hardly a single case among all these veteran-builders of a wife lounging about. They have been as active in all weathers as their husbands."[74] Such couples had good reason to prize long-awaited houses. Tenants in particular, like one longtime inhabitant of Montreal's Verdun, her husband, and three children, aged five, three, and seven months, were delighted to use CMHC mortgages to move, in their case to Lachine's "Dixie" suburb.[75] Their enthusiasm was matched by the York Township resident in Ontario who remembered being "very poor in the depression — 8 people in a 4 room one storey house." She was understandably "really excited — To have a 5 room brick bungalow for the two of us! Such Luxury!!"[76] A Scottish immigrant expressed the same sense of achievement: "We came from a society where houses were scarce, renting was almost impossible unless one had the proper connections, and from a country which had spent 6 years at war. So owning a house in the suburbs was a dream for us, a dream we achieved after only 6 years in Canada."[77]

While new suburbs varied in many particulars,[78] all shared a commitment to the gendered division of labour. Purchase of a home — whether in a highly planned community like Etobicoke's Thorncrest Village with its provision of a wide range of urban services expected by upper-middle-class buyers[79] or in a mass-produced subdivision like Scarborough's Wishing Well Acres, where the one millionth new house constructed after VE-Day was officially opened[80] — was part of a child-centred strategy for many Canadians. As a study by Vancouver's Lower Mainland Regional Planning Board discovered, "to a young family without much money, faced with the alternative of a small apartment in the city . . . it is no small thing to be able to look out of the living-room window at one's children playing in relative freedom with fields and woods beyond them."[81] As a mother of two in Toronto's Iondale Heights suburb explained in 1957, "We moved to the suburbs because of the children. We wanted to give them room to romp, where they wouldn't have to worry about street cars and fiend-driven automobiles. True, we have no museums or art galleries. But the children can go outside and see nature as it is."[82] Such commentators took for granted that greater opportunities for children depended ultimately on maternal supervision.

Finally responsible for child care and house maintenance, modern suburban wives were tethered to their communities in ways that few husbands could match. In 1958 one speaker for a Toronto construction company described the suburban home: "A woman is there all the time, she lives there. A man just boards there: he gets his meals there. She is there all day long."[83] A male architect characterized his own experience of gender relations even more vividly: "I spend every day in my Mobile Room [car] going to and from the women at either end [in the office or in his suburban home]."[84] As these remarks suggest, the suburban house remained first of all a workplace for female residents. For husbands, lengthy commutes and long hours at work, not to mention individual preferences, meant that domestic responsibilities were largely subordinated to the demands of waged work.[85] Nor did the suburbs make joint efforts easy. As one husband recalled:

> Like most of my fellow male suburbanites I was the sole auto driver. I also drove a lot in my job. Rushing home to take a child to cubs or brownies, to take my wife to a class in the city, to drive to hockey practice or to a game, or to be shopping driver when required was a daily task. Work pressures made this more difficult. There were the open spaces to cut, cultivate and shovel. Social evenings required a driver to pick up the sitter, drive into town, return home and drive the sitter home. The automobile was an itching appendage needing constant scratching.[86]

To be sure, some suburban wives always joined their husbands in leaving home for employment. As the expansion of Avon's and other door-to-door sales in these years suggested, earning extra money was never far from many residents' minds.[87] So-called "working" wives shored up families' aspirations to a better standard of living; the husband of a young Bank of Commerce clerk, for instance, was reconciled to her job so she could furnish the house they were building in Saskatoon in 1952.[88] Yet women's ideal primary role remained, especially after babies arrived, in the home. As one resident of a Toronto suburb remembered, her husband "didn't want me to work, and I thought that no one could look after my children as well as I could."[89]

While they may not have remained in the labour market, wives regularly contributed to husbands' careers. Women married to professionals or businessmen often functioned as part of a marital "team," spending hours as unpaid assistants, typing, translating, or entertaining. The wife of a successful academic remembered that "in university circles a wife was expected to entertain — often upwards of 50 people."[90] Another academic spouse found her eyes giving out as she typed the manuscripts that advanced her husband in his profession.[91] Acknowledgement of such contributions forms a regular refrain in scholarly prefaces.

The great majority of wives remained crucially dependent on male wages. Women's financial vulnerability was worsened by the fact that many families purchased suburban homes only by rigorous self-denial. More than one investigator discovered that "Baby sitters were done without, food costs reduced, less spent on clothing, and a hundred and one other small ways discovered to save money. 'I'm not going dancing no more' gave expression certainly to the financial plight of more than one suburban housewife."[92] While such careful juggling of finances was not true of all suburbanites, the strains of budgeting, large or small, were likely to be borne unevenly. Not only did male wage-earners usually have prior right of access to what they commonly held to be "their money,"[93] they frequently had to maintain certain standards as conditions of employment. Women and children could dress, eat, and travel much less well without immediately endangering the family economy.[94]

Suburban houses were the stage on which women explored the meaning of separate spheres. That setting varied greatly depending on income and individual preference, but the introduction of CMHC inspections under the 1954 revision of the Housing Act encouraged the giving way of "individual, custom-built homes" to "mass, speculative development" with standardized shapes, sizes, and configurations.[95] In the late 1940s and 1950s master plans and more stringent municipal zoning by-laws across the country, which represented efforts to control errant developers, also contributed to the increasing uniformity of the emerging suburban landscape.[96] CMHC's support of Canadian Small House competitions after the Second World War,[97] like the *Star Weekly*'s sponsorship of the All Canadian Home in 1959,[98] for all their good intentions, had the same effect. In the heady days of easy sales, developers threw up one imitation after another, differing in little but colour and trim. Most models came as Cape Cods, and, increasingly, as bungalows or split levels. Like the split-level winner of the first coast-to-coast architectural contest in 1953,[99] almost all boasted three bedrooms, an L-shaped living–dining-room combination, and, in most areas of the country, a full basement. Increasingly, too, a rumpus or recreation room appeared below level, which, together with the proliferation of televisions, encouraged families to spend leisure time more privately. In these homes, more comfortable than many had ever encountered, women were to forge the moral basis for postwar Canada.

Female residents were expected and urged to bring uniqueness to uniformity through a careful attention to decoration and design. As one commentator insisted, "The bugaboo of uniformity bothers her not at all, because every woman knows she can work out her own individual design for living with colours and furnishings and personal touches."[100] Their choice of furniture, appliances, art, and even clothes was to transform the identical into the distinguishable, in the process confirming housewives' skills and status. No wonder that practically every issue of popular Canadian women's magazines like *Bride's Book, Canadian Home Journal,*

Canadian Homes and Gardens, and *Chatelaine*, not to mention their American competitors, offered readers ways, thrifty and otherwise, to personalize suburbia. In a Special Issue in March 1955, for example, *Chatelaine* offered lessons on "How to Live in a Suburb," "A Spring Fashion Bazaar for Suburban Living," and "How to Furnish a New Home without Panic Buying." Subscribers consulted such experts but also prided themselves on developing styles that suited their families best.[101] The mistress of a Rexdale, Ontario, bungalow on "a corner-lot so at least it didn't match everything beside it in either direction, but of course, it matched the house on the corner across the street," spoke for a renovating sisterhood when she reflected that "I almost wrecked it trying to create something unique."[102]

Many women soon found more to concern them in the limitations of the environment at large. Conspicuous in their absence from many new developments in the 1940s and early 1950s, before local governments became more demanding, were public spaces and facilities, such as sidewalks, monuments, parks, and cemeteries. A mother of two children settled in a bungalow on Toronto's outskirts typically remembered that "there were no sidewalks and the road was not paved. The mud and dust were a real pain."[103] For many years developers also counted on the open country that surrounded many subdivisions to provide children with nearby recreational space. In time, as the process of urban sprawl accelerated, this resource disappeared, as it did around Scarborough's Wishing Well Acres subdivision in the 1960s, without any provision for its replacement. For women, the presumed mistresses of suburbia, collective provision was almost always curiously lacking. If landscape was any guide, meeting and play were not part of the female mandate.

The location of most commercial shops and services on the periphery or, more occasionally, in the centre of residential development, either in a strip pattern along major roads or in suburban plazas, showed the same lack of attention to women's needs. Patterns of consumption centred increasingly on shopping centres, which first made their appearance in Canada in 1947 in suburban Winnipeg. By 1951, with the construction of Norgate Plaza in Montreal and Park Royal Plaza in West Vancouver, about 46 shopping centres, all poorly served by public transit and demanding access to a private car,[104] drew buyers from surrounding suburbs.

One Don Mills veteran characterized shopping experiences that were not very different from those of the majority of her contemporaries, especially those whose husbands didn't have the option of commuting by train to work: "Walked and pushed baby carriage to most places. Never had a second car — poor bus service especially with 3 children! Little co-operation, wives did not own car — walked to local shops. Traffic was hazardous on highway & only route to major shopping centre (suburbs were designed for the car & most of us had only one which husband used)."[105] Once visitors got there, new plazas, lacking free public space and cultural amenities, offered them little beyond a community based on a common commitment to purchase. As a self-satisfied Canadian retailer put it, "Suburban living, by its basic structure, generates wants and brings latent desires more sharply into focus. The not-so-subtle effect of competitive living is also a potent influence in creating an environment that encourages liberal spending for better living."[106] The domestic and individualistic orientation of women, families' major purchasers, was readily reaffirmed.

While plazas were increasingly influential, door-to-door sales and deliveries were commonplace in the 1940s and 1950s. Phone orders were taken by butchers, grocers, and department stores, and trucks with milk and bakery goods made their way among suburban homes. Avon ladies, who might be members of a local church, and Hoover, Electrolux, Fuller Brush, and Watkins salesmen were also occasional visitors. The latter were described by a former client as canvassing a Montreal suburb "once or twice per year and I always kept their wonderful salve, 'Good for Man or Beast.' Very strong, didn't burn and helped heal cut knees very quickly. They also had wonderful flavourings and food colourings."[107]

In Metropolitan Toronto, another purchaser implied advantages beyond mere convenience: "We liked to see a vegetable man come along the street. Ice, milk and bread were delivered as were beer and pop. The Avon lady and the Fuller Brush man provided some new faces."[108] Such sentiments were shared by a resident of Clarkson's Corners (Mississauga) who recalled, with affection, a milk man who "always poked his head in to say good morning and took the children on his van for a ride." She observed, "Obviously these services were very important. I realize, however, that my mother had far more people calling than I. (She even had a Hellicks coffee man, Duggan's bakery, etc.)."[109] Although they grew less in time as the private automobile undermined their viability, such deliveries helped knit new communities together in ways that more modern shopping alternatives rarely did.

Suburbia's households were also connected by schools and churches. Although it often happened that housing sprawled well beyond the capacity of religious groups and municipalities to ensure even minimum services, by the 1950s their institutions were normally included in the initial planning of developments. Even then they might well be strained to their limits or inconvenient to reach, as with schools offering shift classes or located across busy intersections. For all such shortcomings, as well as their tendency to deal with female clients almost solely in their roles as mothers and wives, such institutions constituted important collective resources to a community lacking common habits of working together. Parent–teacher associations, or home and school groups, were the most effective in mobilizing women, from room mothers to fund-raisers and executive officers.[110] Auxiliaries and Sunday schools were critical for some residents who kept suburban churches expanding in these years.[111] Work with local institutions offered more activist and sociable suburbanites the chance to combine domestic duties with a manageable level of public involvement.

As they had done in other Canadian settings, women wove the fabric of day-to-day life. As one observer noted, "For most of the day while the men are away at work the women run the community. After the bulldozers have pulled out, the spadework to make a real community out of your particular collection of houses has to be done by . . . the homemakers."[112] Women commonly moved beyond their homes through contacts with children and "in turn, the fathers get to know their neighbours through their own ubiquitous wives."[113] Casual meetings, dismissed by critics as "coffee klatches," or even encounters between Avon "ladies" and their clients, might be followed by both intimate friendships and formal associations. These ties helped women cope with limited resources and new environments. Since children were rarely far from mothers' minds, much cooperative activity centred on them. After the war, women in North Burnaby's new subdivisions established "parent–teacher groups . . . in an endeavour to promote better school conditions and assist in providing hot lunches for the children."[114] In Don Mills, where young children were abundant and teenagers rare, women established baby-sitting co-operatives. In Thornhill, Ontario, mothers formed a community kindergarten and encouraged the fathers, who, "though somewhat apathetic at first . . . to contribute some time and energy in making odds and ends of school equipment."[115] In 1955 mothers at North York's York Mills School, alarmed by sexual attacks on local children, created a Parents' Action League.[116] In Etobicoke's Rexdale development, women protested their lack of public transit to local council and to the Toronto Transit Commission. As they explained, "Nearly all of us have children and they have to be taken to the dentist or doctor occasionally. It takes a full day to make the trip and two days to rest up afterwards."[117] Also in 1955, mothers from North York's Livingstone School fought the Board of Education's transfer of pupils to another school.[118] In Clarkson's Corners a Quebecker prompted her neighbours to create French conversation groups and to fund high school scholarships.

Concerns sometimes broadened beyond children to include a variety of community issues. Thorny questions related to sewers, libraries, and garbage disposal provided lessons in collective action and political lobbying. In North York, residents created the North York Women Electors Association on the model of its Toronto counterpart in September 1954.[119] In Etobicoke, a year later, 22 mothers with children in tow from Goldwood Heights subdivision "stormed" a council meeting, demanding "action — not answers" to the problem created by their developer's failure to finish sidewalks, sodding, and ditching.[120] In effect, such women were transforming suburbs into good neighbourhoods. As volunteers they facilitated the creation of everything from schools, hospitals, and churches to libraries.

For all the evidence of activism, however, the majority of women were rarely visible on the public stage. For many, suburbia constituted a period of deep engagement in the day-to-day running of the family. Very few had assistance with household duties, particularly on weekdays, when most husbands were absent. While a few sometimes found substitutes for their own labour in cooperatives or paid help, others, like a Montreal suburbanite, remembered that "even babysitters were all but unavailable (No Teens, no Grannies)."[121] Questioned about their days as mothers of young children, both happy and unhappy veterans of suburbia remember themselves engrossed in time-consuming duties:

> I had helped my mother in bazaars, tag days, processions, etc. etc., fund-raising, church charitable organizations from the time I was knee high. However, once married, I was apolitical. I guess, basically, because I was so very busy [with nine children].[122]
>
> I guess there were clubs and political parties but I really didn't have much time or energy with four small children to get involved. I've always been aware of my own limitations in terms of time and energy.[123]
>
> Not much [leadership from women] in my age group at the time. Too busy at home . . . it was a man's world.[124]
>
> There was no energy or time to do anything about it [feminism].[125]
>
> I didn't participate in politics when my children were small, I was too too too busy. None of my neighbours with children seemed to be involved.[126]

Unless they were especially gregarious, such child-rearing women were likely to devote precious free-time moments to private rather than public pursuits.

To the present day, a baleful mythology associated with postwar suburbs and their female residents persists. Suburban women provided a focus for much contemporary debate about the merits of modern life. In particular, in the minds of critics of mass society who flourished in the years after the Second World War,[127] the suburb emerged as the residential and female expression of the moral bankruptcy they identified in society at large, more particularly in giant corporations, big governments, and the "organization men" who served them.

The most famous indictment from North American feminists was provided by Betty Friedan's *The Feminine Mystique*.[128] This soon-to-be-classic identification of "The Problem That Has No Name" captured the imagination of a generation no longer satisfied with the restricted options of life in suburbia. As one Canadian reader explained:

> I truly considered my genes disturbed until I read Friedan's book. After all, I'd spent my life working to earn, and indeed cherishing, the one compliment that topped them all —"You think like a man."
>
> But I was afraid of that book. I read it in very small snatches, because it stirred me greatly, and I couldn't see any purpose to that. There I was, a relatively uneducated woman with two small children to raise.[129]

More than anyone else, Friedan helped women challenge the egalitarian claim of North American abundance. Ultimately, she argued, and many readers agreed, the gendered experience of suburbia betrayed women, consigning them to subordination and frustration within society and unhappiness within the family. Limited options for women also meant an immeasurably poorer "Free World," a critical point when winning the Cold War was all-important. In Canada, Friedan's dismissal of modern housekeeping as neither sufficiently dignified nor time-consuming to require full-time dedication by wives and mothers was matched by a barrage of popular articles in the 1950s.[130]

Whatever Friedan's insights, her work concentrated on a privileged minority. Her suburban women, pushed by the forces of a commercialized culture, appeared to have made the "great refusal" in rejecting purposeful and independent lives in the public sphere. A considerable amount of women-blaming goes on in *The Feminine Mystique*. As with many of her Canadian imitators, Friedan associated suburban women with the evils of modern society — its secularism, superficiality, and materialism. Her feminism, with its support for broader interpretations and expressions of female ability, gave her message special meaning, but the message itself, like attacks on suburbia from social critics unconcerned about sexual inequality, finally ignored the complexity of female lives.

Nonfeminist critics of modern society routinely targeted female suburbanites. Marshall McLuhan's *The Mechanical Bride: Folklore of Industrial Man* identified "millions of women who live isolated lives from 8:00 to 6:00 p.m."[131] in suburbia as part of the dilemma of modern men. In 1956 in "You Take the Suburbs, I Don't Want Them," the novelist Hugh Garner, flexing his muscles as a home-grown literary "bad boy," rejected a world in which men could not make the rules.[132] Suburbia's psychological failings were brutally diagnosed by the assistant director of Montreal's Mental Hygiene Institute. In 1958 Dr. Alastair MacLeod warned *Chatelaine's* readers that "The suburbs give children fresh air, but take away their fathers. They give women efficient kitchens, but are hard on their femininity and gentleness. They give men pride in providing so handsomely, but drive many of them to drink to make up for their watered-down maleness."[133] This psychiatrist damned suburbs as "matriarchies, manless territories where women cannot be feminine because expediency demands that they control the finances and fix drains and where night-returning men cannot be masculine because their traditional function of ruler and protector has been usurped."[134] While Friedan located suburbia's limitations in the domestic definition of womanhood, few psychiatrists acknowledged that many women needed outlets beyond those provided by purely domestic life.

The indictments of social critics were elaborated most fully in *Crestwood Heights*, a case study of Toronto's Forest Hill, an "inner suburb" built before the Second World War. Dissecting the family lives of an upper-middle-class sample of WASP and Jewish Torontonians, the authors revealed what many critics of mass society feared. Men concentrated on making money, ignoring families' emotional and spiritual needs. Dissatisfied women wielded power in a community in which they were the dominant adults for the daylight hours. Mothers were preoccupied with their offspring, to the detriment of themselves and their children. Both sexes were overly materialistic. The contribution of men and women to the wider society was intrinsically limited. Despite the lack of comparability of this older suburb to what was happening on the periphery of Canadian cities, Crestwood Heights rapidly became the measure by which modern suburbia was judged.[135]

The Royal Architectural Institute of Canada added to the chorus of dismay. Its 1960 *Report* on the design of the residential environment summed up the views of professional architects and representatives of University Women's Clubs and the National Council of Women in its dislike for "the essential identity of houses, the denial of differentiation, built into new suburbs."[136] The *Report* was alert to suburbia's failure to reflect changing Canadian demography. While new buildings took for granted a father in paid employment and a mother at home with two children, many households were very different.[137] The land-eating sprawl of three-bedroom Cape Cods, bungalows, or split levels dependent on private transportation and reflective of a single style of family life was not what all Canadians needed. Preoccupied with aesthetics, however, the *Report* never confronted the problem embodied in the gendered nature of suburban space.

Arguments about the merits of suburban life were not always restricted to polite discourse. Residents of Scarborough's Highland Creek, which their MPP characterized as "a normal Ontario suburban community,"[138] were outraged in 1956 when S.D. Clark, of the University of Toronto, was quoted as accusing them of sexual immorality and hard drinking. The leakage of these observations from a private report to a research group forced him to apologize publicly to Scarborough's residents. Even then there were threats of vigilante justice.[139]

Perhaps chastened by this experience, Clark produced a path-breaking study, *The Suburban Society* (1968), which rejected any simple characterization of suburbia. Dismissing *Crestwood Heights* as unrepresentative in its "culture of a particular urban social class and, in large degree, particular ethnic group,"[140] he championed suburbia's variety and vitality. It was this heterogeneity that Friedan and other critics of modern life, with their focus on middle-class, highly organized communities, had so largely missed. And yet, ironically enough, for all his stress on suburbia's variety, Clark joined critics of mass society in readily sterotyping women. *The Suburban Society* casually dismissed the female resident as "the suburban housewife seeking amusement or instruction in light reading" and the "lone miserable suburban housewife."[141] Making easy generalizations about the "social waste" of women left behind in suburbia,[142] Clark never applied his insight about the complexity of suburban patterns to any consideration of the role of gender. To a significant degree, women continued to be both victims and authors of their own misfortune, keys to the failings of contemporary family life and thus to much of the imperfection of the modern world.

Suburban women, then and today, have their own contributions to make to this debate. In 1959 *Chatelaine*'s readers responded passionately to the attack on suburban women issued by the assistant director of Montreal's Mental Hygiene Institute, Dr. Alastair MacLeod. In more than 300 letters they captured the complexity of women's lives. In all, 42 percent defended women, men, and suburbia itself, one critic bluntly summing up her rejection of the psychiatrist's misogyny as "Bunk." A further 11 percent of respondents blamed the problems of modern life on something other than suburbia, while 8 percent gave it mixed reviews. The remaining 39 percent agreed, more or less, with MacLeod's criticism of suburban women. Most readers were reluctant to limit women to domestic labour as a solution to the ills of modern society. One woman from Rexdale, Ontario, pointed out that many young wives had more than enough business experience and brains to manage the home and its finances. It didn't make sense to "restrict them to the monotonous unthinking roles of mere cooks and floor waxers."[143] Most suburban women did much more and did it well. A few readers, while admitting something was wrong, refused to blame women. A Regina contributor, for instance, argued that women were feeling frustrated and inadequate because their "opportunity for economic contribution has largely been taken from the four walls of her home."[144] The whole tenor of the published answers to MacLeod's condemnation of suburban womanhood suggested a diversity of opinion and experience.

Suburbia's veterans still remain divided about its meaning. In letters, memos, interviews, and answers to a questionnaire about their experience in the suburbs between 1945 and 1960,[145] women, whose families ranged from the well-to-do to the economically marginal, reflected on what those years had meant. Many, like one Etobicoke, Ontario, resident, offered a blunt calculation of benefits: "Suburban life was fine. We had an auto so we weren't isolated from the Toronto scene. It also enabled us immigrants to make friends. I'd do it over again. Everyone benefited . . . When you live a situation you aren't always analyzing it. The decision was economic. I wasn't buying into an image."[146] Like many others, whose satisfaction seemed grounded in happy marriages, this writer argued that suburban life was vital and fulfilling. Helpmate husbands did much to make suburbia a good place for wives.

Favourable assessments also sprang from a recognition that life in the suburbs was a step up in terms of convenience, comfort, and security. Days spent previously as tenants, in too few rooms and without domestic conveniences, could make even modest bungalows feel very good. While not without flaws, suburbs were a good deal better than the alternatives. The benefits for children were stressed repeatedly, but women, like the two speakers below, were likely to convey a strong sense of their own good fortune as well:

> It was the right choice for us . . . We did not want to raise our kids on city streets, although I realize now they did miss out on many things such as museums, libraries, etc. . . . I think all who chose the life benefited from the freer life, the men for a lot of companionship with neighbours . . . It was a happier time because we no longer worried about friends and acquaintances, schoolmates who were overseas and in danger.[147]
>
> Those were good years for us. My husband was getting ahead and I saw myself as a helpmate . . . For children suburbia really worked. They always had playmates and they had multiple parenting . . . [but] Suburbia tended to narrow our vision of the outside world. We thought we had the ideal life . . . We knew little about the world of poverty, culture, crime and ethnic variety. We were like a brand new primer, "Dick and Jane."[148]

In reflecting on their suburban lives, women who counted them successful firmly rejected any portrait of themselves as conformists and insisted that the suburbs worked best for the independent and self-motivated. An artist noted that she and her friends "were already in charge of our lives and didn't feel abused."[149] Whether they were gregarious and heavily involved in the community or took pleasure in quiet family pastimes, positive commentators revealed a strong sense of achievement. Happy children, rewarding relationships with spouses, and strong communities were their trophies.

Cheerful accounts contrasted markedly with those who remembered the suburbs as "hell." Days spent largely alone with demanding infants and lack of support from friends, relatives, and sometimes husbands were to be endured. The result could be desperation. One Ontario survivor captured her predicament, and that of others as well, when she wrote: "I began to feel as if I were slowly going out of my mind. Each day was completely filled with child and baby care and keeping the house tidy and preparing meals. I felt under constant pressure."[150] Some women recollected feeling guilty about such unhappiness: If families were more prosperous than ever and husbands doing their jobs, what right did they have to be less than content? When a desperately lonely neighbour hung her three children in the basement, however, one resident of Don Mills put self-doubts aside and set out to create mothers' groups to compensate for the shortcomings of suburban life.[151]

Critics sometimes observed that dissatisfaction extended beyond their sex. Two women explained: "Certainly didn't work for me. I would have been much happier in row housing . . . It seems to me that everyone loses — Women are isolated. Men don't know their families. Children don't know their fathers."[152] And, "I don't think anybody benefited, exactly. You could say men, but they benefited from marriage, suburbs or not . . . And I think a lot of men were miserable trying to play the part imposed upon them in the wasteland."[153] From the perspective of such veterans, women in particular and society as a whole were the poorer because of the investment on the suburban frontier.

Unlike their contemporaries who relished memories of days nurturing children and husbands, critics yearned for lives that offered them more contact with the wider world, more appreciation of their diverse skills, and more financial independence. For them the suburban landscape entailed an unacceptable restriction on options, a source of frustration, anger, and depression. This group often rejected the domestic ideal embodied in suburbia as soon as possible, ridding themselves of unsatisfactory husbands, moving to more congenial settings, and taking paid employment.

Accounts from suburban women rarely match the image presented by Friedan and the critics of mass society. Their experiences were neither homogeneous nor uncomplicated. They were much more than merely the female counterparts of "organization men." Women were both victims and beneficiaries of a nation's experiment with residential enclaves that celebrated the gendered division of labour. Suburban dreams had captured the hopes of a generation shaken by war and depression, but a domestic landscape that presumed that lives could be reduced to a single ideal inevitably failed to meet the needs of all Canadians after 1945. In the 1960s the daughters of the suburbs, examining their parents' lives, would begin to ask for more.

NOTES

1. See Susan Saegert, "Masculine Cities and Feminine Suburbs: Polarized Ideas, Contradictory Realities," *Women and the American City*, ed. C. Stimpson, E. Dixler, M. Nelson, and K. Yatrakis (Chicago, 1981), 106. The appeal of suburbs was not limited to cities. New resource towns, of which 46 appeared between 1945 and 1957, provided numerous instances of what have been termed "suburbs in search of a town," "suburbs in the wilderness," "suburbia in the bush," "transplanted suburbia," "experiments in conformity," "displaced southern suburbs," and "suburbs without a metropolis." Cited in Margaret P. Nunn Bray's useful overview, "'No Life for a Woman': An Examination and Feminist Critique of the Post–World War II Instant Town with Special Reference to Manitouwadge" (MA thesis, Queen's University, 1989), 46. While produced by many of the same forces, the gendered landscape of the resource town is, however, distinctive. This article explores the suburban experience only as it manifested itself around cities.

2. See, for example, the discussion of gendered space in the provocative studies by Joy Parr, *The Gender of Breadwinners: Women, Men, and Change in Two Industrial Towns, 1880–1950* (Toronto, 1990), and Peter DeLottinville, "Joe Beef of Montreal," *Labour/Le Travailleur* 8/9 (Autumn/Spring 1981/2): 9–40 [reprinted in this volume].

3. Among the major studies, see Kenneth Jackson, *Crabgrass Frontier: The Suburbanization of the United States* (New York, 1985); Robert Fishman, *Bourgeois Utopias: The Rise and Fall of Suburbia* (New York, 1987); Elaine Tyler May, *Homeward Bound: American Families in the Cold War Era* (New York, 1988); Margaret Marsh, *Suburban Lives* (New Brunswick and London, 1990); and Dolores Hayden, *Redesigning the American Dream: The Future of Housing, Work and Family Life* (New York and London, 1984).

4. "Canadian Suburbanization in a North American Context: Does the Border Make a Difference?" *Journal of Urban History* 13, 3 (May 1987): 252–74.

5. Caroline Andrew and Beth Moore Milroy, eds., *Life Spaces: Gender, Household, Employment* (Vancouver, 1988), 4.

6. See Veronica Strong-Boag, *The New Day Recalled: Lives of Girls and Women in English Canada, 1919–1939* (Toronto, 1988).

7. The number of passenger automobiles registered in Canada rose from 1 281 190 in 1941 to 2 105 869 in 1951 to 4 325 682 in 1961. Series T147–194, *Historical Statistics of Canada*, 2nd ed. (Ottawa, 1983).

8. See Charles L. Sanford, "'Woman's Place' in American Car Culture," *The Automobile and American Culture*, ed. David L. Lewis and Laurence Goldstein (Ann Arbor, 1983).

9. See Series Q13–18 to Q75–80, *Historical Statistics of Canada*.

10. See, for example, John Thomas, "How to Stay Married," *Canadian Home Journal* (April 1955): 2–3.

11. For a useful discussion of the impact of the Cold War on sex roles in the United States, see May, *Homeward Bound*.

12. James Lemon, *Toronto since 1918* (Toronto, 1985), 94.

13. See Joyce Hibbert, *The War Brides* (Toronto, 1978), for revealing portraits of the brides who came to Canada.

14. Alice Hooper Beck, "Royal Mother," *Chatelaine* (Jan. 1951): 63. See Hector Bolitho, "The Queen's Conflict: How Can One Woman Fulfill the Dual Role of Monarch and Mother?" ibid. (Feb. 1953): 12–13, 36, 38, 40. See also David Macdonald, "Farewell to the Fifties," *Star Weekly* (2 Jan. 1960): 10–11, 14, who saw the decade as "frantic … an age of anxiety," 24.

15. Dr. K.S. Bernhardt, "Happily Ever After," *Bride's Book* (Fall/Winter 1952): 75.

16. See Fred Edge, "Are Fathers Necessary?" *Canadian Home Journal* (Feb. 1953): 24, 63; John Thomas, "Are Fathers Necessary?" ibid., 24, 63–4, and "Father's a Parent, Too," *Canadian Home and Gardens* (April 1952): 29–31.

17. See Strong-Boag, *New Day*.

18. See J. Ronald Oakley, *God's Country: America in the Fifties* (New York, 1986).

19. Mildred Grade Baker, "Canadian Women and the Suburban Experience, 1945–60: Questionnaire for Residents" (henceforth "Questionnaire"), to author (1991), 8. See also note 147 below.

20. Marjorie Bacon, "Questionnaire," 16.

21. A. Montague, *The Natural Superiority of Women* (New York, 1953), 188. See the favourable assessment in Joan Morris, "The Scientific Truth about 'Male Superiority,'" *Canadian Home Journal* (July 1957): 15, 45.

22. Ibid., 25.

23. See the positive, if cautious, review of Kinsey's work by J.R. Seeley and J. Griffin in *Canadian Welfare* (15 Oct. 1948); the optimistic assessment of the utility of early marriage for women, based on Kinsey's findings, in Miriam Chapin, "Can Women Combine the B.A. and the Baby?" *Saturday Night* (21 Feb. 1948): 24; and the positive attitude to the similarity of male and female sexuality in Eleanor Rumming, "Dr. Kinsey and the Human Female," ibid. (15 Aug. 1953): 7–8. See also Gary Kinsman, *The Regulation of Desire: Sexuality in Canada* (Toronto, 1987), 113–15.

24. See Regina Markell Morantz, "The Scientist as Sex Crusader: Alfred C. Kinsey and American Culture," in *Procreation or Pleasure: Sexual Attitudes in American History*, ed. T.L. Altherr (Malabar, 1983).

25. See "Dr. Kinsey Talks about Women to Lotta Dempsey," *Chatelaine* (Aug. 1949): 10–11, 59–60; and Claire Halliday, "A New Approach to the Problem of Frigidity," *Canadian Home Journal* (June 1956): 9, 69.

26. See "The Age for Marriage," *Chatelaine* (May 1948): 2.

27. Jan E. Dizard and Howard Gadlin, "Family Life and the Marketplace: Diversity and Change in the American Family," in *Historical Social Psychology*, ed. K.J. Gergen and M.M. Gergen (Hillsdale and London, 1984), 292.

28. See, for example, Elsieliese Thorpe, "Does He Resent Your Working?" *Star Weekly* (May 1953), who emphasized the husband's right "to have his wife's undivided attentions at times when he needs to unburden himself, the right to have a companion and a friend when he needs one," 7; Charles Cerami, "Are You Jealous of Your Husband's Job?" ibid. (8 Nov. 1958): 30–41; and J.K. Thomas, "If He Lost His Job …," *Canadian Home Journal* (Feb. 1957): 10–11.

29. Ken Johnstone, "How Do You Rate with Your Husband's Boss?" *Chatelaine* (March 1953): 70. See also the fierce rejection of the role of business helpmate in Mrs. John Doe, "An Open Letter to My Husband's Boss," *Canadian Home Journal* (May 1954): 10–11, 90, 93.

30. Dr. Marion Hilliard, *A Woman Doctor Looks at Love and Life* (Toronto, 1957), 72–73.

31. Full-page ad for Eaton's, *Saturday Night* (9 Aug. 1949): 19.

32. See the response of 2000 members of *Chatelaine*'s Consumers' Council in Mary Juke, "It Makes Married Life Easier," *Chatelaine* (Sept. 1948): 22–23. On television, see Paul Rutherford, *When Television Was Young: Primetime Canada, 1952–1967* (Toronto, 1990), 200–1, which includes a useful discussion of the sexism of broadcasting in these years.

33. S.J. Wilson, *Women, the Family and the Economy* (Toronto, 1972), 19.

34. For discussion of this phenomenon, see Meg Luxton, Harriet Rosenberg, Sedef Arat-Koe, *Through the Kitchen Window: The Politics of Home and Family*, 2nd ed. (Toronto, 1990).

35. Zoe Bieler, "White-Collar Wife," *Chatelaine* (Aug. 1953): 22–4, 37–40.

36. See, for example, Gwyn Le Capelan, "I Worked My Husband's Way through College," *Chatelaine* (April 1949): 4–5. See also the discussion in National Archives of Canada (NA), MG 31, K8, Mattie Rotenberg Papers, vol. 1, folder 66, radio broadcast "Changing Patterns" (Jan. 1954).

37. See Ruth Roach Pierson, "Gender and the Unemployment Insurance Debates in Canada, 1934–1960," *Labour/Le Travail* 25 (Spring 1990): 77–103.

38. See Anita A. Birt, "Married Women, You're Fools to Take a Job," *Chatelaine* (Jan. 1960): 41.

39. Dorothy Manning, "I Quit My Job to Save My Marriage," ibid. (June 1955): 16.

40. Jean Libman Block, "Husbands Should Not Do Housework!" *Star Weekly* (16 Nov. 1957): 6.

41. See the complaint about discrimination against women in Francis Ecker, "Will Married Women Go to War Again?" *Saturday Night* (30 Jan. 1951): 21–3. For a more extended discussion of the policies of the federal government in this area, see Ruth Roach Pierson, *"They're Still Women after All": The Second World War and Canadian Womanhood* (Toronto, 1986), chap. 2.

42. John G. McCulloch, "How to Be Sure of a Happy Marriage," *Bride's Book* (Spring/Summer 1953): 86. See also John K. Thomas, "How to Stay Married: Can Motherhood and Career Mix?" *Canadian Home Journal* (March 1955): 4, 6. For a contemporary assessment of women's own reservations about paid work, especially for mothers with young children, see Department of Labour, "Married Women Workers: The Home Situation," in *Canadian Society: Sociological Perspectives*, ed. B.R. Blishen, F.E. Jones, K.D. Naegele, and J. Porter (New York, 1961), 176.

43. See, for example, John Nash, "It's Time Father Got Back in the Family," *Maclean's* (12 May 1956), 28; S.R. Laycock, "Homosexuality — A Mental Hygiene Problem," *Canadian Medical Association Journal* (Sept. 1950): 247, as cited in Kinsman, *Regulation*, 115; Mary Graham, "Mama's Boy," *Canadian Home Journal* (Oct. 1952): 18–19, 37–39; and Hilliard, *Woman Doctor*, passim. The most famous example of "woman-blaming" in these years was Marynia Farnham and Ferdinand Lundberg, *Modern Woman: The Lost Sex* (1947), with its classic Freudian claim that "anatomy is destiny."

44. Montague, as cited in Robert McKeown, "Women Are the Stronger Sex," *Weekend Magazine, Vancouver Sun* (22 Jan. 1955): 2. See also Dr. Ashley Montague, "Why Men Fall in Love with You," *Chatelaine* (Oct. 1958): 23, 58, 99; Joan Morris, "The Scientific Truth about 'Male Superiority,'" *Canadian Home Journal* (July 1957): 15, 45; and Florida Scott-Maxwell, "Do Men Fear Women?" *Chatelaine* (Nov. 1959): 39, 50, 54–55.

45. See the argument by the anonymous author of "Careers and Marriage Don't Mix," *Saturday Night* (1 Nov. 1949): 32, who concluded that she had been letting her husband down, despite her higher salary of $10 000 a year, by not keeping up the domestic side of their life.

46. *Chatelaine* (March 1959): 214.

47. See J.N. Harris, "One Vacancy!" *Saturday Night* (15 Nov. 1947), 20; E.L. Chicanot, "Juvenile Immigration Will Help Canada," ibid. (6 Dec. 1947): 24, 37; Benjamin Higgins, "Better Strategy and Tactics to Win the Housing War," ibid. (14 Feb. 1948): 6–7; J. Bhaidlow, "Proper Rentals to Ease Housing Predicament," ibid. (17 April 1948): 17, 32; D. Wilensky, "War's Impact on Family Life," *Canadian Welfare* (15 Oct. 1945): 8–16.

48. Canada Mortgage and Housing, *Housing in Canada, 1945–1986: An Overview and Lessons Learned* (Ottawa, 1987), 6.

49. Ibid., 10.

50. Jill Wade, "'A Palace for the Public': Housing Reform and the 1946 Occupation of the Old Hotel Vancouver," *BC Studies* (Spring/Summer 1986): 288–310; "'Squatter Fever' Spreads to Canada," *The Enterprise* (Lansing, ON), 10 Oct. 1946.

51. John Clare, "Where Are the Houses?" *Star Weekly* (8 June 1946): 5.

52. See Dorothy Livesay and Dorothy Macdonald, "Why B.C. Divorces Soar," *Star Weekly* (15 May 1948): 16; and Marjorie Earl, "Canada's Divorce Headache," ibid. (12 June 1948): Section 2, 2.

53. See Canada, Advisory Committee on Reconstruction, Housing and Community Planning, SubCommittee *Report, No. 4* (Ottawa 1944).

54. For an excellent review of policy, see Albert Rose, *Canadian Housing Policies (1935–1980)* (Toronto, 1980).

55. See John Bacher, "From Study to Reality: The Establishment of Public Housing in Halifax, 1930–1953," *Acadiensis* 18, 1 (Autumn 1988): 120–35; and Albert Rose, *Regent Park: A Study of Slum Clearance* (Toronto, 1958).

56. Graduate Students in Community and Regional Planning, *Bridgeview: A Sub/Urban Renewal Study in Surrey, B.C.* (University of British Columbia, 1965).

57. See his *White Niggers of America* (Toronto, 1971). For an equally unflattering description of Ville Jacques Cartier, see John Gray, "Why Live in the Suburbs?" *Maclean's* (1 Sept. 1954): 7–11, 50–52.

58. See Project Planning Associates Ltd., *City of St. John's Newfoundland: Urban Renewal Study* (Toronto, 1961), 6.

59. See David Bettison, *The Politics of Canadian Urban Development*, vol. 1 (Edmonton, 1975), 110.

60. CMHC mortgage assistance was tied to the earnings of the family head; if earnings were too low, then assistance was denied. In low-income areas such as the Maritimes, CMHC loans were correspondingly fewer. For a discussion of the regional implications of CMHC policy, see Atlantic Development Board, *Urban Centres in the Atlantic Provinces* (Ottawa, 1969), 74.

61. Ibid., 76.

62. For a discussion of the impact of mortgaging by government, see Lawrence B. Smith, *The Postwar Canadian Housing and Residential Mortgage Markets and the Role of Government* (Toronto, 1974), chap. 9, and also Rose, *Canadian Housing Policies*, chap. 3. In 1951 single-family construction made up 77.3 percent of all the dominion's housing starts; in 1955, 71.5 percent and in 1960, 61.7 percent. Smith, *Postwar Canadian Housing*, 22–23.

63. S.D. Clark, The Suburban Society (Toronto, 1968), 101.

64. Krisztina Bevilacqua to author, 10 May 1991.

65. Marjorie Bacon, interview with author, 7 June 1991.

66. See John Gray, "A New Life Begins in Winnipeg," *Star Weekly* (9 July 1960): 2–4, 6–7.

67. Lois Strong to author, 29 May 1991.

68. Montreal suburbanite 1, "Questionnaire," 7.

69. See John Weaver, "From Land Assembly to Social Maturity: The Suburban Way of Life of Westdale (Hamilton), Ontario, 1911–1951," *Histoire sociale/Social History* (Nov. 1978): 437.

70. "More Than Half Don Mills Home Owners Professional Men or Executives Survey Shows," *The Enterprise* (Lansing), 26 May 1957.

71. Dottie Walter, "Homes for Tomorrow," *Canadian Home Journal* (June 1945): 30, 33.

72. "Saracinis Will Build 106 Islington Homes," *Etobicoke Press*, 13 April 1950.

73. Rose, *Housing in Postwar Canada*, 168–71.

74. Ronald Hamilton, "You Need a Wife Who Can Saw," *Maclean's* (July 1950): 36.

75. Mildred Grace Baker, "Questionnaire."

76. Helen M. Boneham, "Questionnaire," 5.

77. Catherine Cunningham to author, 14 May 1991.

78. See Clark, *Suburban Society*, 16–18, for his classification of different suburban types. These included "I. The Single-Family Residential Development of the 'Pure' Suburban Type; II. The Semi-Detached Residential Development of the 'Pure' Suburban Type; III. The Single-Family Residential Development in a Built-Up Area; IV. The 'Packaged' or Semi-Packaged Residential Development; V. The Cottage-Type Residential Development; VI. The Residential Development of the 'Pure' Suburban Type, Now Five to Ten Years Old." In the context of this classification, "pure" meant lacking "form and structure" (12) and "packaged" meant growing up "as a result of careful planning and direction" (15).

79. See Collier Stevenson, "City Living in the Country," *Canadian Home Journal* (Nov. 1947): 55–56. For a Scarborough example, see "Guildwood Village on the Move," *The Enterprise* (West Hill) (25 Sept. 1958).

80. "All-Canadian Home Designed from Results of Newspaper Survey," *Canadian Builder* (Jan. 1960): 62, and "Million Mark Reached," ibid. (Oct. 1956): 41. See also "Scarborough Has Canada's Millionth New Home," *The Enterprise* (West Hill) (26 July 1956).

81. The Lower Mainland Regional Planning Board, *The Urban Frontier*, Pt. 2: Technical Report (New Westminster, BC: Oct. 1963): 37.

82. As quoted in William MacEachern, "Suburbia on Trial," *Star Weekly* (18 May 1957): 2. See also, for a continuation of this preoccupation with children, Isabel Dyck, "Integrating Home and Wage Workplace: Women's Daily Lives in a Canadian Suburb," *Canadian Geographer/Le géographie canadien* 33, 4 (1989): 329–41.

83. Mrs. Woods, Saracini Construction, "What the Experts Say about Kitchens," *Canadian Builder* (June 1958): 50.

84. Anthony Adamson, "Where Are the Rooms of Yesteryear?" *Canadian Architect* (June 1958): 74.

85. See, for example, Frank Moritsugu, "Learn How to Relax," *Canadian Homes and Gardens* (Jan. 1955): 7–9, 38–39, 41.

86. Male former resident, Oakridge Acres, London, Ontario, to author, 10 June 1991.

87. See R.D. Magladry, "Door-to-Door Salesmanship Fills the Gap," *Financial Post* 54 (5 March 1960): 13; "Beauty Aid Sales Soar," ibid. (20 Aug. 1960): 1; and J. Schreiner, "Door-to-Door Is a Booming Business," ibid. 55 (30 Dec. 1961): 24.

88. "Wife or Working Girl?" *Bride's Book* (Fall/Winter 1952): 4, 6.

89. Boneham, "Questionnaire," 14.

90. Alaine Barrett Baines, "Questionnaire," 8.

91. Scarborough suburbanite, interview with author, March 1991.

92. Clark, *Suburban Society*, 121.

93. On this male attitude, see Meg Luxton, *More Than a Labour of Love: Three Generations of Women's Work in the Home* (Toronto, 1980), 163–65.

94. On the existence of two standards of living within the family, see the bitter observation in Mrs. John Doe, "An Open Letter to My Husband's Boss."

95. Bettison, *Politics*, 110.

96. As a sign of this interest the Community Planning Association of Canada was created in 1946. See Gerald Hodge, *Planning Canadian Communities* (Toronto and New York, 1986).

97. See the bungalow winner for 1947 in *Etobicoke Press*, 17 March 1947.

98. "First All Canadian Home Completed in Etobicoke," *Star Weekly* (12 Sept. 1959): 14–18.

99. "Home '53," *Canadian Home Journal* (Aug. 1953): 19, 45, 46, 48, 50, 52–53, 58–60.

100. Mary-Ella Macpherson, "Postwar Houses," *Chatelaine* (May 1945): 96.

101. See Betty Alice Marrs Naylor, "Questionnaire."

102. Helen Wallis, "Suburban Experience" (typescript), to author, 3.

103. Boneham, "Questionnaire," 5.

104. John Leaning, "The Distribution of Shopping Centres in Canada," *Canadian Builder* (June 1956): 41–45.

105. Bacon, "Questionnaire," 12.

106. H.J. Barnun, Jr, executive vice-president, Salada-Shirriff-Horsey, Toronto, as cited in "Calls Suburbs Best Place to Develop Retail Sales," *Style Fortnightly* (15 Jan. 1958): 35.

107. Mildred Fox Baker, "Questionnaire," 12.

108. Patricia Margaret Zieman Hughes, "Questionnaire," 12.

109. Alaine Barrett Baines, "Questionnaire," 13.

110. See Eileen Morris, "Your Home-and-School Faces a Crisis," *Chatelaine* (Nov. 1955): 11–13.

111. Between 1947 and 1962, for example, the United Church established 2000 new churches. See Mary Anne MacFarlane, "A Tale of Handmaidens: Deaconesses in the United Church of Canada, 1925 to 1964" (MA thesis, OISE/University of Toronto, 1987), 80.

112. Doris McCubbin, "How to Live in a Suburb," *Chatelaine* (March 1955): 35.

113. See Frank Moritsugu, "The Amazing Don Mills," *Canadian Home and Gardens* (Dec. 1954): 13–19, 55–60, 68.

114. *Vancouver Sun*, 6 Jan. 1951.

115. "Thornhill Women Are Proud of Their Flourishing Nursery School," *The Enterprise* (Lansing), 19 April 1951.

116. "Parents Unite to Catch Man Molesting Children," ibid., 28 April 1955.

117. "1,000 Families Protest Isolation of Rexdale," *Etobicoke Guardian*, 13 Jan. 1955.

118. "Parents Protest Board Moving School Children," *The Enterprise* (Lansing), 2 June 1955.

119. D. Smith, "Don Mills Memo," ibid., 7 Oct. 1954.

120. "Subdivision Problems Cause Angry Mothers to Storm Council Meeting," *Etobicoke Press*, 19 April 1956.

121. Montreal West suburbanite 1, "Questionnaire," 6.

122. Mildred Fox Baker, "Questionnaire," 14.

123. Surrey, BC, suburbanite 1, "Questionnaire," 14.

124. Betty Marrs Naylor, "Questionnaire," 14.

125. Toronto West suburbanite 1, "Questionnaire," 15.

126. Jasper Place, Alberta, suburbanite, "Questionnaire," 14.

127. For one of the few discussions of these critics in Canada, see Rutherford, *When Television Was Young*, esp. chap. 1. For a provocative assessment of the connection between fears about mass society and the maintenance of masculinity, see Barbara Ehrenreich, *The Hearts of Men* (Garden City, NY, 1983).

128. Published in New York in 1963.

129. Wallis, "Suburban Experience," 23.

130. See Richard Roe, "I'm Sending My Wife Back to Work," *Canadian Home Journal* (April 1954): 4–5, 98; Jean Pringle, "How I Broke Out of Solitary Confinement," *Chatelaine* (May 1948): 34; Beverly Gray, "Housewives Are a Sorry Lot," *Chatelaine* (March 1950): 26–27, 37; Isabel T. Dingman, "A Widow Writes an Open Letter to Wives," *Chatelaine* (June 1954): 20–21, 34–35, 37; Dr. Marion Hilliard, "Stop Being Just a Housewife," *Chatelaine* (Sept. 1956): 11, 90; Patricia Clark, "Stop Pitying the Underworked Housewife," *Maclean's* (19 July 1958): 8, 37–38; Jane Hamilton, "Housewives Are Self-Centred Bores," *Star Weekly Magazine* (22 Aug. 1959): 38, 45.

131. Published in New York in 1951. The quote is from page 76.

132. H. Garner, "You Take the Suburbs, I Don't Want Them," *Maclean's* (10 Nov. 1956): 30.

133. Dr. A. MacLeod, "The Sickness of Our Suburbs," *Chatelaine* (Oct. 1958): 23.

134. Ibid., 94–95.

135. See Robert Olson, "What Happened to the Suburb They Called Crestwood Heights?" *Maclean's* (12 Oct. 1957): 24–25, 34–36, 38. The strength of this legacy can be seen in the incorrect identification of Crestwood Heights as Don Mills in McGahan, *Urban Sociology in Canada*, 187.

136. Committee of Inquiry into the Design of the Residential Environment, *Report* (Ottawa 1960), *Journal of the Royal Architectural Institute of Canada* (May 1960): 186.

137. Ibid.

138. "R.E. Sutton Censures Story of 'Carefree' Life at H. Creek," *The Enterprise* (West Hill), 25 Oct. 1956.

139. "There Is No Joy in Highland Creek," *Globe and Mail*, 23 Oct. 1956; "Professor's Report Creates Furor," *The Enterprise* (West Hill), 25 Oct. 1956; and "Letters to the Editor," 1 Nov. 1956.

140. Clark, *Suburban Society*, 6.

141. Ibid., 4.

142. Ibid., 224.

143. Ruth Drysdale, "What Our Readers Say about Suburbia," *Chatelaine* (Jan. 1959): 50.

144. Mrs. J.M. Telford, ibid., 53.

145. Contacts with these women, 32 as of 15 June 1991, are part of an ongoing effort to get in touch with as many women as possible from different types of suburbs in different regions of the country. These women are asked

to specify how they wish to be identified, whether anonymously, by community, or by name, and their choice is reflected in the footnotes to this article. After the completion of a manuscript now entitled "Home Dreams: Women and Canadian Suburbs, 1945–60," these research materials, with certain restrictions on their use, will be deposited in a public archive.

146. Etobicoke suburbanite 1, "Questionnaire," 17.
147. Mildred Fox Baker, "Questionnaire," 17.
148. Metro Toronto suburbanite 1, "Questionnaire," 17.
149. London, Ontario, suburbanite 1, "Questionnaire," 17.
150. Niagara-on-the-Lake suburbanite 1 to author, 10 May 1991.
151. Marjorie Bacon to author, 6 April 1991.
152. Toronto West suburbanite 1, "Questionnaire," 17.
153. Wallis, "Suburban Experience," 27.

Article Thirty-Two

Fatherhood, Masculinity, and the Good Life During Canada's Baby Boom, 1945–1965

Robert Rutherdale

Family historians examining the baby boom years may find it difficult to establish the relationships between how the period was represented and how it was actually experienced. Popular depictions of family life, whether in film, print, or radio or through the new medium of television, projected images usually designed to appeal to wide audiences. While actual experiences varied enormously — in rural and urban settings, among families that were poor or wealthy, newcomer or settled — commercial and popular representations of family life tended to displace reflections of reality with those of an ideal, or constructed, norm. Regardless of local, ethnic, or class differences, mainstream depictions disseminated through the most powerful channels of communication often reflected the aims of consumerism: to create imagined familial contexts for products associated with household formation and consumption. Since the commodification of family life in mass media and advertising helped to promote a very real surge in goods and services consumed by baby boom families, we might expect some distance between images and realities in family life throughout the baby boom years. Conventional depictions of white, middle-class conjugal families served to smooth the edges of a more complex reality at a time when manufacturers and service suppliers competed for increased markets created by unprecedented levels of household formation.[1]

Given their tendency to homogenize family life, hegemonic representations during the baby boom can, nonetheless, provide evidence of shifting tastes, preferences, styles, and values within a commercial mainstream, something often quite distinct from the actual experience of subgroups in Canadian society as a whole. Notions of the ideal, what was expected in the "normal" family, can also influence how a period is remembered, a pattern I encountered frequently while gathering the life stories of men who were fathers in the 1950s and early 1960s.

Source: Robert Rutherdale, "Fatherhood, Masculinity, and the Good Life During Canada's Baby Boom, 1945–1965" from Journal of Family History, 24, 3 (July 1999), pp. 351–73, copyright © 1999 by Sage Publications Inc. Reprinted by Permission of Sage Publications, Inc.

How were the activities of the home handyman, the father on vacation with his family, the baseball coach, or the backyard barbecuer considered masculine in the memories I collected and in samples of journalism typical for the period? The gendered norms delineated in such texts can help us assess for the baby boom generation of husbands and parents what researchers have increasingly approached as evidence of masculine domesticity in histories of fatherhood generally.[2]

The concept of masculine domesticity was first used by Margaret Marsh to describe the adoption of family- and home-centered practices among fathers responding to suburbanization and among the expanded sectors of middle-class men in the wage economy.[3] As a cultural invention, its rise coincided with urban and industrial growth that stretched back well into the nineteenth century. As preconditions, three structural factors permit the emergence of masculine domesticity: family incomes sufficient for a middle-class standard of living, daily work schedules that permit fathers of companionate marriages to return home on a regular basis, and sufficient family living spaces that permit recreational space both inside the home and in the immediate neighborhood. Masculine domesticity was not real feminism but can be best understood as the particular ways men acted within roles associated with home life, from active parenting to household maintenance. It was, as Marsh sees it,

> a model of behavior in which fathers would agree to take on increased responsibility for some of the day-to-day tasks of bringing up children and spending their time away from work in playing with their sons and daughters, teaching them, taking them on trips.

A family man would more often spend his evenings with his wife rather than with his "male cronies."

> While he might not dust the mantel or make the bed except in exceptional circumstances, he would take a significantly greater interest in the details of running the household and caring for the children than his father was expected to.[4]

In American contexts, Marsh traces shifts toward the "domestic man" between mid-century and 1915, while Robert L. Griswold, in *Fatherhood in America*, examines the more family-centered roles that mostly middle-class fathers assumed as part of the new fatherhood of the 1920s.[5]

Part of this study is based on oral histories collected from thirty-four fathers and grandfathers living in Prince George and Abbotsford in the province of British Columbia, men who fathered baby boomers during the 1950s and 1960s. Prince George is centrally located in the northern interior, a timber-rich region that remains heavily dependent on forest product industries. Pulp production began in the early 1960s, drew thousands of young families to the area, and stimulated continued growth in the city from fewer than ten thousand in the mid-1950s to more than fourteen thousand a decade later, before population levels surged in sharp crests toward eighty thousand in the mid-1990s. Growth took place in tandem with the opening of each of three pulp mills and brought with it increased demands for local services. Expanding local infrastructures, from schools and hospitals to shopping and recreational centers, were crucial for newcomers, especially for younger families establishing themselves in the city's new suburban developments. While the timing of Prince George's postwar modernization coincided with trends on both sides of the Canada–U.S. border, it was more intense than most areas and affords an attractive place to study family life on a resource-based "job frontier:" It was, simply put, a city of newcomers, especially during the baby boom.[6]

Population growth in the Abbotsford area, located in the Fraser Valley farm belt, was less dramatic, reflecting the continued importance of agriculture in the region, supplemented by new produce-processing plants and growth in agricultural suppliers.[7] An influx of newcomers throughout the baby boom was nonetheless significant there as well. The 1951 census recorded

15,108 people living in Matsqui, Sumas, and the village of Abbotsford, now amalgamated as a single municipality. By 1966, the figure had jumped to 23,398, a gain of 54.9 percent.[8] Many of the narratives I collected were, of course, concerned with some aspect of household formation, from accounts of marriage and childbirth to how new family homes were acquired or built, in either locale.

This study begins in a time when the idealization of home life can be partly explained as something that had been denied to so many for nearly an entire generation. As Doug Owram has stated in his study of Canada's baby boom, the "idea of home thus had very powerful connotations by the end of the war, ranging from material comfort to renewed relationships, to peace itself." This "romanticized and idealized vision of family," he suggests, was a natural human reaction to years of disruption.[9] Since rising economic prosperity and household formation characterized the period, representations of leisure and consumption in particular were selected as key aspects of historical shifts in masculine domesticity during the postwar era. Forms of masculine domesticity associated with consumption and leisure were intricately connected to significant changes in household demography and to changing family practices.[10]

Relationships between consumption, gender, and household formation can only be partly understood by focusing on the roles played by wives and mothers in the home and marketplace. Veronica Strong-Boag, for example, has considered the conflicts that Canadian women experienced between domestic and paid labor demands that point to part of a larger picture of the gender/power relations shaping how families divided their incomes and time and how they constructed social roles based on sexual difference.[11] Even if attention remains focused on women's domestic roles in postwar homes, the rapid rise in consumption since the late 1940s reflected a host of family practices that intersected with the gendered experiences and responses of fathers as well as of their partners. This work leads us to consider parallel segments of masculine behaviors during the postwar boom years. Widening our consideration of postwar consumerism to include fathers and domestic masculinity as a cultural response — in particular, to consider the preferences and practices of fathers as consumers of goods and services applied to family leisure — can help us gain a broader picture of changes in family life brought about by the economies and culture of postwar consumerism.

The tendency to see mothers at home and fathers at work can obscure the relevance of fatherhood as part of family life. Owram is somewhat guilty of this in suggesting that domestic leisure was dominated by stay-at-home mothers, while fathers remained on the margins, though he notes that their roles as recreational leaders expanded considerably. "The anti-authoritarian views of family life and the accentuation of the sexual division of labour," as he put it,

> meant that children could expect a full-time camp counselor, leisure coordinator, and chauffeur in Mother. Father was present only in the evening and on weekends, but he was much softened when compared to the foreboding figure of Victorian times. Fathers too were supposed to be pals, to take an active part in the world of children and leisure. Thousands of part-time hockey and baseball coaches around the nation testified to the power of this social role.[12]

Although only coaching is mentioned directly here, an important part of our understanding of fatherhood at this time needs to be broadened to consider how fathers refashioned their domestic roles during the period.

What Griswold refers to as an "ideology of breadwinning" among fathers continued to shape gender relations and define their "sense of self, manhood and gender" during the baby boom as in other periods.[13] But the objects and activities on which disposable incomes were spent increased, and new patterns of masculine domesticity emerged. How evidence of this survives as oral histories of fatherhood and family leisure and how it was represented in the print media became a focus for my fieldwork and sampling of the journalistic discourse of the period.

Although breadwinning roles remained a central and defining characteristic of fatherhood, an inquiry directed at how print media depictions and self-representations of fatherhood intersect with experiences of a real past, of cultural ideals shaped by higher consumption levels, can also shed light on what forms masculine domesticity assumed in the period. Fathers too expressed themselves at home, at play, on vacation, and as spouses and parents in pursuit of family or community recreation. And these roles left their own discursive patterns, which survive in memory; in the photographs, illustrations, and advertising copy that circulated during these years; and in popular journalism concerned with family life at that time.

APPROACHES TO THE PRINT MEDIA AND TO THE LIFE STORIES OF FATHERHOOD

In 1955, as the midpoint of the baby boom approached and the dramatic upswing in postwar consumption had become well established, journalist Fred Bodsworth published a general interest piece in *Maclean's* magazine, Canada's most popular English-language weekly, called "The Best Way to Take a Holiday." While it seemed timely and appropriate as an entertaining how-to segment on family automobile camping, replete with statistics on its sudden popularity, it also presented a father's perspective on family adventure and masculinity. After championing its economy (just $2.08 per day for each family member!) and the cohesion it could bring to "team" members, Bodsworth added something, somewhat tongue in cheek, that we might take more seriously, "though I might be a fool for revealing it," as he put it.

> It's a wonderful thing for male prestige. It puts the male back in his traditional role as provider and protector. If you are one of those husbands who bungles every household job and finally stands back humiliated while your wife finishes, you need to take her camping. Setting up a camp looks tough to a woman — to her it belongs with carving-a-home out of the wilderness — but it really isn't that tough at all. In fact, it's a lot easier than mending a leaky faucet, but don't let her find out. Those primitive skills like fire lighting will impress a woman much more than coming home from the office with news that your Whatzit sales are thirty-eight percent higher than the same month last year. For it is one of life's great injustices that, while Man has become thoroughly civilized, Woman still admires him most in a thoroughly uncivilized back-to-nature role.[14]

This depiction, with its ironic portrait of the incompetent father at home or the playful gender-based rivalry between young parents, seemed partly embedded, at least with respect to the possibility of male assertiveness, in family adventure. Like the idealization of home that both wives and husbands engaged in at this time, the idealization of recreation embraced its own mythology, much of which intersected with masculinity and consumption. If not entirely part of the "father's world," family outings depended in part on fathers making that world possible. Finding the good life, on vacation, in tents, boats, cottages, on trains, and even aboard new flights to Europe or some sunny destination, was portrayed in the print media, and in the oral narratives I have recorded, as an important aspect of manful assertiveness.

The style and content of popular journalism that dealt with fatherhood at this time often harmonized with other media messages and images of ideal male parenting. This is particularly true of advertising, considered here as a useful indicator of normative or idealistic depictions designed to appeal to targeted consumers. As generic, commercial forms of representation, images of ideal consumption may have served as models of family life in particular historical contexts, but by no means should they be equated with lived experience. Like Bodsworth's anecdotal account of the family camp out, advertising images in mass-circulating magazines simply suggest how readers were expected to conceive of objects or practices not as reality but as symbols of desire.[15]

A similar point can be made for the use of oral history. As Elizabeth Tonkin has argued, oral narratives are not directed solely by the researcher and the teller but are better understood as cultural constructions embedded in the many norms and ideals that societies create. This "multivocality" of memory is arguably its most significant characteristic. Strictly speaking, as Tonkin notes, oral narratives usually develop as dialogues between researchers and subjects. Many factors shape their construction, and their structures, as she states, are "not reducible to the separate component contributions" of either researchers or their subjects.[16] As a meeting ground between the individual and society, oral histories of fatherhood offer rich sources that transcend individual experience or self-representation. Narratives of fatherhood roles tend to be rooted in languages that also uncover conventional portraits of the ideal man as father, husband, parent, worker, companion, and so on, and the origins of those very ideals need to be historicized.

Memories of fatherhood experiences, usually construed by the teller as individual and unique, tend to be situated within a normative sense of fathers' roles, something researchers should be wary of as both problematic and potentially useful. In generating stories in languages derived from values, attitudes, and beliefs that appeared to be predominant at the time, therefore, the men I interviewed drew self-portraits that can be situated within a more significant collective past. Although many fathers believed that they had led self-directed lives or had formed their opinions independently, I chose to assess memories of fatherhood for both internal and comparative consistencies that suggested societal and cultural influences.[17] From colorful colloquialisms to crisp metaphors, shared and seemingly popular tropes often suggested how certain masculinities were deployed and inscribed in the culture of a previous generation.

Such evidence could be generated at any point in the interview; however, the following questions (introduced toward the end of each session) often provided the best opportunities: "What did you think was important about being a father and why'?" "What did you like/dislike most about it?" "What made a 'good' and a 'bad' father in your day?" "How were you the same as (and different than) your father?" "Did you know other fathers well?" "Did they influence you?" "What worked out well for you as a father?" and "If you had the chance, what would you do differently?" Interviews were tape-recorded and generally required two to three hours to complete. Two fathers participated in follow-up sessions and, for comparative scrutiny, four wives/mothers and two grown children were interviewed separately. These, however, proved superfluous to my main interest in the subjective reconstruction of fatherhood through life stories. Questioning strategies were designed to educe autobiographies that placed narratives in the context of each subject's life cycle.[18] Special attention was also paid to gendered experiences. How, for example, was labor in their childhood families divided between parents? Were brothers and sisters required to do the same or different chores? Portraits of the subjects' own fathers were then developed, conveying impressions of sentiment, power, and the distribution of work in childhood homes.

Recent work in Canada and elsewhere has shed light on how gender relations within families accommodate the demands of work both inside and outside the home.[19] This was often expressed in the narratives I collected concerning sentiments fathers laid claim to, especially when the men I interviewed spoke of the love and respect they had held for their wives as homemakers or when they recalled the need to divide their productive tasks or how they came to be divided. As Raphael Samuel and Paul Thompson suggest, life stories, including those of fathers, can "become a vital document of the construction of consciousness, emphasizing both the variety of experience in any social group, and also how an individual story draws on a common culture."[20] The culture of fatherhood, like other human experiences constructed through generational transmission, both creates and relies on its own sense of the past.

MASCULINITY, FAMILY ADVENTURE, AND THE GOOD LIFE

What Bodsworth called the "best way to take a holiday" leads us to a favorite subject among the men I interviewed: family recreation. Many accounts of vacations placed fathers at the center of constructing some material part of their exercise, if not their occurrence, as a realized aspiration. The precise length of boats and trailers used, the intricacies of cottage construction, and in many cases, the sheer necessity of providing for an annual family trek ran through several narratives. "That was a must — was a holiday every year, somewhere," as Adam Edwards put it.[21] "We bought a small, fifteen-foot trailer, and I had a sixteen-foot boat," David Robson said.[22] "Well, we always . . . " Bob Crawford recalled, "we bought a trailer. Bought a twenty-five-foot Nash way back . . . around '55, '56."[23] "I had a thirty-five horse," Ed Ralston remembered. "It was big enough for the small boat that I built . . . Lotta fun building. Just as much fun as riding it!"[24] Robson's fifteen- and sixteen-footers, Crawford's twenty-five-foot Nashua, and Ralston's thirty-five horsepower outboard were part of a pattern of narrating life stories in androcentric terms.

Self-portraits of family manhood that combined prudence and foresight with the items used in carving out a stake in the good life surfaced repeatedly, both in the oral histories I recorded and in many images of masculine domesticity depicted in recreational advertising. "Here comes Summer!" announced one advertisement for Johnson outboard motors: "be ready with a new quiet Johnson Sea-horse." Featured was an illustration of a man and woman, presumably husband and wife, pulling into a dock with a neat cottage in the background, as a youngster accompanied by a dog ran down to greet them. "Superb engineering and design" in this engine were touted as something that could help make for the "happiest summer ever!"[25] However idealized recreational consumption became, memories of summer were often expressed in gendered terms that included having fun with an outboard motor. "So we'd go to Cultus Lake, and places like that," Jim Black recalled. "We had a new ten horsepower outboard, which put the boat to a very good pace."[26]

It would be a mistake, however, to place fathers at the center of vacation planning and organization in all depictions, whether in print media or in memory. The new masculine domesticity of the baby boom celebrated companionate marriage as the model. And nothing was to be more cooperative, at least as a cultural ideal, as planning the family vacation. By 1963, *Chatelaine* magazine tapped into a well-established industry when it ran a feature in its July issue titled "Family Camping," the "New 'In' Way to Holiday." Listing a plethora of products as the "basics you'll need" to take along, the article urged consumers to accumulate an astonishing array of products for extended outings.

> EXTRAS, for comfort and fun, could range from our 15-foot Fiberglass Dover outboard, with seats that flatten into beds, to the tiny Optimus kerosene stove for indoor cooking. Also handy, 128-ounce Thermos cooler; battery lantern with red flasher signal; small plaid cooler for picnics; transistor radios, one with a shoulder strap and one deluxe model with a short wave band.

Other suggestions included a seven-inch television and a windup razor. Getting away from it all, in part, seemed to mean bringing it all with you. Special recipes for mothers as "camp cooks" were included and readers were advised to "remember, outside appetites appreciate a generous cook."[27]

Yet throughout the baby boom years, many popular representations of the family vacation put fathers in the driver's seat when it came to domestic roles that extended beyond the confines of home. "My work," Joseph N. Bell explained in a *Maclean's* article that ran in August 1957, "frequently sends me on . . . trips, and we feel that, when opportunity permits, the kids should enjoy this broadening influence too." After mention was made of some half-million gas stations, fifty thousand motels, and half a trillion miles of car travel in North America each year, Bell pointed to what he saw as a "curious anomaly." The automobile, "which takes us increasingly away from home, at the same time provides an effective aid to family unity and education. For our family, the car has brought a closer association than seems possible in any other way." As a parent on vacation, Bell seemed to step into a highly involved role as a father, stating that parenting on the road is "just a matter of planning, patience, and psychology once you learn how children think on wheels."[28]

Traveling in the family car also became a central part of how vacations and even weekend outings were remembered by many of the fathers I interviewed. "Course in the summertime," Ron McGregor recalled, "we'd go down to Osoyoos" among other places. "We used to go down to Seattle, Portland, and Long Beach," he said, adding "we used to do a lot of camping."[29] "When the kids were older," Wayne Davis recounted, "we went back to the Prairies. They all went along then." Davis marked those memories with his first new car: "It was in 1965 when we had the first new vehicle we had—a '65 Dodge station wagon, one of those small ones. Took a tent along, and the boys slept in the tent and we slept in the station wagon."[30] Some narratives depicted a sense of adventure with the father in control while the children were thrilled by the scenery along highways, many of which were new or under construction. "The first time we went up the old highway, y'know, the canyon, the kids were scared as hell, 'cause it wasn't wide like it is now," Drew Jackson remembered. "They hid under a blanket on the back seat 'cause you looked right down, y' know, scared as could be."[31]

Casual weekend drives, with dad at the wheel, became a part of family leisure as well. "Sometimes," Ed Ralston noted, "just on a Saturday afternoon, we'd pack up and go for a drive, and then on the way home stop for a hamburger."[32] The car also changed how young parents went to the movies. When asked how free time with the family was spent, for instance, Wayne Davis said,

> Well, go to the movies, we used to. There used to be the drive-in at Chilliwack. You could take small kids in there. . . . You didn't have to worry about babysitting. It was usually movies that would appeal to the kids, as well as us. There used to be one movie down towards Langley, a drive-in down there we went to. And there was one over in Mission, a drive-in, so that's where we did most of our movie-going.[33]

"The exploding ownership of automobiles," as Owram has also noted,

> brought a new possibility. . . . The family could pack itself into the car and herd off to the drive-in, where peanuts, popcorn, and toys could keep the kids amused. 'Bring the Children . . . Come as You Are' was the way one drive-in chain enticed families in 1953. Double features often catered to families by showing a children's movie first; when that was finished, the kids would, parents hoped, drift off to sleep in the back seat.[34]

Masculine domesticity in its many facets included hobbies, sometimes depicted in pursuits of rising cost as well as popularity. "In the era of the forty-hour week," Shirley Mair noted in 1962,

> most workers spend another eighty hours eating, sleeping, grooming and commuting. What's left—forty-eight hours each week—is pure leisure and at a very conservative estimate Canadians are spending three billion dollars a year to outfit themselves for hobbies with which to occupy their leisure.

Although fathers were not the sole consumers in this burgeoning market, from Mair's list of pastimes it seems clear that masculine pursuits were driving most sales to unprecedented levels. "Some radio-controlled model plane hobbyists will spend $600 to get one plane air-borne.

In Canada, five million dollars worth of plastic and wooden modeling kits, ranging in price from twenty-five cents to $200, were sold last year."[35]

Voluntary time spent in coaching, scouting, and other service to youth groups involved fathers in communal parenting roles that extended the time spent with one's children and peers and provided a structure for fathers to participate actively in their children's socialization.[36] On this level, fathers' involvement in community-based parenting can be approached as a set of activities that regulated masculinity for male parents and served to inculcate appropriate forms of recreation within local, community-based parameters. Memories of being in loco parentis, in particular, appeared to involve transmitting principles observed at home to groups of boys from the community.

Throughout the two decades following the war, historical and local circumstances brought an urgency, often acute, to communal parenting, which affected both fathers and mothers. The baby boom, the housing shortage, and rising service and recreational expectations all contributed to putting facilities under stress. Pressing requirements for the new families that poured into cities like Abbotsford and Prince George had to be met, and fathers, as community members, were frequently called on to help as volunteers. As Charles Thompson of Abbotsford recalled, "The community was starting to grow and they needed, y'know, a number of [Boy Scout] troops:'[37] A local professional with good organizational skills, Thompson served on the planning board for Scouts in the Fraser Valley during the movement's rapid growth in the 1960s. In Prince George, Ken Wilson explained how participation in scouting skyrocketed during his years as an organizer at the local and, later, provincial levels.[38]

Coaching too combined a growing need for organized youth recreation with the desire of many fathers to take a more active part in their children's recreation. Advertising images of fathers as expedition leaders also emphasized stalwart men well equipped for masculine adventure in the new era of automobile travel and outdoor recreation. "Long time between quarts, now that I'm using Quaker State," one dad declared as he stood behind his open station wagon as his grinning son knelt in the back with fishing rod cases beside him. The father stood tall and proud, dressed in hiking boots and an outdoor hat with one hand on the open door and the other poised as if to make his point. Masculine domesticity included popular depictions of fathers consuming products that made such outings possible: "Pure Pennsylvania Grade Crude Oil, the world's finest, is super-refined in special ways to make it best for today's engines," this advertisement proclaimed. "Proved superior in every test, in the engine laboratory and on the highway. Try it!"[39]

Father-and-son relationships, especially in hobbies or in outdoor recreation, celebrated a significant aspect of masculine domesticity. Pepsi Cola ran an advertisement in May 1962 with a full-page photograph of a father and son, the boy holding a model airplane while the father held a bottle of Pepsi above copy that read, "Thinking young is a state of mind."[40] One Maclean's cover in February 1957 featured a boy and his dad, presumably dreaming of summer, as they examined a sailboat in a boating store, while others could be seen through the window clearing snow on the street outside.[41]

In many ways, common, everyday practices associated with fatherhood changed dramatically with the economy and with patterns of domestic consumption. Relatively high employment, rising wages, and both the demand and supply of new products associated with recreation, including big-ticket items such as boats, motors, and trailers, all changed what fathers did with their families during their free time. So did television, and so did the weekend or evening chores associated with maintaining the exterior of family properties.

While the arrival of television was an event for the whole family, fathers played a major role in purchasing and installing (or at least overseeing the installation of) the first models. Several spoke of how they managed to get clear reception, despite warnings against buying too soon before transmission stations were set up in their areas. "At the time," Bob Crawford recalled,

> we had a heck of a job getting the guy to bring it. He said, "Well there's just no way you could ever get any reception there. You're too darn low. And there's the mountain on the south of you so that . . . "— yeah. But anyway, he brought it over and they stuck up a temporary television aerial, up on top of the roof, and turned it on. And cripes it just boomed in! King [the nearest station], King was — he said, "It's coming in better than we can get in Mission." So that's how I got the first television set.[42]

For some fathers, becoming one of the first in the neighborhood to own a television set seemed a matter of pride. "We were the only ones in the neighborhood" who owned a set, Ron McGregor recalled. "And all the neighborhood kids used to gather at our place to watch TV. Yeah, I think we were one of the first ones."[43] "We were the first ones in Clayburn to have a television set," Crawford claimed.[44] Once the sight of rooftop antennas became fairly commonplace, fathers easily felt the urge to keep up with this stage of household consumption. "Probably because our friends had them, I guess;' David Robson conceded, he decided to buy one too. "One of these things you gotta keep up with." Like other family members, Robson, a devoted baseball fan, soon found himself spending part of his leisure time in front of the new box.

> Another thing, y'know, was pretty intriguing was the World Series, y'know. Like, you'd listen to the World Series on the radio for years. And then, all of a sudden, well like, when you listen to the radio you imagine what people look like. And now you could see them on TV. It was, it was a big deal to watch.[45]

Like the family car, television sets were a consumer item that fathers took an active part in using as well as in acquiring. Family living spaces that included a television could, at times, be redrawn in gender terms when it came to who watched what. While the whole family might watch a variety of shows, sports programming, including such favorites as *Hockey Night in Canada*, ensured the reconstituting of spectator sports in family homes. Fathers were the prime targets of advertisements sponsored by Canada's leading brewery and petroleum companies.[46]

To approach how household spaces were occupied and used by family members in gendered terms requires consideration both of the interior and exterior property, which in memory and in advertising images represented entirely different domains. Fathers uniformly recalled that they "took care of the yard," particularly when it came to the heavier chores of cutting the grass, raking the leaves, or maintaining the house exterior. Since a significant portion of such tasks was indeed carried out by men as home owners and as consumers, advertising was constructed to match certain products with certain images of masculine domesticity as a cultural ideal.

Masculine domesticity in this period was often portrayed and recalled as a manful assertion of material success directed toward domestic consumption and leisure. Whether in tales of family men in outdoor settings, in expatiations on the number of feet of lake frontage acquired or boat length or horsepower at their command, or in the many advertisements associated with family vacations, the appeal of home ownership, and other forms of family-centered leisure, fathers cast themselves in memory as they had been cast in the print media of their day: as central figures in the provision and enjoyment of the good life. A wide range of advertisements encouraged fathers to participate in family-based consumption, particularly in purchases associated with home maintenance and family-centered leisure. They typically portrayed fathers in active, even creative roles within domestic settings. But they continued to define gendered boundaries through manful forms of recreation and household work within the family circle. Such images supported the expectation that fathers would spend time with their families but in a consumer-based culture that celebrated manliness and postwar consumption in prescribed contexts, from the backyard grass cutter to the vacation traveler.

For the most part, memories of fatherhood during the baby boom seem profoundly influenced by the tastes and values of a comparatively acquisitive period in history. In some cases, however, fathers referred to aspects of their parenthoods in terms of unfavorable, disadvantaged childhood experiences that they strove to overcome. Some drew contrasts between what they remembered as tough, rugged, or even abused childhoods and the measures of success they managed to gain as fathers. Built around notions of self-made men, such narratives might seem in keeping with the usual stories of material advance, of gains fathers proudly recounted that they had achieved for their families in contrast to the circumstances, rooted in the depression, of their own childhoods. But their broader implications, that a contented masculine domesticity did not come easily for some or that their actual experiences of fatherhood differed markedly from fatherhood's most popular images, leads us to consider contradictions in these life stories that challenged the myths of contented domestic masculinity circulating in the print media of that time.

CONFRONTING MYTHS OF HAPPINESS AND SUCCESS

Signs of negative or ambivalent experiences were not uncommon during my fieldwork. Markers, for instance, of fixed gender regimes in marital relations, apparently rooted in male breadwinning, cropped up regularly during interviews.[47] Next to often detailed narratives of working in paid employment, for instance, stood many deprecating, androcentric references to spousal housework. "No, she didn't work," one stated. "She was just a housewife, with the kids."[48] Another maintained that his marriage partner "didn't work. When she had the two children she didn't have a job besides. . . . She just looked after the children and socialized and looked after the house."[49] Some accounts, though rarely explicit in this regard, seemed indicative of patriarchal boundaries. "A father first of all," Sam Taylor said, "has to be a leader. Somebody has to be a leader. If the woman is a leader, the other men laugh at the father, don't they? . . . 'Oh hell, you know who wears the pants in the family,' y'know.' As Taylor developed his stories, often vivid in detail, a deeply rooted yearning to overcome his own father's influence became apparent. He also presented another common theme, his life overcoming scars of the hardships of the depression, and in his case, scars his own father left.

Taylor described his father's drunkenness, how he abused him and ultimately abandoned the family altogether. One poignant memory stood out.

> I can remember running all the way home from that school up here all the way downtown to tell my father that I stood second in the class of forty kids. I never stood second, up that high. And this one girl beat me because she was the school inspector's daughter and got teaching at home and so on. But I stood second. And that big idiot stood there and said, "What the hell good is that, standing second? If you can't stand first, don't stand anything." I expected a dime, or a reward, or a kind word. And then he walks away. I never worked in school after that. He took it out of me in grade five! At eleven years of age, or ten I think it was at the time. He knocked it right out me, right there.

He also said,

> My father was very, very bigoted. And it rubbed off on me. It rubbed off on my brothers. And I had quite a struggle with it all my life. Everybody was a Chink, or a Wop, or a Kike, or a Jap, or a Jew, or y'know, or Bohunk, and y'know. You find yourself repeating those things you see. And now you've got to, oh. It's a struggle. It's a struggle, y'know. It really is. And — your

impressionistic age — you repeat your elders. You don't learn from your little brother or little sister. You learn from ones above you, don't you? This is why it's so important for fathers to be a good role model for their children. And I think I've coped very well.[50]

A sense of pride accompanied his fatherhood memories of minor hockey, when he served as a coach and league organizer. Taylor praised the Canadian Amateur Hockey Association for making him a better coach. He described how he and "a few other dads" got together to reorganize minor hockey in the city and got far more boys into it, while underscoring the difficulty he had appreciating that competition could prevent kids from simply having fun. The son who recalled his father's crushing words, "If you can't stand first, don't stand anything," described a scene behind the bench when one of his young players pleaded with him to ease up on his incessant criticism. "I'm trying to do what you say, coach, but I'm only an eleven-year-old boy."[51] Taylor recalled trying to come to terms with his proper role, given the poor example set for him, and claimed that he succeeded in the end, developing in coaching a sense of fairness that applied equally to his six boys at home.

In Prince George, Roy Gibson remembered his community service as a scoutmaster. His leadership philosophy seemed influenced by a depression-scarred childhood. Gibson's father died when he was nine, leaving him, with his sister and mother, nearly destitute on a small farm in Saskatchewan. As he explained, "I . . . shouldn't say that I felt I was head of the family, but I felt a responsibility. . . . There was no asking for it — put it that way." Later he said, "Growing up in the depression — there was no room for arguing." "You had to look at the facts and take what was there and go from there." Both as a father and a scoutmaster, Gibson felt that self-reliance, more than anything, had to be instilled in boys. He remembered hoping that his hard lessons might serve as their best example. "You were in a corral," he said of his childhood,

> and within that corral certain things had to be done and that was all there was to it. Whether you liked it or not, you did it. Now that's — my years with the scouting movement — this is what I put across to the boys.

His three sons all joined Scouts. He claimed to show no favoritism, but more significantly, he suggested close parallels between the values he espoused as a parent and those he upheld as a scoutmaster. When asked in a general way what good fatherhood was all about, Gibson replied,

> teaching the kids to paddle their own canoe. . . . If you can't take care of yourself nobody else is going to. And yet, they're teaching in the schools, and this I found very difficult to counter in scouting — I was teaching one set of values and they would see another set. And they couldn't make up their minds as to who was right. And it was the older group of boys, basically after they left my group — where they went in Venturers — where you'd see it finally, where the boy made up his mind. And he fell off the fence one way or another. And, if they fell off on my side of the fence, OK, they're still around the community. They're members of the community — some of the others are in jail![52]

David Robson remembers how little time his father was able to spend with him during the depression when he managed a large mill in Mission. "He gave his life to the damn mill," Robson remembered with some bitterness. He also recalled how he became much more involved in parenting and in communal parenting as a baseball coach. "I coached kids' softball for quite a few years," he added later.

> I coached Jimmy a little bit. . . . But Frank, the youngest one, another fellow and we coached their team for about five or six years, I guess, as they went through the ranks. Took them over to Vancouver Island to a tournament one year. It was a way to be with your kids, y'know.[53]

Virtually all of the men I interviewed could draw sharp contrasts, particularly in material terms, between how they grew up and how their children did. "When I grew up, y'know," Robson also recalled,

> like kids didn't have much, y'know. I mean you were lucky to have a set of clothes and a pair of gum boots and — you never had toys. Most kids eventually got around to having a bicycle, which was quite a — y'know if you could have a bicycle when you were in public school, it was quite a feat.[54]

A sense of having done far better than their own fathers could have dreamed of was common-place. "He was a man," Ron McGregor said of his father, "that was, I think, he was very disappointed in life because of his inability to get steady employment, y'know."[55]

Contrasts between the hardships of growing up in the depression and the opportunities they enjoyed as breadwinners in the 1950s and beyond often served to structure their life stories. While most baby boom fathers struggled to get a foothold in the vastly improved economy of the 1950s, their successes as wage earners became a central part of their self-concepts and contributed to the generational perspectives they held of being self-made men. To be sure, they did "do better" than their fathers had. "I think," said Drew Jackson, "I did a lot better than I ever thought I would, y'know."[56] As Ed Ralston put it,

> Right after the war things were not exactly that rosy. But we still, well actually once I moved to the Island, had a regular job, and I could budget better and certain things you could do, look after the family quite well, we didn't really suffer there — we could earn enough money to build a house and get things set and all that.[57]

The rising expectations of the period, something uniformly recalled, were generally cast in contrast to the scarcity of toys, bikes, and other recreational goods available to most children before the war. "But when I get back to my own kids," as Robson put it,

> well I mean they all expected a bike at a certain age. And you might get them a little bike, and then get them a bigger bike and so on, y'know, which is an expensive way to do it. . . . I remember Judy having Barbie dolls, and some of the kids having machine guns and stuff like that, y'know, playing cowboys and Indians.[58]

And yet, what these fathers provided in material terms, as markers of their manhood and respectability, contributed to a sense of change that was not without its critics.

The panacea of television-centered home entertainment wore thin for at least one *Maclean's* contributor that same year. While new sets were still being turned on for the first time across Canada, Vivien Kimber described how she and her husband, Earl, attempted to turn back the clock, at least temporarily.

> Last October my husband and I finally worked up enough courage to try an experiment: we took the TV set out of the house for a month, just to see how (or maybe I should say "if") we and our five children would get along without it.

They were seen, Kimber suggested, as having taken a rather extreme step. "Most of our friends were aghast. You'd have thought we proposed to stop eating for a month instead of just moving a piece of furniture." The television, it seemed, had been their children's pied piper. "In spirit," Kimber related,

> they were wherever the TV set took them. Many a time Earl would come home from work, shout "Hi, kids!" and have to step over the mob watching TV to get to his chair. Only when the program was over would they turn around and look at him in astonishment and say, "Hello, Daddy! When did you come home?"

In many ways, Kimber's account offered readers an idealized portrait of her family's "vacation," their return to a place, however mythologized, of lost, home-centered leisure. Expressed in terms of a fun-seeking, provisional resistance to a television-centered present, set here in 1957, Kimber recounts her husband joining her in restoring those traditional pastimes, as they imagined them, that may have seemed outmoded by the distractions of consumerism in general and television in particular. "Earl and I," she said of their plans, "spent that first evening mapping out what promised to be an exciting vacation at home." She implied, as well, that the recentering of their family away from television helped to secure a more active and, for the children, recognizable place for Earl as their father. The rest of their adventure, predictably enough, recounted how reading, crafts, and other hobbies made their way back into their family routines until they could take back television on their own terms.[59]

By this time, however, the new leisure of the 1950s, much of which was focused on family recreation and consumption, especially weekend consumption, gave popular commentators and columnists openings for the occasional piece of satire. "But I *DON'T WANT* the new leisure," Robert Thomas Allen of *Maclean's* wrote in one of his many humorous columns of the mid-1950s. "I happened to be watching one of my neighbours the other day," Allen stated with his usual satirical lilt,

> as he bored a hole though his window for a TV lead. This took him about five minutes. Then he wandered around with his power drill; looking for something else to drill a hole through, gave up, and slowly worked his way back into the house like a kid on summer holidays trying not to step on cracks in his sidewalk.

Through comical vignettes of flustered fathers in the midst of backyard barbecues, failed workshop projects, and endless reels of home movies, Allen lampooned the new leisure from the ironic pose of a suburban father who witnessed one man sending barbecue smoke into his neighbor's backyard while his counterpart responded by blasting back Beethoven's Fifth Symphony from his new hi-fi. Backyard antics seemed to have become something a satirist could easily poke fun at, as masculine forms of domestic consumption thrust new hobbies into the hands of fathers now plagued by weekend leisure. As Allen put it facetiously,

> Sometimes I think we should all just go back to being frankly bored over the weekend in a stiff, dull, motionless way — the way we used to be on Sunday when we were kids; when we couldn't hammer, saw, shout, or get dirty.[60]

Whether at home engaged in some new hobby or behind the wheel on the annual family vacation trek, fatherhood and leisure attracted the humorist's gaze in these and other pieces with such titles as "How to Train for Your Vacation." "Want a bang-up holiday?" Stuart Trueman asked in the spring of 1955, "then start getting ready now. There's a good chance the family will get so sick of you they'll leave you home." After recounting some fanciful larks, such as deliberately slamming on the car brakes or walking barefoot in the rain to simulate the discomforts of travel, Trueman appealed to dads facing the upcoming summer to

> kindly line up on the right and for the small sum of two dollars you have my new Happy Holidays Kit, complete with informative leaflet, one phonograph record of ocean waves and seagulls (on the opposite side, truck horns honking and a New Year's Eve party in full progress) and three live mosquitoes.[61]

Popular images of the bungling dad, haggard by hobbies or by the amusing discomforts of family travel, stood alongside those of the stalwart adventurer, the proud home owner, and the generous benefactor — the family man who had secured his family's place in the consumer markets and recreational opportunities of a profoundly acquisitive period. This brings us back to connections between representations and reality that opened this discussion. As a revamped cultural ideal, masculine domesticity took shape in the first two decades following the Second World War within an expanding consumer economy that privileged fatherhood by valorizing a variety of home-centered and family-based pursuits from the backyard gardener to the Scout leader or hockey coach. Respectable manhood translated into companionate marriages and involved parenting, not something altogether new. But it also placed new emphasis on gendered aspects of consumption and recreation that moved fathers toward the center of many family- and leisure-based activities, from acquiring the first television to buying a new car or boat or taking the family on vacation. And this did reflect very real and significant shifts in disposable income and domestic buying patterns compared to those of the previous generation.

Oral histories certainly indicate the strong influence this had on shaping memories of being a father at this time. Time and again, stories associated with material accomplishment, especially acquiring objects of leisure and recreation, recalled their acquisition as central to a manful father's role in providing for a dependent family. In uncovering how family men of this era construct their memories, my fieldwork points to the prevalence of shared experiences in a culture of consumption, that fathers knew what was expected of them as prosperous parents and saw much of it as an opportunity to assert themselves as successful family men, not just conform to behaviors designed for particular target markets. The men I interviewed often structured their life stories on perceptions of manful success as home owners, automobile and recreational vehicle owners, television buyers, and cottage builders — accounts of self-made men who lived and worked to afford the ideals of family consumption. Even men's participation in community activities such as scouting and coaching came from gains in leisure time and prosperity after the war. In this way, postwar consumerism survives today as a dominant influence in the social construction of memories connected to masculine domesticity.

Certain memories of fatherhood and the occasional article or column could point to a more complex and ambiguous past or even to critiques of consumer-based family life. Some men who succeeded as fathers in material terms also cast their stories of self-made success within larger narratives that began with abused or deprived childhoods. They recalled spending their years as younger parents trying to overcome the scars of childhood or apply its hard lessons. Many questioned whether gains made in material terms had actually helped spoil the next generation. Moreover, some popular authors lampooned the new leisure, questioned the hold that television had on family recreation, or highlighted concerns that consumer fetishes had become an affront to their sense of days gone by, however pastoral or mythical that sense might have been. At times, the happy blend of masculine domesticity and consumption was challenged, though hardly overthrown. At last, after years of depression and war, able to acquire houses, cars, boats, and cottages, items often beyond the means of their own fathers, the men who shared their life stories with me equated certain forms of consumption with manful assertiveness and lay claim to it in representing themselves as breadwinners and as family men. This appears to have left a profound mark on the masculinity of family men in the generation preceding our own. Future research on fatherhood in this period might do well to consider the influence of consumerism on depictions and histories of masculine domesticity and ideal fatherhood in near-contemporary settings.

NOTES

1. As Doug Owram states in his study of the baby boom in Canada, "The decentralized medium of television perfectly matched the growing suburban needs of families with young children." See Doug Owram, *Born at the Right Time: A History of the Baby Boom in Canada* (Toronto: University of Toronto Press, 1996), 89. For a comprehensive study of the impact of television on popular culture in Canada, see Paul Rutherford, *When Television Was Young: Primetime Canada, 1952–1967* (Toronto: University of Toronto Press, 1990). On stereotypical portraits of the

postwar suburb, see Joanne Meyerowitz, "Introduction: Women and Gender in Postwar America" in *Not June Cleaver: Women and Gender in Postwar America, 1945–1960*, ed. Joanne Meyerowitz (Philadelphia: Temple University Press, 1994). Meyerowitz also cites several simplistic portraits of women and family life in recent college textbooks.

2. For an extended discussion of masculine domesticity, see Ralph LaRossa, *The Modernization of Fatherhood: A Social and Political History* (Chicago: University of Chicago Press, 1997), especially 31–34. LaRossa draws distinctions between *masculine domesticity* and *domestic masculinity*, more than a matter of semantics as he sees it. Like Margaret Marsh, LaRossa sees domestic masculinity as "doing domestic activities in a masculine way." To illustrate, he points to doing child care and housework in a manly or virile manner. Fathers taking their sons hunting for the sake of instilling the masculine virtues of aggressiveness, competitiveness, and dominion over nature would be exhibiting masculine domesticity. So would fathers who did housework the macho way, or the military way, or the corporate capitalist way, since all of these imply either a manly disposition or a manly world.

   This, LaRossa argues, should be separated from domestic masculinity, since "domesticating someone who is masculine is something else." It is, but I might add, a caveat. Boundaries between masculine domesticity and domestic masculinity may be drawn for a particular context but may shift across time. Fathers may do certain things around their families that they see as appropriate for a man, such as reading their children to sleep, that their fathers would not have done. Casting masculine domesticity and domestic masculinity as separate strands for fathers, in other words, tends to essentialize masculinity in fatherhood rather than see it as historically plural and variable.

3. Margaret Marsh, "Suburban Men and Masculine Domesticity, 1870–1915," *American Quarterly* 40 (June 1988): 165–86, and "From Separation to Togetherness: The Social Construction of Domestic Space in American Suburbs, 1840–1915," *Journal of American History* 76 (September 1989): 506–27.

4. Marsh, "Suburban Men and Masculine Domesticity," 166.

5. Robert L. Griswold, *Fatherhood in America: A History* (New York: Basic Books, 1993), especially chap. 5.

6. On demographic change, modernization, and local family/community formation during the baby boom era in Prince George, see Robert Rutherdale, "Approaches to Community Formation and the Family in the Provincial North," *BC Studies*, 104 (winter 1994): 103–260. By 1961, for instance, nearly 80 percent of the city's family dwellings had been built since the end of the Second World War. Figures for the province (51.5 percent) and country (44.2 percent), while much lower, reflect significant corresponding jumps in housing starts (p. 124).

7. On the agricultural industry in the area, which embraced in this period Matsqui, Sumas, and Abbotsford, see John Warnock, "Agriculture and Food Industry," in *After Bennett: A New Politics for British Columbia*, ed. Warren Magnusson et al. (Vancouver: New Star Books, 1986), and David Demeritt, "Visions of Agriculture in British Columbia," *BC Studies* 108 (winter 1995–96): 29–59.

8. *Census of Canada*, vol. 2 (Ottawa: Statistics Canada, 1971), 112, Table 2, Population of Census Subdivisions, 1921–1971, 92–702. Figures combine Abbotsford, Matsqui, and Sumas.

9. Owram, *Born at the Right Time*, 12.

10. On the federal government's role in promoting household improvement prior to 1940, see Margaret Hobbs and Ruth Roach Pierson, "'A kitchen that wastes no steps . . . 'Gender, Class and the Home Improvement Plan, 1936–40," *Histoire Sociale/Social History* 21 (May 1988): 9–37. For the post–World War II period, see Veronica Strong-Boag, "'Their Side of the Story': Women's Voices from Ontario Suburbs, 1945–1965," and Joan Sangster, "Doing Two Jobs: The Wage-Earning Mother, 1945–1970," in *A Diversity of Women: Ontario, 1945–1980*, ed. Joy Parr (Toronto: University of Toronto Press, 1995): 46–74 and 98–134, respectively. On women and appliance shopping, see Joy Parr, "Shopping for a Good Stove: A Parable about Gender, Design and the Market," also in *A Diversity of Women*.

11. Veronica Strong-Boag, "Home Dreams: Women and the Suburban Experiment in Canada, 1945–60," *Canadian Historical Review* 72 (1991): 471–504 [see this volume], and "Canada's Wage-Earning Wives and the Construction of the Middle Class, 1945–60," *Journal of Canadian Studies/Revue d'études Canadiennes* 29 (1994): 5–25.

12. Owram, *Born at the Right Time*, 85–86.

13. Griswold, *Fatherhood in America*, 2.

14. Fred Bodsworth, "The Best Way to Take a Holiday," *Maclean's*, June 11, 1955, 34.

15. A diverse field, advertising continues to attract new research. T. J. Jackson Lear's *Fables of Abundance: A Cultural History of Advertising in America* (New York: Basic Books, 1994) provides a comprehensive and useful survey.

16. Elizabeth Tonkin, *Narrating Our Pasts: The Social Construction of Oral History* (Cambridge: Cambridge University Press, 1992), 67. For perceptive commentaries on the multifaceted nature of authoring in oral history, see Michael Frisch, *A Shared Authority: Essays on the Craft and Meaning of Oral and Public History* (Albany: State

University of New York Press, 1990). See also Paul Thompson, *The Voice of the Past*, 2d ed. (Oxford: Oxford University Press, 1988), and Luisa Passerini, "Mythbiography in Oral History," in *The Myths We Live By*, ed. Raphael Samuel and Paul Thompson (London: Routledge, 1990), 52–53. Recent studies of subjectivity in oral reconstructions of the past abound. In addition to some excellent examples in Samuel and Thompson, and poignant discussion of its many aspects in Tonkin, see Ronald J. Grele, ed., *International Annual of Oral History, 1990: Subjectivity and Multiculturalism in Oral History* (New York: Greenwood, 1992). For a recent application set in British Colombia, see Alexander Freund and Laura Quilici, "Exploring Myths in Women's Narratives: Italian and German Immigrant Women in Vancouver, 1947–1967" *BC Studies*, 105/106 (spring 1995): 159–82.

17. Although the age range of this sample spans just over a generation, all reared offspring were infants, adolescents, or young adults during the mid-1940s to the end of 1960s. This variety permitted consideration of historical change during an extended period of comparatively high fertility and economic growth. Of the thirty-four men interviewed, five were professionals, fourteen were managerial, and fifteen were laborers or in semiskilled positions during their paid working careers. While all had children who grew up in the 1950s and early 1960s, the oldest was born in 1909 and the youngest in 1943.

18. This approach proved most natural in establishing a coherent flow between informants and myself. As well as establishing a useful biographical context, many developed self-portraits that connected aspects of their lives by the end of the interviews that might otherwise have seemed scattered or without foundation. Martine Burgos and J. P. Roos offer useful analysis of this tendency in "Life Stories, Narrativity, and the Search for the Self," *Life Stories/Récits de vie* 5 (1989): 27–38.

19. Canadian historians are beginning to turn their attention to family and gender studies situated in the 1950s and 1960s. In addition to recent work by Veronica Strong-Boag, cited above, see Joy Parr, *The Gender of Breadwinners: Women, Men and Change in Two Industrial Towns, 1880–1950* (Toronto: University of Toronto Press, 1990). On the experience of men, work, and family life, see Mark Rosenfeld, "'She Was a Hard Life': Work, Family, Community and Politics in the Railway Ward of Barrie, Ontario 1900–1960" (Ph.D. thesis, York University, 1990). In addition to Robert L. Griswold's work, also cited above, recent studies in the United States include Elaine Tyler May's *Homeward Bound: American Families in the Cold War Era* (New York: Basic Books, 1988). An extensive sociological literature on American fathers and family life is also available. See, for example, Mirra Komarovsky, *Blue Collar Marriage* (New York: Random House, 1962); Barbara Ehrenreich, *The Hearts of Men: American Dreams and the Flight from Commitment* (Garden City: Anchor, 1983); Scott Coltrane, *Family Man: Fatherhood, Housework, and Gender Equity* (Oxford: Oxford University Press, 1996); and Kathleen Gerson, *No Man's Land: Men's Changing Commitment to Family and Work* (New York: Basic Books, 1993). See also Thomas Dunk, *It's a Man's World: Male Working-Class Culture in Northwestern Ontario* (Montreal: McGill-Queen's University Press, 1991) for an anthropologist's interpretation of male culture in Thunder Bay, Ontario. While conceptual approaches to family and gender now constitute a diverse and growing literature, R. W. Connell's *Gender and Power: Society, the Person and Sexual Politics* (Stanford: Stanford University Press, 1987) and *Masculinities* (Cambridge: Polity, 1995) provide useful theoretical overviews.

20. Samuel and Thompson, *The Myths We Live By*, 2.

21. Interview 32, March 12, 1997 (all informants are identified by pseudonyms).

22. Interview 26, March 5, 1997.

23. Interview 25, March 4, 1997.

24. Interview 31, March 11, 1997.

25. *Maclean's*, April 30, 1955, 38.

26. Interview 22, February 26, 1997.

27. Jessie London et al., "Family Camping . . . New 'in' Way to Holiday," *Chatelaine*, July 1963, 30–34.

28. Joseph N. Bell, "We Travel with Our Kids — And Like It," *Maclean's*, August 3, 1957, 25.

29. Interview 27, March 5, 1997.

30. Interview 29, March 6, 1997.

31. Interview 30, March 11, 1997.

32. Interview 31, March 11, 1997.

33. Interview 29, March 6, 1997.

34. Owram, *Born at the Right Time*, 152.

35. Shirley Mair, "Form Chart on Hobbies: Who's Out in Front in the National Scramble to Find a Newer and Better One," *Maclean's*, January 27, 1962, 19–31.

36. On scouting and organized leisure, see Owram, *Born at the Right Time*, 100–101.

37. Interview 23, March 3, 1997.

38. Interview 5 (pt. 2), March 28, 1995.

39. *Maclean's*, April 2, 1955, 84.

40. Ibid., May 19, 1962, 49.
41. Ibid., February 2, 1957, front cover.
42. Interview 25, March 4, 1997.
43. Interview 27, March 5, 1997.
44. Interview 25, March 4, 1997.
45. Interview 26, March 5, 1997.
46. For a critical examination of the arrival of television in Canada, see Paul Rutherford, *When Television Was Young: Primetime Canada, 1952–1967* (Toronto: University of Toronto Press, 1990).
47. In her work on cultural perception and gender, Sandra Lipsitz Bem has developed an approach to the production of meaning that can be useful when interpreting interview transcripts. Self-awareness and awareness of others, formed and expressed through language, are constituted in gendered terms. In particular, Ben considers masculine consciousness as the product of gendered perception, a cultural lens that distorts, reconfigures, or even omits the presence of women in male-dominated societies. This pattern of thought, or androcentrism, has long dominated men's perceptions of who they are, how they act, and how the world of their experience has evolved. How androcentric perspectives shaped the language, concerns, topics, and assumptions of each life story proved significant in this study, whether fathers discussed parenting, breadwinning, leisure, or consumption. See Sandra Lipsitz Bern, *The Lenses of Gender: Transforming the Debate on Sexual Inequality* (New Haven: Yale University Press, 1993).
48. Interview 8, March 22, 1995.
49. Interview 3, March 6, 1995.
50. Interview 4 (pt. 1), March 9, 1995.
51. Interview 4 (pt. 2), March 15, 1995.
52. Interview 7, March 22, 1995.
53. Interview 26, March 5, 1997.
54. Ibid.
55. Interview 27, March 5, 1997.
56. Interview 30, March 11, 1997.
57. Interview 31, March 11, 1997.
58. Interview 26, March 5, 1997.
59. Vivien Kimber, "What Happened When We Threw Out Our TV Set," *Maclean's*, March 30, 1957, 17–62.
60. Robert Thomas Allen, "But I *DON'T WANT* the New Leisure," Ibid., November 27, 1957, 27–64.
61. Stuart Trueman, "How to Train for Your Vacation," Ibid., April 16, 1955, 48.

Topic Fourteen
Quebec/Canada

Prime Minister Pierre Trudeau reaches to shake hands with Premier René Lévesque of Quebec. The two were at the meeting of First Ministers in Ottawa, November 2, 1981.

Quebec–Canada relations since Confederation in 1867 have largely centred on attempts to find a *modus vivendi* between French-speaking and English-speaking Canadians in an effort to unite the country. This has coincided with the rise of a French-Canadian and an English-Canadian nationalism that have often been in conflict with each other, thus working against the creation of a common Canadian identity.

The differences and intensity of disagreement became particularly noticeable starting in the 1960s with the rise of a Quebec nationalism committed to the separation of the province from Canada. This renewed nationalism coincided with changes within the province of Quebec that were so far ranging that a journalist baptized the new era the "Quiet Revolution." Internally, the Quebec government enacted laws aimed at democratizing political life and increasing the role of the state. It took over jurisdiction of education and health, areas previously controlled by the Roman Catholic Church. It assumed control over the economic and cultural spheres, with the nationalization of hydro-electricity and the establishment of a Ministry of Cultural Affairs respectively. It entered the area of education, enacting a number of language laws designed to strengthen the French language within Quebec by regulating whose children could attend English-language schools in the province. Externally, the Quebec government worked with other provincial governments to overhaul the British North America (BNA) Act so as to establish a new division of power between the federal and the provincial governments. As well, since 1960, successive Quebec provincial governments, even federalist administrations, have fought for greater autonomy from the federal government, including "special status" among the other nine provinces that would in essence recognize Quebec as an autonomous political state within Canada. In the case of sovereignist governments, the aim has been to create a sovereignty-association between Canada and Quebec and, failing to achieve that, independence of Quebec from Canada.

Beginning in World War II, a heightened effort began among English Canadians to find an identity to complement, or counter, a growing Quebec nationalism, and to replace a British-Canadian nationalism, as the formerly close ties with Britain began to weaken. The federal government in Ottawa consciously contributed to the shaping of a new English-Canadian identity through such organizations as the Bureau of Public Information and the National Film Board, both established in 1939, the Wartime Information Board in 1942, and, in the postwar era, the Royal Commission on National Developments in the Arts, Letters and Sciences, (popularly known as the Massey Commission since Vincent Massey chaired the Commission), established in 1949, in hopes of achieving a "pan-Canadian" identity. But the difficulty became finding something unique within English-speaking Canada that all could accept as part of their identity, and that would equally satisfy French Quebeckers.

The following two articles examine Quebec–Canada relations in the context of a growing nationalism among the two founding groups in the period since World War II and in the context of the Quiet Revolution. In "The Quieter Revolution: Evolving Representations of National Identity in English Canada, 1941–1960," José Igartua argues that ethnic-based representations of Canadian identity within English-speaking Canada, one based on the British connection and tradition, the other emphasizing Canada's "bi-racial" nature, persisted in the 1940s and 1950s, but then suddenly disappeared in the 1960s. These were replaced by a belief in the 1960s in "limited identities," based on regional, ethnic, or gender identity as opposed to a national identity, and in the 1970s in a "civic" form of nationalism.

In "Québec-Canada's Constitutional Dossier," Alain-G. Gagnon uses a historical-institutional approach to federal-provincial relations as a context for understanding Quebec–Canada relations. He divides his study into three periods: the historical foundations from 1760 and the establishment of the first constitutional order up to 1960; the period of transition from 1960 to 1982; and from 1982, the year of constitutional repatriation without the consent of Quebec, to the present time. He examines events from the Quebec perspective in an attempt to explain the context for Quebec referendums, the rise of separatist or sovereignist parties both within Quebec and within the Canadian Parliament, and current Quebec–Canada tension.

What are the various representations of national identity that emerged in English Canada in the years between the beginning of World War II and the beginning of the Quiet Revolution? Have constitutional changes since 1960 strengthened or undermined Canadian federalism and a sense of Canadian nationalism?

For the topic of English-Canadian nationalism and identity with Britain, see Carl Berger, *The Sense of Power: Studies in the Ideas of Canadian Imperialism, 1867–1914* (Toronto: University of Toronto Press, 1970). Phillip Buckner examines the continued association of English-Canadian identity with Britain into the 20th century in "The Long Goodbye: English Canadians and the British World," in Phillip Buckner and R. Douglas Francis, eds., *Rediscovering the British World* (Calgary: University of Calgary Press, 2005), pp. 181–207. On the topic of national identity and the Massey Commission, see Paul Litt, *The Muses, the Masses, and the Massey Commission* (Toronto: University of Toronto Press, 1992). A valuable study of identity and Canadian history is Daniel Francis, *National Dreams: Myth, Memory, and Canadian History* (Vancouver: Arsenal Pulp Press, 1997); see as well the essays in Ramsay Cook, *The Maple Leaf Forever: Essays on Nationalism and Politics in Canada* (Toronto: Macmillan, 1971). An earlier but still useful study of the Canadian identity is W. L. Morton, *The Canadian Identity* (Toronto: University of Toronto Press, 1961). See as well Robin Mathews, *Canadian Identity: Major Forces Shaping the Life of a People* (Ottawa: Steel Rail, 1988), and the collection of essays in Association for Canadian Studies, *Canadian Identity: Region, Country, Nation: Selected Proceedings of the 24th Annual Conference of the Association for Canadian Studies* (Montreal: Association for Canadian Studies, 1998). On the historical roots of the Canadian identity, see David V. J. Bell, *The Roots of Disunity: A Study of Canadian Political Culture.* rev. ed. (Toronto: Oxford University Press, 1992). A useful look at English-speaking Canada is Kenneth McRoberts, ed., *Beyond Quebec: Taking Stock of Canada* (Montreal/Kingston: McGill-Queen's University Press, 1995). A collection of essays that looks at English-speaking Canada and its response to an independent Quebec is J. L. Granatstein and Kenneth McNaught, eds., *English Canada Speaks Out* (Toronto: Doubleday Canada, 1991). The memoirs of Keith Spicer, Canada's first commissioner of official languages, *Life Sentences: Memoirs of an Incorrigible Canadian* (Toronto: McClelland and Stewart, 2004) cast an interesting light on English–French relations in Canada in the last third of the 20th century.

For an overview of Quebec in the last half-century, see Kenneth McRoberts, *Quebec: Social Change and Political Crisis*, 3rd ed. (Toronto: McClelland and Stewart, 1988), and for the late 1960s and early 1970s, his *Misconceiving Canada: The Struggle for National Unity* (Toronto: Oxford University Press, 1997). In French, see Y. Belanger, R. Comeau, and C. Metivier, *La Revolution tranquille, 40 ans plus tard: Un bilan* (Montreal: VCB Éditeur, 2000). Other histories include Susan Mann, *The Dream of Nation: A Social and Intellectual History of Quebec* (Montreal/Kingston: McGill-Queen's University Press, 2002 [1983]), chs. 17–20, and Paul-André Linteau et al., *Quebec since 1930* (Toronto: James Lorimer, 1991). M. Behiels, ed., *Quebec since 1945: Selected Readings*, (Toronto: Copp Clark Pitman, 1987) contains useful articles and documents, as does Hubert Guidon, Roberta Hamilton, and John McMullan, eds., *Tradition, Modernity, and Nationhood: Essays on Quebec Society* (Toronto: University of Toronto Press, 1988). On the important topic of Quebec nationalism, see Ramsay Cook, *Canada, Quebec and the Uses of Nationalism*, 2nd ed. (Toronto: McClelland and Stewart, 1995). Alain-G. Gagnon, ed., *Quebec, State and Society*, 3rd ed. (Peterborough, ON: Broadview Press, 2004), and Guy LaForest, *Trudeau and the End of a Canadian Dream*, trans. Paul Leduc Browne and Michelle Weinroth (Montreal/Kingston: McGill-Queen's University Press, 1995) contain valuable essays on Quebec and Canada. For one historian's view after interviewing a number of historians, politicians, and contemporary commentators, see Robert Bothwell, *Canada and Quebec: One Country, Two Histories* (Vancouver: University of British Columbia Press, 1995).

On the Duplessis era, see Conrad Black, *Duplessis* (Toronto: McClelland and Stewart, 1977), and Richard Jones's brief overview in *Duplessis and the Union Nationale Administration*, Canadian Historical Association, Historical Booklet no. 25 (Ottawa: CHA, 1983). The opposition to Premier Maurice Duplessis in the late 1940s and 1950s is analyzed in M. Behiels, *Prelude to Quebec's Quiet Revolution: Liberalism versus Neo-Nationalism, 1945–1960* (Montreal/Kingston: McGill-Queen's University Press, 1985).

For a good overview of the Quiet Revolution, see Jacques Rouillard, "The Quiet Revolution: A Turning Point in Quebec History," in R. Douglas Francis and Donald B. Smith, eds., *Readings in Canadian History: Post-Confederation*, 6th ed. (Toronto: Nelson Thomson Learning, 2002), pp. 440–453. Also consult Dale C. Thomson, *Jean Lesage and the Quiet Revolution* (Toronto: Macmillan, 1984), and articles by Ramsay Cook in his collection *Canada, Quebec, and the Uses of Nationalism*, 2nd ed. (cited above). On the Parti Québécois, see Graham Fraser, *PQ: René Lévesque and the Parti Québécois in Power* (Toronto: Macmillan, 1985). Peter Desbarats's *René* (Toronto: McClelland and Stewart, 1976) reviews the life of the founder of the Parti Québécois. See also Lévesque's *Memoirs* (Toronto: McClelland and Stewart, 1986). On Pierre Elliott Trudeau, see Richard Gwyn, *The Northern Magus* (Toronto: McClelland and Stewart, 1980), and Stephen Clarkson and Christina McCall, *Trudeau and Our Times*, vol. 1, *The Magnificent Obsession* (Toronto: McClelland and Stewart, 1990), and vol. 2, *The Heroic Delusion* (Toronto: McClelland and Stewart, 1994).

Edward McWhinney analyzes the early stages of the constitutional crisis in *Quebec and the Constitution, 1960–1978* (Toronto: University of Toronto Press, 1979), and in his *Canada and the Constitution, 1979–1982: Patriation and the Charter of Rights* (Toronto: University of Toronto Press, 1982). On the post–1982 period, see Alan Cairns, *Charter versus Federalism: The Dilemmas of Constitutional Reform* (Montreal/Kingston: McGill-Queen's University Press, 1992). The aftermath of the first Quebec referendum and the patriation of the BNA Act are discussed in *And No One Cheered: Federalism, Democracy and the Constitution Act*, ed. Keith Banting and Richard Simeon (Toronto: Methuen, 1983). Philosopher Charles Taylor proposes an original analysis of French–English relations in Guy LaForest, ed., *Reconciling the Solitudes: Essays on Canadian Federalism and Nationalism* (Montreal/Kingston: McGill-Queen's University Press, 1993).

Among the many publications bearing on Meech Lake are Michael Behiels, ed., *The Meech Lake Primer: Conflicting Views of the 1987 Constitutional Accord* (Ottawa: University of Ottawa Press, 1989); Andrew Cohen, *A Deal Undone: The Making and Breaking of the Meech Lake Accord* (Vancouver: Douglas and McIntyre, 1990); P. Fournier, *A Meech Lake Post-Mortem: Is Quebec Sovereignty Inevitable?* trans. S. Fischman (Montreal/Kingston: McGill-Queen's University Press, 1991); and R.L. Watts and D.M. Brown, *Options for a New Canada* (Toronto: University of Toronto Press, 1991). Susan Delcourt's *United We Fall: The Crisis of Democracy in Canada* (Toronto: Viking, 1993) looks at the aftermath of the referendum on the Charlottetown Accord in 1992. John F. Conway's *Debts to Pay: English Canada and Quebec from the Conquest to the Referendum*, 2nd ed. (Toronto: James Lorimer, 1996) includes a chapter on the second Quebec referendum of 1995. Dominique Clift has translated the memoirs of Lucien Bouchard as *Lucien Bouchard, On the Record* (Toronto: Stoddart, 1994).

WEBLINKS

Royal Commission on National Development in the Arts, Letters and Sciences
http://www.collectionscanada.ca/massey/index-e.html

The digitized report and recommendations of the Royal Commission on National Development in the Arts, Letters and Sciences, chaired by the Honourable Vincent Massey.

Chapter XIX of the Royal Commission: The National Film Board
http://www.collectionscanada.ca/massey/h5-442-e.html

The National Film Board is the subject of this chapter of the Royal Commission on National Development in the Arts, Letter and Sciences.

The National Film Board of Canada
http://www.nfb.ca/atonf/organisation.php?v=h&lg=en

A detailed history of the National Film Board of Canada.

Pierre Elliot Trudeau
http://www.collectionscanada.ca/primeministers/h4-3375-e.html

A biography of Pierre Elliot Trudeau and some of his selected speeches.

René Lévesque
http://archives.cbc.ca/IDD-1-74-870/people/rene_levesque

A multimedia biography of René Lévesque's political life.

Bill 101
http://archives.cbc.ca/IDD-1-73-1297/politics_economy/bill101

A history of Bill 101 in Quebec as seen in CBC radio and television archives.

Official Languages Act
http://laws.justice.gc.ca/en/O-3.01/90080.html

Full text of the Official Languages Act as passed in 1985.

Clarity Act
http://laws.justice.gc.ca/en/C-31.8/33882.html

Complete text of the Clarity Act as passed by the Government of Canada in 2000.

Article Thirty-Three

The Quieter Revolution: Evolving Representations of National Identity in English Canada 1941–1960

José Igartua

INTRODUCTION

A common view[1] of Canadian[2] nationalism in the twentieth century depicts a slow and gradual evolution: first, an identification with British tradition and culture, then an affirmation of a 'new nationality' in the interwar period, a moment of glory during World War II, a slow succumbing to American influence in the 1950s, a self-questioning in the 1960s, and finally a deliberate reconstruction of national identity in the 1970s. Yet there are two difficulties with this common view. The first is that the historical processes by which the transformation of Canadian identity have occurred remain somewhat elusive. Second, the common view suggests that each of the phases it describes was marked by a dominant definition of Canadian identity. My purpose is to call into question the common view by drawing attention to the polymorphism of the views of Canada that were current in English-speaking Canada and by proposing a more complex sequence for their evolution.

Recent scholarship has been scarce on the issue of English-Canadian representations of Canadian identity. Attention has mainly been drawn to attempts made by some elements in the federal government in the 1940s and 1950s to reshape Canadian identity. W.R. Young has shown how, during the early years of the Second World War, the Wartime Information Board defined as its mandate the edification of a new national sentiment based on a social-democratic ethics.[3] Bourque, Duchastel and Harmony[4] have argued that during the post-war period the federal government appealed to a communal sense of citizenship to fashion a value system founded on egalitarian principles as a justification for introducing welfare programs. Litt has examined the efforts of the Massey Commission to develop a Canadian high culture as a resistance to the invasion of American-dominated popular culture.[5] But few investigations have gone beyond the view from Ottawa.

This paper argues that the common view as well as the recent research neglect to take into account the persistent affirmations of ethnic-based representations of Canadian identity that can be observed in the post-war period. Thus they fail to explain why these affirmations vanished from English-Canadian discourse in the 1960s. We have ignored a revolution even more quiet than Quebec's, a fundamental shift in English-Canadian representations of Canadian identity. This shift in turn conditioned the way in which other representations of national identity within Canada were going to be received by the English-speaking majority.

Two ethnic-based definitions of Canadian identity appear to have permeated political discourse. The first was the definition of Canada as a British nation. Its demise left an ethnic void in English-Canadian representations of Canada. The second major representation of Canadian identity based on ethnicity current in the 1950s emphasized the 'bi-racial' nature of Canada. This view became increasingly difficult to sustain in the 1960s, since recognition of the

Source: José Igartua, "The Quieter Revolution: Evolving Representations of National Identity in English Canada 1941–1960." Paper presented at a joint session of the Canadian Historical Association and the Association for Canadian Studies, St. John's, NFLD, June 8, 1997.

'equality of the two founding races' implicit in this definition of Canada would have required a substantial rearrangement of power within Canadian society. Thus in the early 1960s, it became impossible for Canadian nationalists to counter the concept of a "Quebec nation" with an ethnic form of "Canadian" nationalism, as this would implicitly admit the legitimacy of other forms of ethnically-based nationalism within the Canadian state. The only avenue open to Canadian nationalists was to reject ethnically based definitions of national identity. Since there was no other form of national identity acceptable to them, they had to define Canadian identity as a lack of identity. This constituted a discursive strategy that rejected self-recognition as a legitimate form of political discourse.[6] I would call this the *my name is nobody* posture, in which the concept of 'limited identities' became a defining characteristic of English-Canadian representations of the Canadian nation. A 'civic' form of nationalism was then proposed in the early 1970s. The very roots of civic nationalism lay firmly in British tradition,[7] which made it easier to represent as a 'superior' form of nationalism to counter the 'tribalism' of ethnic-based Quebec nationalism. However, this representation of the nation implicitly contained the same kind of ethical claim to superiority that representations based on the British character of the nation had once explicitly staked,[8] and we may find in this claim some explanation of its lack of appeal in Quebec society.

This paper is in the style of an exploratory essay rather than a research report. What I have just outlined is the general hypothesis with which I want to inquire into the evolution of representations of the Canadian nation in English Canada. I cannot offer a systematic demonstration of the hypothesis in this paper. All I can do at this stage is to indicate the set of questions which are shaping my inquiry, to explain the meaning I give to some key concepts, to indicate where I intend to look, and to offer an introductory exposition of the argument as it relates to the fifteen years between World War II and 1960.

THE FRAMEWORK OF THE INQUIRY

Concepts and Definitions

The questions which are shaping my inquiry concern the representations of national identity in English Canada and how these representations have evolved. I phrase the questions thus because I am not after a single, albeit elusive, English-Canadian identity. I don't believe national identities derive their meaning from some essential character of the nation. The literature on nationalism over the last twenty years has drawn attention to the historically constructed nature of nations and national identities. National identity is a form of collective identification, as are region, gender and class[9]. As such it possesses a number of attributes which have been codified by Charles Tilly as characteristic of public identities. The first is the *relational* nature of such identities. By this Tilly means that identities are located in "connections among individuals and groups rather than in the minds of particular persons or whole populations." Tilly summarizes what he calls the emerging view of public identities as "… not only relational but *cultural* in insisting that social identities rest on shared understandings and their representations. It is *historical* in calling attention to the path-dependent accretion of memories, understandings, and means of action within particular identities. The emerging view, finally, is *contingent* in that it regards each assertion of identity as a strategic interaction liable to failure or misfiring rather than a straightforward expression of an actor's attributes."[10]

Applying Tilly's characterization of public identities to national identity has a number of implications. First, it shows why it is futile to search for the essence of a national identity. Collective identities are not fixed attributes of groups, but are historical constructs liable to evolve as does the nature of the relations within and between groups which give rise to enunciations of identity. Secondly, Tilly's model suggests that identities are enunciated for specific reasons at specific times and for specific purposes. From this it follows that enunciations of national identity will not necessarily be coherent, either internally or over time. Thus it is important to understand the circumstances of such enunciations in order to assess their meaning. Finally, collective identities exist only at the cultural level, that is, as shared representations.

Next, it is important to clarify how I understand the concepts of 'nation,' 'national identity,' and 'English Canada.' A common usage of the word 'nation' in English-language Canadian historiography equates 'nation' with 'country' or 'state.'[11] Thus for instance Granatstein's et al., *Nation: Canada Since Confederation* seems to favour this usage, though its use of the term is occasionally ambiguous.[12] Other historians also give a political connotation to 'nation,' defining it as the locus of conflicts and power struggles among various segments of Canadian society or as a sham designed to hide these struggles.[13] I think neither of these definitions is appropriate to the historical understanding of 'nation.' The first usage seems to view the concept of nation as unproblematic, while the second appears to deny its historical significance. I prefer to follow Benedict Anderson's definition of 'nation' as an 'imagined community,' founded in a *belief* in shared characteristics, a shared past and the hope of a shared future. There are no tangible characteristics of nationhood that are shared by all nations. Instead, nations exist when communities believe in their existence. It follows that they have a historical, rather than an essential, existence: they can be born and they can die, when communities no longer believe in them.

Likewise, national identity, or the definitions which a community gives of itself as a national entity, are historically constructed and thus are liable to evolve over time. The historical question therefore is to discover why certain forms of national identity are born and why certain forms fade away. In the present case, for instance, I am particularly interested in the withering of the definition of Canada as a British nation and in the appearance of the definition of Canada as composed of 'limited identities.' I want to look at these questions not in a polemical manner, but from an ethnographic perspective.

But how can one apprehend 'national identity?' The only handle is to be found in *representations* of identity, that is, statements about what national identity is. These representations are inevitably going to be numerous and their contents will fluctuate according to the purpose for which the statements are made. The important point here, to recall Tillly, is that national identity is a cultural reality defined by shared representations and does not exist outside of these representations. Thus the obvious multifaceted, and *contingent* character of representations of national identity.

I must also explain what I mean by 'English Canada.' It is currently fashionable to state that there is no such thing, that it no longer exists. The argument against the existence of 'English Canada' is a relatively new one: it implies that the *ethnic* or the *cultural* definition of English-Canadian identity no longer has any meaning. This argument is part of current representations of national identity in Canada, which affirm that national identity is (or should be) based on 'civic' rather than 'ethnic' values. Whether ethnic or cultural definitions of Canadian identity still have currency is, of course, a matter for investigation. Yet one cannot deny that these definitions have existed.[14] One aim of my inquiry is to determine for how long and to what extent these definitions were imbedded in definitions of Canadian national identity. So I do not postulate the existence of an unchanging, essential 'English Canada.' For the purposes of my inquiry, I simply use the phrase 'English Canada' to refer to the communicational community, within the Canadian state, whose shared language was and is English. I would argue, following Benedict Anderson again, that this communicational community has existed since newspapers, the telegraph, and the railway ("print capitalism," in his phrase) have defined this communicational space. The focus is on language, rather than on ethnic or cultural origins, though a language of communication rests on the supposed sharing of cultural referents.

Finally, one may well ask, how widely *shared* are the representations which we may be able to identify through various sources? It is a difficult question to answer. One indication is repetition within the communicational community. Another may be occasionally found in opinion surveys, but these seldom phrase explicit questions about the definition of the nation.[15] We are therefore left to rely on the postulate that widespread repetition of certain representations of national identity indicates some form of acceptance of these representations in the population.

Sources

Representations of national identity can be generated for many reasons, and through various media. In order to focus the inquiry, I propose to draw a distinction grounded in the purpose of enunciation. There are first of all *explicit statements* designed to convince the audience as to the nature of national identity. These statements are often polemical and arise mainly in political debate. In the post-war period, a number of political issues have given rise to statements about national identity. The political debates of 1946 about citizenship, the flag, the national anthem, or the name to be given to the July 1st holiday (Dominion Day, Confederation Day, or Canada Day) are a good starting point. Among other occasions for explicit debate one may point to the work of the Massey Commission, the debate over the Diefenbaker Bill of Rights, the Bilingualism & Biculturalism Commission, and the debates over the Official Languages Act and over the Multiculturalism Act.

But there are also occasions where statements about Canadian identity are produced in an incidental manner, in arguments about other issues. These *incidental statements* about Canadian identity are intended to be non-polemical.[16] They are often adduced with the expectation that they are shared by the audience, that they reflect common opinion. For example, newspaper editorials about Empire Day, Victoria Day, Dominion Day, or even New Year's Day occasionally offer such statements about the nature of Canada. Other contexts for the enunciation of non-polemical statements about Canadian identity may include political events such as the retirement of a major political figure, the nomination of a new Governor-General, international crises in which Canada played a prominent role, major celebrations of Canadian achievements, etc. Incidental statements about Canadian identity may also appear, for instance, in pedagogical objectives for the teaching of Canadian history and geography and in the textbooks approved for such purposes.

Representations of national identity may of course appear in other types of discourse than the political discourse cited in the examples mentioned above. Scholarly discourse (e.g., history, political science, geography), as well as literature, art, and sport, [17] can serve as vehicles for the dissemination of representations of national identity. It would be a gigantic task to hunt down systematically all of these representations. I have decided to focus for the moment on political discourse since it appears to offer the most frequent and perhaps the most widely disseminated enunciations of national identity. Schools provide another important channel of dissemination, and scholarly investigations of curricula and textbooks indicate that this will be another fruitful area of inquiry.[18]

Political discourse is by itself a large universe. It is a discourse about politics, not simply the discourse of politicians. Within it one can include, besides the statements of politicians as reported in *Hansard* or in the press, editorials and other expressions of opinion in the press. There is no obvious way to gauge the prevalence of various representations of national identity within the population. We can only hope to be able to identify the more common expressions of national identity and focus our analysis on these. Some indication of the resonance which political discourse finds in the population at large can be provided by an examination of the results of public opinion polls, particularly those which can be submitted to secondary data analysis.[19]

THE EVOLUTION OF REPRESENTATIONS OF NATIONAL IDENTITY IN ENGLISH CANADA, 1941–1960

Let me now turn to a preliminary foray into post-war representations of national identity within the English-speaking communicational community of Canada. My aim is to propose a number of themes from the period's political history as worthy of attention.

The War-Time Effort to Construct a Canadian Identity: A Change of Ethics?

As far as I know, the first deliberate attempts to reshape the definition of Canadian identity occurred during World War II. In 1939, the federal government created the Bureau of Public Information, with the mandate to foster among Canadians (at least among English-speaking Canadians) a common sense of purpose. The Bureau was concerned with uniting the country in the fight against an enemy portrayed as "the antithesis of the real Canadian." To this end it focused on the country's role in the war and attempted to distinguish Canada's interests in the war from those of its allies. Finally, it stressed the need to integrate ethnic communities into the English-speaking majority and called upon the majority to accept members of these communities into a wider sense of 'Canadianism.' Radio as well as print were used to communicate this message of integration. [20]

But these efforts, concludes the student of Canadian war-time propaganda, William R. Young, were not very successful. The public was split in its attitude towards Great Britain: some considered that the British were sacrificing Canadian troops, while others defended the mother country. In 1940, anti-Nazi sentiment threatened to turn into anti-German sentiment and to put German Canadians at risk of witch hunts. Canadians on the West Coast were agitated by the presence of Canadians of Japanese ancestry, and these were forcibly relocated inland. All in all, government propaganda efforts were not able to overcome an ethnically based view of Canada and 'Canadianism' among the English-speaking population. Young cites a 1945 opinion poll in which "English Canadians continued to express dislike of all 'foreigners' and did not believe that citizens of an ethnically 'different' origin could indeed become 'good Canadians'.[21]

The federal government decided in 1942 to intensify its propaganda efforts and created the Wartime Information Board which absorbed the Bureau of Public Information. The new board was composed of leading civil servants such as Lester Pearson, Robert Bryce and Arnold Heeney. In 1943 it was put under the management of John Grierson, who had immigrated from Britain to Canada in 1938 to set up the National Film Board.[22] Before coming to Canada, Grierson had already reflected on the power of his medium of choice, film, to shape society and to inculcate social values.[23] For Grierson, the fight for democracy could only be a fight for a more equitable society, where social justice would entail economic security for the whole population. To him, this was the compelling argument in favour of the war effort. This message could be disseminated among the Canadian population by education, in particular by adult education through radio and discussion groups, and its reception gauged by the scientific method of public opinion polling.[24] The Wartime Information Board used public opinion polls to argue before the government that the population could only be motivated for the war effort by the promise of a better peacetime world, a 'people's world.'[25] One of its main defenders within the government was Brooke Claxton, Parliamentary Assistant to the Prime Minister, who easily equated this new 'people's world' with a Liberal view of the world.

Yet this 'social' view of what being a Canadian stood for did not receive an enthusiastic welcome within the federal Cabinet. Grierson's advocacy of 'central planning' was too much for some members of the Cabinet and in 1944 he was led to resign as manager of operations for the Wartime Information Board. Thereafter the Board's activities were scaled down and its influence in shaping a new definition of Canadian identity lessened. Though "Building a New Social Order for Canada" became the Liberal slogan in the 1945 federal election campaign, it appears to have been more an effort to steal the thunder from the Co-operative Commonwealth Federation (CCF) than to provide a well-defined social blueprint for the post-war period. The definition of Canadian identity promoted by the Wartime Information Board was founded upon the rights of citizens of all categories, but such a definition did not carry the day within the government or throughout the country. The Wartime Information Board, according to Young, "failed in the longer term to accomplish its original purpose of defining a non-political and popular sense of citizenship."[26]

The Ambiguous Nature of the New Canadian Citizenship, 1946

The political debate about the nature of Canadian identity continued in the year following the war. During the 1945 election campaign, Mackenzie King, at the urging of the new Secretary of State, Paul Martin, had promised Canadians to give the country the symbols of nationhood that were still missing, namely its own flag and its own citizenship status. A bill creating a Canadian citizenship was put before the House of Commons in the Fall 1945 session but died on the order paper. It was reintroduced the following Spring and was debated along with other symbolic measures, such as the design for a Canadian flag and the renaming of 'Confederation Day' into 'Canada Day.' Only the citizenship bill made it into law, after a long debate in Parliament and in the press at the heart of which were definitions of Canadian identity. The major feature of the Citizenship bill was to create the legal concept of Canadian citizenship; most of the other clauses of the bill simply codified existing legislation. Most importantly, the bill declared that 'a Canadian citizen is a British subject.'

Basically, two tendencies appeared during the debate about Canadian citizenship in Parliament and in the press. The most vocal tendency defined Canadians as British subjects. The upholding of this 'British' definition of Canadian identity was at the centre of the arguments invoked by the Progressive-Conservative Opposition in the House of Commons as well as by some newspapers in the country.[27] The sponsor of the bill, Secretary of State Paul Martin, was at pains to stress that Canadians would remain British subjects and that the bill did not change the nature of the relationship between Canada and Great Britain.[28]

Proponents of this definition of Canadian identity insisted upon the British tradition of freedom[29] and upon the ability of British immigrants to meld within Canadian society, being familiar with the language and political institutions of the country.[30] British subjects therefore should continue to be given preferential treatment in the process of obtaining Canadian citizenship and any clause in the legislation which would deny them this preferential treatment would be taken as an insult.[31] The British heritage of Canada would be threatened if obstacles were put to the influx of British subjects.

Inversely, some immigrants were judged to be incompatible with Canadian society, for their allegiance to Canada would forever remain doubtful. This was the case of Japanese immigrants or Canadians of Japanese ancestry. The distinction between those who were born here and thus were British subjects and those who came as immigrants mattered little to some Conservative M.P.s from British Columbia. They used the occasion of the debate on the citizenship bill to press the government to deport Canadians of Japanese ancestry or at least to prevent them from returning to the West Coast; one M.P. invoked the 'high Christian point of view' and called upon the Japanese to return to Japan.[32]

There existed, for these Members of Parliament, a definite ethnic hierarchy among Canadian citizens: British subjects (more specifically, British subjects of British ancestry) were at the top of this hierarchy, while Orientals were obviously at the bottom. Where French Canadians ranked within this hierarchy was not always clear: some Conservative M.P.s defined Canada as composed of two major ethnic groups, while others chose to recall what they considered the dubious loyalty of French Canadians during the two World Wars.[33] The 'two founding peoples' were not seen as equal in their devotion to Canada; one was clearly more 'Canadian' than the other.

It was impolitic for the Opposition and for newspapers which supported it to come out against the Citizenship Act. Who after all could refuse to call himself a Canadian citizen? Only the Conservative Member for Broadview, T.L. Church, did so openly.[34] For him there was no need for citizenship legislation. "I am a Canadian, but I also am a British subject. They are both the same and always have been." Church considered the bill the doing of republican elements within Canada. Kindred editorial writers with *The Globe and Mail* and the Ottawa *Citizen* [35] saw the Citizenship Act as part of a concerted assault by 'ultra-nationalists' (i.e., French Canadians) against the symbols and the traditions of the British heritage in Canada; this assault was also aimed at the flag and at Dominion Day. "Taken singly," wrote the *Citizen*, "or even collectively, these nationalist bills are of small consequence; contain little about which any adult mind needs to grow excited. What we dislike about them is what they show of the unseemly haste of certain people in this country, many of them very close to the Government, to rid Canada of anything suggesting the British connection."[36] Thus the lines were drawn. On one side were those who upheld the noblest ideals of British civilization. On the other were narrow-minded busybodies who were anti-British. At stake was the very definition of the country.

A second, very different view of Canadian identity was put forward during the debate concerning the citizenship bill. This second view was voiced mainly by western members of the House of Commons who belonged to the CCF.[37] Theirs was a definition of Canadian identity which included every citizen regardless of color, race, or religion. This 'civic' definition of Canadian identity was stated in their party platform.[38] All Canadians should enjoy the same rights regardless of how they became citizens. CCF Members denounced their Conservative colleagues who demanded the expulsion of the Japanese; they drew attention to the contradictions between their racist views of the Japanese and the universalist principles put forth by John G. Diefenbaker in proposing a Canadian Bill of Rights. The CCF Member for Saskatoon accused the Conservatives of racial pride and of wanting to enjoy a privileged status within Canadian society.[39] This viewpoint was supported by the *Winnipeg Free Press*, which accused Howard Green, the Conservative M.P. for North-Vancouver, of racism and fascism.[40]

These two competing views of what Canada was and of what it should be, the ethnic and the civic views, were skillfully used to defend the Citizenship Act. The government spokesman for the bill, Secretary of State Paul Martin, argued that the bill combined both views of Canadian identity. According to Martin, the Citizenship Act was designed to foster national sentiment, particularly through the clauses which prescribed for new citizens to be cognizant of the rights and duties of citizens and required them to swear allegiance to the Crown and to Canada. "The bill is designed to create a feeling of unity and of solidarity," argued Martin.[41] Yet the bill essentially reaffirmed an 'ethnic' view of Canadian citizenship by maintaining — and even increasing, under Opposition pressure — the privileges of British subjects in obtaining Canadian citizenship. "A Canadian citizen is a British subject" was the key phrase of the bill.

Even so, the citizenship bill revealed divisions within the Cabinet over the issue of Canadian identity.[42] The civil servant mandated to prepare the bill, Gordon Robertson, had underlined that the draft legislation made "as little change as possible" to the existing legal situation. "There is much to be said," he wrote his minister, "for retaining many of the traditional symbols of association that do not conflict or interfere in any way with the essentials of a separate personality and status for members of the Commonwealth."[43] Yet the Cabinet was unenthusiastic and required the reaffirmation of the status of British subjects for Canadians, without which it feared the bill would be defeated in the House of Commons.[44] This indicates the degree to which the 'ethnic' definition of Canadian identity was still shared within the two major Canadian political parties in the aftermath of World War II.

Twin Strands, 1945–1960: One or Two Races?

I would like now to turn to an exploration of the manner in which Canadian identity was represented from 1945 to 1960 in non-polemical discourse. This exploration rests on only two publications and is thus very much tentative in nature even though the publications claimed to have a national audience. Nevertheless, it points to the persistence of ethnic-based representations of national identity: the 'British' view of Canada on the one hand, and the 'bi-racial' view of Canadian identity on the other. These views were more common than the 'civic' view put forth by the CCF. The latter view did not gain much currency in English-speaking Canada before the 1960s.[45]

These two ethnic-based representations of Canadian identity shared a common element, however. This common element was that Canada remained an uncompleted nation. This theme foreshadowed the 'limited identities' of the 1960s, but contained a teleological implication absent in the latter phrase.

I have taken the Toronto *Globe and Mail*, "Canada's national newspaper," as the first source in my exploration. I have scoured its New Year, Empire Day, Victoria Day, and Dominion Day editorial pages to see what representations of Canadian identity were called forth on these symbolic occasions where " . . . a few carefully chosen platitudes . . . ," to quote the paper on one such instance, were the order of the day.[46] The *Globe*'s view of Canadian identity was perhaps best expressed in an editorial on 1 July 1950, entitled "Still a Land of Promise." It defined three major components of Canadian identity: the 'biracial' nature of the country, its belonging to the North American continent, and its British heritage.

> [Canada] has evolved a method whereby biracialism has survived by permitting its two major groups to retain the bases of their culture and yet to co-operate in the management of the country. It has succeeded in being North American without losing its identity in that of its larger and more powerful neighbor; and it has retained its British — and hence its European — connection even while developing an autonomy of its own. It has thus been influential in shaping the growth of the old Empire into the pattern of the new Commonwealth.

Of these three themes, it was the British tradition which most preoccupied the editorial writers on civic holidays. The importance of the British tradition, and the fear of its waning, were frequent topics of Victoria Day editorials. Almost every year, the *Globe and Mail* would reiterate the point. On the occasion of the visit of the Governor General, Viscount Alexander, to Toronto on 24 May 1946, the paper wrote:

> There is more than a little significance in the fact that the visit of Viscount and Lady Alexander coincides with the popular holiday of Victoria Day. No day in calendar recalls more clearly the Imperial association which time has not weakened, but made increasingly valuable . . . the holiday Friday will . . . to some extent make keener their [the people's] understanding of the meaning of the Crown as the bond between the nations of the Commonwealth.[47]

Already, however, according to the paper, Victoria Day was undergoing a transformation which was not wholly welcomed. "There has been a tendency in recent years to convert the day into a holiday to celebrate the Empire," the paper wrote on Victoria Day, 1946, but this tended to obscure the achievements of Canadian and British Victorians, to which the attention of schoolchildren should be directed.[48] It came back to this theme of the transformation of the holiday three years later, but with less reservation, since the Commonwealth embodied the virtues of British tradition: "By popular demand, it [Victoria Day] has become an occasion for celebrating the values and achievements of the British Commonwealth. . . . The active, guiding principle in the Commonwealth has been the spread of liberty and happiness."[49]

But the paper was riled by the federal government's bill to turn the Twenty-Fourth of May into a fixed holiday to be celebrated on the Monday before 25 May.

> Now a generation weak in historic feeling has decided to alter this established custom, and make Victoria Day merely a Monday holiday in the latter part of May. . . . Victoria Day means something which should be cherished, not expunged from public recollection. Even if some do not think of what it means, or do not care, there is value in the keeping of tradition. A nation without a past is a mere collection of people. . . . How shallow we have become, if the past which made us has ceased to matter! How disloyal to our country is this urge to destroy the memory of its roots and traditions![50]

The villain of the piece was the Liberal government in Ottawa, and particularly Prime Minister St. Laurent, who had just added insult to injury by proclaiming 23 May, which in Ontario was celebrated by schoolchildren as Empire Day, as 'Canadian Citizenship Day.'

> Empire Day . . . has been devoted to appropriate ceremonies celebrating Canada's membership in the greatest association of peoples in the history of the world. To Mr. St. Laurent, the miracle of the British Commonwealth and Empire is an embarrassment. It is a thing we should avoid and, if possible, forget. And so in a crass and clumsy move, he is attempting to transform a noble expression of human brotherhood into a narrow and parochial self-aggrandizement. . . . People do not forget their history. It has made them what they are. For any transient politician to attempt to kill a nation's past, to wipe out a people's origins, is an idiotic futility. Mr. St. Laurent might as well give up trying. Our British tie is a great deal stronger than he is. He should remember, too, that if a course is persisted in beyond reason, it produces a reaction which could be very bad because extreme.[51]

The following year, when Victoria Day was for the first time celebrated on the prescribed Monday, the paper's position was expressed in the editorial cartoon, which showed a pioneer in the forefront, labelled 'Our Heritage,' and a Canadian family turning its back to him, facing rather an urban landscape labelled 'Our Country'. The cartoon bore the inscription "In Memory of May 24th 1847–1952."

The complaint about the loss of patriotic fervour and the attacks upon British tradition continued in the latter part of the 1950s. On 23 May 1955, the paper complained that "the word Empire has become taboo," that "most of the fun has been squeezed out of the holiday." "And with the fun, the significance also has tended to disappear. The old songs . . . created a consciousness of unity within Canada, and of Canada's unity within an imperial Commonwealth. Victoria and Empire Day has lost that savor. . . . It is not good for a nation so to slight the truth of its historical beginnings."[52] It continued in the same vein the following year, reflecting that "disrespect for Canada's past (especially that part of it which relates in any way to Britain) is endemic in Ottawa. . . . Forgetting their British past, the people of Canada are forgetting also their Canadian past." This was having a deleterious effect on the nation: "Rub out some of a nation's history, and you might as well rub out all of it."[53] By 1958, the paper seems to have finally accepted the demise of the Twenty-Fourth of May, but it proposed that the civic holiday should honour the new Queen, Elizabeth II. "It would be a fine and gracious thing to make it Elizabeth Day, in fact or in practice or in both."[54]

The *Globe and Mail* also complained occasionally about another attack upon British tradition which gripped Parliament in the Spring of 1946, at the same time as the new citizenship bill was being debated. This was the replacement of the phrase 'Dominion Day' by 'Canada Day,' which had been the object of Bill 8, introduced in March and adopted by the House of Commons in early April. The bill was amended by the Senate and never came back for discussion by the House. But the *Globe and Mail* saw in it another indication that members of the governing party in Ottawa were bent on eliminating all symbols of the British tradition in Canada.

This newspaper has frequently declared that it favors a strong Canadian consciousness. It would favor the abandonment of all hyphenated distinctions between Canadians of different national origins. It favors a recognized Canadian citizenship. It fails to see, however, how any of these things is hindered by the fact that this country is known as 'The Dominion of Canada.' How ridiculous to think of that honorable and historic phrase as an 'outmoded connotation of colonialism!'

A nation without a past is an anomaly. It is as imperfect an entity as a person who has lost his memory. To attempt a deliberate erasure of historical fact is to injure, not augment, national consciousness. . . . There is more than a thread of connection between this strange bill and the clause in the Canadian Citizenship Bill, which would force British subjects from other parts of the world to go through the same form of naturalization which people of non-British nationality are required to accept. The philosophy behind the two is the same. It will be a sorry day for Canadians when legitimate and worthy national pride turns into a species of racial arrogance, which lays about it with hatred or contempt, for all outside our borders. Whether July 1 is called Dominion Day, or Canada Day, is in itself of no great moment. What is significant is the spirit which demands the change.[55]

A few days later, it reprinted a virulent front-page editorial from *Saturday Night*:

Have the members of Parliament no sense at all of the instinctive clinging to the old and traditional which is the essence of the common man's feelings about holidays? . . . Do they think that 11,000,000 inhabitants of Canada are willing to hand over to Mr. Phileas Côté of Matapedia-Matane [the sponsor of the bill in the House of Commons] the right to rename all the cherished days of observance that their ancestors established and they themselves have marked from childhood up?

There is no sense to the proposal to call July the First Canada Day instead of Dominion Day. That date in 1867 was not the beginning of Canada, which existed on June 30 of the same year and had existed for centuries before that. . . . The holiday is the celebration of an event. The event was the establishing of the Dominion. The holiday is and must remain Dominion Day.[56]

The *Globe and Mail* repeated its defense of 'Dominion Day' on 1 July 1948 and again on 1 July 1954:

Fewer than twenty years ago, Canada's leaders were going through all sorts of contortions to minimize our British connection. They felt — why, one cannot guess — that there was something vaguely shameful about it. The war, and events since the war, brought much of that silliness to an end. But wide streaks of it remain; for example, official Ottawa's fear and hatred of the fine word "Dominion".

Canadians, to their credit, do not share that fear and hatred. To the vast majority of them, this is the Dominion of Canada, and today is Dominion Day; and neither of them will ever be anything else. To the vast majority of them, as well, there is reason for quiet satisfaction in their unique relationship with the two great English-speaking nations — bridge, link, interpreter, whatever one may call it.

A subsidiary theme of the Victoria Day editorials was the role of Canada in the creation of the Commonwealth. The advent of responsible government under Queen Victoria was presented as the harbinger of the Commonwealth. "The Victorian era . . . brought forth the most inspired political idea which men have yet evolved; representative self-government under a single Crown, founding the most successful comity of nations in history. For Canadians that invention has special significance, as it was here that its details were first put into effect.[57] It reiterated this idea the next year and came back to it in 1957.[58]

Dominion Day editorials were usually concerned with the uncompleted nature of the Canadian nation. The nation was still divided regionally and ethnically ('racially' was the more usual phrase), but the process of unification was under way. "The land itself, working on the character of the people who have settled it," it wrote on 1 July 1946, "has created its own values, making a new people who are distinctly Canadian. The different regions have each contributed their own outlook and emphasis, the whole evolving from generation to generation into the nation that has yet to be."[59] The tone was slightly less sanguine the following year, when the paper remarked that "[t]rue national unity is not yet ours, however we may try to gloss over the fundamental differences that divide us into provincial and racial camps on domestic issues,"[60] but in successive years the outlook appeared more positive to the paper's editorial writers. In 1948, they wrote on Dominion Day that "[c]omplete unity is not here yet . . . but there are hopeful signs that it is developing." Three years later the paper was hopeful progress was being made: "We have a population drawn from the best of human strains, gradually being woven into a strong, united people. Such a heritage should move our hearts with pride." [61]

A related argument, which John Diefenbaker would later make his hobby horse, was that hyphenated forms of Canadianism prevented the nation from attaining fullness. This was sometimes aimed at immigrant Canadians who sought to preserve their ethnic identity, but it referred mainly, though rarely explicitly, to French Canadians. Yet the *Globe* did not raise this issue directly in its Dominion Day editorials. Besides the condemnation of hyphenated Canadianism already cited in the discussion of the appellation of 'Dominion Day,' the phrase only came up in a commentary upon the coming into force of the new Citizenship Act in January 1947, which was said to " . . . help to eliminate the hyphenated distinctions which mark off some Canadians from others."

During the fifteen years which followed World War II, the *Globe and Mail* stood for the defense of Canada's British heritage. This was seen as the noblest political and cultural heritage a nation could have. The Commonwealth bond was a bond of allegiance to a common ideal of freedom and high moral standards. "[T]he active, guiding principle in the Commonwealth has been the spread of liberty and happiness," it wrote on 24 May 1949.[62] This was the true, 'unhyphenated' nature of Canada. Attacks on symbols of Canada's British heritage, such as the transformation of Victoria Day into a 'Day Off,' or the replacement of 'Dominion Day' by 'Canada Day,' were attacks upon the historical nature of the country, and threatened its 'unity.' Within this united country there was some room for 'biracialism,' but this was only once alluded to in Dominion Day editorials. Clearly this aspect of Canadian identity was secondary, or at least it did not seem to require editorial comment. Instead, it was hoped that 'racial' differences would fade away, and it was clearly expected that this process would mean the adoption of British values by the whole of the population.

Maclean's, another Canadian publication with a claim of national circulation, provides contrasting views from those of the *Globe and Mail*. I systematically examined its editorial pages and have paid attention to columns, guest editorials, opinion pieces and articles which offered representations of Canadian identity. Overall, the magazine offered views that were more 'Canadian' and less 'British' than those of the *Globe and Mail* or, put another way, more 'Liberal' and less 'Conservative.' Much more often than the *Globe and Mail*, it affirmed the 'biracial' character of Canada. On 1 October 1948, an editorial entitled "Two Windows on the World" reminded Canadians that the country was fortunate to have two languages. Arthur Irwin,

Maclean's retiring editor, told an American audience in early 1950 that Canada was ". . . born of compromise between two races, two languages, two cultures. Inevitably he has had to learn that there are always two sides to a case. . . . Culturally, his [the Canadian's] has been the task of trying to span the gap between the Latin and the Anglo-Saxon, between medievalism and modern materialism, Catholicism and Protestantism."[63]

Under Ralph Allen, Irwin's successor, *Maclean's* continued to express similar views on the biracial nature of the country. In March 1950, an editorial suggested that the CBC broadcast French lessons on the English network and English lessons on the French network, since "[b]oth by law and by tradition, Canada is a bilingual country. . . . More and more of us are coming to recognize the positive aspects of our bilingualism." Yet the lack of second-language skills among Canadians meant that, "[t]o a considerable degree, our two great ethnic groups are physically and intellectually apart."[64] On Dominion Day, 1950, the magazine reflected on the "miracle" of Confederation: ". . . four colonies, five regions, two major races, all with a heritage of contempt and hatred for one another, yet all welded into a nation within one long lifetime." Here the 'biracial' character of Canada was joined to its political and regional fragmentation as an original hindrance to unity, but these hindrances had been overcome.[65] Five years later, on the same occasion, it proposed renaming 'Dominion Day' 'Confederation Day,' since the term 'Dominion' had no French translation. "Indeed, it is not too much to say that the use of 'Dominion Day' is a standing insult, no less offensive for being inadvert[ent], to more than one third of all Canadians."[66] In February 1959, it commented on the Heeney report on the federal civil service,[67] which had recommended that civil servants who deal with the public be required to be bilingual in those parts of the country where there was a substantial linguistic minority. It recognized that English-speaking minorities had no difficulty obtaining federal services in their own language, "but thousands of French Canadians deal in their own locality with civil servants who speak no French." It did not flinch at the fact that "[i]n practice, a 'bilingual staff' would mean a French-Canadian staff."

> The suggested change would give French-speaking Canadians a great and often decisive advantage in getting employment and promotion in many branches of the civil service where the English-speaking now predominate. . . . it is the fault of our education in English Canada, and the merit of the French, that we can speak only one language and they can speak two. Perhaps they ought to get the benefit of their superiority. Maybe if they did, there would be less neglect of language in English-Canadian schools.[68]

Thus the magazine was ready to accept the implications of the 'biracial' nature of Canada and recognized the *de facto* inequality between the two main language groups. It offered its own contribution to improving understanding between the two language groups by publishing a special issue on Quebec in May 1959. The editorial which introduced the issue confronted the conflicting claims of heritage and harmony between the two language groups:

> We do not in fact get on very well with each other, we Canadians. Our parliament has found that it cannot even discuss such matters as a national flag or a national anthem because any debate rouses the sleeping dogs of prejudice. . . . We need a proper knowledge of and respect for our past but we also need more knowledge of each other as we really are here and now. This knowledge will confront both of us with some facts we find distasteful, others we may find astonishing, but at least it will give us a foundation on which to build a better understanding. It's the purpose and the hope of this issue of *Maclean's* to contribute to it.[69]

Editorial positions also transpired in *Maclean's* choice of stories. Sometimes the 'biracial' character of Canada was seen as an obstacle to 'national unity.' In 1946 the Honorable Malcolm MacDonald, at the end of his term as British High Commissioner to Canada, considered that there were two major dangers facing Canada: the first one was ". . . any serious quarrel between the French-speaking and the English-speaking Canadians," while the second was a break between Great Britain and the U.S., which would split Canadians according to their preferred affinities.[70] Later in the same year, in an article describing how Canadians differed from Americans, Hugh McLennan wrote that "at the present it is hard to see how Canada can become uniform, with the Province of Quebec in its heart." In 1948, historian Arthur Lower complained about the quality of Canadian education, offering as example the way French was being taught. "I hasten to admit that if French were taken seriously and taught as the language of our fellow countrymen, thousands of zealots in English-speaking Canada would rise up and demand the heads of those who were betraying the English-speaking race."[71]

More often, however, articles in *Maclean's* presented the 'biracial' or bicultural character of Canada as valuable and in need of promotion. In "A Quebecker Speaks Out," Renée Vautelet argued for common history textbooks to foster mutual understanding. For her, citizenship was "biracial." She was concerned, however, ". . . over English Canada's still unresolved division of loyalties . . ." and over Protestant extremists who attacked the Catholic half of the Canadian population.[72] In a photographic essay on Montreal in 1953, Yosuf Karsh ". . . did not see Montreal as a city split into two racial compartments. He found it an amicable if worldly town where two races dovetail neatly together and where, if the inclinations of the flesh are indulged, the needs of the heart and of the spirit are never neglected." In a story about Louis St. Laurent in 1956, Bruce Hutchison wrote : ". . . the supreme duty of any prime minister is to unite the two great Canadian races." Later in the same article Hutchison revealed his fascination with French Canadians. "I do not pretend to understand my French-speaking compatriots. But at least I know them to be a people of peculiar greatness, with many qualities that we lack, a people of profound inner strength, a lovable, kindly people and an essential ingredient of the thing we call Canadianism."[73]

Two years later, in a piece entitled "The Gods Canadians Worship," Arthur Lower hoped that "[i]f those who speak English in Canada and do not find O Canada subversive could link up with those who speak French and join to O Canada the words *Terre de nos aïeux*, there might then be some future for the common country." Lower wished for less bigotry on both sides of the linguistic divide:

> . . . here is a country of two peoples, two ways of life, two cultures. That fact alone gives it any distinction it might happen to possess. The two have lived together for nearly two centuries, never intimately and not often happily, but without flying at each other's throats. That in itself is no mean accomplishment, one to which there are not many parallels elsewhere in the world. They could powerfully reinforce each other — if the more extreme among the French could abandon their touchiness and their lack of interest in everything outside themselves, and if the more extreme among the English their absurd arrogance (what have they to be arrogant about? Second-hand American cars?), their silly notions of racial superiority and their narrow intolerance.[74]

In 1959, Bruce Hutchison visited Quebec to research a piece entitled "The Unconquerable French Canadian." At the beginning of the article he expressed his faith in the 'biracial' character of Canada. "No one but the dual nation of the future had won the battle [of the Plains of Abraham]. And in its unconquerable but still imperfect duality the nation must now reassess, from top to bottom, the marriage of the two races." The article was a perceptive account of changes within French-Canadian society which would erupt in the Quiet Revolution the following year. Its conclusion stressed the positive contribution that 'bi-racialism' had been for Canada:

> Without them [the French Canadians] Canada would be a duller nation, and perhaps it could not have survived as a nation at all against the continental conformity. At any rate, without

them we would have missed our chance of unique achievement, our only great contribution to the world — a workable duality of two distinct peoples, both Canadian, a demonstration of bi-racial living in a race-torn age.

Apart from anything else, that achievement has justified our history since the conquest not of a race, region or nationality but of ourselves jointly. And its product, emerging only in our time, is a new and true nationality.

Hutchison's view of French Canadians was coloured by a concept of 'race' that was a mixture of cultural and physical characteristics. People in Quebec City "... don't look French Canadian any more; they look Canadian and indistinguishable (until you hear their voices) from any others in the nation." Thus a Canadian physical type was emerging. Yet he wondered, "... as I had wondered so often before, [why it was] that the plainest French-Canadian girl always manages to look pretty in spite of nature? Because, I suppose, she has a racial vitality, a feminine instinct, stronger than ours."[75] 'Vitality' still kept the 'races' different.

Both in its editorial writing and in the articles it published, *Maclean's* offered its readers a representation of Canadian identity founded on a positive assessment of its 'bi-racial' nature. It showed goodwill towards Quebec, in spite of the despicable politics of its Premier, Maurice Duplessis, and chided those Canadians who put allegiance to British tradition — or to a narrow Quebec nationalism — ahead of the need for 'bi-racial' harmony within the country. But the other representations it also offered — the uncompleted nation, the nation steeped in British political tradition — were similar to the nexus of representations offered by the *Globe and Mail*, though with different valences.

Like the *Globe and Mail*, *Maclean's* occasionally took up the theme of the uncompleted nation in Dominion Day editorials. On 1 July 1948, it noted that Canadian patriotism "... has been a plant of slow growth. Even now, after 81 Dominion Days, it is a long way from robust maturity. ... As a people we had to be led to accept the idea of nationhood." Yet the editorial ended on a more positive note, reflecting that "... this scattered and divided people has made itself into a nation with its own ideals and its own determinations."[76] It reiterated the same idea for the next Dominion Day celebration, in 1949, exhorting Canadians to be "... Optimists on Canada's Birthday," since they belong to a nation "... whose new strength and new maturity are only half realized even by her own sons."[77] In 1950, it saw the work of 'nation-building' as having been achieved in the 84 years since Confederation.[78]

In 1955 new incidents revealed the fragility of national unity. The CPR was called upon to forgo the name 'Royal Canadian' for its new transcontinental train because some considered it an improper, commercial use of the adjective 'Royal.' "To hear some comments you'd think the whole thing as a conspiracy to bring 'creeping republicanism' to Canada — little short of treason, a sinister plot to undermine the Throne." Symbolic issues such as the flag and the national anthem were still unresolved, and still causing difficulty: "A flag is a symbol of national unity, or it is nothing; to us it has become a symbol of disunity. ... Maybe the time will come when Canada can have a flag, and a national anthem, and a name that we can all agree upon. When that time comes, we'll know we don't really need any of those things — we shall have grown up, at last, without them." The other national railway, the CNR, was not helping national unity: its president, Donald Gordon, was insisting in naming the CNR's new Montreal hotel the Queen Elizabeth rather than Château Maisonneuve. "The argument for Château Maisonneuve are so compelling that it seems incredible they did not prevail in the beginning."[79]

Maclean's editorial depiction of Canada's links with the Great Britain was more nuanced than the *Globe's*. It offered a positive, but not uncritical view of the Commonwealth. In 1950, it regretted the loss of "the spirit and the substance of a community" within the Commonwealth, because the Commonwealth was the one supra-national community that was working. In 1953, it called the Commonwealth "The World's Greatest Asset," since it had, among other things, " . . . saved its member nations from defeat in two world wars."[80] *Maclean's* kept its readers informed on British current events by publishing in each issue Beverley Baxter's "London Letter," which offered the point of view of an expatriate Canadian who had become a Conservative member of the House of Lords. The column ended in July 1960 after 25 years.[81]

The editors did not shy away from occasional critiques of Great Britain. They denounced British intervention in Suez in 1956, calling it " . . . act of callousness and dangerous folly such as Britain has not embarked on in half a century."[82] The Suez crisis had a wrenching effect internally in Canada as well, commented Bruce Hutchison in April 1957. Some considered that it had destroyed Great Britain's reputation as a great nation. Hutchison believed that " . . . few things more important than Suez have ever happened to us in more than three centuries. . . . The first consequence was to split the nation inwardly, as it has seldom been split, between our practical position as a North American nation and our inherited instincts as a child of Europe."[83]

The role of the Crown as symbol of allegiance was viewed positively, but again in a nuanced fashion. In 1954, it lamented the misuse of toasts to the Queen and of the singing of 'God Save the Queen' at banquets. "This is a pity because the Crown still means a good deal to most of the people who live within its orbit. Too much, in fact, to be systematically degraded by routine and meaningless gestures. Let's save the Queen's name for occasions when it stirs the blood, not merely rouses an audience to realize that the time has come to go home or to light up a cigarette." It approved of royal tours, and gave them extensive coverage[84] but regretted that some champions of the monarchy had no tolerance for people who disagreed with them. On the occasion of the Queen's 1959 visit, it remarked: "There is nothing in Canada's constitution or in our nature as a free assembly of human beings that compels all good Canadians to think alike on any subject, including the monarchy and royal visits. In our view the only really regrettable aspect of the latest visit is that far too many of us forgot momentarily that we are not only a monarchy, but a democracy."[85]

In its articles *Maclean's* could reveal the quizzical aspects of the English-Canadian rapport with the monarchy. A long article on the Imperial Order of the Daughters of the Empire, in 1952, recalled the IODE's virulent attachment to British institutions, as manifested in its opposition to the nomination of a Canadian as Governor General " . . . on the grounds that this hinted at 'an insidious and determined plan towards the gradual emergence of a republican state.' The IODE vociferously attacked the decision to discard the Privy Council in London as the final court of Canadian appeal; cried "No!" to the creation of Royal Canadian Corps of Infantry in place of the old regimental order of battle; denounced the Defense Department for discouraging Rule Britannia as the RCN song; howled down the proposal to erase "Royal Mail" from postal trucks, and threw up their hands in horror at the dropping of the word "Dominion" from Canadian statutes."[86] Yet the following year, Blair Fraser reported that Canada had difficulty in filling its allotted number of seats in Westminster Abbey for the Queen's coronation. "Australia has fewer people than Canada, but more Australians than Canadians wanted to come to the Coronation."[87]

Towards the end of the 1950s, *Maclean's* also drew attention to the ethical component of Canadian identity. Bruce Hutchison grew apprehensive at the growing materialism of the country, and its declining sense of compassion. During the Suez and Hungary crises of 1956, " . . . the voice of politics drowned out the voice of compassion" in Canada. Fortunately, " . . . the Canadian people are far more intelligent, more generous and altogether better than they look at present." [88] The editorial page took up the theme later in 1957 in a piece favouring greater immigration into the country.

Within this century Canada has become one of the world's major economic forces as well as a major political force. We can, if we wish, become something indescribably greater than either of these. We can become a moral force of the first dimension. We can show that good will and decency toward one's neighbors, however naïve and out of fashion they may have come to seem, are still good fields for experiment.[89]

The ethical concept of the country in a sense grounded all the other representations of Canada which may be found in the pages of the magazine. The positive attitude towards French Canada, the desire to keep Canada distinct from the United States, the role defined for Canada on the international stage were all based on the virtues of tolerance, justice, and compassion. These were the traits that made Canada a decent nation. *Maclean's* answered in an editorial on 1 July 1952 an inquiry by a German considering emigrating to Canada and wishing to learn what the Canadian character was. "Judge us as Canadians, if you will. But judge us first as human beings, in the clear understanding that we live under no special law which transmits all the virtues and faults in residence here to some monolithic creature of the gods called The Canadian. . . . for we are so proud and fortunate to be Canadians that there are some among us who need reminding that there is no way of being a good Canadian without being a good human being."[90]

Yet *Maclean's*, like the *Globe and Mail*, offered an ethnic-based representation of Canadian identity. The fundamental difference between the two publications was that *Maclean's* did not claim or imply that one of the two main Canadian 'races' was superior to the other. In neither publication could one find any sustained exposition of the concept of 'civic' nationalism as it is understood today.

CONCLUSION

Ethnicity was at the core of most of the representations of Canadian identity in English-speaking Canada that were examined in this paper. There were of course disagreements within the English-language communicational community on the emphasis to be put on the British character of the country and some strenuous resistance, in some quarters, to erasing the symbols of the British connection. But this was a matter of degree, not a profound disagreement as to the nature of the country. This makes the virtual abandonment of the British tradition in the 1960s all the more surprising. Some observers saw this coming in the 1950s and squarely blamed the Liberal government in Ottawa for its deliberate renunciation of Canada's British heritage.[91]

This conclusion is, of course, tentative. The inquiry needs to be extended in at least two directions. First, work on the 1950s needs to be expanded. A much larger sample of newspaper and magazine opinion has to be collected. The actual role of the Liberal government in removing the British connection from the symbolic universe of the country has to be investigated. Other sources of symbolic identification, such as school textbooks, also require examination. Second, attention needs to be focused on the speed with which national symbols were being refashioned in the 1960s. Inquiries similar to those that will bear on the 1950s will have to be conducted for this crucial decade.

Finally, from the conceptual point of view, we can appreciate the usefulness of Tilly's characterization of public identities. Each statement, each representation of identity needs to be carefully situated in its context, relational, cultural, historical and contingent. We can then move away from arguing about *the* Canadian identity and accept representations of national identity as a legitimate object of historical inquiry.

NOTES

1. See Berger, *The Sense of Power* (Toronto: University of Toronto Press, 1970); Mary Vipond, "National Consciousness in English-Speaking Canada in the 1920's: seven essays," Ph.D. thesis, University of Toronto, 1974; Raymond Breton, "From Ethnic to Civic Nationalism: English Canada and Quebec," *Ethnic and Racial Studies*, vol. 11, no 1, (January 1988): 85–102; Philip Resnick, "English Canada: The Nation that Dares Not Speak Its Name," in Kenneth McRoberts, ed., *Beyond Quebec: Taking Stock of Canada* (Montreal: McGill-Queen's University Press, 1995), 84.

2. The term "Canadian" refers to the English-language Canadian communicational community. See definitions below.

3. William R. Young, "Making the Truth Graphic: The Canadian Government's Home Front Information Structure and Programmes during World War II" (Ph.D. thesis, University of British Columbia, 1978).

4. *L'identité fragmentée* (Montreal: Fides, 1996).

5. Paul Litt, *The Muses, the Masses, and the Massey Commission* (Toronto: University of Toronto Press, 1992).

6. See Charles Taylor, "Shared and Divergent Values," in *Reconciling the Solitudes: Essays on Canadian Federalism and Nationalism* (Montreal/Kingston: McGill-Queen's University Press, 1995), 168–169; Margaret Atwood, *Survival: A Thematic Guide to Canadian Literature* (Toronto: Anansi, 1972).

7. See T.H. Marshall, *Citizenship and Social Class, and Other Essays* (Cambridge: University Press, 1950); Liah Greenfeld, *Five Roads to Modernity* (Cambridge: Harvard University Press, 1992).

8. See Sylvie Lacombe, "Race et liberté: l'individualisme politique au Canada, 1896–1920," (Ph.D. thesis, Université de Paris V, 1993).

9. It would be fascinating to speculate as to why there has been such interest among Canadian historians for these other forms of collective identification while national identity remains practically unexplored territory as a field of research.

10. Charles Tilly, "Citizenship, Identity and Social History," *International Review of Social History* 40, Supplement 3 (1995), 5–6.

11. See Joseph Levitt, "Race and Nation in Canadian Anglophone Historiography," *Canadian Review of Studies in Nationalism*, VIII, 1 (Spring 1981): 1–16, for an examination of the writings of some major Canadian historians of the first half of this century.

12. See the third edition, Toronto: McGraw-Hill Ryerson, 1990. The use of 'nation' in the sense of 'state' occurs on p.4: "The new state created by the British North America Act was born on July 1, 1867. . . . Not all inhabitants of the new nation supported its creation." (Formally, the first statement is erroneous: what was created in 1867 was a new arrangement for the governance of Britain's North American colonies, not a new state.) Different meanings occur on p. 7: "In 1838, following the rebellions of the previous year, Lord Durham wrote that he had found two nations warring in the bosom of a single state. Sixty years later, that situation had changed little. . . . If the nation still remained undefined in 1896, the state had come to fulfill the function planned for it in 1964."

13. See for instance Veronica Strong-Boag, "Contested Space: The Politics of Canadian Memory," *Journal of the Canadian Historical Association*, new series, 5 (1994): 5–6. It is revealing that a historian who defines herself as "both a feminist and a nationalist" does not include the question of national identity as part of the 'contested space' she defines as worthy of investigation. She seems to equate the issue of nationalism with old-style political history.

14. See Phillip Buckner, "Whatever happened to the British Empire?" *Journal of the Canadian Historical Association*, new series, 4 (1993): 21–23, 31, on this point.

15. An examination of questions asked by the Canadian Institute for Public Opinion (Gallup) and other polling organizations reveals that questions are usually concretely linked to current issues and are seldom phrased in a general way.

16. They are always, of course, rhetorical.

17. Gerald Friesen has examined the various representations of collective identity to be found around the sport of hockey in a paper given at McGill University in the Fall of 1996.

18. Richard Douglas Wilson, "An inquiry into the interpretation of Canadian history in the elementary and secondary schools textbooks of English and French Canada" (M.A. thesis, McGill University, 1967); Edison Quick, "The Development of Geography and History Curricula in the Elementary Schools of Ontario 1846–1966" (Ph.D. thesis, University of Toronto, 1967); Penney Irene Clark, "'Take It Away, Youth!': Visions of Canadian Identity in British Columbia Social History Textbooks, 1925–1989" (Ph.D. thesis, University of British Columbia, 1995).

19. The Canadian Institute of Public Opinion [Gallup] polls available for this purpose date from the mid 1950s.

20. William R. Young, "Building Citizenship: English Canada and Propaganda during the Second War," *Journal of Canadian Studies*,16, 3–4 (Fall–Winter 1981): 121–132. Quotation is from p.122.

21. Ibid., 124. See also Leslie A. Pal, "Identity, citizenship, and mobilization: The Nationalities Branch and World War Two," *Canadian Public Administration*, 32, 3 (Fall 1989): 407–426.

22. W.R. Young, "Making the Truth Graphic: The Canadian Government's Home Front Information Structure and Programmes during World War II" (Ph.D. dissertation, University of British Columbia, 1978), ch. 2.

23. Kathryn Dodd and Philip Dodd, "Engendering the Nation: British Documentary Film, 1930–1939," in Andrew Higson, ed., *Dissolving Views: Key Writings on British Cinema* (London: Cassell, 1996), 39. I am grateful to Gerald Friesen for this reference.

24. Young, "Making the Truth Graphic." For links with the kindred spirits in the adult education movement, see Gordon Selman, *Citizenship and the Adult Education Movement in Canada* (Vancouver/Toronto: Center for Continuing Education, University of British Columbia/International Council for Adult Education, 1991), ch. 3; Michael R. Welton, "'An Authentic Instrument of the Democratic Process': The intellectual origins of the Canadian Citizens' Forum," *Studies in the Education of Adults*, 18, 1 (1986): 35–49, especially 42–43.

25. Young, "Building Citizenship," 125. Paul Martin entitled his account of the origins of Canada's first Citizenship Act, in 1946, "Citizenship and the People's World." It appeared in William Kaplan, ed., *Belonging: The Meaning and Future of Canadian Citizenship* (Montreal/Kingston: McGill-Queen's University Press, 1993), 64–78.

26. Young, ibid., 130.

27. They were exercised by a clause in the bill which required five years' residency in Canada for British subjects from other parts of the Commonwealth to become Canadian citizens, though existing legislation gave British subjects, no matter where they were born, the right to vote in Canadian elections after one year's residency in the country.

28. Martin indicated in 1993 that he personally would have favoured not including the statement that Canadians were British subjects, as "it left Canada with a mark of inferiority" (Martin, ibid., 74).

29. John G. Diefenbaker, *Debates of the House of Commons*, 1946, 2 April 1946, 514; C.C.I. Merritt, ibid., 11 April 1946, 795.

30. G.R. Pearkes, ibid., 9 April 1946, 702; D. M. Fleming, ibid., 30 April 1946, 1061.

31. Fleming, ibid., 9 April 1946, 691.

32. Pearkes, ibid., 9 April 1946, 704.

33. Fleming; ibid., 9 April 1946, 687, 692; Cockeram, ibid., 9 April 1946, 695–6.

34. Ibid., 21 March 1946, 131; 5 April 1946, 598.

35. "What's in a Name?," *Globe and Mail*, 8 April 1946, 6. All *Globe* editorials cited hereafter appeared on p. 6.

36. "Young Men in a Hurry," *Ottawa Citizen*, 16 April 1946, 8.

37. Some French-Canadian members of the Liberal party also put forward such a view. See Édouard Rinfret, *House of Commons*, 5 April 1946, 596.

38. G.H. Castleden, ibid., 8 April 1946, 720-1.

39. R.R. Knight, ibid., 20 April 1946, 1003.

40. 13 April 1946, 17.

41. Martin, *House of Commons*, 29 April 1946, 1015.

42. This division was also evident in the civil service. Paul Martin had to request the services of Gordon Robertson, then attached to the Prime Minister's office, because his own deputy minister, "who belonged to the old school of empire," was opposed to the idea of a Canadian citizenship (Martin, "Citizenship," 68).

43. National Archives of Canada, MG 31 E87, vol. 2, File 2-7, Gordon Robertson, "Canadian Citizenship Act Notes on Sections,' 14 November 1945, 38; ibid., 20 April 1945, R.G.R./L.F., Memorandum for Paul Martin re: the meaning of British subject.

44. Martin, "Citizenship," 74.

45. A broader examination of newspaper opinion about the Citizenship Act of 1946 revealed that only the *Winnipeg Free Press* adhered to a 'civic' definition of citizenship, but its writers took pain to explain that British subjects would continue to be favoured by the Act. See the series of articles by Grant Dexter, 22–27 March 1946, which seem to have been inspired by Paul Martin.

46. "The Stream Flows Swiftly," 1 July 1947.

47. "Welcome!," 23 May 1946.

48. "Victoria Day," 24 May 1946.

49. "A Commonwealth Day," 24 May 1946.

50. "A Canadian Tradition," 24 May 1952.

51. "Futile and Stupid," 23 May 1952.

52. "Victoria Day," 23 May 1955.

53. "Day Off," 21 May 1956.

54. "Elizabeth Day?," 19 May 1958.

55. "What's in a Name?," 8 April 1946.

56. "Let's Keep Dominion Day." From the Front Page of Saturday Night, 12 April 1946.

57. "Victoria Day," 24 May 1946.

58. "A Commonwealth Day," 24 May 1947; "Victorian Heritage," 20 May 1957.

59. "Two Birthdays," 1 July 1946 [Confederation Day and the centenary of Hamilton].

60. "The Stream Flows Swiftly," 1 July 1947.

61. "Dominion Day," 1 July 1948; "Canada, Our Country," 1 July 1951.

62. "A Commonwealth Day," 24 May 1949.

63. Arthur Irwin, "The Canadian," 1 February 1950, 20, 32, 34-35. Quotation is from p. 34, 35.

64. "Two Windows on the World," Maclean's, 1 October 1948, p.2; "A Lesson for the CBC," 1 March 1950, 2.

65. "Look How Far We've Come — And In Just 84 Years," 1 July 1950, 1.

66. "Let's Call It 'Confederation Day'," 9 July 1955, 2.

67. Personnel Administration in the Public Service: A Review of Civil Service Legislation by the Civil Service Commission of Canada (Ottawa: Queen's Printer, 1959).

68. "It's English Canadians' own fault if 'bilingual' means French-Canadian," 14 February 1959, 4.

69. "Let's stop boasting of national unity and start working on it," 9 May 1959, 9.

70. Malcolm Macdonald, "This Nation Called Canada," 15 May 1946, 43.

71. "Does Our Education Educate?" 15 November 1948, 9, 72–76. Quotation is from p. 72.

72. Renée Vautelet, "A Quebecker Speaks Out," 15 January 1948, 18, 37–39.

73. Bruce Hutchison, "Political Quebec," 18 February 1956, 22, 37, 39–45. Quotations are from p. 40, 44.

74. 25 October 1958, 74.

75. 9 May 1959. Quotations are from 16, 82.

76. "The Long Road to Maturity," 1 July 1948, 1.

77. "Let's Be Optimists on Canada's Birthday," 1 July 1949, 2.

78. "Look How Far We've Come — And In Just 84 Years," 1 July 1950, 1.

79. "It's What's Behind the Symbol that Counts," 2 April 1955, 2; "Donald Gordon and the Château Blunder," 14 May 1955, 2.

80. "The Commonwealth is Chasing Its Own Tail," 1 June 1950, 1; "The Free World's Greatest Asset," 1 June 1953, 2.

81. Beverley Baxter, "Farewell and hail after 25 years," 30 July 1960, 7.

82. "We're not really the heroes of Suez," 22 December 1956.

83. Bruce Hutchison, "For the sake of argument. We're being corrupted by our boom," 13 April 1957, 8, 40-43. Quotation is on p. 40.

84. Special issue of Princess Elizabeth's tour of Canada, 1 October 1951; "June Callwood's story of the Queen's visit," 7 December 1957. However, the 1959 tour was only the subject of a humourous article by Charles Spencer, "The day the queen resigned," 29 August 1959, 2, 39.

85. "Our Ice-Water Loyalty," 1 March 1954, 2; "Why do royal tours make Canadians so belligerent?," 15 August 1959, 4.

86. McKenzie Porter, "The Empire's Dutiful Daughters," 15 August 1952, 10–11, 34–37. Quotation is from p. 34.

87. "Backstage at Ottawa. No Social Climbers in the Abbey," 1 June 1953, special issue on the coronation, 5.

88. "For the sake of argument. We're being corrupted by our boom," 13 April 1957, 8, 40–43. Quotations are from p. 41, 43.

89. "Both parties say 'No' to immigrants but it's not the voice of Canada," 31 August 1957, 4.

90. "Letter to Heinz Weidner," 1 July 1952, 2.

91. See for example John Farthing, Freedom Wears a Crown (Toronto: Kingsford House, 1957). Again, I owe this reference to Gerald Friesen.

Article Thirty-Four

Québec-Canada's Constitutional Dossier

Alain-G. Gagnon

To begin with, Québec is not a province like the others. Adequately accounting for such a political reality necessitates an adapted analytical focus. As such, we employ the notion of the Québec state as a political nation inscribed within a multinational whole and as a historic region in order to highlight Québec's specificity, rather than simply treating Québec as a province, a subordinate government or a political grouping. The latter expressions appear to us as misleading considering the manner in which a large majority of Québecers perceive and define themselves.[1]

There are many ways to address Québec-Canada dynamics in the area of federal-provincial relations. Some researchers have opted for a legal approach . . . while others have chosen to proceed with the study of fiscal federalism (e.g., the Seguin Commission on fiscal imbalance in Canada[2]). The present text will privilege the historical-institutional dimensions of federal-provincial relations with the aim of providing a more encompassing portrait, allowing for a perspective that more effectively accounts for the evolution of power relations between orders of government as well as within the partisan system. We will proceed in three periods: (1) the first period will consider the historical foundations and the establishment of the first constitutional order; (2) the second period is one of transition and covers the years from 1960 to 1982; and (3) the third period extends from 1982, the year of constitutional repatriation without the consent of Québec, to the present time, stressing the rupture with the established constitutional order and the emergence of a new political order.

HISTORICAL FOUNDATIONS AND THE EMERGENCE OF THE FIRST CONSTITUTIONAL ORDER

The founding events of apolitical community are viewed rarely with unanimity. Nevertheless, in the case of Québec it is relatively easy to locate the important dates in which various interpretations are formed according to different political stands. We can identify, up to the 1960s, no less than four fundamental moments: (1) the Conquest of 1759–60 followed by the Surrender of 1763; (2) the Québec Act of 1774; (3) the Rebellions of 1837–1838 followed by the Act of Union in 1840; and (4) the Confederation of 1867. Each of these moments marked the development of Québec's political culture in a notable manner. Indeed, contemporary authors often hark back to them or follow up on them, but rarely are they dismissed.

The great episodes of the Conquest and of the Surrender have frequently been reviewed in analyses centred on Québec-Canada relations. The clashing interpretations advanced respectively by the contentions of those in the *École de Montreal* and the *École de Québec* and, closer to us, in the production of the Radio-Canada televised series titled *Canada: A People's History*, or still further in the exchanges between Gérard Bouchard and John Saul[3] demonstrate the political consequences of targeting one or the other of these two events.

The Québec Act of 1774 constitutes a fundamental moment whose repercussions continue to this day. Some analysts have evoked the desire of Great Britain to prevent an extension to the former French and Catholic possession of its military conflicts with the Americans, who sought to emancipate themselves from their colonizers. Other analysts have advanced more nuanced interpretations, recalling with interest that the passage of the Québec Act would constitute the first imperial statute that recognized a colony's own formal constitution.[4]

In this context, those who identified themselves as *les Canadiens*, and their elites, found themselves with the recognition, on the one hand, of the right to exercise their faith and to use the French language, while on the other, to obtain the re-establishment of the seigneurial regime, the tithe and the use of common law. Indeed, the Québec Act represents an interpretive document whose importance for following generations cannot be ignored.

The relevance of the Québec Act on the legitimacy of Québec's demands within the Canadian federation is in many regards proportional to the significance of the Royal Proclamation of 1763 on the status of Aboriginal nations. At the very least, it probably served to incite the authors of the preliminary report of the Royal Commission on Aboriginal Peoples to establish, in 1995, parallels between the claims of these nations and those of the Québec nation within Canada as a whole.

The events surrounding the rebellions of Lower Canada as well as the Act of Union of 1840 marked the imagination of French Canadians at the time. Moreover, the emergence of republican and liberal ideas in Québec can also be attributed to this period. Nevertheless, the year 1840 does not represent a memorable year for French Canadians as it signified the forced merger of Upper and Lower Canada without the institution of responsible government; it was not until 1848 that this political victory was attained.

It was with the advent of the Union of the two Canadas that French Canadians turned resolutely towards the Church, which provided them with protection and marked the infancy stage of an agreed consociational formula.[5]

In founding the Canadian Confederation in 1867, or what can be designated as the first constitutional order, French and English Canadians agreed on the main tenets of a power-sharing formula. Despite periodic modifications, this constitutional order would continue until repatriation in 1981.

Three interpretations came to the fore during this period: the creation of Canada was interpreted either as an imperial statute, as an agreement between the founding provinces, or as a pact between English Canadians and French Canadians. In Québec, the interpretation that has dominated all debates is centered on dualism, which has given rise to a rich literature concerning constitutional matters. For example, the work of Judge Thomas-Jean-Jacques Loranger, at the start of the 1880s,[6] deserves attention to the extent that it established links to the Québec Act of 1774, and for providing interpretive boundaries with regard to Québec-Canada relations. The main premises of Judge Loranger are summarized in the preliminary report of the Royal Commission on Aboriginal Peoples in 1993:

1. The confederation of the British Provinces was the result of a compact entered into by the provinces and the United Kingdom.
2. The provinces entered into the federal Union with their corporate identity, former constitutions, and all their legislative powers intact. A portion of these powers was ceded to the federal Parliament, to exercise them in common interest of the provinces. The powers not ceded were retained by the provincial legislatures, which continued to act within their own sphere according to their former constitutions, under certain modifications of form established by the federal compact.

3. Far from having been conferred upon them by the federal government, the powers of the provinces are the residue of their former colonial powers. The federal government is the creation of the provinces, the result of their association and of their compact.[7]

Judge Loranger supported his contentions on the basis of continuity in constitutional matters, and reminds us that it is not permissible for political actors to ignore treaties, agreements, and conventions in the elaboration of constitutional reforms. The influence of interpretations advanced by Judge Loranger in the elaboration of Québec's constitutional positions can also be read between the lines in the report of the Royal Commission of Inquiry on Constitutional Problems, the Tremblay Report, which was released by the government of Québec in 1956. The Tremblay report emphasized the notions of provincial autonomy in fiscal and financial domains, coordination between the two orders of government, and the principle of subsidiarity. The report recommended that Québec, as a member-state of the Canadian confederation, is fully responsible for the development of its culture. The Tremblay report allowed for the actualization of the conceptual contentions of Judge Loranger in matters of provincial autonomy, while representing a major source of inspiration for the architects of the Quiet Revolution at a time where a vast program of reforms on the cultural, economic, and social levels were to be elaborated, with the aim of reducing the rift that was developing between Québec and Ontario in particular.

FROM THE QUIET REVOLUTION TO REPATRIATION IN 1982: A PERIOD OF TRANSITION

The start of the 1960s was marked by an impressive political fervour in Québec: the arrival to power of the Liberals of Jean Lesage, the appearance of several third parties, state interventionism, the affirmation of civil society, the rise of the trade union movement and, to limit ourselves to these examples, the first expressions of the Front de Liberation du Québec. Social and political actors sought to redress the structural inequities to which Québec had been subjected over the years and provided Québecers with a context of choice that permitted their affirmation on cultural, political, social, and economic levels.

At the very beginning of the period, the government of Québec attempted to make alliances with the provincial capitals. Moreover, through the initiatives of Premier Jean Lesage, the provincial Premiers began to meet annually with a view to presenting a common front when confronted with unilateral actions by Ottawa in areas of competence that are exclusive to the provinces.

On the constitutional plane, and in response to Québec's demands, the minority Liberal government of Lester B. Pearson decided in 1963 to set up the Laurendeau-Dunton Commission on bilingualism and biculturalism, which provided real meaning to the principle of equality between the two founding peoples.[8] In this context of great fervour, the government of Québec, in concert with the other member-states of the federation, sought to elaborate propositions with the aim of arriving at negotiated agreements with the federal government. This had the particular effect of increasing the frequency of federal-provincial meetings, expanding the range of questions addressed at such encounters and promoting the creation of ministerial committees charged with studying disputed issues.

Subsequently, and inspired by the autonomist doctrine of Judge Loranger, Paul Gérin-Lajoie proposed the external extension of Québec's internal jurisdictions.[9] Québec invested in the international arena and began to establish relations with international organizations and foreign governments, provoking serious conflicts with Ottawa. The government of Québec recognized that foreign policy was a federal jurisdiction, yet argued for its right to act in this domain in cases that were relevant to its own exclusive fields. This approach was particularly effective from 1964–1966, a period in which Québec concluded several agreements related to education, youth, and cultural affairs. Québec's initiatives, combined with efforts in concert with other provincial governments, served to increase the pressure for constitutional reform.

At the time, the establishment of an amending formula constituted a major problem that obstructed constitutional reform. During the Liberal tenure of Jean Lesage (1960–1966), two amending formulas were proposed in Québec, and then rejected. In 1961, Lesage refused the formula proposed by the federal Minister of Justice at the time, Davie Fulton, because the federal government refused to limit the powers that it assumed in 1949, powers that permitted the federal government to unilaterally amend the Constitution in fields of exclusive federal competence. Moreover, Ottawa refused to grant Québec a voice with regard to reforms to central institutions such as the monarchy, the Senate, and the Supreme Court.

In January 1966, the Fulton-Favreau formula, which at the outset was received favourably by all provincial Premiers at the federal-provincial conference of October 1964, would undergo a similar fate with Québec withdrawing its support. This formula would have required the approval of the federal government and all other provincial governments for provisions respecting the division of powers, the use of both official languages, denominational rights in education and representation in the House of Commons. Other provisions respecting the monarchy and Senate representation could be amended by Ottawa with the concurrence of two-thirds of the provinces comprising more than 50 per cent of the Canadian population. Upon reflection, an amending formula based on unanimity was opposed in Québec because it could threaten the possibility of obtaining intergovernmental agreements on culturally sensitive issues, such as language policy, and could discourage any transfer of powers from the federal to the provincial order. With the aim of providing the system with a measure of flexibility, Québec also envisaged a clause regarding delegation of powers that would permit member-states of the federation and Ottawa to delegate, respectively, and under precise conditions, given responsibilities. As it stood, the consent of four provinces and the federal Parliament was necessary, which in effect prevented any bilateral agreement between Québec and Ottawa. The principle of dualism had been supplanted.

The central issue for Québec, however, was not the amending formula, but rather the overhaul of the constitution and a new division of powers.[10] Faced with the prospect of a provincial election, Lesage could not consent to proposals that would run against growing nationalist and autonomist sentiments in the province. Lesage refused to consider repatriation or an amending formula unless this was combined with a clear definition of Québec's powers and responsibilities, as well as the protection of the French language and culture. He thus established the framework that would guide the demands by future Québec governments in discussions concerning constitutional reform.

Afraid of being outflanked by Daniel Johnson of the *Union National* and pressured by the progressive wing within his party, Lesage abandoned any discourse on the equality of provinces in favour of a particular status for Québec. While Lesage was strengthening his autonomist discourse, he also sought to influence decisions of the federal government. In the 1966 Québec budget, the government went so far as to suggest that the province should participate directly in areas of exclusive federal jurisdiction, by participating in the development and execution of fiscal, monetary, and trade policies. The federal government rejected this proposition.

The Lesage government was resolute in pushing for reform, ready to risk an acrimonious relationship with Ottawa if this could enhance Québec's economic and political power and status. In 1964 the Québec government was granted control of its own public pension plan, which gave the province greater fiscal autonomy and allowed for new initiatives without authorization from Ottawa. The Québec pension plan constituted a major gain as it assisted in building the most impressive and durable public investment pool in Canada, the Caisse de dépôt et placement, the gem of Québec's financial institutions. At the time, the federal government attempted unsuccessfully to convince other provinces to follow Québec's lead, so that the latter would not appear to have obtained de facto special status.

The Union Nationale defeated the Liberals in 1966 with the slogan "Equality or independence" and would adopt the same approach with regard to federal-provincial relations, with a greater emphasis initially on nationalist discourse. By making reference to the binational character of Canada and by advancing a project based on distinct status, Premier Daniel Johnson conducted Québec to a new level. Johnson would later rely on his interpretation during the Confederation of Tomorrow Conference in the autumn of 1967, which was convened on the request of the Ontario Premier, John Robarts, who sought a solution to the Canadian malaise. Johnson wanted to obtain firm support from his colleagues, for a commitment recognizing Québec's right to a particular responsibility that would permit Québec to ensure the promotion of French-Canadian culture.

The position adopted by Johnson, and subsequently Jean-Jacques Bertrand (1968–70), tended to concur with the *Report of the Royal Commission of Inquiry on Constitutional Problems* (the Tremblay Commission 1953–1956) that the division of powers and revenues between the provinces and federal government should be based on the Québec interpretation of the British North America Act (BNAA) of 1867. In this perspective, the Union Nationale demanded limits on federal government transfer payments to individuals through pan-Canadian social programs, and complete federal withdrawal if these were run on a shared-cost basis.

Pursuing his demand for constitutional reform, and benefiting from the momentum provided by the Royal Commission of Bilingualism and Biculturalism (the Laurendeau-Dunton Commission 1963–1969), Johnson envisaged a binational solution to Canada's constitutional problems. His proposal was founded on an interpretation of the BNAA as a pact between two founding peoples. The Union Nationale, under Maurice Duplessis, in power in Québec from 1936–1939 and from 1944–1959, had already attempted to protect the division of powers of 1867 from federal encroachment. Under Johnson, the party asked for additional powers to protect francophones within Québec and to some extent those living outside of the province. These modifications were seen to be commensurate with Québec's responsibilities as the primary protector of the French-speaking community in Canada.

Despite constitutional differences, several issues were resolved during the second half of the 1960s. For example, several deals were made with Ottawa on tax revenues, and an opting-out formula was implemented. In addition, Québec started to play an important role in *la francophonie*, while an informal agreement with the federal government allowed Québec to expand the small immigration bureau established during Lesage's mandate into a legitimate department. This departure from established practice paved the way for asymmetrical federalism.

The selection of Pierre Trudeau as leader of the federal Liberal Party in April 1968 and his subsequent election as Prime Minister of Canada in June of that year would change the stakes significantly. His project of constitutional reform lead to much wrangling with the various Québec governments that would follow and, finally, to the repatriation of the constitution in spite of unanimous disagreement by the parties represented in Québec's National Assembly.

Upon his arrival, Pierre Trudeau refused to accord to Québec anything that he was not ready to concede to other member-states of the federation. This did not prevent Johnson from defending the premise that programs such as family allowances, pensions, social assistance, health services, and manpower training were the sole responsibility of the provinces. For Johnson, it was clear that the distinct character of Québec warranted bilateral arrangements between Québec and Ottawa that were not contingent upon the federal government's relations with other provinces. The spending power of the federal government was perceived as having a negative effect on the maintenance of federalism since it did not respect a watertight division of powers between the two orders of government.

Under successive governments, Québec and Ottawa did reach more formal agreements that broadened the province's responsibilities in the areas of immigration and, to a lesser extent, international relations. It should be stressed, however, that neither Ottawa nor the other provinces agreed to constitutional entrenchment of Québec's rights in these domains, conceding only the possibility of making administrative arrangements that are nothing more than reversible deals.

During the 1970s, the Québec government continued its search for greater autonomy by urging that it be given additional powers and the necessary revenues for its exercise. It is in this context that Robert Bourassa, Premier of Québec from 1970–76 and from 1984–93, developed the objectives of profitable federalism, cultural sovereignty, and later, shared sovereignty. It must be noted that Bourassa's priority was not for the entrenchment of Québec's national aspirations in the Canadian Constitution; rather, he sought a revision of the federal system that would assign Québec the requisite powers and resources needed for an affirmation of the bicultural character of Canada. At the Victoria Conference in 1971, political analysts believed that the constitutional debate would be successfully resolved under Bourassa, but the nationalist opposition forces in Québec forced him to retreat, and the agreement was never ratified. The reason given for this reversal was the imprecision of the text, particularly Article 94A, which outlined responsibilities for pensions and other social programs. For Québec, 94A was said to be a test of the extent to which its constitutional partners were willing to push for a significant change in the sharing of powers. Moreover, there was intense political pressure in Québec regarding the proposed amending formula that would have given a veto to Québec, Ontario, to the Western provinces collectively, and one to the Eastern provinces. For Québec, this signalled a vision of Canada without regard for dualism. The package deal proposed by Ottawa failed to guarantee to Québec control over cultural and social policies.

Negotiations resumed in 1975 with the federal government's suggestion that the issue of the division of powers be set aside in favour of a simple patriation with an amending formula. This implied that any discussion of a new division of powers would be the subject of future multilateral and bilateral bargaining among Québec, the other provinces, and the federal government. Ottawa recognized that in modifying the federal sharing of powers, the protection and promotion of linguistic and cultural concerns were of primary interest to Québec, and this was presented at the time as the recognition of Québec's demand for "special status."[11]

In effect, the federal government did not want to give further ammunition to the Parti Québécois, which was rapidly gaining in popularity among the Québec electorate. Québec then made public that it was prepared to accept this approach provided that its linguistic and cultural concerns were entrenched in the Constitution.[12] In exchange for patriation, Bourassa asked that the following provisions be included in a new Constitution: the right for Québec to veto future constitutional amendments; control of policies in the fields of education and culture in the province; the right to opt out of federal programs with compensation; a more important role in immigration, especially aspects dealing with selection and integration of immigrants into Québec society; and limits of the federal government's declaratory and spending powers in areas of provincial jurisdiction.

The federal initiative was accompanied by a threat of unilateral patriation by Ottawa, without the consent of the provinces, prompting the Premier of Québec to call an early election in the fall of 1976. The PQ assumed power on 15 November 1976 with a program of sovereignty-association. Under René Lévesque, the PQ government was committed to acquiring full political sovereignty, accompanied by an economic association (later replaced by the notion of economic union) between Québec and the rest of Canada. The election of an autonomist government under Lévesque in Québec did not change the federal government's inclination to push for the patriation of the Constitution with an amending formula.

In the meantime, the Pepin-Robarts Task Force had received a mandate from the government of Pierre Trudeau to work towards "the elaboration of the means aimed at the reinforcement of Canadian unity."[13] In Pierre Trudeau's estimation, this entailed a centralization of powers to Ottawa. The conclusions of the Pepin-Robarts report rested on three elements: the existence of different regions, the predominance of two cultures, and equality of the two orders of government. The main thrust of the proposed changes was the institutionalization of asymmetrical federalism, which implies that all provinces are not equal, nor are they the same. While avoiding a *de jure* special status for Québec, Québec's special relationship with the rest of Canada was said to be *de facto*, recognized in the arrangements that had been offered to all provinces but in which Québec had been the only participant. The Québec Pension Plan is the most potent example. This recognition of special status and asymmetry was extended to language, with the contention that each province had the right to determine provincial language policy.

Major institutional innovations included proposals for reforming the Senate, an expanded Supreme Court, and the abolition of certain antiquated federal powers, such as the powers of disallowance and reservation. The task force proposed the replacement of the Senate by a Council of the Federation entirely composed of delegates nominated by the provinces. Moreover, seats based on proportional representation would be added to the House of Commons in order to obtain a more equitable representation of political parties. In the area of justice, expanding and dividing the Supreme Court into specialized "benches" designed to address deficiencies in the ability of the courts to rule in various jurisdictions was also among the proposals. Finally, concurrency was proposed for federal declaratory, spending, and emergency powers. In an attempt to reconcile western alienation and Québec nationalism, the task force tackled the issues of provincial autonomy, provincial control over language policy, representation of provincial interests in Ottawa, as well as the status of Québec within the federation.

Failing to deliver the report desired by Trudeau, the task force nevertheless permitted the federal authorities to gain precious time by giving the federal government the possibility of engaging itself simultaneously in the elaboration of its reform project, an initiative set aside during the Québec election in November 1976. Ottawa could then kill two birds with one stone. On the one hand, the political strategists let it be believed that reconciliation could be possible in response to the expectations of the member-states of the federation and, on the other, they were preparing their intended reply by elaborating Bill C-60: A Time for Action. The origins of a Plan A and Plan B approach were emerging.[14]

In 1978, Ottawa introduced Bill C-60, the Constitutional Amendment Bill, containing terms very similar to those of the 1971 Victoria formula. The Bill included intrastate modifications that would strengthen provincial representation at the federal level, as well as a Charter of Rights and Freedoms (which was conceived at the time as an "opt-in" arrangement for the provinces!). According to Bill C-60, these transformations would have involved replacing the Senate with a House of the Federation, with half of its proposed 118 members selected by provincial assemblies and the other half selected by the House of Commons. This would have been accompanied by an entrenched representation of Québec in the Supreme Court, with the right to name three judges. In addition, the ability of the House of the Federation to veto changes to language legislation could be reduced to a 60 day suspensive veto, but could be overturned with the support of two-thirds of the House of Commons.[15]

In a reference decision in 1979, the Supreme Court of Canada ruled that the Parliament of Canada was not empowered to modify itself in a manner that might affect the provinces.

The Court argued that despite the power of amendment in Section 91(1), the House of the Federation, in substituting for the Senate, was affecting an institution that was of interest to the provinces.[16]

The Québec government showed no interest in this new initiative, as it was in the process of preparing its own White Paper, *Québec-Canada: A New Deal* (1979), which argued for the formation of "two communities" where nine provinces would reconstitute Canada and the tenth, that is Québec, would exist as a separate state, on a political level, but would remain tied to Canada in the form of a new economic union. From Québec's perspective, the sovereignty-association option had the advantage of dealing directly with the enduring issue of duality, whereas in the rest of the country it was perceived as ignoring the emerging equality of provinces principle, increasingly popular among less populated provinces outside central Canada.

In May 1979, Canada elected its first Conservative government since 1968. Prime Minister Joe Clark was more disposed than Trudeau towards an acceptance of decentralized federalism, expressed in the conception of Canada as a "community of communities," which was favourable to more harmonious Québec-Canada relations. At the time, Canada was experiencing both a debilitating economic recession and a continuing constitutional crisis. Despite the change in the federal position, the Québec government under René Lévesque remained committed to holding a referendum on sovereignty-association. Then, unexpectedly, the cards were re-shuffled. The Conservative minority government was forced to call an election and the Trudeau Liberals returned to power in February 1980 with a renewed desire to crush the "separatists" and demonstrated little interest in finding solutions to Québec's claims.

During the 1980 referendum campaign, Trudeau challenged Québec "independentists" and sent his Québec-based ministers to campaign for the "No" forces. The Trudeau Liberals had promised that defeat of the referendum would not be interpreted as an endorsement of the status quo, promising to elaborate policies that would respond to Québec's special needs and concerns. Many supporters of this option during the referendum campaign were made to believe that renewed federalism meant an official recognition of Québec as a distinct society/people, and that new powers commensurate with this position would be given to Québec. One will remember that federalists of different persuasions had rallied around Pierre Elliott Trudeau to defeat Québec's claim for sovereignty-association as a new option. Québec's federal MPs, in an ultimate attempt to convince Québecers to vote against the PQ's proposal for independence, claimed that they were putting their seats on the line. This was generally believed to demonstrate the genuine desire of the federal government to accommodate Québec culturally and linguistically.

In 1981, the federal government repatriated the constitution without the consent of Québec. Instead of being granted special recognition, Québec was weakened by the federal order. The move was repudiated in Québec by both federalists and nationalists active on the provincial political scene, including those federalists who sided with Trudeau in May 1980. These federalists felt a sense of betrayal. Trudeau's victory turned sour as opinion leaders who once fought for the federalist cause (such as Claude Ryan, Robert Bourassa, and the business community at large) called for corrective measures to be implemented rapidly in order to keep Canada together.

This episode reveals that the federal government, contrary to what it had promised during the referendum campaign of May 1980, had interpreted the results favouring the federalist option (40 per cent for the "yes" option) as an indication that Québecers desired to remain within the federation, rather than as a mandate for its renewal. Ottawa's stance towards Québec became uncompromising since the so-called "separatists" were deemed to be disorganized and demoralized. Trudeau challenged provincialism and decentralization as outdated principles, and proposed a centralist vision. The PQ was in disarray, the Québec Liberal Party had fought a tough campaign against independence along with Ottawa, the Trudeau Liberals had a majority government, the state of the economy was abysmal, and a neo-liberal ideology was gaining support.

Trudeau lost no time after the referendum and planned a constitutional conference for September 1980. Afraid of a possible unilateral move by Ottawa if talks failed, Québec was busy forging alliances with other provinces. The federal government persisted by introducing, on 2 October 1980, a "Proposed Resolution for Address to Her Majesty the Queen Respecting the Constitution of Canada." Québec and seven other provinces — the Gang of Eight — opposed such action, preparing reference cases in the Québec, Manitoba, and Newfoundland Courts of Appeal that proved disappointing for the provincial forces. Ultimately, the case reached the Supreme Court of Canada, which reached a majority decision. Richard Simeon and Ian Robinson summarize the decision as follows:

> [I]t would be legal for Parliament to act without provincial consent, but that this would still be unconstitutional since it would breach an established convention of substantial provincial consent. . . . Provinces had been warned that if they continued to delay action, Ottawa might move. The only way out was to return to the intergovernmental table. But now there was a critical difference: the convention, said the Court, did not mean unanimity; it required only "substantial consent." Two provinces was clearly not "substantial consent," but one province could no longer stop the process. The groundwork for a settlement without Québec had been laid.[17]

Taking advantage of these circumstances, a constitutional conference was called by Trudeau for November 1981. With the support of the Québec National Assembly and seven provincial Premiers (Ontario and New Brunswick excepted), Premier Lévesque expressed opposition to the central government's plans to reform and patriate the constitution unilaterally. Initially, and strategically, Lévesque agreed to the principle of provincial equality. At the same time, he continued to oppose patriation in the absence of agreement on an amending formula and a new division of powers, demanded that Québec be recognized as a culturally and linguistically distinct society, and asked for the responsibilities and resources that this implied. In return for Québec's acceptance of the equality of provinces notion, the premiers accepted Québec's veto right.

Opposing any form of special status, Trudeau isolated Québec. On 5 November 1981, in the absence of Premier Lévesque, the other premiers agreed to patriation and the entrenchment of a Charter of Rights and Freedoms. With agreement came their preferred amending formula[18] and the right to opt out of the secondary provisions of the Charter. The opting-out (or "notwithstanding") clause ensured the western premiers' support of the package deal. Québec was isolated, with no other course of action but to make use of the notwithstanding clause, which it did systematically until the election of the Québec Liberals in December 1985. The decision to patriate with an entrenched Charter of Rights and Freedoms proved to be a major assault on Québec's vision of federalism in an environment that was growing increasingly hostile to any protective measures. According to most centralist federalists, time would heal everything.[19]

This period of transition that began in the early 1960s with the firm desire to have Québec included as a fundamental element of the Canadian federation proceeds on a note of exclusion, isolation, and the refusal of recognition. During this time, the Canadian constitutional order has been reconsidered without Québec's demands being satisfied.

THE ESTABLISHMENT OF A NEW CONSTITUTIONAL ORDER: 1982 TO THE PRESENT

The imposition of a new constitutional order in 1982 constitutes a break with continuity and disregards the dualist vision as a defining element of the Canadian federation. According to the political philosopher James Tully, the imposition of this new constitutional order has resulted in a situation in which Québec is not free within the Canadian federation for at least three reasons:

1. Other member states of the federation can impose constitutional amendments without its consent;
2. The content of the amending formula, introduced in 1982, renders it virtually impossible, in practice, to amend the Constitution so that Québec be recognized as a nation;

To these two reasons, Tully adds a third following the decision in August 1998 by the Supreme Court on the right of Québec to secede:

3. The Court maintains that phase two of the negotiations, initiated by the attainment of a clear majority in a referendum, subject to a clear question, must be framed in terms of the present amending formula. Therefore, due to the first reason mentioned above, Québec is not bound by this amending formula. Moreover, since Québec's right to initiate constitutional changes is impeded in practice, this phase of negotiations would conclude in an impasse and according to the Court itself, this injustice would legitimize Québec's position of claiming the right to secede unilaterally. Finally, every demand of recognition as a nation . . . implies as a corollary a demand for an amendment to the present amending formula.[20]

The fact that Québec is bound to the present amending formula, which it contests, implies in fact that its rights to propose constitutional changes are not recognized and that its sense of liberty has been unquestionably persecuted. A more in-depth discussion of the decision of the Supreme Court will be provided below.

The Constitution of 1982 has thus resulted in a reduction of democratic space by denying Québec a central place in the Canadian federation. This provided some motivation for the Conservatives of Brian Mulroney, following an election victory in September 1984, to identify a new path to repatriation and reintegrate Québec into the constitutional family with "honour and enthusiasm." Responding to this policy with friendly overtures, René Lévesque decided to re-enter the constitutional fray and spoke of the new situation as representing a "beau risque" for Québec.[21] In May 1985, Lévesque presented the new federal Prime Minister with a "Draft Agreement on the Constitution"[22] that embodied 22 claims made by Québec to settle the constitutional crisis.

These propositions would essentially be re-visited in the constitutional position adopted by Robert Bourassa upon his election victory in Québec in December 1985. The differences were more a question of degree than of kind. The *Péquiste* project, therefore, would serve as a point of departure for the Liberals in the negotiations that followed.[23] It must be noted that between 1981 and 1985, Lévesque, having lost the referendum in May 1980, negotiated from a position of weakness. This changed somewhat when Bourassa, a bona fide federalist, returned as Premier of Québec. The Québec Liberals limited their bottom-line demands to five, as a minimal condition to return to the negotiating table: (1) the explicit recognition of Québec as a distinct society; (2) increased power to Québec in immigration regarding recruitment, administration, and integration of new arrivals; (3) appointment of three Supreme Court judges with expertise in Québec civil law; (4) containment of the federal spending power, and; (5) a full veto for Québec on any new modifications to be made to the Canadian constitution.

The Meech Lake proposals (1987–1990) attempted to deal with most of these claims but failed due, on the one hand, to a lack of openness to difference on the part of the Canadian partners, and on the other, to a reform process (amending formula) that ignored Québec's view of Canadian dualism, as a principal founding partner of the Canadian federation. For Ottawa, the Meech Lake Accord reflected a constant preoccupation with uniformity as an operational principle of Canadian federalism, except for the distinct society clause. By providing all the other provinces that which had been granted to Québec, Ottawa could remove any impression of giving Québec a special status. In turn, the federal government would have obtained a major concession from Québec, as it was willing to recognize for the first time the federal spending power in spheres of exclusive provincial jurisdiction. In Québec, the federal spending power has always been viewed as a federal intrusion, and its acceptance by the Québec government led to great disenchantment among autonomists and nationalists. In the rest of Canada, many observers believed that the distinct society clause would seriously weaken the federal government, for the reason that those provinces choosing not to participate in pan-Canadian programs would be afforded the possibility of opting out with full financial compensation.

As the Meech Lake negotiations began, other interests organized with the aim of defeating Québec's vision of federalism. In the process, Québec's claims became secondary and were depicted as a threat to the rights of First Nations, the equality of provinces and the universality of social programs. The provincial elections of Manitoba, New Brunswick, and Newfoundland provided a platform for leaders to appeal to anti-Québec sentiments. This signalled the failure of the Meech Lake Accord.

Following the failure of the Meech Lake Accord in June 1990, the government of Québec no longer had a mandate to negotiate its reinsertion into the Canadian federation. This resulted in the Québec Liberal party's elaboration of a new policy platform (the Allaire Report) and convinced the Québec government to set up the Commission on the Political and Constitutional Future of Québec (the Bélanger-Campeau Commission). The mandate of this Commission was for a new definition of the political and constitutional arrangements that determined the status of Québec and its relations with other member-states of the federation. This constitutes a unique moment in Canadian history. A province, through its governing party and with the full backing of the official opposition, decided to assess the appropriateness of its continued association with the rest of the country of which it was a founding member, reviving the 1981 unanimity that had condemned unilateral patriation of the BNA Act without Québec's consent.

Following the tabling of the Bélanger-Campeau Report that recommended the setting up of two special National Assembly committees, Bill-150 was enacted to confirm such a proposal. The Québec government intended to maintain pressure on the other governments (provincial and federal) with these two public forums, by forcing a confrontation with the questions of renewed federalism and sovereignty on a daily basis. As a result, the Commission asked that a referendum on the future of Québec in Canada be held no later than 26 October 1992.

In an attempt to regain the initiative, on 24 September 1991, Ottawa released a discussion paper to propose, against all expectations, a restructured federation along the lines of a centralized economic model, and set up a joint Parliamentary Committee (Castonguay-Dobbie, and later Dobbie-Beaudoin) to once more examine the perennial issue of Québec's relations with the rest of Canada.

Contrary to all expectations, the federal government and the nine anglophone provinces reached a consensus on 7 July 1992. The essence of the deal was later confirmed in the 28 August 1992 Consensus Report on the Constitution (Charlottetown Accord). Far from recognizing Québec's distinct status in Canada, and proceeding towards a devolution of powers, the agreement proposed an increase of powers for the central government through the constitutionalization of its spending power, and the strengthening of federal institutions. Instead of transferring powers to the provinces, as has been demanded by Québec, the Charlottetown Accord proposed to make room for the provinces in the Senate and to consolidate the powers of the federal government to intervene in spheres of exclusive provincial jurisdiction. The Accord also included a "Canada clause" that gave equal weight to the distinct society clause, the equality of provinces principle, and the obligation for Canadians and their governments to promote Québec's anglophone minority. Moreover, a major section of the proposed accord dealt with Aboriginal rights to self-government.

The Accord was soundly defeated in Québec (56.7 per cent), as it was in Manitoba (61.6 per cent), in Saskatchewan (55.3 per cent), in Alberta (60.2 per cent), in British Columbia (68.3 per cent), in Nova Scotia (51.3 per cent) and in the Yukon (56.3 per cent). In addition, the Accord was rejected by Aboriginal communities throughout the country, to the great disappointment of the Chief of the Assembly of First Nations, Ovide Mercredi, whose leadership was shaken.

The defeat of the Charlottetown Accord constituted an unprecedented dismissal of the political class, as Canadians throughout the country said No to a package deal cobbled behind closed doors. Defeat also represented a major setback for Robert Bourassa who, according to his closest constitutional advisors, had "caved in" as he failed to defend Québec's traditional demands and political *acquis*. The Québec Premier did not secure even the five minimal conditions of the Meech Lake proposals that were to be met before Québec would agree to re-enter formal constitutional negotiations. In short, Québec had made no gains in the sharing of powers, and saw the centralization of power as being further ensconced, since the federal government could negotiate five-year reversible deals with individual provinces. Moreover, Ottawa confirmed and potentially reinforced its capabilities of intervention in areas of exclusive provincial jurisdiction. It is in this context that the more nationalist wing of the Québec Liberal Party would leave the party to form, under the leadership of Jean Allaire and later Mario Dumont, the *Action Démocratique du Québec*.

The consequences of the failure of the Charlottetown Accord were major for the federal Conservatives in that, having almost achieved reform earlier in their mandate, they were virtually wiped off the map in the 25 October 1993 elections. Québecers also voted in large numbers for the Bloc Québecois, as the party made impressive inroads by winning 54 of the 75 seats in Québec to form Her Majesty's Loyal Opposition in Ottawa. A nationalist party from Québec now occupied a strategic place within the House of Commons itself and could more effectively push for Québec's demands. The victory of the Parti Québecois in the 12 September 1994 election followed, and Jacques Parizeau, strengthened by the presence of the Bloc as an ally of Québec in Ottawa, pursued his intentions in favour of Québec sovereignty.

On the federal side, the governing party of Jean Chrétien proceeded, as though the national question in Québec was of interest to no one, to engage in a major reform project in the area of social programs. The best way to achieve this end was to significantly cut the lifeblood of the provinces, accomplished in February 1995 by the ratification of Bill C-76 that cut transfers to the provinces by a third, by six billion dollars over two years, in the field of health.[24]

It is in this context that a project of sovereignty, based on an economic and eventually a political partnership, was proposed as a solution to deal with the constitutional impasse in terms of Québec's position within the federation. The second referendum in 15 years was called on 30 October 1995, asking Québecers to determine their political future. Unlike the outcome of the 1980 referendum, which saw the No forces gain nearly 60 per cent of the vote, this campaign resulted in 50.6 per cent for the No camp. Moreover, 49.4 per cent of Québecers endorsed the option of sovereignty-partnership with a view to establishing a new political entity in

Québec free to negotiate a new economic and political union with its partners.[25] A slim margin of 54,288 votes separated the two camps, and the referendum signalled somewhat of a victory for democracy, as 94 per cent of registered voters exercised their right to vote.

Reticent as always to any form of accommodation with regards to Québec, Prime Minister Chrétien preferred to maintain the constitutional status quo. In justifying such inertia, Chrétien referred to the notion that citizens were "fed up" with constitutional issues and that their immediate concerns related to more pressing matters of unemployment and the economy. With a certain urgency, and mostly to give the impression that it understood Québec's demands for political recognition, the Chrétien government adopted, by a simple statute, a resolution affirming the distinct character of Québec society within Canada, on December 11, 1995. Furthermore, on 2 February 1996, the federal government added a new obstacle to constitutional reform by superimposing a regional veto right to four territorial groups, consisting of Québec, Ontario, Western Canada, and the Atlantic provinces, onto the provisions already in the Canadian Constitution.[26] These veto rights are not guaranteed constitutionally, as they could be withdrawn following the adoption of a parliamentary statute.

In the same spirit, Ottawa and the Canadian provinces drafted the Calgary Declaration[27] on 14 February 1997, after public consultation among the Canadian population, and reiterated certain principles on which Canadian unity would be based. Having recognized the unique character of Québec society among a large array of conditions so as to undermine its significance, the signatories rejected all forms of asymmetrical federalism and agreed to prioritize one of the jurisdictions exclusive to the provinces, the performance of social programs. Moreover, they agreed that the declaration constitutes a framework for public consultation meant to reinforce the Canadian federation. The door was open for Ottawa to engage Canadians in a project for a social union, a project that had been in the works since the Charlottetown Accord.

The federal regime, notwithstanding a brief period of hesitation under the government of the federal Conservatives from 1984–1993, continued its assault on any form of provincial autonomy and chose to reinforce the new constitutional order of 1982 by establishing the rules of the game on its own. The re-election of a majority Liberal government in 1997, as well as in 2000, would contribute to making the task easier. The approach was simple: if the provinces did not collaborate in the direction desired by Ottawa, their transfers would be cut. The re-election of a sovereigntist majority government in Québec in 1998 did not put an end to the constitutional debates. Moreover, the fact that the provincial Liberals under the leadership of Jean Charest fell short of winning the 1998 election, yet still managed to garner more votes than the Parti Québécois, significantly limited the power of the governing party.

More recent years have been characterized by confrontations between Québec and the federal government. With a strong electoral victory in 1997, the Chrétien government engaged in a full frontal assault on Québec's right to secede. The responses obtained following the Reference case regarding the secession of Québec were not entirely expected by the federal government. Attempting to re-establish the principle of continuity in constitutional discourse, the Supreme Court recognized, as the very basis of the Canadian federation, four main principles: (1) federalism, (2) democracy, (3) constitutionalism and the primacy of law, and (4) the respect for minorities. The Supreme Court underlined, in Sections 84 and 85 of its ruling, that a constitutional modification could permit a province to secede. The Court contends in paragraph 87 that "the results of a referendum have no direct role or legal effect in our constitutional scheme,

[but] . . . it would confer legitimacy on the efforts of the government of Québec to initiate the Constitution's amendment process in order to secede by constitutional means."[28]

If the repatriation of the Constitution in 1982 undermined Québec's liberty of action, as James Tully contends, the Court Ruling allows for some corrective measures. Paragraph 88 constitutes the Gordian knot,

> The clear repudiation by the people of Québec of the existing constitutional order would confer legitimacy on demands for secession, and place an obligation on the other provinces and the federal government to acknowledge and respect that expression of democratic will by entering into negotiations and conducting them in accordance with the underlying constitutional principles . . .

The ruling of the Supreme Court allows for the possibility of relations between Québec and Canada to be more open, for the re-vitalization to some extent of the democratic foundations of the Canadian federation, and paves the way for a possible return to the principle of continuity. The Court stresses that the obligation to negotiate with Québec remains an inalienable right. In paragraph 92, the ruling contends, with some interest, that

> The rights of other provinces and the federal government cannot deny the right of the government of Québec to pursue secession, should a clear majority of the people of Québec choose that goal, so long as in doing so, Québec respects the rights of others.

Contrary to repatriation in 1982, which discredited the Supreme Court in the eyes of many Québecers, the Reference Regarding the Secession of Québec has to some extent restored its credibility. James Tully concurs,

> The condition of liberty of a multinational society rests on the fact that its members remain free to initiate discussions and negotiations with regards to possible amending formulas to the structure of recognition in place and, as a corollary, the other members have the *obligation* to respond to those legitimate demands. A member that seeks recognition as a nation (in a form that is itself open to objection) is free to the extent that the possibilities for discussions, negotiations and amendments are not impeded, in practice, by arbitrary constraints. The Constitution of a society that endures such obstructions can be likened to a strait-jacket or a structure of domination. This situation of an absence of liberty is revealed, in Canada, as much by the case of Québec as that of the First Nations.[29]

What is the situation in Canada? Both the Aboriginal nations and the Québec nation are confronted with situations of domination. The repatriation of the Constitution has led Québec into an era of subjection in terms of its political liberty and the imposition of a new constitutional order.

Without delving deeply into the Clarity Bill (C-20) . . . it is worth noting that we are under an imposition of arbitrary measures by the federal government. This law, to some extent, undercuts the Ruling of the Supreme Court with regards to Québec's right to secede and undermines any desire for constitutional negotiations that Québec may want to pursue.

The re-election of the federal Liberals in the autumn of 2000 and the selection of Bernard Landry to replace Lucien Bouchard as leader of the Québec government in May 2001 did not bode well for any rapprochement between Québec and Canada in the near future. Moreover, while Québec persists in demonstrating that Canadian federalism is a façade, Ottawa continues to undermine the federal condition[30] pertaining to the non-subordination of powers by substituting for them a set of principles that do not take account of Canadian diversity, by imposing an increasing amount of constraining and homogenizing public policies, thus rendering any significant reforms to the federation illusory. Truly helpful reforms would respond to the fundamental expectations of Quebecers with regard to their diversity and would affirm a legitimate context for real choice, which would be supported comprehensively by Quebecers.

CONCLUSION

The federal elections in autumn 2000 have not provided any reason for optimism with regard to the re-establishment of constitutional peace in Canada. The Liberals of Jean Chrétien, having succeeded in securing a majority government for the third consecutive time, feel little urgency in proceeding towards constitutional modifications that would accommodate Québec's demands. It is, therefore, no great surprise that the federal ministers reacted to the recent political program of the Québec Liberal Party, Un projet pour le Québec. Affirmation, autonomie et leadership (2001) with a simple mention that this party did not exercise power in Québec, therefore it did not merit any commentary.

The Canadian condition reduces Québec to merely a province like the others within the federation, which is far from corresponding to the image that Québec projects for itself here as well as on the international scene. Rupturing the founding constitutional order, Québec—Canada relations after repatriation in 1982 have entered a phase of non-recognition and the impoverishing of democratic practices. The ruling of the Supreme Court concerning Québec's right to secede served to widen the realm of the possible, only to be confined and limited by the federal government, which evidently sought to impede the holding of a fundamental debate on the future of the federation.

By constantly ignoring constitutional conventions and denying the existence of the Québec nation, the potential of the government to forge a symbol of identity and to mobilize politically remains doubtful. In short, the Canadian federal experience is not worth pursuing unless the member-states are free to adhere to the federation and all structures of domination are condemned.

NOTES

1. The comments of Andrée Lajoie were very useful in the recasting of this text.
2. See the Commission sur le déséquilibre fiscal, *Pour un nouveau portage des moyens financiers au Canada* (Commission Séguin) (Québec: Bibliothèque nationale du Québec, 2002).
3. See Gérard Bouchard, "La vision siamoise de John Saul," *Le Devoir*, 15 and 17 Jan. 2000; John Saul, "Il n'y a pas de peuple conquis," *Le Devoir*, 22 and 24 Jan. 2000.
4. Hilda Neatby, *The Québec Act: Protest and Policy* (Scarborough: Prentice Hall, 1972); Philip Lawson, *The Imperial Challenge: Québec and Britain in the Age of the American Revolution* (Montreal: McGill-Queen's University Press, 1989).
5. Garth Stevenson, *Community Besieged: The Anglophone Minority and the Politics of Québec* (Montreal: McGill-Queen's University Press, 1999), ch. 2.
6. Thomas-Jean-Jacques Loranger, *Lettres sur l'interprétation de la constitution fédérale: premiere lettre* (Québec: Imprimerie A. Côté et Cie, 1883).
7. Royal Commission on Aboriginal Peoples (RCAP), *Partners in Confederation: Aboriginal Peoples, Self-Government and the Constitution* (Ottawa: Minister of Supply and Services, 1993), 22–23.
8. Every federal party has at one time or another in that decade recognized the concept of two founding peoples as a fundamental principle of the federation. This recognition, however, would vary in significance in the decades that followed.
9. The doctrine recognized and defended the right of provinces to negotiate agreements with international actors or organizations in their fields of jurisdiction.
10. Ironically, Québec accepted the principle of unanimity in 1980 in a last-ditch effort to block the repatriation project proposed by Ottawa.
11. Garth Stevenson, *Unfulfilled Union: Canadian Federalism and National Unity* (Toronto: Gage, 1982), 210.
12. Pierre Elliott Trudeau, "1976 Correspondence to all Provincial Premiers," in Peter Meekison, ed., *Canadian Federalism: Myth or Reality* (Toronto: Methuen, 1977), 140–67.

13. The Task Force on Canadian Unity, *Se retrouver. Observations et recommendations*, vol. 1 (Pepin-Robarts Report) (Ottawa: Official Editor, 1979), 143. Author's translation.

14. This consists of two approaches aimed at "resolving once and for all" the question of Québec: a conciliatory approach and a coercive one following the victory of the PQ in 1994 and the results obtained (nearly 50 per cent of the votes) during the referendum in 1995. We can refer with much interest to the work of the jurist Daniel Turp, notably his work, *La nation bâillonnée: le plan B ou l'offensive d'Ottawa contre le Québec* (Montreal: VLB éditeur, 2000).

15. Douglas Verney, *Three Civilizations, Two Cultures, One State, Canada's Political Traditions* (Durham: Duke University Press, 1986), 367.

16. According to Douglas Verney, the Court supported its decision with the federal White Paper, published in 1965, which recognized the "role of the provinces, even for modifications touching questions that were not exclusive to jurisdictions of the provinces." Author's translation, Verney, *Three Civilizations*, 367.

17. Richard Simeon and Ian Robinson; *State, Society and the Development of Canadian Federalism* (Toronto: University of Toronto Press, 1990), 278.

18. The principal amending formula provided for constitutional changes to be undertaken with the support of seven provinces covering 50 per cent of the Canadian population. The reform of the amending formula was subject to unanimity. This situation was imposed on Québec, which from that moment on had to abide by rules adopted by others, losing all liberty of action in this area.

19. If one is to believe the events that surrounded the celebrations organized by the federal government to mark 20 years of repatriation, in April 2002, federal strategists have not yet regretted their actions, even though the referendum of October 1995 could potentially have represented a fateful moment for the country.

20. James Tully, "Liberté et dévoilement dans les sociétés plurinationales," *Globe*, 2, 2 (1999): 31–32. Author's translation. Also, for a larger analysis, see James Tully, "Introduction," in Alain-G. Gagnon and James Tully, eds., *Multinational Democracies* (Cambridge: Cambridge University Press, 2001) 1–33.

21. For a recent political analysis, see Michel Vastel, "La Charte a 20 ans: Des promesses plusieurs fois repudiées," *Le Soleil*, 17 April 2002, A-6.

22. This document was largely inspired by a document prepared by the Ministry of Intergovernmental Affairs during the first mandate of the PQ government. See *Les positions constitutionnelles du Québec sur le partage des pouvoirs (1960–76)* (Québec: Éditeur officiel du Québec, 1978). For document updated to March 2001, see www.mce.gouv.qc.ca.

23. Before arriving to power, the provincial Liberals had prepared a series of documents that discussed questions for which compromises would have to be negotiated. See *Une nouvelle constitution canadienne*, (1980), also known as the Livre Beige, *Un nouveau leadership pour le Québec*, (1983), and *Maîtriser l'avenir* (1985).

24. See Alain-G. Gagnon and Hugh Segal, "Introduction," in *The Canadian Social Union Without Québec; 8 Critical Analyses* (Montreal: Institute for Research on Public Policy, 2000).

25. Alain-G. Gagnon and Guy Lachapelle, "Québec Confronts Canada: Two Competing Societal Projects Searching for Legitimacy," *Publius*, 26, 3, (1996): 177–91.

26. This indicated to specialists on the issue that the constitutional path had been closed. See Robert Dutrisac, "Une camisole de force," *Le Devoir*, 14 April 2002, G-7.

27. http://www.ccu-cuc.ca/fran/dossiers/calgary.html.

28. *Reference re Secession of Québec*, 2 S.C.R., 1998.

29. James Tully, "Liberté et dévoilement dans les sociétés plurinationales," 30. Author's translation.

30. Donald Smiley, *The Federal Condition in Canada* (Toronto: McGraw-Hill, 1987).

Topic Fifteen

Entering the Twenty-First Century

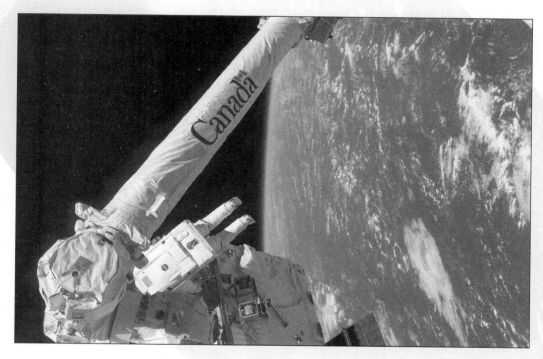

The Canadarm2 (Space Station Remote Manipulator System) is a critical component of the orbiting International Space Station.

As Canada enters the 21st century, it faces a number of challenges whose origins extend back into the 19th and 20th centuries, if not earlier. History helps us to understand how we got to this point in time, as well as, one hopes, provides some guidelines for the future.

The following three articles deal with three major contemporaneous issues at the beginning of the 21st century. In "Aboriginal Peoples in the Twenty-First Century: A Plea for Realism," political scientist Alan C. Cairns provides a tempered discussion on how First Nations and non–First Nations might live together in the future. In the first half of the paper, he looks at the historical evolution of First Nations and non–First Nations relations in Canada as context for studying the current situation, emphasizing that the white paper of 1969, in its heated rejection by the First Nations, unintentionally inaugurated a new era in terms of the federal government's approach to First Nations. A policy of paternalism gave way to a new era in which the federal government came to recognize First Nations rights. Cairns sees this paradigm shift as the Canadian equivalent of the end of colonialism in the overseas territories of the former European empires. The transition was marked by the substitution of the concept of Indians as "wards of the state" to be governed by others as evident in Section 91 (24) of the British North America Act of 1867 with that of "aboriginal peoples of Canada" in Section 35(2) of The Constitution Act of 1982 with their own rights, including the right to self-government. The transition is also evident in the important change in terminology from "Indians" to "First Nations" as the form of identification. He notes, however, that the term "First Nations" should not be construed to mean independence, but rather the recognition of an autonomous people *within* Canada. Cairns argues that this new status offers two roads to the future: self-government through reserves as well as in urban areas. He explores both alternatives and the implications for First Nations and non–First Nations.

In "The Merits of Multiculturalism," philosopher Will Kymlicka examines the success of Canada's policy of multiculturalism, first put forward as an official government policy by the Trudeau government in 1971 and then enacted into law as the Multiculturalism Act by the Mulroney government in 1988. The policy had four aims: to support the cultural development of ethnocultural groups; to help members of ethnocultural groups overcome barriers to full participation in Canadian society; to promote creative encounters and interchange among all ethnocultural groups; and to assist new Canadians in acquiring at least one of Canada's official languages. Kymlicka argues that Canada has succeeded in implementing all four of these objectives, making the policy of multiculturalism a resounding success.

Political scientist Rob Huebert looks at the issue of Canadian sovereignty and security in the Canadian North in "Climate Change and Canadian Sovereignty in the Northwest Passage." He argues that global warming especially in the polar North has serious implications for Canadian control of the Northwest Passage. He explores the implications in terms of the traditional historical argument, the attempt to enclose the Canadian Arctic Archipelago by straight baselines, and the claim that the Inuit's use of the ice in the waterway for their livelihood is the equivalent of claiming the land. A dispute currently exists with Denmark over the tiny Hans Island, located in the channel between Ellesmere Island and northwestern Greenland. This is a very minor concern compared to that posed by the United States. Huebert maintains that the greatest challenge to Canadian sovereignty in the North today comes from the south — just as it did at the time of Confederation with the threat of American annexation of British North America.

What is the nature of the paradigm shift with regards to First Nations that occurred since the white paper of 1969, and what is its impact on First Nations and non–First Nations relations in Canada in the 21st century? Has the policy of multiculturalism helped or hindered the development of a Canadian identity? Does multiculturalism pose certain challenges for Canada as it enters the 21st century? How does global warming in the Arctic affect

Canadian–American relations, thus going to the heart of the issue of Canadian sovereignty and a Canadian identity in North America?

Recent surveys of the history of First Nations in Canada include Olive Patricia Dickason, *Canada's First Nations: A History of Founding Peoples from Earliest Times*, 3rd ed. (Don Mills, ON: Oxford University Press, 2002), and Arthur J. Ray, *I Have Lived Here since the World Began: An Illustrated History of Canada's Native People* rev. ed. (Toronto: Key Porter, 2005 [1996]). Edward S. Rogers and Donald B. Smith, eds., *Aboriginal Ontario* (Toronto: Dundurn Press, 1994), looks at the history of First Nations in Ontario.

For a review of Canadian Indian policy in the early 20th century see E. Brian Titley, *A Narrow Vision: Duncan Campbell Scott and the Administration of Indian Affairs in Canada* (Vancouver: University of British Columbia Press, 1986). Two important summaries of federal Indian policy can be found in Ian A.L. Getty and Antoine S. Lussier, eds., *As Long as the Sun Shines and Water Flows* (Vancouver: University of British Columbia Press, 1983): George F.G. Stanley, "As Long as the Sun Shines and Water Flows: An Historical Comment," pp. 1–26; and John L. Tobias, "Protection, Civilization, Assimilation: An Outline History of Canada's Indian Policy," pp. 39–55. J.R. Miller provides a complete account in *Skyscrapers Hide the Heavens: A History of Indian-White Relations in Canada*, 3rd ed. (Toronto: University of Toronto Press, 2000); see also Noel Dyck, *What Is the Indian "Problem"? Tutelage and Resistance in Canadian Indian Administration* (St. John's: Institute of Social and Economic Research, Memorial University of Newfoundland, 1991). Still valuable for the First Nations' perspective is Harold Cardinal, *The Unjust Society: The Tragedy of Canada's Indians*, reprint (Vancouver: Douglas and McIntyre, 1999).

For First Nations politics in the last 35 years, consult Sally M. Weaver, *Making Canadian Indian Policy: The Hidden Agenda, 1968–1970* (Toronto: University of Toronto Press, 1981); and J. Rick Ponting, ed., *Arduous Journey: Canadian Indians and Decolonization* (Toronto: McClelland & Stewart, 1986). On First Nations self-government see John H. Hylton, ed., *Aboriginal Self-Government in Canada*, 2nd ed. (Saskatoon: Purich Publishing, 1999), and Dan Smith, *The Seventh Fire: The Struggle for Aboriginal Government* (Toronto: Key Porter, 1993). An excellent source book on Aboriginal rights is Bradford W. Morse, ed., *Aboriginal Peoples and the Law: Indian, Métis and Inuit Rights in Canada*, rev. 1st ed. (Ottawa: Carleton University Press, 1989).

Very useful for Canadian–First Nations relations is John Bird, Lorraine Land, and Murray Macadam, eds., *Nation to Nation: Aboriginal Sovereignty and the Future of Canada* (Toronto: Irwin, 2002). Two recent opposing contributions to the subject by political scientists are Alan C. Cairns, *Citizens Plus: Aboriginal Peoples and the Canadian State* (Vancouver: University of British Columbia Press, 2000), and Tom Flanagan, *First Nations? Second Thoughts* (Montreal/Kingston: McGill-Queen's University Press, 2000). A valuable collection of articles on contemporary issues is J.R. Miller, *Lethal Legacy: Current Native Controversies in Canada* (Toronto: McClelland and Stewart, 2004). See as well the articles in David R. Newhouse, Cora J. Voyageur, and Dan Beavon, *Hidden in Plain Sight: Contributions of Aboriginal Peoples to Canadian Identity and Culture* (Toronto: University of Toronto Press, 2005).

Two overviews of Canadian immigration policy are Ninette Kelley and Michael Trebilcock, *The Making of the Mosaic: A History of Canadian Immigration Policy* (Toronto: University of Toronto Press, 1998) and Donald H. Avery, *Reluctant Host: Canada's Response to Immigrant Workers, 1896–1994* (Toronto: McClelland and Stewart, 1995). For a critical view of Canadian immigration, see Daniel Stoffman, *Who Gets In: What's Wrong with Canada's Immigration Policy—And How to Fix It* (Toronto: Macfarlane Walter & Ross, 2002), and Reg Whitaker, *Double Standard: The Secret History of Canadian Immigration* (Toronto: Lester & Orpen Dennys, 1989).

Will Kymlicka's defence of Canada's policy of multiculturalism can be found in greater detail in *Finding Our Way: Rethinking Ethnocultural Relations in Canada* (Toronto: Oxford University Press, 1998), from which the excerpt "The Merits of Multiculturalism" is taken. See as well Andrew Cardozo and Louis Musto, eds., *The Battle over Multiculturalism* (Ottawa: Pearson-Shoyama Institute, 1997); Richard J.F. Day, *Multiculturalism and the History of Canadian Diversity* (Toronto: University of Toronto Press, 2000); and Augie Fleras and Jean Leonard Elliott, *Engaging Diversity: Multiculturalism in Canada,* 2nd ed. (Toronto: Nelson Thomson Learning, 2002). For criticisms of multiculturalism, consult Reginald Bibby, *Mosaic Madness: The Poverty and Potential of Life in Canada* (Toronto: Stoddart, 1990); Neil Bissoondath, *Selling Illusions: The Cult of Multiculturalism in Canada,* rev. ed. (Toronto: Penguin Canada, 2002); and Richard Gwyn, *Nationalism without Walls: The Unbearable Lightness of Being Canadian* (Toronto: McClelland and Stewart, 1995). Vanaja Dhruvarajan's "People of Colour and National Identity in Canada," *Journal of Canadian Studies,* 35, 2 (Summer 2000): 166–175 adds to the debate on multiculturalism and Canadian identity.

Racism and discrimination are examined in Evelyn Kallen, *Ethnicity and Human Rights in Canada,* 2nd ed. (Toronto: Oxford University Press, 1995); B. Singh Bolaria and Peter S. Li, *Racial Oppression in Canada,* 2nd ed. (Toronto: Garamond Press, 1988); Frances Henry, *The Caribbean Diaspora in Toronto: Learning to Live with Racism* (Toronto: University of Toronto Press, 1994); Eleanor Laquian et al., *The Silent Debate: Asian Immigration and Racism in Canada* (Vancouver: Institute of Asian Research, 1998); Frances Henry et al., *The Colour of Democracy: Racism in Canadian Society,* 2nd ed. (Toronto: Harcourt Brace, 2000); and Leo Driedger and Shiva S. Halli, *Race and Racism: Canada's Challenge* (Montreal/Kingston: McGill-Queen's University Press, 2000). An important historiographical work is J.W. Berry and J.A. Lapointe, eds., *Ethnicity and Culture in Canada: The Research Landscape* (Toronto: University of Toronto Press, 1994). An essential work is Paul Robert Magocsi, ed., *Encyclopedia of Canada's Peoples* (Toronto: University of Toronto Press, 1999).

Historical studies on the North include two volumes by Morris Zaslow: *The Opening of the Canadian North, 1870–1914* (Toronto: McClelland & Stewart, 1971), and *The Northward Expansion of Canada, 1914–1967* (Toronto: McClelland & Stewart, 1988). A good overview is William R. Morrison's *True North: The Yukon and Northwest Territories* (Toronto: Oxford University Press, 1998). Post–World War II developments in the North are reviewed in Shelagh D. Grant, *Sovereignty or Security: Government Policy in the Canadian North, 1936–1950* (Vancouver: University of British Columbia Press, 1988), and John David Hamilton, *Arctic Revolution: Social Change in the Northwest Territories, 1935–1994* (Toronto: Dundurn Press, 1994). Essential reading on the sovereignty question is Franklyn Griffiths, ed., *Politics of the Northwest Passage* (Montreal/Kingston: McGill-Queen's University Press, 1987).

WEBLINKS

First Voices
http://www.firstvoices.com/

Sound clips, alphabets, and dictionaries of the languages of the indigenous peoples of Canada.

Aboriginal Canada Portal
http://www.aboriginalcanada.gc.ca/

This portal links to dozens of First Nations organizations in Canada, including the Assembly of First Nations, the Métis National Council, and the Inuit Tapiriit Kanatami.

Delgamuukw v. British Columbia
http://www.lexum.umontreal.ca/csc-scc/en/pub/1997/vol3/html/1997scr3_1010.html

The complete Supreme Court of Canada ruling regarding the case of Delgamuukw v. British Columbia, which among other effects greatly strengthened the use of First Nations oral history as evidence in the Canadian legal system.

Road to Bilingualism
http://archives.cbc.ca/IDD-1-73-655/politics_economy/bilingualism/

A series of video and radio files detailing the origins of Canada's bilingual policy and its controversial existence.

Canadian Charter of Rights and Freedoms
http://laws.justice.gc.ca/en/charter/index.html

The Canadian Charter of Rights and Freedoms.

Statistics Canada: Ethnic Diversity Survey
http://www.statcan.ca:8096/bsolc/english/bsolc?catno=89-593-X

A statistical look at ethnic diversity in Canada based on the 2001 census.

Article Thirty-Five

Aboriginal Peoples in the Twenty-First Century: A Plea for Realism

Alan C. Cairns

I do not expect the arguments in this paper, especially those in the last half, to convince all who read or heard this presentation. In fact, if I fail to convince you, I may have succeeded in the much more important task of contributing to a discussion. The Aboriginal policy field has too many converts and too few discussions in which we listen to each other. Converts and discussion have an uneasy relationship: basically, each is the other's most feared opponent. At the turn of the century, converts and ideologies can look after themselves; discussion, however, needs help. Hence the following pages.

This paper has a single objective — to clarify the debate about how Aboriginal and non-Aboriginal peoples are to live together in the future. We cannot be successfully forward-looking, however, without understanding the past that has shaped us. The first half of the paper, accordingly, focusing as it does largely on the last half of the century, establishes how we got to 'now.' Now is defined as the post-1969 White Paper (Canada 1969) era, in which, I argue, there are two roads to the future — the self-government route based on Aboriginal nations and the urban route.

Source: Alan C. Cairns. "Aboriginal Peoples in the Twenty-First Century: A Plea for Realism" from *The Canadian Distinctiveness into the XXIst Century*, University of Ottawa Press, 2003. pp.135–163. © University of Ottawa Press, 2003. Reprinted by permission the University of Ottawa Press.

This is the era of Aboriginal nationalism; of Oka; of the Royal Commission on Aboriginal Peoples (RCAP); of major advances by Aboriginal peoples in the *Constitution Act*, 1982; of a huge increase in the number of Aboriginal post-secondary graduates; of the dramatic growth of the urban Aboriginal population; of the dawning recognition that Aboriginal communities, especially First Nations, are not going to disappear as believers in assimilation once thought; of the birth of Nunavut (1999); and of many other developments, most of which would have been inconceivable fifty years ago. This background underlines the reality that ours is a new era — that indeed we are creating a new Canada — and that we desperately need more understanding if we are to avoid major policy errors.

Of the many issues needing attention, I have selected the coexistence of the two roads to the future mentioned above. The last half of the paper, grandiosely subheaded "a plea for realism," tries to disentangle the issues posed by this apparent choice, to stick-handle through the claims of both the advocates and opponents of each route. I conclude that the debate is poorly conducted and that both roads will be with us for the foreseeable future. We need more information and analysis and less ideology if we are to make progress in one of the most politicized and conflict-filled policy areas on our agenda. (The paper focuses disproportionately on status Indians because neither Inuit nor Métis [with only eight small settlements in northern Alberta] confront the choice between the urban and the self-government route to the same degree.)

FROM PATERNALISM TO ABORIGINAL NATIONALISM

No dialogue between Indians and the federal government preceded the release of that government's 1969 White Paper which proposed ending the separate status of Indian people and their assimilation into Canadian society. This act of paternalism was repudiated by the organized opposition of Indian peoples, led by the Indian Chiefs of Alberta (Indian Chiefs of Alberta 1970). The subsequent withdrawal of the White Paper was more than the defeat of a particular policy initiative. The historic federal policy of assimilation was in ruins. Since then, it has been generally assumed that Indian communities would survive as such — that they would have a distinct, ongoing communal existence in Canada (Weaver 1990). Thirty years after the White Paper's defeat, Canadians are still grappling with that new reality.

Since then, the federal government has lost or given up its leadership role. Initially, it appeared that the policy of assimilation had been cast in the dustbin of discarded experiments. For the first decade after the White Paper's withdrawal, the relevant actors repositioned themselves behind the vague consensus that assimilation, at least as a conscious policy, was dead, and that the emerging policy question was how Indian peoples — as peoples — or, as the terminology evolved, as nations — should be fitted into the Canadian constitutional order. In the period leading up to the *Constitution Act*, 1982, Inuit and Métis emerged and made independent claims for recognition and self-government. This foreshadowed the new constitutional category "Aboriginal Peoples of Canada," defined in the *Constitution Act*, 1982, s. 35(2), as including Indian, Inuit, and Métis.

Increasingly, initiatives in the broad field of Aboriginal policy came from Aboriginal organizations, particularly the National Indian Brotherhood, later renamed the Assembly of First Nations, which spoke for the legal status Indian population living on reserves. Its voice, and that of other Aboriginal organizations, was strengthened by a fortuitous convergence of factors.

The federal government policy of funding the major Aboriginal organizations — which commenced in the early 1970s, on the premise that the poverty, small populations, and geographical diffusion of Aboriginal peoples would otherwise marginalize them in democratic politics — gave them not only a voice but ultimately a unique status among the claimants for government attention. They quickly came to be much more than the standard interest group speaking for a particular clientele or cause. As the major Aboriginal associations acquired confidence, they decisively distanced themselves from the proliferating ethnic associations which represented the ethnocultural communities gathered under the official policy of multiculturalism. They represented not ethnic minorities, but nations.

The nation label gained sustenance from the opening up of the Constitution in response to Francophone nationalism in Québec, particularly following the victory of the Parti Québécois in the 1976 provincial election. This placed the question of Canada's future on the bargaining table. What kind of people were Canadians? What revised institutional arrangements and constitutional reforms were appropriate for a country increasingly separated from Europe, with an immigration policy that was transforming the face of major metropolitan centres, one that confronted a Québec nationalist challenge to its very survival, and one with indigenous peoples no longer willing to accept their marginalization? The opening up of the Constitution was quickly seen as providing an arena in which Aboriginal peoples could advance their claims for recognition, self-government, and an end to their stigmatized marginalization.

Trudeau's assertion "Everything is up for grabs" was a direct response to a reinvigorated, assertive Québec nationalism. Aboriginal peoples successfully inserted themselves into constitutional politics and made major gains in the Constitution Act, 1982. Simultaneously, their self-description as nations gathered momentum. The National Indian Brotherhood renamed itself the Assembly of First Nations. The 1983 Penner Committee, with its ringing advocacy of self-government for Indian peoples in its report, systematically employed the term nation in a clear response to the messages of Indian spokespersons who appeared before it (Canada 1983). The language of nationalism clearly added symbolic legitimacy to claims for recognition and special treatment.

This was evident in the four Aboriginal constitutional conferences, 1983 to 1987 (Schwartz 1986), primarily focusing on the inherent right of self-government. The conferences gave additional proof of, and stimulus to, the emerging distinct status of Aboriginal peoples. Aboriginal associations participated almost as bargaining equals of the federal and provincial governments on the other side of the table. Their goal was to carve out a separate category of constitutional space for the implementation of the inherent right of self-government. No other interest groups that flourished in democratic, pluralistic politics, whether representing women, disabled persons, Italian Canadians, or others, were given similar recognition.

The rhetoric surrounding the concept of nation became the standard terminology used to identify Aboriginal peoples. Indians became 'First Nations' in a clear attempt to gain historical priority and a stronger legitimacy than that of the two founding nations of French and English newcomers. The Métis also employed the self-identifying, status-raising label of nation as, to a lesser extent, did the Inuit. Perhaps, however, the most decisive indication of the status-enhancing capacity of the nation terminology was the dramatic diffusion of such self-labelling among Indian bands themselves. By 1999, about 30 per cent of over 600 Indian bands had added nation to their official name. Most of them had populations well under one thousand people (Canada 1985, 1990, 1999).

The language of nationalism changes the nature of Aboriginal policy discussions. The term nation easily, almost automatically, leads to a justification for an ongoing future existence, and therefore for the policy tools to achieve that goal. Nation attracts the supportive attention of prominent political theorists — Will Kymlicka, Sam LaSelva, Charles Taylor, Jim Tully — in a way that the term 'villages' would not. They add a certain philosophical legitimacy to Aboriginal nationalism and to the consequences that logically attach to that labelling. Nation, inevitably and desirably in the eyes of its proponents, stresses an internal within-group solidarity, while stressing the 'otherness' of the non-Aboriginal majority.

This otherness is reinforced by the widespread employment of the language of colonialism to describe the history of Aboriginal/non-Aboriginal relations from which an escape is sought. The colonial analogy is a dramatic reminder that the relation of indigenous people to the Canadian majority from the last half of the nineteenth century to the present has *always* been massively influenced by international trends — particularly the world of empire and of its ending. In the former, when a handful of European states ruled much of humanity, the wardship status of Indian peoples — their marginalization — their subjection to the demands of a majority confident of its own cultural superiority — did not have to be argued in terms of first principles — it was simply assumed. Canadian rule over indigenous peoples — most dramatically in the case of status Indians — was simply a spillover from the larger world of empire outside Canada.

The implicit international support in the imperial era for wardship for Indians, for their exclusion from the franchise until 1960, for leaving Inuit (then Eskimo) isolated and forgotten, and for the marginalization of the Métis, evaporated when empire ended. When the British left India, the French handed over power in Senegal, the Dutch lost control of Indonesia, and the Portuguese finally succumbed to exhaustion and retreated from Angola and Mozambique, the message flowing across Canadian borders no longer justified hierarchy with Aboriginal peoples at the base, whether hierarchy was conceived in cultural or racial terms.

The international system was no longer a club of white states. The Commonwealth — now a multicultural, multiracial association — contrasted dramatically with the older view of the white dominions as Britain overseas. The United Nations was transformed into a multiracial institution, with European states in a minority, after the collapse of European empires and the emergence of more than a hundred new states. The United Nations launched a crusade against colonialism and racism that inevitably challenged the legitimacy of white leadership over indigenous peoples in settler colonies — even if that leadership was dressed up in the language of trusteeship and guardianship.

We can argue, therefore, that the emergence of Aboriginal nationalism was overdetermined. It fed on the opening up of the Canadian Constitution; on the demise of European empires and the subsequent transformations in the international system; on the funding of Aboriginal associations by the federal government; on the defeat of the White Paper; and on the contagious, world-wide diffusion of nationalism among indigenous peoples. The simultaneous emergence of indigenous nationalism in Australia (Aborigines) and New Zealand (Maori) as well as in Canada, underlines the international forces at work. Those wishing to understand Aboriginal nationalism in Canada, accordingly, must look outward beyond domestic, within-Canada causes to embrace changes in the international environment. To look inwardly only at our domestic selves blinds us to the fact that indigenous peoples around the globe learn and borrow from each other. There is, in other words, an indigenous international.

The colonial analogy drawn from the international arena and the widespread diffusion of the label nation were appropriate yet, at the same time, potentially misleading. Colonialism was clearly a reasonable description of the system of alien rule and the displacement of Indian peoples onto reserves, thought of as schools for their civilization. It was somewhat less appropriate for Inuit and Métis, in that they were not subject to a separate administrative system, nor subjected to the same degree of cultural assault as Indians. On the other hand, they too were marginalized, defined as backward, and not considered to be full, ordinary citizens.

Colonialism, however, is also misleading. The end of colonialism in yesterday's world of the demise of the European empires resulted in independence. The new flag of a new country was raised, and the international community acquired a new member. The ending of colonialism in Canada, however, does not usher in independence but requires a rapprochement with the majority — the working out of arrangements that combine self-government where land-based Aboriginal communities exist with membership in the Canadian community of citizens. Colonialism focuses attention on the self-rule dimension, but it positively deflects attention from the rapprochement dimension, which requires a positive collaboration with yesterday's oppressor. Therefore, it contributes to a misunderstanding of the requirements of a workable reconciliation.

Nation is also Janus-faced. It is status-raising for those who employ it. It speaks to a positive sense of belonging and to a people's desire for a continuing future existence. For peoples whose difference has been reinforced by their treatment by the majority society, the attribution of nation is a logical if not inevitable response to their situation, especially for land-based communities. The term nation, however, can be misleading. Nation is a potent word that presupposes population sizes and self-government capacities that are beyond small populations of several hundred or several thousand people. The accompanying nation-to-nation theme, the key concept in the analysis of the RCAP report (Canada 1996), also misleads as it inevitably conjured up an image of Canada as an international system. It suggests autonomous, discrete actors bargaining the terms of their separate coexistence. If, however, "within Canada" means anything, the reality is that a part is rearranging its relationship with the whole of which it is a part. In other words, when federal and provincial governments are bargaining their future relations with an Aboriginal nation in a land claims/self-government negotiation for example, the members of the latter group are also and simultaneously represented as citizens by the federal and provincial governments. If this is not so, the whole system of voting and elections in federal and provincial politics and the receipt of standard federal and provincial services are based on a misunderstanding — an assertion that would find minimal support.

It is possible, and perhaps probable, that the leading players in public discussions realize that the language of colonialism, of nation, and of nation-to-nation in the Canadian context does not carry the same meaning and consequences in Canada as it did in Algeria or Kenya. There may be a tacit understanding on both sides of the table that these terms — colonialism, nation, and nation-to-nation — have a more limited, restricted meaning than the full sense of the words suggests. Even so, their use adds a potential element of confusion to our attempts to work out our relations with each other. The increasingly common description of Canada as a multinational country normally fails to mention that the Québec nation is some 7,000 times larger than the average Aboriginal nation proposed by the RCAP. Further, the RCAP figures — average nation size of 5,000–7,000 people — are not a current reality, but a goal that can only be achieved by aggregating small bands into larger units, a goal certain to generate considerable resistance. We cannot think clearly if we forget such realities.

Nor can we think clearly if we overlook the constitutional changes and judicial decisions that have provided indigenous peoples with constitutional support for their aspirations. The Constitution Act, 1982, declared that "The existing aboriginal and treaty rights of the aboriginal peoples of Canada are hereby recognized and affirmed," and "In this Act 'aboriginal peoples of Canada' includes the Indian, Inuit and Métis peoples of Canada," (s. 35(1) and (2)). This constitutional affirmation was, in effect, a repudiation of the original British North America Act, 1867, which in s. 91(24) simply treated Indians as a subject of federal jurisdiction, indicating that their constitutional recognition had nothing to do with their rights, but simply with which government had authority over them. Section 91(24) presupposed wards who, for their own sake, had to be governed by others. Section 35(1), by contrast, identified the rights of peoples that are to be recognized and affirmed. Section 35(2) created a new constitutional category, "aboriginal peoples of Canada," which inevitably generated pressures from the least favoured member of the category — the Métis — who achieved a constitutional recognition in 1982 they had long sought — access to state-provided, positive benefits, available to status Indian peoples. The move from s. 91(24) (1867) to s. 35 (1982), from wards to rights holders, was the domestic equivalent of the end of colonialism in the overseas territories of the former European empires. That domestic equivalent, of course, falls short of independence. The new status to which it leads is to be "within Canada."

The courts, which historically had played a limited role in affirming Aboriginal rights, made important contributions in the post-White Paper decades. Two decisions — Calder (1973) (*Calder v. AG BC*, [1973] SCR 313) and Delgamuukw (1997) (*Delgamuukw v. BC*, [1997] 3 SCR 1010) — underline the judicial contribution, which can be followed in more detail in any of the standard case books in Canadian constitutional law. In Calder, the Supreme Court dismissed an application by the Nishga (now Nisga'a) Indians of northwestern British Columbia for formal recognition of their Aboriginal title based on their immemorial occupation of the land. Six of the seven judges, however, recognized the concept of Aboriginal title, three of whom suggested that their Aboriginal title had not been extinguished. Subsequently, the Trudeau government announced a land claims policy, which is the origin of the modern land claims settlements already completed and of the many negotiations, especially in British Columbia, that are now underway.

In *Delgamuukw*, the Supreme Court confirmed that Aboriginal title existed in British Columbia and that it constitutes a right to the land itself, not just to traditional uses such as hunting. The Court also held that oral history should be included in the evidence legitimately before the Court. Both of these strands of *Delgamuukw* have profoundly transformed the treaty process in British Columbia by dramatically enhancing the bargaining resources of First Nations negotiators.

THE PERVASIVE IMPACT OF NATIONALISM

The emergence of Aboriginal nationalism and the response to it are highlighted in some of the key events of the past decade and a half listed below. This brief and elementary listing — all that space limitations allow — is neither exhaustive nor faithful to the complexities behind the events, but it will serve to underline the temper of the present era.

- The role of Elijah Harper in preventing debate on the Meech Lake Accord in the Manitoba legislature, just as the three-year ratification clock was running out in 1990, was a crucial factor in the defeat of the accord. Harper's role, backed by enthusiastic First Nations support, symbolized the willingness of First Nations — if their own demands were not met — to defeat a major constitutional effort to bring Québec back into the constitutional family with, in Prime Minister Mulroney's words, honour and enthusiasm.
- The Oka crisis of 1990, as well as other, less dramatic, indicators of frustration and anger expressed in road blocks, occupations, and demonstrations, underlined the growing tension in Aboriginal/non-Aboriginal relations.
- The massive, five-volume report of the Royal Commission on Aboriginal Peoples, released in 1996, its policy recommendations and its governing nation-to-nation theme, confirmed that the status quo was not viable. The RCAP Report is a document of Aboriginal nationalism.
- The establishment of the BC Treaty Commission in 1993, following the century-long denial by British Columbia governments that Aboriginal title was a continuing reality, suggested that even the most obdurate provincial government could not prevail against the combination of politicized First Nations claims and a supportive Supreme Court jurisprudence of Aboriginal and treaty rights.

- The passage of the Nisga'a treaty in 2000, in spite of a deeply divisive debate in British Columbia, including a court challenge, suggested that Aboriginal nationalism could be accommodated within Canadian federalism.
- The emergence of Nunavut in 1999 as a quasi-province with an Inuit majority was an even more symbolic indication of the possibility of finding common ground. On the other hand, the confrontation between Québec and Aboriginal nationalism, particularly of the northern Cree and Inuit, over the territorial integrity of Québec should it secede from Canada, underlined the limits of compromise, and confirmed that Aboriginal nationalism would be a major player and a major complication if Canada was threatened with a split.
- Nationalism, defined as the unwillingness to forget, and the willingness to pursue claims for redress for past maltreatment was a supportive factor in the emergence into public attention of the history of sexual and physical abuse in residential schools and the pursuit of claims for compensation by thousands of former students. These claims, which threaten devastating financial impacts on the major churches involved in what a recent scholar described as *A National Crime* in his history of residential schools (Milloy 1999), only surfaced when yesterday's paternalism was displaced by assertive nationalism.

The recognition and accommodation of Aboriginal nationalism *within Canada* is one of the most difficult, high-priority tasks confronting Canadian policy-makers. "Within Canada" indicates that the goal is not only to recognize Aboriginal difference but also to generate a positive identification with, and participation in, the Canadian community of citizens. Aboriginal nationalism is not enough. It has to be supplemented by a shared citizenship with other Canadians if our living together is to go beyond a wary coexistence.

THE SPIRIT OF THE TIMES—THEN AND NOW

Cumulatively, the preceding suggest a profound transformation in the spirit of the times from the conventional assumptions of forty years ago; in different language, the self-consciousness of the major players has been transformed; their very identities differ; non-Aboriginals no longer assume an unchallenged authority to be in charge, while Aboriginal peoples sense the possibility that this time historical momentum may be on their side. Differently phrased, Aboriginal peoples now occupy the moral high ground once occupied by the majority society that had justified its former leadership role, by virtue of the superior civilization it was assumed to be spreading. These changes in mood, in temperament, in identity, in consciousness, in confidence, and in taken-for-granted assumptions about who was in charge, and about what a desirable future would look like are not easily pinned down, yet they are fundamental components of where we are.

This profound transformation is best illustrated by the fate of the rhetoric of assimilation. Formerly the trademark of the non-Aboriginal liberal/left progressives in the middle of the twentieth century, it recently re-emerged on the right end of the spectrum in the Reform party and its successor, the Canadian Alliance, as a reaction against the policy thrust toward special treatment and a constitutionalized third order of Aboriginal governments. Now, however, the liberal/left end of the spectrum passionately opposes the assimilation it formerly supported; it now sees that assimilation is an unacceptable expression of cultural arrogance and ethnocentrism.

Assimilation was formerly the policy of the progressives. The Saskatchewan Co-operative Commonwealth Federation (CCF) under Tommy Douglas and Woodrow Lloyd, 1944–64, was a passionate advocate of assimilation well before the 1969 White Paper (Pitsula 1994). Some of this was a spillover from Afro-American pressure to join the mainstream in the United States, a perspective that saw American blacks seeking to 'get in' as anticipating what Canadian Indians would seek when their Martin Luther King belatedly emerged. Assimilation also drew sustenance from the belief that industrial civilization was the great leveller of cultural difference. Anthropologists took it for granted that assimilation was both the inevitable and desirable goal toward which we were heading. (Loram and McIlwraith 1943). Against such a powerful tendency, resistance was seen as futile. More generally, of course, assimilation had been the historic policy of the Canadian state since Canada was founded.

Support for assimilation has now drifted to the right end of the political spectrum. Preston Manning (Manning 1992), Stockwell Day — now succeeded by Stephen Harper — have replaced Tommy Douglas. Mel Smith (Smith 1995), Tom Flanagan (Flanagan 2000), and others now defend in a very different political-intellectual climate the ideas that attracted Trudeau and the team which produced the White Paper (Canada 1969). The tone of contemporary advocates of assimilation is, of necessity, different from the tone of its supporters of thirty to fifty years ago. Yesterday's advocates wrote and spoke with the easy authority that history was on their side. Contemporary advocates are not so sure. They frequently assert that they write against an unsympathetic climate of political correctness that challenges their right to speak. Other authors have noted the inhibitions which attend speaking out against what they detect as a political consensus behind the overall thrust toward recognition and implementation of the inherent right of self-government (Cairns 2000: 14–16 for references).[1]

This is another example of the changing spirit of the times; forty years ago, in the Hawthorn report of the mid-sixties (Hawthorn 1966–67) and in the 1969 White Paper, treaties were considered of marginal importance. Trudeau, indeed, found it inconceivable that one section of society could have a treaty with another part of society, declaring that "we must all be equal under the laws and we must not sign treaties amongst ourselves" (Trudeau 1969). Now, the RCAP report informs the reader that treaties are the key, the fundamental instrument for regulating relationships between Aboriginal and non-Aboriginal peoples (Cairns 2000:134–136 for a discussion).

Observing the erosion of yesterday's conventional wisdom too easily leads to a complacent arrogance among the supporters of today's conventional wisdom, convinced that they have arrived at truth. A much better lesson would be a reminder that we, too, will be seen, in hindsight, as yesterday's conventional wisdom.

SOME CHARACTERISTICS OF THE PRESENT DEBATE

The present dialogue or debate has the following characteristics. First, there is now a burgeoning literature. Any reasonably sized bookstore currently stocks a sizeable collection of books under the rubric of Native studies. The media now devotes considerable attention to Aboriginal issues. The *National Post*, which gives extensive coverage to Aboriginal issues, vigorously and recurrently attacks special status and espouses assimilation. Aboriginal issues are one of the staples of Jeffrey Simpson, the leading national affairs columnist for the *Globe and Mail* (Simpson 1998; 1999; 2000). Polar positions are now expressed in the national party system. The Reform and the Canadian Alliance analysis of the Aboriginal policy area closely mirror the assumptions behind the 1969 White Paper (Reform Party of Canada 1995; Cairns 2000: 72).

Second, there are prominent Aboriginal participants in the public dialogue. They include the major national and provincial Aboriginal associations whose leaders are often skilled in getting media coverage. They conduct research and publish major position papers. They are joined by a small but growing cadre of Aboriginal scholars in law and other disciplines. Their work receives practical sustenance from Native studies departments, Native studies associations, and specialized journals of Native Studies. They have already made major contributions to our collective search for improved understanding. Their numbers and importance will increase with the dramatic increase in number of Aboriginal graduates of post-secondary institutions.

Third, there is now an extensive university-based community of scholars whose focus is Aboriginal issues. Research is not monolithic — contrast, for example, on the non-Aboriginal side the work of Jim Tully (Tully 1995) and Tom Flanagan (Flanagan 2000), or on the Aboriginal side John Borrows (Borrows 1999), Taiaiake Alfred (Alfred 1999), and Mary Ellen Turpel-Lafond who now sits on the bench of the Provincial Court of Saskatchewan (Turpel 1989–90).

Given the above welcome diversity, it remains true that the major contemporary academic contributions to the debate come from an influential cadre of university law professors, who have taken on the task of enlarging the constitutional space for Aboriginal self-government. Their goal is to provide a legal rationale for the maximum jurisdictional autonomy for the Aboriginal governments of the future. They are unquestionably the major academic contributors to public discourse. Their importance is magnified by the role of the courts in the evolution of Aboriginal rights. Their contributions are supplemented by political scientists, anthropologists, and historians. Each of these disciplines brings different strengths and weaknesses to Aboriginal studies and to Aboriginal policy.

The conclusion is irresistible that the dominant role of legal scholars is defining the issues at stake, in fleshing out a rights-based discourse, and in contributing to a leading role for the courts has contributed to Aboriginal gains. On the other hand, academic legal contributors in this policy area show little concern for Canadian citizenship as a uniting bond, or more generally, for what will hold us together, and show much less interest in the 50 per cent of the Aboriginal population in urban areas, whose concerns are less amenable to the language of rights.[2]

A PLEA FOR REALISM

It is perhaps inevitable that Canadians — be they Aboriginal and non-Aboriginal, citizens and scholars — disagree on where we should go. We still hear the voices of assimilators and their antithesis — those who describe our future as coexisting solitudes maintaining a possibly friendly possibly cool distance from one another. There is another slightly different divide between advocates of a nation-to-nation relationship — competing solidarities who engage in a domestic version of international relations — and others who stress the necessity, at least at one level of our relationship, of a common citizenship as the contemporary source of the empathy that makes us feel responsible for each other. Each of these divides and the rhetoric that sustains them could easily consume the remainder of these pages. It would be a worthwhile task to explore the plausibilities, the exaggerations, the kernels of truth, and the simplifications that attend each side of the above divides. Each divide, in its own way, is at the very centre of our present search for understanding.

I have decided to focus on a different divide, or contrast, in the remaining pages — one which deserves more attention that it has received. This discussion will turn on two roads to the future: that of Aboriginal peoples in landed communities on the path to self-government and that of urban Aboriginals. The pressure and temptation when confronting two roads is to assume the necessity of choosing one, to set the two roads as rivals, to imply that those who have not chosen 'our' road can only have done so because of some false consciousness which clouds their reasoning, to suggest that the urban Aboriginal is somehow betraying Aboriginality by subjecting him/herself to the perils of cultural contagion that will eat away at

Aboriginal difference that should be cherished and protected, or to intimate that the travellers on the self-government road overestimate the possibility of cultural renewal and economic viability for small nations distanced from urban centres.

I prefer not to take sides, but rather to try to think my way through both of these routes to the future, on the premise that there are advantages and disadvantages to each. To condemn one or the other I view as an unhelpful ideological position at this stage of our understanding and evolution.

TWO ROADS TO THE FUTURE

We have more information and analysis now than ever before to inform our policy decisions. Formerly, non-Aboriginals dominated the policy discussions of Aboriginal issues. This was especially true for status Indians. By definition wards are, after all, objects of policy determined by paternal authorities, not participants in its making. For the last thirty years, in contrast, we have had a dialogue with extensive and growing Aboriginal participation. The scholarly community studying Aboriginal issues is now dramatically larger than even a quarter of a century ago. Non-Aboriginals still dominate the field, but scholarly contributions from Aboriginal academics are on the increase. Further, non-Aboriginal academics are aware that their scholarly authority no longer flows automatically from their skin colour. These are all positive developments. Nevertheless, I argue that our understanding is imperfect, that there are immense gaps in our knowledge, that ideology plays too prominent a role, and that the inevitable politicization of a field in which nationalism and the response to it is the dominant focus often gets in the way of realism.

Whether we speak of Aboriginal policy writ large to include Indians, Inuit, and Métis or focus only on the status Indian population — the largest of the constitutionally recognized "Aboriginal peoples" — the reality is that there are two roads to the future — the self-government road and the urban route. This is obvious from even a casual acquaintance with elementary demographic data — half of the Aboriginal people live in urban centres.[3]

Amazingly, the coexistence of these alternative futures, which should be thought of as contemporary, is consistently, if not almost systematically, overlooked or deprecated by those who have cast their votes either for the nation-government route and who see urban life as a distraction or a threat, or by those who see self-government as slowing down the desirable migration to the job opportunities of the city. I argue for acceptance of the coexistence of these two roads to the future, coupled with the belief that each road merits the attention of policy-makers and analysts.

My reasons are elementary. Both roads exist and, as noted above, have about the same number of travellers. Of the status Indian population 42 per cent live off reserve, and 58 per cent live either on reserve (54 per cent) or on crown (4 per cent) land (1996 figures, Canada 1997b: xiv). When Métis and Inuit are included, about half of the Aboriginal population overall is urban. Generally speaking, these two roads lead to different goals. The self-government option, especially when it is practised with competence and integrity, can be a valuable instrument for cultural retention and renewal. The urban option, by its very nature, is more attuned to participation in non-Aboriginal society, with the resultant probability of higher income, less unemployment, and so on. Neither of these goals deserves to be deprecated as such — to be defined as unworthy, as representing an irrational choice. To opt for urban life is not an act of betrayal. To remain in an Aboriginal community, in part because that is where 'home' is, is not to opt for the past.

The fact that both routes exist and that they serve different purposes suggests that they should not be judged by the same criteria. Cultural survival and the modernization of tradition may be the appropriate and priority criteria for judging self-governing nations. Economic opportunities and higher incomes and other pursuits congenial to urban living are the appropriate criteria for assessing Aboriginal urban life. When the RCAP Report foresaw a future in which Aboriginal peoples would be proportionally represented in such prestigious professions as "doctors . . . biotechnologists . . . computer specialists . . . professors, archaeologists and . . . other careers" (Canada 1996, 3: 501) it was not referring to options available in small rural nations. To compare small rural nations with urban settings in terms of their respective capacities to sustain such professions would be to cook the books in favour of urban life. Equally, however, to make cultural renewal the prime criterion for judging the relative merits of urban living and self-governing nations is to predetermine the outcome against the urban setting. Each road to the future should be judged in terms of criteria appropriate to its virtues. This does not mean that economic criteria are irrelevant to judging self-government, nor that cultural criteria have no place in judging the urban situation, but that their relative significance varies according to the setting.

Clarity is not helped by attaching scarce words to one or the other route. 'Assimilation,' brandished as an aggressive description of the consequences of urban living — sometimes of course by its non-Aboriginal supporters — stigmatizes Aboriginals in the city. Assimilation implies losing oneself in someone else's culture. Further, since assimilation was the official, historical policy of the Canadian state, to be accused of having been assimilated suggests succumbing to a policy initially premised on the inferiority of Indian cultures. Of course, assimilation rhetoric often presupposes that an Aboriginal identity can only survive if it manifests itself in vastly different behaviours and beliefs from those of the non-Aboriginal majority. This is simply simplistic social psychology. Identity divergence and cultural convergence are obviously compatible. Is this not what has happened among the Québec Francophone majority? Culturally, convergence of values with Anglophone Canada is well advanced compared to half a century ago. On the other hand, a nationalist identity is unquestionably stronger. This, however, is not to suggest that identity loss never occurs, or to deny that after several generations of intermarriage in urban settings, individuals may retain only a sliver of Aboriginal culture and be happy with what and who they have become. To say that this could never happen is a form of blindness. To assert that it will not be allowed to happen is to deny individual choice. However, my large point remains — a modernizing, urban Aboriginality is perfectly compatible with the retention of a strong Aboriginal identity.

Equally unhelpful are scarce words attached to the separate existence of Indian communities. In the assimilation era, reserves were pejoratively referred to as the Gulag Archipelago, as representative of apartheid, and as equivalent to displaced persons camps. More recently, given the drive to self-government, they have been criticized as making "race the constitutive factor of the political order" and as "based on a closed racial principle" (Flanagan 2000: 194). These are all rhetorical devices to foreclose debate. Indian communities, unlike provincial communities, will be closed communities in the minimum sense of controlling their own membership. To describe them as "race based" (Gibson 2000), however, is not helpful, given the high rate of intermarriage. Further, at the present time, only about 5 per cent of Indian bands employ "blood quantum" criteria for membership and they were reproved by RCAP (Canada 1996, 2 (1): 237–40).

The existence of two roads to the future constitutes the fundamental reality against which should be judged the adequacy of the distribution of attention, of research, and in general, of all attempts to throw light on where we are and might go. From nearly every perspective, the urban dimension of Aboriginality is relegated to secondary importance, when it is not completely ignored. The recurrent use of the colonial analogy contributes to the neglect of the urban situation. The language of nation fits poorly with urban Aboriginals; the possibilities for self-government are limited. Accordingly, since neither nation (as the actor to battle colonialism) nor significant powers of self-government (the purpose of the struggle) make as much sense in the urban setting, urban Aboriginals remain largely outside the purview of one of the most potent organizing labels in contemporary disclosure. They are, therefore, naturally overlooked. The leading role of the academic legal community includes paying scant attention to the urban situation, which, in truth, does not lend itself as readily to analysis in terms of Aboriginal rights. Further, the urban setting lacks a compelling, simplifying focus equal to the appeal of nationalism and self-government as self-evident good causes for scholars to support. The urban scene presents a host of discrete practical problems that resist consolidation under a single rubric.

Indeed, when the heady language of nationalism, of treaties, of inherent rights to self-government, and of nation-to-nation relations casts its aura over one route to the future — self-government and cultural renewal — the second, urban route, which can easily be portrayed negatively in terms of youth gangs, Aboriginal ghettos in the urban core, language loss, and high rates of intermarriage, can be seen as an embarrassment. Indeed, it may even be seen as the road that obviously should not have been taken.

The nation and self-government focus of academics simply duplicates the historical operational bias of the federal department of Indian Affairs which, in administering the Indian Act, 1985, concentrated overwhelmingly on reserve-based Indian communities. The focus on Indian land-based communities is reinforced by the fact that the strongest and most visible national Aboriginal organization, the Assembly of First Nations (AFN), rests squarely on the Indian bands/nations, whose status is governed by the Indian Act, 1985. For nearly twenty years, the most visible Aboriginal leader has been the Grand Chief of the AFN.

The favourable bias toward Aboriginal (especially Indian) nations and their self-government is graphically underlined by the RCAP Report, that is dominated by the nation-to-nation theme, contrasted with what it portrays as a "rootless urban existence" (Canada 1996, 2 (2): 1023). This negative judgment of the urban situation supports the focus on nation and on self-government as its servant for the task of cultural renewal. Alternatively, the nation preference, supported by a global ethnic revival and by a colonial analysis that sees self-government as the culmination of the anti-colonial struggle, requires a negative view of urban Aboriginal life, seen as getting in the way of the movement of history.

From these perspectives, urban Aboriginal life is distinctly unpromising. Urban Aboriginals come from too many diverse nations to coalesce into a sharing, self-governing group even if they had a coherent land base, which they do not. Further, urban Aboriginal life is, by definition, the setting for increased cultural contact leading both to to cultural erosion and the diminishing use of native languages and traditional customs. From the cultural perspective, therefore, urban living is easily viewed as a threat, not as a promise, and those who choose it are seen by its critics as, in a sense, lost to the cause.

Further, especially in the major cities of western Canada, but not confined to them, the Aboriginal concentration in urban core areas has depressing ghetto characteristics. Crime, drug abuse, youth gangs, violence, and prostitution are widespread (LaPrairie 1995). Recent reports speak of normlessness; of a fractured social fabric; and "the emergence of Canada's first US-style slum" in Winnipeg, evident to even a "casual visitor," and becoming evident in "other Prairie cities" (Mendelson and Battle 1999: 25; National Association of Friendship Centres and the Law Commission of Canada 1999: 63–5).

In the absence of some countervailing evidence, the preceding passages would constitute an almost unanswerable condemnation of the urban route. There is, however, another side.

The RCAP outlined numerous positive features of urban life. The employment situation is superior; incomes are markedly higher; urban Indian people have the highest life expectancy among Aboriginal peoples; various indicators of social breakdown are much higher for the on-reserve compared to the non-reserve population (Cairns 2000: chap. 4). As well, preliminary findings of the Department of Indian Affairs Research and Analysis Directorate, based on 1991 data, reported a marked advantage for off-reserve status Indians in terms of life expectancy, educational attainment, and per capital income. Life expectancy was 4.6 years longer and per capita income 50 per cent higher (Beavon and Cooke 1998). Evelyn Peters reported "a significant urban Aboriginal population earning a good income" of $40,000 or more in 1990 (Peters 1994: 28 and Table 15).

These trends feed on the truly dramatic increase in the number of Aboriginal post-secondary graduates. In the late 1950s, there were only a handful of Indian university students. In 1969, there were fewer than 800 Aboriginal post-secondary graduates. Now, more than 150,000 Aboriginal people have completed or are in post-secondary education (Borrows 1999: 75). There was an increase in the number of Inuit and Indian students enrolled in post-secondary institutions of nearly 750 per cent from the numbers in 1977–1978 to the more than 27,000 reported in 1999–2000 (Canada 1997a: 36 and 2001: 33).[4]

This dramatic educational expansion, and the urbanization to which it will contribute, will almost certainly increase the out-marriage rate (see also Clatworthy and Smith 1992: 36). In a recent study employing five-year data ending in December 1995, the overall out-marriage rate was 33 per cent, ranging from 22.8 per cent out-marriage on reserve to 57.4 per cent off-reserve. In general, the smaller the reserve population, the higher the out-marriage rate (Canada 1997b: 21–3).

It is implausible to assume not only that this educational explosion can be contained but also that most graduates can have satisfying lives and find meaningful employment in small-self-governing nations with a weak private sector. This remains largely true even if, by a process of consolidation, the average population of self-governing nations is raised to the viable level of 5,000–7,000, as advocated by the RCAP.

Further, as John Borrows argues, Aboriginal peoples should seek to influence the overall structure of the larger society through vigorous participation. For Borrows, to think of Indianness, or more broadly Aboriginality, as restricted to self-governing, small national communities is to be condemned to a limited and partial existence. Borrows argues, in effect, that the expression of a modernizing Aboriginality should be diffused throughout society in politics, culture, the professions, and so on. He denies that Aboriginality is a fixed thing; he is obviously open to a selective incorporation of values and practices of non-Aboriginal society. As he says, "Identity is constantly undergoing renegotiation. We are traditional, modern, and post-modern people" (Borrows 1999: 77). Accordingly, the self-governing component of Aboriginal futures, while important, is by itself not enough. Neither, however, is the urban route.

Hundreds (sixty to eighty if RCAP hopes for consolidation are realized — more if they are not) of small, self-governing native communities will be scattered across the land, wielding jurisdictions proportionate to their capacity and desire. They are not about to disappear in any foreseeable future. Aboriginal and treaty rights "recognized and affirmed" in the Constitution Act, 1982 s. 35(1), cannot be removed by anything short of a constitutional amendment, the pursuit of which would be an unthinkable act of constitutional aggression. The relocation of communities is not possible. Dispossession of lands and setting band members adrift is not a policy choice. A ruthless cutting of benefits to encourage exodus is neither humane nor an available option. Any expeditious attempt to wind down the existence of small, self-governing nations would arouse an opposition that could not be overcome in a democratic society. Such a policy cannot be implemented; even if it could, to do so would be undesirable. The result would be a rapid exodus to the city that would add many more individuals to the dark side of urban life and would exacerbate the developing Aboriginal urban crisis while adding few success stories.

If we eliminate the pipe dreams of assimilation advocates from the spectrum of available policies, we are left with about half the Aboriginal population living in small, self-governing communities: these communities are not going to go away. They are sustained not only by inertia and by the fact that they are home, but their survival is buttressed by Aboriginal and treaty rights. The powerful force of nationalism can be mobilized on their behalf. Although limited by small populations, the availability of self-government provides some leverage for Aboriginal peoples to shape the terms of interaction with the majority society.

Further, Canadians through their governments are now engaged in major efforts to respond to Indian land claims where Aboriginal title still exists — most visibly in British Columbia, but also in Québec and Atlantic Canada. Discussions are underway to enlarge the land and resource base of many First Nations. When the preceding efforts are coupled with various attempts to increase economic activity on Indian reserves, the continuing significance and presence of self-governing Aboriginal communities is one of the taken-for-granteds of the Canadian future.

Neither the self-government route nor the urban route is an easy road to an unblemished, positive future for Aboriginal peoples or for their relations with their non-Aboriginal neighbours. The urban route, as already indicated, holds out the disturbing possibility in several metropolitan centres of becoming a Canadian version of those American cities that have a black middle class coexisting with a black ghetto. The Canadian parallel of an urban Aboriginal middle class and an Aboriginal ghetto could undermine the civility and social stability of a number of Canada's major metropolitan centres.

There is no easy answer to this unhappy prospect. The present relative inattention to the chequered reality of urban Aboriginal life is, however, obviously damaging. Since it would be arrogant of me to make specific recommendations, that would almost inevitably be either obvious, platitudinous, or superficial, I will restrict myself to the observation that we have studies and a literature that is helpful. *Seen But Not Heard: Native People in the Inner City*, by LaPrairie, is an excellent analysis, replete with policy suggestions and references to the pertinent literature (LaPrairie 1994).

The route of self-governing nations, even if there were no more outstanding claims and if existing lands and resources were significantly supplemented, will not produce across-the-board successes — healthy, Aboriginal communities, functioning democratically, whose members have standards of living comparable with neighbouring non-Aboriginal communities. Most communities are small; many are isolated; and the politics of which are often dominated by kinship relations in circumstances where the public sector is large and the private sector weak. Conditions are therefore often not propitious for victories over poverty, anomie, and existing inequalities.

The RCAP Report launched a comprehensive package of proposals, too detailed to be listed here, to improve the quality of Aboriginal life in every major dimension. Achievement of these goals, the report argued, required an extensive reallocation of lands and resources, economic opportunity expenditures, major improvements in housing and community infrastructure, dramatically enhanced educational opportunities and attainments, including training 10,000 Aboriginal professionals in health and social services within ten years, and much more (Canada 1996, 5: 213).

The RCAP Report proposed a massive increase in annual public spending, rising to an additional $1.5 to $2 billion in year five, to be sustained over a number of years (Canada 1996, 5: 56). Elsewhere the report wrote of an investment of up two billion a year for twenty years (Canada 1996, 5: 60). This was defined as a "good investment for all Canadians" (Canada 1996, 5: 55), as after fifteen to twenty years the positive benefits of these expenditures would generate a net gain, that would benefit both Aboriginal people and other Canadians and their governments (Canada 1996, 5: 57). This cost-benefit analysis is surely at best somewhere between an educated guess and a leap of faith. Even assuming the translation of RCAP proposals into government policy, many Aboriginal nations will remain impoverished, welfare dependent, and anomic.

Canada does not have a clean slate. The legacy of history cannot be wished away. The present distribution of Aboriginal peoples in towns, cities, reserves, in Nunavut, and elsewhere is not going to be transformed by depopulating the reserves, or Nunavut, or Métis settlements in Alberta by a massive migration to urban settings. But it is equally the case that the urban Aboriginal presence is not a passing phase to be repudiated by a massive return to various homelands. Many Aboriginals in the city have no homelands or, it they do, have no desire to return. Both these realities will confront Canadians in any middle range future we care to visualize. There will always be movement of individuals back and forth for a multitude of reasons. Where self-government successes occur, those nations may receive a net inflow, if the would-be returnees are welcomed (Canada 1997b: 5). Conversely, if positive urban Aboriginal role models become more frequent, urban life may become more of a beacon — seen as a plausible choice to make.

The coexistence of alternative futures should be viewed positively. Since the two routes do not have the same advantages — cultural renewal may be more likely in self-governing contexts and economic gains for individuals more predictable in urban settings — each route acts as a check against the other. They are complementary rivals, especially for those who have homelands to which they can return.

In these circumstances, the task of the state is to encourage both successful adaptation of individuals to urban life and community success stories in self-governing nations.

POLICY FOR THE FUTURE

Sound future policy requires an evolving understanding of what is developing in two different contexts. A series of natural experiments is unfolding at this very moment. There are hundreds of nation-renewing experiments already, or soon to be, underway. What works and what does not, and why? Multiple experiments are underway in urban settings too, and their significance will surely deepen and more innovations will occur as more urban governments and politicians are seized of the complexities, the dangers, and the possibilities created by the urban Aboriginal population.

If, by constant monitoring, we were made aware of what works and what does not, we could facilitate the diffusion of successful practices among both Aboriginal and non-Aboriginal governments. Achievement of this goal will require independent monitoring bodies to examine and report on both roads to the future. Similar proposals have surfaced in previous inquiries. The Hawthorn Report of 1966–67 proposed an Indian Progress Agency with the task of "preparing an annual progress report on the condition of the Indian people of Canada" to include, *inter alia*, educational, legal, economic, and social data and analysis (Hawthorn 1966, 1: 402–3). The purpose was to improve the quality of policy-making and public discussion and hence, in general, to act as a constant reminder of what remains to be done.

Thirty years later, the RCAP proposed an independent Aboriginal Peoples Review Commission headed by an Aboriginal chief commissioner, with most of the other commissioners and staff also to be Aboriginal. The Commission's task would be to monitor and report annually on progress being made "to honour and implement existing treaties . . . in achieving self-government and providing an adequate lands and resource base for Aboriginal peoples . . . in improving the social and economic well-being for Aboriginal people; and . . . in honouring governments' commitments and implementing" RCAP recommendations (Canada 1996, 5: 19–20). The Commission's focus would be broad. It would include "the activities of provincial and territorial governments within its review" (Canada 1996, 5: 19). The essential task would be to act as a watchdog to see that non-Aboriginal governments do not slacken in their endeavours. Judging the performance of Aboriginal governments does not appear as part of its mandate, however, though some monitoring might indirectly be undertaken by RCAP's proposed Aboriginal Government Transition Centre, which would be assigned to various tasks to facilitate successful transitions to self-government (Canada 1996, 5: 167–69). The Transition Centre would presumably have only minimal, if any, interest in Aboriginal peoples in urban settings.

The proposal offered here is more complex than that proposed in either Hawthorn or the RCAP. The recommendation is for two monitoring agencies. Implicitly they would be providing annual material to facilitate the comparison between an urban route and a self-government route. Explicitly, they will provide ongoing commentary and analysis — in the one case on the probably hundreds of self-government experiments underway and in the other on the developing indicators of achievements and shortfalls in urban Aboriginal life.

Surely such an ongoing set of monitoring and analyzing reports would reduce the ideology that dominates contemporary discussion. How these agencies should be institutionalized and how their analyses should be disseminated to have maximum effect would have to be worked out. The proposal may seem threatening, even paternalistic, especially to self-governing nations. Relatively soon, and possibly even immediately, however, the staffs of these agencies will have Aboriginal majorities. This is not the time for specifics, but rather for throwing out an idea for public discussion. Those who resist the proposal should suggest alternative means by which we can profitably learn from the fact that we are in the early stages of major policy experiments in areas where our ignorance is vast. To reduce that ignorance is to reduce the cost it imposes on Aboriginal peoples. Some will deny that these are experiments and thus there is nothing to learn, but such claims are not believable. Others might argue that if self-government is an inherent right, the manner of its exercise should be immune from public scrutiny. Such a claim will only survive if evidence of misgovernment is rare or sporadic, which is implausible given the number of small nations potentially involved and the immense problems and temptations they will encounter.

Both routes — the self-government and the urban — place the Aboriginal future directly within Canada. Even the largest unit of self-government, Nunavut, is clearly fully within Canada and deeply dependent on external funding. This will be overwhelmingly true for First Nations. They cannot realistically isolate themselves from the provincial, territorial, and Canadian contexts in which they live. Only 5 per cent of the Indian bands — 30 out of 623 — have on reserve populations of more than 2,000; 405 of 623 bands have on reserve populations of less than 500. There are 111 bands with on reserve populations of less than one hundred (Indian and Northern Affairs Canada 1997: xvi). The RCAP reports that a "disproportionate number of Aboriginal people live in small, remote, and northern communities" (Canada 1996, 5: 39). The RCAP recognized that the jurisdictions they are capable of wielding are severely limited, so the commissioners recommended aggregating bands to produce an average size of 5,000 to 7,000 for the sixty to eighty nations they hoped would emerge. These are still small populations, with a limited capacity to deliver services. Their populations, therefore, will be heavily dependent on federal and provincial governments for many services; the services they will receive from their own governments can only be provided if their governments are recipients of large infusions of outside monies. This double dependence makes it imperative that individual members of self-governing nations be thought of as full Canadian citizens in the psychological and sociological sense of the term. It is for this reason that the Hawthorn Report of the mid-1960s coined the phrase "Citizens plus" as an appropriate description of the place of Indian peoples in Canadian society. (Inuit and Métis were outside Hawthorn's terms of reference.) If Aboriginal individuals and the communities where they live are seen as strangers proclaiming "we are not you," the danger arises that the majority will agree that "they are not us." We must constantly work towards a common citizenship to support the "we" group that sustains our responsibility for each other. This will provide the secure basis for pursuing the "plus" dimension of Aboriginal Canadians.

Recognition as members of the Canadian community of citizens is equally necessary for Aboriginals in the city. Intermingled with non-Aboriginal neighbours, with at best only limited self-government possibilities, their links to municipal, provincial, and federal government will be crucial to their quality of life.

In both cases, therefore, it is essential that Aboriginal people be thought of as fellow citizens. In contemporary, democratic Western societies, citizenship provides the bonds of solidarity. Empathy weakens when citizenship erodes. At a certain point in the erosion, we see each other as strangers, owing little to each other.

If this thesis is accepted, one responsibility of our governors and of the major Aboriginal organizations will be to work constantly for a reconciliation between Aboriginal nationalism and Canadian citizenship. This is also an appropriate, indeed urgent, responsibility for scholars who wish to influence the course of events. The RCAP, the most elaborate inquiry into indigenous peoples and their relation to the majority society ever undertaken, failed in this task. The idea and reality of Aboriginal nations and nationalism crowded out that of Canadian citizenship. Discussion of the former was fulsome, passionate, and repeated. Discussion of the latter — mention is perhaps more accurate — was infrequent and typically lukewarm, except when claims for equality apropos the receipt of services were made. Thus, the shared rule dimension of Canadian federalism — participation in the Canadian practice of self-government via elections and Parliament — was little more than an afterthought. Access of Aboriginal governments to section 36 equalization payments did not receive the standard justification that it is a response to our common shared citizenship; instead it was justified on the weak claim that we share an economy.

In other words, the RCAP, the most exhaustive inquiry ever undertaken of Aboriginal and non-Aboriginal relations in Canada, failed to ask the elementary question "What will hold us together?" and thus the RCAP failed to answer it. This is a mistake that should not be repeated.

CONCLUSION

Realism suggests the following:

- There are two roads to the future: the nation or self-government road and the urban route; both require the attention of policymakers.
- Both roads can be thought of as natural experiments that need to be carefully monitored so we can learn from success and avoid the needless repetition of policy errors. Accordingly, two monitoring, analyzing, reporting agencies should be established to reduce the number of gaps in our knowledge.
- Both roads are clearly within Canada. Canada is not just a box or container, but a political community bound together by a solidarity based on citizenship. Aboriginal peoples must be part of, not outside, that community. A nation-to-nation description of who we are is insufficient. Aboriginal nationhood and Canadian citizenship should not be seen as rivals, but as complementary patterns of belonging to a complex political order. If we recognize only our diversities, "we" will become an uncaring aggregation of solitudes.

NOTES

1. The politicization of this policy area generates unusually polemical scholarly debates, as well as exchanges between authors and reviewers that threaten civility.
2. An important research project remains to be undertaken to 1) identify the changing relation between Aboriginal peoples and those who study them, and 2) assess the shifting relative influence of various disciplines. The hegemony of law is less than a quarter of a century old. Such a study should also track the emergent, growing role of indigenous scholars in the major disciplines. In doing so, it should also note their distribution among the three categories of Aboriginal people — Indian, Inuit, and Métis.
3. As always, there are exceptions to a simple contrast between self-governing nations and urban life, where nation has limited salience. There are urban reserves and urban nations. Further, some, albeit limited options for self-government can be made available to urban Aboriginals. Nevertheless, the contrast between self-government for Aboriginal nations and an urban existence is sufficiently real to focus discussion around these two alternative visions of the future.
4. Aboriginal students in post-secondary programs are much more likely than other Canadians to select trade and non-university programs than university programs — 76 per cent to 24 per cent for registered Indians; 70 per cent to 30 per cent for other Aboriginal students, compared to 58 per cent to 42 per cent for other Canadians (1991 figures) (Santiago 1997: 14–16).

Article Thirty-Six

The Merits of Multiculturalism

Will Kymlicka

In 1971 Canada embarked on a unique experiment by declaring a policy of official "multiculturalism." According to Pierre Trudeau, the prime minister who introduced it in the House of Commons, the policy had four aims: to support the cultural development of ethnocultural groups; to help members of ethnocultural groups overcome barriers to full participation in Canadian society; to promote creative encounters and interchange among all ethnocultural groups; and to assist new Canadians in acquiring at least one of Canada's official languages.[1] This policy was officially enshrined in law in the 1988 Multiculturalism Act.

Although the multiculturalism policy was first adopted by the federal government, it was explicitly designed as a model for other levels of government, and it has been widely copied. "Multiculturalism programs" can now be found not just in the multiculturalism office in Ottawa, but also at the provincial and municipal levels of government and in a wide range of public and private institutions, including schools and businesses.

Such programs are now under attack, perhaps more so today than at any time since 1971. In particular, they are said to be undermining the historical tendency of immigrant groups to integrate, encouraging ethnic separatism, putting up "cultural walls" around ethnic groups, and thereby eroding our ability to act collectively as citizens. It is understandable that Canadians have had anxieties about multiculturalism, and it would be a mistake to ascribe all of them to xenophobia or prejudice. The process of integrating immigrants from very different backgrounds, including every conceivable race, religion, and language group, who share little in common, is never easy, and historically Canada has been fortunate in having avoided serious ethnic conflict. Canadians have naturally worried that any dramatic change in our approach to integration — such as the adoption of the multiculturalism policy — would change this dynamic, igniting ethnic separatism and conflict.

Thus it is worth having a vigorous discussion about multiculturalism. So far, though, the debate has generated much more heat than light. One reason is that it has been carried on without enough attention to the empirical evidence; as we will see, the critics of multiculturalism are simply uninformed about the consequences of the policy.

But defenders of multiculturalism, including the federal government itself, must also share part of the blame. Virtually every study of the policy in Canada has concluded that it has been "barely explained at all to the Canadian public," and that "no serious effort was made by any senior politician to define multiculturalism in a Canadian context."[2] Insofar as the policy has been defended, the usual approach has been simply to invoke "cultural diversity" and "tolerance," as if these were self-evidently or unqualifiedly good things. In fact, both diversity and tolerance have limits. Diversity is valuable, but only if it operates within the context of certain common norms and institutions; otherwise it can become destabilizing. Similarly, tolerance is a virtue, but only within certain boundaries; otherwise it can threaten principles of equality and individual rights. It is on these questions of the limits or boundaries of multiculturalism that defenders have been strangely inarticulate.

As a result, the debate over multiculturalism in the last few years has taken on an air of unreality. On the one hand, uninformed critics level unfounded charges of ethnocultural separatism, without regard for the evidence; on the other hand, defenders invoke "diversity" and "tolerance" as a mantra, without explaining the common institutions and principles that define the context within which diversity and tolerance can flourish.

To bring some order to this confusion, I will focus on the evidence regarding the impact of multiculturalism since its adoption in 1971, to show that critics of the policy are indeed misinformed.

THE DEBATE

The debate over multiculturalism has heated up recently, largely because of two best-selling critiques: Neil Bissoondath's *Selling Illusions: The Cult of Multiculturalism in Canada* (1994) and Richard Gwyn's *Nationalism without Walls: The Unbearable Lightness of Being Canadian* (1995).[3] Bissoondath and Gwyn make very similar claims about the results of the policy. In particular, both argue that multiculturalism has promoted a form of ethnic separatism among immigrants. According to Bissoondath, multiculturalism has led to "undeniable ghettoization."[4] Instead of promoting integration, it encourages immigrants to form "self-contained" ghettos "alienated from the mainstream," and this ghettoization is "not an extreme of multiculturalism but its ideal: a way of life transported whole, a little outpost of exoticism preserved and protected." He approvingly quotes Arthur Schlesinger's claim that multiculturalism reflects a "cult of ethnicity" that "exaggerates differences, intensifies resentments and antagonisms, drives even deeper the awful wedges between races and nationalities," producing patterns of "self-pity and self-ghettoization" that lead to "cultural and linguistic apartheid."[5] According to Bissoondath, multiculturalism policy does not encourage immigrants to think of themselves as Canadians; even the children of immigrants "continue to see Canada with the eyes of foreigners. Multiculturalism with its emphasis on the importance of holding on to the former or ancestral homeland, with its insistence that *There* is more important than *Here*, encourages such attitudes."

Gwyn makes the same claim, in very similar language. He argues that "official multiculturalism encourages apartheid, or to be a bit less harsh, ghettoism."[6] The longer multiculturalism policy has been in place, "the higher the cultural walls have gone up inside Canada."

Multiculturalism encourages ethnic leaders to keep their members "apart from the mainstream," practising "what can best be described as mono-culturalism." In this way the Canadian state "encourages these gatekeepers to maintain what amounts, at worst, to an apartheid form of citizenship."

Bissoondath and Gwyn are hardly alone in these claims; they are repeated endlessly in the media. To take just one example, Robert Fulford recently argued in *The Globe and Mail* that the policy encourages people to maintain a "freeze-dried" identity, reducing intercultural exchange and relationships, and that time will judge it to be one of Canada's greatest "policy failures."[7]

It is important — indeed urgent — to determine whether such claims are true. Surprisingly, however, neither Bissoondath nor Gwyn provides any empirical evidence for his views. In order to assess their claims, therefore, I have collected some statistics that may bear on the question of whether multiculturalism has promoted ethnic separatism, and discouraged or impeded integration. I will start with evidence from within Canada, comparing ethnic groups before and after the adoption of the multiculturalism policy in 1971. I will then consider evidence from other countries, particularly countries that have rejected the principle of official multiculturalism, to see how Canada compares with them.

THE DOMESTIC EVIDENCE

How has the adoption of multiculturalism in 1971 affected the integration of ethnic groups in Canada? To answer this question requires some account of what "integration" involves. It is one of the puzzling features of the Gwyn and Bissoondath critiques that neither defines exactly what he means by integration. However, we can piece together some of the elements they see as crucial: adopting a Canadian identity rather than clinging exclusively to one's ancestral identity; participating in broader Canadian institutions rather than participating solely in ethnic-specific institutions; learning an official language rather than relying solely on one's mother tongue; having inter-ethnic friendships, or even mixed marriages, rather than socializing entirely within one's ethnic group. Such criteria do not form a comprehensive theory of "integration," but they seem to be at the heart of Gwyn's and Bissoondath's concerns about multiculturalism, so they are a good starting point.

Let us begin with the most basic form of integration: the decision of an immigrant to become a Canadian citizen. If the Gwyn/Bissoondath thesis were true, one would expect naturalization rates to have declined since the adoption of multiculturalism. In fact, naturalization rates have increased since 1971.[8] This is particularly relevant because the economic incentives to naturalize have lessened over the last 25 years. Canadian citizenship is not needed in order to enter the labour market in Canada, or to gain access to social benefits. There are virtually no differences between citizens and permanent residents in their civil rights or social benefits; the right to vote is the only major legal benefit gained by naturalization.[9] The primary reason for immigrants to take out citizenship, therefore, is that they identify with Canada; they want to formalize their membership in Canadian society and to participate in the political life of the country.

Moreover, if we examine which groups are most likely to naturalize, we find that it is the "multicultural groups"— immigrants from nontraditional source countries, for whom the multiculturalism policy is most relevant — that have the highest rates of naturalization. By contrast, immigrants from the United States and United Kingdom, who are not seen in popular discourse as "ethnic" or "multicultural" groups, have the lowest rates of naturalization.[10] In other words, those groups that are most directly affected by the multiculturalism policy have shown the greatest desire to become Canadian, while those that fall outside the multiculturalism rubric have shown the least desire to become Canadian.

Let's move now to political participation. If the Gwyn/Bissoondath thesis were true, one would expect the political participation of ethnocultural minorities to have declined since the adoption of multiculturalism in 1971. After all, political participation is a symbolic affirmation of citizenship, and reflects an interest in the political life of the larger society. Yet there is no evidence of decline in such participation.[11] To take one relevant indicator, between Confederation and the 1960s, in the period prior to the adoption of multiculturalism, ethnic groups became increasingly underrepresented in Parliament, but since 1971 the trend has been reversed, so that today they have nearly as many MPs as one would expect, given their percentage of the population.[12]

It is also important to note the way ethnocultural groups participate in Canadian politics. They do not form separate ethnic-based parties, either as individual groups or as coalitions, but participate overwhelmingly within pan-Canadian parties. Indeed, the two parties in Canada that are closest to being ethnic parties were created by and for those of French or English ancestry: the Parti/Bloc Québécois, whose support comes almost entirely from Quebeckers of French ancestry, and the Confederation of Regions Party, whose support came almost entirely from New Brunswickers of English Loyalist ancestry.[13] Immigrants themselves have shown no inclination to support ethnic-based political parties, and instead vote for the traditional national parties.

This is just one indicator of a more general point: namely, that immigrants are overwhelmingly supportive of, and committed to protecting, the country's basic political structure. We know that, were it not for the "ethnic vote," the 1995 referendum on secession in Quebec would have succeeded. In that referendum, ethnic voters overwhelmingly expressed their commitment to Canada. More generally, all the indicators suggest that immigrants quickly absorb and accept Canada's basic liberal-democratic values and constitutional principles, even if their home countries are illiberal or nondemocratic.[14] As Freda Hawkins put it, "the truth is that there have been no riots, no breakaway political parties, no charismatic immigrant leaders, no real militancy in international causes, no internal political terrorism . . . immigrants recognize a good, stable political system when they see one."[15] If we look at indicators of legal and political integration, then, we see that since the adoption of multiculturalism in 1971 immigrants have been more likely to become Canadians, and more likely to participate politically. And when they participate, they do so through pan-ethnic political parties that uphold Canada's basic liberal-democratic principles.

This sort of political integration is the main aim of a democratic state. Yet from the point of view of individual Canadians, the most important forms of immigrant integration are probably not political, but societal. Immigrants who participate in politics may be good democratic citizens, but if they can't speak English or French, or are socially isolated in self-contained ethnic groups, then Canadians will perceive a failure of integration. So let us shift now to two indicators of societal integration: official language acquisition and intermarriage rates.

If the Gwyn/Bissoondath thesis were true, one would expect to find that the desire of ethnocultural minorities to acquire official language competence has declined since the adoption of multiculturalism. If immigrant groups are being "ghettoized," are "alienated from the mainstream," and are attempting to preserve their original way of life intact from their homeland, then presumably they have less reason than they did before 1971 to learn an official language.

In fact, demand for classes in English and French as second languages (ESL; FSL) has never been higher, and actually exceeds supply in many cities. According to the 1991 Census, 98.6 percent of Canadians report that they can speak one of the official languages.[16] This figure is staggering when one considers how many immigrants are elderly and/or illiterate in their mother tongue, and who therefore find it extremely difficult to learn a new language. It is especially impressive given that the number of immigrants who arrive with knowledge of an official language has declined since 1971.[17] If we set aside the elderly — who make up the majority of the Canadians who cannot speak an official language — the idea that there is a general decrease in immigrants' desire to learn an official language is absurd. The overwhelming majority do learn an official language, and insofar as such skills are lacking, the explanation is the lack of accessible and appropriate ESL/FSL classes, not lack of desire.[18]

Another indicator worth looking at is intermarriage rates. If the Gwyn/Bissoondath thesis were true, one would expect intermarriage to have declined since the adoption of a policy said to have driven "even deeper the awful wedges between races and nationalities" and to have encouraged groups to retreat into "monocultural" ghettoes and hide behind "cultural walls." In fact, intermarriage rates have consistently increased since 1971. There has been an overall decline in endogamy, both for immigrants and for their native-born children. Moreover, and equally important, we see a dramatic increase in social acceptance of mixed marriages.[19] Whereas in 1968 a majority of Canadians (52 percent) disapproved of Black–white marriages, the situation is now completely reversed, so that by 1995 an overwhelming majority (81 percent) approved of such marriages.[20]

Unlike the previous three indicators of integration, intermarriage is not a deliberate goal of government policy; it is not the business of governments either to encourage or to discourage intermarriage. But changes in intermarriage rates are useful as indicators of a broader trend that is a legitimate government concern: namely, the extent to which Canadians feel comfortable living and interacting with members of other ethnic groups. If Canadians feel comfortable living and working with members of other groups, inevitably some people will become friends with, and even lovers of, members of other ethnic groups. The fact that intermarriage rates have gone up is important, therefore, not necessarily in itself, but rather as evidence that Canadians are more accepting of diversity. And we have direct evidence for this more general trend. Canadians today are much more willing to accept members of other ethnic groups as co-workers, neighbours, or friends than they were before 1971.[21]

Other indicators point to the same trends. For example, despite Gwyn's and Bissoondath's rhetoric about the proliferation of ethnic "ghettos" and "enclaves," studies of residential concentration have shown that permanent ethnic enclaves do not exist in Canada. Indeed, "it is scarcely sensible to talk of 'ghettos' in Canadian cities."[22] What little concentration does exist is more likely to be found among older immigrant groups, like the Jews and Italians, whose arrival preceded the multiculturalism policy. Groups that have arrived primarily after 1971, such as Asians and Afro-Caribbeans, exhibit the least residential concentration.[23]

In short, whether we look at naturalization, political participation, official language competence, or intermarriage rates, we see the same story. There is no evidence to support the claim that multiculturalism has decreased the rate of integration of immigrants, or increased the separatism or mutual hostility of ethnic groups. As Orest Kruhlak puts it, "irrespective of which variables one examines, including [citizenship acquisition, ESL, mother-tongue retention, ethnic association participation, intermarriage or] political participation, the scope of economic involvement, or participation in mainstream social or service organizations, none suggest a sense of promoting ethnic separateness."[24]

THE COMPARATIVE EVIDENCE

We can make the same point another way. If the Bissoondath/Gwyn thesis were correct about the ghettoizing impact of our official multiculturalism policy, we would expect Canada to perform worse on these indicators of integration than other countries that have not adopted such a policy. Both Gwyn and Bissoondath contrast the Canadian approach with the American, which exclusively emphasizes common identities and common values, and refuses to provide public recognition or affirmation of ethnocultural differences. If Canada fared worse than the United States in terms of integrating immigrants, this would provide some indirect support for the Bissoondath/Gwyn theory.

In fact, however, Canada fares better than the United States on virtually any dimension of integration. Its naturalization rates are almost double those of the United States.[25] Canada's rates of political participation and official language acquisition are higher, and its rates of residential segregation are lower.[26] In addition Canadians show much greater approval for intermarriage. In 1988, when 72 percent of Canadians approved of interracial marriages, only 40 percent of Americans approved, and 25 percent felt they should be illegal![27] And ethnicity is less salient as a determinant of friendship in Canada than in the United States.[28]

On every indicator of integration, then, Canada with its multiculturalism policy, fares better than the United States, with its repudiation of multiculturalism. We would find the same story if we compared Canada with other immigrant countries that have rejected multiculturalism in favour of an exclusive emphasis on common identities — such as France.[29] Canada does better than these other countries not only in actual rates of integration, but also in the day-to-day experience of ethnic relations. In a 1997 survey, people in twenty countries were asked whether they agreed that "different ethnic groups get along well here." The percentage of those agreeing was far higher in Canada (75 percent) than in the United States (58 percent) or France (51 percent).[30]

This should not surprise us, since Canada does better than virtually any other country in the world in the integration of immigrants. The only comparable country is Australia, which has its own official multiculturalism policy — one largely inspired by Canada's, although of course it has been adapted to Australia's circumstances.[31] The two countries that lead the world in the integration of immigrants are countries with official multiculturalism policies. They are much more successful than any country that has rejected multiculturalism.

In short, there is no evidence to support the claim that multiculturalism is promoting ethnic separateness or impeding immigrant integration. Whether we examine the trends within Canada since 1971 or compare Canada with other countries, the conclusion is the same: the multiculturalism program is working. It is achieving what it set out to do: helping to ensure that those people who wish to express their ethnic identity are respected and accommodated, while simultaneously increasing the ability of immigrants to integrate into the larger society. Along with our fellow multiculturalists in Australia, Canadians do a better job of respecting ethnic diversity while promoting societal integration than citizens of any other country.

EXPLAINING THE DEBATE

This finding raises a genuine puzzle. Why do so many intelligent and otherwise well-informed commentators agree that multiculturalism policy is impeding integration? Part of the explanation is that many critics have simply not examined the actual policy to see what it involves. For example, both Gwyn and Bissoondath claim that, in effect, multiculturalism tells new Canadians that they should practise "monoculturalism," preserving their inherited way of life intact while avoiding interacting with or learning from the members of other groups, or the larger society.[32] If this were a plausible interpretation of the policy's aims, it would be only natural to assume that ethnocultural separatism is increasing in Canadian society.

In reality, as the government's documents make clear, the main goals of multiculturalism policy (and most of its funding) have been to promote civic participation in the larger society and to increase mutual understanding and cooperation between the members of different ethnic groups. Unfortunately, neither Gwyn nor Bissoondath quotes or cites a single document published by the multiculturalism unit of the federal government — not one of its annual reports, demographic analyses, public education brochures, or program funding guidelines. Their critiques are thus double unreal. They describe a (nonexistent) policy of promoting "monoculturalism" among ethnocultural groups, and then blame it for a (nonexistent) trend toward "apartheid" in Canadian society. They have invented a nonexistent policy to explain a nonexistent trend.

But if the Bissoondath and Gwyn accounts are so ill-informed, why have they been so influential? Both books were generally well reviewed, and often praised for their insight into ethnocultural relations in Canada. Why were so many Canadians persuaded by their claims about growing ethnocultural separatism, even though these claims had no empirical support, and indeed are contradicted by the evidence? Why were so many Canadians persuaded by their mistaken characterization of the policy?

Part of the answer, I think, is that defenders of the policy have been strangely inarticulate. The federal government has not clearly explained the aims of the policy, nor has it provided criteria for evaluating its success. Even though the policy has been demonstrably successful, the government itself has made little attempt to demonstrate its success; so far as I can tell, it has never attempted to gather together the various findings on integration discussed in this chapter, or to monitor them systematically so as to measure changes in integration over time.

Collecting and publicizing this sort of information would provide Canadians with the tools to question and deflate the exaggerated claims and misinformed critiques we find in Gwyn and Bissoondath. Yet even if this information were more widely available, it would likely not entirely alleviate public anxiety about multiculturalism. Lack of information cannot, by itself, explain public attitudes. In the absence of information, why do so many Canadians assume that multiculturalism has had negative consequences? Why are they fearful of multiculturalism, rather than confident about it?

Part of the problem may be that Canadians have no clear sense of the limits of multiculturalism. They are not sure that certain "non-negotiable" principles or institutions will be protected and upheld, even if they conflict with the desires or traditions of some immigrant groups. Canadians are not averse to multiculturalism within limits, but they want to know that those limits exist. They value diversity, but they also want to know that this diversity will be expressed within the context of common Canadian institutions, and that it doesn't entail acceptance of ethnic separation. Similarly, Canadians are generally tolerant, but they also believe that some practices, such as clitoridectomy, are intolerable, and they want to know that they won't be asked to "tolerate" the violation of basic human rights.

So long as Canadians feel insecure about the limits of multiculturalism, publicizing statistics about the beneficial effects of multiculturalism will have only limited success in changing public attitudes. The statistics may look good today, but what about tomorrow? Perhaps the policy has worked until now to promote integration, but only because the full "logic" of multiculturalism has not yet been implemented. Perhaps the logic of multiculturalism is to undermine the very idea that there are any principles or institutions that all citizens must respect and adhere to. It is this sort of insecurity that explains, at least in part, the popularity of the Bissoondath/Gwyn account. Until defenders of multiculturalism explain its limits, these sorts of critiques will continue to strike a chord among Canadians, touching deeply felt anxieties about ethnocultural relations.

I think it is possible to address these concerns. In order to do so, however, we need to understand how multiculturalism fits into a larger set of government policies regarding ethnocultural relations in Canada. It is precisely this larger context that is typically ignored in debates about multiculturalism. Both critics and defenders of multiculturalism often talk as if the adoption of the policy in 1971 ushered in an entirely new era in ethnic relations in Canada, overturning the government policies developed over the previous 150 years of immigration. This is a very misleading picture. In many respects, the government policies that encourage the historical integration of immigrants remain firmly in place. After all, multiculturalism is not the only — or even the primary — government policy affecting the place of ethnic groups in Canadian society; it is just one small piece of the pie. Many aspects of public policy affect these groups, including policies relating to naturalization, education, job training and professional accreditation, human rights and anti-discrimination law, civil service employment, health and safety, even national defence. It is these other policies that are the major engines of integration, for they encourage, pressure, even legally force immigrants to take steps toward integrating into Canadian society.

The idea that multiculturalism promotes ethnic separateness stems in large part, I think, from a failure to see how multiculturalism fits into this larger context of public policy. When we do situate multiculturalism within this larger context, we see that it is not a rejection of integration, but a renegotiation of the terms of integration — a renegotiation that was in general not merely justified but overdue.

NOTES

1. Trudeau in *House of Commons Debates*, 8 Oct. 1971: 8545–6.
2. Freda Hawkins, *Critical Years in Immigration: Canada and Australia Compared* (Montreal: McGill-Queen's University Press, 1989), p. 221.
3. Neil Bissoondath, *Selling Illusions: The Cult of Multiculturalism in Canada* (Toronto: Penguin, 1994); Richard Gwyn, *Nationalism without Walls: The Unbearable Lightness of Being Canadian* (Toronto: McClelland and Stewart, 1995).
4. The passages quoted in this paragraph can be found on pages 111, 110, 98, and 133 of *Selling Illusions*.
5. Schlesinger, *The Disuniting of America* (New York: Norton, 1992), p. 138. According to his analysis, the United States is witnessing the "fragmentation of the national community into a quarrelsome spatter of enclaves, ghettoes, tribes . . . encouraging and exalting cultural and linguistic apartheid" (137–38). Bissoondath argues that the same process is occurring in Canada.
6. The passages quoted in this paragraph are from pages 274, 8, and 234 of *Nationalism without Walls*.
7. Robert Fulford, "Do Canadians Want Ethnic Heritage Freeze-Dried?," *The Globe and Mail*, 17 Feb. 1997.
8. Citizenship and Immigration Canada, *Citizenship and Immigration Statistics* (Ottawa: Public Works, 1997), Table G2 and Table 1.
9. The remaining differences between citizens and permanent residents relate to (a) minority language rights; (b) protection against deportation; and (c) access to a few sensitive bureaucratic positions, none of which are relevant to most immigrants.
10. The average length of residence before naturalization is 7.61 years, with immigrants from the UK taking the longest (13.95 years); immigrants from China, Vietnam, and the Philippines all take under five years on average (Citizenship Registrar, Multiculturalism and Citizenship Canada, 1992). In 1971, only 5 percent of the Americans eligible to take out citizenship in Canada chose to do so. See Karol Krotki and Colin Reid, "Demography of Canadian Population by Ethnic Group," in *Ethnicity and Culture in Canada: The Research Landscape*, ed. J.W. Berry and Jean Laponce (Toronto: University of Toronto Press, 1994), p. 26.
11. For surveys of the political participation of ethnocultural groups in Canadian politics, see the three research studies in Kathy Megyery, ed., *Ethnocultural Groups and Visible Minorities in Canadian Politics: The Question of Access*, vol. 7 of the Research Studies of the Royal Commission on Electoral Reform and Party Financing (Ottawa: Dundurn Press, 1991); Jean Laponce, "Ethnicity and Voting Studies in Canada: Primary and Secondary Sources 1970–1991" in Berry and Laponce, eds., *Ethnicity and Culture*, pp. 179–202; and Jerome Black

and Aleem Lakhani, "Ethnoracial Diversity in the House of Commons: An Analysis of Numerical Representation in the 35th Parliament," *Canadian Ethnic Studies* 29, 1 (November 1997): 13–33.

12. Daiva Stasiulus and Yasmeen Abu-Laban, "The House the Parties Built: (Re)constructing Ethnic Representation in Canadian Politics" in Megyery, ed., *Ethnocultural Groups*, p. 14; cf. Alain Pelletier, "Politics and Ethnicity: Representation of Ethnic and Visible-Minority Groups in the House of Commons," in ibid., pp. 129–30.

13. Geoffrey Martin, "The COR Party of New Brunswick as an 'Ethnic Party,'" *Canadian Review of Studies in Nationalism* 23, 1 (1996): 1–8.

14. For evidence of the quick absorption of liberal-democratic values by immigrants, see James Frideres, "Edging into the Mainstream: Immigrant Adults and their Children" in *Multiculturalism in North America and Europe: Comparative Perspectives on Interethnic Relations and Social Incorporation in Europe and North America*, ed. S. Isajiw (Toronto: Canadian Scholars' Press, 1997); Jerome Black, "The Practice of Politics in Two Settings: Political Transferability among Recent Immigrants to Canada," *Canadian Journal of Political Science* 20, 4 (1987): 731–53. Studies show that students born outside Canada, as well as students for whom English was not a first or home language, knew and valued their rights as much as their Canadian-born, English-speaking counterparts. See, for example, Charles Ungerleider, "Schooling, Identity and Democracy: Issues in the Social-Psychology of Canadian Classrooms" in *Educational Psychology: Canadian Perspectives*, ed. R. Short et al., (Toronto: Copp Clark, 1991), p. 204–5.

15. Hawkins, *Critical Years*, p. 279.

16. Some 63 percent of immigrants have neither English nor French as their mother tongue, yet only 309 000 residents in the 1991 Census couldn't speak an official language. Most of these were elderly (166 000 were over 55). See Brian Harrison, "Non Parlo né inglese, né francese" (Statistics Canada: Census of Canada Short Article Series, #5, September 1993).

17. Derrick Thomas, "The Social Integration of Immigrants," in *The Immigration Dilemma*, ed. Steven Globerman (Vancouver: Fraser Institute, 1992): 224.

18. Susan Donaldson, "Un-LINC-ing Language and Integration: Future Directions for Federal Settlement Policy" (M.A. thesis, Department of Linguistics and Applied Language Studies, Carleton University, 1995).

19. Morton Weinfeld, "Ethnic Assimilation and the Retention of Ethnic Cultures," in Berry and Laponce, eds., *Ethnicity and Culture*, pp. 244–45.

20. Jeffrey Reitz and Raymond Breton, *The Illusion of Difference: Realities of Ethnicity in Canada and the United States* (Toronto: C.D. Howe Institute, 1994), p. 80; Leo Driedger, *Multi-Ethnic Canada: Identities and Inequalities* (Toronto: Oxford University Press, 1996), p. 277.

21. Driedger, *Multi-Ethnic Canada*, p. 263.

22. John Mercer, "Asian Migrants and Residential Location in Canada," *New Community* 15, 2 (1989): 198.

23. Thomas, "Social Integration," pp. 240, 247.

24. Orest Kruhlak, "Multiculturalism: Myth versus Reality," unpublished paper prepared for the Institute for Research on Public Policy project "Making Canada Work: Towards a New Concept of Citizenship" (1991), p. 10.

25. For example, the naturalization rate of immigrants who arrived in the United States in 1977 is around 37 percent. The comparable rate in Canada is between 70 percent and 80 percent, and is much higher in some multicultural groups (e.g., 95 percent of the Vietnamese refugees have become citizens). For a comparative study of naturalization policies and trends, see Dilek Cinar, "From Aliens to Citizens: A Comparative Analysis of Rules of Transition," in *From Aliens to Citizens: Redefining the Legal Status of Immigrants*, ed. Rainer Baubock (Aldershot: Avebury, 1994), p. 65. For the case of Vietnamese "boat people" in Canada, see Frideres, "Edging into the Mainstream."

26. Krotki and Reid, "Demography", p. 40.

27. Reitz and Breton, *The Illusion of Difference*, pp. 80–81.

28. Ibid., p. 60.

29. See Cinar, "From Aliens to Citizens," p. 65; Stephen Castles and Mark Miller, *The Age of Migration: International Population Movements in the Modern World* (London: Macmillan, 1993), pp. 220–21; Sarah Wayland, "Religious Expression in Public Schools: Kirpans in Canada, Hijab in France," *Ethnic and Racial Studies* 20, 3 (1997): 545–61.

30. Angus Reid, *Canada and the World: An International Perspective on Canada and Canadians*. The polling data is available on the Angus Reid Web site at www.angusreid.com. Australia came second on this question, with 71 percent of respondents agreeing that ethnic groups get along well in Australia.

31. As Freda Hawkins notes, multiculturalism was adopted in both countries in the 1970s "for the same reasons and with the same objectives" (*Critical Years*, p. 214). And they have evolved in similar directions since the 1970s,

from an emphasis on cultural maintenance to issues of public participation and institutional accommodation. For a detailed comparison of their origins, see Hawkins, "Multiculturalism in Two Countries: The Canadian and Australian Experience," *Review of Canadian Studies* 17, 1 (1982): 64–80. For a more up-to-date account, see James Jupp, *Explaining Australian Multiculturalism* (Canberra: Centre for Immigration and Multicultural Studies, Australian National University, 1996), and Stephen Castles, "Multicultural Citizenship in Australia," in *Citizenship and Exclusion*, ed. Veit Bader (London: St. Martin's Press, 1997).

32. Similarly, Fulford argues that the multiculturalism policy disapproves of inter-marriage and interethnic friendships ("Do Canadians Want Ethnic Heritage Freeze-Dried?").

Article Thirty-Seven

Climate Change and Canadian Sovereignty in the Northwest Passage

Rob Huebert

The most recent report from the Intergovernmental Panel on Climate Change (IPCC) reports that the Arctic region is especially sensitive to the dynamics of warming temperatures.[1] The most recent scientific evidence strongly suggests that the Arctic is experiencing warming at a rate greater than almost any other region of the globe. This is evidenced by the thickness of the ice cover; the occurrence of both the melting and freezing of the Arctic Ocean and its surrounding waterways; and from the samples of ice cores.[2] Observations made by northern Aboriginal peoples also lend credence to the evidence that the Arctic is warming up.[3] Insects have been reported much further north than is the norm. Changes in animal migration patterns have also been reported.[4] Both northern Aboriginal peoples and scientists have reported significant changes in the hunting patterns of predators such as the polar bear. For example, Ian Sterling, one of the world's leading experts on the North American polar bear, has noted that the polar bear population inhabiting the Hudson Bay region has become smaller.[5] He attributes this to the earlier melting of the ice cover on Hudson Bay, which has made it more difficult for the bears to hunt seal. The Canadian Ice Services of Environment Canada has noted that the ice cover has decreased since the mid-1970s.[6] Satellite data show that the ice cover has steadily been decreasing.

THE PROBLEM: CLIMATE CHANGE AND THE ICE COVER

Not all scientists agree that climate change is the cause of these changes in the Arctic. Some researchers suggest that the ice is thinning because of fluctuations in wind patterns and not as a result of increased temperatures.[7] However, those who suggest that climate change and the resulting impact of global warming have not occurred or have not affected ice levels in the Arctic are in the distinct minority. The consensus is that climate change increases average temperatures in the Arctic regions which, in turn, causes the ice cover to melt.

Source: Rob Huebert, "Climate Change and Canadian Sovereignty in the Northwest Passage," *ISUMA: Canadian Journal of Policy Research*, 2, 4 (Winter 2001): 86–94. Used with permission.

INCREASED INTEREST IN THE CANADIAN NORTH

There are limited signs of renewed interest in shipping through the Northwest Passage. At the end of the Cold War, ecotourist voyages began to enter the Passage, but only between five and ten partial or complete voyages a year. To date, only icebreakers or ice-strengthened vessels have made the voyage in this capacity, and the companies responsible have requested the Canadian government's permission. Every company that used these vessels to transit the Passage has requested the Canadian Government's permission. Most of these voyages have been without incident. However, in 1996, the *Hanseatic* went aground on a sand bar near Cambridge Bay.[8] Although only a minor oil leak occurred, the grounding was severe enough to require the vessel's complete evacuation as well as the removal of most of its stores to facilitate its removal from the sand bar.

In 1999, the first non-American passage for commercial shipping purposes took place when a Russian company sold a floating dry dock based in Vladivostok. Its new owners decided to move the dock to Bermuda. With the aid of a Russian icebreaker and an ocean-going tug, the dry dock was successfully towed through the Passage. This use of the Passage to avoid storms in the open ocean demonstrated its advantage for international shipping should the ice be reduced. The fact that the dry dock was then almost lost in a storm off Newfoundland seemed to confirm the benefits of sheltered waters of the Passage route.

Also in 1999, a Chinese research vessel visited Tuktoyaktuk. While the Canadian embassy in Beijing had been informed of the Chinese plan to send a vessel to the western Arctic, local Canadian authorities were not informed. Consequently, local officials were considerably surprised when the Chinese arrived in Tuktoyaktuk. The voyage of the Chinese vessel demonstrated the limited Canadian surveillance capabilities. Canadian officials did not learn of the vessel's entry into Canadian waters until it actually arrived.

The U.S. Navy has begun to examine the issue of conducting surface vessel operations in Arctic waters. In April 2001, the U.S. Navy organized a symposium on the subject. This strongly suggests that it perceives the possibility of an ice-free Arctic where it may be required to operate and has begun to give the subject serious thought.

New multilateral efforts to prepare for increased maritime traffic in the Arctic have also begun in the 1990s. An initiative of the Canadian Coast Guard led a group of Arctic coastal states and relevant international shipping companies to meet in 1993 to develop what is now known as the Polar Code.[9] The meetings were intended to develop a common set of international standards governing the construction and operation of vessels that would operate in Arctic waters. To a large degree, these talks represented the Canadian Coast Guard's effort to initiate discussions in anticipation of increased shipping in the region. Unfortunately, the United States State Department has attempted to derail the negotiations for reasons that are not clear. Substantial progress was made when the discussions involved officials from the various Coast Guards. However, as the talks began to lead to an agreement, the American State Department became involved, and several elements of the American position were altered, including initial acceptance of developing a mandatory agreement and accepting the inclusion of Antarctic shipping. Although the other participants have accepted the changes in the American position, the Americans have still been reluctant to advance the negotiations.

While each of these events by themselves can be dismissed as interesting but unimportant events, when considered as a whole they indicate an upward trend in interest in Canadian Arctic waters. Furthermore, it is expected that there will be an increase in activity associated with the development of oil and gas deposits in this region. All things considered, the Canadian Arctic is becoming busy, and as it becomes increasingly ice free, it will become even busier.

THE CANADIAN CLAIM

The melting of the ice that covers the Northwest Passage gives rise to questions about the impact this has on Canadian claims of sovereignty. There is no question about the status of the land territory that comprises the Canadian Arctic archipelago. All conflicting land claims were settled in the 1930s,[10] with the sole exception of a dispute over the ownership of a small island between Baffin Island and Greenland named Hans Island. The government of Denmark contests the Canadian claim of ownership. The only relevance of this claim is its impact on the determination of the maritime boundary line between Canada and Greenland in the Davis Strait. Canadian claims of sovereignty of its Arctic areas with respect to maritime boundaries have resulted in three disputes. Canada disagrees with both the United States and Denmark over the maritime boundaries that border Alaska and Greenland respectively. Neither dispute will be influenced by reduced ice conditions.

It is a third dispute, concerning Canada's claim over the international legal status of the Northwest Passage, which will be adversely affected by a reduction of ice cover in the Passage. The Canadian government's official position is that the Northwest Passage is Canadian historical internal waters. This means that Canada assumes full sovereignty over the waters and thereby asserts complete control over all activity within them. The Government of Canada's most comprehensive statement to this end was made by then Secretary of State for External Affairs, Joe Clark, in the House of Commons on September 10, 1985. In that declaration, he included the following statement:

> Canada's Sovereignty in the Arctic is indivisible. It embraces land, sea, and ice. It extends without interruption to the seaward-facing coasts of the Arctic Islands. These Islands are joined and not divided by the waters between them. They are bridged for most of the year by ice. From time immemorial Canada's Inuit people have used and occupied the ice as they have used and occupied the land.[11]

The Department of Foreign Affairs has not issued any further official statements regarding the Passage since 1985. Following the end of the Cold War, the department's main focus in the north has been the development of new international institutions. These include the Arctic Environmental Protection Strategy and the Arctic Council. Both bodies are important new developments, but their focus has been based almost exclusively on sustainable development.[12] In June 2000, the department issued a "new" Arctic foreign policy statement listing four main objectives. The second objective was to "assert and ensure the preservation of Canada's sovereignty in the North."[13] However, the document does not discuss how Canada will assert and enforce its sovereignty. The only statement on the topic is that the "public concern about sovereignty issues has waned" and that "globalization has also altered the exercise of state sovereignty, partly through the development of a web of legally binding multilateral agreements, informal agreements and institutions."[14] There is no explanation or justification as to how these assessments are reached.

The department has had little to say about the impact of climate change on Canadian claims. One of the few comments on the subject was made by an official from the Legal Affairs Bureau in a presentation in Whitehorse on March 19, 2001 regarding Canadian sovereignty in the Arctic. Much of his focus was on the impact of climate change. Although his discussion is not official policy, it nevertheless provides the most current understanding of the position of the Department of Foreign Affairs. He argued that Canadian sovereignty over the waterways of the Canadian Arctic did not depend on the ice cover of the region, but that

> Canada's view, then and now, is that since the 1880 deed transfer [of the Arctic archipelago from the U.K. to Canada], the waters of the Arctic Archipelago have been Canada's internal

waters by virtue of historical title. These waters have been used by Inuit, now of Canada, since time immemorial. Canada has unqualified and uninterrupted sovereignty over the waters.[15]

The official also noted that Canada has not relied on the concept of "ice as land" to support its claim of sovereignty. This is due in part to the differences between pack ice and shelf ice. Pack ice is "dynamic and ever-changing" and is therefore "unsuitable for legal analysis as being dry land." Shelf ice, while potentially more useful in determining boundaries, is not particularly useful to Canadian claims in that the four main ice shelves of the Canadian Arctic are on the northern border of Baffin Island, and therefore, are not pertinent to the issue of the Northwest Passage. Thus, he concluded that "even if the ice were to melt, Canada's legal sovereignty would be unaffected."[16] In conclusion, he argues "[S]overeignty over the marine areas is based on law, not on the fact that waters in question frequently are covered by ice. The waters between the lands and the islands are the waters of Canada by virtue of historical waters."[17]

There are several problems with this line of argument that are unrelated to the issue of ice use. First, the claim that these waters are internal by virtue of historical title is in doubt. A study by one of the leading Canadian legal jurists, Donat Pharand, has demonstrated the weakness of the use of this line of argumentation. In his major study of the issue he concludes that "[i]t is highly doubtful that Canada could succeed in proving that the waters of the Canadian Arctic Archipelago are historical internal waters over which it has complete sovereignty."[18] Pharand supports this conclusion with two sets of arguments. First, the use of the legal concept of historical waters has diminished in recent years. It is unlikely that it would be persuasive in an international court. Second, the requirements for proving historical waters are exacting. These include "exclusive control and long usage by the claimant State as well as acquiescence by foreign States, particularly those clearly affected by the claim."[19] Pharand argues this has not been the case for Canadian Arctic waters. Canada has not dedicated the resources to demonstrate exclusive control, and the foreign States with an interest, i.e., the United States and the European Union, have not acquiesced. Although Canada may make a claim that the Arctic waters are historical waters, Pharand convincingly argues that this claim would likely not withstand an international challenge.

The Canadian foreign affairs official also argued that the Government of Canada's decision in 1986 to enclose the Canadian Arctic Archipelago by straight baselines ensures that the waters within the straight baselines are internal. The weakness of this argument lies in the timing of the Canadian declaration. Canada implemented straight baselines around the Arctic on January 1, 1986. However, in 1982, it had signed the United Nations Law of the Sea Convention (UNCLOS), in which article 8(2) states that a State cannot close an international strait by declaring straight baselines.[20] Therefore, the Canadian government's claim that drawing straight baselines gives it the international legal right to claim jurisdiction over international shipping in these waters is also unlikely to withstand an international challenge.

The Foreign Affairs official offered a strong argument that the condition of the ice is not an important element of the Canadian claim. However, this is not entirely true. As stated earlier, the September 10, 1985 statement by Joe Clark clearly connects ice conditions to sovereignty. The statement provides that the islands of the Arctic are "joined and not divided by the waters between them. They are bridged for most of the year by ice." The statement continues that "[f]rom time immemorial Canada's Inuit people have used and occupied the ice as they have used and occupied the land."[21] The intent of the Government of Canada in issuing this statement is clear. The ice cover makes the Northwest Passage unique by virtue of the inhabitation of the Inuit on the ice. Thus, the ice can be considered more as land than water. Following this logic, the Government is obviously making the case that international law as it pertains to international straits does not apply. Since this statement remains as the definitive statement on Canadian Arctic sovereignty, it is clear that any new statements to the contrary are not accurate.

The Canadian legal position has been challenged. Both the United States and the European Union have indicated that they do not accept Canadian claims of sovereignty over the waters of the Canadian Arctic archipelago. However, neither the United States nor the European Union pushed their challenge as long as ice conditions precluded any economically viable international shipping. This hesitation will likely diminish as the ice melts, and this is the crux of the problem facing Canada.

THE AMERICAN AND EUROPEAN POSITION

The United States and the European Union position is that, contrary to Canadian claims, the Northwest Passage is an international strait. The Americans in particular do not accept the argument that ice cover makes a difference for the international legal definition of an international strait. The Americans have always maintained that the International Court of Justice's ruling in the Strait of Corfu case is applicable for the Northwest Passage. In that case, the Court ruled that an international strait is a body of water that joins two international bodies of water, and has been used by international shipping.[22] The United States argues that the Northwest Passage joins two international bodies of water and has been used for international shipping, albeit a very small number of transits.

Historically, the United States has posed the greatest challenge to Canadian claims of sovereignty. In 1969 and in 1970, the *Manhattan*, on behalf of Humble Oil, transited the Northwest Passage without seeking the Government of Canada's permission. The *Manhattan* was an ice-strengthened super tanker which could transit the Northwest Passage only with the assistance of icebreakers, and even then, ice conditions made the voyage very difficult and expensive.[23] In 1985, the American icebreaker, *Polar Sea*, was sent through the Passage without the Canadian government's permission. Though not designed to challenge Canadian claims of sovereignty, the voyage led to a significant diplomatic dispute.[24] However, to maintain good American–Canadian relations, an agreement was reached regarding future transits by American icebreakers. The 1988 agreement on Arctic co-operation between the Government of the United States of America and the Government of Canada required the United States to request Canadian consent for any future transit of the Passage by American government icebreakers.[25] However, both governments agreed to disagree on the actual status of the Passage. When the agreement was reached, the United States had only two icebreakers capable of such a passage. Since then, the Americans have built one more icebreaker, which invoked the agreement to transit the Passage in 2000.

In addition to the United States, the United Kingdom, acting on behalf of the European Community, issued a diplomatic protest against Canadian efforts in 1985 to enclose its Arctic waters as internal waters by using straight baselines.[26] The Europeans have kept their protests low key, preferring to allow the Americans to take the more active position. But by issuing a demarche against the Canadian claim, they have given notice that they have not acquiesced to Canadian claims of sovereignty.

SIGNIFICANCE OF THE DISPUTE

The difference between the Canadian position and that of the United States and the European Union is in the issue of control. If the Passage is Canadian internal waters as maintained by Canada, Canada has sovereign control over any activity, both foreign and domestic, that occurs in those waters. On the other hand, if the Northwest Passage is an international strait, then

Canada cannot unilaterally control international shipping in it. Therefore, Canada would be unable to deny passage to any vessel that meets international standards for environmental protection, crew training and safety procedures. As these standards are set by the International Maritime Organization (IMO), Canada cannot set different standards, especially those which impose more demanding requirements.

However, Canada could invoke more exacting environmental standards through the United Nations Law of the Sea Convention (UNCLOS). Article 234, the ice-covered waters clause, allows a State to pass legislation that exceeds international standards for any ice-covered waters within its 200-mile Exclusive Economic Zone (EEZ). The Canadian clause, as it is referred to since Canada was its main proponent, states

> Coastal States have the right to adopt and enforce non-discriminatory laws and regulations for the preservation, reduction and control of marine pollution from vessels in ice-covered areas within the limits of the exclusive economic zone, where particularly severe climatic conditions and the presence of ice covering such areas for most of the year create obstructions or exceptional hazards to navigation, and pollution of the marine environment could cause major harm to or irreversible disturbance of the ecological balance. Such laws and regulations shall have due regard to navigation and the protection and preservation of the marine environment based on the best available scientific evidence.[27]

It is important to note that the article does not give the coastal State the right to deny passage. Rather it bestows the right to the coastal State to pass its own domestic legislation for environmental protection rather than being bound by international standards. Such legislation can be more demanding than that of existing international agreements.

It is interesting that despite the fact that Canada drafted the clause and was originally a strong supporter of the entire Convention, it has not ratified the Convention.[28] The Government of Canada has stated that it accepts most of the Convention as customary international law. However, while it has continued to issue vague statements that it someday intends to ratify the Convention, there is no evidence as to when or if this will actually happen.

Although the issue of sovereignty invokes strong nationalistic feelings for Canadians, the reality is that after Canada and the United States signed the Arctic Cooperation Agreement in 1988, which controls the passage of American icebreakers, and continued to officially ignore the transit of American nuclear-powered submarines through Canadian northern waters, there was little incentive to revisit the issue. As long as ice conditions remained hazardous to commercial shipping, there was little incentive for any country, the United States included, to challenge the Canadian position. However, if ice conditions become less hazardous, then this situation changes drastically. The main attraction of the Northwest Passage is obvious. It substantially shortens the distance from Asia to the east coast of the United States and Europe. It is more than 8,000 kilometres shorter than the current route through the Panama Canal, and would significantly shorten the voyage for vessels that are too large to fit through the Canal and must sail around the Cape Horn. The voyage of the *Manhattan* demonstrated that the Passage can accommodate supertankers of at least 120,000 tons. The shorter distance means substantial savings for shipping companies, which translates into reduced costs for the products that are shipped. It is easy to see why an ice-free Northwest Passage, even for a limited time, would be of tremendous interest to major international shipping companies as well as the countries that avail themselves of their services.

It is impossible to know who will make the first challenge. While it is reasonable to suspect that it might be either an American or a European vessel, it could also be from another country. For example, Japan has shown considerable interest in Arctic navigation in the 1990s. It was a major partner in a multi-year million-dollar study of navigation through the Russian

Northern Sea Route (also known as the Northeast Passage).[29] The Japanese also were interested in buying the Canadian ice-strengthened oil tanker, *Arctic*, when the Canadian government put it up for sale. Perhaps even more telling is the amount of money that the Japanese put into polar research and development that is now substantial and continues to increase.[30] While the Japanese have never issued a statement of their view of the status of the Northwest Passage, it is clear that they would gain if it became a functioning international strait. Oil from both Venezuela and the Gulf of Mexico would then be cheaper to ship to Japan.

CANADIAN EFFORTS TO ASSERT AND MAINTAIN SOVEREIGNTY

It would appear that Canada should be now giving serious thought to how it can best respond to the prospects of any future challenges. Unfortunately there is little indication that this is happening. Instead, it appears that the Government continues to downgrade its existing limited capabilities. The two main government agencies with important roles in the protection and maintenance of Canadian international interests in the Arctic are the Department of National Defence (DND) and the Canadian Coast Guard (CCG). Both are continuing to see their northern capabilities reduced.

While the Department of National Defence has begun to consider the impact of a diminished ice cover, budget cuts forced it to eliminate most of its activities devoted to northern sovereignty. The previous Commander of Northern Area initiated a working group of relevant federal and territorial departments, called the Arctic Security Interdepartmental Working Group, which has been meeting twice a year since May 1999. The group shares both information and concerns and has raised the issue of climate change several times. However, it has almost no resources of its own and can only act as a means of co-ordination and networking.

Also at the initiative of the former Commander of Northern Area, DND recently assessed its capabilities in the north. The assessment found that Canada had limited resources that could be used in the northern area, and that the cost of any equipment and programs to remedy this shortcoming would be extremely expensive. The department concluded that given its constrained budget, resources would be allocated to more immediate priorities. It did note that projects could be developed to improve surveillance capabilities if funding was available.[31]

Financial cutbacks to the department have resulted in the elimination of most programs that gave Canada a presence in the North. Northern deployments of naval assets to Canadian northern waters, termed NORPLOYS, ended in 1990. Northern sovereignty overflights by Canadian long-range patrol aircraft (CP-140/CPI40A Aurora and Arcturus) were reduced in 1995 to one overflight per year and will soon be totally eliminated. The recently acquired Victoria class submarines do not have the capability to operate in Arctic waters. In fact, none of the Canadian naval units can operate in northern waters due to their thin hulls and the risk of ice damage.

The one exception to the cutbacks is the recent expansion of the number of Ranger Patrols. The Canadian government is increasing the number of serving Rangers from 3,500 to 4,800 by 2008.[32] However, although the Rangers can assert a presence in the north, they are a militia unit comprising northern inhabitants who can travel a moderate distance with snowmobiles.

In short, the ability of the Department of Defence to demonstrate a presence in the North is severely limited. The recently concluded defence study does suggest that it may be possible to improve surveillance with future technological developments including High Frequency Surface Wave Radar, rapidly deployable undersea surveillance systems and the use of UAVs (unmanned aerial vehicles-drones). While each system would prove useful for surveillance and presence in the North, none is currently being considered for deployment and all are still in the research and development phase. These technologies are unlikely to be purchased anytime soon.

The Canadian Coast Guard has the greatest responsibility for monitoring the Arctic region. Recently moved from the Department of Transport to the Department of Fisheries and Oceans, the CCG operates a fleet of icebreakers in the Arctic, consisting of two heavy icebreakers and three medium icebreakers. The most recent icebreaker, the *Henry Larsen* was added in 1987, but the fleet is heavily tasked and is ageing. A prolonged refit between 1988 and 1993 resulted in the extension of the operating life of the largest icebreaker, *Louis St. Laurent*. However, the vessel will soon be reaching the end of its operational life. There are no plans to build any new icebreakers in the immediate future.

Following the 1969–1970 voyage of the *Manhattan*, the Trudeau Government enacted the *Arctic Waters Pollution Prevention Act*,[33] creating a 100-mile environmental protection zone within Canadian Arctic waters. AWPPA regulations forbid the discharge of any fluids or solid wastes into the Arctic waters and set design requirements for vessels. Upon entering Canadian Arctic waters, vessels are requested to register through NORDREG, a voluntary, not mandatory, reporting system operated by the coast guard that all vessels (Canadian and otherwise) are requested to use when operating in Canadian Arctic waters. While such a system works reasonably well when few vessels enter the Northwest Passage, it is clear that it will not work when the number of voyages increases due to ice reduction. Consideration has been given to make NORDREG mandatory, but there has been no further action on this front.

The voluntary nature of NORDREG poses an obvious challenge to Canada's commitment to its claims. If Canada is serious about its statements that the waters of the Arctic Archipelago are internal waters, then there should be no question about its ability to enforce its rules and requirements. Yet, by making the system voluntary, the message internationally is that Canada questions its own ability to enforce its claim.

Canada does not have the capability to demonstrate a meaningful presence in its Arctic waters. So long as ice conditions in the north do not change, then this is not a significant problem. However, as the ice melts, it will become a serious problem.

THE INTERNATIONALIZATION OF THE NORTHWEST PASSAGE

Would it really matter if Canada lost an international challenge to its claim of sovereignty? The Canadian government is on record as stating that it does support international shipping through the Passage as long as Canadian regulations are followed.[34] The issue, then, is the type of regulations to be followed. Canada could claim that regardless of the status of the Passage, it retains the right to pass environmental regulations based on article 234 of UNCLOS. The problem with this argument is that the Canadian Government has not ratified the Convention. Therefore, the question is whether Canada could claim the rights provided by the article without ratifying the Convention.

The Canadian Coast Guard's efforts to formulate a Polar Code to govern the construction and operation of shipping in Arctic waters are designed to ensure that any international rules will have significant Canadian input. Canada, along with Russia, has played a key role in developing the technical requirements contained in the code.[35] On the other hand, these efforts may send the message that Canada expects to lose the ability to develop regulations unilaterally. Thus, there are signs that a new regime for regulating the international system is developing beyond Canada's control. Such a regime is likely to leave Canada facing tremendous challenges if, and when, shipping develops.

First, traditional security problems of an international waterway will arise. An examination of waterways in southeast Asia indicates that increased shipping can result in increased smuggling and other associated crimes. The deserted coastlines of northern Canada could be used for a host of illegal activities such as drug and human smuggling. It is also likely that smuggling of other goods, such as diamonds and fresh water could also take place. To control such potential problems, Canada will have to improve its surveillance and policing capabilities substantially.

The spread of new and exotic diseases is also a potential problem. Crews of most vessels come from southern countries and may carry strains of diseases to which northern Canadians have a low tolerance or to which they have not been exposed. Thus the risk of a disease outbreak could increase as shipping increases.

Even if Canada implements strong environmental regulations, the probability of an accident will increase with the corresponding increase of ship traffic. As the *Exxon Valdez* accident demonstrated, the grounding of a large vessel in northern waters will produce an ecological disaster. Currently, Canada is ill-equipped for even a moderate grounding, as was clearly demonstrated in 1996 when the *Hanseatic* grounded off Cambridge Bay.[36] The *Hanseatic* was successfully evacuated due only to the favourable weather conditions and the availability of local commercial pilots and planes. It is doubtful the grounding could have been responded to as successfully in a more isolated location and with severe weather conditions.

The lifestyle of Canada's northern Aboriginal people will be substantially affected by international shipping. Traditional hunting and trapping will be severely dislocated by the twin impact of global warming and the passages of large vessels. The influx of large numbers of foreigners associated with the new shipping will also affect their traditional way of life. Opportunities for employment will be available, but only for northerners with the right skills.

Nevertheless, there are some advantages to the melting of the Northwest Passage. Singapore has demonstrated that with the proper planning, geographical location on an international strait can bring substantial economic benefits. Vessels transiting the Passage would require certain services that could be provided by Canadian settlements. For example, Tuktoyaktuk and Iqaluit could conceivably become important ports of call if their port facilities were substantially improved.

CONCLUSIONS

Will climate change result in the melting of the Northwest Passage for some parts of the year? Will international shipping interests then attempt to take advantage of the more benign conditions? Will the Canadian status regarding the Passage be challenged? Will Canada be prepared? The evidence for the first is mounting. The question that remains is how fast these changes will occur and when the Passage will become economically viable for shipping interests. It is logical that international shipping interests will wish to take advantage if and when this happens. Canada can expect to face a challenge when this occurs. It is becoming apparent that the Canadian position will probably not be successful given the current low levels of Canadian activity in the region. But even if Canadian claims of sovereignty are upheld, pressure to allow the passage of international shipping will remain. Regardless of the nature of the international status, it is clear that Canada will face tremendous challenges in adapting to the opening of the Passage. The challenge that now faces Canada is to become aware of these possibilities and to begin taking action to prepare for them.

NOTES

1. Intergovernmental Panel on Climate Change, *Climate Change 2001: The Scientific Basis. A Report of Working Group I of the Intergovernmental Panel on Climate Change* (2001), PP- 2.2.5–2.2.6. [http://www.ipcc.sh/].

2. O.M. Johannessen, E.V. Shalina and M.W. Miles, "Satellite Evidence for an Arctic Sea Ice Cover in Transformation," *Science*, Vol. 286 (1999), pp. 1937–39; D.A. Rothrock, Y. Yu, and G.A. Maykut, "Thinning of the Arctic Sea-Ice Cover," *Geophysical Research Letters*, Vol. 26, no. 23 (December 1999), pp. 3469–3472; and M.J. Serreze, J. Walsh, F. Chapin, T. Osterkamp, M. Dyurgerov, V. Romanovsky, W. Oechel, J. Morrison, T. Zhang and R.G. Berry, "Observational Evidence of Recent Changes in Northern High-Latitude Environment," *Climate Change*, Vol. 46 (2000), pp. 159–207.

3. S. McKibbon, "Inuit Elders Say the Arctic Climate is Changing," *Nunatsiaq News* (June 2, 2000).

4. R. Bowkett, "Clear Signs of Global Warming: Dandelions at the Arctic Circle," *Anglican Journal*, Vol. 123, no. 8 (October 1997), p. 7; M. Nichols and D. Huffam, "The Heat Is On: A Crisis Is in the Making as Canada Confronts Its Commitment to Drastically Reduce Greenhouse-Gas Emissions," *Maclean's* (February 21, 2000), p. 48

5. I. Stirling, "Running out of Ice?" *Natural History*, Vol. 109, no. 2 (March 2000), p. 92.

6. J. Falkingham, "Sea Ice in the Canadian Arctic in the 21st Century," (September 2000) (unpublished paper).

7. B. Webber, "Arctic Sea Ice Is Not Melting: New Research," *Canadian Press* (April 24, 2001).

8. F. McCague "High Arctic Grips a Cruise Ship: Hundreds Evacuate by Dinghies as Tugs Try to Free the *Hanseatic*," *Alberta Report*, Vol. 2, no. 40 (September 16, 1996), p. 15.

9. L. Brigham, "Commentary: An International Polar Navigation Code for the Twenty-First Century," *Polar Record*, Vol. 33, no. 187 (1997), p. 283.

10. E. Franckx, Maritime *Claims in the Arctic* (Dordrecht: Martinus Nijhoff Publishers, 1993), pp. 71–74.

11. External Affairs Canada, *Statements* and *Speeches*, "Policy on Canadian Sovereignty" (September 10, 1985).

12. R. Huebert, "New Directions in Circumpolar Cooperation: Canada, The Arctic Environmental Protection Strategy, and the Arctic Council," *Canadian Foreign Policy*, Vol. 5, no. 2 (Winter 1998), pp. 37–57.

13. Department of Foreign Affairs and International Trade, *The Northern Dimension of Canada's Foreign Policy* (n.d.), p. 2.

14. *Ibid.*, p.5.

15. M. Gaillard, Legal Affairs Bureau, Department of Foreign Affairs and International Trade, "Canada's Sovereignty in Changing Arctic Waters," (March 19, 2001), Whitehorse, Yukon.

16. *Ibid.*, p.4.

17. *Ibid.*, p. 5.

18. D. Pharand, *Canada's Arctic Waters in International Law* (Cambridge: Cambridge University Press, 1988), p. 251.

19. *Ibid.*

20. United Nations, The Law of the Sea, *United Nations Convention on the Law of the Sea with Index and Final Act of the Third United Nations Conference on the Law of the Sea (UNCLOS)* (New York: United Nations, 1983), p. 4.

21. *Op. cit.*, External Affairs, note 11 at p. 2.

22. *Corfu Channel Case* [1949] ICJ, Rep.4.

23. D. McRae, "The Negotiation of Article 234," in F. Griffiths (ed.), *Politics of the Northwest Passage* (Kingston and Montreal; McGill-Queen's University Press, 1987), pp. 98–114.

24. R. Huebert, "Polar Vision or Tunnel Vision: The Making of Canadian Arctic Waters Policy," *Marine Policy*, Vol. 19, no. 4 (1995), pp. 343–363.

25. *Agreement between the Government of the United States of America and the Government of Canada on Arctic Cooperation*, (January 11, 1988).

26. R. Huebert, "Steel Ice and Decision-Making. The Voyage of the Polar Sea and its Aftermath: The Making of Canadian Northern Foreign Policy," (Halifax: Dalhousie Unversity, 1993), p. 331. (Unpublished thesis).

27. *Op. cit., UNCLOS*, note 20 at p. 84.

28. Canada remains one of only a handful of countries that have not ratified the Convention. Currently 135 States have ratified. The few that have not are either landlocked and/or a developing State. The United States is the only other major country that has not ratified. United Nations, Ocean and Law of the Sea Home Page, "Convention and Implementing Agreement," July 31, 2001 [http://www.un.org/Depts/los/losconv1.htm].

29. INSROP, International Northern Sea Route Programme, June 1993–March 1994. [http:www.fni.no/insrop/#Overview].

30. Natural Sciences and Engineering Research Council of Canada (NSERC) and Social Sciences and Humanities Research Council of Canada (SSHRC), *From Crisis to Opportunity: Rebuilding Canada's Role in Northern Research*

2000: Final Report to NSERC and SSHRC from the Task Force on Northern Research (Ottawa: NSERC and SSHRC, 2000), p. 12; B. Wuethrich, "New Center Gives Japan an Arctic Toehold," *Science*, vol. 285 (September 17, 1999), p. 1827.

31. A. Mitrovica, "Military Admits It Can't Detect Arctic Intruders," *Globe and Mail* (March 17, 2001), p. A3.
32. DND, VCDS, "Reserves and Cadets: Canadian Rangers." [http://www.rangers.dnd.ca/rangers/intro_e.asp].
33. *Arctic Water Pollution Prevention Act* 1970 [R.S.C. 1985 (1st Supp.) C.2, (1st Supp.) S.1.]
34. The most recent statement by the Government of Canada on the issue of shipping in the Northwest Passage can be found in its response to the Special Committee of the Senate and House of Commons on Canada's International Relations (Hockin Simard Report). See Department of External Affairs, Canada's *International Relations: Response of the Government of Canada to the Report of the Special Joint Committee of the Senate and the House of Commons* (December 1986), p. 32.
35. L. Brigham, "Commentary: An International Polar Navigation Code for the Twenty-First Century," *Polar Record*, vol. 33, no. 187 (1997), p. 283.
36. *Op. cit.*, McCague, note 8 at p. 15

CONTRIBUTORS

Peter Bakker is a researcher in the Department of Linguistics at the University of Aarhus, Denmark.

Jean Barman is a professor in the Department of Educational Studies at the University of British Columbia in Vancouver.

Will Bird (1891–1984) joined the 193rd Battalion, Nova Scotia in 1916 and fought with the 42nd Battalion, the Black Watch of Canada. He was awarded a military medal for bravery in the capture of Mons, on the night of 10–11 November 1918.

Bettina Bradbury teaches in the History Department at York University and in Women's Studies, Glendon College, York University.

Alan C. Cairns is Adjunct Professor of Political Science at the University of Waterloo and Professor Emeritus in the Political Science Department at the University of British Columbia, where he taught from 1960 to 1995.

J. Terry Copp teaches Canadian history at Wilfrid Laurier University in Waterloo, Ontario.

Peter deLottinville is an archivist at the National Archives of Canada in Ottawa.

W.J. Eccles (1917–1998) taught Canadian history at the University of Toronto.

E. Jane Errington is a professor of history at the Royal Military College of Canada in Kingston, Ontario.

Alain-G. Gagnon is a professor in the Department of Political Science at the Université du Québec à Montréal where he holds the Canada Research Chair in Quebec and Canadian Studies.

J.L. Granatstein taught Canadian history at York University, Toronto, from 1966 to 1995, and is Distinguished Research Professor of History Emeritus. He served as the director and CEO of the Canadian War Museum (1998–2001).

Allan Greer teaches Canadian history at the University of Toronto.

Naomi Griffiths taught Canadian history at Carleton University in Ottawa. She is now retired.

Ronald G. Haycock is professor of Military History and War Studies at the Royal Military College of Canada in Kingston, Ontario.

Rob Huebert teaches in the Department of Political Science and at the Centre for Military and Strategic Studies, University of Calgary.

José Igartua teaches history at l'Université du Quebec à Montreal.

Will Kymlicka is a professor of Philosophy at Queen's University in Kingston, Ontario.

David Lee is a historian with Historical Services Branch, National Historic Sites Directorate, Parks Canada, Canadian Heritage in Hull, Quebec.

Elizabeth Mancke teaches in the Department of History at the University of Akron in Ohio.

Ged Martin formerly held the chair of Canadian Studies at the University of Edinburgh and is now retired.

Cecilia Morgan teaches in the Department of Theory and Policy Studies in Education at the Ontario Institute for Studies in Education at the University of Toronto.

Howard Palmer (1946–1991) taught Canadian history at the University of Calgary.

Frits Pannekoek is president of Athabasca University in Alberta.

Adele Perry holds the Canada Research Chair in Western Canadian Social History at the University of Manitoba.

Harald E.I. Prins teaches anthropology at Kansas State University at Manhattanville, Kansas.

John A. Rohr is professor of Public Administration at the Centre for Public Administration and Policy at Virginia Polytechnic Institute and State University.

Paul Romney has taught at the Center for Canadian Studies in the School of Advanced International Studies, John Hopkins University, and currently works as a freelance writer.

Robert Rutherdale teaches in the Department of History and Philosophy at Algoma University College, Laurentian University, Sault Ste Marie, Ontario.

Irene Spry (1907–1998) was Economics Professor Emerita at the University of Ottawa.

James W. St.G. Walker teaches Canadian history at the University of Waterloo.

A. Blair Stonechild is head of Indigenous Studies, First Nations University of Canada, in Regina.

Veronica Strong-Boag is a Canadian historian working in Women's Studies and Educational Studies at the University of British Columbia in Vancouver.

Bruce G. Trigger teaches in the Department of Anthropology at McGill University in Montreal.

Sylvia Van Kirk taught Canadian history at the University of Toronto, and is now Professor Emerita.

Reg Whitaker is Distinguished Research Professor Emeritus at York University and currently teaches Political Science at the University of Victoria.

Wendy Wickwire teaches history in the Department of History at the University of Victoria.

PHOTO CREDITS

INDEX